Western Movies

Western Movies

A TV and Video Guide to 4200 Genre Films

Michael R. Pitts

McFarland & Company, Inc., Publishers
Jefferson, North Carolina, and London

Library of Congress Cataloguing-in-Publication Data

Pitts, Michael R.
Western movies.

Bibliography: p. 521
Includes index.
1. Western films – Catalogs. I. Title.
PN1995.9.W4P58 1986   016.79143'09'093278   85-31014

ISBN 0-89950-195-8 (acid-free natural paper)

Printed in the United States of America

McFarland & Company, Inc., Publishers
Box 611 Jefferson NC 28640

For Angela

Table of Contents

Introduction

Without doubt the Western film has been the most popular and enduring motion picture genre since the turn of the century. It has been estimated that over 20,000 Western films have been churned out over the years and despite the dearth of many new Westerns in recent years the genre itself continues unabated in popularity.

This television and video guide to Western movies includes 4,189 feature Westerns generally available to the viewing public. This availability includes television, 16mm, 8mm and Super 8mm film; videocassettes and videodiscs. The intent of this book, therefore, is to provide the Western film viewer with a comprehensive handbook of films available plus a fair amount of information about them.

Each entry includes film title, release company and year, running time and whether the film is in black and white or color; a thorough cast listing, plot synopsis and brief critical review. Video sources are also provided for several hundred titles. The following abbreviations are used in the entries:

B/W	Black/White
D	Director
SC	Script
V	Video Source
VD	VideoDisc Source

Only feature films (running four reels or 40 minutes or more) are included in the text; there are no XXX-rated movies. Running times on films may vary according to source. When films have been edited (mainly for television) both the original and TV running times are included. Thus an entry with a listing such as 54 (74) minutes means the edited running time is 54 minutes while the original running time is 74 minutes.

In the area of casts it should be noted that sometimes spellings vary (i.e., Jimmie or Jimmy Aubrey) and actors' sons often drop the "Jr." (e.g. Lon Chaney, Jr., Noah Beery, Jr., and Alan Hale, Jr.) in the later years of their careers.

An important point, I believe, regarding any book such as this one is that opinions on movies are purely subjective and should be taken for just that and nothing more. What appeals to one person will not appeal to another. Thus the critical remarks herein are nothing more than suggestions for the reader and are not the final word. Too many books on movies, particularly Westerns, laud or castigate a film without regard to the viewers' likes or dislikes. Films are for fun. I hope the reader will find this book enjoyable reading as well as a useful reference tool.

As stated, I have included suggested video sources for several hundred films, as an aid to video collectors. These suggestions are hardly all-encompassing nor are they timeless. New titles are added almost daily to the ever-growing list of Western films on videocassettes and videodiscs. The author and publisher of this book have not knowingly included any video titles from any source which might be in copyright violation. Source listings are based solely on company catalogs and press releases.

This book is intended to include all aspects of the Western genre and not just the shoot-'em-up film. Thus in these pages will be found northwoods dramas, south-of-the-border action, frontier sagas and foreign films that either deal with the American frontier or have plot ingredients indigenous to the Western.

The author would appreciate any additions, corrections or comments regarding this volume, sent in care of the publisher.

In closing, I would especially like to thank my wife, Carolyn, for helping in the difficult task of alphabetizing the book's entries. Thanks for their help are also extended to the Academy of Motion Picture Arts and Sciences' Film Information Service, The American Film Institute Mayer Library (Barbara Malone), John Cocchi, Dennis Deas, Tim Ferrante, Reinhold Haase, Gary Kramer, Buck Rainey, the Motion Picture, Broadcasting and Recorded Sound Division of the Library of Congress (Katharine Loughney and

Cooper C. Graham), Richard Bojarski, Bertil Lundgren, Ray White, Lone Ranger Television/Wrather Corporation (Kathy Leslie), the New York Public Library Performing Arts Research Center (Dorothy L. Swerdlove and David E. Bartholomew), and George W. Gersich. Special thanks to George A. Katchmer and George F. Geltzer for their help in researching obscure silent titles. Special mention should also be made of the late Don Miller, who helped serve as an inspiration for this volume.

Pleasant reading, good viewing and happy trails.

Michael R. Pitts

Western Feature Films

A

1 Abilene Town. United Artists, 1946. 89 minutes B/W. D: Edwin L. Marin. SC: Harold Shumate. WITH Randolph Scott, Ann Dvorak, Edgar Buchanan, Rhonda Fleming, Lloyd Bridges, Helen Boyce, Howard Freeman, Richard Hale, Jack Lambert, Hank Patterson, Eddy Waller, Dick Curtis. A sheriff tries to stop range fights between settlers and cattlemen in Kansas after the Civil War. Good Randolph Scott star vehicle.

2 Abilene Trail. Monogram, 1951. 54 minutes B/W. D: Lewis D. Collins. SC: Harry Fraser. WITH Whip Wilson, Andy Clyde, Noel Neill, Tommy Farrell, Steve Clark, Dennis Moore, Marshall Reed, Lee Roberts, Milburn Morante, Ted Adams, Bill Kennedy, Stanley Price, Lyle Talbot. Two suspected horse thieves come to the aid of a young rancher who is having trouble driving his herd to market. Although the "B" Western was in decline in the early 1950s, this Whip Wilson outing is solid.

3 Ace High. Paramount, 1969. 120 minutes Color. D-SC: Giuseppe Colizzi. WITH Terence Hill, Eli Wallach, Bud Spencer, Brock Peters, Kevin McCarthy, Steffan Zacharias, Livio Lorenzon, Tiffany Hoyveld, Remo Capitani, Armando Bandini, Isa Foster, Rick Boyd. Sentenced to hang, an outlaw is offered a chance to save his life. Hard-fo-follow Italian oater with the usual violent touches. Made as **Il Quattro dell'Ave Maria** and issued in Great Britain as **Revenge at El Paso.**

4 The Ace of Clubs. Rayart, 1926. 60 minutes B/W. D: J. P. McGowan. SC: G. A. Durlam. WITH Al Hoxie, Peggy Montgomery, Minna Redman, Andrew Waldron, Jules Cowles, Charles "Slim" Whitaker, Frank Ellis, Mutt (dog). A girl comes West to live with her two uncles who are cattle rustlers and one of them tries to kill a neighboring rancher with whose mother the girl is staying. Slapped together, rock-bottom Al Hoxie vehicle; the silent Western at its worst.

5 Aces and Eights. Puritan, 1936. 62 minutes B/W. D: Sam Newfield. SC: George A. Durlam. WITH Tim McCoy, Luana Walters, Wheeler Oakman, Rex Lease, John Merton, Chares Stevens, Joe Girard, Jimmie Aubrey, Earle Hodgins, J. Frank Glendon, Frank Ellis. A gambler is out to fleece the populace in a small town. Slow-paced Tim McCoy outing saved by the star's fine performance as a gambler. V: Discount Video.

6 Aces Wild. Commodore, 1936. 57 minutes B/W. D: Harry Fraser, SC: Monroe Talbot. WITH Harry Carey, Gertrude Messinger, Phil Dunham, Roger Williams, Fred "Snowflake" Toones, Ed Cassidy, Chuck Morrison, Theodore Lorch, William McCall. A newspaper editor is threatened by outlaws when he tries to stop their activities. Low budget but nicely done Harry Carey film. V: Cumberland Video.

7 Across the Badlands. Columbia, 1950. 55 minutes B/W. D: Fred F. Sears. SC: Barry Shipman. WITH Charles Starrett, Smiley Burnette, Helen Mowery, Stanley Andrews, Robert Wilke, Harmonica Bill, Dick Elliott, Hugh Prosser, Robert W. Cavendish, Charles Evans, Paul Campbell, Richard Alexander. The general manager of a railroad calls in a lawman to investigate constant attacks on the line's surveying crews. Well done entry in the "Durango Kid" series.

8 Across the Great Divide. Pacific International, 1977. 101 minutes Color. D-SC: Stewart Raffill. WITH Robert Logan, Heather Rattray, Mark Edward Hall, George "Buck" Flower, Hal Bokar, Frank F. Salsedo, Fernando Celis, Loren Ewing, Tiny Brooks, James Elk, Stanley Cowley. In 1876 two orphans and a vagabond brave the harsh elements of the West to trek to Oregon so the youngsters can claim inherited land. Too long and a bit draggy but nice scenery.

9 Across the Plains. Associated Independent Producers, 1928. 55 minutes B/W. D-SC: Robert J. Horner. WITH Pawnee Bill Jr. (Ted Wells), Ione Reed, Martha Barclay, Jack Richardson, Boris Bullock, Cliff Lyons. A crooked lawman tries to hang a ranch foreman for shooting a gambler in a crooked poker game but a saloon girl comes to his rescue. Bottom rung entry in the very low grade "Pawnee Bill Jr." silent series.

10 Across the Plains. Monogram, 1939. 57 minutes B/W. D: Spencer Gordon Bennet. SC: Robert Emmett (Tansey). WITH Jack Randall, Joyce Bryant, Frank Yaconelli, Hal Price, Dennis Moore, Glenn Strange, Robert Card, Bud Osborne, Dean Spencer, Wylie Grant. As youngsters, two brothers are separated and years later they meet again but this time they are on opposite sides of the law. The hackneyed plot does not help this average Jack Randall vehicle.

11 Across the Rio Grande. Monogram, 1949. 55 minutes B/W. D: Oliver Drake. SC: Ronald Davidson. WITH Jimmy Wakely, Dub Taylor, Reno Browne, Riley Hill, Dennis Moore, Kenne Duncan, Ted Adams, Myron Healey, Bud Osborne, Polly (Bergen) Burgin, Bob Curtis, Carol Henry, Boyd Stockman. A young lawyer becomes involved with border ore smuggling. Typical Jimmy Wakely musical western enhanced by sidekick Dub Taylor.

12 Across the Sierras. Columbia, 1941. 58 minutes B/W. D: D. Ross Lederman. SC: Paul Franklin. WITH Bill Elliott, Richard Fiske, Luana Walters, Dub Taylor, Dick Curtis, LeRoy Mason, Ruth Robinson, Art Mix, John Dilson, Milton Kibbee, Ralph Peters, Tex Cooper, Eddie Laughton, Edmund Cobb, Tom London, James Pierce. Wild Bill Hickok plans to settle down in the Oklahoma Territory but gets involved with an old friend on the wrong side of the law and a badman he once sent to jail. Surprisingly austere "Wild Bill Hickok" series entry with Dick Curtis stealing the show as villainous Mitch Carew; a very good programmer.

13 Across the Wide Missouri. Metro-Goldwyn-Mayer, 1951. 79 minutes Color. D: William A. Wellman. SC: Talbot Jennings. WITH Clark Gable, Ricardo Montalban, John Hodiak, Adolphe Menjou, J. Carrol Naish, Jack Holt, Alan Napier, George Chandler, Richard Anderson, Henri Letondal, Douglas Fowley, Maria Elena Marques, Louis Niccolletti Whitmore,

Russell Simpson, John Hartman, Frankie Darro. Story of the opening of the trail west from St. Louis in the 19th century. Well done and actionful; good entertainment.

Adios see **The Lash**

14 Adios, Amigo. Atlas, 1976. 87 minutes Color. D-SC: Fred Williamson. WITH Fred Williamson, Richard Pryor, James Brown, Robert Phillips, Mike Henry, Victoria Jee, Lynne Jackson, Suhaila Farhat, Thalmus Rasulala, Liz Treadwell. A con man and his fall guy ply their trade in the Old West. Nice comedy.

15 Adios Gringo. Explorer Film/Fono Roma/Trebal Film C.C.-Les Films Corona, 1965. 97 minutes Color. D: George Finlay (Giorgio Stegani). SC: George Finlay, Jerez & Villerot. WITH Giuliano Gemma (Montgomery Wood), Evelyn Stewart (Ida Galli), Roberto Camardiel, Peter Cross, Jesus Puente, Grant Laramy, Jean Martin, Dax Dean, Monique Saint Clare. A rancher, cheated out of his cattle and forced to kill a man in self-defense, sets out to find the man who can prove his innocence. Not bad for this type of European fare.

16 Adios, Sabata. United Artists, 1971. 104 minutes Color. D: Gianfranco Parolini (Frank Kramer). SC: Renato Izzo & Gianfranco Parolini. WITH Yul Brynner, Dean Reed, Pedro Sanchez, Gerard Herter, Sal Borgese, Franco Fantasia, Joseph Persuad, Gianni Rizzo, Salvatore Billa, Massimo Carocci, Antonio Gardoli. A gunslinger is induced to aid antigovernment rebels in Mexico but he is also lured by a shipment of buried gold. Typical Spanish-Italian western with Yul Brynner, instead of Lee Van Cleef, in the title role, as Van Cleef starred in this film's predecessor **Sabata** (q.v.) as well as its sequel **The Return of Sabata** (q.v.). Original title: **Indio Black.**

17 Advance to the Rear. Metro-Goldwyn-Mayer, 1964. 97 minutes Color. D: George Marshall. SC: Samuel A. Peeples. WITH Glenn Ford, Stella Stevens, Melvyn Douglas, Jim Backus, Joan Blondell, Andrew Prine, Jesse Pearson, Alan Hale, James Griffith, Whit Bissell, Michael Pate, Yvonne Craig, Chuck Roberson, Bill Troy, Frank Mitchell, Harlan Warde, Paul Langton, Charles Horvath, Eddie Quillan, Paul Smith, Harvey Stephens, Gregg Palmer. During the Civil War a group of misfit raw recruits are mistakenly ordered by the Union army to guard a shipment of gold. A comedy that is only average but the cast is good despite the material.

18 An Adventure of the Texas Kid: Border Ambush. United International, 1954. 60 minutes B/W. D: Robert Tansey. SC: Robert Emmet (Tansey). WITH Hugh Hooker, John Laurenz, Pamela Blake, Monte Blue, Terry Frost. Two undercover operatives run into trouble with outlaws led by a corrupt lawyer, in this telefeature made up of two unsold pilot films. Probably one of Robert Tansey's last, or nearly last, ventures.

19 The Adventurer of Tortuga. Liber Film, 1965. 100 minutes Color. D: Luigi Capuano. SC: De Riso & Poggi. WITH Guy Madison, Nadia Gray, Rik Battaglia, Inge Schoner, Mino Doro, Aldo Bufi Landi, Andrea Aureli, Giulio Marchetti, Linda Sini. A pirate is at odds with a Spanish governor for the hand of a beautiful Indian princess, the niece and heiress of a very wealthy man. Mediocre dubbed costume actioner from Italy originally issued as **L'Avventuriero della Torgua** (The Adventurer from Tortuga).

20 Adventures in Silverado. Columbia, 1948. 75 minutes B/W. D: Phil Karlson. SC: Kenneth Gamet, Tom Kilpatrick & Joe Pagano. WITH William Bishop, Gloria Henry, Edgar Buchanan, Forrest Tucker, Edgar Barrier, Irving Bacon, Joseph Crehan, Paul E. Burns, Patti Brady, Fred Sears, Joe Wong, Charles Kane, Eddy Waller, Netta Parker, Trevor Bardette. Traveling west, author Robert Louis Stevenson is on a stage robbed by a masked highwayman called "The Monk" and when the stage driver is accused of being in cahoots with the badman he sets out to capture him. Well done action drama based on Stevenson's story "Silverado Squatters."

21 The Adventures of Bullwhip Griffin. Buena Vista, 1967. 110 minutes Color. D: James Nielson. SC: Lowell S. Hawley. WITH Roddy McDowall, Suzanne Pleshette, Karl Malden, Harry Guardino, Richard Haydn, Hermoine Baddeley, Bryan Russell, Liam Redmond, Cecil Kellaway, Joby Baker, Mike Mazurki, Alan Carney, Parley Baer, Arthur Hunnicutt, Dub Taylor, Pedro Gonzalez-Gonzalez, Gil Lamb, Burt Mustin, Dave Willock, John Qualen. A young Boston boy and his stuffy butler head west for California to hunt for gold. Nicely done and amusing take-off on the Western genre.

22 The Adventures of Don Coyote. United Artists, 1947. 65 minutes B/W. D: Reginald LeBorg. SC: Bob Williams & Ralph Cohn. WITH Frances Rafferty, Richard Martin, Marc Cramer, Bennie Bartlett, Frank Fenton, Byron Fougler, Eddie Parker, Pierce Lyden, Frank McCarroll, Val Carlo. Two caballeros try to help a girl whose ranch is being attacked by outlaws. Entertaining little "B" outing.

23 The Adventures of Frank and Jesse James. Republic, 1948. 13 Chapters B/W. D: Fred C. Brannon & Yakima Canutt. SC: Franklyn Adreon, Sol Shor & Basil Dickey. WITH Clayton Moore, Noel Neill, Steve Darrell, George J. Lewis, Stanley Andrews, John Crawford, Sam Flint, House Peters Jr., Dale Van Sickel, Tom Steele, James Dale, I. Stanford Jolley, Gene (Roth) Stutenroth, Lane Bradford, George Chesebro, Jack Kirk, Steve Clark, Dub Taylor, Carey Loftin, Frank Ellis, Art Dillard, Fred Graham, Guy Teague, Joe Yrigoyen, Eddie Parker, Bud Osborne, Rosa Turich, David Sharpe, Bob Reeves, Kenneth Terrell, Bud Wolfe. A crooked mine foreman tries to prevent Frank and Jesse James from repaying their robbery debts from a gold mine they operate with a man and his daughter. Action Republic cliffhanger.

24 The Adventures of Frontier Fremont. Sunn Classic, 1976. 85 minutes Color. D: Richard Friedenberg. SC: David O'Malley. WITH Dan Haggerty, Denver Pyle, Norman Goodman, Tony Mirrati. In 1835 a man decides to live in the wilderness and has to overcome many hardships before finding happiness in the wild. Low budget but nicely entertaining family-oriented adventure feature.

25 The Adventures of Grizzly Adams at Beaver Dam. NBC-TV, 1981. 60 minutes Color. WITH Dan Haggerty, Denver Pyle, Don Shanks. A mountain man tries to stop a family of beavers from building a dam which he fears will flood his valley home. Entertaining segment from the TV series "The Life and Times of Grizzly Adams" (NBC-TV, 1977-78) and issued as a feature to the video market. Filmed in the high Uinta Mountain Range of Utah.

26 The Adventures of Grizzly Adams:

Blood Brothers. NBC-TV, 1980. 60 minutes Color. WITH Dan Haggerty, Denver Pyle, Don Shanks. Trying to live in the wild after being falsely accused of a crime, a man meets an Indian brave who becomes his blood brother. Okay segment of the TV series "The Life and Times of Grizzly Adams" (NBC-TV, 1977-78) made available as a video feature.

27 The Adventures of the Masked Phantom. Equity, 1939. 59 minutes Color. D: Charles Abbott. SC: Joseph O'Donnell & Clifford Sanforth. WITH Monte Rawlins, Betty Burgess, Larry Mason (Art Davis), Sonny LaMont, Merrill McCormack, Matty Kemp, Jack Ingram, Curley Dresden, Boots (Dog), Thunder (horse). A law officer hides his face behind a mask in order to hunt down outlaws smuggling stolen gold plates out of a mine with low grade ore. Unbelievably campy curio; a delight for lovers of such fare. V: Video Images.

28 The Adventures of Neeka. Wrather Corporation, 1968. 75 minutes Color. D: Dick Moder. SC: Robert Schaefer & Eric Freiwald. WITH Lassie, Mark Miranda, Robert Rockwell, Jed Allan, R. G. Armstrong, John Harmon. An orphaned Alaskan Indian boy, now the adopted son of a rancher, has a series of adventures with Lassie including a night in a ghost town, the injuring of a horse when he drives his dad's truck, and helping a reclusive old man. Well done family fare made up of three segments of the "Lassie" (CBS-TV, 1954-71) series.

29 Adventures of Red Ryder. Republic, 1940. 12 Chapters B/W. D: William Witney & John English. SC: Franklyn Adreon, Ronald Davidson, Norman S. Hall, Barney A. Sarecky & Sol Shor. WITH Don "Red" Barry, Noah Beery, Tommy Cook, Maude Pierce Allen, Vivian Coe, Harry Worth, Hal Taliaferro, William Farnum, Robert Kortman, Carleton Young, Ray Teal, Gene Alsace, Gayne Whitman, Hooper Atchley, John Dilson, Lloyd Ingraham, Charles Hutchinson, Gardner James, Wheaton Chambers, Lynton Brent, Edward Hearn, Dickie Jones, Matty Roubert, Roy Brent, Ed Cassidy, William Benedict, Curley Dresden, Joe De La Cruz, Bud Geary, Jack Rockwell, Post Parks, Fred Burns, Dan White, Kenneth Terrell, Reed Howes, Budd Buster, Ed Brady, Augie Gomez, Al Taylor, Frank Conklin, Walter James, Ernest Sarracino, Bob Burns, Jack Kirk, James Fawcett, Duke Green, Art Dillard, Art Mix, David Sharpe, Joe Yrigoyen, Bill Yrigoyen, William Nestel, James Carlisle, Max Waizman, Chester Conklin, Edward Hearn, Jack O'Shea, Robert Wilke, Chick Hannon, Rose Plummer. A crooked banker murders several citizens in his efforts to seize land to be used by the railroad and after he kills Red Ryder's father, Red and his pal Little Beaver vow revenge. Top notch Republic cliffhanger which made Don Barry a genre star; well worth watching.

30 The Adventures of the Tucson Kid. Tucson Kid Productions, 1953. 50 minutes Color. D-SC: Edward D. Wood Jr. WITH Tom Keene, Tom Tyler, Lyle Talbot, Kenne Duncan, Harvey B. Dunne, Don Nagel, Edward D. Wood Jr. The story of the Tucson Kid, also called the Crossroads Avenger, an insurance claims adjuster in the West. Made up of two unsold "The Crossroads Avenger" television series pilots starring Tom Keene in the title role, originally considered for theatrical release in the late 1950s, these two films are sometimes tied together as a feature at Ed Wood film festivals.

31 Adventures of the Wilderness Family. Pacific International, 1975. 100 minutes Color. D-SC: Stewart Raffill. WITH Robert Logan, Susan Damante Shaw, Hollye Holmes, Ham Larsen, George "Buck" Flower, William Cornford. A modern-day family rejects civilization and moves to the rugged Rocky Mountains. Big moneymaking family film which is slight on plot but heavy on visuals and is well done. Two sequels followed: **The Further Adventures of the Wilderness Family** and **Mountain Family Robinson** (q.v.).

32 Africa—Texas Style! Paramount, 1967. 109 minutes Color. D: Andrew Marton. SC: Andy White. WITH Hugh O'Brian, John Mills, Nigel Green, Tom Nardini, Adrienne Corri, Ronald Howard, Charles Hayes, Haley Mills. A rancher in Kenya hires two American cowpokes to try to save African wildlife by the herding and domesticating of wild animals, but a fellow rancher tries to ruin the plan. Although this African-set Western has a lot of promise it fails to deliver much in the way of entertainment although it served as the basis for the television series "Cowboy in Africa" (ABC-TV, 1967-68) with Chuck Conners starring and Tom Nardini and Ronald Howard as regulars.

33 Against a Crooked Sky. Cinema Shares, 1976. 100 minutes Color. D: Earl Bellamy.

SC: Eleanor Lamd & Douglas Stewart. WITH Richard Boone, Stewart Petersen, Henry Wilcoxon, Clint Ritchie, Shannon Farnon, Geoffrey Land, Vincent St. Cyr. After his teenage sister is kidnapped by Indians and his parents give her up for dead, a young boy sets out with an old trapper and tries to find her. Nicely made and picturesque family-oriented feature.

34 Al Jennings of Oklahoma. Columbia, 1950. 77 minutes Color. D: Ray Nazarro. SC: George Bricker. WITH Dan Duryea, Gale Storm, Dick Foran, Gloria Henry, Guinn Williams, Raymond Greenleaf, Stanley Andrews, John Ridgely, James Millican, Harry Shannon, Robert Bice, Helen Brown, George J. Lewis, Jimmie Dodd, Edwin Parker, James Griffith, William Phillips, John Dehner, Charles Meredith, William Norton Bailey, Louis Jean Heydt, Harry Cording, Myron Healey, George Lloyd, Hank Patterson, George Chesebro, Earle Hodgins, John R. Hamilton, Harry Tyler, Guy Beach, Boyd Stockman. The story of Oklahoma native Al Jennings who is forced to give up his law practice and soon becomes a famous outlaw. Highly fabricated, but entertaining, version of Al Jennings' life, based on his book, with a fine performance by Dan Duryea in the title role.

35 The Alamo. United Artists, 1960. 192 minutes Color. D: John Wayne. SC: James Edward Grant. WITH John Wayne, Richard Widmark, Laurence Harvey, Richard Boone, Frankie Avalon, Carlos Arruza, Patrick Wayne, Linda Cristal, Joan O'Brien, Chill Wills, Joseph Calleia, Ken Curtis, Hank Worden, Denver Pyle, Aissa Wayne, Julian Trevino, Jester Hairston, Veda Ann Borg, Olive Carey, Wesley Lau, Tom Hennessey, Bill Henry, John Dierkes, Guinn Williams, Jack Pennick, Fred Graham, Chuck Roberson, Boyd "Red" Morgan, Ruben Padilla. The story leading up to the heroic sacrifice of the men at the Alamo, which led to the independence of Texas from Mexico. Too long and detailed but still a magnificent effort with excellent work by its stars and well-staged battle sequences. V: Blackhawk, Cumberland Video. VD: Blackhawk.

36 Alaska. Monogram, 1944. 76 minutes B/W. George Archainbaud. SC: George Wallace Sayre, Harrison Orkow & Malcolm Stuart Boyland. WITH Kent Taylor, Marga-

ret Lindsay, Dean Jagger, John Carradine, Nils Asther, Iris Adrian, George Cleveland, Dewey Robinson, Lee "Lasses" White, John Rogers, John Maxwell, Warren Jackson. A prospector trying to hold off claim jumpers is unjustly accused of murder and given three days to find the real killer. Nicely done version of Jack London's short story "Flush of Gold."

37 Alaskan Safari. American National Enterprises, 1968. 120 minutes Color. D-SC: Arthur R. Dubs. WITH Arthur R. Dubs (narrator). Documentary on Alaska including its animal life, mountains and giant ice packs. Well done and entertaining nature film, followed by **White Fury** (q.v.).

38 Alias Billy the Kid. Republic, 1946. 54 minutes B/W. D: Thomas Carr. SC: Earle Snell & Betty Burbridge. WITH Sunset Carson, Peggy Stewart, Roy Barcroft, Tom London, Russ Whiteman, Tom Chatterton, Tex Terry, Pierce Lyden, Stanley Price, Ed Cassidy. A ranger lets a convicted murderer escape from jail so he can trail him to his gang but the man gets away and the ranger becomes involved with a female outlaw leader. Lots of action but not much else in this average Sunset Carson programmer.

39 Alias Jesse James. United Artists, 1959. 92 minutes Color. D: Norman McLeod. SC: William Bowers & Daniel B. Beauchamps. WITH Bob Hope, Rhonda Fleming, Wendell Corey, Jim Davis, Hugh O'Brian, Ward Bond, James Arness, Roy Rogers, Fess Parker, Gail Davis, James Garner, Gene Autry, Jay Silverheels, Bing Crosby, Gary Cooper, Gloria Talbott, Will Wright, Mary Young, Sid Melton, George E. Stone, James Burke, Joseph Vitale, Lyle Latell, Harry Tyler, Mike Mazurki, Mickey Finn, Nestor Paiva, Emory Parnell, I. Stanford Jolley, Richard Alexander, Oliver Blake, Jack Lambert, Ethan Laidlaw, Glenn Strange, J. Anthony Hughes, Iron Eyes Cody. An insurance agent is sent west to protect Jesse James after the company discovers it has a policy on the outlaw and the agent is mistaken for a gunman. Highly amusing Bob Hope vehicle loaded with genre guest stars.

40 Alias John Law. Supreme, 1935. 54 minutes B/W. D: Robert North Bradbury. SC: Forbes Parkhill. WITH Bob Steele, Roberta Gale, Earl Dwire, Jack Rockwell, Buck Connors, Bob McKenzie, Roger

Williams, Steve Clark, Horace Murphy. A young man returns home to claim land where oil has been discovered while an outlaw gang leader also masquerades as the heir. Bob Steele fans will like this actionful and entertaining Supreme series outing.

41 Alias Smith and Jones. Universal/ABC-TV, 1971. 90 minutes Color. D: Gene Levitt. SC: Matthew Howard & Glen A. Larson. WITH Peter Deuel, Ben Murphy, Forrest Tucker, Susan Saint James, James Drury, Jeanette Nolan, Earl Holliman, John Russell, Bill Fletcher, Bill McKinney, Peter Brocco, Sid Haig, Jon Shank. Two outlaws are given amnesty if they agree to bring in a vicious outlaw gang. Adequate TV comedy Western feature which was the pilot for the "Alias Smith and Jones" series (ABC-TV, 1971-73).

42 Alias the Badman. Tiffany, 1931. 66 minutes B/W. D: Phil Rosen. SC: Earle Snell. WITH Ken Maynard, Virginia Brown Faire, Frank Mayo, Charles King, Lafe McKee, Robert Homans, Irving Bacon, Ethan Allen, Earl Dwire, Jack Rockwell, Jim Corey. A cowboy pretending to be an outlaw in order to catch the man who murdered his father falls in love with a girl whose father is a suspected cattle rustler. Good Ken Maynard star vehicle.

43 The Alien Encounters. Gold Key, 1976. 90 minutes Color. D-SC: James T. Flocker. WITH Augie Tribuck, Matt Boston, Phil Catalli, Bonnie Henry, Patricia Hunt, Lukas Jackson, Chris Lee Jackson, Amy Dalton. In the desert country, a man tries to locate persons who have had encounters with alien beings. Slow moving and poorly made, the film even manages to make its intriguing plot premise dull; desert scenery its only interest.

Alien Thunder see **Dan Candy's Law**

44 All Mine to Give. Universal-International/RKO Radio, 1957. 102 minutes Color. D: Allen Reisner. SC: Dale Eunson & Katherine Eunson. WITH Glynis Johns, Cameron Mitchell, Rex Thompson, Patty McCormack, Ernest Truex, Hope Emerson, Alan Hale (Jr.), Sylvia Field, Ralph Sanford, Steven Wooten, Butch Bernard, Yolanda White, Terry Ann Ross, Roy Engel, Ellen Corby, Reta Shaw, Royal Dano, Rita Johnson, Margaret Brayton. In frontier Wisconsin a pioneer family struggles to survive. Heart-warming

and very well done family movie; recommended.

45 Allegheny Uprising. RKO Radio, 1939. 81 minutes B/W. D: William A. Seiter. SC: P. J. Wolfson. WITH Claire Trevor, John Wayne, George Sanders, Brian Donlevy, Wilfried Lawson, Robert Barrat, John F. Hamilton, Moroni Olsen, Eddie Quillan, Chill Wills, Ian Wolfe, Wallis Clark, Monte Montague, Eddy Waller, Clay Clement, Olaf Hytten, Charles Middleton, Douglas Spencer, Bud Osborne. A frontiersman goes against his colony's commanding officer and goes after a crooked trader whose selling weapons to the Indians is threatening peace. John Wayne-Claire Trevor's follow-up film to **Stagecoach** (q.v.) is set in the pre-Revolutionary War period and is based on fact, making it all the more interesting. British title: **The First Rebel.** V: Blackhawk, Nostalgia Merchant.

46 Along Came Jones. RKO Radio, 1945. 90 minutes B/W. D: Stuart Heisler. SC: Nunnally Johnson. WITH Gary Cooper, Loretta Young, William Demarest, Dan Duryea, Frank Sully, Russell Simpson, Arthur Loft, Willard Robertson, Don Costello, Ray Teal, Walter Sande, Lane Chandler, Frank Cordell, Tommy Coates, Tony Roux, Erville Alderson, Paul Sutton, Ernie Adams, Paul E. Burns, Chris-Pin Martin, Ralph Dunn, John Merton, Lee Phelps, Robert Kortman, Frank McCarroll, Hank Bell. A cowboy is mistaken for a hunted outlaw and becomes the target of both the posse looking for the outlaw and by the badman himself. Gary Cooper produced and starred in this International Pictures' feature with tepid results.

47 Along the Great Divide. Warner Brothers, 1951. 88 minutes B/W. D: Raoul Walsh. SC: Walter Doniger & Lewis Meltzer. WITH Kirk Douglas, Virginia Mayo, John Agar, Walter Brennan, Ray Teal, Hugh Sanders, Morris Ankrum, James Anderson, Charles Meredith, Lane Chandler, Kenneth MacDonald, Steve Clark, Carl Harbaugh, Zon Murray, Sam Ash, Steve Darrell, Al Ferguson, Guy Wilkerson. A sheriff who feels responsible for his father's death sets out to bring a prisoner back to stand trial and along the way faces opposition from the man's daughter as well as a posse who wants to kill the prisoner. Nicely done film, full of suspense and well acted, especially by Virginia Mayo as the prisoner's pretty daughter.

48 Along the Mohawk Trail. International Television Corporation (ITC), 1964. 89 minutes B/W. D: Sam Newfield, WITH John Hart, Lon Chaney, Bill Walsh, Stan Francis. A frontiersman and his Indian friend try to help the people of a small community to stop a man who has set himself up as dictator. Paste-up of three episodes of the Canadian-filmed syndicated television series "Hawkeye and the Last of the Mohicans" (1957) which was issued directly to TV.

49 Along the Navajo Trail. Republic, 1945, 54 (66) minutes B/W. D: Frank McDonald. SC: Gerald Geraghty. WITH Roy Rogers, George "Gabby" Hayes, Dale Evans, Estelia Rodriguez, Douglas Fowley, Nestor Paiva, Emmett Vogan, Roy Barcroft, Sam Flint, Bob Nolan & The Sons of the Pioneers, David Cota, Ed Cassidy, Tex Terry, Budd Buster. Cowboy Roy Rogers aids pioneers and gypsies against land grabbers. Dull doing except for the exciting climax.

50 Along the Oregon Trail. Republic, 1947. 64 minutes Color. D: R. G. Springsteen. SC: Earle Snell. WITH Monte Hale, Adrian Booth, Max Terhune, Clayton Moore, Roy Barcroft, Foy Willing & The Riders of the Purple Sage, Will Wright, LeRoy Mason, Tom London, Forrest Taylor, Kermit Maynard, Wade Crosby. A cowboy finds himself at odds with a madman who wants to build an empire for himself in the West. Average Monte Hale outing helped by color and sidekick Max Terhune.

51 Along the Rio Grande. RKO Radio, 1941. 61 minutes B/W. D: Edward Killy. SC: Arthur V. Jones & Morton Grant. WITH Tim Holt, Ray Whitley, Emmett Lynn, Robert Fiske, Betty Jane Rhodes, Hal Taliaferro, Carl Stockdale, Slim Whitaker, Monte Montague, Ruth Clifford, Ernie Adams. In order to avenge the murder of their ex-boss, three men assume the guise of outlaws and go into Mexico and join the gang responsible for the killing. Typically good Tim Holt star vehicle with Ray Whitley making his first appearance in the role of Smokey.

52 Along the Sundown Trail. Producers Releasing Corporation, 1942. 59 minutes B/W. D: Peter Stewart (Sam Newfield). SC: Arthur St. Clair. WITH Bill Boyd, Art Davis, Lee Powell, Julie Duncan, Charles King, Karl Hackett, Howard Masters, John Merton, Jack Ingram, Kermit Maynard, Herman Hack, Frank Ellis, Ted Adams, Al St. John, Reed Howes, Art Dillard, Tex Palmer, Curley Dresden, Steve Clark, Hal Price, Jimmie Aubrey. A trio of lawmen are on the trail of outlaws who are trying to rob a tungsten mine. Typical low grade entry in PRC's "Frontier Marshal" series. V: Video Connection, Cassette Express.

53 Alvarez Kelly. Columbia, 1966. 116 minutes Color. D: Edward Dmytryk. SC: Franklin Coen & Elliott Arnold. WITH William Holden, Richard Widmark, Janice Rule, Patrick O'Neal, Victoria Shaw, Roger C. Carmel. Richard Rust, Arthur Franz, Donald (Don "Red") Barry, Harry Carey Jr., Mauritz Hugo, Robert Morgan, Stephanie Hill, Paul Lukather, Clint Ritchie. An adventurer leads a herd of cattle East to sell to the Union army during the Civil War but he is kidnapped by Confederates who want the herd for their army. Fairly entertaining Western which could have been better. V: Columbia Pictures Home Entertainment.

54 Ambush. Metro-Goldwyn-Mayer, 1949. 89 minutes B/W. D: Sam Wood. SC: Marguerite Roberts. WITH Robert Taylor, John Hodiak, Arlene Dahl, Don Taylor, Jean Hagen, Bruce Cowling, Leon Ames, John McIntire, Pat Moriarity, Charles Stevens, Chief Thundercloud, Ray Teal, Robin Short, Richard Bailey. A scout finds himself at odds with a cavalry captain when he is assigned to bring back a girl captured by renegade Indians. The MGM gloss somewhat helps this average "A" budget outing.

55 Ambush at Cimarron Pass. 20th Century-Fox, 1958. 70 minutes B/W. D: Jodie Copelan. SC: Richard G. Taylor & John K. Butler. WITH Scott Brady, Margia Dean, Clint Eastwood, Irving Bacon, Frank Gerstle, Dirk London, Baynes Barron, Keith Richards, John Merrick. A rancher, once a Confederate, teams up with a group of soldiers in order to thwart an Indian attack. Arid feature mainly of interest in that it provided Clint Eastwood with his first major film role in a Western.

56 Ambush at Tomahawk Gap. Columbia, 1953. 73 minutes Color. D: Fred Sears. SC: David Lang. WITH John Hodiak, David Brian, Maria Elena Marques, John Derrell, Ray Teal, John Qualen, Otto Hullett, Percy Helton, Trevor Bardette, John Doucette. Four convicts escape from jail to prove their innocence and become involved in an Indian attack. Well done and suspenseful.

57 Ambush Trail. Producers Releasing Corporation, 1946. 59 minutes B/W. D: Harry Fraser. SC: Elmer Clifton. WITH Bob Steele, Syd Saylor, Lorraine Miller, I. Stanford Jolley, Charles King, Bob Cason, Budd Buster, Kermit Maynard, Frank Ellis, Ed Cassidy. A rancher comes to the aid of his friends as they oppose a desperado who is after their lands. Cheaply made PRC oater that is saved by star Bob Steele. V: Video Connection.

58 Ambush Valley. Reliable, 1936. 57 minutes B/W. D: Raymond Samuels (Bernard B. Ray). SC: Bennett Cohen. WITH Bob Custer, Victoria Vinton, Vane Calvert, Eddie Phillips, Wally Wales, Oscar Gahan, Ed Cassidy, Denver Dixon, Wally West, Roger Williams, John Elliott. A lawman finds himself opposing the views of his future father-in-law who threatens to kill nestors who settle on his land. Low grade Bob Custer outing.

59 American Empire. United Artists, 1942. 82 minutes B/W. D: William McGann. SC: J. Robert Bren, Gladys Atwater & Ben Grauman Kohn. WITH Richard Dix, Preston Foster, Frances Gifford, Leo Carrillo, Guinn Williams, Robert Barrat, Jack LaRue, Cliff Edwards, Chris-Pin Martin, Richard Webb, William Farnum, Hal Taliaferro, Tom London, Guy Rodin. Two partners build a cattle empire in Texas despite personal problems between them over a girl and their battles with a Mexican bandit leader. Highly entertaining and well made film with especially good work by Richard Dix, Preston Foster and Leo Carrillo, the latter as the bandit leader. V: Cassette Express.

60 The Americano. RKO Radio, 1955. 85 minutes B/W. D: William Castle. SC: Guy Trosper. WITH Glenn Ford, Frank Lovejoy, Cesar Romero, Ursula Theiss, Abbe Lane, Rodolfo Hoyos, Tom Powers, Dan White, Frank Marlowe. A Texas cowboy is sent to Brazil to deliver prize Brahma bulls and there runs into outlaws as well as a pretty girl. Typical mid-1950s theatrical oater set in Brazil instead of the Old West.

61 Among Vultures. Rialto-Film/Jadran-Film/Atlantis-Film, 1964. 98 minutes Color. D: Alfred Vohrer. SC: Eberhard Keindorff & Johanna Sibelius. WITH Stewart Granger, Pierre Brice, Elke Sommer, Gotz George, Walter Barnes, Mario Girotti, Renato Baldini, Sieghardt Rupp, Louis Velle, Mila Blach. Frontier scout Old Surehand and his Indian friend Winnetou lead a wagon train carrying the daughter of a diamond dealer and the girl is kidnapped by outlaws masquerading as Indians. Flavorful screen adaptation of Karl May's novel with Stewart Granger very good as Old Surehand. Made in West Germany as **Unter Geirn** (Among Vultures) and issued in the United States in 1966 by Columbia as **Frontier Hellcat.**

62 And Now Miguel. Universal, 1966. 95 minutes Color. D: James B. Clark. SC: Ted Sherdeman & Jane Klove. WITH Pat Cardi, Guy Stockwell, Clu Gulagher, Michael Ansara, Joe De Santis, Pilar Del Rey, Peter Robbins, Buck Taylor, James Hall, Emma Tyson. A young boy longs to go with his father into the mountains for the summer grazing of their sheep herd but it takes an artist to teach him the meaning of patience in growing up. Nicely done period piece set in the Southwest.

63 Angel and the Badman. Republic, 1947. 100 minutes B/W. D-SC: James Edward Grant. WITH John Wayne, Gail Russell, Harry Carey, Bruce Cabot, Irene Rich, Lee Dixon, Stephen Grant, Tom Powers, Paul Hurst, Olin Howlin, John Halloran, Joan Barton, Craig Woods, Marshall Reed, Hank Worden, Pat Flaherty. An outlaw on the run is reformed by the love of a devout Quaker girl. Fine John Wayne star vehicle; the type of fare that Harry Carey and Bill Hart did in the silent era. V: Capital Home Video, Video Dimensions, Cumberland Video.

64 The Animals. Levitt-Pickman, 1971. 86 minutes Color. D: Ron Joy. SG: Hy Mizrahi. WITH Henry Silva, Keenan Wynn, Michele Carey, John Anderson, Joseph Turkel, Pepper Martin, Bobby Hall, Peter Hellmann, William Bryant, Peggy Stewart. A young school teacher is raped by five thugs after they hold up the stagecoach she is riding and the girl vows revenge against the men. Brutal oater which had limited theatrical release. British title: **Five Savage Men.**

65 Annie Get Your Gun. Metro-Goldwyn-Mayer, 1950. 107 minutes Color. D: George Sidney. SC: Sidney Shelton. WITH Betty Hutton, Howard Keel, Louis Calhern,

J. Carrol Naish, Edward Arnold, Keenan Wynn, Benay Venuta, Clinton Sunderberg, James H. Harrison, Chief Yowlachie, Lee Tung Foo, William Tannen, Anne O'Neal, John Hamilton, Edward Earle, Marjorie Wood, Frank Wilcox, John Mylong, Carl Sepulveda, Carol Henry, Fred Gilman. Annie Oakley rises from backwoods target practice to the top sharpshooter with Buffalo Bill Cody's Wild West Show as she tries to win the man of her dreams. Lively screen adaptation of the Irving Berlin musical which starred Ethel Merman and Ray Middleton on Broadway.

66 Annie Oakley. RKO Radio, 1935. 90 minutes B/W. D: George Stevens. SC: Joel Sayre & John Twist. WITH Barbara Stanwyck, Preston Foster, Melvyn Douglas, Pert Kelton, Moroni Olsen, Andy Clyde, Chief Thundercloud, Delmar Watson. The story of a tomboy crack sharpshooter who falls in love with the world's top marksman and then becomes the featured attraction of Buffalo Bill Cody's Wild West Show. Highly fictional account of the life of Annie Oakley, but still pleasant entertainment. V: Nostalgia Merchant.

67 Another Man, Another Chance. United Artists, 1977. 132 minutes Color. D: Claude Lelouch. SC: Jacques Lefrancois (Claude Lelouch). WITH James Caan, Genevieve Bujold, Francie Huster, Jennifer Warren, Susan Tyrrell, Rossie Harris. A young woman comes to the West in 1880 with a photographer who dies suddenly and she meets and marries a widowed veterinarian. Well acted and visually interesting retelling of director Claude Lelouch's **A Man and a Woman** (Allied Artists, 1966), this time set in the Old West. Made in France as **Un Autre Homme, Une Autre Chance.** Alternate title: **Another Man, Another Woman.**

Another Man, Another Woman see **Another Man, Another Chance**

68 Any Gun Can Play. Golden Eagle, 1968. 105 minutes Color. D: Enzo G. Castellari. SC: Enzo G. Castellari, Romolo Guerrieri, George Simmonelli & Fabio Carpi. WITH George Hilton, Edd Byrnes, Gilbert Roland, Kareen O'Hara, Pedro Sanchez, Gerard Herter. Three men, a bandit, a stranger and a banker, all join forces so they can divide a fortune in stolen gold. Better than average Italian Western made so by the strong macho performance of Gilbert Roland as one

of the lead players. Released in Italy in 1967 as **Vado...l'Ammazo e Torno** (I'll Go...I'll Kill Him, and Come Back) by Fida Cinematografica.

69 Apache. United Artists, 1954. 91 minutes Color. D: Robert Aldrich. SC: James R. Webb. WITH Burt Lancaster, Jean Peters, John McIntire, Charles (Bronson) Buchinsky, John Dehner, Paul Guifoyle, Ian MacDonald, Walter Sande, Morris Ankrum, Monte Blue. A peaceful Indian gives up his pacifist ways to combat the U. S. Cavalry when the rights of his people are threatened. Not a very remarkable film with supporting players Charles Bronson and Monte Blue more impressive than star Burt Lancaster. VD: Blackhawk.

70 Apache Ambush. Columbia, 1955. 68 minutes B/W. D: Fred F. Sears. SC: David Lang. WITH Bill Williams, Richard Jaeckel, Alex Montoya, Movita, Adele August, Tex Ritter, Ray Corrigan, Ray Teal, Don C. Harvey, James Griffith, James Flavin, George Chandler, Forrest Lewis, George Keymas, Victor Millan, Harry Lauter, Bill Hale, Robert Foulk. While leading a cattle drive to Texas after the Civil War, an ex-Union soldier is faced with trouble from marauding Indians and renegade Confederates. Average outing of interest because of Tex Ritter and Ray Corrigan in supporting roles.

71 Apache Chief. Lippert, 1949. 60 minutes B/W. D: Frank McDonald. SC: Gerald Green & Leonard Picker. WITH Alan Curtis, Tom Neal, Russell Hayden, Carol Thurston, Fuzzy Knight, Francis McDonald, Trevor Bardette, Roy Gordon, Charles Soldani. Two Indian brothers, one peaceful and one warlike, oppose each other to see who will lead their tribe. Low budget Lippert outing of interest because of its three stars.

72 Apache Drums. Universal, 1951. 75 minutes Color. D: Hugh Fregonese. SC: David Chandler. WITH Stephen McNally, Coleen Gray, Willard Parker, Arthur Shields, James Griffith, Armando Silvestre, Georgia Backus, Clarence Muse, James Best, Ray Bennett. After being run out of a small town by a corrupt official, a gambler returns there to help the people fight off an Indian attack. Despite budget trappings, this outing is not of much interest.

Apache Fury see Fury of the Apaches

73 Apache Gold. Columbia, 1963. 91 (111) minutes Color. D: Harald Reinl. SC: Harald G. Petersson. WITH Lex Barker, Pierre Brice, Mario Adorf, Marie Versini, Ralf Walter, Walter Barnes, Mavid Popovic, Dunja Rajter, Chris Howland. A frontiersman and his Indian friend try to protect Indians from marauding whites who are after their gold. Actionful outing in the Karl May series from West Germany, based on the author's 1893 novel Winnetou, Der Rote Gentleman. Alternate title: **Winnetou the Warrior.** West German title: **Winnetou I.**

74 The Apache Kid. Republic, 1941. 56 minutes B/W. D: George Sherman. SC: Eliot Gibbons & Richard Murphy. WITH Don "Red" Barry, Lynn Merrick, LeRoy Mason, Robert Fiske, John Elliott, Forbes Murray, Monte Montague, Al St. John, Fred "Snowflake" Toones, Charles King, Frank Brownlee, John Cason, Cactus Mack, Kenne Duncan, Hal Price, Buddy Roosevelt. A young adventurer leads a wagon train of friends and neighbors westward to Oregon but finds out that the trip was instigated by his crooked uncle, who has a government contract to build a road. Nicely done Don Barry star vehicle with pretty Lynn Merrick adding to the entertainment.

75 The Apache Kid's Escape. Horner Productions, 1930. 50 minutes B/W. D: Robert J. Horner. WITH Jack Perrin, Josephine Hill, Fred Church, Virginia Ashcroft, Henry Rocquemore, Bud Osborne. An outlaw masquerades as a cowpoke and helps a friend who is in trouble, even giving up the girl he loves. Tattered early talkie mainly of curio value.

Apache Massacre see Face to the Wind

76 Apache Rifles. 20th Century-Fox, 1964. 92 minutes Color. D: William Witney. SC: Kenneth Gamet & Richard Schayer. WITH Audie Murphy, Michael Dante, Linda Lawson, L. Q. Jones, Ken Lynch, John Archer, Charles Watts, Hugh Sanders. A Cavalry captain in Arizona in 1879 is sent out to capture marauding Indians who have been slaughtering miners and settlers. Actionful Audie Murphy vehicle somewhat hurt by stock footage and mediocre plot.

77 Apache Rose. Republic, 1947. 54 (75) minutes Color. D: William Witney.

SC: Gerald Geraghty. WITH Roy Rogers, Dale Evans, Bob Nolan & The Sons of the Pioneers, Olin Howlin, George Meeker, Russ Vincent, Minerva Urecal, LeRoy Mason, Terry Frost, Tex Terry, John Laurenz. Oil wildcatter Roy Rogers discovers rich oil deposits on a Mexican ranch but the owner is heavily in debt to a man who tries to kill the owner's cousin, who owns half-interest in the land. Average Roy Rogers entry enhanced by Trucolor.

78 Apache Territory. Columbia, 1958. 75 minutes B/W. D: Ray Nazarro. SC: Charles R. Marion & George W. George. WITH Rory Calhoun, Barbara Bates, John Dehner, Carolyn Craig, Leo Gordon, Myron Healey, Frank De Kova, Reg Parton, Bob Woodward, Thomas Pittman. While crossing the desert, a drifter comes across a girl who is the sole survivor of a wagon train attack and he joins her in fighting attacking Indians. Average but fairly interesting Rory Calhoun vehicle.

79 Apache Trail. Metro-Goldwyn-Mayer, 1943. 66 minutes B/W. D: Richard Thorpe. SC: Maurice Geraghty. WITH Lloyd Nolan, Donna Reed, William Lundigan, Ann Ayars, Connie Gilchrist, Chill Wills, Miles Mander, Gloria Holden, Ray Teal, Grant Withers, Fuzzy Knight, Trevor Bardette, Frank M. Thomas, George Watts. After their ceremonial grounds are desecrated by whites, Indians go on the warpath and innocent settlers face the consequences. Curio M-G-M oater from the World War II era with a fine cast and fast direction.

80 Apache Uprising. 20th Century-Fox/ CBS-TV, 1956. 45 minutes B/W. WITH Richardo Montalban, John Lupton, Rita Moreno, John Conte. A scout is assigned to convince an Apache chief to stop his attacks on the U. S. mail carriers. Originally an episode of "The 20th Century-Fox Hour" on CBS-TV, this interesting telefeature was based on the movie **Broken Arrow** (q.v.) and served as the pilot for the "Broken Arrow" (ABC-TV, 1956-60) television series.

81 Apache Uprising. Paramount, 1966. 90 minutes Color. D: R. G. Springsteen. SC: Harry Sanford. WITH Rory Calhoun, Corinne Calvet, John Russell, Lon Chaney, Gene Evans, Richard Arlen, Robert H. Harris, Arthur Hunnicutt, DeForrest Kelley, George Chandler, Johnny Mack Brown, Jean Parker, Abel Fernandez,

Don "Red" Barry. A diverse group of stage passengers head for a way station where a robbery is set to occur as Indians near for an attack. Better-than-average A. C. Lyles Western with a good cast, highlighted by Lon Chaney as the happy-go-lucky stage driver.

82 Apache War Smoke. Metro-Goldwyn-Mayer, 1952. 67 minutes B/W. D: Harold Kress. SC: Jerry Davis. WITH Gilbert Roland, Glenda Farrell, Robert Horton, Barbara Ruick, Gene Lockhart, Henry (Harry) Morgan, Patricia Tierani, Hank Worden, Myron Healey, Emmett Lynn, Argentia Brunetti, Bobby Blake, Douglass Dumbrille. Bandits head for a way station after robbing a stagecoach only to find the station is about to be attacked by Indians. Well done MGM Western with a strong performance by Gilbert Roland in a good-badman role.

83 Apache Warrior. 20th Century-Fox, 1957. 73 minutes B/W. D: Elmo Williams. SC: Kurt Keumann & Eric Norden. WITH Keith Larsen, Jim Davis, Rodolfo Acosta, John Miljan, Eddie Little Sky, Michael Carr, George Keymas, Lane Bradford, Eugenia Paul, Damian O'Flynn, Ray Kellogg, Allan Nixon, Karl Davis, Boyd Stockman. An Indian scout for the Army turns renegade when his brother is killed and his former white brother is forced to hunt him down. Fairly interesting outing with good performances by Keith Larsen as the renegade, Jim Davis as the hunter and Rodolfo Acosta as the Indian really responsible for the trouble.

84 Apache Woman. American Releasing Corporation, 1955. 83 minutes B/W. D: Roger Corman. SC: Lou Rusoff. WITH Lloyd Bridges, Joan Taylor, Lance Fuller, Morgan Jones, Paul Birch, Paul Dubov, Jonathan Hale, Dick Miller, Chester Conklin. A government agent investigates several mysterious deaths blamed on Indians on a reservation. Roger Corman's second Western is a low grade affair but moves well and should satisfy his followers.

Apache's Last Battle see **Old Shatterhand**

85 The Appaloosa. Universal, 1966. 98 minutes Color. D: Sidney J. Furie, SC: James Bridges & Roland Kibbee. WITH Marlon Brando, Anjanette Comer, John Saxon, Emilio Fernandez, Alex Montoya, Miriam Colon, Rafael Campos, Frank Silvera, Argentia Brunetti, Larry Mann.

A prize horse is stolen from a cowboy and he heads into the Mexican wilderness at the turn of the century to retrieve it. Slow moving and not very interesting Marlon Brando vehicle highlighted by good photography.

86 The Apple Dumpling Gang. Buena Vista, 1975. 100 minutes Color. D: Norman Tokar. SC: Don Tait. WITH Bill Bixby, Susan Clark, Don Knotts, Tim Conway, David Payne, Slim Pickens, Harry Morgan, Clay O'Brien, Brad Savage, Irish Adrian. A gambler becomes the guardian of three homeless children and he tries to get rich by pulling off a fantastic bank robbery. Well-done Walt Disney comedy-western highlighted by the antics of Don Knotts and Tim Conway.

87 The Apple Dumpling Gang Rides Again. Buena Vista, 1979. 89 minutes Color. D: Bernard McEveety. SC: Don Talt. WITH Tim Conway, Don Knotts, Tim Matheson, Kenneth Mars, Elyssa Davalos, Jack Elam, Robert Pine, Harry Morgan, Ruth Buzzi, Audrey Totter, Richard X. Slattery, John Crawford, Cliff Osmond, Ted Gehring. Two bumblers are hunted throughout the West as outlaws. Mediocre sequel to **The Apple Dumpling Gang** (q.v.). V: Disney Home Video.

88 Arctic Flight. Monogram, 1952, 78 minutes B/W. D: Lew Landers. WITH Wayne Morris, Lola Albright, Alan Hale Jr., Carol Thurston, Phil Tead, Tom Richards, Anthony Carson, Kenneth MacDonald, Paul Bryar, Dale Van Sickel. An Alaskan bush pilot is hired by a big-game hunter to fly him to an area to supposedly hunt polar bears but actually the man is a Soviet spy. Well done little action melodrama with good location footage.

89 Arctic Fury. RKO Radio, 1949. 61 minutes B/W. D-SC: Norman Dawn. WITH Del Cambre, Eve Miller, Gloria Petroff, Merrill McCormack, Fred Smith. A plane carrying a doctor to a plague-ridden village crashes in the Arctic and the doctor fights the elements to survive. Slapped together programmer also called **Tundra.**

90 Arctic Manhunt. Universal-International, 1949. 69 minutes B/W. D: Ewing Scott. SC: Oscar Brodney & Joel Malone. WITH Mikel Conrad, Carol Thurston, Wally Cassell, Helen Brown, Harry Harvey, Chet Huntley, Paul E. Burns, Quianna.

Insurance agents are on the trail of an ex-convict who has fled to Alaska with money taken from a robbery. Low budget actioner based on director Ewing Scott's book Narana of the North.

91 Arena. Metro-Goldwyn-Mayer, 1953. 83 minutes Color. D: Richard Fleischer. SC: Harold Jack Bloom. WITH Gig Young, Jean Hagen, Polly Bergen, Henry (Harry) Morgan, Barbara Lawrence, Robert Horton, Lee Aaker, Lee Van Cleef, Marilee Phelps, Jim Hayward, George Wallace, Stuart Randall, Morris Ankrum. A rodeo star lets success go to his head and this causes the near-failure of his marriage. Mediocre modern-day oater highlighted by rodeo footage from the annual Fiesta de los Vaqueros in Tucson, Arizona.

92 Arizona. Columbia, 1940. 127 minutes B/W. D: Wesley Ruggles. SC: Claude Binyon. WITH Jean Arthur, William Holden, Warren William, Regis Toomey, Paul Harvey, George Chandler, Byron Foulger, Porter Hall, Colin Tapley, Edgar Buchanan, Griff Barnett, Paul Lopez, Frank Darien, Syd Saylor, Addison Richards, Carleton Young. A young Arizona girl, with the aid of a young man from Missouri, sets out to battle corrupt elements in running a successful freight business and setting up a large cattle ranch. Entertaining "A" budget oater that is much too long, with a nice villainous portrayal by Warren William.

93 Arizona Bound. Monogram, 1941. 57 minutes B/W. D: Spencer Gordon Bennet. SC: Jess Bowers (Adele Buffington). WITH Buck Jones, Tim McCoy, Raymond Hatton, Luana Walters, Dennis Moore, Tristram Coffin, Kathryn Sheldon, Gene Alsace, Slim Whitaker, Artie Ortego, I. Stanford Jolley, Horace Murphy, Hal Price, Jack Daley. Three retired U.S. marshals on special assignment each take on different guises as they come into a small town to find out who is the leader of a gang of stagecoach robbers. The first of eight films in the "Rough Riders" series and a good kickoff for the popular teaming of Buck Jones, Tim McCoy and Raymond Hatton. V: Video Connection, Discount Video.

94 Arizona Bushwackers. Paramount, 1968. 86 minutes Color. D: Lesley Selander. SC: Steve Fisher. WITH Howard Keel, Yvonne De Carlo, John Ireland, Marilyn Maxwell, Scott Brady, Brian Donlevy, Barton MacLane, James Craig, Reg Parton,

Monte Montana, Eric Cody, Roy Rogers Jr. During the Civil War, a Confederate officer becomes the sheriff of a small Arizona town and uncovers a gun runner who has been dealing with the local Indians. Well-done A. C. Lyles Western highlighted by the usual veteran cast with narration by James Cagney.

Arizona Colt see **The Man From Nowhere**

95 The Arizona Cowboy. Republic, 1950. 57 minutes. D: R. G. Springsteen. SC: Bradford Ropes. WITH Rex Allen, Teala Loring, Gordon Jones, Minerva Urecal, James Cardwell, Roy Barcroft, Stanley Andrews, Harry Cheshire, Edmund Cobb, Joseph Crehan, Steve Darrell, Douglas Evans, John Elliott, Chris-Pin Martin, Frank Reicher, George Lloyd, Lane Bradford. After service in World War II, a cowboy becomes the top attraction in a rodeo but bad guys falsely accuse him of being involved in a robbery. Rex Allen's starring debut in this film is a good one and he became known by the monicker of the film's title. V: Cumberland Video.

96 Arizona Cyclone. Universal, 1941. 57 minutes B/W. D: Ray Taylor. SC: Sherman Lowe. WITH Johnny Mack Brown, Fuzzy Knight, Nell O'Day, Kathryn Adams, Herbert Rawlinson, Dick Curtis, Buck Moulton, Glenn Strange, Jack Clifford, Kermit Maynard, Frank Ellis, Carl Sepulveda, Chuck Morrison, Robert Strange, The Notables. The driver for a freight line tries to find out who murdered his boss over a telegraph hauling contract. Well done Johnny Mack Brown entry shackled by a trio of mediocre songs.

97 Arizona Days. Syndicate, 1928. 50 minutes B/W. D: J. P. McGowan. SC: Mack V. Wright. WITH Bob Custer, Peggy Montgomery, J. P. McGowan, John Lowell Russell, Mack V. Wright, Jack Ponder. A cowboy working for the cattlemen's association pretends to be an outlaw in order to join a rustling gang and finds a local rancher doing the same thing. Fairly actionful Bob Custer silent vehicle.

98 Arizona Days. Grand National, 1937. 56 minutes B/W. D: John English. SC: Lindsley Parsons. WITH Tex Ritter, Eleanor Stewart, Syd Saylor, Snub Pollard, Ed Cassidy, William Faversham, Forrest Taylor, Glenn Strange, Horace Murphy, Earl Dwire, Budd Buster, Salty Holmes, William Desmond, Tex Palmer. A drifter joins a traveling minstrel show which is burned by outlaws and the man becomes a tax collector in order to replace the show's equipment and has a showdown with the man responsible for the fire. Entertaining Tex Ritter outing. V: Video Communications.

99 Arizona Frontier. Monogram, 1940. 55 minutes B/W. D: Al Herman. SC: Robert Emmett (Tansey). WITH Tex Ritter, Arkansas Slim Andrews, Evelyn Finley, Frank LaRue, Tristram Coffin, Gene Alsace, Richard Cramer, James Pierce, Jim Thorpe, Hal Price, Sherry Tansey, Chick Hannon, Art Wilcox & His Arizona Rangers. A government agent is sent to investigate a series of Indian raids and becomes convinced that the commander of the local army post is actually behind the lawlessness. Filmed in Arizona, this Tex Ritter star vehicle is a pretty good one with Tex singing a couple of songs, including "Red River Valley."

100 Arizona Gang Busters. Producers Releasing Corporation, 1940. 57 minutes B/W. D: Peter Stewart (Sam Newfield). SC: Joseph O'Donnell & William Lively. WITH Tim McCoy, Pauline Haddon, Lou Fulton, Ted Adams, Forrest Taylor, Otto Reichow, Julian Rivero, Arno Frey, Kenne Duncan, Carl Mathews, Ben Corbett, Frank Ellis, Curley Dresden. A cowboy in Arizona uncovers a Nazi fifth column group and he sets out to destroy them. Nicely entertaining Tim McCoy vehicle, given its poverty row origins.

101 Arizona Gunfighter. Republic, 1937. 58 minutes B/W. D: Sam Newfield. SC: George Plympton. WITH Bob Steele, Jean Carmen, Ted Adams, Ernie Adams, Lew Meehan, Steve Clark, John Merton, Karl Hackett, Frank Ball, Sherry Tansey, Jack Kirk, Hal Price, Budd Buster, Horace Carpenter, Tex Palmer, Allen Greer, Oscar Gagan. A cowboy sets out to find the man who murdered his father. Entertaining and well-done series oater with the usual Bob Steele plot motif.

102 The Arizona Kid. Davis Distributing, 1928. 50 minutes B/W. D-SC: Horace B. Carpenter. WITH Art Acord, Carol Lane, Cliff Lyons, Lynn Sanderson, Bill Conant, George Hollister, Horace B. Carpenter, James Tromp, Al Hoxie, Star (horse), Rex (dog). A U. S. marshal pretends to be a foppish bandit in order to round up a gang who has robbed an

express shipment and taken its guard and his daughter hostage. Fast paced but low grade Art Acord vehicle, one of his last and hardly one of his best. Retitled: **Pursued.**

103 The Arizona Kid. Fox, 1930. 90 minutes B/W. D: Alfred Santell. SC: Ralph Block. WITH Warner Baxter, Mona Maris, Carol(e) Lombard, Theodore Von Eltz, Arthur Stone, Solidad Jiminez, Walter P. Lewis, Jack Herrick, Wilfred Lucas, Hank Mann, James Gibson, Larry McGrath, De Sacia Mooers. Posing as a romantic Mexican miner, a bandit carries out his illegal activities while romancing many girls until he falls for an Eastern girl who is actually married. Slow moving early talkie in which Warner Baxter carries on his Cisco Kid-like tradition.

104 The Arizona Kid. Republic, 1939. 54 (61) minutes B/W. D: Joseph Kane. SC: Luci Ward & Gerald Geraghty. WITH Roy Rogers, George "Gabby" Hayes, Dorothy Sebastian, Stuart Hamblen, Sally March, David Kerwin, Earl Dwire, Peter Fargo, Fred Burns, Ed Cassidy, Jack Ingram, Ted Mapes, Frank McCarroll. During the Civil War Roy and Gabby fight for the South and oppose a guerilla leader who is allied with Roy's pal. Good action sequences and minor songs in this well-done film with an effective performance by Stuart Hamblen as a pseudo-Quantrill.

105 The Arizona Legion. RKO Radio, 1939. 58 minutes B/W. D: David Howard. SC: Oliver Drake. WITH George O'Brien, Lorraine Johnson (Laraine Day), Chill Wills, Carlyle Moore Jr., Edward Le Saint, Harry Cording, Tom Chatterton, William Royle, Glenn Strange, Monte Montague, Bob Burns, John Dilson, Lafe McKee, Guy Usher, Robert Kortman, Wilfred Lucas, Jim Mason, Art Mix. An undercover agent, at a cavalry post commanded by a former friend who no longer trusts him, is assigned to expose a corrupt official. Highly competent and entertaining George O'Brien opus.

106 Arizona Mahoney. Paramount, 1936. 61 minutes B/W. D: James Hogan. SC: Robert Yost & Stuart Anthony. WITH Joe Cook, Robert Cummings, June Martel, Larry "Buster" Crabbe, Marjorie Gateson, Fred Kohler, John Miljan, Dave Chasen, Irving Bacon, Richard Carle, Billy Lee, Fuzzy Knight, Si Jenks. An Eastern tenderfoot is falsely accused of being an outlaw but the true crook proves his innocence. Standard "B" outing from Zane Grey's Stairs of Sand which was first filmed under that title in 1929 by Paramount with Wallace Beery, Jean Arthur, Phillips Holmes and Fred Kohler. Reissue title: **Arizona Thunderbolt.**

107 Arizona Manhunt. Republic, 1951. 60 minutes B/W. D: Fred C. Brannon. SC: William Lively. WITH Michael Chapin, Eilene Janssen, James Bell, Lucille Barkley, Roy Barcroft, John Baer, Harry Harvey, Stuart Randall, Ted Cooper. A group of youngsters aid an old sheriff and his deputy in defeating a gang of outlaws. Mediocre entry in the "Rough Ridin' Kids" series not helped much by the Republic sheen.

Arizona Mission see **Gun the Man Down**

108 Arizona Raiders. Paramount, 1936. 54 minutes B/W. D: James Hogan. SC: Robert Yost & John Drafft. WITH Larry "Buster" Crabbe, Marsha Hunt, Raymond Hatton, Jane Rhodes, Grant Withers, Johnny Downs, Don Rowan, Arthur Aylesworth, Richard Carle, Herbert Heywood, Petra Silva. A gunman comes to the aid of settlers who are being terrorized by a gang of outlaws in early Arizona. Fair "B" actioner based on Zane Grey's Raiders of Spanish Peaks. Reissued as **Bad Men of Arizona.** V: Video Communications, Discount Video.

109 Arizona Raiders. Columbia, 1965. 88 minutes B/W. D: William Witney. SC: Alex Gottlieb, Mary Willingham & Willard Willingham. WITH Audie Murphy, Michael Dante, Ben Cooper, Buster Crabbe, Gloria Talbott, Ray Stricklyn, Red Morgan, George Keymas, Willard Willingham, Fred Graham. After the Civil War a former member of Quantrill's Raiders joins the newly formed Arizona Rangers in hunting down his former gang members who have been raiding the settlements in the area. Better-than-average Audie Murphy vehicle not hurt by William Witney's direction or a good supporting cast.

110 The Arizona Ranger. RKO Radio, 1948. 63 minutes B/W. D: John Rawlins. SC: Norman Houston. WITH Tim Holt, Jack Holt, Nan Leslie, Richard Martin, Steve Brodie, Paul Hurst, Robert Bray, Jim Nolan, Richard Benedict, William Phipps, Harry Harvey. Two new rangers join forces with an old-time lawman in defeating a gang of outlaws. Typically

good Tim Holt outing enhanced by the casting of Jack Holt as the veteran ranger.

111 Arizona Roundup. Monogram, 1942. 56 minutes B/W. D: Robert Emmett Tansey. SC: Robert Emmett (Tansey) & Frances Kavanaugh. WITH Tom Keene, Hope Blackwood, Frank Yaconelli, Sugar Dawn, Jack Ingram, Steve Clark, Nick Moro, Tom Seidel, Hal Price, I. Stanford Jolley, Ed Cassidy, Tex Palmer, Gene Alsace, Fred Hoose, Horace B. Carpenter, James Sheridan. A federal agent goes to work for a rancher selling wild horses to the government and sets out to break up a combine formed by two crooks. Okay Tom Keene star vehicle.

112 Arizona Stagecoach. Monogram, 1942. 58 minutes B/W. D: S. Roy Luby. SC: Arthur Hoerl. WITH Ray Corrigan, John King, Max Terhune, Nell O'Day, Kermit Maynard, Charles King, Carl Mathews, Slim Whitaker, Steve Clark, Frank Ellis, Roy Harris (Riley Hill), Jack Ingram, Stanley Price, Forrest Taylor, Richard Cramer, Eddie Dean. The Ranger Busters try to help a man wrongly accused of murder by hunting for the real killer. Actionful entry in The Ranger Busters series (the last with the original trio of Corrigan, King and Terhune) but one that is hurt by too much stock footage and forced comedy.

113 Arizona Territory. Monogram, 1950. 56 minutes B/W. D: Wallace Fox. SC: Adele Buffington. WITH Whip Wilson, Andy Clyde, Nancy Saunders, Dennis Moore, John Merton, Carl Mathews, Ted Adams, Carol Henry, Bud Osborne, Frank Austin. A lawman is on the trail of counterfeiters who are transferring fake currency to merchants in the East. Average Whip Wilson vehicle.

114 The Arizona Terror. Tiffany, 1931. 64 minutes B/W. D: Phil Rosen. Sc: John Francis (Jack) Natteford. WITH Ken Maynard, Lina Basquette, Hooper Atchley, Nena Quartaro, Michael Visaroff, Murdock MacQuarrie, Charles King, Tom London, Edmund Cobb, Fred Burns, Jack Rockwell, Jim Corey. Falsely accused of murder, a man is saved by a rancher and his daughter and soon becomes aware of a plot to take over the man's land. Nicely done early sound feature, actionful with nice locations and Michael Visaroff is especially good as a good-badman character.

115 Arizona Terror. Republic, 1942, 56 minutes B/W. D: George Sherman. SC: Doris Schroeder & Taylor Cavan. WITH Don "Red" Barry, Lynn Merrick, Al St. John, Reed Hadley, Rex Lease, John Maxwell, Frank Brownlee, Lee Shumway, Tom London, John Merton, Fred "Snowflake" Toones, Curley Dresden, Herman Hack. Two cowboys come to the aid of area ranchers who are being terrorized and heavily taxed by a tyrant who claims the land they have settled belongs to him via a Spanish land grant. The old saw about an ancient land grant is given a fresh airing here and the end result is lots of fast action.

Arizona Thunderbolt see **Arizona Mahoney**

116 Arizona Trail. Universal, 1943. 57 minutes B/W. D: Vernon Keays. SC: William Lively. WITH Tex Ritter, Fuzzy Knight, Dennis Moore, Janet Shaw, Johnny Bond & His Red River Valley Boys, Jack Ingram, Erville Alderson, Joseph Greene, Glenn Strange, Dan White, Art Fowler, Roy Brent, George Gray, William Yip, Ray Jones, Bill Wolfe. A young man returns home to find his dad battling land-grabbers and he joins in the fight. Fairly well done Tex Ritter vehicle.

117 Arizona Whirlwind. Monogram, 1944. 59 minutes B/W. D: Robert Tansey. SC: Frances Kavanaugh. WITH Ken Maynard, Hoot Gibson, Bob Steele, Myrna Dell, Ian Keith, Donald Stewart, Charles King, Karl Hackett, George Chesebro, Dan White, Frank Ellis, Chief Soldani, Charley Murray Jr. A trio of U. S. marshals come to a small town to combat a crooked banker who is behind a diamond smuggling ring. Nicely done entry in "The Trail Blazers" series with lots of action and good humor; Ken Maynard's last film in the series.

118 The Arizona Wildcat. 20th Century-Fox, 1939. 68 minutes B/W. D: Herbert I. Leeds. SC: Barry Trivers & Jerry Cady. WITH Jane Withers, Leo Carrillo, Pauline Moore, Henry Wilcoxon, William Henry, Douglas Fowley, Ethienne Girardot, Harry Woods. After he is falsely accused of a crime, a former bandit is helped by his adopted daughter in exposing a crooked sheriff and an outlaw gang. Another venture out West with Jane Withers and strictly for her fans.

119 The Arizonian. RKO Radio, 1935. 75 minutes B/W. D: Charles Vidor. SC: Dudley Nichols. WITH Richard Dix, Margot Grahame, Preston Foster, Louis Calhern, James Bush, Ray Mayer, Francis Ford, J. Farrell MacDonald, Joseph Sawyer, Edward Van Sloan, Robert Kortman, Ted Oliver, Willie Best, Etta McDaniel, Jim Thorpe, Hank Bell. An honest lawman sets out to protect his brother and girl friend by cleaning up a small town run by a crook. Very entertaining Richard Dix vehicle and one of the best high budget oaters of the 1930s.

120 Arkansas Judge. Republic, 1941. 72 minutes B/W. D: Frank McDonald. SC: Dorrell McGowan & Stuart McGowan. WITH The Weaver Brothers and Elviry, Roy Rogers, Pauline Moore, Spring Byington, Frank M. Thomas, Veda Ann Borg, Monte Blue, Eily Malyon, Loretta Weaver, Minerva Urecal, Harrison Greene, Frank Darien, Russell Hicks, Edwin Stanley. A working woman is accused of a crime actually committed by the daughter of a judge, the man who wrongly accused the woman. Vehicle for the corn comedy and music of The Weaver Brothers and Elviry, with Roy Rogers along for bait; humorous.

121 Arrow in the Dust. Allied Artists, 1954. 80 minutes Color. D: Lesley Selander. SC: Don Martin. WITH Sterling Hayden, Coleen Gray, Keith Larsen, Tom Tully, Lee Van Cleef, Tudor Owen, Jimmy Wakely, John Pickard, Carleton Young. A Cavalry soldier deserts his unit but in his flight he comes across a dying officer and assumes his identity which he later uses when he takes command of a wagon train under siege from Indians. Rather well done action drama nicely helmed by Lesley Selander with Jimmy Wakely singing "The Weary Stranger."

122 Arrowhead. Paramount, 1953. 105 minutes Color. D-SC: Charles Marquis Warren. WITH Charlton Heston, Jack Palance, Katy Jurado, Brian Keith, Mary Sinclair, Milburn Stone, Richard Shannon, Lewis Martin, Frank De Kova, Robert Wilke, Peter Coe, John Pickard, Pat Hogan, Mike Ragan, Chick Hannon, James Burke. In the Southwest a Cavalry officer and the chief of the Tonto Apaches are at odds when the Indians refuse to sign a peace treaty and the officer is ordered to consummate such a signing. Fairly entertaining feature greatly aided by the work of Heston and Palance in the lead roles.

As I Rode Down to Laredo see **Return of the Gunfighter**

123 At Gunpoint. Allied Artists, 1955. 81 minutes Color. D: Alfred Werker. SC: Daniel B. Ullman. WITH Fred MacMurray, Dorothy Malone, Walter Brennan, Tommy Rettig, Skip Homeier, John Qualen, Harry Shannon, Whit Bissell, Irving Bacon, Jack Lambert, Frank Ferguson, James Anderson, John Pickard, Charles Morton, Anabel Shaw, Rick Vallin, Kim Charney, Mimi Gibson, James Griffith, Harry Lauter, Byron Foulger, Keith Richards, Lyle Latell, Barbara Woodell, Gertrude Astor, Harry Strang. A businessman is forced to kill a hold-up man during a robbery and he finds himself deserted by his friends and aided only by his pretty wife when the dead man's killer brother vows revenge against him. Tame take-off of **High Noon** (q.v.) with nice work by a good cast. V: NTA Home Entertainment.

124 The Avenger. Aywon, 1924. 50 minutes B/W. D: Charles R. Seeling. WITH Guinn Williams. A cowboy tries to prove to the girl he loves that her other suitor, a real estate agent, is a crook. Low grade poverty row actioner for fans of Guinn "Big Boy" Williams.

125 The Avenger. Columbia, 1931. 65 minutes B/W. D: Roy William Neill. SC: George Morgan & Jack Townley. WITH Buck Jones, Dorothy Revier, Ed Piel, Otto Hoffman, Sidney Bracey, Edward Hearn, Walter Percival, Paul Fix, Frank Ellis, Al Taylor, Slim Whitaker. Taking on the guise of a Mexican bandit, a man sets out to take revenge on a gang who murdered his family. Buck Jones' sixth sound film is a good one with a nice south of the border setting and the star is quite good in his Mexican disguise. Remade as **Vengeance of the West** (q.v.) in 1942.

126 The Avenger. B.R.C./Estela Films, 1966. 92 minutes Color. D: Ferdinando Baldi. SC: Franco Rossetti & Ferdinando Baldi. WITH Franco Nero, Cole Kitosch, Elisa Montes, Livio Lorenzon, Jose Suarez, Jose Guardiola. Trying to avenge the murder of his father, a man finds out the killer is the father of his younger half-brother. Fair Italian horse opera, a bit on the slow side. Released in Italy as **Texas Addio** (Goodbye Texas).

127 The Avengers. Republic, 1950. 90 minutes B/W. D: John Auer. WITH John Carroll, Adele Mara, Mona Maris, Fernando Lamas, Roberto Airaldi, Jorge Villoldo, Vivian Ray. When settlers are attacked by bandits in South America, the heroic Don Careless rides to their rescue and avenges the murder of his father. Okay South American "Western" based on the novel **Don Careless** by Rex Beach.

128 The Avenging. Comworld Pictures, 1981. 91 minutes Color. D-SC: Lyman Dayton. WITH Michael Horse, Efrem Zimbalist Jr., Matt Stetson, Sherry Hursey, Taylor Lacher, Joseph Running Fox, Cam Clarke, Brenda Venus, Dan August, Dorothy Romero. A well-educated half-breed finds himself the victim of racial persecution and accused of horse stealing. Passable horse opera with good work by Efrem Zimbalist Jr.

129 The Avenging Rider. RKO Radio, 1943. 55 minutes B/W. D: Sam Nelson. SC: Harry O. Hoyt. WITH Tim Holt, Cliff Edwards, Ann Summers, Davison Clark, Norman Willis, Karl Hackett, Earle Hodgins, Ed Cassidy, Kenne Duncan, Bud Osborne, Robert Kortman, Guy Usher, Lloyd Ingraham, David Sharpe. A man sets out to clear himself and his buddy of the murder of his partner in a gold mine operation. Good Tim Holt vehicle with nice sidekick support from Cliff "Ukulele Ike" Edwards.

130 Avenging Waters. Columbia, 1936. 56 minutes B/W. D: Spencer Gordon Bennet. SC: Nate Gatzert. WITH Ken Maynard, Beth Marion, John Elliott, Zella Russell, Ward Bond, Wally Wales, Tom London, Edmund Cobb, Buffalo Bill Jr., Glenn Strange, Edward Hearn, Buck Moulton, Cactus Mack. A cowboy leading a cattle herd to be sold to a rancher runs into a range feud over fencing rights. Pretty good Ken Maynard action entry, slightly marred by some mediocre processing shots involving the climactic flood.

B

131 Back in the Saddle. Republic, 1941. 54 (73) minutes B/W. D: Lew Landers. SC: Richard Murphy & Jesse Lasky Jr. WITH Gene Autry, Smiley Burnette, Mary Lee, Edward Norris, Jacqueline Wells (Julie Bishop), Addison Richards, Arthur Loft, Edmund Cobb, Reed Howes,

Stanley Blystone, Curley Dresden, Fred "Snowflake" Toones, Frank Ellis, Jack O'Shea, Herman Hack, Bob Burns. A cowpoke inherits a ranch and he finds it is rich in copper, causing a local boom, but crooks are soon after his property. Fairly actionful Gene Autry outing with heavy emphasis on songs.

132 Back to God's Country. Canadian Photoplays/First National, 1919. 60 minutes B/W. D: David M. Hartford. SC: James Oliver Curwood. WITH Nell Shipman, Wheeler Oakman, Wellington Palyter, Ralph Laidlaw, Charles Arling. A husky dog comes to the aid of a girl who is being chased by a lecherous crook. Interesting silent adaptation of James Oliver Curwood's story "Wapi the Walrus" with especially good photography and scenery; filmed in northern Canada. V: Classic Video Cinema Collectors Club.

133 Back to God's Country. Universal-International, 1953. 78 minutes Color. D: Joseph Pevney. SC: Tom Reed. WITH Rock Hudson, Steve Cochran, Marcia Henderson, Hugh O'Brian, Chubby Johnson, Tudor Owen, John Cliff, Bill Radovich, Arthur Space, Pat Hogan. Carrying a cargo of valuable furs, a sea captain and his wife land in a remote Canadian harbor where a villainous trader plots to steal the furs, murder the man and take his wife. Color and the villainy of Steve Cochran greatly help this adaptation of the James Oliver Curwood story.

134 Back Trail. Monogram, 1948. 54 minutes B/W. D: Christy Cabanne. SC: J. Benton Cheney. WITH Johnny Mack Brown, Raymond Hatton, Mildred Coles, Ted Adams, Pierce Lyden, Jimmy Horne Jr., Snub Pollard, Marshall Reed, Bob Woodward, Carol Henry, George Morrell. A saloon owner is blackmailing a banker for a crime he did not commit and the banker asks for help from a special investigator for the State Protective League. Another in the long series of oaters with Johnny Mack Brown at Monogram; average.

135 Backfire. Aywon, 1922. 50 minutes B/W. D-SC: Alvin J. Neitz (Alan James). WITH Jack Hoxie, Florence Gilbert, George Sowards, Lew Meehan, William Lester, William Gould, Bert Rollins, Nellie Anderson, Poke Williams. A cowboy and his pal are framed for the murder of a Wells Fargo agent during a holdup, the crime actually being committed by a gang headed by a corrupt ranch

foreman. Very actionful Jack Hoxie silent feature which will please his fans.

136 Backlash. Universal-International, 1956. 84 minutes Color. D: John Sturges. SC: Bordon Chase. WITH Richard Widmark, Donna Reed, William Campbell, John McIntire, Barton MacLane, Edward Platt, Harry Morgan, Robert Wilke, Reg Parton, Robert Foulk, Roy Roberts. After five other men die in an Indian attack, the survivor is hunted by a posse because they think he has escaped with a fortune in gold. Entertaining oater done in the typically good John Sturges fashion.

137 Backtrack. Universal, 1969. 97 minutes Color. D: Earl Bellamy. SC: Borden Chase. WITH James Drury, Neville Brand, Doug McClure, Rhonda Fleming, Ida Lupino, Fernando Lamas, Peter Brown, William Smith, Philip Carey, Royal Dano, Gary Clarke, Randy Boone, L. Q. Jones, Carol Byron, Ross Elliott, Hal Baylor, George Savalas, Alberto Morin, Ruben Moreno, Teresa Terry, Priscilla Garcia. On the way to Mexico to get a prize bull four Texas Rangers become involved with bandits. Tacky compilation of episodes of "The Virginian" and "Laredo" television series issued theatrically.

138 Bad Bascomb. Metro-Goldwyn-Mayer, 1946. 112 minutes B/W. D: S. Sylvan Simon. SC: William Lipman & Grant Garrett. WITH Wallace Beery, Margaret O'Brien, Marjorie Main, J. Carrol Naish, Frances Rafferty, Marshall Thompson, Russell Simpson, Warner Anderson, Don Curtis, Connie Gilchrist, Sara Haden, Renie Riano, Henry O'Neill, Frank Darien. Two bandits take refuge with a group of Mormons and one pays them back by stealing their money while the other remains to aid them during an Indian attack. Fans of Wallace Beery, Margaret O'Brien and Marjorie Main will go for this one.

139 Bad Company. Paramount, 1972. 93 minutes Color. D: Robert Benton. SC: David Newman & Robert Benton. WITH Jeff Bridges, Barry Brown, Jim Davis, David Huddleston, John Savage, Jerry Houser, Damon Cofer, Geoffrey Lewis, Ed Lauter, John Quade, Jean Allison, Charles Tyner, Claudia Bryar, Todd Martin. Two draft dodgers head West on a robbery spree and are hounded by a relentless lawman during the Civil War. Underrated Western greatly helped by Jim Davis as the sheriff.

140 Bad Day at Black Rock. Metro-Gold-wyn-Mayer, 1955. 81 minutes Color. D: John Sturges. SC: Millard Kaufman & Don McGuire. WITH Spencer Tracy, Robert Ryan, Anne Francis, Dean Jagger, Walter Brennan, John Ericson, Ernest Borgnine, Lee Marvin, Russell Collins, Walter Sande. A one-armed man arrives in a small Western town and uncovers a secret which upsets the inhabitants. Excellent modern-day Western, well made, acted and directed.

141 Bad Lands. RKO Radio, 1939. 70 minutes B/W. D: Lew Landers. SC: Clarence Upson Young. WITH Robert Barrat, Noah Beery Jr., Guinn Williams, Robert Coote, Douglas Walton, Andy Clyde, Addison Richards, Paul Hurst, Francis Ford, Francis McDonald, Jack (John) Payne. An Army officer leads a small group of men into the desert after renegade Indians and the soldiers are soon being picked off one by one. Modest but entertaining little "B" drama which shows Lew Landers was not just a hack director; Western remake of **The Lost Patrol** (RKO Radio, 1934).

142 The Bad Man. First National, 1930. 90 minutes B/W. D: Clarence Badger. SC: Howard Estabrook. WITH Walter Huston, Dorothy Revier, James Rennie, O. P. Heggie, Sidney Blackmer, Marion Byron, Guinn Williams, Arthur Stone, Edward Lynch, Harry Semels, Erville Alderson, Myrna Loy. A Mexican bandit comes to the aid of a man who once saved his life when the man is about to lose his ranch. Early talkie mainly of interest to Walter Huston fans. First filmed in 1923 by Associated First National with Jack Mulhall, Holbrook Blinn and Enid Bennett.

143 The Bad Man. Metro-Goldwyn-Mayer, 1941. 70 minutes B/W. D: Richard Thorpe. SC: Wells Root. WITH Wallace Beery, Lionel Barrymore, Laraine Day, Ronald Reagan, Henry Travers, Chris-Pin Martin, Tom Conway, Chill Wills, Nydia Westman, Charles Stevens. An elderly ranch owner is forced to depend on an old friend, a bandit with a price on his head, to help him save his ranch from crooks. This third screen version of Porter Emerson Browne's play is basically a vehicle for the delightful hamming of Wallace Beery and Lionel Barrymore.

Bad Man from Big Bend see **Swing, Cowboy, Swing**

144 Bad Man from Red Butte. Universal, 1940. 58 minutes B/W. D: Ray Taylor. SC: Sam Robins. WITH Johnny Mack Brown, Fuzzy Knight, Bob Baker, Anne Gwynne, Lloyd Ingraham, Lafe McKee, Bill Cody Jr., Roy Barcroft, Norman Willis, Earle Hodgins, Myra McKinney, Art Mix, Texas Jim Lewis & His Lone Star Cowboys. Arriving in a small Western town, a cowboy is mistaken for his twin brother, who is a killer. Average Johnny Mack Brown oater.

145 The Bad Man of Brimstone. Metro-Goldwyn-Mayer, 1937. 89 minutes B/W. D: J. Walter Reuben. SC: Maurice Rapf & J. Walter Reuben. WITH Wallace Beery, Virginia Bruce, Dennis O'Keefe, Joseph Calleia, Lewis Stone, Guy Kibbee, Guinn Williams, Cliff Edwards, Noah Beery, Charley Grapewin, Arthur Hohl, John Qualen, Robert Barrat, Art Mix. When an old-time outlaw finds out that a young man is really his son it completely changes his life. Wallace Beery fans will like this one but everyone else will find it overly sentimental.

146 Bad Man of Deadwood. Republic, 1941. 54 (61) minutes B/W. D: Joseph Kane. SC: Joseph R. Webb. WITH Roy Rogers, George "Gabby" Hayes, Carol Adams, Sally Payne, Henry Brandon, Herbert Rawlinson, Hal Taliaferro, Jay Novello, Monte Blue, Horace Murphy, Ralf Harolde, Jack Kirk, Yakima Canutt, Curley Dresden, Fred Burns, Lynton Brent, Lloyd Ingraham, George Lloyd, Robert Frazer, Archie Twitchell, Karl Hackett, Harry Harvey, Eddie Acuff, Tom London, Jack Rockwell, Ernie Adams, Jack O'Shea, George Morrell, Wally West, Bob Woodward, Horace Carpenter, Harrison Greene. Trying to get away from his unlawful past, a young man joins a medicine show as a sharpshooter and in a small town he becomes allied with citizens who are opposed to a group of businessmen who are terrorizing them in order to keep out competition. Very good Roy Rogers series entry with a big supporting cast of familiar faces.

Bad Man of Harlem see **Harlem on the Prairie**

147 Bad Man's River. Scotia International, 1972. 89 (100) minutes Color. D: Eugenio (Gene) Martin. SC: Eugenio Martin & Philip Yordan. WITH Lee Van Cleef, Gina Lollobrigida, James Mason, Simon Andreu, Eduardo Fajarado, Diana Lorys.

In 1905 an outlaw gang is hired by a Mexican revolutionary leader to blow up a safe but the gang gets involved with a pretty woman and a double-cross. This Spanish-Italian-French coproduction does not know whether to be a Western or a comedy and it fails miserably at both. Filmed in Spain as **El Hombre del Rio Malo** by Zurbano Films/Apollo Films/ Jacques Roitfeld.

Bad Men of Arizona see **Arizona Raiders** (1936)

148 Bad Men of the Border. Universal, 1945. 56 minutes B/W. D: Wallace Fox. SC: Adele Buffington. WITH Kirby Grant, Fuzzy Knight, Armida, John Eldredge, Barbara Sears, Francis McDonald, Soledad Jiminez, Edward Howard, Edmund Cobb, Pierce Lyden, Gene (Roth) Stutenroth, Roy Brent, Glenn Strange, Ethan Laidlaw, Charles Stevens. A U. S. marshal masquerading as an outlaw and a female Mexican agent investigating a counterfeiting ring join forces to bring in the crooks. If one can overlook the implausible plot, Kirby Grant's initial series vehicle for Universal is acceptable entertainment.

149 Bad Men of the Hills. Columbia, 1942. 58 minutes B/W. D: William Berke. SC: Luci Ward. WITH Charles Starrett, Russell Hayden, Cliff Edwards, Luana Walters, Alan Bridge, Guy Usher, Joel Friedkin, Norma Jean Wooters, John Shay, Richard Botiller, Art Mix, Jack Ingram, Ben Corbett, Carl Sepulveda, Frank Ellis, John Cason. Crooks try to murder a young man investigating a marshal's murder but he is befriended by the residents of a lawless town who are actually ranchers who are opposed to the murderous crooks. A complicated plot and lots of action make this Starrett-Hayden vehicle pleasant viewing.

150 Bad Men of Missouri. Warner Brothers, 1941. 71 minutes B/W. D: Ray Enright. SC: Charles Grayson. WITH Dennis Morgan, Jane Wyman, Wayne Morris, Arthur Kennedy, Victor Jory, Alan Baxter, Walter Catlett, Howard Da Silva, Faye Emerson, Russell Simpson, Virginia Brissac, Erville Alderson, Hugh Sothern, Sam McDaniel, Dorothy Vaughn, William Gould, Ann Todd, Roscoe Ates. The story of the Younger Brothers and how they were pushed into a life of crime by carpetbaggers in Missouri after the Civil War. Entertaining but complete fiction about an historical subject.

151 Bad Men of Thunder Gap. Producers Releasing Corporation, 1943. 60 minutes B/W. D: Albert Herman. SC: Elmer Clifton. WITH James Newill, Dave O'Brien, Guy Wilkerson, Janet Shaw, Jack Ingram, Charles King, Tom London, Michael Vallon, Lucille Vance, I. Stanford Jolley, Bud Osborne, Jimmie Aubrey, Cal Shrum's Rhythm Rangers, Artie Ortego. When outlaws plague a small town, members of the Texas Rangers set out to stop them. Dull entry in "The Texas Rangers" series. Reissued in 1947 by Eagle Lion as **Thundergap Outlaws.**

152 Bad Men of Tombstone. Allied Artists, 1949. 74 minutes B/W. D: Kurt Neumann. SC: Jay Monaghan. WITH Barry Sullivan, Marjorie Reynolds, Broderick Crawford, Fortunio Bonanova, Guinn Williams, John Kellogg, Mary Newton, Louis Jean Heydt, Virginia Carroll, Dick Wessell, Claire Carleton, Ted Hecht, Harry Cording, Lucien Littlefield, Harry Hayden, Olin Howlin, Robert Barrat, Julie Gibson, Joseph Crehan, Ted Mapes, Rory Mallison, Ted French, Douglas Fowley, Dennis Hoey, Morris Ankrum, Tom Fadden, Billy Gray. During the Gold Rush era a young man sets out to make his fortune but instead turns to a life of crime. Average outing from Monogram, which had just turned into Allied Artists, but the results are still the same.

153 The Badge of Marshal Brennan. Allied Artists, 1959. 74 minutes B/W. D: Albert C. Gannaway. SC: Thomas G. Hubbard. WITH Jim Davis, Arleen Whelan, Carl Smith, Lee Van Cleef, Louis Jean Heydt, Marty Robbins, Harry Lauter, Douglas Fowley, Lawrence Dobkin. An outlaw, on the run, is mistaken for a dead marshal and goes up against an evil land baron. Entertaining low budget entry with a good performance from Jim Davis in the lead.

154 The Badlanders. Metro-Goldwyn-Mayer, 1958. 85 minutes Color. D: Delmer Daves. SC: Richard Collins. WITH Alan Ladd, Ernest Borgnine, Katy Jurado, Claire Kelly, Kent Smith, Nehemiah Persoff, Anthony Caruso, Robert Emhardt, Adam Williams, Ford Rainey, John Day. At the turn of the century two men plan to rob gold from an Arizona mine while each plans to doublecross the other. Fairly good oater which is a Western remake of **The Asphalt Jungle** (MGM, 1950).

155 Badlands of Dakota. Universal, 1941. 74 minutes B/W. D: Alfred E. Green. SC: Gerald Geraghty. WITH Robert Stack, Ann Rutherford, Broderick Crawford, Frances Farmer, Richard Dix, Hugh Herbert, Lon Chaney Jr., Fuzzy Knight, Andy Devine, Addison Richards, Samuel S. Hinds, Eddie Dew, Kermit Maynard, Hank Bell, Charles King, Bradley Page, Carleton Young, Glenn Strange, Don Barclay, Emmett Vogan, Willie Fung, Edward Fielding, The Jesters. In Deadwood, a crooked saloon owner sends his younger brother to bring home his fiancee and the two fall in love. Nicely made Universal Western with Frances Farmer (as Calamity Jane) and Richard Dix (as Wild Bill Hickok) stealing the show.

156 Badlands of Montana. 20th Century-Fox, 1957. 75 minutes B/W. D-SC: Daniel B. Ullman. WITH Rex Reason, Margia Dean, Beverly Garland, Keith Richards, Emile Meyer, William Phipps, Stanley Farrar, John Pickard, Ralph Peters, Paul Newlan, Russ Bender, Jack Kruschen. Two friends, one a marshal and the other the member of an outlaw gang, are forced into a showdown. Arid, mediocre oater of little entertainment value.

157 Badman's Country. Warner Brothers, 1958. 68 minutes B/W. D: Fred F. Sears. SC: Orville Hampton. WITH George Montgomery, Neville Brand, Buster Crabbe, Karin Booth, Gregory Walcott, Malcolm Atterbury, Russell Johnson, Richard Devon, Morris Ankrum, Dan Riss, Lewis Martin, Fred Graham, John Harmon, William Bryant. Sheriff Pat Garrett joins forces with Wyatt Earp, Bat Masterson and Buffalo Bill Cody when he goes against Butch Cassidy and his cohorts. Familiar faces add zest to this otherwise average oater. Title song is sung by The Mellowmen.

158 Badman's Gold. Eagle Lion Classics, 1951. 58 minutes B/W. D: Robert Tansey. SC: Robert Emmet (Tansey) & Alyn Lockwood. WITH John Carpenter, Alyn Lockwood, Kenne Duncan, Emmett Lynn, Jack Daly, Daish (Dog). When a series of robberies take place on a stage line carrying gold shipments, a marshal is called in to investigate. Independent oater made on a shoestring and it looks it.

159 Badman's Territory. RKO Radio, 1946. 98 minutes B/W. D: Tim Whelan. SC: Jack Natteford & Luci Ward. WITH Randolph Scott, Ann Richards, George "Gabby" Hayes, Lawrence Tierney, Tom Tyler, Steve Brodie, John Halloran, Phil Warren, William Moss, James Warren, Isabel Jewell, Morgan Conway, Nestor Paiva, Chief Thundercloud, Ray Collins, Virginia Sale, Andrew Tombes, Harry Holman, Richard Hale, Emory Parnell, Ethan Laidlaw, Kermit Maynard, Bud Osborne. A marshal is at a loss about how to control a group of notorious outlaws who have taken refuge in a town outside government jurisdiction. Highly entertaining and well produced Randolph Scott vehicle with a good supporting cast.

160 Baker's Hawk. Doty-Dayton, 1976. 105 minutes Color. D: Lyman D. Dayton. SC: Dan Greer & Hal Harrison Jr. WITH Clint Walker, Burl Ives, Diane Baker, Alan Young, Lee H. Montgomery, Taylor Lacher, Bruce M. Fisher, Cam Clarke, Danny Bouaduce, Phil Hoover, Brian Williams. A young boy learns about growing up when he aids an injured hawk and helps his father fight crooks. Overlong but fairly interesting outdoor actioner.

161 Ballad of a Bounty Hunter. United Picture/Trebol Film, 1970. 83 minutes Color. D: Joaquin L. Romero Marchent. SC: Joaquin L. Romero Marchent, Giovanni Simonelli & Victor Aux. WITH James Philbrook, Norma Bengell, Simon Andrew, Luis Induni, Emilio Caba, Alfonso Rojas, Maria Silva, Alvaro de Luna, Angel Ortiz. A bounty hunter falls in love with a young girl and then is forced to hunt down her brother. Low budget actioner, a Spanish-Italian coproduction originally called **Lo Non Pardono. . .Uccido.**

162 Ballad of a Gunfighter. Parade, 1964. 84 minutes B/W. D-SC: Bill Ward. WITH Marty Robbins, Joyce Redd, Bob Barron, Nestor Paiva, Michael Davis, Laurette Luez, Gene Davis, Traveler (Horse). An outlaw's plan to rob a stage is foiled by another man who not only takes the bandit's gold but also his girl. Marty Robbins' first starring feature is a low budget affair but his fans will love it, especially when he sings "El Paso" and "San Angelo."

163 The Ballad of Ben and Charlie. Jupiter, 1972. 118 minutes Color. D: Michele Lupo. SC: Sergio Donati. WITH Giuliano Gemma, George Eastman, Marisa Mell, Vittorio Congia, Giancomo Rossi Stuart. Two petty crooks become wanted men and form a gang and find themselves hunted by both the law and the lawless. Somewhat tongue-in-cheek spaghetti oater is fun to watch. Issued in Italy as **Amico, Stammi Lontano Almeno un Palmo** and also called **Ben and Charlie.**

164 The Ballad of Cable Hogue. Warner Brothers, 1970. 120 minutes Color. D: Sam Peckinpah. SC: John Crawford & Edmund Penny. WITH Jason Robards, Stella Stevens, David Warner, Strother Martin, Slim Pickens, L. Q. Jones, Peter Whitney, R. G. Armstrong, Gene Evans, William Mims, Kathleen Freeman, Vaughn Taylor, James Anderson. A prospector is left in the desert by his partners to die but he survives and eventually builds a depot station around a waterhole and becomes prosperous. Overrated Sam Peckinpah feature which rambles a bit too much but is fairly entertaining.

165 The Ballad of Gregorio Cortez. PBS-TV, 1982. 99 minutes Color. D: Robert M. Young. SC: Victor Villasenor. WITH Edward James Olmos, Tom Bower, James Gammon, Bruce McGill, Brion James, Pepe Serna, Alan Vint, Tim Scott, Michael McGuire, Jack Kehoe, Barry Corbin, Rosana DeSoto, Victoria Plata, William Sanderson. In 1901 a Mexican cowboy who has shot the lawman who killed his brother tries to elude a 600-man posse across the Texas desert. Grim and somewhat slow, but fairly good made-for-public-TV movie which was given theatrical release in 1983 by Embassy Pictures.

166 The Ballad of Josie. Universal, 1968. 102 minutes Color. D: Andrew V. McLaglen. SC: Harold Swanton. WITH Doris Day, Peter Graves, George Kennedy, Andy Devine, William Talman, David Hartman, Guy Raymond, Karen Jensen, Robert Lowery, Paul Fix. In 1890 a widow tries to build up a rundown ranch to raise sheep and this starts a feud with cattlemen. Dud Doris Day Western that is supposed to be funny but is not.

167 Bandido. United Artists, 1956. 92 minutes Color. D: Richard Fleischer. SC: Earl Fenton. WITH Robert Mitchum, Ursula Thiess, Gilbert Roland, Zachary Scott, Rodolfo Acosta, Henry Brandon, Douglas Fowley, Victor Junco, Jose I. Torvay. Arriving in Mexico in 1916 to sell weapons during the revolution there, an American adventurer finds himself up against a trecherous rival. Robert Mitchum and Zachary Scott, as the rivals, and Gilbert Roland, as the revolutionary

leader, make this a fast moving and highly watchable feature.

168 Bandit King of Texas. Republic, 1949. 60 minutes B/W. D: Fred C. Brannon. SC: Olive Cooper. WITH Allan "Rocky" Lane, Eddy Waller, Helen Stanley, Harry Lauter, Jim Nolan, Robert Bice, John Hamilton, Lane Bradford, George Lloyd, Steve Clark, I. Stanford Jolley, Richard Emory, Danni Nolan. A government investigator is after racketeers who sell bogus land to settlers and then murder them for their money. Fast moving Allan Lane vehicle.

169 Bandit Queen. Lippert, 1950. 71 minutes B/W. D: William Berke. SC: Victor West & Budd Lesser. WITH Barbara Britton, Willard Parker, Philip Reed, Barton MacLane, Martin Garralaga, John Merton, Jack Ingram, Victor Kilian, Thurston Hall, Jack Perrin, Chuck Roberson, Margia Dean, Angie (Angelo Rossitto), Paul Martin, Pepe Hern, Lalo Rios, Mike Conrad, Carl Pitti, Hugh Hooker. When vicious land grabbers murder her family in Old California a young girl takes on the guise of a masked crusader and leads a vigilante group against the killers. Passable Lippert entry with plenty of action and pretty Barbara Britton as an added asset.

170 Bandit Ranger. RKO Radio, 1942. 64 minutes B/W. D: Lesley Selander. SC: Bennett Cohen & Morton Grant. WITH Tim Holt, Cliff Edwards, Joan Barclay, Kenneth Harlan, LeRoy Mason, Glenn Strange, Jack Rockwell, Frank Ellis, Robert Kortman, Bud Geary, Dennis Moore, Ernie Adams, Russell Wade, Tom London, Lloyd Ingraham. When he finds a dying Ranger, a man takes on the guise of a lawman to save the Ranger's daughter from a murder-kidnap plot. Good drama interpolated with action and a workmanlike cast provide entertainment in this Tim Holt entry.

171 The Bandit Trail. RKO Radio, 1941. 60 minutes B/W. D: Edward Killy. SC: Norton S. Parker. WITH Tim Holt, Ray Whitley, Janet Waldo, Lee "Lasses" White, Morris Ankrum, Roy Barcroft, J. Farrell Holmes, Eddy Waller, Glenn Strange, Frank Ellis, Guy Usher, Jack Clifford, Bud Osborne, John Merton, Bud Geary, Lew Meehan, Terry Frost, Carl Stockdale, James Farley, Al Ferguson. A man and his two pals become outlaws after the murder of the man's father but when he falls in love with a pretty girl the trio go to the right side of the law and round up an outlaw gang. Typically solid Tim Holt RKO vehicle.

172 The Bandits. Conrad-Zacharias, 1979. 89 minutes Color. D: Robert Conrad & Alfred Zacharias. WITH Robert Conrad, Antonio Aguilar, Jan-Michael Vincent, Pilar Pellicar, Maria Duval, Roy Jenson, Pedro Armendariz Jr., Manuel Lopez Ochoa. A Mexican saves three cowpokes from being hanged and they accompany him to his homeland where they have a series of adventures. Average actioner filmed in Mexico in 1966 as **Los Bandidos** (The Bandits).

173 Bandits of Dark Canyon. Republic, 1947. 59 minutes B/W. D: Philip Ford. SC: Bob Williams. WITH Allan "Rocky" Lane, Eddy Waller, Bob Steele, Roy Barcroft, Linda Johnson, John Hamilton, Francis Ford, Eddie Acuff, LeRoy Mason, Gregory Marshall. When a mine owner is falsely accused of killing his foreman, he escapes with the help of friends and they try to find the real murderer. Better than average Allan Lane entry, mainly because Bob Steele is the co-star.

174 Bandits of El Dorado. Columbia, 1949. 56 minutes B/W. D: Ray Nazarro, SC: Barry Shipman. WITH Charles Starrett, Smiley Burnette, George J. Lewis, Fred Sears, Clayton Moore, Mustard & Gravy, John Dehner, Jock (Mahoney) O'Mahoney, John Doucette, Max Wagner, Henry Kulky. A government investigator fakes the murder of a Texas Ranger in order to become wanted so he can find out how criminals are escaping across the border into Mexico. Fairly good "Durango Kid" series outing.

175 Bandits of the Badlands. Republic, 1945. 55 minutes B/W. D: Thomas Carr. SC: Doris Schroeder. WITH Sunset Carson, Peggy Stewart, Si Jenks, Monte Hale, John Merton, Forrest Taylor, Jack Ingram, Fred Graham, Robert Wilke, Tex Terry, Jack O'Shea, Jack Kirk, Horace B. Carpenter, Charles Stevens, Marshall Reed. When his brother is murdered by outlaws in retaliation for his having killed one of their members during a holdup, a ranger resigns from the force and takes on the guise of an escaped convict to track down the killer. Fast paced and entertaining Sunset Carson vehicle.

176 Bandits of the West. Republic, 1953. 54 minutes B/W. D: Harry Keller, SC: Gerald Geraghty. WITH Allan "Rocky"

Lane, Eddy Waller, Cathy Downs, Roy Barcroft, Trevor Bardette, Ray Montgomery, Byron Foulger, Harry Harvey, Robert Bice. When outlaws try to sabotage a gas company, a U. S. marshal is sent to stop the disturbance. Despite fast declining production values in the genre in the early 1950s, this Allan Lane entry is well made, fast and more than watchable.

177 Bandolero! 20th Century-Fox, 1968. 106 minutes Color. D: Andrew V. McLaglen. SC: James Lee Barrett. WITH James Stewart, Dean Martin, Raquel Welch, George Kennedy, Andrew Prine, Will Geer, Denver Pyle, Tom Heaton, Rudy Diaz, Sean McClory, Harry Carey Jr., Donald (Don "Red") Barry, Guy Raymond, Perry Lopez, Jock Mahoney, Big John Hamilton, Dub Taylor, John Mitchum, Joseph Patrick Cranshaw, Roy Barcroft, Bob Adler. Masquerading as a hangman, a man saves his brother and their outlaw gang and then flees south of the border with a pretty hostage. Okay entertainment with good production values and likable stars. VD: Blackhawk.

178 The Bang Bang Kid. Ajay Films, 1967. 90 minutes Color. D: Stanley Prager. SC: Howard Beck. WITH Guy Madison, Tom Bosley, Sandra Milo, Riccardo Garrone, Jose Maria Caffarel, Dianik Zurakowska, Giustino Durano. A bumbler finds himself in a small town lorded over by a notorious gunman but saved by a gun-toting robot. Surprisingly amusing Old West parody coproduced by the U.S., Italy and Spain.

179 Banjo Hackett. Columbia/NBC-TV, 1976. 100 minutes Color. D: Andrew V. McLaglen. SC: Ken Trevey. WITH Don Meredith, Ike Eisenmann, Chuck Connors, Jennifer Warren, Dan O'Herlihy, Jeff Corey, Gloria De Haven, L. Q. Jones, Jan Murray, Anne Francis, Slim Pickens, David Young, Richard Young, Stan Haze. In 1880 a horse trader and his orphaned nephew wander the frontier looking for the boy's prize horse which has been stolen by a bounty hunter. Run-of-the-mill television feature which was a pilot for a series that did not sell. Original title: **Banjo Hackett: Roamin' Free.**

Banjo Hackett: Roamin' Free see **Banjo Hackett**

180 Bar 20. United Artists, 1943. 54 minutes B/W. D: Lesley Selander. SC: Morton Grant, Norman Houston & Michael

Wilson. WITH William Boyd, Andy Clyde, Dustine Farnum, George Reeves, Victor Jory, Douglas Fowley, Betty Blythe, Robert Mitchum, Francis McDonald, Earle Hodgins, Buck Bucko. Hopalong Cassidy, California Carlson and Lin Bradley try to help a girl and her mother after they lose their valuables in a holdup with the chief suspects being the girl's fiancee and his best man. Fairly good Hopalong Cassidy series entry that is somewhat draggy in spots with Robert Mitchum having a large role as a ranch owner.

181 Bar 20 Justice. Paramount, 1938. 54 (70) minutes B/W. D: Lesley Selander. SC: Arnold Belgard & Harrison Jacobs. WITH William Boyd, George ("Gabby") Hayes, Russell Hayden, Paul Sutton, Gwen Gaze, Pat O'Brien, Joseph DeStefani, William Duncan, Walter Long, H. Bruce Mitchell, John Beach. Hopalong Cassidy tries to help a girl in reopening her mine while a crook tries to keep it closed so he can get all its ore. Entertaining Hopalong Cassidy series entry.

182 Bar 20 Rides Again. Paramount, 1935. 54 (62) minutes B/W. D: Howard Bretherton. SC: Doris Schroeder & Gerald Geraghty. WITH William Boyd, James Ellison, Jean Rouverol, George ("Gabby") Hayes, Harry Worth, Frank McGlynn Jr., Howard Lang, Ethel Wales, Paul Fix, J. P. McGowan, Joe Rickson, Al St. John, John Merton, Frank Layton, Chill Wills & His Avalon Boys. The boys from the Bar 20 ranch find themselves up against a land baron who fancies himself another Napoleon. The third feature in the Hopalong Cassidy series and one of the very best; highly recommended.

183 Bar Z Bad Men. Republic, 1937. 57 minutes B/W. D: Sam Newfield. SC: George Plympton. WITH Johnny Mack Brown, Lois January, Tom London, Ernie Adams, Dick Curtis, Jack Rockwell, Milburn Morante, Horace Murphy, Budd Buster, Frank Ellis, George Morrell, Tex Palmer, Horace Carpenter, Art Dillard, Oscar Gahan. When he is falsely accused of rustling a fellow rancher's cattle, a man seeks out the real culprits. Typically good Johnny Mack Brown Republic vehicle with a cast of familiar faces.

184 Barbarosa. Universal, 1982. 90 minutes Color. D: Fred Schepisi. SC: William D. Wittliff. WITH Gary Busey, Willie Nelson, Gilbert Roland, Isela Vega, Danny De La Paz, George Voskovec, Alma Mar-

tinez, Howland Chamberlain, Wolf Muser, Kai Wulf, Harry Caesar, Sharon Compton, Roberto Contreros, Luis Contreros, Sonia De Leon, Joanelle Romera. A young farm boy, on the run for the accidental killing of his brother-in-law, is befriended by a notorious outlaw who teaches him how to survive. Offbeat oater, which got little theatrical release, is not bad but it's not good either, although Willie Nelson is very likable in the title role and Gilbert Roland is powerful as the vengeful patron. VD: RCA. V: Blackhawk.

185 Barbary Coast. United Artists, 1935. 91 minutes B/W. D: Howard Hawks. SC: Ben Hecht & Charles MacArthur. WITH Miriam Hopkins, Edward G. Robinson, Joel McCrea, Walter Brennan, Frank Craven, Brian Donlevy, Otto Hoffman, Rollo Lloyd, Donald Meek, Harry Carey, Robert Gray, Clyde Cook, J. M. Kerrigan, Matt McHugh, Wong Chung, Russ Powell, Frederik Vogeding, David Niven, Edward Gargan, Herman Bing, Tom London, Heinie Conklin, Art Miles, Charles West. In San Francisco in 1849, a dance hall queen throws over a corrupt gambling house operator for an honest, but broke, young man. Fast paced and highly entertaining period piece with a bevy of fine performances.

186 The Barbary Coast. Paramount/ABC-TV, 1975. 100 minutes Color. D: Bill Bixby. SC: Douglas Heyes. WITH William Shatner, Dennis Cole, Charles Aidman, Michael Ansara, Neville Brand, Bobbi Jordan, Richard Kiel, John Vernon, Lynda Day George, Leo Gordon, Boy Hoy, Terry Lester, Simon Scott, Todd Martin, Charles Picerni, Michael Carr, Bill Bixby. When a Confederate officer sets up an extortion plot he finds himself opposed by a casino owner and a government agent in San Francisco in the 1860s. Moderately sustaining telefeature which served as the pilot for the "Barbary Coast" (ABC-TV, 1975-76) series which starred William Shatner and Doug McClure.

187 Barbary Coast Gent. Metro-Goldwyn, Mayer, 1944. 87 minutes B/W. D: Roy Del Ruth. SC: William R. Lipman, Grant Garrett & Harry Ruskin. WITH Wallace Beery, Binnie Barnes, John Carradine, Bruce Kellogg, Frances Rafferty, Chill Wills, Noah Beery, Henry O'Neill, Ray Collins, Morris Ankrum, Donald Meek, Addison Richards, Harry Hayden, Paul E. Burns, Paul Hurst, Victor Kilian, Cliff Clark, Louise Beavers, Robert Emmett O'Connor, Ray Teal, Earle Hodgins, Jack

Norton, Harry Shannon, Fred "Snowflake" Toones, Byron Foulger, Lee Phelps, Anne O'Neal, James Farley, Edgar Dearing. In the 1890s a likable crook makes a quick getaway from San Francisco and goes to Nevada where he plans to sell phoney mining stock but to his surprise he reforms. Fun Wallace Beery vehicle.

188 The Bargain. Paramount, 1914. 50 minutes B/W. D: Reginald Barker. SC: William H. Clifford & Thomas H. Ince. WITH Clara Williams, J. Barney Sherry, William S. Hart, J. Frank Burke, James Dowling. A notorious bandit is injured while trying to rob a stage and is rescued by a rancher and nursed back to health by his pretty daughter, with whom the bandit falls in love. William S. Hart's first feature, in which he is third billed as the outlaw, is a good silent effort. V: Classic Video Cinema Collectors Club.

189 The Baron of Arizona. Lippert, 1950. 97 minutes B/W. D-SC: Samuel Fuller. WITH Vincent Price, Ellen Drew, Beulah Bondi, Reed Hadley, Vladimir Sokoloff, Robert Barrat, Robin Syort, Barbara Woodell, Tina Rome, Margia Dean, Edward Keane, Gene Roth, Karen Kester, Joseph Green, Fred Kohler Jr., Tristam Coffin, I. Stanford Jolley, Terry Frost, Angelo Rossitto, Zachary Uaconeilli, Wheaton Chambers, Stuart Holmes, Jonathan Hale, Stanley Price, Sam Flint, Richard Cramer. A clerk in the Arizona land office spends years falsifying documents in order to prove that he is the legal heir to thousands of acres in Arizona. Top notch work by Vincent Price, in the title role, Ellen Drew and director-scripter Samuel Fuller make this historical-based film worth watching.

190 Barricade. Warner Brothers, 1950. 75 minutes Color. D: Peter Godfrey. SC: William Sackheim. WITH Dane Clark, Raymond Massey, Ruth Roman, Robert Douglas, Morgan Farley, Walter Loy, George Stern, Robert Griffin, Frank Marlowe, Tony Martinez. Two outlaws come to the rescue of the denizens of a mining camp who are under the ruthless control of a tyrant. Fairly good programmer.

191 Barricade on the Big Black. NBC-TV, 1957. 54 minutes B/W. SC: Anthony Spinner. WITH Richard Crenna, Mary LaRoche, Andrew Duggan, George Galbreth. An Indian-hating Army lieutenant finds himself falling in love with the white wife of a hostile warrior. Originally telecast

March 27, 1957 as a segment of "Matinee Theatre" on NBC-TV, this drama is available to television as a feature film.

192 The Barrier. Paramount, 1937. 90 minutes B/W. D: Lesley Selander. SC: Bernard Shubert, Harrison Jacobs & Mordaunt Shairp. WITH Leo Carrillo, Jean Parker, James Ellison, Otto Kruger, J. M. Kerrigan, Robert Barrat, Andy Clyde, Sally Martin, Sara Haden, Addison Richards, Allen Davies. When her true background is revealed to the man who loves her, a young girl decides to join her father, an Alaskan sea captain. Filmed at Washington's Mount Baker National Forest, this drama from the Rex Beach novel is an above average programmer. First filmed in 1926 by Metro-Goldwyn-Mayer with Norman Kerry, Henry B. Walthall, Lionel Barrymore and Marceline Day.

193 Barquero. United Artists, 1970. 115 minutes Color. D: Gordon Douglas. SC: George Schenck & William Marks. WITH Lee Van Cleef, Warren Oates, Kerwin Matthews, Forrest Tucker, Mariette Hartley, Marie Gomez, Armando Silvestre, John Davis Chandler, Harry Lauter, Brad Weston, Craig Littler, Ed Bakey, Richard Lapp. A ferryman has to protect his job against bandits and when the gang wipes out a small Mexican town he sets out to hunt them down. Actionful but extremely violent and bloody oater, in the style Lee Van Cleef did in Europe.

194 The Battle of Apache Pass. Universal-International, 1951. 85 minutes Color. D: George Sherman. SC: Gerald Drayson Adams. WITH John Lund, Jeff Chandler, Beverly Tyler, Susan Cabot, Bruce Cowling, John Hudson, James Best, Regis Toomey, Richard Egan, Hugh O'Brian, William Reynolds, Jay Silverheels, Tommy Cook, Jack Elam, Richard Garland, Jack Ingram, John Baer. An Army major and the Indian chief Cochise try to work together to keep the renegade Geronimo from slaughtering settlers. Jeff Chandler repeats his Cochise role from **Broken Arrow** (q.v.) but this melodrama is no competition for that genre classic.

195 Battle of Greed. Crescent, 1937. 59 minutes B/W. D: Howard Higgins, SC: John T. Neville. WITH Tom Keene, Gwynne Shipman, James Bush, Jimmy Butler, Budd Buster, Lloyd Ingraham, Bob Callahan, Henry Rocquemore, Rafael Bennett, Robert Fiske, Carl Stockdale, William Worthington. A young man becomes involved in treachery following the discovery of the Comstock Lode in Virginia City. One of the pseudo-historical Westerns in Tom Keene's Crescent series, this one even includes Mark Twain in the adventure; average for the series.

196 Battle of Rogue River. Columbia, 1954. 71 minutes Color. D: William Castle. SC: Douglas Heyes. WITH George Montgomery, Martha Hyer, Richard Denning, John Crawford, Emory Parnell, Michael Granger, Bill Bryant, Charles Evans, Lee Roberts, Steve Ritch, Frank Sully, Bill Hale, Jimmy Lloyd, Willis Bouchey. Settlers in Oregon in 1850 want statehood but this cannot be accomplished without the signing of a peace treaty with local Indians and a man sets out to accomplish the mission. Producer Sam Katzman must have spent the budget on Technicolor because the title battle is not much although the film entertains adequately.

197 The Battles of Chief Pontiac. Realart, 1952. 71 minutes B/W. D: Felix Feist. SC: Jack DeWitt. WITH Lex Barker, Lon Chaney, Helen Westcott, Berry Kroeger, Roy Roberts, Larry Chance, Katherine Warren, Ramsey Hill, Guy Teague, James Fairfax, Abner George. In the early 1760s a ranger tries to arrange a peace treaty between the British and Chief Pontiac only to find out that a Hessian renegade is selling guns to the Indians. Cheaply made and historically inaccurate but not bad entertainment.

198 Battlin' Buckaroo. Anchor, 1924. 60 minutes B/W. D-SC: Allan J. Nietz. WITH Bill Patton, Peggy O'Day, Andrew Waldron, Lew Meehan, Anthony Freendenthall, Fred Hank. A nestor loves a rancher's daughter and gets the blame when the old man is cheated by his crooked foreman. Interesting as an opportunity to see a starring Bill Patton (whose screen personality was like that of a silent Jimmy Wakely) vehicle but otherwise the film is low grade although actionful with nice photography (by Marvin Hughes) and desert locales.

199 Battling Marshal. Astor, 1950. 55 minutes B/W. D: Oliver Drake. SC: Rose Kreves. WITH Sunset Carson, Pat Starling, Lee Roberts, Forrest Matthews, Al Terry, A. J. Baxley, Richard Bartell, Bob Curtis, Pat Gleason, Stephen Keyes, Don Gray, Dale Carson, William Val, Buck Buckley, Joe Hiser. Two federal marshals arrive in a small town to investigate attempts made on the life of a rancher. Very low grade Sunset Carson vehicle. V: Sunland Enterprises, Cassette Express.

200 Battling with Buffalo Bill. Universal, 1931. 12 Chapters B/W. D: Ray Taylor. SC: George Plympton & Ella O'Neal. WITH Tom Tyler, Lucile Browne, Rex Bell, William Desmond, Francis Ford, Yakima Canutt, Chief Thundercloud, Franklyn Farnum, Joe Bonomo, Art Mix, Bud Osborne, John Beck, George Regas, Jim Thorpe, Bobby Nelson, Edmund Cobb, Fred Humes. Scout Buffalo Bill Cody comes to the aid of a young girl whose father's mine is sought by a crook and his gang who have incited Indian attacks. Not much history here but there is plenty of action to make up for it in this cliffhanger.

201 Bearheart of the Great Northwest. Pathe-Alpha, 1964. 75 minutes Color. D: Rand Brooks. WITH Marshall Reed, Fritz Feld, Joey Young. When his master is killed in the Canadian timber country a dog sets out to get the murderers. Obscure, but pleasant, north woods family film. Alternate title: **Beartooth.**

202 The Bears and I. Buena Vista, 1974. 89 minutes Color. D: Bernard McEveety. SC: John Whedon. WITH Patrick Wayne, Chief Dan George, Andrew Duggan, Michael Ansara, Robert Pine, Val De Vargas, Hal Baylor. A Vietnam war veteran moves to the North Woods where he becomes embroiled in a dispute between Indians and settlers. This Walt Disney production is only average but the scenery is nice.

Beartooth see **Bearheart of the Great Northwest**

203 The Beast of Hollow Mountain. United Artists, 1956. 80 minutes Color. D: Edward Nassour & Ismael Rodriguez. SC: Robert Hill. WITH Guy Madison, Patricia Medina, Eduardo Noriega, Carlos Rivas, Marjo Navarro, Pascual Garcia Pena, Margarito Luna. When cattle begin disappearing from his ranch a man sets out to find out why and discovers a huge dinosaur. Taken from a story by Willis O'Brien, this film combines the horror and Western genres, but not very well. Filmed in Mexico as **El Monstruo de la Montana Hueca** by Peliculas Rodriguez.

204 Beau Bandit. RKO Productions, 1930. 68 minutes B/W. D: Lambert Hillyer. SC: Wallace Smith. WITH Rod La Rocque,

Mitchell Lewis, Doris Kenyon, Walter Long, Charles Middleton, George Duryea (Tom Keene/Richard Powers), James Donlan, Charles Brinley, Barney Furey, Bill Patton, Kenneth Cooper, Bob Erickson, Gordon Jones, Walt Robbins, Ben Corbett. A notorious bandit plans to rob a bank but becomes enamoured with a pretty girl only to find she is being sought after by the owner of the bank he planned to rob. This early sound oater, definitely a curio today, was even considered old-fashioned at the time of its release.

205 The Beautiful Blonde from Bashful Bend. 20th Century-Fox, 1949. 77 minutes Color. D-SC: Preston Sturges. WITH Betty Grable, Cesar Romero, Rudy Vallee, Olga San Juan, Sterling Holloway, Hugh Herbert, El Brendel, Porter Hall, Danny Jackson, Emory Parnell, Al Bridge, Chris-Pin Martin, Pati Behrs, Margaret Hamilton, J. Farrell MacDonald, Richard Hale, Georgia Caine, Esther Howard, Harry Hayden, Chester Conklin, Torben Meyer, Dewey Robinson, Richard Kean, Harry Tyler, Dudley Dickerson, Russell Simpson, Marie Windsor, Mary Monica McDonald. After a run-in with the law, a gun-toting girl goes to a small town where she is mistaken for the new school marm but she soon runs afoul of crooks. Bland Preston Sturges "comedy" which was a box office bust when it was issued, although a good cast (Rudy Vallee is especially good) does its best.

206 Beauty and the Bandit. Monogram, 1946. 77 minutes B/W. D: William Nigh. SC: Charles Belden. WITH Gilbert Roland, Ramsay Ames, Martin Garralaga, Frank Yaconelli, Vida Aldana, George J. Lewis, William Gould, Dimas Sotello, Felipe Turich, Glenn Strange, Alex Montoya, Artie Ortego. The Cisco Kid joins forces with a beautiful female bandit who is fighting corrupt officials. Nicely done "Cisco Kid" series adventure for which star Gilbert Roland wrote additional dialogue; the film is greatly helped by the presence of the luscious Ramsay Ames as a female Robin Hood.

207 Before the White Man Came. FC, 1921. 50 minutes B/W. D: John Maple. SC: William E. Wing. The story of the American Indian and how the tribes lived in the West before the arrival of white settlers. Rather interesting, if somewhat crude, semi-documentary feature made in the Big Horn Mountains of Montana and Wyoming with the cooperation of the Crow Indians (the film has an all-Indian cast) who had adopted director John Maple into their tribe. Production was made in association with the Department of Indian Affairs and endorsed by the Department of the Interior. V: Film Classic Exchange.

208 Belle Le Grand. Republic, 1951. 90 minutes B/W. D: Allan Dwan. SC: D. D. Beauchamp. WITH Vera Ralston, John Carroll, William Ching, Muriel Lawrence, Hope Emerson, Grant Withers, Stephen Chase, John Qualen, Henry (Harry) Morgan, Charles Cane, Thurston Hall, Marietta Canty, Glen Vernon, Don Beddoe, Isabel Randolph, John Holland, Frank Wilcox, Paul Maxey, Pierre Watkin, John Hart, Edward Keane, Russell Hicks, Sam Flint, Ed Cassidy, John Hamilton, Perry Ivins, William Schallert, Maude Eburne, Carl "Alfalfa" Switzer, Queenie Smith, Peter Brocco, Hal Price, Dick Elliott, Andrew Tombes, Eddie Parks, Fred Hoose, James Kirkwood, John Wengraft, Howard Negley, Ruth Robinson, Gino Corrado, Thomas Browne Henry, James Arness, Eddie Dunn, Emory Parnell, Chester Clute. In Virginia City a lady gambler marries a no-account she loves despite the fact the man has a yen for her younger sister. Big production, good supporting cast, empty script—mediocre film.

209 Belle of the Yukon. RKO Radio, 1944. 84 minutes B/W. D: William A. Seiter. SC: James Edward Grant. WITH Randolph Scott, Gypsy Rose Lee, Dinah Shore, Bob Burns, Charles Winninger, William Marshall, Guinn Williams, Robert Armstrong, Florence Bates, Wanda McKay, Edward Fielding, Charles Soldani. A crooked gambling hall proprietor in the Yukon during the time of the gold rush finally becomes an honest man to make his sweetheart happy. Fairly actionful adventure film with an emphasis on music and comedy.

210 Belle Starr. 20th Century-Fox, 1941. 87 minutes B/W. D: Irving Cummings. SC: Lamar Trotti. WITH Randolph Scott, Gene Tierney, Dana Andrews, Shepperd Strudwick, Elizabeth Patterson, Chill Wills, Louise Beavers, Olin Howland, Paul Burns, Joseph Sawyer, Joseph Downing, Charles Trowbridge, Howard Hickman, James Flavin, Charles Middleton, Matthew "Stymie" Beard, Mae Marsh, Kermit Maynard, Franklyn Farnum, Cecil Weston. After the Civil War, a Confederate guerilla leader and his bandit-wife wage a private war against local carpetbaggers. Not much fact in this screen biography of Belle Starr but who cares when there's Gene Tierney to look at?

211 Belle Starr. CBS-TV, 1980. 97 minutes Color. D: John A. Alonzo. SC: James Lee Barrett. WITH Elizabeth Montgomery, Cliff Potts, Michael Cavanaugh, Fred Ward, Jesse Vint, Allan Vint, Geoffrey Lewis. Another retelling of the tale of Belle Starr, this time showing her as a rebellious female who deserts her lover to ride with the likes of the James, Dalton and Younger brothers. Like its theatrical predecessor this film has little foundation in fact but Elizabeth Montgomery is good in the title role.

212 Belle Starr's Daughter. 20th Century-Fox, 1947. 85 minutes B/W. D: Lesley Selander. SC: W. R. Burnett. WITH George Montgomery, Rod Cameron, Ruth Roman, Wallace Ford, Charles Kemper, William Phipps, Edith King, Chris-Pin Martin, Jack Lambert, J. Farrell MacDonald. A marshal is blamed for the murder of the notorious Belle Starr and the outlaw's daughter comes to town to avenge her mother's death. Better than average outlaw yarn aided by its trio of stars, steady direction and a good script.

213 Bells of Capistrano. Republic, 1942. 54 (73) minutes B/W. D: William Morgan. SC: Lawrence Kimble. WITH Gene Autry, Smiley Burnette, Virginia Grey, Lucien Littlefield, Morgan Conway, Claire DuBrey, Charles Kane, Joe Strauch Jr., Marla Shelton, Tristram Coffin, Jay Novello, Al Bridge, Eddie Acuff, Jack O'Shea, Julian Rivero, William Forrest, Ken Christy, Dick Wessell, Guy Usher, Ralph Peters, Joe McGuinn, Terrisita Osta, Howard Hickman, William Kellogg, Peggy Satterlee, Frankie Marvin, Ray Jones. Singer Gene Autry and his crew join a rodeo which is targeted for destruction by a rival outfit. Gene Autry's last pre-World War II oater is on the sluggish side.

214 Bells of Coronado. Republic, 1950. 54 (67) minutes Color. D: William Witney. SC: Sloan Nibley. WITH Roy Rogers, Dale Evans, Grant Withers, Foy Willing & The Riders of the Purple Sage, Pat Brady, Clifton Young, Robert Bice, Stuart Randall, Leo Cleary, John Hamilton, Edmund Cobb, Rex Lease, Lane Bradford. Insurance investigator Roy Rogers tries to find missing uranium ore thought to be sought after by a foreign power. Good action and an entertaining storyline

make this an above average later Roy Rogers feature.

215 Bells of Rosarita. Republic, 1945. 54 (68) minutes B/W. D: Frank McDonald. SC: Jack Townley. WITH Roy Rogers, George "Gabby" Hayes, Dale Evans, Adele Mara, Grant Withers, Bob Nolan & The Sons of the Pioneers, Roy Barcroft, Earle Hodgins, Addison Richards, Janet Martin, Syd Saylor, Ed Cassidy, Kenne Duncan, Rex Lease, Robert Wilke, Ted Adams, Wally West, The Robert Mitchell Boychoir, Helen Talbot, Poodles Hanneford, Hank Bell, Eddie Kane, Tom London, Marin Sais, Sam Ash, Barbara Elliott, Mary McCarty; Guest stars: Bill Elliott, Allan Lane, Robert Livingston, Don "Red" Barry, Sunset Carson. Movie star Roy Rogers tries to keep a circus from being taken over by crooks and he calls in several other cowboy heroes to help him. Interesting Roy Rogers outing with too much music and pretty Adele Mara stealing the acting honors. V: Cassette Express, Discount Video.

216 Bells of San Angelo. Republic, 1947. 54 (71) minutes Color. D: William Witney, SC: Sloan Nibley. WITH Roy Rogers, Dale Evans, Andy Devine, John McGuire, Olaf Hytten, David Sharpe, Fritz Leiber, Hank Patterson, Fred "Snowflake" Toones, Eddie Acuff, Bob Nolan & The Sons of the Pioneers, Dale Van Sickel, Buck Bucko. Border investigator Roy Rogers is after the gang which is smuggling silver across the Mexican border. Fairly entertaining Roy Rogers entry not bogged down with too much music. V: Video Connection, Cumberland Video.

217 Bells of San Fernando. Screen Guild, 1947. 74 minutes B/W. D: Terry Morse. SC: Jack DeWitt & Renault Duncan (Duncan Renaldo). WITH Donald Woods, Gloria Warren, Monte Blue, Shirley O'Hara, Byron Foulger, Paul Newlan, Anthony Warde, Claire Du Brey, Gordon Clark, Angelo Rossitto. An evil man takes control of a small town in Spanish California and rules like a tyrant until he is opposed by an Irish immigrant. Cheaply made but entertaining "B" feature.

218 Below the Border. Monogram, 1942. 57 minutes B/W. D: Howard Bretherton. SC: Jess Bowers (Adele Buffington). WITH Buck Jones, Tim McCoy, Raymond Hatton, Linda Brent, Charles King, Dennis Moore, Roy Barcroft, Ted Mapes, Bud Osborne, Eva Puig, Merrill McCormack, Jack Rockwell. Three lawmen assume various guises as they head to the Mexican border to put a stop to a gang of cattle rustlers who have stolen jewels from a girl whose fiancee has become involved with the gang. Another entry in "The Rough Riders" series which will suit Jones-McCoy-Hatton fans just fine.

219 Bend of the River. Universal, 1952. 91 minutes Color. D: Anthony Mann. SC: Borden Chase. WITH James Stewart, Julia(e) Adams, Arthur Kennedy, Rock Hudson, Lori Nelson, Jay C. Flippen, Henry (Harry) Morgan, Chubby Johnson, Royal Dano, Stepin Fetchit, Howard Petrie, Jack Lambert, Frank Ferguson, Frances Bavier, Cliff Lyons, Lillian Randolph, Britt Wood, Gregg Barton, Philo McCullough, Donald Kerr, Denver Dixon. A former border raider saves a man from hanging and the two end up leading a train of fruit farmers to Oregon and along the way they fight hostile Indians. Big, brawling oater which is nicely produced; good entertainment.

220 Beneath Western Skies. Republic, 1944. 56 minutes B/W. D: Spencer Gordon Bennet. SC: Albert DeMond & Bob Williams. WITH Robert Livingston, Smiley Burnette, Effie Laird, Joe Strauch Jr., LeRoy Mason, Kenne Duncan, Bud Geary, Jack Kirk, Tom London, Frank Jacquet, Jack Ingram, Budd Buster, Robert Wilke, Tom Steele, Herman Hack, Carl Sepulveda. A sheriff sets out to stop a gang of outlaws but a blow to the head causes him to have amnesia which ends up making him a tool of the outlaws. One of three "John Paul Revere" oaters which Bob Livingston did at Republic in the mid-1940s; quite watchable.

221 Best of the Badmen. RKO Radio, 1951. 84 minutes Color. D: William D. Russell. SC: Robert Hardy Andrews & John Twist. WITH Robert Ryan, Claire Trevor, Jack Buetel, Robert Preston, Walter Brennan, Bruce Cabot, John Archer, Lawrence Tierney, Barton MacLane, Tom Tyler, Robert Wilke, John Cliff, Lee MacGregor, Emmett Lynn, Carleton Young, Byron Foulger, Larry Johns, Harry Woods, William Tannen, Ed Max, David McMahon, Everett Glass. A Union officer takes Jesse James, the Ringo Kid and the Younger Brothers into custody only to be framed on a murder charge by a crooked detective. All-star galloper is quite good and one that will warm the heart of any genre fan.

222 Between Fighting Men. World Wide,

1932. 60 minutes B/W. D: Forrest Sheldon. SC: Betty Burbridge & Forrest Sheldon. WITH Ken Maynard, Ruth Hall, Wallace MacDonald, Josephine Dunn, Albert J. Smith, Walter Law, James Bradbury Jr., John Pratt, Charles King, Edmund Cobb, Jack Rockwell, Jack Kirk, Bud McClure, Roy Bucko, Jack Ward. Two men try to stop a range war by stopping sheep herders from moving their herds through town and at the same time they become rivals for a pretty girl. Very pleasant Ken Maynard vehicle with good use of comedy and surprisingly little action. V: Cumberland Video.

223 Between Men. Supreme, 1935. 59 minutes B/W. D: Robert North Bradbury. SC: Charles Francis Royal. WITH Johnny Mack Brown, Beth Marion, William Farnum, Earl Dwire, Lloyd Ingraham, Frank Ball, Harry Downing, Horace Carpenter, Forrest Taylor, Bud Osborne, Sherry Tansey, Milburn Morante, Artie Ortego. A young man heads West to find the rejected daughter of the man who raised him and not only finds her but his real father who had gone West after he thought the boy had been killed. Complicated plotline, good performances and competent production make this one add up to pleasing entertainment; the fist fight between Brown and Farnum is a corker with Farnum more than holding his own.

224 Beyond the Border. Producers Distributing Corporation, 1925. 55 minutes B/W. D: Scott R. Dunlap. SC: Harvey Gates. WITH Harry Carey, Mildred Harris, Tom Santschi, Jack Richardson, William Scott. A lawman brings in his girl's brother who has been falsely accused of a crime only to find a local crook has taken his job. Entertaining Harry Carey silent film.

225 Beyond the Last Frontier. Republic, 1943. 57 minutes B/W. D: Howard Bretherton. SC: John K. Butler & Morton Grant. WITH Eddie Dew, Smiley Burnette, Lorraine Miller, Robert Mitchum, Harry Woods, Kermit Maynard, Ernie Adams, Richard Cramer, Jack Kirk, Wheaton Chambers, Jack Rockwell, Cactus Mack, Art Dillard, Tom Steele, Henry Wills, Curley Dresden. In an effort to stop border gun runners, the Texas Rangers have one of their own men infiltrate the gang. The first of two films which starred Eddie Dew in the "John Paul Revere" series, this fails to do much other than have the hero take a backseat to villain Bob Mitchum.

226 Beyond the Law. Syndicate, 1930. 60 minutes B/W. D: J. P. McGowan. SC: G. A. Durlam. WITH Robert Frazer, Louise Lorraine, Lane Chandler, Charles King, Jimmy Kane, William Walling, Franklyn Farnum, Harry Holden, George Hackathorne, Ed Lynch, Robert Graves, Al St. John. Two cowpokes ride into a region where the law is in cahoots with a hoodlum who hires a famous road agent to run ranchers off their lands. Fast moving early sound film that is poorly recorded, includes too much stock footage and has two inane musical numbers by a group of singing soldiers.

227 Beyond the Law. Columbia, 1934. 60 minutes B/W. D: D. Ross Lederman. SC: Harold Shumate. WITH Tim McCoy, Shirley Grey, Lane Chandler, Addison Richards, Dick Rush, Harry Bradley, Morton Laverre (John Merton). When a girl's father is sent to prison for a murder committed during a holdup, a railroad detective, who believes him innocent, sets out to find the real culprits. Good Tim McCoy programmer made as a part of his non-Western action series for Columbia but basically a genre entry.

228 Beyond the Law. Sancrosiap/Roxy Film, 1968. 78 minutes Color. D: Giorgio Stegani. SC: Giorgio Stegani, Fernando Di Leo. WITH Lee Van Cleef, Antonio Sabato, Lionel Stander, Graziella Granata, Bud Spencer, Ann Smyrner, Herbert Fox, Carlo Gaddi, Enzo Fiermonte, Gordon Mitchell, Hans Elwenspoek, Gunther Stoll, Carlo Pedersoli. A notorious bandit and his two cohorts rob a stage and the bandit later befriends a man who saves his life and in a small town the bandit is made sheriff and must protect a money shipment from a gang of vicious holdup men. Violent but well made Lee Van Cleef vehicle which was made in Italy as **Al Di La Della Legge.** Issued in the U. S. in 1973 by Cinema Shares.

229 Beyond the Pecos. Universal, 1945. 59 minutes B/W. D: Lambert Hillyer. SC: Bennett Cohen. WITH Rod Cameron, Eddie Dew, Fuzzy Knight, Jennifer Holt, Ray Whitley & His Bar-Six-Cowboys, Gene Roth, Robert Homans, Jack Ingram, Frank Jacquet, Henry Wills, Jack Rockwell, Jim Thorpe, Dan White, Al Ferguson, Forrest Taylor, William Desmond, Herman Hack, Artie Ortego. Two men from feuding families fight over rich oil land rights and the love of a pretty girl. Stout Rod Cameron vehicle nicely helmed by veteran director Lambert Hillyer.

230 Beyond the Purple Hills. Columbia, 1950. 70 minutes B/W. D: John English. SC: Norman S. Hall. WITH Gene Autry, Pat Buttram, Jo Dennison, Don Beddoe, James Millican, Don Kay Reynolds, Hugh O'Brian, Robert Wilke, Roy Gordon, Harry Harvey, Gregg Barton, Ralph Peters, Frank Ellis, John Cliff, Sandy Sanders, Merrill McCormack, Tex Terry, Maudie Prickett, Pat O'Malley, Herman Hack, Cliff Barnett, Frank O'Connor, Frankie Marvin, Bobby Clark, Boyd Stockman, Lynton Brent. An acting sheriff is forced to arrest his pal when the latter's father is murdered but the lawman believes his friend is innocent. Adequate Gene Autry series actioner.

231 Beyond the Rio Grande. Big 4, 1930. 60 minutes B/W. D: Harry S. Webb. SC: Carl Krusada. WITH Jack Perrin, Franklyn Farnum, Charline Burt, Emma Tansey, Buffalo Bill Jr., Pete Morrison, Henry Roquemore, Edmund Cobb, Henry Taylor. When his partner robs a bank a man is falsely blamed for the crime and is forced to head south of the border. Pretty fair early talkie which will appeal to fans of Jack Perrin and Franklyn Farnum.

232 Beyond the Rockies. RKO Radio, 1932. 60 minutes B/W. D: Fred Allen. SC: Oliver Drake. WITH Tom Keene, Rochelle Hudson, Julian Rivero, Hank Bell, Ernie Adams, William Welsh, Ted Adams, Tom London, Marie Wells. When cattle rustling becomes a problem in a part of Texas the government sends an undercover agent to investigate. David O. Selznick was the executive producer of this oater which is well made and moves fast although Tom Keene, as usual for his RKO series, is a bit too gung-ho as the hero.

233 Beyond the Sacramento. Columbia, 1940. 58 minutes B/W. D: Lambert Hillyer. SC: Luci Ward. WITH Bill Elliott, Evelyn Keyes, Dub Taylor, John Dilson, Bradley Page, Frank LaRue, Norman Willis, Steve Clark, Jack Clifford, Don Beddoe, Art Mix, Bud Osborne, George McKay, Olin Francis, Tex Cooper, Ned Glass. Settlers in California are plagued by lawlessness and a lone man arrives to try to put a stop to the terrorism. Fast paced Bill Elliott vehicle with good direction by Lambert Hillyer and nice work by Evelyn Keyes as the heroine.

234 The Big Bonanza. Republic, 1945. 68 minutes B/W. D: George Archainbaud. SC: Dorrell McGowan, Stuart McGowan

& Paul Gengelin. WITH Richard Arlen, Robert Livingston, Jane Frazee, George "Gabby" Hayes, Lynne Roberts, Bobby Driscoll, J. M. Kerrigan, Russell Simpson, Frank Reicher, Cordell Hickman, Roy Barcroft, Fred Kohler Jr., Charles King, Jack Rockwell, Henry Wills, Fred Graham, Dan White, Robert Wilke, Monte Hale. During the Civil War a Union soldier is wrongly accused of cowardice and goes west where he meets up with a friend, a gambling house proprietor who actually framed him on the false charge. Top grade Republic actioner which is benefitted by the performances of Richard Arlen and Bob Livingston as the good and bad guys.

235 Big Boy Rides Again. Beacon, 1935. 55 minutes B/W. D: Al Herman. SC: William Nolte. WITH Guinn Williams, Connie Bergen, Charles K. French, Lafe McKee, Victor Potel, Bud Osborne, William Gould, Augie Gomez. A young man returns home to aid his father in protecting a buried treasure, only to have his dad killed and himself kidnapped by the murderer. Cheaply made but fast moving and entertaining Big Boy Williams vehicle.

236 Big Calibre. Supreme, 1935. 58 minutes B/W. D: Robert North Bradbury. SC: Perry Murdock. WITH Bob Steele, Peggy Campbell, Georgia O'Dell, Earl Dwire, Bill Quinn, John Elliott, Forrest Taylor, Perry Murdock, Si Jenks, Frank Ball, Frank McCarroll, Blackie Whiteford. When he is falsely accused of killing his own father, a rancher is nearly lynched by the locals before he escapes and proves his innocence. Bob Steele is on the run again in this oater, which is not a typical one in that a grotesque chemist uses gas to kill his victims.

237 The Big Cat. Eagle-Lion, 1949. 75 minutes Color. D: Phil Karlson. SC: Morton Grant. WITH Preston Foster, Lon McCallister, Forrest Tucker, Peggy Ann Garner, Skip Homeier, Sara Holden, Irving Bacon, Gene Reynolds. The long time hatred of two men for each other over a girl is triggered by the arrival of the girl's son in a Utah valley plagued by a rampaging cougar and a deadly drought. Better-than-average outdoor melodrama helped by nice location scenery and a good cast.

238 The Big Country. United Artists, 1958. 156 minutes Color. D: William Wyler. SC: James R. Webb, Sy Bartlett & Robert Wilder. WITH Gregory Peck, Jean Simmons, Charlton Heston, Burl Ives, Carroll Baker, Charles Bickford, Alfonso Bedoya, Chuck Connors, Chuck Hayward, Buff Brady, Jim Burk, Dorothy Adams, Chuck Roberson, Bob Morgan, John McKee, Jay Slim Talbot. A one-time sea captain arrives in the West to marry a rancher's daughter and finds himself in the middle of a feud over water rights. Sprawling Western which is splendidly made but overblown and verbose.

A Big Deal at Dodge City see **A Big Hand for the Little Lady**

239 The Big Gundown. Columbia, 1968. 90 minutes Color. D: Sergio Sollima. SC: Sergio Donati & Sergio Sollima. WITH Lee Van Cleef, Tomas Milian, Fernando Sancho, Luisa Rivelli, Nieves Navarro, Benito Stefanelli, Walter Barnes, Angel Del Pozo, Maria Granada, Lanfranco Ceccarelli, Roberto Camardiel. A famous Texas hunter gets on the trail of a Mexican accused of raping and murdering a small girl but as the search continues the man begins to realize he is being used to cover up another crime. Handsomely made feature starring Lee Van Cleef which was popular on both sides of the Atlantic; tremendous Ennio Morricone music score. Released in Italy, where it was filmed, in 1967 as **La Resa Dei Conti** (Account Rendered) by P.E.A./Tulio De Micheli.

240 A Big Hand for the Little Lady. Warner Brothers, 1966. 95 minutes Color. D: Fielder Cook. SC: Sidney Carroll. WITH Henry Fonda, Joanne Woodward, Jason Robards, Paul Ford, Charles Bickford, Burgess Meredith, Kevin McCarthy, Robert Middleton, John Qualen, James Kenny, Allen Collins, Jim Boles, Gerald Michenaud, Virginia Gregg, Chester Conklin, Ned Glass, Mae Clarke, James Griffith, Noah Keene, Milton Selzer, Louise Glenn, William Cort. Trying to rid her husband of his compulsive gambling habit, and recoup his losses, a woman enters a showdown in five-card poker in Laredo in 1896. Somewhat of a genre takeoff, this production is amusing and well done. Also called **A Big Deal at Dodge City.**

241 Big Jack. Metro-Goldwyn-Mayer, 1949. 85 minutes B/W. D: Richard Thorpe. SC: Gene Fowler, Marin Borowsky, Otto Van Eyss & Robert Thoere. WITH Wallace Beery, Richard Conte, Marjorie Main, Edward Arnold, Vanessa Brown, Clinton Sundberg, Charles Dingle, Clem Bevans, Jack Lambert, Will Wright, William Phillips, Syd Saylor. In Colonial times a man and a woman make a living as road agents until they are reformed by a righteous doctor. Fairly good Wallace Beery vehicle with emphasis on humor; this is Beery's last film and he looks in poor health.

242 Big Jake. National General, 1971. 110 minutes Color. D: George Sherman. SC: Harry Julian Fink & R. M. Fink. WITH John Wayne, Maureen O'Hara, Richard Boone, Patrick Wayne, Chris Mitchum, Bobby Vinton, Bruce Cabot, Glenn Corbett, Harry Carey Jr., John Doucette, Jim Davis, John Agar, Gregg Palmer, Robert Warner, Jim Burke, John Ethan Wayne, Virginia Capers, William Walker, Jerry Gatlin, Tom Henessy, Don Epperson, Everett Creach, Jeff Wingfield, Hank Worden, Jerry Summers, Chuck Roberson, Bernard Fox, Roy Jenson. When his grandson is kidnapped by a gang of outlaws, a rich land owner sets out to rescue him. Typically good John Wayne film with plenty of action and a good plot. Working title: **The Million Dollar Kidnapping.**

243 The Big Land. Warner Brothers, 1957. 98 minutes Color. D: Gordon Douglas. SC: David Dortort & Martin Rackin. WITH Alan Ladd, Virginia Mayo, Edmond O'Brien, Anthony Caruso, Julie Bishop, John Qualen, Don Castle, David Ladd, Jack Wrather Jr., George J. Lewis, James Anderson, Don Kelly, Charles Watts. When businessmen try to cheat cattlemen and farmers in the post-Civil War era the two unite and attempt to build a railroad spur which will connect them with better markets. Good Alan Ladd entry with fine production values.

The Big North see **The Wild North**

244 Big Red. Buena Vista, 1962. 89 minutes Color. D: Norman Tokar. SC: Louis Pelletier. WITH Walter Pidgeon, Gilles Payant, Emile Genest, Janette Bertrand, Doris Lussier, Rolland Bedard, George Bouvier, Teddy Burns Goulet. An orphaned boy comes to live at the ranch of a wealthy dog fancier and he develops a rapport with a previously incorrigible dog. Highly watchable Disney family film made in Canada.

245 The Big Show. Republic, 1936. 59 minutes B/W. D: Mack V. Wright. SC: Dorrell McGowan & Stuart McGowan. WITH Gene Autry, Smiley Burnette, Kay Hughes, Max Terhune, Sally Payne, William Newell, Charles Judels, Rex

King, Harry Worth, Mary Russell, Christine Maple, Jerry Larkin, Jack O'Shea, Slim Whitaker, George Chesebro, Edward Hearn, Cliff Lyons, The Sons of the Pioneers, Tracy Layne, Jack Rockwell, Frankie Marvin, Cornelius Keefe, Horace Carpenter, Frances Morris, Richard Beach, Art Mix, I. Stanford Jolley, Sally Rand, The SMU 50, The Light Crust Doughboys, The Beverly Hillbillies, The Jones Boys. When a stuck-up cowboy hero refuses to appear at a rodeo his stunt double takes the assignment in his place and becomes mixed up with gangsters and eventually wins screen stardom for himself. Very entertaining Gene Autry feature filmed at the Texas Centennial Exposition with a plethora of country and western acts; Max Terhune's screen debut. V: Cumberland Video.

246 The Big Sky. RKO Radio, 1952. 122 (140) minutes B/W. D: Howard Hawks. SC: Dudley Nichols. WITH Kirk Douglas, Dewey Martin, Elizabeth Threatt, Arthur Hunnicutt, Buddy Baer, Steven Geray, Hank Worden, Jim Davis, Henri Letondal, Robert Hunter, Booth Colman, Paul Frees, Frank De Kova, Guy Wilkerson, Cliff Clark, Fred Graham, George Wallace, Max Wagner, Charles Regan, Sam Ash, Don Beddoe, Jim Hayward, Anthony Jochim, Nolan Leary, Frank Lackteen, Ray Hyke, Eugene Borden, Veola Vonn, Cactus Mack, Crane Whitley. Two pals head west and join a fur-trapping expedition and along the way both fall in love with an Indian girl. Sprawling adaptation of A. B. Guthrie Jr.'s novel; cuts for TV make it more watchable.

247 The Big Sombrero. Columbia, 1949. 82 minutes Color. D: Frank McDonald. SC: Olive Cooper. WITH Gene Autry, Elena Verdugo, Stephen Dunne, George J. Lewis, Vera Marshe, William Edmunds, Martin Garralaga, Gene (Roth) Stutenroth, Neyle Morrow, Bob Cason, Pierce Lyden, Jose Alvarado, Alex Montoya, Joe Kirk, Artie Ortego, Joe Dominguez. A cowboy tries to stop a crook from marrying a girl for her ranch, which the man wants to sell. Finely done and entertaining Gene Autry opus.

248 The Big Stampede. Warner Brothers, 1932. 54 minutes B/W. D: Tenny Wright. SC: Kurt Kempler. WITH John Wayne, Noah Beery, Mae Madison, Luis Alberni, Berton Churchill, Paul Hurst, Sherwood Bailey, Frank Ellis, Hank Bell, Lafe McKee. A deputy sheriff enlists the help of a bandit in opposing a ranch owner who kills lawmen so his men can rustle cattle. Pleasing early John Wayne vehicle with usual larger-than-life villainy of Noah Beery. Remake of Ken Maynard's **Land Beyond the Law** (First National, 1927) and remade under that title by Warner Brothers in 1936 with Dick Foran.

249 The Big Trail. United Artists, 1930. 110 (158/125) minutes B/W. D: Raoul Walsh. SC: Jack Peabody, Marie Boyle & Florence Postal. WITH John Wayne, Marguerite Churchill, Tyrone Power Sr., El Brendel, Tully Marshall, David Rollins, Ian Keith, Frederick Burton, Russ Powell, Charles Stevens, Helen Parrish, Louise Carver, William V. Mong, Dodo Newton, Jack Peabody, Ward Bond, Marcia Harris, Marjorie Leet, Emslie Emerson, Frank Rainboth, Andy Shufford, Gertrude Van Lent, Lucille Van Lent, DeWitt Jennings, Alphonse Ethier, Chief Big Tree. While leading a wagon train west a young wagonmaster plans to avenge the murder of a trapper friend by one of the travelers. Originally shot in both 35mm and 70mm, this expansive production is a delight to the eye as well as providing John Wayne with a fine first starring film role. It is hard to understand why this film was not more popular than it was when first released. Recommended.

250 The Big Trees. Warner Brothers, 1952. 89 minutes Color. D: Felix Feist. SC: John Twist & James R. Webb. WITH Kirk Douglas, Eve Miller, Patrice Wymore, Edgar Buchanan, John Archer, Alan Hale Jr., Roy Roberts, Charles Meredith, Harry Cording, Ellen Corby, William Challee, Lester Sharp, Mel Archer, Duke Watson, Lillian Bond, Vicki Raaf, Kay Marlow, Sue Casey, Ann Stuart, Art Millan, Iris Adrian, William Vedder. An unscrupulous timber man gets into the confidence of a valley of settlers so he can destroy their redwood trees and sell them for timber. Color adds a good touch to this lumbering yarn although "hero" Kirk Douglas is none-too-likable in the lead. V: Discount Video, Cumberland Video, Budget Video.

251 Bigfoot. Ellman Enterprises/Gemini-American/Western-International, 1971. 94 minutes Color. D: Robert Slatzer. SC: Robert Slatzer & James Gordon White. WITH Chris Mitchum, Joi Lansing, John Carradine, Ken Maynard, Lindsay Crosby, James Craig, Judy Jordan, John Mitchum, Joy Wilkerson, Doodles Weaver, Dorothy Keller, Noble "Kid" Chissell, Nick Raymond, James Stellar, Lois Red

Elk, Lonesome Fawn. When her plane crashes in Northern California a girl is captured by an ape-like creature and a rescue party saves the girl while a peddler makes plans to exhibit the creature. Combination of horror and Western genres for the drive-in trade; interesting because of special billed Ken Maynard as a storekeeper.

252 Billy Jack. Warner Brothers, 1971. 112 minutes Color. D: T. C. Frank (Delores Taylor). SC: Frank Christina & Teresa Christina. WITH Tom Laughlin, Delores Taylor, Clark Howard, Bert Freed, Julie Webb, Kenneth Tobey, Victor Izay, Debbie Schock, Stan Rice, Teresa Kelly, John McClune, Katy Moffatt. When the existence of a freedom school for runaway teenagers on an Indian reservation in Arizona is threatened by the citizens of a small town, a halfbreed Vietnam veteran comes to the school's aid. Fans of the "Billy Jack" series should like this feature but others beware of this violent peace-preaching outing.

253 Billy the Kid. Metro-Goldwyn-Mayer, 1930. 90 minutes B/W. D: King Vidor. SC: Wanda Tuchock & Lawrence Stallings. WITH John (Johnny) Mack Brown, Wallace Beery, Kay Johnson, Wyndham Standing, Karl Dane, Russell Simpson, Blanche Frederici, Roscoe Ates, Warner Richmond, James Marcus, Nelson McDowell, Jack Carlyle, John Beck, Christopher Martin, Soledad Jiminzez, Don Coleman, Lucille Powers, Hank Bell. Billy the Kid murders a cattle baron in revenge for the death of a pal, then gets married, but he and his bride are trailed by his friend, Sheriff Pat Garrett, and a posse. Early talkie shot in widescreen process is something of a novelty today but it is definitely worth a look. TV Title: **The Highwayman Rides.**

254 Billy the Kid. Metro-Goldwyn-Mayer, 1941. 95 minutes B/W. D: David Miller. SC: Gene Fowler. WITH Robert Taylor, Brian Donlevy, Ian Hunter, Mary Howard, Gene Lockhart, Henry O'Neill, Frank Puglia, Cy Kendall, Connie Gilchrist, Ethel Griffies, Chill Wills, Guinn Williams, Olive Blakeney, Lon Chaney Jr., Frank Conlan, Mitchell Lewis, Dick Curtis, Ted Adams, Earl Gunn, Frank Dunn, Grant Withers, Joe Yule, Carl Pitti, Arthur Housman, Lew Harvey, Priscilla Lawson, Kermit Maynard, Slim Whittaker, Ray Teal, George Chesebro, Frank Hagney, Edwin Brady, Tom London. A long-time friend of outlaw Billy the Kid is forced to hunt him down when Billy kills a corrupt rancher who had murdered his pal. A remake of the 1930 **Billy the Kid** (q.v.) this outing is only fair and for some odd reason Pat Garrett is called Jim Sherwood.

255 Billy the Kid in Santa Fe. Producers Releasing Corporation, 1941. 64 minutes B/W. D: Peter Stewart (Sam Newfield). SC: Joseph O'Donnell. WITH Bob Steele, Al St. John, Rex Lease, Dennis Moore, Marin Sais, Karl Hackett, Steve Clark, Hal Price, Charles King, Frank Ellis, Dave O'Brien, Kenne Duncan, Curley Dresden. A crook falsely accuses Billy the Kid of a killing and he escapes to Santa Fe where he makes an alliance with a man whose brother was hanged by the crook. Run-of-the-mill PRC oater, fast and furious but not overly good.

256 Billy the Kid in Texas. Producers Releasing Corporation, 1940. 52 minutes B/W. D: Sam Newfield. SC: Joseph O'Donnell. WITH Bob Steele, Terry Walker, Al St. John, Carleton Young, Charles King, John Merton, Frank LaRue, Slim Whitaker, Curley Dresden, Tex Palmer, Merrill McCormack, Denver Dixon, Bob Woodward, Sherry Tansey, Herman Hack. Escaping from New Mexico, Billy the Kid thwarts a robbery and becomes the sheriff of a small town only to find his brother is the head of the area's outlaw gang. Low grade but actionful.

257 Billy the Kid Outlawed. Producers Releasing Corporation, 1940. 52 minutes B/W. D: Peter Stewart (Sam Newfield). SC: Oliver Drake. WITH Bob Steele, Louise Currie, Al St. John, Carleton Young, John Merton, Ted Adams, Joe McGuinn, Walter McGrail, Hal Price, Kenne Duncan, Reed Howes, George Chesebro, Steve Clark, Budd Buster, Sherry Tansey. In Lincoln County, New Mexico, Billy the Kid and his pals are outlawed by a corrupt lawman who is in cahoots with local crooks who are planning a big swindle. The first of a half dozen "Billy the Kid" features starring Bob Steele for PRC, this feature is fairly good considering its origins.

Billy the Kid, Sheriff of Sage Valley see **Sheriff of Sage Valley**

258 Billy the Kid Trapped. Producers Releasing Corporation, 1942. 59 minutes B/W. D: Sherman Scott (Sam Newfield). SC: Oliver Drake & Joseph O'Donnell. WITH Buster Crabbe, Al St. John, Anne

Jeffreys, Bud McTaggart, Glenn Strange, Walter McGrail, Ted Adams, Jack Ingram, Milton Kibbee, Eddie Phillips, Budd Buster, Jack Kenney, Jimmie Aubrey, Wally West, Bert Dillard, Kenne Duncan, George Chesebro, Carl Mathews, Richard Cramer, Curley Dresden, Horace Carpenter, Jim Mason, Hank Bell, Oscar Gahan, Herman Hack. Three outlaws claim to be Billy the Kid and his cohorts and they attack a sheriff but the real Billy rescues the lawman and then sets out to round up the culprits. Another in the long-running "Billy the Kid-Billy Carson" series at PRC with Buster Crabbe; average.

259 Billy the Kid vs. Dracula. Embassy, 1966. 89 minutes Color. D: William Beaudine. SC: Carl K. Hittleman. WITH John Carradine, Chuck Courtney, Melinda Plowman, Virginia Christine, Walter Janovitz, Bing Russell, Lenni Geer, Roy Barcroft, Olive Carey, Mannie Landman, Marjorie Bennett, George Cisar, Charlita, William Forrest, Richard Reeves, Harry Carey Jr., Max Kelvin, Jack Williams, William Challee. Billy the Kid is a foreman of a ranch whose nubile young owner is the lecherous object of Count Dracula, who poses as the girl's uncle. As bad as it sounds with Dracula in bat form even flying around in the daylight! V: Video Images.

260 Billy the Kid Wanted. Producers Releasing Corporation, 1941. 64 minutes B/W. D: Sherman Scott (Sam Newfield). SC: Fred Myton. WITH Buster Crabbe, Al St. John, Dave O'Brien, Choti Sherwood, Glenn Strange, Charles King, Slim Whitaker, Howard Masters, Joel Newfield, Budd Buster, Frank Ellis, Curley Dresden, Wally West. Billy the Kid hides out at the home of a rancher friend to elude a posse who framed him for a crime and he and the man fake a feud in order to capture the villains. Cheaply made but entertaining Buster Crabbe-Al St. John vehicle.

261 Billy the Kid's Fighting Pals. Producers Releasing Corporation, 1941. 62 minutes B/W. Sherman Scott (Sam Newfield). SC: George Plympton. WITH Bob Steele, Al St. John, Phyllis Adair, Hal Price, Carleton Young, George Chesebro, Forrest Taylor, Budd Buster, Julian Rivero, Wally West, Ray Henderson, Curley Dresden, Ed Piel Sr., Art Dillard. When a sheriff is murdered, Billy the Kid gets the murdered man's lookalike to pose as him so Billy can capture the killer. Low grade but okay; Bob Steele as Billy the Kid.

262 Billy the Kid's Gun Justice. Producers Releasing Corporation, 1940. 59 minutes B/W. D: Peter Stewart (Sam Newfield). SC: Joseph O'Donnell. WITH Bob Steele, Louise Currie, Al St. John, Carleton Young, Charles King, Rex Lease, Kenne Duncan, Forrest Taylor, Ted Adams, Al Ferguson, Karl Hackett, Ed Peil, Julian Rivero, Joe McGuinn, George Morrell, Blanca Fisher. Billy the Kid and his pals come to the aid of area ranchers who have bought properties only to find a crook has diverted the local water supply. Bob Steele fans will like this "Billy the Kid" series entry but overall it is on the tacky side.

Billy the Kid's Law and Order see **Law and Order** (1942)

263 Billy the Kid's Range War. Producers Releasing Corporation, 1941. 58 minutes B/W. D: Peter Stewart (Sam Newfield). SC: William Lively. WITH Bob Steele, Al St. John, Joan Barclay, Rex Lease, Carleton Young, Milton Kibbee, Karl Hackett, Ted Adams, Julian Rivero, John Ince, Buddy Roosevelt, Ralph Peters, Alden Chase, Howard Masters, George Chesebro, Charles King, Steve Clark, Tex Palmer. Billy the Kid is blamed for several murders by a steamboat line owner who is trying to stop construction on a stageline road. Better-than-average Billy the Kid actioner.

264 Billy the Kid's Roundup. Producers Releasing Corporation, 1941. 58 minutes B/W. Sherman Scott (Sam Newfield). SC: Fred Myton. WITH Buster Crabbe, Al St. John, Carleton Young, Joan Barclay, Glenn Strange, Dick Curtis, Slim Whitaker, John Webster, Charles King, John Elliott, Dennis Moore, Kenne Duncan, Curley Dresden, Richard Cramer, Wally West, Tex Palmer, Tex Cooper, Horace Carpenter, Jim Mason. The sheriff of a small town is murdered and Billy the Kid urges the female operator of a newspaper to use her business to combat the villains. Okay Buster Crabbe–Billy the Kid entry.

265 Billy the Kid's Smoking Guns. Producers Releasing Corpration, 1942. 63 minutes B/W. D: Sherman Scott (Sam Newfield). SC: George Milton. WITH Buster Crabbe, Al St. John, Joan Barclay, Dave O'Brien, John Merton, Milton Kibbee, Ted Adams, Frank Ellis, Karl Hackett, Budd Buster, Joel Newfield, Slim Whitaker, Bert Dillard. When a gang of hoodlums tries to force ranchers off their land by means of overcharging them for goods

and even murder, Billy the Kid and Fuzzy Q. Jones step in to aid the settlers. Plenty of action and shooting in this PRC feature.

266 Billy Two Hats. United Artists, 1974. 97 minutes Color. D: Ted Kotcheff. SC: Alan Sharp. WITH Gregory Peck, Desi Arnaz Jr., Jack Warden, David Huddleston, Sian Barbara Allen, John Pearce, Dawn Little Sky, W. Vincent St. Cyr, Henry Medicine Hat, Zev Berlinsky, Anthony Scott. An old Irishman befriends a half-breed Indian boy and the two are chased by a relentless lawman for robbing a bank. Western filmed in Israel with Gregory Peck making it palatable in his offbeat characterization as the Irish rogue.

267 Birth of a Legend. Gold Key, 1973. 96 minutes Color. An orphaned coyote, who has learned to herd sheep instead of hunting them, is mistaken by a Navajo Indian for the reincarnation of his sheepherder grandfather. Entertaining docudrama. Also called **Navajo Coyote.**

268 Bite the Bullet. Columbia, 1975. 131 minutes Color. D-SC: Richard Brooks. WITH Gene Hackman, Candice Bergen, James Coburn, Jan-Michael Vincent, Ian Bannen, Ben Johnson, John McLiam, Jerry Gatlin, Robert Donner, Robert Hoy, Dabney Coleman, Paul Stewart, Jean Willes, Sally Kirkland, Buddy Van Horn. A number of cowboys and adventurers enter an endurance horse race over 600 miles of badlands in 1908 for a $2,000 prize. Well produced but overlong Western which Ben Johnson steals with his poignant performance which should have won him a second Oscar. V: RCA/Columbia.

269 Bitter Creek. Allied Artists, 1954. 74 minutes B/W. D: Thomas Carr. SC: George Waggner. WITH William Elliott, Beverly Garland, Veda Ann Borg, Carleton Young, Claude Akins, John Harmon, John Pickard, Jim Hayward, Forrest Taylor, Mike Ragan, Zon Murray, John Larch, Florence Lake, Earle Hodgins, Jane Easton, Joe Devlin. When his rancher brother is shot in the back a man sets out to avenge the murder. Later Bill Elliott film that is compact, well acted and nicely scripted.

270 Bitter Springs. British Empire Films, 1950. 86 minutes B/W. D: Ralph Smart. SC: W. P. Lyescomb & M. Danischewsky. WITH Tommy Trinder, Chips Rafferty, Gordon Jackson, Jean Blue, Charles Tingwell, Nonnie Piper, Nicky Yardley,

Michael Pate, Henry Murdock. In frontier Australia a sheepherder and his family face danger from attacking aborigines. Well made and exciting Australian drama also called **Savage Justice.**

271 Black Aces. Universal, 1937. 59 minutes B/W. D: Buck Jones. SC: Frances Guihan. WITH Buck Jones, Kay Linaker, Robert Frazer, Charles King, Red Mackaye, W. E. Laurence, Raymond Brown, Robert Kortman, Bernard Phillips, Frank Campeau, Charles LeMoyne, Arthur Van Zlyke, Bob McKenzie. When outlaws rustle his cattle a rancher goes out to roundup the gang. Buck Jones produced and directed this entry in his Universal series and the results are good.

272 Black Arrow. Columbia, 1944. 15 Chapters B/W. D: B. Reeves Eason. SC: Sherman Lowe, Jack Stanley, Leighton Brill & Royal K. Cole. WITH Robert Scott, Adele Jergens, Kenneth MacDonald, Robert Williams, Charles Middleton, Martin Garralaga, George J. Lewis, Chief Thundercloud, Nick Thompson, George Navarro, I. Stanford Jolley, Harry Harvey, John Laurenz, Dan White, Eddie Parker, Stanley Price, Ted Mapes, Iron Eyes Cody. An Indian brave, who is actually white, is run off the reservation for refusing to take revenge for the murder of his supposed father and he tries to prevent warfare when crooks try to steal gold from Indian lands. Mediocre cliffhanger.

273 Black Bandit. Universal, 1938. 60 minutes B/W. D: George Waggner. SC: Joseph West. WITH Bob Baker, Marjorie Reynolds, Hal Taliaferro, Jack Rockwell, Forrest Taylor, Glenn Strange, Arthur Van Slyke, Carleton Young, Dick Dickinson, Rex Downing. Two twin boys are separated when they are young and when they meet again as grown men one is a sheriff and the other an outlaw wanted for murder. Good production values add greatly to this Bob Baker series entry.

274 Black Bart. Universal, 1948. 80 minutes Color. D: George Sherman. SC: Luci Ward, Jack Natteford & William Bowers. WITH Yvonne De Carlo, Dan Duryea, Jeffrey Lynn, Percy Kilbride, Lloyd Gough, Frank Lovejoy, Don Beddoe, John McIntire, Ray Walker, Soledad Jiminez, Eddy Waller, Anne O'Neal, Chief Many Treaties, Douglas Fowley, Paul Maxey, Milton Kibbee, Ray Harper, Eddie Acuff, Ray Teal, Russ Conway, Ray Bennett, George Douglas, Reed

Howes, Everett Shields. On a tour of the West, dancer Lola Montez becomes involved with the famous highwayman Black Bart, who masquerades as a rancher, and she tries to reform him. Dan Duryea, in the title role, and Yvonne De Carlo, as Lola Montez, and color, add zest to this fast-moving Western fantasy.

275 Black Cyclone. Pathe, 1925. 70 minutes B/W. D: Fred Jackman. SC: H. M. Walker & Malcolm Stuart Boylan. WITH Rex (horse), Guinn Williams, Kathleen Williams, Christian Frank; Killer, Pest, Lady (horses). A wild stallion, rescued from quicksand by a cowboy, aids his new master in fighting a crook as well as rescuing his mate from the herd led by a killer stallion. Good actionful silent adventure based on Hal Roach's story.

276 The Black Dakotas. Columbia, 1954. 68 minutes Color. D: Ray Nazarro. SC: Roy Buffum & DeVallon Scott. WITH Gary Merrill, Wanda Hendrix, John Bromfield, Noah Beery Jr., Fay Roope, Howard Wendell, Robert Simon, James Griffith, Richard Webb, Peter Whitney, Clayton Moore, Jay Silverheels, George Keymas, Robert Griffin, Frank Wilcox. In order to steal money from the Sioux Indians and start an Indian uprising to cover their escape, two men kill a Sioux emissary. A good cast and color can do little to save this mundane bow-and-arrows "B" outing.

277 Black Eagle. Columbia, 1948. 76 minutes B/W. D: Robert Gordon. SC: Edward Huebsch & Hal Smith. WITH William Bishop, Virginia Patton, Gordon Jones, James Bell, Trevor Bardette, Will Wright, Edmund McDonald, Paul E. Burns, Harry V. Cheshire, Al Eben, Ted Mapes, Richard Talmadge. A young man who tries to avoid trouble finds himself involved with a crooked livestock agent. Average action programmer.

278 Black Eagle of Santa Fe. International Television Corporation, 1966. 86 minutes Color. D: Ernst Hofbauer. SC: Jack Lewis. WITH Brad Harris, Tony Kendall, Joachim Hansen, Horst Frank, Pinkas Braun. A power hungry rancher tries to goad the Comanches into war so he can steal their lands but two young men try to thwart his machinations. Typically violent West German-French-Italian coproduction filmed in West Germany by Rapid-Film was **Die Schwarzen Adler Von Santa Fe** and originally running 93 minutes. V: Marketing Film.

The Black Ghost   36

The Black Ghost see The Last Frontier
(1932)

279 Black Gold. Allied Artists, 1947.
90 minutes B/W. D: Phil Karlson. SC:
Agnes Christine Johnson. WITH Anthony
Quinn, Katherine De Mille, Elyse Knox,
Kane Richmond, Moroni Olsen, Ducky
Louie, Darryl Hickman, Raymond Hatton,
Thurston Hall. An Indian couple discover
oil on their land and become millionaires
and begin breeding horses, one of which
wins the Kentucky Derby. Well-intentioned
feature which is badly hurt by poor production values.

280 Black Gold. Warner Brothers, 1963.
76 minutes B/W. D: Leslie H. Martinson.
SC: Bob Duncan & Wanda Duncan. WITH
Philip Carey, Diane McBain, Claude
Akins, James Best, Fay Spain, William
Phipps, Dub Taylor, Ken Mayer, Iron-Eyes
Cody, Vincent Barbi, Rusty Westcoatt.
When a ruthless oil tycoon plans to cheat
a girl out of her oil-rich lands his foreman
works to stop his plans. Rather typical
modern-day oil drilling drama.

281 Black Hills. Eagle Lion, 1947. 60
minutes B/W. D: Ray Taylor. SC: Joseph
Poland. WITH Eddie Dean, Roscoe Ates,
Shirley Patterson, Terry Frost, Andy
Parker & The Plainsmen, Steve Drake,
William Fawcett, Nina Bara, Lane Bradford, Lee Morgan, George Chesebro,
Bud Osborne, Steve Crane, Carl Mathews,
Eddie Parker. A man kills a rancher
who has discovered a rich gold vein on
his land but is thwarted by a lawman
and his pal. Poor Eddie Dean vehicle,
except for some good songs.

282 Black Hills Ambush. Republic, 1952.
54 minutes B/W. D: Harry Keller. SC:
M. Coates Webster & Ronald Davidson.
WITH Allan "Rocky" Lane, Eddy Waller,
Leslye Banning, Roy Barcroft, Michael
Hall, John Vosper, Ed Cassidy, John
Cason, Michael Barton. When a gang
of raiders terrorize a frontier area a
U. S. marshal is called in to bring the
gang to justice. Typical but okay Allan
Lane series entry.

283 The Black Hills Express. Republic,
1943. 56 minutes B/W. D: John English.
SC: Norman Hall & Fred Myton. WITH
Don "Red" Barry, Wally Vernon, Ariel
Heath, George Lewis, William Halligan,
Hooper Atchley, Charles Miller, Pierce
Lyden, Jack Rockwell, Robert Kortman,
Al Taylor, LeRoy Mason, Milton Kibbee,
Wheaton Chambers, Marshall Reed, Curley

Dresden, Frank Ellis, Carl Sepulveda,
Ray Jones. A famous outlaw is given
a month's immunity by the law when
the manager of the Black Hills division
of the Wells Fargo wants him to round
up the gang holding up the company's
express lines. Quite good Don Barry
vehicle heaped with action and nice
emoting.

284 Black Horse Canyon. Universal-
International, 1954. 82 minutes Color.
D: Jesse Hibbs. SC: Geoffrey Homes.
WITH Joel McCrea, Mari Blanchard,
Murvyn Vye, Irving Bacon, Ewing Mitchell,
John Pickard, Henry Wills. A long-time
cowpoke and the niece of a cattle breeder
join forces to capture a rebellious black
stallion but are opposed by a neighboring
rancher. Easy going oater for Joel McCrea
fans.

285 Black Market Rustlers. Monogram,
1943. 58 minutes B/W. D: S. Roy Luby.
SC: Patricia Harper. WITH Ray Corrigan,
Dennis Moore, Max Terhune, Evelyn
Finley, Steve Clark, Glenn Strange, Carl
Sepulveda, George Chesebro, Frank Ellis,
Hank Worden, John Merton, Hal Price,
Stanley Price, Wally West, Carl Mathews,
Tex Cooper, Claire McDowell. The Range
Busters are sent by the government to
stop a gang which is rustling cattle and
killing ranchers while supplying beef
for the black market. Pretty good entry
in The Range Busters series helped by
a trick-riding heroine Evelyn Finley.

Black Mountain Stage see Riders of
   Black Mountain

286 Black Noon. CBS-TV/Columbia,
1971. 73 minutes Color. D: Bernard Kowalski. SC: Andrew J. Fenady. WITH Roy
Thinnes, Yvette Mimieux, Ray Milland,
Lynn Loring, Henry Silva, Gloria Grahame,
William Bryant, Buddy Foster, Hank
Worden. A circuit riding preacher and
his wife arrive in a small Western town
which is infested by a weird religious
cult and an evil gunfighter. Combination
of the Western and horror genres is pretty
well handled in this television movie.

287 Black Patch. Warner Brothers, 1957.
83 minutes B/W. D: Allen H. Miner. SC:
Leo Gordon. WITH George Montgomery,
Diane Brewster, Leo Gordon, Tom Pittman,
House Peters Jr., Lynn Cartwright,
Sebastian Cabot, Peter Brocco, Strother
Martin, George Trevino. After the Civil
War, the sheriff of a small town is accused
of killing a bank robber, the husband

of the girl he once loved, and taking the bank loot and hiding it. This George Montgomery vehicle is not nearly as good as it should be and tends to be mundane.

288 Black Rodeo. Cinerama, 1972. 87 minutes Color. D-SC: Jeff Kanew. WITH Woody Strode, Muhammad Ali, Bud Bramwell, Cleo Hearn, Skeets Henderson, Rocky Watson, Lisa Bramwell. Various noted black rodeo performers appear in a rodeo staged in New York City in this documentary which also includes comments by black personalities as well as some background on black history. For those interested in the subject matter.

289 Black Spurs. Paramount, 1965. 81 minutes Color. D: R. G. Springsteen. SC: Steve Fisher. WITH Rory Calhoun, Linda Darnell, Scott Brady, Lon Chaney, Terry Moore, Richard Arlen, Bruce Cabot, Patricia Owens, Jerome Courtland, James Best, DeForest Kelley, James Brown, Joseph Hoover, Manuel Padilla, Robert Carricart, Joe Forte, Lorraine Bendix, Jeanne Baird, Guy Wilkerson, Read Morgan, Chuck Roberson, Reg Parton, Roy Jenson. A cowboy gains the alliance of several important people in a small Western town in a scheme to make a nearby community so wild that the railroad will bypass it and build in this town. Not one of A. C. Lyles' best but still nice to see for all its veteran players.

290 Black Star. Ambrosiana Cinematografia, 1966. 93 minutes Color. D-SC: Giovanni Grimaldi. WITH Robert Woods, Elga Andersen, Renato Rossini, Franco Lantieri, Jane Tilden, Andrea Scotti, Harald Wolff. A gambler-banker rides roughshod over a town in Mexico but his authority is threatened by the arrival of a mysterious man who begins defending the people the villain is trying to control. Robert Woods is a Robin Hood of the Old West, Italian-style in this violent sagebrusher originally called **Starblack.**

291 The Black Whip. 20th Century-Fox, 1956. 77 minutes B/W. D: Charles Marquis Warren. SC: Orville Hampton. WITH Hugh Marlowe, Coleen Gray, Adele Mara, Angie Dickinson, Richard Gilden, Strother Martin, Paul Richards, Charles Gray, Patrick O'Moore, Sheb Wooley, John Pickard, Harry Landers, Howard Culver. When they rescue a quartet of dance-hall girls in a Western town, two brothers find themselves up against a whip-yielding badman. Mundane and rather pointless oater.

292 Blackjack Ketchum, Desperado. Columbia, 1956. 76 minutes B/W. D: Earl Bellamy. SC: Luci Ward & Jack Natteford. WITH Howard Duff, Victor Jory, Maggie Mahoney, Angela Stevens, David Orrick, William Tannen, Ken Christy, Martin Garralaga, Don C. Harvey, Pat O'Malley, Ralph Sanford, Charles Wagenheim. A famous outlaw wants to live a peaceful life but in order to do so he is forced to fight against a gang of cattle thieves. Howard Duff is fine in the title role in this otherwise average outing.

293 Blazing Across the Pecos. Columbia, 1948. 55 minutes B/W. D: Ray Nazarro. SC: Norman S. Hall. WITH Charles Starrett, Smiley Burnette, Patricia White, Chief Thunder Cloud, Paul Campbell, Charles Wilson, Thomas Jackson, Pat O'Malley, Jock Mahoney, Frank McCarroll, Pierce Lyden, Paul Conrad, Jack Ingram, Red Arnnall & The Western Aces. When outlaws try to start an Indian uprising against local settlers the Durango Kid tries to stop them. Actionful and well written "Durango Kid" saga.

Blazing Arrows <u>see</u> Fighting Caravans

294 Blazing Bullets. Monogram, 1951. 51 minutes B/W D: Wallace Fox. SC: George Daniels. WITH Johnny Mack Brown, Lois Hall, House Peters Jr., Stanley Price, Dennis Moore, Edmund Cobb, Milburn Morante, Forrest Taylor, Ed Cassidy, Carl Mathews. A U. S. marshal tries to find a man who has been kidnapped along with his gold bullion, since the man's daughter's fiancee is suspected of the crime. Mild action show.

295 The Blazing Forest. Paramount, 1952. 90 minutes Color. D: Edward Ludwig. SC: Lewis R. Foster & Winston Miller. WITH John Payne, Susan Morrow, Richard Arlen, Agnes Moorehead, William Demarest, Roscoe Ates, Lynne Roberts, Ewing Mitchell, Walter Reed, Jim Davis, Joey Ray, Joe Garcia, Brett Houston, Max Wagner. A logger is contracted by a woman to cut timber on her northwoods land and he falls in love with her pretty niece but has troubles with his no-account brother. Handsome production with especially good work by Susan Morrow as the city-yearning young girl and Richard Arlen as the no-good brother.

296 Blazing Frontier. Producers Releasing Corporation, 1943. 61 minutes B/W. D: Sam Newfield. SC: Patricia Harper. WITH Buster Crabbe, Al St. John, Marjorie Manners, Milton Kibbee, I. Stanford

Jolley, Kermit Maynard, Frank Hagney, George Chesebro, Frank Ellis, Hank Bell, Jimmie Aubrey. When settlers and railroad officials begin fighting over rights-of-way, Billy Carson and Fuzzy Q. Jones discover that land agents are the cause of the trouble. Another entry in the Billy Carson series; low grade and fast. V: Video Connection.

297 Blazing Guns. Monogram, 1943, 55 minutes B/W. D: Robert Tansey, SC: Frances Kavanaugh. WITH Ken Maynard, Hoot Gibson, Kay Forrester, LeRoy Mason, Lloyd Ingraham, Roy Brent, Charles King, Weldon Heyburn, Dan White, Frank Ellis, Kenne Duncan, Emmett Lynn. Two U. S. marshals are called into a small town where a gang of thugs are stealing land in order to put together a cattle empire. Slickly done and well-directed entry in "The Trail Blazers" series.

298 Blazing Justice. Spectrum, 1936. 60 minutes B/W. D: Albert Herman. SC: Zara Tazil. WITH Bill Cody, Gertrude Messinger, Gordon Griffith, Mil Moranti (Milburn Morante), Budd Buster, Frank Yaconelli, Charles Tannen. After bringing in two wanted criminals, a cowboy is falsely accused of stealing money belonging to a rancher. Awkward, dull Bill Cody vehicle with about enough plot to fill a slow two reeler.

299. Blazing Saddles. Warner Brothers, 1974. 94 minutes Color. D: Mel Brooks. SC: Mel Brooks, Norman Steinberg, Andrew Bergman, Richard Pryor & Alan Unger. WITH Cleavon Little, Gene Wilder, Slim Pickens, David Huddleston, Liam Dunn, Alex Karras, John Hillerman, George Furth, Madeline Kahn, Harvey Korman, Mel Brooks, Carol Arthur, Dom DeLuise, Don Megowan, Burton Gilliam, Count Basie, Harvey Parry, Tom Steele. A black man, recently on a chain gang, becomes the sheriff of a Western town and must face local prejudice as well as dishonest state officials out to take over the territory. Every cliche imaginable is kidded in this comedy oater which varies in quality from very funny to distasteful to boring. The best part of the film comes at the beginning when Frankie Laine sings the title song. V: Warners Home Video.

300 Blazing Six Shooters. Columbia, 1940. 61 minutes B/W. D: Joseph H. Lewis. SC: Paul Franklin. WITH Charles Starrett, Iris Meredith, Bob Nolan & The Sons of the Pioneers, Dick Curtis, Al Bridge, George Cleveland, Henry Hall, Stanley Brown, John Tyrell, Eddie Laughton, Francis Walker, Edmund Cobb, Bruce Bennett. A cowboy tries to stop a crook from cheating an old man out of his ranch since the land contains a rich silver deposit. Fair Charles Starrett series vehicle.

301 Blazing Sixes. Warner Brothers, 1937. 55 minutes B/W. D: Noel Smith. SC: John T. Neville. WITH Dick Foran, Helen Valkis, John Merton, Myra McKinney, Kenneth Harlan, Glenn Strange, Wilfred Lucas, Henry Otho, Milton Kibbee, Gordon Hart, Bud Osborne, Artie Ortego, Jack Mower, Gene Alsace, Frank Ellis, Cactus Mack. A government agent is assigned to capture outlaws who have been robbing gold shipments and in order to accomplish his mission the agent masquerades as a bandit. Pleasing Dick Foran entry with the star handling the action well in addition to singing a few ditties.

302 Blazing Stewardesses. Independent-International, 1975. 85 minutes Color. D: Al Adamson. SC: Samuel M. Sherman & John R. D'Amato. WITH Yvonne De Carlo, Robert Livingston, Don "Red" Barry, The Ritz Brothers (Harry & Jimmy Ritz), Geoffrey Land, Regina Carrol, Connie Hoffman, T. A. King, Lon Bradshaw, John Shank, David Sharpe. Three stewardesses come to the rescue of a rancher friend who is being robbed by his crooked foreman who is in cahoots with the local madam romancing the rancher. Forgetting the brief opening sex scenes, this film is a mild, amusing tribute to the Westerns of yore, complete with a masked hero and a score made up of Gordon Zahler's music; lots of fun. Harry and Jimmy Ritz were last minute replacements for The Three Stooges (Moe Howard, Joe Da Rita, Emil Sitka). V: Super Video.

303 The Blazing Sun. Columbia, 1950. 70 minutes B/W. D: John English. SC: Jack Townley. WITH Gene Autry, Pat Buttram, Lynne Roberts, Anne Gwynne, Edward Norris, Kenne Duncan, Alan Hale Jr., Gregg Barton, Steve Darrell, Tom London, Sandy Sanders, Frankie Marvin, Bob Woodward, Boyd Stockman, Lewis Martin, Virginia Carroll, Sam Flint, Charles Coleman, Pat O'Malley, Almira Sessions, Nolan Leary, Chris Allen. Lawman Gene Autry is on the trail of a duo of bank robbers. Okay modern-day oater.

304 Blazing the Overland Trail. Columbia, 1956. 15 Chapters B/W. D: Spencer Gordon Bennet. SC: George Plympton. WITH Lee Roberts, Dennis Moore, Norma Brooks, Gregg Barton, Don C. Harvey, Lee Morgan, Pierce Lyden, Ed Coch, Reed Howes, Kermit Maynard, Al Ferguson. A crooked rancher organizes a gang to raid the overland trail but he is opposed by an army scout and a Pony Express agent. Tacky cliffhanger, the final such film made in the U. S. and a sad finale to a grand genre.

305 Blazing the Western Trail. Columbia, 1946. 60 minutes B/W. D: Vernon Keays. SC: J. Benton Cheney. WITH Charles Starrett, Tex Harding, Dub Taylor, Carole Matthews, Bob Wills & The Texas Playboys, Alan Bridge, Nolan Leary, Virginia Sale, Steve Clark, Mauritz Hugo, Ethan Laidlaw, Edmund Cobb, Frank LaRue, Forrest Taylor, Francis Walker, Bud Nelson, Budd Buster, Ted Mapes, John Tyrell. The Durango Kid comes to the aid of a stagecoach operator who is being forced out of business by a rival who wants a monopoly on the business. Pretty good "Durango Kid" episode.

Blazing Trail see **Guns for Hire**

306 The Blazing Trail. Columbia, 1949. 56 minutes B/W. D: Ray Nazarro. SC: Barry Shipman. WITH Charles Starrett, Smiley Burnette, Marjorie Stapp, Hank Penny & Slim Duncan, Jack O'Mahoney (Jock Mahoney), Steve Darrell, Fred Sears, Steve Pendleton, Robert Malcolm, Trevor Bardette, John Cason, Frank McCarroll, John Merton, Merrill McCormack. A sheriff and a newspaper editor believe that fraud exists when a rancher is killed and his will leaves only a worthless mine to one brother while the other gets the rest of his property. A fair "Durango Kid" series film.

307 Blindman. 20th Century-Fox, 1972. 105 minutes Color. D: Ferdinando Baldi. SC: Vincenzo Cerami, Piero Anchisi & Tony Anthony. WITH Tony Anthony, Ringo Starr, Agneta Eckemyr, Lloyd Battista, Magda Konopka, Raf Baldassarie, David Dreyer. A blind gunman sets out to stop a ruthless Mexican bandit who had kidnapped fifty mail order brides. Typically violent spaghetti Western, coproduced by Tony Anthony, with more nudity than usual for this type of fare.

308 The Blocked Trail. Republic, 1943. 56 minutes B/W. D: Elmer Clifton. SC: John K. Butler & Jacquin Frank. WITH Bob Steele, Tom Tyler, Jimmie Dodd, Helen Deverall, George J. Lewis, Walter Soderling, Kermit Maynard, Pierce Lyden, Carl Mathews, Hal Price, Budd Buster, Earle Hodgins, Bus Osborne, Al Taylor, Art Dillard, Bud Geary. The Three Mesquiteers are suspected of killing an eccentric man and they set out to expose the real killer as well as his motive. A mystery motif with the killing of the miner only witnessed by his horse makes this "Three Mesquiteers" entry a bit different from others in the series.

309 Blood and Guns. Filamerica, 1968. 90 minutes Color. D: Guilio Petroni. SC: Guilio Petroni & Franco Solinas. WITH Tomas Milian, Orson Welles, John Steiner, Jose Torres, Luciano Casamonica, Anna Maria Lanciaprima, Giancarlo Badessi. During the Mexican revolution of 1917 government soldiers and a young English doctor both want revenge on an illiterate peon who is leading a small group in rebellion. Typically hard to follow and violent Italian oater originally issued as **Tepepa** and **Viva la Revolucion.**

310 Blood and Steel. Independent Pictures, 1925. 60 minutes B/W. D: J. P. McGowan. SC: George Plympton. WITH Helen Holmes, William Desmond, Robert Edeson, Mack V. Wright, Albert J. Smith, Ruth Stonehouse, C. L. Sherwood, Paul Walters, Walter Fitzroy. An engineer is hired to aid in the completion of a railroad and he finds out a rival company plans to sabotage the project. This teaming of action stars Helen Holmes and William Desmond provides its quota of thrills.

311 Blood Arrow. 20th Century-Fox, 1958. 78 minutes B/W. D: Charles Marquis Warren. SC: Fred Freiberger. WITH Scott Brady, Phyllis Coates, Paul Richards, Don Haggerty, Rocky Shahan, Patrick O'Moore, Jeanne Bates, John Dierkes. When her people need a serum a Mormon girl treks through hostile enemy country to get it and she is exposed to Indian attacks. Pretty mundane outing although Phyllis Coates does well by the role of the serum-seeking girl.

312 Blood for a Silver Dollar. Teleworld, 1965. 92 minutes Color. D: Kelvin Jackson Paget. SC: George Finley & Kelvin Jackson Paget. WITH Montgomery Wood, Evelyn Stewart, Peter Cross, John MacDouglas, Frank Farrel, Tor Altmayer, Max Dean, Andrew Scott, Nicholas St. John, Benny Reeves, Frank Liston, Jean Martin, Peter

Surtess, Benny Farber. After the defeat of the South in the Civil War two men head West where they eventually are forced into a gunfight with each other and the one who survives sets out to revenge the death of his brother. Very violent Italian oater made by Fono Roma/ Dorica/Explorer/Les Films Corona as **Un Dollaro Bucato** (A Dollar With a Hole In It).

313 Blood on the Arrow. Allied Artists, 1964. 91 minutes Color. D: Sidney Salkow. SC: Robert E. Kent. WITH Dale Robertson, Martha Hyer, Wendell Corey, Dandy Curran, Paul Mantee, Ted de Corsia, Elisha Cook, Tom Reese. A man who is a prisoner of the Army ends up being the only survivor of an Indian attack and he takes refuge with a couple, at a trading post, whose son has been kidnapped by the Indians who demand rifles as his ransom. None-too-interesting Indians-on-the-warpath feature; looks like something that should have been made a decade before in black and white.

314 Blood on the Moon. RKO Radio, 1948. 88 minutes B/W. D: Robert Wise. SC: Lillie Hayward. WITH Robert Mitchum, Barbara Bel Geddes, Robert Preston, Walter Brennan, Phyllis Thaxter, Frank Faylen, Tom Tully, Charles McGraw, Clifton Young, Tom Tyler, George Cooper, Richard Powers (Tom Keene), Bud Osborne, Zon Murray, Robert Bray, Al Ferguson, Ben Corbett, Joe Devlin, Erville Alderson, Chris-Pin Martin, Robert Malcolm, Ruth Brennan, Harry Carey Jr., Hal Taliaferro, Iron Eyes Cody, Al Murphy. When his rustler-pal hires a gunfighter to run a girl and her father off their ranch either by persuasion or cattle theft, the gunman finds himself falling for the girl. Studio-bound oater should have been more interesting but it is greatly helped by its trio of stars, especially Robert Mitchum. V: Nostalgia Merchant.

315 Blood River. Constantin, 1966. 93 minutes Color. D: Piero Pierotti. SC: Piero Pierotti & Arpad de Riso. WITH Alan Steel, Toni Sailer, Mario Petri, Birgit Heiberg, Wolfgang Lukschy, Dada Gallotti, Elisabetta Fanti. Two men are hired to protect an Inca treasure but outlaws steal it and when one of the men is killed by them the other goes in pursuit. Fair West German-made Western originally issued in Europe as **Samson und der Schatz der Inkas** (Samson and the Treasure of the Incas).

316 Blood Shack. Program Releasing, 1971. 55 minutes Color. D: Wolfgang Schmidt (Ray Dennis Steckler). SC: Christopher Edwards. WITH Carolyn Brandt, Ron Haydock, Jason Wayne, Laurel Spring, John Bates, Steve Edwards, Linda Steckler, Laura Steckler. A woman inherits a ranch which is said to be plagued by a monster. All this modern-day outing offers is a slim, slim budget, a few murders and some rodeo action. Alternate title: **The Chooper.** V: Program Releasing Corporation.

317 Blowing Wild. Warner Brothers, 1953. 90 minutes Color. D: Hugo Fregonese. SC: Philip Yordan. WITH Gary Cooper, Barbara Stanwyck, Ruth Roman, Anthony Quinn, Ward Bond, Ian MacDonald, Richard Karlan, Juan Garcia. A wildcatter puts up all of his money in hopes of striking it rich with a gusher while his ex-love, now the wife of an oil tycoon, wants to renew their relationship. Filmed in Mexico, this steamy oil fields drama promises far more than it delivers; Frankie Laine sings the title song.

318 Blue. Paramount, 1968. 113 minutes Color. D: Silvio Narizzano. SC: Meade Roberts & Ronald M. Cohen. WITH Terence Stamp, Joanna Pettet, Karl Malden, Ricardo Montalban, Anthony Costello, Joe De Santis, James Westerfield, Stathis Giallelis, Carlos East, Robert Lipton, Kevin Corcoran. Raised by a Mexican bandit, a young man finds himself resented by the bandits' three sons and distrusted by Americans as well as Mexicans. Big, expensive Western which proves that foreign genre directors cannot improve their craft in Hollywood; not much of a film.

319 Blue Blazes Rawden. Paramount-Artcraft, 1918. 55 minutes B/W. D: William S. Hart. SC: J. G. Hawks. WITH William S. Hart, Maude George, Gertrude Claire, Robert McKim, Robert Gordon, Hart (Jack) Hoxie. A lumber camp worker wins a saloon in a bet and is forced to shoot and kill the owner but is later reformed by the mother of the man he shot. Another frontier morality play by William S. Hart; good entertainment. V: Classic Video Cinema Collectors Club.

320 Blue Canadian Rockies. Columbia, 1952. 58 minutes B/W. D: George Archainbaud. SC: Gerald Geraghty. WITH Gene Autry, Pat Buttram, Gail Davis, Carolina Cotton, Russ Ford, Tom London, Mauritz Hugo, Don Beddoe, Gene Roth, John

Merton, David Garcia, Bob Woodward, Billy Wilkerson, The Cass County Boys. Sent to Canada by his employer to stop the man's daughter from marrying a no-good, Gene Autry finds the girl has turned her home into a dude ranch and game preserve but the place is plagued with a series of murders. Compact and interesting Gene Autry film. V: Blackhawk, NTA Home Entertainment.

321 Blue Montana Skies. Republic, 1939. 54 (56) minutes B/W. D: B. Reeves Eason. SC: Gerald Geraghty. WITH Gene Autry, Smiley Burnette, June Storey, Harry Woods, Tully Marshall, Al Bridge, Glenn Strange, Dorothy Granger, Edmund Cobb, Jack Ingram, John Beach, Elmo Lincoln, Walt Shrum & His Colorado Hillbillies, Allan Cavan, Buffalo Bill Jr. (Jay Wilsey). When fur thieves begin smuggling pelts into the United States, the government sends a young man to trace the origins of the activities and round up the gang. Fairly good Gene Autry vehicle with a well-written script and ingratiating music interludes.

322 Blue Steel. Monogram, 1934. 54 minutes B/W. D-SC: Robert North Bradbury. WITH John Wayne, Eleanor Hunt, George ("Gabby") Hayes, Ed Peil Sr., Yakima Canutt, George Cleveland, George Nash, Lafe McKee, Hank Bell, Earl Dwire. A U. S. marshal is on the trail of the Polka Dot bandit and he and a fellow sheriff come to the aid of a girl whose father has been murdered by the bandit. Good John Wayne-Lone Star Western with atmospheric opening sequence at a hotel during a thunderstorm when a robbery takes place. V: Electric Video, Capital Home Video, Video Dimensions.

323 Bobbie Jo and the Outlaw. American-International, 1976. 88 minutes Color. D: Mark Lester. SC: Vernon Zimmerman. WITH Marjoe Gortner, Lynda Carter, Jesse Vint, Peggy Stewart, Merrie Lynn Ross, Gerrit Graham. Believing he is the reincarnation of Billy the Kid, a young punk sets out to live up to his beliefs. Really bad modern-day Western.

324 The Boiling Point. Allied, 1932. 70 minutes B/W. D: George Melford. SC: Donald W. Lee, Harry Neumann & Tom Gallaghan. WITH Hoot Gibson, Helen Foster, Skeeter Bill Robbins, Lafe McKee, Tom London, George ("Gabby") Hayes, Wheeler Oakman, William Nye, Charles Bailey, Billy Bletcher, Frank Ellis, Lew Meehan, Hattie McDaniel, Bob Burns, Art Mix, Merrill McCormack, Artie Ortego. A young man is sent to a neighbor's ranch and told to hold his temper for a month or lose an inheritance but once there he gets into a fight over a girl. Slow moving Hoot Gibson vehicle. V: Video Communications.

325 The Bold Caballero. Republic, 1936. 69 minutes Color. D-SC: Wells Root. WITH Robert Livingston, Heather Angel, Sig Rumann, Robert Warwick, Ian Wolfe, Emily Fitzroy, Charles Stevens, Walter Long, Ferdinand Munier, King (Chris-Pin) Martin, John Merton, Jack Kirk, Slim Whitaker, George Plues, Chief Thundercloud, Carlos De Valdez. In Old Spanish California a young man takes on the guise of the masked avenger Zorro to stop the tyranny of local crooked officials. The initial sound Zorro feature is a low budget effort but enhanced by Magna Color, fast action and an ingratiating performance by Bob Livingston as Zorro. V: Video Connection, Video Dimensions, Cassette Express.

326 The Bold Frontiersman. Republic, 1948. 60 minutes B/W. D: Philip Ford. SC: Bob Williams. WITH Allan "Rocky" Lane, Eddy Waller, Roy Barcroft, Fred Graham, John Alvin, Francis McDonald, Ed Cassidy, Edmund Cobb, Harold Goodwin, Jack Kirk, Kenneth Terrell, Marshall Reed, Al Murphy. A government investigator resorts to trickery in order to capture an outlaw and his gang. Standard Allan Lane Republic film. V: Cumberland Video.

327 The Boldest Job in the West. Promofilm, 1971. 101 minutes Color. D-SC: Jose Antonio de la Loma. WITH Mark Edwards, Carmen Sevilla, Fernando Sancho, Charley Bravo, Piero Lulli, Yvan Verella. A gang plans to carry off the robbery of a small town bank but everything goes wrong. Slight Italian Western which showed the genre was badly slipping at this time. Italian title: **El Mas Fabulosi Golpe del Far West.** Alternate title: **Nevada.**

328 Bonanza Town. Columbia, 1951. 56 minutes B/W. D: Fred F. Sears. SC: Barry Shipman & Bart Forswell. WITH Charles Starrett, Smiley Burnette, Fred F. Sears, Luther Crockett, Slim Duncan, Myron Healey, Charles Horvath, Ted Jordan, Al Wyatt, Marshall Reed, Vernon Dent, Paul McGuire. The Durango Kid is on the trail of an outlaw who was thought to be dead but who is actually hiding in a small town and in cahoots with the corrupt town boss. Average "Durango Kid" actioner.

329 The Boogens. Jensen Farley Pictures/ Taft International, 1982. 95 minutes Color. D: James L. Conway. SC: David O'Malley & Bob Hunt. WITH Rebecca Balding, Fred McCarren, Anne-Marie Martin, Jeff Harland, John Crawford, Med Flory, Jon Lormer, Peg(gy) Stewart, Scott Wilkinson, Marcia Reider. The reopening of a silver mine in a remote Utah town results in the letting loose of prehistoric monsters buried there since a 1912 disaster. Eerie horror-Western provides shivers for fans.

330 Boom Town. Metro-Goldwyn-Mayer, 1940. 116 minutes B/W. D: Jack Conway. SC: John Lee Mahin. WITH Clark Gable, Claudette Colbert, Spencer Tracy, Hedy Lamarr, Frank Morgan, Lionel Atwill, Chill Wills, Marion Martin, Minna Gombell, Joe Yule, Horace Murphy, Roy Gordon, Richard Lane, Casey Johnson, George Lessey, Sara Haden, Frank Orth, Frank McGlynn Jr., Curt Bois, Dick Curtis. Two partners strike it rich in the oil fields but soon part over money and a woman. Big, brawling and high budget film which was voted one of the top ten films in 1940 by the Film Daily poll does not hold up too well today but who cares with Hedy Lamarr around to look at?

331 Boot Hill. Film Ventures, 1971. 87 minutes Color. D-SC: Giuseppe Colizzi. WITH Terence Hill, Bud Spencer, Eduardo Ciannelli, Woody Strode, Victor Buono, Lionel Stander. Under the cover of a circus a man escapes from jail and is joined by two others as they seek revenge against an outlaw gang. Rather complicated and somewhat hard-to-follow spaghetti Western issued in Italy in 1969 as **La Collina Degli Stivali** (The Hill of Boots).

332 Boot Hill Bandits. Monogram, 1942. 58 minutes B/W. D: S. Roy Luby. SC: Arthur Durlam. WITH Ray Corrigan, John King, Max Terhune, Jean Brooks, John Merton, Glenn Strange, I. Stanford Jolley, Steve Clark, Richard Cramer, George Chesebro, Budd Buster, Milburn Morante, Jimmie Aubrey, Carl Mathews, Tex Palmer, Merrill McCormack, Hank Bell, Horace B. Carpenter, Charles King. The Range Busters arrive in a small town plagued by a series of Wells Fargo gold shipment robberies and try to find out who is behind the lawlessness. Muddled entry in The Range Busters series, although Glenn Strange is grand as a murderous prospector.

333 Boothill Brigade. Republic, 1937. 58 minutes B/W. D: Sam Newfield. SC: George Plympton. WITH Johnny Mack Brown, Claire Rochelle, Dick Curtis, Horace Murphy, Frank La Rue, Ed Cassidy, Bobby Nelson, Frank Ball, Steve Clark, Frank Ellis, Lew Meehan, Jim Corey, Tex Palmer, Sherry Tansey. A bad man holds the mortgage on a rancher's land and forces him to do his bidding which upsets the man's daughter and her fiancee, the foreman. Final film in Johnny Mack Brown's series for A. W. Hackel; above average and actionful.

334 Boots and Saddles. Republic, 1937. 59 minutes B/W. D: Joseph Kane. SC: Oliver Drake. WITH Gene Autry, Smiley Burnette, Judith Allen, Guy Usher, Gordon (William) Elliott, John Ward, Frankie Marvin, Chris-Pin Martin, Stanley Blystone, Bud Osborne, Merrill McCormack. Ranch foreman Gene Autry becomes involved with the pretty daughter of an Army colonel when he sells horses to the service but he finds a rival horse dealer is out to stop his business. Although actionful, this Gene Autry opus is somewhat hampered by a complicated plot. V: Video Dimensions, Blackhawk, Nostalgia Merchant.

335 Boots of Destiny. Grand National, 1937. 56 minutes B/W. D: Arthur Rosson. SC: Philip White. WITH Ken Maynard, Claudia Dell, Vince Barnett, Walter Patterson, Martin Garralaga, George Morell, Fred Cordova, Ed Cassidy, Carl Mathews, Wally West. A cowboy is put in jail when the local sheriff thinks he is a famous bandit after buried treasure on a girl's ranch. Low budget effort but beefy Ken Maynard could still carry a film and this one is more than passable. The title refers to traces of clay on the villain's boots, which causes his capture.

336 The Border. Universal/RKO, 1982. 107 minutes Color. D: Tony Richardson. SC: Deric Washburn, Walon Green & David Freeman. WITH Jack Nicholson, Valerie Perrine, Harvey Keitel, Warren Oates, Jeff Morris, Dirk Blocker, Lonny Chapman, Elpidia Carillo, Shannon Wilcox. A U. S.-Mexican border guard finds himself caught in the middle with the smuggling of aliens across the border. Not a very good movie.

337 Border Badmen. Producers Releasing Corporation, 1945. 59 minutes B/W. D: Sam Newfield. SC: George Milton. WITH Buster Crabbe, Al St. John, Lorraine Miller, Marilyn Gladstone, Charles King, Marin Sais, Budd Buster, Bud Osborne, John Cason, Ray Bennett, Archie Hall, Robert Kortman. Fuzzy thinks he is the heir to an estate and on the way to claim it he and Billy Carson are arrested by a gang led by a man who wants the estate for himself. Seedy but actionful Billy Carson outing made entertaining by Al St. John's many pratfalls.

338 Border Bandits. Monogram, 1946. 58 minutes B/W. D: Lambert Hillyer. SC: Frank Young. WITH Johnny Mack Brown, Raymond Hatton, Rosa Del Rosario, Riley Hill, John Merton, Tom Quinn, Frank LaRue, Steve Clark, Charles Stevens, Bud Osborne, Terry Frost, I. Stanford Jolley, Ray Jones. Two U. S. marshals come to the aid of a girl whose father has been robbed of valuable jewels. Typically actionful Johnny Mack Brown-Raymond Hatton Monogram series entry.

339 Border Brigands. Universal, 1935. 58 minutes B/W. D: Nick Grinde. SC: Stuart Anthony. WITH Buck Jones, Lona Andre, Fred Kohler, Frank Rice, Edward Keane, J. P. McGowan, Hank Bell, Alan Bridge, Lew Meehan. When his brother is murdered by a gang leader who escapes across the border into the U. S., a Mountie quits the force and heads south to get revenge. Another good outing for Buck Jones in his Universal series.

340 Border Buckaroos. Producers Releasing Corporation, 1943. 61 minutes B/W. D-SC: Oliver Drake. WITH Dave O'Brien, James (Jim) Newill, Guy Wilkerson, Christine McIntyre, Eleanor Counts, Charles King, Jack Ingram, Ethan Laidlaw, Michael Vallon, Kenne Duncan, Reed Howes, Kermit Maynard, Bud Osborne. Mistaken for three outlaws in a town where a murder has just been committed, three lawmen join up with the outlaw gang to find out its leader. Typical entry in PRC's "Texas Rangers" series.

341 Border Caballero. Puritan, 1936. 54 minutes B/W. D: Sam Newfield. SC: Joseph O'Donnell. WITH Tim McCoy, Lois January, Ralph Byrd, Ted Adams, J. Frank Glendon, Earle Hodgins, John Merton, Bob McKenzie, Oscar Gahan, Bill Patton, Frank McCarroll, Tex Phelps, George Morrell, Jack Evans, Ray Henderson. A medicine show sharpshooter, a former federal agent, rejoins the service when his pal and former coworker is murdered by an outlaw gang he had infiltrated. Well done and actionful Tim McCoy vehicle.

342 Border Cafe. RKO Radio, 1937. 67 minutes B/W. D: Lew Landers. SC: Lionel Houser. WITH Harry Carey, John Beal, Armida, Walter Miller, Marjorie Lord, J. Carrol Naish, Lee Patrick, Paul Fix, George Irving, Leona Roberts, Max Wagner, Alec Craig. In order to rehabilitate himself a young man goes West and he ends up fighting outlaws to save a community. Pretty good RKO "B+" effort with a sturdy performance by Harry Carey.

343 Border Devils. Artclass, 1932. 60 minutes B/W. D: William Nigh. SC: Harry C. (Fraser) Crist. WITH Harry Carey, Kathleen Collins, Niles Welch, Ray Gallagher, Olive Gordon, Murdock McQuarrie, George ("Gabby") Hayes, Al Smith, Maston Williams, Art Mix. Falsely accused of a crime, a man breaks jail to prove his innocence. Good Harry Carey vehicle.

344 Border Feud. Producers Releasing Corporation, 1947. 54 minutes B/W. D: Ray Taylor. SC: Joseph O'Donnell. WITH Lash LaRue, Al St. John, Ian Keith, Gloria Marlen, Kenneth Ferrell, Ed Cassidy, Bob Duncan, Brad Slaven, Mikel Conrad, Bud Osborne, Frank Ellis, Richard Cramer, Casey MacGregor. Sheriffs Cheyenne Davis and Fuzzy Q. Jones are at odds with a mysterious outlaw called "The Tiger" and Cheyenne masquerades as the outlaw in order to get the goods on him and his gang. Actionful Lash LaRue outing which moves fast but is not of much interest.

345 Border G-Man. RKO Radio, 1938. 60 minutes B/W. D: David Howard. SC: Oliver Drake & Bernard McConville. WITH George O'Brien, Laraine (Day) Johnson, Ray Whitley, John Miljan, Rita LeRoy, Edgar Dearing, William Stelling, Edward Keane, Bob Burns, Ethan Laidlaw, Hugh Sothern. Posing as a ranch foreman, an FBI agent tries to find out who is heading a smuggling ring along the West Coast. Action-packed George O'Brien series oater, one of his best. Ray Whitley sings "Back in the Saddle Again" (which he cowrote with Gene Autry, who used it as his theme song) in this one.

346 Border Guns. Awyon, 1935. 55 minutes B/W. D: Robert L. Horner. WITH Bill

Cody, Franklyn Farnum, Janet Morgan (Blanche Mehaffey), George Chesebro, Fred Church, William Desmond, Jimmie Aubrey, Wally Wales. A cowpoke is aided by a notorious gunman in stopping outlaws from taking over range land. Crude and vapid, helped only by Franklyn Farnum's bravura performance as the good-badman.

347 Border Incident. Metro-Goldwyn-Mayer, 1949. 95 minutes B/W. D: Anthony Mann. SC: John C. Higgins & George Zuckerman. WITH George Murphy, Ricardo Montalban, Howard Da Silva, James Mitchell, Arnold Moss, Alfonso Bedoya, Teresa Celli, Charles McGraw, Jose Torvay, John Ridgely, Arthur Hunnicutt, Sig Rumann, Otto Waldis. The story of U. S. Immigration agents trying to put a stop to the smuggling of Mexicans into this country across the Texas-Mexican border. Good expose, if somewhat violent, of modern-day slave trade.

Border Land see **Borderland**

348 Border Law. Columbia, 1931. 63 minutes B/W. D: Louis King. SC: Stuart Anthony. WITH Buck Jones, Lupita Tovar, Frank Rice, Jim Mason, Don Chapman, Louis Hickus, F. R. Smith, John Wallace, Bob Burns, Glenn Strange, Fred Burns, Art Mix. When his brother is murdered in a fight a cowboy vows revenge. Excellent Buck Jones vehicle. Remade as **The Fighting Ranger** (q.v.) in 1934, also starring Buck Jones.

349 The Border Legion. Paramount, 1930. 80 minutes B/W. D: Otto Brower & Edwin F. Knoff. SC: Percy Heath & Edward E. Paramore Jr. WITH Richard Arlen, Jack Holt, Fay Wray, Eugene Pallette, Stanley Fields, E. H. Calvert, Ethan Allen, Syd Saylor. In Idaho an outlaw gang rescues a young cowboy about to be hanged for a crime committed by one of the gang members and in gratitude the man agrees to join them. Well done early sound version of the 1916 Zane Grey novel which Goldwyn first filmed in 1919 with Hobart Bosworth and Paramount remade in 1924 with Antonio Moreno.

350 The Border Legion. Republic, 1940. 54 (58) minutes B/W. D: Joseph Kane. SC: Olive Cooper & Louis Stevens. WITH Roy Rogers, George "Gabby" Hayes, Carol Hughes, Joseph Sawyer, Maude Eburne, Jay Novello, Hal Taliaferro, Dick Wessell, Paul Porcasi, Robert Emmett Keane, Ted Mapes, Fred Burns, Post Parks, Art Dillard, Chick Hannon, Charles Baldra. A New York doctor heads to Idaho a wanted fugitive, after taking the blame for a crime committed by his girl's brother, and ends up joining an outlaw gang in order to bring them to justice. Pretty good Roy Rogers film although it bears little resemblance to the Zane Grey work. TV title: **West of the Badlands.**

Border Lust see **Lust to Kill**

351 Border Menace. Awyon, 1936. 55 minutes B/W. D: Jack Nelson. SC: Robert L. Horner. WITH Bill Cody, Miriam Rice, George Chesebro, Jimmie Aubrey, Benny Corbett, Frank Clark, Jim Donnelly. A secret service agent (called "The Shadow") tries to prevent a crooked banker and his henchman from cheating a man and his daughter out of their oil lands. Rock bottom cinema and probably one of the very worst "B" Westerns ever produced.

352 Border Outlaws. United International/ Eagle-Lion, 1950. 59 minutes B/W. D: Richard Talmadge. SC: Arthur Hoerl. WITH Spade Cooley, Maria Hart, Bill Edwards, Bill Kennedy, George Slocum John Laurenz, Douglas Wood, Bud Osborne, John Carpenter, The Metzetti Brothers. Authorities post a big reward for the capture of the "Phantom Rider" who is wanted for smuggling drugs. Another attempt at sagebrush stardom by country swing bandleader Spade Cooley which mainly belongs to Bill Edwards but mostly it is just plain bad. Richard Talmadge not only directed but he coproduced and appeared as one of the Metzetti Brothers. V: Cassette Express.

353 Border Patrol. Pathe, 1928. 5 reels. D: James P. Hogan. SC: Finis Fox. WITH Harry Carey, Kathleen Collins, Richard Tucker, Phillips Smalley, James Neil, James Marcus. A U. S.-Mexican border patrolman falls in love with a girl not knowing she is being used by a band of crooks which include her father. Modern day Western with much footage in El Paso, Texas, containing lots of comedy and well photographed chase sequences.

354 Border Patrol. United Artists, 1943. 54 (64) minutes B/W. D: Lesley Selander. SC: Michael Wilson. WITH William Boyd, Andy Clyde, Jay Kirby, Russell Simpson, Claudia Drake, Cliff Parkinson, George Reeves, Pierre Lyden, Duncan Renaldo, Robert Mitchum, Earle Hodgins, Charles

Stevens, Merrill McCormack. Texas Rangers, Hopalong Cassidy, California Carlson and Johnny Travers try to help a girl find out who killed a mine operator and uncover a crooked judge who leads the gang who murdered the man. Good, exciting "Hopalong Cassidy" entry with Russell Simpson excellent as the crooked judge.

355 The Border Patrolman. 20th Century-Fox, 1936. 60 minutes B/W. D: David Howard. SC: Dan Jarrett & Bennett Cohen. WITH George O'Brien, Polly Ann Young, Roy (LeRoy) Mason, Mary Doran, Smiley Burnette, Tom London, Al Hill, Murdock McQuarrie, John St. Polis, Cyril Ring, William P. Carlton, Martin Garralaga, Chris-Pin Martin. A wealthy family retains a border patrolman to keep their spoiled daughter in line but the girl goes to Mexico and becomes involved with an international jewel theft ring and the patrolman has to come to her rescue. Spritely George O'Brien oater interpolating both comedy and action.

356 Border Phantom. Republic, 1937. 58 minutes B/W. D: S. Roy Luby. SC: Fred Myton. WITH Bob Steele, Harley Wood, Don Barclay, Karl Hackett, Horace Murphy, Miki Morita, John Peters, Perry Murdock, Frank Ball, Hans Joby. A cowpoke and his tenderfoot pal stumble onto a girl whose professor uncle has been murdered. Mystery element provides zest to this exciting Bob Steele vehicle; Harley Wood is the leading lady.

357 Border Rangers. Lippert, 1950. 57 minutes B/W. D: William Berke. SC: Victor West & William Berke. WITH Don ("Red") Barry, Robert Lowery, Wally Vernon, Pamela Blake, Lyle Talbot, Bill Kennedy, John Merton, George Keymas, Tom Kennedy, Eric Norden, Bud Osborne. A gang of outlaws hold up a bank and a Texas Ranger takes on the guise of a bandit to arrange their capture. Fast moving but rather cheap later Don Barry starring effort.

358 Border River. Universal-International, 1954. 81 minutes Color. D: George Sherman. SC: William Sackheim & Louis Stevens. WITH Joel McCrea, Yvonne De Carlo, Pedro Armendariz, Howard Petrie, Erika Nordin, Alfonso Bedoya, George J. Lewis, Nacho Galindo, Ivan Triesault, George Wallace, Martin Garralaga, Lane Chandler, Charles Horvath, Britt Wood, Fred Beir, Monte Montague, Pilar Del Rey. Near the end of the Civil War, a Confederate officer crosses the Rio Grande River into Zona Libre, a territory separated from Mexico, to buy weapons from a self-serving general. Colorful outing that provides good entertainment.

359 Border Romance. Tiffany, 1930. 60 minutes B/W. D: Richard Thorpe. SC: John Francis (Jack) Natteford. WITH Armida, Don Terry, Marjorie "Babe" Kane, Victor Potel, Wesley Barry, Nita Martan, Frank Glendon, Harry Von Meter, William Costello. Three cowpokes have their cattle stolen by a notorious Mexican bandit and one of them romances a girl to find out the whereabouts of the thief although he really loves a pretty senorita. This oater was not much even when it was first issued, other than as a starring vehicle for the then-popular actress Armida, and today it is a dated curio.

360 Border Roundup. Producers Releasing Corporation, 1942. 57 minutes B/W. D: Sam Newfield. SC: Stephen Worth. WITH George Houston, Al St. John, Smokey (Dennis) Moore, Patricia Knox, Charles King, I. Stanford Jolley, Ed Peil Sr., Jimmie Aubrey, John Elliott, Dale Sherwood, Nick Thompson, Frank Ellis, Curley Dresden, Lynton Brent. The Lone Rider comes to the aid of a friend who has been framed for murder by crooks wanting a gold mine. Good entry in "The Lone Rider" series. TV title: **The Lone Rider in Border Roundup.**

361 Border Saddlemates. Republic, 1952. 57 minutes B/W. D: William Witney. SC: Albert DeMond. WITH Rex Allen, Mary Ellen Kay, Slim Pickens, Forrest Taylor, Roy Barcroft, Jimmy Moss, Zon Murray, Keith McConnell, Bud Osborne, The Republic Rhythm Riders. A government agent is sent to a small town on the Canadian border to doctor silver foxes and uncovers a crooked scheme. The "B" Western was on its way out by the time this Rex Allen effort came along and the decline shows. V: Cumberland Video.

362 Border Sheriff. Universal, 1926. 55 minutes B/W. D-SC: Robert North Bradbury. WITH Jack Hoxie, Olive Hasbrouck, S. E. Jennings. Gilbert "Pee Wee" Holmes, Buck Moulton, Tom Lingham, Bert De Marc, Frank Rice, Floyd Criswell, Leonard Trainer. A sheriff, working incognito, becomes the ally of a wealthy rancher who he suspects is the head of a narcotics smuggling operation. Colorful Jack Hoxie film which shows why he was so popular in the 1920s.

363 Border Treasure. RKO Radio, 1950. 60 minutes B/W. D: George Archainbaud. SC: Norman Houston. WITH Tim Holt, Jane Nigh, Richard Martin, John Doucette, House Peters Jr., Inez Cooper, Julian Rivero, Kenneth MacDonald, Vince Barnett, David Leonard. A young woman collects a great amount of money for charity which is stolen from her by an outlaw gang and a cowboy sets out in pursuit to retrieve the loot. Quality entry in the Tim Holt-RKO series.

364 Border Vengeance. Aywon, 1925. 60 minutes B/W. D: Harry S. Webb. SC: Forrest Sheldon. WITH Jack Perrin, Minna Redman, Vondell Darr, Jack Richardson, Josephine Hill, Leonard Clapham. A cowboy fights for a girl and a mine with a gambler and his gang. Low grade silent offering.

365 Border Vengeance. Willis Kent, 1935. 57 minutes B/W. D: Ray Heinz. WITH Reb Russell, Mary Jane Carey, Clarence Geldert, Kenneth MacDonald, June Bupp, Ed Phillips, Norman Feusier, Ben Corbett, Narty Joyce, Slim Whitaker, Fred Burns, Pat Harmon, Glenn Strange, Eddie Parker, Bart Carre, Silvertip Baker, Bud Pope, Bill Gillis, Hank Bell, Rex Bell, Monte Montana, Mabel Strickland. A rodeo performer gets mixed up in a revenge plot set up by the man who forced his family off their land by trumping up a fake murder charge against them. Exceedingly poor Reb Russell vehicle with lots of stock rodeo footage; of some interest, however, because of the brief rodeo appearances by Rex Bell and Monte Montana.

366 Border Vigilantes. Paramount, 1941. 62 minutes B/W. D: Derwin Abrahams, SC: J. Benton Cheney. WITH William Boyd, Russell Hayden, Andy Clyde, Victor Jory, Frances Gifford, Morris Ankrum, Ethel Wales, Tom Tyler, Hal Taliaferro, Jack Rockwell, Britt Wood, Hank Worden, Hank Bell, Edward Earle, Al Haskell, Curley Dresden, Chuck Morrison, Ted Wells. Hopalong Cassidy and pals Lucky and California head to a border mining locale to try and stop raids by an outlaw gang. Formula, but entertaining, "Hopalong Cassidy" series entry.

367 Border Wolves. Universal, 1938. 57 minutes B/W. D: Joseph H. Lewis. SC: Norton S. Parker. WITH Bob Baker, Constance Moore, Fuzzy Knight, Dickie Jones, Frank Campeau, Glenn Strange, Ed Cassidy, Oscar O'Shea, Jack Montgomery, Willie Fung, Dick Dorrell, Frank Ellis, Hank Bell, Jack Kirk, Ed Brady, Jack Evans. During the time of the California gold rush a man is falsely accused of criminal activities and sets out to clear himself. Some fancy camerawork from director Joseph H. Lewis and star Bob Baker's pleasant personality and songs make this one add up to a more than passable outing.

368 Borderland. Paramount, 1937. 54 (82) minutes B/W. D: Nate Watt. SC: Harrison Jacobs. WITH William Boyd, James Ellison, George ("Gabby") Hayes, Stephen Morris (Morris Ankrum), Charlene Wyatt, John Beach, Nora Lane, George Chesebro, Trevor Bardette, Earle Hodgins, Al Bridge, John St. Polis, Slim Whitaker, Cliff Parkinson, Karl Hackett, Robert Walker, Frank Ellis, Ed Cassidy, J. P. McGowan, Jack Evans. Hopalong Cassidy pretends to take up the side of the lawless in order to aid the Texas Rangers and the Mexican Secret Service in capturing a notorious border badman called "The Fox." Overlong but acceptable "Hopalong Cassidy" feature.

Borderland Rangers see **The Man from God's Country** (1924)

369 Borderline. Universal, 1950. 88 minutes B/W. D: William A. Seiter. SC: Devery Freeman. WITH Fred MacMurray, Claire Trevor, Raymond Burr, Roy Roberts, Morris Ankrum, Jose Torvay, Charles Lane, Don Diamond, Nacho Galindo. A narcotics agent and a newspaperwoman team to track down dope smugglers on the Mexican border. Ho-hum feature which unsuccessfully treads a thin line between comedy and drama.

370 Borderline. Associated Film Distribution, 1980. 106 minues Color. D: Jerrold Freeman. SC: Steve Kline & Jerrold Freeman. WITH Charles Bronson, Bruno Kirby, Bert Remsen, Michael Lerner, Kenneth McMillan, Ed Harris, Karmin Murcelo, Enrique Castillo, A. Wilford Brimley, Norman Alden, James Victor, John Ashton, Lawrence Casey, Charles Cyphers. When a fellow border patrolman is murdered while investigating the smuggling of aliens into the U. S., a man sets out to avenge the murder and stop the illegal traffic in humans. Taut and well executed Charles Bronson thriller. V: Cumberland Video.

371 Bordertown Gunfighters. Republic, 1944. 56 minutes B/W. D: Howard Bretherton. SC: Norman S. Hall. WITH Bill Elliott, George "Gabby" Hayes, Anne Jeffreys, Ian Keith, Harry Woods, Roy Barcroft, Bud Geary, Karl Hackett, Charles King, Carl Sepulveda, Edward Keane, Frank McCarroll, Wheaton Chambers, Ken Terrell, Neal Hart, Frosty Royce, Marshall Reed, Bill Woolf. Wild Bill Elliott is assigned to a small town where a lottery racket is in operation and when he gets there he tries to break up the gang and also finds romance. Typically fast moving Bill Elliott Republic entry.

372 Bordertown Trail. Republic, 1944. 55 minutes B/W. D: Lesley Selander. SC: Bob Williams & Jesse Duffy. WITH Smiley Burnette, Sunset Carson, Ellen Lowe, Weldon Heyburn, Jack Luden, Addison Richards, Francis McDonald, John James, Jack Kirk, Harry Willis, Jack O'Shea, Neal Hart, Chick Hannon, Robert Wilke. The U. S. Border Patrol finds itself up against a gang of smugglers in cahoots with a self-serving politician. Early actionful Sunset Carson entry with as many plot twists as fights with one-time genre star Jack Luden in a supporting role as Sunset's brother.

373 Born Reckless. Warner Brothers, 1959. 79 minutes B/W. D: Howard Koch. SC: Richard Landau & Aubrey Schenck. WITH Mamie Van Doren, Jeff Richards, Arthur Hunnicutt, Carol Ohmart, Tom Duggan, Tex Williams, Donald (Don "Red") Barry, Nacho Galindo, Orlando Rodrigues, Johnny Olenn & Group. Rodeo drama about a champion performer and his beautiful blonde girlfriend. Title pretty much tells all in this rodeo outing.

374 Born to Battle. Pathe, 1927. 5 reels B/W. D: Allan J. Neitz. SC: L. V. Jefferson. WITH Bill Cody, Barbara Luddy, Sheldon Lewis, Frank McGlynn Jr., Olin Francis, Ralph Yearsley, Nora Cecil, J. P. Lockney, Lew Meehan, Sailor Sharkey. A half-crazed woman wants revenge on the man who killed her husband and the man's daughter is in love with a cowpoke whose uncle wants the feud to continue so he can get control of both of the feuding parties' ranches. Silent Bill Cody feature with a complicated plot, quite a bit of slapstick comedy and the star doing some nice stunt riding as well as using a bullwhip.

375 Born to Battle. Reliable, 1935. 58 minutes B/W. D: Harry S. Webb. SC: Rose Gordon & Carl (Krusada) Hartman.

WITH Tom Tyler, Jean Carmen, Earl Dwire, Julian Rivero, Nelson McDowell, William Desmond, Richard Alexander, Charles King, Ralph Lewis, Ben Corbett, Jimmie Aubrey, Roger Williams, Robert Walker, George Morrell, Blackie Whiteford. A wild living cowboy is bailed out of jail by a representative of the cattlemen's association and assigned the task of locating a notorious rustler and his gang. Actionful, but shoddy, Tom Tyler film.

376 Born to Buck. A.N.E., 1968. 93 minutes Color. WITH Casey Tibbs; Henry Fonda, Rex Allen (narrators). Documentary about rodeo champion Casey Tibbs breeding his own bucking broncos on the Teton Sioux Indian reservation in South Dakota, then driving his herd of some 400 wild horses halfway across the state and back to his ranch. A different kind of film with fine scenic values.

377 Born to the Saddle. Astor, 1953. 73 minutes Color. D: William Beaudine. SC: Adele Buffington. WITH Donald Woods, Leif Erickson, Karen Morley, Rand Brooks, Chuck Courtney, Glenn Strange, Dolores Priest, Fred Kohler Jr., Dan White, Milton Kibbee, Boyd Davis. A young boy is befriended by a man who hires him to train a horse for an important race although the man is really a gambler and the race has been fixed. Astor's low production values do little to enhance this Western racing drama.

378 Born to the West. Paramount, 1937. 59 minutes B/W. D: Charles Barton. SC: Stuart Anthony & Robert Yost. WITH John Wayne, Johnny Mack Brown, Marsha Hunt, John Patterson, Syd Saylor, Monte Blue, Lucien Littlefield, Nick Lukats, James Craig, Jack Kennedy, Vester Pegg, Earl Dwire, Jim Thorpe, Jennie Boyle, Alan Ladd, Jack Daley, Lee Prather. A cowboy and his pal wander into a small town and go to work for a cattleman and the cowboy falls for his boss' girl and is framed by crooks. Fairly interesting Zane Grey outing with nice scenic locales. Re-released as **Hell Town.**

379 Borrowed Trouble. United Artists, 1948. 54 (60) minutes B/W. D: George Archainbaud. SC: Charles Belden. WITH William Boyd, Andy Clyde, Rand Brooks, Elaine Riley, John Kellogg, Earle Hodgins, Cliff Clark, Helen Chapman, John Parrish, Herbert Rawlinson, Don Haggerty. An old maid school teacher tries to stop a saloon owner from keeping his business open adjacent to her school. Amusing "Hopalong Cassidy" entry enhanced by nice performances.

380 The Boss Cowboy. Superior, 1934. 51 minutes B/W. D: Denver Dixon (Victor Adamson) SC: B. Burdoge. WITH Buddy Roosevelt, Frances Morris, Sam Pierce, Fay McKenzie, Bud Osborne, George Chesebro, Lafe McKee, William McCormick, Allen Holbrook, Clyde McClary. A ranch foreman falls for two girls, one of whom is being robbed by her foreman, who is a wanted killer. Pretty poor stuff.

381 Boss Nigger. Dimension, 1974. 87 minutes Color. D: Jack Arnold. SC: Fred Williamson. WITH Fred Williamson, D'Urville Martin, William Smith, Barbara Leigh, R. G. Armstrong, Don "Red" Barry, Carmen Hayworth, Ben Zeller. Two black bounty hunters take over a small town as the marshal and deputy and capture an outlaw gang. Violent black oater directed by the somewhat highly regarded director Jack Arnold.

382 Boss of Boomtown. Universal, 1944. 56 minutes B/W. D: Ray Taylor. SC: William Lively. WITH Rod Cameron, Tom Tyler, Fuzzy Knight, Vivian Austin, Ray Whitley, Jack Ingram, Robert Barron, Marie Austin, Max Wagner, Sam Flint, Richard Alexander, Forrest Taylor, Beverlee Mitchell. Two buddies ride into a brawling Western town where they come up against the city boss and also find romance. Rod Cameron's first genre starring vehicle is an entertaining one and it will appeal to fans because Tom Tyler is costarred and the two make a good duo.

383 Boss of Bullion City. Universal, 1941. 61 minutes B/W. D: Ray Taylor. SC: Arthur St. Claire & Victor McLeod. WITH Johnny Mack Brown, Fuzzy Knight, Nell O'Day, Maria Montez, Harry Woods, Melvin Lang, Richard Alexander, Earle Hodgins, Karl Hackett, Frank Ellis, Tex Terry, Kermit Maynard. A ruthless man rules his town with an iron hand and a lawman is called in to put a stop to his reign. Well produced entry in the Johnny Mack Brown series; of interest to Maria Montez fans because she played the second female lead, the role of a girl who hero-worships Brown.

384 The Boss of Hangtown Mesa. Universal, 1942. 59 minutes B/W. D: Joseph H. Lewis. SC: Oliver Drake. WITH Johnny

Mack Brown, Fuzzy Knight, William Farnum, Rex Lease, Helen Deverell, Hugh Prosser, Jimmy Wakely, The Pals of the Golden West, Nora Lou Martin, Robert Barron, Michael Vallon, Fred Kohler Jr., Henry Hall. When a man working for the telegraph company is robbed by an outlaw, a sheriff is assigned to clean up a lawless town. Typically plotted entry in the Johnny Mack Brown Universal series but this one has a plethora of music.

385 Boss of Lonely Valley. Universal, 1937. 60 minutes B/W. D: Ray Taylor. SC: Frances Guihan. WITH Buck Jones, Muriel Evans, Harvey Clark, Walter Miller, Lee Phelps, Ted Adams, Matty Fain, Ezra Pallette, Dickie Howard. A crooked town boss obtains land through fraud and a cowboy arrives in the area and puts a stop to his unlawful activities. Buck Jones produced this entry in his Universal series, a fairly good effort based on Forrest Brown's novel.

386 Boss of Rawhide. Producers Releasing Corporation, 1943. 60 minutes B/W. D-SC: Elmer Clifton. WITH Dave O'Brien, Jim (James) Newill, Guy Wilkerson, Nell O'Day, Ed Cassidy, Jack Ingram, Charles King, Billy Bletcher, George Chesebro, Robert Hill, Dan White, Lucille Vance, Robert Kortman. The Texas Rangers are sent to an area where mysterious killings have been taking place and they uncover a gang who has unlawfully set up toll gates across range land. Another fast but cheap entry in PRC's "The Texas Rangers" series.

387 The Boss Rider of Gun Creek. Universal, 1936. 60 minutes B/W. D: Lesley Selander. SC: Frances Guihan. WITH Buck Jones, Muriel Evans, Harvey Clark, Tom Chatterton, Josef Swickard, Lee Phelps, Ernest Hilliard, Mahlon Hamilton, Alphonse Ethier, Edward Hearn. A man convicted of a murder he did not commit escapes from prison and takes on the guise of his lookalike in order to clear himself. Buck Jones plays a dual role in this entertaining entry in his Universal series.

388 Both Barrels Blazing. Columbia, 1945. 57 minutes B/W. D: Derwin Abrahams. SC: William Lively. WITH Charles Starrett, Tex Harding, Dub Taylor, Pat Parrish, Emmett Lynn, Alan Bridge, The Jesters, Dan White, Edward Howard, Jack Rockwell, Charles King, Robert Barron, Mauritz Hugo, Bud Nelson, John

Cason, Bert Dillard, Tex Palmer. A crook uses an old panhandler as a front for shipping stolen gold and a Texas Ranger, alias the Durango Kid, is on his trail. Fair entry in the "Durango Kid" series.

389 The Bounty Hunter. Warner Brothers, 1954. 79 minutes Color. D: Andre De Toth. SC: Winston Miller. WITH Randolph Scott, Dolores Dorn, Marie Windsor, Howard Petrie, Harry Antrim, Robert Keys, Ernest Borgnine, Dub Taylor, Tyler McDuff, Archie Twitchell, Paul Picerni, Phil Chambers, Mary Lou Holloway, Charles Delaney, Fess Parker. A bounty hunter is on the trail of three killers who pretend to be average citizens. Randolph Scott fans will love this hard, relentless chase film which also features a fight sequence between heroine Dolores Dorn and saloon gal Marie Windsor.

390 The Bounty Killer. Embassy, 1965. 92 minutes Color. D: Spencer Gordon Bennet. SC: R. Alexander & Leo Gordon. WITH Dan Duryea, Rod Cameron, Audrey Dalton, Richard Arlen, Buster Crabbe, Fuzzy Knight, Johnny Mack Brown, Bob Steele, G. M. "Bronco Billy" Anderson, Peter Duryea, Eddie Quillan, Norman Willis, Edmund Cobb, I. Stanford Jolley, Frank Lackteen, Dan White, Grady Sutton, Emory Parnell, Red Morgan, Tom Kennedy. A dude from the East is forced to defend himself against an outlaw gang and when he kills the lot of them he is turned into a vicious bounty hunter. Production values and script are none-too-great but nobody really cares with all of the veteran genre stars and character players which populate this Alex Gordon production; Buster Crabbe is particularly good as a vicious outlaw.

391 The Bounty Man. ABC-TV/ABC Circle Films, 1972. 74 minutes Color. D: John Llewellyn Moxey. SC: Jim Byrnes. WITH Clint Walker, Richard Basehart, John Ericson, Margot Kidder, Gene Evans, Arthur Hunnicutt, Rex Holman, Wayne Sutherlin, Paul Harper, Dennis Cross. Two rival bounty hunters track a young outlaw to an isolated valley and then find themselves being attacked by the outlaw's vicious gang. This telefeature shows just how good TV movies can be when some care is taken with them.

392 Bowery Buckaroos. Monogram, 1947. 66 minutes B/W. D: William Beaudine. SC: Tim Ryan & Edmond Seward. WITH Leo Gorcey, Huntz Hall, Bobby Jordan, Gabriel Dell, Billy Benedict, David Gorcey, Julie Gibson, Bernard Gorcey, Minerva Urecal, Jack Norman (Norman Willis), Russell Simpson, Chief Yowlachie, Iron Eyes Cody, Rose Turich, Sherman Sanders, Billy Wilkerson, Jack O'Shea, Bud Osborne. When drugstore owner Louis is accused of murder the Bowery Boys go West to track down the real killer. Average Bowery Boys series entry which will please their fans.

393 The Boy From Oklahoma. Warner Brothers, 1954. 88 minutes Color. D: Michael Curtiz. SC: Frank Davis & Winston Miller. WITH Will Rogers Jr., Nancy Olson, Lon Chaney, Anthony Caruso, Sheb Wooley, Merv Griffin, Clem Bevans, Louis Jean Heydt, Wallace Ford, Slim Pickens, Harry Lauter, James Griffith, Charles Watts, John Cason, Guy Teague, Tom Monroe, George Chesebro, George Lloyd, John Weldon, Forrest Taylor, Jack Daly, Guy Wilkerson, Britt Wood, Frank Marlowe, Emile Avery, Bud Osborne, Charles Waggenheim, Tyler MacDuff, Denver Pyle, Ted Mapes. An easy-going law student finds himself the sheriff of a rough town which he manages to clean up with the urging of a pretty girl, the daughter of his murdered predecessor. Pleasant semi-funny Western which is a good vehicle for Will Rogers Jr.

394 The Boy Who Talked to Badgers. Buena Vista, 1975. 100 minutes Color. D: Gary Nelson. WITH Christian Juttner, Carl Betz, Salome Jens, Denver Pyle (narrator). A young boy has the ability to communicate with animals and he runs away from home to the wilds of Canada where his life is endangered. Well made Walt Disney family film originally telecast as a two-part segment of the Disney TV series on NBC-TV.

395 Boy's Ranch. Metro-Goldwyn-Mayer, 1946. 97 minutes Color. D: Roy Rowland. SC: William Ludwig. WITH James Craig, Butch Jenkins, Skippy (Skip) Homeier, Dorothy Patrick, Ray Collins, Darryl Hickman, Sharon McManus, Minor Watson, Arthur Space, Robert Emmett O'Connor, Moroni Olsen, Geraldine Wall. An ex-baseball player, trying to raise two orphans on his cattle ranch, makes it possible for delinquent boys to rehabilitate themselves by working there. Somewhat dated juvenile-oriented film which may appeal to youngsters.

396 Brand of Fear. Monogram, 1949. 56 minutes B/W. D: Oliver Drake. SC:

Basil Dickey. WITH Jimmy Wakely, Dub Taylor, Gail Davis, Tom London, Ray Whitley, Marshall Reed, William Ruhl, William Norton Bailey, Boyd Stockman, Dee Cooper, Frank McCarroll, Holly Bane, Bob Curtis, Myron Healey, Bob Woodward, Denver Dixon, Ray Jones. A cowpoke falls in love with a beautiful girl only to discover she is the daughter of an ex-convict. Jimmy Wakely's singing and a good supporting cast make this one passable.

397 Brand of Hate. Supreme, 1934. 63 minutes B/W. D: Lewis D. Collins. SC: John F. (Jack) Natteford. WITH Bob Steele, Lucille Brown(e), William Farnum, George ("Gabby") Hayes, Archie Ricks, James Flavin, Charles K. French, Jack Rockwell, Mickey Rentschler. A rancher is forced to harbor his cattle stealing half-brother and his pals while the man's daughter is in love with the son of a neighboring rancher, the young man trying to investigate the cattle thefts. Somewhat average Bob Steele vehicle with an actionful finale and a fine cast.

398 Brand of the Devil. Producers Releasing Corporation, 1944. 62 minutes B/W. D: Harry Fraser. SC: Elmer Clifton. WITH Dave O'Brien, Jim (James) Newill, Guy Wilkerson, Ellen Hall, Charles King, I. Stanford Jolley, Reed Howes, Budd Buster, Karl Hackett, Kermit Maynard, Ed Cassidy. An outlaw gang called "The Brand of the Devil" has been plaguing ranchers and the Texas Rangers trio come to their aid. Another cheap entry (number fourteen) in PRC's "The Texas Rangers" series and the last one for James Newill.

399 Brand of the Outlaws. Supreme, 1936. 60 minutes B/W. D-SC: Robert North Bradbury. WITH Bob Steele, Margaret Marquis, Jack Rockwell, Charles King, Virginia True Boardman, Ed Cassidy, Frank Ball, Robert Kortman, Bud Osborne. After saving the life of a lawman, a cowboy joins up with a gang not knowing they are cattle rustlers and the sheriff captures him and brands him an outlaw and he sets out to prove his innocence. Actionful and well done Bob Steele film.

400 Branded. Columbia, 1931. 61 minutes B/W. D: D. Ross Lederman. SC: Randall Faye. WITH Buck Jones, Ethel Kenton, Wallace MacDonald, Al Smith, Fred Burns, Philo McCullough, John Oscar, Robert Kortman, Clark Burroughs, Sam McDaniel. Inheriting a ranch, a man

becomes involved with a pretty neighbor whose crooked foreman plans to rustle his cattle. Good Buck Jones series film.

401 Branded. Paramount, 1951. 95 minutes Color. D: Rudolph Mate. SC: Sidney Boehm & Cyril Hume. WITH Alan Ladd, Mona Freeman, Charles Bickford, Robert Keith, Joseph Callem, Peter Hansen, Tom Tully, Milburn Stone, Martin Garralaga, Edward Clark, John Butler, John Berkes. Outlaws find a man in the wilderness and come up with a scheme to use him in bilking a rancher by making the man think this is his long-lost son. There is enough action and romance in this Alan Ladd film to satisfy most genre followers.

402 Branded a Coward. Supreme, 1935. 57 minutes B/W. D: Sam Newfield. SC: Richard Martinsen. WITH Johnny Mack Brown, Billie Seward, Roger Williams, Syd Saylor, Lloyd Ingraham, Yakima Canutt, Lee Shumway, Frank McCarroll, Rex Downing, Robert Kortman, Ed Piel Sr., Joe Girard. After seeing his parents killed when he was a boy, a young man overcomes his fear of gunmen and becomes a marshal and sets out to find a criminal, who turns out to be his long-lost brother. Johnny Mack Brown's first series Western, a good one despite low production values.

403 Branded Men. Tiffany, 1931. 70 minutes B/W. D: Phil Rosen. SC: Earle Snell. WITH Ken Maynard, June Clyde, Charles King, Irving Bacon, Donald Keith, Jack Rockwell, Hooper Atchley, Edmund Cobb, Slim Whitaker, Billy Bletcher, Al Taylor, Bud McClure. A cowboy and his pals all join the side of the law in order to round up a bad man and his outlaw gang. Standard Ken Maynard vehicle without the fast pace of some of his other features. V: Discount Video.

404 The Brass Legend. United Artists, 1956. 79 minutes B/W. D: Gerd Oswald. SC: Don Martin. WITH Hugh O'Brian, Nancy Gates, Raymond Burr, Reba Tassell, Donald MacDonald, Robert Burton, Eddie Firestone, Stacy Harris, Norman Leavitt, Russell Simpson. When a young boy aids him in the capture of a vicious killer, a sheriff tries to save the lad when the badman sets out for revenge. Average oater with future TV stars Hugh O'Brian (as the sheriff) and Raymond Burr (as the bad guy) to recommend it.

405 The Bravados. 20th Century-Fox, 1958. 98 minutes Color. D: Henry King.

SC: Philip Yordan. WITH Gregory Peck, Joan Collins, Stephen Boyd, Albert Salmi, Henry Silva, Kathleen Gallant, Barry Coe, George Voskovec, Herbert Rudley, Lee Van Cleef, Andrew Duggan, Ken Scott, Gene Evans, Joe Da Rita, Robert Adler, Robert Griffin. Wanting vengeance for the rape and murder of his wife, a man sets out to kill the men who committed the crime and after a time realizes he has become no better than those he is hunting. Austere but very good film with Gregory Peck excellent as the hunter and Joe Da Rita (later one of The Three Stooges) giving a surprisingly harrowing performance as the "hangman."

406 Brave Warrior. Columbia, 1952. 73 minutes Color. D: Spencer Gordon Bennet. SC: Robert E. Kent. WITH Jon Hall, Christine Larson, Jay Silverheels, Michael Ansara, Harry Cording, James Seay, George Eldredge, Leslie Denison, Rory Mallison, Rusty Westcoatt. Peace between settlers and Indians in Indiana is threatened in 1811 by the interference of the British. Not even Technicolor can help this dull Sam Katzman production.

407 Braveheart. Producers Distributing Corporation, 1925. 60 minutes B/W. D: Alan Hale. SC: Mary O'Hara. WITH Rod LaRocque, Lillian Rich, Robert Edeson, Arthur Housman, Frank Hagney, Jean Acker, Tyrone Power, Sally Rand, Henry Victor. An Indian brave goes to college to study law in order to defend his tribe's fishing rights and there he becomes a top athlete but in order to save a friend he ends up in disgrace. Well done silent feature, presented by Cecil B. DeMille.

408 The Bravos. ABC-TV/Universal, 1972. 100 minutes Color. D: Ted Post. SC: Christopher Knopf & Ted Post. WITH George Peppard, Pernell Roberts, Belinda Montgomery, L. Q. Jones, George Murdock, Barry Brown, Dana Elcar, John Kellogg, Bo Svenson, Vincent Van Patten, Clint Ritchie, Randolph Mantooth, Joaquin Martinez. After the Civil War an officer is assigned to command a small Western post but troubles with the Indians arise and his small son is kidnapped. There is nothing special about this made-for-TV Western, despite a good story premise.

409 The Brazen Bell. Universal, 1963. 74 minutes Color. D: James Sheldon. WITH James Drury, Lee J. Cobb, George C. Scott, Doug McClure, Gary Clarke, Pippa Scott, Roberta Shore, Anne Meacham, Royal Dano, John Davis Chandler, Robert J. Stevenson, Ross Elliott, Kay Stewart, Justin Smith, Walter Matthews, Lester Maxwell, Rick Murray. A frightened school teacher attempts to escape the harsh realities of the West but in a forced showdown proves he can stand up and fight. Pretty good drama originally telecast October 17, 1962 as an episode of "The Virginian" (NBC-TV, 1962-70) series and issued theatrically abroad.

410 Breakheart Pass. United Artists, 1976. 95 minutes Color. D: Tom Gries. SC: Alistair MacLean. WITH Charles Bronson, Ben Johnson, Richard Crenna, Jill Ireland, Charles Durning, Ed Lauter, David Huddleston, Roy Jenson, Casey Tibbs, Archie Moore, Joe Kapp, Read Morgan, Robert Rothwell, Rayford Barnes, Scott Newman, Bill McKinney, Eddie Little Sky, Robert Tessier. Masquerading as a cowardly prisoner, an undercover agent is put on a train in an effort to expose gun runners. Alistair MacLean adapted his novel to the screen for this film, a taut Western-mystery. VD: Blackhawk.

411 Breakout. NBC-TV/Universal, 1970. 93 minutes Color. D: Richard Irving. SC: Sy Gomberg. WITH James Drury, Red Buttons, Kathryn Hays, Woody Strode, Sean Garrison, Victor Meyerlink, Bert Freed, Mort Mills, William Mims, Harold J. Stone, Don Wilbanks, Kenneth Tobey, Ric Roman. A criminal works out a master plan to escape from a mountain prison camp to be near his wife and the half-million dollars he has hidden but the plan is endangered by a small boy lost in the snowy area. Well done TV movie.

412 Breed of the Border. Monogram, 1933. 58 minutes B/W. D: Robert North Bradbury. SC: Harry O. Jones. WITH Bob Steele, Marion Byron, George ("Gabby") Hayes, Ernie Adams, Wilfred Lucas, Henry Rocquemore, Fred Cavens, Robert Cord, Perry Murdock, John Elliott, Hal Price, Horace B. Carpenter, Blackie Whiteford, Ray Jones. A race car driver and his pal join forces with a female government undercover agent to track down smugglers working along the Mexican border. Complicated but actionful Bob Steele vehicle with some nice fencing scenes between the star and Fred Cavens.

413 Breed of the West. Big 4, 1930. 5 reels. D: Alvin J. Neitz (Alan James).

The Bride

WITH Wally Wales, Virginia Browne Faire, Buzz Barton, Robert Walker, Lafe McKee, Bobby Dunn, George Gerwin, Hank (Bell) Cole, Edwin (Edmund) Cobb, Art Mix, Frank Ellis, Slim Andrews. A ranch hand is in love with the boss' daughter but has a rival in the ranch foreman, who plans to rob the old man. More romance than action in this poorly made Wally Wales film.

The Bride Comes to Yellow Sky see **Face to Face**

414 Bridger. ABC-TV/Universal, 1976. 100 minutes Color. D: David Lowell Rich. SC: Merwin Gerard. WITH James Wainwright, Ben Murphy, Dirk Blocker, John Anderson, William Windom, Sally Field, Margarita Cordova, Tom Middleton, X Brands. Jim Bridger is commissioned by President Andrew Jackson to open a trail from the Rocky Mountains to the West Coast in forty days in order to obtain the land for the U. S. Fair historical drama with John Anderson as Andrew Jackson being its best moments.

415 Brigham. Yordan-Yeaman, 1977. SC: Philip Yordan. WITH Maurice Grandmaison, Charles Moll. The story of the Mormon Church from the time of Joseph Smith through the Indian Wars of the 1850s. This low budget effort was redone and reissued in 1978 but its only bookings were sparse ones in the mountain states.

Brigham Young see **Brigham Young, Frontiersman**

416 Brigham Young, Frontiersman. 20th Century-Fox, 1940. 114 minutes B/W. D: Henry Hathaway. SC: Lamar Trotti. WITH Tyrone Power, Linda Darnell, Dean Jagger, Jane Darwell, Brian Donlevy, John Carradine, Mary Astor, Vincent Price, Jean Rogers, Ann Todd, Willard Robertson, Moroni Olsen, Marc Lawrence, Stanley Andrews, Frank Thomas, Fuzzy Knight, Dickie Jones, Selmer Jackson, Russell Simpson, Arthur Aylesworth, Chief Big Tree, Claire Du Brey, Tully Marshall, Davison Clark, Dick Rich, Edwin Maxwell, Edmund MacDonald, Charles Halton, Lee Shumway, Charles Middleton, Frank LaRue, Cecil Watson, Ruth Robinson. The trek of the Mormons to Salt Lake, from the death of Joseph Smith in Illinois to the final establishment of the Mormon colony in Utah, is retold in this historical drama. Very well-done, with a great performance by Dean Jagger in the title role; recommended.

417 Brighty of Grand Canyon. Feature Film Corporation of America, 1967. 92 minutes Color. D-SC: Norman Foster. WITH Joseph Cotten, Pat Conway, Dick Foran, Karl Swenson, Dandy Curran, Jiggs (burro). When his master is murdered a little burro meets a famed hunter, a boy and Theodore Roosevelt, as he brings the killer to justice. Location filming and a good story make this pleasant entertainment.

418 Brimstone. Republic, 1949. 90 minutes Color. D: Joseph Kane. SC: Thames Williams. WITH Rod Cameron, Adrian Booth, Forrest Tucker, Walter Brennan, Jack Holt, Jim Davis, James Brown, Guinn Williams, Jack Lambert, Will Wright, David Williams, Harry V. Cheshire, Hal Taliaferro, Herbert Rawlinson, Stanley Andrews, Charlita. A lawman is sent to a territory where cattle rustling is rampant and he finds out that his friend, now a crooked sheriff, is working with a rancher and his two sons in the thefts. Actionful, brutal Western which is far above average.

Broadway to Cheyenne see **From Broadway to Cheyenne**

419 Broken Arrow. 20th Century-Fox, 1950. 93 minutes Color. D: Delmer Daves. SC: Michael Blankfort. WITH James Stewart, Jeff Chandler, Debra Paget, Basil Ruysdael, Arthur Hunnicutt, Will Geer, Joyce MacKenzie, Raymond Bramley, Jay Silverheels, Argentina Brunetti, Jack Lee, Robert Adler, Harry Carter, Robert Griffin, Billy Wilkerson, Mickey Kuhn, Charles Soldani, Iron Eyes Cody, John Doucette, Trevor Bardette. After the Civil War an Indian agent, who eventually marries an Indian maiden, tries to bring peace between the government and the Chiricahua Apaches lead by Cochise. Highly colorful and entertaining Western.

420 Broken Lance. 20th Century-Fox, 1954. 96 minutes Color. D: Edward Dmytryk. SC: Richard Murphy. WITH Spencer Tracy, Jean Peters, Robert Wagner, Richard Widmark, Katy Jurado, Hugh O'Brian, Carl Benton Reid, Eduard Franz, Earl Holliman, E. G. Marshall, Philip Ober, Robert Burton, Robert Adler, Robert Grandlin, Harry Carter, Nacho Galindo, Julian Rivero, Edmund Cobb, Russell Simpson, King Donovan, George E. Stone, Paul Kruger. Following his second marriage, an aging Western land baron begins to feel that his empire is crumbling due to conflicts with his sons. Western remake of **House of Strangers** (20th Century-Fox, 1949), this is a powerful and well acted film.

421 The Broken Land. 20th Century-Fox, 1962. 60 minutes Color. D: John Bushelman. SC: Edward Lasko. WITH Kent Taylor, Jody McCrea, Dianna Darrin, Robert Sampson, Gary Sneed, Don Orlands, Jack Nicholson, Bud Pollard. A small Western town is ruled by a sadistic sheriff who is at odds with a trio of young people who finally enlist the aid of the lawman's deputy in bringing about his downfall. Compact oater with an impressive performance by Kent Taylor as the sheriff.

422 Broken Sabre. Columbia, 1966. 89 minutes Color. D: Bernard McEveety. SC: Jameson Brewer. WITH Chuck Connors, Kamala Devi, Peter Breck, MacDonald Carey, John Carradine, Wendell Corey, Rochelle Hudson, Robert Q. Lewis, Cesar Romero, Patrick Wayne, William Bryant, Steve Malo, H. M. Wynant, John Lormer, Jay Jostyn, Montie Plyler. A man is convicted of being a coward during the Battle of Bitter Creek and he tries to prove himself in the Arizona Frontier country after being dismissed from the service. This feature was made up of several segments of the "Branded" (NBC-TV, 1965-66) and issued theatrically in Great Britain.

423 The Broken Star. United Artists, 1956. 82 minutes B/W. D: Lesley Selander. SC: John C. Higgins. WITH Howard Duff, Lita Baron, Bill Williams, Henry Calvin, Douglas Fowley, Addison Richards, Joel Ashby, John Pickard, William Phillips, Dorothy Adams. A deputy marshal claims he killed a man in self-defense when he really murdered him for his gold. Interesting plot does not help this average oater.

424 Bronco Billy. Warner Brothers, 1980. 119 minutes Color. D: Clint Eastwood. SC: Dennis Hackim. WITH Clint Eastwood, Sondra Locke, Geoffrey Lewis, Scatman Crothers, Bill McKinney, Sam Bottoms, Dan Vadis, Sierra Pecheur, Walter Barnes, Hank Worden. An heiress with a bad temper, deserted by her husband, reluctantly joins a rag-tag Wild West show as the head showman's assistant. Beautifully done serio-comedy which nicely captures the dream image of the cowboy hero. V: Warners Home Video.

425 Bronco Buster. Universal-International, 1952. 80 minutes Color. D: Budd Boet-

ticher. SC: Horace McCoy & Lillie Hayward. WITH John Lund, Scott Brady, Joyce Holden, Chill Wills, Don Haggerty, Casey Tibbs, Dan Poore. A veteran rodeo rider befriends a young man and teaches him his trade only to become his rival both in work and romance. Not bad but the rodeo sequences are superior to the plot.

426 The Bronze Buckaroo. Sack Amusements, 1938. 60 minutes B/W. D-SC: Richard C. Kahn. WITH Herb Jeffreys, Spencer Williams, Rellie Hardin, Artie Young, Clarence Brooks, F. E. Miller, The Four Tunes. A cowboy and his pal go to a ranch to help a girl whose father has been bushwhacked and the cowpoke sets out to find the culprit. Interesting curio with an all-black cast starring singing hero Herb Jeffreys; filmed at N. B. Murray's black dude ranch near Victorville, California. V: Budget Video.

427 Brother of the Wind. Sun International, 1973. 91 minutes Color. D: Dick Robinson. SC: John Mahon & John Champion. WITH Dick Robinson, Leon Ames (narrator). A mountain man finds his life of solitude changing after he adopts four motherless wolf cubs. Filmed in the forests of the Canadian Rockies, this heartwarming feature is a treat for the eye.

428 Brothers Blue. Warner Brothers, 1973. 81 minutes Color. D: Luigi Bazzoni. WITH Jack Palance, Tina Aumont, Antonio Falsi. In order to stop crooks from taking over the West a gang stages a series of holdups but they are tracked by a hired gunman. Jack Palance's fans should go for this Italian actioner issued originally in that country in 1971 by Felix Cinematografica as **A Few Happy Days of the Brothers Ken.** Also called **The Short and Happy Life of the Brothers Blue.**

429 Brothers in the Saddle. RKO Radio, 1949. 60 minutes B/W. D: Lesley Selander. SC: Norman Houston. WITH Tim Holt, Richard Martin, Steve Brodie, Virginia Cox, Carol Forman, Richard Powers, Stanley Andrews, Robert Bray, Francis McDonald, Emmett Vogan, Monte Montague. Two brothers go to the opposite sides of the law, with one becoming a gambler who sinks deeper into crime despite the help given him by his sibling. A fast moving and exciting Tim Holt film.

430 The Brothers O'Toole. CVD/American National Enterprises, 1973. 94 minutes

Color. D: Richard Erdman. SC: Tim Kelly & Marion Hargrove. WITH John Astin, Pat Carroll, Hans Conreid, Lee Meriwether, Allyn Joslyn, Jesse White, Richard Jury, Steve Carlson, Richard Erdman, Miranda Barry, Jacques Hampton. Two shiftless brothers come to a small Colorado town and one is mistaken for a notorious highwayman and sentenced to be hanged. Dull, terrible Western-comedy.

431 The Brute and the Beast. American-International, 1968. 87 minutes Color. D: Lucio Fulci. SC: Fernando Di Leo. WITH Franco Nero, George Hilton, Nino Castelnuovo, Lyn Shane, John McDouglas, Rita Franchetti, Aysanoa Runachaugua, Tchang Yu. A man returns home and eventually gets the aid of his brother in fighting a corrupt man and his sons who have taken over their ranch. Brutal and violent Italian oater originally issued in 1966 as **Tempo di Massacro** (Time of Massacre) by Mega Film/Colt Produzioni Cinematografiche/L. F. Produzioni Cinematografiche.

432 Brute Corps. General Film Corporation, 1972. 90 minutes Color. D: Jerry Jameson. SC: Mike Kars & Abe Polsky. WITH Paul Carr, Jennifer Billingsley, Joseph Kaufmann, Alex Rocco, Michael Pataki, Charles Macaulay, Roy Jenson, Felton Perry, Joseph Bernard, Parker West. While on a camping trip in rural Mexico, a young American couple meet a group of mercenaries with tragic results. Violent modern-day Western which may be cut for TV.

433 Buchanan Rides Alone. Columbia, 1958. 78 minutes Color. D: Budd Boetticher. SC: Charles Lang Jr. WITH Randolph Scott, Craig Stevens, Barry Kelley, Jennifer Holden, Tol Avery, Peter Whitney, Manual Rojab, William Leslie, Don C. Harvey, L. Q. Jones, Robert Anderson, Joe De Santis, Nacho Galindo, Roy Jenson, Frank Scannell, Terry Frost, Riley Hill, Al Wyatt, Barbara James. A Texan rides into a border town and befriends a Mexican who has opposed the tyrant who runs the area and trouble results. One of the rather highly regarded features that Randolph Scott, Harry Joe Brown and Budd Boetticher made in the late 1950s and one that deserves its reputation.

434 Buck and the Preacher. Columbia, 1972. 102 minutes Color. D: Sidney Poitier. SC: Ernest Kinoy. WITH Sidney Poitier, Harry Belafonte, Cameron Mitchell, Ruby Dee, Denny Miller, Nita Talbot, John Kelly, Tony Brubaker, James McEachin, Clarence Muse, Ken Menard, Julie Robinson. A trail guide taking ex-slaves West so they can homestead is forced to ally himself with a con-man preacher when their journey is threatened by bounty hunters who want to return the people back to the South as cheap labor. Interesting premise does not unfold well in this black oater which has far more talk than action. V: RCA/Columbia.

435 Buck Benny Rides Again. Paramount, 1940. 82 minutes B/W. D: Mark Sandrich. SC: William Morrow & Edmund Belion. WITH Jack Benny, Ellen Drew, Andy Devine, Phil Harris, Dennis Day, Eddie "Rochester" Anderson, Don Wilson, Virginia Dale, Lillian Cornel, Theresa Harris, Kay Linaker, Ward Bond, Morris Ankrum, Charles Lane, James Burke. Radio comedian Jack Benny tries to win a girl's affections by showing her that he is an all-American cowboy. Frequently very funny comedy with lots of help from Benny's radio crew; perhaps Jack Benny's best film.

436 Buckaroo from Powder River. Columbia, 1947. 55 minutes B/W. D: Ray Nazarro. SC: Norman S. Hall. WITH Charles Starrett, Smiley Burnette, Eve Miller, Forrest Taylor, The Cass County Boys, Paul Campbell, Doug Coppin, Philip Morris, Casey MacGregor, Ted Adams, Ethan Laidlaw, Frank McCarroll, Kermit Maynard, Roy Butler, Phil Arnold. An outlaw gang leader plans to counterfeit government bonds his gang stole in a bank holdup but his nephew, in love with the sheriff's daughter, will not go along with the scheme and his uncle plans to have him murdered. Entertaining "Durango Kid" series segment.

437 Buckaroo Sheriff of Texas. Republic, 1951. 60 minutes B/W. D: Philip Ford. SC: Arthur Orloff. WITH Michael Chapin, Eilene Janssen, James Bell, Hugh O'Brian, Steve Pendleton, Tristram Coffin, William Haade, Selmer Jackson, Ed Cassidy, Eddie Dunn. A group of young children help to bring in a notorious outlaw. First of four films in the "Rough Ridin' Kids" series which showed that the business of the law in the Old West was best left to grownups.

438 Buckskin. Paramount, 1968. 97 minutes Color. D: Michael Moore. SC: Steve Fisher. WITH Barry Sullivan, Joan Caulfield, Wendell Corey, Lon Chaney, John Russell, Barbara Hale, Bill Williams,

Richard Arlen, Gerald Michenaud, Barton MacLane, Aki Aleong, Michael Larrain, Leo Gordon, George Chandler, Emile Meyer, Robert Riordan, Manuela Thiess. A territorial marshal opposes the activities of a Montana land baron who is trying to drive off remaining settlers around a small town by diverting their water supply. Except for the veteran players there is not much to recommend A. C. Lyles' final Paramount Western.

439 Buckskin Frontier. United Artists, 1943. 74 minutes B/W. D: Lesley Selander. SC: Norman Houston. WITH Richard Dix, Jane Wyatt, Lee J. Cobb, Victor Jory, Albert Dekker, Lola Lane, Max Baer, Joseph Sawyer, George Reeves, Francis McDonald. A man opposes corruption in a Western town in the 1860s when businessmen try to stop the building of the railroad to further their cattle empire. Big, action-filled Harry Sherman production with a well-conceived shoot-out finale.

440 The Buckskin Lady. United Artists, 1957. 66 minutes B/W. D: Carl K. Hittleman. SC: David Lang & Carl K. Hittleman. WITH Patricia Medina, Richard Denning, Gerald Mohr, Henry Hull, Robin Short, Richard Reeves, Dorothy Adams, Hank Worden, Frank Sully, George Cisar, Louis Lettieri, Byron Foulger, John Dierkes. A lady gambler, who supports her drunken doctor father, falls for the new medico in town but her gunman boyfriend objects. Okay action programmer.

441 Buffalo Bill. 20th Century-Fox, 1944. 90 minutes Color. D: William A. Wellman. SC: Aeneas MacKenzie, Clements Reipley & Cecile Kramer. WITH Joel McCrea, Maureen O'Hara, Linda Darnell, Thomas Mitchell, Edgar Buchanan, Anthony Quinn, Moroni Olsen, Frank Fenton, Matt Briggs, George Lessey, Frank Orth, George Chandler, Chief Many Treaties, Chief Thundercloud, Sidney Blackmer, Evelyn Beresford, Cecil Watson, Fred Graham, Harry Tyler, Arthur Loft, Syd Saylor, Robert Homans, John Dilson, Edwin Stanley. The story of Buffalo Bill Cody, from his days as a Cavalry scout to the time he became a famous showman and the owner of the most authentic wild west show in America. Entertaining but basically glossy picture of a legend.

442 Buffalo Bill. Bianco, 1964. 95 minutes Color. D: Mario Costa (J. W. Fordson). SC: Stresa & Martino. WITH Gordon Scott, Mario Brega, Catherine Ribeiro,

Jan Hendricks, Piero Lulli, Roldano Lupi, Hans von Borsady, Carlo Rustichelli. To stop the attacks on whites led by Yellow Hand, President Grant sends Buffalo Bill Cody to a Western fort and there the scout finds out that a trader has been responsible for supplying the Indians with firearms. Handsomely made European treatment of an American historical subject, although none-too-accurate. Made in Italy by Filmes/Corona/Gloria Film as **Buffalo Bill, l'eroe Del Far West** (Buffalo Bill, Hero of the West).

443 Buffalo Bill and the Indians, or Sitting Bull's History Lesson. United Artists, 1976. 123 minutes Color. D: Robert Altman. SC: Alan Rudolph & Robert Altman. WITH Paul Newman, Burt Lancaster, Joel Grey, Kevin McCarthy, Harvey Keitel, Allan Nicholls, Geraldine Chaplin, John Considine, Robert Doqui, Mike Kaplan, Bert Remsen, Bonnie Leaders, Denver Pyle, Will Sampson, Pat McCormick, Shelley Duvall. Buffalo Bill Cody uses fraud and treachery to build a reputation for himself as an Indian fighter and a frontiersman. Filmed in Canada and supposedly a Bicentennial presentation, this Robert Altman production is dull and pointless. V: Key Video.

444 Buffalo Bill in Tomahawk Territory. United Artists, 1952. 66 minutes B/W. D: Bernard B. Ray. SC: Sam Neuman & Nat Tanchuck. WITH Clayton Moore, Arkansas Slim Andrews, Sharon Dexter, Chief Yowlachie, Chief Thundercloud, Rodd Redwing, Charles Hughes, Eddie Phillips, Tom Hubbard, Helena Dare, Charles Harvey. When outlaws try to steal lands from the Indians Buffalo Bill Cody and his sidekick come to the rescue. Low grade actioner although Clayton Moore is fine in the title role.

445 Buffalo Bill on the U. P. Trail. Sunset, 1926. 60 minutes B/W. D: Frank S. Mattison. WITH Roy Stewart, Kathryn McGuire, Cullen Landis, Sheldon Lewis, Earl Metcalfe, Milburn Morante, Hazel Howell, Fred De Silva, Felix Whitefeather, Jay Morley, Eddie Harris, Dick LaReno, Harry Fenwick. Buffalo Bill and his pal plan to build a town along a railroad route but run into trouble when they prevent a town locator from buying into their plans. Standard, but actionful, silent "historical" feature. Also called **With Buffalo Bill on the U. P. Trail.**

446 Buffalo Bill Rides Again. Screen Guild, 1947. 70 minutes B/W. D: Bernard

B. Ray. SC: Barney Sarecky & Frank Gilbert. WITH Richard Arlen, Jennifer Holt, Lee Shumway, Gil Patrick, Edmund Cobb, Ed Cassidy, Ted Adams, Charles Stevens, Chief Many Treatries, Holly Bane, Frank McCarroll, Carl Matthews, George Sherwood, Fred Graham, Frank O'Connor, Dorothy Curtis, Shooting Star. Buffalo Bill Cody comes to the aid of a girl and her father whose ranch is being sought by fur thieves. This low budget quickie is a fast moving affair with stars Richard Arlen and Jennifer Holt helping to make it more than passable entertainment.

447 Buffalo Gun. Globe, 1962. 72 minutes B/W. D: Albert C. Gannaway. SC: A. L. Milton. WITH Wayne Morris, Webb Pierce, Marty Robbins, Carl Smith, Mary Ellen Kay, Donald (Don "Red") Barry, Douglas Fowley, Harry Lauter, Ed Crandall, Bill Coontz, Chris Little, Charles Sallon. Three singing government agents are sent West to investigate the thefts of shipments to the Indians. Cheaply made oater which capitalizes on its three country-western singers in starring roles; Wayne Morris' final film.

Buffalo Stampede see **The Thundering Herd**

448 Bugles in the Afternoon. Warner Brothers, 1952. 85 minutes Color. D: Roy Rowland. SC: Geoffrey Homes & Harry Brown. WITH Ray Milland, Helena Carter, Hugh Marlowe, Forrest Tucker, Barton MacLane, George Reeves, James Millican, Gertrude Michael, Stuart Randall, William Phillips, Hugh Beaumont, Dick Rich, John Pickard, John War Eagle, Sheb Wooley, Charles Evans, Nelson Leigh, Ray Montgomery, Virginia Brissac, John Doucette, Bud Osborne, Harry Lauter, Bob Steele, Mary Adams. Branded a coward during the Civil War, a cavalry sergeant meets an old rival in the Dakota Territory and plans to settle an old score on the eve of the Little Big Horn battle. Average cavalry outing with big budget trappings.

449 The Bull of the West. Universal, 1965. 78 minutes Color. D: Paul Stanley & Jerry Hopper. WITH James Drury, Charles Bronson, Lee J. Cobb, Lois Nettleton, Bob Random, George Kennedy, Vito Scotti, Diane Roter, Doug McClure, Randy Boone. An embittered man tries to make his ranch a success without the aid of others. An episode of the TV series "The Virginian" (NBC-TV, 1962-70),

issued as a feature in Europe in 1970. This film is an unofficial remake of **Man Without a Star** and **A Man Called Gannon** (q.v.).

450 Bulldog Courage. Puritan, 1935. 60 minutes. D: Sam Newfield. SC: Joseph O'Donnell & Frances Guihan. WITH Tim McCoy, Joan Woodbury, Karl Hackett, John Elliott, Ed Cassidy, Edmund Cobb, George Morrell, Paul Fix, Jack Rockwell, Bud Osborne. Twenty years before his father was cheated out of a gold mine and a young man returns home to even the score with the crook who caused his father's death. Highly competent and exciting Tim McCoy actioner with good direction from Sam Newfield. V: Thunderbird.

451 Bullet and the Flesh. Ultima/Hesperia/ Cineurope, 1964. 85 minutes Color. D-SC: Marino Girolami (Fred Wilson). WITH Rod Cameron, Patricia Viterbo, Thomas Moore, Dan Harrison, Carol Brown, Manuelo Lupo, Julio Pena, Piero Lulli, Marco Mariani, George Lynn, Franco Latni, Enzo Girolami. A lumber king plans to plunder Cherokee timberland while his daughter falls in love with an Indian chief. Pretty good Italian-made oater with a good performance by Rod Cameron in the starring role. Made as **I Sentieri Dell'Odio** (Paths of Hate) and also called **Bullet in the Flesh** on television.

452 Bullet Code. RKO Radio, 1940. 58 minutes B/W. D: David Howard. SC: Doris Schroeder. WITH George O'Brien, Virginia Vale, Harry Woods, Slim Whitaker, Robert Stanton (Kirby Grant), Walter Miller, William Haade, Bob Burns, Howard Hickman, Lew Meehan, Bob McKenzie, Jack C. Smith, Cactus Mack. A cowboy, who mistakenly thinks he killed his pal, goes to work for the dead man's father and sister, who are having their cattle rustled. Handsome entry in George O'Brien's RKO series.

453 Bullet for a Badman. Universal, 1964. 80 minutes Color. D: R. G. Springsteen. SC: Mary Willingham & Willard Willingham. WITH Audie Murphy, Darren McGavin, Ruta Lee, Beverly Owen, Skip Homeier, George Tobias, Alan Hale (Jr.), Bob Steele, Edward C. Platt, Mort Mills, Kevin Tate, Buff Brady. The happiness of a man and his wife is threatened when her ex-husband, who deserted her for the life of an outlaw, swears revenge on them. Competently done and more than passable Audie Murphy film.

454 Bullet for a Stranger. Flora Film/ National Cinematografica, 1971. 94 minutes Color. D: Anthony Ascott (Guiliano Carminio). SC: E. B. Clucher. WITH Gianni Garko, William Berger, Christopher Chittel, John Fordyce, Ugo Fancareggi, Franco Ressel, Ivano Staccioll, Nello Pazzafini, Gianni Di Benedetto, Ugo Adinolfi. A mysterious stranger helps two young men whose family is being threatened by an extortionist. Rather entertaining Italian actioner, one of a string of films with Gianni Garko as the mysterious stranger. Issued in Italy as **Gli Fumavano le Colt...Lo Chiamavano Camposanto** (His Pistols Smoked...They Call Him Cemetery).

455 A Bullet for Billy the Kid. Associated Distributors Producers (ADP), 1963. 61 minutes Color. D: Rafael Baledon. SC: Raymond Obon. WITH Gaston (Santos) Sands, Steve Brodie, Lloyd Nelson, Marla Blaine, Richard McIntyre, Rita Mace. When he goes up against corrupt forces, young Billy the Kid soon finds himself the target of an assassin's bullet. Hacked-up U. S. release version of a Mexican film, issued here by Jerry Warren, known for such scissors-and-paste efforts from Mexican features as **Attack of the Mayan Mummy** (ADP, 1964) and **Face of the Screaming Werewolf** (ADP, 1965).

456 A Bullet for Sandoval. UMC Pictures, 1970. 96 minutes Color. D: Julio Buchs. SC: Ugo Guerro, Jose Luis Martinez Molla, Frederic De Urratia & Julio Buchs. WITH George Hilton, Ernest Borgnine, Gustavo Rojo, Alberto De Mendoza, Leo Anchoriz, Annabella Incontrera, Antonio Pico, Jose Manuel Martin, Manuel De Blas, Manuel Miranda. During the Civil War, a Confederate soldier comes to Mexico to find his wife dead and he and his infant son are driven out by her father and when the baby dies of hunger the man swears revenge against his father-in-law. Violent and actionful Spanish-Italian coproduction issued in 1969 in Italy as **Quei Disperati Che Puzzano de Sudore e di Morte** (Those Desperate Men, Smelling of Sweat and Death) by Leoen/Daiano/Atlantida.

457 A Bullet for the General. Avco-Embassy, 1966. 95 minutes Color. D: Damiano Damiani. SC: Salvatore Laurani. WITH Gian Maria Volonte, Klaus Kinski, Martine Beswick, Lou Castel, Bianca Manini, Jaimie Fernandez, Andrea Checci, Jose Manuel Martin, Spartaco Conversi, Joaquin Parra, Aldo Sambrell. During the Mexican Revolution a government agent is hired to kill a revolutionary army general and to do so he gains the loyalty of a guerilla leader. Made in Italy as **Quien Sabe?**, this is an above average European Western.

Bullet in the Flesh see **Bullet and the Flesh**

458 A Bullet is Waiting. Columbia, 1954. 82 minutes Color. D: John Farrow. SC: Thames Williamson & Casey Robinson. WITH Rory Calhoun, Jean Simmons, Stephen McNally, Brian Aherne. A resolute lawman treks through the desert with his prisoner and the two become stranded with an old man and his daughter. Highly intriguing psychological Western, heavy on characterization by its compact cast.

459/60 Bullets and Saddles. Monogram, 1943. 56 minutes B/W. D: Anthony Marshall. SC: Elizabeth Beecher. WITH Ray Corrigan, Dennis Moore, Max Terhune, Julie Duncan, Budd Buster, Rose Plummer, Forrest Taylor, Glenn Strange, Steve Clark, John Merton, Ed Cassidy, Joe Garcia, Silver Harr, Carl Mathews, Robert Kortman, Tom London. The Range Busters are called into an area to stop a crooked businessman who is trying to get control with his gang of outlaws. Final entry in "The Range Busters" series is on the anemic side, using footage from the earlier entry **Fugitive Valley** (q.v.).

461 Bullets Don't Argue. Walter Manley Productions, 1965. 93 minutes Color. D: Manfred Rieger (Mike Perkins). SC: Manuel Waller & Donald Mooch. WITH Rod Cameron, Dick Palmer, Vivi Bach, Kai Fisher, Angel Aranda, Horst Frank, Hans Nielsen, Ludwig Duran. On his wedding day, Sheriff Pat Garrett is forced to give chase to two outlaw brothers who have robbed the town bank and killed area citizens. One of the earliest, and best, of the European Westerns; full of lively action and helped by a strong performance by Rod Cameron as Pat Garrett. The film also includes one of Ennio Morricone's best, and sadly underrated, scores. Originally made by Jolly/Trio/Constantin as **Die Letzen Zwei Vom Rio Bravo** (The Last Two from Rio

Bravo), the film is also known as **Guns Don't Argue.**

462 Bullets for Bandits. Columbia, 1942, 55 minutes B/W. D: Wallace Fox. SC: Robert Lee Johnson. WITH Bill Elliott, Tex Ritter, Dorothy Short, Frank Mitchell, Forrest Taylor, Ralph Theodore, Edythe Elliott, Eddie Laughton, Joe McGuinn, Tom Moray, Art Mix, Harry Harvey, Hal Taliaferro, John Tyrell, Bud Osborne. Wild Bill Hickok comes to the aid of a woman rancher whose property is sought by a crook. Somewhat uneven entry in the Bill Elliott-Tex Ritter starring series.

463 Bullets for Rustlers. Columbia, 1940. 58 minutes B/W. D: Sam Nelson. SC: John Rathmell. WITH Charles Starrett, Lorna Gray, Bob Nolan & The Sons of the Pioneers, Ken Curtis, Kenneth Mac-Donald, Jack Rockwell, Ed LeSaint, Francis Walker, Eddie Laughton, Lee Prather, Hal Taliaferro. A cattlemen's association undercover agent pretends to be a rustler in order to join a gang he is trying to stop. Actionful Charles Starrett film.

464 Bullwhip!. Allied Artists, 1956. 80 minutes Color. D: Harmon Jones. SC: Adele Buffington. WITH Guy Madison, Rhonda Fleming, James Griffith, Don Beddoe, Peter Adams, Dan Sheridan, Burt Nelson, Al Terry, Hank Worden, Barbara Woodell, Rhys Williams, Jay Reynolds, Tim Graham, Rick Vallin. In order to control a trading firm, a badman forces a cowpoke to either marry the girl who is to inherit the business or face hanging over a false murder charge. Average Guy Madison vehicle; Frankie Laine sings the title song with more conviction than there is in the film itself.

465 Burning Gold. Republic, 1936. 58 minutes B/W. D: Sam Newfield. SC: Stuart Anthony. WITH Bill (William) Boyd, Judith Allen, Frank Mayo, Lloyd Ingraham, Fern Emmett. An oil driller gets rich from a well only to lose it in a fire. Poor stuff.

466 The Burning Hills. Warner Brothers, 1956. 94 minutes Color. D: Stuart Heisler. SC: Irving Wallace. WITH Tab Hunter, Natalie Wood, Skip Homeier, Eduard Franz, Earl Holliman, Claude Akins, Ray Teal, Frank Puglia, Hal Baylor,

Tyler MacDuff, Rayford Barnes. On the run from cattle thieves, a young man finds shelter with a half-breed girl and they fall in love. Average outing which its stars can do little to help.

467 Bury Me Not on the Lone Prairie. Universal, 1941. 61 minutes B/W. D: Ray Taylor. SC: Sherman Lowe & Victor McLeod. WITH Johnny Mack Brown, Fuzzy Knight, Nell O'Day, Kathryn Adams, Harry Cording, Jack Rockwell, Ernie Adams, Ed Cassidy, Don House, Lee Shumway, Pat O'Brien, Frank O'Connor, William Desmond, Bud Osborne, Slim Whitaker, Kermit Maynard, Robert Kort-man, Jim Corey, Charles King, Ethan Laidlaw, Frank Ellis, Jimmy Wakely & His Rough Riders. After the killing of his brother and a girl's brother, a mining engineer sets out to get the mur-derer. Good Johnny Mack Brown series entry with both action and music.

468 The Bushwackers. Realart, 1952. 70 minutes B/W. D-SC: Rod Amateau & Thomas Gries. WITH John Ireland, Wayne Morris, Lawrence Tierney, Dorothy Malone, Lon Chaney, Myrna Dell, Frank Marlowe, Bill Holmes, Jack Elam, Bob Wood, Charles Trowbridge, Stuart Randall, George Lynn, Norman Leavitt, Eddie Parks, Ted Jordan, Kit Guard. At the end of the Civil War, a soldier returns home to Missouri to find a ruthless man and his daughter have gained control of the territory. Cheaply done Jack Broder production which is helped somewhat by its cast.

469 Butch and Sundance: The Early Years. CBS-TV, 1979. 100 minutes Color. D: Richard Lester. SC: Allan Burns. WITH Tom Berenger, William Katt, Jeff Corey, John Schuck, Michael C. Gwynne, Peter Weller, Brian Dennehy, Jill Eikenberry. The story of how Butch Cassidy and the Sundance Kid met and teamed up as outlaws. Average TV movie detailing the lives of **Butch Cassidy and the Sun-dance Kid** (q.v.).

470 Butch Cassidy and the Sundance Kid. 20th Century-Fox, 1969. 110 minutes Color. D: George Roy Hill. SC: William Goldman. WITH Paul Newman, Robert Redford, Katharine Ross, Strother Martin, Henry Jones, Jeff Corey, George Furth, Cloris Leachman, Ted Cassidy, Kenneth

Mars, Donnelly Rhodes, Jody Gilbert, Timothy Scott, Don Keefer, Nelson Olmstead, Paul Bryar, Charles Akins, Eric Sinclair, Pery Helton. The hijinks of outlaws Butch Cassidy and Harry "The Sundance Kid" Longbaugh, along with the Kid's girlfriend, Etta Place, are told, from their various robberies to a spree in New York City to their trip to Bolivia, where they are chased by law officers. Glamourized account of the two lawbreakers which was very popular when released and still holds up for its entertainment value. V: 20th Century-Fox Video, Blackhawk. VD: Blackhawk.

471 Butterfly. Analysis Film Releasing, 1981. 108 minutes Color. D: Matt Cimber. SC: John Goff & Matt Cimber. WITH Pia Zadora, Stacy Keach, James Franciscus, Edward Albert, Orson Welles, Lois Nettleton, Stuart Whitman, June Lockhart, Ed McMahon, Paul Hampton, George "Buck" Flower, Ann Dare, Guy Gault, John O'Connor White, Peter Jason, John Goff. In 1937 the caretaker of a closed Nevada silver mine lusts after a teenage girl he believes to be his daughter. Mediocre screen adaptation of James M. Cain's sizzling novel; Orson Welles' self-indulgent performance as the local judge has to be seen to be believed. About the only interest to genre fans is the use of Johnny Bond's recording of "Silver on the Sage."

472 Buzzy and the Phantom Pinto. Ellkay, 1941. 55 minutes B/W. D: Richard C. Kahn. SC: E. C. Robertson. WITH Buzzy Henry, Dave O'Brien, Dorothy Short, George Morrell, Sven Hugo Borg, Milburn Morante, Frank Marlo, Harry Norman, Don Kelly, Philip Arnold. A young cowpoke and a ranch foreman set out to capture an elusive horse. Second and last entry in the Buzzy Henry starring series; a mediocre affair. Also called **Phantom Pinto.** Reissued in 1948 by Astor as **Western Terror.** V: Cassette Express.

473 Buzzy Rides the Range. Ellkay, 1940, 60 minutes B/W. D: Richard C. Kahn. SC: E. C. Robertson. WITH Buzzy Henry, Dave O'Brien, Claire Rochelle, George Morrell, George Eldridge, Frank Marlo, Don Kelly. A young boy teams with a range detective to track down outlaws. So-so independent feature intended as the first of a series to star juvenile Robert "Buzzy" (later Buzz) Henry but followed only with **Buzzy and the Phantom Pinto** (q.v.) the next year.

C

474 The Cactus Kid. Reliable, 1935. 56 minutes B/W. D: Harry S. Webb. SC: Carl Krusada. WITH Jack Perrin, Jayne Regan, Slim Whitaker, Tom London, Fred Humes, Wally Wales, Philo McCullough, Joe de la Cruz, Tina Menard, Kit Guard, Lew Meehan, George Chesebro, Gordon DeMain, George Morrell. When his partner is murdered a cowboy sets out to get revenge. Poorly done Jack Perrin vehicle.

475 Cahill, United States Marshal. Warner Brothers, 1973. 103 minutes Color. D: Andrew V. McLaglen. SC: Harry Julian Fink & Rita M. Fink. WITH John Wayne, George Kennedy, Gary Grimes, Neville Brand, Clay O'Brien, Marie Windsor, Morgan Paull, Dan Vadis, Royal Dano, Scott Walker, Denver Pyle, Jackie Coogan, Rayford Barnes, Dan Kemp, Harry Carey Jr., Walter Barnes, Paul Fix, Pepper Martin, Vance Davis, Chuck Roberson, Ken Wolger, Hank Worden, James Nusser, Murray MacLeod, Hunter Von Leer. A duty-bound U. S. marshal neglects his two sons in deference to duty and when he goes after a gang of robbers he finds out the boys are mixed up in the crime. Not one of John Wayne's better outings but still good entertainment. V: Warners Home Video.

Cain's Cutthroats see **Cain's Way**

476 Cain's Way. M.D.A. Associates, 1970. 95 minutes Color. D: Kent Osborne. SC: Wilton Denmark. WITH Scott Brady, John Carradine, Robert Dix, Don Epperson, Adair Jamison, Darwin Jaston, Bruce Kimball, Teresa Thaw, Willis Martin. Seven bikers in a small modern Western town find themselves transported back to the West of the 1870s. Overly violent and cheaply made film which combines the genres of the Western and fantasy, none-too-successfully. Also issued as **Cain's Cutthroats.**

477 Calaboose. United Artists, 1943. 45 minutes B/W. D: Hal Roach Jr. SC: Arnold Belgard. WITH Jimmy Rogers, Noah Beery Jr., Mary Brian, Marc Lawrence, Bill Henry, Paul Hurst, William B. Davidson, Jean Porter, Iris Adrian, Sarah Edwards. Two cowboy pals come to the aid of a sheriff and his daughter in opposing a big-city gangster. One of a brief series of featurettes starring

Jimmy Rogers (son of Will Rogers) and Noah Berry Jr., this film is an average affair.

478 Calamity Jane. Warner Brothers, 1953. 101 minutes Color. D: David Butler. SC: James O'Hanlon. WITH Doris Day, Howard Keel, Philip Carey, Allyn Ann McLerie, Dick Wesson, Paul Harvey, Chubby Johnson, Gale Robbins. The wildest and best shooting girl in the West decides to tame the heart of Marshal Wild Bill Hickok. Musical hokum about Calamity Jane and Wild Bill Hickok makes for good light entertainment and there's the song "Secret Love" for additional recommendation.

479 Calamity Jane and Sam Bass. Universal, 1949. 85 minutes Color. D: George Sherman. SC: Maurice Geraghty. WITH Yvonne De Carlo, Howard Duff, Dorothy Hart, Willard Parker, Norman Lloyd, Marc Lawrence, Houseley Stevenson, Milburn Stone, Clifton Young, John Rodney, Roy Roberts, Ann Doran, Charles Cane, Walter Baldwin, Paul Maxey, George Carleton, Harry Harvey, Jack Ingram, Francis McDonald, Douglas Walton, Nedrick Young, Russ Conway, Pierce Lyden, I. Stanford Jolley, Stanley Blystone, Roy Butler, Frank McCarroll, Bob Perry. When his prize horse is killed by crooks, Sam Bass takes to a life of crime and meets Calamity Jane, but prefers the sister of a sheriff. Surprisingly good film, although mostly fiction, with Yvonne De Carlo and Howard Duff in top form as the leads.

480 California. Paramount, 1946. 97 minutes Color. D: John Farrow. SC: Frank Butler & Theodore Strauss. WITH Ray Milland, Barbara Stanwyck, Barry Fitzgerald, George Coulouris, Albert Dekker, Anthony Quinn, Frank Faylen, Gavin Muir, James Burke, Eduardo Ciannelli, Roman Bohnen, Argentina Burnetti, Howard Freeman, Julia Faye. During the Gold Rush a wagon master with a past and a shady lady become involved in a scheme set up by crooks to keep California from attaining statehood. Fans of the stars will like this feature but otherwise beware; the color helps.

481 California. American-International, 1963. 86 minutes B/W. D: Hamil Petroff. SC: James West. WITH Jock Mahoney, Faith Domergue, Michael Pate, Susan Seaforth, Rodolfo Hoyos, Penny Santon, Nestor Paiva, Felix Locher, Charles Horvath. In California in 1841 the people revolt against Mexican oppression and ask the U. S. for statehood. Actionful but cheaply-made oater which Jock Mahoney fans will enjoy.

482 California Conquest. Columbia, 1952. 79 minutes Color. D: Lew Landers. SC: Robert E. Kent. WITH Cornel Wilde, Teresa Wright, Alfonso Bedoya, Lisa Ferraday, Eugene Iglesias, John Dehner, Ivan Lebedeff, Tito Renaldo, Renzo Cesana, Baynes Barron, Rico Alaniz, Alex Montoya, Hank Patterson, George Eldredge. A young nobleman aids the Spanish government when the Russians try to lay claim to California. Mild account of a little known aspect of California history; from producer Sam Katzman.

483 California Firebrand. Republic, 1948. 63 minutes Color. D: Philip Ford. SC: J. Benton Cheney & John K. Butler. WITH Monte Hale, Adrian Booth, Paul Hurst, Tristram Coffin, Foy Willing & The Riders of the Purple Sage, Alice Tyrell, Douglas Evans, LeRoy Mason, Sarah Edwards, Dan Sheridan, Duke York, Lanny Rees. Disguised as a notorious outlaw, a cowboy investigates a series of mining claim thefts. Adventuresome Monte Hale opus, enhanced by Trucolor.

484 California Frontier. Columbia, 1938. 55 minutes B/W. D: Elmer Clifton. SC: Monroe Schaff & Arthur Hoerl. WITH Buck Jones, Carmen Bailey, Milburn Stone, Jose Perez, Soledad Jiminez, Stanley Blystone, Carlos Villarios, Glenn Strange, Paul Ellis, Ernie Adams, Forrest Taylor. When Mexican ranchers are forced off their lands by crooks the government sends an army captain to California to stop the injustice. Buck Jones' final Columbia series film is an okay effort but not up to the standards of some of his early features.

485 California Gold Rush. Republic, 1946. 54 minutes B/W. D: R.G. Springsteen. SC: Bob Williams. WITH Bill Elliott, Bobby Blake, Alice Fleming, Peggy Stewart, Russell Simpson, Dick Curtis, Kenne Duncan, Monte Hale, Tom London, Joel Friedkin, Wen Wright, Jack Kirk, Budd Buster, Bud Osborne, Neal Hart, Frank Ellis, Herman Hack, Dickie Dillon. In order to save a stage line from outlaws, Red Ryder takes on the guise of a killer called the Idaho Kid. Pretty good outing in the "Red Ryder" series.

486 California Gold Rush. NBC-TV, 1981. 100 minutes Color. D: Jack B. Hively.

SC: Tom Chapman & Roy London. WITH Robert Hays, John Dehner, Henry Jones, Ken Curtis, Gene Evans, Victor Mohica, Coleman Creel, Cliff Osmond. Writer Bret Harte comes West in 1849 and becomes involved with Captain John Sutter and the California Gold Rush. Fairly good "Classics Illustrated" TV movie based on the Bret Harte stories "The Luck of Roaring Camp" and "The Outcasts of Poker Flat." V: VCI Home Video.

California in 1878 see **Fighting Thru, or California in 1878**

487 California in '49. Arrow, 1925. 60 minutes B/W. D: Jacques Jaccard. SC: Karl Coolidge. WITH Edmund Cobb, Neva Gerber, Charles Brinley, Ruth Royce, Wilbur McGaugh, Yakima Canutt, Clark Coffey. Captain John Sutter and his friends plan to build an empire in California and after aiding the snowbound Donner party he helps Mexican-American settlers in revolting against the Mexican government. Fast moving silent actioner, taken from the 1924 Arrow serial **Days of '49.**

488 California Joe. Republic, 1943. 55 minutes B/W. D: Spencer Gordon Bennet. SC: Norman S. Hall. WITH Don "Red" Barry, Helen Talbot, Wally Vernon, Terry Frost, Twinkle Watts, Edward Earle, LeRoy Mason, Charles King, Pierce Lyden, Edmund Cobb, Karl Hackett, Robert Kortman, Edward Keane, Tom London, Jack O'Shea, Robert Wilke. During the Civil War, corrupt politicians plan to make California into a separate empire and a Union soldier masquerades under the guise of California Joe to thwart their plan. Typically actionful Don Barry series entry. V: Cumberland Video.

489 California Mail. Warner Brothers, 1936. 56 minutes B/W. D: Noel Smith. SC: Harold Buckley & Roy Chanslor. WITH Dick Foran, Linda Perry, Edmund Cobb, Tom Brower, James Farley, Gene Alsace, Glenn Strange, Bob Woodward, Wilfred Lucas, Fred Burns, Milton Kibbee, Edward Keane, Jack Kirk, Lew Meehan, Tex Palmer, The Sons of the Pioneers. Crooks try to obtain a mail contract and when three stagecoach lines have the same bids on it a race is staged to decide the winner. Nicely paced Dick Foran entry with some songs by the star along with The Sons of the Pioneers, then including Roy Rogers.

California Outpost see **Old Los Angeles**

490 California Passage. Republic, 1950. 90 minutes B/W. D: Joseph Kane. SC: James Edward Grant. WITH Forrest Tucker, Adele Mara, Estelia Rodriguez, Jim Davis, Bill Williams, Paul Fix, Rhys Williams, Francis McDonald, Eddy Waller, Peter Miles, Charles Kemper, Charles Stevens, Iron Eyes Cody, Alan Bridge, Ruth Brennan. A girl falls in love with a saloon owner although the man accidentally killed her brother and despite the fact he has been accused of robbing a stage, the crime being committed by his crooked partner. Pretty interesting "A" budget oater with Forrest Tucker as the good guy for a change.

491 The California Trail. Columbia, 1933. 67 minutes B/W. D: Lambert Hillyer. SC: Jack Natteford. WITH Buck Jones, Helen Mack, Emile Chautard, George Humbert, Charles Stevens, Evelyn Sherman, Chris-Pin Martin, Carmen LaRoux, Carlos Villarios, Augie Gomez, John Paul Jones, Allan Garcia, Robert Steele, Juan DuVal. An American scout comes to the aid of a village in old Mexico which is being ruled by two ruthless brothers who want to cheat the people out of their lands. Well made Buck Jones vehicle highlighted by a good story and direction.

492 The Californian. 20th Century-Fox, 1937. 61 minutes B/W. D: Gus Meins. SC: Gilbert Wright. WITH Ricardo Cortez, Marjorie Weaver, Katherine De Mille, Maurice Black, Morgan Wallace, Nigel de Brulier, Ann Gillis, Helen Holmes, James Farley, George Regas, Pierre Watkin, Edward Keane, Gene Reynolds, Richard Botiller, Tom Forman, Bud Osborne, Monte Montague, William Fletcher. Sent to Spain by his father to become a gentleman, a man returns home to find the area plagued by crooks. Fair programmer adaptation of the Zane Grey work. TV title: **Gentleman from California.**

493 Call of the Canyon. Republic, 1942. 54 (71) minutes B/W. D: Joseph Santley, SC: Olive Cooper. WITH Gene Autry, Smiley Burnette, Ruth Terry, Joe Strauch Jr., Thurston Hall, Cliff Nazarro, Dorothea Kent, Bob Nolan & The Sons of the Pioneers, Edmund McDonald, Marc Lawrence, John Holland, Eddy Waller, Budd Buster, Frank Jacquet, Lorin Baker, Johnny Duncan, Ray Bennett, Anthony Marsh, Fred Santley, Frank Ward, Earle Hodgins, John Harmon, Al Taylor, Frankie Marvin,

Bob Burns, Charles Williams, Joy Barton. While in the big city trying to get fair prices for ranchers from a meat packer, Gene Autry becomes involved with a pretty radio singer and when he gets back home he finds out Frog has rented their ranch to her. Very actionful and entertaining Gene Autry musical oater.

494 Call of the Desert. Syndicate, 1930. 5 reels B/W. D: J. P. McGowan. SC: Sally Winters & Barney Williams. WITH Tom Tyler, Sheila Le Gay, Cliff Lyons, Bud Osborne, Bobby Dunn. Two men go into the desert to look for a gold mine claim left to one of them by his father and the other man steals the claim. Fairly entertaining and fast moving Tom Tyler film with interesting opening scenes of snow in the desert. Originally issued with a music score but no dialogue.

495 Call of the Forest. Lippert, 1949. 74 minutes B/W. D: John Link. WITH Robert Lowery, Ken Curtis, Chief Thundercloud, Martha Sherill, Charles Hughes, Tom Hanley, Fred Gildart, Eula Guy, Black Diamond (horse), Jimmy (crow), Beady (Raccoon), Ripple (deer), Fuzzy (bear). The adventures of a young boy and the animals he befriends in the great north woods. Pleasant youth-oriented feature with Robert Lowery, Ken Curtis and Chief Thundercloud along for genre buffs.

496 The Call of the Klondike. Rayart, 1926. 45 minutes B/W. D: Oscar Apfel. SC: John F. Natteford. WITH Gaston Glass, Dorthy Dwan, Earl Metcalfe, Sam Allen, William Lowery, Olin Francis, Harold Holland, Jimmie Aubrey, Lightning Girl (dog). A girl and her father rescue a mining engineer in the Klondike and later in Alaska the man, now a miner accused of murdering his partner, escapes from jail to save the girl from the advances of a crook. Okay silent melodrama.

497 Call of the Klondike. Monogram, 1950. 67 minutes B/W. D: Frank McDonald. SC: Charles Lang. WITH Kirby Grant, Anne Gwynne, Lynne Roberts, Tom Neal, Russell Simpson, Paul Bryar, Duke York, Pat Gleason. A Mountie and a girl search for the latter's missing father and when they find a lost gold mine are attacked by outlaws. One of several Monogram films with Kirby Grant based on James Oliver Curwood stories and slightly better than most in the group.

498 Call of the Mesquiteers. Republic, 1938. 54 minutes B/W. D: John English.

SC: Luci Ward. WITH Robert Livingston, Ray Corrigan, Max Terhune, Lynne Roberts, Sammy McKim, Earle Hodgins, Eddy Waller, Maston Williams, Eddie Hart, Pat Gleason, Roger Williams, Warren Jackson, Hal Price, Frank Ellis, Curley Dresden, Jack Ingram, Ralph Peters, Ethan Laidlaw, Tom Steele, Al Taylor. The Three Mesquiteers find themselves falsely accused of robbing a train and committing murder and set out to clear their names. Another good, actionful entry in "The Three Mesquiteers" series.

499 Call of the Prairie. Paramount, 1936. 54 (65) minutes B/W. D: Howard Bretherton. SC: Doris Schroeder & Nernon Smith. WITH William Boyd, James Ellison, Muriel Evans, George ("Gabby") Hayes, Chester Conklin, Al Bridge, Hank Mann, Willie Fung, Howard Lang, Al Hill, John Merton, Jim Mason, Chill Wills & His Avalon Boys. An outlaw gang frames Johnny Nelson for a series of crimes but Hopalong Cassidy comes to his rescue. Fine entry in the "Hopalong Cassidy" series.

500 Call of the Rockies. Columbia, 1938. 54 minutes B/W. D: Alan James. SC: Ed Earl Repp. WITH Charles Starrett, Iris Meredith, Donald Grayson, Bob Nolan & The Sons of the Pioneers, Dick Curtis, Ed Le Saint, Edmund Cobb, Art Mix, John Tyrell, George Chesebro, Glenn Strange, Jack Rockwell. A cowboy comes to the aid of a young woman who is in debt and about to lose her ranch to a crooked land dealer. Another entertaining entry in Charles Starrett's long-running Columbia series.

501 Call of the Rockies. Republic, 1944. 58 minutes B/W. D: Lesley Selander. SC: Bob Williams. WITH Smiley Burnette, Sunset Carson, Ellen Hall, Kirk Alyn, Harry Woods, Frank Jacquet, Charles Williams, Jack Kirk, Tom London, Robert Kortman, Edmund Cobb, Jack O'Shea, Rex Lease, Frank McCarroll, Bud Geary, Robert Wilke, Kit Guard, Carl Sepulveda, Horace Carpenter. Two freight haulers lose their cargo and find out that a mine owner and a doctor are in cahoots in a plan to get control of all of the mines in the area. Sunset Carson's first starring film (he took second billing to Smiley Burnette) is a fast-paced rip-snorter and what the star lacks in the thespian department he more than makes up for in his ability to fight and ride.

502 Call of the West. Columbia, 1930. 70 minutes B/W. D: Albert Ray. SC:

Colin Clements. WITH Dorothy Revier, Matt Moore, Katherine Clark Ward, Tom O'Brien, Alan Roscoe, Victor Potel, Nick De Ruiz, Joe De La Cruz, Blanche Rose, Bud Osborne. A cabaret entertainer falls in love with a rancher while in Texas and they get married but when he joins a posse to track down rustlers she returns to New York City where she is romanced by her former suitor. Early talkie mainly for the curious.

503 Call of the Wild. United Artists, 1935. 91 minutes B/W. D: William A. Wellman. SC: Gene Fowler & Leonard Praskins. WITH Clark Gable, Loretta Young, Jack Oakie, Reginald Owen, Frank Conroy, Sidney Toler, Charles Stevens, Katherine De Mille, James Burke, John T. Murray, Bob Perry, Sid Grauman, Herman Bing, Wade Boteler, John Ince, Syd Saylor, Joan Woodbury, Arthur Aylesworth, Buck (dog). Two men search for gold in the frozen Klondike and one finds love while both are threatened by a vicious claim jumper. Highly watchable version of the Jack London story which has more romance than London; Reginald Owen is a delight as the bad guy.

504 Call of the Wild. Intercontinental Releasing Corporation, 1973. 102 minutes Color. D: Ken Annakin. SC: Hubert Frank & Tibor Reves. WITH Charlton Heston, Michele Mercier, Maria Rohm, George Eastman, Raymond Harmstorf, Friedhelm Lehmann, Horst Heuck, Sancho Garcia. An adventurer and his dog travel over the northernmost parts of the Pacific from the waters of Alaska to the gold fields of the Yukon where they see men driven by the greed of wealth. West German production of Jack London's novel, filmed in Finland and somewhat weakened by its handling of the material. Issued in West Germany in 1973 as **Ruf Der Wildnis** by CCC Filmkunst.

505 Call of the Wild. NBC-TV, 1976. 100 minutes Color. D: Jerry Jameson. SC: James Dickey. WITH John Beck, Bernard Fresson, John McLiam, Michael Pataki, Penelope Windust, Billy Green Bush, Johnny Tillotson, Ray Guth, Dennis Burkley. In 1903 a young prospector and a veteran trapper face the wilds of the Yukon in search of gold. Pretty good telefilm version of the Jack London story.

Call of the Wilderness see **Trailing the Killer**

506 Call of the Yukon. Republic, 1938. 70 minutes B/W. D: B. Reeves Eason. SC: Gertrude Orr & William Bartlett. WITH Richard Arlen, Beverly Roberts, Lyle Talbot, Ray Mala, Garry Owen, Ivan Miller, James Lono, Emory Parnell, Al St. John, Anthony Hughes, Nina Campana, Buck (dog). A trapper and a woman writer, along with two dogs, search for gold and a story in the wilds of the Yukon. Entertaining adventure yarn with many animals and some nice avalanche footage.

507 Callaway Went Thataway. Metro-Goldwyn-Mayer, 1951. 81 minutes B/W. D-SC: Norman Panama & Melvin Frank. WITH Fred MacMurray, Dorothy McGuire, Howard Keel, Jesse White, Fay Roope, Natalie Schaefer, Douglas Kennedy, Elisabeth Fraser, Johnny Indrisane, Stan Freberg, Don Haggerty, Dorothy Andre, Glenn Strange, Mae Clarke, Hugh Beaumont, Earle Hodgins, Clark Gable, Elizabeth Taylor, Esther Williams. Two advertising agents resurrect the old films of a forgotten cowboy star and he becomes popular again on television but when he cannot be found a double is used to make more movies. A delightful spoof of the "Hopalong Cassidy" craze of the early 1950s with Howard Keel as both the drunken, woman-chasing cowboy star and as his real-life cowboy double. Well worth seeing.

508 The Calling of Dan Matthews. Columbia, 1936. 63 minutes B/W. D: Phil Rosen. SC: Dan Jarrett, Don Swift & Karl Brown. WITH Richard Arlen, Charlotte Wynters, Douglass Dumbrille, Mary Kornman, Donald Cook, Carlyle Blackwell Jr. A militant clergymen tries to fight corruption and gangsters in the modern-day West. Fairly good programmer from Harold Bell Wright's novel.

Call to Glory see **Ride to Glory**

509 Calling Wild Bill Elliott. Republic, 1943. 55 minutes B/W. D: Spencer Gordon Bennet. SC: Anthony Coldeway. WITH Bill Elliott, George "Gabby" Hayes, Anne Jeffreys, Buzz Henry, Fred Kohler Jr., Roy Barcroft, Herbert Heyes, Charles King, Frank Hagney, Bud Geary, Lyndon Brent, Frank McCarroll, Burr Caruth, Forbes Murray, Ted Mapes, Herman Hack, Yakima Canutt. In order to catch a corrupt cattle baron, Wild Bill Elliott poses as the governor of a new territory. First film in Bill Elliott's Republic series, this is a fast moving adventure, short on plot but heavy on fights, chases, etc.

510 Campbell's Kingdom. Lopert, 1958. 102 minutes Color. D: Ralph Thomas. SC: Robin Estridge & Hammond Innes. WITH Dirk Bogarde, Stanley Baker, Michael Craig, Barbara Burray, James Robertson Justice, Athene Seyler, Robert Brown, John Laurie, Sidney James, Mary Merrall, George Murcell, Ronald Brand, Finlay Currie, Peter Illing, Stanley Maxted, Gordon Tanner, Richard McNamara. In the Canadian Rockies, a land owner is at odds with a man who wants to build a huge dam. British-made adventure film, produced in Canada, which is highly entertaining. Released in Great Britain in 1957 by the Rank Organization.

511 Canadian Mounties vs. Atomic Invaders. Republic, 1953. 12 Chapters. D: Franklin Adreon. SC: Ronald Davidson. WITH Bill Henry, Susan Morrow, Arthur Space, Dale Van Sickel, Pierre Watkin, Mike Ragan, Stanley Andrews, Harry Lauter, Hank Patterson, Edmund Cobb, Gayle Kellogg, Tom Steele, Jean Wright. The Canadian Mounted Police are on the trail of a gang of foreign agents who are mysteriously working in the upper reaches of Canada. Slow moving cliffhanger, re-edited into a 100 minute TV feature called **Missile Base at Taniak.**

512 Canadian Pacific. 20th Century-Fox, 1949. 95 minutes Color. D: Edwin L. Marin. SC: Jack DeWitt & Kenneth Gamet. WITH Randolph Scott, Jane Wyatt, Nancy Olson, J. Carrol Naish, Victor Jory, Robert Barrat, Walter Sande, Don Haggerty, Brandon Rhodes, Mary Kent, John Parrish, John Hamilton, Richard Wessel, Howard Negley. An advance man for the westward moving railroad is romantically interested in a female doctor and a frontier gal and is opposed by Indians and trappers who do not want the railroad moving further west. Handsome Randolph Scott epic in Cinecolor.

513 The Canadians. 20th Century-Fox, 1961. 85 minutes Color. D-SC: Burt Kennedy. WITH Robert Ryan, John Dehner, Torin Thatcher, Teresa Stratas, Burt Metcalfe, John Sutton, Jack Creley, Scott Peters, Richard Alden, Michael Pate. Following the Custer massacre, the Sioux Indians move into Canada and there a trio of Mounties convince them to remain peaceful or be driven back south of the border. Fairly colorful Mountie yarn which wastes opera singer Teresa Stratas in the role of an Indian squaw.

514 Cannon. CBS-TV, 1971. 100 minutes Color. D: George McGowan. SC: Ed Hume. WITH William Conrad, Vera Miles, J. D. Cannon, Lynda Day (George), Barry Sullivan, Keenan Wynn, Murray Hamilton, Earl Holliman, John Fiedler, Lawrence Pressman, Ross Hagen. In a small modern-day Western town a private detective uncovers local corruption while trying to help an ex-girlfriend accused of murdering her husband. Entertaining TV movie which was the pilot for the popular "Cannon" (CBS-TV, 1971-76) series.

515 Canon for Cordoba. United Artists, 1970. 104 minutes Color. D: Paul Wendkos. SC: Stephen Kandell. WITH George Peppard, Giovanna Ralli, Raf Vallone, Peter Duel, Don Gordon, Nico Minardos, John Russell, Francine York, John Larch, Charles Stainaker, John Clark, Gabrielle Tinti, Hans Meyer. An Army intelligence officer and a small group of men attempt to recover canons stolen from General Pershing's army by Mexican revolutionaries. Average action production which attempts to imitate the European oaters of the period.

516 Can't Help Singing. Universal, 1944. 95 minutes B/W. D: Frank Ryan. SC: Lewis R. Foster & Frank Ryan. WITH Deanna Durbin, Robert Paige, Akim Tamiroff, David Bruce, June Vincent, Ray Collins, Olin Howlin, Leonid Kinsky, Clara Blandick, Thomas Gomez, Andrew Tombes, George Cleveland, Edward Earle, Almira Sessions, Chester Conklin. In 1849 a young girl, over her father's objections, heads to California to marry an Army lieutenant but finds romance along the trail. Spritely musical-comedy-Western which will delight Deanna Durbin fans.

517 Canyon Ambush. Monogram, 1952. 53 minutes B/W. D: Lewis Collins. SC: Joseph Poland. WITH Johnny Mack Brown, Lee Roberts, Phyllis Coates, Dennis Moore, Hugh Prosser, Marshall Reed, Denver Pyle, Pierce Lyden, Carol Henry, Stanley Price, Frank Ellis, Russ Whiteman. A government agent comes to a small town to help the local sheriff and concerned citizens in combating a gang led by a masked rider. Fair entertainment is provided in this Johnny Mack Brown oater, the star's final series production.

518 Canyon City. Republic, 1943. 56 minutes B/W. D: Spencer Gordon Bennet. SC: Robert Yost. WITH Don "Red" Barry, Helen Talbot, Wally Vernon, Twinkle Watts, LeRoy Mason, Pierce Lyden,

Forbes Murray, Ed Piel Sr., Eddie Gribbon, Tom London, Morgan Conway, Emmett Vogan, Stanley Andrews, Roy Barcroft, Jack Kirk, Kenne Duncan, Bud Geary, Bud Osborne, Hank Worden. The Nevada Kid aids citizens in their fight against an Eastern gangster out to steal their lands. Not the best of Don Barry's outings, especially with little Twinkle Watts along as some kind of a sidekick.

519 Canyon Crossroads. United Artists, 1955. 83 minutes B/W. D: Alfred Werker. SC: Emmett Murphy & Leonard Heideman. WITH Richard Basehart, Phyllis Kirk, Stephen Elliott, Russell Collins, Charles Wagenheim, Richard Hale, Tommy Cook. A man searches for uranium deposits in Utah as a group of crooks are out to get the claim before he can record its location. Taut modern-day film which uses helicopters more than horses.

520 Canyon Hawks. Big 4, 1930. 55 minutes B/W. D-SC: Allan J. Neitz. WITH Yakima Canutt, Buzz Barton, Rene Borden, Wally Wales, Robert Walker, Bob Reeves, Cliff Lyons, Bobby Dunn. A man befriends a girl and her brother and sells them land for their sheep herd and he comes to the girl's rescue when she is kidnapped by a badman. Low grade early talkie which should appeal to Yakima Canutt's fans because it provides him with a starring role.

521 Canyon of Missing Men. Syndicate, 1930. 5 reels B/W. D: J. P. McGowan. SC: George H. Williams. WITH Tom Tyler, Sheila LeGay, Bud Osborne, Tom Forman, J. P. McGowan, Cliff Lyons, Bobby Dunn, Arden Ellis. An outlaw gang member falls for a rancher's daughter and he betrays the gang when they try to kidnap the girl and hold her for ransom. This silent Tom Tyler entry is only fair with mostly outdoor shots and a slight story.

522 Canyon Passage. Universal, 1946. 99 minutes Color. D: Jacques Tourneur. SC: Ernest Pascal. WITH Dana Andrews, Susan Hayward, Brian Donlevy, Patricia Roc, Hoagy Carmichael, Ward Bond, Andy Devine, Stanley Ridges, Lloyd Bridges, Fay Holden, Victor Cutler, Tad Devine, Denny Devine, Onslow Stevens, Rose Hobart, Dorothy Peterson, Halliwell Hobbes, James Cardwell, Ray Teal, Virginia Patton, Francis McDonald, Erville Alderson, Ralph Peters, Jack Rockwell, Gene Roth, Karl Hackett, Jack Clifford, Richard Alexander, Chief Yowlachie, Wallace Scott, Peter Whitney, Harry Shannon, Chester Clute, Frank Ferguson, Eddie Dunn, Harlan Briggs, Rex Lease, Jack Ingram. A store owner-mule freight hauler and a crooked gambling banker both love the same girl in the rugged Oregon country of 1856. Beautifully produced feature showing both the glory and harshness of frontier life; a very good motion picture.

523 Canyon Raiders. Monogram, 1951. 54 minutes B/W. D: Lewis D. Collins. SC: Jay Gilgore. WITH Whip Wilson, Fuzzy Knight, Phyllis Coates, Jim Bannon, Bill Kennedy, Barbara Woodell, I. Stanford Jolley, Marshall Reed, Riley Hill. Two ranchers try to stop crooks who have rustled 500 horses and plan to sell them to the army with forged bills of sale. There is enough action to carry along this Whip Wilson vehicle.

524 Canyon River. Allied Artists, 1956. 80 minutes Color. D: Harmon Jones. SC: Daniel F. Ullman. WITH George Montgomery, Marcia Henderson, Peter Graves, Richard Eyer, Walter Sande, Robert Wilke, Alan Hale, John Harmon, Jack Lambert, William Fawcett. The foreman of a cattle drive from Oregon to Wyoming has his life saved by the head of a gang of outlaws but when the bandits attack the trail drive he is forced to fight them. Average oater helped by George Montgomery and color.

525 Captain Apache. Scotia International, 1971. 95 minutes Color. D: Alexander Singer. SC: Philip Yordan & Milton Sperling. WITH Lee Van Cleef, Carroll Baker, Stuart Whitman, Percy Herbert, Elisa Montes, Tony Vogel, Charles Stalnaker, Charlie Bravo, Faith Clift, Dan Van Husen, D. Pollock, Hugh McDermott, George Margo, Jose Bodalo. When an Indian commissioner is murdered an Apache warrior is assigned by the Army to find out who committed the killing. British-produced oater with all the violence of continental Westerns.

526 Captain John Smith and Pocahontas. United Artists, 1953. 75 minutes Color. D: Lew Landers. SC: Aubrey Wisberg & Jack Pollexfen. WITH Anthony Dexter, Jody Lawrence, Alan Hale (Jr.), Robert Clarke, Stuart Randall, James Seay, Philip Van Zandt, Shepard Menken, Douglass Dumbrille, Anthony Eustral, Henry Rowland, Franchesca di Scaffa, Joan Nixon. Captain John Smith tries to establish a colony in Virginia despite opposition from others who want to hunt for gold or use it as a base for privateering, and he tries to make peace with the Indians only to be captured. Colorful romantic history about the supposed love affair between Captain John Smith and Indian maiden Pocahontas; average entertainment.

527 Captain Thunder. Warner Brothers, 1930. 66 minutes B/W. D: Alan Crosland. SC: Gordon Rigby & William K. Wells. WITH Victor Varconi, Fay Wray, Charles Judels, Don Alvarado, Robert Elliott, Natalie Moorehead, Bert Roach, Frank Campeau, Robert Emmett Keane, John Sainpolis. A dashing Mexican bandit comes to the aid of a young man who tries to capture him when the man's pretty fiancee is forced to marry a rival. Early talkie curio for fans of that era.

528 Captive of Billy the Kid. Republic, 1952. 54 minutes B/W. D: Fred C. Brannon. SC: M. Coates Webster & Richard Wormer. WITH Allan "Rocky" Lane, Penny Edwards, Grant Withers, Clem Bevans, Roy Barcroft, Mauritz Hugo, Frank McCarroll. Outlaws are after a treasure hidden by Billy the Kid and a marshall sets out to round up the gang and uncovers the loot. Nicely paced entry in the Allan Lane Republic series; his fans will like it.

529 The Capture. RKO Radio, 1950. 81 minutes B/W. D: John Sturges. SC: Niven Busch. WITH Lew Ayres, Teresa Wright, Victor Jory, Duncan Renaldo, Jacqueline White, Jimmy Hunt, Barry Kelley, William Bakewell, Milton Parsons. A detective feels he may have killed the wrong man in a robbery attempt and sets out to reinvestigate the case. Modern day feature with much of its footage in rural Mexico; good viewing.

530 The Capture of Grizzly Adams. NBC-TV, 1982. 100 minutes Color. D-SC: Arthur Heinemann. WITH Dan Haggerty, Kim Darby, Chuck Connors, Noah Beery, Keenan Wynn. A mountain man is faced with a fake murder charge by those who want to see him out of the way. Average TV movie based on the 1976 feature film **The Life and Times of Grizzly Adams** (q.v.) and the 1977-78 NBC-TV program of the same title.

531 The Caravan Trail. Producers Releasing Corporation, 1946. 57 minutes Color. D: Robert Emmett (Tansey). SC: Frances Kavanaugh. WITH Eddie Dean, Emmett Lynn, Al "Lash" LaRue, Jean Carlin, Robert Malcolm, Charles King, Robert Barron, Forrest Taylor, Bob Duncan, Jack O'Shea, Terry Frost, George Chesebro, Bud Osborne, Lee Roberts, Wylie Grant, Lee Bennett, Lloyd Ingraham. The leader of a wagon train of settlers enlists the aid of an outlaw gang leader in stopping landgrabbers who have stolen the pioneers' homesteads. Passable Eddie Dean vehicle which helped launch Lash LaRue into his own series; best when Eddie Dean sings "Wagon Wheels."

532 The Cariboo Trail. 20th Century-Fox, 1950. 81 minutes Color. D: Edwin L. Marin. SC: Frank Gruber. WITH Randolph Scott, Karin Booth, George "Gabby" Hayes, Bill Williams, Douglas Kennedy, Jim Davis, Dale Robertson, Mary Stuart, James Griffith, Lee Tung Foo, Anthony Hughes, Mary Kent, Ray Hyke, Jerry Root, Cliff Clark, Fred Libby, Dorothy Adams, Michael Barret, Smith Ballew. While searching for a location for a cattle ranch in northwest Canada, a cattleman discovers gold. Typically good Randolph Scott feature with beautiful locations.

533 Carolina Cannonball. Republic, 1955. 74 minutes B/W. D: Charles Lamont. SC: Barry Shipman. WITH Judy Canova, Andy Clyde, Ross Elliott, Sig Rumann, Leon Askin, Jack Kruschen, Frank Wilcox, Roy Barcroft. A group of bumbling foreign spies capture an atomic-controlled missile and they end up causing it to land on a girl's ranch. Later, but still typical Judy Canova corn-fare, which will appeal to her fans.

534 Carolina Moon. Republic, 1940. 54 (65) minutes B/W. D: Frank McDonald. SC: Winston Miller. WITH Gene Autry, Smiley Burnette, June Storey, Mary Lee, Eddy Waller, Hardie Albright, Texas Jim Lewis & His Texas Cowboys, Frank Dale, Terry Nibert, Robert Fiske, Etta McDaniel, Paul White, Fred Ritter, Ralph Sanford, Jack Kirk. Rodeo performers Gene Autry and Frog Millhouse try to help a man and his daughter who are about to be cheated out of their prize horse by crooks but the girl believes Gene is in league with the hoodlums. Too long and fairly vapid Gene Autry vehicle.

535 Caryl of the Mountains. Reliable, 1936. 60 minutes B/W. D: Bernard B. Ray. SC: Tom Gibson. WITH Rin-Tin-Tin Jr., Francis X. Bushman Jr., Lois Wild(e), Joseph Swickard, Earl Dwire, Robert Walker, George Chesebro, Steve Clark, Jack Hendricks. A Mountie and his faithful

German shepherd dog are on the trail of an outlaw. Low budget quickie for fans of the Royal Mounted; supposedly based on James Oliver Curwood.

536 Carry on Cowboy. Anglo-Amalgamated/Filmways, 1966. 95 minutes Color. D: Gerald Thomas. SC: Talbot Rothwell. WITH Sidney James, Kenneth Williams, Joan Sims, Jim Dale, Percy Herbert, Angela Douglas, Davy Kaye, Bernard Bresslaw, Charles Hawtrey, Peter Butterworth, Sydney Bromley, Sally Douglas, Joan Pertwee, Edina Ronay, Peter Gilmore, Garry Colleano. The evil Rumpo Kid kills the sheriff and takes over the town of Stodge City before being faced by a marshal from the British Sanitary Engineers. Typical loony entry in the British "Carry On..." series. Also called **The Rumpo Kid.**

537 Carson City. Warner Brothers, 1953. 87 minutes Color. D: Andre De Toth. SC: Sloan Nibley & Winston Miller. WITH Randolph Scott, Lucille Norman, Raymond Massey, Richard Webb, James Millican, Larry Keating, George Cleveland, William Haade, Thurston Hall, Vince Barnett, Don Beddoe, Jack Woody, James Smith, Guy Tongue, Billy Vincent, Ida Moore, Sarah Edwards, Edgar Dearing, Russ Clark, Iris Adrian, Nick Thompson, Frank McCarroll, Post Parks, Jack Daley, Mickey Simpson, Edmund Cobb, John Halloran, Mikel Conrad, Zon Murray, House Peters Jr., Rory Mallinson, Ray Bennett, Karen Hale, Stanley Blystone, Stanley Andrews, Richard Reeves, George Eldredge, Charles Evans, Kenneth MacDonald, George Sherwood, Pierce Lyden, Les O'Pace. A railroad boss is at odds with a miner and a young girl who do not want him to continue the construction of his railroad. Rugged Randolph Scott oater; well worth watching.

538 Carson City Cyclone. Republic, 1943. 55 minutes B/W. D: Howard Bretherton. SC: Norman S. Hall. WITH Don "Red" Barry, Lynn Merrick, Noah Beery, Emmett Lynn, Bryant Washburn, Stuart Hamblen, Roy Barcroft, Bud Osborne, Jack Kirk, Bud Geary, Curley Dresden, Reed Howes, Tom London, Frank Ellis, Horace Carpenter, Ed Cassidy, Tom Steele, Jack O'Shea, Frank McCarroll, Roy Brent. During a court trial a young lawyer is accused of bribing a witness and he sets out to find out who is the real culprit. More than passable Don Barry entry with good villainy from Noah Beery.

539 The Carson City Kid. Republic, 1940. 54 (57) minutes B/W. D: Joseph Kane. SC: Robert Yost & Gerald Geraghty. WITH Roy Rogers, George "Gabby" Hayes, Bob Steele, Noah Beery Jr., Pauline Moore, Francis McDonald, Hal Taliaferro, Arthur Loft, Chester Gan, Paul Hurst, George Rosener, Hank Bell, Ted Mapes, Jack Ingram, Jack Kirk, Jack Rockwell, Art Dillard, Hal Price, Yakima Canutt, Kit Guard, Curley Dresden, Oscar Gahan. In Senora in 1849 gambling house owner Jessop is sought by the bandit The Carson City Kid, who believes the gambler was responsible for the murder of his younger brother. Top notch Roy Rogers' series entry dominated by villain Bob Steele, who is given special billing. Film also includes the song "Sonora Moon."

540 Carson City Raiders. Republic, 1948. 60 minutes B/W. D: Yakima Canutt. SC: Earle Snell. WITH Allan "Rocky" Lane, Eddy Waller, Beverly Jones, Frank Reicher, Hal Landon, Steve Darrell, Harold Goodwin, Dale Van Sickel, Edmund Cobb, Holly Bane, Robert Wilke, Herman Hack. A U. S. marshal sets out to aid in the capture of a man's murderer but the man's son is out to avenge the killing himself. Another fine entry in the Allan Lane Republic series, with lots of story movement from director Yakima Canutt.

541 Cassidy of the Bar 20. Paramount, 1938. 54 (56) minutes B/W. D: Lesley Selander. SC: Norman Houston. WITH William Boyd, Russell Hayden, Frank Darien, Nora Lane, Robert Fiske, John Elliott, Margaret Marquis, Carleton Young, Gertrude W. Hoffman, Gordon Hart, Ed Cassidy. The Bar 20 trio go to the aid of Hoppy's ex-sweetheart and come up against a crooked landowner. Mediocre entry in the "Hopalong Cassidy" series.

542 Cast a Long Shadow. United Artists, 1959. 82 minutes B/W. D: Thomas Carr. SC: Martin G. Goldsmith & John McGreevy. WITH Audie Murphy, Terry Moore, John Dehner, James Best, Denver Pyle, Ann Doran, Robert Foulk, Rita Flynn, Wright King. Troubled by the fact that he is illegitimate, a young man turns to the bottle but when given the responsibility of tending a ranch he begins to make something of his life. None-too-interesting Audie Murphy vehicle.

543 The Castaway Cowboy. Buena Vista, 1974. 91 minutes Color. D: Bernard McEveety. SC: Don Tait. WITH James Garner,

The Cat 68

Vera Miles, Robert Culp, Eric Shea, Shug Fisher, Elizabeth Smith, Gregory Sierra, Manu Tupou. A cowboy shipwrecked in Hawaii meets a young widow and her son whose land is being sought by a bad man, and he proceeds to turn her land into a cattle ranch. Pleasant Walt Disney outing with the Old West transferred to Hawaii. V: Disney Home Video.

544 The Cat. Embassy, 1966. 87 minutes Color. D: Ellis Kadison. SC: William Redlin & Laird Koenig. WITH Roger Perry, Peggy Ann Garner, Barry Coe, Dwayne Redlin, George "Shug" Fisher, Ted Darby, John Todd Roberts, Richard Webb, Les Bradley. A young boy looking for a wildcat observes a rustler murder a forest ranger. Pleasant family film.

545 Cat Ballou. Columbia, 1965. 96 minutes Color. D: Elliott Silverstein. SC: Walter Newman. WITH Lee Marvin, Jane Fonda, Michael Callan, Dwayne Hickman, Nat "King" Cole, Stubby Kaye, Tom Nardini, John Marley, Reginald Denny, Jay C. Flippen, Arthur Hunnicutt, Bruce Cabot, Burt Mustin, Paul Gilbert, Harvey Clark, Oscar Blank. A timid schoolmarm comes West and soon becomes a wanted outlaw who teams with a drunken gunman to take on his notorious gunfighter brother. Overrated comedy which does not hold up well although Lee Marvin's Oscar-winning performance is still worth watching. V: Columbia Pictures Home Entertainment.

546 Catlow. Metro-Goldwyn-Mayer, 1971. 101 minutes Color. D: Sam Wanamaker. SC: Scott Finch & J. J. Griffith. WITH Yul Brynner, Richard Crenna, Daliah Lavi, Leonard Nimoy, Jo Ann Pflug, Jeff Corey, David Ladd, Bessie Love, Michael Delano, Julian Mateos. While trying to steal two million dollars in gold from a pack train, an outlaw is forced to avoid his marshal-friend and a bounty hunter, both of whom are after him. Average genre entry filmed in Spain.

547 Cattle Annie and Little Britches. Universal, 1981. 95 minutes Color. D: Lamont Johnson. SC: David Eyre & Robert Ward. WITH Burt Lancaster, Rod Steiger, John Savage, Diane Lane, Amanda Plummer, Scott Glenn, Michael Conrad. Two feisty young girls track down the remnants of the once-notorious Doolin-Dalton gang and urge them to continue their life of lawlessness. Pleasant tongue-in-cheek actioner filmed in Mexico.

548 Cattle Drive. Universal-International, 1951. 77 minutes Color. D: Kurt Neumann. SC: Jack Natteford & Lillie Hayward. WITH Joel McCrea, Dean Stockwell, Chill Wills, Leon Ames, Henry Brandon, Bob Steele, Howard Petrie, Griff Barnett, Chuck Roberson. The sheltered young son of a railroad tycoon learns life's values as he goes with a veteran cowboy on a cattle drive across the desert. A different kind of a Western and one that is quite entertaining.

549 Cattle Empire. 20th Century-Fox, 1958. 83 minutes Color. D: Charles Marquis Warren. SC: Andre Boehm & Eric Norden. WITH Joel McCrea, Gloria Talbott, Phyllis Coates, Don Haggerty, Bing Russell, Paul Brinegar, Hal K. Dawson, Richard Shannon, Charles Gray, Patrick O'Moore, Steve Raines, Nesdon Booth, Bill Hale, Howard Culver, Bill McGraw. When it becomes imperative to get their cattle to market a group of citizens ask a cattle boss, a man they once sent to jail, to lead their herd and he agrees but plans to double-cross them. Entertaining Joel McCrea oater with several neat plot twists.

550 Cattle King. Metro-Goldwyn-Mayer, 1963. 88 minutes Color. D: Tay Garnett. SC: Thomas Thompson. WITH Robert Taylor, Joan Caulfield, Robert Loggia, Robert Middleton, Larry Gates, Malcolm Atterbury, William Windom, Virginia Christie, Ray Teal, Richard Devon, Robert Ivers, Maggie Pierce, John Mitchum. In 1883 in Wyoming Territory a rich rancher wants to have fenced-in ranges but other cattlemen oppose this and the situation becomes so tense that President Chester A. Arthur is forced to intervene. Fairly interesting Western with a novel plot, but Larry Gates looks nothing like Chester A. Arthur.

551 Cattle Queen. United International, 1951. 72 minutes B/W. D-SC: Robert Emmett Tansey. WITH Maria Hart, Drake Smith, William Fawcett, Robert Gardette, John Carpenter, Edward Clark. The head of a ranch, a young woman, battles for her rights as she aids the town in cleaning up lawlessness with the aid of paroled criminals. Sparse actioner starring whip-carrying Maria Hart.

552 Cattle Queen of Montana. RKO Radio, 1954. 88 minutes Color. D: Allan Dwan. SC: Robert Blees & Howard Estabrook. WITH Barbara Stanwyck, Ronald

Reagan, Gene Evans, Lance Fuller, Anthony Caruso, Jack Elam, Yvette Dugay, Morris Ankrum, Chubby Johnson, Myron Healey, Rodd Redwing, Paul Birch, Byron Foulger, Burt Mustin, Roy Gordon. An Army undercover agent comes to the aid of a woman rancher after her father is murdered by a renegade white and his Indian accomplice. Filmed in SuperScope near the Glacier National Park, this oater has little interest for anyone outside fans of its two stars. V: Disney Home Video.

553 The Cattle Raiders. Columbia, 1938. 61 minutes B/W. D: Sam Nelson. SC: Joseph Poland & Ed Earl Repp. WITH Charles Starrett, Donald Grayson, Iris Meredith, The Sons of the Pioneers, Dick Curtis, Allen Brook, Ed LeSaint, Edmund Cobb, George Chesebro, Art Mix, Ed Coxen, Steve Clark, Alan Sears, Ed Piel, Jim Thorpe, Hank Bell, Blackie Whiteford, Jack Clifford, Frank Ellis, Curley Dresden, Merrill McCormack, George Morrell, Bob Burns, Wally West, Forrest Taylor, Horace B. Carpenter, Jim Mason, Clem Horton. A man is falsely accused of murder by a pal who is deeply in debt to a crooked cattle dealer. Actionful Charles Starrett vehicle.

554 Cattle Stampede. Producers Releasing Corporation, 1943. 59 minutes B/W. D: Sam Newfield. SC: Joseph O'Donnell. WITH Buster Crabbe, Al St. John, Frances Gladwin, Charles King, Ed Cassidy, Hansel Warner, Ray Bennett, Frank Ellis, Steve Clark, Roy Brent, John Elliott, Budd Buster, Hank Bell, Tex Cooper, Ted Adams, Frank McCarroll, Ray Jones, George Morrell. Billy Carson and Fuzzy Q. Jones come to the aid of a cattleman who is caught in the middle of a range war. Crude but fans of the series will like this one.

555 The Cattle Thief. Columbia, 1936. 57 minutes B/W. D: Spencer Gordon Bennet. SC: Nate Gatzert. WITH Ken Maynard, Geneva Mitchell, Ward Bond, Roger Williams, Jim (James) Marcus, Sheldon Lewis, Edward Cecil, Jack Kirk, Edward Hearn, Glenn Strange, Al Taylor, Dick Rush, Bud McClure, Jack King. An agent for the cattlemen's association masquerades as a dimwit peddler to get the goods on an outlaw gang trying to cheat ranchers out of their land. Good Ken Maynard vehicle with the star showing just how good he could be in a character role in playing the peddler. Inside joke: the name of the owner of the Bottleneck

Ranch in the film is Carl Pierson, a well known editor and sometimes film director.

556 Cattle Town. Warner Brothers, 1952. 71 minutes B/W. D: Noel Smith. SC: Tom Blackburn. WITH Dennis Morgan, Rita Moreno, Philip Carey, Paul Picerni, Amanda Blake, George O'Hanlon, Ray Teal, Jay Novello, Robert Wilke, Sheb Wooley, Charles Meredith, Merv Griffin, Boyd Morgan. When trouble erupts between cattlemen and a land baron a gunfighter is brought in to restore peace. Throwaway Dennis Morgan vehicle made on the cheap.

557 Caught. Paramount, 1931. 71 minutes B/W. D: Edward Sloman. SC: Agnes Brand Leahy & Kenne Thompson. WITH Richard Arlen, Frances Dee, Louise Dresser, Syd Saylor, Edward J. LeSaint, Tom Kennedy, Martin Burton, Marcia Manners, Guy Oliver, Charles K. French, Jim Mason, Jack Clifford. An Army lieutenant is on the trail of saloon owner Calamity Jane, who is wanted for a series of crimes. Dresser gives interesting true-to-life unglamorous portrayal of Calamity Jane.

558 Cavalier of the West. Artclass, 1931. 65 minutes B/W. D-SC: J. P. McCarthy. WITH Harry Carey, Kane Richmond, Carmen LaRoux, Paul Panzer, Ted Adams, George ("Gabby") Hayes, Ben Corbett, Maston Williams, Carlotta Monti. When war between Indians and whites is imminent, an Army captain sets out to restore peace. Early talkie with Harry Carey that will be of interest to his fans, but basically it is a low-grade effort.

559 Cavalry. Republic, 1936. 63 minutes B/W. D: Robert North Bradbury. SC: George Plympton. WITH Bob Steele, Frances Grant, Karl Hackett, William Welch, Earl Ross, Hal Price, Ed Cassidy, Perry Murdock, Budd Buster, Earl Dwire, William Desmond, Horace B. Carpenter. After the Civil War a group attempts to form a separate state in the West and the Army sends a cavalry officer to stop them. Good Bob Steele effort, well paced with a literate script.

560 Cavalry Command. Parade, 1963. 86 minutes Color. D-SC: Eddie Romero. WITH John Agar, Richard Arlen, Myron Healey, Alica Vergel, Pancho Magalone, William Phipps, Eddie Infante. During the American occupation of the Philippines in 1902, cavalry troops who befriend the people are resisted by a guerilla leader. So-so Philippine-made oater interesting because of its trio of stars.

561 Cavalry Scout. Allied Artists, 1951. 78 minutes Color. D: Lesley Selander. SC: Dan Ullman & Thomas Blackburn. WITH Rod Cameron, Audrey Long, Jim Davis, James Millican, James Arness, John Doucette, William Phillips, Stephen Chase, Rory Mallinson, Eddy Waller, Paul Bryar. When two Gatling guns and other weapons are stolen from an Army arsenal, a civilian scout is assigned to track down the guns and their captors. Fast moving oater which will pass muster for Rod Cameron fans.

562 Cave of the Outlaws. Universal-International, 1951. 75 minutes Color. D: William Castle. SC: Elizabeth Wilson. WITH MacDonald Carey, Alexis Smith, Edgar Buchanan, Victor Jory, Hugh O'Brian, Houseley Stevenson, Charles Horvath. An ex-convict searches for gold hidden in a Wells Fargo holdup and on his trail, also looking for the loot, are an investigator and a crooked miner. Mediocre oater which should have been a lot better considering its fairly interesting plot and cast.

The Century Turns see **Hec Ramsey**

563 The Challenge of Rin Tin Tin. Burt Leonard Productions, 1957. 90 minutes B/W. D: Robert G. Walker. WITH Rin Tin Tin V, James Brown, Lee Aaker, Joseph Sawyer, Rand Brooks. An orphaned boy and his dog, both adopted as honorary troopers by the cavalry soldiers of Fort Apache, aid the cavalry and nearby citizens against lawlessness in the old West. Enjoyable telefeature culled from segments of "The Adventures of Rin Tin Tin" (ABC-TV, 1954-59) television series.

564 The Challenge of the MacKennas. Picturmedia, 1969. 101 minutes Color. D: Leon Klimovsky. SC: Viaderk & Mulargia. WITH John Ireland, Robert Woods, Annabella Incontrera, Robert Camardiel, Daniela Giordano. A rancher rules his family and land with an iron hand but begins to meet opposition from a gunman as well as his own family members. Typically violent spaghetti actioner. Made in Italy by Filmar/Atlantida Films.

565 Challenge of the Range. Columbia, 1949. 56 minutes B/W. D: Ray Nazarro. SC: Ed Earl Repp. WITH Charles Starrett, Smiley Burnette, Paula Raymond, William (Billy) Halop, Steve Darrell, Henry Hall, Robert Filmer, George Chesebro, John McKee, Frank McCarroll, John Cason, Kermit Maynard, Edmund Cobb, Ray

Bennett, Cactus Mack, The Sunshine Boys, Jock Mahoney. The Durango Kid tries to sort out problems when ranchers accuse each other of various acts of lawlessness. High class entry in the popular "The Durango Kid" series.

566 Challenge to be Free. Pacific International, 1976. 88 minutes Color. D: Tay Garnett & Ford Beebe. SC: Chuck Keen, Anne Bosworth & Tay Garnett. WITH Mike Mazurki, Jimmy Kane, Fritz Ford, Vic Christy, Tay Garnett, John McIntire (Narrator). A trapper who loves animals is hunted by the law through the Yukon after he accidentally kills a trooper. Filmed in the Yukon in 1972 as **The Mad Trapper,** this somewhat crude feature makes for good entertainment, especially for the scenery and Mike Mazurki in the title role.

Challenge to Survive see **Land of No Return**

567 Champions of Justice. Wrather Corporation, 1956. 75 minutes Color. D: Earl Bellamy & Oscar Rudolph. SC: Thomas Seller, Doane Hoag, Robert E. Schaefer, Eric Friewald & Robert Leslie Bellem. WITH Clayton Moore, Jay Silverheels, Allen Pinson, Wayne Burson, Myron Healey, Dennis Moore, David Sharpe, Harry Strang, Don C. Harvey, Steve Raines, George Barrows, Robert Humans, Sydney Mason, Watson Downs, Dan Barton, Walt LaRue, Brad Jackson, Florence Lake, Carlos Vera, Linda Wrather, Tom Noel, Byron Foulger, Kathryn Riehl, Nolan Leary, William Fawcett, Zon Murray. The Lone Ranger and Tonto are almost hung for a murder committed by an outlaw gang and they also try to keep a boy from going to the wrong side of the law and unravel the mystery of a man's murder. Well done telefilm from "The Lone Ranger" (ABC-TV, 1949-57) series from the episodes "The Angel and the Outlaw," "Blind Witness" and "Clover in the Dust."

568 The Charge at Feather River. Warner Brothers, 1953. 96 minutes Color. D: Gordon Douglas. SC: James R. Webb. WITH Guy Madison, Frank Lovejoy, Vera Miles, Helen Westcott, Dick Wesson, Onslow Stevens, Steve Brodie, Ron Hagerthy, Fay Roope, Neville Brand, Henry Kulky, Lane Chandler, Fred Carson, James Brown, Ben Corbett, Ralph Brooke, Carl Andre, Fred Kennedy, Dub Taylor. Two women are kidnapped by Indians and the cavalry rescues them only to start an uprising. Nothing special in this oater, originally issued in 3-D.

569 Charley-One-Eye. Paramount, 1973. 96 minutes Color. D: Don Chaffey, SC: Keith Leonard. WITH Richard Roundtree, Roy Thinnes, Nigel Davenport, Jill Pearson, Aldo Sambrell, Rafael Albaicin, Alex Davion, Johnny Sekka, Madeline Hinde, Patrick Mower, Imogene Hassall, Edward Woodward, William Mervyn, David Lodge. An army deserter and a wounded Indian join forces to survive in the desert but find themselves the victims of bounty hunters. There is far more drama than action in this British-produced Western.

570 Charlie Cobb: Nice Night for a Hanging. NBC-TV/Universal, 1977. 100 minutes Color. D: Richard Michaels. SC: Peter S. Fischer. WITH Clu Gulager, Ralph Bellamy, Blair Brown, Christopher Connelly, Pernell Roberts, Stella Stevens, Carmen Matthews, George Furth, Tricia O'Neil. A private detective is hired by a rancher to return a girl he believes is his lost daughter, while the man's wife and her cohorts work to stop the detective. Mediocre TV Western which was the pilot for a series that failed to sell.

571 Charlie, The Lonesome Cougar. Buena Vista, 1970. 75 minutes Color. D: Winston Hibler. SC: Jack Speirs. WITH Rex Allen (narrator), Ron Brown, Brian Russell, Linda Wallace, Jim Wilson, Clifford Peterson, Lewis Sample, Edward C. Moller. Members of a northwoods logging camp befriend a small cougar. Very pleasant Disney family film.

572 Charro! National General, 1969. 98 minutes Color. D-SC: Charles Marquis Warren. WITH Elvis Presley, Ina Balin, Victor French, Barbara Werle, Solomon Sturges, Lynn Kellogg, Paul Brinegar, James Sikking, Harry Landers, Tony Young, James Almanazar, Charles H. Gray, Rodd Redwing, Gary Walbert, Duane Grey, John Pickard, J. Edward McKinley, Robert Luster, Chrisa Lang, Robert Karnes. In a small border town, a one-time outlaw must face the members of his former gang while romancing the pretty saloon owner. Elvis Presley tries his best in the title role (he sings only the title song) but is defeated by the production itself.

573 Chato's Land. United Artists, 1972. 92 minutes Color. D: Michael Winner. SC: Gerald Wilson. WITH Charles Bronson, Jack Palance, Richard Basehart, James Whitmore, Simon Oakland, Ralph Waite, Richard Jordan, Victor French, William Watson, Roddy McMillan, Paul Young, Lee Patterson, Rudy Ugland, Raul Castro, Sonia Rangan, Clive Endersby, Peter Dyneley, Hugh McDermott. When an Indian is forced to kill a lawman, a posse murders his family and then sets out after him only to find themselves the hunted rather than the hunters. Well-made Western reworking of **The Lost Patrol** (RKO Radio, 1935) which was shot in Spain. Originally released at 100 minutes.

574 Check Your Guns. Eagle Lion, 1948. 55 minutes B/W. D: Ray Taylor. SC: Joseph O'Donnell. WITH Eddie Dean, Roscoe Ates, Nancy Gates, George Chesebro, Andy Parker & The Plainsmen, I. Stanford Jolley, Mikel Conrad, Lane Bradford, Terry Frost, Mason Wynn, Dee Cooper, William Fawcett, Ted Adams, Budd Buster, Wally West. Wandering into a small town a man soon becomes its sheriff and sets out to stop an outlaw gang. Passable Eddie Dean musical vehicle.

575 Cherokee Flash. Republic, 1945. 58 minutes B/W. D: Thomas Carr. SC: Betty Burbridge. WITH Sunset Carson, Linda Stirling, Roy Barcroft, Bud Geary, Fred Graham, Tom London, John Merton, Frank Jacquet, Joe McGuinn, Pierce Lyden, James Lynn, Edmund Cobb, Bud Osborne, Bill Woolf, Hank Bell, George Chesebro, Chick Hannon. A man's adopted father, once a famous outlaw, is blamed for a robbery committed by his ex-gang and his son sets out to clear him. Another actionful outing from Sunset Carson with Roy Barcroft as a good guy for a change.

576 Cherokee Strip. Warner Brothers, 1937. 55 minutes B/W. D: Noel Smith. SC: Joseph K. Watson & Luci Ward. WITH Dick Foran, Jane Bryan, David Carlyle, Helen Valkis, Edmund Cobb, Gordon Hart, Joseph Crehan, Frank Faylen, Milton Kibbee, Jack Mower, Tom Brower, Walter Soderling, Tommy Bupp, Glenn Strange, Bud Osborne, Ben Corbett, Artie Ortego, Jack Kirk. Settlers are out to get free land in the Oklahoma Territory and take part in the land rush with a cowboy having his horse lamed by a man who wants to get the land he plans to claim. Better-than-average Dick Foran outing, thanks to the plot and song "My Little Buckaroo."

577 Cherokee Strip. Paramount, 1940. 86 minutes B/W. D: Lesley Selander. SC: Norman Houston & Bernard McConville. WITH Richard Dix, Florence Rice,

Victor Jory, Andy Clyde, William Henry, Tom Tyler, George E. Stone, Morris Ankrum, Charles Trowbridge, Douglas Fowley, Addison Richards, Hal Taliaferro, William Haade, Ray Teal, Jack Rockwell, Tex Cooper, A newly appointed lawman tries to bring order to the town of Goliath in the Cherokee Strip. Entertaining Richard Dix vehicle that is well produced and actionful.

578 Cherokee Uprising. Monogram, 1950. 60 minutes B/W. D: Lewis D. Collins. SC: Dan Ullman. WITH Whip Wilson, Andy Clyde, Lois Hall, Iron Eyes Cody, Sam Flint, Forrest Taylor, Marshall Reed, Chief Yowlachie, Lee Roberts, Stanley Price, Lyle Talbot, Edith Mills. A government agent tries to get to the bottom of the causes behind a threatened Indian uprising. Standard, but more than passable, Whip Wilson vehicle.

579 Chetan, Indian Boy. Autoren, 1972. 94 minutes Color. D-SC: Hark Bohn. WITH Marquard Bohm, Dschingis Bowakow, Willi Schultes. In the northwest wilderness a shepherd frees an Indian boy held captive by a farmer who comes searching for them. Well made and entertaining West German feature issued in that country as **Tschetan.**

580 Cheyenne. Warner Brothers, 1947. 100 minutes B/W. D: Raoul Walsh. SC: Alan LeMay & Thomas Williamson. WITH Dennis Morgan, Jane Wyman, Janis Paige, Bruce Bennett, Alan Hale, Arthur Kennedy, John Ridgely, Barton MacLane, Tom Tyler, Bob Steele, John Compton, John Alvin, Monte Blue, Ann O'Neal, Tom Fadden, Britt Wood. While trying to capture an outlaw a gambler falls in love with the man's wife. A good cast and steady direction greatly aid this Warner Brothers effort. TV title: **The Wyoming Kid.**

581 Cheyenne Autumn. Warner Brothers, 1964. 145 minutes Color. D: John Ford. SC: James R. Webb. WITH Richard Widmark, Carroll Baker, James Stewart, Karl Malden, Edward G. Robinson, Sal Mineo, Dolores Del Rio, Ricardo Montalban, Gilbert Roland, Arthur Kennedy, Elizabeth Allen, John Carradine, Patrick Wayne, Victor Jory, Mike Mazurki, George O'Brien, Sean McClory, Judson Pratt, Carmen D'Antonio, Ken Curtis, Walter Baldwin, Shug Fisher, Nancy Hsueh, Chuck Roberson, Harry Carey Jr., Ben Johnson, Jimmy O'Hara, Chuck Hayward, Lee Bradley, Walter Reed, Willis Bouchey,

Carleton Young, Denver Pyle, John Qualen, Dan Borzage, Dean Smith, Bing Russell. Nearly 300 Cheyenne Indians try to return to their homes in the Dakotas from their Oklahoma reservation and they are pursued by the cavalry. Although not a totally successful film, John Ford's final Western is more hit than miss; it is nice to see George O'Brien again and Mike Mazurki excels in a part which Victor McLaglen would have done two decades before.

582 Cheyenne Cyclone. Willis Kent, 1932. 57 minutes B/W. D: Armand L. Schaefer. SC: Oliver Drake. WITH Lane Chandler, Connie LaMont, Frankie Darro, Edward Hearn, J. Frank Glendon, Henry Rocquemore, Yakima Canutt, Marie Quillan, Jay Hunt, Charles "Slim" Whitaker, Jack Kirk, Hank Bell. Stranded in a small town with an acting troupe, a cowboy goes to work for a rancher who is about to lose his cattle herd to a crook. Rawboned actioner, although Lane Chandler is a likable Western hero.

583 The Cheyenne Kid. RKO Radio, 1933. 54 minutes B/W. D: Robert Hill. SC: Kenne Thompson. WITH Tom Keene, Mary Mason, Roscoe Ates, Alan Bridge, Otto Hoffman, Allan Roscoe, Anderson Lawler. An easy-going cowboy is blamed for a murder and sets out to reveal the real killer. Likable Tom Keene series entry. V: Thunderbird.

584 The Cheyenne Kid. Monogram, 1940. 50 minutes B/W. D: Raymond K. Johnson. SC: Tom Gibson. WITH Jack Randall, Louise Stanley, Kenneth (Kenne) Duncan, Frank Yaconelli, Reed Howes, Charles King, George Chesebro, Forrest Taylor, Tex Palmer. A notorious outlaw tries to reform and goes to work for a cattleman but crooks try to frame him on a murder and rustling charge. Fairly entertaining Jack Randall series vehicle.

585 Cheyenne Rides Again. Victory, 1937. 56 minutes B/W. D: Robert Hill. SC: Basil Dickey. WITH Tom Tyler, Lucille Browne, Jimmie Fox, Lon Chaney Jr., Roger Williams, Ed Cassidy, Theodore Lorch, Bud Pope, Francis Walker, Carmen LaRoux, Jed Martin, Slim Whitaker, Bob Hill, Merrill McCormack, Oscar Gahon, Jack C. Smith, Wilbur McCauley. A detective for the cattlemen's association tries to pass himself off as an outlaw in order to infiltrate an outlaw gang. Actionful oater in Tom Tyler's Victory series—heavy on outdoor scenes.

586 Cheyenne Roundup. Universal, 1942. 59 minutes B/W. D: Ray Taylor. SC: Elmer Clifton & Bernard McConville. WITH Johnny Mack Brown, Tex Ritter, Fuzzy Knight, Jennifer Holt, Harry Woods, Roy Barcroft, Robert Barron, Budd Buster, Gil Patrick, The Jimmy Wakely Trio (Jimmy Wakely, Johnny Bond, Scotty Harrell), William Desmond, Kenne Duncan, Kermit Maynard, Budd Buster, Carl Mathews. A bad man tries to kill a lawman who is after him and is himself killed and his good twin infiltrates a gang, masquerading as his outlaw brother, in order to clean up the territory. Satisfactory Johnny Mack Brown-Tex Ritter remake of **Bad Man from Red Butte** (q.v.) with a good song, "On the Rainbow Trail." V: Video Connection.

587 The Cheyenne Social Club. National General, 1970. 103 minutes Color. D: Gene Kelly. SC: James Lee Barrett. WITH James Stewart, Henry Fonda, Shirley Jones, Sue Anne Langdon, Elaine Devry, Robert Middleton, Arch Johnson, Dabbs Greer, Jackie Russell, Jackie Joseph, Sharon De Bord, Richard Collier, Charles Tyner, Jean Willes, Robert Wilke, Carl Reindel, J. Pat O'Malley, Jason Wingreen, John Dehner, Hal Baylor, Charlotte Stewart, Albert Morin, Myron Healey, Warren Kemmerling, Dick Johnstone, Red Morgan, Bill Davis, Richard Alexander. Two lowbrow cowpokes find themselves the owner of a brothel and having to defend the honor of their "girls." Fairly pleasant Western comedy, noted as the final screen teaming of James Stewart and Henry Fonda.

588 Cheyenne Takes Over. Eagle Lion, 1947. 56 minutes B/W. D: Ray Taylor. SC: Arthur E. Orloff. WITH Lash LaRue, Al St. John, Nancy Gates, George Chesebro, Lee Morgan, John Merton, Steve Clark, Bob Woodward, Marshall Reed, Budd Buster, Carl Mathews, Dee Cooper, Brad Slaven, Hank Bell. U. S. marshals Cheyenne Davis and Fuzzy Q. Jones come to the aid of a girl who saw a man murder another over a ranch. A draggy drama with mediocre production values dominated by George Chesebro as the bad guy.

589 Cheyenne Wildcat. Republic, 1944. 56 minutes B/W. D: Lesley Selander. SC: Randall Faye. WITH Bill Elliott, Bobby Blake, Alice Fleming, Peggy Stewart, Francis McDonald, Roy Barcroft, Tom London, Tom Chatterton, Kenne Duncan, Bud Geary, Jack Kirk, Bud Osborne, Robert Wilke, Rex Lease, Tom Steele, Forrest Taylor, Franklyn Farnum, Horace Carpenter, Frank Ellis, Steve Clark, Bob Burns, Jack O'Shea. Red Ryder and Little Beaver come to the aid of citizens in Cheyenne whose bank is being sought by a crook from the East. Nicely done entry in the "Red Ryder" series.

590 Chief Crazy Horse. Universal, 1955. 86 minutes Color. D: George Sherman. SC: Gerald Drayson Adams & Franklin Coen. WITH Victor Mature, Suzan Ball, John Lund, Ray Danton, Keith Larsen, Paul Guifoyle, David Janssen, Robert Warwick, James Millican, Morris Ankrum, Donald Randolph, Robert F. Simon, Stuart Randall, Pat Hogan, Dennis Weaver, John Peters, Henry Wills, Charles Horvath, David Miller. Young brave Crazy Horse believes in the old prophecy that a warrior will defeat the whites and he proves it to be true by defeating General Custer. Predictable oater focusing on the famous Indian chief with Victor Mature stalwart in the title role. British title: **Valley of Fury.**

591/92 A Child of the Prairie. Aywon, 1924. 45 minutes B/W. D-SC: Tom Mix. WITH Tom Mix, Louella Maxam, Baby Norma, Edward J. Brady, Leo Maloney, Fay Robinson, Frank Campeau. A gambler steals the wife and child of a rancher and the little girl grows up to be reunited with her father who wants revenge on the badman. Fairly interesting silent Tom Mix film actually made up of two of his early Selig two reelers.

593 China 9, Liberty 37. Lorimar/Titanus/ Compagnia Europea Cinematographica, 1978. 102 minutes Color. D: Monte Hellman. SC: Jerry Harvey & Douglas Verturelli. WITH Warren Oates, Fabio Testi, Jenny Agutter, Sam Peckinpah, Isabel Mestres, Gianrico Tondinelli, Franco Interlenghi, Carlos Bravo, Helga Line, Paco Benlloch, Richard C. Adams, Sydney Lassick, Natalie Kim, Luis Prendes, Yvonne Sentis, Frank Clement, Matthieu Ettori, David Thompson, Ramano Puppo, Tony Brandt, Piero Fondi, Luciano Sapdoni, Daniel Panes, Jose Murillo, Raphael Albaicon, Luis Barboo. Saved from execution by corrupt railroad tycoons, a man is sent to murder a former gunman for his land and finds the intended victim's young wife is willing to help him. Well acted but rather tiresome Italian-Spanish coproduction. Ronee Blakley sings the title theme. The film's title is a trail sign.

Chinchero see **The Last Movie**

594 Chino. Intercontinental Releasing Corporation, 1976. 98 minutes Color. D: John Sturges. SC: Dino Maiuri, Massimo De Rita & Clair Huffaker. WITH Charles Bronson, Jill Ireland, Vincent Van Patten, Marcel Bozzuffi, Melissa Chimenti, Fausto Tozzi, Ettore Manni, Adolfo Thous, Florencia Amarilla, Corrado Gaida, Diana Lorys. In 1880 a half-breed horse raiser befriends a teenage boy who helps him on his ranch but their life is interrupted when the man falls in love with the sister of a neighbor who vows to destroy him. Entertaining and colorful Charles Bronson film, made in Spain and issued abroad in 1973 by CIC as **The Valdez Horses.**

595 Chip of the Flying U. Universal, 1939. 55 minutes B/W. D: Ralph Staub. SC: Larry Rhine & Andrew Bennison. WITH Johnny Mack Brown, Bob Baker, Fuzzy Knight, Doris Weston, Forrest Taylor, Anthony Warde, Karl Hackett, Henry Hall, Claire Whitney, Ferris Taylor, Kermit Maynard, Cecil Kellogg, The Texas Rangers, Hank Bell, Harry Tenbrook, Chester Conklin, Victor Potel, Hank Worden, Charles K. French, Budd Buster, Frank Ellis. Foreign agents rob a bank and shoot its president and the foreman of a nearby ranch is blamed for the crime. Entertaining, but highly unfaithful, adaptation of Berta Muzzy Bower's chestnut which was first filmed by Selig in 1914 as a Tom Mix vehicle. In 1920 Bud Osborne starred as Chip in **The Galloping Dude** and in 1926 Hoot Gibson played Chip under the original title.

596 The Chisholms. CBS-TV, 1979. 270 minutes Color. D: Mel Stuart. SC: Evan Hunter. WITH Robert Preston, Rosemary Harris, Ben Murphy, Brian Kerwin, Jimmy Van Patten, Stacey Nelkin, Susan Swift, Charles Frank, Glynnis O'Connor, Sandra Griego, David Hayward, Anthony Zerbe, Brian Keith, Doug Kershaw, Tom Taylor, Gavin Troster, Dean Hill, David Allen, Don Shanks. The story of a pioneer family's journey from Virginia to Wyoming and their eventual settlement in California. Originally telecast as a three-part miniseries, this well-done drama was issued theatrically in a shorter version in 1979 by New Line International Releasing.

597 Chisum. Warner Brothers, 1970. 110 minutes Color. D: Andrew V. McLaglen. SC: Andrew J. Fenady. WITH John Wayne, Forrest Tucker, Christopher George, Pamela McMyler, Geoffrey Deuel, Ben Johnson, Glenn Corbett, Bruce Cabot, Andrew Prine, Patric Knowles, Richard Jaeckel, Lynda Day (George), John Agar, Lloyd Battista, Robert Donner, Ray Teal, Edward Faulkner, Ron Soble, John Mitchum, Glenn Langan, Alan Baxter, Alberto Morin, William Bryant, Pedro Armendariz Jr., Christopher Mitchum, Abraham Sofaer, Gregg Palmer, Chuck Roberson, Hank Worden, Ralph Volkie, Pedro Gonzales Gonzales, John Pickard. New Mexico cattle country baron John Chisum opposes crooks who are trying to steal his lands, resulting in the famous Lincoln County Cattle Wars. Big, brawling John Wayne oater; quite entertaining and one of his last really exciting vehicles. V: Cumberland Video.

The Chooper see **Blood Shack**

598 The Christmas Kid. Producers Releasing Organization, 1967. 87 minutes Color. D: Sidney Pink. SC: Jim Henaghan & R. Rivero. WITH Jeffrey Hunter, Louis Hayward, Gustavo Rojo, Perla Cristal, Luis Prendes, Reginald Gilliam, Fernando Hilbeck, Jack Taylor, Eric Chapman, Carl Rapp. A loner, rebelling against society, finds himself as he tries to stop a corrupt gambler from taking over a town. Cheaply made European oater of chief interest because of stars Jeffrey Hunter and Louis Hayward.

599 Christmas Mountain. Gold Coast, 1980. 90 minutes Color. D: Pierre De Moro. WITH Slim Pickens, Mark Miller, Barbara Stanger, Tina Minard, Fran Ryan, John Hart. Caught in the mountains during a blizzard an aging cowboy learns the true meaning of Christmas when he finds shelter with a widow and her children. Somewhat obscure, but pleasant, holiday fare.

600 Chuka. Paramount, 1967. 105 minutes Color. D: Gordon Douglas. SC: Richard Jessup. WITH Ernest Borgnine, John Mills, Luciana Paluzzi, James Whitmore, Angela Dorian (Victoria Vetri), Louis Hayward, Michael Cole, Hugh Reilly, Barry O'Hara, Joseph Sirola, Marco Antonio, Gerald York, Lucky Carson. A gunman comes to a small fort to tell its Indian-hating soldiers that unless the Indians are given food there will be warfare. Interesting concept that is not totally successful, resulting in a mediocre feature.

601 Cimarron. RKO Radio, 1931. 131 minutes B/W. D: Wesley Ruggles. SC: Howard Estabrook. WITH Richard Dix, Irene Dunne, Estelle Taylor, Nance O'Neil, William Collier Jr., Roscoe Ates, George E. Stone, Stanley Fields, Robert McWade, Edna May Oliver, Frank Darien, Eugene Jackson, Dolores Brown, Gloria Vonic, Otto Hoffman, William Orlamond, Frank Beal, Nancy Dover, Helen Parish, Donald Dillaway, Junior Johnson, Douglas Scott, Lillian Lane, Henry Roquemore, Nell Craig, Robert McKenzie, Robert Kortman, Dennis O'Keefe, William Janney. A young girl marries a drifter-gunfighter and they get in the Oklahoma land rush but go their separate ways, she becoming a newspaper editor and later a Congresswoman, while he dies as an oil worker. This film won three Oscars, including best film and script, but today this initial adaptation of Edna Ferber's novel is dated, but still worth viewing.

602 Cimarron. Metro-Goldwyn-Mayer, 1960. 140 minutes Color. D: Anthony Mann. SC: Arnold Schulman. WITH Glenn Ford, Maria Schell, Anne Baxter, Arthur O'Connell, Russ Tamblyn, Mercedes McCambridge, Vic Morrow, Robert Keith, Charles McGraw, Harry Morgan, David Opatoshu, Aline MacMahon, Lili Darvas, Edgar Buchanan, Mary Wickes, Royal Dano, L. Q. Jones, George Brelin, Vladimir Sokoloff, Helen Westcott, Ivan Triesault, Eddie Little Sky, Dawn Little Sky. A man with wanderlust and a pretty girl meet and wed and move to the Oklahoma Territory where they eventually split up, her to become a success while he drifts into obscurity. Indifferent remake of the Edna Ferber novel, relying too much on color and modern film techniques and not enough on the original novel.

603 The Cimarron Kid. Universal-International, 1951. 84 minutes Color. D: Ted Richmond. SC: Louis Stevens. WITH Audie Murphy, Beverly Tyler, James Best, Yvette Dugay, John Hudson, Leif Erickson, Noah Beery Jr., John Hubbard, Hugh O'Brian, Palmer Lee (Gregg Palmer), Rand Brooks, William Reynolds, Roy Roberts, David Wolfe, John Bromfield, Frank Silvera, Richard Garland, Eugene Baxter. A gunman, who leads a gang of bank robbers, falls in love with a girl who tries to get him to give up his life of crime. Average Audie Murphy vehicle, helped by Technicolor.

604 Circle Canyon. Superior, 1934. 48 minutes B/W. D: Victor Adamson (Denver Dixon). SC: B. R. Tuttle. WITH Buddy Roosevelt, June Mathews, Clarise Woods, Robert Williamson, Allen Holbrook, Clyde McClary, Harry Leland. A cowboy arrives in an area where two outlaw gangs are opposing each other. Bottom rung Buddy Roosevelt film.

605 Circle of Death. Willis Kent, 1935. 60 minutes B/W. D: J. Frank Glendon. WITH Monte Montana, Tove Lindan, Henry Hall, Yakima Canutt, Ben Corbett, J. Frank Glendon, Jack Carson, John Ince, Princess Ah-Tee-Ha, Richard Botiller, Chief Standing Bear, Slim Whitaker, Hank Bell, Budd Buster, Bart Carre, George Morrell, Olin Francis, Marin Sais, Bob Burns. The son of an Indian chief, actually a white boy rescued by braves years before following a massacre, aids a rancher who is being blackmailed by crooks who believe there is gold on his land. Near the bottom of the barrel but still worth a watch to see the great Monte Montana in his only starring Western. V: Video Dimensions.

606 The Cisco Kid. Fox, 1931. 60 minutes B/W. D: Irving Cummings. SC: Alfred A. Cohn. WITH Warner Baxter, Edmund Lowe, Conchita Montenegro, Nora Lane, Frederick Burt, Willard Robertson, James Bradbury Jr., Jack Dillon, Charles Stevens, Chris-Pin Martin, Douglas Haig, Marilyn Knowlden. The Cisco Kid steals $5,000 to help a girl pay off her ranch and that same amount is placed on his head as reward money. Pleasing followup to Warner Baxter's Academy Award winning performance at the Cisco Kid in **In Old Arizona** (q.v.).

607 The Cisco Kid and the Lady. 20th Century-Fox, 1940. 73 minutes B/W. D: Herbert I. Leeds. SC: Frances Hyland. WITH Cesar Romero, Marjorie Weaver, Chris-Pin Martin, George Montgomery, Virginia Field, Robert Barrat, Harry

Green, John Beach, Ward Bond, J. Anthony Hughes, James Burke, Harry Hayden, James Flavin, Ruth Warren, Gloria Ann White. The Cisco Kid gets involved with a man trying to steal a gold mine as well as an orphaned baby and a girl who loves another man. First of a half-dozen "Cisco Kid" adventures with Cesar Romero in the title role; this film is too long on romance (and running time) and too short on action.

608 The Cisco Kid Returns. Monogram, 1945. 64 minutes B/W. D: John P. McCarthy. SC: Betty Burbridge. WITH Duncan Renaldo, Martin Garralaga, Roger Pryor, Cecilia Callejo, Anthony Warde, Fritz Leiber, Vicky Lane, Jan Wiley, Sharon Smith, Cy Kendall, Eva Puig, Bud Osborne, Bob Duncan, Carl Mathews. The Cisco Kid and Pancho suspect a respected businessman of being behind a series of crimes. Duncan Renaldo's first appearance as "The Cisco Kid" is a standard affair but will appeal to his fans. TV title: **The Daring Adventurer.**

609 City of Badmen. 20th Century-Fox, 1953. 82 minutes Color. D: Harmon Jones. SC: George W. George & George F. Slavin. WITH Dale Robertson, Jeanne Crain, Richard Boone, Lloyd Bridges, Carole Mathews, Carl Betz, Whitfield Connor, Hugh Sanders, Rodolfo Acosta, Pasquel Garcia Pena, Harry Carter, Robert Adler, John Doucette, Alan Dexter, Don Haggerty, Leo Gordon, Gil Perkins, John Day, James Best, Richard Cutting, Douglas Evans, Kit Carson, Barbara Fuller, Anthony Jochim, George Melford, George Selk (Budd Buster), Charles Tannen. When the heavyweight championship boxing bout between James J. Corbett and Bob Fitzsimmons is staged in Carson City, Nevada, in 1897, outlaws plan to steal the box office receipts. Pretty good Western-crime melodrama highlighted by a restaging of the famous fight.

610 The Civilized Men. NBC-TV/Universal, 1969. 74 minutes Color. WITH Robert Stack, Jack Kelly, Rod Cameron, Jill St. John, Kaz Garas, Susan Saint James. A former F.B.I. agent, now the senior editor of a news magazine, travels to Florida to investigate modern-day cattle rustling on ranches there. Very good telefeature, originally telecast November 28, 1969 as a segment of the series "The Name of the Game" (NBC-TV, 1968-72).

611 Clancy of the Mounted. Universal, 1933. 12 Chapters B/W. D: Ray Taylor.

SC: Basil Dickey, Harry O. Hoyt & Ella O'Neill. WITH Tom Tyler, Jacqueline Wells (Julie Bishop), Earl McCarthy, William Desmond, Rosalie Roy, W. L. Thomas, Leon Duval, Francis Ford, Tom London, Edmund Cobb, William Thorne, Al Ferguson, Fred Humes, Frank Lackteen, Monte Montague, Steve Clemente. Crooks after a dead man's gold mine frame a Mountie's brother on a murder charge and the lawman is assigned to bring him to trial. Tom Tyler fans will love this action packed cliffhanger.

612 Clash of the Wolves. Warner Brothers, 1925. 60 minutes B/W. D: Noel Mason Smith. SC: Charles A. Logue. WITH Rin Tin Tin, June Marlowe, Charles Farrell, Heinie Conklin, Will Walling, Pat Hartigan. A half-dog, half-wolf, leader of a wolf pack, has a price on his head but is befriended by a borax prospector who he aids against a rival. Actionful Rin Tin Tin vehicle; good entertainment.

613 Claws. Alaska Pictures, 1977. 90 minutes Color. D: Richard Bansbach & R. E. Pierson. SC: Chuck D. Keen & Brian Russell. WITH Myron Healey, Leon Ames, Jason Evers, Anthony Caruso, Carla Layton, Glenn Sipes. A killer grizzly bear plagues the northwoods area and hunters set out to destroy the beast. Beautifully photographed adventure melodrama made in Alaska and somewhat similar to **Grizzly** (q.v.).

614 Clearing the Range. Allied, 1931. 65 minutes B/W. D: Otto Brower. SC: Jack Natteford. WITH Hoot Gibson, Sally Eilers, Hooper Atchley, Robert Homans, Edward Piel, George Mendoza, Edward Hearn, Maston Williams, Eva Grippon. A cowpoke tries to find out who killed his brother and he takes on two guises to do so: a pacificist and that of the bandit El Capitan. Slow moving, nicely photographed (by Ernest Miller) with good fight sequences.

615 Climb an Angry Mountain. NBC-TV/Warner Brothers, 1972. 100 minutes Color. D: Leonard Horn. SC: Joseph Cavelli & Sam Rolfe. WITH Fess Parker, Marj Dusay, Arthur Hunnicutt, Barry Nelson, Stella Stevens, Joe Kapp, Clay O'Brien, Jewel Branch, Richard Brian Harris, Casey Tibbs, Kenneth Washington, J. C. McElroy. An Indian, running from the law, kidnaps a sheriff's son and heads up California's Mount Shasta, with the sheriff and a New York City policeman, at odds over police procedure, in pursuit.

Better-than-average telefeature with nice scenic values.

616 Cocaine Cowboys. International Harmony, 1979. 87 minutes Color. D: Ulli Lommel. SC: Ulli Lommel, S. Compton, T. Sullivan & V. Bockris. WITH Jack Palance, Tom Sullivan, Andy Warhol, Suzanna Love, Esther Bedham-Faran, Winnie Hollmann, Richard Young, Toni Manafo, Richard Bassett, Pete Huckabee, The Cowboy Island Band. A rock group with few playdates decides to make a living as cowboys, only they rustle dope instead of cattle. Strictly amateur night at Andy Warhol's house, where his dud was filmed.

617 The Cockeyed Cowboys of Calico County. Universal, 1970. 97 minutes Color. D: Tony Leader. SC: Ranald MacDougall. WITH Dan Blocker, Nanette Fabray, Jim Backus, Wally Cox, Jack Elam, Jack Cassidy, Henry Jones, Stubby Kaye, Mickey Rooney, Noah Beery, Marge Champion, Donald (Don "Red") Barry, Hamilton Camp, Tom Basham, Iron Eyes Cody, James McCallion, Byron Foulger, Ray Ballard. Fearing they will lose their blacksmith, who sent for a mail order bride who did not arrive, the citizens of a Western town try to find him a bride. Made for TV but first issued to theatres, this is a dull Western comedy.

618 Code of the Cactus. Victory, 1939. 57 minutes B/W. D: Sam Newfield. SC: Edward Halperin. WITH Tim McCoy, Dorothy Short, Dave O'Brien, Ben Corbett, Ted Adams, Alden Chase, Forrest Taylor, Bob Terry, Slim Whitaker, Frank Wayne, Kermit Maynard, Art Davis, Carl Mathews, Carl Sepulveda, Jimmie Aubrey, Clyde McClary, Jack King. Ranchers enlist the aid of lawman Lightnin' Bill Carson to help stop a gang of rustlers who use trucks to steal their cattle. Cheaply made but fast moving Tim McCoy vehicle.

619 Code of the Fearless. Spectrum, 1939. 56 minutes B/W. D: Raymond K. Johnson. SC: Fred Myton. WITH Fred Scott, Claire Rochelle, John Merton, Walter McGrail, George Sherwood, Harry Harvey, William Woods, Don Gallaher, Roger Williams, Carl Mathews, Frank LaRue, Gene Howard, James "Buddy" Kelly, Art Mix. A Texas Ranger pretends to be drummed out of the service in order to infiltrate an outlaw gang. The same old plot does nothing for this average Fred Scott vehicle, nor do a trio of mediocre songs. V: Discount Video.

620 Code of the Outlaw. Republic, 1942. 57 minutes B/W. D: John English. SC: Barry Shipman. WITH Bob Steele, Tom Tyler, Rufe Davis, Melinda Leighton, Weldon Heyburn, Don Curtis, John Ince, Kenne Duncan, Phil Dunham, Chuck Morrison, Carleton Young, Al Taylor, Robert Frazer, Richard Alexander, Forrest Taylor, Jack Ingram, Wally West, Ed Piel Sr., Bud Osborne, Hank Worden, Cactus Mack. An outlaw responsible for the theft of a mine payroll is hunted by The Three Mesquiteers. Typically fast entry in the Republic series with its likable trio stars, but not as good as those of yore.

Code of the Plains see The Renegade

621 Cody of the Pony Express. Columbia, 1950. 15 Chapters B/W. D: Spencer Gordon Bennet. SC: David Matthews, Lewis Clay & Charles Condon. WITH Jock O'Mahoney (Mahoney), Dickie Moore, Peggy Stewart, William Fawcett, Tom London, Helena Dare, George J. Lewis, Pierce Lyden, Jack Ingram, Rick Vallin, Frank Ellis, Ross Elliott, Ben Corbett, Rusty Wescoatt. The army assigns an undercover agent to find out who is behind a series of stagecoach raids, actually the work of a crooked lawyer and his gang who work for an eastern syndicate out to corral transportation routes. Passable Columbia cliffhanger.

622 Code of the Prairie. Republic, 1944. 56 minutes B/W. D: Spencer Gordon Bennet. SC: Albert Demond & Anthony Coldeway. WITH Smiley Burnette, Sunset Carson, Peggy Stewart, Weldon Heyburn, Tom Chatterton, Roy Barcroft, Bud Geary, Tom London, Jack Kirk, Tom Steele, Robert Wilke, Frank Ellis, Rex Lease, Henry Wills, Kenneth Terrell, Charles King, Nolan Leary, Hank Bell, Karl Hackett, Jack O'Shea, Horace Carpenter. A cowboy and his photographer pal come to the aid of a girl and her father, who plan to start a newspaper in a small town, but are opposed by an outlaw gang, actually led by the town barber. Nifty Sunset Carson actioner with Smiley Burnette along for some fun as the photographer. V: Cumberland Video.

623 Code of the Range. Columbia, 1936. 55 minutes B/W. D: C. C. Coleman Jr. SC: Ford Beebe. WITH Charles Starrett, Mary Blake, Ed Coxen, Allan Cavan, Ed Peil, Edmund Cobb, Ed LeSaint, Ralph McCullough, George Chesebro, Art Mix, Albert J. Smith. Cattlemen are at odds with each other over allowing sheepmen to use range land for grazing their herds and a crooked saloon owner attempts to inflame the situation for his own financial gain. Quite good Charles Starrett vehicle which is very well written.

624 Code of the Rangers. Monogram, 1938. 56 minutes B/W. D: Sam Newfield. SC: Stanley Roberts. WITH Tim McCoy, Judith Ford, Rex Lease, Wheeler Oakman, Frank LaRue, Roger Williams, Zeke Clements, Kit Guard, Frank McCarroll, Jack Ingram, Budd Buster, Ed Piel, Hal Price, Herman Hack. Two brothers belong to the Texas Rangers but one of them joins forces with outlaws and it is up to the other brother to bring him to justice. Steadily actionful Tim McCoy film with good-bad guy work by Wheeler Oakman.

625 Code of the Saddle. Monogram, 1947. 53 minutes B/W. D: Thomas Carr. SC: Eliot Biggons. WITH Johnny Mack Brown, Raymond Hatton, Kay Morley, Riley Hill, William Norton Bailey, Zon Murray, Gary Garrett, Ken Duncan Jr., Ted Adams, Bud Osborne, Boyd Stockman, Ray Jones, Chick Hannon. A rancher is killed and two cowboys who are visiting him and his daughter set out to find the real killer, although a neighbor has been accused of the crime by the local sheriff. A good story enhances this Johnny Mack Brown vehicle.

626 Code of the Silver Sage. Republic, 1950. 60 minutes B/W. D: Fred C. Brannon. SC: Arthur Orloff. WITH Allan "Rocky" Lane, Eddy Waller, Kay Christopher, Roy Barcroft, Rex Lease, Lane Bradford, William Ruhl, Richard Emory, Forrest Taylor, Kenne Duncan, Hank Patterson, John Butler. A madman has plans to become dictator of the Arizona Territory and a U. S. cavalry lieutenant is sent to stop him. Another good vehicle for Allan Lane; full of action and an interesting storyline.

627 Code of the West. RKO Radio, 1947. 57 minutes B/W. D: William Berke. SC: Norman Houston. WITH James Warren, Debra Allen, John Laurenz, Steve Brodie, Robert Clarke, Carol Forman, Rita Lynn, Harry Woods, Raymond Burr, Harry Harvey, Phil Warren, Emmett Lynn. Two cowboys come to the aid of a man and his daughter who try to open an honest bank but are opposed by a corrupt town boss. Okay James Warren vehicle based on the Zane Grey story.

628 Cold River. Shapiro, 1979. 94 minutes Color. D-SC: Fred G. Sullivan. WITH Suzanne Weber, Pat Petersen, Richard Jaeckel, Robert Earl Jones, Brad Sullivan, Elizabeth Hubbard, Augusta Dabney. Modern-day outdoor adventure film about a man and a woman and their attempts to tame a raging river. Nice locations make this a pleasant adaptation of William Judson's best seller.

629 Cole Younger, Gunfighter. Allied Artists, 1958. 78 minutes Color. D: R. G. Springsteen. SC: Daniel Mainwaring. WITH Frank Lovejoy, Abby Dalton, James Best, Jan Merlin, Douglas Spencer, Frank Ferguson, Myron Healey, George Keymas, Dan Sheridan, John Mitchum, Ainslie Pryor. In Texas in the early 1870s a man gets a reputation as a gunfighter for his opposition to corrupt lawmen. Frank Lovejoy handles the title role well and the film moves along at a good clip.

630 Colorado. Republic, 1940. 54 (57) minutes B/W. D: Joseph Kane. SC: Louis Stevens & Harrison Jacobs. WITH Roy Rogers, George "Gabby" Hayes, Pauline Moore, Milburn Stone, Maude Eburne, Hal Taliaferro, Vestor Pegg, Fred Burns, Lloyd Ingraham, Jay Novello, Tex Palmer, Joseph Crehan, Ed Cassidy, Robert Fiske, Stanley Andrews. During the Civil War, a Union lieutenant is sent to Denver with his sidekick to find out what is causing trouble with the Indians. Good Roy Rogers drama, fast paced and well played with a fine desert finale.

631 Colorado Ambush. Monogram, 1951. 51 minutes B/W. D: Lewis Collins. SC: Myron Healey. WITH Johnny Mack Brown, Lois Hall, Myron Healey, Tommy Farrell, Christine McIntyre, Lyle Talbot, Lee Roberts, Marshall Bradford, John Hart. A ranger investigates the murders of three Wells Fargo men and finds out that a man supplying horses to the freight hauler is also giving information to a hotel hostess. Myron Healey wrote the script for this one and he also plays a dastardly villain, the highlight of this more than passable Johnny Mack Brown entry.

632 Colorado Kid. Republic, 1937. 60 minutes B/W. D: Sam Newfield. SC: Charles Francis Royal. WITH Bob Steele, Marion Weldon, Karl Hackett, Ted Adams, Ernie Adams, Frank LaRue, Horace Murphy, Kenne Duncan, Budd Buster, Frank Ball, John Merton, Horace B. Carpenter, Wally West. When he is unjustly accused of murder a cowboy escapes from jail to find the real killer. Pretty actionful Bob Steele vehicle.

633 Colorado Pioneers. Republic, 1945. 57 minutes B/W. D: R. G. Springsteen. SC: Earle Snell. WITH Bill Elliott, Bobby Blake, Alice Fleming, Roy Barcroft, Bud Geary, Billy Cummings, Freddie Chapman, Frank Jacquet, Tom London, Monte Hale, Buckwheat Thomas, George Chesebro, Emmett Vogan, Tom Chatterton, Ed Cassidy, Fred Graham, Horace Carpenter, Bill Woolf, Jack Rockwell, George Morrell, Jack Kirk, Roger Williams, Richard Lydon. A group of tough city kids, sent to the West to be reformed, aid Red Ryder in stopping a rancher after the Duchess' land. An out-of-the-ordinary plot gives some zest to this "Red Ryder" segment.

634 Colorado Ranger. Lippert, 1950. 57 minutes B/W. D: Thomas Carr. SC: Ron Ormond & Maurice Tombragel. WITH James Ellison, Russell Hayden, Fuzzy Knight, Raymond Hatton, Betty (Julie) Adams, Tom Tyler, George J. Lewis, John Cason, Stanley Price, Dennis Moore, George Chesebro, Bud Osborne, Gene Roth, I. Stanford Jolley, Stephen Carr, Jimmie Martin, Joseph Richards. Shamrock and Lucky come to Shamrock's family ranch for his late mother's inheritance and they find that his stepfather has been kidnapped. Arid entry in the James Ellison-Russell Hayden series for Lippert with little to recommend it except its cast. TV title: **Guns of Justice.**

635 Colorado Serenade. Producers Releasing Corporation, 1946. 68 minutes Color. D: Robert Emmett Tansey. SC: Frances Kavanaugh. WITH Eddie Dean, Roscoe Ates, May Kenyon, David Sharpe, Forrest Taylor, Dennis Moore, Abigail Adams, Warner Richmond, Lee Bennett, Robert McKenzie, Bob Duncan, Charles King, Bud Osborne. Two cowboys save a judge who is about to be ambushed and later learn that one of the would-be killers is actually the judge's son who refuses to believe that the judge is really his father. Very actionful Eddie Dean vehicle, one of the better ones in his PRC/Eagle Lion series.

636 Colorado Sundown. Republic, 1952. 67 minutes B/W. D: William Witney. SC: Eric Taylor & William Lively. WITH Rex Allen, Mary Ellen Kay, Slim Pickens, June Vincent, Fred Graham, John Daheim, Louise Beavers, Chester Clute, Clarence Straight, The Republic Rhythm Riders. While trying to help a friend to keep a ranch he inherited, a fellow rancher is accused of murder. Nicely done Rex Allen entry, with emphasis on lots of movement.

637 Colorado Sunset. Republic, 1939. 54 (61) minutes B/W. D: George Sherman. SC: Betty Burbridge & Stanley Roberts. WITH Gene Autry, Smiley Burnette, June Storey, Barbara Pepper, Larry "Buster" Crabbe, Robert Barrat, William Farnum, Patsy Montana, Frankie Marvin, Purnell B. Pratt, Kermit Maynard, Jack Ingram, Elmo Lincoln, Ethan Laidlaw, Fred Burns, Jack Kirk, Budd Buster, Ed Cassidy, Slim Whitaker, Murdock McQuarrie, Ralph Peters, The CBS-KMBC Texas Rangers. A musical troupe buys a cattle ranch but the herd turns out to be milk cows and they find themselves being pressured by crooks to join a combine. Pretty fair Gene Autry vehicle.

638 Colorado Territory. Warner Brothers, 1949. 94 minutes B/W. D: Raoul Walsh. SC: John Twist & Edmund H. North. WITH Joel McCrea, Virginia Mayo, Dorothy Malone, Henry Hull, John Archer, James Mitchell, Morris Ankrum, Basil Ruysdael, Frank Puglia, Ian Wolfe, Harry Woods, Houseley Stevenson, Victor Kilian, Oliver Blake. An outlaw escapes from jail and meets his girlfriend and the two try to escape but are trapped by a posse in a mountain area. Raoul Walsh's Western remake of his gangster classic **High Sierra** (Warner Brothers, 1941); a very good motion picture. Remade again by Warners in 1955 as a gangster film and called **I Died a Thousand Times.**

639 Colorado Trail. Columbia, 1938. 55 minutes B/W. D: Sam Nelson. SC: Charles Francis Royal. WITH Charles Starrett, Irish Meredith, Bob Nolan & The Sons of the Pioneers, Ed Le Saint, Al Bridge, Robert Fiske, Dick Curtis, Hank Bell, Ed Peil, Edmund Cobb, Jack Clifford, Richard Botiller. A young man joins cattlemen in a range war with his father on the opposite side. Pretty fair Charles Starrett film.

640 Colt Comrades. United Artists, 1943. 54 (67) minutes B/W. D: Lesley Selander. SC: Michael Wilson. WITH William Boyd, Andy Clyde, Jay Kirby, George Reeves, Gayle Lord, Earle Hodgins, Victor Jory, Douglas Fowley, Herbert Rawlinson, Robert Mitchum. Crooks frame Hopalong Cassidy as a cattle rustler and he sets out to prove his innocence. Standard entry in the "Hopalong Cassidy" series.

641 Colt .45. Warner Brothers, 1950. 74 minutes Color. D: Edwin L. Marin. SC: Thomas Blackburn. WITH Randolph Scott, Ruth Roman, Zachary Scott, Lloyd Bridges, Alan Hale, Ian MacDonald, Chief Thundercloud, Luther Crockett, Walter Coy, Charles Evans, Buddy Roosevelt, Hal Taliaferro, Art Miles, Barry Reagan, Howard Negley, Paul Newland, Aurora Navarro, Franklyn Farnum, Ed Peil Sr., Jack Watt, Carl Andre, Ben Corbett, Artie Ortego, Bob Burrows, William Steele. When his gun samples are stolen by an outlaw, a gun salesman is accused of being a member of the gang and sets out to capture the bad man and prove his own innocence. Pretty good Randolph Scott opus with Zachary Scott helping as the outlaw. TV title: **Thunder Cloud.**

642 Column South. Universal-International, 1953. 84 minutes Color. D: Frederick De Cordova. SC: William Sackheim. WITH Audie Murphy, Joan Evans, Robert Sterling, Ray Collins, Palmer Lee (Gregg Palmer), Ralph Moody, Dennis Weaver, Johnny Downs, Russell Johnson, Bob Steele, Jack Kelly, Ray Montgomery, Richard Garland, James Best, Ed Rand. In order to prevent fighting between the Indians and Army troops, agitated by an intolerant captain, a young lieutenant tries to help the Navajos before they are forced into war. Fairly interesting Audie Murphy cavalry actioner.

643 Comanche. United Artists, 1956. 87 minutes Color. D: George Sherman. SC: Carl Krueger. WITH Dana Andrews, Kent Smith, Linda Cristal, John Litel, Henry Brandon, Nestor Paiva, Mike Mazurki, Stacey Harris, Lowell Gilmore, Reed Sherman. In order to stop skirmishes along the United States and Mexican border, and to bring lasting peace with the Indians, two scouts are assigned the job of finding the Comanche chief and offer him a peace promise. Director George Sherman infuses quite a bit of action into this oater to cover up a mundane story.

644 Comanche Station. Columbia, 1960. 74 minutes Color. D: Budd Boetticher. SC: Burt Kennedy. WITH Randolph Scott, Nancy Gates, Skip Homeier, Richard Rust, Rand Brooks, Dyke Johnson, Foster Hood, Joe Molina, Vince St. Cyr, John Patrick Noland. A man enlists the aid of three outlaws in helping him track

down his wife who has been captured by Indians. Entertaining Randolph Scott film, exceedingly well made and paced.

645 Comanche Territory. Universal-International, 1950. 76 minutes Color. D: George Sherman. SC: Oscar Brodney & Lewis Meltzer. WITH Maureen O'Hara, Macdonald Carey, Will Geer, Charles Drake, Pedro de Cordoba, Ian MacDonald, Rick Vallin, Parley Baer, James Best, Edmund Cobb, Glenn Strange, Iron Eyes Cody. When outlaws try to steal lands belonging to the Indians because of rich silver deposits, frontiersman Jim Bowie comes to the rescue of his red brothers. Historical fiction which is basically romantic pap.

646 The Comancheros. 20th Century-Fox, 1961. 107 minutes Color. D: Michael Curtiz (& John Wayne, uncredited). SC: James Edward Grant & Clair Huffaker. WITH John Wayne, Stuart Whitman, Ina Balin, Nehemiah Persoff, Lee Marvin, Michael Ansara, Patrick Wayne, Bruce Cabot, Joan O'Brien, Jack Elam, Edgar Buchanan, Guinn Williams, Bob Steele, Henry Daniell, Richard Devon, Steve Baylor, John Dierkes, Roger Mobley, Luisa Triana, Iphigenie Castiglioni, Aissa Wayne, George J. Lewis, Gregg Palmer, Don Brodie, Jon Lormer, Phil Arnold, Alan Carney, Ralph Volkie, Dennis Cole. A captain in the Texas Rangers teams with a gambler to thwart gun runners and then to carry a consignment of weapons to the stronghold of the comancheros, white men working with the Indians. Top notch John Wayne vehicle with lots of action and good humor. V: CBS/Fox, Blackhawk, Cumberland Video. VD: Blackhawk.

647 The Comeback Trail. Dynamic Entertainment, 1982. 76 minutes Color. D-SC: Harry Hurwitz. WITH Buster Crabbe, Chuck McCann, Ina Balin, Robert Staats, Jara Kahout, Henny Youngman, Professor Irwin Corey, Monti Rock III, Joe Franklin, Lenny Schultz, Hugh Hefner, Mike Gentry. Two crooked movie producers hire a once famous cowboy star to appear in their film, only they plan to kill him off to collect insurance money. This comedy was originally made in 1970 and got some release in Canada in 1979 by International Film Distributors as **Crazy Movie.** Except for Buster Crabbe, who is quite good as one-time cowboy star Duke Montana, the film is a real bust.

648 Come on Cowboys. Republic, 1937. 54 (59) minutes B/W. D: Joseph Kane. SC: Betty Burbridge. WITH Robert Livingston, Ray Corrigan, Max Terhune, Maxine Doyle, Ed Piel, Horace Murphy, Ann Bennett, Ed Cassidy, Roger Williams, Willie Fung, Fern Emmett, Yakima Canutt, Merrill McCormack, Al Taylor, George Plues, Milburn Morante, Carleton Young, George Morrell, Ernie Adams, Jim Corey, Jack Kirk. When an old pal from the circus gets mixed up with crooks the Three Mesquiteers come to his rescue. Actionful series entry from "The Three Mesquiteers" with some big-top excitement thrown in for good measure. V: Cumberland Video.

649 Come On, Danger. RKO Radio, 1932. 60 minutes B/W. D: Robert Hill. SC: Bennett Cohen. WITH Tom Keene, Julie Haydon, Roscoe Ates, Robert Ellis, Wade Boteler, William Scott, Harry Tenbrook, Bud Osborne, Roy Stewart, Frank Lackteen, Nell Craig, Monte Montague. A ranger and his pal set out to capture the killer of the ranger's brother but he soon finds out that the gang leader he is after is a girl who has been framed for the crime. Mature and well executed Tom Keene film.

650 Come On, Danger! RKO Radio, 1942. 58 minutes B/W. D: Edward Killy. SC: Norton S. Parker. WITH Tim Holt, Frances Neal, Ray Whitley, Lee "Lasses" White, Karl Hackett, Bud McTaggert, Glenn Strange, Davidson Clark, John Elliott, Slim Whitaker, Henry Rocquemore, Evelyn Dickson, Kate Harrington. A Texas Ranger is assigned to bring in the female leader of a gang of outlaws and after she is wounded he discovers that a crooked tax collector is actually behind all the trouble. Remake of the 1932 Tom Keene film, this Tim Holt vehicle is not as good as the original but it is still more that passable entertainment.

651 Come On, Rangers. Republic, 1938. 54 (57) minutes B/W. D: Joseph Kane. SC: Gerald Geraghty & Jack Natteford. WITH Roy Rogers, Mary Hart, Raymond Hatton, J. Farrell MacDonald, Purnell B. Pratt, Harry Woods, Bruce MacFarlane, Lane Chandler, Chester Gunnels, Lee Powell, Robert Kortman, George (Montgomery) Letz, Frank McCarroll, Chick Hannon, Jack Kirk, Al Taylor, Horace B. Carpenter, Robert Wilke, Al Ferguson, Allan Cavan, Ben Corbett, Burr Caruth. Due to a lack of money the Texas Rangers are disbanded and crooks begin pouring into the state under the control of a crooked senator who is actually behind a protection organization using a gang of raiders. Very entertaining and well made Roy Rogers vehicle.

652 Come On, Tarzan. World Wide, 1932. 61 minutes B/W. D-SC: Alan James. WITH Ken Maynard, Merna Kennedy, Kate Campbell, Niles Welch, Roy Stewart, Ben Corbett, Robert Kortman, Jack Rockwell, Nelson McDowell, Jack Mower, Edmund Cobb, Robert Walker, Hank Bell, Slim Whitaker, Jim Corey, Blackjack Ward, Al Taylor, Bud McClure. A ranch foreman at odds with his pretty female boss fights crooks who are killing horses to be used as dog food. A bit different for Ken Maynard, but still a good film. V: Video Dimensions.

653 Comes a Horseman. United Artists, 1978. 118 minutes Color. D: Alan J. Pakula. SC: Dennis Lynton Clark. WITH Jane Fonda, James Caan, Jason Robards, George Grizzard, Richard Farnsworth, Jim Davis, Mark Harmon, Macon McCalman, Basil Hoffman, James Kline, James Keach, Clifford A. Pellon. Small ranchers in the 1940s in Colorado are being squeezed out by a land-hungry man. Standard, but well made, oater filmed in Colorado's Wet Mountain Valley and sporting a good performance by Richard Farnsworth as Dodger. V: 20th Century-Fox Video. VD: Blackhawk.

654 Comin' At Ya! Filmways, 1981. 91 minutes Color. D: Ferdinando Baldi. SC: Lloyd Battista, Wolf Lowenthal & Gene Quintano. WITH Tony Anthony, Gene Quintano, Victoria Abil, Ricardo Palacios, Gordon Lewis. Two evil brothers working the white slave trade kidnap a cowboy's girlfriend and then leave her to die in the desert. Lumbering 3-D spaghetti Western produced by star Tony Anthony.

655 Comin' Round the Mountain. Republic, 1936. 55 minutes B/W. D: Mack V. Wright. SC: Oliver Drake, Dorrell McGowan & Stuart McGowan. WITH Gene Autry, Smiley Burnette, Ann Rutherford, LeRoy Mason, Raymond Brown, Ken Cooper, Tracy Layne, Robert McKenzie, John Ince, Frank Lackteen, Jim Corey, Al Taylor, Steve Clark, Frank Ellis, Hank Bell, Richard Botiller. Gene Autry comes to the aid of a young girl, a ranch owner, who has had money stolen from her. Well made Gene Autry vehicle.

656 The Command. Warner Brothers, 1953. 88 minutes Color. D: David Butler. SC: Russell Hughes & Samuel Fuller. WITH Guy Madison, Joan Weldon, James Whitmore, Carl Benton Reid, Harvey Lembeck, Ray Teal, Bob Nichols, Don Shelton, Gregg Barton, Red Morgan. An Army captain leads his troops and civilians through the Wyoming Territory, battling Indians and smallpox, in order to take possession of the area. Fairly good adaptation of James Warner Bellah's novel.

657 Companeros! 20th Century-Fox, 1971. 118 minutes Color. D: Sergio Corbucci. SC: Dino Maiuri, Massimo De Rita, Fritz Ebert & Sergio Corbucci. WITH Franco Nero, Jack Palance, Tomas Milian, Fernando Rey, Iris Beben, Francisco Bodalo, Eduardo Fajardo, Karin Schubert, Luizi Pernice, Alvarado De Luna, Jesus Fernandez, Claudio Scarchilli, Lorenzo Robeldo, Giovanni Petti, Gerard Tichy, Giovanni Pulone. A mercenary from Sweden works as a gun runner in revolution-torn Mexico at the turn of the century. Fans of Franco Nero and Jack Palance may find some interest in this overlong, bloody spaghetti Western.

658 The Concentratin' Kid. Universal, 1930. 60 minutes B/W. D: Arthur Rosson. SC: Harold Tarshis. WITH Hoot Gibson, Kathryn Crawford, Duke R. Lee, Jim Mason, Robert E. Homans. A cowboy in love with a radio singer he has never met bets his pals he can win her or he will give them a radio. Fun early talkie from Hoot Gibson who also served as its producer.

659 The Conquering Horde. Paramount, 1931. 76 minutes B/W. D: Edward Sloman. SC: Grover Jones & William McNutt. WITH Richard Arlen, Fay Wray, George Mendoza, Ian MacLaren, Claude Gillingwater, James Durkin, Claire Ward, Charles Stevens, Arthur Stone, Frank Rice, Ed Brady, Robert Kortman, Harry Cording, John Elliott. After the Civil War, a Texan returns home to help in the rebuilding of his state but finds himself in opposition to carpetbaggers. Old-fashioned oater, a bit on the slow-moving side but fans of Richard Arlen will want to view it. Made in 1924 by Paramount as **North of '36.**

660 The Conquerors. RKO Radio, 1932. 88 minutes B/W. D: William A. Wellman. SC: Robert Lord. WITH Richard Dix, Ann Harding, Edna May Oliver, Julie Haydon, Guy Kibbee, Donald Cook, Harry Holman, Skeets Gallagher, Walter Walker, Wally Albright Jr., Marilyn Knowlden, Jason Robards, Jed Prouty, E. H. Calvert, J. Carrol Naish, Robert Greig, Elizabeth Patterson. A young couple marry and go West where they start a bank which proliferates into a banking empire which survives three panics. One of William A. Wellman's most underrated features, this film spans the half-century between the 1870s and 1932 with Richard Dix particularly good as the empire builder. TV title: **Pioneer Builders.**

661 Conquest of Cheyenne. Republic, 1946. 54 minutes B/W. D: R. G. Springsteen. SC: Earle Snell. WITH Bill Elliott, Bobby Blake, Alice Fleming, Peggy Stewart, Jay Kirby, Milton Kibbee, Tom London, Emmett Lynn, Kenne Duncan, George Sherwood, Frank McCarroll, Jack Kirk, Tom Chatterton, Ted Mapes, Jack Rockwell. A corrupt banker is after a pretty girl's oil lands and he accuses a young man of kidnapping her and Red Ryder comes to the rescue. Another well-made entry in the "Red Ryder" series, handled well by director R. G. Springsteen.

662 Conquest of Cochise. Columbia, 1953. 70 minutes Color. D: William Castle. SC: Arthur Lewis & DeVallon Scott. WITH Robert Stack, John Hodiak, Joy Page, Rico Alaniz, Fortunio Bonanova, Edward Colemans, Alex Montoya, Steve Ritch, Carol Thurston, Rodd Redwing, Robert E. Griffith, Joseph Waring. In the 1850s Cavalry officers are sent to New Mexico to keep the peace and stop the raids of Cochise and his braves. Nothing special about this color oater.

663 Coogan's Bluff. Universal, 1968. 100 minutes Color. D: Don Siegel. SC: Herman Miller, Dean Riesner & Howard Rodman. WITH Clint Eastwood, Susan Clark, Lee J. Cobb, Tisha Sterling, Don Stroud, Betty Field, Tom Tully, Melodie Johnson, James Edwards, Rudy Diaz, David Doyle, Marjorie Bennett. An Arizona deputy sheriff comes to New York City to track down and extradite a killer. Sturdy, actionful Clint Eastwood melodrama, which his fans will love. V: MCA.

664 Copper Canyon. Paramount, 1950. 83 minutes Color. D: John Farrow. SC: Jonathan Latimer. WITH Ray Milland, Hedy Lamarr, Macdonald Carey, Mona Freeman, Harry Carey Jr., Frank Faylen, Hope Emerson, Taylor Holmes, Peggy Knudsen, James Burke, Percy Helton,

Philip Van Zandt, Francis Pierlot, Erno Verebes, Paul Lees, Robert Watson, George Backus, Ian Wolfe, Robert Kortman, Nina Mae McKinney, Len Hendry, Earle Hodgins, Robert Stephenson, Buddy Roosevelt, Julia Faye, Joe Whitehead, Hank Bell, Ethan Laidlaw, Russell Kaplan, Alan Dinehart III, Rex Lease, Stanley Andrews, Kit Guard, Stuart Holmes. In the post-Civil War West a former soldier joins a carnival as a sharp-shooter and meets a beautiful woman. Glossy oater without much interest although Hedy Lamarr is nice on the eye.

665 Copper Sky. 20th Century-Fox, 1957. 79 minutes B/W. D: Charles Marquis Warren. SC: Eric Norden. WITH Jeff Morrow, Coleen Gray, Strother Martin, Paul Brinegar, John Pickard, Patrick O'Moore, Rocky Shahan, Rush Williams, Rodd Redwing. A drunken ex-soldier and a school teacher survive an Indian massacre of a small town and the duo trek across the desert to the nearest outpost. Stars Jeff Morrow and Coleen Gray try hard but the arid script defeats them.

666 Cornered. Columbia, 1932. 60 minutes B/W. D: B. Reeves Eason. SC: Wallace MacDonald. WITH Tim McCoy, Raymond Hatton, Noah Beery, Shirley Grey, Niles Welch, Claire McDowell, Walter Long, Walter Brennan, Wheeler Oakman, Robert Kortman, Edmund Cobb, Tom London, Lloyd Ingraham, Charles King, John Elliott, Art Mix, Merrill McCormack, Artie Ortego, Jim Corey, Ed Piel Sr., Ray Jones, Jack Evans, Blackie Whiteford. A sheriff and a ranch foreman both like the same girl but when her father is murdered the ranch foreman is blamed for the crime but escapes from jail and gets involved with an outlaw gang. Well made and very good Tim McCoy vehicle dominated by madman villain Noah Beery who says there are two things worth living for: "To kill and be killed" and "to get revenge."

667 Coroner Creek. Columbia, 1948. 90 minutes Color. D: Ray Enright. SC: Kenneth Gamet. WITH Randolph Scott, Marguerite Chapman, George Macready, Sally Eilers, Edgar Buchanan, Barbara Reed, Wallace Ford, William Bishop, Forrest Tucker, Joseph Sawyer, Russell Simpson, Douglas Fowley, Lee Bennett, Forrest Taylor, Phil Schumacher, Warren Jackson. A cowpoke, with the help of a pretty hotel owner, plans revenge on the man responsible for the death of his girl. High grade Randolph scott color opus.

668 Corpus Christi Bandits. Republic, 1945. 55 minutes B/W. D: Wallace Grissell. SC: Norman S. Hall. WITH Allan "Rocky" Lane, Helen Talbott, Twinkle Watts, Tom London, Francis McDonald, Jack Kirk, Roy Barcroft, Kenne Duncan, Robert Wilke, Ed Cassidy, Emmett Vogan, Neal Hart, Horace Carpenter, Hal Price, Frank Ellis, Frank McCarroll, Henry Wills. A pilot learns the story of how his grandfather became an outlaw due to carpetbaggers after the Civil War. A different kind of plot adds some zest to this above average Allan Lane vehicle.

669 Cotter. Gold Key, 1973. 94 minutes Color. D: Paul Stanley. WITH Don Murray, Carol Lynley, Rip Torn, Sherry Jackson. When he loses his job in a rodeo due to drink, an Indian returns home only to be blamed for the murder of a rich rancher and to be chased by a lynch mob. Nicely done, although somewhat obscure, modern-day oater.

670 Cougar. Sidney A. Snow Productions, 1933. 70 minutes B/W. WITH Jay Bruce. An expedition heads into California's Caly Hills in search of mountain lions and other game. Good vintage documentary.

671 Cougar Country. Gold Key, 1970. 91 minutes Color. WITH Ernest Wilkinson, Whiskers (cougar). A cougar, over a two-year span, grows from a cub to a powerful hunter. Filmed in southern Colorado, this outdoor adventure is ideal family fare.

Count Your Blessings see **Face to the Wind**

672 Count the Clues. Wrather Corporation, 1956. 75 minutes Color. D: Earl Bellamy & Oscar Rudolph. SC: Doane Hoag, Wells Root, Robert E. Schaefer & Eric Friewald. WITH Clayton Moore, Jay Silverheels, Allen Pinson, Wayne Burson, Richard Crane, Claire Carleton, Bud Osborne, William Challee, Rand Brooks, Slim Pickens, Mickey Simpson, Steven Ritch, House Peters Jr., Jason Johnson, Frank Scanner, Gordon Mills, Paul Engle, Barbara Knudsen, Sydney Mason, Walt LaRue, Ron Hagerthy, Lee Roberts John Beradino, Tudor Owen, Carlos Vera, Brad Morrow, Baynes Barron. The Lone Ranger and Tonto fight blackmailers, aid a man against outlaws and chase a bank robbery gang into the badlands. Entertaining "Lone Ranger" tele-feature made up of three 1956-57 segments of the popular ABC-TV series; the original episodes were "Wooden Rifle," "Sheriff of Smoketree" and "Ghost Town Fury."

673 Count the Hours. RKO Radio, 1953. 76 minutes B/W. D: Don Siegel. SC: Doane R. Hoag. WITH Teresa Wright, MacDonald Carey, Dolores Moran, Adele Mara, Edgar Barrier, John Craven, Jack Elam, Ralph Sanford, Ralph Dumke. A ranch hand is falsely accused of murdering the couple he works for and his wife and a district attorney try to prove his innocence. Taut modern-day oater shot in only nine days; worth viewing.

674 Count Three and Pray. Columbia, 1955. 102 minutes Color. D: George Sherman. SC: Herb Meadows. WITH Van Heflin, Joanne Woodward, Philip Carey, Raymond Burr, Allison Hayes, Myron Healey, Nancy Kulp, James Griffith, Richard Webb, Kathryn Givney, Robert Burton, Vince Townsend, John Carson, Jean Willes, Adrienne Marden, Steve Raines, Jimmy Hawkins, Juney Ellis. After the Civil War a man with a past becomes the pastor in a small frontier town and he becomes enamoured with an orphaned girl. Okay melodrama with good dramatics from its stars.

675 The Country Beyond. 20th Century-Fox, 1936. 69 minutes B/W. D: Eugene Forde. SC: Lamar Trotti & Adele Commandini. WITH Rochelle Hudson, Paul Kelly, Robert Kent, Alan Hale, Alan Dinehart, Matt McHugh, Andrew Tombes, Paul McVey, Claudia Coleman, Holmes Herbert, Buck (dog). A girl and her dog aid two Mounties in the capture of a murderous fur thief. Followup to **Call of the Wild** (q.v.) this is a more than satisfactory north country "B" outing.

676 The Courage of Kavil, the Wolf Dog. NBC-TV, 1980. 100 minutes Color. D: Peter Carter. WITH Ronny Cox, John Ireland, Linda Sorenson, Andrew Ian McMillan, Chris Wiggins. Taken from his family, a champion sled dog undergoes the arduous trek of 2,000 miles through the Alaskan wilderness to return to them. Average TV movie fare with nice scenery.

677 Courage of the North. Stage & Screen, 1935. 55 minutes B/W. D-SC: Robert Emmett (Tansey). WITH John Preston, June Love, William Desmond, Tom London, Jimmie Aubrey, Charles King, James Sheridan (Sherry Tansey), Jim Thorpe, Dynamite (horse), Captain (dog). A gang of fur thieves are working in the north country and are tracked by the Mounties. Low budget northwoods affair with good photography by Bydron Baker and little else.

678 Courage of the West. Universal, 1937. 56 minutes B/W. D: Joseph H. Lewis. SC: Norton S. Parker. WITH Bob Baker, Lois January, J. Farrell MacDonald, Fuzzy Knight, Carl Stockdale, Harry Woods, Albert Russell, Charles K. French, Oscar Gahan, Richard Cramer, Jack Montgomery, Thomas Monk, Buddy Cox. Outlaws have been robbing Wells Fargo messengers and express offices and the Rangers are assigned to stop them. Bob Baker's first starring series oater is a fairly fast affair, helped by a good script and direction.

679 Courageous Avenger. Supreme, 1935. 58 minutes B/W. D: Robert North Bradbury. SC: Charles Francis Royal. WITH Johnny Mack Brown, Helen Erickson, Warner Richmond, Ed Cassidy, Frank Ball, Eddie Parker, Forrest Taylor, Bob Burns, Earl Dwire. A sheriff tries to track down the murderer of a young man driving a silver wagon and he finds out that outlaws are tapping a silver vein and using forced prisoners as miners. Average Johnny Mack Brown series entry with a rather novel plot.

680 The Court-Martial of General George Armstrong Custer. NBC-TV/Warner Brothers, 1977. 100 minutes Color. D: Glenn Jordan. WITH Brian Keith, James Olson, Ken Howard, Blythe Danner, Stephen Elliot, Richard Dysart, Nicholas Coster, J. D. Cannon, William Daniels, James Ray. Teledrama about what might have occurred had General Custer survived the Battle of the Little Big Horn. Based on Douglas C. Jones' book, this telefeature was originally shown on "The Hallmark Hall of Fame" on NBC-TV on December 1, 1977 and will be of interest to history buffs.

681 Courtin' Trouble. Monogram, 1948. 58 minutes B/W. D: Ford Beebe. SC: Ronald Davidson. WITH Jimmy Wakely, Dub Taylor, Virginia Belmont, Leonard Penn, Steve Clark, Marshall Reed, House Peters Jr., Frank LaRue, Bob Woodward, Bud Osborne, Boyd Stockman, Bill Bailey, Bill Potter, Bill Hale, Carol Henry, Don Weston, Louis Armstrong, Arthur Smith. A singing cowboy returns home to find warfare between businessmen and cattle ranchers. Fair Jimmy Wakely musical opus with an actionful second half.

682 The Covered Wagon. Paramount, 1923. 60 minutes B/W. D: James Cruze. SC: Jack Cunningham. WITH J. Warren Kerrigan, Lois Wilson, Ernest Torrence, Charles Ogle, Ethel Wales, Alan Hale, Tully Marshall, Guy Oliver, Johnny Fox, Tim McCoy. In 1848 two wagon trains leave Kansas City for Oregon but one of the trains gets cut off from the main convoy and heads for the California gold rush. One of the all-time great Westerns highlighted by its semi-documentary style and Karl Brown's photography; a must see for all genre followers. V: Film Cassic Exchange.

683 Covered Wagon Days. Republic, 1940. 54 (56) minutes B/W. D: George Sherman. SC: Earle Snell. WITH Robert Livingston, Raymond Hatton, Duncan Renaldo, Kay Griffith, George Douglas, Ruth Robinson, Paul Marion, John Merton, Tom Chatterton, Guy D'Ennery, Tom London, Reed Howes, Jack Kirk, Al Taylor, Lee Shumway, Edward Earle, Richard Alexander, Edward Hearn, Art Mix, Frank McCarroll, Herman Hack, Kenneth Terrell, Tex Palmer, Jack Montgomery. The Three Mesquiteers get mixed up with silver smugglers when a crooked businessman, the head of the smuggling operation, tries to force one of their uncles to sell his silver mine. Pretty fair south-of-the border "Three Mesquiteers" segment.

684 Covered Wagon Raid. Republic, 1950. 60 minutes B/W. D: R. G. Springsteen. SC: M. Coates Webster. WITH Allan "Rocky" Lane, Eddy Waller, Lyn Thomas, Alex Gerry, Byron Barr, Dick Curtis, Marshall Reed, Pierce Lyden, Sherry Jackson, Rex Lease, Lester Dorr, Lee Roberts, Wee Willie Keeler. A cowboy is on the trail of a vicious outlaw gang terrorizing a small community. Nicely done Allan Lane action film.

685 Covered Wagon Trails. Syndicate, 1930. 50 minutes B/W. D: J. P. McGowan. SC: Sally Winters. WITH Bob Custer, Phyllis Bainbridge, Perry Murdock, Charles Brinley, Martin Cichy, J. P. McGowan. Lawman Smoke Sanderson is on the trail of a gang of crooks working along the Mexican border and in the process he falls for the sister of a gang member. Without being hampered by dialogue, Bob Custer comes across fairly well in this silent effort with a music score.

686 Covered Wagon Trails. Monogram, 1940. 52 minutes B/W. D: Raymond K. Johnson. SC: Tom Gibson. WITH Jack Randall, Sally Cairns, Lafe McKee, David Sharpe, Budd Buster, Glenn Strange, Hank Bell, Kenne Duncan, Frank Ellis, George Chesebro, Carl Mathews, Edward Hearn, Art Mix, Jack Montgomery, Frank McCarroll. A cowboy opposes corrupt cattlemen who are trying to stop settlers from farming the range. So-so Jack Randall vehicle.

687 Cow Country. Allied Artists, 1953. 82 minutes B/W. D: Lesley Selander. SC: Tom W. Blackburn. WITH Edmond O'Brien, Helen Westcott, Robert Lowery, Barton MacLane, Peggie Castle, Robert Barrat, James Millican, Don Beddoe, Robert Wilke, Raymond Hatton, Chuck Courtney, Steve Clark, Rory Mallinson, Marshall Reed, Tom Tyler, Sam Flint, Jack Ingram, George J. Lewis. In Texas in the Panhandle region in the 1880s ranchers struggle to keep their spreads despite drought and depression. Downbeat oater that is well made and worth watching.

688 Cow Town. Columbia, 1950. 70 minutes B/W. D: John English. SC: Gerald Geraghty. WITH Gene Autry, Gail Davis, Harry Shannon, Jock (Mahoney) O'Mahoney. Clark "Buddy" Burroughs, Harry Harvey, Steve Darrell, Sandy Sanders, Ralph Sanford, Bud Osborne, Robert Hilton, Ted Mapes, Charles (Chuck) Roberson, House Peters Jr. When he supports the use of barbed wire on the range to end rustling, Gene Autry finds he is disliked by a pretty girl rancher and in the middle of range warfare. Actionful Gene Autry vehicle with several good songs, including "Down in the Valley" and "Powder Your Face With Sunshine." V: Blackhawk.

689 Cowboy. Columbia, 1958. 92 minutes Color. D: Delmer Daves. SC: Edmund H. North. WITH Glenn Ford, Jack Lemmon, Anna Kashfi, Brian Donlevy, Dick York, Victor Manuel Mendoza, Richard Jaeckel, King Donovan, Vaughn Taylor, Donald Randolph, James Westerfield, Frank de Kova, Buzz Henry, William Leslie, Guy Wilkerson. A young hotel clerk in the 1870s joins up with a cattle drive and is toughened into a man, with the help of the trail boss. Delightful drama, most realistic and entertaining.

690 Cowboy. CBS-TV, 1983. 100 minutes Color. D: Jerry Jameson. SC: Stanley Cherry, Carole Cherry and Dennis Capps.

WITH James Brolin, Annie Potts, Randy Quaid, Ted Danson, George DeCenzo. A former teacher returns home to find that crooks are after his ranch. Made-for-television modern Western which holds up pretty well.

691 The Cowboy. Lippert, 1954. 69 minutes Color. D: Elmo Williams. SC: Lorraine Williams. WITH Tex Ritter, William Conrad, John Dehner, Lawrence Dobkin (narrators). The history and present day existence of the American cowboy, shown on the trail, at roundups, rodeos, festivals, etc. An exceedingly good documentary on the American cowboy and one that is well worth viewing; in addition to partially narrating the film Tex Ritter sings "Dodge City Trail" on the soundtrack.

692 The Cowboy and the Bandit. Superior, 1935. 57 minutes B/W. D: Al Herman. SC: Jack Jeyne. WITH Rex Lease, Janet Morgan (Blanche Mehaffey), Bobby Nelson, Richard Alexander, Wally Wales, William Desmond, Bill Patton, Franklyn Farnum, Art Mix, Lafe McKee, Ben Corbett, George Chesebro, Victor Potel, Jack Kirk. When a gang of crooks are after her land, a young widow is aided by a fun-loving cowboy. Cheaply produced Rex Lease vehicle for fans of curio oaters.

693 The Cowboy and the Blonde. 20th Century-Fox, 1941. 68 minutes B/W. D: Ray McCarey. SC: Walter Bullock. WITH Mary Beth Hughes, George Montgomery, Alan Mowbray, Robert Conway, John Miljan, Richard Lane, Robert Emmett Keane, Minerva Urecal, Fuzzy Knight, George O'Hara. A real-life cowboy tries to become a Western star but fails his screen test and ends up romancing a beautiful blonde star. Fans of stars Carole Landis and George Montgomery will like this outing, but others beware.

694 The Cowboy and the Indians. Columbia, 1949. 68 minutes B/W. D: John English. SC: Dwight Cummins & Dorothy Yost. WITH Gene Autry, Sheila Ryan, Frank Richards, Hank Patterson, Jay Silverheels, Claudia Drake, George Nokes, Charles Stevens, Alex Frazer, Frank Lackteen, Chief Yowlachie, Lee Roberts, Nolan Leary, Maudie Prickett, Harry Macklin, Charles Quigley, Gilbert Alonzo, Roy Gordon, Jose Alvarado, Ray Beltram, Felipe Gomex, Iron Eyes Cody, Shooting Star, Romere Darling, Evelyn Finley. A young brave is blamed when the chief of the Navajo tribe is murdered by a trader and his men but rancher Gene

Autry tries to prove the man's innocence. A good script highlights this Gene Autry film and in it Gene sings a quartet of songs, including "Here Comes Santa Claus."

695 The Cowboy and the Kid. Universal, 1936. 58 minutes B/W. D: Ray Taylor. SC: Frances Guihan. WITH Buck Jones, Dorothy Revier, Billy Burrud, Harry Worth, Charles LeMoyne, Dick Rush, Lafe McKee, Robert McKenzie, Burr Caruth, Eddie Lee, Kernan Cripps. A fun-loving cowboy blames himself for the death of a rancher and he decides to raise the man's orphaned son. Good Buck Jones vehicle with a fine mixture of drama, comedy and pathos.

696 The Cowboy and the Lady. United Artists, 1938. 91 minutes B/W. D: H. C. Potter. SC: Sonya Levien. WITH Gary Cooper, Merle Oberon, Patsy Kelly, Walter Brennan, Fuzzy Knight, Mabel Todd, Henry Kolker, Harry Davenport, Emma Dunn, Walter Walker, Berton Churchill, Charles Richman, Frederick Vogeding, Arthur Hoyt, Ernie Adams, Russ Powell, Jack Baxley, Johnny Judd. The snobbish daughter of a presidential candidate meets and falls in love with a lanky rodeo cowboy. Samuel Goldwyn's teaming of Gary Cooper and Merle Oberon in this Western-comedy is basically a dated bore.

697 The Cowboy and the Senorita. Republic, 1944. 54 (78) minutes B/W. D: Joseph Kane. SC: Gordon Kahn. WITH Roy Rogers, Mary Lee, Dale Evans, Guinn Williams, Bob Nolan & The Sons of the Pioneers, John Hubbard, Hal Taliaferro, Jack Kirk, Fuzzy Knight, Dorothy Christy, Lucien Littlefield, Jack O'Shea, Rex Lease, Lynton Brent, Julian Rivero, Robert Wilke, Wally West. Two cowpokes are falsely accused of kidnapping a young girl and when she gives them a job on her ranch they discover that crooks are after high grade gold in her late father's mine. Passable Roy Rogers entry with Guinn Williams a good comedy sidekick but hampered by mediocre songs and production numbers.

698 Cowboy Canteen. Columbia, 1944. 72 minutes B/W. D: Lew Landers. SC: Paul Gangelin & Felix Adler. WITH Charles Starrett, Jane Frazee, Vera Vague, Guinn Williams, Dub Taylor, Max Terhune, Emmett Lynn, Edythe Elliott, Bill Hughes, John Tyrell, Jeff Donnell, Dick Curtis, The Mills Brothers, Jimmy Wakely &

His Saddle Pals, Chickie & Buck, Roy Acuff & His Smokey Mountain Boys & Girls, The Tailor Maids. A ranch owner joins the Army and finds his newly hired hands are all female and the service soon sends him back home to help establish a canteen. Musically this is an interesting item but plotwise it is pretty thin.

699 Cowboy Cavalier. Monogram, 1948. 57 minutes B/W. D: Derwin Abrahams. SC: Ronald Davidson & J. Benton Cheyney. WITH Jimmy Wakely, Dub Taylor, Jan Bryant, Douglas Evans, Claire Whitney, William Ruhl, Steve Clark, Milburn Morante, Bud Osborne, Carol Henry, Bob Woodward. The stage and freight line operated by a young woman is being harassed by bandits and a singing cowboy and his pal come to her rescue. Typically low grade and not-very-entertaining Jimmy Wakely series entry.

700 Cowboy Commandos. Monogram, 1943. 55 minutes B/W. D: S. Roy Luby. SC: Elizabeth Beecher. WITH Ray Corrigan, Dennis Moore, Max Terhune, Evelyn Finley, Johnny Bond, Budd Buster, John Merton, Edna Bennett, Steve Clark, Bud Osborne, Frank Ellis, Hank Bell, Denver Dixon, Artie Ortego, George Chesebro, Ray Jones, Carl Sepulveda. The Range Busters uncover a nest of Nazis who are trying to sabotage the production of a magnesium mine. Delightful entry in "The Range Busters" series; this is the one where Johnny Bond sings "I'll Shoot the Fueher, Sure as Shootin'."

701 The Cowboy Counsellor. Allied, 1932, 62 minutes B/W. D: George Melford. SC: Jack Natteford. WITH Hoot Gibson, Sheila Mannors, Skeeter Bill Robbins, Bobby Nelson, Fred Gilman, Jack Rutherford, William Humphreys, Gordon De Main, Merrill McCormack, Al Bridge, Frank Ellis. A frontier lawyer is at odds with a gang of crooks. Leisurely paced and somewhat humorous Hoot Gibson vehicle, lacking a budget necessary to make it really good.

702 The Cowboy from Sundown. Monogram, 1940. 58 minutes B/W. D: Spencer Gordon Bennet. SC: Roland Lynch & Robert Emmett (Tansey). WITH Tex Ritter, Pauline Haddon, Roscoe Ates, Carleton Young, George Pembroke, Dave O'Brien, Patsy Moran, Tristram Coffin, Chick Hannon, Arkansas Slim Andrews, Bud Osborne, Glenn Strange, Wally West, Sherry Tansey. A sheriff is forced to quarantine area cattle due to hoof and mouth disease and this angers ranchers who have to get their herds to market or lose their ranches to the local banker who holds the mortgages. A fairly interesting plot helps this Tex Ritter outing.

703 Cowboy Holiday. Beacon, 1934. 57 minutes B/W. D: Robert Hill. SC: Rock Hawley (Robert Hill). WITH Guinn Williams, Janet Chandler, Julian Rivero, Richard Alexander, John Elliott, Alma Chester, Frank Ellis, Julia Bejarano. A man disguised as a Mexican bandit is causing a great deal of lawlessness along the border and a cowboy sets out to bring him to justice. Cheaply made but rugged, and often amusing, Guinn "Big Boy" Williams film.

704 Cowboy in the Clouds. Columbia, 1943. 55 minutes B/W. D: Benjamin Kline. SC: Elizabeth Beecher. WITH Charles Starrett, Dub Taylor, Julie Duncan, Jimmy Wakely, Hal Taliaferro, Charles King, Lane Chandler, Davidson Clark, Dick Curtis, Ed Cassidy, Ted Mapes, John Tyrell, Paul Zarema, The Jesters. A cowboy fights for his country by joining the Civil Air Patrol and combating enemy agents. Topical and well done.

705 The Cowboy Millionaire. Fox, 1935. 74 minutes B/W. D: Edward Cline. SC: George Waggoner & Dan Jarrett. WITH George O'Brien, Evelyn Bostock, Edgar Kennedy, Alden Chase, Maude Allen, Dan Jarrett, Lloyd Ingraham, Thomas Curran. Coming to a dude ranch for a vacation, a young titled English girl falls in love with a cowboy and after many misunderstandings they eventually get together. As much of a romantic comedy as a Western, this outing will appeal to George O'Brien fans.

Cowboy Roundup see **Ride 'em Cowboy** (1936)

706 Cowboy Serenade. Republic, 1942. 54 (66) minutes B/W. D: William Morgan. SC: Olive Cooper. WITH Gene Autry, Smiley Burnette, Fay McKenzie, Cecil Cunningham, Rand Brooks, Addison Richards, Tristram Coffin, Arkansas Slim Andrews, Melinda Leighton, Johnny Berkes, Forrest Taylor, Hank Worden, Si Jenks, Ethan Laidlaw, Hal Price, Bud Wolfe, Forbes Murray, Bud Geary, Frankie Marvin, Tom London, Kenneth Terrell, Ken Cooper. When professional gamblers get control of a cattle herd Gene Autry sets out to retrieve the beef. Fair Gene Autry vehicle with some good music.

707 The Cowboy Star. Columbia, 1936. 56 minutes B/W. D: David Selman. SC: Frances Guihan. WITH Charles Starrett, Iris Meredith, Si Jenks, Marc Lawrence, Ed Peil, Wally Albright, Ralph McCullough, Landers Stevens, Dick Terry, Winifred Hari, Nick Copeland, Lew Meehan. Wanting a rest, a cowboy film star goes to a small town incognito and there proves himself a real-life hero. Breezy and entertaining tongue-in-cheek jab at the "B" Western genre; lots of fun for fans.

708 The Cowboys. Warner Brothers, 1972. 121 minutes Color. D: Mark Rydell. SC: Irving Ravetch, Harriet Frank Jr. & William Dale Jennings. WITH John Wayne, Roscoe Lee Browne, Bruce Dern, Colleen Dewhurst, Slim Pickens, A. Martinez, Alfred Barker Jr., Nicholas Beauvy, Steve Benedict, Robert Carradine, Norman Howells Jr., Stephen Hudis, Sean Kelly, Clay O'Brien, Sam O'Brien, Mike Pyeat, Lonny Chapman, Sarah Cunningham, Charles Tyner, Allyn Ann McLerie, Matt Clark, Jerry Gatlin, Tap Canutt, Chuck Courtney, Henry Wills, Joe Yrigoyen, Casey Tibbs, Chuck Roberson. When his drovers all leave, a big cattleman rounds up a group of boys and has them help him drive his herd to market. Handsomely made and very good, although violent, John Wayne vehicle; recommended. Frank De Kova as Chief Joseph was cut from the final release print. The film served as the source for the television series "The Cowboys" (ABC-TV, 1974) starring Jim Davis in the John Wayne role. V: Warners Home Video.

709 Cowboys from Texas. Republic, 1939. 57 minutes B/W. D: George Sherman. SC: Oliver Drake. WITH Robert Livingston, Raymond Hatton, Duncan Renaldo, Carole Landis, Betty Compson, Ethan Laidlaw, Yakima Canutt, Walter Willis, Ed Cassidy, Bud Osborne, Charles King, Forbes Murray, Horace Murphy, Henry Strang, Jack Kirk, David Sharpe, Lew Meehan, Jack O'Shea, Charles Miller, Ivan Miller. When cattle ranchers and homesteaders declare war over open range, the Three Mesquiteers try to bring the matter to a peaceful solution. Another speedy entry in the long-running series based on William Colt MacDonald's literary characters.

710 Coyote Trails. Reliable, 1935. 60 minutes B/W. D: Bernard B. Ray. SC: Rose Gordon. WITH Tom Tyler, Alice Dahl, Ben Corbett, Lafe McKee, Richard Alexander, Slim Whitaker, George Chesebro, Lew Meehan, Jack Evans, Art Dillard, Jimmie Aubrey, Bud McClure, Tex Palmer, Phantom (horse). Two cowboys try to capture a stallion who they believe has been falsely accused of rustling a rancher's horses. The story has been done both before and since and usually much better than in this shoddy Tom Tyler film.

711 Crashing Broadway. Monogram, 1933. 61 minutes B/W. D: John P. McCarty. SC: Wellyn Totman. WITH Rex Bell, Doris Hill, Harry Bowen, Charles King, George ("Gabby") Hayes, Ann Howard, Blackie Whiteford, Perry Murdock, Henry Rocquemore, Gordon De Main, Tex Palmer, George Morrell. Heading East for the first time, a cowpoke runs into trouble with hoodlums in the big city. Rather typical breezy Rex Bell vehicle. V: Video Connection.

712 Crashin' Through. Anchor, 1924. 50 minutes B/W. D: Robert J. Horner, SC: Alvin J. Neitz. WITH Jack Perrin, Aline Goodwin, Jack Richardson, Steve Clements, Dick La Reno, Jean Riley, Taylor Graves. Wanting to sell his ranch to a man who wants real Western wildness, a man plans such a masquerade only to have a real outlaw gang arrive on the scene. Fun tongue-in-cheek silent actioner.

713 Crashing Thru. Grand National, 1939. 60 minutes B/W. D: Elmer Clifton. SC: Sherman Lowe. WITH James Newill, Jean Carmen, Warren Hull, Dave O'Brien, Milburn Stone, Robert Frazer, Walter Byron, Stanley Blystone, Joe Gerard, Earle Douglas, Ted Adams, Roy Barcroft, Iron Eyes Cody. A brother and sister plan to hijack a gold shipment, but are opposed by Renfrew of the Mounties. Final entry in the "Renfrew of the Mounted" series for Grand National and a pleasant closing.

714 Crashing Thru. Monogram, 1949. 58 minutes B/W. D: Ray Taylor. SC: Adele Buffington. WITH Whip Wilson, Andy Clyde, Christine Larson, Kenne Duncan, Tristram Coffin, George J. Lewis, Jan Bryant, Virginia Carroll, Steve Darrell, Jack Richardson, Tom Quinn, Dee Cooper, Boyd Stockman, Bob Woodward. An undercover insurance agent poses as a murdered ranger to trap the gang responsible for the killing. Whip Wilson's first series vehicle is a well written and produced affair greatly aided by a fine supporting cast.

Crazy Movie see **The Comeback Trail**

715 The Crimson Trail. Universal, 1935. 56 minutes B/W. D: Al Rabock. SC: Jack Natteford. WITH Buck Jones, Polly Ann Young, Carl Stockdale, Charles K. French, Ward Bond, Robert Kortman, Bud Osborne, Paul Fix, Robert Walker. Two rival ranchers are running against each other in an election and one of them is shot and his nephew tries to find the culprit and along the way falls in love with the other man's daughter. Somewhat complicated, but appealing Buck Jones fare.

716 Cripple Creek. Columbia, 1952. 78 minutes Color. D: Ray Nazarro. SC: Richard Shayer. WITH George Montgomery, Karin Booth, Jerome Courtland, William Bishop, Richard Egan, Don Porter, John Dehner, Roy Roberts, George Cleveland, Byron Foulger, Cliff Clark, Harry Cording. When outlaws steal shipments from gold mines, two government agents try to uncover the culprits by pretending to be bandits. Average George Montgomery oater; nothing special.

717 Crooked River. Lippert, 1950. 55 minutes B/W. D: Thomas Carr. SC: Ron Ormond & Maurice Tombragel. WITH James Ellison, Russell Hayden, Betty (Julie) Adams, Fuzzy Knight, Raymond Hatton, Tom Tyler, George J. Lewis, John Cason, Stanley Price, Stephen Carr, Dennis Moore, George Chesebro, Bud Osborne, Jimmie Martin, Cliff Taylor, Helen Gibson, Carl Mathews, George Sowards. A cowboy finds out that his folks have been brutally murdered and he sets out to catch the culprits. A fine cast can do nothing to save this poor, and last, entry in the James Ellison-Russell Hayden series for Lippert, the film being loaded with stock footage from an old Bob Steele film. TV title: **The Last Bullet.**

718 The Crooked Trail. Supreme, 1936. 60 minutes B/W. D: S. Roy Luby. SC: George Plympton. WITH Johnny Mack Brown, Lucille Browne, John Merton, Charles King, Ted Adams, Dick Curtis, John Van Pelt, Ed Cassidy, Horace Murphy, Earl Dwire, Artie Ortego, Hal Price. A man saves two men from thirst in the desert and when he later becomes a sheriff he refuses to believe one of them is a thief. Johnny Mack Brown stars as the quick-on-the-draw lawman.

719 Crossed Trails. Monogram, 1948. 60 minutes B/W. D: Lambert Hillyer.

SC: Colt Remington. WITH Johnny Mack Brown, Raymond Hatton, Kathy Frye, Lynne Carver, Douglas Evans, Steve Clark, Ted Adams, Zon Murray, Pierce Lyden, Milburn Morante, Frank LaRue, Mary MacLaren, Pierce Lyden, Henry Hall, Bud Osborne, Artie Ortego. A young girl is the heir to a ranch with valuable water rights and her guardian, who refuses to sell the land, is jailed on a false murder charge. Entertaining Johnny Mack Brown-Raymond Hatton series entry.

720 Crossfire. RKO Radio, 1933. 55 minutes B/W. D: Otto Brower. SC: Tom McNamara. WITH Tom Keene, Betty Furness, Edgar Kennedy, Lafe McKee, Charles K. French, Edward Phillips, Murdock McQuarrie, Stanley Blystone. A soldier returns home to the West after World War I to find gangsters working the range. Tom Keene's final RKO film is okay but its plot was nothing new.

721 Cry Blood Apache. Golden Eagle, 1970. 82 minutes Color. D: Jack Starrett. SC: Sean MacGregor. WITH Jody McCrea, Dan Kemp, Jack Starrett, Don Henley, Robert Tessier, Carolyn Stellar, Joel McCrea. An old-timer recalls an event from his youth involving a feud between whites and Indians just after the Mexican-American war. Anemic actioner enhanced only by Joel McCrea's brief cameo.

Cry For Me, Billy see **Face to the Wind**

722 A Cry in the Wilderness. ABC-TV/ Universal, 1974. 74 minutes Color. D: Gordon Hessler. SC: Stephen Knarpf & Elinor Knarpf. WITH George Kennedy, Joanna Pettet, Lee H. Montgomery, Collin Wilcox-Horne, Liam Dunn, Roy Poole, Bing Russell, Irene Tedrow, Robert Brubaker, Anne Seymour, Paul Sorenson. After being bitten by a rabid skunk, a farmer tries to protect his family by chaining himself inside a barn, only to learn that a flood is coming. Fairly suspenseful outing made for television.

723 Cry of the Wild. American National Enterprises, 1974. 91 minutes Color. D: Bill Mason. Documentary on wolves, both at large and in captivity, telling of their habits and exposing many myths about these supposedly savage beasts. Director Bill Mason also did the camera work for this documentary, which is quite entertaining.

724 Cry to the Wind. Sebastian International Pictures, 1979. 90 minutes Color.

D: Robert W. Davison. SC: David James Nielsen. WITH Sheldon Woods, Cameron Garnick. A young man sets out to conquer the wilderness and learns how to survive and respect his surroundings. Capable adventure yarn, lots of scenic values.

725 The Culpepper Cattle Company. 20th Century-Fox, 1972. 92 minutes Color. D: Dick Richards. SC: Eric Berovici & Gregory Prentiss. WITH Gary Grimes, Billy Green Bush, Luke Askew, Bo Hopkins, Geoffrey Lewis, Wayne Sutherlin, John McLiam, Matt Clark, Raymond Guth, Anthony James, Charles Martin Smith, Larry Finley, Bob Morgan, Jan Burrell, Gregory Sierra, Royal Dano, Hal Needham, Jerry Gatlin. A teenager becomes a part of a trail drive and the hardships along the way teach him to be a man. Fairly good dramatic outing, a bit on the violent side.

726 Curse of the Headless Horseman. DLM, 1972. 80 minutes Color. D: John Kirkland. SC: Kenn Riche. WITH Ultra Violet, Marland Proctor, Don Carrara, Claudia Ream, B. G. Fisher, Margo Dean, Lee Byers, Joe Cody. A doctor inherits a ranch where a headless horseman is said to ride out to take revenge on the eight gunmen who murdered him. Very low grade horror tale in a Western setting.

727 Curtain Call at Cactus Creek. Universal, 1950. 86 minutes Color. D: Charles Lamont. SC: Howard Dimsdale. WITH Donald O'Connor, Gale Storm, Walter Brennan, Vincent Price, Eve Arden, Chick Chandler, Joseph Sawyer, Harry Shannon, Rex Lease, I. Stanford Jolley. A stage-struck stagehand with an acting troupe in the Old West accidentally captures a local bank robber. Amusing satire helped by an eager cast.

728 Custer of the West. Cinerama, 1967. 146 minutes Color. D: Robert Siodmak & Irving Lerner. SC: Bernard Gordon & Julian Halvey. WITH Robert Shaw, Mary Ure, Jeffrey Hunter, Ty Hardin, Robert Ryan, Charles Stalnaker, Robert Hall, Lawrence Tierney, Kieron Moore, Marc Lawrence. After being a hero in the Civil War, George Armstrong Custer is given a command in the West, where he must deal with warring Indians and army rivals. Fairly accurate rendering of the Custer story, filmed in Spain. Also called **A Good Day For Fighting.**

729 Custer's Last Fight. Ince, 1912. 55 minutes B/W. D: Thomas H. Ince. SC: Richard V. Spencer. WITH Francis Ford. The story of the final showdown between General Custer and Sitting Bull at the Little Big Horn River. This early Thomas H. Ince silent production is considered one of the first really good Westerns and it is well worth viewing; originally a three reeler, it was expanded to feature length when reissued in 1925 by Quality Amusements.

730 Custer's Last Stand. Stage & Screen, 1936. 65 (91) minutes B/W. D: Elmer Clifton. SC: George A. Durlam, Eddy Graneman & Bob Lively. WITH Rex Lease, Jack Mulhall, Ruth Mix, Dorothy Gulliver, William Farnum, Lona Andre, Reed Howes, Bobby Nelson, Frank McGlynn Jr., William Desmond, Helen Gibson, Nancy Casell, Chief Thundercloud, Josef Swickard, Creighton Hale, George Chesebro, Milburn Morante, Ted Adams, George Morrell, Robert Walker, Walter James, Cactus Mack, Budd Buster, Carl Mathews, Artie Ortego, Franklyn Farnum, Lafe McKee, Allen Greer, James Sheridan, Ken Cooper, Chief Big Tree, Iron Eyes Cody. A scout for General Custer tries to aid settlers who are being attacked by Indians led by a renegade who is after an Indian medicine arrow which is the clue to a hidden Indian treasure. Lots of stock footage in this feature version of the 15 chapter serial. Film is dull and poorly made and paced, saved only by its large veteran cast with George Chesebro a standout as a dishonest soldier turned good. V: Video Connection.

731 Cutter's Trail. CBS-TV/CBS Studio Center, 1970. 100 minutes Color. D: Vincent McEveety. SC: Paul Savage. WITH John Gavin, Marisa Pavan, Beverly Garland, Joseph Cotten, J. Carrol Naish, Nehemiah Persoff, Manuel Padilla Jr., Shug Fisher, Ken Swofford, Victor French, Bob Random, Robert Totten, Tom Brown. The marshal returns to Santa Fe to find the town pillaged by an outlaw gang and only a young Mexican mother and her small son will help him track the marauders. Fairly acceptable television oater, which originally ran 75 minutes and was expanded for subsequent showings.

732 Cut-Throats Nine. United International, 1973. 90 minutes Color. D: Joaquin L. Romero Merchant. SC: Santiago Moncada & Joaquin L. Romero Merchant. WITH Robert Hundar, Emma Cohen, Alberto Dalbos, Manuel Jejada, Ricardo Diaz, Carlos Romero Marchant. A Union army sergeant and his pretty daughter lead criminals on a 400 mile journey to a government owned gold mine so the convicts can work it for the Union cause during the Civil War. One of the better spaghetti actioners, this one originally produced by Films Triunfo in Spain.

733 Cyclone Cavalier. Rayart, 1925. 55 minutes B/W. D: Albert S. Rogell. SC: Krag Johnson & Burke Jenkins. WITH Reed Howes, Carmelita Geraghty, Wilfred Lucas, Jack Mower, Eric Mayne, Johnny Sinclair, Ervin Renard. A young man is sent to a Central American republic where he falls in love with the president's daughter and tries to thwart a palace revolution. Low budget silent actioner and a chance to see Reed Howes in a starring role.

734 Cyclone Fury. Columbia, 1951. 54 minutes B/W. D: Ray Nazarro. SC: Barry Shipman & Ed Earl Repp. WITH Charles Starrett, Smiley Burnette, Fred F. Sears, Clayton Moore, Robert Wilke, Louis Lettieri, George Chesebro, Frank O'Connor, Merle Travis & His Bronco Busters. An agent sent to insure the delivery of horses to the government gets suspicious after a rancher is murdered. Fairly good "Durango Kid" series film.

735 The Cyclone Kid. Big 4, 1931. 60 minutes B/W. D: J. P. McGowan. SC: George Morgan. WITH Caryl Lincoln, Buzz Barton, Francis X. Bushman Jr., Ted Adams, Lafe McKee, Blackie Whiteford. A ranch foreman, in love with the boss' daughter, is aided by a young boy in opposing outlaws. Poor low grade affair.

736 The Cyclone Kid. Republic, 1942. 56 minutes B/W. D: George Sherman. SC: Richard Murphy. WITH Don "Red" Barry, Lynn Merrick, John James, Alex Callam, Joel Friedkin, Slim Andrews, Rex Lease, Joe McGuinn, Monte Montague, Frank LaRue, Edmund Cobb, Budd Buster, Hal Price, Jack Rockwell, Jack O'Shea, Curley Dresden, Bob Woodward. When his lawyer brother comes West and finds out his true activities, a gunman turns on his crooked cattle baron boss. Typically good Don Barry series entry with a plot that is a bit hard to take, but the action compensates.

737 Cyclone of the Saddle. Superior, 1935. 53 minutes B/W. D: Elmer Clifton. SC: Elmer Clifton & George Merrick. WITH Rex Lease, Janet Chandler, Bobby Nelson, William Desmond, Yakima Canutt,

Art Mix, Chief Thundercloud, Helen Gibson, Milburn Morante, George Chesebro, The Range Ranglers, Chief Standing Bear. When an outlaw gang causes trouble with settlers and Indians the army assigns an officer to stop them. Poor production values detract from this Rex Lease vehicle.

738 Cyclone on Horseback. RKO Radio, 1941. 60 minutes B/W. D: Edward Killy. SC: Norton S. Parker. WITH Tim Holt, Marjorie Reynolds, Ray Whitley, Lee "Lasses" White, Dennis Moore, Harry Worth, Monte Montague, John Dilson, Lew Kelly, Terry Frost, Slim Whitaker. Three cowpokes come to the aid of a pretty girl and her brother whose attempt to string a telegraph wire, in order to win a contract, is being thwarted by hoodlums. Well paced and actionful Tim Holt film, with an especially exciting finale.

739 Cyclone Prairie Rustlers. Columbia, 1944. 55 minutes B/W. D: Benjamin Kline. SC: Elizabeth Beecher. WITH Charles Starrett, Dub Taylor, Jimmie Davis, Constance Worth, Jimmy Wakely & His Saddle Pals, Robert Fiske, Clancy Cooper, Ray Bennett, I. Stanford Jolley, Edward M. Phillips, Edmund Cobb, Forrest Taylor, Paul Zaremba, Ted Mapes. A cowboy and his pals try to stop Nazis from sabotaging cattle, crops and equipment in the West. Topical and quite actionful Charles Starrett vehicle.

740 The Cyclone Ranger. Spectrum, 1935. 60 minutes B/W. D: Robert Hill. SC: Oliver Drake. WITH Bill Cody, Nena Quartero, Eddie Gribbon, Soledad Jiminez, Earle Hodgins, Zara Tazil, Donald Reed, Colin Chase, Budd Buster. An outlaw is befriended by a blind woman and he pretends to be her son who was killed by a posse. Sentimental, but mediocre, Bill Cody vehicle.

D

741 Dakota. Republic, 1945. 82 minutes B/W. D: Joseph Kane. SC: Lawrence Hazard. WITH John Wayne, Vera Hruba Ralston, Walter Brennan, Ward Bond, Mike Mazurki, Ona Munson, Hugo Haas, Olive Blakeney, Nicodemus Stewart, Paul Fix, Grant Withers, Robert Livingston, Olin Howlin, Pierre Watkin, Robert Barrat, Jonathan Hale, Bobby Blake, Paul Hurst, Eddy Waller, Sarah Padden, Jack LaRue,

George Cleveland, Selmer Jackson, Claire DuBrey, Roy Barcroft, Cliff Lyons, Fred Graham, Linda Stirling. An ex-soldier and his heiress wife head West to the Dakotas where she owns land on which a railroad is to be built and they find themselves at odds with two crooks trying to force farmers off their properties. Big, brawling oater is not nearly as good as it should have been, but is more than passable, especially for the Duke's fans. V: Cumberland Video, NTA Home Entertainment.

742 Dakota Incident. Republic, 1956. 88 minutes Color. D: Lewis R. Foster. SC: Frederick Louis Fox. WITH Linda Darnell, Dale Robertson, John Lund, Ward Bond, Skip Homeier, Regis Toomey, Irving Bacon, John Doucette, Whit Bissell, William Fawcett, Malcolm Atterbury, Charles Horvath. Passengers on a stagecoach are attacked by Indians and must defend themselves as well as settle their own differences. Interesting premise but none-too-interesting production.

743 The Dakota Kid. Republic, 1951. 60 minutes B/W. D: Philip Ford. SC: William Lively. WITH Michael Chapin, Eilene Janssen, James Bell, Margaret Field, Robert Shayne, Roy Barcroft, Danny Morton, Mauritz Hugo, House Peters Jr., Lee Bennett. A group of youngsters aid the law in rounding up an outlaw gang. One of quartet of features in the "Rough Ridin' Kids" series and just as mediocre as the others.

744 Dakota Lil. 20th Century-Fox, 1950. 88 minutes Color. D: Lesley Selander. SC: Maurice Geraghty. WITH George Montgomery, Rod Cameron, Marie Windsor, John Emery, Wallace Ford, Jack Lambert, Larry Johns, Marion Martin, James Flavin, J. Farrell MacDonald. A Treasury agent is on the trail of a team of counterfeiters in the Old West. Pleasing outing with nice performances in the leading roles.

745 Dallas. Warner Brothers, 1950. 94 minutes Color. D: Stuart Heisler. SC: John Twist. WITH Gary Cooper, Ruth Roman, Steve Cochran, Raymond Massey, Barbara Payton, Leif Erickson, Antonio Moreno, Jerome Cowan, Reed Hadley, Will Wright, Monte Blue, Byron (Brian) Keith, Gil Donaldson, Zon Murray. In Post-Civil War Texas, a former Confederate sets out to take revenge on the carpetbaggers who murdered his family. Big budget Gary Cooper opus which hits the entertainment mark; Barbara Payton is good as heroine Ruth Roman's pal.

746 The Dalton Gang. Lippert, 1949. 59 minutes B/W. D-SC: Ford Beebe. WITH Don ("Red") Barry, Robert Lowery, Betty (Julie) Adams, James Millican, Byron Foulger, J. Farrell MacDonald, Greg McClure, George J. Lewis, Marshall Reed, Ray Bennett, Lee Roberts, Dick Curtis, Stanley Price, Cactus Mack. Two lawmen set out to round up the infamous Dalton gang. Outside of the stars there is not much to recommend this pedestrian effort. TV title: **The Outlaw Gang.**

747 The Dalton Girls. United Artists, 1957. 71 minutes B/W. D: Reginald LeBorg. SC: Maurice Tombragel. WITH Merry Anders, Penny Edwards, John Russell, Lisa Davis, Sue George, Johnny Western, Malcolm Atterbury, Douglas Henderson, Red Morgan, Ed Hinton. After the Dalton Gang is stopped by the law, several young female relatives band together and form their own outlaw coterie. Director Reginald LeBorg and the cast tries hard but the cheap production values don't help matters in this pedestrian effort.

748 The Dalton's Women. Western Adventures, 1950. 80 minutes B/W. D: Thomas Carr. SC: Ron Ormond & Maurice Tombragel. WITH Tom Neal, Pamela Blake, Jack Holt, Lash LaRue, Al St. John, Jacqueline Fontaine, Raymond Hatton, Lyle Talbot, Tom Tyler, J. Farrell MacDonald, Terry Frost, Stanley Price, Bud Osborne, Lee Bennett. A saloon owner is in cahoots with an outlaw gang which is terrorizing a small town, but U. S. marshals are on their trail. Notorious stitched-together oater is at its best when taken as a curio, otherwise it is pretty poor stuff.

749 The Daltons Ride Again. Universal, 1945. 70 minutes B/W. D: Ray Taylor. SC: Roy Chanslor & Paul Gangelin. WITH Alan Curtis, Lon Chaney, Kent Taylor, Noah Beery Jr., Martha O'Driscoll, Jess Barker, Thomas Gomez, John Litel, Walter Sande, Douglass Dumbrille, Virginia Brissac, Milburn Stone, Stanley Andrews, Fern Emmett, Cyril Delevanti, Wheaton Chambers, Davidson Clark, Jack Rockwell, Robert Wilke, Dick Dickinson, George Chesebro, Paul Birch, Ed Cassidy, Ethan Laidlaw, Henry Hall. The story of the exploits of the Dalton brothers outlaw gang is told by the only survivor of the Coffeyville, Kansas, shootout. Compact and very entertaining "B" outing, with the four stars doing excellent work as the Daltons.

750 Dan Candy's Law. Cinerama Releasing Corporation/American-International, 1973. 95 minutes Color. D: Claude Fournier. SC: George Malko. WITH Donald Sutherland, Chief Dan George, Kevin McCarthy, Jean Duceppe, Francine Rocette, Jack Creely. After his partner is killed, a Mountie sets out to track down the Indian accused of the crime but he eventually finds that he is the hunted instead of the hunter. Nice scenery highlight this otherwise tiresome Canadian feature. Also called **Alien Thunder.**

751 Danger Ahead. Monogram, 1940. 60 minutes B/W. D: Ralph Staub. SC: Edward Halperin. WITH James Newill, Dorothea Kent, Dave O'Brien, Guy Usher, Maude Allen, Harry Depp, John Dilson, Earl Douglas. Renfrew and the Mounties are at odds with a stubborn girl who refuses to aid them in capturing an outlaw gang wanted for murder. Okay entry in the "Renfrew of the Royal Mounted" series. V: Cumberland Video.

752 Danger Patrol. RKO Radio, 1937. 60 minutes B/W. D: Lew Landers. SC: Helen Vreeland & Hilda Vincent. WITH Sally Eilers, John Beal, Harry Carey, Frank M. Thomas, Crawford Weaver, Lee Patrick, Edward Gargan, Paul Guifoyle, Solly Ward. Working as a nitro shooter in the oil fields, a young medical student falls in love with the daughter of the man who is training him. Sturdy oil drilling saga with good work by Harry Carey as the mentor-father.

753 Danger Trails. Beacon/First Division, 1935. 62 minutes B/W. D: Robert Hill. SC: Rock Hawley (Robert Hill). WITH Guinn Williams, Marjorie Gordon, Wally Wales, Edmund Cobb, John Elliott, George Chesebro, Steve Clark, Ace Cain. A young man, educated in the East, sets out to take revenge on the outlaw gang who murdered his family. Cheaply made but entertaining Guinn "Big Boy" Williams vehicle for which the star wrote the original story.

754 Danger Valley. Monogram, 1938. 58 minutes B/W. D: Robert North Bradbury. SC: Robert Emmett (Tansey). WITH Jack Randall, Lois Wilde, Charles King, Hal Price, Frank LaRue, Chick Hannon, Earl Dwire, Ernie Adams, Tex Palmer, Merrill McCormack, Oscar Gahan, Denver Dixon, Sherry Tansey, Jimmie Aubrey, Glenn Strange, Bud Osborne. Two cowpokes come upon a ghost town where an old man has discovered gold but is being harrassed by an outlaw gang. Passable Jack Randall singing Western.

755 The Dangerous Days of Kiowa Jones. ABC-TV/Metro-Goldwyn-Mayer, 1966. 100 minutes Color. D: Alex March. SC: Frank Fenton & Robert W. Thompson. WITH Robert Horton, Diane Baker, Sal Mineo, Nehemiah Persoff, Gary Merrill, Robert H. Harris, Lonny Chapman, Royal Dano, Zalman King, Harry Dean Stanton, Val Avery. A dying marshal asks a man to transport two criminals to jail and along the way the trio must elude bounty hunters. Early network telefeature is on the mediocre side and failed to sell as a series.

756 Dangerous Nan McGrew. Paramount, 1930. 62 minutes B/W. D: Malcolm St. Clair. SC: Paul Gerard Smith & Pierre Collings. WITH Helen Kane, Victor Moore, James Hall, Stuart Erwin, Frank Morgan, Roberta Robinson, Louise Closser Hale, Allan Forrest, John Hamilton, Robert Milash. A girl working in a medicine show is stranded in the Canadian northwest and ends up capturing a bank robber. Vintage Helen Kane vehicle with songs will satisfy the curious, but genre fans beware.

757 Dangerous Odds. Independent Pictures, 1925. 50 minutes B/W. D: William J. Craft. WITH Bill Cody, Eileen Sedgwick, Milton Fahrney, Claude Payton, Monte Collins, Al Hallett. When the bank manager who has withdrawn funds for his ranch is murdered a man is accused of the crime and escapes a lynch party to prove his innocence. Okay Bill Cody silent film, but nothing special.

758 Dangerous Venture. United Artists, 1947 54 (59) minutes B/W. D: George Archainbaud. SC: Doris Schroeder. WITH William Boyd, Andy Clyde, Rand Brooks, Fritz Leiber, Douglas Evans, Harry Cording, Betty Alexander, Francis McDonald, Neyle Morrow. Hopalong Cassidy gets caught in the middle of Indian warfare caused by archaeologists who are trying to locate a sacred Indian treasure. Dull, arid film with implausible story and cheap sets helped only by Fritz Leiber as the Indian chief.

759 Dangers of the Canadian Mounted. Republic, 1948. 12 Chapters B/W. D: Fred C. Brannon & Yakima Canutt. SC: Franklyn Adreon, Basil Dickey, Sol Shor & Robert G. Walker. WITH Jim Bannon, Virginia Belmont, Anthony Warde,

Dorothy Granger, Dale Van Sickel, Tom Steele, I. Stanford Jolley, Phil Warren, Lee Morgan, James Dale, Ted Adams, John Crawford, Jack Clifford, Eddie Parker, Frank O'Connor, Kenneth Terrell, Robert Wilke, Marshall Reed, House Peters Jr., Holly Bane, Ted Mapes, Jack Kirk, Al Taylor, Harry Cording, Bud Wolfe, Roy Bucko, David Sharpe. Canadian Mounties are on the trail of a gang of crooks who are after a hidden Chinese treasure in the north country. Mediocre cliffhanger which will appeal mainly to genre fans. TV feature title: **R.C.M.P. and the Treasure of Genghis Khan** (100 minutes).

760 Daniel Boone. RKO Radio, 1936. 77 minutes B/W. D: David Howard. SC: David Jarrett. WITH George O'Brien, Heather Angel, John Carradine, Ralph Forbes, Clarence Muse, George Regas, Dickie Jones, Huntley Gordon, Harry Cording, Aggie Herring, Crauford Kent, Keith Richard. The story of Daniel Boone leading settlers across the Cumberland Mountains in 1775 to settle in what is now Kentucky, and their encounters with hostile Indians led by the evil Simon Girty. Very fine historical drama with George O'Brien making an excellent Daniel Boone and John Carradine equally good as the villainous Girty. Well worth seeing. V: Blackhawk.

761 Daniel Boone Thru the Wilderness. Sunset, 1926. 60 minutes B/W. D: Frank S. Mattison. WITH Roy Stewart, Kathleen Collins. Daniel Boone leads settlers into the wilderness to set up a new settlement and meets opposition from Indians. Compact actioner also known as **With Daniel Boone in the Wilderness.**

762 Daniel Boone, Trail Blazer. Republic, 1956. 76 minutes Color. D: Albert C. Gannaway & Ismael Rodrigues. SC: Tom Hubbard & Jack Patrick. WITH Bruce Bennett, Lon Chaney, Faron Young, Damion O'Flynn, Ken Dibbs, Jacqueline Evans, Freddy Fernandez, Nancy Rodman, Fred Kohler Jr., Lee Morgan. Another telling of how Daniel Boone led his people from North Carolina to establish the fort at Boonesborough in Kentucky and their fights with the Indians, renegade French and Tories. Partially filmed in Mexico, this historical outing is more than passable with Bruce Bennett making a stalwart Daniel Boone and Lon Chaney an excellent Chief Blackfish, although country singer Faron Young is miscast as scout Callaway.

763 Daredevils of the West. Republic, 1943. 12 Chapters B/W. D: John English. SC: Ronald Davidson, Basil Dickey, Joseph O'Donnell, Joseph Poland & William Lively. WITH Allan Lane, Kay Aldridge, Eddie Acuff, William Haade, Robert Frazer, Ted Adams, George J. Lewis, Stanley Andrews, Jack Rockwell, Charles Miller, John Hamilton, Budd Buster, Kenneth Harlan, Kenne Duncan, Rex Lease, Chief Thundercloud, Eddie Parker, Ray Jones, Chief Many Treaties, Tom Steele, Jack O'Shea, George Magrill, Pierce Lyden, George Plues, Edmund Cobb, Al Taylor, Frank McCarroll, Tom London, George Pembrook, Ed Cassidy, Herbert Rawlinson, Tex Cooper, Charles Soldani, Crane Whitley, Augie Gomez. A young man comes to the aid of a girl whose stage line is being threatened by mysterious attacks. Exciting Republic serial.

The Daring Adventurer see **The Cisco Kid Returns**

764 The Daring Caballero. Monogram, 1950. 60 minutes B/W. D: Wallace Fox. SC: Betty Burbridge. WITH Duncan Renaldo, Leo Carrillo, Kippee Valez, Charles Halton, Pedro De Cordoba, Stephen Chase, Edmund Cobb, David Leonard, Frank Jacquet, Mickey Little. The Cisco Kid and his pal Pancho (dubbed as Chico and Pablo) come to the aid of a banker falsely convicted of robbery and murder. More than adequate "Cisco Kid" series programmer. TV title: **Guns of Fury.** V: Video Communications.

765 Daring Danger. Columbia, 1932. 60 minutes B/W. D: D. Ross Lederman. SC: Michael Trevelyan. WITH Tim McCoy, Alberta Vaughn, Wallace MacDonald, Robert Ellis, Edward J. LeSaint, Bobby Nelson, Max Davidson, Richard Alexander, Vernon Dent, Murdock McQuarrie, Edmund Cobb, Art Mix. A crook tries to starve an old man and his daughter off their range and a cowboy and a cattlemen's agent come to their rescue. This Tim McCoy vehicle is a bit on the slow moving side but it is entertaining and has a good finale.

766 Dark Command. Republic, 1940. 94 minutes B/W. D: Raoul Walsh. SC: Lionel Hosier & F. Hugh Herbert. WITH Claire Trevor, John Wayne, Walter Pidgeon, Roy Rogers, George "Gabby" Hayes, Porter Hall, Marjorie Main, Raymond Walburn, Joseph Sawyer, Helen MacKellar, J. Farrell MacDonald, Trevor

Bardette, Harry Woods, Glenn Strange, Alan Bridge, Jack Rockwell, Ernie Adams, Edward Hearn, Edmund Cobb, Hal Taliaferro, Yakima Canutt, Ben Alexander, Tom London, Cliff Lyons. During the Civil War, a Kansas school teacher becomes the leader of a notorious band of guerillas and he is also at odds with a sheriff over the girl they both love. Big, thrilling Republic production which is probably the best screen version of Quantrill's Raiders, despite the fact the character is called Will Cantrell here. Well worth viewing. V: Cumberland Video, NTA Home Entertainment.

767 Dark Mountain. Paramount, 1944. 66 minutes B/W. D: William Berke. SC: Maxwell Shane. WITH Robert Lowery, Ellen Drew, Regis Toomey, Eddie Quillan, Elisha Cook Jr., Byron Foulger, Walter Baldwin. A young woman marries a gangster instead of the forest ranger who truly loves her. Very well made and actionful Pine-Thomas production.

768 The Darkening Trail. Mutual, 1915. 62 minutes B/W. D: William S. Hart. SC: C. Gardner Sullivan. WITH William S. Hart, Enid Markey, Louise Glaum, George Fisher, Nona Thomas, Milton Ross, Roy Laidlaw. In the Yukon a cad marries a girl but soon loses interest in her but his chief rival still cares for her. Interesting, and very sombre, early William S. Hart silent film, directed by Hart. V: Classic Video Cinema Collections Club.

769 A Daughter of the Sioux. Davis Distributing, 1925. 55 minutes B/W. D: Ben Wilson. SC: George W. Pyper. WITH Ben Wilson, Neva Gerber, Robert Walker, Fay Adams, William Lowery, Rhody Hathaway. A government surveyor suspects a young Indian girl of giving information about fortifications to renegade braves. Low budget silent actioner from the team of Ben Wilson and Neva Gerber.

770 Daughter of the West. Film Classics, 1949. 77 minutes Color. D: Harold Daniels. SC: Irving R. Franklyn & Raymond L. Schrock. WITH Martha Vickers, Philip Reed, Donald Woods, James J. Griffith, Tommy Cook, Pedro De Cordoba, William Farnum, Milton Kibbee, Marion Carney, Anthony Barr. A young woman working on an Indian reservation tries to help the Navajos when a corrupt agent tries to steal their copper lands. Low grade but entertaining Western.

771 The Daughters of Joshua Cabe. ABC-TV, 1972. 74 minutes Color. D: Philip Leacock. SC: Paul Savage. WITH Buddy Ebsen, Karen Valentine, Lesley Ann Warren, Sandra Dee, Don Stroud, Henry Jones, Jack Elam, Leif Erickson, Michael Anderson Jr., Paul Koslo, Ron Soble. When a new homesteading law requires a man to have children in order to hold onto his lands, a veteran trapper hires three girls with tainted pasts to be his daughters. Fairly amusing Western telefilm satire. Sequel: **The Daughters of Joshua Cabe Return** (q.v.).

772 The Daughters of Joshua Cabe Return. ABC-TV, 1975. 74 minutes Color. D: David Lowell Rich. SC: Kathleen Hite. WITH Dan Dailey, Dub Taylor, Ronnie Troup, Christina Hart, Brooke Adams, Kathleen Freeman, Carl Betz, Arthur Hunnicutt, Terry Wilson, Robert Burton. When three girls are hired by an old trapper to pose as his daughters, they are outsmarted when the father of one of them kidnaps her and holds her for ransom. Sequel to **The Daughters of Joshua Cabe** (q.v.), this telefeature amounts to little more than low grade entertainment.

773 Davy Crockett and the River Pirates. Buena Vista, 1956. 81 minutes Color. D: Norman Foster. SC: Tom Blackburn & Norman Foster. WITH Fess Parker, Buddy Ebsen, Jeff York, Kenneth Tobey, Clem Bevans, Irvin Ashkenazy, Mort Mills, Paul Newlan, Frank Richards, Walter Catlett, Douglass Dumbrille. In 1810 Davy Crockett and pal Georgie Russell agree to a flatboat race with Big Mike Fink, the self-styled "King of the (Ohio) River." Fictional, enjoyable, followup to **Davy Crockett, King of the Wild Frontier,** and like its predecessor was first shown on Walt Disney's TV program (as a two-part episode) before successful theatrical release; Jeff York is grand as Big Mike Fink. V: Walt Disney Home Video.

774 Davy Crockett, Indian Scout. United Artists, 1950. 71 minutes B/W. D: Lew Landers. SC: Richard Schayer. WITH George Montgomery, Ellen Drew, Philip Reed, Noah Beery Jr., Paul Wilkerson, John Hamilton, Chief Thundercloud, Kenne Duncan, Ray Teal, Jimmy Moss, Vera Marshe. Davy Crockett is the leader of a wagon train which is attacked by Indians with the chief's daughter working as a spy. Tepid pseudo-historical oater with good work by George Montgomery in the title role. TV title: **Indian Scout.**

775 Davy Crockett, King of the Wild Frontier. Buena Vista, 1955. 93 minutes Color. D: Norman Foster. SC: Tom Blackburn. WITH Fess Parker, Buddy Ebsen, Basil Ruysdael, Hans Conreid, William Bakewell, Kenneth Tobey, Pat Hogan, Helen Stanley, Nick Cravat, Don Megowan, Mike Mazurki, Jeff Thompson, Henry Joyner, Benjamin Hornbuckle, Hal Youngblood, Jim Maddux, Robert Booth, Eugene Brindel, Ray Whitetree, Campbell Brown. The story of Davy Crockett, from his days as an Indian fighter with Andrew Jackson, through his serving in Congress and his final heroic stand at the Alamo. Although historically glossy, this feature made from three segments of Walt Disney's TV series is dandy entertainment and was the cause of the 1950s' Davy Crockett phenomena. Sequel: **Davy Crockett and the River Pirates** (q.v.). V: Walt Disney Home Video.

776 Dawn at Socorro. Universal-International, 1954. 80 minutes Color. D: George Sherman. SC: George Zuckerman. WITH Rory Calhoun, Piper Laurie, David Brian, Kathleen Hughes, Alex Nicol, Edgar Buchanan, Mara Corday, Skip Homeier, Roy Roberts, James Millican, Lee Van Cleef, Stanley Andrews, Richard Garland, Paul Brinegar, Philo McCullough, Forrest Taylor. A reformed gunman, waiting in a small town for a train, is forced into one last shootout. Predictable but entertaining.

777 Dawn on the Great Divide. Monogram, 1942. 70 minutes B/W. D: Howard Bretherton. SC: Jess Bowers (Adele Buffington). WITH Buck Jones, Raymond Hatton, Mona Barrie, Rex Bell, Robert Lowery, Harry Woods, Christine McIntyre, Betty Blythe, Robert Frazer, Tristram Coffin, Jan Wiley, Roy Barcroft, Dennis Moore, Steve Clark, Reed Howes, Bud Osborne, I. Stanford Jolley, Artie Ortego, George Morrell, Milburn Morante, Ray Jones. Three buddies lead a wagon train of munitions for the railroad but two brothers plan to hijack the train and hire an outlaw gang to dress as Indians in order to put the blame on the local tribe. Buck Jones' final film is short on action but has an interesting plot and a very fine cast. V: Discount Video.

778 The Dawn Rider. Monogram, 1935. 56 minutes B/W. D-SC: Robert North Bradbury. WITH John Wayne, Marion Burns, Yakima Canutt, Reed Howes, Denny Meadows (Dennis Moore), Bert Dillard, Jack Jones, James Sheridan. A man sets out to capture the robber who murdered his father and becomes involved with the man's pretty sister. Typical John Wayne-Lone Star vehicle, next to the last in the series before Republic took over the Paul Malvern production releases. Remade as **Western Trails** (q.v.). V: Discount Video.

779 The Dawn Trail. Columbia, 1930. 60 (66) minutes B/W. D: Christy Cabanne. SC: John T. Neville. WITH Buck Jones, Miriam Seegar, Charles Morton, Charles King, Hank Mann, Erville Alderson, Edward J. LeSaint, Vester Pegg, Slim Whitaker, Bob Burns, Buck Connors. In an area plagued by a cattlemen-sheepmen war, a sheriff must hold his girl's brother for murder. Excellent Buck Jones early talkie.

780 Day of Anger. National General, 1969. 109 minutes Color. D: Tonino Valerii. SC: Ernesto Gastaldi, Tonino Valerii & Renzo Genta. WITH Lee Van Cleef, Giuliano Gemma, Walter Rilla, Christa Linder, Ennio Balboa, Lukas Ammann, Andrea Bosic, Pepe Calvo, Giorgio Gargiullo, Anna Orso, Benito Stefanelli. A gunslinger befriends a young man and the two take over a town to get money owed to the gunman but eventually the younger one learns to dislike his mentor's ways. Not one of Lee Van Cleef's better efforts but still has enough action and violence to please fans of this kind of fare. Issued in Italy in 1967 by Sancrosia/Cornoa/KG Divina Films as I **Giorni Dell'Ira** (The Days of Wrath).

781 A Day of Fury. Universal-International, 1956. 78 minutes Color. D: Harmon Jones. SC: James Edmiston & Oscar Brodney. WITH Dale Robertson, Jock Mahoney, Mara Corday, Carl Benton Reid, Jan Merlin, John Dehner, Dayton Lummis, Sheila Bromley. Seeing the decline of lawlessness in the Old West, a young rebel tries to terrorize a small town. A bit different plotline adds some interest to this oater.

782 Day of the Animals. Film Ventures International, 1977. 95 minutes Color. D: William Girdler. SC: William Norton. WITH Christopher George, Leslie Nielsen, Lynda Day George, Richard Jaeckel, Michael Ansara, Ruth Roman, Andrew Stevens, Gil Lamb, Jon Cedar, Paul Mantee. A group of hikers are attacked by a variety of animals in the wilderness after going mad from the damage done to the Earth's ozone layer. Fairly competent combination of the Western and sci-fi genres with a pleasingly adept score by Lal Shifrin. Also called **Something Is Out There**. V: Film Ventures.

783 Day of the Bad Man. Universal, 1958. 82 minutes Color. D: Harry Keller. SC: Lawrence Roman. WITH Fred MacMurray, Joan Weldon, John Ericson, Robert Middleton, Marie Windsor, Edgar Buchanan, Skip Homeier, Eduard Franz. A circuit judge sentences a man to be hanged and in order for the sentence to be carried out he must hold off the man's brothers, who plan to rescue him. Passable low budget entry.

784 Day of the Evil Gun. Metro-Goldwyn-Mayer, 1968. 93 minutes Color. D: Jerry Thorpe. SC: Charles Marquis Warren & Eric Bercovici. WITH Glenn Ford, Arthur Kennedy, Dean Jagger, Pilar Pellicer, John Anderson, Paul Fix, Nico Minardos, Dean Stanton, Parley Baer, Barbara Babcock, James J. Griffith. Two enemies join together to rescue the wife and children of one of them, who have been taken captive by Indians. Fairly exciting and entertaining big budget outing.

785 Day of the Outlaw. United Artists, 1959. 90 minutes B/W. D: Andre De Toth. SC: Philip Yordan. WITH Robert Ryan, Burl Ives, Tina Louise, Alan Marshal, Nehemiah Persoff, David Nelson, Venetia Stevenson, Donald Elson, Helen Westcott, Robert Cornthwaite, Jack Lambert, Lance Fuller, Frank De Kova, Paul Wexler, William Schallert, Arthur Space, Betsy Jones Moreland, Elisha Cook, George Ross. An outlaw gang, with their injured leader, rides into a small town and are detained there by a blizzard. Better-than-average melodrama; well done.

786 Days of Adventure, Dreams of Gold. William Bronson, 1975. 60 minutes Color. D: William Bronson & Denver Sutton. WITH Hal Holbrook (narrator). Documentary on the last gold rush in the Yukon Territory in 1897. Historical buffs will like this one.

787 Days of Buffalo Bill. Republic, 1946. 56 minutes B/W. D: Thomas Carr. SC: William Lively & Doris Schroeder. WITH Sunset Carson, Peggy Stewart, Tom London, James Craven, Rex Lease, Edmund Cobb, Eddie Parker, Michael Sloan, Jay Kirby, George Chesebro, Ed Cassidy, Tex Cooper, Kit Guard. A cowpoke and his buddy are framed for murder and run from a posse in order to prove their innocence. Buffalo Bill Cody is nowhere to be seen in this outing, but Sunset Carson fans will like it anyway.

788 Days of Jesse James. Republic, 1939. 54 (63) minutes B/W. D: Joseph Kane. SC: Jack Natteford. WITH Roy Rogers, George "Gabby" Hayes, Pauline Moore, Donald (Don "Red") Barry, Harry Woods, Arthur Loft, Wade Boteler, Ethel Wales, Scotty Beckett, Harry Worth, Glenn Strange, Olin Howlin, Monte Blue, Jack Rockwell, Fred Burns, Bud Osborne, Jack Ingram, Carl Sepulveda, Lynton Brent, Pasquel Perry, Eddie Acuff, Horace Carpenter. A railroad detective is on the trail of Jesse James and runs afoul of an opportunistic sheriff and a crooked banker who commit a series of robberies and put the blame on the famous outlaw. Excellent Roy Rogers feature in which Don Barry steals the show as Jesse James.

789 Days of Old Cheyenne. Republic, 1943. 55 minutes B/W. D: Elmer Clifton. SC: Norman S. Hall. WITH Don "Red" Barry, Lynn Merrick, Herbert Rawlinson, William Haade, Emmett Lynn, Robert Kortman, William Ruhl, Nolan Leary, Kenne Duncan, Eddie Parker, Bob Reeves, Art Dillard. A young man aids citizens in battling a corrupt political leader in Wyoming Territory. Typically actionful Don Barry vehicle.

790 The Dead Don't Dream. United Artists, 1948. 54 (62) minutes B/W. D: George Archainbaud. SC: Francis Rosenwald. WITH William Boyd, Andy Clyde, Rand Brooks, John Parrish, Leonard Penn, Mary Tucker, Francis McDonald, Richard Alexander, Bob Gabriel, Stanley Andrews, Forbes Murray, Don Haggerty. Hoppy, California and Lucky are at a ranch trying to find out who has killed a number of the owner's relatives. Good atmospheric mystery angle makes this one of the better of the later "Hopalong Cassidy" series films.

791 Dead Man's Gold. Screen Guild, 1948. 60 minutes B/W. D: Ray Taylor. SC: Moree Herring & Gloria Welsch. WITH Lash LaRue, Al St. John, Peggy Stewart, John Cason, Terry Frost, Lane Bradford, Pierce Lyden, Steve Keys, Cliff Taylor, Britt Wood, Marshall Reed, Bob Woodward. Two men arrive in Gold Valley to help a buddy but they run into outlaws and find their friend has been murdered. Fans of Lash LaRue-Al St. John will certainly enjoy this entry in their series.

792 Dead Man's Gulch. Republic, 1943, 56 minutes B/W. D: John English. SC: Norman S. Hall & Robert Williams. WITH Don "Red" Barry, Lynn Merrick, Rex Lease, Emmett Lynn, Clancy Cooper, Bud McTaggart, Jack Rockwell, Pierce Lyden, Lee Shumway, Robert Frazer, Robert Fiske. A one-time pony express rider finds that he is being used by crooks to help cheat ranchers on freight rates. Another good entry in the Republic Don Barry series.

793 Dead Man's Trail. Monogram, 1952. 59 minutes B/W. D: Lewis D. Collins. SC: Joseph Poland. WITH Johnny Mack Brown, James Ellison, Barbara Allen, I. Stanford Jolley, Terry Frost, Lane Bradford, Gregg Barton, Richard Avonde, Dale Van Sickel, Stanley Price. The brother of an outlaw, who has been murdered by his own gang, aids a sheriff in tracking down the badmen and recovering stolen money. Fair Johnny Mack Brown outing and his last film with James Ellison.

794 Dead or Alive. Producers Releasing Corporation, 1944. 56 minutes B/W. D: Elmer Clifton. SC: Harry Fraser. WITH Tex Ritter, Dave O'Brien, Guy Wilkerson, Marjorie Clements, Charles King, Rebel Randall, Ray Bennett, Reed Howes, Bud Osborne, Henry Hall, Ted Mapes. Three lawmen, using various guises, come to the aid of a judge who asks them to clean up an outlaw gang after a girl's ranch. Lots of action but crudely made with cheap sets and a mundane plot. Among the songs sung by Tex Ritter are "I'm Gonna Leave You Like I Found You" and "Don't Care Since You Said Goodbye."

795 Deadline. Columbia, 1931. 60 minutes B/W. D-SC: Lambert Hillyer. WITH Buck Jones, Loretta Sayers, Robert Ellis, Raymond Nye, Ed Brady, Knute Erickson, George Ernest, Harry Todd, Jack Curtis, James Farley, Robert Kortman. A quick-tempered cowboy is paroled from jail but soon finds himself in trouble with area outlaws. Exceedingly good Buck Jones vehicle thanks to a literate script and good production values.

796 Deadline. Astor, 1948. 57 minutes B/W. D: Oliver Drake. SC: C. O. (Oliver) Drake. WITH Sunset Carson, Pat Starling, Al Terry, Pat Gleason, Lee Roberts, Steven Keyes, Frank Ellis, Forrest Matthews, Robert Curtis, Philip Arnold, Joe Hiser, Don Grey, Buck Monroe, Al Wyatt. While making his final run before

the use of the telegraph, a Pony Express rider uncovers a plot by a rancher to force a company out of business and steal its lands for his own profit. Low grade and very boring Sunset Carson vehicle.

797 Deadlock. Cinerama, 1970. 94 minutes Color. D-SC: Roland Klick. WITH Mario Adorf, Anthony Dawson, Marquard Bohm, Mascha Elm Rabben. After pulling off a robbery two bandits meet in a deserted mining town to divide their loot but an old miner tries to steal it from them. Interesting West German drama.

798 The Deadly Companions. Pathe-America, 1961. 90 minutes Color. D: Sam Peckinpah. SC: A. S. Fleischman. WITH Maureen O'Hara, Steve Cochran, Brian Keith, Chill Wills, Strother Martin, Will Wright, John Hamilton, Jim O'Hara. When a former soldier accidentally shoots a boy he agrees to lead his funeral procession across the desert in Apache Territory so his mother can prove the dead boy's legitimacy. Austere oater; slow moving but not without interest.

799 The Deadley Trackers. Warner Brothers, 1973. 104 minutes Color. D: Barry Shear. SC: Lukas Heller. WITH Rod Taylor, Richard Harris, Al Lettieri, Neville Brand, William Smith, Paul Benjamin, Pedro Armendariz Jr., Kelly Jean Peters, Sean Marshal, Red Morgan, William Bryant. When outlaws rob the local bank and murder the banker's wife and son, a peaceful man sets out on the quest of avenging the crimes. Despite a good plotline, this Western is a misfire and will not likely please genre fans. Also called **Killbrand** and **Riata.**

800 Deadwood Dick. Columbia, 1940. 15 Chapters B/W. D: James W. Horne. SC: Wyndham Gittens, Morgan B. Cox, George Morgan & John Cutting. WITH Don Douglas, Lorna Gray (Adrian Booth), Harry Harvey, Marin Sais, Lane Chandler, Jack Ingram, Charles King, Ed Cassidy, Robert Fiske, Lee Shumway, Edmund Cobb, Ed Piel, Edward Hearn, Karl Hackett, Roy Barcroft, Bud Osborne, Joe Girard, Tom London, Kenne Duncan, Yakima Canutt, Fred Kelsey, Ed Cecil, Kit Guard, Al Ferguson, Franklyn Farnum, Jim Corey, Eddie Featherston, Charles Hamilton, Constantine Romanoff. Deadwood Dick, a mysterious figure of the plains, aided by Wild Bill Hickok, tries to thwart the nefarious activities of "The Skull" and his gang which has been terrorizing the area around Deadwood, South Dakota. Well done Columbia cliff-hanger which will delight serial lovers.

801 Deadwood Pass. Monarch/Freuler, 1933. 61 minutes B/W. D: J. P. McGowan. SC: John Wesley Patterson & Oliver Drake. WITH Tom Tyler, Wally Wales, Alice Dahl, Lafe McKee, Edmund Cobb. Slim Whitaker, Merrill McCormack, Carlotta Monti, Buffalo Bill Jr., Duke Lee, Blackie Whiteford, Bill Nestell, Bud Osborne. A government agent poses as the notorious outlaw "The Hawk" in order to find out where his gang has hidden stolen loot. Fast moving and action-ful Tom Tyler film; one of his better series vehicles.

802 Deadwood '76. Fairway-International, 1965. 94 minutes Color. D: James Landis. SC: Arch Hall Jr. & William Watters (Arch Hall). WITH Arch Hall Jr., Melissa Morgan, Jack Lester, William Watters (Arch Hall), Robert Dix, Rex Marlow, John Bryant, Barbara Moore, Red Morgan, John Cardos, Little Jack Little. When he heads to the Dakotas to take part in the Gold Rush, an ex-soldier is mistaken for Billy the Kid. Wild Bill Hickok, Calamity Jane, Sam Bass and Chief Crazy Horse are just a few of the historical characters who show up in this inane film which has to be seen to be believed.

803 Deaf Smith and Johnny Ears. Metro-Goldwyn-Mayer, 1973. 91 minutes Color. D: Paolo Carara. SC: Harry Esses & Oscar Saul. WITH Anthony Quinn, Franco Nero, Pamela Tiffin, Ira Furstenberg, Franco Grazios, Renato Romano, Adolfo Castretti. Two pals try to stop a would be dictator from taking over the newly founded Republic of Texas in 1836. Medi-ocre European Western which does have good interplay between the title characters played by Anthony Quinn and Franco Nero.

804 Death Goes North. Warwick Films, 1939. 56 minutes B/W. D: Frank McDonald. SC: Edward R. Austin. WITH Rin-Tin-Tin Jr., Edgar Edwards, Dorothy Bradshaw, Jameson Thomas, Walter Byron, Arthur Kerr, James McGrath. A Mountie and his dog set out to bring in a killer in the Canadian north woods. Well made and entertaining Canadian-produced programmer issued in that country in 1938 by Columbia.

805 Death Hunt. 20th Century-Fox, 1981. 97 minutes Color. D: Peter Hunt. SC:

Michael Craig & Mark Victor. WITH Charles Bronson, Lee Marvin, Andrew Stevens, Carl Weathers, Ed Lauter, Angie Dickinson, Scott Hylands, Henry Beckman, William Sanderson, Jon Cedar, James McConnell, Len Lesser, Dick Davalos, Murray Chapin, James McIntire, Rayford Barnes. In the Yukon Territory in 1931 a reclusive trapper is forced to commit murder and is hunted over the frozen wastes by a resolute Mountie and a vicious posse. Nice pictorial fact-based film, similar to **Challenge to be Free** (q.v.), colorful and entertaining. V: 20th Century-Fox Video, Cumberland Video.

806 Death of a Gunfighter. Universal, 1969. 100 minutes Color. D: Allen Smithee (Robert Totten & Donald Siegel). SC: Joseph Calvelli. WITH Richard Widmark, Lena Horne, Carroll O'Connor, John Saxon, Kent Smith, David Opatoshu, Jacqueline Scott, Morgan Woodward, Larry Gates, Dub Taylor, Victor French, Michael McGreevey, Darleen Carr, Mercer Harris, James O'Hara, Harry Carey Jr., Jimmy Lydon. An old-time marshal tries to prevent the citizens of his town from taking his job away from him. Somewhat interesting Western which was originally made for television but instead was given theatrical release.

807 Death Rides a Horse. United Artists, 1969. 114 minutes Color. D: Guilio Petroni. SC: Luciano Vincenzoni. WITH John Philip Law, Lee Van Cleef, Luigi Pistilli, Anthony Dawson, Jose Torres, Mario Brega, Carla Cassola, Archie Savage, Spoletini. Fifteen years after the brutal murder of his parents a man sets out to find the killers and joins forces with an ex-convict believing he may know the whereabouts of the murderers. Over-long, but actionful, Italian Western; mainly for Lee Van Cleef fans. Issued in Europe in 1967 by P.E.C. as **Da Uomo a Uomo** (As Man to Man).

808 Death Rides the Plains. Producers Releasing Corporation, 1943. 56 minutes B/W. D: Sam Newfield. SC: Joseph O'Don-nell. WITH Robert Livingston, Al St. John, Nica Doret, Ray Bennett, I. Stanford Jolley, George Chesebro, John Elliott, Kermit Maynard, Slim Whitaker, Karl Hackett, Frank Ellis, Ted Mapes, Jimmie Aubrey, Dan White. A rancher offers to sell his land and then kills the buyers for their money and the Lone Rider stum-bles onto his activities and sets out to stop him. Good entry in PRC's "Lone Rider" series.

Death Rides 100

809 Death Rides the Range. Colony, 1940. 58 minutes B/W. D: Sam Newfield. SC: William Lively. WITH Ken Maynard, Fay McKenzie, Ralph Peters, Julian Rivero, Charles King, John Elliott, William Costello, Swen Hugo Borg, Michael Vallen, Richard Alexander, Bud Osborne, Murdock McQuarrie, Wally West. A cowboy and his pal find themselves at odds with foreign agents who are after a helium gas deposit. An interesting plot and plenty of action make this later Ken Maynard vehicle a must-see for his fans.

810 Death Sentence. B. L. Vision, 1967. D-SC: Mario Lanfranchi. WITH Richard Conte, Robin Clarke, Adolfo Celi, Tomas Milian, Enrico Maria Salerno. A young gunman sets out to take revenge on the men who killed his brother in a robbery some years before. Typically violent spaghetti Western helped by some good acting by Richard Conte and Adolfo Celi. Italian title: **Sentenza di Morte** (Sentence of Death).

811 Death Valley. Screen Guild, 1946. 70 minutes Color. D: Lew Landers. SC: Doris Schroeder. WITH Nat Pendleton, Helen Gilbert, Robert Lowery, Sterling Holloway, Barbara Reed, Russell Simpson, Paul Hurst, Dick Scott, Stan(ley) Price, Bob Benton. A man buys a fake gold claim map in Death Valley and the lure of gold there drives him mad. Well done adventure melodrama with added attraction of being filmed on location in Cinecolor.

812 Death Valley. Universal, 1982. 87 minutes Color. D: Dick Richards. SC: Richard Rothstein. WITH Paul Le Mat, Catherine Hicks, Stephen McHattie, A. Wilford Brimley, Peter Billingsley, Edward Herrmann, Jack O'Leary. A woman, her young son and her boyfriend travel through the desert on a vacation and run into a murderous psychopath. Modern-day Western is only fairly suspenseful but genre fans will like seeing a good display of Ken Maynard film clips. V: MCA.

813 Death Valley Gunfighter. Republic, 1949. 60 minutes B/W. D: R. G. Springsteen. SC: Bob Williams. WITH Allan "Rocky" Lane, Gail Davis, Eddy Waller, Jim Nolan, William Henry, Harry Harvey, Mauritz Hugo, George Chesebro, Forrest Taylor, Lane Bradford. While looking into a payroll robbery, a peace officer is attacked by outlaws. Typically good Allan Lane Republic vehicle.

814 Death Valley Manhunt. Republic, 1943. 55 minutes B/W. D: John English. SC: Norman W. Hall & Anthony Coldeway. WITH Bill Elliott, George "Gabby" Hayes, Anne Jeffreys, Weldon Heyburn, Herbert Heyes, Davidson Clark, Pierce Lyden, Jack Kirk, Bud Geary, Marshall Reed, Charles Murray Jr., Edward Keane, Curley Dresden. Brought out of retirement by an oil company to look into the sabotage of their wells in Death Valley, Wild Bill Elliott sets out to track down the man behind the problems. Highly competent Bill Elliott vehicle with lots of action and a good script. V: Cumberland Video.

815 Death Valley Outlaws. Republic, 1941. 54 minutes B/W. D: George Sherman. SC: Don Ryan, Jack Lait Jr. WITH Don "Red" Barry, Lynn Merrick, Rex Lease, Bob McKenzie, Milburn Stone, Karl Hackett, Jack Kirk, Fred "Snowflake" Toones, Robert Kortman, Curley Dresden, John Cason, Griff Barnett, Lee Shumway, Reed Howes, George J. Lewis, Harry Strang, Michael Owen, Wally West. When his brother is missing, a young man sets out to find him and becomes involved with a lawless gang. Nice going for Don Barry in this early Republic film.

816 Death Valley Rangers. Monogram, 1943. 59 minutes B/W. D: Robert Tansey. SC: Robert Emmett (Tansey), Francis Kavanaugh & Elizabeth Beecher. WITH Ken Maynard, Hoot Gibson, Bob Steele, Linda Brent, Weldon Heyburn, Bryant Washburn, Glenn Strange, Forrest Taylor, Karl Hackett, Charles King, George Chesebro, John Bridges, Al Ferguson, Steve Clark, Wally West. The Trail Blazers trio try to aid a town against a gang of gold shipment robbers by having Bob masquerade as an outlaw and join the gang. Good "Trail Blazers" series entry which moves very quickly with the three heroes in good form.

817 Decision at Sundown. Columbia, 1957. 95 minutes Color. D: Budd Boetticher. SC: Charles Lang Jr. WITH Randolph Scott, John Carroll, Karen Steele, Valerie French, Noah Beery Jr., John Archer, Andrew Duggan, James Westerfield, John Litel, Ray Teal, Vaughn Taylor, Richard Deacon, H. M. Wynant, Guy Wilkerson, Bob Steele, Abel Fernandez, Reed Howes, Jim Hayward. A man searches for three years for the man who stole his wife and he finds him in a small town just as he is about to marry a local girl. Highly competent and brooding Western; one of Randolph Scott's best.

818 Deep in the Heart of Texas. Universal, 1942. 62 minutes B/W. D: Elmer Clifton. SC: Grace Norton. WITH Johnny Mack Brown, Tex Ritter, Jennifer Holt, Fuzzy Knight, William Farnum, Harry Woods, Kenneth Harlan, Pat O'Malley, Eddie Polo, Earle Hodgins, Roy Brent, Edmund Cobb, Rod Cameron, The Jimmy Wakely Trio (Jimmy Wakely, Johnny Bond, Scotty Harrell), Budd Buster, Frank Ellis. A man returns home as the commissioner of public affairs and finds himself at odds with his father, the leader of a guerilla band. Good drama, action, and nice music makes this one fine viewing.

819 Deep Valley. Warner Brothers, 1947. 104 minutes B/W. D: Jean Negulesco. SC: Salka Vietrel & Stephen Morehouse Avery. WITH Ida Lupino, Dane Clark, Wayne Morris, Fay Bainter, Henry Hull, Willard Robertson. The life of a bitter and lonely farm girl changes when she meets an escapee from a chain gang. Downbeat and brooding drama which makes for good entertainment.

820 The Deerslayer. Cameo Distributing, 1923. 60 minutes B/W. D: Arthur Wellin. SC: Robert Heymann. WITH Emil Mamelok, Bela Lugosi, Herta Heden, Gottfried Kraus, Edward Eyseneck, Margot Sokolowska. Hawkeye and his Indian blood brother Chingachgook aid British settlers harassed by the French and Indians in upper New York state. Picturesque, but jumbled, German silent version of the James Fenimore Cooper novel originally issued in Europe in 1920 by Luna Film as **Lederstrumpf** (Leatherstocking); heavily cut but still worth seeing for Bela Lugosi's performance as Chingachgook.

821 The Deerslayer. Republic, 1943. 67 minutes B/W. D: Lew Landers. SC: P. S. Harrison & E. B. Derr. WITH Bruce Kellogg, Jean Parker, Larry Parks, Warren Ashe, Wanda McKay, Yvonne De Carlo, Addison Richards, Robert Warwick, Johnny Michaels, Philip Van Zandt, Trevor Bardette, Chief Many Treaties. Natty Bumppo, the Deerslayer, comes to the aid of a tribe whose pretty princess is coveted by a rival Huron brave who burns their village and kidnaps the maiden. Tacky presentation of the James Fenimore Cooper story; for the record, Republic issued this independent production from producers P. S. Harrison and E. B. Derr, who also wrote the script.

822 The Deerslayer. 20th Century-Fox, 1957. 78 minutes Color. D-SC: Kurt Neumann. WITH Lex Barker, Forrest Tucker, Cathy O'Donnell, Rita Moreno, Jay C. Flippen, Carlos Rivas, John Halloran, Joseph Vitale, Rocky Shahan, Carol Henry. Hawkeye and his Mohican blood brother try to avert an Indian war when they find out that a white man, living on an isolated island fort with his two daughters, is a scalp hunter. Colorful adaptation of the James Fenimore Cooper novel.

823 The Deerslayer. NBC-TV/Schick Sunn Classics, 1978. 74 minutes Color. D: Dick Friedenbert. SC: S. S. Schweitzer. WITH Steve Forrest, Ned Romero, John Anderson, Victor Mohica, Joan Prather, Charles Dierkop, Brian Davies, Ted Hamilton, Madeline Stowe, Ruben Moreno, Alma Bettran. When an Indian chief's lovely daughter is kidnapped by a rival tribe, Hawkeye and Chingachgook come to their aid. "Classics Illustrated" TV version of the Cooper novel; pretty good viewing. Follow-up to the previous year's **The Last of the Mohicans** (q.v.).

Deliver Us from Evil see **Running Wild**

824 Deliver Us from Evil. ABC-TV, 1973. 78 minutes Color. D: Boris Sagal. SC: Jack B. Sowards. WITH George Kennedy, Jan-Michael Vincent, Bradford Dillman, Jim Davis, Charles Aidman, Jack Weston, Allen Pinson. Five men on a hiking trip in the mountains run across an injured skykacker with $600,000 and they kill him and then fall out among themselves. Fairly entertaining TV feature.

825 A Demon for Trouble. Supreme, 1934. 58 minutes B/W. D: Robert Hill. SC: Jack Natteford. WITH Bob Steele, Gloria Shea, Walter McGrail, Don Alvarado, Lafe McKee, Nick Stuart, Carmen LaRoux, Perry Murdock, Blackie Whiteford, Jimmie Aubrey. A cowboy uncovers a murder plot in which land buyers are murdered and their money stolen after they have purchased range land. Very good Bob Steele vehicle.

826 Denver and the Rio Grande. Paramount, 1952. 89 minutes Color. D: Byron Haskin. SC: Frank Gruber. WITH Edmond O'Brien, Sterling Hayden, Dean Jagger, Laura Elliott, Lyle Bettger, J. Carrol Naish, ZaSu Pitts, Tom Powers, Robert Barrat, Paul Fix, Don Haggerty, James Burke. Two rival companies compete in the building of the Denver and Rio Grande railroad in the 1870s. Competent oater with a good script and cast.

827 The Denver Kid. Republic, 1948. 60 minutes B/W. D: Philip Ford. SC: Bob Williams. WITH Allan "Rocky" Lane, Eddy Waller, Carole Gallagher, William Henry, Douglas Fowley, Rory Mallinson, George Lloyd, George Meeker, Emmett Vogan, Hank Patterson, Tom Steele. A border patrol agent is after a notorious murderer. Nicely staged Allan Lane vehicle.

The Deputies see **Law of the Land**

828 Deputy Marshal. Lippert, 1949. 75 minutes B/W. D-SC: William Berke. WITH Frances Langford, Jon Hall, Dick Foran, Julie Bishop, Russell Hayden, Joseph Sawyer, Clem Bevans, Vince Barnett, Mary Gordon, Kenne Duncan, Stanley Blystone, Wheaton Chambers, Forrest Taylor, Ted Adams. A lawman is on the trail of gunmen brothers and a map belonging to the railroad. Outside of the cast, there is not a whole lot to recommend this pedestrian oater.

829 Desert Bandit. Republic, 1941. 54 minutes B/W. D: George Sherman. SC: Eliot Gibbons & Bennett Cohen. WITH Don "Red" Barry, Lynn Merrick, James Gilette, William Haade, Dick Wessell, Tom Chatterton, Robert Strange, Curley Dresden, Jim Corey, Merrill McCormack, Charles King, Jack Montgomery, Jack O'Shea, Tom Ewell. Texas Rangers are on the trail of a band of gun smugglers. Very actionful outing in the Republic-Don Barry series. V: Cumberland Video.

830 Desert Gold. Paramount, 1936. 58 minutes B/W. D: James Hogan. SC: Stuart Anthony & Robert Yost. WITH Larry "Buster" Crabbe, Robert Cummings, Marsha Hunt, Tom Keene, Monte Blue, Raymond Hatton, Glenn (Leif) Erickson, Walter Miller, Frank Mayo, Philip Morris. An outlaw gang leader tries to kidnap a girl who is loved by a soldier and his Eastern friend. Sturdy programmer adaptation of the Zane Grey novel first filmed by Paramount in 1926 with Neil Hamilton, Shirley Mason, Robert Frazer and William Powell.

831 Desert Guns. Beaumont, 1936. 60 minutes B/W. D: Charles Hutchison. SC: Jacques Jaccard. WITH Conway Tearle, Margaret Morris, Charles K. French, Budd Buster, William Gould, Marie Werner, Kate Brinker, Duke Lee, Art Felix, Slim Whitaker, Bull Montana. A lawman pretends to be a girl's long-lost brother in order to save her inheritance from crooks. Stilted poverty row Conway Tearle series vehicle, although the star makes a good genre hero even in his 50s. V: Cassette Express.

832 The Desert Horseman. Columbia, 1946. 57 minutes B/W. D: Ray Nazarro. SC: Sherman Lowe. WITH Charles Starrett, Smiley Burnette, Adelle Roberts, Richard Bailey, John Merton, Walt Shrum & His Colorado Hillbillies, George Morgan, Tommy Coates, Jack Kirk, Bud Osborne, Riley Hill. Falsely accused of robbing an army payroll, a captain takes on the alias of the Durango Kid to clear himself and find the real culprit. Fairly good "Durango Kid" series entry.

833 Desert Justice. Atlantic, 1936. 60 minutes B/W. D: Lester Williams (William Berke). SC: Gordon Phillips & Lewis Kingdom. WITH Jack Perrin, Maryan Downing, Warren Hymer, David Sharpe, Dennis Meadows (Dennis Moore), Roger Williams, Budd Buster, William Gould, Fred "Snowflake" Toones, Earl Dwire, Starlight (horse), Braveheart (dog). Border patrolman Casey is on the trail of a gang of smugglers. Cheaply made, but Jack Perrin is a pleasing player.

834 Desert of Lost Men. Republic, 1951. 54 minutes B/W. D: Harry Keller. SC: M. Coates Webster. WITH Allan "Rocky" Lane, Mary Ellen Kay, Irving Bacon, Roy Barcroft, Ross Elliott, Cliff Clark, Red Morgan, Kenneth MacDonald. A deputy marshal sets out to track down and capture an outlaw gang made up of notorious badmen from all over the West. Interesting plot adds zest to this Allan Lane opus.

835 Desert Passage. RKO Radio, 1952. 61 minutes B/W. D: Lesley Selander. SC: Norman Houston. WITH Tim Holt, Richard Martin, Joan Dixon, Walter Reed, Clayton Moore, Dorothy Patrick, John Dehner, Lane Bradford, Denver Pyle, Francis McDonald. After he is paroled from prison, a man sets out to find hidden bank robbery money but he is trailed by a crooked lawyer and a gunman. Tim Holt's final "B" film is a good one with a literate script and fine acting.

836 Desert Patrol. Republic, 1938. 60 minutes B/W. D: Sam Newfield. SC: Fred Myton. WITH Bob Steele, Marion Weldon, Rex Lease, Ted Adams, Forrest Taylor, Budd Buster, Steve Clark, Jack Ingram, Tex Palmer. After a fellow ranger is killed, a member of the Texas Rangers sets out to get the smuggling gang who murdered him. The revenge plot is typical for a Bob Steele oater and this one is a good entry in his series for A. W. Hackel.

837 The Desert Phantom. Supreme, 1936. 66 minutes B/W. D: S. Roy Luby. SC: Earle Snell. WITH Johnny Mack Brown, Sheila Mannors, Ted Adams, Karl Hackett, Hal Price, Nelson McDowell, Charles King, Forrest Taylor. A man is hired by a girl to protect her ranch, which is being raided by an outlaw gang. Cheaply made but more than passable Johnny Mack Brown entry for producer A. W. Hackel.

838 Desert Pursuit. Monogram, 1952. 71 minutes B/W. D: George Blair. SC: W. Scott Darling. WITH Wayne Morris, Virginia Grey, Anthony Caruso, George Tobias, Gloria Talbott, Emmett Lynn, Frank Lackteen, John Doucette, Robert Bice. A prospector and a fortune-hunting girl are hunted by an outlaw gang as they search for gold hidden in the California desert. Low budget but entertaining "B" outing.

839 The Desert Rider. Sunset, 1923. 45 minutes B/W. D: Robert North Bradbury. WITH Jack Hoxie, Evelyn Nelson, Frank Rice, Claude Peyton, Tom Lingham, Walter Wilkinson. A cowboy finds a dying miner and plans to take care of his young son and at the same time find the man's claim and bring in his killer. Somewhat drawn out, but still entertaining, Jack Hoxie silent affair, although not one of his better efforts.

840 The Desert Trail. Monogram, 1935. 54 minutes B/W. D: Cullen Lewis. SC: Lindsley Parsons. WITH John Wayne, Mary Kornman, Paul Fix, Eddie Chandler, Carmen LaRoux, Al Ferguson, Lafe McKee, Henry Hall. A rodeo star and his gambler pal are falsely accused of having committed a hold-up and set out to clear their names and catch the culprits. A bit stilted, but still pleasing Lone Star production. V: Video Dimensions.

841 Desert Vengeance. Columbia, 1931. 55 minutes B/W. D: Louis King. SC: Stuart Anthony. WITH Buck Jones, Barbara Bedford, Douglas Gilmore, Al Smith, Ed Brady, Buck Connors, Gilbert "Pee Wee" Holmes, Slim Whitaker, Robert Ellis, Bob Fleming, Joe Girard, Barney Bearsley. A bandit who runs a remote town stronghold falls in love with a girl

who deceives him but he saves her when she is left to die in the desert by her partner and the two face an attack by a rival gang. The plot is a bit different for a Buck Jones film but overall the picture is quite good.

842 Desert Vigilante. Columbia, 1949. 56 minutes B/W. D: Fred F. Sears. SC: Earle Snell. WITH Charles Starrett, Smiley Burnette, Peggy Stewart, Tristram Coffin, The Georgia Crackers, Mary Newton, George Chesebro, Jack Ingram, Paul Campbell, Tex Harding, I. Stanford Jolley, Ted Mapes. A government agent is on the trail of silver smugglers working along the Mexican border and he meets a pretty girl whose uncle has been killed by the band. Mediocre "Durango Kid" series film.

843 A Desert Wooing. Paramount, 1918. 55 minutes B/W. D: Jerome Storm. WITH Enid Bennett, Jack Holt, Donald Mac-Donald, John P. Lockney, Charles Spere, Elinor Hancock. A woman in need of money sells her pretty daughter in marriage to a rugged rancher and the girl eventually learns to love her husband. Thomas H. Ince supervised this curio which will be of interest to Jack Holt fans.

844 The Deserter. Triangle, 1916. 59 minutes B/W. D: Walter Edwards. SC: R. V. Spencer. WITH Charles Ray, Rita Stanwood, Wedgwood Nowell, Hazel Belford, Joseph Dowling. A soldier is spurned by a colonel's daughter and after a fight with another soldier deserts his post but eventually proves that he is a hero in a fight with Indians. Fairly actionful silent drama.

845 The Deserter. Paramount, 1971. 99 minutes Color. D: Burt Kennedy. SC: Clair Huffaker. WITH Bekim Fehmiu, Richard Crenna, Chuck Connors, Ricardo Montalban, Brandon De Wilde, Slim Pickens, Albert Salmi, Woody Strode, Patrick Wayne, Ian Bannen, John Huston. A cavalryman deserts from the Army to carry on a one-man war against the Apaches for the mutilation of his wife. Passable actioner but nothing more.

846 The Desperado. Allied Artists, 1954. 82 minutes B/W. D: Thomas Carr. SC: Geoffrey Homes. WITH Wayne Morris, Beverly Garland, James Lydon, Dabbs Greer, Rayford Barnes, Lee Van Cleef, Nestor Paiva, Roy Barcroft, John Dierkes, I. Stanford Jolley, Florence Lake. A young lawman teams with an outlaw to oppose the carpetbagger government in Texas in 1870. Nicely done "B" outing and one of the last series Westerns.

847 The Desperado Trail. Constantin, 1965. 93 minutes Color. D: Harald Reinl. SC: Harald G. Petersson. WITH Lex Barker, Pierre Brice, Rik Battaglia, Ralf Wolter, Carl Lange, Sophie Hardy. Land specualtors try to get Indians on the warpath to steal their lands but Shatterhand and Winnetou try to stop them. Familiar but very entertaining West German oater in the Karl May series. Released in Europe by Rialto/Jadran-Film as **Winnetou III.**

848 The Desperadoes. Columbia, 1943. 85 minutes Color. D: Charles Vidor. SC: Robert Carson. WITH Randolph Scott, Claire Trevor, Glenn Ford, Evelyn Keyes, Edgar Buchanan, Raymond Walburn, Guinn Williams, Irving Bacon, Porter Hall, Joan Woodbury, Glenn Strange, Bernard Nedell, Ethan Laidlaw, Slim Whitaker, Edward Pawley, Chester Clute. A lawman reforms a young hellion and the two team to round up an outlaw gang. Well made and quite entertaining.

849 The Desperadoes. Columbia, 1969. 90 minutes Color. D: Henry Levin. SC: Walter Brough. WITH Vincent Edwards, Jack Palance, George Maharis, Neville Brand, Sylvia Syms, Christian Roberts, Kate O'Mara. After the Civil War a father and his three sons go West and lead an outlaw band but one son deserts and marries and settles down only to find his land invaded by his own family. Fairly interesting and entertaining oater.

850 The Desperadoes Are in Town. 20th Century-Fox, 1956. 78 minutes B/W. D: Kurt Neumann. SC: Earle Snell & Kurt Neumann. WITH Robert Arthur, Kathy Nolan, Rhys Williams, Rhodes Reason, Dave O'Brien, Kelly Thordsen, Mae Clarke, Robert Osterloh. When a former outlaw befriends a young man and is then killed by two ex-partners, the young man sets out to revenge his death. Uninteresting and dull.

851 Desperadoes of Dodge City. Republic, 1948. 60 minutes B/W. D: Philip Ford. SC: Bob Williams. WITH Allan "Rocky" Lane, Eddy Waller, Mildred Coles, Tristram Coffin, Roy Barcroft, William Phipps, James Craven, John Hamilton, Ed Cassidy, House Peters Jr., Dale Van Sickel, Ted Mapes. An outlaw gang is out to stop a wagon train of settlers. Mystery element helps this Allan Lane vehicle.

852 Desperadoes of the West. Republic, 1950. 12 Chapters. D: Fred C. Brannon. SC: Ronald Davidson. WITH Richard Powers (Tom Keene), Judy Clark, Roy Barcroft, I. Stanford Jolley, Lee Phelps, Lee Roberts, Cliff Clark, Edmund Cobb, Dale Van Sickel, Tom Steele, Sandy Sanders, John Cason, Guy Teague, Bud Osborne, Stanley Blystone, Chuck Hayward, Frank O'Connor, George Chesebro, Art Dillard, Holly Bane, Duke Taylor, Cactus Mack, Ken Cooper, Dennis Moore, Steve Clark, Chick Hannon, Mauritz Hugo, Al Taylor, Bob Reeves, Eddie Parker, Fred Kohler Jr., Harold Goodwin, Jack Ingram, Augie Gomez, Merrill McCormack. A crook and his outlaw gang try to prevent ranchers from successfully drilling for oil so he can get the lease on their oil rich properties for his eastern syndicate bosses. Action filled Republic cliffhanger starring Tom Keene.

853 Desperadoes' Outpost. Republic, 1952. 54 minutes B/W. D: Philip Ford. SC: Albert DeMond & Arthur Orloff. WITH Allan "Rocky" Lane, Eddy Waller, Roy Barcroft, Myron Healey, Lyle Talbot, Claudia Barrett, Lee Roberts, Lane Bradford, Ed Cassidy. When a number of stagecoaches are mysteriously sabotaged, a government agent sets out to find the culprits. Another good entry in the Allan Lane series.

854 Desperate Chance. Rayart, 1926. 55 minutes B/W. D: J. P. McGowan. SC: Charles Saxton. WITH Bob Reeves, Ione Reed, Leon De La Mothe, Charles "Slim" Whitaker, Gypsy Clarke, Harry Hurley. Two men set out to get even with a businessman who has harmed them and when he is murdered one of them is accused of the crime. Low grade silent Bob Reevers actioner.

855 Desperate Mission. ABC-TV/20th Century-Fox, 1971. 98 minutes Color. D: Earl Bellamy. SC: Jack Guss & Richard Collins. WITH Ricardo Montalban, Slim Pickens, Rosey (Roosevelt) Grier, Ina Balin, Earl Holliman, Miriam Colon, Jim McMullan, Armando Silvestre, Robert Wilke, Anthony Caruso, Charles Horvath, Barbara Turner. A bandit aids the locals in Spanish California in fighting outlaws and crooked government officials. Another telling of the story of Joaquin Murieta, with Ricardo Montalban good in the title role, but overall a mediocre film. Initially released abroad in 1970 as **Joaquin Murieta** and **Murieta.**

856 Desperate Search. Metro-Goldwyn-Mayer, 1953. 73 minutes B/W. D: Joseph H. Lewis. SC: Walter Doniger. WITH Howard Keel, Jane Greer, Keenan Wynn, Robert Burton, Lee Aaker, Linda Lowell, Michael Dugan, Elaine Stewart, Jonathan Cott, Jeff Richards, Dick (Richard) Simmons. After his children are stranded in the Canadian northwoods following a plane crash, a man sets out to find them. Low budget but well done and exciting drama.

Desperate Siege see **Rawhide** (1950)

857 Desperate Trails. Universal, 1939. 58 minutes B/W. D: Albert Ray. SC: Andrew Bennison. WITH Johnny Mack Brown, Bob Baker, Fuzzy Knight, Frances Robinson, Russell Simpson, Clarence Wilson, Bill Cody Jr., Ralph Dunn, Charles Stevens, Ed Cassidy, Horace Murphy, Fern Emmett, Frank Ellis, Frank McCarroll, Cliff Lyons, Eddie Parker. A crooked sheriff and banker are behind a group of night riders who are trying to rustle a girl's horses. Johnny Mack Brown's first Universal series film and it is a good one.

858 Desperate Women. NBC-TV, 1978. 100 minutes Color. D: Earl Bellamy. SC: Jack B. Sowards. WITH Susan Saint James, Dan Haggerty, Ronee Blakley, Ann Dusenberry, Susan Mayers, Randy Powell, Max Gail, Michael Delano, Taylor Larcher, Tiger Williams, Bob Hoy, James Griffith, Rudy Diaz, John Crawford, Clint Ritchie, William Vaughan, Ed Fury. Three women prisoners and two orphaned children are left in the desert with an Army deserter and they team with a gunman to oppose an outlaw gang. Passable TV movie, nothing more.

859 Destry. Universal, 1955. 95 minutes Color. D: George Marshall. SC: Felix Jackson, Edmund H. North & D. D. Beauchamp. WITH Audie Murphy, Mari Blanchard, Lyle Bettger, Lori Nelson, Thomas Mitchell, Edgar Buchanan, Wallace Ford, Mary Wickes, Alan Hale Jr., Lee Aaker, Trevor Bardette, Walter Baldwin. A shy young man becomes the sheriff of a rough town and falls for a saloon singer. The third screen version of the Max Brand story; not bad but hardly as good as the two earlier versions of **Destry Rides Again** (q.v.).

860 Destry Rides Again. Universal, 1932. 64 minutes B/W. D: Ben Stoloff. SC: Richard Schayer & Robert Keith. WITH Tom Mix, Claudia Dell, Stanley Fields, ZaSu Pitts, Earle Fox, Ed Piel Sr., Francis Ford, Frederick Howard, George Ernest, John Ince, Ed LeSaint, Charles K. French. A cowboy intends to clean up a corrupt town by running for sheriff but crooks frame him on a murder charge. Tom Mix's first sound feature and it is a good one, proving why he is one of the all-time great stars of the genre. TV title: **Justice Rides Again.** V: Cassette Express.

861 Destry Rides Again. Universal, 1939. 94 minutes B/W. D: George Marshall. SC: Felix Jackson, Gertrude Purcell & Henry Myers. WITH Marlene Dietrich, James Stewart, Mischa Auer, Charles Winninger, Brian Donlevy, Allen Jenkins, Warren Hymer, Irene Hervey, Una Merkel, Tom Fadden, Samuel S. Hinds, Lillian Yarbo, Edmund MacDonald, Billy Gilbert, Virginia Brissac, Ann Todd, Dickie Jones, Jack Carson, Joe King, Harry Cording, Richard Alexander, Bill (Steele) Gettinger, Minerva Urecal, Bob McKenzie, Billy Bletcher, Lloyd Ingraham, Bill Cody Jr., Harry Tenbrook, Chief Big Tree, Philo McCullough. A young tenderfoot is drafted into becoming marshal of a rough town and falls under the spell of a seductive saloon singer. Remake of the Max Brand novel which still holds up well today, mainly for James Stewart's performance as Destry and for Marlene Dietrich's singing "See What the Boys in the Backroom Will Have."

862 The Devil and Miss Sarah. ABC-TV/Universal, 1971. 73 minutes Color. D: Michael Caffey. SC: Calvin Clements. WITH Gene Barry, James Drury, Janice Rule, Charles McGraw, Slim Pickens, Logan Ramsey, Donald Moffat. A young couple take a gunman to the nearest law and along the way the badman uses his hypnotic powers to take possession of the young wife. There is not much to recommend this TV made horror-Western.

863 The Devil Horse. Pathe, 1926. 50 minutes B/W. D: Fred Jackman. SC: Hal Roach. WITH Rex (horse), Yakima Canutt, Gladys Morrow, Robert Kortman, Roy Clements, Fred Jackson, Killer (horse). A man, the sole survivor of an Indian massacre as a boy, is aided by a wild stallion in rescuing a major's daughter who has been kidnapped by a renegade Indian. Very actionful silent feature.

864 The Devil Horse. Mascot, 1932. 12 Chapters B/W. D: Otto Brower. SC: George

Morgan, Barney A. Sarecky, George Plympton & Wyndham Gittens. WITH Harry Carey, Noah Beery, Frankie Darro, Greta Granstedt, Barrie O'Daniels, Ed Peil, Jack Mower, Al Bridge, Jack Byron, J. Paul Jones, Carli Russell, Lou Kelley, Dick Dickinson, Lane Chandler, Fred Burns, Yakima Canutt, Ken Cooper, Wes Warner, Al Taylor, Apache (horse). A man tries to capture a wild horse and in doing so kills a forest ranger and the man's brother swears revenge and enlists the aid of a boy who has run with the wild horse herd since he was a child. There is plenty of action in this Nat Levine production but genre purists may be put out by excessive "cheat" footage. Also issued in a feature version. V: Cassette Express.

865 Devil on Horseback. Grand National, 1936. 71 minutes B/W. D-SC: Crane Wilbur. WITH Lili Damita, Fred Keating, Del Campo. Tiffany Thayer, Jean Chatburn, Renee Torres, Juan Torena, Blanca Visher. A visiting radio star and her troupe are kidnapped and held for ransom by a Central American ranch owner. Dull comedy-drama shot in Hirlicolor by producer George A. Hirliman.

866 The Devil Riders. Producers Releasing Corporation, 1943. 59 minutes B/W. D: Sam Newfield. SC: Joseph O'Donnell. WITH Buster Crabbe, Al St. John, Patti McCarthy, Charles King, John Merton, Kermit Maynard, Frank LaRue, Jack Ingram, George Chesebro, Ed Cassidy, Al Ferguson, Frank Ellis, Bert Dillard, Bud Osborne, Artie Ortego, Herman Hack. A crooked lawyer and his pal are after land the government has designated for a stage route and Billy the Kid helps the stage company owner combat the villain. Okay PRC entry in its "Billy the Kid" series.

867 The Devil's Bedroom. Allied Artists, 1963. 72 minutes B/W. D: L. Q. Jones. SC: Claude Hall & Morgan Woodward. WITH John Lupton, Valerie Allen, Dick Jones, Alvy Moore. When they find out a property is located on a valuable oil deposit, a couple tries to drive the owner insane in order to obtain his ranch. Obscure effort from the production team of Alvy Moore and L. Q. Jones.

868 Devil's Canyon. RKO Radio, 1953. 92 minutes Color. D: Alfred Werker. SC: Frederick Hazlitt Brennan & Harry Essex. WITH Virginia Mayo, Dale Robertson, Stephen McNally, Arthur Hunnicutt,

Robert Keith, Jay C. Flippen, George J. Lewis, Whit Bissell, Morris Ankrum, James Bell, William Phillips, Earl Holliman, Irving Bacon. After killing two men in self-defense, a marshal is railroaded into prison where he becomes involved in a riot. Offbeat Western; not without interest.

869 Devil's Doorway. Metro-Goldwyn-Mayer, 1950. 84 minutes B/W. D: Anthony Mann. SC: Guy Trosper. WITH Robert Taylor, Paula Raymond, Louis Calhern, Marshall Thompson, James Mitchell, Edgar Buchanan, Rhys Williams, Spring Byington, James Millican, Fritz Leiber, Chief Big Tree. A Shoshone Indian who fought for the North during the Civil War and honored for bravery, returns home to find he has to fight to save his people's lands. Robert Taylor is quite good as the Indian brave and this outing is well worth viewing.

870 The Devil's Mistress. Emerson, 1968. 66 minutes Color. D-SC: Orville Wanzer. WITH Joan Stapleton, Robert Gregory, Forest Westmoreland, Douglas Warren, Oren Williams, Arthur Resley. Four cowboys murder a man and take his wife as their servant and she sets out to take revenge on them. Low budget effort filmed in New Mexico.

871 The Devil's Partner. Mutual/Truart, 1926. 50 minutes B/W. D-SC: Frederick Becker. WITH Edward Hearn, Nancy Deaver, Philo McCullough, Carl Stockdale, Florence Lee, Will Walling, Harvey Clark, Billie Lattimer, Fred Beker, Hayden Stevenson. The leader of a rustling gang has a romantic rival framed for a crime and then kidnaps the girl. Poverty row silent actioner which should please genre fans.

872 The Devil's Partner. American-International/Filmgroup, 1962. 61 minutes B/W. D: Charles Rondeau. SC: Stanley Clements & Laura Mathews. WITH Ed Nelson, Richard Crane, Edgar Buchanan, Jean Allison, Spencer Carlisle, Byron Foulger, Claire Carleton. When his uncle dies, a young man comes to a small Western town and mysterious things begin to happen. Low budget, and low grade, horror-Western which was originally filmed in 1958.

873 The Devil's Playground. United Artists, 1946. 54 (62) minutes B/W. D: George Archainbaud. SC: Doris Schroeder. WITH William Boyd, Andy Clyde, Rand Brooks,

Elaine Riley, Robert Elliott, Joseph J. Greene, Francis McDonald, Ned Young, George Eldredge, Earle Hodgins, Everett Shields, John George, Glenn Strange. Hoppy, California and Lucky try to help a girl who is hunted by a crooked judge who wants her "friend's" gold. Lots of action, a good story and nice locations in this later "Hopalong Cassidy" entry.

874 The Devil's Rain. Bryanston, 1975. 86 minutes Color. D: Robert Fuest. SC: Gabe Essoe, James Ashton & Gerald Hopman. WITH Ernest Borgnine, Eddie Albert, William Shatner, Ida Lupino, Tom Skeritt, Joan Prather, Keenan Wynn, Woodrow Chambliss, George Sawaya, Lisa Todd, Claudio Brook, Anton LaVey, John Travolta, Robert Wallace, Erika Carlson, Tony Cortez. A man finds himself the victim of a cult of devil worshippers in a Western town. Awful horror film set in the modern-day West.

875 Devil's Saddle Legion. Warner Brothers, 1937. 52 minutes B/W. D: Bobby Connolly. SC: Ed Earl Repp. WITH Dick Foran, Anne Nagel, Willard Parker, Granville Owen, Carlyle Moore Jr., Gordon Hart, Max Hoffman Jr., Glenn Strange, Frank Orth, Jack Mower, Milton Kibbee, George Chesebro, Ray Bennett, Dick Botiller, Bud Osborne, Art Mix, Artie Ortego, Ben Corbett. A young man is falsely accused of being an outlaw gang leader and is sent to work on a gang building a dam which is designed to divert water needed by ranchers. More than passable entry in Dick Foran's Warner Brothers series.

The Devil's Spawn see **The Last Gunfighter**

876 The Devil's Trail. Columbia, 1942. 61 minutes B/W. D: Lambert Hillyer. SC: Robert Lee Johnson. WITH Bill Elliott, Tex Ritter, Eileen O'Hearn, Noah Beery, Frank Mitchell, Ruth Ford, Art Mix, Joel Friedkin, Joe McGuinn, Edmund Cobb, Tristram Coffin, Paul Newland, Steve Clark, Sarah Padden, Bud Osborne, Stanley Brown, Buck Moulton. During the period when the slavery question was raised in Kansas, a federal marshal tries to aid his pal Wild Bill Hickok who has been falsely accused of murder. Top notch effort in the Bill Elliott-Tex Ritter series with writer Robert Lee Johnson adapting the screenplay from his story "The Town in Hell's Backyard"; a grand performance by Noah Beery as villain Bull McQuade.

877 The Diamond Trail. Monogram, 1932. 60 minutes B/W. D: Harry Fraser. SC: Harry Fraser & Sherman Lowe. WITH Rex Bell, Frances Rich, Lloyd Whitlock, Bud Osborne, Norman Feusier, Jerry Storm, John Webb Dillon, Billy West, Harry LaMont. A New York City reporter infiltrates a band of jewel thieves who head West to murder a cattleman who has worked as a go-between for the gang. Only fair.

878 Dig That Uranium. Allied Artists, 1956. 61 minutes B/W. D: Edward Bernds. SC: Elwood Ullman & Bert Lawrence. WITH Leo Gorcey, Huntz Hall, Bernard Gorcey, Mary Beth Hughes, Raymond Hatton, Myron Healey, Richard Powers (Tom Keene), Harry Lauter, Francis McDonald, David Gorcey, Bennie Bartlett, Paul Fierro, Frank Jenks, Don C. Harvey, Carl "Alfalfa" Switzer. The Bowery Boys buy a mine in Nevada but when they arrive to claim it they find themselves at odds with crooks. Typically amusing outing in the "Bowery Boys" series.

879 Dirty Dingus Magee. Metro-Goldwyn-Mayer, 1970. 79 (91) minutes Color. D: Burt Kennedy. SC: Tom Waldman, Frank Waldman & Joseph Heller. WITH Frank Sinatra, George Kennedy, Anne Jackson, Lois Nettleton, Jack Elam, Michele Carey, John Dehner, Henry Jones, Harry Carey Jr., Paul Fix, Donald (Don "Red") Barry, Mike Wagner, Terry Wilson, Tom Fadden, Lisa Todd, Carol Anderson, Grady Sutton. A small-time crook and saddle tramp has his troubles in a Western town with a dumb sheriff, woman mayor-madam, Indians and the Army. Unfunny Western spoof, badly cut for TV release.

880 Dirty Little Billy. Columbia, 1972. 100 minutes Color. D: Stan Dragoti. SC: Charles Moss & Stan Dragoti. WITH Michael J. Pollard, Lee Purcell, Richard Evans, Charles Aidman, Dran Hamilton, Willard Sage, Josip Elic, Mills Watson, Alex Wilson, Ronnie Graham, Dick Stahl, Gary Busey, Doug Dirksen, Cherie Franklin, Dick Van Patten, Rosary Nix, Frank Welker. The story of the early years of Billy the Kid and how he got into a life of crime. Low class biopic not likely to appeal to genre followers.

881 The Dirty Outlaws. Transvue, 1971. 103 minutes Color. D-SC: Franco Rossetti. WITH Chip Gorman (Andrea Giordana), Rosemarie Dexter, Franco Giornelli, Dana Ghia, Aldo Berti, Giovanni Petrucci,

John Janos Bartha. A man tries to pass himself off as a blindman's son in order to get gold buried in a deserted town but he soon finds an outlaw gang is also after the riches. Another in the long line of violent spaghetti Westerns. Originally issued in Italy in 1967 by Daiano/ Leone Film as **El Desperado** (The Desperado).

882 The Disciple. Ince/Triangle, 1915. 60 minutes B/W. D: William S. Hart & Clifford Smith. WITH William S. Hart, Dorothy Dalton, Robert McKim, Charles French, Thelma Salter. In a small Western town a new "sky pilot" loses his wife to a gambler and denounces God only to return to the faith when his small daughter becomes sick. Well done silent William S. Hart morality film with none of the slickness associated with later genre movies. V: Classic Video Cinema Collectors Club.

Disciples of Death see **Enter the Devil**

883 Distant Drums. Warner Brothers, 1951. 101 minutes Color. D: Raoul Walsh. SC: Niven Busch & Martin Rackin. WITH Gary Cooper, Mari Aldon, Richard Webb, Ray Teal, Arthur Hunnicutt, Robert Barrat, Clancy Cooper, Dan White, Lee Roberts, Gregg Barton, Sheb Wooley. An Indian fighter leads troops to the Florida Everglades to put down a Seminole uprising. Filmed in Florida, this is hardly one of Gary Cooper's better genre outings.

884 A Distant Trumpet. Warner Brothers, 1964. 116 minutes Color. D: Raoul Walsh. SC: John Twist. WITH Troy Donahue, Suzanne Pleschette, James Gregory, Diane McBain, William Reynolds, Claude Akins, Kent Smith, Judson Pratt, Bartlett Robinson, Bobby Bare, Richard X. Slattery, Guy Eltsosis, Larry Ward, Mary Patton, Russell Johnson, Lane Bradford. At a frontier cavalry post, an officer falls in love with a lieutenant's wife and when the man is killed, the officer's fiancee arrives on the scene just as an Indian attack is imminent. Raoul Walsh's final film is hardly a deserving swan song.

885 Django. B.R.C./Tecisa, 1965. D: Sergio Corbucci. SC: Franco Rossetti & Jose G. Maesso. WITH Franco Nero, Loredana Nusciak, Jose Bodalo, Angel Alvarez, Eduardo Fajardo, Jimmy Douglas, Simone Arrag, Ivan Scratuglia. A mysterious stranger arrives in a small border town during a battle between Mexicans and American soldiers and he takes off

with gold belonging to the Mexican army. First film in the Italian produced "Django" series; very violent.

886 Django Shoots First. FIDA Cinematografica, 1966. 95 minutes Color. D: Alberto De Martino. SC: Alberto De Martino, Continenza, Capriccioli, Capri, Flamini & Simonelli. WITH Glenn Saxon, Fernando Sancho, Ida Galli, (Evelyn Stewart), Alberto Lupo, Nando Gazzolo, Lee Burton, Erika Blanc. A crooked banker frames his partner for a crime he did not commit and the man is killed by a bounty hunter and his son sets out to get revenge. Another outing in the Italian-produced "Django" series, originally released as **Django Spara Per Primo** (Django Shoots First).

887 Djurado. Studio T/Compagnia Cinematografica Astro, 1966. 90 minutes Color. D-SC: Gianni Narzisi (John Farrell). WITH Montgomery Clark, Scilla Gabel, Margaret Lee, Mary Jordan, Isarco Ravaioli. A gambler arrives in a small border town and wins half interest in a saloon and then begins to oppose a local murderous tyrant. Less than average Italian Western.

888 Doc. United Artists, 1971. 96 minutes Color. D: Frank Perry. SC: Pete Hamill. WITH Stacy Keach, Faye Dunaway, Harris Yulin, Mike Witney, Denver John Collins, Dan Greenberg, Penelope Allen, Hedy Sontag, Bruce M. Fisher, James Green, Richard MacKenzie, John Scanlon, Antonia Rey, John Bottoms, Philip Shafer, Marshall Efron, Fred Dennis, Mart Hulswit, Gene Collins. Hard-drinking, tubercular Doc Holliday joins forces with prostitute Kate Elder and the two end up aiding Wyatt Earp in his battle with the Clanton clan. Murky and basically boring re-telling of the Wyatt Earp-Doc Holliday story.

889 Dodge City. Warner Brothers, 1939. 104 minutes Color. D: Michael Curtiz. SC: Robert Buckner. WITH Errol Flynn, Olivia de Havilland, Ann Sheridan, Bruce Cabot, Frank McHugh, Alan Hale, John Litel, Henry Travers, Henry O'Neill, Victor Jory, Guinn Williams, Bobs Watson, William Lundigan, Gloria Holden, Douglas Fowley, Georgia Caine, Charles Halton, Ward Bond, Cora Witherspoon, Russell Simpson, Monte Blue, Nat Carr, Clem Bevans, Joseph Crehan, Thurston Hall, Chester Clute. An Irish soldier of fortune becomes the sheriff of Dodge City and is determined to make the area safe for homesteaders. Colorful Errol Flynn opus is short on story but big on action and color. V: Blackhawk, VD: Blackhawk.

Dollars For a Fast Gun see **$100,000 For Lassiter**

890 Domino Kid. Columbia, 1957. 74 minutes B/W. D: Ray Nazarro. SC: Kenneth Gamet. WITH Rory Calhoun, Kristine Miller, Andrew Duggan, Yvette Dugay, Peter Whitney, Robert Burton, James J. Griffith, Roy Barcroft, Denver Pyle, Ray Corrigan, Eugene Iglesias. Returning home to Texas after the Civil War, a man finds his father and brother have been murdered and he sets out to find the killers. Star Rory Calhoun wrote the original story on which this fairly entertaining "B" is based.

891 Don Daredevil Rides Again. Republic, 1951. 12 Chapters B/W. D: Fred C. Brannon. SC: Ronald Davidson. WITH Ken Curtis, Aline Towne, Roy Barcroft, Lane Bradford, Robert Einer, John Cason, I. Stanford Jolley, Hank Patterson, Lee Phelps, Sandy Sanders, Guy Teague, Tom Steele, Michael Ragan, Cactus Mack, Art Dillard, Bud Osborne, Saul Gorss, Gene (Roth) Stutenroth, James Magill, David Sharpe, Charles Horvath, Dale Van Sickel, Jack Ingram, George Lloyd, Carey Loftin, Art Dillard, Forrest Taylor, Don C. Harvey, Tex Terry, Bob Reeves, Chick Hannon, Herman Hack, Joe Phillips, Roy Bucko. A homesteader takes on the guise of the masked Don Daredevil to stop a political boss who is trying to run settlers off their land by claiming an old land grant is a fake. This cliffhanger has a good plot but too much footage from earlier Republic outings.

892 Don Q, Son of Zorro. United Artists, 1925. 113 minutes B/W. D: Donald Crisp. SC: Lotta Woods. WITH Douglas Fairbanks, Mary Astor, Jack McDonald, Donald Crisp, Stella De Lanit, Warner Oland, Jean Hersholt, Albert MacQuarrie, Lottie Pickford Forrest, Charles Stevens, Tote Du Crow, Martha Franklin, Juliette Belanger, Roy Coulson, Enrique Acosta. Sent to Spain by his father, Don Diego, a young Californian falls in love with a pretty girl and gets involved in court intrigue. Actionful Douglas Fairbanks diversion, a sequel to his **The Mark of Zorro.** V: Video Yesteryear, Morecraft Films/Penguin Video.

893 Don Ricardo Returns. Producers Releasing Corporation, 1946. 63 minutes B/W. D: Terry Morse, SC: Jack DeWitt & Renault Duncan (Duncan Renaldo). WITH Fred Colby, Isabelita, Martin Garralaga, Paul Newton, Claire DuBrey, David Leonard, Anthony Warde, Michael Visaroff. When he finds out he has been declared legally dead and that his cousin has taken his place, a Spanish don masquerades as a peon and seeks the aid of a mission priest in proving his inheritance. Pleasant outing from PRC.

894 Donner Pass: The Road to Survival. NBC-TV/Schick Sunn Classics, 1978. 100 minutes Color. D: James L. Conway. SC: S. S. Schweitzer. WITH Robert Fuller, Andrew Prine, Michael Callan, Diane McBain, John Anderson, John Doucette, Cynthia Eilbacher, Royal Dano, Gregory Walcott, Lance LeGault, Whit Bissell, Peg(gy) Stewart, Reid Cruickshanks, Robert Carricart, Rudy Diaz, John Hansen, George Barrows. A wagon train is stranded in the mountains during a blizzard and the inhabitants are eventually forced into cannibalism. Despite its subject matter, this "Classics Illustrated" TV movie is a pretty good film. V: Embassy Home Entertainment.

895 Don't Fence Me In. Republic, 1945. 54 (71) minutes B/W. D: John English. SC: Dorrell McGowan, Stuart McGowan & John K. Butler. WITH Roy Rogers, George "Gabby" Hayes, Dale Evans, Robert Livingston, Moroni Olsen, Arthur Space, Bob Nolan & The Sons of the Pioneers, Marc Lawrence, Lucille Gleason, Andrew Tombes, Paul Harvey, Douglas Fowley, Stephen Barclay, Edgar Dearing, Helen Talbot, Tom London. A woman magazine writer uncovers the fact that an old man was once a famous outlaw which gets him into trouble until he finds a killer and collects a reward. Better than average Roy Rogers vehicle which mainly belongs to Gabby Hayes. One interesting sequence has Gabby in a funeral parlor pretending to be dead while The Sons of the Pioneers sing "Headin' for the Last Roundup," while another sequence has him using a bullwhip, pre-Lash LaRue.

896 The Doolins of Oklahoma. Columbia, 1949. 90 minutes B/W. D: Gordon Douglas. SC: Kenneth Gamet. WITH Randolph Scott, Louise Allbritton, George Macready, John Ireland, Virginia Huston, Charles Kemper, Noah Beery Jr., Dona Drake, Robert Barrat, Lee Patrick, Griff Barnett, Frank Fenton, Jock Mahoney, James Kirkwood, Robert Osterloh, Virginia

Brissac, John Sheehan. An ex-outlaw attempts to go straight but his brothers continue their lawless ways and the entire family ends up being hunted by a sheriff and his posse. Well staged Randolph Scott vehicle; quite good.

897 Doomed at Sundown. Republic, 1937. 60 minutes B/W. D: Sam Newfield. SC: George Plympton. WITH Bob Steele, Lorraine Hayes (Laraine Day), Warner Richmond, David Sharpe, Earl Dwire, Horace B. Carpenter, Sherry Tansey, Harold Daniels, Budd Buster, Jack Kirk, Horace Murphy, Charles King, Lew Meehan, Jack Ingram. When his father is murdered by an outlaw gang, a cowpoke pretends to be an outlaw also in order to infiltrate the gang. Bob Steele is again on the trail of his father's murderer and this one will provide lots of thrills for his legion of fans.

898 Doomed Caravan. Paramount, 1941. 54 (62) minutes B/W. D: Lesley Selander. SC: Johnston McCulley & J. Benton Cheney. WITH William Boyd, Russell Hayden, Andy Clyde, Minna Gombell, Morris Ankrum, Georgia Hawkins, Trevor Bardette, Pat J. O'Brien, Raphael Bennett, Jose Luis Tortosa, Ed Cassidy. Hoppy and the Bar 20 boys agree to help a woman whose freight wagon has been raided but he becomes suspicious when she calls in the cavalry, actually a group of outlaws. Good "Hopalong Cassidy" series entry, very well done and exciting.

The Doomed Ranch see **Fury of the Apaches**

Doomsday see **Drummer of Vengeance**

Double Identity (1940) see **River's End** (1940)

Double Identity (1941) see **Hurricane Smith**

899 Down Dakota Way. Republic, 1949. 67 minutes Color. D: William Witney. SC: John K. Butler & Sloan Nibley. WITH Roy Rogers, Dale Evans, Pat Brady, Monte Montana, Foy Willing & The Riders of the Purple Sage, Elizabeth Risdon, Byron Parr, James Cardwell, Roy Barcroft, Emmett Vogan. When hoof-and-mouth disease is diagnosed in his cattle, a rancher hires a gunman to kill the veterinarian who made the diagnosis before he is forced to lose his herd. Nicely plotted and actionful Roy Rogers vehicle. V: NTA Home Entertainment.

900 Down Laredo Way. Republic, 1953. 54 minutes B/W. D: William Witney. SC: Gerald Geraghty. WITH Rex Allen, Slim Pickens, Dona Drake, Marjorie Lord, Roy Barcroft, Clayton Moore, Judy Nugent, Percy Helton, Zon Murray. A gang of diamond smugglers get away with a series of robberies until they are hunted by a rodeo star. Good direction and a fast moving script add up to good entertainment in this Rex Allen opus.

901 Down Mexico Way. Republic, 1941. 77 minutes B/W. D: Joseph Santley. SC: Olive Cooper & Albert Duffy. WITH Gene Autry, Smiley Burnette, Fay McKenzie, Harold Huber, Sidney Blackmer, Joseph Sawyer, Andrew Tombes, Murray Alper, Arthur Loft, Duncan Renaldo, Paul Fix, Julian Rivero, Ruth Robinson, Thornton Edwards, Eddie Dean, The Herrera Sisters. Three cowpokes are on the trail of a group of crooks who bilk townspeople out of money on the pretext of producing a movie in their community. Pleasant Gene Autry film with a good script and nice songs (i.e., "South of the Border," "Maria Elena" and the title tune).

902 Down Missouri Way. Producers Releasing Corporation, 1946. 73 minutes B/W. D: Josef Berne. SC: Sam Neuman. WITH Martha O'Driscoll, John Carradine, Eddie Dean, William Wright, Roscoe Ates, Renee Godfrey, Mabel Todd, Eddie Craven, Chester Clute, Will Wright, Paul Scardon. A wind-bag movie producer wants to make a film about an intelligent mule and finds one at a Missouri college. Not much to recommend this so-called comedy except for the fact that Eddie Dean sings a half-dozen tunes.

903 Down Rio Grande Way. Columbia, 1942. 57 minutes B/W. D: William Berke. SC: Paul Franklin. WITH Charles Starrett, Russell Hayden, Britt Wood, Rose Anne Stevens, Norman Willis, Davidson Clark, Edmund Cobb, Budd Buster, Paul Newlan, William Desmond, Jim Corey, Steve Clark, Forrest Taylor, Ed Piel, John Cason, Art Mix, Kermit Maynard, Frank McCarroll. Two cowboys get involved with the movement for independence in Texas. Slim production values hurt the overall effectiveness of this pseudo-historical Charles Starrett vehicle.

904 Down Texas Way. Monogram, 1942. 57 minutes B/W. D: Howard Bretherton. SC: Jess Bowers (Adele Buffington). WITH Buck Jones, Tim McCoy, Raymond

Hatton, Luana Walters, Dave O'Brien, Lois Austin, Harry Woods, Glenn Strange, Tom London, Jack Daley. An outlaw gang has a young woman pose as the widow of a murdered man in order to claim his ranch, which rightfully belongs to his son. Good entry in the popular "Rough Riders" series, with a complicated, but interesting, plot. V: Video Connection.

905 Down the Wyoming Trail. Monogram, 1939. 62 minutes B/W. D: Al Herman. SC: Peter Dixon & Roger Merton. WITH Tex Ritter, Mary Brodel, Horace Murphy, Bobby Lawson, Charles King, Bob Terry, Jack Ingram, Earl Douglas, Frank LaRue, Ernie Adams, Ed Coxen, Jean Southern, Charles Sargent, The Northwesterners. A cowpoke is on the trail of an outlaw gang planning to drive their herd of stolen cattle through a mountainous area. Fair Tex Ritter vehicle benefitting from scenic locales and nice songs.

906 Dragoon Wells Massacre. Allied Artists, 1957. 88 minutes Color. D: Harold Schuster. SC: Oliver Drake & Warren Douglas. WITH Barry Sullivan, Dennis O'Keefe, Mona Freeman, Katy Jurado, Sebastian Cabot, Jack Elam, Trevor Bardette, Hank Worden, Warren Douglas, John War Eagle. In 1860 a diverse group of people, including outlaws and lawmen, are cornered in a fort about to be attacked by Indians. Well staged and highly entertaining oater.

907 Drango. United Artists, 1957. 92 minutes B/W. D: Hall Bartlett & Jules Bricken. SC: Hall Bartlett. WITH Jeff Chandler, Joanne Dru, Julie London, Ronald Howard, Donald Crisp, John Lupton, Morris Ankrum, Helen Wallace, Walter Sande, Parley Baer, Charles Horvath, Mimi Gibson, Paul Lukather, Damian O'Flynn, Katherine Warren, Chubby Johnson, Milburn Stone, Edith Evanson. After the Civil War a Union officer is assigned to govern a town he was once forced to plunder. Fairly entertaining yarn.

908 Draw! Home Box Office Premiere Films, 1984. 100 minutes Color. D: Steven H. Stern. SC: Stanley Mann. WITH Kirk Douglas, James Coburn, Alexandra Bastedo, Graham Jarvis, Derek McGrath, Jason Michas, Len Birman. A once-famous outlaw is forced to shoot a lawman in a small town and he takes a girl hostage while the citizens demand his capture by a respected, but drunken, lawman. Made-for-pay-TV feature is only average despite good work by its two stars and fine production trappings.

909 Drift Fence. Paramount, 1936. 56 minutes B/W. D: Otho Lovering. SC: Robert Yost & Stuart Anthony. WITH Larry "Buster" Crabbe, Katherine DeMille, Tom Keene, Benny Baker, Glenn (Leif) Erickson, Stanley Andrews, Richard Carle, Irving Bacon, Effie Ellsler, Jan Duggan, Walter Long, Chester Gan, Richard Alexander, Bud Fine, Jack Pennick. A dude has a wrangler take over his identity in order to take control of a ranch he has inherited. Very well done "B" adaptation of the Zane Grey novel; Benny Baker is quite good as tenderfoot Jim Traft. Reissued as **Texas Desperadoes.** V: Video Connection.

910 The Drifter. Willis Kent, 1932. 60 minutes B/W. D: William O'Connor. SC: Oliver Drake. WITH William Farnum, Noah Beery, Phyllis Barrington, Charles Sellon, Bruce Warren, Russell Hopton, Ann Brody, Ynez Seabury. A man gets involved in a lumber feud not knowing one of the leaders is his brother. Pretty good low budget affair highlighted by stars William Farnum and Noah Beery.

911 The Drifter. Producers Releasing Corporation, 1944. 64 minutes B/W. D: Sam Newfield. SC: Patricia Harper. WITH Buster Crabbe, Al St. John, Carol Parker, Kermit Maynard, Jack Ingram, Roy Brent, George Chesebro, Ray Bennett, Jimmie Aubrey, Slim Whitaker, Wally West. Billy Carson impersonates a sharpshooter, the leader of an outlaw gang, in order to find out who is really behind a series of robberies. Interesting plot, mundane execution.

912 The Driftin' Kid. Monogram, 1941. 55 minutes B/W. D: Robert Emmett Tansey. SC: Robert Emmett (Tansey) & Frances Kavanaugh. WITH Tom Keene, Betty Miles, Frank Yaconelli, Arkansas Slim Andrews, Stanley Price, Gene Alsace, Glenn Strange, Steve Clark, Sherry Tansey, Fred Hoose, Frank McCarroll, Wally West. Outlaws plan to kill a horse rancher for his ranch and government contract and a federal agent is sent to investigate the theft of his cattle and the two men turn out to be lookalikes. Okay entry in the Tom Keene Monogram series.

913 Driftin' River. Producers Releasing Corporation, 1946. 57 minutes B/W. D: Robert Emmett Tansey. SC: Frances Kavanaugh. WITH Eddie Dean, Shirley Patterson, Roscoe Ates, Lee Bennett, William Fawcett, Dennis Moore, Lottie Harrison, Forrest Taylor, Robert Callahan,

Lee Roberts, Don Murphy, The Sunshine Boys. Two cowpokes join a gang of cattle rustlers to capture those responsible for the massacre of an army platoon carrying money to buy a girl's herd of horses. Slow drama aided by pretty Shirley Patterson and Eddie Dean's singing of the title tune and "Way Back in Oklahoma."

914 Drifting Along. Monogram, 1946. 60 minutes B/W. D: Derwin Abrahams. SC: Adele Buffington. WITH Johnny Mack Brown, Raymond Hatton, Lynne Carver, Douglas Fowley, Smith Ballew, Milburn Morante, Steve Clark, Marshall Reed, Jack Rockwell, Terry Frost, Lynton Brent, Curt Barrett & The Trailsmen, Harry V. Cheshire, Ted Mapes, Ted French, Hollywood Exhibition Square Dancers, Thornton Edwards. A ranch foreman learns that his pretty boss's fiancée is actually a cattle rustler. Fairly good outing in the Johnny Mack Brown-Raymond Hatton series at Monogram, with a quartet of tunes including Johnny's singing a number.

915 Drifting Westward. Monogram, 1939. 57 minutes B/W. D: Robert Hill. SC: Robert Emmett (Tansey). WITH Jack Randall, Frank Yaconelli, Edna Duran, Julian Rivero, Stanley Blystone, Octavio Giraud, Dave O'Brien, Sherry Tansey, Carmen Bailey, Dean Spencer. Crooks are after a hidden silver mine map and a man sends for a friend to help him stop the raids on his home and he takes on the guise of a killer hired by the two crooks so he can find out what they really want. Pretty good Jack Randall series film.

916 Drop Them or I'll Shoot. Films Marceau, 1969. 90 minutes Color. D-SC: Sergio Corbucci. WITH Johnny Hallyday, Francoise Fabian, Silvy Fennec, Serge Marquand, Mario Adorf, Gaston Moschin. A man opposes outlaws plaguing the people of a small town. Italian actioner offers little but lots of violence. Original title: **Le Specialisti** (The Specialist).

917 Drum Beat. Warner Brothers, 1954. 111 minutes Color. D-SC: Delmer Daves. WITH Alan Ladd, Audrey Dalton, Marisa Pavan, Charles Bronson, Robert Keith, Rodolfo Acosta, Warner Anderson, Elisha Cook Jr., Anthony Caruso, Richard Gaines, Edgar Stehli, Hayden Rorke, Frank De Kova, Isabel Jewell, Perry Lopez, Willis Bouchey, George J. Lewis, Frank Ferguson. In 1869 President Grant appoints a peace commissioner to negotiate a treaty with renegade Indians. Good action film with Charles Bronson giving a fine performance as the Indian leader. V: Cumberland Video.

918 Drum Taps. World Wide, 1932. 61 minutes B/W. D: J. P. McGowan. SC: Alan James. WITH Ken Maynard, Dorothy Dix, Hooper Atchley, Alan Bridge, Charles Stevens, Junior Coughlan, Harry Semels, Jim Mason, Slim Whitaker, Neal Hart, Art Mix, Kermit Maynard, Leo Willis, Boy Scout Troop 107. A cowboy aids the boy scouts in trying to thwart land grabbers. A good Ken Maynard series entry with an exciting climax. V: Discount Video, Video Dimensions.

919 Drummer of Vengeance. Times Film, 1974. 90 minutes Color. D-SC: Paul Paget (Mario Gariazzo). WITH Ty Hardin, Rossano Brazzi, Craig Hill, Gordon Mitchell, Rosalba Neri, Edda de Benedetta. After an outlaw gang murders his wife and children a man seeks revenge but finds the going rough when he finds out their leader is a sheriff. Fair British-Italian co-production, better for its performances than plot. Made in 1972 as **Doomsday.**

920 Drums Across the River. Universal-International, 1954. 78 minutes Color. D: Nathan Juran. SC: John K. Butler. WITH Audie Murphy, Lisa Gaye, Lyle Bettger, Walter Brennan, Mara Corday, Hugh O'Brian, Jay Silverheels, Regis Toomey, Morris Ankrum, James Anderson, George Wallace, Bob Steele, Lane Bradford, Emile Meyer, Gregg Barton, Howard McNear, Kenneth Terrell. A young man mistakenly joins a group of gold hunters who go into Indian Territory and he soon sees the error of his ways and joins with his father in trying to restore peace. Fairly actionful Audie Murphy vehicle.

921 Drums Along the Mohawk. 20th Century-Fox, 1939. 103 minutes Color. D: John Ford. SC: Lamar Trotti & Sonya Levien. WITH Claudette Colbert, Henry Fonda, Edna May Oliver, Eddie Collins, John Carradine, Doris Bowden, Jessie Ralph, Arthur Shields, Robert Lowery, Roger Imhof, Francis Ford, Ward Bond, Kay Linaker, Russell Simpson, Chief Big Tree, Spencer Charters, Arthur Aylesworth, Si Jenks, Jack Pennick, Charles Tannen, Paul McVey, Clarence Wilson, Edwin Maxwell, Clara Blandick. A young married couple struggles against adversity and Tories in the Mohawk Valley at the start of the Revolutionary War. A great John Ford classic, a must-see film.

922 Drums in the Deep South. RKO Radio, 1951. 87 minutes Color. D: William Cameron Menzies. SC: Philip Yordan & Sidney Harmon. WITH James Craig, Barbara Payton, Guy Madison, Barton MacLane, Craig Stevens, Tom Fadden, Robert Osterloh, Taylor Holmes, Lewis Martin, Peter Brocco, Dan White, Robert Easton, Louis Jean Heydt, Myron Healey. Two friends, who love the same girl, find themselves on opposite sides as General Sherman marches through Georgia. Mediocre Civil War yarn greatly enhanced by Lionel Lindon's photography.

923 Drums of Destiny. Crescent, 1937. 64 minutes B/W. D: Ray Taylor. SC: Roger Whatley & John T. Neville. WITH Tom Keene, Edna Lawrence, Budd Buster, Rafael Bennett, Robert Fiske, David Sharpe, John Merton, Carlos De Valdez, Chief Flying Cloud. In West Florida in 1815 a cavalry captain plans to go into Spanish Florida to put down Creek Indian attacks, an action contrary to government policy. Well done entry in Crescent's historical series starring Tom Keene.

924 The Drylanders. Columbia/National Film Board of Canada, 1963. 70 minutes B/W. D: Donald Haldane. SC: M. Charles Cohen. WITH Frances Hyland, James Douglas, Lester Nixon, Mary Savage, William Fruete, Don Francks, Irena Mayeska. In 1907 a man takes his wife and sons west to homestead in Canada and there they fight the elements to survive and build a new life. Reasonably good entertainment; Canada's National Film Board's first feature film.

925 The Duchess and the Dirtwater Fox. 20th Century-Fox, 1976. 104 minutes Color. D: Melvin Frank. SC: Barry Sandler, Jack Rose & Melvin Frank. WITH George Segal, Goldie Hawn, Conrad Janis, Thayer David, Jennifer Lee, Roy Jenson, Pat Ast, Sid Gould, Bob Hoy, E. J. Andre, Richard Farnsworth, John Alderson, Prentiss Rowe, Jerry Gatlin. A crooked gambler is forced to team with a dancehall girl when they head for the desert with stolen loot. Less than mediocre genre "comedy" for fans of its two stars only.

926 Duck, You Sucker. United Artists, 1972. 121 (139) minutes Color. D: Sergio Leone. SC: Sergio Leone, Sergio Donati & Luciano Vincenzoni. WITH Rod Steiger, James Coburn, Romolo Valli, Maria Monti, Rik Battaglia, Franco Graziosi, Domingo Antoine, Goffredo Pistoni, Roy Bosier,

John Frederick. During the Mexican Revolution in 1913-14 a foreigner aids a local revolutionary while planning a bank robbery. Big Italian-made oater mainly for fans of Sergio Leone. Issued in Italy in 1971 as **Giu la Testa** (Down With Your Head) by Rafran/San Marco/Miura Film and running 158 minutes. TV title: **A Fistful of Dynamite.**

927 Dude Bandit. Allied, 1933. 62 minutes B/W. D: George Melford, SC: Jack Natteford. WITH Hoot Gibson, Gloria Shea, Hooper Atchley, Skeeter Bill Robbins, Neal Hart, Lafe McKee, Gordon DeMain, Fred Burns, Art Mix, Fred Gilman, George Morrell, Merrill McCormack. Pretending to be a dimwit, a man investigates the murder of a friend and finds out that a crooked banker is responsible and the cowpoke takes on the guise of a bandit to stop him. A rather rambling production with Gibson doing a character similar to the one in **Spirit of the West** (q.v.). Skeeter Bill Robbins was a most annoying sidekick.

928 Dude Cowboy. RKO Radio, 1941. 59 minutes B/W. D: David Howard. SC: Morton Grant. WITH Tim Holt, Marjorie Reynolds, Louise Currie, Ray Whitley, Lee "Lasses" White, Helen Holmes, Eddie Kane, Eddie Dew, Byron Foulger, Glenn Strange, Tom London, Lloyd Ingraham. An agent of the Treasury Department's Secret Service goes slumming on a dude ranch in order to break up a counterfeiting operation. Highly entertaining Tim Holt film.

929 The Dude Goes West. Allied Artists, 1948. 86 minutes B/W. D: Kurt Neumann. SC: Richard Sale & Mary Loos. WITH Eddie Albert, Gale Storm, Gilbert Roland, James Gleason, Binnie Barnes, Barton MacLane, Douglas Fowley, Tom Tyler, Harry Hayden, Chief Yowlachie, Sarah Padden, Catherine Doucet, Edward Gargan, Frank Yaconelli, Olin Howlin, Dick Elliott, Lee "Lasses" White, Si Jenks, George Meeker, Ben Weldon. A shopkeeper from the Bowery becomes a sharpshooter and heads West where he goes up against an outlaw gang. Very pleasant Western comedy with a good cast.

930 Dude Ranch. Paramount, 1931. 72 minutes B/W. D: Frank Tuttle. SC: Percy Heath, Grover Jones & Lloyd Corrigan. WITH Jack Oakie, Stuart Erwin, Mitzi Green, June Collyer, Eugene Pallette, Charles Sellon, Guy Oliver. In order to impress a girl, an actor goes to a dude ranch where he poses as a cowboy. Antique early talkie is still fun.

931 The Dude Ranger. Fox, 1934. 68 minutes B/W. D: Edward F. Cline. SC: Barry Barringer. WITH George O'Brien, Irene Hervey, Syd Saylor, LeRoy Mason, Henry Hall, Jim Mason, Lloyd Ingraham, Earl Dwire, Si Jenks, Lafe McKee, Hank Bell, Jack Kirk. After inheriting a ranch in Arizona from his uncle, a young man finds out it is being plagued by rustlers. Entertaining adaptation of Zane Grey's story. V: Video Dimensions.

932 The Dude Wrangler. Sono Art-World Wide, 1930. 60 minutes B/W. D: Richard Thorpe. SC: Robert N. Lee. WITH Lina Basquette, George Duryea (Tom Keene/ Richard Powers), Francis X. Bushman, Clyde Cook, Sojin, Margaret Seddon, Ethel Wales, Wilfred North, Alice Davenport, Virginia Sale, Julia Swayne Gordon, Louis Payne, Fred Parker, Aileen Carlyle, Jack Richardson. A young man borrows the money to buy a dude ranch but one of the guests plots to sabotage the operation so he can impress the girl they both want. Interesting early talkie for Tom Keene fans.

933 Dudes Are Pretty People. United Artists, 1942. 46 minutes B/W. D: Hal Roach Jr. SC: Louis Kaye. WITH Jimmy Rogers, Noah Beery Jr., Marjorie Woodworth, Paul Hurst, Marjorie Gateson, Russell Gleason, Grady Sutton, Bob Gregory, Frank Moran. Two cowboys work at a dude ranch and one of them falls for a girl who already has a boyfriend. Silly opener for the brief series of featurettes starring Jimmy Rogers and Noah Beery Jr.

934 Due Mafiosi Nel Far West (Two Mafiamen in the Far West). Fida/Epoca Film, 1964. 102 minutes Color. D-SC: Giorgio Simonelli. WITH Franco Franchi, Ciccio Ingrassi, Aroldo Tieri, Helene Chanel, Fernando Sancho, Anna Casares, Aldo Giuffre, Felix De Fauce, Alfredo Rizzo. Two Italians inherit a Texas goldmine and get mixed up with outlaws. Silly Italian comedy with the team of Franchi & Ingrassi.

935 Due Sergenti Del Generale Custer (The Two Sergeants of General Custer). Fida Cinematografica/Balcazar, 1965. 97 minutes Color. D-SC: Giorgio Simonelli. WITH Franco Franchi, Ciccio Ingrassia, Fernando Sancho, Margaret Lee, Moira Orfei, Aroldo Tieri, Riccardo Garrone, Ernesto Calindri. Two Italians are mourned as cowards at Fort Alamo when in reality they are deserters who redeem themselves by spying on the Confederate army. Inane Italian comedy-Western.

936 Duel at Apache Wells. Republic, 1957. 70 minutes B/W. D: Joseph Kane. SC: Bob Williams. WITH Anna Maria Alberghetti, Ben Cooper, Jim Davis, Harry Shannon, Francis McDonald, Bob Steele, Frank Puglia, Argentina Brunetti, Ian MacDonald, John Dierkes, Ric Roman, Dick Elliott. A young man returns home to face the crook who murdered his father and stole his lands. Fairly satisfying oater with Jim Davis good as the villain and Bob Steele as his vicious henchman.

937 Duel at Diablo. United Artists, 1966. 103 minutes B/W. D: Ralph Nelson. SC: Marvin H. Albert & Michael M. Grilikhes. WITH James Garner, Sidney Poitier, Bibi Andersson, Dennis Weaver, Bill Travers, William Redfield, John Hoyt, John Crawford, John Hubbard, Kevin Coughlin, Jay Ripley, Jeff Cooper, Ralph Bahnsen, Bobby Crawford, Richard Lapp, Dawn Little Sky, Eddie Little Sky, Al Wyatt, Phil Schumacher, Richard Farnsworth, Joe Finnegan, Bill Hart. A diverse group of people travel through the desert with a convoy of munitions as they face the threat of Indian attack. Surprisingly good accounting of an old plot ploy.

938 Duel at Silver Creek. Universal-International, 1952. 77 minutes Color. D: Donald Siegel. SC: Gerald Dryson Adams & Joseph Hoffman. WITH Audie Murphy, Faith Domergue, Stephen McNally, Susan Cabot, Gerald Mohr, Lee Marvin, Eugene Iglesias, James Anderson, Walter Sande, George Eldredge. Coming to town to do some gambling, the Silver Kid finds himself teaming with the sheriff to stop a gang of murdering claim jumpers. Fast-paced and lots of fun.

939 Duel At the Rio Grande. Teleworld, 1964. 93 minutes B/W. D: Mario Gaiano. WITH Sean Flynn, Danielle de Metz, Folco Lulli, Armando Calvo. A young man returns home to Mexico to find his father has been murdered by a dictator and he leads a band of revolutionaries to stop the tyrant. Mediocre reworking of the Zorro theme with Sean Flynn only average in an attempt to recreate the swashbuckling image of his father, Errol Flynn. Original Title: **Il Segno di Zorro.**

Duel in Durango see Gun Duel in Durango

940 Duel in the Sun. Selznick Releasing, 1946. 138 minutes Color. D: King Vidor (& uncredited Otto Brower, William Dieterle, Sidney Franklin, William Cameron Menzies, David O. Selznick & Josef von Sternberg). SC: David O. Selznick & Oliver H. P. Garrett. WITH Jennifer Jones, Gregory Peck, Joseph Cotten, Lionel Barrymore, Lillian Gish, Walter Huston, Herbert Marshall, Charles Bickford, Joan Tetzel, Harry Carey, Otto Kruger, Sidney Blackmer, Tilly Losch, Scott McKay, Butterfly McQueen, Francis McDonald, Victor Milian, Griff Barnett, Frank Cordell, Dan White, Steve Dunhill, Lane Chandler, Lloyd Shaw, Bert Roach, Si Jenks, Hank Worden, Rose Plummer, Guy Wilkerson, Lee Phelps, Al Taylor, Robert McKenzie, Charles Dingle, Orson Welles (narrator). As their senator-land baron father battles the railroad over building track on his land, two brothers fight it out over a half-breed girl. Very bad "epic" Western from David O. Selznick, which is still worth a look just to see how big budget producers can bungle a project.

941 Duel on the Mississippi. Columbia, 1955. 72 minutes Color. D: William Castle. SC: Gerald Drayson Adams. WITH Lex Barker, Patricia Medina, Warren Stevens, Craig Stevens, John Dehner, Ian Keith, Chris Alcaide, John Mansfield, Celia Lovsky, Lou Merrill, Mel Welles, Jean Del Val, Baynes Barron, Vince M. Townsend Jr. In 1820s New Orleans a young man goes into bondage so his planter father will not go to jail and eventually he stops raids on sugar plantations by bayou renegades. Standard costume programmer which moves along at a speedy clip.

942 Dugan of the Badlands. Monogram, 1931. 66 minutes B/W. D-SC: Robert North Bradbury. WITH Bill Cody, Andy Shuford, Blanche Mehaffey, Earl Dwire, Ethan Laidlaw, Julian Rivero, John Elliott. A cowboy adopts a young boy whose father has been killed and together they aid a lawman in tracking down a crooked deputy. Fair first entry in the "Bill and Andy" series.

943 Durango Valley Raiders. Republic, 1938. 60 minutes B/W. D: Sam Newfield. SC: George Plympton. WITH Bob Steele, Louise Stanley, Karl Hackett, Forrest Taylor, Ted Adams, Steve Clark, Horace Murphy, Jack Ingram, Ernie Adams, Budd Buster, Frank Ball. A young cowpoke gets involved with people trying to fight an outlaw gang and he discovers that the local sheriff is the culprit behind the terrorism. Plenty of action in this nicely done Bob Steele oater. V: Cumberland Video.

944 Dynamite Canyon. Monogram, 1941. 58 minutes B/W. D: Robert Emmett Tansey. SC: Robert Emmett (Tansey) & Frances Kavanaugh. WITH Tom Keene, Evelyn Finley, Arkansas Slim Andrews, Sugar Dawn, Stanley Price, Kenne Duncan, Gene Alsace, Fred Hoose, Tom London. When an outlaw gang leader murders two men over a copper deposit, a ranger is sent to investigate and masquerades as an outlaw named Trigger Jones in order to join the gang. Pretty fair entry in Tom Keene's last Monogram series.

945 Dynamite Jim. Balcazar, 1966. 86 minutes Color. D: Alfonso Balcazar. WITH Luis Davila, Fernando Sancho, Rosalba Neri, Maria Pia Conte. During the Civil War a Northern colonel tries to bring a gold shipment from Mexico to aid the Union cause but along the way some of his men get greedy. Fairly interesting Spanish-made oater.

946 Dynamite Joe. Seven Film/Hispamer, 1966. 94 minutes Color. D: Antonio Margheriti. SC: Maria Del Carmin Martinez. WITH Rick Van Nutter, Halina Zalewska, Mercedes Caracuel, Renato Baldini, Barta Barry, Aldo Cecconi, Alfonso Rocas, Mario De Grassi, Santiago Rivero. Special agent Dynamite Joe Ford is given the assignment, by a senator, to protect government gold shipments from attacking Comancheros. Better-than-average spaghetti Western.

947 Dynamite Pass. RKO Radio, 1950. 61 minutes B/W. D: Lew Landers. SC: Norman Houston. WITH Tim Holt, Richard Martin, Lynne Roberts, Regis Toomey, Robert Shayne, Don C. Harvey, Cleo Moore, John Dehner, Don Haggerty, Ross Elliott, Denver Pyle. Fearing the competition, a toll-road owner sets out to stop the building of a new road. Well done Tim Holt vehicle. V: Nostalgia Merchant.

948 Dynamite Ranch. World Wide, 1932. 60 minutes B/W. D: Forrest Sheldon. SC: Barry Barrington & Forrest Sheldon. WITH Ken Maynard, Ruth Hiatt, Alan Roscoe, Jack Perrin, Arthur Hoyt, Al Smith, John Beck, George Pierce, Lafe McKee, Martha Mattox, Edmund Cobb,

Charles LeMoyne, Cliff Lyons, Kermit Maynard. When a train is robbed during a fake stop a playful cowpoke is blamed for the crime and escapes from jail to prove his innocence. Okay Ken Maynard series affair. V: Discount Video.

E

Each Man for Himself see **The Ruthless Four**

949 The Eagle and the Hawk. Paramount, 1950. 104 minutes Color. D: Lewis R. Foster. SC: Geoffrey Homes & Lewis R. Foster. WITH John Payne, Rhonda Fleming, Dennis O'Keefe, Thomas Gomez, Fred Clark, Frank Faylen, Eduardo Noriega, Grandon Rhodes, Walter Reed, Margaret Martin. The government sends two law enforcers to Mexico in the 1860s in an attempt to stop the plot to make Maximilian the emperor of Mexico. Mildly entertaining historical fiction.

950 The Eagle's Brood. Paramount, 1935. 54 (59) minutes B/W. D: Howard Bretherton. SC: Doris Schroeder & Harrison Jacobs. WITH William Boyd, James Ellison, Joan Woodbury, William Farnum, Addison Richards, George ("Gabby") Hayes, Frank Shannon, Dorothy Revier, Paul Fix, John Merton. When outlaws murder a young couple and kidnap their child, Hopalong Cassidy comes to the rescue. Second film in the "Hopalong Cassidy" series and a portent of the good things to come.

951 The Eagle's Claw. Aywon, 1924. 50 minutes B/W. D: Charles R. Seeling. WITH Guinn Williams. When he inherits a mine a young man becomes the target of attacks from an old enemy. Cheap silent effort which will be of interest to fans of Guinn "Big Boy" Williams.

952 80 Steps to Jonah. Warner Brothers, 1969. 107 minutes Color. D: Gerd Oswald. SC: Frederic Louis Fox. WITH Wayne Newton, Diana Ewing, Jo Van Fleet, Keenan Wynn, R. G. Armstrong, Slim Pickens, Mickey Rooney, Sal Mineo, Brandon Cruz, Teddy Quinn, Susan Mathews, Dennis Cross, James Bacon, Erin Moore, Butch Patrick. On the run from the law, a young man finds his way to a ranch for blind children and there he changes his life. Okay drama although singer Wayne Newton is somewhat miscast in the lead role.

953 El Cisco. Filmepoca, 1966. 90 minutes Color. D-SC: Sergio Bergonzelli. WITH William Berger, George Wang, Antonella Murgia, Tom Felleghy, Nino Vingelli, Cristina Gajoni, Renato Chiantoni. El Cisco, a man unjustly accused of a crime and with a price on his head, foils a bank robbery attempt by a deputy sheriff in league with Mexican bandits but ends up being blamed for that crime. Somewhat involved, but fair Italian oater with a good score by Bruno Nicolai.

954 El Condor. National General, 1970. 98 minutes Color. D: John Guillermin. SC: Larry Cohen & Steven Carabatsos. WITH Jim Brown, Lee Van Cleef, Mariana Hill, Patrick O'Neal, Elisha Cook, Iron Eyes Cody, Imogen Hassall, Gustavo Rojo, Florencio Amarilla, Julio Pena, John Clark. Two men go to Mexico with plans to steal the gold of Maximilian, which is hidden in the fort at El Condor. Veteran director Andre De Toth produced this foreign-filmed oater, which is fair entertainment.

955 El Diablo Rides. Metropolitan, 1939. 55 minutes B/W. D: Ira Webb. SC: Carl Krusada. WITH Bob Steele, Claire Rochelle, Carleton Young, Ted Adams, Kit Guard, Robert Walker. A cowboy finds himself in the middle of a range war between cattlemen and sheep herders. Low grade but actionful Bob Steele film.

956 El Dorado. Paramount, 1967. 127 minutes Color. D: Howard Hawks. SC: Leigh Brackett. WITH John Wayne, Robert Mitchum, James Caan, Charlene Holt, Michele Carey, Arthur Hunnicutt, R. G. Armstrong, Edward Asner, Paul Fix, Christopher George, Robert Donner, John Gabriel, Jim Davis, Marina Chane, Anne Newman, Johnny Crawford, Robert Rothwell, Adam Roarke, Chuck Courtney, Bill Henry, Nacho Galindo, Victoria George, John Mitchum. An aging gunfighter aids his sheriff pal in opposing a corrupt land baron. Entertaining reworking of **Rio Bravo** (q.v.), although not up to the previous effort. V: Blackhawk, Cumberland Video. VD: Blackhawk.

957 El Dorado Pass. Columbia, 1948. 56 minutes B/W. D: Ray Nazarro. SC: Earle Snell. WITH Charles Starrett, Smiley Burnette, Elena Verdugo, Steve Darrell, Rory Mallinson, Shorty Thompson & His Saddle Rockin' Rhythm, Ted Mapes, Blackie Whiteford, Stanley Blystone, Harry Vejar, Russell Meeker, Gertrude Chorre. Framed for a crime he did not commit, a cowboy escapes from jail and takes on his Durango Kid guise and aids a Mexican rancher and his daughter who have been robbed of money they planned to use to buy cattle. Passable "Durango Kid" series segment.

958 El Paso. Paramount, 1948. 101 minutes Color. D-SC: Lewis R. Foster. WITH John Payne, Gail Russell, Sterling Hayden, George "Gabby" Hayes, Dick Foran, Henry Hull, Mary Beth Hughes, Eduardo Noriega, H. B. Warner, Catherine Craig, Arthur Space, Bobby Ellis, Peggy McIntyre, Chief Yowlachie, Steven Geray, Lawrence Tibbett Jr. In Texas after the Civil War a young lawyer learns that the gun is the only way to rid the area of lawlessness. Standard but entertaining big budget actioner.

959 The El Paso Kid. Republic, 1946. 54 minutes B/W. D: Thomas Carr. SC: Norman Sheldon. WITH Sunset Carson, Marie Harmon, Robert Filmer, Wheaton Chambers, Zon Murray, John Carpenter, Hank Patterson, Edmund Cobb, Tex Terry, Robert Wilke, Ed Cassidy. After leaving an outlaw gang over a killing, a young man is made the town's sheriff and eventually redeems himself for his past. Although a good rider and fighter, Sunset Carson was a mediocre actor at best and this does not help the proceedings.

960 El Paso Stampede. Republic, 1953. 53 minutes B/W. D: Harry Keller. SC: Arthur E. Orloff. WITH Allan "Rocky" Lane, Phyllis Coates, Eddy Waller, Stephen Chase, Roy Barcroft, Edward Clark, Tom Monroe, Stanley Andrews, William Tannen, John Hamilton. During the Spanish-American War rustlers hijack cattle intended for the army and the government sends special agent Rocky Lane to investigate. None-too-interesting outing with lots of stock footage and re-use of the old chestnut of having cattle hidden in a valley behind a waterfall. Trivia fans: a picture of Grant Withers is used to portray unseen rustler Jose Delgado.

961 El Puro. Filmar Cinematografica, 1972. 89 minutes Color. D: Fabrizio Gianni. SC: Ignacio Iquino, Eduardo Mullargia & Fabrizio Gianni. WITH Robert Woods, Rosalba Neri, Maurizio Bonuglia, Mario Brega, Mariangela Giordano, Aldo Berti, Attilio Cottesio, Fabrizio Gianni, Gustavo Re. After accepting a reward to bring in an outlaw alive, a young cowboy is forced to shoot the wanted man. A later spaghetti Western, but just as violent as its predecessors. Italian title: **La Taglia E Pia l'Umo, l'Animazzo Io, El Puro.** French title: **El Puro, La Rancon Est Pour Toi.**

El Rancho Grande see **Rancho Grande**

962 El Topo (The Mole). ABKCP/Producciones Panicas, 1971. 123 minutes Color. D-SC: Alexandro Jodorowsky. WITH Alexandro Jodorowsky, Brontis Jodorowsky, Maria Lorenzio, David Silva, Paula Romo, Jacqueline Luis, Robert John. A mysterious figure rides through the desert and meets a woman who urges him to search out and kill four sharp-shooting masters. Strange, ambiguous and extremely violent Mexican film which has become popular on the Midnight Movie circuit but is not likely to appeal to the average filmgoer.

963 The Electric Horseman. Universal/Columbia, 1979. 120 minutes Color. D: Sydney Pollack. SC: Robert Garland & Paul Gaer. WITH Robert Redford, Jane Fonda, Willie Nelson, Valerie Perrine, John Saxon, Nicholas Coster, Allan Arbus, Wilford Brimley. A faded rodeo star heads to his desert hideout after one of his "deals" fails to work out and he is sought out by a TV reporter and the two fall in love. Lackluster outing that is too long to be interesting although Willie Nelson is just fine as the "hero's" pal. V: Universal 8.

964 Emperor of the North Pole. 20th Century-Fox, 1973. 118 minutes Color. D: Robert Aldrich. SC: Christopher Knopf. WITH Lee Marvin, Ernest Borgnine, Keith Carradine, Charles Tyner, Malcolm Atterbury, Simon Oakland, Harry Caesar, Hal Baylor, Matt Clark, Elisha Cook, Joe Di Reda, Liam Dunn, Daine Dye, Robert Foulk, James Goodwin, Ray Guth, Sid Haig, Karl Lukas, Edward McNally, John Steadman, Vic Tayback, Dave Willock. A hobo carries out a personal vendetta against a train foreman who brutally murders those trying to get free rides on his train. Very violent melodrama; Marty Robbins sings the title song, "A Man and a Train."

965 Empty Holsters. Warner Brothers, 1937. 62 minutes B/W. D: B. Reeves Eason. SC: John T. Neville. WITH Dick Foran, Pat Wathall, Edmund Cobb, Glenn Strange, George Chesebro, J. P. McGowan, Milton Kibbee, Emmett Vogan, Art Mix, Artie Ortego, Earl Dwire, Jack Mower,

Ben Corbett, Merrill McCormack. After he is released from prison where he was falsely sent on charges of robbery and murder, a cowboy sets out to clear his name by finding the real culprit. Old story is given plenty of fast action in this retelling.

966 Empty Saddles. Universal, 1936. 62 minutes B/W. D: Lesley Selander. SC: Franches Guihan. WITH Buck Jones, Louise Brooks, Harvey Clark, Niles Welch, Gertrude Astor, Frank Campeau, Charles Middleton, Lloyd Ingraham, Claire Rochelle, Robert Adair, Ben Corbett, Earl Askam. Crooks start a war between cattle ranchers and sheepmen and a cowboy tries to put a stop to the feuding. Well mounted Buck Jones vehicle of double interest because of Louise Brooks as the leading lady.

967 The Enchanted Valley. Eagle Lion, 1948. 72 minutes B/W. D: Robert Emmett Tansey. SC: Frances Kavanaugh. WITH Alan Curtis, Anne Gwynne, Charles Grapewin, Donn Gift, Joseph Crehan, Joseph Devlin, Al (Lash) LaRue, John Bleifer, Rocky Camron, Jerry Riggio. A young man's happy existence is interrupted by the arrival of two bandits and their woman companion. Average programmer.

968 End of a Gun. CBS-TV/20th Century-Fox, 1957. 45 minutes B/W. WITH Richard Conte, John Barrymore Jr., Marilyn Erskine, Lyle Bettger, John Conte. A famous gunman, who wants to lead a peaceful life, is forced into still another showdown. TV adaptation of **The Gunfighter** (q.v.), this telefeature was originally shown as a segment of "The 20th Century-Fox Hour" on CBS-TV on January 9, 1957.

969 End of the Rope. NBC-TV, 1957. 54 minutes Color. SC: Sheldon Stark. WITH John Barrymore Jr., Susan Oliver, George Peppard, Norma Moore, Parley Baer, John Conte. A man finds himself in an Arizona town where the populace is wanting to lynch him. Telefeature originally shown as an episode of "Matinee Theatre" (NBC-TV, 1955-58) on April 1, 1957.

970 End of the Trail. Columbia, 1932. 60 minutes B/W. D: D. Ross Lederman. SC: Stuart Anthony. WITH Tim McCoy, Luana Walters, Wheeler Oakman, Wally Albright, Lafe McKee, Wade Boteler, Chief White Eagle. A soldier, forced out of the army after being falsely accused

of giving guns to the Indians, goes to live with the Arapahoes after his adopted son is killed but eventually thwarts a massacre. Exceedingly well done film which is not hurt by a tacked-on happy ending, perhaps Tim McCoy's finest film.

971 End of the Trail. Columbia, 1936. 70 minutes B/W. D: Erle C. Kenton. SC: Harold Shumate. WITH Jack Holt, Louise Henry, Guinn Williams, Douglass Dumbrille, George McKay, Gene Morgan, John McGuire, Ed Le Saint, Frank Shannon, Erle C. Kenton, Hank Bell, Art Mix, Blackie Whiteford, Blackjack Ward, Edgar Dearing. Two friends, who have grown up together, are on opposite sides of the law and both are in love with the same girl. Top notch Jack Holt feature with an adult theme; very well done.

972 Enemy of the Law. Producers Releasing Corporation, 1945. 59 minutes B/W. D-SC: Harry Fraser. WITH Tex Ritter, Dave O'Brien, Guy Wilkerson, Kay Hughes, Jack Ingram, Charles King, Frank Ellis, Kermit Maynard, Henry Hall, Karl Hackett, Ed Cassidy, Ben Corbett. The Texas Rangers track down a gang, who years before robbed a safe and hid the loot, in order to recover the money and capture the outlaws. A rather dull "Texas Rangers" series entry with a meandering plot, somewhat saved by Tex Ritter singing "Teach Me to Forget" and "You Will Have to Pay."

973 Enter the Devil. Artists International, 1971. 86 minutes Color. D-SC: Frank Q. Dobbs & David Cass. WITH Josh Bryant, Irene Kelly, David Cass, Carle Benson, Linda Rascoe, John Martin, Nodris Dominque, Wanda Wilson, Ed Geldert, Happy Shahan. An anthropologist looking for cult sub-cultures in the Texas desert comes across a group of devil worshippers. Mediocre horror feature originally called **Disciples of Death.**

974 Epitaph for a Fast Gun. Jack H. Harris, 1967. 82 minutes Color. D: Nick Nostro. SC: Astrain Bada. WITH Michael Riva, Diana Garson, Albert Farley, Indio Gonzales, Jack Rocks. An aging sheriff teams with the young man, who loves his daughter, in cleaning up a tough town. Average Italian-Spanish concoction originally issued by Cineproduzioni Associate/ I.F.I.S.A. as **Un Dollaro Di Fuoco** (A Dollar of Fire).

975 Escape from Fort Bravo. Metro-Goldwyn-Mayer, 1953. 98 minutes Color.

D: John Sturges. SC: Frank Fenton.
WITH William Holden, Eleanor Parker,
John Forsythe, William Demarest, William
Campbell, John Lupton, Richard Anderson,
Polly Bergen, Carl Benton Reid. During
the Civil War, a woman manages to help
her Confederate fiancée and fellow prisoners escape from the Yankees, only
to find themselves under attack by hostile
Indians. A good story and a compact
cast make this interesting viewing.

976 Escape from Red Rock. 20th Century-
Fox, 1958. 79 minutes B/W. D-SC: Edward
Bernds. WITH Brian Donlevy, Eileen
Janssen, Gary Murray, Jay C. Flippen,
William Phipps, Michael (Myron) Healey,
Nesdon Booth, Rick Vallin, Dan White,
Andre Adoree, Courtland Shepard, Tina
Menard, Zon Murray, Ed Hinton, Frosty
Royce, Frank Richards, Hank Patterson,
Eileen Stevens, Frank Marlowe, Dick
Crockett, Sailor Vincent. A young rancher,
in order to save his brother's life, is
forced to take part in a robbery by the
latter's gang, and to escape a posse he
flees into the desert with his girlfriend
although Indians are on the warpath.
Entertaining and actionful oater with
good work by Brian Donlevy as the gang
leader, Myron Healey as a vicious gang
member and Eilene Janssen as the girl.

977 Escape in the Desert. Warner Brothers,
1945. 81 minutes B/W. D: Edward A.
Blatt. SC: Thomas Job. WITH Philip
Dorn, Helmut Dantine, Alan Hale, Jean
Sullivan, Irene Manning, Samuel S. Hinds,
Bill Kennedy, Kurt Kreuger, Rudolph
Anders, Hans Schumann. A flier tries
to capture an escaped Nazi he spots
in an Arizona desert cafe. Mediocre
reworking of **The Petrified Forest** (q.v.).

Escondido see **A Minute to Pray, a
Second to Die**

978 Escort West. United Artists, 1959.
75 minutes B/W. D: Francis D. Lyon.
SC: Leo Gordon & Fred Hartsook. WITH
Victor Mature, Elaine Stewart, Faith
Domergue, Reba Waters, Noah Beery
Jr., Leo Gordon, Rex Ingram, John Hubbard, Harry Carey Jr., Slim Pickens,
Roy Barcroft, William Ching, Ken Curtis,
X Brands, Chuck Hayward, Charles Soldani,
Claire DuBrey. An ex-Confederate soldier
and his small daughter head West after
the Civil War and are snubbed by a Union
wagon train but they later find the two
female survivors of the train, which
had been attacked by Indians. Competent
but only average sagebrush outing.

979 Eureka Stockade. British-Pathe,
1949. 103 minutes B/W. D-SC: Harry
Watt. WITH Chips Rafferty, Gordon
Jackson, Peter Illing, Peter Finch. In
Australia in 1853 miners fight for the
right to hunt for gold, the events leading
to the designing of the nation's first
flag. Exciting and well produced frontier
melodrama from J. Arthur Rank.

980 Everybody's Dancin! Lippert, 1950.
67 minutes B/W. D: William Berke. SC:
Bob Nunes & Spade Cooley. WITH Spade
Cooley, Dick (Richard) Lane, Hal Derwin,
James Millican, Lyle Talbot, Michael
Whalen, Sid Melton, The Sons of the
Pioneers, Roddy McDowell, Adele Jergens,
James Ellison, Russell Hayden, Barbara
Woodell, Ginny Jackson, Tex Cromer,
Bobby Hyatt, Chuy Reyes Orchestra.
Crooks are out to get a ballroom owner's
business and several show business stars
come to his rescue. Cheaply made but
flavorful Western musical.

981 Everyman's Law. Supreme, 1936.
61 minutes B/W. D: Albert Ray. SC:
Earle Snell. WITH Johnny Mack Brown,
Beth Marion, Frank Campeau, Roger
Gray, Lloyd Ingraham, John Beck, Horace
Murphy, Richard Alexander, Slim Whitaker,
Ed Cassidy, Jim Corey, George Morrell.
A trio of lawmen pretend to be hired
guns in order to get the goods on a rancher
who is harassing homesteaders. A good
entry in Johnny Mack Brown's Supreme
series.

982 Evil Roy Slade. NBC-TV/Universal,
1972. 100 minutes Color. D: Jerry Paris.
SC: Garry Marshall & Jerry Belson. WITH
John Astin, Edie Adams, Dick Shawn,
Milton Berle, Pamela Austin, Mickey
Rooney, Dom DeLuise, Henry Gibson,
Arthur Batanides, Larry Hankin, Milton
Frome, Luana Anders, Robert Liberman,
Connie Sawyer, Pat Morita, Leonard
Barr. A notorious outlaw tries to mend
his ways when he falls in love with an
innocent school teacher but he is plagued
by a sheriff out to capture him. Poorly
conceived and executed Western comedy.

983 An Eye for an Eye. Embassy, 1966.
92 minutes Color. D: Michael Moore.
SC: Bing Russell & Sumner Williams.
WITH Robert Lansing, Pat(rick) Wayne,
Slim Pickens, Gloria Talbott, Paul Fix,
Strother Martin, Henry Wills, Jerry Gatlin,
Rance Howard, Clint Howard. An ex-
bounty hunter is out to get the men who
murdered his wife and son and enlists
the aid of another man to help him as

both are physically handicapped. An interesting plot adds some life to this feature.

984 Eyes of Texas. Republic, 1948. 54 (70) minutes Color. D: William Witney. SC: Sloan Nibley. WITH Roy Rogers, Lynne Roberts, Andy Devine, Bob Nolan & The Sons of the Pioneers, Nana Bryant, Roy Barcroft, Danny Morton, Francis Ford, Stanley Blystone. A rancher turns his spread into a camp for war-orphaned youngsters but outlaws are also after the land. Okay entry in Roy Rogers' series; fast on action and good use of color. V: Video Connection.

F

985 The Fabulous Texan. Republic, 1947. 96 minutes B/W. D: Edward Ludwig. SC: Lawrence Hazard & Horace McCoy. WITH William Elliott, John Carroll, Catherine McLeod, Andy Devine, Albert Dekker, Jim Davis, Ruth Donnelly, Russell Simpson, James Brown, George Beban, Tommy Kelly, Johnny Sands, Harry Davenport, John Miles, Robert Coleman, Robert Barrat, Douglass Dumbrille, Reed Hadley, Roy Barcroft, Frank Ferguson, Glenn Strange, Selmar Jackson, Harry V. Cheshire, Harry Woods, Karl Hackett, John Hamilton, Pierre Watkin, Ed Cassidy, Tristram Coffin, Stanley Andrews, Olin Howlin, Kenneth MacDonald, Jack Ingram, Ted Mapes, Pierce Lyden, Al Ferguson, Ethan Laidlaw, Ray Teal, Franklyn Farnum. When the carpetbaggers take over Texas after the Civil War, a man is forced to become a bandit in order to defend himself and his rights. Very well done William Elliott film with a top notch cast of character actors.

986 Face of a Fugitive. Columbia, 1959. 81 minutes Color. D: Paul Wendkos. SC: David T. Chantler & Daniel B. Ullman. WITH Fred MacMurray, Lin McCarthy, Dorothy Green, Alan Baxter, Myrna Fahey, James Coburn, Francis De Sales, Gina Gillespie, Paul Burns, Buzz Henry, James Gavin, Hal K. Dawson, Harrison Lewis. When he is falsely accused of murder, a man takes on a new identity in another town, but he finds he cannot shake his past. Fairly entertaining oater with Fred MacMurray good as the fugitive.

987 Face to Face. RKO Radio, 1952. 92 minutes B/W. D: Bretaigne Windust.

SC: James Agee. WITH Robert Preston, Marjorie Steele, Minor Watson, Dan Seymour, Olive Carey, James Agee. A man brings his young bride to a small Western town where they plan to settle down. Dull adaptation of the Stephen Crane story "The Bride Comes to Yellow Sky" makes up one-half of this feature film, the other half being James Mason in Joseph Conrad's "The Secret Sharer."

988 Face to the Wind. Warner Brothers, 1974. 93 minutes Color. D: William A. Graham. SC: David Markson. WITH Cliff Potts, Xochitl, Harry Dean Stanton, Don Wilbanks, Woodrow Chambliss, James Gammon, Roy Jenson, William Carstens, Richard Breeding. When a young drifter meets and falls in love with an Indian maiden the two find themselves the object of hate and violence. Obscure and violent oater which was first issued in 1972 as **Cry for Me, Billy.** Alternate titles: **Apache Massacre, Count Your Blessings** and **The Long Tomorrow.**

989 Fade-In. Paramount, 1968. 93 minutes Color. D: Allen Smithee (Jud Taylor). SC: Jerry Ludwig & Mart Crowley. WITH Burt Reynolds, Barbara Loden, Patricia Casey, Noam Pitlik, James Hampton, Joseph Perry, Lawrence Heller, Wage Tucker, Sally Kirkland, George Savalas, Jason Heller, Jud Taylor. During the filming of the movie **Blue** (q.v.) a cowboy working as an extra falls in love with an attractive film editor. This film received no official release and was made simultaneously with **Blue** by co-producer Silvio Narizzano, who directed the former film; nothing special but watchable.

990 Fair Warning. Fox, 1931. 74 minutes B/W. D: Alfred Werker. SC: Ernest Pascal. WITH George O'Brien, Louise Huntington, Mitchell Harris, George Brent, Nat Pendleton, Willard Robertson, Ernie Adams, John Sheehan, Erwin Connelly, Alphonse Ethier. A cowboy tries to prove that two men were responsible for the robbery of a saloon. Entertaining George O'Brien "B plus" actioner.

991 The Falcon Out West. RKO Radio, 1944. 64 minutes B/W. D: William Clemens. SC: Billy Jones & Morton Grant. WITH Tom Conway, Carole Gallagher, Barbara Hale, Joan Barclay, Cliff Clark, Minor Watson, Don Douglas, Edward Gargan, Lyle Talbot, Lee Trent, Perc Launders, Wheaton Chambers, Chief Thundercloud, Robert Anderson, Edmund Glover, Rosemary La Blanche, Elaine Riley, Shirley

O'Hara, Patti Brill, Bert Roach, Norman Willis, Kernan Cripps, Slim Whitaker, William Nestell. When a wealthy Texas rancher is murdered in New York City, detective Tom Lawrence, alias The Falcon, goes to the man's ranch in Texas in order to uncover the killer. Nicely done entry in the "Falcon" series with a good Western flavor.

992 False Colors. United Artists, 1943. 54 (65) minutes B/W. D: George Archainbaud. SC: Bennett Cohen. WITH William Boyd, Andy Clyde, Jimmy Rogers, Tom Seidel, Claudia Drake, Douglass Dumbrille, Robert Mitchum, Glenn Strange, Pierce Lyden, Roy Barcroft, Sam Flint, Earle Hodgins, Elmer Jerome, Tom London, Dan White, George Morrell, Bob Burns. One of the Bar 20 wranglers inherits a ranch but is soon killed and Hoppy agrees to look after the place and the dead man's sister, but a crooked banker, who was behind the murder, is out to get the land for himself. Excellent photography (by Russell Harlan), a good plot and nice action makes this a good "Hopalong Cassidy" entry.

993 False Paradise. United Artists, 1948. 54 (60) minutes B/W. D: George Archainbaud. SC: Harrison Jacobs & Doris Schroeder. WITH William Boyd, Andy Clyde, Rand Brooks, Elaine Riley, Joel Friedkin, Cliff Clark, Kenneth MacDonald, Don Haggerty, Richard Alexander, William Norton Bailey, Zon Murray, George Eldredge. Hoppy and pals California Carlson and Lucky Jenkins come to the aid of ranchers whose silver-rich lands are being sought by a crooked banker who holds their mortgages. Last theatrical entry in the "Hopalong Cassidy" series and a long way from the best.

994 Fancy Pants. Paramount, 1950. 92 minutes Color. D: George Marshall. SC: Edmund Hartman & Robert O'Brien. WITH Bob Hope, Lucille Ball, Bruce Cabot, Lea Penman, Hugh French, Eric Blore, Joseph Vitale, John Alexander, Norma Varden, Virginia Keiley, Colin Keith-Johnston, Joe Wong. A high-class British butler is hired by a newly rich Western girl to bring culture to her community. Okay remake of **Ruggles of Red Gap** (q.v.) with the star billed as "Mr. Robert Hope."

995 Fangs of Fate. Chesterfield, 1925. 60 minutes B/W. D-SC: Horace B. Carpenter. WITH Bill Patton, Dorothy Donald, Ivor McFadden, Beatrice Allen, William Bertram, Merrill McCormick, Tex Starr, Carl Silvera. An outlaw goes straight for the sake of a girl and when his old gang refuses to quit he becomes a deputy sheriff to capture them. Fairly good silent horse opera, although Bill Patton is a rather staid hero.

996 Fangs of the Arctic. Monogram, 1953. 63 minutes B/W. D: Rex Bailey. SC: Bill Raynor & Warren Douglas. WITH Kirby Grant, Lorna Hansen, Warren Douglas, Leonard Penn, Richard Avonde, Robert Sherman, John Close, Roy Gordon, Kit Carson, Chinook (dog). A Mountie and his husky dog are on the trail of crooks who are engaged in illegal trapping. Passable production of the James Oliver Curwood story, made on the cheap.

997 Fangs of the Wild. Astor/Metropolitan, 1941. 55 minutes B/W. D: Raymond K. Johnson. SC: R. D. Pearsall. WITH Rin-Tin-Tin Jr., Dennis Moore, Luana Walters, Tom London, Mae Busch, Theodore (Ted) Adams, George Chesebro, James (Jimmie) Aubrey, Bud Osborne, George Morrell, Martin Spellman. A federal investigator and his trusty dog try to find out who is behind the thefts of silver foxes from breeding ranches. Fast paced and somewhat scenic poverty row actioner.

998 Fangs of the Wild. Lippert, 1954. 71 minutes B/W. D: William F. Claxton. SC: Orville Hampton & William F. Claxton. WITH Charles Chaplin Jr., Onslow Stevens, Margia Dean, Freddie Ridgeway, Phil Tead, Robert Stevenson, Buck (dog). A young boy witnesses a murder in the north woods but he cannot convince his father about what he saw and he soon becomes the target of the murderer. Cheaply made but scenic and quite entertaining little "B" drama. TV title: **Follow the Hunter.**

999 The Far Country. Universal, 1955. 96 minutes Color. D: Anthony Mann. SC: Borden Chase. WITH James Stewart, Ruth Roman, Corinne Calvet, Walter Brennan, John McIntire, Jay C. Flippen, Harry Morgan, Steve Brodie, Connie Gilchrist, Robert Wilke, Chubby Johnson, Royal Dano, Jack Elam, Kathleen Freeman, Guy Wilkerson, John Doucette, Eddy Waller, Eugene Borden, Robert Foulk, Paul Bryar, Edwin Parker. A loner and his pal take their cattle herd by boat to Alaska and find lots of trouble in the mining camps there. Big budget and quite entertaining oater.

1000 The Far Frontier. Republic, 1948. 54 (67) minutes Color. D: William Witney. SC: Sloan Nibley. WITH Roy Rogers, Gail Davis, Andy Devine, Francis Ford, Roy Barcroft, Clayton Moore, Foy Willing & The Riders of the Purple Sage, Lane Bradford, Edmund Cobb, Holly Bane, Clarence Straight, Tom London. Two men smuggle gangsters who have been deported back into the United States and they plan to buy out a rancher but are thwarted by Roy Rogers and pal Cookie Bullfincher. A pretty good action feature in which the villains and supporting cast dominate the film in deference to star Roy Rogers. V: NTA Home Entertainment.

1001 The Far Horizons. Paramount, 1955. 108 minutes Color. D: Rudolph Mate. SC: Winston Miller & Edmund H. North. WITH Fred MacMurray, Charlton Heston, Donna Reed, Barbara Hale, William Demarest, Alan Reed, Eduardo Noriega, Larry Pennell, Argentina Brunetti, Ralph Moody, Herbert Heyes, Lester Matthews, Helen Wallace, Walter Reed, Voltaire Perkins, Joe Canutt. The story of the Meriwether Lewis-William Clark expedition into the recently purchased Louisiana Territory. Colorful but highly fictional account of the famous trek with Donna Reed badly miscast as Sacajawea.

1002 The Far Out West. Universal, 1967. 87 minutes Color. D: Joe Connelly. SC: George Tibbles. WITH Ann Sheridan, Ruth McDevitt, Douglas V. Fowley, Gary Vinson, Carole Wells, Robert Lowery, Morgan Woodward, Lon Chaney, Marc Cavel, Leo Gordon, Jay Silverheels, Alex Henteloff, Stanley Adams, Lee Patrick, Charles Meredith, Gil Lamb, Quinn O'Hara, Fred Williams, George Murdock, Bill Oberlin, Willis Bouchey. A gun-toting frontier family is at odds with a greedy saloon owner and his hired gunman. Rather amusing telefeature sewn together from episodes of the television series "Pistols 'n Petticoats" (CBS-TV, 1967-68).

1003 Fargo. Monogram, 1952. 69 minutes B/W. D: Lewis Collins. SC: Joseph Poland & Jack DeWitt. WITH Bill Elliott, Phyllis Coates, Myron Healey, Fuzzy Knight, Arthur Space, Robert Wilke, Jack Ingram, Terry Frost, Robert Bray, Tim Ryan, Florence Lake, Stanley Andrews, Richard Reeves, Gene Roth. After his brother is murdered by a cattleman, a man returns to North Dakota and begins helping the small ranchers in fencing off the range,

thus starting a range war. Nicely done tale of barbed wire being introduced on the range.

1004 Fargo Express. World Wide/Fox, 1933. 61 minutes B/W. D: Alan James. SC: Alan James & Earle Snell. WITH Ken Maynard, Helen Mack, Paul Fix, William Desmond, Roy Stewart, Jack Rockwell, Claude Payton, Joe Rickson, Hank Bell, Bud McClure. A cowboy tries to help a young man who has robbed the Fargo Express because he loves the bandit's pretty sister. Pretty good Ken Maynard vehicle.

1005 The Fargo Kid. RKO Radio, 1940. 63 minutes B/W. D: Edward Killy. SC: W. C. Tuttle. WITH Tim Holt, Jane Drummond, Ray Whitley, Emmett Lynn, Cy Kendall, Ernie Adams, Paul Fix, Paul Scardon, Glenn Strange, Mary MacLaren, Dick Hogan, Carl Stockdale, Harry Harvey, Lee Phelps. A young man is mistaken for an outlaw and two crooked businessmen try to hire him to kill a man so they can get his ore-rich land from the intended victim's widow. Well done remake of **The Cheyenne Kid** (q.v.).

1006 Fast Bullets. Reliable, 1936. 59 minutes B/W. D: Henri Samuels (Harry S. Webb). SC: Carl Krusada & Rose Gordon. WITH Tom Tyler, Rex Lease, Margaret Nearing, Alan Bridge, William Gould, Robert Walker, Slim Whitaker, Jimmie Aubrey, Nelson McDowell, Lew Meehan, George Chesebro, Charles King. A government ranger is on the trail of smugglers and enlists the help of a gang member whose pretty sister is the object of the gang leader's affections. Pretty low grade Tom Tyler effort.

1007 Fast on the Draw. Lippert, 1950. 57 minutes B/W. D: Thomas Carr. SC: Maurice Tombragel & Ron Ormond. WITH James Ellison, Russell Hayden, Raymond Hatton, Fuzzy Knight, Betty (Julie) Adams, Tom Tyler, George J. Lewis, John Cason, Dennis Moore, Judith Webster, Bud Osborne, Helen Gibson, Stanley Price, Ray Jones, I. Stanford Jolley, Cliff Taylor. Texas Rangers are after a dishonest landowner and one of them poses as an outlaw in order to get the goods on the bad man. Tacky production which wastes a good cast. TV title: **Sudden Death.**

1008 The Fastest Guitar Alive. Metro-Goldwyn-Mayer, 1967. 88 minutes Color. D: Michael Moore. SC: Robert E. Kent.

WITH Roy Orbison, Sammy Jackson, Maggie Pierce, Joan Freeman, Lyle Bettger, John Doucette, Patricia Donohue, Ben Cooper, Douglas Kennedy, Len Hendry, Iron Eyes Cody, Victoria Carroll, Maria Korda. Near the end of the Civil War, Confederate spies steal gold from the U. S. mint in San Francisco and when they find out the war is over they have to replace the money without being detected. Sam Katzman cheapie made to exploit the popularity of singer Roy Orbison and with the latter singing plenty of songs, the film will please his fans.

1009 The Fastest Gun Alive. Metro-Goldwyn-Mayer, 1956. 89 minutes B/W. D: Russell Rouse. SC: Frank D. Gilroy & Russell Rouse. WITH Glenn Ford, Jeanne Crain, Broderick Crawford, Russ Tamblyn, Allyn Joslyn, Leif Erickson, John Dehner, Noah Beery Jr., J. M. Kerrigan, Rhys Williams, Virginia Gregg, Chubby Johnson, John Doucette, William Phillips, Paul Birch. A peaceful storekeeper, who was once a famous gunfighter, is forced into a showdown with a bad man who threatens to destroy the man's town. The old saw about the ex-gunfighter trying to live down his past is nicely retold in this entertaining feature.

1010 Female Artillery. ABC-TV/Universal, 1973. 73 minutes Color. D: Marvin Chomsky. SC: Bud Freeman. WITH Dennis Weaver, Ida Lupino, Sally Ann Howes, Linda Evans, Lee Harcourt Montgomery, Albert Salmi, Nina Foch, Anna Navarro, Charles Dierkop, Robert Sorrells, Bobby Eilbacher. An outlaw steals gold from another gang and hides it in a wagon train consisting of women who find the loot and blackmail the man into taking them to a fort. None-too-amusing Western comedy, which wastes a nice cast.

1011 The Female Bunch. Dalia, 1972. 86 minutes Color. D: Al Adamson & John Cardos. SC: Jale Lockwood & Brent Nimrod. WITH Russ Tamblyn, Jenifer Bishop, Lon Chaney, Nesa Renet, Geoffrey Land, Regina Carrol, Don Epperson, John Cardos, Albert Cole, A'Lesha Lee, Jackie Taylor, Leslie MacRae, William Bonner, Bobby Clark. A group of hell raising girls work with a one-time movie stuntman in smuggling drugs over the U. S.-Mexican border. Violent modern-day oater of interest only because it was Lon Chaney's final film appearance.

1012 Fence Riders. Monogram, 1950. 57 minutes B/W. D: Wallace Fox. SC:

Eliot Gibbons. WITH Whip Wilson, Andy Clyde, Reno Browne, Riley Hill, Myron Healey, Ed Cassidy, Terry Frost, Frank McCarroll, George DeNormand, Holly Bane, John Merton, Buck Bailey. A cowboy and his pal come to the aid of a pretty rancher whose cattle are being rustled. Okay Whip Wilson series outing.

1013 The Ferocious Pal. Principal, 1934. 55 minutes B/W. D: Spencer Gordon Bennet. SC: Joe Roach. WITH Ruth Sullivan, Gene Toler, Robert Manning, Tom London, Grace Wood, Edward Cecil, Kazan (dog). A boy and his dog help a man and a girl fight crooks. Exceedingly low budget juvenile programmer.

1014 The Feud Maker. Republic, 1938. 60 minutes B/W. D: Sam Newfield. SC: George Plympton. WITH Bob Steele, Marion Weldon, Karl Hackett, Frank Ball, Budd Buster, Lew Meehan, Roger Williams, Forrest Taylor, Steve Clark, Lloyd Ingraham, Sherry Tansey, Wally West. A cowpoke tries to stop a crook who has instigated a feud between ranchers and homesteaders. Typically actionful Bob Steele oater in his A. W. Hackel series.

1015 Feud of the Range. Metropolitan, 1939. 55 minutes B/W. D: Harry S. Webb. SC: Carl Krusada. WITH Bob Steele, Gertrude Messinger, Jean Cranford, Richard Cramer, Frank LaRue, Bob Burns, Budd Buster, Jack Ingram, Charles King, Denver Dixon, Carl Mathews. A badman instigates a feud on the range in order to obtain land and a cowboy sets out to stop him. Cheap Bob Steele outing for Harry S. Webb, which is loaded with stock footage. Also called **Feud on the Range.**

1016 Feud of the Trail. Victory, 1937. 56 minutes B/W. D: Robert Hill. SC: Basil Dickey. WITH Tom Tyler, Harley Wood, Milburn Morante, Roger Williams, Lafe McKee, Richard Alexander, Slim Whitaker, Jim Corey. A family which belongs to the grange has its gold stolen by crooks and a cowboy sets out to recover the money. Very, very cheaply made Sam Katzman production, which does nothing to enhance Tom Tyler.

1017 Feud of the West. Diversion, 1936. 62 minutes B/W. D: Harry Fraser. SC: Phil Dunham. WITH Hoot Gibson, Joan Barclay, Buzz Barton, Reed Howes, Robert Kortman, Ed Cassidy, Nelson McDowell, Roger Williams, Allen Greer, Richard

Cramer. A rodeo rider is hired by a rancher to get evidence on the gang who killed his son and nephew and the cowpoke ends up being accused of murder and is forced to head for the hills. The lack of good production values hurt this Hoot Gibson vehicle for producer Walter Futter.

Feud on the Range see **Feud of the Range**

1018 A Few Bullets More. RAF Industries, 1969. 90 minutes Color. D-SC: Julio Buchs. WITH Peter Lee Lawrence, Gloria Milland, Fausto Tozzi, Dianik Zuratowska. Seventeen-year-old Billy Bonney becomes a fugitive when he kills the man who raped his mother and he seeks refuge with Pat Garrett, a friend of his late father, but eventually turns to a life of crime. Violent Italian retelling of the Billy the Kid saga; for fans only. Issued in Italy in 1967 by Kinesis/Aitor Film as ...**E Divenne Il Piu Spietato Bandito Del Sud** (...And He Became the Most Ruthless Bandit in the South).

1019 A Few Dollars for Django. Italian, 1966. 87 minutes Color. D: Leon Klimovsky. SC: Manuel Sebares & Tito Carpi. WITH Antonio De Teffe (Anthony Steffen), Gloria Osuna, Frank Wolff, Enzo Girolami, Thomas Moore, Joe Kammell, Alfredo Rojas, Angel Ter. A bounty hunter tracks down a gang of killers in old Montana. Violent Italian western for fans of the genre only. Original title: **Pochi Dollari Per Django.** TV Title: **A Few Dollars for Gypsy.**

1020 The Fiddlin' Buckaroo. Universal, 1933. 63 minutes B/W. D: Ken Maynard. SC: Nate Gatzert. WITH Ken Maynard, Gloria Shea, Fred Kohler, Frank Rice, Jack Rockwell, Jack Mower, Bob McKenzie, Joe Girard, Slim Whitaker, Pascale Perry, Frank Ellis, Roy Bucko, Buck Bucko, Bud McClure, Hank Bell, Jack Kirk, Robert Walker, Clem Horton. Arrested for supposedly aiding an outlaw gang in a robbery, an undercover government agent breaks jail when the gang kidnaps a rancher's pretty daughter. A bit on the slow side with too much music, this film was also produced, as well as directed, by star Ken Maynard.

1021 The Fiend Who Walked the West. 20th Century-Fox, 1958. 101 minutes B/W. D: Gordon Douglas. SC: Harry Brown & Philip Yordan. WITH Hugh O'Brian, Robert Evans, Dolores Michaels, Linda Cristal, Stephen McNally, Edward Andrews,

Ron Ely, Ken Scott, Emile Meyer, Gregory Morton, Georgia Simmons. A madman escapes from prison and goes on a killing spree and his cellmate is allowed to escape in order to stop him. Exceedingly brutal film.

1022 $50,000 Reward. Davis Distributing, 1924. 49 minutes B/W. D: Clifford S. Elfelt. SC: Frank Howard Clark. WITH Ken Maynard, Esther Ralston, Bert Lindley, Ed Peil Sr., Lillian Leighton, Charles Newton, Frank Whitson. A cowboy inherits a ranch where a dam is to be built and a crooked banker wants the land for himself. Ken Maynard's first series film is an exciting affair and one which launched his genre career. V: Blackhawk.

1023 The Fighter. United Artists, 1952. 78 minutes B/W. D: Herbert Kline. SC: Aben Kendall & Herbert Kline. WITH Richard Conte, Vanessa Brown, Lee J. Cobb, Frank Silvera, Roberta Haynes, Hugh Sanders, Claire Carleton, Martin Garralaga, Argentina Brunetti, Rodolfo Hoyos Jr., Margaret Padilla. After his family is murdered in the Mexican Revolution in 1910, a young man takes up boxing in order to get money to buy weapons for guerillas. Pretty good screen version of Jack London's story "The Mexican."

Fighters in the Saddle see **Fighters of the Saddle**

1024 Fighters of the Saddle. Davis, 1929. 50 minutes B/W. WITH Art Acord, Peggy Montgomery, John Lowell, Tom Bay, Betty Carter, Lynn Sanderson, Cliff Lyons, Jack Ponder. The owner of a land company wants a ranch for a county road expansion and frames a young girl and her brother who have leased the property. Cheaply made Art Acord vehicle (one of his final films) but it should please his many fans. Alternate title: **Fighters in the Saddle.**

1025 Fightin' Jack. Goodwill, 1926. 40 minutes B/W. D: Louis Chaudet. SC: Peggene Olcott. WITH Bill Bailey, Hazel Deane, Frona Hale, John Byron, Sailor Sharkey, Herma Cordova. A cowboy rescues a girl after falling from a cliff but he soon finds out that a crook and his gang are after her ranch. Fast action and nice scenery make up for a mediocre story in this silent Bill Bailey vehicle.

1026 Fighting Bill Carson. Producers Releasing Corporation, 1945. 55 minutes B/W. D: Sam Newfield. SC: Louise Rosseau.

WITH Buster Crabbe, Al St. John, Lorraine Miller, Kay Hughes, I. Stanford Jolley, Kermit Maynard, Bob Cason, Budd Buster, Bud Osborne, Charles King. Billy Carson and pal Fuzzy Q. Jones rescue a girl from a stagecoach holdup only to later discover that she is part of the outlaw gang. Average entry in PRC's "Billy Carson" series.

1027 Fighting Bill Fargo. Universal, 1942. 58 minutes B/W. D: Ray Taylor. SC: Paul Franklin, Dorcas Cochran & Arthur V. Jones. WITH Johnny Mack Brown, Fuzzy Knight, Jeanne Kelly, Kenneth Harlan, Nell O'Day, Ted Adams, James Blaine, Al Bridge, The Eddie Dean Trio, Robert Kortman, Earle Hodgins, Tex Palmer, Harry Tenbrook, Kermit Maynard, Blackie Whiteford, Merrill McCormack, Bud Osborne. A man returns home to help his sister run his late father's newspaper and he becomes involved with crooks trying to control the election of the town's sheriff. Rather good Johnny Mack Brown entry with songs by Eddie Dean and his trio.

1028 Fighting Caballero. Superior/First Division, 1935. 59 minutes B/W. D: Elmer Clifton. SC: Elmer Clifton & George Merrick. WITH Rex Lease, Dorothy Gulliver, George Chesebro, Robert Walker, Wally Wales, Earl Douglas, Milburn Morante, George Morrell, Carl Mathews, Franklyn Farnum, Paul Ellis. A cowboy comes to the aid of a silver mine owner being harrassed by an outlaw gang. Cheaply made Rex Lease film.

1029 Fighting Caravans. Paramount, 1931. 91 minutes B/W. D: Otto Brower & David Burton. SC: Edward G. Paramore Jr., Kenne Thompson & Agnes Brand Leahy. WITH Gary Cooper, Lily Damita, Ernest Torrence, Fred Kohler, Tully Marshall, Eugene Pallette, Roy Stewart, May Boley, James Farley, James Marcus, Eve Southern, Donald Mackenzie, Syd Saylor, E. Alyn Warren, Frank Campeau, Charles Winninger, Frank Hagney, Jane Darwell, Irving Bacon, Harry Semels, Iron Eyes Cody, Merrill McCormick, Tiny Sanford, Chief Big Tree. A young wagonmaster and his two pals lead a wagon train of pioneers across the plains, fighting outlaws and Indians. Better-than-average actioner which had footage used later in **Wagon Wheels** (q.v.). TV title: **Blazing Arrows.**

1030 The Fighting Champ. Monogram, 1932. 56 minutes B/W. D: J. P. McCarthy.

SC: Wellyn Totman. WITH Bob Steele, Arletta Duncan, Kit Guard, George Chesebro, George ("Gabby") Hayes, Charles King, Henry Rocquemore, Lafe McKee, Frank Ball, Si Jenks. A cowboy who foils a stage holdup is drafted into fighting a traveling boxer. A well staged boxing match highlights this Bob Steele actioner which also has a good performance by George Chesebro as an oily fight manager.

1031 The Fighting Code. Columbia, 1934. 65 minutes B/W. D-SC: Lambert Hillyer. WITH Buck Jones, Diane Sinclair, Niles Welch, Ward Bond, Richard Alexander, Louis Natheux, Alf James, Erville Alderson, Gertrude Howard, Robert Kortman, Charles Brinley, Buck Moulton. A cowboy tries to find out who killed a girl's father. Excellent Buck Jones vehicle enhanced by its mystery motif.

1032 The Fighting Cowboy. Superior, 1933. 58 minutes B/W. D: Denver Dixon (Victor Adamson). SC: L.V. Jefferson. WITH Buffalo Bill Jr., Genee Boutell, Allen Holbrook, William Ryno, Marin Sais, Tom Palky, Bart Carre, Jack Evans, Boris Bullock, Ken Brocker, Betty Butler, Clyde McClary. An investigator stops a bad man from stealing an old miner's tungsten claim, as well as his pretty daughter. About as shoddy as a film can be.

1033 The Fighting Deputy. Spectrum, 1937. 60 minutes B/W. D: Sam Newfield. SC: William Lively. WITH Fred Scott, Al St. John, Phoebe Logan, Marjorie Beebe, Charles King, Lafe McKee, Frank LaRue, Eddie Holden, Sherry Tansey, Jack C. Smith, Chick Hannon, Jack Evans. A cowboy takes over his dad's lawman job to hunt down the man who ambushed him only to find out the culprit is his fiancée's long-lost brother. Although the plot is not much, this outing is fairly well staged and Fred Scott makes a grand singing cowboy cavalier.

1034 The Fighting Fool. Columbia, 1932. 58 minutes B/W. D: Lambert Hillyer. SC: Frank Clark. WITH Tim McCoy, Marceline Day, Mary Carr, Robert Ellis, Ethel Wales, Dorothy Granger, Robert Kortman, Arthur Rankin, Harry Todd, William V. Mong. A cowboy is on the trail of an outlaw gang led by a masked phantom. Rather slow going in this Tim McCoy film.

1035 Fighting for Justice. Columbia, 1932. 60 minutes B/W. D: Otto Brower.

SC: Robert Quigley. WITH Tim McCoy, Joyce Compton, Hooper Atchley, William Norton Bailey, Lafe McKee, Walter Brennan, Harry Todd, Harry Cording, Robert Frazer, Murdock McQuarrie, William V. Mong, Charles King. Crooks kill a man who has just bought a cattle ranch belonging to another man, and the latter must clear himself of the charge of murder. A good script and effective action make this a good Tim McCoy vehicle.

1036 Fighting Frontier. RKO Radio, 1943. 57 minutes B/W. D: Lambert Hillyer. SC: J. Benton Cheney & Norton S. Parker. WITH Tim Holt, Cliff Edwards, Ann Summers, Eddie Dew, William Gould, Davidson Clark, Slim Whitaker, Tom London, Monte Montague, Jack Rockwell, Bud Osborne, Russell Wade. An undercover agent is assigned by the governor to join an outlaw gang in order to get the goods on its leader. Good entry in Tim Holt's long-running and high-grade RKO series.

1037 Fighting Fury. J. D. Trop, 1934. 61 minutes B/W. D: Robert Hill. SC: Myron Dattlebaum. WITH John King, Bonita Baker, Tom London, Lafe McKee, Philo McCullough, Bart Carre, Del Morgan, Jack Donovan, Kazan (dog), Cactus (horse). Kazan the wonder dog and Cactus, a beautiful white stallion, aid a cowboy called the Lone Ranger as he opposes an outlaw gang. Low grade actioner produced by John King (not the later John "Dusty" King of "Range Busters" fame), the owner-trainer of Kazan.

1038 The Fighting Gringo. RKO Radio, 1939. 59 minutes B/W. D: David Howard. SC: Oliver Drake. WITH George O'Brien, Lupita Tovar, Lucio Villegas, William Royle, Glenn Strange, Slim Whitaker, LeRoy Mason, Mary Field, Martin Garralaga, Richard Botiller, Bill Cody, Cactus Mack, Chris-Pin Martin, Ben Corbett, Forrest Taylor, Hank Bell. The leader of a group of hired guns becomes involved in the rescue of a gold shipment from bandits and in trying to aid a man save his ranch. Lots of fast and furious action in this George O'Brien vehicle.

1039 Fighting Hero. Reliable, 1934. 55 minutes B/W. D: Harry S. Webb. SC: Carl Krusada & Rose Gordon. WITH Tom Tyler, Renee Borden, Edward Hearn, Richard Botiller, Ralph Lewis, Murdock McQuarrie, Nelson McDowell, Tom London, George Chesebro, Rosa Rosanova, J. P. McGowan, Lew Meehan, Chuck Baldra,

Jimmie Aubrey. An undercover agent pretends to be a wanted man in order to round up a crook and his gang. Low grade, tacky and hard to follow Tom Tyler vehicle.

1040 The Fighting Kentuckian. Republic, 1949. 100 minutes B/W. D-SC: George Waggner. WITH John Wayne, Vera Ralston, Philip Dorn, Oliver Hardy, Marie Windsor, John Howard, Hugo Haas, Odette Myrtil, Grant Withers, Paul Fix, Mae Marsh, Jack Pennick, Mickey Simpson, Fred Graham, Mabelle Koenig, Shy Waggner, Crystal White, Hank Worden, Charles Cane, Cliff Lyons, Chuck Roberson. In Alabama in 1818 a Kentucky rifleman falls in love with a pretty French girl and uncovers a plot to deprive the French of their lands. Not John Wayne's best by any means but still an entertaining outing with Oliver Hardy quite good as Duke's bumbling pal. V: Cumberland Video, NTA Home Entertainment.

1041 The Fighting Lawman. Allied Artists, 1953. 71 minutes B/W. D: Thomas Carr. SC: Dan Ullman. WITH Wayne Morris, Virginia Grey, John Kellogg, Harry Lauter, Myron Healey, John Pickard, Rick Vallin, Dick Rich. When a quartet of outlaws rob a bank, a deputy marshal sets out to capture them and becomes involved with a woman who wants the stolen loot. Well written and acted drama which belies its small budget.

1042 The Fighting Legion. Universal, 1930. 75 minutes B/W. D: Harry J. Brown. SC: Bennett Cohen. WITH Ken Maynard, Dorothy Dwan, Ernie Adams, Stanley Blystone, Frank Rice, Harry Todd, Robert Walker, Jack Fowler, Les Bates, Bill Nestel, Slim Whitaker. A crooked cattleman, in cahoots with a corrupt banker, murders a Texas Ranger and then tries to lay the blame on the cowpoke who romances the girl he wants. This Ken Maynard part-talkie is a bit overlong and somewhat stagy at times but overall it provides good entertainment.

1043 Fighting Luck. Rayart, 1926. 50 minutes B/W. D: J. P. McGowan. WITH Bob Reeves, Ione Reed, William Ryno, Lew Meehan. A hired gunman is wounded by an outlaw and his gang and later he falls for a rancher's daughter who is kidnapped by the badman. This silent poverty row actioner is lots of fun to view.

1044 Fighting Mad. Monogram, 1939. 60 minutes B/W. D: Sam Newfield. SC:

George Rosenor & John Rathmell. WITH James Newill, Sally Blane, Dave O'Brien, Benny Rubin, Milburn Stone, Walter Long, Warner Richmond, Ted Adams, Chief Thundercloud, Horace Murphy. Bandits capture a girl who has witnessed a robbery and the Mounties come to her rescue. Okay entry in the "Renfrew of the Mounted" series with nice locales. Also called **Renfrew of the Mounted in Fighting Mad.**

1045 Fighting Man of the Plains. 20th Century-Fox, 1949. 94 minutes Color. D: Edwin L. Marin. SC: Frank Gruber. WITH Randolph Scott, Jane Nigh, Bill Williams, Victor Jory, Douglas Kennedy, Joan Taylor, Barry Kroeger, Rhys Williams, Barry Kelley, James Todd, Paul Fix, James Millican, Burk Symon, Dale Robertson, Herbert Rawlinson, J. Farrell MacDonald, Harry V. Cheshire, James Griffith, Tony Hughes, John Hamilton, John Halloran, Cliff Clark, Anthony Jochim, James Harrison, Matt Willis. A notorious gunman sets out to find the man who killed his brother and ends up as the sheriff of a lawless town. Another entertaining action feature from Randolph Scott.

1046 The Fighting Marshal. Columbia, 1931. 60 minutes B/W. D: D. Ross Lederman. SC: Frank Clark. WITH Tim McCoy, Dorothy Gulliver, Matthew Betz, Mary Carr, Pat O'Malley, Ed Le Saint, Lafe McKee, Dick Dickinson, Harry Todd, Ethan Laidlaw, Lee Shumway, Blackie Whiteford. Escaping from prison before he receives his reprieve, a man takes on the identity of a marshal and helps clean up an outlaw gang before finally hearing the news of his official innocence of a crime for which he was wrongly jailed. Nice going in this actionful Tim McCoy vehicle.

1047 Fighting Mustang. Astor, 1948. 60 minutes B/W. D: Oliver Drake. SC: Rita Ross. WITH Sunset Carson, Pat Starling, Al Terry, Polly McKay, William Val, Forrest Matthews, Joe Hiser, Lee Roberts, Felice Raymond, Bob Curtis, Stephen Keyes, Tex Wilson, Al Ferguson, Hugh Hooker, Dale Harrison, Little Joe's Wranglers. Two rangers stationed near the badlands try to combat an outlaw gang stealing wild horses. Tattered Sunset Carson vehicle. V: Sunland Enterprises.

1048 The Fighting Parson. Allied, 1933. 70 minutes B/W. D-SC: Harry Fraser. WITH Hoot Gibson, Marceline Day, Robert Frazer, Stanley Blystone, Skeeter Bill Robbins, Charles King, Jules Cowan, Phil Dunham, Ethel Wales, Frank Nelson, Frank Ellis, Merrill McCormack, Horace B. Carpenter, Blackie Whiteford, J. Farrell MacDonald. Two men, kicked off of a ranch when falsely accused of dishonesty, arrive in a small town run by crooks and one of them takes on the guise of a minister in order to fight the gang. Overlong and slow moving Hoot Gibson vehicle.

1049 Fighting Pioneers. Resolute, 1935. 54 minutes B/W. D: Harry Fraser. SC: Harry Fraser & Chuck Roberts. WITH Rex Bell, Ruth Mix, Buzz Barton, Stanley Blystone, Earl Dwire, John Elliott, Chief Thundercloud, Roger Williams, Guate Mozin, Chuck Morrison, Chief Standing Bear, Francis Walker, Bob Burns, Blackjack Ward. Gun runners are stirring up trouble between Indians and whites and a cavalry officer enlists the aid of the chief's daughter in stopping the trouble. Low grade but probably the best of the quartet of Rex Bell-Ruth Mix-Buzz Barton vehicles for Resolute.

1050 The Fighting Ranger. Columbia, 1934. 60 minutes B/W. D: George B. Seitz. SC: Harry O. Hoyt. WITH Buck Jones, Dorothy Revier, Frank Rice, Ward Bond, Bradley Page, Paddy O'Flynn, Art Smith, Frank LaRue, Jack Wallace, Bud Osborne, Lew Meehan, Denver Dixon, Jim Corey, Steve Clemente, Frank Ellis, Mozelle Britton. A ranger quits the service and heads to Mexico in order to round up a murderous outlaw gang. Actionful remake of Buck Jones' **Border Law** (q.v.).

1051 The Fighting Ranger. Monogram, 1948. 57 minutes B/W. D: Lambert Hillyer. SC: Ronald Davidson. WITH Johnny Mack Brown, Raymond Hatton, Christine Larson, Marshall Reed, Steve Clark, I. Stanford Jolley, Bob Woodward, Eddie Parker, Milburn Morante. A ranger finds out that a man framed his cousin for murder in order to inherit his ranch and he gets a job on the spread in order to capture the culprit. Another passable entry in Johnny Mack Brown's Monogram series.

1052 The Fighting Redhead. Eagle Lion,

1949. 55 minutes Color. D: Lewis D. Collins. SC: Paul Franklin & Jerry Thomas. WITH Jim Bannon, Don Kay Reynolds, Peggy Stewart, Emmett Lynn, Marin Sais, John Hart, Lane Bradford, Forrest Taylor, Lee Roberts, Bob Duncan, Sandy Sanders, Billy Hammond, Ray Jones. Red Ryder helps a girl capture cattle rustlers who murdered her homesteader father. Average entry in the revival of the "Red Ryder" series.

1053 Fighting Renegade. Victory, 1939. 60 minutes B/W. D: Sam Newfield. SC: William Lively. WITH Tim McCoy, Joyce Bryant, Dave O'Brien, Ben Corbett, Budd Buster, Forrest Taylor, Ted Adams, Reed Howes, John Elliott, Carl Mathews. Using a Mexican disguise, a man sets out to clear himself of a six-year-old murder charge. Average outing, fast but with low production values. Tim McCoy, as Bill Carson, wears a Mexican disguise throughout the film.

The Fighting 7th see **Little Big Horn**

1054 Fighting Shadows. Columbia, 1935. 60 minutes B/W. D: David Selman. SC: Ford Beebe. WITH Tim McCoy, Robert (Bob) Allen, Geneva Mitchell, Ward Bond, Si Jenks, Otto Hoffman, Ed Le Saint, Bud Osborne, Ethan Laidlaw. A Northwest Mounted Police constable is assigned to find out who is behind a gang of fur thieves. Well done Tim McCoy film, aided by good scenery, a tight script and nice photography (by George Meehan).

1055 The Fighting Sheriff. Columbia, 1931. 67 minutes B/W. D: Louis King. SC: Stuart Anthony. WITH Buck Jones, Loretta Sayers, Robert Ellis, Harlan Knight, Paul Fix, Lillian Worth, Nena Quartero, Clarence Muse, Lillian Leighton. A sheriff loves a young girl but she turns against him when his crooked rival tells her that the lawman killed her brother, who was riding with a gang led by the crook. One of Buck Jones' best early talkies; a good film.

1056 The Fighting Stallion. Eagle Lion, 1950. 62 minutes Color. D: Robert Tansey. SC: Frances Kavanaugh. WITH Bill Edwards, Doris Merrick, Forrest Taylor, Rocky Camron, John Carpenter, Maria Hart, Don C. Harvey, Bob Cason, Merrill McCormack. A war veteran, who is

going blind, captures and trains a wild stallion and the horse later saves his life during a forest fire. Cheaply made but actionful melodrama for the juvenile trade.

1057 The Fighting Texan. Ambassador, 1937. 59 minutes B/W. D: Charles Abbott. SC: Joseph O'Donnell. WITH Kermit Maynard, Elaine Shepard, Frank LaRue, Budd Buster, Ed Cassidy, Bruce Mitchell, Murdock McQuarrie, Art Miles, Merrill McCormack, Blackie Whiteford, Wally West, John Merton, Bob Woodward. When his new partner is killed, a rancher accuses a rival rancher and his daughter of being involved in the murder. Somewhat complicated, but still entertaining Kermit Maynard vehicle.

1058 Fighting Through. Willis Kent/Cristo, 1934. 55 minutes B/W. D-SC: Harry Fraser. WITH Reb Russell, Lucille Lund, Yakima Canutt, Edward Hearn, Chester Gan, Steve Clemento, Bill Patton, Frank McCarroll, Ben Corbett, Hank Bell, Slim Whitaker, Nelson McDowell, Wally Wales, Lew Meehan, Jack Kirk, Jack Jones, Chuck Baldra. Two cowpokes become friends when one saves the other's life after a framed card game and the two get a job on a girl's ranch and save her from kidnappers. Low grade but actionful Reb Russell vehicle.

1059/60 Fighting Thru or California in 1878. Tiffany, 1930. 61 minutes B/W. D: William Nigh. SC: Jack (John Francis) Natteford. WITH Ken Maynard, Jeannette Loff, Wallace MacDonald, Carmelita Geraghty, William L. Thorne, Charles King, Fred Burns, William Nestell, Art Mix, Chuck Baldra, Jack Kirk, Bud McClure, Jim Corey, Tommy Bay, Jack Fowler. A gold miner is accused of killing his partner but finds out a gambler and a saloon girl are the real culprits. Fairly standard Ken Maynard early talkie with a somewhat involved plot.

1061 Fighting to Live. Principal, 1934. 60 minutes B/W. D: Eddie (Edward F.) Cline. SC: Robert Ives. WITH Marion Shilling, Gaylord (Steve) Pendleton, Reb Russell, Eddie Phillips, Lloyd Ingraham, Henry Hall, John Strohback, Bruce Mitchell, Captain & Lady (dogs). Two dogs, muzzled and left to die in the desert, are hunted by a posse for stealing chickens but are defended by a young lawyer.

Crude juvenile-oriented programmer, poorly photographed and recorded.

1062 The Fighting Trooper. Ambassador, 1934. 57 minutes B/W. D: Ray Taylor. SC: Forrest Sheldon. WITH Kermit Maynard, Barbara Worth, Walter Miller, Robert Frazer, LeRoy Mason, George Regas, Charles Delaney, Joe Girard, George Chesebro, Charles King, Artie Ortego, Lafe McKee, Milburn Morante, Gordon DeMain, Nelson McDowell, George Morrell, Merrill McCormack. A Mountie goes after a gang of crooks in this Northwest melodrama from James Oliver Curwood's story "Footprints." Kermit Maynard's first talkie starrer and his initial entry in the Mountie series he did for producer Maurice Conn; good film. V: Video Dimensions.

1063 Fighting Valley. Producers Releasing Corporation, 1943. 62 minutes B/W. D-SC: Oliver Drake. WITH James Newill, Dave O'Brien, Guy Wilkerson, Patti McCarthy, John Merton, Robert Bice, Stanley Price, Mary MacLaren, John Elliott, Charles King, Dan White, Carl Mathews, Curley Dresden, Jimmie Aubrey. The Texas Rangers step in to help a man who is having ore from his smelting mine stolen by hijackers. Typical entry in PRC's "Texas Rangers" series.

1064 The Fighting Vigilantes. Producers Releasing Corporation, 1947. 61 minutes B/W. D: Ray Taylor. SC: Robert Churchill. WITH Lash LaRue, Al St. John, Jennifer Holt, George Chesebro, Lee Morgan, Marshall Reed, Steve Clark, Carl Mathews, Russell Arms, John Elliott. Two marshals come to a Western town to find out who is causing all the violence and murders and they pose as vigilantes in order to get to the bottom of the crimes. Mostly dull going except for an exciting climax.

The Fighting Westerner see **Rocky Mountain Mystery**

1065 Fighting With Kit Carson. Mascot, 1933. 12 Chapters B/W. D: Armand L. Schaefer & Colbert Clark. SC: Jack Natteford, Barney A. Sarecky, Colbert Clark & Wyndham Gittens. WITH Johnny Mack Brown, Noah Beery, Betsy King Ross, Tully Marshall, Robert Warwick, William Farnum, Lane Chandler, Noah Beery Jr., Edward Hearn, Edmund Breese, Lafe McKee, Ernie Adams, Al Bridge, Reed Howes, Jack Mower, Maston Williams, Iron Eyes Cody, Frank Ellis, Slim Whitaker, DeWitt Jennings. A crooked

trader, the leader of the gang called the Mystery Riders, is after government gold stolen in a pack train massacre and he is opposed by scout Kit Carson. Slow moving and none-too-entertaining cliffhanger; Johnny Mack Brown's first serial. V: Video Dimensions.

1066 The Final Hour. Universal, 1963. 74 minutes Color. D: Robert Douglas. WITH Lee J. Cobb, James Drury, Doug McClure, Ulla Jacobsson, Gary Clarke, Roberta Shore, Jacques Aubuchon, Bert Freed, Don Galloway, Dean Fredericks, Myron Healey, Sheldon Allman, Ross Elliott, Whit Bissell, Richard Garland, Peter Mamakos, Ted Knight, Anthony Jochim. Trouble erupts between ranchers and imported Polish miners over the affections of a girl. Entertaining feature which was originally telecast as a segment of "The Virginian" (NBC-TV, 1962-70) TV series on May 5, 1963.

1067 Find a Place to Die. Gadabout Gaddis Productions, 1971. 100 minutes Color. D: Anthony Ascott (Giuliano Carmineo). SC: Hugo Fregonese & Ralph Grave. WITH Jeffrey Hunter, Pascale Petit, Piero Lulli, Daniela Giordano, Gianni Pallavicini, Nello Pazzafini, Aldo Lastretti, Reza Fahzeli. Outlaws attack a gold mine, wounding the husband of a woman. She goes for help and brings back an assorted group of men, some of whom plan to steal the loot. Exceedingly violent spaghetti Western originally issued in Italy in 1968 by Aico Film as **Joe...Cercati un Posto per Morire** (Joe...Look for a Place to Die).

1068 Finger on the Trigger. Allied Artists, 1966. 87 minutes Color. D: Sidney Pink. SC: Luis De Los Arcos & Sidney Pink. WITH Rory Calhoun, James Philbrook, Todd Martin, Silvia Solar, Brad Talbot, Leo Anchoriz, Jorge Rigaud, Eric Chapman, John Clarke, Fernando Bilboa. Former Civil War soldiers, both Union and Confederate, search for Southern gold hidden in a fort but are forced to unite when an Indian attack is threatened. Dubious Spanish-made oater; for Rory Calhoun fans only.

1069 The Firebrand. 20th Century-Fox, 1962. 63 minutes B/W. D: Maury Dexter. SC: Harry Spalding. WITH Kent Taylor, Valentin De Vargas, Lisa Montell, Joe Raciti, Chubby Johnson, Barbara Mansell, Troy Melton, Fred Krone, Sid Haig, Felix Locher, Jerry Summers, Allen Jaffe. The leader of a group of Mexican bandits goes on a killing spree when he finds out that an ex-follower caused the murders of members of his gang. Supposedly based on the exploits of Joaquin Murieta, this compact oater provides good entertainment.

1070 Firebrand Jordan. Big 4, 1930. 60 minutes B/W. D: Alvin J. Neitz. SC: Carl Krusada. WITH Lane Chandler, Aline Goodwin, Yakima Canutt, Sheldon Lewis, Marguerite Ainslee, Tom London, Lew Meehan, Frank Yaconelli, Alfred Hewston, Fred Harvey, Cliff Lyons. A cowboy on the trail of counterfeiters meets a girl whose father is missing and who is being compromised by a man the cowpoke suspects as being a gang member. Low class early talkie.

1071 Firebrands of Arizona. Republic, 1944. 55 minutes B/W. D: Lesley Selander. SC: Randall Faye. WITH Smiley Burnette, Sunset Carson, Peggy Stewart, Earle Hodgins, Roy Barcroft, LeRoy Mason, Tom London, Jack Kirk, Rex Lease, Charles Morton, Bud Geary, Robert Wilke, Fred "Snowflake" Toones, Pierce Lyden, Budd Buster, Bob Burns, Jack O'Shea, Hank Bell. Sunset Carson and pal Frog Millhouse, a hypochondriac, are on their way to see a doctor when the law mistakes Frog for his lookalike, outlaw Beefsteak Disco. Thanks to Smiley Burnette in a dual role and lots of action with good direction from Lesley Selander, this Sunset Carson film is a cut above average.

1072 Firecreek. Warner Brothers/Seven Arts, 1968. 104 minutes Color. D: Vincent McEveety. SC: Calvin Clements. WITH James Stewart, Henry Fonda, Inger Stevens, Gary Lockwood, Dean Jagger, Ed Begley, Jay C. Flippen, Jack Elam, James Best, Barbara Luna, Jacqueline Scott, Brooke Bundy, J. Robert Porter, Morgan Woodward, John Qualen, Louise Latham, Kevin Tate, Christopher Shea. The sheriff of a small town finds that he must defend his citizens against a gang of rowdies and their cold-blooded leader. This James Stewart-Henry Fonda film promises a lot more entertainment than it provides; average at best.

1073 The First Texan. Allied Artists, 1956. 82 minutes Color. D: Byron Haskin. SC: Daniel B. Ullman. WITH Joel McCrea, Felicia Farr, Jeff Morrow, Wallace Ford, Abraham Sofaer, Jody McCrea, Chubby Johnson, Dayton Lummis, Rodolfo Hoyos, William Hopper, Roy Roberts, Frank Puglia, James Griffith, Nelson Leigh.

The story of Sam Houston and how he wanted no part of the Texas fight for freedom until President Andrew Jackson urges him to take the lead in making Texas independent of Mexican rule. Fine film study of Sam Houston with Joel McCrea very good in the title role.

1074 The First Traveling Saleslady. RKO Radio, 1956. 92 minutes Color. D: Arthur Lubin. SC: Stephen Longstreet & Devery Freeman. WITH Ginger Rogers, Carol Channing, Barry Nelson, James Arness, Robert F. Simon, Frank Wilcox, Dan White, Harry V. Chesire, John Eldredge, Clint Eastwood, Ed Cassidy, Fred Essler. After a Broadway show is closed because some of her corsets are used in a number, a corset designer and her secretary head West to sell barbed wire and run into all kinds of trouble. Ginger Rogers and Carol Channing try hard but nothing can help this dull Western comedy, which was originally written for Mae West.

1075 Fish Hawk. JAD Films International, 1980. 95 minutes Color. D: Donald Shebib. SC: Blanche Hanalis. WITH Will Sampson, Charlie Fields, Geoffrey Bowes, Mary Pirie, Don Francks, Chris Wiggins. A young boy becomes the friend of a drunken Indian and he helps the man to give up the bottle and find happiness in life. G-rated fare which is only average; filmed in Canada.

1076 A Fistful of Dollars. United Artists, 1964. 96 minutes Color. D: Bob Robertson (Sergio Leone). SC: Sergio Leone & Duccio Tessari. WITH Clint Eastwood, Marianne Koch, Gian Maria Volonte, Wolfgang Lukschy, S. Rupp, Antonio Prieto, Pepe Calvo, Benny Reeves. A stranger rides into a border town and finds two factions at war and decides to make money by heating up the rivalry. Filmed in Italy as **Per un Pugno di Dollari** (For a Fistful of Dollars), this feature started the popular "Spaghetti Western" craze of the 1960s. The film, which started Clint Eastwood on his climb to international stardom, is a refashioning of the Japanese film **Yojimbo** (1961) but is not nearly as good as its followup, **For a Few Dollars More** (q.v.). V: 20th Century-Fox Video. VD: RCA.

A Fistful of Dynamite see **Duck, You Sucker**

1077 Five Bloody Graves. Independent-International, 1970. 98 minutes Color. D: Al Adamson. SC: Robert Dix. WITH

Robert Dix, Scott Brady, Jim Davis, John Carradine, Paula Raymond, John Cardos, Tara Ashton, Ken Osborne, Vicki Volante, Denver Dixon, Ray Young, Julie Edwards, Fred Meyers, Maria Pola, Gene Raymond (narrator). A notorious gunman is on the trail of a gun runner who is selling munitions to warring Indians. Low grade and violent oater, mainly interesting for its cast. TV title: **Gun Riders.** V: Blackhawk.

1078 Five Bold Women. Citation, 1960. 82 minutes Color. D: Jorge Lopez Portillo. SC: Mortimer Braus & Jack Pollexfen. WITH Jeff Morrow, Merry Anders, Irish McCalla, Guinn Williams, Kathy Marlowe, Jim Ross, Dee Carroll. The husband of one of five women being taken to prison attacks the lawmen transporting the women and they escape, only to later be threatened by Indians. Passable low budget oater.

1079 Five Card Stud. Paramount, 1968. 103 minutes Color. D: Henry Hathaway. SC: Marguerite Roberts. WITH Dean Martin, Robert Mitchum, Inger Stevens, Roddy McDowall, Katherine Justice, John Anderson, Ruth Springford, Yaphet Kotto, Denver Pyle, Bill Fletcher, Whit Bissell, Ted De Corsia, Don Collier, Roy Jenson, Boyd "Red" Morgan, Jerry Gatlin, Chuck Hayward, Louise Lorimer, Hope Summers. A sheriff teams with a gun-toting preacher to find a man who plans to murder five gamblers who hanged their sixth player. Mystery element added to the leads makes this a good time for genre buffs.

1080 Five Giants From Texas. Miro Cinematografica/Balcazar, 1966. 90 minutes Color. D: Aldo Florio. SC: Aldo Florio, Alfonso Balcazar & Jose L. De La Loma. WITH Guy Madison, Monica Randall, Vidal Molina, Molino Rojo, Vassill Karamesinis, Giovanni Cianfriglia, Manuel Martin, Gianni Solaro. Several years after their friend is murdered by bandits hired by his wife's jealous cousins, five men arrive from Texas to take revenge. Violent oater mainly for Guy Madison fans. An Italian-Spanish coproduction issued in Italy as **I Cinque Della Vendetta** (Five for Revenge) and in Spain as **Los Cunco de la Venganza** (Five for Vengeance).

1081 Five Guns to Tombstone. United Artists, 1962. 71 minutes B/W. D: Edward L. Cahn. SC: Richard Schayer. WITH James Brown, John Wilder, Walter Coy,

Robert Karnes, Joe Haworth, Quent Sondergaard, Boyd "Red" Morgan, Jon Locke, Della Sharman, Gregg Palmer, Willis Bouchey, John Eldredge, Jeff De-Benning, Boyd Stockman, Al Wyatt, Bob Woodward. A reformed gunslinger finds out his outlaw brother is trying to lure him back to lawlessness by framing him for a crime he did not commit. Standard programmer with good work by James Brown in the lead.

1082 Five Guns West. American Releasing, 1955. 79 minutes B/W. D: Roger Corman. SC: R. Wright Campbell. WITH John Lund, Dorothy Malone, Touch (Michael) Connors, Jonathan Haze, Paul Birch, Jack Ingram, Larry Thor. Five murderers get out of prison when they join the Confederate army and they are assigned to steal gold from a Union stagecoach, but after they commit the robbery they decide to keep the loot. Roger Corman's first directorial effort is a passable affair.

1083 The Five Man Army. Metro-Goldwyn-Mayer, 1970. 105 minutes Color. D: Don Taylor. SC: Dario Argento & Marc Richards. WITH Peter Graves, James Daly, Bud Spencer, Tetsuro Tamba, Nino Castelnuovo, Daniela Giordano, Marc Lawrence, Claudio Gora, Annabella Andreoli, Carlo Alighiero, Jack Stuart, Jose Torres, Marino Mase. In 1914 five men team to rob a half-million dollars in gold from a train with four of them wanting the loot for themselves while the fifth wants it for the Mexican Revolution. Italian-made feature which provides some good excitement. Italian title: **Un Esercito di 5 Uomini.**

1084 $5,000 on One Ace. International Germania/Balcazar/FIDA, 1966. 91 minutes Color. SC: Alfonso Balcazar. SC: Alessandro Continenza & Helmut Harum. WITH Robert Wood, Fernando Sancho, Maria Sebalt, Jack Stewart, Norman Preston, Hans Neilsen, Helmut Schmidt. A gambler wins part of a ranch from a man he is forced to kill and with his new partners, a brother and sister, he has to fight a land-grabbing blackmailer to keep the ranch. Typical European Western from the mid-1960s, short on plot and long on violence. German title: **Die Gejagten der Sierra Nevada.**

1085 The Flame of New Orleans. Universal, 1941. 79 minutes B/W. D: Rene Clair. SC: Norman Krasna. WITH Marlene Dietrich, Bruce Cabot, Roland Young, Mischa Auer, Andy Devine, Frank Jenks,

Eddie Quillan, Laura Hope Crews, Franklin Pangborn, Theresa Harris, Clarence Muse, Melville Cooper, Ann Revere, Bob Evans, Emily Fitzroy, Virginia Sale, Dorothy Adams, Anthony Marlowe, Gitta Alpar, Reed Hadley, Gus Schilling, Bess Flowers. In 1841 a girl comes to New Orleans seeking a rich husband and ends up falling in love with a riverboat captain after a fling with the town's richest man. Marlene Dietrich fans will go for this film which provides solid entertainment but not lots of action.

Flame of Sacramento see **In Old Sacramento**

1086 Flame of the Barbary Coast. Republic, 1945. 91 minutes B/W. D: Joseph Kane. SC: Borden Chase. WITH John Wayne, Ann Dvorak, Joseph Schildkraut, William Frawley, Virginia Grey, Russell Hicks, Jack Norton, Paul Fix, Manart Kippen, Eve Lynne, Marc Lawrence, Butterfly McQueen, Rex Lease, Hank Bell, Al Murphy, Adele Mara, Emmett Vogan. A Montana cowboy is fleeced of his money by a San Francisco gambling house owner and he returns to set up a rival saloon and take the man's girl, only to have his fortunes interrupted by the San Francisco earthquake. Okay John Wayne vehicle which is not up to his usual "A" efforts. V: Cumberland Video, NTA Home Entertainment.

1087 Flame of the West. Monogram, 1945. 71 minutes B/W. D: Lambert Hillyer. SC: Adele Buffington. WITH Johnny Mack Brown, Raymond Hatton, Joan Woodbury, Douglass Dumbrille, Lynne Carver, Harry Woods, John Merton, Riley Hill, Steve Clark, Bud Osborne, Jack Rockwell, Ray Bennett, Tom Quinn, Jack Ingram, Eddie Parker, John Cason, Frank McCarroll, Hal Price, Ted Mapes, Kermit Maynard, Pee Wee King & His Golden West Cowboys, Horace Carpenter. A pacifistic doctor, thought a coward by his girlfriend, takes up his guns when the sheriff is murdered by gamblers. One of Johnny Mack Brown's best Westerns; highly recommended.

1088 Flaming Bullets. Producers Releasing Corporation, 1945. 59 minutes B/W. D-SC: Harry Fraser. WITH Tex Ritter, Dave O'Brien, Guy Wilkerson, Patricia Knox, Charles King, I. Stanford Jolley, Bud Osborne, Kermit Maynard, Richard Alexander, Bob Duncan, Dan White. A lawman pretends to be a wanted outlaw in order to capture a gang which murders wanted criminals to collect the reward money. Tex Ritter's last entry in PRC's "Texas Rangers" series and an okay effort with the star singing a couple of tunes.

1089 Flaming Feather. Paramount, 1952. 77 minutes Color. D: Ray Enright. SC: Gerald Drayson Adams & Frank Gruber. WITH Sterling Hayden, Arleen Whelan, Forrest Tucker, Barbara Rush, Richard Arlen, Victor Jory, Edgar Buchanan, Carol Thurston, Ian MacDonald, George Cleveland, Robert Kortman, Ethan Laidlaw, Paul Burns, Ray Teal, Nacho Galindo, Frank Lackteen, Donald Kerr. A group of vigilantes sets out to rescue a girl who has been captured by renegade Indians and is being held in Montezuma Castle. Well written and actionful Western.

1090 Flaming Frontier. 20th Century-Fox, 1958. 70 minutes B/W. D: Sam Newfield. SC: Louis Stevens. WITH Bruce Bennett, Jim Davis, Don Garrard, Paisley Maxwell, Cecil Linder, Bill Walsh, Larry Mann, Peter Humphreys, Ben Lennick. When trouble develops between the whites and Sioux Indians, a half-breed Sioux Cavalry officer tries to intervene but runs into prejudice. Cheaply made effort filmed in Canada.

1091 Flaming Frontier. Warner Brothers-Seven Arts, 1968. 93 minutes Color. D: Alfred Vohrer. SC: Eberhard Keindorff, Johanna Sibelius & Fred Denger. WITH Stewart Granger, Pierre Brice, Letitia Roman, Larry Pennell, Mario Girotti, Wolfgang Lukschy, Erik Schumann, Paddy Fox, Aleksandar Gavric, Vladimir Hedar, Dusco Janicijevic, Hermina Pipinic, Jelena Jovanovic. When an Indian chief's son is murdered by a gang of outlaws, frontiersman Old Surehand enlists the aid of his Apache blood brother Winnetou to help him avert a war. Sturdy West German oater with Stewart Granger and Pierre Brice good as Surehand and Winnetou. Issued in Europe in 1965 by Rialto/Jadran as **Old Surehand.**

1092 Flaming Frontiers. Universal, 1938. 15 Chapters B/W. D: Ray Taylor & Alan James. SC: Wyndham Gittens, Paul Perez, Basil Dickey, George Plympton & Ella O'Neill. WITH Johnny Mack Brown, Ralph Bowman (John Archer), Eleanor Hansen, Charles Middleton, James Blaine, Charles Stevens, William Royle, Horace Murphy, Michael Slade, John Rutherford, Chief Thundercloud, Roy Barcroft, Eddy Waller, Ed Cassidy, Karl Hackett, Iron Eyes Cody, Pat O'Brien, Earle Hodgins, J. P.

McGowan, Jim Corey, Frank Ellis, Hank Bell, Horace B. Carpenter, Tom Steele, Slim Whitaker, Frank LaRue, Al Bridge, Blackjack Ward, Ferris Taylor, Bob Woodward, Helen Gibson, George Plues. An Indian scout comes to the aid of a young woman who is being courted by a crook who wants to marry her for her father's gold mine. There is not much logic in this serial but this is made up for by endless action. V: Video Connection, Cassette Express.

1093 Flaming Gold. RKO Radio, 1934. 54 minutes B/W. D: Ralph Ince & Merian C. Cooper. SC: Van Nest Polglase. WITH Bill (William) Boyd, Pat O'Brien, Mae Clarke, Rollo Lloyd, Helen Ware. A man is sent to rural Mexico by an oil company to put a rival out of business. Confusing melodrama.

1094 Flaming Guns. Universal, 1932. 57 minutes B/W. D: Arthur Rosson. SC: Jack Cunningham. WITH Tom Mix, Ruth Hall, William Farnum, George Hackathorne, Clarence Wilson, Bud Osborne, Duke Lee, Gilbert "Pee Wee" Holmes, Bill Steele, Fred Burns, Slim Whitaker. Assigned to run a ranch, a cowboy finds opposition from the crusty owner as well as an outlaw gang. The weakest of Tom Mix's Universal series, this film was a remake of Hoot Gibson's silent feature **The Buckaroo Kid** (Universal, 1926).

1095 Flaming Lead. Colony, 1939. 57 minutes B/W. D: Sam Newfield. SC: Joseph O'Donnell. WITH Ken Maynard, Eleanor Stewart, Dave O'Brien, Ralph Peters, Walter Long, Tom London, Carleton Young, Reed Howes, Kenne Duncan, John Merton, Carl Mathews, Bob Terry. A cowboy comes to the aid of a rancher who is about to lose an Army contract for horses due to constant rustling. One of the best of Ken Maynard's later films with a good story and lots of movement.

1096 Flaming Star. 20th Century-Fox, 1960. 101 minutes Color. D: Donald Siegel, SC: Claire Huffaker & Nunnally Johnson. WITH Elvis Presley, Barbara Eden, Steve Forrest, Dolores Del Rio, John McIntire, Rodolfo Acosta, Karl Swenson, Ford Rainey, Richard Jaeckel, Anne Benton, L. Q. Jones, Douglas Dick, Tom Reese, Roy Jenson, Virginia Christine, Rodd Redwing, Perry Lopez, Tom Fadden, The Jordanaires. A family gets caught in the middle of an Indian war and the son, a half-breed, must choose loyalty between either whites or Indians. Elvis Presley is quite good as the half-breed in this well-done melodrama which many consider his finest film.

1097 Flap. Warner Brothers, 1970. 105 minutes Color. D: Carol Reed. SC: Clair Huffaker. WITH Anthony Quinn, Shelley Winters, Claude Akins, Victor Jory, Victor French, Tony Bill, Rodolfo Acosta, Anthony Caruso, Susana Miranda, William Mims, John War Eagle, Rudy Diaz, Pedro Regas. A renegade Indian claims the city of Phoenix actually belongs to him. Film tries to show the plight of American Indians but despite Anthony Quinn's performance it cannot decide whether it is a comedy or a tragedy. British title: **The Last Warrior.**

1098 Flashing Guns. Monogram, 1947. 59 minutes B/W. D: Lambert Hillyer. SC: Frank H. Young. WITH Johnny Mack Brown, Raymond Hatton, Jan Bryant, Riley Hill, James Logan, Douglas Evans, Ted Adams, Gary Garrett, Edmund Cobb, Ray Jones, Jack O'Shea, Steve Clark, Frank LaRue, Jack Rockwell, Bob Woodward. A sheriff comes to the aid of a rancher and his daughter when a banker, who wants the man's land for silver ore on it, has the rancher's loan payment stolen before it can be brought to the bank. Routine but entertaining Johnny Mack Brown film.

1099 Flashing Steeds. Chesterfield, 1925. 60 minutes B/W. D: Horace B. Carpenter. WITH Bill Patton, Dorothy Donald, Merrill McCormack, Ethel Childers, Alfred Hewston, Dick La Reno, Harry O'Connor. A government agent tries to stop two swindlers, masquerading as British nobility, from stealing a retired sea captain's valuable black pearl. Cheap silent Bill Patton vehicle.

1100 Flesh and the Spur. American-International, 1956. 80 minutes B/W. D: Edward L. Cahn. SC: Charles B. Griffith & Mark Hanna. WITH John Agar, Marla English, Touch (Michael) Connors, Raymond Hatton, Joyce Meadows, Kenne Duncan, Maria Monay, Frank Lackteen, Richard Alexander, Kermit Maynard, Bud Osborne, Buddy Roosevelt, Michael Harris, Mel Gaines. While searching for the killer of his twin brother, a cowboy meets a girl and a gunfighter who lead him into outlaw territory. Well modulated Alex Gordon production makes for good entertainment.

Flight from Adventure see Tales of
Adventure

1101 Flowing Gold. Warner Brothers,
1940. 82 minutes B/W. D: Alfred E. Green.
SC: Kenneth Gamet. WITH John Garfield,
Frances Farmer, Pat O'Brien, Raymond
Walburn, Cliff Edwards, Tom Kennedy,
Granville Bates, Jody Gilbert, Edward
Pawley, Frank Mayo, William Marshall,
Virginia Sale, John Alexander. A young
drifter goes to work on an oil drilling
operation and soon becomes the foreman's
rival for the affections of the boss' daughter. Actionful oil field melodrama with
good performances from the leads and
fine comedy support from Raymond
Walburn, Cliff Edwards, Tom Kennedy
and Jody Gilbert.

Follow the Hunter see **Fangs of the
Wild**

1102 Fool's Gold. United Artists, 1946.
64 minutes B/W. D: George Archainbaud.
SC: Doris Schroeder. WITH William Boyd,
Andy Clyde, Rand Brooks, Jane Randolph,
Robert Emmett Keane, Stephen Barclay,
Forbes Murray, Harry Cording, Earle
Hodgins, Wee Willie Davis, Ben Corbett,
Fred "Snowflake" Toones, Bob Bentley.
An army lieutenant, who deserted when
summoned for court martial, is captured
by outlaws and Hopalong Cassidy agrees
to help his colonel father rescue him.
Entertaining entry in the long-running
"Hopalong Cassidy" series.

1103 For a Few Dollars More. United
Artists, 1965. 125 minutes Color. D:
Sergio Leone. SC: Luciano Vincenzoni
& Sergio Leone. WITH Clint Eastwood,
Lee Van Cleef, Gian Maria Volonte,
Jose Egger, Rosemarie Dexter, Mara
Krup, Klaus Kinski, Mario Brega, Aldo
Sambrell, Luigi Pistilli, Robert Camardiel,
Benito Stefanelli, Luis Rodriguez, Panos
Papadopulos. Two bounty hunters form
an uneasy alliance as they track down
the leader of a vicious outlaw gang.
Sergio Leone's followup to **A Fistfull
of Dollars** (q.v.) is a better film, mainly
because Lee Van Cleef is along to add
some life to the proceedings. Filmed
in Italy as **Per Quaiche Dollaro In Piu.**
VD: RCA/Columbia.

1104 For Some Dollars Less. Panda Cine-
matografica, 1966. 90 minutes Color.
D: Mario Mattoli. SC: Sergio Corbucci,
Bruno Corbucci & Mario Guerra. WITH
Lando Buzzanca, Raimondo Vianello,
Gloria Paul, Valeria Ciangottini, Ellio

Pandolfi, Lucia Modungo, Angela Lue,
Tony Renis. Trying to replace missing
funds at his bank, a cashier teams with
his gambler cousin in a scheme which
puts him in jail while his cousin gambles
away the reward money he collected
on him. Silly Italian Western-comedy,
issued there as **Per Qualche Dollaro
In Meno** (For a Few Dollars Less).

1105 For the Love of Mike. 20th Century-
Fox, 1960. 84 minutes Color. D: George
Sherman. SC: D. D. Beauchamp. WITH
Richard Basehart, Stuart Erwin, Danny
Bravo, Arthur Shields, Armando Silvestre,
Elsa Cardenas, Rex Allen, Michael Steckler. A young Indian boy finds an injured
colt and nurses him back to health and
then trains him for a race so he can
use his winnings for a new church. Minor
but entertaining family fare.

1106 For the Service. Universal, 1936.
65 minutes B/W. D: Buck Jones. SC:
Isadore Bernstein. WITH Buck Jones,
Beth Marion, Fred Kohler, Clifford Jones,
Edward Keane, Frank McGlynn, Ben
Corbett, Chief Thundercloud. In Indian
territory a government agent tries to
outwit an outlaw gang. Pretty actionful
Buck Jones vehicle produced and directed
by the star.

1107 For the Taste of Killing. Hercules
Cinematografica/Montana Films, 1966.
89 minutes Color. D: Tonino Valeri. SC:
Victor Auz. WITH Craig Hill, George
Martin, Fernando Sancho, Peter Carter,
Diana Martin, Frank Ressel, Rada Rassimov, Graham Sotty, George Wang,
Jose Marco. A bounty hunter who only
hunts for convoys of stolen gold is encour-
aged to bet his own money that a local
bank will not be successfully robbed.
Another in the long line of Italian-made
oaters with Craig Hill playing a character
called "Lanky Fellow." Original title:
Per Il Gusto di Uccidere (For the Taste
of Killing). British title: **A Taste for
Killing.**

1108 Forbidden Trail. Columbia, 1932.
71 minutes B/W. D: Lambert Hillyer.
SC: Milton Krims. WITH Buck Jones,
Barbara Weeks, Mary Carr, George Cooper,
Ed Brady, Frank Rice, Al Smith, Frank
LaRue, Wallis Clark, Tom Forman, Dick
Rush. A cowboy arrives in a small town
and tries to aid a girl newspaper editor
in fighting a local rustler-land grabber.
Too much comedy makes this Buck Jones
vehicle a bit draggy although it does
have an exciting finale.

1109 The Forbidden Trail. Sunset, 1923. 50 minutes B/W. D-SC: Robert North Bradbury. WITH Jack Hoxie, Evelyn Nelson, Frank Rice, William Lester, Joe McDermott, Tom Lingham, Steve Clemento. On the trail of his father's killer, a man falls in love with a girl who he believes is the murderer's daughter. Fast moving and entertaining Jack Hoxie silent film.

1110 Forbidden Trails. Monogram, 1941. 60 minutes B/W. D: Robert North Bradbury. SC: Jess Bowers (Adele Buffington). WITH Buck Jones, Tim McCoy, Raymond Hatton, Dave O'Brien, Tristram Coffin, Christine McIntyre, Charles King, Glenn Strange, Lynton Brent, Hal Price, Richard Alexander, Jerry Sheldon. The Rough Riders come to the aid of a mine owner who is being forced to sign a hauling contract. Fast action entry in the fine "Rough Riders" series.

1111 Forbidden Valley. Universal, 1938. 67 minutes B/W. D-SC: Wyndham Gittens. WITH Noah Beery Jr., Frances Robinson, Robert Barrat, Fred Kohler, Henry Hunter, Samuel S. Hinds, Stanley Andrews, Spencer Channing, Charles Stevens, Margaret McWade, John Ridgely. After growing up in a secret canyon, a young man sets out to round up a herd of wild horses and take them to market, but rustlers steal the herd. Nicely done adventure drama.

1112 The Forest Rangers. Paramount, 1942. 87 minutes Color. D: George Marshall. SC: Harold Shumate. WITH Fred MacMurray, Paulette Goddard, Susan Hayward, Lynne Overman, Albert Dekker, Eugene Pallette, Regis Toomey, Rod Cameron, Clem Bevans, James Brown, Kenneth Griffith, Keith Richards, William Cabanne, George Chandler, Tim Ryan, Lee Phelps, Chester Clute, Pat West, Sarah Edwards, Jimmy Conlin, Robert Kent, Jack Mulhall, George Turner, Robert Kortman, Perc Launders. A forest ranger marries a wealthy girl and his ex-love tries to prove to him that he made a mistake. Technicolor, lots of action and a forest fire help to make up for a mundane plot.

1113 Forlorn River. Paramount, 1937. 56 minutes B/W. D: Charles Barton. SC: Stuart Anthony & Robert Yost. WITH Larry "Buster" Crabbe, June Martel, Harvey Stephens, John Patterson, Chester Conklin, Lew Kelly, Syd Saylor, William Duncan, Rafael Bennett, Lee Powell,

Robert Homans, Purnell Pratt, Merrill McCormack, Vester Pegg. A cowboy is on the trail of a wily outlaw who has framed him for a crime he did not commit. Nicely done version of the Zane Grey story, made as a silent in 1926 with Jack Holt. TV title: **River of Destiny.** V: Sunland Enterprises.

1114 Fort Apache. RKO Radio, 1948. 127 minutes B/W. D: John Ford. SC: Frank S. Nugent. WITH John Wayne, Henry Fonda, Shirley Temple, Pedro Armendariz, John Agar, Ward Bond, Irene Rich, George O'Brien, Anna Lee, Victor McLaglen, Dick Foran, Jack Pennick, Guy Kibbee, Grant Withers, Miguel Inclan, Mae Marsh, Movita Castenada, Francis Ford, Frank Ferguson, Mickey Simpson, Ray Hyke, Mary Gordon, Hank Worden, Archie Twitchell, William Forrest, Cliff Clark, Fred Graham, Philip Keiffer, Ben Johnson. An arrogant lieutenant is at odds with a captain at a remote Army post which is threatened by an Indian uprising. Classic John Ford cavalry drama; well worth seeing. V: VID America, Blackhawk, Nostalgia Merchant, Cumberland Video.

1115 Fort Bowie. United Artists, 1958. 80 minutes B/W. D: Howard W. Koch. SC: Maurice Tombragel. WITH Ben Johnson, Kent Taylor, Jan Harrison, Jana Davi, Larry Chance, Ian Douglas, Peter Mamakos, Jerry Frank, Johnny Western, Ed Hinton, Barbara Parry. A fort commander believes an officer is romancing his wife while the two men face the danger of an Indian attack. Ben Johnson and Kent Taylor bring some life to this actionful programmer.

1116 Fort Courageous. 20th Century-Fox, 1965. 72 minutes B/W. D: Lesley Selander. SC: Richard Landau. WITH Fred Beir, Donald (Don "Red") Barry, Hanna Landy, Harry Lauter, Walter Reed, Michael Carr, Fred Krone, George Sawaya, Joseph Partridge, Cheryl MacDonald. A courtmartialed sergeant takes over the command of a fort beleagured by Indian attacks. Low budget affair of interest to fans of Don "Red" Barry.

1117 Fort Defiance. United Artists, 1951. 81 minutes Color. D: John Rawlins. SC: Louis Lantz. WITH Dane Clark, Ben Johnson, Peter Travey, Tracey Roberts, Dennis Moore, George Cleveland, Ralph Sanford, Iron Eyes Cody, Craig Woods, Dick Elliott. Relationships build between several people at a fort about to be attacked by Navajo Indians. Interesting "B" melodrama with more emphasis on characterization than action.

1118 Fort Dobbs. Warner Brothers, 1958. 90 minutes B/W. D: Gordon Douglas. SC: Burt Kennedy & George W. George. WITH Clint Walker, Virginia Mayo, Brian Keith, Richard Eyer, Russ Conway, Michael Dante. A widow and her young son are escorted through Indian country by a man the woman believes killed her husband. Well done oater with fine performances by Clint Walker and Virginia Mayo.

1119 Fort Dodge Stampede. Republic, 1951. 60 minutes B/W. D: Harry Keller. SC: Richard Wormer. WITH Allan "Rocky" Lane, Mary Ellen Kay, Roy Barcroft, Chubby Johnson, Trevor Bardette, Bruce Edwards, Wesley Hudman, William Forrest, Chuck Roberson, Rory Mallinson, Jack Ingram, Kermit Maynard. A deputy sheriff is forced to give up his badge when he goes on the trail of an outlaw gang after $30,000 in hidden loot. Another actionful and well scripted entry in Allan Lane's Republic series.

1120 Fort Massacre. United Artists, 1958. 80 minutes Color. D: Joseph M. Newman. SC: Martin N. Goldsmith. WITH Joel McCrea, Forrest Tucker, Susan Cabot, John Russell, Anthony Caruso, Robert Osterloh, Denver Pyle, Rayford Barnes, Guy Prescott, Irving Bacon, Claire Carleton, Francis McDonald, George N. Neise. A cavalry sergeant leads a band of soldiers who are constantly being attacked by warring Indians. This oater is a nice combination of both action and characterization; well done.

1121 Fort Osage. Monogram, 1952. 72 minutes Color. D: Lesley Selander. SC: Dan Ullman. WITH Rod Cameron, Jane Nigh, Douglas Kennedy, Morris Ankrum, John Ridgely, William Phipps, I. Stanford Jolley, Dorothy Adams, Francis McDonald, Myron Healey, Lane Bradford, Iron Eyes Cody, Barbara Woodell, Russ Conway. A scout is hired to lead a wagon train West but he soon finds out the people who hired him are the cause of an Indian uprising. Considering those involved, this oater is a bit of a disappointment.

1122 Fort Savage Raiders. Columbia, 1951. 54 minutes B/W. D: Ray Nazarro. SC: Barry Shipman. WITH Charles Starrett, Smiley Burnette, John Dehner, Trevor Bardette, Peter Thompson, Fred Sears, John Cason, Frank Griffin, Sam Flint,

Dusty Walker. The Durango Kid and his two pals set out to track down an Army deserter and his gang which has been raiding the countryside. Well made "Durango Kid" series episode with a sympathetic villain excellently played by John Dehner.

1123 Fort Ti. Columbia, 1953. 73 minutes Color. D: William Castle. SC: Robert E. Kent. WITH George Montgomery, Joan Vohs, Irving Bacon, James Seay, Ben Astar, Phyllis Fowley, Howard Petrie, Lester Matthews, Louis Merrill. In 1759 the British send Rogers' Rangers to join the English in fighting the French and Indians at Fort Ticonderoga. This low budget Sam Katzman outing covers the same ground as **Northwest Passage** (q.v.) but is not nearly as well done; shown in 3-D.

1124 Fort Utah. Paramount, 1967. 83 minutes Color. D: Lesley Selander. SC: Steve Fisher & Andrew Craddock. WITH John Ireland, Virginia Mayo, Scott Brady, John Russell, Robert Strauss, James Craig, Richard Arlen, Jim Davis, Donald (Don "Red") Barry, Harry Lauter, Read Morgan, Reg Parton, Eric Cody. An Indian agent and a cowboy are forced to defend a wagon train from an Indian attack. Not too good A. C. Lyles oater although the cast is worth watching.

1125 Fort Vengeance. Allied Artists, 1953. 75 minutes Color. D: Lesley Selander. SC: Dan Ullman. WITH James Craig, Rita Moreno, Keith Larsen, Reginald Denny, Morris Ankrum, Guy Kingsford, Paul Marion, Emory Parnell, Charles Irwin. Two men, one of whom is wanted by the law, go to Canada and join the Mounties and become involved with fur thieves, an Indian uprising and romance. Colorful action melodrama.

1126 Fort Worth. Warner Brothers, 1951. 80 minutes Color. D: Edwin L. Marin. SC: John Twist. WITH Randolph Scott, David Brian, Phyllis Thaxter, Helena Carter, Dick Jones, Ray Teal, Paul Picerni, Emerson Treacy, Bob Steele, Lawrence Tolan, Walter Sande, Chubby Johnson. A newspaperman comes to Fort Worth via wagon train and starts a newspaper which accuses the train's trail boss of committing a murder on the orders of the town's leading citizen. Okay "A" melodrama.

1127 Fort Yuma. United Artists, 1955. 78 minutes Color. D: Lesley Selander. SC: Danny Arnold. WITH Peter Graves,

Joan Vohs, Joan Taylor, Abel Fernandez, Stanley Clements, John Pickard, Addison Richards, John Hudson, Bill Phillips. When a homesteader kills the chief of the Apaches, the Indians go on the warpath. Average action melodrama which moves along at a good clip.

1128 Fort Yuma Gold. Gala, 1969. 100 minutes Color. D: Kelvin Jackson Padget (Giorgio Ferroni). SC: Augusto Finocchi & Massimiliano Capriccioli. WITH Montgomery Wood (Giuliano Gemma), Dan Vadis, Jacques Sernas, Jose Calvo, Sophie Daumier, Angel Del Pozo. At the end of the Civil War a Southern major plans to attack his own country's fort in order to get its gold. Another in the almost endless string of violent spaghetti Westerns. Issued in Italy in 1966 as **Per Pochi Dollari Ancora** (For a Few Extra Dollars) by Fida Cinematografica/Epoca Film; an Italian-French-Spanish coproduction.

1129 40 Graves for 40 Guns. Boxoffice International, 1971. 95 minutes Color. D: Paul Hunt. SC: Steve Fisher. WITH Robert Padilla, Stanley Adams, Richard Rust, Mahita Saint Duvall, Rita Rogers, Steven Oliver, David Eastman, Rockne Tarkington, Michael Christina, Owen Orr, Michael Green. An outlaw gang heads south of the border and raids a small Mexican town and carries off a priceless gold cross only to be relentlessly pursued by the Mexican army. Violent low budget actioner filmed in Arizona as **El Salvejo** (The Savage). Alternate title: **Machismo - 40 Graves for 40 Guns.** Reissued in 1977 by Sun Productions as **The Great Gundown.**

1130 Forty Guns. 20th Century-Fox, 1957. 80 minutes B/W. D-SC: Samuel Fuller. WITH Barbara Stanwyck, Barry Sullivan, Dean Jagger, John Ericson, Gene Barry, Robert Dix, Paul Dubov, Ziva Rodann, Hank Worden, Neyle Morrow, Chuck Roberson, Chuck Hayward, Eve Brent. A tough woman who has appointed herself the ruler of Tombstone, Arizona, finds opposition from an ex-gunfighter, now working for the U. S. attorney general, and his brothers. Film is interesting for Barbara Stanwyck's work in the leading role and will also appeal to Sam Fuller followers.

1131 40 Guns to Apache Pass. Columbia, 1967. 95 minutes Color. D: William Witney. SC: Willard Willingham & Mary Willingham. WITH Audie Murphy, Kenneth Tobey, Michael Burns, Laraine Stephens, Robert

Brubaker, Kay Stewart, Kenneth MacDonald, Byron Morrow, Willard Willingham, Ted Gehring, Jackson Beck. When Cochise and his braves declare war, a cavalry captain leads settlers to safety and then goes on the hunt for the traitor who sold the Indians stolen rifles. Average Audie Murphy film.

1132 Forty-Niners. Monarch/Freuler, 1932. 49 minutes B/W. D: J. P. McCarthy. SC: F. McGrew Willis. WITH Tom Tyler, Betty Mack, Alan Bridge, Gordon Wood, Fern Emmett, Mildred Rogers, Fred Ritter, Frank Ball, Florence Wells. A cowboy tries to help a wagon train going westward and facing trouble from outlaws and a buffalo stampede. Compact, but crudely made, Tom Tyler vehicle.

1133 The Forty-Niners. Allied Artists, 1954. 71 minutes B/W. D: Thomas Carr. SC: Dan Ullman. WITH Bill Elliott, Virginia Grey, Henry (Harry) Morgan, John Doucette, Lane Bradford, I. Stanford Jolley, Denver Pyle, Ralph Sanford, Gregg Barton, Harry Lauter, Earle Hodgins. In order to find out the identities of three men involved in a killing, a marshal takes on the guise of a murderer. Well done Bill Elliott film.

1134 Forty Thieves. United Artists, 1944. 54 (60) minutes B/W. D: Lesley Selander. SC: Michael Wilson & Bernie Kamins. WITH William Boyd, Andy Clyde, Jimmy Rogers, Louise Currie, Douglass Dumbrille, Kirk Alyn, Herbert Rawlinson, Robert Frazer, Glenn Strange, Jack Rockwell, Robert Kortman, Hal Taliaferro. A crooked election results in Hopalong Cassidy losing his job as the town's sheriff and he sets out to track down those responsible for stuffing the ballot boxes. Cheaply made but actionful entry in the "Hopalong Cassidy" series and the last one produced by Harry Sherman.

1135 Four Dollars for Revenge. GAR Film, 1966. 88 minutes Color. D: J. Warren. SC: Garrone, Di Nardo & Vari. WITH Robert Woods, Chia Arlen, Jack Stuart, Dan Vadis, Jose Torres, Rosy Zichel, John Douglas, Dick Regan, Angelo Infanti, Antonio Casas. At the end of the Civil War a Confederate colonel hides a fortune in gold and it is wanted by a Mexican bandit as well as a young lieutenant who is sent by the Army to retrieve the loot. Violent Italian-Spanish oater which will appeal to fans of this sub-genre. Original title: **Deguejo.**

Four Faces 138

1136 Four Faces West. United Artists, 1948. 90 minutes B/W. D: Alfred E. Green. SC: Graham Baker. WITH Joel McCrea, Frances Dee, Charles Bickford, Joseph Calleia, William Conrad, Martin Garralaga, Raymond Largay, John Parrish, Dan White, Davison Clark, Eva Novak, Houseley Stevenson, Sam Flint, Forrest Taylor, George McDonald. A man robs a bank to get money to save his father's ranch and he is pursued by a sheriff and is helped by a railroad nurse and a saloon keeper. Entertaining but fairly non-violent oater with fine performances. British title: **They Passed This Way.**

1137 Four Fast Guns. Universal-International, 1960. 74 minutes B/W. D: William Hole Jr. SC: James Edmiston & Dallas Goultois. WITH James Craig, Martha Vickers, Edgar Buchanan, Brett Halsey, Paul Richards, Richard Martin, John Swift. When a gunman is hired to rid a small town of its lawless element, he is forced into a showdown with his own brother. Nothing special about this average oater.

1138 Four for Texas. Warner Brothers, 1963. 124 minutes Color. D: Robert Aldrich. SC: Allan Weiss. WITH Frank Sinatra, Dean Martin, Anita Ekberg, Ursula Andress, Victor Buono, Charles Bronson, Richard Jaeckel, Eric Connor, Nick Dennis, Mike Mazurki, Wesley Addy, Marjorie Bennett, Jack Elam, Fritz Feld, Percy Helton, Jonathan Hale, Jack Lambert, Paul Langton, Bob Steele, Virginia Christie, Ellen Corby, Ralph Volkie, The Three Stooges (Moe Howard, Larry Fine, Joe Da Rita), Teddy Buckner & His All Stars, Barbara Payton. Two feuding con-men become involved with a crooked banker and they join forces to thwart his nefarious plans. Poorly conceived Western comedy with only villains Victor Buono and Charles Bronson and a lot of fine character actors to recommend it.

1139 Four Guns to the Border. Universal-International, 1954. 83 minutes Color. D: Richard Carlson. SC: George Van Marter & Franklin Coen. WITH Rory Calhoun, Colleen Miller, George Nader, Walter Brennan, Nina Foch, John McIntire, Charles Drake, Jay Silverheels, Nestor Paiva, Mary Field, Reg Parton. After holding up a bank an outlaw gang comes to the aid of an ex-gunman and his daughter, who are being attacked by Indians. Slightly different story makes this oater acceptable entertainment; directed by actor Richard Carlson.

1140 Four Rode Out. ADA Films/Sagittarius Productions, 1969. 99 minutes Color. D: John Peyser. WITH Sue Lyon, Pernell Roberts, Leslie Nielsen, Julian Mateos, Albert Salmi, Maria Martin, Bob Hall, John Clark. When falsely accused of robbing a bank and committing murder, a lawman heads into the desert with his girlfriend and a Pinkerton agent. Mediocre actioner filmed in Spain.

1141 The Fourth Horseman. Universal, 1932. 63 minutes B/W. D: Hamilton McFadden. SC: Jack Cunningham. WITH Tom Mix, Margaret Lindsay, Fred Kohler, Raymond Hatton, Rosita Marstini, Edmund Cobb, Richard Cramer, Herman Nolan, Paul Shawhan, Donald Kirke, Harry Allan, Duke Lee, C. E. Anderson, Helene Millard, Martha Mattox, Buddy Roosevelt, Frederick Howard, Grace Cunard, Walter Brennan, Pat Harmon, Hank Mann, Jim Corey, Delmar Watson, Fred Burns, Bud Osborne, Harry Tenbrook, Charles Sullivan, Augie Gomez. A cowboy tries to help a girl save her ghost town property because irrigation will recultivate the area but he finds out outlaws are using it as a hideout. Entertaining and well made Tom Mix series vehicle.

1142 The Foxes of Harrow. 20th Century-Fox, 1947. 117 minutes B/W. D: John M. Stahl. SC: Wanda Tuchock. WITH Rex Harrison, Maureen O'Hara, Richard Haydn, Victor McLaglen, Vanessa Brown, Patricia Medina, Gene Lockhart, Charles Irwin, Hugo Haas, Roy Roberts, Dennis Hoey, Marcel Journet, Helen Crozier, Sam McDaniel, Libby Taylor, Renee Beard, Suzette Marbin, Percy William Ward, Clear Nelson Jr., James Lagano, Dorothy Adams, Celia Lovsky, Eugene Borden, Gordon Clark, Robert Emmett Keane, Bernard DeRoux, Frederick Burton, Wee Willie Davis, Randy Stuart. In New Orleans in 1820 a gambler woos and weds a society belle only to leave her. Colorful frontier soap opera based on the Frank Yerby novel.

1143 Foxfire. Universal-International, 1955. 93 minutes Color. D: Joseph Pevney. SC: Ketti Frings. WITH Jane Russell, Jeff Chandler, Dan Duryea, Mara Corday, Robert F. Simon, Frieda Inescort, Barton MacLane, Charlotte Wynters, Eddy Waller, Celia Lovsky, Arthur Space, Phil Chambers, Robert Bice, Vici Raaf, Grace Lenard, Guy Wilkerson, Lillian Bronson, Dabbs Greer, Hal K. Dawson, Billy Wilkerson, Charles Soldani. A pretty socialite marries a Western mining engineer and his quest for gold almost destroys their marriage. Murky melodrama with Jeff Chandler doing a good job singing the title song.

1144 Freighters of Destiny. RKO Radio, 1931. 60 minutes B/W. D: Fred Allen. SC: Adele Buffington. WITH Tom Keene, Barbara Kent, Frank Rice, Mitchell Harris, Fred Burns, Slim Whitaker, Billy Franey, Frederick Burton. A young man becomes involved in leading a wagon train carrying pioneers westward. Well produced entry in Tom Keene's RKO oater series.

1145 Frenchie. Universal-International, 1951. 80 minutes Color. D: Louis King. SC: Oscar Brodney. WITH Joel McCrea, Shelley Winters, Paul Kelly, Elsa Lanchester, John Russell, Marie Windsor, John Emery, George Cleveland, Regis Toomey, Paul E. Burns, Frank Ferguson, Lawrence Dobkin. After her father is murdered by a gunman, a girl returns to a Western town and opens a saloon and plans to revenge his death. Mediocre Western based on Max Brand's "Destry Rides Again."

1146 The Friendly Persuasion. Allied Artists, 1956. 140 minutes Color. D: William Wyler. SC: Jessamyn West. WITH Gary Cooper, Dorothy McGuire, Marjorie Main, Anthony Perkins, Richard Eyer, Phyllis Love, Robert Middleton, Mark Richman, Walter Catlett, Richard Hale, Joel Fluellen, Theodore Newton, John Smith, Mary Carr, Edna Skinner, Russell Simpson, Charles Halton, Everett Glass, Richard Garland, James Dobson, John Compton, James Seay, Diane Jergens, Ralph Sanford, Nelson Leigh, William Schallert, John Craven, Frank Jenks, Frank Hagney. In Indiana during the Civil War, a Quaker must choose between his religious beliefs and taking revenge on the man who murdered his friend. Exceedingly good screen version of Jessamyn West's novel.

1147 The Friendly Persuasion. ABC-TV/ International Television Productions/Allied Artists, 1975. 100 minutes Color. D: Joseph Sargent. SC: William P. Wood. WITH Richard Kiley, Shirley Knight, Clifton James, Michael O'Keefe, Kevin O'Keefe, Tracie Savage, Sparky Marcus, Paul Benjamin, Erik Holland, Maria Grimm, Bob Minor. During the Civil War a Quaker couple jeopardize themselves and their family when they harbor two runaway slaves. Television remake of the Jessamyn West book; pretty good for TV.

1148 Frisco Kid. Warner Brothers, 1935. 77 minutes B/W. D: Lloyd Bacon. SC: Warren Duff & Seton I. Miller. WITH James Cagney, Margaret Lindsay, Ricardo Cortez, Lily Damita, Donald Woods, Barton MacLane, George E. Stone, Addison Richards, Joseph King, Robert McWade, Joseph Crehan, Robert Strange, Joseph Sawyer, Fred Kohler, Edward McWade, Claudia Coleman, John Wray, Lee Phelps, Don Barclay, Jack Curtis, Milton Kibbee, Karl Hackett, Wilfred Lucas, James Farley, Charles Middleton, Landers Stevens, Frank Sheridan, Edward Keane, Ed LeSaint, Dick Rush, William Desmond, Helene Chadwick. When he opposes gambling on the Barbary Coast, a sailor emerges as a kingpin only to be threatened by vigilantes. Warner Brothers' answer to Samuel Goldwyn's **Barbary Coast** ('35) (q.v.) is nothing more than an imitation.

1149 The Frisco Kid. Warner Brothers, 1979. 122 minutes Color. D: Robert Aldrich. SC: Michael Elias & Frank Shaun. WITH Gene Wilder, Harrison Ford, Ramon Bieri, Val Bisoglio, George Ralph DiCenzo, Leo Fuchs, Penny Peyser, William Smith, Jack Somack, Cliff Pellow, Allan Rich. In 1850 a penniless Polish Orthodox Rabbi teams with a good-hearted outlaw en route to head his new congregation in San Francisco. Lame, overlong genre comedy.

1150 Frisco Sal. Universal, 1945. 63 minutes B/W. D: George Waggner. SC: Curt Siodmak & Gerald Geraghty. WITH Susanna Foster, Alan Curtis, Turhan Bey, Andy Devine, Thomas Gomez, Collette Lyons, Samuel S. Hinds, Fuzzy Knight, Ernie Adams, George Lloyd. After her brother is murdered, a singer from New England comes to California to avenge the deed. Film vehicle for signer-actress Susanna Foster; basically for her fans.

1151 Frisco Tornado. Republic, 1950. 61 minutes B/W. D: R. G. Springsteen. SC: M. Coates Webster. WITH Allan "Rocky" Lane, Eddy Waller, Martha Hyer, Stephen Chase, Ross Ford, Maurita Hugo, Lane Bradford, Hal Price, Rex Lease, George Chesebro, Edmund Cobb, Bud Geary. Outlaws force ranchers to submit to a protection racket and a U. S. marshal sets out to break up the illegal activities. Another fast moving entry in the Allan Lane series.

1152 From Broadway to Cheyenne. Monogram, 1932. 62 minutes B/W. D: Harry

Fraser. SC: Wellyn Totman. WITH Rex Bell, Marceline Day, Robert Ellis, Roy D'Arcy, Gwen Lee, George ("Gabby") Hayes, Huntley Gordon, Matthew Betz, John Elliott. Two cowpokes head East to the big city and run into trouble with hoodlums and romance. Title tells all in this average Rex Bell actioner.

1153 From Hell to Texas. 20th Century-Fox, 1958. 100 minutes Color. D: Henry Hathaway. SC: Robert Buckner & Wendell Mayes. WITH Don Murray, Diane Varsi, Chill Wills, Dennis Hopper, R. G. Armstrong, Jay C. Flippen, Margo, John Larch, Ken Scott, Rodolfo Acosta, Harry Carey Jr., Jose Torvay, Malcolm Atterbury. After accidentally killing the son of a rancher, a young man heads into the desert, pursued by the dead man's father and two brothers, and he is helped by a rancher and his tomboy daughter. Colorful and entertaining film which is strong on characterization.

1154 From Noon Till Three. United Artists, 1976. 99 minutes Color. D-SC: Frank D. Gilroy. WITH Charles Bronson, Jill Ireland, Douglas V. Fowley, Stan Haze, Damon Douglas, Betty Cole, Don "Red" Barry, Sonny Jones, Hector Morales, Howard Brunner. When she thinks her third-rate outlaw lover has been killed, a pretty widow writes a book about their three-hour romance and he becomes a legend. Excellent Western satire which is probably Charles Bronson's most underrated film.

1155 Frontier Agent. Monogram, 1945. 56 minutes B/W. D: Vernon Keays. SC: Norman S. Hall. WITH Johnny Mack Brown, Raymond Hatton, Reno Blair, Kenneth MacDonald, Dennis Moore, Riley Hill, Frank LaRue, Ted Adams, William Ruhl, Lane Bradford, Bob Woodward, Boyd Stockman. A land promoter tries to sabotage the completion of a telegraph line and a trouble-shooter for the company comes to the aid of a rancher who is using his own money to complete the line. Actionful entry in Johnny Mack Brown's Monogram series, with a good script to boot.

1156 Frontier Badmen. Universal, 1943. 80 minutes B/W. D: William McGann & Ford Beebe. SC: Gerald Geraghty & Morgan B. Cox. WITH Robert Paige, Anne Gwynne, Noah Beery Jr., Diana Barrymore, Leo Carrillo, Lon Chaney, Andy Devine, Thomas Gomez, Tex Ritter, William Farnum, Frank Lackteen, Robert

Homans, Tom Fadden, Norman Willis, Arthur Loft, Jack Rockwell, Stanley Price, Carl Sepulveda, William Desmond, Gil Patrick, Eddy Waller, Charles Wagenheim, Frank Austin, William Ruhl, Fern Emmett, George Eldredge, Earle Hodgins, Bob Reeves, Kermit Maynard. In 1869 a cattleman organizes an exchange for the sale of various herds after a syndicate has taken over the cattle trade arriving in Texas over the Chisholm Trail. Authentic-looking oater from Ford Beebe with a good script, excellent cast and plenty of action; well above average.

1157 Frontier Crusader. Producers Releasing Corporation, 1940. 63 minutes B/W. D: Peter Stewart (Sam Newfield). SC: William Lively. WITH Tim McCoy, Dorothy Short, Forrest Taylor, Ted Adams, John Merton, Lou Fulton, Karl Hackett, Hal Price, Kenne Duncan, Frank LaRue, George Chesebro, Frank Ellis, Carl Mathews, Reed Howes, Lane Bradford, Sherry Tansey. A mysterious rider arrives on the scene as outlaws plan to rob a mine payroll in order to get control of the mine. Well written and effective Tim McCoy vehicle.

1158 Frontier Days. Spectrum, 1934. 61 minutes B/W. D: Robert Hill. SC: James Shawkey. WITH Bill Cody, Ada Ince, Wheeler Oakman, Franklyn Farnum, Lafe McKee, William Desmond, Bill Cody Jr., Vic Potel, Bob McKenzie. The town's leading citizen (banker, justice of the peace, lawyer) wants a man's ranch and has him killed and a cowboy named The Pinto Kid is blamed and tries to clear himself. Slow moving Bill Cody vehicle hampered by sub-par production values.

1159 Frontier Feud. Monogram, 1945. 54 minutes B/W. D: Lambert Hillyer. SC: Jess Bowers (Adele Buffington). WITH Johnny Mack Brown, Raymond Hatton, Christine McIntyre, Dennis Moore, Jack Ingram, Lloyd Ingraham, Mary MacLaren, Steve Clark, Jack Rockwell, Eddie Parker, Terry Frost, Frank LaRue, Ted Mapes, Charles King, Edmund Cobb, Stanley Price, Dan White, Lynton Brent. Two ranchers arrive in a small Arizona town to find a rancher about to be lynched for the murder of his rival. Okay entry in Johnny Mack Brown's Monogram series.

Frontier Fighters see **Western Cyclone**

1160 Frontier Fugitives. Producers Releasing Corporation, 1945. 58 minutes B/W.

D: Harry Fraser. SC: Elmer Clifton. WITH Tex Ritter, Dave O'Brien, Guy Wilkerson, Lorraine Miller, I. Stanford Jolley, Jack Ingram, Frank Ellis, Jack Hendricks, Charles King, Karl Hackett, Budd Buster, Robert Kortman. In Indian territory The Texas Rangers get mixed up with a crook who kills a man for his hidden furs and then find out he is associated with a corrupt Indian agent. A rambling and draggy film saved only by Tex Ritter singing "Too Late to Worry, Too Blue to Cry," "I'll Wait for You, Dear" and "Long Time Gone."

1161 Frontier Fury. Columbia, 1943. 55 minutes B/W. D: William Berke. SC: Betty Burbridge. WITH Charles Starrett, Roma Aldrich, Arthur Hunnicutt, Jimmie Davis & His Singing Buckaroos, Johnny Bond, Clancy Cooper, I. Stanford Jolley, Edmund Cobb, Bruce Bennett, Ted Mapes, Bill Wilkerson, Stanley Brown, Joel Friedkin, Frank LaRue, Lew Meehan, Chief Yowlachie. When funds belonging to Indians are stolen the agent is fired and he tries to find the real robbers. Fair Charles Starrett actioner.

1162 Frontier Gal. Universal, 1945. 84 minutes Color. D: Charles Lamont. SC: Michael Fessier & Ernest Pagano. WITH Yvonne De Carlo, Rod Cameron, Andy Devine, Fuzzy Knight, Sheldon Leonard, Andrew Tombes, Beverly Sue Simmons, Clara Blandick, Frank Lackteen, Claire Carleton, Eddie Dunn, Harold Goodwin, Jan Wiley, Rex Lease, George Eldredge, Jack Ingram, Joseph Haworth, Lloyd Ingraham, Joan Shawlee, Jack O'Shea, Billy Engle, Cliff Lyons, Eddie Borden, William Desmond, Kit Guard. After a one-night honeymoon with a fiery French girl, a man returns home from prison to find his wife a saloon owner and he is the father of a little girl. Colorful, brawling, rambling oater which will more than satisfy fans of its two stars. British title: **The Bride Wasn't Willing.**

1163 Frontier Gambler. Associated Releasing Corporation, 1956. 75 minutes B/W. D: Sam Newfield. SC: Orville Hampton. WITH John Bromfield, Coleen Gray, Jim Davis, Kent Taylor, Margia Dean, Veda Ann Borg, Tracey Roberts, Stanley Andrews, Roy Engel, Frank Sully, Pierce Lyden, Rick Vallin, John Merton. When the woman ruler of a small town is murdered, and her ex-lover accused of the crime, a deputy marshal is sent to investigate. Good script and a quartet of fine stars help this low budget entry.

1164 Frontier Gun. 20th Century-Fox, 1959. 70 minutes B/W. D: Paul Landres. SC: Stephen Kandel. WITH John Agar, Joyce Meadows, Barton MacLane, Robert Strauss, Morris Ankrum, James Griffith, Lyn Thomas, Leslie Bradley, Doodles Weaver, Mike Ragan (Holly Bane), Claire DuBrey. A young man rides into a small town and is soon made an unwilling sheriff as he must stand up to the town bosses, a gambler and a saloon-owner. Average oater.

1165 Frontier Gunlaw. Columbia, 1946. 60 minutes B/W. D: Derwin Abrahams. SC: Bennett Cohen. WITH Charles Starrett, Tex Harding, Dub Taylor, Jean Stevens, Al Trace & His Silly Symphonies, Jack Guthrie, Weldon Heyburn, Jack Rockwell, Frank LaRue, John Elliott, Robert Kortman, Stanley Price, William Nestell, Hank Worden, John Tyrell. The Durango Kid gets on the trail of a band of outlaws called "The Phantoms" which have been robbing area ranchers. Pretty fair entry in the popular "Durango Kid" series.

Frontier Hellcat see **Among Vultures.**

Frontier Horizon see **The New Frontier** (1939)

1166 Frontier Investigator. Republic, 1949. 60 minutes B/W. D: Fred C. Brannon. SC: Robert Williams. WITH Allan "Rocky" Lane, Eddy Waller, Clayton Moore, Gail Davis, Roy Barcroft, Robert Emmett Keane, Marshall Reed, Francis Ford, Claire Whitney, Harry Lauter, Tom London, George Lloyd. A lawman is on the trail of a killer who murders victims with a special telescopic device mounted on his rifle. There is plenty of action in this Allan Lane outing. V: Cumberland Video.

1167 Frontier Justice. First Division/Grand National, 1936. 58 minutes B/W. D: Robert McGowan. SC: W. Scott Darling. WITH Hoot Gibson, Jane Barnes, Richard Cramer, Franklyn Farnum, Lloyd Ingraham, Joe Girard, Fred "Snowflake" Toones, Roger Williams, George Yoeman, John Elliott, Lafe McKee. A man returns home to find his father has been committed to an asylum and their ranch is under heavy mortgage and suffering from rustling raids. Complicated but entertaining Hoot Gibson vehicle but the low budget hurts. V: Thunderbird.

1168 Frontier Law. Universal, 1943. 59 minutes B/W. D-SC: Elmer Clifton.

WITH Russell Hayden, Fuzzy Knight, Jennifer Holt, Dennis Moore, Johnny Bond & His Red River Valley Boys, Jack Ingram, Hal Taliaferro, George Eldredge, I. Stanford Jolley, Frank LaRue, James Farley, Michael Vallon, Tex Cooper. Two cowboys ride into an area plagued by cattle rustling and find a pal is working for the culprit behind the gang. Fair Universal programmer in which star Russell Hayden replaced an ailing Tex Ritter.

1169 Frontier Marshal. Fox, 1934. 66 minutes B/W. D: Lewis Seiler. SC: William Conselman & Stuart Anthony. WITH George O'Brien, Irene Bentley, George E. Stone, Alan Edwards, Ruth Gillette, Berton Churchill, Frank Conroy, Ward Bond, Ed LeSaint, Russell Simpson, Jerry Foster. A lawman arrives in Tombstone, Arizona, where the crooked mayor controls all the dishonest elements and has killed his banking partner. First screen version of Stuart N. Lake's novel Wyatt Earp, Frontier Marshal (although Earp is called Michael Wyatt here) and it is a good film.

1170 Frontier Marshal. 20th Century-Fox, 1939. 71 minutes B/W. D: Allan Dwan. SC: Sam Hellman. WITH Randolph Scott, Nancy Kelly, Cesar Romero, Binnie Barnes, John Carradine, Edward Norris, Eddie Foy Jr., Ward Bond, Lon Chaney Jr., Tom Tyler, Chris-Pin Martin, Joseph Sawyer, Del Henderson, Harry Hayden, Ventura Ybarra, Si Jenks, Gloria Roy, Pat O'Malley, Charles Stevens, Harry Woods, Richard Alexander, Hank Mann, Ed LeSaint, Heinie Conklin, George Melford, Fern Emmett, Kathryn Sheldon, Ferris Taylor, Arthur Aylesworth, Eddie Dunn, Philo McCullough, Ethan Laidlaw. Sheriff Wyatt Earp, with the help of Doc Holliday, sets out to bring law and order to the town of Tombstone, Arizona. Second screen version of the Stuart N. Lake novel contains excellent recreation of the shootout at the O.K. Corral.

1171 Frontier Outlaws. Producers Releasing Corporation, 1944. 58 minutes B/W. D: Sam Newfield. SC: Joseph O'Donnell. WITH Buster Crabbe, At St. John, Frances Gladwin, Marin Sais, Charles King, Jack Ingram, Kermit Maynard, Ed Cassidy, Emmett Lynn, Budd Buster, Frank Ellis. An outlaw gang is attempting to control a valley and when Billy Carson opposes them the crooks have him framed for murder. Another typically low grade but entertaining entry in PRC's "Billy Carson" series.

1172 Frontier Outpost. Columbia, 1950. 55 minutes B/W. D: Ray Nazarro. SC: Barry Shipman. WITH Charles Starrett, Smiley Burnette, Lois Hall, Steve Darrell, Fred Sears, Hank Penny & Slim Duncan, Robert Wilke, Paul Campbell, Jock (Mahoney) O'Mahoney, Bud Osborne, Chuck Roberson, Pierre Watkin, Dick Wessell, Everett Glass. The Durango Kid robs a stage carrying a government gold shipment so the money would not be stolen by outlaws. Rather jumbled episode.

1173 The Frontier Phantom. Western Adventure/Realart, 1952. 55 minutes B/W. D: Ron Ormond. SC: Maurice Tombragel & June Carr. WITH Lash LaRue, Al St. John, Virginia Herrick, Archie Twitchell, Clarke Stevens, Bud Osborne, Cliff Taylor, Kenne Duncan, George Chesebro, Sandy Sanders, Buck Garrett, Jack O'Shea, Frank Ellis, Roy Butler, Larry Barton. Two U. S. marshals attempt to uncover the ringleader of a counterfeiting outfit and one of them, in order to get in good with the bad man, takes on the guise of his outlaw brother, the Frontier Phantom. Lash LaRue's final starring series Western is an exciting and actionful outing.

1174 Frontier Pony Express. Republic, 1939. 54 (58) minutes B/W. D: Joseph Kane. SC: Norman S. Hall. WITH Roy Rogers, Mary Hart, Raymond Hatton, Edward Keane, Noble Johnson, Monte Blue, Donald Dillaway, William Royle, Ethel Wales, Bud Osborne, George (Montgomery) Letz, Charles King, Fred Burns, Jack Kirk, Ernie Adams, Hank Bell, Jack O'Shea. In 1861 a crooked senator plans to set up his own republic in California by pretending to aid the Confederacy in getting hold of the state via the Pony Express. A very entertaining Roy Rogers film with the songs "Rusty Spurs" and "My Old Kentucky Home."

1175 Frontier Revenge. Screen Guild/ Western Adventure, 1948. 58 minutes B/W. D-SC: Ray Taylor. WITH Lash LaRue, Al St. John, Peggy Stewart, Jim Bannon, Ray Bennett, Sarah Padden, Jimmie Martin, Jack Hendricks, Lee Morgan, Sandy Sanders, Billy Dix, Cliff Taylor, Steve Raines, Bud Osborne, George Chesebro, Kermit Maynard, Jack Evans. Lash and Fuzzy pose as two famous outlaws in order to join up with an outlaw gang which has been terrorizing a small town, and to unmask the gang leader. Okay action drama in Lash LaRue's series for producer Ron Ormond.

1176 Frontier Scout. Grand National, 1938. 62 minutes B/W. D: Sam Newfield. SC: Frances Guihan. WITH George Houston, Beth Marion, Al St. John, Dave O'Brien, Guy Chase, Jack Ingram, Jack C. Smith, Dorothy Fay, Slim Whitaker, Kenne Duncan, Carl Mathews, Kit Guard, Bob Woodward, Walter Byron, Budd Buster, Frank LaRue, Minerva Urecal, Mantan Moreland, Roger Williams, Joe Girard. Wild Bill Hickok aids local ranchers plagued by cattle rustlers and Indian raids. George Houston's first Western, in which he plays Wild Bill Hickok, is a sturdy affair which will please his fans.

1177 Frontier Town. Grand National, 1938. 60 minutes B/W. D: Ray Taylor. SC: Lindsley Parsons. WITH Tex Ritter, Ann Evers, Snub Pollard, Horace Murphy, Charles King, Forrest Taylor, Jack C. Smith, Ed Cassidy, Karl Hackett, Lynton Brent, Don Marion, Hank Worden, John Elliott, Jimmy LeFieur's Saddle Pals. Despite the events being fixed by a gang of crooks, a singing cowboy tries to win the big prize money at a rodeo. Cheaply made but fairly exciting Tex Ritter vehicle, helped by Tex singing a few good songs.

1178 Frontier Uprising. United Artists, 1961. 68 minutes B/W. D: Edward L. Cahn. SC: Owen Harris. WITH Jim Davis, Nancy Hadley, Ken Mayer, Nestor Paiva, Don O'Kelly, Stuart Randall, David Renard, Tudor Owen, Addison Richards, Jan Arvan, Sid Kane, Barbara Mansell. A wagon train heads West to California unaware that the U. S. and Mexico are at war and the Mexicans, who control California, have made an alliance with the local Indians. Small budget, but more than passable drama with Jim Davis doing a good job as the frontier scout leading the wagon train.

1179 Frontier Vengeance. Republic, 1940. 54 minutes B/W. D: Nate Watt. SC: Bennett Cohen & Barry Shipman. WITH Don "Red" Barry, Betty Moran, George Offerman Jr., Ivan Miller, Yakima Canutt, Kenneth MacDonald, Cindy Walker, Griff Barnett, Jack Lawrence, Fred "Snowflake" Toones, Obed Packard. When a crooked stage line owner tries to run a rival company, owned by a young girl, out of business, a stage driver steps in to help the young lady. Typically breezy Don Barry Republic film.

1180 Frontiers of '49. Columbia, 1939. 54 minutes B/W. D: Joseph Levering.

SC: Nate Gatzert. WITH Bill Elliott, Luana de Alcaniz, Hal Taliaferro, Charles King, Slim Whitaker, Al Ferguson, Jack Walters, Octavio Girard, Carlos Villarias, Jose de la Cruz, Kit Guard, Bud Osborne, Jack Ingram, Lee Shumway, Ed Cassidy, Tex Palmer. Two government men are sent to California in 1848 to stop the dictatorial activities of a crook who has forced many Spanish ranchers off their lands. Compact and actionful Bill Elliott vehicle.

1181 The Frontiersman. Paramount, 1938. 54 (74) minutes B/W. D: Lesley Selander. SC: Norman Houston & Harrison Jacobs. WITH William Boyd, George ("Gabby") Hayes, Russell Hayden, Evelyn Venable, William Duncan, Clara Kimball Young, Charles (Tony) Hughes, Dickie Jones, Roy Barcroft, Emily Fitzroy, John Beach, George Morrell, Jim Corey. A crook, who is in love with a school teacher, rustles Bar 20 cattle and then murders his partner. A mediocre entry in the "Hopalong Cassidy" series, interesting only for appearances by silent stars William Duncan (as Buck Peters) and Clara Kimball Young. Contains useless filler of the Saint Brendan Boys Choir in a school sequence. Reissued by Film Classics.

1182 The Fugitive. Monogram, 1933. 61 minutes B/W. D: Harry Fraser. SC: Harry O. Jones (Harry Fraser). WITH Rex Bell, Cecilia Parker, George ("Gabby") Hayes, Robert Kortman, Tom London, Gordon DeMain, Theodore Lorch, Dick Dickinson, Earl Dwire, George Nash. A cowboy is falsely accused of a crime and is forced to run from the law until he can prove his innocence. Low budget Rex Bell vehicle.

1183 The Fugitive. RKO Radio, 1947. 104 minutes B/W. D: John Ford. SC: Dudley Nichols. WITH Henry Fonda, Dolores Del Rio, Pedro Armendariz, Ward Bond, Leo Carrillo, J. Carrol Naish, Robert Armstrong, John Qualen, Fortunio Bonanova, Chris-Pin Martin, Michael Inclan, Fernando Fernandez, Jose Torvay. A priest who supports the revolutionary cause in Mexico is hunted by the police and he is befriended by a man who later turns him in for money. Low key John Ford film which will please Henry Fonda fans.

1184 Fugitive from Sonora. Republic, 1943. 55 minutes B/W. D: Howard Bretherton. SC: Norman S. Hall. WITH Don "Red" Barry, Lynn Merrick, Wally Vernon, Harry

Cording, Ethan Laidlaw, Frank McCarroll, Pierce Lyden, Kenne Duncan, Karl Hackett, Slim Whitaker, Art Dillard. A one-time outlaw comes to a small town and tries to stop the war between homesteaders and cattlemen. Another good entry in Don Barry's Republic series; this one introduced Barry's long-time comedy sidekick, Wally Vernon.

1185 Fugitive of the Plains. Producers Releasing Corporation, 1943. 56 minutes B/S. D: Sam Newfield. SC: George W. Sayre. WITH Buster Crabbe, Al St. John, Maxine Leslie, Jack Ingram, Kermit Maynard, Karl Hackett, Hal Price, Budd Buster, Artie Ortego, Carl Sepulveda. Billy the Kid and Fuzzy Q. Jones come to the aid of a young girl forced into lawlessness by crooks. Standard "Billy the Kid" series entry. Reissued in 1947 by Eagle Lion in a 38 minute edited version called **Raiders of Red Rock.**

1186 Fugitive Valley. Monogram, 1941. 60 minutes B/W. D: S. Roy Luby. SC: John Vlahos & Robert Finkle. WITH Ray Corrigan, John King, Max Terhune, Julie Duncan, Glenn Strange, Robert Kortman, Tom London, Reed Howes, Ed Brady, Carl Mathews, Ed Piel Sr., Doye O'Dell, Frank McCarroll. In Arizona an outlaw gang led by "The Whip" terrorizes the countryside and The Range Busters get into the gang in order to stop them. Okay "Range Busters" series entry with a bit too much humor although Glenn Strange and Robert Kortman are just great in villainous roles.

1187 The Furies. Paramount, 1950. 109 minutes B/W. D: Anthony Mann. SC: Charles Schnee. WITH Barbara Stanwyck, Walter Huston, Wendell Corey, Gilbert Roland, Judith Anderson, Thomas Gomez, Beulah Bondi, Albert Dekker, John Bromfield, Wallace Ford, Blanche Yurka, Louis Jean Heydt, Frank Ferguson, Movita, Myrna Dell, Charles Evans. A stubborn self-made cattle rancher clashes with the strong-willed daughter he cannot control. None-too-interesting psychological oater with lots of hidden undertones for those with a symbolic bent.

1188 The Further Adventures of the Wilderness Family. Pacific International, 1978. 105 minutes Color. D: Frank Zuniga. SC: Arthur R. Dubs. WITH Robert Logan, Susan Damante Shaw, Hollye Holmes, Ham Larsen, George "Buck" Flowers, Brian Cutler. A modern-day family, having deserted the big city for the pioneer

life in the Rocky Mountains, further experiences the joys and tribulations of their new life by going through a harsh winter. The second film in a three-part series and just as good as the others. Preceded by **The Adventures of the Wilderness Family** (q.v.) and followed by **Mountain Family Robinson** (q.v.). Also called **Wilderness Family, Part Two.**

1189 Fury at Furnace Creek. 20th Century-Fox, 1948. 88 minutes B/W. D: H. Bruce Humberstone. SC: Charles G. Booth. WITH Victor Mature, Coleen Gray, Glenn Langan, Reginald Gardiner, Albert Dekker, Fred Clark, Charles Kemper, Robert Warwick, George Cleveland, Roy Roberts, Willard Robertson, Griff Barnett, Frank Orth, J. Farrell MacDonald, Jay Silverheels, Robert Adler, Mauritz Hugo, Howard Negley, Harry Carter, Harlan Briggs, Si Jenks, Guy Wilkerson, Edmund Cobb, Kermit Maynard, Paul Newlan, Ted Mapes, George Chesebro, Al Hill, Minerva Urecal, Ray Teal, Alan Bridge, Oscar O'Shea, Jerry Miley. A young man tries to prove his father was not the cause of a massacre and uncovers proof that three no-accounts were the real culprits. Routine oater with Victor Mature trying hard as the young avenger.

1190 Fury at Gunsight Pass. Columbia, 1956. 68 minutes B/W. D: Fred F. Sears. SC: David Lang. WITH David Brian, Neville Brand, Richard Long, Lisa Davis, Kathleen Warren, Percy Helton, Morris Ankrum, Addison Richards, Joe Forte, Wally Vernon, Paul E. Burns, Frank Fenton, James Anderson, George Keymas, Robert Anderson. When a wedding halts their attempt to rob a small town bank, an outlaw gang decides to take over the town. An out-of-the-ordinary storyline adds some spice to this low budget entry produced by Wallace MacDonald.

1191 Fury at Sundown. United Artists, 1957. 75 minutes B/W. D: Gerd Oswald. SC: Jason James. WITH John Derek, John Smith, Carolyn Craig, Nick Adams, Gage Clarke, Robert Griffin, Malcolm Atterbury, Rusty Lane, Frances Morris, Tyler McDuff, Robert Adler, Norman Leavitt, Ken Christy. A one-time outlaw is called a coward for refusing to use a gun but when an outlaw takes his girl as an escape hostage, the man comes to her defense. Brooding oater with fine performances.

1192 Fury in Paradise. Filmmakers/Alfonso Sanchez-Tello, 1956. 77 minutes Color.

D-SC: George Bruce. WITH Peter Thompson, Carlos Rivas, Rea Iturbi, Eduardo Noreiga, Felipe Nolan, Claud Brooks. An American tourist in Mexico nearly ends up facing a firing squad after becoming involved with a man and his pretty daughter who are in a revolution plot. Low budget actioner filmed in Mexico.

1193 Fury of the Apaches. Castilla, 1965. 84 minutes Color. D: Antonio Roman. WITH Frank Latimore, Ken Clark, Yvonne Bastion, George Gordon, Liza Moreno. When a rancher and his pretty wife have troubles with a vicious neighbor, a young cowboy aids them in the struggle. Adequate Spanish-made oater. Also called **Apache Fury** and **The Doomed Ranch.**

1194 Fury River. Metro-Goldwyn-Mayer, 1962. 74 minutes B/W. D: Jacques Tourneur, Alan Crosland Jr., Joe Waggner & Otto Lang. WITH Keith Larsen, Buddy Ebsen, Don Burnett, Philip Tonge, Lisa Davis, Larry Chance, Jim Hayward, Pat Hogan, Lisa Gaye. Rogers' Rangers search for a waterway to the ocean while they battle the French and Indians in frontier Canada. Telefeature from episodes of the "Northwest Passage" (NBC-TV, 1958-59) teleseries and issued theatrically abroad; average.

1195 Fuzzy Settles Down. Producers Releasing Corporation, 1944. 60 minutes B/W. D: Sam Newfield. SC: Louise Rousseau. WITH Buster Crabbe, Al St. John, Patti McCarthy, Charles King, John Merton, Frank McCarroll, Hal Price, John Elliott, Ed Cassidy, Robert Hill, Ted Mapes, Tex Palmer. Billy Carson and Fuzzy Q. Jones capture two notorious outlaws and Fuzzy uses his portion of the reward money to buy a newspaper in a town where the people want a telegraph line in order to break up a gang of rustlers. Low grade but quite entertaining.

G

1196 The Gal Who Took the West. Universal, 1949. 84 minutes Color. D: Frederick De Cordova. SC: William Bowers & Oscar Brodney. WITH Yvonne De Carlo, Scott Brady, Charles Coburn, John Russell, Myrna Dell, James Millican, Clem Bevans, Bob Stevenson, Houseley Stevenson, Robin Short, Russell Simpson, John Litel, James Todd, Edward Earle, Jack Ingram,

Francis McDonald, Glenn Strange, William Tannen, Steve Darrell, Pierce Lyden, Ross Elliott, John James, Howard Negley, Charles Cane, William Haade, Louise Lorimer, Forrest Taylor, Paul Brinegar, House Peters Jr., Russ Whiteman, Roger Moore, Forbes Murray, Gary Teague. An opera singer comes to Arizona in the 1890s and two feuding brothers both fall in love with her. Serio-comedy Western is not good on either count; mediocre.

1197 The Gallant Defender. Columbia, 1935. 60 minutes B/W. D: David Selman. SC: Ford Beebe. WITH Charles Starrett, Joan Perry, Harry Woods, Ed LeSaint, Jack Clifford, Al Bridge, George Chesebro, Edmund Cobb, Frank Ellis, Jack Rockwell, Tom London, Stanley Blystone, The Sons of the Pioneers, Lew Meehan, Merrill McCormack, Glenn Strange, Al Ferguson, Slim Whitaker, Bud Osborne, George Billings. A cowboy comes to the aid of homesteaders who are being harrassed by cattlemen who do not want them to homestead their range. Charles Starrett's initial series film is a sturdy affair enhanced by Ford Beebe's fine script.

1198 The Gallant Fool. Monogram, 1933. 61 minutes B/W. D: Robert North Bradbury. SC: Robert North Bradbury & Harry O. (Fraser) Jones. WITH Bob Steele, Arletta Duncan, John Elliott, Theodore Lorch, Perry Murdock, George ("Gabby") Hayes, George Nash, Pascale Perry. After being falsely accused of murder, a man takes refuge in a circus with his small son. Nicely done and actionful Bob Steele vehicle.

1199 The Gallant Legion. Republic, 1948. 88 minutes B/W. D: Joseph Kane. SC: Gerald Adams. WITH William Elliott, Adrian Booth, Joseph Schildkraut, Bruce Cabot, Andy Devine, Jack Holt, Adele Mara, Grant Withers, James Brown, Hal Taliaferro, Russell Hicks, Herbert Rawlinson, Marshall Reed, Harry Woods, Roy Barcroft, Bud Osborne, Hank Bell, Jack Ingram, George Chesebro, Noble Johnson, Rex Lease, John Hamilton, Emmett Vogan, Trevor Bardette, Gene Roth, Ferris Taylor, Iron Eyes Cody, Kermit Maynard, Jack Kirk, Merrill McCormack, Fred Kohler, Glenn Strange, Tex Terry, Joseph Crehan, Lester Sharpe. When a crooked politician tries to split Texas in half by disbanding the Texas Rangers, a ranger tries to stop him and is aided by a girl reporter. Very fine William Elliott vehicle, strong in story, action and cast.

1200 Galloping Dynamite. Ambassador, 1937. 58 minutes B/W. D: Harry Fraser. SC: Sherman Lowe & Charles Condon. WITH Kermit Maynard, Ariane Allen, John Merton, John Ward, Stanley Blystone, David Sharpe, Earl Dwire, Francis Walker, Tracy Layne, Bob Burns, Allen Greer, Budd Buster. A Texas Ranger finds out that three crooks have murdered his prospector brother in order to gain a ranch on which a valuable gold vein runs. Kermit Maynard joins the legion of singing cowboys in this average entry in his Ambassador series. V: Video Dimensions.

1201 Galloping On. Action/Weiss Brothers/ Artclass, 1925. 50 minutes B/W. D: Richard Thorpe. SC: Frank L. Ingraham & Betty Burbridge. WITH Wally Wales, Jessie Cruzon, Louise Lester, Charles Whittaker, Richard Belfield, Gretchen Waterman, Art Phillips, Lawrence Underwood. A man returns home after being falsely sent to prison and he finds out the crook who framed him wants to send him back to jail. With the aid of a young girl he sets out to get evidence against the crook, who is the town banker. A good silent "B" entry with a top notch performance by Wally Wales in the lead role.

1202 Galloping Romeo. Monogram, 1933. 60 minutes B/W. D: Robert North Bradbury. SC: Harry O. (Fraser) Jones. WITH Bob Steele, Doris Hill, George ("Gabby") Hayes, Frank Ball, Ernie Adams, Lafe McKee, Ed Brady, George Nash, Earl Dwire. A young man teams with an old-timer to prove his innocence when he is falsely accused of a crime. Entertaining Bob Steele vehicle, but the film is hurt somewhat by excessive footage from the star's previous films.

1203 Galloping Through. Sunset, 1923. 50 minutes B/W. D: Robert North Bradbury. WITH Jack Hoxie, Priscilla Banner, William Lester, Lorraine Lorimer, William McCall, Tom Lingham, Janet Ford, Scout (horse). A cowboy aids a homesteader family in which the man is falsely accused of a crime. Well done early Jack Hoxie vehicle—his fans will like it.

1204 Galloping Thru. Monogram, 1932. 58 minutes B/W. D: Lloyd Nosler. SC: Wellyn Totman. WITH Tom Tyler, Betty Mack, Alan Bridge, Si Jenks, Stanley Blystone, G. D. Woods, John Elliott, Artie Ortego. A man returns home to see his father murdered and he tries to find the culprit. Low grade, but action-ful, Tom Tyler vehicle.

1205 Galloping Thunder. Columbia, 1946. 54 minutes B/W. D: Ray Nazarro. SC: Ed Earl Repp. WITH Charles Starrett, Smiley Burnette, Adelle Roberts, Merle Travis & His Bronco Busters, Richard Bailey, Edmund Cobb, Kermit Maynard, Ray Bennett, Curt Barrett, John Merton, Nolan Leary, Budd Buster, Forrest Taylor, Gordon Harrison. Outlaws are preventing ranchers from shipping their mustang herds to the government for army use and an agent, who is really the Durango Kid, is sent to investigate. Only a passable effort in the "Durango Kid" series.

The Gambler see **Kenny Rogers as the Gambler**

1206 The Gambler from Natchez. 20th Century-Fox, 1954. 88 minutes Color. D: Henry Levin. SC: Gerald Drayson Adams & Irving Wallace. WITH Dale Robertson, Debra Paget, Kevin McCarthy, Thomas Gomez, Lisa Davis, Douglas Dick, John Wengraf, Jay Novello, Woody Strode, Peter Mamakos, Donald Randolph. When his father is falsely accused of cheating at cards and is gunned down by three men, a young man sets out to avenge the murder. Entertaining frontier drama set in the 1840s.

1207 The Gambler Wore a Gun. United Artists, 1961. 66 minutes B/W. D: Edward L. Cahn. SC: Owen Harris. WITH Jim Davis, Merry Anders, Mark Allen, Addison Richards, Don Dorrell, Robert Anderson, Keith Richards, John Craig, Charles Cane, Joe McGuinn, Boyd "Red" Morgan, Boyd Stockman, Jack Kenney, Brad Trumbull. An honest gambler buys a ranch but cannot take possession of it because the owner died before signing the final papers, and in trying to help the man's children the gambler finds out the ranch is being used by crooks for hiding stolen cattle. Competent programmer remake of **The Lone Gun** (q.v.).

1208 The Gambling Terror. Republic, 1937. 60 minutes B/W. D: Sam Newfield. SC: George Plympton & Fred Myton. WITH Johnny Mack Brown, Iris Meredith, Charles King, Ted Adams, Earl Dwire, Dick Curtis, Horace Murphy, Bobby Nelson, Frank Ellis, Frank Ball, Budd Buster, Lloyd Ingraham, Sherry Tansey, Steve Clark, George Morrell, Art Dillard, Tex Palmer, Jack Montgomery. A man pretends to be a gambler in order to stop a crook who is running a cattle protection racket. Okay entry in Johnny Mack Brown's series for A. W. Hackel.

147   Gangs

1209 Gangs of Sonora. Republic, 1941. 56 minutes B/W. D: John English. SC: Albert DeMond & Doris Schroeder. WITH Robert Livingston, Bob Steele, Rufe Davis, June Johnson, Bud McTaggart, Helen MacKellar, Robert Frazer, William Farnum, Budd Buster, Hal Price, Wally West, Bud Osborne, Bud Geary, Jack Kirk, Griff Barnett, Curley Dresden. The Three Mesquiteers come to the aid of newspaperwoman Kansas Kate after a crooked rival tries to take over her business. Pleasant outing for "The Three Mesquiteers."

1210 Gangster's Den. Producers Releasing Corporation, 1945. 55 minutes B/W. D: Sam Newfield. SC: George Plympton. WITH Buster Crabbe, Al St. John, Sidney Logan, Charles King, I. Stanford Jolley, Emmett Lynn, Kermit Maynard, Ed Cassidy, George Chesebro, Karl Hackett, Bob Cason, Michael Owen, Wally West. Billy Carson and pal Fuzzy Q. Jones set out to stop a crook from trying to take over a girl's land. Good Billy Carson series entry with Charles King not playing the villain for a change; here he is a lovable drunk in a brief barroom sequence. Fuzzy tells Charlie he is "big and ugly enough" to be his bodyguard and Charlie replies, "I was a pretty baby." Asked if he wants the job, Charlie asks what it pays. "All your drinks and grub," Fuzzy answers. "Do you want the job?" "Forget the grub and I do," says Charlie.

1211 Gangsters of the Frontier. Producers Releasing Corporation, 1944. 58 minutes B/W. D-SC: Elmer Clifton. WITH Tex Ritter, Dave O'Brien, Guy Wilkerson, Patti McCarty, Harry Harvey, Betty Miles, I. Stanford Jolley, Marshall Reed, Clarke Stevens, Charles King, Ted Mapes. The Texas Rangers come to a small town which has been taken over by two brothers, who have escaped from prison and are forcing the townspeople to work in the local mines. Dreary entry in "The Texas Rangers" series although Tex Ritter does do well by a trio of songs, including "Please Remember Me" and "Ride, Ranger, Ride." British title: **Raiders of the Frontier.**

1212 Garden of Evil. 20th Century-Fox, 1954. 100 minutes Color. D: Henry Hathaway. SC: Frank Fenton. WITH Gary Cooper, Susan Hayward, Richard Widmark, Hugh Marlowe, Cameron Mitchell, Rita Moreno, Victor Manuel Mendoza. A woman hires three soldiers of fortune to find her husband who has disappeared into the Mexican gold fields. Fans of the stars will have a good time with this steamy melodrama.

1213 The Gas House Kids Go West. Producers Releasing Corporation, 1947. 62 minutes B/W. D: William Beaudine. SC: Robert E. Kent, Robert A. McGowan & Eugene Conrad. WITH Chili Williams, John Sheldon, Carl "Alfalfa" Switzer, Vince Barnett, Bennie Bartlett, Tommy Bond, Emory Parnell, William Wright, Lela Bliss, Ronn Martin, Ray Dalcianne, Rudy Wissler. A group of kids wins a trip to California and are to deliver a car to a dealer but they find out the auto has been stolen. Typical low grade entry in PRC's "Gas House Kids" series.

1214 The Gatling Gun. Ellman Enterprises, 1971. 93 minutes Color. D: Robert Gordon. SC: Joseph Van Winkle & Mark Hanna. WITH Guy Stockwell, Robert Fuller, Barbara Luna, Woody Strode, Patrick Wayne, Pat Buttram, John Carradine, Phil Harris, Judy Jordan, Carlos Rivas, Tommy Cooke, Steve Conte. A Cavalry officer and his men must protect a gatling gun and a westward-bound family from marauding Indians. Actionful tale with good battle scenes.

1215 The Gaucho. United Artists, 1928. 95 minutes B/W. D: F. Richard Jones. SC: Lotta Woods. WITH Douglas Fairbanks, Lupe Velez, Geraine Greer, Eve Southern, Gustav von Seyffertitz, Michael Vavitch, Charles Stevens, Nigel De Brulier, Albert MacQuarrie, Mary Pickford. A gaucho is turned over to the law by the girl who loves him because she becomes jealous of his interest in a "miracle girl." Actionful Douglas Fairbanks silent film.

1216 Gaucho Serenade. Republic, 1940. 66 minutes B/W. D: Frank McDonald. SC: Betty Burbridge & Bradford Ropes. WITH Gene Autry, Smiley Burnette, June Storey, Mary Lee, Duncan Renaldo, Cliff Severn Jr., Lester Matthews, Smith Ballew, Joseph Crehan, William Ruhl, Wade Boteler, Ted Adams, Fred Burns, Julian Rivero, George Lloyd, Ed Cassidy, Olaf Hytten, Fred "Snowflake" Toones, Jack Kirk, Harry Strang, Hank Worden, Jim Corey, Tom London, Walter Miller, Frankie Marvin. Gene Autry and his pals get involved with a group of show girls and a pompous singing cowboy. Exceedingly slow moving and actionless Gene Autry vehicle. Reissue title: **Keep Rollin'.**

1217 Gauchos of El Dorado. Republic, 1941. 56 minutes B/W. D: Lester Orleback. SC: Earle Snell. WITH Bob Steele, Tom Tyler, Rufe Davis, Lois Collier, Duncan Renaldo, Yakima Canutt, Norman Willis, Rosina Galli, William Ruhl, Edmund Cobb, Eddie Dean, Terry Frost, John Merton, Si Jenks, Ted Mapes, Bob Woodward, Horace Carpenter, Tony Roux, Ray Bennett. A dishonest banker tries to cheat local citizens but is opposed by The Three Mesquiteers. Another fast moving entry in the long-running Republic series.

1218 The Gay Amigo. United Artists, 1949. 62 minutes B/W. D: Wallace Fox. SC: Doris Schroeder. WITH Duncan Renaldo, Leo Carrillo, Armida, Joseph Sawyer, Fred Kohler Jr., Walter Baldwin, Kenneth MacDonald, George DeNormand, Clayton Moore, Fred Crane, Helen Servis, Bud Osborne, Sam Flint, Beverly Jons, Al Ferguson, David Sharpe. The Cisco Kid and Pancho are blamed by the cavalry for a series of robberies that have actually been committed by a gang disguised as Mexicans and masterminded by two corrupt businessmen. This "Cisco Kid" theatrical release is a fast moving dual biller.

1219 The Gay Buckaroo. Allied, 1932. 61 minutes B/W. D: Phil Rosen, SC: Philip Graham White. WITH Hoot Gibson, Merna Kennedy, Roy D'Arcy, Ed Piel Sr., Charles King, Lafe McKee, Sidney DeGrey, The Hoot Gibson Cowboys. A rancher and a gambler are rivals for the love of a pretty girl. This Hoot Gibson opus is definitely on the slow side.

1220 The Gay Caballero. Fox, 1932. 60 minutes B/W. D: Alfred Werker. SC: Barry Connors & Philip Klein. WITH George O'Brien, Victor McLaglen, Conchita Montenegro, Linda Watkins, C. Henry Gordon, Weldon Heyburn, Willard Robertson, Wesley Giraud. A college football hero returns to his Western ranch home to find that a crooked Mexican cattle baron has taken control of his family and its money. Well made and entertaining George O'Brien vehicle.

1221 The Gay Caballero. 20th Century-Fox, 1940. 57 minutes B/W. D: Otto Brower. SC: Albert Duffy & John Larkin. WITH Cesar Romero, Sheila Ryan, Chris-Pin Martin, Robert Sterling, Janet Beecher, Edmund McDonald, Jacqueline Dalya, Hooper Atchley, G. Montague Shaw, Ethan Laidlaw. The Cisco Kid comes to the aid of a young girl who is being swindled out of her ranch by two crooks. Delightful "Cisco Kid" series entry which moves along at a fast clip.

1222 The Gay Cavalier. Monogram, 1946. 65 minutes B/W. D: William Nigh. SC: Charles B. Belden. WITH Gilbert Roland, Ramsay Ames, Martin Garralaga, Nacho Galindo, Helen Gerald, Drew Allen, Tristram Coffin, Iris Flores, John Merton, Frank LaRue, Ray Bennett, Artie Ortego, Pierre Andre. When a rancher is plagued by outlaw attacks the Cisco Kid comes to his defense. Gilbert Roland is dashing as the Cisco Kid, Ramsay Ames is nice to look at and the Roland-Tristram Coffin sword fight is exciting, but overall this "Cisco Kid" series entry is too long and only passable entertainment.

1223 The Gay Desperado. United Artists, 1936. 88 minutes B/W. D: Rouben Mamoulian. SC: Wallace Smith. WITH Nino Martini, Ida Lupino, Leo Carrillo, Harold Huber, Mischa Auer, Stanley Fields, James Blakeley, Paul Hurst, Adrian Rosley, Alan Garcia, Frank Puglia, Michael Visaroff, Chris-Pin Martin, Harry Semels. A Mexican bandit, influenced by American gangster movies, kidnaps a singing caballero and a feisty heiress and her fiancee. Picturesque musical-comedy spoof of the Western and gangster film genres; pleasant entertainment.

1224 Gene Autry and the Mounties. Columbia, 1951. 70 minutes B/W. D: John English. SC: Norman S. Hall. WITH Gene Autry, Pat Buttram, Elena Verdugo, Carleton Young, Herbert Rawlinson, Richard Emory, Trevor Bardette, Francis McDonald, Jim Frasher, Gregg Barton, House Peters Jr., Jody Gilbert, Nolan Leary, Boyd Stockman, Teddy Infuhr, Billy Gray, Roy Butler, Chris Allen. Two Montana marshals join forces with a Mountie to bring in a bank robber. Average, but scenic, Gene Autry vehicle.

1225 General Custer at Little Big Horn. Sunset, 1926. 60 minutes B/W. D: Harry Fraser. SC: Carrie E. Rawles & L. V. O'Connor. WITH Roy Stewart, Helen Lynch, Edmund Cobb, John Beck, Arthur Morrison, Nora Lindley, Andre Farneur. Historical romance surrounding the Custer Massacre with a scout and an evil army captain romancing a pioneer girl and the captain being the cause of the Indian uprising. Considering its limited budget, this silent is a pretty good film. Also called **With General Custer at Little**

Big Horn and With Custer at Little Big Horn.

1226 Gentle Annie. Metro-Goldwyn-Mayer, 1944. 80 minutes B/W. D: Andrew Martin. SC: Lawrence Hazard. WITH James Craig, Donna Reed, Marjorie Main, Barton Mac-Lane, Morris Ankrum, Henry (Harry) Morgan, Paul Langton. A woman and her two sons commit a series of robberies and are tracked by a marshal disguised as a bum. Low key and highly entertaining little film with Marjorie Main stealing the show as the outlaw gang leader.

1227 The Gentleman from Arizona. Monogram, 1939. 71 minutes Color. D: Earl Haley. SC: Earl Haley & Jack O'Donnell. WITH John King, J. Farrell MacDonald, Joan Barclay, Craig Reynolds, Ruthie Reece, Johnny Morris, Nora Lane, Doc Pardee. A drifting cowboy wanders into a ranch for a job and ends up entering a big horse race. Innocuous little programmer shot in the early Cinecolor process.

Gentleman from California see **The Californian**

1228 The Gentleman from Texas. Monogram, 1946. 55 minutes B/W. D: Lambert Hillyer. SC: J. Benton Cheney. WITH Johnny Mack Brown, Raymond Hatton, Claudia Drake, Reno Blair, Christine McIntyre, Tristram Coffin, Marshall Reed, Ted Adams, Frank LaRue, Steve Clark, Terry Frost, Tom Carter, Jack Rockwell, Lynton Brent, Pierce Lyden, Curt Barrett & The Trailsmen, George Morrell, Artie Ortego, Wally West. Two lawmen come to a small town where a crook has bullied the population and has taken over the area. Nicely done Johnny Mack Brown entry with Tristram Coffin especially good as the bad man.

1229 Gentlemen with Guns. Producers Releasing Corporation, 1946. 51 minutes B/W. D: Sam Newfield. SC: Fred Myton. WITH Buster Crabbe, Al St. John, Patricia Knox, Steve Darrell, George Chesebro, Karl Hackett, Budd Buster, Frank Ellis, George Morrell. When Fuzzy Q. Jones refuses to sell the water rights to his land, a crook has him framed for murder and Billy Carson has to come to his rescue. Not one of the better entries in the long-running "Billy Carson" series at PRC.

1230 Geronimo. Paramount, 1939. 89 minutes B/W. D-SC: Paul H. Sloane. WITH Preston Foster, Ellen Drew, Andy Devine, William Henry, Ralph Morgan,

Gene Lockhart, Marjorie Gateson, Kitty Kelly, Monte Blue, Addison Richards, Pierre Watkin, Joseph Crehan, Chief Thundercloud, Joe Dominguez, William Haade, Ivan Miller, Frank M. Thomas, Syd Saylor, Richard Denning, Steve Gaylord, Francis Ford, Russell Simpson, Archie Twitchell. An Army captain tries to stop war between the whites and Indians. Trite melodrama made up mostly of stock footage and despite the title, Geronimo (Chief Thundercloud) is barely in evidence.

1231 Geronimo. United Artists, 1962. 101 minutes Color. D: Arnold Laven. SC: Pat Fielder. WITH Chuck Connors, Kamala Devi, Ross Martin, Pat Conway, Adam West, Enid Jaynes, Lawrence Dobkin, Denver Pyle, Armando Silvestre, John Anderson, Joe Higgins, Robert Hughes, Mario Navarro, Bill Hughes, James Burk. After bad treatment from a crooked Indian agent, Geronimo puts together a small band of braves and plans to attack the U. S. cavalry. Anemic telling of the Geronimo story with little to recommend it.

1232 Geronimo's Revenge. Buena Vista, 1965. 61 minutes Color. D: James Neilson & Harry Keller. SC: D. P. Harmon. WITH Tom Tryon, Darryl Hickman, Betty Lynn, Brian Corcoran, Onslow Stevens, Harry Carey Jr., Allan Lane, Pat Hogan, Charles Maxwell, James Edwards, Annette Gorman, Jay Silverheels. A Texas Ranger tries to aid the chief of the Natchez Indians when Geronimo disobeys his orders and goes on the warpath. Standard actioner originally telecast as a segment of the "Texas John Slaughter" series on Walt Disney's ABC-TV program on March 4, 1960 and issued abroad theatrically.

1233 Get Mean. Strange Films, 1976. 90 minutes Color. D: Ferdinando Baldi. SC: Lloyd Battista & Wolfe Lowenthal. WITH Tony Anthony, Lloyd Battista, Diana Lorys, Raf Balthasar. A lone cowboy singlehandedly attacks a fortress, the stronghold of the man who has been trying to kill him, and ends up finding a treasure. Outlandish and violent spaghetti actioner.

1234 Ghost City. Monogram, 1932. 60 minutes B/W. D: Harry Fraser. SC: Wellyn Totman. WITH Bill Cody, Andy Shuford, Helen Forrest, Walter Miller, Charles King, Walter Shumway, Al Taylor, Kate Campbell, Jack Carlisle, Thomas Curran. A cowboy comes to the aid of a girl who is trying to obtain her rightful gold field inheritance from a crook. Fair Bill Cody-Andy Shuford series vehicle.

1235 Ghost Guns. Monogram, 1944. 60 minutes B/W. D: Lambert Hillyer. SC: Frank H. Young. WITH Johnny Mack Brown, Raymond Hatton, Evelyn Finley, John Merton, Tom Quinn, Sarah Padden, Marshall Reed, Ernie Adams, Jack Ingram, Frank LaRue, Steve Clark, John Cason, George Morrell, Riley Hill. Crooks want a valley because a railroad spur will be built there and they start killing off ranchers and rustling cattle before being thwarted by two marshals. Good entry in Johnny Mack Brown's Monogram series.

1236 Ghost of Hidden Valley. Producers Releasing Corporation, 1946. 56 minutes B/W. D: Sam Newfield. SC: Ellen Coyle. WITH Buster Crabbe, Al St. John, Jean Carlin, John Meredith, John Cason, Charles King, Jimmie Aubrey, George Morrell, Bert Dillard, Karl Hackett, Silver Harr, Zon Murray. Cattle rustlers use a range belonging to a young married couple to hide stolen herds but soon Billy Carson and Fuzzy Q. Jones are on their trail. Average entry in the "Billy Carson" series.

1237 Ghost of Zorro. Republic, 1959. 72 minutes B/W. D: Fred C. Brannon. SC: Royal Cole, William Lively & Sol Shor. WITH Clayton Moore, Pamela Blake, Roy Barcroft, George J. Lewis, Gene Roth, John Crawford, I. Stanford Jolley, Steve Clark, Steve Darrell, Dale Van Sickel, Tom Steele Marshall Reed, Jack O'Shea, Holly Bane, Bob Reeves, Eddie Parker, Stanley Blystone, Joe Yrigoyen, George Chesebro, Charles King, Kenneth Terrell, Robert Wilke, Art Dillard, Frank Ellis. When crooks try to stop the construction of a telegraph line, a descendant of Don Diego takes on the guise of Zorro to stop them. Feature version of the 1949 twelve chapter serial of the same title, fast moving but a bit hard to follow.

1238 Ghost Patrol. Puritan, 1936. 56 minutes B/W. D: Sam Newfield. SC: Joseph O'Donnell. WITH Tim McCoy, Claudia Dell, Walter Miller, Wheeler Oakman, Lloyd Ingraham, Dick Curtis, Slim Whitaker, Artie Ortego, Art Dillard. A scientist invents a ray machine which outlaws use to bring down mail shipment planes so they can rob them. The sci-fi element adds some zest to this fast moving Tim McCoy vehicle. V: Video Communications.

1239 The Ghost Rider. Superior/First Division, 1935. 56 minutes B/W. D: Jack Levine. SC: John West. WITH Rex Lease, Ann Carol, William Desmond, Franklyn Farnum, Art Mix, Bill Patton, Denver Dixon, Lloyd Ingraham, Bobby Nelson, Blackie Whiteford, Roger Williams, Eddie Parker, Lafe McKee. A deputy sheriff on the trail of outlaws finds himself being aided by a ghostly masked phantom. Cheap Louis Weiss production which is enhanced by the mystery ploy.

1240 The Ghost Rider. Monogram, 1943. 54 minutes B/W. D: Wallace Fox. SC: Jess Bowers (Adele Buffington). WITH Johnny Mack Brown, Raymond Hatton, Beverly Boyd, Harry Woods, Charles King, Edmund Cobb, Bud Osborne, Milburn Morante, George Morrell, Tom Seidel, Artie Ortego. A marshal on the trail of the man who murdered his father joins with an outlaw gang to find the killer. The first of the long-running Johnny Mack Brown-Raymond Hatton series for Monogram and this entry put the showcase off to a good start.

Ghost Riders of the West see **The Phantom Rider** (1946)

1241 Ghost Town. Commodore, 1936. 60 minutes B/W. D: Harry Fraser. SC: Monroe Talbot. WITH Harry Carey, Ruth Findlay, Jane Novak, David Sharpe, Lee Shumway, Ed Cassidy, Roger Williams, Earl Dwire, Phil Dunham, Chuck Morrison, Sonny (horse). Claim jumpers are after a mine and a cowboy comes to the aid of its owner. Cheaply made but entertaining Harry Carey film for producer William Berke.

1242 Ghost Town. United Artists, 1956. 75 minutes B/W. D: Allen Miner. SC: Jameson Brewer. WITH Kent Taylor, John Smith, Marian Carr, John Doucette, William Phillips, Serena Sande, Gary Murray. When a stage arrives at a way station which has been raided by Indians, the passengers decide to head for a ghost town in order to avoid the hostilities. Low budget but more than passable oater.

1243 Ghost Town Gold. Republic, 1936. 54 minutes B/W. D: Joseph Kane. SC: John Rathmell & Oliver Drake. WITH Robert Livingston, Ray Corrigan, Max Terhune, Kay Hughes, Yakima Canutt, Frank Hagney, LeRoy Mason, Burr Caruth, Robert Kortman, Milburn Morante, Horace Murphy, Earle Hodgins, Ed Piel Sr., Harry Harvey, Hank Worden, Bud Osborne,

Bob Burns, I. Stanford Jolley, Wally West. The Three Mesquiteers are on the trail of an outlaw gang which hides its stolen loot in a ghost town. Second entry in the popular Republic series "The Three Mesquiteers," based on the William Colt MacDonald characters, and the first one with the great Max Terhune as Lullaby Joslin (and, of course, Elmer Sneezewood); solid entertainment. V: Video Connection.

1244 Ghost Town Law. Monogram, 1942. 62 minutes B/W. D: Howard Bretherton. SC: Jess Bowers (Adele Buffington). WITH Buck Jones, Tim McCoy, Raymond Hatton, Virginia Carpenter, Murdock McQuarrie, Charles King, Howard Masters, Ben Corbett, Tom London. While investigating the murders of two fellow lawmen, The Rough Riders help a woman whose brother has mysteriously disappeared. The mystery element and good staging help make this an entertaining entry in Monogram's "The Rough Riders" series.

1245 Ghost Town Renegades. Producers Releasing Corporation, 1947. 58 minutes B/W. D: Ray Taylor. SC: Patricia Harper. WITH Lash LaRue, Al St. John, Jennifer Holt, Jack Ingram, Terry Frost, Steve Clark, Lane Bradford, Lee Roberts, William Fawcett, Henry Hall. Crooks are after a property with gold on it and when the Cheyenne Kid and Fuzzy Q. Jones try to stop them the outlaws murder a man and frame Cheyenne for the crime. Pretty good actionful outing for Lash LaRue. V: Thunderbird.

1246 Ghost Town Riders. Universal, 1938. 54 minutes B/W. D: George Waggner. SC: Joseph West (George Waggner). WITH Bob Baker, Fay Shannon, George Cleveland, Hank Worden, Forrest Taylor, Glenn Strange, Jack Kirk, Martin Turner, Reed Howes, Murdock McQuarrie, Merrill McCormack, George Morrell, Frank Ellis, Oscar Gahan, Tex Phelps. Two cowboys with a herd of horses come across a ghost town where a gang plans to take over and start a fake gold boom. Pretty good Bob Baker series entry, predating some of director George Waggner's later horror efforts at Universal.

1247 Ghost Valley. RKO Radio, 1932. 54 minutes B/W. D: Fred Allen. SC: Adele Buffington. WITH Tom Keene, Merna Kennedy, Buck Moulton, Kate Campbell, Harry Bowen, Mitchell Harris, Harry Semels, Ted Adams, Al Taylor, Slim Whitaker. Mysterious happenings begin when a girl and her step-brother inherit a gold mine and a cowboy tries to help them. Eerie atmosphere aids this Tom Keene vehicle.

1248 Ghost Valley Raiders. Republic, 1940. 54 minutes B/W. D: George Sherman. SC: Bennett Cohen. WITH Don "Red" Barry, Lona Andre, LeRoy Mason, Tom London, Jack Ingram, Horace Murphy, Ralph Peters, Curley Dresden, Yakima Canutt, John Beach, Bud Osborne, Al Taylor, Jack Montgomery, Fred Burns. Trying to capture a notorious stagecoach robber, a cowboy takes on another identity. Fast moving early entry in Don Barry's Republic series, the film shows why he quickly established himself as one of the genre's most popular and durable players.

1249 Giant. Warner Brothers, 1956. 197 minutes Color. D: George Stevens. SC: Fred Guiol & Ivan Moffat. WITH Elizabeth Taylor, Rock Hudson, James Dean, Carroll Baker, Chill Wills, Mercedes McCambridge, Jane Withers, Sal Mineo, Robert Nichols, Dennis Hopper, Elsa Cardenas, Fran Bennett, Earl Holliman, Paul Fix, Judith Evelyn, Carolyn Craig, Rodney (Rod) Taylor, Alexander Scourby, Monte Hale, Mary Ann Edwards, Charles Watts, Maurice Jara, Victor Millan, Sheb Wooley, Ray Whitley, Tina Menard, Mickey Simpson, Noreen Nash, Guy Teague, Max Terhune, Ray Bennett, Barbara Barrie, George Dunne, Slim Talbot, Tex Driscoll. A wealthy Texas ranger marries a strong-willed woman and they face problems with worker discontent and an ambitious foreman who becomes a rich oilman. Very lengthy but good adaptation of Edna Ferber's novel which now has a cult following.

1250 The Giant Gila Monster. Hollywood Pictures, 1959. 74 minutes B/W. D: Ray Kellogg. SC: Jay Simms. WITH Don Sullivan, Lisa Simone, Pat Reaves, Shug Fisher, Jerry Cortwright, Beverly Thurman, Clarke Browne, Pat Simmons, Fred Graham, Grady Vaughn, Howard Ware, Don Flourney, Bob Thompson. The denizens of a desert town in New Mexico are terrorized by a giant lizard. El cheapo production from producer Ken Curtis, complete with a silly (and non-scary) blow-up monster.

1251 The Girl and the Gambler. RKO Radio, 1939. 63 minutes B/W. D: Lew Landers. SC: Joseph A. Fields & Clarence Upson Young. WITH Leo Carrillo, Steffi Duna, Tim Holt, Donald MacBride, Chris-

Pin Martin, Paul Fix, Julian Rivero, Frank Puglia, Esther Muir, Paul Sutton, Charles Stevens, Frank Lackteen, Edward Raquello, Henry Rocquemore. A young American falls in love with a Mexican girl who is also being wooed by a revolutionary leader. The leader rescues the young man from jail on the girl's promise that she will marry the revolutionary. Okay remake of **The Dove** (United Artists, 1927) which RKO had also done in 1932 as **Girl of the Rio** (q.v.), also with Leo Carrillo in the Pancho Villa-type role of the revolutionary.

1252 Girl from Alaska. Republic, 1942. 54 (75) minutes B/W. D: Nick Grinde. SC: Edward T. Lowe & Robert Ormond Case. WITH Ray Middleton, Jean Parker, Jerome Cowan, Robert Barrat, Ray Mala, Francis McDonald, Raymond Hatton, Milton Parsons, Nestor Paiva. A man who is wanted by the law becomes involved with crooks in Alaska who try to use him to cheat a girl out of her gold claim. Robert Ormond Case co-adapted this screen version of his story, "The Golden Portage," and the result is a pretty good melodrama.

1253 The Girl from Calgary. Monogram, 1932. 66 minutes B/W. D: Phil Whitman. SC: Leon D'Usseau. WITH Fifi D'Orsay, Paul Kelly, Astrid Allwyn, Robert Warwick, Eddie Fetherston, Edwin Maxwell. A pretty rodeo champion from Canada sets her eye on the man she plans to marry. Standard light-hearted action programmer.

1254 Girl from God's Country. Republic, 1940. 54 minutes B/W. D: Sidney Salkow. SC: Elizabeth Meehan, Robert Lee Johnson & Malcolm Stuart Boylan. WITH Chester Morris, Jane Wyatt, Charles Bickford, Mala, Kate Lawson, John Bleifer, Mamo Clark, Ferike Boros, Don Zelaya, Clem Bevans, Edward Gargan, Spencer Charters, Thomas Jackson, Victor Potel, Si Jenks, Gene Morgan, Ace (dog). A doctor is hunted by the law for the mercy killing of his father and he is aided by a pretty nurse in Alaska. Fairly pleasing drama.

1255 The Girl from San Lorenzo. United Artists, 1950. 59 minutes B/W. D: Derwin Abrahams. SC: Ford Beebe. WITH Duncan Renaldo, Leo Carrillo, Jane Adams, Leonard Penn, Edmund Cobb, David Sharpe, Lee Phelps, Bill Lester, Don C. Harvey, Byron Foulger. Outlaws carry out a series of stage robberies and place the blame on the Cisco Kid and Pancho.

This final theatrical release in "The Cisco Kid" series is an actionful affair.

1256 Girl in the Woods. Republic, 1957. 71 minutes B/W. D: Tom Gries. SC: Oliver Crawford & Marcel Klauber. WITH Forrest Tucker, Maggie Hayes, Barton MacLane, Diana Francis, Murvyn Vye, Paul Langton, Joyce Compton, Kim Charney, Mickey Finn, Bartlett Robinson, George Lynn. A veteran lumberman comes to work for a new outfit and trouble errupts with a rival outfit and over a young girl. Cheaply made but passably entertaining north woods melodrama.

1257 The Girl of the Golden West. First National, 1930. 100 minutes B/W. D: John Francis Dillon. SC: Waldemar Young. WITH Ann Harding, James Rennie, Harry Bannister, Ben Hendricks Jr., J. Farrell MacDonald, George Cooper, Johnny Walker, Richard Carlyle, Arthur Stone, Arthur Houseman, Norman McNeil, Fred Warren, Joe Girard, Newton House, Princess Noola, Chief Yowlachie. A pretty saloon owner falls in love with a notorious bandit and wins his freedom in a poker game with a lawman. Fair first sound version of the David Belasco play, remade in a much better version in 1938 (q.v.) with Jeannette MacDonald and Nelson Eddy. Filmed in 1923 by Associated First National with J. Warren Kerrigan, Sylvia Breamer, Russell Simpson and Rosemary Theby.

1258 The Girl of the Golden West. Metro-Goldwyn-Mayer, 1938. 120 minutes Sepia. D: Robert Z. Leonard. SC: Isabel Dawn & Boyce McGrew. WITH Jeanette MacDonald, Nelson Eddy, Walter Pidgeon, Leo Carrillo, Buddy Ebsen, Cliff Edwards, Leonard Penn, Priscilla Lawson, Bob Murphy, Olin Howland, Billy Bevan, Brandon Tynan, H. B. Warner, Monty Woolley, Charles Grapewin, Noah Beery, Bill Cody Jr., Ynez Seabury, Victor Potel, Nick Thompson, Chief Big Tree, Russell Simpson, Curley Wright, Pegro Regas, Alberto Morin, Joe Dominguez, Frank McGlynn, Cy Kendall, E. Alyn Warren, Hank Bell, Francis Ford, Richard Tucker. A young girl competes in a battle of wits with a sheriff who is after her bandit lover. David Belasco's 1905 evergreen is brought to the screen for the fourth time (Cecil B. DeMille filmed the first version in 1915 and First National did remakes in 1923 and 1930, the latter with Ann Harding and James Rennie) but not even a score by Gus Kahn and Sigmund Romberg can save the aged story; for Jeanette MacDonald and Nelson Eddy fans.

1259 The Girl of the Rio. RKO Radio, 1932. 69 minutes B/W. D: Herbert Brenon. SC: Elizabeth Meehan. WITH Delores Del Rio, Leo Carrillo, Norman Foster, Ralph Ince, Lucille Gleason, Edna Murphy, Stanley Fields, Frank Campeau. A beautiful Mexican cabaret entertainer falls in love with a gambler and has to gamble for his life with an outlaw. Fairly charming Delores Del Rio vehicle from Willard Mack's play "The Dove" and first made under that title in 1928 with Norma Talmadge, Gilbert Roland and Noah Beery, and issued by United Artists, remade in 1939 as **The Girl and the Gambler** (q.v.).

1260 Girl Rush. RKO Radio, 1944. 65 minutes B/W. D: Gordon Douglas. SC: Robert E. Kent. WITH Alan Carney, Wally Brown, Frances Langford, Robert Mitchum, Vera Vague (Barbara Jo Allen), Paul Hurst, Patti Brill, Sarah Padden, Cy Kendall, John Merton, Diana King, Rita Corday, Elaine Riley, Rosemary La Planche, Daun Kennedy, Virginia Belmont, Michael Vallon, Sherry Hall, Kernan Cripps, Wheaton Chambers, Chilli Williams, Ernie Adams, Dale Van Sickel, Kenneth Terrell, Bud Osborne, Byron Foulger. When all their patrons head to the gold fields during the 1849 gold rush, a show troupe follows them to entertain the miners. Average Western musical-comedy.

1261 Git Along Little Doggies. Republic, 1937. 60 minutes B/W. D: Joseph Kane. SC: Dorrell McGowan & Stuart McGowan. WITH Gene Autry, Smiley Burnette, Judith Allen, William Farnum, Weldon Heyburn, The Maple City Four, Carleton Young, Will & Gladys Ahern, Willie Fung, The Cabin Kids, G. Raymond Nye, Frankie Marvin, George Morrell, Horace Carpenter, Earl Dwire, Lynton Brent, Jack Kirk, Al Taylor, Frank Ellis, Jack C. Smith, Murdock McQuarrie, Oscar Gahan, Monte Montague, Sam McDaniel, Eddie Parker, Bob Burns. Oil drillers vie with cattlemen over range land while Gene Autry tries to clear up the conflict and romance a banker's daughter. Pleasant Gene Autry vehicle with its blend of songs and action. V: Cumberland Video.

1262 The Glory Guys. United Artists, 1965. 112 minutes Color. D: Arnold Laven. SC: Sam Peckinpah. WITH Tom Tryon, Harve Presnell, Michael Anderson Jr.,

Senta Berger, James Caan, Andrew Duggan, Slim Pickens, Peter Breck, Jeanne Cooper, Laurel Goodwin, Adam Williams, Erik Holland, Wayne Rogers, Alice Backes. A soldier, with a troop of untrained recruits, is ordered by his superiors to do battle with rampaging Sioux Indians. Filmed in Mexico, this oater is a pedestrian drama with little to recommend it.

1263 The Glory Trail. Crescent, 1937. 64 minutes B/W. D: Lynn Shores. SC: John T. Neville. WITH Tom Keene, Joan Barclay, E. H. Calvert, Frank Melton, William Royle, Walter Long, Allen Greer, William Crowell, Harve Foster, Ann Hovey, John Lester Johnson, Etta McDaniel, James Bush. Following the Civil War a cowboy takes part in the settlement of the West and the events leading to the Bozeman Massacre. Colorful historical drama in the series produced by E. B. Derr.

1264 Go West. Metro-Goldwyn-Mayer, 1940. 80 minutes B/W. D: Edward Buzzell. SC: Irving Brecher. WITH The Marx Brothers (Groucho, Harpo, Chico), John Carroll, Diana Lewis, Robert Barrat, Walter Woolf King, June MacCloy, George Lessey, Mitchell Lewis, Tully Marshall, Clem Bevans, Joe Yule, Arthur Houseman. Three zanies head West to reclaim a land deed stolen by a crook. None-too-good Marx Brothers film which is not much of a satire and certainly not much of a Western. For diehard Marx Brothers fans only.

1265 Go West, Young Girl. ABC-TV/ Columbia, 1978. 74 minutes Color. D: Alan J. Levi. SC: George Yanok. WITH Karen Valentine, Sandra Will, Stuart Whitman, Richard Jaeckel, Michael Bell, Cal Bellini, David Dukes, Charles Frank, Richard Kelton, William Larsen, John Quade, Gregg Palmer, Pepe Callahan. Two young women, a New England writer and a cavalry officer's widow, team up to go in search of Billy the Kid. Fairly amusing Western comedy made for TV.

1266 Go West, Young Lady. Columbia, 1941. 70 minutes B/W. D: Frank R. Strayer. SC: Richard Flournoy & Karen DeWolf. WITH Penny Singleton, Glenn Ford, Ann Miller, Charles Ruggles, Allen Jenkins, Onslow Stevens, Bob Wills & His Texas Playboys, Edith Meiser, Bill Hazlett. A saloon-keeper sends for his nephew who turns out to be a pretty young lady who gets into a series of misadventures. Tepid Western musical-comedy which is better for Penny Singleton's singing and Ann Miller's dancing than for its plotline.

1267 God Forgives, I Don't!. American-International, 1969. 101 minutes Color. D: Giuseppe Colizzi. SC: Giuseppe Colizzi & Gumersndo Mollo. WITH Terence Hill, Frank Wolff, Bud Spencer, Gina Rovere, Jose Manuel Martin, Tito Garcia, Paco Sanz, Giovanna Lenzi. A gunman and an insurance detective join forces to find loot hidden by a brutal gunman who they believe is dead but who is actually on their trail. Slow moving Italian oater, issued in Europe in 1967 by Rono Cinematografica/P.C.F.S.A. Filmed as **Dio Perdona...Io No.**

1268 God Holds the Bullet. Danny Film, 1967. 90 minutes Color. D: Amerigo Anton. SC: Mario Amendola. WITH Robert Mark, Larry Ward, Gordon Mitchell, Elina De Witt, Fabrizio Moroni, Andrea Bosic, Albert Farley, Benjamin May, Tony Rogers, Mary Land. A mysterious fiddler, actually a wanted man, arrives in a small town and falls in love with a girl whose family is in the middle of a deadly feud. Lots of slaughter and other violence are the main ingredients in this European import. Issued in Italy in 1966 by Regalfilm as **Uccidi O Muori** (Kill or Die).

1269 God's Country. Action Pictures/ Screen Guild, 1946. 62 minutes Color. D: Robert Tansey. SC: Frances Kavanaugh. WITH Robert Lowery, Helen Gilbert, William Farnum, Buster Keaton, Si Jenks, Stanley Andrews, Trevor Bardette, Estelle Zarco, Juan Reyes, Al Ferguson, Sandy McTavish, Howard King, Turk Monroe, Old Tarr, White Cloud. On the lam from the law, a man and his pals come to the north country and get involved in helping a girl and her father save their forest from a dishonest lumber company boss. Nice color and a good James Oliver Curwood story make this very pleasant entertainment.

1270 God's Country and the Man. Syndicate, 1931. 59 minutes B/W. D: John P. McCarthy. SC: Wellyn Totman. WITH Tom Tyler, Lillian Bond, Alan Bridge, Andy Shuford, Jack Perrin, Ted Adams, Gordon De Main, Slim Whitaker, Fern Emmett. A Texas ranger and his former outlaw sidekick try to bring to justice a murderous outlaw gang leader. Fairly good Tom Tyler early talkie with Alan Bridge as the fiddle playing killer.

1271 God's Country and the Man. Monogram, 1937. 56 minutes B/W. D: Robert North Bradbury. SC: Robert Emmett (Tansey). WITH Tom Keene, Betty Compson, Charlotte Henry, Charles King, Billy Bletcher, Eddie Parker, Robert McKenzie, Merrill McCormack, Sherry Tansey. A man is on the trail of the gang leader who murdered his father. Tom Keene's first Monogram film is a pretty sturdy outing despite stock footage from **The Trail Beyond** (q.v.).

1272 God's Country and the Woman. Warner Brothers, 1937. 71 minutes Color. D: William Keighley. SC: Norman Reilly Raine. WITH George Brent, Beverly Roberts, Barton MacLane, Robert Barrat, Alan Hale, Joseph King, El Brendel, Joseph Crehan, Addison Richards, Roscoe Ates, Billy Bevan, Bert Roach, Victor Potel, Mary Treen, Herbert Rawlinson, Harry Hayden, Pat Moriarity, Max Wagner, Susan Fleming, Eily Malyon. A playboy comes to the north woods to manage a lumber company and becomes involved in a business dispute with the female owner of a rival business. Okay action drama which was originally assigned to Bette Davis, who refused to appear in it.

1273 God's Gun. Cannon Films, 1977. 90 minutes Color. D-SC: Frank Kramer (Gianfranco Parolini). WITH Lee Van Cleef, Jack Palance, Christopher George, Lynda Day George, Leif Garrett, Robert Lipton, Cody Palance. A gunman and his five gang members terrorize a small town until one man stands up to them. Fairly actionful oater filmed in Israel.

1274 The Godchild. ABC-TV/Metro-Goldwyn-Mayer, 1974. 78 minutes Color. D: John Badham. SC: Ron Bishop. WITH Jack Palance, Jack Warden, Keith Carradine, Ed Lauter, Jose Perez, Bill McKinney, Jesse Vint, Fionnuala Flanagan, John Quade, Simon Deckard, Ed Bakey, Kermit Murdock. Three Civil War deserters rob a bank and head into the desert, being pursued by cavalry and Indians, and they find a dying woman and agree to deliver her newborn baby to safety. Not bad television adaptation of the oft-filmed Peter B. Kyne story, "Three Godfathers."

1275 Goin' South. Paramount, 1978. 101 minutes Color. D: Jack Nicholson. SC: Al Ramus, Charles Shyer & Alan Mendel. WITH Jack Nicholson, Mary Steenburgen, Christopher Lloyd, Veronica Cartwright,

155   Goin' to Town

John Belushi, Richard Bradford, Lucy Lee Flippen, Jeff Morris, Danny De Vito, Tracey Walter, Gerald H. Reynolds, Luana Anders, George W. Smith, Ed Begley Jr., Britt Leack, R. L. Armstrong, Dennis Fimple. In order to save himself from the gallows a crook agrees to marry a pretty spinster but she turns out to be a stern taskmaster. Dull going.

1276 Goin' to Town. Paramount, 1935. 74 minutes B/W. D: Alexander Hall. SC: Mae West. WITH Mae West, Paul Cavanagh, Gilbert Emery, Marjorie Gateson, Ivan Lebedeff, Fred Kohler, Monroe Owsley, Grant Withers, Luis Alberni, Tito Coral, Lucio Villegas, Mona Rico, Wade Boteler, Paul Harvey, Joe Frye, Adrienne D'Ambricourt, Bert Roach, Tom London, Syd Saylor, Irving Bacon, Francis Ford, Dewey Robinson, Julian Rivero, Stanley Price, Morgan Wallace, Tom Ricketts, J. P. McGowan, Jack Pennick, James Pierce, Leonid Kinsky, Lew Kelly, James Cowles, George Guhl, Virginia Hammond, Nell Craig, Cyril Ring, Frank Mundin. A dance hall singer marries a rich cattle baron and when he dies she inherits all of his money and tries to become socially prominent. Typically bawdy and funny Mae West vehicle.

1277 Gold. Majestic, 1932. 58 minutes B/W. D: Otto Brower, SC: W. Scott Darling. WITH Jack Hoxie, Alice Day, Hooper Atchley, Tom London, Robert Kortman, Lafe McKee, Matthew Betz, Jack Clifford, Jack Byron, Jack Kirk, Dynamite (horse). A cowpoke shares a gold claim with a man who is murdered and the man's daughter blames him for the crime, so he sets out to find the real culprit. Dull and slow moving, the film contains a most austere finale with villain Hooper Atchley tied to a wagon and disguised as an intended victim and being gunned down by his own men.

1278 Gold Fever. Monogram, 1952. 63 minutes B/W. D: Leslie Goodwins. SC: Edgar B. Anderson Jr. & Cliff Lancaster. WITH John Calvert, Ann Cornell, Ralph Morgan, Gene Roth, Tom Kennedy, Judd Holdren, George Morrell. A young man puts up the money for an old prospector to work a hidden claim but crooks get wind of their operations and try to take over. Star John Calvert produced this cheaply made melodrama.

1279 Gold is Where You Find It. First National, 1938. 90 minutes Color. D:

Michael Curtiz. SC: Warren Duff & Robert Buckner. WITH George Brent, Olivia de Havilland, Claude Rains, Margaret Lindsay, John Litel, Marcia Ralston, Barton MacLane, Tim Holt, Sidney Toler, Henry O'Neill, Willie Best, Robert McWade, George ("Gabby") Hayes, Harry Davenport, Russell Simpson, Clarence Kolb, Moroni Olsen, Granville Bates, Robert Homans, Eddy Chandler. When gold is discovered on California farmland a terrible feud erupts between ranchers and miners. Elaborate and actionful melodrama.

1280 Gold Mine in the Sky. Republic, 1938. 54 (60) minutes B/W. D: Joseph Kane. SC: Betty Burbridge & Jack Natteford. WITH Gene Autry, Smiley Burnette, Carol Hughes, Craig Reynolds, Cupid Ainsworth, LeRoy Mason, Frankie Marvin, Robert Homans, Eddie Cherkose, Ben Corbett, Milburn Morante, Jim Corey, George Guhl, Jack Kirk, Fred "Snowflake" Toones, The Stafford Sisters, J. L. Franks' Golden West Cowboys, George (Montgomery) Letz, Charles King, Lew Kelly, Joe Whitehead, Earl Dwire, Maudie Prickett, Al Taylor, Art Dillard. Gene Autry is made the administrator of a ranch belonging to a wild-spending girl and when he refuses to turn the place into a dude ranch her crooked boyfriend hires Chicago gangsters to kill Gene. Interesting Gene Autry vehicle with enough action and music, plus a good plot, to entertain his fans.

1281 Gold of the Seven Saints. Warner Brothers, 1961. 88 minutes Color. D: Gordon Douglas. SC: Leigh Brackett & Leonard Freeman. WITH Clint Walker, Roger Moore, Leticia Roman, Robert Middleton, Chill Wills, Gene Evans, Roberto Contreras, Jack C. Williams, Art Stewart. Two trappers find a gold strike but end up being chased across the desert by marauders. Utah location shooting is this film's main interest.

1282 Gold Raiders. United Artists, 1951. 56 minutes B/W. D: Edward Bernds. SC: Daniel Elwood Ullman & William Lively. WITH George O'Brien, The Three Stooges, (Moe Howard, Larry Fine, Shemp Howard), Sheila Ryan, Clem Bevans, Monte Blue, Lyle Talbot, John Merton, Al Baffert, Hugh Hooker, Bill Ward, Fuzzy Knight, Dick Crockett, Roy Canada. An ex-marshal sells miners insurance to protect their gold shipments while three zanies with a traveling variety store end up chasing the crooks. Fans of The Three Stooges will like this one.

The Gold Rush

156

1283 The Gold Rush. United Artists, 1925. 85 minutes B/W. D-SC: Charles Chaplin. WITH Charles Chaplin, Georgia Hale, Mack Swain, Tom Murray, Betty Morrissey, Malcolm Waite, Henry Bergman. The Lone Prospector finds adventure in the Klondike as he falls for a saloon girl and helps a friend to reclaim a stolen gold mine. Chaplin's classic comedy is as fresh today as it was when originally released; highly recommended. V: Film Classic Exchange.

1284 Gold Rush Maisie. Metro-Goldwyn-Mayer, 1940. 82 minutes B/W. D: Edwin L. Marin. SC: Betty Reinhardt & Mary C. McCall Jr. WITH Ann Sothern, Lee Bowman, Virginia Weidler, John F. Hamilton, Mary Nash, Slim Summerville, Scotty Beckett, Irving Macon, Louis Mason, Victor Kilian, Wallace Reed Jr., Clem Bevans, John Sheehan, Charles Judels, Virginia Sale. An out-of-work entertainer ends up at a mining camp and joins a poor family in searching for gold but soon softens a local rancher and takes up farming. Definitely one of the lesser entries in MGM's long running "Maisie" series.

1285 The Golden Eye. Monogram, 1948. 69 minutes B/W. D: William Beaudine. SC: Scott Darling. WITH Roland Winters, Wanda McKay, Mantan Moreland, Victor Sen Young, Bruce Kellogg, Tim Ryan, Evelyn Brent, Ralph Dunn, Lois Austin, Forrest Taylor, Lee "Lasses" White, Edmund Cobb, John Merton, Tom Tyler, George L. Spaulding, Jean Fong, Richard Loo. Charlie Chan is called to an Arizona mine to aid a man who has been injured and he uncovers a smuggling ring. Atmospheric "Charlie Chan" series entry in Western setting. Also called **The Mystery of the Golden Eye.**

1286 Golden Girl. 20th Century-Fox, 1951. 108 minutes Color. D: Lloyd Bacon. SC: Walter Bullock, Charles O'Neal & Gladys Lehman. WITH Mitzi Gaynor, Dale Robertson, Dennis Day, James Barton, Una Merkel, Raymond Walburn, Gene Sheldon, Carmen D'Antonio, Michael Ross, Harry Carter, Lovyss Bradley, Emory Parnell, Luther Crockett, Harris Brown, Kermit Maynard, Robert Nash, Jessie Arnold. In California during the Civil War actress Lotta Crabtree finds herself falling in love with a man who turns out to be a Confederate spy. Pleasant entertainment due more to its musical numbers than its plot.

1287 The Golden Stallion. Mascot, 1927. 55 minutes B/W. D: Harry S. Webb. SC: Carl Krusada & William Lester. WITH Maurice "Lefty" Flynn, Molly Malone, Joe Bonomo, Josef Swickard, Burr McIntosh, Billy Franey, Tom London, White Fury (horse). A Mountie tries to stop an outlaw gang from capturing a horse which has the clue to a fabulous treasure branded in its neck. Enjoyable feature version of the ten chapter serial of the same title.

1288 The Golden Stallion. Republic, 1949. 67 minutes Color. D: William Witney. SC: Sloan Nibley. WITH Roy Rogers, Dale Evans, Estelita Rodriguez, Pat Brady, Foy Willing & The Riders of the Purple Sage, Chester Conklin, Douglas Evans, Greg McClure, Frank Fenton, Dale Van Sickel, Clarence Straight, Karl Hackett. A horsetrader comes across a band of diamond smugglers who use a herd of wild horses to smuggle gems across the Mexican border. Actionful film with good photography, marred by inane Pat Brady and "Nellybelle." V: NTA Home Entertainment.

1289 The Golden Trail. Monogram, 1940. 52 minutes B/W. D: Al Herman. SC: Rolland Lynch, Robert Emmett (Tansey) & Roger Merton. WITH Tex Ritter, Arkansas Slim Andrews, Ina Guest, Patsy Moran, Gene Alsace, Stanley Price, Warner Richmond, Eddie Dean, Forrest Taylor, Frank LaRue, Chuck Morrison, Chick Hannon, Tex Palmer, Denver Dixon, Sherry Tansey, James Pierce, Hal Price, Ernie Adams, Richard Cramer, Bill Wells. A mining town is controlled by murderous crooks who want two miners out of the way and they try to do so by planting false evidence on them. Pretty fair Tex Ritter film with Tex singing a song he co-wrote, "Gold is Where You Find It."

1290 The Golden West. Fox, 1932. 74 minutes B/W. D: David Howard. SC: Gordon Rigby. WITH George O'Brien, Janet Chandler, Marion Burns, Onslow Stevens, Julia Swayne Gordon, Everett Corrigan, Edmund Breese, Sam West, Arthur Pierson, Bert Hanlon, Hattie McDaniel, Charles Stevens, Stanley Blystone, George Regas, Dorothy Ward, Sam Adams, Ed Dillon, Chief Big Tree, John War Eagle. After his father is killed by Indians, a young man becomes a member of the tribe and he grows up hating whites and leads an attack on settlers. Fine screen adaptation of the Zane Grey novel.

1291 Goldtown Ghost Raiders. Columbia, 1953. 59 minutes B/W. D: George Archainbaud. SC: Gerald Geraghty. WITH Gene Autry, Smiley Burnette, Gail Davis, Kirk Rile, Carleton Young, Neyle Morrow, Denver Pyle, John Doucette, Steve Conte. A frontier circuit judge must decide if a man must go back to prison for killing his ex-partner a second time, since the victim actually survived the first attempt. Pretty fair Gene Autry vehicle enhanced by a good storyline.

1292 Good Day for a Hanging. Columbia, 1958. 85 minutes Color. D: Nathan Juran. SC: Daniel B. Ullman & Maurice Zimm. WITH Fred MacMurray, Maggie Hayes, Robert Vaughn, Joan Blackman, James Drury, Edmond Ryan, Wendell Holmes, Stacy Harris, Kathyn Card, Emile Meyer, Bing Russell, Russell Thorson, Denver Pyle, Phil Chambers, Howard McNear, Rusty Swope, Harry Lauter, Greg Barton, Tom London, William Fawcett, Bob Bice. A lawman brings in a wanted killer only to discover the townspeople do not care if the man stands trial or not, as they believe him innocent. Well done, but neglected, oater.

A Good Day for Fighting see **Custer of the West**

1293 The Good Guys and the Bad Guys. Warner Brothers, 1969. 90 minutes Color. D: Burt Kennedy. SC: Ronald M. Cohan & Dennis Shryack. WITH Robert Mitchum, George Kennedy, David Carradine, Tina Louise, Douglas V. Fowley, Lois Nettleton, Martin Balsam, John David Chandler, John Carradine, Marie Windsor, Dick Peabody, Kathleen Freeman, Jimmy Murphy, Garrett Lewis, Nick Dennis. A has-been lawman and his long-time outlaw foe, who has been discarded by his gang, join forces to thwart a train robbery. Fanciful oater comedy with fine work by Mitchum and Kennedy in the lead roles.

1294 The Good, the Bad and the Ugly. United Artists, 1968. 155 minutes Color. D: Sergio Leone. SC: Sergio Leone & Luciano Vincenzoni. WITH Clint Eastwood, Lee Van Cleef, Eli Wallach, Aldo Giuffre, Chelo Alonso, Rada Rassimov, Silvana Bacci, Mario Brega, Luigi Pistilli, Enzo Petito, Al Mulloch. Three Civil War veterans form an uneasy alliance as they search for a cash box full of gold which was hidden in an unmarked grave. Overrated and overlong, this is still probably the most famous of the Italian West-

erns and it is not without interest, especially for Lee Van Cleef's performance as the sadist killer. Filmed in Italy in 1966 as **Il Buono, il Brutto, il Cattivo** (The Good, the Bad, the Wicked) by P.E.A. VD: RCA/Columbia. V: Blackhawk.

Gone with the West see **Little Moon and Jud McGraw**

1295 Gordon of Ghost City. Universal, 1933. 12 Chapters B/W. D: Ray Taylor. SC: Ella O'Neill, Basil Dickey, George Plympton, Harry O. Hoyt & Het Mannheim. WITH Buck Jones, Madge Bellamy, Walter Miller, William Desmond, Francis Ford, Edmund Cobb, Tom Ricketts, Hugh Enfield, Bud Osborne, Dick Rich, Ethan Laidlaw, Jim Corey, Bill Steele, Artie Ortego. When a mysterious masked figure and an outlaw gang try to gain control of a gold strike in a small town a man is hired to bring peace to the area. Fast paced and highly entertaining cliffhanger which was Buck Jones' initial serial; his fans will love it.

1296 Grand Canyon. Screen Guild, 1949. 69 minutes B/W. D: Paul Landres. SC: Jack Harvey & Milton Luban. WITH Richard Arlen, Mary Beth Hughes, Reed Hadley, James Millican, Olin Howlin, Grady Sutton, Joyce Compton, Charlie Williams, Margia Dean, Stanley Price, Holly Bane. A movie director connives to make a film on location in the Grand Canyon and he discovers a local prospector and elevates him to stardom. Pretty bad Robert Lippert production (which mentions the company name at every opportunity) and not even star Richard Arlen can save it.

1297 Grand Canyon Trail. Republic, 1948. 54 (67) minutes Color. D: William Witney. SC: Gerald Geraghty. WITH Roy Rogers, Andy Devine, Jane Frazee, Robert Livingston, Roy Barcroft, James Finlayson, Emmett Lynn, Foy Willing & The Riders of the Purple Sage, Charles Coleman, Kenneth Terrell, Zon Murray. In a ghost town Roy Rogers and pal Cookie Bullfincher try to combat a crook who is trying to find the location of a vein of silver. Good blend of action, comedy and suspense with Robert Livingston a fine villain and Jimmy Finlayson proving slapstick comedy relief as the local sheriff.

1298 Grandpa Goes to Town. Republic, 1940. 54 minutes B/W. D: Gus Meins. SC: Jack Townley. WITH James Gleason, Lucille Gleason, Ralph Gleason, Harry

Davenport, Lois Ranson, Maxie Rosenbloon, Tommy Ryan, Ledda Godoy, Noah Beery, Douglas Meins, Gary Owen, Ray Turner, Lee "Lasses" White, Walter Miller, Emmett Lynn, Joe Caits, Arturo Godoy. When a family inherits a bankrup hotel in a Nevada ghost town the false rumor of a gold strike causes a boom. Adequate entry in "The Higgins Family" series.

1299 The Grand Duel. Cinema Shares, 1974. 92 minutes Color. D: Giancarlo Santi. SC: Ernesto Gastaldi. WITH Lee Van Cleef, Peter O'Brien, Marc Mazza, Klaus Grunberg, Horst Frank, Jess Hahn. A veteran gunfighter becomes the self-appointed protector of a young man who is being sought by an outlaw gang for the murder of their leader. Another typically violent Western from Europe with Lee Van Cleef, although this one uses the mystery element to good effect. This Italian-French-West German coproduction was made in 1972 as **Il Grande Duello** (The Grand Duel).

1300 Granny Get Your Gun. Warner Brothers, 1940. 56 minutes B/W. D: George Amy. SC: Kenneth Gamet. WITH May Robson, Margot Stevenson, Harry Davenport, Hardie Albright, Clem Bevans, William B. Davidson, Clay Clement, Arthur Aylesworth, Granville Bates, Ann Todd, Vera Lewis, Max Hoffman, Archie Twitchell, Walter Wilson, Nat Carr. When her granddaughter is falsely accused of murder, a woman returns to Nevada, where she made a fortune as a gold miner, to find the real culprit. Slim adaptation of Erle Stanley Gardner's "Case of the Dangerous Dowager" although May Robson and Harry Davenport are delightful in the lead roles.

Grass Lands see **Hex**

1301 Grayeagle. American-International, 1977. 104 minutes Color. D-SC: Charles B. Pierce. WITH Ben Johnson, Alex Cord, Lana Wood, Iron Eyes Cody, Jack Elam, Paul Fix, Jacob Daniels, Charles B. Pierce. When an Indian brave kidnaps his daughter, a rancher goes in search of her and eventually learns a startling truth. Murky and over-long drama helped by a good cast.

1302 Greaser's Palace. Cinema 5, 1972. 91 minutes Color. D-SC: Robert Downey. WITH Allan Arbus, Albert Henderson, Elsie Downey, Luana Anders, Woodrow Chambliss, Michael Sullivan, James Antonio, George Morgan, Ron Nealy, Larry Moyer, John Paul Hudson, Jackson Haynes,

Lawrence Wolf, Alex Hitchcock, Pablo Ferro, Toni Basil, Stan Gottlieb, Herve Vellechaize, Rex King, Joe Madden, Don Smolen, Donald Calfe. In a sleezy Western town a gunman comes to realize he is really Jesus Christ and begins performing miracles. Lowjinks feature full of "inside humor."

1303 The Great Adventure. Pacific International, 1976. 87 minutes Color. D: Paul Elliotts (Gianfranco Baldanello). SC: Jay Anson & Elliot Geisinger. WITH Jack Palance, Joan Collins, Fred Romer (Fernando Romero), Elisabetta Virgili, Manuel de Blas, Remo de Angelis. Stranded in the Alaskan Rockies, a young boy finds companionship and protection with a faithful dog. Average adventure tale loosely based on Jack London; made in Europe.

1304 The Great Adventures of Wild Bill Hickok. Columbia, 1938. 15 Chapters B/W. D: Mack V. Wright & Sam Nelson. SC: George Rosener, Charles Arthur Powell & George Arthur Durlam. WITH Gordon (Bill) Elliott, Monte Blue, Carole Wayne, Frankie Darro, Dickie Jones, Sammy McKim, Kermit Maynard, Roscoe Ates, Monty Collins, Reed Hadley, Chief Thundercloud, Mala, Walter Wills, J. P. McGowan, Eddy Waller, George Chesebro, Alan Bridge, Slim Whitaker, Walter Miller, Lee Phelps, Robert Fiske, Earle Hodgins, Earl Dwire, Ed Brady, Ray Jones, Edmund Cobb, Art Mix, Hal Taliaferro, Blackie Whiteford. Abilene marshall Wild Bill Hickok organizes a group of youngsters into a group called the "Flaming Arrows" to aid him in combating renegade phantom raiders trying to stop a cattle drive from Texas over the Chisholm Trail. Well made and exciting cliffhanger which launched Bill Elliott to genre stardom.

1305 The Great Alaskan Mystery. Universal, 1944. 13 Chapters B/W. D: Ray Taylor & Lewis D. Collins. SC: Maurice Tombragel & George H. Plympton. WITH Milburn Stone, Marjorie Reynolds, Edgar Kennedy, Samuel S. Hinds, Martin Kosleck, Ralph Morgan, Joseph Crehan, Fuzzy Knight, Harry Cording, Anthony Warde. An expedition heads to Alaska hoping to find an old mine containing ore for a new weapon but one of the expedition is actually an enemy agent. Actionful wartime cliffhanger.

1306 The Great American Cowboy. American National Enterprises/Sun International,

1974. 90 minutes Color. D: Keith Merrill.
SC: Douglas Kent Hall. WITH Joel McCrea
(narrator), Larry Mahan, Phil Lyne, Elias
Arriola. The story of the year-long quest
for the world's rodeo championship between
veteran star Larry Mahan and young
competitor Phil Lyne. Academy Award
winning documentary which contains
exciting rodeo footage and pleasing narration by Joel McCrea.

1307 The Great American Indian. Doty-
Dayton, 1974. 90 minutes Color. D: Keith
Merrill. The story of the American Indian,
how they live today and their history
and heritage. Well done documentary
from the people who made **The Great
American Cowboy** (q.v.).

1308 The Great American Wilderness.
Bill Burrud Productions, 1977. 95 minutes
Color. D: Barry Clark. WITH Marvin
Miller (narrator). A travelog of the wilderness areas of America, including the
Great Plains, the Rocky Mountains, deserts
of the Southwest and the Arctic. Just
the type of fare which will please nature
lovers.

1309 The Great Bank Robbery. Warner
Brothers-Seven Arts, 1969. 98 minutes
Color. D: Hy Averback. SC: William
Peter Blatty. WITH Kim Novak, Zero
Mostel, Clint Walker, Claude Akins,
Akim Tamiroff, Larry Storch, John Ander-
son, Sam Jaffe, Mako, Elisha Cook Jr.,
Ruth Warrick, John Fiedler, John Larch,
Peter Whitney, Norman Alden, Grady
Sutton, Bob Steele, Mickey Simpson,
Guy Wilkerson, Burt Mustin, Philo McCul-
lough, William Zuckert, Jerry Summers.
A woman and her friends pose as church
leaders in a small town but they really
plan to rob a bank built by the notorious
James, Dalton and Younger brothers.
Pretty poor Western comedy.

1310 The Great Barrier. Gaumont-British,
1937. 84 minutes B/W. D: Milton Rosmer.
SC: Michael Barringer & Milton Rosmer.
WITH Richard Arlen, Lilli Palmer,
Antoinette Cellier, J. Farrell MacDonald,
Barry MacKay. A former gambler becomes
a railroad builder and helps in the construction of a rail line across the Canadian
wilderness. British financed and Canadian
filmed, this film encompassed a trite
drama with some good action sequences.
Alternate title: **Secret Barriers.**

1311 The Great Call of the Wilderness.
American National Enterprises, 1976.
95 minutes Color. WITH Larry Jones.

In the American Northwest, a man fights
to build a large natural preserve for
the local animal life. Another okay drama
for outdoors fans.

1312 Great Day in the Morning. RKO
Radio, 1956. 92 minutes Color. D: Jacques
Tourneur. SC: Lesser Samuels. WITH
Virginia Mayo, Robert Stack, Ruth Roman,
Alex Nicol, Raymond Burr, Leo Gordon,
Regis Toomey, Peter Whitney, Dan White,
Donald McDonald. During the gold rush
in Colorado, trouble develops not only
between gold hunters but also between
those wishing to leave the union and
those opposed to leaving. Colorful adap-
tation of Robert Hardy Andrews' novel.

1313 The Great Divide. First National,
1929. 73 minutes B/W. D: Reginald Barker.
SC: Fred Myton & Paul Perez. WITH
Dorothy Mackaill, Ian Keith, Myrna Loy,
Lucien Littlefield, Creighton Hale, George
Fawcett, Claude Gillingwater, Roy
Stewart, Ben Hendricks Jr., Jean Laverty,
Marjorie Kane. An arrogant Eastern
girl vacations in the West with her friends
and her fiancee and finds herself being
courted by a mine owner. Picturesque
early talkie from William Vaugh Moody's
1909 play and first filmed in 1925 by
Metro-Goldwyn Pictures with Alice Terry,
Conway Tearle and Wallace Beery.

The Great Gundown see **40 Graves
for 40 Guns**

1314 The Great Jesse James Raid. Lippert,
1953. 73 minutes Color. D: Reginald
LeBorg. SC: Richard Landau. WITH Willard
Parker, Barbara Payton, Tom Neal, Wallace
Ford, James Anderson, Jim Bannon,
Richard Cutting, Barbara Woodell, Marin
Sais, Earle Hodgins, Joan Arnold, Steve
Pendleton, Rory Mallinson. A "retired"
Jesse James agrees to join Bob Ford
in stealing gold hidden in a closed mine
tunnel. Tawdry melodrama made to get
box office mileage out of the romance
between plump Barbara Payton and Tom
Neal, although neither has much to do
in the proceedings.

1315 The Great K&A Train Robbery.
Fox, 1926. 53 minutes B/W. D: Lewis
Seiler. SC: John Stone. WITH Tom Mix,
Dorothy Dwan, William Walling, Harry
Grippe, Carl Miller, Ed Piel, Curtis Mc-
Henry. A railroad detective disguises
himself as a bandit in order to board
a train plagued by robberies to unmask
the culprits. Grand Tom Mix and Tony
silent Western; very entertaining. V:
Glenn Photo.

1316 The Great Locomotive Chase. Buena Vista, 1956. 85 minutes Color. D: Francis D. Lyon. SC: Lawrence S. Watkin. WITH Fess Parker, Jeffrey Hunter, Jeff York, John Lupton, Eddie Firestone, Kenneth Tobey, Don Megowan, Claude Jarman Jr., Harry Carey Jr., Lennie Geer, Stan Jones, Slim Pickens, Morgan Woodward, Harvey Hester. A Union spy leads a group of volunteers into the South disguised as Confederates and their plan is to steal a train and take it north. Fine Disney action drama.

1317 The Great Man's Lady. Paramount, 1942. 90 minutes B/W. D: William A. Wellman. SC: W. L. River. WITH Barbara Stanwyck, Joel McCrea, Brian Donlevy, Katherine Stevens, Thurston Hall, Lloyd Corrigan, Lillian Yarbo, Damian O'Flynn, Charles Lane, George Chandler, Anna Q. Nilsson, George P. Huntley, Milton Parsons, Etta McDaniel, Mary Treen, Helen Lynd, Lucien Littlefield, Frank M. Thomas, William B. Davidson, Fred "Snowflake" Toones, John Hamilton. A young girl falls in love with a man who wants to build an oil empire but eventually he loses her to a gambler. Interesting performances aid this rather stilted saga.

1318 The Great Meadow. Metro-Goldwyn-Mayer, 1931. 75 minutes B/W. D: Charles Brabin. SC: Elizabeth Roberts. WITH Eleanor Boardman, Johnny Mack Brown, Lucille LaVerne, Anita Louise, Gavin Gordon, Guinn Williams, Russell Simpson, Sarah Padden, Helen Jerome Eddy. Pioneers form a wagon train and travel from Virginia to settle new lands in Kentucky. Dated historical melodrama with some good action sequences and an early genre role for Johnny Mack Brown as the wagon master.

1319 The Great Missouri Raid. Paramount, 1951. 83 minutes Color. D: Gordon Douglas. SC: Frank Gruber. WITH Macdonald Carey, Ellen Drew, Wendell Corey, Ward Bond, Bruce Bennett, Bill Williams, Anne Revere, Edgar Buchanan, Louis Chastland, Louis Jean Heydt, Barry Kelly, James Millican, Guy Wilkerson, Ethan Laidlaw, Tom Tyler, Paul Fix, James Griffith, Steve Pendleton, Paul Lees. The James and Younger brothers are forced onto the wrong side of the law after they are treated badly by Union soldiers after the Civil War. Color is a big help in this otherwise pedestrian effort.

1320 The Great Northfield, Minnesota Raid. Universal, 1972. 91 minutes Color. D-SC: Philip Kaufman. WITH Cliff Robertson, Robert Duvall, Luke Askew, R. G. Armstrong, Dana Elcar, Donald Moffatt, John Pearce, Matt Clark, Barry Brown, Wayne Sutherlin, Robert H. Harris, Jack Manning, Elisha Cook, Royal Dano, Mary-Robin Redd, Bill Callaway, Craig Curtis, Nolan Leary, Henry Hunter, Valda Hansen. When they fail to get amnesty from the law, the James and Younger brothers plan to pull off a big robbery in Northfield, Minnesota. Interesting account of the famous outlaws' last big bungle with good performances from the leads.

1321 The Great Scout and Cathouse Thursday. American-International, 1976. 102 minutes Color. D: Don Taylor. SC: Richard Shapiro. WITH Lee Marvin, Oliver Reed, Robert Culp, Elizabeth Ashley, Kay Lenz, Strother Martin, Sylvia Miles, Howard Platt, Leticia Robles, Erika Carlson, Ana Verdugo. When his partner steals the money from their gold strike and becomes a wealthy and influential citizen, the victim tries to ruin his ex-partner. Western comedy is bawdy and has its moments but mostly it is rather dull.

1322 The Great Sioux Massacre. Columbia, 1965. 91 minutes Color. D: Sidney Salkow. SC: Fred C. Dobbs (Marvin Gluck). WITH Joseph Cotten, Darren McGavin, Philip Carey, Julie Sommars, Nancy Kovack, John Matthews, Michael Pate, Don Haggerty, Frank Ferguson, Stacy Harris, Iron Eyes Cody, House Peters Jr., John Napier, William Tannen. The events leading up to General Custer's last stand at the Little Big Horn River are recounted in this melodrama. Average oater which adds nothing new to the already familiar historical event.

1323 The Great Sioux Uprising. Universal-International, 1953. 80 minutes Color. D: Lloyd Bacon. SC: Melvin Levy, J. Robert Bren & Gladys Atwater. WITH Jeff Chandler, Faith Domergue, Lyle Bettger, Stacy Harris, Walter Sande, Clem Fuller, Glenn Strange, Ray Bennett, Chares Arnt, Peter Whitney, John War Eagle, Stephen Chase, Rosa Rey. A former Army officer becomes friends with Chief Red Cloud and he stops rustlers from causing the Sioux nation to go on the warpath. Competent entertainment in this average bow-and-arrows oater.

1324 The Great Stagecoach Robbery. Republic, 1945. 54 minutes B/W. D: Lesley

Selander. SC: Randall Faye. WITH Bill Elliott, Bobby Blake, Alice Fleming, Francis McDonald, Don Costello, Sylvia Arslan, Bud Geary, Leon Tyler, Henry Wills, Hank Bell, Robert Wilke, John James, Tom London, Horace Carpenter, Grace Cunard, Freddie Chapman. A young man plans to follow in the footsteps of his famous outlaw father but his actions are opposed by Red Ryder. Only average.

1325 The Great Train Robbery. Republic, 1941. 54 (61) minutes B/W. D: Joseph Kane. SC: Olive Cooper, Garnett Weston & Robert T. Shannon. WITH Bob Steele, Claire Carleton, Milburn Stone, Helen MacKeller, Si Jenks, Monte Blue, Hal Taliaferro, George Guhl, Jay Novello, Dick Wessell, Yakima Canutt, Lew Kelly, Guy Usher. A railroad detective is assigned to locate a train, carrying a money shipment, which disappeared while en route. Although it bears no relation to the 1903 classic, this outing is a clever blend of action, mystery and the Western genre.

1326 Green Grass of Wyoming. 20th Century-Fox, 1948. 89 minutes Color. D: Louis King. SC: Martin Berkeley. WITH Peggy Cummins, Charles Coburn, Robert Arthur, Lloyd Nolan, Burl Ives, Geraldine Wall, Robert Adler, Will Wright, Richard Garrick, Charles Tannen. Two rival families both breed and raise trotting horses and the boy and girl from each family end up finding romance. Juvenile outing which is fairly entertaining.

1327 The Grey Fox. United Artists, 1983. 90 minutes Color. D: Philip Borsos. SC: John Hunter. WITH Richard Farnsworth, Jackie Burroughs, Wayne Robson, Ken Pogue, Timothy Webber, Gary Reineke. After thirty years in prison an old-time outlaw decides to become a train robber. Leisurely paced Western filmed in Canada with a grand performance by Richard Farnsworth as the outlaw.

1328 The Grey Vulture. Davis Distributing, 1926. 50 minutes B/W. D: Forrest Sheldon. SC: George Hively. WITH Ken Maynard, Hazel Deane, Sailor Sharkey, Boris Bullock, Fred Burns, Nancy Zann, Whitehorse, Olive Trevor, Marie Woods, Flora Matiland, Dorothy Dodd, Fern Lorraine. A cowboy, who falsely believes he murdered a man, goes to work for a rancher, falls in love with his daughter and saves his boss's stolen cattle. Entertaining Ken Maynard silent vehicle.

Gringo (1965) see **Gunfight at Red Sands**

1329 Gringo. Cemofilm, 1968. 89 minutes Color. D: Frank Corlish (Mario Amendola). SC: Bruno Corbucci & Mario Amendola. WITH Brian Kelly, Fabrizio Moroni, Keenan Wynn, Folco Lulli, Erica Blanc, Gigi Bonos, Gianni Pallavicino. A wealthy Mexican land baron hires a gunman to bring back his son who has joined an American outlaw band but the gunman soon discovers the boy is actually the man's wife's illegitimate son and that his employer plans to torture the boy. Exceedingly violent Italian oater originally called **Spara Gringo, Spara.** Alternate titles: **Rainbow** and **The Longest Hunt.**

1330 Grizzly. Film Ventures International, 1976. 91 minutes. D: William Girdler. SC: Harvey Flaxman & David Sheldon. WITH Christopher George, Andrew Prine, Richard Jaeckel, Joan McCall, Joe Dorsey. A giant grizzly bear murders two teenage girls in an amusement park and three men try to hunt him down before he attacks again. Fairly suspenseful horror-Western with the bad bear being the main interest. TV title: **Killer Grizzly.**

1331 The Grizzly and the Treasure. Gold Key, 1974. 98 minutes Color. D: James T. Flocker. WITH Scott Beach (Narrator), Andrew Gordon, Robert Sheble, Susan Bucklinie, Terry Bough, Mark Ostrander. A man takes his wife and young son to Alaska in search of gold and they suffer many hardships as a result, including a blizzard. Satisfying G-rated family entertainment feature.

1332 The Groom Wore Spurs. Universal-International, 1950. 80 minutes B/W. D: Richard Whorf. SC: Robert Carson, Robert Libott & Frank Burt. WITH Ginger Rogers, Jack Carson, Joan Davis, Stanley Ridges, James Brown, John Litel, Victor Sun Yung, Mira McKinney, Gordon Nelson, George Meader, Kemp Niver, Robert B. Williams, Richard Whorf. When her cowboy-star husband is falsely accused of murder a lawyer helps him in proving his innocence. Fun comedy with some behind-the-scenes looks at the fantasy of cowboy moviemaking.

1333 Guardian of the Wilderness. Sunn Classics Pictures, 1977. 112 minutes Color. D: David O'Malley. SC: Casey Conlon & Charles E. Sellier Jr. WITH Denver Pyle, John Dehner, Ken Berry, Cheryl Miller, Don Shanks, Cliff Osmond, Jack Kruschen, Ford Rainey, Norman Fell, Prentiss Rowe, Brett Palmer, Melissa Jones, Yosemite (bear), Hardtack (Rhodesian Ridgeback). After recovering his health in the wilderness, a man carries out his fight to save the great sequoia trees in the Yosemite valley from being cut by timberjacks. This film tells the true story of Galen Clark, the man responsible for making the Yosemite Valley a national refuge; it is quite entertaining. Alternate TV title: **Mountain Man.**

1334 Guilty Trails. Universal, 1938. 57 minutes B/W. D: George Waggner. SC: Joseph West (George Waggner). WITH Bob Baker, Marjorie Reynolds, Hal Taliaferro, Georgia O'Dell, Jack Rockwell, Carleton Young, Glenn Strange, Murdock McQuarrie, Jack Kirk, Tom London, Tex Palmer. A crooked banker stages a fake bank robbery in order to steal a girl's proof of inheritance of a ranch and a lawman tries to aid her. Pretty fair Bob Baker vehicle highlighted by the song "Ring Around the Moon Tonight."

1335 The Gun and the Pulpit. ABC-TV, 1974. 74 minutes Color. D: Daniel Petrie. SC: William Bowers. WITH Marjore Gortner, Slim Pickens, David Huddleston, Geoffrey Lewis, Estelle Parsons, Pamela Sue Martin, Jeff Corey, Karl Swenson, Jon Lormer, Robert Phillips, Larry Ward, Joan Goodfellow, Walter Barnes, Melanie Fullerton, Steve Tackett, Jason Clark, Ron Nix. A gunman on the run takes on the guise of a minister and in a small town he stands up to a local tyrant. Standard TV movie enhanced by a good cast.

1336 Gun Battle at Monterey. Allied Artists, 1957. 74 minutes B/W. D: Carl K. Hittleman & Sidney A. Franklin Jr. SC: Jack Leonard & Lawrence Resner. WITH Sterling Hayden, Pamela Duncan, Ted de Corsia, Mary Beth Hughes, Lee Van Cleef, Charles Cane, Byron Foulger, Mauritz Hugo, I. Stanford Jolley, Michael Vallon. After he is bushwacked by his friend and left for dead, an outlaw recovers and sets out to take revenge on the man. Cheaply made melodrama with some good scenic locations. Alternate title: **Gun Battle of Monterey.**

Gun Battle of Monterey see **Gun Battle at Monterey**

1337 Gun Belt. United Artists, 1953. 77 minutes Color. D: Ray Nazarro. SC: Richard Schayer & Jack DeWitt. WITH George Montgomery, Tab Hunter, Helen Westcott, John Dehner, William Bishop, Jack Elam, Hugh Sanders, Willis Bouchey, James Millican, Bruce Cowling, Boyd

Stockman, Douglas Kennedy, Boyd "Red" Morgan, William Philips, Joe Hayworth, Chuck Roberson. A once famous gunfighter wants to get married and settle down but his former gang implicates him in a crime. More than passable entertainment with strong work by George Montgomery as the ex-gunman.

1338 Gun Brothers. United Artists, 1956. 79 minutes B/W. D: Sidney Salkow. SC: Gerald Drayson Adams. WITH Buster Crabbe, Ann Robinson, Neville Brand, Michael Ansara, Walter Sande, Lita Milan, James Seay, Roy Barcroft, Slim Pickens, Dorothy Ford. A man sets up his own homestead and his ex-outlaw brother, trying to reform, joins him but they are soon attacked by the brother's former partner and gang. Fairly entertaining oater which will satisfy Buster Crabbe fans.

1339 Gun Code. Producers Releasing Corporation, 1940. 57 minutes B/W. D: Peter Stewart (Sam Newfield). SC: Joseph O'Donnell. WITH Tim McCoy, Inna Gest, Lew Fulton, Dave O'Brien, Alden Chase, Carleton Young, Ted Adams, Robert Winkler, George Chesebro, Jack Richardson, John Elliott, Stephen Chase, Carl Mathews. A federal agent is sent to a small town to stop a protection racket. Low budget affair with Tim McCoy giving a good account as the stern agent.

1340 Gun Duel in Durango. United Artists, 1957. 73 minutes B/W. D: Sidney Salkow. SC: Louis Stevens. WITH George Montgomery, Ann Robinson, Steve Brodie, Bobby Clark, Frank Ferguson, Donald (Don "Red") Barry, Henry Rowland, Denver Pyle, Mary Treen, Red Morgan, Al Wyatt, Joe Yrigoyen. Trying to go straight, an ex-outlaw is forced to shoot it out with his former gang in order to be able to reform. Mediocre oater greatly aided by star George Montgomery. TV title: **Duel in Durango.**

1341 Gun Fever. United Artists, 1958. 81 minutes B/W. D: Mark Stevens. SC: Stanley H. Silverman. WITH Mark Stevens, John Lupton, Larry Storch, Jana Davi, Aaron Saxon, Jerry Barclay, Norman Frederic, Clegg Hoyt, Jean Inness, Russell Thorson, Michael Hinn, Iron Eyes Cody, Cyril Delevanti, George Selk. When his father is murdered a young boy sets out to find the killer, not realizing he is a close family friend. Okay actioner for Mark Stevens fans.

1342 Gun Fight. United Artists, 1961. 68 minutes B/W. D: Edward L. Cahn. SC: Gerald Drayson Adams & Richard Schayer. WITH James Brown, Joan Staley, Gregg Palmer, Ron Soble, Ken Mayer, Charles Cooper, Walter Coy, James Panrell, Andy Albin, Jon Locke, John Damler, Robert Nash, Jack Kenney, Frank Eldredge, Gene Coogan, Bill Koontz, Boyd Stockman, Bob Woodward. An ex-soldier heads West to join his brother in ranching only to find out he is actually an outlaw. Fair dual biller for James Brown fans.

1343 Gun for a Coward. Universal, 1957. 88 minutes Color. D: Abner Biberman. SC: R. Wright Campbell. WITH Fred MacMurray, Jeffrey Hunter, Janice Rule, Chill Wills, Dean Stockwell, Josephine Hutchinson, Betty Lynn, Iron Eyes Cody, Robert Hoy, Jane Howard, John Larch, Paul Birch, Bob Steele, Frances Morris, Marjorie Stapp. A successful rancher has trouble with his two sons, one being a hothead and the other branded a coward. Nothing new in this psychological approach to the genre.

1344 Gun Fury. Columbia, 1953. 83 minutes Color. D: Raoul Walsh. SC: Irving Wallace & Roy Huggins. WITH Rock Hudson, Donna Reed, Philip Carey, Roberta Haynes, Lee Marvin, Neville Brand, Leo Gordon, Ray Thomas, Forrest Lewis, John Cason, Pat Hogan, Mel Welles, Post Park. A man, his girlfriend and an Indian kidnap the fiancée of another man who goes after them. Originally issued in 3-D, this Arizona-made oater is a colorful outing.

1345 Gun Glory. Metro-Goldwyn-Mayer, 1957. 89 minutes Color. D: Roy Rowland. SC: William Ludwig. WITH Stewart Granger, Rhonda Fleming, Chill Wills, Steve Rowland, James Gregory, Jacques Aubuchon, Arch Johnson, William Fawcett, Carl Pitti, Lane Bradford, Rayford Barnes, Ed Mundy, Gene Coogan, Michael Dugan, Jack Montgomery, Bud Osborne, May McAvoy, Charles Herbert, Steve Widders. An ex-gunman returns to his hometown only to be shunned by the citizens until they are threatened by another gunslinger. Stewart Granger is good in the lead but the story, based on Philip Yordan's novel Man of the West, is only passable.

1346 Gun Grit. Atlantic, 1936. 60 minutes B/W. D: Lester Williams (William Berke). SC: Gordon Phillips. WITH Jack Perrin, Ethel Beck, David Sharpe, Jimmie Aubrey,

Ed Cassidy, Earl Dwire, Horace Murphy, Roger Williams, Ralph Peters, Frank Hagney, Oscar Gahan, Budd Buster, Starlight (horse), Braveheart (Dog). Big city racketeers head West to sell protection to cattlemen and an FBI agent is sent to stop the racket. Low grade film with lots of Hollywood locales; Jack Perrin is a pleasant player.

1347 The Gun Hawk. Allied Artists, 1963. 92 minutes Color. D: Edward Ludwig. SC: Jo Heims. WITH Rory Calhoun, Rod Cameron, Ruta Lee, Rod Lauren, Morgan Woodward, Robert Wilke, John Litel, Rodolfo Hoyos, Lane Bradford, Lee Bradley. A notorious gunman tries to prevent a younger gunfighter from continuing his life of crime. Stars Rory Calhoun and Rod Cameron make this one interesting.

1348 Gun in His Hand. CBS-TV/20th Century-Fox, 1956. 45 minutes B/W. WITH Robert Wagner, Debra Paget, Charles Drake, Ray Collins, Royal Dano, John Conte. When he takes part in a bank robbery with his father and the latter is killed, a young man tries to redeem himself in the eyes of the law by hunting the other robbers. Telefeature originally shown as a segment of "The 20th Century-Fox Hour" (CBS-TV, 1955-57) on April 4, 1956.

1349 Gun Justice. Universal, 1933. 62 minutes B/W. D: Alan James. SC: Robert Quigley. WITH Ken Maynard, Cecilia Parker, Hooper Atchley, Walter Miller, Jack Rockwell, Francis Ford, Fred McKaye, William Dyer, Jack Richardson, Ed Coxen, William Gould, Sheldon Lewis, Lafe McKee, Ben Corbett, Bob McKenzie, Horace B. Carpenter, Frank Ellis, Hank Bell, Bud McClure, Roy Bucko, Buck Bucko, Pascale Perry, Cliff Lyons, Blackjack Ward. Crooks murder a man for his ranch and then hire a lookalike to impersonate his nephew, who has inherited one-half of the property. Ken Maynard also produced this fairly actionful drama. V: Video Connection.

1350 Gun Law. Majestic, 1933. 59 minutes B/W. D: Lewis D. Collins. SC: Lewis D. Collins & Oliver Drake. WITH Jack Hoxie, Betty Boyd, J. Frank Glendon, Mary Carr, Harry Todd, Edmund Cobb, Ben Corbett, Paul Fix, Richard Botiller, Bob Burns, Horace B. Carpenter, Jack Kirk. Lawmen are on the trail of the notorious Sonora Kid, who has been terrorizing the Arizona countryside. A good chance to take a look at star Jack Hoxie in one of his half-dozen talking films; fairly good entertainment.

1351 Gun Law. RKO Radio, 1938. 60 minutes B/W. D: David Howard. SC: Oliver Drake. WITH George O'Brien, Rita Oehman, Ray Whitley, Paul Everton, Ward Bond, Francis McDonald, Edward Pawley, Robert Glecker, Frank O'Connor, Hank Bell, Paul Fix, Ethan Laidlaw, Lloyd Ingraham, Bob Burns, Jim Mason, Neal Burns, Ken Card. When a series of stagecoach holdups occur, a U. S. marshal takes on the guise of an outlaw to capture the culprits. Highly exciting and actionful; a remake of **West of the Law** (Film Bookings Office, 1928) starring Tom Tyler, and **The Reckless Rider** (Willis Kent, 1932), a Lane Chandler vehicle.

1352 Gun Law Justice. Monogram, 1949. 54 minutes B/W. D: Lambert Hillyer. SC: Basil Dickey. WITH Jimmy Wakely, Dub Taylor, Jane Adams, Ray Whitley, John James, Myron Healey, I. Stanford Jolley, Lee Phelps, Edmund Cobb, Bud Osborne, Carol Henry, Tom Chatterton, Bob Curtis, Zon Murray, Eddie Majors, Herman Hack, Merrill McCormack, George Morrell, Ray Jones. A singing cowboy and his pal try to aid an outlaw gang leader who is trying to live on the right side of the law. Okay Jimmy Wakely singing vehicle.

1353 Gun Lords of Stirrup Basin. Republic, 1937. 60 minutes B/W. D: Sam Newfield. SC: George Plympton & Fred Myton. WITH Bob Steele, Louise Stanley, Karl Hackett, Ernie Adams, Frank LaRue, Frank Ball, Steve Clark, Lew Meehan, Frank Ellis, Jim Corey, Budd Buster, Lloyd Ingraham, Jack Kirk, Horace Murphy, Milburn Morante, Bobby Nelson, Tex Palmer, Horace B. Carpenter. Outlaws ignite a feud between two families but the plan is thwarted when a boy and girl from each family fall in love. Actionful Bob Steele vehicle for producer A. W. Hackel. TV title: **Gunlords of Stirrup Basin.**

1354 Gun Packer. Monogram, 1938. 49 minutes B/W. D: Wallace Fox. SC: Robert Emmett (Tansey). WITH Jack Randall, Louise Stanley, Charles King, Barlowe Borland, Raymond Turner, Lloyd Ingraham, Lowell Drew, Ernie Adams, Glenn Strange, Forrest Taylor, Curley Dresden, Sherry Tansey. A lawman investigates a series of stage holdups and finds the bandits are using the gold to salt a mine in a

planned swindle. Compact and one of the better Jack Randall series films.

Gun Play (1935) see **Lucky Boots**

1355 The Gun Ranger. Republic, 1937. 60 minutes B/W. D: Robert North Bradbury. SC: George Plympton. WITH Bob Steele, Eleanor Stewart, Hal Taliaferro, John Merton, Ernie Adams, Earl Dwire, Budd Buster, Frank Ball, Horace Murphy, Lew Meehan, Horace B. Carpenter, Jack Kirk, George Morrell, Tex Palmer. When a girl's father is killed, a ranger tries to find the murderer. Exciting and well-done Bob Steele film.

Gun Riders see **Five Bloody Graves**

1356 Gun Runner. Monogram, 1949. 56 minutes B/W. D: Lambert Hillyer. SC: J. Benton Cheney. WITH Jimmy Wakely, Dub Taylor, Noel Neill, Mae Clarke, Kenne Duncan, Steve Clark, Marshall Reed, Ted Adams, Bud Osborne, Carol Henry, Bob Woodard, Ray Whitley, Ray Jones. A woman is illegally smuggling guns to local Indians and a cowboy wants to stop her. Not a bad film and well-done in its modest way—it just needs a star!

1357 Gun Smoke. Paramount, 1931. 66 minutes B/W. D: Edward Sloman. SC: Grover Jones & William McNutt. WITH Richard Arlen, Mary Brian, William Boyd, Eugene Pallette, Louise Fazenda, Charles Winninger, James "Junior" Durkin, J. Carrol Naish, Dawn O'Day (Anne Shirley), Guy Oliver, Brooks Benedict, William V. Mong, Willie Fung. Gangsters take over a small Western town but are opposed by a cowboy and his pals. Interesting interpolation of the oater and gangster genres with Richard Arlen as the hero and William Boyd as the lead villain.

1358 Gun Smoke. Monogram, 1945. 60 minutes B/W. D: Howard Bretherton. SC: Frank Young. WITH Johnny Mack Brown, Raymond Hatton, Jennifer Holt, Riley Hill, Wen Wright, Ray Bennett, Steve Clark, Bob Cason, Roy Butler, Frank Ellis, Marshall Reed, Chick Hannon. Two marshals find a stagecoach in which all of the passengers have been killed and they discover that an outlaw gang was after Indian gold relics. Interesting plot for this entry in the Monogram series with Johnny Mack Brown and Raymond Hatton.

1359 Gun Smugglers. RKO Radio, 1948. 62 minutes B/W. D: Frank McDonald.

SC: Norman Houston. WITH Tim Holt, Martha Hyer, Richard Martin, Gary Gray, Paul Hurst, Douglas Fowley, Robert Warwick, Don Haggerty, Frank Sully, Robert Bray. A small boy, who is in the custody of an honest man, is used by gun smugglers in a plot to fleece the guardian. Average outing in Tim Holt's RKO series.

1360 Gun Street. United Artists, 1962. 67 minutes B/W. D: Edward L. Cahn. SC: Sam C. Freddle. WITH James Brown, Jean Willes, Mel Flory, John Clarke, John Pickard, Peggy Stewart, Sandra Stone, Warren Kemmerling, Neston Booth, Herb Armstrong. A sheriff tries to stop a convict from murdering the man who sent the convict to prison and then married his wife. Pretty fair programmer.

1361 Gun Talk. Monogram, 1947. 57 minutes B/W. D: Lambert Hillyer. SC: J. Benton Cheney. WITH Johnny Mack Brown, Raymond Hatton, Christine McIntyre, Geneva Gray, Douglas Evans, Wheaton Chambers, Frank LaRue, Ted Adams, Carol Mathews, Zon Murray, Carol Henry, Bill Hale, Boyd Stockman. While searching for his missing cousin, a man thwarts a stage robbery and becomes involved in capturing the crooks. A rather complicated plot enhances this otherwise routine oater.

1362 The Gun That Won the West. Columbia, 1955. 71 minutes Color. D: William Castle. SC: James R. Gordon. WITH Dennis Morgan, Paula Raymond, Richard Denning, Chris O'Brien, Robert Bice, Michael Morgan, Roy Gordon, Howard Wright, Richard Cutting, Kenneth MacDonald, Howard Negley. In Wyoming, the Cavalry and its scouts use a new weapon to restore the peace with local Indians. Title refers to the Springfield Rifle in this competent actioner.

1363 Gun the Man Down. United Artists, 1956. 78 minutes B/W. D: Andrew V. McLaglen. SC: Burt Kennedy. WITH James Arness, Angie Dickinson, Robert Wilke, Emile Meyer, Don Megowan, Michael Emmett, Harry Carey Jr. After being wounded in a robbery, an outlaw gang member is deserted by his cohorts and he swears to get revenge on them. Average mid-1950s theatrical oater aided by a good plot and nice cast. TV title: **Arizona Mission.**

1364 Gun Town. Universal, 1946. 53 minutes B/W. D: Wallace Fox. SC: William

Lively. WITH Kirby Grant, Fuzzy Knight, Lyle Talbot, Louise Currie, Claire Carleton, Dan White, Ray Bennett, Earle Hodgins, George Morrell, Tex Cooper, Merrill McCormack. Two cowpokes come to the aid of a female stage line owner who is being harrassed by outlaws who are actually being lead by her fiancee. Compact Kirby Grant series vehicle with fine villainous work by Lyle Talbot.

Guns A' Blazing see **Law and Order** (1932)

Guns of Fury see **The Daring Caballero**

1365 Guns and Guitars. Republic, 1936. 54 (56) minutes B/W. D: Joseph Kane. SC: Dorrell McGowan & Stuart McGowan. WITH Gene Autry, Smiley Burnette, Dorothy Dix, Earle Hodgins, J.P. MaGowan, Tom London, Charles King, Frankie Marvin, Jack Rockwell, Ken Cooper, Harrison Greene, Eugene Jackson, Pascale Perry, Bob Burns, Tracy Layne, Jack Kirk, George Morrell, Sherry Tansey, Jack Evans, George Plues, Denver Dixon, Wes Warner, Jim Corey. In an area plagued by cattle rustling, cattle fever and quarantines, Gene Autry arrives with a medicine show and tries to put a stop to lawlessness by running for sheriff. Top-grade Gene Autry oater with nice songs and a strong plot—a good film.

Guns Don't Argue see **Bullets Don't Argue**

1366 Guns for Hire. Willis Kent, 1932. 59 minutes B/W. D-SC: Oliver Drake. WITH Lane Chandler, Sally Darling, Neal Hart, Yakima Canutt, John Ince, Slim Whitaker, Jack Rockwell, Ben Corbett, Steve Clemente, Bill Patton, Hank Bell, John P. McGuire, Frances Morris, Nelson McDowell, John Bacon, Edward Porter, Roy Bucko, Buck Bucko, Bud McClure, Gene Alsace, Bud Pope, Jack O'Shea, Ray Jones. A gunman joins forces with a rancher fighting crooks, but finds out the other side employs the man who taught him his trade. A low budget but still entertaining Lane Chandler film; fans can see silent star Neal Hart in a major role as the rival gunman. TV title: **Blazing Trail.**

1367 Guns in the Dark. Republic, 1937. 56 minutes B/W. D: Sam Newfield. SC: Charles Francis Royal. WITH Johnny Mack Brown, Claire Rochelle, Syd Saylor, Ted Adams, Frank Ellis, Budd Buster, Merrill McCormick, Richard Cramer,

Jack C. Smith, Dick Curtis, Roger Williams, Steve Clark, Jim Corey, Julian Madison, Slim Whitaker, Lew Meehan, Tex Palmer, Oscar Gahan, Sherry Tansey, Chick Hannon. After a man mistakenly thinks he killed his pal in a Mexican saloon brawl, he returns to the U.S. to work for a girl who has a contract to build a dam, but the dam's operations are being sabotaged by a gang of rustlers. Interesting Johnny Mack Brown vehicle with all kinds of subplots, including drug smuggling.

1368 Guns of a Stranger. Universal, 1973. 91 minutes Color. D: Robert Hinkle. SC: Charles W. Aldridge. WITH Marty Robbins, Chill Wills, Dovie Beams, Steve Tackett, Shug Fisher, Ronny Robbins, Melody Hinkle, Charles Aldridge. A singing drifter rides into a small Western town and has a profound effect on the lives of its citizens. Tepid oater starring country favorite Marty Robbins. Monte Hale was originally scheduled to appear in this feature.

1369 Guns of Diablo. Metro-Goldwyn-Mayer, 1964. 79 minutes Color. D: Boris Sagal. SC: Bernie Giler. WITH Charles Bronson, Susan Oliver, Kurt Russell, Jan Merlin, John Fiedler, Douglas Fowley, Raymond Barnes, Morris Ankrum, Russ Conway. The head of a wagon train stops at a small town and becomes involved with a former adversary and an ex-love. Telefeature from the television series "The Travels of Jamie McPheeters" (ABC-TV, 1963-64), is well made and finely acted by Charles Bronson.

1370 Guns of Fort Petticoat. Columbia, 1957. 82 minutes Color. D: George Marshall. SC: Walter Doniger. WITH Audie Murphy, Kathryn Grant, Hope Emerson, Jeff Donnell, Jeanette Nolan, Sean McClory, James Griffith, Madge Meredith, Ernestine Wade, Peggy Maley, Isobel Elson, Kim Charney, Ray Teal, Nestor Paiva, Charles Horvath. During the Civil War, a lieutenant is about to be court-martialed so he deserts and heads West where he comes across a band of women in Texas, whose husbands are away fighting in the war, and he trains them to defend their settlement against attacking Indians. Highly entertaining Audie Murphy vehicle with nice support from Hope Emerson.

1371 Guns of Hate. RKO Radio, 1948. 62 minutes B/W. D: Lesley Selander. SC: Norman Houston & Ed Earl Repp. WITH Tim Holt, Richard Martin, Nan Leslie, Steve Brodie, Myrna Dell, Tony Barrett, Jason Robards, Robert Bray, Jim Nolan. When crooks try to steal a gold mine, two cowboys find themselves involved in the dispute. Standard Tim Holt series outing.

Guns of Justice see **Colorado Ranger**

1372 Guns of Nevada. Cineproduzioni Associate/I.F.I.S.A., 1965. 93 minutes Color. D-SC: Ignacio Iquino. WITH George Martin, Audrey Amber, Katya Loritz, John McDouglas, Stan Bart. A man falls in love with two women, one a mine owner and the other a saloon proprietor, and he opposes a crooked engineer trying to steal the first woman's mine. Passable Italian-Spanish coproduction originally called **La Sfida Degli Implacabili** (Challenge by the Implacable Ones).

1373 Guns of San Sebastian. Metro-Goldwyn-Mayer, 1967. 111 minutes Color. D: Henri Verneuil. SC: James R. Webb. WITH Anthony Quinn, Anjanette Comer, Charles Bronson, Sam Jaffe, Silvia Pinal, Jorge Martinez de Hoyos, Jaime Fernandez, Pedro Armendariz Jr., Rosa Furman, Leon Askin, Ivan Desny. An outlaw is mistaken for a priest and helps a small Mexican village defeat a gang of outlaws. Weak Anthony Quinn vehicle; the star does his best as does Charles Bronson as the leader of the Yaqui Indians.

1374 Guns of the Law. Producers Releasing Corporation, 1944. 56 minutes B/W. D-SC: Elmer Clifton. WITH James Newill, Dave O'Brien, Guy Wilkerson, Jack Ingram, Robert Kortman, Robert Barron, Frank McCarroll, Charles King, Budd Buster, Bud Osborne. A crooked lawyer and his gang try to steal a valuable property by running a family off of it and the Texas Rangers trio come to the rescue. Low-grade entry in the popular "Texas Rangers" series from PRC.

1375 Guns of the Magnificent Seven. United Artists, 1969. 106 minutes Color. D: Paul Wendkos. SC: Herman Hoffman. WITH George Kennedy, Monte Markham, James Whitmore, Reni Santoni, Bernie Casey, Joe Don Baker, Scott Thomas, Michael Ansara, Frank Silvera, Tony Davis, Wende Wagner, Luis Rivera, Fernando Rey, Sancho Garcia. A gunslinger and a half-dozen hired cohorts agree to spring a Mexican revolutionary leader from prison so he can resume his cause. Very actionful third entry in the popular "Magnificent Seven" series.

1376 Guns of the Pecos. Warner Brothers-First National, 1937. 56 minutes B/W. D: Noel Smith. SC: Harold Buckley. WITH Dick Foran, Anne Nagel, Gordon (William) Elliott, Gordon Hart, Joseph Crehan, Eddie Acuff, Robert Middlemass, Monte Montague, Gaby Fay (Holden), Milton Kibbee, Bud Osborne, Bob Burns, Douglas Wood, Glenn Strange, Gene Alsace, Bob Woodward, Frank McCarroll, Jack Kirk, Ray Jones. Rustlers murder an Army major who is purchasing horses for the service and Texas Rangers are assigned to track down the killers. Fair entry in Dick Foran's Warner Brothers series.

1377 Guns of the Timberland. Warner Brothers, 1960. 91 minutes Color. D: Robert D. Webb. SC: Joseph Petracca. WITH Alan Ladd, Jeanne Crain, Gilbert Roland, Frankie Avalon, Lyle Bettger, Noah Beery Jr., Regis Toomey, Johnny Seven, Alana Ladd, Verna Felton, George Selk, Paul E. Burns, Henry Kulky. Ranchers and townspeople oppose the action of loggers who are clearing the land with the aid of a government grant. Colorful feature with an interesting plot line centered on business interests versus ecology.

1378 A Gunfight. Paramount, 1971. 90 minutes Color. D: Lamont Johnson. SC: Harold Jack Bloom. WITH Kirk Douglas, Johnny Cash, Jane Alexander, Raf Vallone, Karen Black, Eric Douglas, Dana Elcar, Robert Wilke, Keith Carradine, Paul Lambert, Philip L. Mead, John Wallwork. Two aging gunmen are forced into a showdown in a small town and they decide to charge admission to the event. Offbeat oater which is badly hampered by Johnny Cash's performance in one of the leads.

1379 Gunfight at Comanche Creek. Allied Artists, 1963. 90 minutes Color. D: Frank McDonald. SC: Edward Bernds. WITH Audie Murphy, Ben Cooper, Coleen Miller, DeForrest Kelley, Jan Merlin, John Hubbard, Damian O'Flynn, Susan Seaforth. A detective is hired to stop an outlaw gang and he ingratiates himself into the band and sets out to uncover its mysterious leader. Mundane Audie Murphy vehicle.

1380 The Gunfight at Dodge City. United Artists, 1959. 81 minutes Color. D: Joseph M. Newman. SC: Daniel B. Ullman & Martin M. Goldsmith. WITH Joel McCrea, Julia (Julie) Adams, John McIntire, Nancy Gates, Richard Anderson, James Westerfield, Walter Coy, Wright King, Don

Haggerty, Harry Lauter, Myron Healey, Mauritz Hugo, Henry Kulky. Bat Masterson is asked to take over the job as the sheriff of a Western town only to discover the citizens do not approve of his trying to clean out the lawless element. Nicely done melodrama with Joel McCrea making a grand Bat Masterson.

1381 Gunfight at Red Sands. Screen Gems, 1965. 97 minutes Color. D: Riccardo Blasco. SC: Alfredo Antonini & Riccardo Blasco. WITH Richard Harrison, Mikaela, Giacomo Rossi Stuart. When his adopted brother is murdered by outlaws and their gold stolen by them, a Mexican miner's adopted son seeks revenge on the three killers. Pretty good Spanish-made oater with a fine music score by Ennio Morricone. Made in 1963 as *Gringo.*

1382 Gunfight at Sandoval. Buena Vista, 1963. 74 minutes B/W. D: Harry Keller. WITH Tom Tryon, Dan Duryea, Lyle Bettger, Beverly Garland, Norma Moore, Harry Carey Jr., Judson Pratt. A Texas ranger hunts down an outlaw gang who murdered his pal when he tried to stop them from robbing a bank. Well done actioner issued theatrically in Europe although in this country it was shown on Walt Disney's TV program on ABC-TV as "Showdown at Sandoval," on January 23, 1959, a part of the "Texas John Slaughter" mini-series.

1383 Gunfight at the O.K. Corral. Paramount, 1957. 122 minutes Color. D: John Sturges. SC: Leon Uris. WITH Burt Lancaster, Kirk Douglas, Rhonda Fleming, Jo Van Fleet, John Ireland, Lyle Bettger, Frank Faylen, Earl Holliman, Ted de Corsia, Dennis Hopper, Whit Bissell, George Mathews, John Hudson, DeForrest Kelley, Martin Milner, Kenneth Tobey, Lee Van Cleef, Joan Camden, Olive Carey, Brian Hutton, Nelson Leigh, Jack Elam, Don Castle, Dennis Moore, Ethan Laidlaw, William Norton Bailey, Joe Forte. Wyatt Earp teams with Doc Holliday to oppose the notorious Ike Clanton and his outlaw sons. Still another retelling of the showdown at the O.K. Corral, colorful but historically empty. Frankie Laine sings the title song. VD: RCA. V: Blackhawk.

1384 Gunfight in Abilene. Universal, 1967. 86 minutes Color. D: William Hale. SC: Bernie Giler & John D. F. Black. WITH Bobby Darin, Emily Banks, Leslie Nielsen, Donnelly Rhodes, Don Galloway, Frank McGrath, Michael Sarrazin, Barbara

Werle, Johnny Seven, William Phipps, William Mims, Don Dubbins. During the Civil War, the ex-sheriff of Abilene becomes afraid of guns and when he returns home the townspeople want him to take over his old job. Competent actioner starring pop singer Bobby Darin in a dramatic role.

1385 The Gunfighter. 20th Century-Fox, 1950. 84 minutes B/W. D: Henry King. SC: William Bowers & William Sellers. WITH Gregory Peck, Helen Westcott, Millard Mitchell, Jean Parker, Karl Malden, Skip Homeier, Anthony Ross, Verna Felton, Ellen Corby, Richard Jaeckel, Alan Hale Jr., John Pickard, Angela Clarke, Cliff Clark, Alberto Morin, Kenneth Tobey, Michael Brandon, Ferris Taylor, Hank Patterson, Mae Marsh, Kim Spaulding, Harry Shannon, Houseley Stevenson, James Millican. A famous gunman, pursued by the brothers of his latest victim, returns to the town where his ex-wife and son now live as he tries to start a new life. Top notch melodrama with fine writing and performances; a near classic of the genre.

1386 The Gunfighters. Columbia, 1947. 87 minutes Color. D: George Waggner. SC: Alan LeMay. WITH Randolph Scott, Barbara Britton, Dorothy Hart, Bruce Cabot, Charles Grapewin, Steven Geray, Forrest Tucker, Charles Kemper, Grant Withers, John Miles, Griff Barnett. A former gunman becomes a wrangler on a ranch where the owner's daughter is in love with a murderer. Fine screen adaptation of Zane Grey's Twin Sombreros with Randolph Scott returning to the author whose material gave him screen stardom more than a decade before.

1387 Gunfighters of Casa Grande. Metro-Goldwyn-Mayer, 1965. 92 minutes Color. D: Roy Rowland. SC: Borden Chase & Clarke Reynolds. WITH Alex Nicol, Jorge Mistral, Dick Bentley, Steve Rowland, Phil Posner, Maria Granada, Diana Lorys, Mercedes Alonso. A notorious outlaw enlists the aid of other crooks in pulling off a big cattle theft but tries to double-cross his cohorts. Spanish-made oater which got good distribution in the U. S.; average. Produced in 1964 as Los Pistoleros de Casa Grande.

1388 Gunfighters of the Northwest. Columbia, 1954. 15 Chapters B/W. D: Spencer Gordon Bennet. SC: Arthur Hoerl, Royal K. Cole & George Plympton. WITH Jack (Jock) Mahoney, Clayton Moore, Phyllis

Coates, Don C. Harvey, Marshall Reed, Rodd Redwing, Lyle Talbot, Tom Farrell, Terry Frost, Lee Roberts, Joe Allen Jr., Gregg Barton, Chief Yowlachie, Pierce Lyden. A Mountie is faced with marauding Indians and an avalanche in the great northwest. Lame cliffhanger, although its three stars do the best they can with the tired material.

1389 Gunfire. Resolute, 1934. 56 minutes B/W. D: Harry Fraser. SC: Harry C. (Fraser) Crist. WITH Rex Bell, Ruth Mix, Buzz Barton, Milburn Morante, Theodore Lorch, Philo McCullough, Ted Adams, Lew Meehan, Willie Fung, Mary Jane Irving, Jack Baston, Fern Emmett, Howard Hickey, Chuck Morrison, Mary Jo Ellis, William Demarest, Slim Whitaker. Rivals frame a rancher on a murder charge but a cowboy and an Eastern girl come to his aid. Low grade Rex Bell actioner.

1390 Gunfire. Lippert, 1950. 60 minutes B/W. D: William Berke. SC: William Berke & Victor West. WITH Don Barry, Robert Lowery, Wally Vernon, Pamela Blake, Gaylord (Steve) Pendleton, Tommy Farrell, Leonard Penn, Dean Reisner. Claude Stroud, Steve Conte, Robert Anderson, William Norton Bailey. A man who is a look-alike for Frank James begins a series of holdups using the James name and the real Frank James comes out of seclusion to stop him. Low budget affair enhanced by excellent work by Don Barry in dual roles.

1391 Gunfire at Indian Gap. Republic, 1957. 70 minutes B/W. D: Joe (Joseph) Kane. SC: Barry Shipman. WITH Vera Ralston, Anthony George, George Macready, Barry Kelley, John Doucette, George Keymas, Chubby Johnson, Glenn Strange, Dan White, Steve Warren, Chuck Hicks, Sarah Selby. At a remote relay station, three outlaws are after a shipment of gold and a half-breed girl. Cheap Vera Ralston vehicle with the star too old for the part.

Gunlords of Stirrup Basin see **Gun Lords of Stirrup Basin**

1392 The Gunman. Monogram, 1952. 52 minutes B/W. D: Lewis D. Collins. SC: Fred Myton. WITH Whip Wilson, Fuzzy Knight, Phyllis Coates, Rand Brooks, Terry Frost, I. Stanford Jolley, Lane Bradford, Gregg Barton, Russ Whiteman, Richard Avonde. Citizens of an outlaw-ridden area send to Texas Territory for a marshal and his deputy to help them. Anemic Whip Wilson film.

1393 The Gunman from Bodie. Monogram, 1941. 62 minutes B/W. D: Spencer Gordon Bennet. SC: Jess Bowers (Adele Buffington). WITH Buck Jones, Tim McCoy, Raymond Hatton, Christine McIntyre, Dave O'Brien, Robert Frazer, Charles King, Lynton Brent, Max Walzman, Jerry Sheldon, Jack King, Earl Douglas, Warren Jackson, Billy Carro, Frederick Gee, John Merton, Frank LaRue, Gene Alsace. A man masquerades as a gunman to find out who is killing families near a small town and he is aided by a U. S. marshal and a ranch owner's cook. Actionful Rough Riders series entry which does not reveal the trio until its finale; Buck Jones and Tim McCoy share the spotlight here while Raymond Hatton has little to do.

1394 Gunman in Town. Devon Film/ Copercines, 1970. 99 minutes Color. D: Anthony Ascott (Giuliano Carmineo). SC: Tito Carpi. WITH Gianni Garko, Susan Scott, Piero Lulli, Nieves Navarro, Massimo Serato, Jose Jaspe. A gunman breaks a convicted murderer out of jail and returns him to the site of the crime to see that justice is carried out. Fairly interesting entry in the Italian "Sartana" series with a good music score by Bruno Nicolai. Italian title: **Una Nuvola de Polvere...Un Grido di Morte...Ariva Sartana** (A Cloud of Dust...A Cry of Death... Sartana is Coming).

1395 Gunman's Code. Universal, 1946. 55 minutes B/W. D: Wallace Fox. SC: William Lively. WITH Kirby Grant, Fuzzy Knight, Jane Adams, Danny Morton, Bernard Thomas, Karl Hackett, Charles Miller, Frank McCarroll, Dan White, Artie Ortego, Jack Montgomery. Two Wells Fargo agents arrive in a small town trying to capture an outlaw gang which has been attacking the company's stagecoaches. Pretty fair actioner in the Kirby Grant-Universal series.

1396 Gunman's Walk. Columbia, 1958. 97 minutes Color. D: Phil Karlson. SC: Frank Nugent. WITH Van Heflin, Tab Hunter, Kathryn Grant, James Darren, Mickey Shaugnessy, Robert F. Simon, Edward Platt, Ray Teal, Paul Birch, Will Wright, Bert Convy, Paul E. Burns, Paul Bryar, Everett Glass, Dorothy Adams. A rancher tries to raise his two sons to walk the straight and narrow but there is a personality clash and one of them

ends up killing his brother's girl. Okay psychological oater with Van Heflin excelling as the patriarch.

1397 Gunmen from Laredo. Columbia, 1959. 67 minutes Color. D: Wallace MacDonald. SC: Clarke Reynolds. WITH Robert Knapp, Kana Davi, Walter Coy, Paul Birch, Don C. Harvey, Clarence Straight, Ron Hayes, Charles Horvath, Jean Moorehead, X Brands. With the aid of an Indian girl, a rancher escapes from jail and gets on the trail of the men who framed him and murdered his wife. Low grade outing from producer-director Wallace MacDonald, who acted in Tim McCoy's Columbia films in the 1930s.

1398 Gunmen of Abilene. Republic, 1950. 60 minutes B/W. D: Fred C. Brannon. SC: M. Coates Webster. WITH Allan "Rocky" Lane, Eddy Waller, Donna Hamilton, Roy Barcroft, Peter Brocco, Selmer Jackson, Duncan Richardson, Don C. Harvey, Don Dillaway, George Chesebro, Steve Clark. An outlaw gang plots to steal a gold shipment but is opposed by an undercover deputy marshal. Another good and actionful Allan Lane vehicle.

1399 Gunmen of the Rio Grande. Allied Artists, 1965. 86 minutes Color. D: Tulio Demicheli. SC: Gene Luotto. WITH Guy Madison, Madeline Lebeau, Carolyn Davys, Massimo Serato, Gerard Tichy, Fernando Sancho, Olivier Hussenot. Taking on the guise of a drifter, Wyatt Earp comes to a small Western town to help a girl whose silver interests are being sought by a ruthless mine owner. Pretty good actioner from Europe which will please Guy Madison's fans since he portrays Wyatt Earp. British title: **Duel at Rio Bravo**. Made in Italy as **Jennie Lees Ha Una Nuova Pistola** by West-Film/Flora Film/Illama Films/Pathe-Cinema.

1400 Gunners and Guns. Beaumont, 1935. 57 minutes B/W. D: Jerry Callahan & Robert Hoyt. SC: Ruth Runell. WITH Black King (horse), Edwin (Edmund) Cobb, Edna Aselin, Edward Allen Biby, Eddie Davis, Ned Norton, Lois Glaze, Felix Vallee, Jack Cheatham, Ruth Runell, Frank Walker. A ranch foreman is falsely accused of murdering his dude ranch owner boss, the deed actually done by men who were once part of a gang lead by the rancher. Bottom-of-the-barrel actioner which does include a beautiful horse as its star as well as giving one a chance to see Edmund Cobb in a starring role in a sound film. Given brief release in 1934 by Fred Thompson Productions as **Racketeer Round-Up** with new footage added for general release the next year. V: Cassette Express.

1401 Gunning for Justice. Monogram, 1948. 60 minutes B/W. D: Ray Taylor. SC: J. Benton Cheney. WITH Johnny Mack Brown, Raymond Hatton, Max Terhune, Evelyn Finley, House Peters Jr., Ted Adams, I. Stanford Jolley, Bud Osborne, Dan White, Bob Woodard, Carol Henry, Boyd Stockman, Dee Cooper, Artie Ortego. A man and his pals find a map which shows the location of gold hijacked during the Civil War and try to find it. **The Good, the Bad and the Ugly** it is not but this Monogram outing is a pleasant affair.

1402 Gunning for Vengeance. Columbia, 1946. 56 minutes B/W. D: Ray Nazarro. SC: Ed Earl Repp. WITH Charles Starrett, Smiley Burnette, Marjean Neville, Curt Barrett & The Trailsmen, Robert Kortman, George Chesebro, Frank LaRue, Lane Chandler, Phyllis Adair, Robert Williams, Jack Kirk, John Tyrell, Nolan Leary, Frank Fanning. The Durango Kid comes to the aid of a small girl whose father has been bushwacked by a gang who has been extorting protection money from area ranchers. Fairly good "Durango Kid" series entry.

1403 Gunplay. RKO Radio, 1951. 61 minutes B/W. D: Lesley Selander. SC: Ed Earl Repp. WITH Tim Holt, Richard Martin, Joan Dixon, Marshall Reed, Robert Bice, Robert Wilke, Mauritz Hugo, Harper Carter, Jack Hill. The father of a young boy is murdered and the youngster is befriended by two cowpokes who set out to find the killer. Solid entertainment is provided by this later Tim Holt vehicle. V: Nostalgia Merchant.

1404 Gunpoint. Universal, 1966. 86 minutes Color. D: Earl Bellamy. SC: Mary Willingham & Willard Willingham. WITH Audie Murphy, Joan Staley, Warren Stevens, Edgar Buchanan, Denver Pyle, Royal Dano, Nick Dennis, William Bramley, Kelly Thordsen, David Macklin, Morgan Woodward, Robert Pine, Mike Ragan. An outlaw gang robs a train and kidnaps a saloon girl and the sheriff of a small town forms a posse and chases them into New Mexico Territory. Pretty interesting Audie Murphy vehicle enhanced by a good script.

1405 Gunsight Ridge. United Artists, 1957. 85 minutes B/W. D: Francis D. Lyon. SC: Talbot Jennings & Elizabeth Jennings. WITH Joel McCrea, Joan Weldon, Mark Stevens, Darlene Fields, Addison Richards, Carolyn Craig, Robert Griffin, Slim Pickens, I. Stanford Jolley, George Chandler, Herbert Vigran, Jody McCrea, Martin Garralaga, Cindy Robbins. The citizens in the Arizona Territory hire a new deputy marshal to stop a series of robberies and he finds out that supposedly respectable citizens are behind the outrages. Fast moving Joel McCrea vehicle that is sure to satisfy his legion of followers.

1406 Gunslinger. American Releasing Corporation, 1956. 78 minutes Color. D: Roger Corman. SC: Mark Hanna & Charles B. Griffith. WITH John Ireland, Beverly Garland, Allison Hayes, Martin Kingsley, Jonathan Haze, Chris Alcaide, Dick Miller, Bruno Ve Sota, William Schallert, Margaret Campbell. When her marshal husband is murdered a woman takes over the job and the crooked saloon boss hires a gunman to kill her. Early six-day Roger Corman cheapie which is rather appealing.

1407 Gunslingers. Monogram, 1950. 55 minutes B/W. D: Wallace Fox. SC: Adele Buffington. WITH Whip Wilson, Andy Clyde, Reno Browne, Dennis Moore, Riley Hill, George Chesebro, Sarah Padden, Bill Kennedy, Hank Bell, Steve Clark, Carl Mathews, Frank McCarroll, Reed Howes, Carol Henry, George DeNormand, Frank Ellis, Ray Jones. A saloon owner wants to foreclose on the properties of drought-stricken ranchers in order to sell their lands to the railroad, and he fixes a scheme to have a rancher hung for rustling but the man is defended by a drifting cowboy. Well done Whip Wilson film with an involved plotline.

1408 Gunsmoke. Universal-International, 1953. 79 minutes Color. D: Nathan Juran. SC: D. D. Beauchamp. WITH Audie Murphy, Susan Cabot, Paul Kelly, Charles Drake, Mary Castle, Jack Kelly, Jesse White, William Reynolds, Chubby Johnson, Edmund Cobb, Clem Fuller. An outlaw is hired to run a family off a ranch but instead takes over the spread, rounds up the cattle for market and falls in love with the owner's pretty daughter. Somewhat offbeat and nicely done.

1409 Gunsmoke in Tucson. Allied Artists, 1958. 79 minutes Color. D: Thomas Carr.

SC: Paul Leslie Peil & Robert Joseph.
WITH Mark Stevens, Forrest Tucker,
Gale Robbins, Vaughn Taylor, Kevin
Hagen, Bill Henry, Richard Reeves, Gail
Kobe, George Keymas, Zon Murray,
John Ward, John Cliff. In the Arizona
Territory turbulence between a cattle
baron and settlers erupts causing a show-
down between a marshal and his outlaw
brother. Rather routine oater with good
performances from the two stars.

1410 Gunsmoke Mesa. Producers Releasing
Corporation, 1944. 59 minutes B/W.
D: Harry Fraser. SC: Elmer Clifton.
WITH James Newill, Dave O'Brien, Guy
Wilkerson, Patti McCarthy, Jack Ingram,
Kermit Maynard, Robert Barron, Richard
Alexander, Roy Brent, Michael Vallon,
Jack Rockwell. The Texas Rangers trio
witness a murder and when they report
it they are arrested for the crime and
are forced to break jail to find the real
murderers. Fairly interesting outing
in the PRC "Texas Rangers" series.

1411 Gunsmoke Ranch. Republic, 1937.
54 (56) minutes B/W. D: Joseph Kane.
SC: Oliver Drake & Jack Natteford.
WITH Robert Livingston, Ray Corrigan,
Max Terhune, Julia Thayer (Jean Carmen),
Kenneth Harlan, Sammy McKim, Oscar
& Elmer, Yakima Canutt, Burr Caruth,
Horace B. Carpenter, Robert Walker,
Jack Ingram, Jack Kirk, Jack Padjan,
Fred "Snowflake" Toones, John Merton,
Robert McKenzie, Ed Piel Sr., Fred Burns.
When settlers are nearly ruined by a
flood, a crooked politician sets out to
steal their lands but is thwarted by The
Three Mesquiteers. Exciting entry in
the very popular "The Three Mesquiteers"
series.

1412 Gunsmoke Trail. Monogram, 1938.
57 minutes B/W. D: Sam Newfield. SC:
Fred Myton. WITH Jack Randall, Louise
Stanley, Al St. John, John Merton, Henry
Rocquemore, Ted Adams, Alan Bridge,
Glenn Strange, Hal Price, Harry Strang,
Kit Guard, Jack Ingram, Slim Whitaker,
Art Dillard, Carleton Young, Sherry
Tansey, George Morrell, Oscar Gahan,
Blackjack Ward. A cowboy aids a girl
whose property is wanted by a murderer
who is pretending to be her uncle. Better
than average Jack Randall series vehicle
with a fine supporting cast.

1413 Gypsy Colt. Metro-Goldwyn-Mayer,
1954. 72 minutes Color. D: Andrew Marton.
SC: Martin Berkeley. WITH Donna
Corcoran, Ward Bond, Frances Dee,

Larry Keating, Lee Van Cleef, Nacho
Galindo, Rodolfo Hoyos, Peggy Maley,
Joe Dominguez. Drought causes a couple
to sell their daughter's prize racing horse
to a faraway stable and the loyal animal
undertakes the 500-mile journey to return
home. Heartwarming family film which
is a reworking of **Lassie Come Home**
(Metro-Goldwyn-Mayer, 1943).

H

1414 Hail to the Rangers. Columbia,
1943. 57 minutes B/W. D: William Berke.
SC: Gerald Geraghty. WITH Charles
Starrett, Leota Atcher, Arthur Hunnicutt,
Bob Atcher, Norman Willis, Lloyd Bridges,
Ted Adams, Ernie Adams, Tom London,
Davison Clark, Jack Kirk, Edmund Cobb,
Budd Buster, Art Mix, Eddie Laughton,
Richard Botiller. An ex-ranger comes
to the aid of a rancher pal who is about
to lose his range to an influx of home-
steaders. The plot twist of having the
homesteaders as the bad guys adds some
zest to this Charles Starrett actioner.

1415 Hair Trigger Casey. Atlantic, 1936.
59 minutes B/W. D: Harry S. Fraser.
SC: Monroe Talbot. WITH Jack Perrin,
Betty Mack, Wally Wales, Fred "Snowflake"
Toones, Ed Cassidy, Robert Walker,
Phil Dunham, Denny Meadows (Dennis
Moore). A cowboy tries to put a stop
to a smuggling gang working along the
U. S.-Mexican border. Better-than-average
Jack Perrin vehicle for producer William
Berke, with plenty of suspense and some
good comedy.

1416 Half-Breed. Hampton, 1973. 90
minutes Color. D: Harald Philipp. SC:
Fred Denger. WITH Lex Barker, Pierre
Brice, Ralf Wolter, Gotz George, Walter
Barnes. A half-breed girl inherits her
father's gold mine and outlaws kidnap
her but Old Shatterhand and his Apache
blood brother Winnetou come to her
rescue. Sturdy actioner in the Karl May
series. West German title: **Winnetou
Und Has Halbblut Apantaschi** (Winnetou
and the Half-Blood Apantaschi); originally
released in West Germany in 1966 by
Rialto/Jadran Film.

1417 The Half-Breed. RKO Radio, 1952.
81 minutes Color. D: Stuart Gilmore.
SC: Harold Shumate & Richard Wormser.
WITH Robert Young, Janis Carter, Jack
Buetel, Barton MacLane, Reed Hadley,

Porter Hall, Connie Gilchrist, Sammy White, Damian O'Flynn, Frank Wilcox, Charles Delaney, Tom Monroe. Crooked profiteers incite a half-breed Apache into leading his tribe against white settlers in Arizona. Average oater outing which should have been better than it turned out.

1418 Halfway to Hell. Pathe-Alpha, 1962. 75 minutes B/W. D: Denver Dixon (Victor Adamson). WITH Lyle Felice, Carroll Montour, Sergio Virell, Rick Adams (Al Adamson). At the time of the Pancho Villa rebellion in Mexico in 1902, the daughter of a wealthy family falls in love with an aide to the revolutionary leader. Last feature film directed by the legendary Denver Dixon, this production was partially filmed in Mexico and may have been made as early as 1957.

1419 The Hallelujah Trail. United Artists, 1965. 167 minutes Color. D: John Sturges. SC: John Gay. WITH Burt Lancaster, Lee Remick, Jim Hutton, Pamela Tiffin, Donald Pleasence, Brian Keith, Martin Landau, John Anderson, John Dehner, Tom Stern, Robert Wilke, Jerry Gatlin, Larry Duran, Jim Burk, Dub Taylor, John McKee, Helen Kleeb, Noam Pitlik, Carl Pitti, Bill Williams, Marshall Reed, Carroll Adams, Ted Markland. In the winter of 1867 an army officer is assigned to take a shipment of whiskey to Denver and his detail is beset by several groups, including Indians and a gang of female temperance workers. Thin, overlong Western comedy which is not very good.

1420 The Halliday Brand. United Artists, 1957. 79 minutes B/W. D: Joseph H. Lewis. SC: George W. George & George S. Slavin. WITH Joseph Cotten, Viveca Lindfors, Betsy Blair, Ward Bond, Bill Williams, Christopher Dark, Jeanette Nolan, Jay C. Flippen, John Dierkes, Glenn Strange, I. Stanford Jolley, Jay Lawrence, George Lynn, John Halloran, Michael Hinn. A wealthy rancher rides roughshod over his family, but trouble develops with his son when he allows a mob to hang his daughter's half-breed lover. Surprisingly appealing psychological Western with an excellent performance by Joseph Cotten as the patriarch.

1421 Hands Across the Border. Republic, 1944. 54 (73) minutes B/W. D: Joseph Kane. SC: Bradford Ropes & J. Benton Cheney. WITH Roy Rogers, Ruth Terry, Guinn Williams, Bob Nolan & The Sons of the Pioneers, Onslow Stevens, Mary Treen, Joseph Crehan, Duncan Renaldo, LeRoy Mason, Janet Martin, The Wiere Brothers, Roy Barcroft, Frederick Burton, Julian Rivero, Kenne Duncan, Jack O'Shea, Jack Kirk, Curley Dresden. Roy Rogers is forced to ride Trigger in a race to win a cavalry contract after a crook deprives an honest rival of the contract. Fairly actionful film with plot subordinate to the songs and containing a big musical finale.

1422 Hands Across the Rockies. Columbia, 1941. 55 minutes B/W. D: Lambert Hillyer. SC: Paul Franklin. WITH Bill Elliott, Mary Daily, Dub Taylor, Kenneth Mac-Donald, Frank LaRue, Donald Curtis, Tom Murray, Stanley Brown, Slim Whitaker, Harrison Greene, Art Mix, Eddy Waller, Hugh Prosser, Edmund Cobb, John Tyrell, George Morrell, Kathryn Bates, Eddie Laughton, Ethan Laidlaw, Buck Moulton. Wild Bill Hickok and his pal Cannonball search for the murderer of the latter's father and they come to a small town where a girl, a witness to the crime, is being forced to marry the man who did the deed. Pretty actionful Bill Elliott film.

1423 Hang 'em High. United Artists, 1968. 114 minutes Color. D: Ted Post. SC: Leonard Freeman & Mel Goldberg. WITH Clint Eastwood, Inger Stevens, Ed Begley, Pat Hingle, Ben Johnson, Charles McGraw, Ruth White, Bruce Dern, Alan Hale, Arlene Golonka, Bob Steele, James Westerfield, Dennis Hopper, L. Q. Jones, Michael O'Sullivan, James MacArthur, Bert Freed, Russell Thorsen, Rick Gates, Bruce Scott, Tod Andrews, Roy Glenn, Paul Sorenson, Jack Ging. When a man is unjustly lynched by a group of men for a crime he did not commit, he is saved and sets out to take revenge on those who tried to kill him. Fairly successful attempt by Hollywood to imitate the feel of then-popular European oaters with a strong performance by Bob Steele as the only repentant hangman. VD: RCA/Columbia.

1424 The Hanged Man. ABC-TV, 1974. 74 minutes Color. D: Michael Caffey. SC: Ken Trevey. WITH Steve Forrest, Cameron Mitchell, Sharon Acker, Dean Jagger, Will Geer, Barbara Luna, Rafael Campos, Brendon Boone, Bobby Eilbacher, Ray Teal, Steve Marlo, John Mitchum, William Bryant, Hank Worden, John Pickard. A one-time gunfighter survives his own hanging and turns to the side of the law, coming to the aid of a woman whose silver mine is being sought by a crooked land baron. Better-than-average oater made for television.

1425 The Hanging Tree. Warner Brothers, 1959. 106 minutes Color. D: Delmer Daves. SC: Wendell Mayes & Halsted Welles. WITH Gary Cooper, Maria Schell, Karl Malden, Ben Piazza, George C. Scott, Karl Swenson, Virginia Gregg, John Dierkes, King Donovan, Slim Talbot, Guy Wilkerson, Bud Osborne, Annette Claudier, Clarence Straight. In a rough gold mining settlement, a doctor trying to forget his past falls in love with a girl he nurses back to health. Colorful, better-than-average, but not a totally successful oater, best at showing the raw frontier. Marty Robbins sings the title song.

1426 The Hangman. Paramount, 1959. 86 minutes B/W. D: Michael Curtiz. SC: Dudley Nichols. WITH Robert Taylor, Tina Louise, Fess Parker, Jack Lord, Mickey Shaughnessey, Gene Evans, Shirley Harmer, James Westerfield, Mabel Albertson, Lucille Curtis. A deputy marshal is on the trail of a wanted man and he tracks him to a small town where he finds the citizens are shielding the man. Offbeat and rather interesting oater with a solid performance by Robert Taylor as marshal.

1427 Hangman's Knot. Columbia, 1952. 84 minutes Color. D-SC: Roy Huggins. WITH Randolph Scott, Donna Reed, Claude Jarman Jr., Frank Faylen, Glenn Langan, Richard Denning, Lee Marvin, Jeanette Nolan, Clem Bevans, Ray Teal, Guinn Williams, Monte Blue, John Call, Reed Howes, Edward Earle, Post Park, Frank Hagney, Frank Yaconelli. In the closing days of the Civil War, a Confederate detachment is ordered to attack a Union outfit transporting gold, and after the successful effort the men learn the war is over and the ordering officer wanted the money for himself. Highly competent Randolph Scott vehicle with a good cast and plotline.

1428 Hannah Lee. Realart, 1953. 79 minutes Color. D-SC: John Ireland & Lee Garmes. WITH Macdonald Carey, Joanne Dru, John Ireland, Stuart Randall, Frank Ferguson, Ralph Dumke, Don Haggerty, Tom Powers, Tristram Coffin, Norman Leavitt, Peter Ireland. Cattlemen hire a notorious gunman to rid their lands of settlers but he is opposed by the local sheriff and a woman who runs the local cafe. Cheap Jack Broder production based on Mackinlay Kantor's story, the film was originally issued in 3-D. Alternate title: **Outlaw Territory.**

1429 Hannie Caulder. Paramount, 1972. 85 minutes Color. D: Burt Kennedy. SC: Z. X. Jones (Burt Kennedy & David Haft). WITH Raquel Welch, Robert Culp, Stephen Boyd, Ernest Borgnine, Jack Elam, Strother Martin, Christopher Lee, Diana Dors. A woman wants to take revenge on the murderous bank robbery gang who raped her and murdered her husband. Better than one might expect considering the plot and the star.

1430 Hard Day at Blue Nose. M.P.C./Stonehenge, 1974. 66 minutes Color. D: Herbert Kenwith. WITH John Astin, Patty Duke Astin, Philip Carey, Royal Dano. On vacation at a dude ranch in Nevada, a New York detective gets involved in solving the murder of a woman guest. Obscure feature which has had three late night playdates on ABC-TV.

1431 Hard Hombre. Allied, 1931. 65 minutes B/W. D: Otto Brower. SC: Jack Natteford. WITH Hoot Gibson, Lina Basquette, Skeeter Bill Robbins, Mathilde Comont, Jessie Arnold, Raymond Nye, Christian Frank, Jack Byron, Bob Burns, Glenn Strange, Tiny Sanford. When crooks threaten his mother's property a cowboy comes to her rescue. Typically fanciful Hoot Gibson vehicle.

1432 The Hard Man. Columbia, 1957. 80 minutes Color. D: George Sherman. SC: Leo Katcher. WITH Guy Madison, Valerie French, Lorne Greene, Barry Atwater, Robert Burton, Rudy Bond, Trevor Bardette, Rickie Sorenson, Frank Richards, Myron Healey, Renata Vanni. While investigating the murder of a rancher who had refused to sell out to a cattle baron, a deputy marshal finds himself falling in love with the murdered man's widow. Somewhat offbeat oater with a psychological tinge; entertaining.

1433 A Hard Road to Vengeance. NBC-TV/Universal, 1973. 98 minutes Color. WITH Richard Boone, Stuart Whitman, Ruth Roman, Keenan Wynn, Rita Moreno, Harry Morgan, Rick Lenz, Sharon Acker. A one-time lawman comes to a small town to clear his name of a thirteen-year-old murder charge. Telefilm which was originally an episode of producer Jack Webb's "Hec Ramsey" (NBC-TV, 1972-74) series and originally telecast November 25, 1973.

1434 Hard Rock Harrigan. Fox, 1935. 70 minutes B/W. D: David Howard. SC: Raymond L. Schrock & Dan Jarrett. WITH George O'Brien, Irene Hervey, Fred Kohler, Dean Benton, Frank Rice, Victor Potel, Olin Francis, William Gould, George Humbert, Edward Keane, Lee Shumway, Glenn Strange, Jack Kirk, Lee Phelps, Curley Dresden. Two tunnel drillers find they are in love with the same girl and fight to win her affections. Solid entertainment with George O'Brien, based on the Zane Grey story. Alternate title: **Hardrock Harrigan.**

1435 Hardcase. ABC-TV, 1972. 74 minutes Color. D: John Llewellyn Moxey. SC: Harold Jack Bloom & Sam Rolfe. WITH Clint Walker, Stefanie Powers, Pedro Armendariz Jr., Alex Karras, Luis Mirando, Martin LaSalle, E. Lopez Rojas. A drifter returns home to find his ranch has been sold and his wife has disappeared. He runs across a gang of Mexican revolutionaries and finds her with its leader. Well directed and not-too-bad oater considering its plot.

1436 Harlem on the Prairie. Associated Features, 1938. 54 minutes B/W. D: Sam Newfield. SC: Fred Myton & Flourney E. Miller. WITH Herb Jeffries, Flourney E. Miller, Mantan Moreland, Connie Harris, Maceo Sheffield, William Spencer Jr., George Randall, Nathan Curry, The Four Tones, Edward Brandon, James Davis, The Four Blackbirds. A black cowboy tries to stop a crooked Los Angeles cop from cheating club owners. Interesting curio, and one of a trio of all-black features starring Herb Jeffries; worth a look. Alternate title: **Bad Man of Harlem.**

1437 Harlem Rides the Range. Hollywood Pictures, 1939. 58 minutes B/W. D: Richard C. Kahn. SC: Spencer Williams & F. E. Miller. WITH Herb Jeffries, Spencer Williams, Lucius Brooks, F. E. Miller, Artie Young, Clarence Brooks, Tom Southern, The Four Tunes, John Thomas. A cowboy tries to stop a crook from getting control of his girl's father's radium mine. All-black Western starring crooner Herb Jeffries. V: Budget Video.

1438 The Harmony Trail. Walt Mattox, 1944. 57 minutes B/W. D: Robert Emmett (Tansey). SC: Frances Kavanaugh. WITH Ken Maynard, Max Terhune, Eddie Dean, Rocky Camron (Gene Alsace), Ruth Roman, Glenn Strange, Robert McKenzie, Charles King, Bud Osborne, Dan White, Hal Price. A lawman calls on three pals to aid him in capturing a gang who robbed the local bank. Ken Maynard's last "B" film is a low budget but fairly interesting affair in which Eddie Dean croons "On the Banks of the Sunny San Juan" (which he cowrote with Glenn Strange). Reissued in 1947 by Astor as **White Stallion.**

1439 Harpoon. Screen Guild, 1948. 83 minutes B/W. D: Ewing Scott. SC: Girard Smith & Ewing Scott. WITH John Bromfield, Alyce Louis, James Cardwell, Patricia Garrison, Jack George, Edgar Hinton, Frank Hagney, Holly Bane, Ruth Castle, Grant Means, Sally Davis, Alex Sharp, Lee Roberts, James Martin, Willard Jillson, Gary Garrett. In the 1880s in Alaska a young man seeks revenge against his father's enemies. Okay action drama.

1440 Harry Tracy—Desperado. IMC/Isram, 1982. 100 minutes. D: William A. Graham. SC: David Lee Henry. WITH Bruce Dern, Helen Shaver, Michael C. Gwynne, Gordon Lightfoot. Harry Tracy, known as a friend of the poor and as a gallant toward women, finds himself becoming a legendary outlaw and relentlessly hunted by the law. Fairly entertaining biopic filmed in Canada.

1441 The Harvey Girls. Metro-Goldwyn-Mayer, 1946. 101 minutes Color. D: George Sidney. SC: Edmund Beloin & Nathaniel Curtis. WITH Judy Garland, John Hodiak, Ray Bolger, Preston Foster, Angela Lansbury, Virginia O'Brien, Kenny Baker, Marjorie Main, Chill Wills, Cyd Charisse, Selena Royle, Jack Lambert, Ruth Brady, Edward Earle, Morris Ankrum, William "Bill" Phillips, Ben Carter, Norman Leavitt, Horace (Stephen) McNally, Catherine McLeod, Virginia Hunter, Mitchell Lewis, Jack Clifford, Vernon Dent, Robert Emmett O'Connor, Paul Newlan. Westward expansion brings railroad restaurants to various communities and the waitresses bring civilization to the areas' inhabitants. Dated musical best remembered for the song "On the Atchinson, Topeka and the Santa Fe," which was popularized on record by Kate Smith.

1442 Hate for Hate. Metro-Goldwyn-Mayer, 1968. 79 minutes Color. D: Domenico Paolella. SC: Bruno Corbucci & Fernando Di Leo. WITH Antonio Sabato, John Ireland, Fernando Sancho, Gloria Milland, Mirko Ellis, Nadia Marconi. In the Southwest two men join forces to escape to Mexico with gold sought after by a Mexican revolutionary leader. Another well made but violent oater from Italy, issued there in 1967 by West Film as **Odio Per Odio** (Hate for Hate).

1443 The Haunted. A. B. Enterprises/ International Film Industries, 1977. 85 minutes Color. D-SC: Michael De Gaetano. WITH Virginia Mayo, Aldo Ray, Jim Negele, Ann Michelle. A family in Arizona's Superstition Mountain finds itself haunted by the spirit of a dead Indian woman who places a vengeful spirit in the body of their young daughter. Somewhat obscure gothic/Western tale worth viewing for stars Virginia Mayo and Aldo Ray. V: Direct Video.

1444 Haunted Gold. Warner Brothers, 1932. 58 minutes B/W. D: Mack V. Wright. SC: Adele Buffington. WITH John Wayne, Sheila Terry, Erville Alderson, Harry Woods, Otto Hoffman, Martha Mattox, Blue Washington, Slim Whitaker, Jim Corey, Ben Corbett, Bud Osborne. A young man and his friend go to a deserted mine in the desert which was half-owned by his father, and they find a spooky situation with the partner's daughter there along with crooks who are after hidden gold. The "Cat and the Canary" of "B" Westerns, this film is well done and atmospheric with footage from Ken Maynard's silent **The Phantom City** (First National, 1928), of which it is a remake. Trivia buffs: the statue of the Maltese Falcon appears in one scene where heroine Sheila Terry plays the organ. V: Video Connection, Cassette Express.

1445 The Haunted Mine. Monogram, 1951. 60 minutes B/W. D: Derwin Abrahams. SC: Frank Young. WITH Johnny Mack Brown, Raymond Hatton, Linda Johnson, Riley Hill, Claire Whitney, John Merton, Marshall Reed, Terry Frost, Lynton Brent, Ray Bennett, Frank LaRue, Ray Jones. Crooks are out to steal a mine from its lady owners and a U. S. marshal is called in to find out who has been murdering those interested in the property. A mystery background adds some flavor to this otherwise pedestrian oater.

1446 Haunted Ranch. Monogram, 1943. 57 minutes B/W. D: Robert Tansey. SC: Elizabeth Beecher. WITH John King, David Sharpe, Max Terhune, Julie Duncan, Rex Lease, Charles King, Bud Osborne, Budd Buster, Steve Clark, Glenn Strange, Tex Palmer, Fred "Snowflake" Toones, Carl Mathews, Jimmie Aubrey, Hank Bell, Jim Corey. The Range Busters come to the aid of a girl whose ranch is being besieged by crooks who are after a hidden treasure. Spooky atmosphere adds some life to this "Range Busters" effort. V: Blackhawk, Cassette Express.

1447 Haunted Trails. Monogram, 1949. 60 minutes B/W. D: Lambert Hillyer. SC: Adele Buffington. WITH Whip Wilson, Andy Clyde, Reno Browne, Dennis Moore, I. Stanford Jolley, Myron Healey, John Merton, Mary Gordon, William Ruhl, Steve Clark, Milburn Morante, Eddie Majors, Bud Osborne, Bill Potter, Carl Mathews, Thornton Edwards, Chuck Roberson, Carol Henry, Ben Corbett. A man is on the trail of outlaws who murdered his brother and finds the gang trying to take control of a ranch using an imposter to pose as the late owner's brother. One of the best in the Whip Wilson series.

1448 Have a Good Funeral My Friend. Flora Film, 1971. 90 minutes Color. D: Anthony Ascott. SC: G. Simonelli & Gianviti. WITH John (Gianni) Garko, Antonio Vilar, Daniela Giordano, Ivano Staccioli, Helga Line, Luis Hinduni, Franco Pesce, Rick Boyd, George Wang, Franco Ressel. A gunman arrives in a small town looking for a swindler and finds the man's niece is being beset by two prominent townsmen who are after a vein of gold discovered by her uncle. Fairly interesting spaghetti oater in the popular "Sartana" series. Italian title: **Buono Funerale, Amigos!...Paga Sartana** (A Good Funeral, Friends!...Sartana is Paying).

1449 Hawaiian Buckaroo. 20th Century-Fox/Principal, 1938. 60 minutes B/W. D: Ray Taylor. SC: Dan Jarrett. WITH Smith Ballew, Evelyn Knapp, Harry Woods, Benny Burt, George Regas, Carl Stockdale, Pat O'Brien, Fred "Snowflake" Toones. A crooked realtor sells a cowboy some worthless ranch land in Hawaii and the man is then forced to take a job on a girl's ranch. The Hawaiian setting (the movie was made in California) makes this "B" effort a bit different but the plot is pretty mundane.

The Hawk see **The Phantom of Santa Fe**

1450 The Hawk of Powder River. Eagle Lion/Producers Releasing Corporation, 1948. 54 minutes B/W. D: Ray Taylor. SC: George Smity. WITH Eddie Dean, Roscoe Ates, Jennifer Holt, June Carlson, Eddie Parker, Terry Frost, Lane Bradford, Carl Mathews, Ted French, Steve Clark, Tex Palmer, Charles King, Marshall Reed, Andy Parker & The Plainsmen. A cowboy and his pal find themselves at odds with an outlaw gang led by "The

Hawk," who turns out to be a beautiful woman. Despite footage from earlier Eddie Dean features, this film was one of the star's better later PRC starring efforts and Jennifer Holt is quite good in the villainous title role.

1451 Hawk of the Hills. Pathe, 1927. 10 Chapters B/W. D: Spencer Gordon Bennet. SC: George Arthur Gray. WITH Allene Ray, Walter Miller, Frank Lackteen, Paul Panzer, Wally Oettel, Jack Pratt, Jack Ganzhorn, Parks Jones, Fred Dana, Evangeline Russell, George Magrill, Chief White Horse. A notorious Montana outlaw raids mining claims but one of his gang betrays him to protect a pretty girl the badman plans to murder. Fun filled action-mystery silent cliffhanger.

1452 Hawk of the Wilderness. Republic, 1938. 12 Chapters B/W. D: William Witney & John English. SC: Barry Shipman, Rex Taylor & Norman Hall. WITH Herman Brix (Bruce Bennett), Mala, Monte Blue, Jill Martin, Noble Johnson, William Royle, Tom Chatterton, George Eldredge, Patrick J. Kelly, Dick Wessel, Fred "Snowflake" Toones. On a lost island north of the Bering Strait, a young man, the son of a dead explorer, tries to save the natives who raised him from murderous treasure seekers. Extremely actionful and entertaining Republic serial. Re-edited 100 minute TV feature version: **Lost Island of Kioga.**

1453 The Hawk of Wild River. Columbia, 1952. 54 minutes B/W. D: Fred F. Sears. SC: Howard J. Green. WITH Charles Starrett, Smiley Burnette, Jack (Jock) Mahoney, Clayton Moore, Eddie Parker, Jim Diehl, Lane Chandler, Syd Saylor, John Cason, LeRoy Johnson, Jack Carry, Sam Flint, Donna Hall. Two government men are sent to a small town to stop the lawlessness caused by a gang led by "The Hawk," a desperado using a bow and arrow. Fast moving "Durango Kid" series film.

1454 Hawmps!. Mulberry Square, 1976. 113 (126) minutes Color. D: Joe Camp. SC: William Bickley, Michael Warren & Joe Camp. WITH James Hampton, Christopher Connelly, Slim Pickens, Jack Elam, Denver Pyle, Gene Conforti, Mimi Maynard, Lee deBroux, Herbert Vigran, Jesse Davis, Frank Inn, Mike Travis, Larry Swartz, Tiny Wells, Dick Drake, Henry Kendrick, Don Starr, Cynthia Smith, Roy Gunzburg, Rex Janssen, Catherine Hearne, Larry Strawbridge, James Weir, Alvin Wright, Lee Tiplitsky, Joey Camp, Perry Martin, Richard Lundin, Charles Starkey. A remote Army post is chosen as the training ground for the use of camels as mounts in the desert. Fairly amusing genre spoof; well made. V: Children's Video Library.

1455 He Rides Tall. Universal, 1964. 84 minutes B/W. D: R. G. Springsteen. SC: Charles W. Irwin & Robert Creighton Williams. WITH Tony Young, Dan Duryea, Jo Morrow, Madlyn Rhue, R. G. Armstrong, Joel Fluellen, Carl Reindel, Mickey Simpson, George Murdock, Michael Carr, George Petrie, Bob Steele. On the eve of his wedding a marshall must tell his foster-father that he was forced to gun down his son. Fairly good dramatic Western which is held together by Dan Duryea's smooth performance as the villain.

1456 Headin' East. Columbia, 1937. 67 minutes B/W. D: Ewing Scott. SC: Ethel LaBlanche & Paul Franklin. WITH Buck Jones, Ruth Coleman, Donald Douglas, Elaine Arden, Shemp Howard, Earle Hodgins, John Elliott, Stanley Blystone, Frank Faylen, Dick Rich, Al Herman, Harry Lash. When gangsters try to take advantage of lettuce growers a rancher comes to the big city to stop them. Somewhat out-of-the-ordinary Buck Jones vehicle but of interest to his followers.

1457 Headin' for God's Country. Republic, 1937. 78 minutes B/W. D: William Morgan. SC: Elizabeth Meehan & Houston Branch. WITH William Lundigan, Virginia Dale, Harry Davenport, Harry Shannon, Addison Richards, J. Frank Hamilton, Eddie Acuff, Wade Crosby, Skelton Knaggs, John Bleifer, Eddy Waller, Charlie Lung, Ernie Adams, Eddie Lee, James B. Leong, Anna Q. Nilsson. To get even with the people in an Alaskan village, a prospector tells them the U. S. is at war. Fairly interesting "B" outing; topical when issued.

1458 Headin' for the Rio Grande. Grand National, 1936. 60 minutes B/W. D: Robert North Bradbury. SC: Robert Emmett (Tansey). WITH Tex Ritter, Eleanor Stewart, Warner Richmond, Syd Saylor, Snub Pollard, Charles King, Earl Dwire, Forrest Taylor, William Desmond, Charles K. French, Bud Osborne, Budd Buster, Tex Palmer, Jack C. Smith, Sherry Tansey, Jim Mason, Ed Cassidy. A cowboy brings a wounded cattleman into a town controlled by an outlaw and is promptly jailed for murder. Tex Ritter's second feature is good and he sings songs, including the title tune and "Night Herding Song." V: Cumberland Video.

Morgan, Ray Middleton, R. G. Armstrong, Robert Pratt, Dick Van Patten, Perry Lopez, Dennis Rucker, Bill Vint. An aging gunfighter at the turn of the century agrees to work as the deputy to a young, college-trained lawman. Okay pilot to the "Hec Ramsey" (NBC-TV, 1972-74) which starred Richard Boone in the title role. Alternate TV title: **The Century Turns.**

1476 Heir to Trouble. Columbia, 1935. 59 minutes B/W. D: Spencer Gordon Bennet. SC: Nate Gatzert. WITH Ken Maynard, Joan Perry, Harry Woods, Wally Wales, Martin Faust, Harry Brown, Dorothy Wolbert, Fern Emmett, Pat O'Malley, Art Mix, Frank Yaconelli, Hal Price, Frank LaRue, Jim Corey, Lafe McKee, Jack Rockwell, Slim Whitaker, Bud McClure, Artie Ortego. When he adopts the small son of his late saddle pal, a cowboy runs into trouble with a rival who wants to steal his girl as well as his mining property. Fair Ken Maynard vehicle but a bit slim on coherent plot.

1477 Heldorado. Republic, 1946. 54 (70) minutes B/W. D: William Witney. SC: Gerald Geraghty & Julian Zimet. WITH Roy Rogers, George "Gabby" Hayes, Dale Evans, Paul Harvey, Rex Lease, LeRoy Mason, Eddie Acuff, Bob Nolan & The Sons of the Pioneers, Clayton Moore, Steve Darrell, Doye O'Dell, Charles Williams, John Bagni, Barry Mitchell. In Las Vegas ranger Roy Rogers joins the local sheriff and government investigators in trying to track down racketeers passing thousand dollar bills which have not been subject to taxes. Better than average Roy Rogers entry for the mid-1940s period.

1478 Hell Bent for Leather. Universal-International, 1960. 82 minutes Color. D: George Sherman. SC: Christopher Knopf. WITH Audie Murphy, Felicia Farr, Stephen McNally, Robert Middleton, Rad Fulton, Jan Merlin, Herbert Rudley, Malcolm Atterbury, Allan Lane, John Qualen, Bob Steele, Eddie Little Sky. A man is ambushed by a wanted murderer and ends up being arrested by a reward-hungry sheriff who claims he is the real wanted killer. Fair Audie Murphy vehicle.

1479 Hell Canyon Outlaws. Republic, 1957. 72 minutes B/W. D: Paul Landres. SC: Allan Kaufman & Max Glandbard. WITH Dale Robertson, Brian Keith, Rossana Rory, Dick Kallman, Don Megowan, Mike Lane, Buddy Baer, George Pembroke,

Tom Hubbard. A sheriff is forced to take on an outlaw gang which has taken control of a small town. Actionful oater from Republic's last days.

1480 Hell-Fire Austin. Tiffany, 1932. 70 minutes B/W. D: Forrest Sheldon. SC: Betty Burbridge. WITH Ken Maynard, Ivy Merton, Nat Pendleton, Jack Perrin, Charles LeMayne, Lafe McKee, Allan Roscoe, William Robyns, Fargo Bussey, Jack Rockwell, Jack Ward, Bud McClure, Lew Meehan, Ben Corbett, Slim Whitaker, Jim Corey, Jack Pennick. Two men return home to Texas after World War I and receive a poor welcome, eventually landing in jail. They are paroled when one agrees to ride a horse in a cross-country race. Well written and actionful Ken Maynard vehicle; good entertainment. V: Discount Video.

Hell Town see **Born to the West**

1481 The Hellbenders. Avco-Embassy, 1967. 92 minutes Color. D: Sergio Corbucci. SC: Albert Band & Ugo Liberatore. WITH Joseph Cotten, Norma Bengell, Julian Mateos, Aldo Sambrell, Angel Aranda, Gino Pernice, Claudio Gora, Maria Martin. Following the Civil War a Confederate colonel refuses to accept the South's defeat and he attempts to form an army to continue the war. Highly actionful but statical Italian oater with a fine performance by Joseph Cotten as the madman colonel. Made in 1966 by Alba Cinematografica/Tecisa as **I Crudeli** (The Cruel Ones).

1482 Hellfire. Republic, 1949. 90 minutes Color. D: R. G. Springsteen. SC: Dorrell McGowan & Stuart McGowan. WITH William Elliott, Marie Windsor, Forrest Tucker, Jim Davis, H. B. Warner, Grant Withers, Paul Fix, Emory Parnell, Esther Howard, Jody Gilbert, Harry Woods, Denver Pyle, Trevor Bardette, Dewey Robinson, Harry Tyler, Roy Barcroft, Hank Worden, Kenneth MacDonald, Eva Novak, Richard Alexander, Louis Faust, Edward Keane. A gunman is redeemed by religion and wants to build a church but finds himself opposed by a crook as he tries to reform a woman outlaw. Exceedingly good William Elliott vehicle, the type of fare William S. Hart made in the silent days, with an excellent performance by Marie Windsor as the wanted woman.

1483 Hellgate. Lippert, 1952. 87 minutes B/W. D-SC: Charles Marquis Warren.

WITH Sterling Hayden, Joan Leslie, Ward Bond, James Arness, Peter Coe, John Pickard, Robert Wilke, Richard Emory, Marshall Bradford, Sheb Wooley, Rory Mallinson, Timothy Carey, Rodd Redwing, Stanley Price. A man is falsely sent to prison and he takes part in an aborted prison break but eventually redeems himself in the eyes of the law. Low budget, but credible, refashioning of the story of Dr. Samuel Mudd, first filmed by 20th Century-Fox in 1936 as the excellent **The Prisoner of Shark Island.**

1484 Hellhounds of the Plains. Goodwill, 1927. 60 minutes B/W. WITH Yakima Canutt, Neva Gerber, Lafe McKee, Al Ferguson, Bud Osborne, Cliff Lyons. A cowboy opposes a gang of horse thieves which is being led by his boss's renegade son. The young man also blackmails his half-sister, the girl loved by the cowboy. Low grade but fast paced Yakima Canutt silent vehicle.

1485 The Hellions. Columbia, 1961. 79 minutes Color. D: Ken Annakin. SC: Harold Swanton, Patrick Kirwan & Harold Ruth. WITH Richard Todd, Anne Aubrey, Jamie Uys, Marty Wilde, Lionel Jeffries, James Booth, Al Mulock, Colin Blakely, Ronald Fraser, Zena Walker, George Moore, Bill Brewer, Jan Bruyns, Lorna Cowell. In 1860s South African Transvaal a man and his sons arrive in a small town intent in seeking revenge against a lawman. Fairly interesting British film containing all the necessary Western plot ingredients.

1486 Hello Trouble. Columbia, 1932. 67 minutes B/W. D-SC: Lambert Hillyer. WITH Buck Jones, Lina Basquette, Wallace MacDonald, Spec O'Donnell, Ruth Warren, Otto Hoffman, Ward Bond, Frank Rice, Russell Simpson, Alan Roscoe, Al Smith, King Baggott, Bert Roach, Walter Brennan, Morgan Galloway. A Texas Ranger on the trail of a trio of cattle rustlers kills one of them and then finds out it is his friend and he quits the service, only to get involved in finding the killer of a rancher friend. Somewhat slow moving and erratic Buck Jones vehicle, but still solid entertainment.

1487 Hell's Crossroads. Republic, 1957. 73 minutes Color. D: Franklin Adreon. SC: John K. Butler & Barry Shipman. WITH Stephen McNally, Peggie Castle, Robert Vaughn, Barton MacLane, Harry Shannon, Henry Brandon, Douglas Kennedy, Grant Withers, Myron Healey, Frank Wilcox, Jean Howell, Morris Ankrum.

A member of the James Gang wants to reform but his cohorts try to foil his efforts. Average oater with an extremely good cast.

1488 Hell's Heroes. Universal, 1930. 65 minutes B/W. D: William Wyler. SC: Tom Reed. WITH Charles Bickford, Raymond Hatton, Fred Kohler, Fritzi Ridgeway, Maria Alba, Jose de la Cruz, Buck Connors, Walter James. Three outlaws flee a posse into the desert and come across a dying woman and agree to take her newborn infant to its father. This first sound version of Peter B. Kyne's oft-filmed novel The Three Godfathers is a sturdy affair which still holds up well.

1489 Hell's Hinges. Triangle, 1915. 55 minutes B/W. D: William S. Hart & Charles Swickard. SC: C. Gardner Sullivan. WITH William S. Hart, Clara Williams, Louise Glaum, Jack Standing, Alfred Hollingsworth, Robert McKim, J. Frank Burke, Robert Kortman, Leo Willis, Jean Hersholt, John Gilbert. A crooked gambler hires a bad man to stop the work of the new town minister but the gunman falls for the clergyman's sister and tries to aid his cause. Top notch William S. Hart film; a faithful recreation of the old West with plenty of action and violence. V: Classic Video Cinema Collectors Club.

1490 Hell's Outpost. Republic, 1954. 90 minutes B/W. D: Joseph Kane. SC: Kenneth Gamet. WITH Rod Cameron, Joan Leslie, John Russell, Chill Wills, Jim Davis, Kristine Miller, Ben Cooper, Taylor Holmes, Barton MacLane, Ruth Lee, Oliver Blake. A war veteran comes to a small town determined to work his mining claim and he is opposed by a crooked banker. Rugged drama with Rod Cameron a sturdy hero and John Russell a bad, bad villain.

1491 Henry Goes Arizona. Metro-Goldwyn-Mayer, 1939. 66 minutes B/W. D: Edwin L. Marin. SC: Florence Ryerson & Milton Merlin. WITH Frank Morgan, Virginia Weidler, Guy Kibbee, Slim Summerville, Douglas Fowley, Owen Davis Jr. When a broke actor inherits his brother's ranch, a gang of outlaws tries to take it for themselves. Well made genre comedy programmer.

Hercules and the Treasure of the Incas see **Lost Treasure of the Aztecs**

1492 Heritage of the Desert. Paramount, 1932. 63 minutes B/W. D: Henry Hathaway.

SC: Harold Shumate & Frank Partos. WITH Randolph Scott, Sally Blane, J. Farrell MacDonald, David Landau, Gordon Westcott, Guinn Williams, Vince Barnett, Susan Fleming, Charles Stevens, Fred Burns. A young man, raised by a desert rancher, tries to stop a claim jumper from taking his property. Adequate screen adaptation of the Zane Grey novel, which Paramount first filmed in 1924 with Bebe Daniels, Lloyd Hughes, Ernest Torrence and Noah Beery. Reissue title: **When the West Was Young.**

1493 Heritage of the Desert. Paramount, 1939. 74 minutes B/W. D: Lesley Selander. SC: Norman Houston. WITH Donald Woods, Evelyn Venable, Russell Hayden, Robert Barrat, Sidney Toler, C. Henry Gordon, Willard Robertson, Paul Guilfoyle, Paul Fix, John Miller, Reginald Barlow. An Easterner comes West to claim an inheritance and becomes mixed up with outlaws. Very fine third screen version of the Zane Grey work.

1494 Heroes of Fort Worth. Fenix Film, 1964. 90 minutes B/W. D: Herbert Martin. SC: Eduardo Manzanos. WITH Edmund Purdom, Priscilla Steele, Paul Paget, Aurora Julia, Isarco Ravaioli, Umberto Raho, Miguel Del Castillo, Eduardo Pajardo. After the Civil War a group of Confederates head to Mexico to enlist the aid of Emperor Maximilian in restarting their cause, but they meet opposition at a Western fort. Actionful spaghetti oater with lots of historical ingredients but little fact. Issued in Italy as **La Carica Del 7 Cavalleggeri** (The Charge of the Seventh).

1495 Heroes of the Alamo. Columbia, 1938. 74 minutes B/W. D: Harry S. Fraser. SC: Ruby Wentz. WITH Earle Hodgins, Lane Chandler, Rex Lease, Roger Williams, Ed Piel Sr., Julian Rivero, Jack C. Smith, Bruce Warren, Ruth Findlay, Lee Valianos, William Costello, Steve Clark, Sherry Tansey, Denver Dixon, George Morrell, Tex Cooper, Oscar Gahan, Ben Corbett. Stephen Austin fights for the independence of Texas from Mexico and Texans under Colonel William Travis fight Santa Anna's army at the Alamo and are massacred, thus beginning the final drive for Texas independence. Pretty good independent film originally issued by Anthony J. Xydias' Sunset Pictures in 1937 and picked up by Columbia the next year. Alternate title: **Remember the Alamo.**

1496 Heroes of the Hills. Republic, 1938. 56 minutes B/W. D: George Sherman. SC: Betty Burbridge & Stanley Roberts. WITH Robert Livingston, Ray Corrigan, Max Terhune, Priscilla Lawson, LeRoy Mason, James Eagles, Roy Barcroft, Carleton Young, Forrest Taylor, Maston Williams, John Beach, Roger Williams, Kit Guard, Jack Kirk, Curley Dresden. The Three Mesquiteers turn their ranch into a work farm for prison trustees but when they try to get neighboring ranchers to go along with the program a crooked contractor tries to stop them. Another fine and exciting entry in Republic's "The Three Mesquiteers" series.

1497 Heroes of the Range. Columbia, 1936. 58 minutes B/W. D: Spencer Gordon Bennet. SC: Nate Gatzert. WITH Ken Maynard, June Gale, Harry Woods, Harry Ernest, Robert Kortman, Bud McClure, Tom London, Bud Osborne, Frank Hagney, Jack Rockwell, Lafe McKee, Wally Wales, Buffalo Bill Jr., Bud Jamison, Bob Reeves. A cowboy comes to the aid of a pretty girl whose brother is in the clutches of an outlaw gang. Delightfully fun Ken Maynard vehicle; this is the one where Ken tries to masquerade as an outlaw and when the crooks ask him to prove his identity he says, "I know what ye want," and proceeds to play the fiddle and sing.

1498 Heroes of the Saddle. Republic, 1940. 54 (59) minutes B/W. D: William Witney. SC: Jack Natteford. WITH Robert Livingston, Raymond Hatton, Duncan Renaldo, Patsy Lee Parsons, Loretta Weaver, Byron Foulger, Vince Barnett, William Royle, Reed Howes, Al Taylor, Kermit Maynard, Tex Terry, Matt McHugh, Harrison Greene. When money belonging to an orphanage is reported stolen, The Three Mesquiteers investigate and find the institution is being run by crooks. Modern-day setting somewhat detracts from the overall effectiveness of this oater.

1499 Heroes of the West. Universal, 1932. 12 Chapters B/W. D: Ray Taylor. SC: George Plympton, Basil Dickey, Joe Roach & Ella O'Neill. WITH Noah Beery Jr., Diane Duval (Julie Bishop), Onslow Stevens, William Desmond, Martha Mattox, Philo McCullough, Harry Tenbrook, Frank Lackteen, Edmund Cobb, Jules Cowles, Francis Ford, Grace Cunard, Chief Thunderbird. A contractor moves to Wyoming with his daughter and son to fulfill his contract to complete the transcontinental railroad, and with the aid of an engineer he opposes crooks trying to sabotage his operations. Fair Universal serial with a more interesting cast than plot. V: Cassette Express.

1500 Hex. 20th Century-Fox, 1973. 90 minutes Color. D: Leo Garen. SC: Leo Garen & Steve Katz. WITH Keith Carradine, Robert Walker, Hilarie Thompson, Tina Herazo, Scott Glenn, Gary Busey, John Carradine, Mike Combs, Doria Cook, Patricia Ann Porter. After World War I a motorcycle gang becomes involved with the occult in a small Western town, after a mysterious girl casts a spell on them. Fair combination of the horror-Western genres. Also called **Grass Lands.**

1501 Hi Gaucho! RKO Radio, 1936. 60 minutes B/W. D: Thomas Atkins. SC: Adele Buffington. WITH John Carroll, Steffi Duna, Rod LaRoque, Montagu Love, Ann Codel, Tom Ricketts, Paul Porcasi. A South American cowboy prefers a pretty Castillian senorita to taking part in a long-standing family feud. Fair comedy-action programmer.

1502 Hiawatha. Allied Artists, 1952. 80 minutes Color. D: Kurt Neumann. SC: Arthur Strawn & Dan Ullman. WITH Vincent Edwards, Yvette Dugay, Keith Larsen, Morris Ankrum, Gene Iglesias, Ian MacDonald, Stuart Randall, Katherine Emery, Stephen Chase, Armando Silvestre, Michael Tolan, Richard Bartlett, Michael Granger, Robert Bice. The chief of one Indian tribe tries to bring peace with his people's long-time foes. Walter Mirisch's production is an adaptation of Henry Wadsworth Longfellow's poem but it is on the dull side.

1503 Hidden Danger. Monogram, 1948. 55 minutes B/W. D: Ray Taylor. SC: J. Benton Cheney & Eliot Gibbons. WITH Johnny Mack Brown, Raymond Hatton, Max Terhune, Christine Larson, Myron Healey, Marshall Reed, Kenne Duncan, Edmund Cobb, Steve Clark, Milburn Morante, Carol Henry, Bill Hale, Boyd Stockman, Bill Potter, Bob Woodward. A crook heading a cattlemen's protective group persuades local ranchers to sell cattle to him but he pays less than the market price and his activities are soon opposed by a lawman. Last Johnny Mack Brown series entry with Raymond Hatton; average.

1504 Hidden Gold. Universal, 1932. 60 minutes B/W. D: Arthur Rosson. SC:

Jack (John) Natteford & James Milhauser. WITH Tom Mix, Judith Barrie, Raymond Hatton, Eddie Gribbon, Donald Kirke, Wallis Clark, Roy Moore. A cowboy goes to jail to get in good with an outlaw gang who has hidden the loot from a robbery. This is not one of Tom Mix's better sound films.

1505 Hidden Gold. Paramount, 1940. 54 (61) minutes B/W. D: Lesley Selander. SC: Jack Mersereau & Gerald Geraghty. WITH William Boyd, Russell Hayden, Britt Wood, Ruth Rogers, Roy Barcroft, Minor Watson, Ethel Wales, Lee Phelps, George Anderson, Jack Rockwell, Eddie Dean, Raphael Bennett, Walter Long, Robert Kortman, Merrill McCormack. Hopalong Cassidy becomes the foreman of a ranch and is at odds with a crook who wants to steal a gold mine from a man who was once his outlaw partner. Pretty fair outing in the Hoppy series. V: Video Connection.

1506 Hidden Guns. Republic, 1956. 66 minutes B/W. D: Albert C. Gannaway. SC: Sam Roeca & Albert C. Gannaway. WITH Richard Arlen, Bruce Bennett, John Carradine, Faron Young, Angie Dickinson, Lloyd Corrigan, Damian O'Flynn, Irving Bacon, Tom Hubbard, Guinn Williams, Edmund Cobb, Ben Welden, Gordon Terry, Bill Coontz, Ron Kennedy. A sheriff and his son try to save their small town from a crooked gambler, his henchman and their hired killers. Fairly good "B" outing with nice work from the trio of veteran stars.

1507 Hidden Valley. Monogram, 1932. 60 minutes B/W. D: Robert North Bradbury. SC: Wellyn Totman. WITH Bob Steele, Gertrude Messinger, Francis McDonald, Ray Haller, John Elliott, Arthur Miller, V. L. Barnes, Dick Dickinson, George ("Gabby") Hayes, Tom London, Captain Verner L. Smith. A cowboy is at odds with a gang of crooks searching for a treasure hidden in a peaceful valley. Pretty good Bob Steele vehicle with a mystery plot plus some dirigible sequences.

1508 Hidden Valley Outlaws. Republic, 1944. 56 minutes B/W. D: Howard Bretherton. SC: John K. Butler & Bob Williams. WITH Bill Elliott, George "Gabby" Hayes, Anne Jeffreys, Roy Barcroft, Kenne Duncan, John James, Charles Miller, Budd Buster, Tom London, LeRoy Mason, Earle Hodgins, Yakima Canutt, Fred "Snowflake" Toones, Jack Kirk, Tom

183 The High Country

Steele, Bud Geary, Frank McCarroll, Ed Cassidy, Robert Wilke, Cactus Mack, Forbes Murray, Frank O'Connor. A vicious outlaw gang terrorizes a small town in the southwest but a marshal comes to the rescue. Fast moving and highly entertaining "Wild Bill" Elliott film.

1509 The High Country. Crown-International, 1981. 101 minutes Color. D: Harvey Hart. SC: Bud Townsend. WITH Timothy Bottoms, Linda Purl, George Sims, Bill Berry, Jim Lawrence, Walter Mills, Paul Jolicoeur, Dick Butler, Elizabeth Alderton, Barry Graham, John Duthie, Marsha Stonehouse. An escaped convict persuades an illiterate girl to take him into Alberta's high country in order to elude the law. Fair drama but nothing exceptional. V: Vestron Video.

1510 High Country Pursuit. Dove Cinema, 1981. 90 minutes Color. SC: R. Jon Emr. WITH Stuart Whitman, Ben Johnson, Will Sampson, Slim Pickens, Amy Botwinick, Dale Robinette. Two rugged men and an Indian warrior team to find the men who stole their women. Actionful and colorful pursuit film with nice locales.

1511 High Hell. Paramount, 1958. 87 minutes B/W. D: Burt Balaban. SC: Irene Tunich. WITH John Derek, Elaine Stewart, Patrick Allen, Jerold Wells, Al Mulock, Rodney Burke, Colin Croft, Nicholas Stuart. A man reaches his mountain mine and finds his wife there with his partner. The three are soon snowed in for the winter. Brooding, British-made melodrama.

1512 High Lonesome. Eagle Lion, 1950. 81 minutes Color. D-SC: Alan LeMay. WITH John Barrymore Jr., Chill Wills, Lois Butler, Christine Miller, John Archer, Basil Ruysdael, Jack Elam, Dave Kashner. A young man becomes involved with two escaped convicts out to commit a murder. Fairly involved psychological melodrama.

1513 High Noon. United Artists, 1952. 84 minutes B/W. D: Fred Zinneman. SC: Carl Foreman. WITH Gary Cooper, Thomas Mitchell, Lloyd Bridges, Katy Jurado, Grace Kelly, Otto Kruger, Lon Chaney, Henry (Harry) Morgan, Ian MacDonald, Eve McVeagh, Harry Shannon, Lee Van Cleef, Robert Wilke, Sheb Wooley, Tom London, Ted Stanhope, Larry Blake, William Phillips, Jeanne Blackford, William Newell, Lucien Prival, Guy Beach, Howland Chamberlin, Morgan Farley, Virginia

Christine, Virginia Farmer, Jack Elam, Paul Dubov, Harry Harvey, Tim Graham, Nolan Leary, Tom Greenway, Dick Elliott, John Doucette. On the eve of his marriage, a veteran marshall must face three killers without the aid of the town's citizens. Classic Western drama with a number of excellent performances; still, the film would be slow indeed if it were not for Tex Ritter's singing of the title song. V: Blackhawk.

1514 High Noon, Part Two: The Return of Will Kane. CBS-TV, 1980. 100 minutes Color. D: Jerry Jameson. WITH Lee Majors, David Carradine, Pernell Roberts, J. A. Preston, Michael Pataki, Katherine Cannon, Britt Leach, Frank Campanella, M. Emmet Walsh. An ex-lawman, now a rancher, protects a man wanted by a marshal and is forced to take up his guns to defend the man. Average TV followup to the classic **High Noon** (q.v.).

1515 High Plains Drifter. Universal, 1973. 105 minutes Color. D: Clint Eastwood. SC: Ernest Tidyman. WITH Clint Eastwood, Verna Bloom, Marianna Hill, Mitchell Ryan, Jack Ging, Stefan Gierasch, Ted Hartley, Billy Curtis, Geoffrey Lewis, Walter Barnes, Paul Brinegar, Dan Vadis, Jack Kosslyn, Belle Mitchell, John Mitchum, Pedro Regas. A gunman is hired by the citizens of a small town to protect them against a gang of killers but they begin to wonder if their new sheriff is really mortal. Fairly entertaining oater which seems to be a cross between the spaghetti Westerns from Europe and a genre spoof. V: CIC Video, MCA.

1516 High Voltage. Pathe, 1929. 60 minutes B/W. D: Howard Higgin. SC: James Gleason & Kenyon Nicholson. WITH William Boyd, Owen Moore, Carol(e) Lombard, Diane Ellis, Billy Bevan, Phillips Smaley. During a snowstorm, bus passengers are marooned in a small church in the High Sierras and one of them, a girl going to jail, falls for a lineman who is actually a wanted man. Although disliked by the critics when first issued this early talkie holds up rather well.

1517 High, Wide and Handsome. Paramount, 1937. 112 minutes B/W. D: Rouben Mamoulian. SC: Oscar Hammerstein II. WITH Irene Dunne, Randolph Scott, Dorothy Lamour, Elizabeth Patterson, Raymond Walburn, Akim Tamiroff, Charles Bickford, Ben Blue, William Frawley, Alan Hale, Irving Pichel, Stanley Andrews, James Burke, Roger Imhof, Lucien Littlefield, Purnell B. Pratt, Edward Gargan. A circus star marries an oil driller and they become involved with farmers in Pennsylvania in 1859 who try to save their oil lands from the railroads. Big budget musical which is on the bland side.

The Highwayman Rides see **Billy the Kid** (1930)

1518 Hills of Oklahoma. Republic, 1950. 67 minutes B/W. D: R. G. Springsteen. SC: Olive Cooper & Victor Arthur. WITH Rex Allen, Fuzzy Knight, Elizabeth Fraser, Elizabeth Risdon, Roscoe Ates, Rex Lease, Robert Karns, Robert Emmett Keane, Trevor Bardette, Lee Phelps, Edmund Cobb, Ted Adams, Lane Bradford, Johnny Downs, Michael Carr. Rustlers try to steal a cattle herd being led to market by the head of the cattleman's protective group. Average entry in Rex Allen's series for Republic.

1519 Hills of Old Wyoming. Paramount, 1937. 54 (79) minutes B/W. D: Nate Watt. SC: Maurice Geraghty. WITH William Boyd, George ("Gabby") Hayes, Russell Hayden, Gail (Ann) Sheridan, Stephen Morris (Morris Ankrum), Clara Kimball Young, Earle Hodgins, Steve Clemente, Chief Big Tree, John Beach, George Chesebro, Jim Mason. Hoppy, Windy and Lucky oppose crooks trying to blame Indians for rustling cattle. Colorful "Hopalong Cassidy" feature with plenty of action and the lovely title song later associated with Eddie Dean. Russell Hayden's first film in the series in the role of Lucky Jenkins.

1520 The Hills of Utah. Republic, 1951. 70 minutes B/W. D: John English. SC: Gerald Geraghty. WITH Gene Autry, Pat Buttram, Elaine Riley, Onslow Stevens, Denver Pyle, Donna Martell, William Fawcett, Harry Lauter, Tom London, Kenne Duncan, Sandy Sanders, Teddy Infuhr, Lee Morgan, Boyd Stockman, Stanley Price, Bob Woodward, Tommy Ivo, Billy Griffith. A frontier doctor arrives in a small town to find out who killed his father and becomes embroiled in a feud between a local mine operator and ranchers. Entertaining Gene Autry vehicle with more emphasis on drama than songs. V: Blackhawk.

1521 The Hills Run Red. United Artists, 1967. 89 minutes Color. D: Lee W. Beaver (Carlo Lizzani). SC: Dean Craig (Mario Pierotti). WITH Thomas Hunter, Henry Silva, Dan Duryea, Nando Gazzolo, Nicoletta Machiavelli, Gianna Serra, Loris Loddi, Geoffrey Copleston, Paolo Magalotti, Tiberio Mitri, Vittorio Bonos, Mirko Valentin. A mysterious gunman comes to the aid of a former prisoner who is out to get his ex-partner who sent him to jail and then kept the payroll money they had possessed. Fast moving and violent Italian oater held together by Dan Duryea's work as the gunslinger. Issued in Europe in 1966 as **Un Fiume Di Dollari** (A River of Dollars).

Hired Gun see **The Last Gunfighter**

1522 The Hired Gun. Metro-Goldwyn-Mayer, 1957. 64 minutes B/W. D: Ray Nazarro. SC: David Lang & Buckley Angell. WITH Rory Calhoun, Anne Francis, Vincent Edwards, John Litel, Chuck Connors, Robert Burton, Guinn Williams, Reg Parton. A lawman bringing a young woman back to a small town to hang for a murder becomes convinced of her innocence and tries to find the real killer. Compact and entertaining little drama.

1523 The Hired Man. Universal, 1971. 98 minutes Color. D: Peter Fonda. SC: Alan Sharp. WITH Peter Fonda, Warren Oates, Verna Bloom, Robert Pratt, Severn Darden, Ted Markland, Rita Rogers, Megan Denver. After being away from home for seven years a man returns to work for his ex-wife and daughter and then sets out to free a buddy being held prisoner by outlaws. Uneven drama which is fairly well acted.

1524 His Brother's Ghost. Producers Releasing Corpration, 1945. 50 minutes B/W. D: Sam Newfield. SC: George Plympton. WITH Buster Crabbe, Al St. John, Charles King, Karl Hackett, Archie Hall, Frank McCarroll, Bud Osborne, Bob Cason, Roy Brent, George Morrell. After being ambushed by outlaws, a man sends for his lookalike and after his death the bad men see the impersonator and think it is the man's ghost. Typical cheap "Billy Carson" series entry slightly distinguished by Al St. John's work in a dual role, showing how good he could be in a dramatic part. V: Cumberland Video.

1525 His Fighting Blood. Ambassador, 1935. 60 minutes B/W. D: John English. SC: Joseph O'Donnell. WITH Kermit Maynard, Polly Ann Young, Paul Fix, Ben Hendricks Jr., Ted Adams, Joseph Girard, Frank LaRue, John McCarthy, Frank O'Connor, Charles King, Jack

Cheatham, Ed Cecil, Theodore (Ted) Lorch, The Singing Constables. When his brother takes part in a crime, a man goes to jail for him but the latter gets in with a gang and the brother, who becomes a Mountie upon his release, sets out to stop the outlaws. Pretty fair Kermit Maynard actioner featuring two songs by a group called The Singing Constables, made up of Glenn Strange, Chuck Baldra and Jack Kirk, traditional genre bad guys.

1526 Hit and Run. Universal, 1924. 45 minutes B/W. D: Edward Sedgwick. SC: Edward Sedgwick & Raymond L. Schrock. WITH Hoot Gibson, Marion Harland, Cyril Ring, Harold Goodwin, DeWitt Jennings, Mike Donlin, William A. Steele. A baseball player from a desert town is signed by a major team and he romances the team's scout's daughter, and he and the girl are kidnapped by crooks out to fix the world series. Pleasant comedy combinations of the Western film and baseball; for Hoot Gibson fans.

1527 Hit the Saddle. Republic, 1937. 54 (61) minutes B/W. D: Mack V. Wright. SC: Oliver Drake. WITH Robert Livingston, Ray Corrigan, Max Terhune, Rita (Hayworth) Cansino, Yakima Canutt, J. P. McGowan, Ed Cassidy, Sammy McKim, Harry Tenbrook, Robert Smith, Ed Boland, Jack Kirk, George Plues, Robert Smith, Bob Burns, Russ Powell, Alan Cavan, George Morrell, Budd Buster, Kernan Cripps. The Three Mesquiteers have a falling out when Stony falls for a gold-digging fandango dancer but they reunite to fight a gang rustling wild horses in a protected area. Average entry in the popular "The Three Mesquiteers" series. V: Cassette Express.

1528 Hitched. NBC-TV/Universal, 1973. 73 minutes Color. D: Boris Sagal. SC: Richard Alan Simmons. WITH Sally Field, Tim Matheson, Neville Brand, Slim Pickens, John Fiedler, Denver Pyle, John McLiam, Kathleen Freeman, Don Knight, Bo Svenson, Bill Zuckert, Charles Lane. A couple of newly married youngsters out West find themselves the victims of a crooked scheme. Sub-par TV movie, sequel to **Lock, Stock and Barrel** (q.v.).

1529 Hittin' The Trail. Grand National, 1937. 58 minutes B/W. D: Robert North Bradbury. SC: Robert Emmett (Tansey). WITH Tex Ritter, Jerry Bergh, Tommy Bupp, Earl Dwire, Jack C. Smith, Heber Snow (Hank Worden), Ed Cassidy, Snub Pollard, Archie Ricks, Charles King, Ray Whitley & The Range Ramblers, Tex Ritter's Tornados, Smokey (dog). A cowboy innocently becomes involved with rustlers and is arrested and to prove his innocence he sets out to capture the gang. Okay Tex Ritter yarn although the series was beginning to show signs of excess economic measures by this time. Tex Ritter sings a half-dozen songs, including "Blood on the Saddle."

Hi-Yo Silver see **The Lone Ranger** (1938)

1530 Hoedown. Columbia, 1950. 64 minutes B/W. D: Ray Nazarro. SC: Barry Shipman. WITH Eddy Arnold, Jeff Donnell, Jock (Mahoney) O'Mahoney, Guinn Williams, Carolina Cotton, Fred F. Sears, Don C. Harvey, Charles Sullivan, Douglas Fowley, Ray Walker, Harry Harvey, The Pied Pipers, The Oklahoma Wranglers (The Willis Brothers). A cowboy film star comes to a dude ranch and finds bank robbers are hiding there. Fun country music-Western musical with a good job by Jock Mahoney as the cowboy hero.

1531 Hollywood Barn Dance. Screen Guild, 1947. 72 minutes B/W. D: Bernard B. Ray. SC: Dorothy Knox Martin. WITH Ernest Tubb, Helen Royce, Earle Hodgins, Frank McGlynn, Dotti Hackett, Pat Combs, Jack Guthrie, Phil Arnold, Cyril Ring. When a country band accidentally burns down the hometown church where they are rehearsing, they go on the road to earn the money to rebuild the house of worship and get mixed up with a crooked promoter and his pretty daughter. Cheap musical made to cash-in on Ernest Tubb's popularity.

1532 Hollywood Cowboy. RKO Radio, 1937. 65 minutes B/W. D: Ewing Scott. SC: Dan Jarrett & Ewing Scott. WITH George O'Brien, Cecilia Parker, Maude Eburne, Joe Caits, Frank Milan, Charles Middleton, Lee Shumway, Walter De Palma, Al Hill, William Royle, Al Herman, Frank Hagney, Dan Wolheim, Slim Balch, Sid Jordan, Lester Dorr, Harold Daniels. While taking a vacation in a small Western town, a cowboy film star becomes aware of local ranchers being cheated by the local protective association and he tries to right the wrong. Very good George O'Brien vehicle with a nice mixture of comedy and action. Reissue and TV title: **Wings Over Wyoming.** V: Thunderbird.

1533 Hollywood Round-Up. Columbia, 1937. 63 minutes B/W. D: Ewing Scott.

A Holy Terror

SC: Joseph Hoffman & Monroe Shaff. WITH Buck Jones, Helen Twelvetrees, Grant Withers, Shemp Howard, Dickie Jones, Eddie Kane, Monty Collins, Warren Jackson, Lester Dorr, Lee Shumway, Edward Keane, George Beranger. A stuntman is fired because of the jealousy of the film's star and he gets a job with another movie company but ends up a fall guy when they rob the local bank. Pretty fair Buck Jones vehicle with some nice kidding of the Hollywood scene.

1534 A Holy Terror. Fox, 1931. 53 minutes B/W. D: Irving Cummings. SC: Ralph Brock. WITH George O'Brien, Sally Eilers, Rita LaRoy, James Kirkwood, Humphrey Bogart, Stanley Fields, Robert Warwick, Richard Tucker, Earl Pinegree. When his father is murdered in Wyoming a polo-playing playboy heads West to find the culprits. Entertaining George O'Brien vehicle based on a Max Brand story.

1535 Hombre. 20th Century-Fox, 1967. 110 minutes Color. D: Martin Ritt. SC: Irving Ravetch & Harriet Frank Jr. WITH Paul Newman, Fredric March, Richard Boone, Diane Cilento, Cameron Mitchell, Barbara Rush, Margaret Blye, Peter Lazer, Martin Balsam, Skip Ward, Frank Silvera, Val Avery, David Canary. A white man, raised by the Apaches, learns to dislike his fellow passengers aboard a stagecoach but when they are attacked by outlaws he is forced to defend them. Average psychological action melodrama. V: Blackhawk.

1536 Home from the Hill. Metro-Goldwyn-Mayer, 1960. 150 minutes Color. D: Vincent Minnelli. SC: Harriet Frank Jr. & Irving Ravetch. WITH Robert Mitchum, Eleanor Parker, George Peppard, George Hamilton, Everett Sloane, Luana Patten, Anne Seymour, Constance Ford, Ken Renard, Ray Teal, Guinn Williams, Charlie Briggs, Hilda Haynes, Denver Pyle, Dan Sheridan, Orville Sherman, Dub Taylor, Stuart Randall, Tom Gilson, Rev. Duncan Gray Jr., Joe Ed Russell, Burt Mustin. A wealthy Texas land baron is estranged from his wife and illegitimate son and is hunted by a man who thinks he seduced his young daughter. Powerful psychological melodrama with an excellent performance by Robert Mitchum as the rich landowner.

1537 Home in Oklahoma. Republic, 1946. 54 (72) minutes B/W. D: William Witney. SC: Gerald Geraghty. WITH Roy Rogers, George "Gabby" Hayes, Dale Evans, Carol Hughes, George Meeker, Arthur

Space, Frank Reicher, Claire Carleton, Bob Nolan & The Sons of the Pioneers, Lanny Rees, Ruby Dandridge. A rancher is murdered and his fortune is left to a young boy, and Roy Rogers and a newspaper woman try to find the killer. An exciting and well directed film with a good mystery angle.

1538 Home in Wyomin'. Republic, 1942. 54 (67) minutes B/W. D: William Morgan. SC: Robert Tasker & M. Coates Webster. WITH Gene Autry, Smiley Burnette, Fay McKenzie, Olin Howlin, Chick Chandler, Joe Strauch Jr., Forrest Taylor, James Seay, George Douglas, Charles Lane, Hal Price, Bud Geary, Ken Cooper, Jean Porter, James McNamara, Kermit Maynard, Rex Lease, Roy Butler, Billy Benedict, Cyril Ring, Spade Cooley, Ted Mapes, Jack Kirk, William Kellogg, Betty Farrington, Tom Hanlon, Lee Shumway. Gene Autry becomes involved in helping the owner of a rodeo straighten out his wayward son. Good Gene Autry opus enhanced by a mystery angle and based on a story by detective fiction master Stuart Palmer.

1539 Home on the Prairie. Republic, 1939. 54 (58) minutes B/W. D: Jack Townley. SC: Arthur Powell & Paul Franklin. WITH Gene Autry, Smiley Burnette, June Storey, George Cleveland, Jack Mulhall, Walter Miller, Gordon Hart, Hal Price, Earle Hodgins, Ethan Laidlaw, John Beach, Jack Ingram, Bob Woodward, Sherven Brothers Rodeoliers. Crooks cause a girl's ranch to be quarantined by placing their own sick cattle on the place while they try to ship the rest of the diseased herd to market before the hoof-and-mouth disease is discovered. Standard Gene Autry entry.

1540 Home on the Range. Paramount, 1935. 54 minutes B/W. D: Arthur Jacobson. SC: Ethel Doherty & Grant Garrett. WITH Jackie Coogan, Randolph Scott, Evelyn Brent, Dean Jagger, Addison Richards, Fuzzy Knight, Howard Wilson, Phillip Morris, Albert Hart, Allen Wood, Richard Carle, Ralph Remley, C. L. Sherwood, Clara Lou Sheridan, Francis Sayles, Jack Clark, Joe Morrison, Alfred Delcambre. A gang of crooks are out to shoot a valuable racing pony belonging to two brothers. Surprisingly inferior adaptation of Zane Grey's Code of the West.

1541 Home on the Range. Republic, 1946. 55 minutes Color. D: R. G. Springsteen. SC: Betty Burbridge. WITH Monte Hale, Adrian Booth, Bob Nolan & The Sons of the Pioneers, Bobby Blake, LeRoy Mason, Roy Barcroft, Kenne Duncan, Tom Chatterton, Budd Buster, Jack Kirk, John Hamilton. A rancher wants to protect the wildlife in his area and his ideas place him at odds with local cattlemen. Monte Hale's first starring effort is only average.

1542 The Homesteaders. Allied Artists, 1953. 60 (62) minutes B/W. D: Lewis D. Collins. SC: Sol Theil & Milton Raison. WITH Bill Elliott, Robert Lowery, Barbara Allen, George Wallace, Emmett Lynn, Buzz Henry, Rick Vallin, Stanley Price, William Fawcett, James Seay, Tom Monroe, Ray Walker. Crooks are after a wagon train carrying dynamite for the Army and the two Oregon homesteaders leading the train stop them. Well above average "B" outing; well done.

1543 Homesteaders of Paradise Valley. Republic, 1947. 54 (59) minutes B/W. D: R. G. Springsteen. SC: Earle Snell. WITH Allan Lane, Bobby Blake, Martha Wentworth, Ann Todd, Gene (Roth) Steutenroth, John James, Mauritz Hugo, Emmett Vogan, Milton Kibbee, Tom London, Edythe Elliott, George Chesebro, Ed Cassidy, Jack Kirk, Herman Hack. When homesteaders try to build a dam in their new valley home they are opposed by two brothers. Average entry in the "Red Ryder" series.

1544 Hondo. Warner Brothers, 1953. 83 minutes Color. D: John Farrow. SC: James Edward Grant. WITH John Wayne, Geraldine Page, Ward Bond, Michael Pate, James Arness, Rodolfo Acosta, Leo Gordon, Tom Irish, Lee Aaker, Paul Fix, Rayford Barnes. An ex-gunman in the Southwest comes across a widow and her small son living on a ranch about to be attacked by Indians. Fine psychological oater mixed with action and nicely adapted from the Louis L'Amour story.

1545 Hondo and the Apaches. Metro-Goldwyn-Mayer, 1967. 85 minutes Color. D: Lee H. Katzin. SC: Andrew J. Fenady. WITH Robert Taylor, Ralph Taeger, Kathie Browne, Randy Boone, Michael Rennie, Noah Beery, Gary Clarke, Gary Merrill, John Smith, Buddy Foster, Michael Pate, Victor Lundin, Jim Davis, Steve Marlo, John Pickard, William Bryant. A loner takes an assignment from the army to keep peace with the Indians and becomes involved with a mine owner

who meets the son he has never seen. Issued abroad theatrically, this telefeature was the pilot for the TV series "Hondo" (ABC-TV, 1967).

1546 Honeychile. Republic, 1951. 89 minutes Color. D: R. G. Springsteen. SC: Jack Townley & Charles E. Roberts. WITH Judy Canova, Eddie Foy Jr., Alan Hale, Walter Catlett, Roy Barcroft, Claire Carleton, Karolyn Grimes, Brad Morrow, Leonid Kinsky, Fuzzy Knight, Gus Schilling, Irving Bacon, Roscoe Ates, Ida Moore, Sarah Edwards, Emory Parnell, Dick Elliott, Dick Wessell. A song publisher thinks the tune written by a hick girl was actually done by a famous composer. Typical Judy Canova outing for her fans; others beware.

1547 The Honkers. United Artists, 1972. 101 minutes Color. D: Steve Ihnat. SC: Steve Ihnat & Stephen Lodge. WITH James Coburn, Lois Nettleton, Slim Pickens, Anne Archer, Jim Davis, Joan Huntington, Richard Anderson, Ramon Bieri, Ted Eccles, Mitchell Ryan, Wayne McLaren, John Harmon, Richard O'Brien, Pitt Herbert, Larry Mahan, Chuck Henson, Jerry Gatlin. A once-famous rodeo star tries to make a comeback to impress his son and rewin his estranged wife. Actionful but not very involving character study.

1548 Honky Tonk. Metro-Goldwyn-Mayer, 1941. 105 minutes B/W. D: Jack Conway. SC: Marguerite Roberts & John Sanford. WITH Clark Gable, Lana Turner, Claire Trevor, Frank Morgan, Marjorie Main, Albert Dekker, Chill Wills, Henry O'Neill, John Maxwell, Morgan Wallace, Douglas Wood, Betty Blythe, Hooper Atchley, Harry Worth, Veda Ann Borg, Dorothy Granger, Sheila Darcy, Cy Kendall, Erville Alderson, John Farrell, Don Barclay, Ray Teal, Esther Muir, Ralph (Francis X. Jr.) Bushman, Art Miles, Anne O'Neal, Russell Hicks, Henry Roquemore, Lew Harvey. The nice daughter of the town drunk falls in love with a crooked gambler who has taken over a small Western town. Big budget vehicle for Clark Gable and Lana Turner is only average screen fare.

1549 Honky Tonk. NBC-TV/Metro-Goldwyn-Mayer, 1974. 74 minutes Color. D: Don Taylor. SC: Douglas Heyes. WITH Richard Crenna, Stella Stevens, Will Geer, Margot Kidder, John Dehner, Geoffrey Lewis, Gregory Sierra, Robert Casper, Dub Taylor, Dennis Fimple, John Quade,

Richard Evans, Richard Stahl. A con man comes to Nevada in the 1880s to take advantage of the gold strikes in the various boom towns. Fairly good reworking of the 1941 theatrical release; made-for-television.

1550 Honor of the Mounted. Monogram, 1932. 60 minutes B/W. D-SC: Harry Fraser. WITH Tom Tyler, Cecilia Ryland, Francis McDonald, Charles King, Tom London, Stanley Blystone, William Dyer, Arthur Millet, Gordon (DeMain) Wood, Theodore (Ted) Lorch. A Mountie is blamed for a crime but proves his innocence and sets out to get the real criminal. Tom Tyler is in the north country again but the results are only passable.

1551 Honor of the Range. Universal, 1934. 61 minutes B/W. D: Alan James. SC: Nate Gatzert. WITH Ken Maynard, Cecilia Parker, Fred Kohler, James Marcus, Frank Hagney, Eddie Barnes, Franklyn Farnum, Jack Rockwell, Albert J. Smith, Slim Whitaker, Ben Corbett, Fred McKaye, Wally Wales, Jack Kirk, Hank Bell, Art Mix, Lafe McKee, Bill Patton, Bud McClure, Nelson McDowell, Pascale Perry, Blackjack Ward, Roy Bucko, Buck Bucko, Fred Burns, Jim Corey, Cliff Lyons. A sheriff is on the trail of an outlaw who is actually his crooked look-alike brother. Ken Maynard, who produced this series outing, handles the dual roles of the hero and villain quite well.

1552 Honor of the West. Universal, 1939. 58 minutes B/W. D: George Waggner. SC: Joseph West (George Waggner). WITH Bob Baker, Marjorie Bell (Marge Champion), Carleton Young, Jack Kirk, Dick Dickinson, Frank O'Connor, Reed Howes, Glenn Strange, Forrest Taylor, Murdock MacQuarrie. A sheriff on the trail of a gang of rustlers finds out his girl's brother is involved with the outlaws. Plenty of action plus some nice songs make this one of the better Bob Baker films.

1553 Hop-A-Long Cassidy. Paramount, 1935. 54 (63) minutes B/W. D: Howard Bretherton. SC: Doris Schroeder. WITH William Boyd, James Ellison, Paula Stone, Kenneth Thompson, Robert Warwick, Charles Middleton, Frank McGlynn Jr., George ("Gabby") Hayes, Jim Mason, Frank Campeau, Ted Adams, Willie Fung, Franklyn Farnum, John Merton, Wally West. The foreman of the Bar 20 ranch, Hopalong Cassidy, tries to find out who

is behind a series of rustling attempts as his boss tries to keep his water rights. Initial entry in the "Hopalong Cassidy" series is a leisurely effort, short on action but entertaining with a very fine performance by George "Gabby" Hayes. Reissued as **Hopalong Cassidy Enters** by Screen Guild. TV title: **Hopalong Cassidy Enters.**

Hopalong Cassidy Enters see Hop-A-Long Cassidy

1554 Hopalong Cassidy Returns. Paramount, 1936. 54 (71) minutes B/W. D: Nate Watt. SC: Harrison Jacobs. WITH William Boyd, George ("Gabby") Hayes, Gail (Ann) Sheridan, Evelyn Brent, Stephen Morris (Morris Ankrum), William Janney, Irving Bacon, Grant Richards, John Beck, Ernie Adams, Al St. John, Ray Whitley. After his editor friend is ambushed and killed Hoppy takes over as sheriff of a small town and finds himself at odds with a female saloon owner, whose life he saved, and who wants to control the town for the gold in a nearby mine. One of the very best in the "Hopalong Cassidy" series with a good story, cast, locations and some very fine camera angles.

Hopalong Enters see Hop-A-Long Cassidy

1555 Hopalong Rides Again. Paramount, 1937. 54 (67) minutes B/W. D: Lesley Selander. SC: Norman Houston. WITH William Boyd, George ("Gabby") Hayes, Russell Hayden, William Duncan, Lois Wilde, Billy King, Nora Lane, Harry Worth, John Rutherford, Ernie Adams, Frank Ellis, John Beach, Artie Ortego, Ben Corbett. A rustler uses the guise of a professor hunting dinosaur bones in order to steal Bar 20 cattle. Fairly actionful entry in the "Hopalong Cassidy" series with a good scene of a wagon buried by an avalanche.

1556 Hoppy Serves a Writ. United Artists, 1943. 69 minutes B/W. D: George Archainbaud. SC: Gerald Geraghty. WITH William Boyd, Andy Clyde, Jay Kirby, Victor Jory, George Reeves, Jan Christy, Hal Taliaferro, Forbes Murray, Byron Foulger, Earle Hodgins, Roy Barcroft, Ben Corbett, Robert Mitchum, Art Mix. Hopalong Cassidy arrives in Mesa City in order to stop a murder and gets involved with a gang of rustlers and their corrupt boss. Pretty good entry in the "Hopalong Cassidy" series featuring a good scrap between Hoppy and villain Victor Jory. V: Cumberland Video.

189   Hoppy's Holiday

1557 Hoppy's Holiday. United Artists, 1947. 54 (60) minutes B/W. D: George Archainbaud. SC: J. Benton Cheney, Bennett Cohen & Ande Lamb. WITH William Boyd, Andy Clyde, Rand Brooks, Andrew Tombes, Jeff Corey, Mary Ware, Leonard Penn, Donald Kirk, Holly Bane, Gil Patrick, Frank Henry. While in town for a celebration, California accidentally is given loot stolen in a robbery and Hoppy sets out to find the real criminals after his pal is arrested for the crime. Only average entry in the "Hopalong Cassidy" series which does contain a neat climax of the outlaws using a horseless carriage for a getaway.

1558 Horizons West. Universal, 1952. 81 minutes Color. D: Budd Boetticher. SC: Louis Stevens. WITH Robert Ryan, Julia (Julie) Adams, Rock Hudson, John McIntire, Judith Braun, Raymond Burr, James Arness, Frances Bavier, Dennis Weaver, Tom Powers, Rodolfo Acosta, John Hubbard, Douglas Fowley, Walter Reed, Raymond Greenleaf, Tom Monroe, Dan White, John Harmon, Robert Bice, Dan Moore, Mae Clarke, Alberto Morin, Peter Mamakos, Eddie Parker, Monte Montague, Forbes Murray, Buddy Roosevelt. Two brothers return from the Civil War and one becomes a sheriff while the other takes to a life of crime. So-so oater which is well acted.

A Horse Called Comanche see **Tonka**

1559 The Horse Soldiers. United Artists, 1959. 119 minutes Color. D: John Ford. SC: John Lee Mahin & Martin Rackin. WITH John Wayne, William Holden, Constance Towers, Althea Gibson, Hoot Gibson, Anna Lee, Russell Simpson, Stan Lee, Carleton Young, Basil Ruysdael, Willis Bouchey, Ken Curtis, O. Z. Whitehead, Judson Pratt, Denver Pyle, Strother Martin, Hank Worden, Walter Reed, Jack Pennick, Fred Graham, Chuck Hayward, Charles Seel, Stuart Holmes, Major Sam Harris, Richard Cutting, Bing Russell, William Leslie, Ron Haggerty, William Forrest, Fred Kennedy, Bill Henry, Dan Borzage. During the Civil War a Union outfit, led by two feuding leaders, makes a daring move into the Confederacy to cut communication lines. Big budget production which will satisfy fans of John Wayne and William Holden; Hoot Gibson has a nice supporting role.

1560 Horsemen of the Sierras. Columbia, 1949. 56 minutes B/W. D: Fred F. Sears. SC: Barry Shipman. WITH Charles Starrett,

Smiley Burnette, Lois Hall, Tommy Ivo, T. Texas Tyler, John Dehner, Jason Robards, Dan Sheridan, Jock (Mahoney) O'Mahoney, George Chesebro, Al Wyatt. While trying to find out who murdered a government surveyor, an undercover agent gets involved in a feud between two families. Standard "Durango Kid" drama.

1561 Hostile Country. Lippert, 1950. 61 minutes B/W. D: Thomas Carr. SC: Ron Ormond & Maurice Tombragel. WITH Jimmie (James) Ellison, Russell Hayden, Fuzzy Knight, Raymond Hatton, Betty (Julie) Adams, Tom Tyler, George J. Lewis, John Cason, Stanley Price, Bud Osborne, Dennis Moore, George Chesebro, Stephen Carr, Jimmie Martin, I. Stanford Jolley, Ray Jones, J. Farrell MacDonald. Shamrock and Lucky come to a territory for Shamrock to take over half-interest in his stepfather's ranch and they get involved in a range feud. Some interesting camera work highlights this better-than-average entry in the James Ellison-Russell Hayden series for Lippert; the film still is not very interesting although John Cason and Tom Tyler are good as the villainous Brady boys. TV title: **Outlaw Fury.**

1562 Hostile Guns. Paramount, 1967. 91 minutes Color. D: R. G. Springsteen. SC: Steve Fisher & Sloan Nibley. WITH George Montgomery, Yvonne De Carlo, Tab Hunter, Brian Donlevy, John Russell, Leo Gordon, Robert Emhardt, Pedro Gonzales Gonzales, James Craig, Richard Arlen, Emile Meyer, Donald Barry, Fuzzy Knight, William Fawcett, Joe Brown, Reg Parton, Read Morgan, Eric Cody. A sheriff and his deputy lead a prison wagon through hostile country and are stalked by an outlaw gang with a score to settle with the lawman. Mediocre A. C. Lyles production which wastes its fine cast.

The Hot Horse see **Once Upon a Horse**

1563 Hot Lead. RKO Radio, 1951. 60 minutes B/W. D: Stuart Gilmore. SC: William Lively. WITH Tim Holt, Richard Martin, Joan Dixon, Ross Elliott, John Dehner, Stanley Andrews, Robert Wilke, Kenneth MacDonald, Paul Marion, Lee MacGregor, Paul E. Burns. To gain information on gold shipments, an outlaw gang substitutes one of its members in place of the local telegrapher. Average entry in the Tim Holt series for RKO.

1564 Hot Lead and Cold Feet. Buena Vista, 1978. 90 minutes Color. D: Robert Butler. SC: Joe McEveety, Arthur Alsberg & Don Nelson. WITH Jim Dale, Karen Valentine, Don Knotts, Jack Elam, Darren McGavin, John Williams, Warren Vanders, Debbie Lytton, Michael Sharrett, Dave Cass, Richard Wright, Don "Red" Barry, Jimmy Van Patten, Gregg Palmer, Ed Bakey, John Steadman, Eric Server, Paul Lukather, Hap Lawrence, Robert Rothwell, Dallas McKennon, Stanley Clements, Don Brodie, Warde Donovan, Brad Weston, Art Burke. Three brothers try to win a town in an obstacle race, opposing the dishonest activities of the community's mayor. Fair, but fast moving, Disney comedy oater.

1565 Hour of the Gun. United Artists, 1967. 101 minutes Color. D: John Sturges. SC: Edward Anhalt. WITH James Garner, Jason Robards, Robert Ryan, Albert Salmi, Charles Aidman, Steve Ihnat, Michael Tolan, Frank Converse, Sam Melville, Austin Willis, Richard Bull, Larry Gates, Karl Swenson, Bill Fletcher, Robert Phillips, Jon Voight, William Schallert, Lonnie Chapman, Monte Markham, William Windom, Edward Anhalt, Walter Gregg, David Perna, Jim Sheppard, Jorge Russek. Wyatt Earp and Doc Holliday give chase to Ike Clanton and the survivors of the gunfight at the O.K. Corral. Mediocre followup by director John Sturges to his earlier **Gunfight at the O.K. Corral** (q.v.).

1566 How the West Was Won. Metro-Goldwyn-Mayer, 1962. 162 minutes Color. D: John Ford, Henry Hathaway & George Marshall. SC: James R. Webb. WITH John Wayne, James Stewart, Gregory Peck, Carroll Baker, George Peppard, Henry Fonda, Carolyn Jones, Karl Malden, Robert Preston, Debbie Reynolds, Richard Widmark, Eli Wallach, Walter Brennan, Raymond Massey, David Brian, Agnes Moorehead, Spencer Tracy (narrator), Harry Morgan, Andy Devine, Russ Tamblyn, Ken Curtis, Lee J. Cobb, Brigid Bazlen, Mickey Shaughnessy, Lee Van Cleef, Karl Swenson, Jack Lambert, Christopher Dark, Jay C. Flippen, Joseph Sawyer, James Griffith, Claude Johnson, Walter Reed, Carleton Young, Rodolfo Acosta, Dean Stanton, Kim Charney, Bing Russell, Gene Roth, Clinton Sundberg, Walter Burke, John Larch, Edward J. McKinley, Barry Harvey, Jamie Ross, Mark Allen, Craig Duncan, Charles Briggs, Paul Bryar, Tudor Owen, Chuck Roberson, Boyd "Red" Morgan, Beulah Archuletta. The saga of western migration from the late 1830s to 1889 as seen through the eyes of three generations of pioneers. Vast, brawling story of the development of the American West which is well acted by a big cast. The best sequence is probably Henry Hathaway's "The Rivers" with Walter Brennan stealing the show as a river pirate.

1567 How the West Was Won. ABC-TV/Metro-Goldwyn-Mayer, 1977. 300 minutes Color. D: Burt Kennedy & Daniel Mann. WITH James Arness, Eva Marie Saint, Bruce Boxleitner, Anthony Zerbe, Don Murray, Brit Lind, William Kirby Cullen, Kathryn Holcomb, Vicki Schreck, Royal Dano, John Dehner, Jack Elam, David Huddleston, Robert Padilla, Richard Angarola, Bridget Hanley, Parley Baer, Paul Fix. The adventures of an Eastern family and their mountain man uncle as they try to settle in the West after the death of the family's father. This fine telefeature was originally telecast in three parts and is the followup to the popular TV feature **The Macahans** (q.v.).

1568 The Howards of Virginia. Columbia, 1940. 117 minutes B/W. D: Frank Lloyd. SC: Sidney Bochman. WITH Cary Grant, Martha Scott, Sir Cedric Hardwicke, Alan Marshal, Richard Carlson, Paul Kelly, Irving Bacon, Elizabeth Risdon, Anne Revere, Tom Drake, Phil Taylor, Rita Quigley, Libby Taylor, Richard Gaines, George Houston, Sam McDaniel, Virginia Sale, Ralph Byrd, Dickie Jones, Buster Phelps, Wade Boteler, Mary Field, R. Wells Gordon, Charles Francis, Olaf Hytten, Emmett Vogan, J. Anthony Hughes, Lane Chandler, Brandon Hurst, Alan Ladd, Pat Somerset, James Westerfield. The story of a young man who marries into a wealthy Virginia family and against his wife's wishes joins the colonial cause during the Revolutionary War. Overlong tale of the Revolution which does have an authentic look. George Houston plays George Washington.

1569 Hud. Paramount, 1963. 112 minutes B/W. D: Martin Ritt. SC: Irving Ravetch & Harriet Frank Jr. WITH Paul Newman, Melvyn Douglas, Patricia Neal, Brandon De Wilde, Whit Bissell, John Ashley, Crahan Denton, Val Avery, Sheldon Allman, Pitt Herbert, Peter Brooks, Curt Conway, Yvette Vickers, George Petrie, David Kent, Monty Montana, Carl Saxe, Sharyn Hillyer. A young man is torn between the love of his grandfather and the man's rebellious son, who he wants to emulate. Stark, well acted modern Western; for fans of such fare.

1570 Hudson's Bay. 20th Century-Fox, 1940. 95 minutes B/W. D: Irving Pichel. SC: Lamar Trotti. WITH Paul Muni, Gene Tierney, Laird Cregar, John Sutton, Virginia Field, Vincent Price, Nigel Bruce, Montagu Love, Morton Lowry, Robert Greig, Chief Thundercloud, Frederick Worlock, Ian Wolfe, Chief Big Tree, Jody Gilbert, Jean Del Val, Eugene Borden, Constant Franke, John Rogers, Reginald Sheffield. Banished to Canada, an Englishman joins forces with two French fur trappers to form the Hudson's Bay Company for the export of furs. Another in Darryl F. Zanuck's historical film series and one of the weakest and least historically accurate.

1571 Human Targets. Big 4, 1932. 55 minutes B/W. D: J. P. McGowan. SC: George Morgan. WITH Rin-Tin-Tin Jr., Buzz Barton, Francis X. Bushman Jr., Nancy Price, Tom London, Edmund Cobb, Ted Adams, Leon Kent, John Ince, Edgar Lewis, Pauline Parker, Helen Gibson, Franklyn Farnum. A young boy, a dog and a cowboy fight for a gold claim against crooks. Surprisingly well done oater from poverty row.

Hunt to Kill see **The White Buffalo**

1572 The Hunting Party. United Artists, 1971. 102 minutes Color. D: Don Medford. SC: William Norton, Gilbert Alexander & Lou Morheim. WITH Oliver Reed, Candice Bergen, Gene Hackman, Simon Oakland, Ronald Howard, Mitchell Ryan, L. Q. Jones. G. D. Spradlin, Bernard Kay, William Watson, Rayford Barnes, Ralph Brown, Marian Collier, Max Slaten, Carlos Bravo, Emilio Rodrigues, Deal Selmier, Ritchie Adams, Eugenio Escudero. An outlaw and his gang kidnap a woman thinking she is a school teacher who can teach them to read, but she turns out to be the wife of a land baron who comes after them with his men. A thin story and too much violence make this a poor viewing bet.

1573 Hurricane Horseman. Willis Kent, 1931. 50 minutes B/W. D: Armand L. Schaefer. SC: Oliver Drake. WITH Lane Chandler, Marie Quillan, Walter Miller, Yakima Canutt, Lafe McKee, Richard Alexander. A gunsmith comes to the aid of a pretty senorita held for ransom by an outlaw gang. Mediocre Lane Chandler vehicle for producer Willis Kent.

1574 Hurricane Smith. Republic, 1941. 68 minutes B/W. D: Bernard Vorhaus. SC: Robert Presnell. WITH Ray Middleton, Jane Wyatt, Harry Davenport, J. Edward Bromberg, Henry Brandon, Charles Trowbridge, Frank Darien, Howard Hickman, Emmett Vogan. When he is falsely accused of theft, a cowboy escapes and assumes a new life and marries only to find that someone from the past has recognized him. Republic's one attempt at making Ray Middleton a Western star was not a success due to a paltry script rather than the presence of Ray Middleton, who was a fine actor and singer. TV title: **Double Identity.**

I

1575 I Killed Geronimo. Eagle Lion, 1950. 63 minutes B/W. D: John Hoffman. SC: Sam Neuman & Nat Tanchuck. WITH James Ellison, Virginia Herrick, Chief Thundercloud, Smith Ballew, Dennis Moore, Ted Adams, Myron Healey, Luther Crockett, Jean Andren. An Army captain sets out to track down outlaws supplying arms to the Indians and ends up in hand-to-hand combat with Geronimo. Extremely cheap outing with little entertainment value.

1576 I Killed Wild Bill Hickok. Associated Artists/Wheeler Company, 1956. 63 minutes B/W. D: Richard Talmadge. SC: John Carpenter. WITH John (Carpenter) Forbes, Helen Westcott, Tom Brown, I. Stanford Jolley, Denver Pyle, Frank Carpenter, Virginia Gibson. A man arrives in town with his daughter to sell horses to the Army but in a gunfight the girl is killed. He sets out to get revenge by killing Wild Bill Hickok. Tiny budget outing from producer John Carpenter (who also plays the lead role of Johnny Rebel, billed as John Forbes) which seeks to prove that the legendary Wild Bill Hickok was really a bad guy who deserved his fate.

1577 I Married Wyatt Earp. NBC-TV, 1983. 100 minutes Color. D: Michael O'Herlihy. SC: I. C. Rappaport. WITH Marie Osmond, Bruce Boxleitner, John Bennett Perry, Jeffrey DeMunn, Allison Arngrim, Ross Martin, Ron Manning. A young woman arrives in the town of Tombstone and wins the love of marshal Wyatt Earp and sees him through the famed gunfight at O.K. Corral. Based on the memoirs of Josephine Marcus Earp, this TV film is just another recounting of the famed gun battle; average.

1578 I Shot Billy the Kid. Lippert, 1950. 58 minutes B.W. D: William Berke. SC: Ford Beebe & Orville Hampton. WITH Don Barry, Robert Lowery, Wally Vernon, Tom Neal, Judith Allen, Wendy Lee, Barbara Woodell, Richard Lane, Sid Nelson, Archie Twitchell, John Merton, Bill Kennedy. The story of Billy the Kid, from his first crime to the final shootout with Sheriff Pat Garrett. Don Barry is very good in the title role of this low budget but entertaining outing.

1579 I Shot Jesse James. Lippert/Screen Guild, 1949. 83 minutes B/W. D-SC: Samuel Fuller. WITH John Ireland, Preston Foster, Barbara Britton, J. Edward Bromberg, Victor Kilian, Barbara Woodell, Tom Tyler, Reed Hadley, Tommy Noonan, Byron Fougler, Eddie Dunn. The story of Bob Ford, the man who murdered Jesse James, and how his life declined after the famous incident, even to losing the girl he loves. Fairly interesting low budget entry with a fine performance by Tom Tyler as Frank James.

1580 I Will Fight No More Forever. ABC-TV, 1975. 74 minutes Color. D: Richard T. Heffron. SC: Jeb Rosebrook & Theodore Strauss. WITH James Whitmore, Ned Romero, Sam Elliott, John Kauffman, Emilio Delgado, Nick Ramus, Linda Redfearn, Frank Salsedo, Vincent St. Cyr, Delroy White. In 1877 Chief Joseph of the Nez Percés Indian tribe refuses to go to a reservation and instead tries to lead his people to Canada, but is opposed by the U.S. Army. Well done TV movie which will appeal to history buffs.

1581 Ice Palace. Warner Brothers, 1960. 143 minutes Color. D: Vincent Sherman. SC: Harry Kleiner. WITH Richard Burton, Robert Ryan, Carolyn Jones, Martha Hyer, Ray Danton, Diane McBain, Karl Swenson, Shirley Knight, Barry Kelley, Sheridan Comerate, George Takei, Steve Harris, Sam McDaniel, I. Stanford Jolley, John Bleifer, Judd Holdren. Two men battle over two women and the issue of statehood for Alaska, over several decades. There is not much to recommend this overlong soap opera except some fairly good performances.

1582 Idaho. Republic, 1943. 54 (70) minutes B/W. D: Joseph Kane. SC: Roy Chanslor & Olive Cooper. WITH Roy Rogers, Smiley Burnette, Bob Nolan & The Sons of the Pioneers, Virginia Grey, Harry Shannon, Ona Munson, Dick Purcell, Onslow Stevens, Arthur Hohl, Hal Taliaferro, Tristram Coffin, Roy Barcroft, Tom London, Rex Lease, Jack Ingram, James Bush, The Robert Mitchell Boychoir. A judge, who was once an outlaw, is blackmailed by two hoodlums and a female gambling house owner when he refuses to help them rob a bank. Good Roy Rogers series entry. V: Video Connection.

1583 The Idaho Kid. Colony, 1936. 54 minutes B/W. D: Robert F. Hill. SC: George Plympton. WITH Rex Bell, Marion Shilling, David Sharpe, Earl Dwire, Lafe McKee, Lane Chandler, Charles King, Phil Dunham, Dorothy Woods, Herman Hack, Ed Cassidy, George Morrell, Jimmie Aubrey, Sherry Tansey, Richard Botiller. A young man returns home to stop a long-time feud between his real father and the man who raised him. Nice Paul Malvern production highlighted by Rex Bell's good performance in the title role.

1584 I'm from the City. RKO Radio, 1938. 66 minutes B/W. D: Ben Holmes. SC: Nicholas T. Barrows, Robert St. Clair & John Grey. WITH Joe Penner, Lorraine Kruger, Richard Lane, Paul Guilfoyle, Kay Sutton, Ethan Laidlaw, Lafe McKee, Edmund Cobb, Katherine Sheldon. A young man, with the aid of a crooked manager, becomes a famous trick rider. Typical Joe Penner comedy from RKO and one that will satisfy his fans.

1585 In a Colt's Shadow. Warner Brothers, 1967. 86 minutes Color. D-SC: Gianni Brimaldi. WITH Stephen Forsyth, Conrado Sanmartin, Anne Sherman, Graham Sooty. Two gunmen work together but are at odds because one of them is in love with the daughter of the other one. Lots of violence and action in this dubbed Italian-Spanish coproduction. Made in Italy in 1965 as **All'ombra di una Colt.** TV title: **In the Shadow of a Colt.**

1586 In Early Arizona. Columbia, 1938. 53 minutes B/W. D: Joseph Levering. SC: Nate Gatzert. WITH Bill Elliott, Dorothy Gulliver, Harry Woods, Art Davis, Jack Ingram, Franklyn Farnum, Charles King, Ed Cassidy, Slim Whitaker, Frank Ellis, Al Ferguson, Bud Osborne, Lester Dorr, Tom London, Kit Guard, Jack O'Shea, Frank Ball, Tex Palmer, Sherry Tansey, Dick Dorrell, Oscar Gahan, Buzz Barton, Jess Cavan, Symona Boniface.

A peaceful man takes up the gun and badge in order to clean up a town controlled by outlaws. Bill Elliott's first starring series oater is a corker, with plenty of action and a good script and one of the best roundups of genre bad guys in the history of the "B" Western.

1587 In Line of Duty. Monogram, 1931. 60 minutes B/W. D: Bert Glennon. SC: G.A. Durlam. WITH Sue Carol, Noah Beery, Francis McDonald, James Murray, Richard Cramer, Frank Seider, Henry Hall. A Mountie sets out to bring a man in on a murder charge but finds out the fugitive is his girl's father. Dual biller quickie of interest mainly to fans of Northwest Mountie movies.

1588 In Old Amarillo. Republic, 1951. 67 minutes B/W. D: William Witney. SC: Sloan Nibley. WITH Roy Rogers, Estelita Rodriguez, Penny Edwards, Pinky Lee, Roy Barcroft, Pierre Watkin, Ken Howell, Elisabeth Risdon, William Holmes, Alan Bridge, Kermit Maynard, The Roy Rogers Riders. When families are hard hit by drought, Roy Rogers tries to bring in a scientific rainmaker but is opposed by a crook who wants to buy the ranchers' cattle cheap so he can start a meat packing plant. This is one of the poorer efforts by Roy Rogers from the latter part of his Republic series.

1589 In Old Caliente. Republic, 1939. 54 (57) minutes B/W. D: Joseph Kane. SC: Norman Houston & Gerald Geraghty. WITH Roy Rogers, Mary Hart, George "Gabby" Hayes, Jack LaRue, Katherine De Mille, Frank Puglia, Harry Woods, Merrill McCormack, Paul Marion, Ethel Wales. After being falsely accused of betraying his employer (a wealthy Spanish landowner) a young man joins a wagon train of immigrants and soon discovers who is trying to steal all of the landowner's cattle. Better than average Roy Rogers film enhanced by attractive seaside locations. V: Video Connection.

1590 In Old California. Republic, 1942. 88 minutes B/W. D: William McGann. SC: Gertrude Purcell & Frances Hyland. WITH John Wayne, Binnie Barnes, Albert Dekker, Helen Parrish, Patsy Kelly, Edgar Kennedy, Dick Purcell, Harry Shannon, Charles Halton, Emmett Lynn, Bob McKenzie, Milton Kibbee, Paul Sutton, Anne O'Neal, Frank McGlynn, Hooper Atchley, Jack O'Shea, Ruth Robinson, Frank Jacquet, Jack Kirk, Lynne Carver, Horace B. Carpenter, James Morton, Olin Howlin, Chester Conklin, Ralph Peters, Forrest Taylor, Richard Alexander, Donald Curtis, George Lloyd, Stanley Blystone, Slim Whitaker, Frank Ellis, Frank Hagney, Bud Osborne, Guy Usher, Minerva Urecal, Martin Garralaga, Rex Lease, Karl Hackett, Art Mix, Robert Homans, Merrill McCormack, Ed Brady. A pharmacist comes to Sacramento to set up practice but is at odds with the town boss over a girl. Rather tame John Wayne outing; not one of his better features. V: Cumberland Video, NTA Home Entertainment.

1591 In Old Cheyenne. Sono-Art/World Wide, 1931. 60 minutes B/W. D: Stuart Paton. SC: Betty Burbridge. WITH Rex Lease, Dorothy Gulliver, Jay Hunt, Harry Woods, Harry Todd, Slim Whitaker. A cowboy comes to the aid of a beautiful horse blamed for rustling activities actually carried out by a crooked ranch foreman. Cheap Rex Lease vehicle with a plot used many times, both before and after this outing.

1592 In Old Cheyenne. Republic, 1941. 54 (58) minutes B/W. D: Joseph Kane. SC: Olive Cooper. WITH Roy Rogers, George "Gabby" Hayes, Joan Woodbury, J. Farrell MacDonald, Sally Payne, William Haade, Hal Taliaferro, Billy Benedict, George Rosenor, Jack Kirk, Bob Woodward, Jim Corey, Cactus Mack, George Lloyd, Jack O'Shea, Ed Piel Sr., Merrill McCormack, Ted Mapes, Fred Burns, Ben Corbett. The New York Inquirer sends reporter Roy Rogers to Wyoming to report on a range war between cattlemen and an outlaw gang leader. A good Roy Rogers entry which has the star becoming engaged to Spanish dancer Joan Woodbury at the finale.

1593 In Old Colorado. Paramount, 1941. 54 (66) minutes B/W. D: Howard Bretherton. SC: J. Benton Cheney, Norton S. Parker & Russell Hayden. WITH William Boyd, Russell Hayden, Andy Clyde, Margaret Hayes, Morris Ankrum, Sarah Padden, Cliff Nazarro, Stanley Andrews, James Seay, Morgan Wallace, Weldon Heyburn, Glenn Strange, Eddy Waller, Philip Van Zandt, Henry Wills, Curley Dresden. Hoppy is sent to buy cattle from a woman rancher who is feuding with a fellow landowner and he soon realizes that a crook is after both spreads. Typically good "Hopalong Cassidy" entry with a fine cast, good locations and entertaining story.

In Old Los Angeles see Old Los Angeles

1594 In Old Mexico. Paramount, 1938. 54 (62) minutes B/W. D: Edward D. Venturini. SC: Harrison Jacobs. WITH William Boyd, George ("Gabby") Hayes, Russell Hayden, Paul Sutton, Allan Garcia, Jan Clayton, Trevor Bardette, Betty Amann, Glenn Strange, Anna Demetrio, Tony Roux, Fred Burns. In New Mexico, Hoppy, Lucky and Windy are after a bandit leader called "The Fox" who is leading a band of rustlers. Leisurely paced "Hopalong Cassidy" outing with nice location scenery. V: Video Communications.

1595 In Old Montana. Spectrum, 1939. 60 minutes B/W. D: Raymond K. Johnson. SC: Jackson Parks, Homer King Gordon, Raymond K. Johnson & Barney Hutchison. WITH Fred Scott, Jean Carmen, John Merton, Harry Harvey, Walter McGrail, Wheeler Oakman, Gene Howard, Frank LaRue, Allan Cavan, Jane Keckley, Richard Cramer, James Kelly, Carl Mathews. A medicine show entertainer stops to visit his dad and finds the area is in a range war between sheepherders and cattlemen. Passably good Fred Scott vehicle with several nice songs to help it along.

1596 In Old Monterey. Republic, 1939. 54 (73) minutes B/W. D: Joseph Kane. SC: Gerald Geraghty, Dorrell McGowan & Stuart McGowan. WITH Gene Autry, Smiley Burnette, George "Gabby" Hayes, June Storey, The Hoosier Hot Shots, Sarie & Sally, The Ranch Boys, Stuart Hamblen, Billy Lee, Jonathan Hole, Robert Warwick, William Hall, Eddy Conrad, Curley Dresden, Victor Cox, Ken Carson, Robert Wilke, Hal Price, Tom Steele, Jack O'Shea, Rex Lease, Edward Earle, Jim Mason, Fred Burns, Dan White Frank Ellis, Jim Corey. An army sergeant is sent West to convince ranchers and townspeople to support the army's request for land to be used for bomb maneuver practice. Patriotic actioner with Gene Autry in uniform; fairly good entertainment.

1597 In Old New Mexico. Monogram, 1945. 62 minutes B/W. D: Phil Rosen. SC: Betty Burbridge. WITH Duncan Renaldo, Martin Garralaga, Gwen Kenyon, Norman Willis, Lee "Lasses" White, Pedro de Cordoba, Frank Jacquet, Bud Osborne, Artie Ortego, Edward Earle, James Farley. The Cisco Kid and pal Pancho come to the aid of a nurse accused of murder.

Pretty fair "Cisco Kid" series entry; this is one of those films where Cisco and Pancho are redubbed as Chico and Pablo in TV prints.

In Old Oklahoma see War of the Wildcats

1598 In Old Sacramento. Republic, 1946. 89 minutes B/W. D: Joseph Kane. SC: Francis Hyland & Frank Gruber. WITH William Elliott, Constance Moore, Hank Daniels, Ruth Donnelly, Eugene Pallette, Lionel Stander, Jack LaRue, Grant Withers, Bobby Blake, Charles Judels, Paul Hurst, Victoria Horne, Dick Wessel, Hal Taliaferro, Jack O'Shea, Marshall Reed, Eddy Waller, William Haade, Boyd Irwin, Lucien Littlefield, Ethel Wales, William B. Davidson, Ellen Corby, Fred Burns, Elaine Lange. A gambler who is being hunted by vigilantes sets out to clean up the lawless element in Sacramento. Bill Elliott's first "A" film; a good one. Reissued as **Flame of Sacramento.**

1599 In Old Santa Fe. Mascot, 1934. 60 (64) minutes B/W. D: David Howard & (uncredited) Joseph Kane. SC: Colbert Clark. WITH Ken Maynard, Evelyn Knapp, H. B. Warner, Kenneth Thomson, George ("Gabby") Hayes, Gene Autry, Lester "Smiley" Burnette, Frankie Marvin, Wheeler Oakman, George Chesebro, Jack Rockwell, Jim Corey, Jack Kirk, Edward Hearn, Frank Ellis, Horace B. Carpenter, George Burton. A cowboy who races his horse for a living loses the animal in a crooked race at a dude ranch. Gangsters, out to steal the ranch owner's gold, frame him on a murder charge. Well-made and exciting Ken Maynard vehicle with a good story and plenty of action. Gene Autry is impressive in his first screen role as he sings a couple of songs as the entertainer at the dude ranch.

1600 In the Days of the Thundering Herd. Selig, 1914. 41 minutes B/W. D: Colin Campbell. SC: Gordon Willets. WITH Tom Mix, Bessie Eyton, Princess Red Wing, Wheeler Oakman, John Bowers, Major Gordon Lillie (Pawnee Bill), Sally Madison. When a cowboy and his sweetheart are captured by Indians, they are forced to fight off the whole tribe in order to gain freedom. Actionful Tom Mix silent film from his Selig days; it will please his fans but it lacks the finesse of his later Fox efforts.

In the Shadow of a Colt see In a Colt's Shadow

1601 Incident at Phantom Hill. Universal, 1966. 88 minutes Color. D: Earl Bellamy. SC: Frank Nugent. WITH Robert Fuller, Dan Duryea, Jocelyn Lane, Tom Simcox, Linden Chiles, Claude Akins, Noah Beery, Paul Fix, Denver Pyle, William Phipps, Don Collier, Mickey Finn. Two men and a girl trek through the desert in search of hidden gold and battle the elements, hostile Indians and themselves. Pretty good action thriller with an impressive performance by Dan Duryea.

1602 The Incredible Rocky Mountain Race. NBC-TV/Sunn Classics, 1977. 100 minutes Color. D: James L. Conway. SC: Tom Chapman & David O'Malley. WITH Christopher Connelly, Forrest Tucker, Larry Storch, Jack Kruschen, Mike Mazurki, Parley Baer, Whit Bissell, Bill Zuckert, Don Haggerty, Sam Edwards, Sandy Gibbon, William Kazele, John Hansen, Robert Easton, David O'Malley, Allen Wood. Long-time rivals Mark Twain and Mike Fink engage in a cross-country, no-holds-barred, race from Missouri to California. Satisfying Western spoof. V: VCI Home Video.

1603 Indian Agent. RKO Radio, 1948. 65 minutes B/W. D: Lesley Selander. SC: Norman Houston. WITH Tim Holt, Noah Beery Jr., Richard Martin, Nan Leslie, Lee "Lasses" White, Richard Powers, Harry Woods, Claudia Drake, Robert Bray, Bud Osborne, Iron Eyes Cody. A cowboy finds that a dishonest Indian agent has been selling food intended for the reservation, causing the Indians to nearly starve. Good entry in Tim Holt's RKO series.

1604 The Indian Fighter. United Artists, 1955. 88 minutes Color. D: Andre De Toth. SC: Frank Davis & Ben Hecht. WITH Kirk Douglas, Elsa Martinelli, Walter Matthau, Walter Abel, Diana Douglas, Eduard Franz, Alan Hale, Lon Chaney, Elisha Cook, Michael Winkelman, Harry Landers, William Phipps, Buzz Henry, Ray Teal, Frank Cady, Hank Worden, Lane Chandler. The leader of a wagon train gets a treaty from the local Indian chief to let his train pass peacefully through Indian lands to Oregon, but two villains soon have the Indians on the warpath. Colorful and actionful film with a rather slight plotline.

Indian Love Call see **Rose Marie** (1936)

1605 Indian Paint. Eagle-American Films/ Crown-International, 1965. 91 minutes Color. D-SC: Norman Foster. WITH Johnny Crawford, Jay Silverheels, Pat Hogan, Robert Crawford Jr., Robert Crawford Sr., George J. Lewis, Joan Hollmark. A young Indian boy tries to tame a beautiful wild horse to keep him from joining a wild herd. Okay juvenile-oriented feature.

Indian Scout see **Davy Crockett, Indian Scout**

1606 Indian Uprising. Columbia, 1952. 74 minutes Color. D: Ray Nazarro. SC: Kenneth Gamet & Richard Schayer. WITH George Montgomery, Audrey Long, Carl Benton Reid, Eugene Iglesias, Jo Baer, Joseph Sawyer, Eddy Waller, Douglas Kennedy, Robert Shayne, Miguel Inclan, Hugh Sanders, Hank Patterson, Robert Griffith, Fay Roope, Robert Dover. A cavalry captain who is facing a court-martial ends up trying to stop an Indian attack led by Geronimo. Okay action outing enhanced by Super Cinecolor.

Indio Black see **Adios, Sabata**

1607 Inside Straight. Metro-Goldwyn-Mayer, 1951. 89 minutes B/W. D: Gerald Mayer. SC: Guy Trosper. WITH David Brian, Arlene Dahl, Barry Sullivan, Mercedes McCambridge, Paula Raymond, Claude Jarman Jr., Lon Chaney, John Hoyt, Roland Winters, Barbara Billingsley, Hayden Rourke, Jerry Hartleben, Dale Hartleben, Lou Nova, Richard Hale, Percy Helton, John R. Hamilton, Marshall Bradford, Matt Moore, Cameron Grant, William Lewis, Sherry Hall, Philo Mc-Cullough, George Sherwood, Jack Shea, James Pierce, Harry Lauter, Mae Clarke, Richard Alexander, Dewey Robinson, John Bryant, Mitchell Lewis. In San Francisco in the 1870s a crooked gambler cheats everyone he can in order to become rich and then finds it all without worth. Told mostly in flashbacks, this melodrama is an adequate affair, nothing more.

1608 The Invasion of Johnson County. NBC-TV, 1976. 100 minutes Color. D: Jerry Jameson. SC: Nicholas E. Bachr. WITH Bill Bixby, Bo Hopkins, John Hillerman, Billy Green Bush, Stephen Elliott, Lee DeBroux, M. Emmet Walsh, Mills Watson, Alan Fudge, Luke Askew, Edward Winter, David Donner, Ted Gehring. When land-grabbers and their hired guns try to steal land from small ranchers, two men, an Easterner and a cowboy, team to stop them. Actionful TV movie.

1609 Invitation to a Gunfighter. United Artists, 1964. 92 minutes Color. D: Richard Wilson. SC: Elizabeth Wilson & Richard Wilson. WITH Yul Brynner, Janice Rule, Brad Dexter, Alfred Ryder, Mike Kellin, George Segal, Clifford David, Pat Hingle, Bert Freed, Curt Conway, Clifton James, Clarke Gordon, Strother Martin, Arthur Peterson. A small Western town hires a gunman to get rid of a local killer but the plan develops a surprise twist. Too much talk and not enough action in this oater.

1610 The Iron Horse. Fox, 1924. 119 minutes B/W. D: John Ford. SC: Charles Kenyon. WITH George O'Brien, Madge Bellamy, Cyril Chadwick, Fred Kohler, Gladys Hulette, James Marcus, J. Farrell MacDonald, James Welch, Walter Rogers, George Waggoner, Jack Padjan, Charles O'Malley, Charles Newton, Charles Edward Bull, Colin Chase, Delbert Mann, Chief Big Tree, Chief White Spear, Ed Piel, James Gordon, Winston Miller, Peggy Cartwright, Stanhope Wheatcroft, Frances Teague, Will Walling. A young man searches for his father's killer and ends up romancing his childhood sweetheart, the daughter of a builder of the Transcontinental Railroad. One of the truly great classic Westerns, this silent melodrama is well worth viewing. V: Classic Video Cinema Collectors Club.

1611 The Iron Mistress. Warner Brothers, 1952. 110 minutes Color. D: Gordon Douglas. SC: James Webb. WITH Alan Ladd, Virginia Mayo, Joseph Calleia, Phyllis Kirk, Alf Kjellin, Douglas Dick, Anthony Caruso, Ned Young, Don Beddoe, Robert Emhardt, Richard Carlyle, Jay Novello, George J. Lewis, Darla Massey. The story of Jim Bowie, his invention of the famous knife and his love for a girl who tries to take advantage of him. Mediocre historical drama although Virginia Mayo is quite good as the ruthless girl.

1612 Iron Mountain Trail. Republic, 1953. 54 minutes B/W. D: William Witney. SC: Gerald Geraghty. WITH Rex Allen, Slim Pickens, Nan Leslie, Grant Withers, Roy Barcroft, Alan Bridge, Forrest Taylor, George Lloyd, John Hamilton, Koko (horse). Post office inspector Rex Allen is sent to find out why mail is lost in clipper ship transportation, with a race between a stagecoach and a clipper ship being sabotaged. Nothing outstanding although henchman Roy Barcroft does have a pet monkey.

1613 The Iron Rider. Goodwill, 1926. 60 minutes B/W. D: Jacques Jaccard. WITH Yakima Canutt, Villa Vale, Elsie Benham, Jim Corey, Lee Sepulveda, Alfred Houston, Nelson McDowell, Boy (horse), Lad (dog). A cowpoke who wants to get married gets into trouble with a gambler when he is cheated out of his horse trying to win enough money to set up housekeeping. Below average silent oater which is greatly helped by good acting by star Yakima Canutt who also does a lot of fine trick riding and stunt work.

1614 The Iron Sheriff. United Artists, 1957. 73 minutes B/W. D: Sidney Salkow. SC: Seeleg Lester. WITH Sterling Hayden, Constance Ford, John Dehner, Kent Taylor, Darryl Hickman, Walter Sande, Frank Ferguson, King Donovan, Mort Mills, Peter Miller, Kathy Nolan, I. Stanford Jolley, Will Wright, Ray Walker, Bob Williams. When his son is accused of robbery and murder the local sheriff believes he is innocent and tries to prove his belief. Strong "B" Western which is well acted by a good cast.

1615 The Iroquois Trail. United Artists, 1950. 85 minutes B/W. D: Phil Karlson. SC: Richard Schayer. WITH George Montgomery, Brenda Marshall, Glenn Langan, Reginald Denny, Monte Blue, Sheldon Leonard, Paul Cavanagh, Holmes Herbert, Dan O'Herlihy, John Doucette. During the French and Indian War a scout aids the British in their attempt to wrest control of the St. Lawrence-Hudson river valleys from the French. None-too-accurate historical melodrama with more talk than action.

1616 Ishi: The Last of His Tribe. NBC-TV, 1978. 150 minutes Color. D: Robert Ellis Miller. SC: Dalton Trumbo & Christopher Trumbo. WITH Dennis Weaver, Eloy Phil Casados, Devon Erickson, Geno Silva, Joseph Running Fox, Lois Red Elk, Gregory Norman Cruz, Arliene Nofchissey Williams, Michael Medina, Peter Brandon. The story of the last Yahi Indian who was discovered by an anthropologist in northern California in 1911. Well done TV film.

1617 It Can Be Done Amigo. Atlantida/ Terzafilms, 1973. 95 minutes Color. D: Maurizio Lucidi. SC: Rafael Azcona. WITH Jack Palance, Bud Spencer, Francisco Rabal, Renato Cestie, Dany Saval. A bounty hunter and his sister pursue a man who has dishonored the girl, with the latter being put in charge of a small boy who is about to inherit a ranch which may contain oil deposits. Amusing, rambling Spanish-made oater with little bloodshed. Spanish title: **En El Oeste Se Puede Hacer...Amigo.**

1618 It Happened Out West. 20th Century-Fox, 1937. 59 minutes B/W. D: Howard Bretherton. SC: Earle Snell. WITH Paul Kelly, Judith Allen, Johnny Arthur, LeRoy Mason, Nina Compana, Steve Clemento, Frank LaRue, Reginald Barlow. Crooks try to cheat a girl out of her milk cow ranch when a silver vein is discovered on the property. Well done Sol Lesser production; an adaptation of the Harold Bell Wright novel.

1619 It's a Big Country. Metro-Goldwyn-Mayer, 1951. 89 minutes B/W. D: Richard Thorpe, John Sturges, Charles Vidor, Don Weis, Clarence Brown, William A. Wellman & Don Hartman. WITH Ethel Barrymore, Keefe Brasselle, Gary Cooper, Nancy Davis (Reagan), Van Johnson, Gene Kelly, Janet Leigh, Marjorie Main, Fredric March, George Murphy, William Powell, S. Z. Sakall, Lewis Stone, James Whitmore, Keenan Wynn, Leon Ames, Angela Clarke, Bobby Hyatt, Sharon McManus, Elisabeth Risdon, Bill Baldwin, Mickey Martin, William H. Welsh, Ned Glass, Sherry Hall, Fred Santley, Henry Sylvester, Roger Moore, Roger Cole, Harry Stanton, Benny Burt. Stories of several Americans, showing the greatness of this country, with Gary Cooper hosting a segment entitled "Texas," in which he brags about the lone star state backed by newsreel footage. Fairly entertaining family fare.

1620 The Ivory-Handled Gun. Universal, 1935. 60 minutes B/W. D: Ray Taylor. SC: John T. Neville. WITH Buck Jones, Charlotte Wynters, Walter Miller, Carl Stockdale, Frank Rice, Joseph Girard, Robert Kortman, Stanley Blystone, Lafe McKee, Lee Shumway, Charles King, Ben Corbett, Eddie Phillips, Niles Welch. Two men involved in a long-standing feud are on opposite sides when rustlers begin stealing sheep. Good Buck Jones vehicle with a surprise finale.

J

1621 J. W. Coop. Columbia, 1972. 112 minutes Color. D-SC: Cliff Robertson.

WITH Cliff Robertson, Geraldine Page, Christina Farrare, R. G. Armstrong, R. L. Armstrong, John Crawford, Wade Crosby, Marjorie Durant Dye, Paul Harper, Son Hooker, Richard Kennedy, Bruce Kirby, Claude Stroud. After a decade in prison, a one-time rodeo performer decides to return to the circuit to become the all-around cowboy, but finds the times and ways of the sport have changed. Cliff Robertson does a good job in the title role and he is equally good as the film's director and scripter.

Jack London's Klondike Fever see **Klondike Fever**

Jack London's Tales of Adventure see **Tales of Adventure**

1622 Jack McCall, Desperado. Columbia, 1953. 76 minutes Color. D: Sidney Salkow. SC: John O'Dea. WITH George Montgomery, Angela Stevens, Douglas Kennedy, James Seay, Eugene Iglesias, William Tannen, Jay Silverheels, John Hamilton, Selmer Jackson, Stanley Blystone, Gene Roth, Joe McGuinn. During the Civil War, a Southerner joins the Union army but he is framed on a charge of giving information to the enemy and is convicted of treason and sentenced to die, but escapes to find the man who framed him. Pretty good Sam Katzman production.

1623 Jack Slade. Allied Artists, 1953. 90 minutes B/W. D: Harold Schuster. SC: Warren Douglas. WITH Mark Stevens, Dorothy Malone, Barton MacLane, John Litel, Paul Langton, Harry Shannon, John Harmon, Jim Bannon, Lee Van Cleef, Ron Hargrave. A rebellious young man grows up to become a noted lawman but he eventually turns against the woman he loves and becomes a criminal. Fairly interesting account of a good man gone bad although Mark Stevens' Jack Slade must be the grimiest leading man in movie history.

1624 The Jackals. 20th Century-Fox, 1967. 93 minutes Color. D: Robert D. Webb. SC: Lamar Trotti & Austin Medford. WITH Vincent Price, Dana Ivarson, Robert Gunner, Bob Courtnet, Bill Brewer, Johnny Whitney. The gold rush in 1883 in South Africa's Transvaal area brings a quartet of bank robbers who try to steal the gold of an old prospector and his pretty granddaughter. Rather obscure South African reworking of **Yellow Sky** (q.v.) with a good performance by Vincent Price as the aged prospector.

1625 Jackass Mail. Metro-Goldwyn-Mayer, 1942. 80 minutes B/W. D: Norman McLeod. SC: Lawrence Hazard. WITH Wallace Beery, Marjorie Main, J. Carrol Naish, Dick Curtis, William Haade, Darryl Hickman, Robert Cavanaugh, Joe Yule, Esther Howard. An old-time badman is pursued by the woman owner of a mail wagon team and saloon, but escaping from a hanging party he stops a robbery and becomes a hero. Highly pleasant Wallace Beery-Marjorie Main vehicle which will delight their fans.

1626 Jaguar. Republic, 1956. 66 minutes B/W. D: George Blair. SC: John Fenton Murray & Benedict Freedman. WITH Sabu, Chiquita, Barton MacLane, Jonathan Hale, Touch (Michael) Connors, Jay Novello, Fortunio Bonanova, Nacho Galindo, Rodd Redwing, Pepe Hern. In order to keep others away from rich oil deposits, an old prospector uses the guise of a jaguar to eliminate his competitors. El cheapo programmer for which Mickey Rooney was an associate producer.

1627 The James Brothers of Missouri. Republic, 1950. 12 Chapters. D: Fred C. Brannon. SC: Royal Cole, William Lively & Sol Shor. WITH Keith Richards, Robert Bice, Noel Neill, Roy Barcroft, Patricia Knox, Lane Bradford, Gene Roth, John Hamilton, Edmund Cobb, Hank Patterson, Dale Van Sickel, Tom Steele, Lee Roberts, Frank O'Connor, Marshall Reed, Wade Ray, Nolan Leary, David Sharpe, Art Dillard, John Crawford, Post Parks, Duke Taylor, Al Ferguson, Cactus Mack, Tommy Coats, Kenneth Terrell, Robert Wilke, Forrest Burns, Herman Hack, Chick Hannon, Chuck Roberson, Bud Wolfe, Frosty Royce, Rocky Shahan. Using aliases, the James brothers join an ex-gang member's freight line and when he is murdered by rivals they agree to help his sister run the line and capture the culprits. Fair Republic cliffhanger.

1628 James Michener's Dynasty. NBC-TV, 1976. 100 minutes Color. D: Lee Phillips. SC: Sidney Carroll. WITH Sarah Miles, Stacy Keach, Harris Yulin, Harrison Ford, Amy Irving, Granville Van Dusen, Charles Weldon, Gerrit Graham, Stanley Clay, Tony Swartz, John Carter, Stephanie Faulkner, Rayford Barnes, Sari Price, Norbert Schiller, Ian Wolfe, Guy Raymond, Don Eitner, James Houghton, J. Jay Saunders, William Challee, Francis De Sales, Dennis Larson. In frontier Ohio of the 1820s a man, his wife and brother-in-law turn a family business into a financial empire. Pretty fair TV movie; well acted.

1629 Jaws of Justice. Principal, 1933. 58 minutes B/W. D: Spencer Gordon Bennet. SC: Joseph Anthony Roach. WITH Kazan (dog), Richard Terry (Jack Perrin), Ruth Sullivan, Robert Walker, Gene Tolar, Lafe McKee. In the north country a Mountie and his loyal dog team bring in an outlaw. Fast moving but poverty-stricken outdoor melodrama.

1630 The Jayhawkers. Paramount, 1959. 100 minutes Color. D: Melvin Frank. SC: Melvin Frank, Joseph Petracca, Frank Fenton & A. I. Bezzerides. WITH Jeff Chandler, Fess Parker, Nicole Maurey, Henry Silva, Herbert Rudley, Leo Gordon. An outlaw gang leader is pursued by a man determined to capture him but they both fall for the same woman. Tepid melodrama from the team of Norman Panama and Melvin Frank.

1631 Jeep Herders. Astor, 1949. 46 minutes B/W. D-SC: Richard Talmadge & Harvey Perry. WITH John Day, June Carlson, Pat Michaels, Steve Clark, Ashley Cowan, Slim Gaut, Paul Bradley, Dale Van Sickel, Tom Steele, Saul Gorss, Richard Fitch, Fred Kennedy, Frank McCarroll, Victor Metzetti. Returning home from World War II a man finds his ranch without workers—they have gone to nearby oil fields for higher wages—so he hires his war buddies from a convalescent hospital to help him run the homestead. Low-grade programmer with plenty of action and stunts. Originally issued by Planet in 1946 in 16mm.

1632 Jeepers Creepers. Republic, 1939. 67 minutes B/W. D: Frank McDonald. SC: Dorrell McGowan & Stuart McGowan. WITH The Weavers (Leon, Frank, June & Loretta), Roy Rogers, Maris Wrixon, Billy Lee, Lucien Littlefield, Thurston Hall, Johnny Arthur, Milton Kibbee, Ralph Sanford, Dan White. A backwoods family is cheated out of their land by a rich industrialist and they set out to get it back and humanize him in the process. Fun homespun programmer with the pleasing title tune and Roy Rogers as the sheriff.

1633 Jeremiah Johnson. Warner Brothers, 1972. 108 minutes Color. D: Sidney Pollack. SC: John Milius & Edward Anhalt. WITH Robert Redford, Will Geer, Stefan Gierasch, Allyn Ann McLerie, Charles

Tyner, Paul Benedict, Matt Clark, Joaquin Martinez. The story of a man who becomes a recluse in the wilderness, learning to survive against the environment and an Indian curse. Somewhat interesting adventure melodrama which is too long but will satisfy Robert Redford fans. V: Warners Home Video.

1634 Jesse James. 20th Century-Fox, 1939. 105 minutes Color. D: Henry King. SC: Nunnally Johnson. WITH Tyrone Power, Henry Fonda, Nancy Kelly, Randolph Scott, Henry Hull, Slim Summerville, J. Edward Bromberg, Brian Donlevy, John Carradine, Donald Meek, John Russell, Jane Darwell, Charles Tannen, Claire Du Brey, Willard Robertson, Paul Sutton, Ernest Whitman, Paul Burns, Spencer Charters, Arthur Aylesworth, Lon Chaney, Charles Halton, George Chandler, Erville Alderson, Harry Tyler, George Breakston, John Elliott, Virginia Brissac, Don Douglas, Ed LeSaint, Wylie Grant, Harry Holman, Ethan Laidlaw, Charles Middleton, James Flavin, George O'Hara. The story of Jesse and Frank James and how they became outlaws after their mother was ruthlessly murdered by carpetbaggers in post-Civil War Missouri. Although historically inaccurate, this is a highly entertaining, well made, and finely acted drama; recommended. In the silent days Fred Thompson also starred in a feature called **Jesse James** (Paramount, 1927).

1635 Jesse James at Bay. Republic, 1941. 54 (56) minutes B/W. D: Joseph Kane. SC: James R. Webb. WITH Roy Rogers, George "Gabby" Hayes, Sally Payne, Pierre Watkin, Hal Taliaferro, Gale Storm, Roy Barcroft, Jack Kirk, Jack O'Shea, Billy Benedict, Rex Lease, Ed Piel Sr., Jack Rockwell, Curley Dresden, Hank Bell, Fern Emmett, Budd Buster, Lloyd Ingraham, Karl Hackett, Fred Burns, Kit Guard. When the railroad and a crooked banker try to cheat farmers out of their land, the local law sends for Jesse James to help in the crisis. Entertaining historical fiction with Roy Rogers in a dual role, Jesse James and gambler Clint Burns.

1636 Jesse James Jr. Republic, 1942. 56 minutes B/W. D: George Sherman. SC: Richard Murphy, Taylor Cavan & Doris Schroeder. WITH Don "Red" Barry, Lynn Merrick, Al St. John, Douglas Walton, Robert Kortman, Kal Hackett, Lee Shumway, Stanley Blystone, Jack Kirk, George Chesebro, Frank Brownlee, Forbes Murray, Jim Corey, Kermit Maynard. A young

man tries to thwart crooks who are trying to destroy a telegraph headquarters. Fun and actionful Don Barry film with good comedy support from Al St. John. TV title: **Sundown Fury.**

1637 Jesse James Meets Frankenstein's Daughter. Embassy, 1966. 82 minutes Color. D: William Beaudine. SC: Carl K. Hittleman. WITH Estelita, John Lupton, Jim Davis, Cal Bolder, Steven Geray, Narda Onyx, Felipe Turich, Rosa Turich, Raymond Barnes, William Fawcett, Nestor Paiva, Dan White, Page Slattery, Roger Creed. A female descendant of Dr. Frankenstein uses one of the doctor's artificial brains to turn Jesse James' henchman into a monster. Poorly conceived and made Western-horror exploitation thriller issued on a double bill with **Billy the Kid vs. Dracula** (q.v.).

1638 Jesse James Rides Again. Republic, 1947. 13 Chapters B/W. D: Fred C. Brannon & Thomas Carr. SC: Franklin Adreon, Basil Dickey, Jesse Duffy & Sol Shor. WITH Clayton Moore, Linda Stirling, Roy Barcroft, John Compton, Tristram Coffin, Tom London, Holly Bane, Edmund Cobb, Gene Roth, LeRoy Mason, Ed Cassidy, Dave Anderson, Eddie Parker, Tom Steele, Dale Van Sickel, Robert Blair, Ted Mapes, Tex Terry, Gil Perkins, Tex Palmer, Emmett Lynn, Charles Morton, Duke Taylor, Monte Montague, Lee Shumway, Herman Hack, Chuck Roberson, Carl Sepulveda, Kenneth Terrell, Pascale Perry, Chester Conklin, Tommy Coats, George Chesebro, Bud Wolfe, Tom Chatterton, Charles King, Robert Riordan, Howard Mitchell, Richard Alexander, Keith Richards. Fleeing from the law for a crime he did not commit, Jesse James and a pal arrive in an area being plagued by attacks by masked raiders after oil. Rather typical later Republic cliffhanger with a good cast.

1639 Jesse James vs. The Daltons. Columbia, 1954. 65 minutes Color. D: William Castle. SC: Robert E. Kent & Samuel Newman. WITH Brett King, Barbara Lawrence, James Griffith, Bill Phillips, John Cliff, Rory Mallinson, William Tannen, Richard Garland, Nelson Leigh. Believing he is Jesse James' son, a man finds himself in a shootout with the Dalton brothers. Cheap 3-D production from Sam Katzman.

1640 Jesse James' Women. United Artists, 1954. 83 minutes Color. D: Donald Barry. SC: D. D. Beauchamp. WITH Don Barry, Jack Buetel, Peggie Castle, Lita Baron,

Joyce Rhed, Betty Brueck, Laura Lee, Sam Keller. The James gang plan to rob a small town but end up getting involved in romance. Don "Red" Barry directed and starred in this low budget hijinks which is more laughable than actionful.

1641 Jessi's Girls. Manson Distributing, 1975. 84 minutes Color. D: Al Adamson. SC: Budd Donnelly. WITH Sondra Currie, Geoffrey Land, Ben Frank, Rod Cameron, Regina Carrol, Jenifer Bishop, Ellen Stern, Joe Cortese, Jon Shank, Biff Yeager, Gavin Murrell, Rigg Kennedy, William Hammer, Hugh Warden, Joe Arrowsmith, John Durren. In 1879 newlyweds are attacked by an outlaw gang. The husband is murdered, the wife is raped, shot and left for dead, but she is rescued by an old prospector who teaches her to survive and she sets out to get revenge on the killers. Tacky and violent; Rod Cameron, as the prospector, is its only interest. Alternate title: **Wanted Woman.**

1642 Jiggs and Maggie Out West. Monogram, 1950. 66 minutes B/W. D: William Beaudine. SC: Barney Gerard & Adele Buffington. WITH Joe Yule, Renie Riano, Tim Ryan, Jim Bannon, Riley Hill, Pat Golden, June Harrison, Henry (Kulky) Kulkowich, Terry McGinnis, Billy Griffith, George McManus. Jiggs and Maggie head West when Maggie inherits a ranch and a goldmine but a crook wants the mine for himself. Pleasant screen adaptation of the long-running comic strip "Bringing Up Father" with the strip's author, George McManus, appearing as himself; good fun.

Joaquin Murieta see **Desperate Mission**

1643 Joe Dakota. Universal-International, 1957. 79 minutes Color. D-SC: Samuel Fuller. WITH Jock Mahoney, Luana Patten, Charles McGraw, Barbara Lawrence, Claude Akins, Lee Van Cleef, Anthony Caruso, Paul Birch, George Dunn, Steve Darrell, Rita Lynn, Gregg Barton, Jeanne Wood, Junie Ellis, Anthony Jochim. A man arrives in a small town where the people are cold and unfriendly. He tries to humanize them and instill respect for themselves and their community. A different kind of oater which succeeds more than it fails; Jock Mahoney is fine in the lead and the supporting cast is very good.

1644 Joe Kidd. Universal, 1972. 88 minutes Color. D: John Sturges. SC: Elmore

Leonard. WITH Clint Eastwood, Robert Duvall, John Saxon, Don Stroud, Stella Garcia, James Wainwright, Paul Koslo, Gregory Walcott, Dick Van Patten, Lynne Marta, John Carter, Pepe Hern, Chuck Hayward, Buddy Van Horn. Mexicans invade a small town and a powerful land baron hires a drifter-gunman to stop them. Another in the line of features which pushed Clint Eastwood into super stardom; a little better than mediocre.

1645 Joe Panther. Artists Creation, 1976. 110 minutes Color. D-SC: Paul Krasny. WITH Brian Keith, Ricardo Montalban, Ray Tracey, A. Martinez, Cliff Osmond, Alan Feinstein, Lois Red Elk. A young Indian brave, against great adversity, tries to make a life for himself in a modern-day world and still hold on to his Indian heritage. Okay drama.

1646 Johnny Concho. United Artists, 1956. 85 minutes B/W. D: Don McGuire. SC: David Harmon & Don McGuire. WITH Frank Sinatra, Phyllis Kirk, Keenan Wynn, Wallace Ford, William Conrad, Dorothy Adams, Christopher Dark, Howard Petrie, Harry Bartell, Willis Bouchey, Robert Osterloh, Jean Byron, Leo Gordon, Claude Akins, John Qualen, Ben Wright, Dan Russ. A cowardly bully lives in the glory of his gunman brother until the latter is killed. Then he must learn to be a man and face up to another gunfighter. Frank Sinatra is good in the title role of this otherwise average oater.

1647 Johnny Firecloud. Entertainment Ventures, 1975. 90 minutes Color. D: William A. Castleman. WITH Victor Mohica, David Canary, Frank De Kova. Returning home from the Army, an Indian finds out his ex-girlfriend's town boss father, and the local sheriff, are harassing his tribe. Low budget, little seen, modern-day oater.

1648 Johnny Guitar. Republic, 1954. 110 minutes Color. D: Nicholas Ray. SC: Philip Yordan. WITH Joan Crawford, Sterling Hayden, Scott Brady, Mercedes McCambridge, Ward Bond, Ben Cooper, Ernest Borgnine, John Carradine, Royal Dano, Frank Ferguson, Paul Fix, Rhys Williams, Ian MacDonald, Will Wright, John Maxwell, Robert Osterloh, Frank Marlowe, Trevor Bardette, Sumner Williams, Sheb Wooley, Denver Pyle, Clem Harvey. A ruthless woman who runs a saloon in a small town is reunited with her gunman ex-lover who must defend her against her enemies, including a nearby town boss and a female cattle raiser. Tough, symbolic oater is probably the only film Joan Crawford made to be lionized by the pointed-heads, but overall it is mostly on the dull side. V: Blackhawk.

1649 Johnny Hamlet. Transvue, 1972. 91 minutes Color. D: Enzo G. Castellari. SC: Bruno Corbucci, Tito Carpi & Enzo G. Castellari. WITH Chip Gorman (Andrea Giordana), Gilbert Roland, Francoise Prevost, Gabriella Grimaldi, Horst Frank, Enio Girolami, Pedro Sanchez, Stefania Careddu. A young man returns home after the Civil War only to find his father is dead and that his mother has married his uncle. Violent Italian oater which is a refashioning of William Shakespeare's tragedy "Hamlet." The feature was made in 1968 as **Quella Sporca Storia Del West** (The Dirty Story of the West) by Daiano Film/Leone Film.

Johnny Oro see **Ringo And His Golden Pistol**

1650 Johnny Reno. Paramount, 1966. 83 minutes Color. D: R. G. Springsteen. SC: Steve Fisher. WITH Dana Andrews, Jane Russell, Lon Chaney, John Agar, Lyle Bettger, Tom Drake, Richard Arlen, Tracy Olsen, Paul Daniel, Dale Van Sickle, Robert Lowery, Reg Parton, Rodd Redwing, Charles Horvath, Chuck Hicks, Edmund Cobb. A sheriff brings an accused killer of an Indian chief's son into a small town for trial but finds most of the people support the prisoner. Average A. C. Lyles production enhanced by good performances from its veteran cast.

1651 Johnny Tiger. Universal, 1966. 100 minutes Color. D: Paul Wendkos. SC: Paul Crabtree & R. John Hough. WITH Robert Taylor, Geraldine Brooks, Chad Everett, Brenda Scott, Marc Lawrence, Ford Rainey, Carol Seflinger, Steven Wheeler, Pamela Melendez, Deanna Lund. In Florida, a half-breed Seminole youth, in love with his teacher's pretty daughter, must decide whether to take over the leadership of his diminishing tribe or try a new life for himself. Cheaply made but adequate modern-day drama with a fine performance by Robert Taylor as the dedicated teacher.

1652 Johnny Tremain. Buena Vista, 1957. 80 minutes Color. D: Robert Stevenson. SC: Tom Blackburn. WITH Hal Stalmaster, Luana Patten, Jeff York, Sebastian Cabot, Richard Beymer, Walter Sande, Rusty Lane, Whit Bissell, Will Wright, Virginia Christine, Walter Coy, Geoffrey Toone, Ralph Clanton, Gavin Gordon, Lumsden Hare, Anthony Ghazlo Jr., Charles Smith. In 1773 a young silversmith's apprentice loses his job and becomes involved with the Sons of Liberty, leading to the Revolutionary War. Good Walt Disney family film filled with lots of history. V: Disney Home Video.

1653 Johnny Yuma. Clover Films, 1967. 99 minutes Color. D: Romolo Guerrieri. SC: Fernando Di Leo. WITH Mark Damon, Rosalba Neri, Lawrence Dobkin, Louis Vanner, Fidel Gonzales, Gus Harper, Leslie Daniel, Dada Gallotti, Gianni Solaro, Nando Poggi, Frank Liston. A young man inherits his uncle's ranch but finds out the man was ordered killed by his young wife. Very violent and bloody oater made in Italy in 1966.

1654 Jory. Avco-Embassy, 1972. 97 minutes Color. D: Jorge Fons. SC: Gerald Herman & Robert Irving. WITH John Marley, B. J. Thomas, Robby Benson, Brad Dexter, Claudio Brook, Ben (Benny) Baker, Patricia Aspilaga, Todd Martin, Linda Purl, Anne Lockhart, Betty Sheridan, Ted Markland. A teenage boy sets out to take revenge on the men who murdered his father and friends. Made in Mexico, this oater was issued theatrically only on an experimental basis but it is a fairly good outing which marked Robby Benson's screen debut and includes a fine performance by Benny Baker as the man behind the killings.

1655 Journey Through Rosebud. Avco-Embassy, 1972. 92 minutes Color. D: Tom Gries. SC: Albert Ruben. WITH Robert Forster, Kristoffer Tabori, Victoria Racimo, Eddie Little Sky, Roy Jenson, Wright King, Larry Pennell, Robert Kornwaithe, Steve Shemayne. A draft dodger hides from the law in an Indian reservation where he gets involved in the politics of the inhabitants and their troubles with the government. Tepid antiwar, pro-Indian feature filmed in South Dakota.

1656 Journey to Shiloh. Universal, 1968. 101 minutes Color. D: William Hale. SC: Gene Coon. WITH James Caan, Michael Sarrazin, Brenda Scott, Paul Petersen, Don Stroud, Michael Burns, Michael Vincent, Harrison Ford, John Doucette, Noah Beery, Tisha Sterling, James Gammon, Clark Gordon, Robert Pine, Wesley Lau, Chet Stratton, Bing Russell, Lane Bradford, Rex Ingram, Myron Healey,

Eileen Wesson. A group of young men in 1862 Texas head East to join the Confederate Army without any idea as to what they are fighting for or the actual meaning of war. A good premise went awry in this rambling and none-too-satisfying melodrama.

1657 Juarez. Warner Brothers, 1939. 132 minutes B/W. D: William Dieterle. SC: John Huston, Aeneas MacKenzie & Wolfgang Reinhardt. WITH Paul Muni, Bette Davis, Brian Aherne, Claude Rains, John Garfield, Donald Crisp, Gale Sondergaard, Joseph Calleia, Gilbert Roland, Henry O'Neill, Pedro de Cordoba, Montagu Love, Harry Davenport, Walter Fenner, Alex Leftwich, Robert Warwick, John Miljan, Irving Pichel, Walter Kingsford, Monte Blue, Louis Calhern, Vladimir Sokoloff, Georgia Caine, Hugh Sothern, Fred Malatesta, Carlos de Valdez, Frank Lackteen, Bill Wilkerson, Frank Reicher, Holmes Herbert, Egon Brecher, Mickey Kuhn, Noble Johnson, Martin Garralaga, Grant Mitchell, Charles Halton. The story of the rise of Mexican revolutionary leader Benito Juarez, during the time Louis Napoleon tried to establish Maximilian as the emperor of Mexico. Overlong and basically boring, mainly due to Paul Muni's stoical performance as Juarez, although Bette Davis and Brian Aherne are fine as Carlotta and Maximilian.

1658 Jubal. Columbia, 1956. 101 minutes Color. D: Delmer Daves. SC: Russell S. Hughes & Delmer Daves. WITH Glenn Ford, Ernest Borgnine, Rod Steiger, Valerie French, Felicia Farr, Basil Ruysdael, Noah Beery Jr., Charles Bronson, John Dierkes, Jack Elam, Robert Burton, Robert Knapp, Juney Ellis, Don C. Harvey, Guy Wilkerson, Larry Hudson, Mike Lawrence, Buzz Henry. A man is forced to shoot his best friend when falsely accused of having an affair with the man's wife, but finds love with a religious girl who hides him from a posse. Taut psychological oater which is of interest due to its cast rather than its steamy plot.

1659 Jubilee Trail. Republic, 1954. 103 minutes Color. D: Joseph Kane. SC: Bruce Manning. WITH Vera Ralston, Joan Leslie, Forrest Tucker, John Russell, Ray Middleton, Pat O'Brien, Buddy Baer, Jim Davis, Barton MacLane, Richard Webb, James Millican, Nina Varela, Martin Garralaga, Charles Stevens, Nacho Galindo, Don Beddoe, John Holland, William Haade, Alan Bridge, John Halloran, Stephen

Chase, Dan White, Eugene Borden, Rodolfo Hoyos, Bud Wolfe, Paul Stader, Marshall Reed, Maurice Jara, Rosa Turich, Manuel Lopez, Perry Lopez, Claire Carleton, Victor Sen Yung, Edward Colmans, George Navarro, Grant Withers, Frank Puglia, Pepe Hern, Glenn Strange, Felipe Turich, Joe Dominguez, Emil Sitka, Emmett Lynn, Tex Terry, Rocky Shahan, Chuck Hayward, Jack O'Shea, Jack Elam, Tina Menard, Buzz Henry. A woman wanted for murder travels West with a young girl and her baby, the latter being kidnapped by the girl's dead husband's crooked brother. Big, brawling adaptation of Gwen Bristow's popular novel provides good screen fare.

1660 Judgment Book. Beaumont, 1935. 61 minutes B/W. D: Charles Hutchinson. SC: E. J. Thornton. WITH Conway Tearle, Bernadine Hayes, Howard Lang, Richard Cramer, William Gould, Jack Pendleton, Roy Rice, Jimmie Aubrey, Ray Gallagher, Dick Rush, Blackie Whiteford, Francis Walker, Edward Clayton. When his newspaper editor uncle is murdered by ruthless cattlemen intent on dominating a small town, a man comes West to take over the business and oppose the lawless. Pretty fair Conway Tearle vehicle if you can accept the star (then in his 50s) as a young man.

1661 Junction City. Columbia, 1952. 54 minutes B/W. D: Ray Nazarro. SC: Barry Shipman. WITH Charles Starrett, Smiley Burnette, Jack (Jock) Mahoney, Kathleen Case, John Dehner, Steve Darrell, George Chesebro, Anita Castle, Mary Newton, Robert Bice, Hal Price, Hal Taliaferro, Chris Alcaide, Bob Woodward, Frank Ellis, Joel Friedkin, Harry Tyler. The Durango Kid comes to the aid of a stage driver who has been falsely accused of kidnapping his fiancee, who is actually in hiding to prevent her guardians from killing her for the rich mine she has inherited. Passable "Durango Kid" film from late in the series.

1662 Junior Bonner. Cinerama Releasing, 1972. 100 minutes Color. D: Sam Peckinpah. SC: Jed Rosebrook. WITH Steve McQueen, Robert Preston, Ida Lupino, Ben Johnson, Joe Don Baker, Barbara Leigh, Mary Murphy, Bill McKinney, Sandra Deel, Donald Barry, Dub Taylor, Charles Gray, Matthew Peckinpah, Sundown Spencer, Rita Garrison, Casey Tibbs. A rodeo circuit performer returns home to take part in a local rodeo and tries to re-establish his relationships with his estranged parents. Nicely done melodrama of rodeo life.

1663 Just Pals. Fox, 1920. 50 minutes B/W. D: John Ford. SC: Paul Schofield. WITH Buck Jones, Helen Ferguson, George E. Stone, Duke R. Lee, William Buckley, Edwin Booth Tilton, Eunice Murdock, Burt Apling, Slim Padgett, Pedro Leone, Ida Tenbrook, John J. Cooke. A town loafer is made into a he-man when he befriends a young vagabond boy. Well made and entertaining early Buck Jones silent film.

1664 Just Tony. Fox, 1922. 58 minutes B/W. D-SC: Lynn Reynolds. WITH Tom Mix, Claire Adams, J. P. Lockney, Duke Lee, Frank Campeau, Walt Robbins. A cowboy saves a beautiful wild mustang from men who want to beat it. The horse later returns the favor by saving the cowboy and a rancher's daughter from trouble. Tom Mix's beautiful horse Tony is spotlighted in this delightfully actionful silent oater.

1665 Justice of the Range. Columbia, 1935. 58 minutes B/W. D: David Selman. SC: Ford Beebe. WITH Tim McCoy, Billie Seward, Ward Bond, Guy Usher, Ed Le-Saint, Alan Sears, Jack Rockwell, Jack Rutherford, George ("Gabby") Hayes, Bill Patton, Stanley Blystone, Earl Dwire, Dick Rush, J. Frank Glendon, Frank Ellis, Tom London, Bud Osborne, Richard Botiller. A cowboy is hired to find out who is behind local cattle rustling but when a ranch foreman is murdered he is accused of the crime and sets out to clear himself. Very fine entry in Tim McCoy's Columbia series with a good script and fine performances from the cast.

1666 Justice of the West. Wrather Corporation, 1956. 75 minutes Color. D: Earl Bellamy & Oscar Rudolph. SC: Robert Schaefer, Eric Friewald, Walter A. Thompkins & Robert Leslie Bellem. WITH Clayton Moore, Jay Silverheels, Allen Pinson, Wayne Burson, Terry Frost, Denver Pyle, Bill Henry, Joseph Crehan, House Peters Jr., Tom Steele, Steven Ritch, Russell Sanders, Robert Burton, Henry Rowland, Ric Roman, Ron Hagerthy, John Beradino, Mickey Simpson, Tudor Owen, Will Wright, James D. Parnell, Gary Lee Marshall. The Lone Ranger and Tonto track down a stolen million dollar gold shipment, hunt marauders who murder an elderly sheriff and try to save a man from being hanged for a robbery he did not commit.

Good "The Lone Ranger" (ABC-TV, 1949-57) telefilm made up of the series segments "No Handicap," "Quicksand" and "Outlaw Masquerade."

Justice Rides Again see **Destry Rides Again** (1932)

K

1667 Kangaroo. 20th Century-Fox, 1951. 84 minutes Color. D: Lewis Milestone. SC: Harry Kleiner. WITH Maureen O'Hara, Peter Lawford, Richard Boone, Finlay Currie, Chips Rafferty, Letty Graydon, Charles Tingwell, Ron Whelan, John Fegan, Guy Doleman, Reg Collins. Two Americans in Australia become involved with murder, a beautiful woman and a cattle drive. The Australian scenery is the main asset of this otherwise mundane Down Under oater.

1668 The Kansan. United Artists, 1943. 79 minutes B/W. D: George Archainbaud. SC: Harold Shumate. WITH Richard Dix, Jane Wyatt, Victor Jory, Albert Dekker, Eugene Pallette, Robert Armstrong, Clem Bevans, Rod Cameron, Francis McDonald, Willie Best, Glenn Strange, Douglas Fowley, Jack Norton, Eddy Waller, Ray Bennett, Sam Flint, Merrill McCormack, Jack Mulhall. A frontiersman is hired to rid a town of the James gang but ends up fighting the corrupt town officials who hired him. Actionful and entertaining Richard Dix vehicle. V: Cassette Express.

1669 Kansas Cyclone. Republic, 1941. 54 (58) minutes B/W. D: George Sherman. SC: Oliver Drake & Doris Schroeder. WITH Don "Red" Barry, Lynn Merrick, Dorothy Sebastian, William Haade, Milton Kibbee, Harry Worth, Jack Kirk, Forrest Taylor, Charles Moore, Eddie Dean, Reed Howes, Guy Usher, Ed Piel Sr., Yakima Canutt, Cactus Mack, Bob Woodward, Tex Terry, George J. Lewis, Buddy Roosevelt. Outlaws attacking Wells Fargo shipments are hunted by a U. S. marshal determined to stop the holdups. Another fast moving and actionful entry in Don Barry's Republic series.

1670 Kansas Pacific. Allied Artists, 1953. 73 minutes Color. D: Ray Nazarro. SC: Dan Ullman. WITH Sterling Hayden, Eve Miller, Barton MacLane, Harry Shannon, Reed Hadley, Tom Fadden, Douglas

Fowley, Irving Bacon, Myron Healey, James Griffith, Clayton Moore, Jonathan Hale, Bob Keys. An engineer tries to fashion the building of the Kansas Pacific Railroad during the Civil War but the project is plagued by Confederate guerilla activities. Pretty fare oater with good work by Clayton Moore in a villainous role.

1671 The Kansas Raiders. Universal-International, 1950. 80 minutes Color. D: Ray Enright. SC: Robert L. Richards. WITH Audie Murphy, Brian Donlevy, Marguerite Chapman, Scott Brady, Tony Curtis, Richard Arlen, Richard Long, James Best, John Kellogg, Dewey Martin, George Chandler, Charles Delaney, Richard Egan, David Wolfe, Mira McKinney, Sam Flint, Buddy Roosevelt, Larry Mc-Grath, Ed Piel Sr. The James Brothers join the guerilla band led by William Quantrill during the Civil War. Jesse James cares for Quantrill when he is blinded, and the outlaw leader returns the favor by saving Jesse's life. Colorful and well acted, but historically empty.

1672 Kansas Territory. Monogram, 1952. 60 (65) minutes B/W & Sepiatone. D: Lewis D. Collins. SC: Daniel Ullman. WITH Bill Elliott, Peggy Stewart, Lane Bradford, Marshall Reed, I. Stanford Jolley, House Peters Jr., Lyle Talbot, Terry Frost, John Hart, William Fawcett. Fuzzy Knight, Stanley Andrews, Lee Roberts, Ted Adams, Pierce Lyden. A man wrongfully wanted on an old charge returns home to avenge the death of his brother. Very well done with a good story, cast and action.

1673 The Kansas Terrors. Republic, 1939. 54 (57) minutes B/W. D: George Sherman. SC: Jack Natteford & Betty Burbridge. WITH Robert Livingston, Raymond Hatton, Duncan Renaldo, Jacqueline Wells (Julie Bishop), Howard Hickman, George Douglas, Frank Lackteen, Myra Marsh, Yakima Canutt, Ruth Robinson, Artie Ortego, Richard Alexander, Merrill McCormack, Curley Dresden, Al Haskell. Mesquiteers Stony Brooke and Rusty Joslin take on the job of delivering horses from the government to a small Caribbean island. There they team with Rico in defeating a tyrant. Although the plot is fairly interesting, the sudden change of locale and characters does not help this "Three Mesquiteers" series entry.

1674 Kate Bliss and the Ticker Tape Kid. ABC-TV, 1978. 100 minutes Color.

D: Burt Kennedy. SC: William Bowers & John Zodorow. WITH Suzanne Pleshette, Don Meredith, Harry Morgan, David Huddleston, Tony Randall, Burgess Meredith, Buck Taylor, Jerry Hardin, Gene Evans, Don Collier, Alice Hirson, Harry Carey Jr., Don "Red" Barry. Around 1900 a lady detective from the East gets on the trail of a masked renegade and his band who are opposed to a British land baron after a rancher's property. Surprisingly well done tongue-in-cheek TV movie.

1675 Kazan. Columbia, 1949. 65 minutes B/W. D: Will Jason. SC: Arthur A. Ross. WITH Stephen Dunne, Lois Maxwell, Joseph Sawyer, Roman Bohnen, George Cleveland, John Dehner, Ray Teal, Loren Gage. Stolen by crooks, a huge sled dog escapes and sets out to find his master. Fair programmer adaptation of the James Oliver Curwood novel.

Keep Rollin' see **Gaucho Serenade**

1676 Kelly. Paramount/Famous Players Film Corporation, 1981. 93 minutes Color. D: Christopher Chapman. SC: Robert Logan. WITH Robert Logan, Twyla-Dawn Vokins, George Clutesi, Elaine Natee, Doug Lennox, Alec Willows, Dan Granier, Jack Leaf, Mona Cozart. A young girl with a perceptual handicap goes to Canada to live with her bush pilot father. Nice scenery and a fair amount of action makes this Canadian production okay viewing.

1677 Kenny Rogers As the Gambler. CBS-TV, 1980. 105 minutes Color. D: Dick Lowry. SC: Jim Byrnes. WITH Kenny Rogers, Bruce Boxleitner, Clu Gulager, Harold Gould, Christine Belford, Lee Purcell, Lance LeGault, Ronnie Scribner, Bruce M. Fischer. In the Southwest, a gambler returns to the town where his son and the woman he never married live, although an enemy waits there for him. Based on the Grammy-winning song, this TV movie should please Kenny Rogers fans. Also called **The Gambler.**

1678 Kenny Rogers As the Gambler—The Adventure Continues. CBS-TV, 1983. 200 minutes Color. D: Dick Lowry. SC: Jim Byrnes. WITH Kenny Rogers, Linda Evans, Bruce Boxleitner, Mitchell Ryan, Charlie Fields, Harold Gould, Cameron Mitchell, Gregory Sierra, Ken Swofford, Paul Koslo, David Hedison, Johnny Crawford, Brian James, Robert Hoy. A gambler, whose son has been kidnapped by outlaws, joins forces with his buddy and a female bounty hunter to track down the gang. Leisurely TV film (telecast originally in parts); a followup to the earlier **Kenny Rogers As the Gambler** (q.v.).

1679 The Kentuckian. United Artists, 1955. 104 minutes Color. D: Burt Lancaster. SC: A. B. Guthrie Jr. WITH Burt Lancaster, Dianne Foster, Diana Lynn, John McIntire, Una Merkel, Walter Matthau, John Carradine, Donald MacDonald, John Litel, Rhys Williams, Edward Norris, Lee Erickson, Clem Bevans, Lisa Ferraday, Douglas Spencer, Paul Wexler. In the 1820s, a man and his son head West to the Texas Territory but along the way they are sidetracked by two pretty women, a servant girl and a school teacher, and a corrupt town boss. Okay frontier drama with adequate entertainment value. V: Blackhawk.

1680 Kentucky Rifle. Howco-International, 1956. 80 minutes Color. D: Carl K. Hittleman. SC: Carl K. Hittleman & Lee J. Hewitt. WITH Chill Wills, Lance Fuller, Cathy Downs, Henry Hull, Jess Barker, Jeanne Cagney, Sterling Holloway, John Pickard, John Alvin, I. Stanford Jolley, Rory Mallinson, George Keymas. Due to breakdowns, people are forced to leave a wagon train in Comanche Territory and later find their travel is impeded by the Indians who want their cargo of rifles. Cheap production values hurt this otherwise adequate wagon train tale. Stanley Price served as the dialogue coach for this feature for which Ira S. Webb was the executive producer.

Kettle Creek see **Mountain Justice**

1681 The Kid and the Killers. Cinema Shares, 1979. 90 minutes Color. D: Ralph Bluemke. SC: Ralph Bluemke & John Garces. WITH Jon Cypher, John Garces, Gerry Ross, Elida Alicia, Ralph Bluemke, Jamie Delgado, Joel Douglas, Susan Douglas, Gino Eqcclo, Eduardo Mosquera, Hector Rojas, Dan Ross. Two bandits take refuge with a young boy and his sister. One of them rapes and murders the girl and takes off with stolen loot while the boy and the other outlaw team to get him. Meandering drama enhanced by its rural Mexico locales.

1682 Kid Blue. 20th Century-Fox, 1973. 100 minutes Color. D: James Frawley. SC: Edwin Shrake. WITH Dennis Hooper, Warren Oates, Peter Boyle, Ben Johnson, Lee Purcell, Janice Rule, Ralph Waite, Clifton James, Jose Torvay, Mary Jackson, Howard Hessman, Jay Varela, Emmett Walsh. A hellion outlaw tries to settle down in a small Texas town at the turn of the century but finds it rough going, especially after his friend's wife seduces him. None-too-amusing genre spoof filmed in Mexico.

1683 The Kid Comes Back. Warner Brothers, 1938. 61 minutes B/W. D: B. Reeves Eason. SC: George Bricker. WITH Wayne Morris, June Travis, Barton MacLane, James Robbins, Joseph Crehan, Dickie Davis, Maxie Rosenbloom, Frank Otto, David Carlyle, Herbert Rawlinson, Robert Homans, Ken Niles. In order to raise money to save his ranch a cowboy turns to prize fighting and ends up falling in love with a rival's sister. Fast paced action programmer with genre elements only in the beginning before turning into a total boxing film.

1684 Kid Courageous. Supreme, 1935. 53 minutes B/W. D-SC: Robert North Bradbury. WITH Bob Steele, Renee Borden, Kit Guard, Arthur Loft, Jack Powell, Lafe McKee, Vane Calvert, Perry Murdock, John Elliott, Barry Seury. After a series of thefts, a man travels West to discover the robber and ends up saving a pretty girl from a marriage she does not want. Cheaply made but fast moving and highly entertaining Bob Steele film.

1685 The Kid from Amarillo. Columbia, 1951. 56 minutes B/W. D: Ray Nazarro. SC: Barry Shipman. WITH Charles Starrett, Smiley Burnette, Harry Lauter, Fred F. Sears, Don Megowan, Jerry Scroggins & The Cass County Boys, Scott Lee, Guy Teague, Charles Evans, George J. Lewis, Henry Kulky, George Chesebro. Two U. S. Treasury agents head to the Mexican border to capture a gang of clever silver smugglers. Fair actioner in the "Durango Kid" series.

1686 The Kid from Arizona. Cosmos, 1931. 55 minutes B/W. D: Robert J. Horner. SC: Robert Walker. WITH Jack Perrin, Josephine Hill, Robert Walker, George Chesebro, Henry Rocquemore, Ben Corbett. A marshal is sent to the badlands to stop raids by marauding Indians. Any connection between this film and entertainment is purely accidental.

1687 The Kid from Broken Gun. Columbia, 1952. 56 minutes B/W. D: Fred F. Sears. SC: Ed Earl Repp & Barry Shipman. WITH Charles Starrett, Smiley Burnette, Jack

(Jock) Mahoney, Angela Stevens, Tristram Coffin, Myron Healey, Pat O'Malley, Helen Mowery, Chris Alcaide, John Cason, Mauritz Hugo, Edgar Dearing, Eddie Parker, Charles Horvath, Edward Hearn. Two men arrive in a small town to aid their pal, an ex-fighter, who has been falsely accused of robbery and murder. Sturdy series finale to "The Durango Kid."

1688 The Kid from Gower Gulch. Friedgen, 1950. 57 minutes B/W. D: Oliver Drake. SC: Elmer (Clifton) S. Pond. WITH Spade Cooley, Wanda Cantlon, Bob Gilbert, Billy Dix, Jack Baxley, "Little" Joe Hiser, William Val. A Hollywood Western star who has no talent as a Westerner is roped into representing a ranch at a local rodeo and must take a crash course in being a cowboy. One of the most incredibly cheap oaters of all time—even the stock shots don't match. Must be seen to be believed!

1689 The Kid from Santa Fe. Monogram, 1940. 57 minutes B/W. D: Raymond K. Johnson. SC: Carl Krusada. WITH Jack Randall, Claire Rochelle, Forrest Taylor, Clarene Curtis, Tom London, George Chesebro, Dave O'Brien, Jimmie Aubrey, Kenne Duncan, Steve Clark, Carl Mathews, Buzz Barton, Tex Palmer. The Sante Fe Kid aids a sheriff in tracking down a gang of smugglers. Fair Jack Randall vehicle.

1690 The Kid from Texas. Metro-Goldwyn-Mayer, 1939. 71 minutes B/W. D: S. Sylvan Simon. SC: Florence Ryerson & Albert Mannheimer. WITH Dennis O'Keefe, Florence Rice, Anthony Allan, Jessie Ralph, Buddy Ebsen, Virginia Dale, Robert Wilcox, Jack Carson, Helen Lynd, J. M. Kerrigan, Tully Marshall. A polo-playing cowboy comes East, becomes the manager of a Long Island estate and falls in love with the daughter of the proprietor of a wild west show. Humorous programmer.

1691 The Kid from Texas. Universal-International, 1950. 78 minutes Color. D: Kurt Neumann. SC: Robert Hardy Andrews & Karl Lamb. WITH Audie Murphy, Gale Storm, Albert Dekker, Shepperd Strudwick, Will Geer, William Talman, Martin Garralaga, Robert Barrat, Walter Sande, Frank Wilcox, Dennis Hoey, Ray Teal, Don Haggerty, Paul Ford, Zon Murray, Rosa Turich, Pilar Del Rey, Harold Goodwin. Billy the Kid goes to work for a rancher. When the man does not sell his produce at the prices a rival wants him to, he is murdered and Billy goes berserk and vows revenge. Not much history in this Audie Murphy vehicle but there is plenty of action.

1692 The Kid Ranger. Supreme, 1936. 57 minutes B/W. D-SC: Robert North Bradbury. WITH Bob Steele, Joan Barclay, William Farnum, Earl Dwire, Charles King, Lafe McKee, Frank Ball, Buck Moulton. On the trail of a gang of outlaws, a ranger accidentally shoots the wrong man. Another fast action entry in Bob Steele's lengthy series for producer A. W. Hackel.

1693 The Kid Rides Again. Producers Releasing Corporation, 1943. 57 minutes B/W. D: Sherman Scott (Sam Newfield). SC: Fred Myton. WITH Buster Crabbe, Al St. John, Iris Meredith, Glenn Strange, Charles King, I. Stanford Jolley, Ed Peil Sr., Ted Adams, Slim Whitaker, Karl Hackett, Kenne Duncan, Curley Dresden, Snub Pollard, John Merton. Billy the Kid is arrested for a train robbery he did not commit and he breaks out of jail to catch the real culprits, who he finds posing as honest ranchers. Typically fast and cheap entry in the Buster Crabbe-Al St. John series of PRC.

1694 Kid Rodelo. Paramount, 1966. 91 minutes B/W. D: Richard Carlson. SC: Jack Natteford. WITH Don Murray, Janet Leigh, Broderick Crawford, Richard Carlson, Jose Nieto, Julia Pena, Miguel Del Castillo, Emilio Rodriguez. After spending a year in jail for being in the company of an outlaw, an embittered man sets out to find the hidden $50,000 in gold he was accused of stealing. Based on a story by Louis L'Amour, this is just another adequately made oater filmed in Spain during the 1960s.

1695 Kid Vengeance. Cannon Films, 1977. 94 minutes Color. D: Joe Manduke. SC: Budd Robbins & Jay Telfer. WITH Lee Van Cleef, Jim Brown, John Marley, Leif Garrett, Glynnis O'Connor, Matt Clark, Timothy Scott. When outlaws murder his folks and abduct his sister, a young man seeks to get revenge and rescue the girl. Overly violent oater filmed in Israel.

1696 The Kid's Last Ride. Monogram, 1941. 55 minutes B/W. D: S. Roy Luby. SC: Earle Snell. WITH Ray Corrigan, John King, Max Terhune, Luana Walters, Edwin Brian, Al Bridge, Glenn Strange,

Frank Ellis, John Elliott, George Havens, Tex Palmer, George Morrell, Carl Mathews. A crook blackmails a young man into telling him the whereabouts of the hiding places of ranchers' cattle sale money and the Range Busters arrive pretending to help the bad man. Fair production in "The Range Busters" series that is a bit draggy and uninteresting. Songs include John King's warbling of "Call of the Wild," Ray Corrigan and John King doing a bit of "Home on the Range" and the trio, plus Elmer, singing "It's All a Part of the Game."

Kill Johnny R see **Who Killed Johnny R?**

1697 Kill Or Be Killed. Rizzoli Films, 1968. 90 minutes Color. D: Amerigo Anton (Tanio Boccia). SC: Mario Amendola. WITH Robert Mark, Gordon Mitchell, Elina De Witt, Fabrizio Moroni, Andrea Bosic, Albert Farley, Benjamin May, Tony Rogers, Mary Land. Posing as an elderly violin-playing barfly, a gunman becomes involved in a feud between two families. Typically violent European oater made in Italy in 1966 as **Uccidi O Muori.**

1698 Kill Them All and Come Back Home. Fanfare, 1970. 93 minutes Color. D: Enzo G. Castellari. SC: Tito Carpi, Enzo G. Castellari & Romero Hernandez. WITH Chuck Connors, Frank Wolff, Ken Wood, Franco Citti, Leo Anchoriz, Alberto Dell'Acqua, Hercules Cortes, John Bartha, Furio Meniconi. An escaped prisoner-of-war during the Civil War takes part in the robbery of gold from an ammunition depot and when he is double-crossed and left for dead by the mastermind of the heist, he plans to get revenge. Another in the long line of complicated and bloody European oaters. Made in Italy in 1968 as **Ammazzali Tutti E Torna Solo** (Go and Kill Everybody and Come Back Alone).

Killbrand see **The Deadly Trackers**

Killer Grizzly see **Grizzly**

1699 Kimberley Jim. Embassy, 1965. 81 minutes Color. D-SC: Emil Nofal. WITH Jim Reeves, Madeleine Usher, Clive Parnell, Arthur Swemmer, Mike Holt, Tromp Terre'blanche, Vonk de Ridder, David Van Der Walt, June Neethling, George Moore, The Blue Boys. Two crooked gamblers win a diamond mine in a poker game they have fixed but find the mine is worthless. Pleasant South African musical Western which will appeal most to Jim Reeves fans.

1700 The King and Four Queens. United Artists, 1956. 86 minutes Color. D: Raoul Walsh. SC: Margaret Fitts & Richard Alan Simmons. WITH Clark Gable, Eleanor Parker, Jo Van Fleet, Jean Willes, Barbara Nichols, Sara Shane, Roy Roberts, Arthur Shields, Jay C. Flippen. A soldier of fortune is after gold buried by four men and in the search he finds himself in the company of the men's lovely wives. Hardly Clark Gable's best vehicle but not nearly as bad as often stated and is, in fact, fairly good.

1701 King of Dodge City. Columbia, 1941. 63 minutes B/W. D: Lambert Hillyer. SC: Gerald Geraghty. WITH Bill Elliott, Tex Ritter, Dub Taylor, Judith Linden, Guy Usher, Rick Anderson, Kenneth Harlan, Pierce Lyden, Francis Walker, Harrison Greene, Jack Rockwell, Edmund Cobb, George Chesebro, Tristram Coffin, Steve Clark, Jack Ingram, Ned Glass, George Morrell, Horace B. Carpenter, Ted Mapes. A former lawman and a roving sheriff team to oppose a crook and his gang who are trying to take over a Kansas town in 1861. Steady Bill Elliott-Tex Ritter outing but not one of their better vehicles.

1702 King of the Arena. Universal, 1933. 62 minutes B/W. D-SC: Alan James. WITH Ken Maynard, Lucille Browne, John St. Polis, Robert Kortman, James Marcus, Michael Visaroff, Frank Rice, Jack Rockwell, Bobby Nelson, Edgar "Blue" Washington, Jack Mower, Iron Eyes Cody, Edward Coxen, Lafe McKee, Fred McKaye, William Walker, William Steele, Helen Gibson, Pascale Perry, Bud McClure, Horace B. Carpenter, Buck Bucko, Jack Kirk, Chief Big Tree, Artie Ortego, Merrill McCormack, Bob Burns. A one-time circus performer, now a Texas Ranger on the hunt for a vicious outlaw called the "Black Death," rejoins the circus which seems to be the main locale of the badman's operations. Ken Maynard produced this interesting actioner with its authentic circus background.

1703 King of the Bullwhip. Western Adventure, 1951. 59 minutes B/W. D: Ron Ormond. SC: Jack Lewis & Ira Webb. WITH Lash LaRue, Al St. John, Jack Holt, Anne Gwynne, Tom Neal, Dennis Moore, George Lewis, Michael Whalen, Willis

Houck, Cliff Taylor, Frank Jaquet, Jimmie Martin, Roy Butler, Hugh Hooker, Tex Cooper. A bank president sends for two U. S. marshals to aid his town in combating a mysterious masked bandit called El Azote. Well done Lash LaRue vehicle with interesting camera work and brutal fight sequences, especially the opening and climactic ones involving whips. V: Cassette Express.

1704 King of the Cowboys. Republic, 1943. 54 (67) minutes B/W. D: Joseph Kane. SC: Oliver Cooper & J. Benton Cheney. WITH Roy Rogers, Smiley Burnette, Bob Nolan & The Sons of the Pioneers, Peggy Moran, Gerald Mohr, Dorothea Kent, Lloyd Corrigan, James Bush, Russell Hicks, Irving Bacon, Stuart Hamblen, Emmett Vogan, Eddie Dean, Forrest Taylor, Dick Wessell, Jack Kirk, Edward Earle, Yakima Canutt, Charles King, Jack O'Shea. Roy Rogers and his pals try to smash a sabotage ring fronted by a fake mind-reader and a governor's assistant. Film does not live up to its title although it is fairly interesting. V: NTA Home Entertainment, Cassette Express.

1705 King of the Forest Rangers. Republic, 1946. 12 Chapters B/W. D: Spencer Gordon Bennet & Fred C. Brannon. SC: Albert DeMond, Basil Dickey, Jesse Duffy & Lynn Perkins. WITH Larry Thompson, Helen Talbot, Stuart Hamblen, Anthony Warde, LeRoy Mason, Scott Elliott, Tom London, Walter Soderling, Bud Geary, Harry Strang, Ernie Adams, Eddie Parker, Jack Kirk, Tom Steele, Dale Van Sickel, Stanley Blystone, Marin Sais, Buddy Roosevelt, Robert Wilke, Sam Ash, Carey Loftin, Jay Kirby, Joe Yrigoyen, Kenneth Terrell, Bud Wolfe, Wheaton Chambers, Rex Lease, Charles Sullivan, David Sharpe. A Forest Ranger uncovers a plot by an amateur scientist to steal treasure buried in ancient Indian ruins in a national park. Pretty interesting cliffhanger but light on production values.

1706 King of the Grizzlies. Buena Vista, 1970. 93 minutes Color. D: Ron Kelly. SC: Jack Speirs. WITH John Yesno, Chris Wiggins, Hugh Webster, Jack Van Evera, Winston Hibler (narrator). A young Cree Indian boy raises a bear cub but when the animal grows up he is faced with the beast while alone in the wilds. Average Walt Disney studios production with some nice outdoor material; filmed in the Canadian Rockies.

1707 King of the Lumberjacks. Warner Brothers, 1940. 58 minutes B/W. D: William Clemens. SC: Crane Wilbur. WITH John Payne, Gloria Dickson, Stanley Fields, Joseph Sawyer, Victor Kilian, Earl Dwire, Herbert Heywood, G. Pat Collins, John Sheehan, Pat West, Nat Carr, Jack Mower, John Miller. Two men battle over a pretty girl and a lumber contract in the north woods. Adequate "B" action melodrama.

1708 King of the Mounties. Republic, 1942. 12 Chapters B/W. D: William Witney. SC: Ronald Davidson, Joseph Poland, William Lively, Joseph O'Donnell & Taylor Davan. WITH Allan Lane, Peggy Drake, Gilbert Emery, Russell Hicks, George Irving, Abner Biberman, William Vaughn, Nestor Paiva, Bradley Page, Douglass Dumbrille, William Bakewell, Duncan Renaldo, Francis Ford, Jay Novello, Anthony Warde, Norman Nesbitt, John Hiestand, Allen Jung, Paul Fung, Arvon Dale, Kenneth Terrell, Duke Taylor, Harry Cording, Carleton Young, Tom Steele, Hal Taliaferro, Stanley Price, Tommy Coats, Bob Jamison, Jack Kenney, Forrest Taylor, David Sharpe. A Mountie uncovers a plot by three enemy agents who are devising the Axis invasion of North America. Actionful Republic cliffhanger followup to **King of the Royal Mounted** (q.v.).

1709 King of the Pecos. Republic, 1936. 54 minutes B/W. D: Joseph Kane. SC: Bernard McConville, Dorrell McGowan & Stuart McGowan. WITH John Wayne, Muriel Evans, Cy Kendall, Jack Clifford, J. Frank Glendon, Herbert Heywood, Arthur Aylesworth, John Beck, Mary McLaren, Bradley Metcalfe Jr., Yakima Canutt, Edward Hearn, Earl Dwire, Tex Palmer, Jack Kirk. A law student seeks revenge on the crook who murdered his parents a decade earlier because they would not give up their land. Fast moving John Wayne vehicle highlighted by Cy Kendall's portrayal of the crafty villain.

1710 King of the Rodeo. Universal, 1929. 60 minutes B/W. D: Henry MacRae. SC: B. M. Bower. WITH Hoot Gibson, Kathryn Crawford, Joseph W. Girard, Bodil Rosing, Charles K. French, Harry Todd, Slim Summerville, Jack Knapp, Monte Montague. The "new Chip of the Flying U" is thrown off his family ranch by his father for refusing to return to college. He joins a rodeo and becomes a headliner before becoming involved with thieves, and eventually he is reunited with his family. Lots of action and rodeo footage in this Hoot Gibson feature, one of the star's last silent films.

1711 King of the Royal Mounted. 20th Century-Fox, 1936. 61 minutes B/W. D: Howard Bretherton. SC: Earle Snell. WITH Robert Kent, Rosalind Keith, Jack Luden, Alan Dinehart, Frank McGlynn, Grady Sutton, Arthur Loft. A Canadian Mountie tries to stop a gang after a scientist's invention. Average programmer based on Zane Grey's comic strip and remade four years later by Republic as a serial (q.v.).

1712 King of the Royal Mounted. Republic, 1940. 12 Chapters B/W. D: William Witney & John English. SC: Franklyn Adreon, Sol Shor, Barney A. Sarecky, Norman S. Hall & Joseph Poland. WITH Alan Lane, Lita Conway, Robert Kellard, Robert Strange, Herbert Rawlinson, Harry Cording, Bryant Washburn, Budd Buster, Stanley Andrews, John Davidson, John Dilson, Paul McVey, Lucien Prival, Norman Willis, Tony Paton, Kenneth Terrell, Charles Thomas, Ted Mapes, Major Sam Harris, George Plues, Richard Simmons, Wallace Reid Jr., William Justice, John Bagni, Earl Gunn, Curley Dresden, George DeNormand, Bud Geary, Tommy Coats, Dale Van Sickel, Bob Jamison, Al Taylor, David Sharpe, William Stahl. A Mountie discovers enemy foreign agents are working in the north country trying to locate a valuable mineral and he sets out to stop them. Anti-Axis serial has plenty of action. Issued in a feature version in 1942 called **The Yukon Patrol.**

1713 King of the Sierras. Grand National, 1938. 55 minutes B/W. D: Samuel Diege. SC: W. Scott Darling. WITH Rex, Sheik (horses), Hobart Bosworth, Harry Harvey Jr., Frank Campeau, Harry Harvey, Jack Lindell. An old man tells a small boy the story of how a stallion tries to protect his harem of mares from a rival. Fair low budget production.

1714 King of the Texas Rangers. Republic, 1941. 12 Chapters B/W. D: William Witney & John English. SC: Ronald Davidson, Norman S. Hall, Joseph Poland, William Lively & Joseph O'Donnell. WITH Slingin' Sammy Baugh, Neil Hamilton, Pauline Moore, Duncan Renaldo, Charles Trowbridge, Kermit Maynard, Roy Barcroft, Kenne Duncan, Jack Ingram, Monte Montague, Iron Eyes Cody, Hooper Atchley, Ed Cassidy, Buddy Roosevelt, David Sharpe, Herbert Rawlinson, Frank Darien, Robert O. Davis, Monte Blue,

Stanley Blystone. Joe Forte, Lucien Prival. When his father, a captain in the Texas Rangers, is murdered by enemy agents a young man joins the Rangers and uncovers saboteurs working along the Mexican border. Football hero Sammy Baugh proved to be a mediocre serial hero but silent film star Neil Hamilton nearly salvages this cliffhanger as the villainous traitor.

1715 The King of the Wild Horses. Pathe, 1924. 45 minutes B/W. D: Fred Jackman. SC: Carl Himm. WITH Rex (horse), Charles Parrott, Edna Murphy, Sidney DeGray, Leon Barry, Pat Hartigan, Frank Butler, Sidney D'Albrook. A cowboy, who is in love with the ranch owner's pretty daughter, captures a wild stallion who aids him in trying to stop the rustling of the ranch's cattle. Hal Roach wrote the story for this adventure for Rex, the wild stallion, who would also star for him in such outings as **Black Cyclone** and **The Devil Horse** (qq.v.); actionful entertainment.

1716 King of the Wild Horses. Columbia, 1933. 62 minutes B/W. D: Earl Haley. SC: Fred Myton. WITH Rex (horse), William Janney, Dorothy Appleby, Wallace MacDonald, Harry Semels, Art Mix, Ford West, King & Lady (horses). A cowboy tames a wild horse who has been mistreated by badmen. Okay juvenile fare.

1717 King of the Wild Horses. Columbia, 1947. 79 minutes B/W. D: George Archainbaud. SC: Brenda Weisberg. WITH Preston Foster, Gail Patrick, Bill Sheffield, Guinn Williams, Buzz Henry, Charles Kemper, Patti Brady, John Kellogg, Ruth Warren. A young boy befriends and tames a wild stallion. Average boy and horse drama with good scenic values.

1718 King of the Wild Stallions. Monogram, 1942. 63 minutes B/W. D: Edward Finney. SC: Sherman Lowe & Arthur St. Clair. WITH Chief Thundercloud, Chief Yowlachie, Dave O'Brien, Barbara Felker, Rick Vallin, Sally Cairns, Ted Adams, Gordon DeMain, Forrest Taylor, Bill Wilkerson, Chief Many Treaties, Iron Eyes Cody, George Sky Eagle, Joe Cody, Charles Brunner. A ranch foreman tries to aid some Indians in capturing a beautiful stallion, the leader of a herd of wild horses. Competent followup to **Silver Stallion** but filled with stock footage.

1719 King of the Wild Stallions. Allied Artists, 1959. 75 minutes Color. D: R. G. Springsteen. SC: Ford Beebe. WITH

George Montgomery, Diane Brewster, Edgar Buchanan, Emile Meyer, Byron Foulger, Denver Pyle, Dan Sheridan, Rory Mallinson, Jerry Hartleben. A widow and her son fight to save their ranch from a crooked rival and are aided by a cowboy and a wild stallion. Charming little drama provides good entertainment.

1720 Kingdom of the Spiders. Dimension, 1977. 95 minutes Color. D: John "Bud" Cardos. SC: Richard Robinson & Alan Caillou. WITH William Shatner, Tiffany Bolling, Woody Strode, Altovise Davis, Joe Ross, Hoke Howell, Marcy Lafferty, Roy Engel, Lieux Dressler, David McLean, Natasha Ryan, Adele Malis. In the Arizona desert a veterinarian and an entomologist discover that tarantulas, with venom five times more toxic than normal, have formed an army and plan to attack a small town. Harrowing thriller with nicely done shock ending.

1721 Kiss of Fire. Universal-International, 1955. 87 minutes Color. D: Joseph M. Newman. SC: Franklyn Coen & Richard Collins. WITH Jack Palance, Barbara Rush, Rex Reason, Martha Hyer, Alan Reed, Leslie Bradley, Lawrence Dobkin, Pat Hogan, Henry Rowland. A Spanish princess travels to the New World and falls in love with a soldier and refuses to return home when she is named queen. Colorful but empty nonsense set in Spanish America.

1722 The Kissing Bandit. Metro-Goldwyn-Mayer, 1948. 102 minutes Color. D: Laslo Benedek. SC: Isobel Lennart & John Briard Harding. WITH Frank Sinatra, Kathryn Grayson, J. Carrol Naish, Mildred Natwick, Ricardo Montalban, Ann Miller, Cyd Charisse, Mikhail Rasummy, Clinton Sundberg, Carleton Young, Edna Skinner, Vicente Gomez, Henry Mirelez, Nick Thompson, Joe Dominguez, Alberto Morin, Pedro Regas, Julian Rivero, Mitchell Lewis, Byron Foulger. In Old California a young man takes over his father's position as head of a group of daring highwaymen. There is not much to recommend this overlong, dull musical Western.

1723 Kit Carson. United Artists, 1940. 96 minutes B/W. D: George B. Seitz. SC: George Bruce. WITH Jon Hall, Lynn Bari, Dana Andrews, Harold Huber, Ward Bond, Renie Riano, Clayton Moore, Rowena Cook, Raymond Hatton, Harry Strang, C. Henry Gordon, Lew Merrill, Stanley Andrews, Edwin Maxwell, Peter Lynn, William Farnum, Charles Stevens. Frontier

scout Kit Carson leads a wagon train through Indian country as he and a cavalry officer fight over the same girl. There is nothing special or historically accurate about this so-called biopic, but it does entertain. V: Nostalgia Merchant.

1724 Klondike. Monogram, 1932. 68 minutes B/W. D: Phil Rosen. SC: Tristan Tupper. WITH Lyle Talbot, Thelma Todd, Tully Marshall, Henry B. Walthall, Ethel Wales, George ("Gabby") Hayes, Myrtle Steadman, Pat O'Malley, Jason Robards, Lafe McKee, Frank Hawks, Priscilla Dean. A doctor on the run from the law manages to turn his life around in the Klondike. Entertaining programmer with a fine cast including a small part by famous aviator Frank Hawks. Remade as **Klondike Fury** (q.v.).

1725 Klondike Annie. Paramount, 1936. 77 minutes B/W. D: Raoul Walsh. SC: Mae West. WITH Mae West, Victor McLaglen, Philip Reed, Helen Jerome Eddy, Harry Beresford, Harold Huber, Lucille Webster Gleason, Conway Tearle, Esther Howard, Soo Young, John Rogers, Ted Oliver, Lawrence Grant, Gene Austin, Vladimir Bykoff, Tetsu Komai, James Burke, George Walsh, Chester Gan, Jack Daley, Jack Wallace, Philo McCullough. After killing a man in self-defense, a woman heads to Alaska. To avoid the law she takes on the identity of a deceased evangelist and, when she arrives, sets up a Settlement House. Funny and quite entertaining Mae West vehicle with some good songs written by Gene Austin.

1726 Klondike Fever. CFI, 1980. 106 minutes Color. D: Peter Carter. SC: Charles Israel & Martin Lager. WITH Rod Steiger, Angie Dickinson, Lorne Greene, Jeff East, Barry Morse, Lisa Langlois, Robin Gammell, Michael Hogan, Gordon Pinsent, Sherry Lewis, D. D. Winters. The story of writer Jack London during his days in the Klondike during the gold rush. Average adventure drama with little historical importance. Also called **Jack London's Klondike Fever.**

1727 Klondike Fury. Monogram, 1942. 68 minutes B/W. D: William K. Howard. SC: Henry Blankfort & Tristan Tupper. WITH Edmund Lowe, Lucille Fairbanks, Bill Henry, Ralph Morgan, Mary Forbes, Jean Brooks, Vince Barnett, Clyde Cook, Robert Middlemass, John Roche, Monte Blue, Kenneth Harlan. After having lost faith in his ability, a doctor redeems himself in the Klondike after performing a successful operation. Entertaining and very well done remake of **Klondike** (q.v.).

1728 Klondike Kate. Columbia, 1943. 64 minutes B/W. D: William Castle. SC: Houston Branch & M. Coates Webster. WITH Ann Savage, Glenda Farrell, Tom Neal, Constance Worth, Sheldon Leonard, Lester Allen, George Cleveland, George McKay, Dan Seymour. During the gold rush in Alaska in the late 1890s a young hotel owner is nearly lynched for a murder he did not commit. Based on the true story of Kate Rockwell Matson, this "B" effort fails to deliver much entertainment.

1729 Knight of the Plains. Spectrum, 1938. 57 minutes B/W. D: Sam Newfield. SC: Fred Myton. WITH Fred Scott, Al St. John, Marion Weldon, Richard Cramer, John Merton, Frank LaRue, Lafe McKee, Emma Tansey, Steve Clark, Carl Mathews, Sherry Tansey, Jimmie Aubrey, George Morrell, Cactus Mack, Tex Palmer, Olin Francis, Bob Burns, Budd Buster. A cowboy comes to the aid of settlers who are being harrassed by rustlers and land grabbers. Entertaining Fred Scott musical oater; a Stan Laurel production.

1730 Knights of the Range. Paramount, 1940. 68 minutes B/W. D: Lesley Selander. SC: Norman Houston. WITH Russell Hayden, Jean Parker, Victor Jory, Britt Wood, J. Farrell MacDonald, Morris Ankrum, Ethel Wales, Rad Robinson, Raphael Bennett, Ed Cassidy, Eddie Dean, The King's Men. A young man gets involved with outlaws but switches to the right side of the law to aid a girl and her father in Oklahoma's Cimarron country. Well done entertainment by producer Harry Sherman, from the novel by Zane Grey.

1731 Konga, The Wild Stallion. Columbia, 1940. 65 minutes B/W. D: Sam Nelson. SC: Harold Shumate. WITH Fred Stone, Rochelle Hudson, Richard Fiske, Eddy Waller, Robert Warwick, Don Beddoe, Carl Stockdale, George Cleveland, Burr Caruth. When a man shoots his favorite horse, a rancher kills the man and is sent to jail. Years later he is reunited with the horse who has been cared for by his daughter. Simple but entertaining tale enhanced by Fred Stone's performance as the rancher.

1732 Kung Fu. ABC-TV/Warner Brothers, 1972. 75 minutes Color. D: Jerry Thorpe.

SC: Ed Spielman & Howard Friedlander. WITH David Carradine, Barry Sullivan, Albert Salmi, Wayne Maunder, Benson Fong, Keye Luke, Philip Ahn, Richard Loo, Victor Sen Yung, Keith Carradine, Radames Pera, Roy Fuller, Robert Ito, John Leoning, David Chow. Running away from murder charges in China, a Chinese-American kung fu expert comes to America and opposes the exploitation of railroad workers in the West. Highly popular TV movie which helped to start the kung fu movie craze as well as serve as pilot for the "Kung Fu" (ABC-TV, 1972-75) series.

L

1733 Lacy and the Mississippi Queen. NBC-TV/Paramount, 1978. 74 minutes Color. D: Robert Butler. SC: Kathy Donnell & Madeline DeMaggio-Wagner. WITH Kathleen Lloyd, Debra Feuer, Edward Andrews, Jack Elam, Matt Clark, Les Lannom, Christopher Lloyd, James Keach, Anthony Palmer, David Byrd, Alvy Moore, Sandy Ward, Elizabeth Rogers, David Comford, Cliff Pellow, Robert Casper. Two sisters, who are direct opposites, team to hunt down train robbers they believe killed their father. Just passable TV movie actioner.

1734 Lad: A Dog. Warner Brothers, 1962. 98 minutes Color. D: Aram Avakian & Leslie Martinson. SC: Lillie Hayward & Robert O. Hodes. WITH Peter Breck, Peggy McCay, Carroll O'Connor, Angela Cartwright, Maurice Dallimore, Alice Pearce, Jack Daly, Charles Fredericks, Tim Graham, Lillian Buyeff, Lad (dog). The story of how a beautiful collie brings happiness to the life of a small crippled girl. Pleasant screen adaptation of Albert Payson Terhune's novel.

1735 Lady for a Night. Republic, 1942. 87 minutes B/W. D: Leigh Jason. SC: Isabel Dawn & Boyce De Gaw. WITH Joan Blondell, John Wayne, Ray Middleton, Philip Merivale, Blanche Yurka, Edith Barrett, Leonid Kinsky, Hattie Noel, Montagu Love, Carmel Myers, Dorothy Burgess, Guy Usher, Ivan Miller, Patricia Knox, Dewey Robinson, The Hall Johnson Choir. A riverboat entertainer yearns for social position and she throws over her gambler lover to marry an impoverished planter. Fairly interesting post-Civil War story with good work by Joan

Blondell in the title role although John Wayne is subordinate as the gambler. V: Cumberland Video.

1736 The Lady from Cheyenne. Universal, 1941. 87 minutes B/W. D: Frank Lloyd. SC: Kathryn Scola & Warren Duff. WITH Loretta Young, Robert Preston Edward Arnold, Frank Craven, Gladys George, Jessie Ralph, Stanley Fields, Willie Best, Samuel S. Hinds, Spencer Charters, Clare Verdera, Alan Bridge, Joseph Sawyer, Ralph Dunn, Harry Cording, Marion Martin, Gladys Blake, Sally Payne, Iris Adrian, June Wilkins, Erville Alderson, Emmett Vogan, Roger Imhoff, William B. Davidson, James Kirkwood, Emory Parnell, Dorothy Granger, Richard Alexander, Griff Barnett, Esther Howard. In Wyoming a pretty school teacher tries to start a school in a wild town and at the same time obtain the voting rights for women. Production about early women's liberation activities is fun to view.

Lady from Frisco see **Rebellion**

1737 Lady from Louisiana. Republic, 1941. 82 minutes B/W. D: Bernard Vorhaus. SC: Vera Caspary, Michael Hogan & Guy Endore. WITH John Wayne, Ona Munson, Ray Middleton, Henry Stephenson, Helen Westley, Jack Pennick, Dorothy Dandridge, Shimen Ruskin, Jacqueline Dalya, Paul Scardon, James C. Morton, Maurice Costello. In old New Orleans a lawyer tries to destroy a corrupt gang and ends up falling in love with the gangleader's daughter. Rather interesting period melodrama with John Wayne as the crusader. V: Cumberland Video, NTA Home Entertainment.

1738 The Lady from Texas. Universal-International, 1951. 78 minutes Color. D: Joseph Pevney. SC: Gerald Drayson Adams & Connie Lee Bennett. WITH Howard Duff, Mona Freeman, Josephine Hull, Gene Lockhart, Craig Stevens, Ed Begley, Barbara Knudson, Lane Bradford, Chris-Pin Martin, Kenneth Patterson, Jay C. Flippen. Crooks try to declare insane a woman whose husband was killed in the Civil War. A cowboy and a girl come to her aid. Delightful Western comedy.

1739 The Lady Is My Wife. NBC-TV/Universal, 1967. 49 minutes Color. WITH Jean Simmons, Bradford Dillman, Alex Cord. In a small mining town, following the Civil War, a gambler and a cowboy play a game of mounted pool for each

other's possessions. Originally telecast February 1, 1967 as a segment of the "Bob Hope Chrysler Theatre" (NBC-TV, 1963-67), this fair outing has been issued to TV as a feature film.

1740 A Lady Takes a Chance. RKO Radio, 1943. 86 minutes B/W. D: William A. Seiter. SC: Robert Ardrey. WITH Jean Arthur, John Wayne, Charles Winninger, Phil Silvers, Mary Field, Don Costello, John Philliber, Grady Sutton, Grant Withers, Hans Conreid, Peggy Carroll, Ariel Heath, Sugar Geise, Joan Blair, Tom Fadden, Eddy Waller, Nina Quartaro, Cy Kendall, Charles D. Brown, Butch & Buddy, The Three Peppers. An eastern girl with three unacceptable suitors heads West and is romanced by a rodeo rider. Dated and mundane genre comedy.

1741 Land Beyond the Law. Warner Brothers, 1937. 58 minutes B/W. D: B. Reeves Eason. SC: Luci Ward & Joseph K. Watson. WITH Dick Foran, Linda Perry, Wayne Morris, Irene Franklin, Gordon Hart, Joseph King, Cy Kendall, Frank Orth, Glenn Strange, Harry Woods, Milton Kibbee, Edmund Cobb, Henry Otho, Tom Brower, Paul Panzer, Julian Rivero, Artie Ortego, Jim Corey, Bud Osborne, Wilfred Lucas, Gene Alsace, Frank McCarroll. A rancher finds himself in trouble with the law when, by mistake, he gets mixed up with a band of outlaws. Pretty good Dick Foran series entry, briskly directed by B. Reeves "Breezy" Eason.

Land of Fury see **The Seekers**

1742 Land of Hunted Men. Monogram, 1943. 58 minutes B/W. D: S. Roy Luby. SC: Elizabeth Beecher. WITH Ray Corrigan, Dennis Moore, Max Terhune, Phyllis Adair, Charles King, John Merton, Ted Mapes, Frank McCarroll, Forrest Taylor, Steve Clark, Fred "Snowflake" Toones, Carl Sepulveda. The Range Busters are on the trail of an outlaw gang which has been terrorizing the countryside. Ray Corrigan returned to the "Range Busters" series in this entry and Dennis Moore joined as the third member, but otherwise mediocre.

1743 The Land of Missing Men. Tiffany, 1930. 60 minutes B/W. D: J. P. McCarthy, SC: J. P. McCarthy & Bob Quigley. WITH Bob Steele, Al St. John, Edward Dunn, Caryl Lincoln, Al Jennings, Fern Emmett, Emilio Fernandez, Noah Hendricks, C. R. Dufau, S. S. Simon. Two cowpokes falsely accused of a stage holdup rescue a girl from another coach and then infiltrate an outlaw gang in order to capture the real culprits. Bob Steele's fans will like this rather interesting early talkie.

1744 Land of Missing Men. Monogram, 1938. 53 minutes B/W. D: Alan James. SC: Joseph O'Donnell. WITH Jack Randall, Louise Stanley, Herman Brix (Bruce Bennett), Walt Shrum & His Colorado Hillbillies, Dickie Jones, Bob Burns, Wheeler Oakman, John Merton, Lane Chandler, Rex Lease, Ernie Adams. A rancher calls in a pal to aid him in a range war with two crooks who are after all the area land. Okay Jack Randall vehicle enhanced by a fine cast.

1745 Land of No Return. International Picture Show, 1981. 84 minutes Color. D-SC: Kent Bateman. WITH Mel Torme, William Shatner, Donald Moffat, Caesar (eagle), Romulus (wolf). A television animal trainer crashes his private plane in the wilds of Utah and tries to survive with only the aid of his pet eagle. Not much here but the scenery. Alternate titles: **Challenge to Survive** and **Snowman.**

1746 Land of the Lawless. Monogram, 1947. 60 minutes B/W. D: Lambert Hillyer. SC: J. Benton Cheney. WITH Johnny Mack Brown, Raymond Hatton, Christine McIntyre, Tristram Coffin, June Harrison, Marshall Reed, I. Stanford Jolley, Steve Clark, Edmund Cobb, Roy Butler, Cactus Mack, Gary Garrett, Ben Corbett, Carl Sepulveda. A man arrives in a small town and finds his best friend murdered. He joins a prospector in ridding the town of a corrupt female saloon boss and her crooked cohort. Pretty good action entry in Johnny Mack Brown's Monogram series.

1747 Land of the Open Range. RKO Radio, 1942. 60 minutes B/W. D: Edward Killy. SC: Morton Grant. WITH Tim Holt, Ray Whitley, Janet Waldo, Lee "Lasses" White, Hobart Cavanaugh, Lee Bonnell, Roy Barcroft, John Elliott, Frank Ellis, Tom London. An outlaw dies and his will states that a large tract of land he owned can only be homesteaded by ex-convicts. A young deputy tries to stop the lawlessness they cause. A different kind of plotline adds some interest to this Tim Holt vehicle.

1748 Land of the Outlaws. Monogram, 1944. 58 minutes B/W. D: Lambert Hillyer. SC: Joseph O'Donnell. WITH Johnny Mack Brown, Raymond Hatton, Nan Halliday, Stephen Keyes, Hugh Prosser,

Charles King, John Merton, Steve Clark, Art Fowler, Tom Quinn, Ray Elder, Chick Hannon, Bob Cason, Kansas Moehring, George Morrell, Ben Corbett. A marshal is on the trail of the outlaws behind the hijacking of ore shipments. Pretty fair action entry in the Monogram-Johnny Mack Brown series.

1749 Land of the Six Guns. Monogram, 1940. 54 minutes B/W. D: Raymond K. Johnson. SC: Tom Gibson. WITH Jack Randall, Louise Stanley, Kenne Duncan, Glenn Strange, Bud Osborne, George Chesebro, Jack Perrin, Steve Clark, Frank LaRue, Carl Mathews, Jimmie Aubrey. A lawman buys a ranch but finds it being used by rustlers bringing in cattle from Mexico. Poor Jack Randall vehicle.

1750 Land of Wanted Men. Monogram, 1932. 60 minutes B/W. D-SC: Harry Fraser. WITH Bill Cody, Andy Shuford, Sheila Mannors, Gibson Gowland, Frank Lackteen, James Marcus, Jack Richardson. An outlaw gets a job as a lawman in country where sheep are being introduced on cattle range land. Routine Bill Cody-Andy Shuford series vehicle.

1751 Land Raiders. Columbia, 1970. 101 minutes Color. D: Nathan Juran. SC: Ken Pettus. WITH Telly Savalas, George Maharis, Arlene Dahl, Janet Landgard, Jocelyn Lane, George Coulouris, Guy Rolfe, Phil Brown, Marcella St. Amant, Paul Picerni, Robert Carricart, Gustavo Rojo, Fernando Rey, Ben Tatar, John Clark, Charles Stahlnaker, Susan Harvey. A young man and a girl survive a wagon train massacre by Indians. The attack was caused by the man's brother, who is a town boss who pays for Indian scalps. Spanish-made, violent oater is basically a mediocre genre outing.

1752 Landrush. Columbia, 1946. 54 minutes B/W. D: Vernon Keays. SC: Michael Simmons. WITH Charles Starrett, Smiley Burnette, Doris Houck, Emmett Lynn, Ozie Waters & His Colorado Rangers, Bud Geary, Stephen Barclay, Robert Kortman, George Chesebro, Bud Osborne, Ted French, George Russell, George Hoey, Ethan Laidlaw, Johnny Tyrell, Russell Meeker, Roy Butler. Outlaws try to keep settlers off of land recently opened for settlement but the Durango Kid sets out to stop the outlaws. More than passable "Durange Kid" segment.

1753 Laramie. Columbia, 1949. 56 minutes B/W. D: Ray Nazarro. SC: Barry Shipman.

WITH Charles Starrett, Smiley Burnette, Elton Britt, Fred Sears, Tommy Ivo, Marjorie Stapp, Robert Wilke, Myron Healey, Shooting Star, Jay Silverheels, Jim Diehl, Ethan Laidlaw, Bob Cason, George Lloyd, Rodd Redwing, Nolan Leary. When an evil Army scout selling rifles to the Indians kills a chief, warfare nearly errupts and the Durango Kid tries to stop impending bloodshed. Mediocre "Durango Kid" film.

1754 The Laramie Kid. Reliable, 1935. 57 minutes B/W. D: Harry S. Webb. SC: Carl Krusada & Rose Gordon. WITH Tom Tyler, Alberta Vaughn, Al Ferguson, Murdock McQuarrie, George Chesebro, Snub Pollard, Steve Clark, Artie Ortego, Jimmie Aubrey, Wally Wales, Nelson McDowell, Budd Buster. A cowboy gives himself up so his girl's father can collect the reward to pay off his ranch so the girl will not be forced into marriage with the banker she does not love. The production is as bad as the plot in this Tom Tyler vehicle.

1755 Laramie Mountains. Columbia, 1952. 53 minutes B/W. D: Ray Nazarro. SC: Barry Shipman. WITH Charles Starrett, Smiley Burnette, Jack (Jock) Mahoney, Fred F. Sears, Marshall Reed, Rory Mallinson, Zon Murray, John War Eagle, Robert Wilke, Chris Alcaide. A government Indian agent tries to prevent warfare after several attacks on the cavalry and he finds out the trouble has been caused by dishonest scouts. Fair "Durango Kid" series segment.

1756 The Laramie Trail. Republic, 1944. 54 minutes B/W. D: John English. SC: J. Benton Cheney. WITH Robert Livingston, Smiley Burnette, Linda Brent, George J. Lewis, John James, Emmett Lynn, Leander de Cordova, Slim Whitaker, Bud Osborne, Bud Geary, Kenne Duncan, Roy Barcroft, Marshall Reed. Arriving at a Spanish hacienda, a man and his pal try to aid a young man falsely accused of murder. Last entry in the "John Paul Revere" series is a nifty outing with nicely atmospheric mystery touches; well worth viewing.

Lariats' End see **Mystery Brand**

1757 Lasca of the Rio Grande. Universal, 1931. 60 minutes B/W. D: Edward Laemmle. SC: Randall Faye. WITH Johnny Mack Brown, Leo Carrillo, Dorothy Burgess, Slim Summerville, Frank Campeau, Chris-Pin Martin, Tom London, John Ince, Jim Corey. A Texas Ranger and a Mexican bandit both love a dance hall girl. When she kills a man in self-defense, the lawman lets her go. Early talkie is more of a curio than anything else for genre fans.

1758 The Lash. First National, 1930. 75 minutes B/W. D: Frank Lloyd. SC: Bradley King. WITH Richard Barthelmess, Mary Astor, Marian Nixon, James Rennie, Fred Kohler, Robert Edeson, Barbara Bedford, Erville Alderson. A young man returns home to Old California from school and finds crooks have taken over the area. He sets out to stop them with daring raids, earning the nickname of "El Puma." Entertaining early talkie which moves at a good clip although it now appears somewhat dated. Original title: **Adios.**

1759 The Lash of the Law. Goodwill, 1926. 50 minutes B/W. D: Paul Hurst. SC: Al Jennings & Jay Inman Kane (Joseph Kane). WITH Bill Bailey, Alma Rayford, Dick LaReno, Marcel Perez, Bud Osborne, Milton Fahrney, Roy Watson. A cowboy on the trail of an outlaw gang comes to the aid of a boy and girl brutalized by their stepfather. Well made silent programmer; worth viewing.

Lassie's Adventures in the Gold Rush see **The Painted Hills**

1760 Lassie's Great Adventure. 20th Century-Fox, 1963. 103 minutes B/W. D: William Beaudine. SC: Monroe Manning & Charles O'Neal. WITH Lassie, Jon Provost, June Lockhart, Hugh Reilly, Richard Simmons, Richard Kiel, Walter Stocker. Lassie and her young master are carried away in a hot air balloon which takes them to the wilds of Canada where an Indian decides to make the boy a replacement for his son. Very well done family drama taken from four segments of the "Lassie" (CBS-TV, 1954-71) TV series and issued theatrically both here and abroad. Who says William Beaudine was not a good director?

1761 The Last Bandit. Republic, 1949. 80 minutes Color. D: Joseph Kane. SC: Thomas Williamson. WITH William Elliott, Adrian Booth, Forrest Tucker, Andy Devine, Jack Holt, Grant Withers, Minna Gombell, Virginia Brissac, Louis Faust, Stanley Andrews, Martin Garralaga, Joseph Crehan, Charles Middleton, Rex Lease, Emmett Lynn, Gene Roth, George Chesebro, Hank Bell, Jack O'Shea, Steve

Clark, Tex Terry. A reformed outlaw tries to go straight as an express agent but he runs afoul of a saloon singer and his crooked brother, who is planning a big gold heist by robbing the local railroad. Pretty good William Elliott action film; quite colorful.

The Last Bullet see **Crooked River**

1762 The Last Challenge. Metro-Goldwyn-Mayer, 1967. 105 minutes Color. D: Richard Thorpe. SC: John Sherry & Robert Emmett Ginna. WITH Glenn Ford, Angie Dickinson, Chad Everett, Gary Merrill, Jack Elam, Delphi Lawrence, Royal Dano, Kevin Hagen, Florence Sundstrom, Marian Collier, Robert Sorrells, Frank McGrath, John Milford. A once famous gunman takes on a life of leisure as the sheriff of a small town until a young punk arrives to gun him down. Clichéd story does nothing to aid this rather pedestrian feature.

1763 The Last Command. Republic, 1955. 110 minutes Color. D: Frank Lloyd. SC: Warren Duff. WITH Sterling Hayden, Anna Maria Alberghetti, Richard Carlson, Arthur Hunnicutt, Ernest Borgnine, J. Carrol Naish, Ben Cooper, John Russell, Jim Davis, Virginia Grey, Eduard Franz, Otto Kruger, Russell Simpson, Roy Roberts, Slim Pickens, Hugh Sanders. Jim Bowie and his followers join the Texas fight for independence from Mexico and become martyrs at the Alamo. Very fine account of the fall of the Alamo with well-staged battle sequences.

1764 The Last Day. NBC-TV/Paramount, 1975. 100 minutes Color. D: Vincent McEveety. SC: Jim Byrnes & Steve Fisher. WITH Richard Widmark, Christopher Connelly, Robert Conrad, Gene Evans, Richard Jaeckel, Tim Matheson, Barbara Rush, Tom Skerrit, Loretta Swit, Morgan Woodward, Kathleen Cody, Jon Locke, Bryan O'Byrne, Harry Morgan (narrator). When the Dalton gang threatens to rob the town bank, a retired gunman is forced to take up his guns again. Nicely entertaining telefeature from producer A. C. Lyles.

1765 Last Days of Boot Hill. Columbia, 1947. 55 minutes B/W. D: Ray Nazarro. SC: Norman S. Hall. WITH Charles Starrett, Smiley Burnette, Virginia Hunter, Paul Campbell, The Cass County Boys, Mary Newton, Bill Free, J. Courtland Lytton, Robert Wilke, Alan Bridge, Tex Harding. The supposedly dead Durango

Kid is on the trail of gold stolen by an outlaw, now the foreman of a ranch. Tacky "Durango Kid" series entry mostly made up of footage from the earlier series film **Both Barrels Blazing** (q.v.), thus accounting for the appearance of Tex Harding who had been out of the series for almost two years when this entry was issued.

1766 The Last Frontier. RKO Radio, 1932. 12 Chapters B/W. D: Spencer Gordon Bennet. SC: George Plympton & Robert F. Hill. WITH Creighton (Lon Jr.) Chaney, Dorothy Gulliver, Mary Jo Desmond, Francis X. Bushman Jr., Joe Bonomo, Slim Cole, Judith Barrie, Richard Neil, William Desmond, LeRoy Mason, Yakima Canutt, Pete Morrison, Claude Peyton, Fritzi Fern, Bill Nestell, Ben Corbett, Fred Burns, Frank Lackteen. A crusading frontier newspaper editor takes on the guise of a hooded avenger in fighting an outlaw gang after gold on settlers' lands. RKO Radio's only cliffhanger is a slow affair although Lon Chaney's fans will like it. Also issued in a 65 minute feature version called **The Black Ghost.**

1767 The Last Frontier. Columbia, 1955. 98 minutes Color. D: Anthony Mann. SC: Philip Yordan & Russell S. Hughes. WITH Victor Mature, Guy Madison, Robert Preston, Anne Bancroft, James Whitmore, Russell Collins, Peter Whitney, Pat Hogan, Manuel Donde, Guy Williams, Mickey Kuhn, William Calles, Jack Pennick. Three frontier scouts find themselves at odds with a know-it-all fort commander who leads his men into a massacre by the Indians. Fairly colorful and actionful frontier saga. TV title: **Savage Wilderness.**

1768 Last Frontier Uprising. Republic, 1947. 67 minutes Color. D: Lesley Selander. SC: Harvey Gates. WITH Monte Hale, Adrian Booth, Foy Willing & The Riders of the Purple Sage, James Taggert, Roy Barcroft, Edmund Cobb, Philip Van Zandt, John Ince, Frank O'Connor, Bob Blair, Doye O'Dell. A young man buying horses for the government finds himself up against a gang of horse thieves. Predictable but still enjoyable Monte Hale film.

1769 The Last Gun. British Lion, 1964. 88 minutes Color. D-SC: Serge Bergen (Sergio Berganzelli). WITH Cameron Mitchell, Carl Mohner, Celina Cely. When a town is threatened by gunmen, an ex-gunfighter is forced to strap on his guns for one final shootout. Cameron Mitchell is the chief interest as the protagonist of this Spanish-produced oater, originally called **Jim II Primo**. British title: **Killer's Canyon**.

1770 The Last Gunfighter. Joseph Brenner, 1961. 56 minutes B/W. D-SC: Lindsay Shontref. WITH Don Borisenko, Tass Tory, Jay Shannon, Michael Zenon, Ken James, Gordon Clark, James (Hagan) Beggs, Art Janoff, James Barron, Mike Conway. A gunman is hired by ranchers to protect them against a land baron but trouble soon develops over a woman. Tattered, violent actioner filmed in Canada in 1959. Alternate titles: **Hired Gun** and **The Devil's Spawn**.

1771 The Last Hard Man. 20th Century-Fox, 1976. 98 minutes Color. D: Andrew V. McLaglen. SC: Guerdon Trueblood. WITH Charlton Heston, James Coburn, Barbara Hershey, Christopher Mitchum, Michael Parks, Jorge Rivero, Larry Wilcox, Morgan Paul, Thalmus Rasulala, Robert Donner, John Quade. In order to get revenge on the sheriff who sent him to jail an outlaw and his gang kidnap the lawman's young daughter. Sturdy actioner with good entertainment value.

1772 The Last Horseman. Columbia, 1944. 58 minutes B/W. D: William Berke. SC: Ed Earl Repp. WITH Russell Hayden, Dub Taylor, Bob Wills & The Texas Playboys, Ann Savage, John Maxwell, Frank LaRue, Nick Thompson, Ted Mapes, Forrest Taylor, Curley Dresden. Crooks plan to rob a bank and use an innocent female bank teller to aid them but a cowboy and his pals save the day. Lots of action and music help this Russell Hayden vehicle.

1773 The Last Hunt. Metro-Goldwyn-Mayer, 1956. 108 minutes Color. D-SC: Richard Brooks. WITH Robert Taylor, Stewart Granger, Lloyd Nolan, Debra Paget, Russ Tamblyn, Constance Ford, Joe De Santis, Ainslie Pryor, Terry Wilson, Ralph Moody, Fred Graham, Ed Lonehill, Dan White, William Phillips, Jerry Martin, Roy Barcroft, Rosemary Johnston. A rancher, whose cattle herd has been destroyed by rampaging buffalos, teams with a sadistic hunter to destroy the animals. Very good psychological Western interpolated with nice action and mostly filmed in Custer State Park in South Dakota.

1774 The Last Movie. Universal, 1971. 108 minutes Color. D: Dennis Hopper. SC: Stewart Stern. WITH Dennis Hopper,

Stella Garcia, Julie Adams, Peter Fonda, John Alderman, Michael Anderson Jr., Daniel Ades, Tom Baker, Rod Cameron, Severn Darden, Roy Engel, Fritz Ford, Samuel Fuller, George Hill, Kris Kristofferson, John Phillip Law, Ted Markland, Tomas Milian, Sylvia Miles, Jim Mitchum, Michelle Phillips, Robert Rothwell, Dean Stockwell, Russ Tamblyn, Dennis Stock, Don Gordon, Clint Kimbrough, Warren Finnerty. A cowboy-stuntman, who enjoys violence for its own sake, goes to Peru to work in a Western movie and stays there only to end up as a sacrifice by the natives. Extremely unpleasant and disappointing feature which wastes a good cast. Alternate title: **Chinchero**.

1775 The Last Musketeer. Republic, 1952. 67 minutes B/W. D: William Witney. SC: Arthur Orloff. WITH Rex Allen, Mary Ellen Kay, Slim Pickens, James Anderson, Boyd "Red" Morgan, Monte Montague, Michael Hall, Alan Bridge, Stan Jones, The Republic Rhythm Riders. On a cattle buying trip, a cowboy stops in a small town to aid the citizens who have been plagued by a gang of outlaws. Typical Rex Allen vehicle with the usual amount of action.

1776 Last of the Badmen. Allied Artists, 1957. 80 minutes Color. D: Paul Landres. SC: Daniel B. Ullman & David Chandler. WITH George Montgomery, Keith Larsen, James Best, Douglas Kennedy, Robert Foulk, Tom Greenway, Meg Randall, Willis Bouchey, Michael Ansara, Addison Richards, John Doucette, Harlan Warde. When outlaws kill a detective, his agency sends two operatives West to round up the gang. Okay action drama.

1777 The Last of the Clintons. Ajax, 1935. 64 minutes B/W. D: Harry Fraser. SC: Weston Edwards. WITH Harry Carey, Betty Mack, Del Gordon, Victor Potel, Earl Dwire, Ruth Findlay, Tom London, Slim Whitaker, Ernie Adams, Lafe McKee. An outlaw gang has been plaguing the countryside and a range detective pretends to be an outlaw to infiltrate the gang. Cheap production values do not help this oater but Harry Carey fans will go for it anyway.

1778 Last of the Comanches. Columbia, 1953. 85 minutes Color. D: Andre De Toth. SC: Kenneth Gamet. WITH Broderick Crawford, Barbara Hale, Lloyd Bridges, Johnny Stewart, Mickey Shaughnessy, George Mathews, Hugh Sanders, Ric Roman, Chubby Johnson, Martin Milner,

Milton Parsons, Jack Woody, John War Eagle, Carleton Young. The six surviving members of a cavalry unit attacked by Indians join the passengers of a stagecoach in staving off the Comanches. Tired oater which is a reworking of **Sahara** (Warner Brothers, 1943).

1779 Last of the Desperados. Associated Film Distributors, 1955. 75 minutes B/W. D: Sam Newfield. SC: Orville Hampton. WITH James Craig, Jim Davis, Margia Dean, Barton MacLane, Myrna Dell, Bob Steele, Stanley Clements, Brad Johnson, Herbert Vigran, Thomas Browne Henry. After the final shootout with Billy the Kid, sheriff Pat Garrett finds that he is now more of a hunted man than was his outlaw adversary. Actionful and different "B" oater; Charles King shows up at the start of the film via stock footage.

1780 Last of the Duanes. Fox, 1930. 55 minutes B/W. D: Alfred L. Werker. SC: Ernest Pascal. WITH George O'Brien, Lucille Brown, Myrna Loy, Walter McGrail, James Bradbury Jr., Nat Pendleton, Blanche Frederici, Frank Campeau, Jim Mason, Lloyd Ingraham, Willard Robertson. Complications arise for a cowboy after he saves a girl from a badman, when the latter's wife falls for him. Slow moving adaptation of the Zane Grey novel with songs added. First filmed in 1919 by Fox with William Farnum and the studio remade it in 1924 as a Tom Mix vehicle. Filmed simultaneously with the George O'Brien vehicle was a Spanish-language version called **El Ultimo de Los Vargas,** directed by David Howard, with George J. Lewis.

1781 Last of the Duanes. 20th Century-Fox, 1941. 55 minutes B/W. D: James Tinling. SC: Irving Cummings Jr. & William Couselman Jr. WITH George Montgomery, Lynne Roberts, Eve Arden, Francis Ford, George E. Stone, William Farnum, Joseph Sawyer, Truman Bradley, Russell Simpson, Don Costello, Harry Woods, Andrew Tombes, Tom London, Tim Ryan, Lane Chandler, Arthur Aylesworth, Ann Carter, Harry Hayden, Walter McGrail, Russ Clark, Lew Kelly, Jack Stoney, Tom Murray, Syd Saylor. A man sets out to avenge the murder of his father and gets an unjust reputation as a gunman. Fifth filming of the Zane Grey novel is an okay "B" effort which helped George Montgomery on his road to stardom.

1782 The Last of the Fast Guns. Universal-International, 1958. 82 minutes Color. D: George Sherman. SC: David P. Harmon. WITH Jock Mahoney, Gilbert Roland, Linda Cristal, Eduard Franz, Lorne Greene, Carl Benton Reid, Edward Platt, Eduardo Noreigo, Jorge Trevino, Lee Morgan, Richard Cutting. A gunman heads into Mexico to find the missing brother of the man who hired him for the job. Pretty good action drama with fine work from stars Jock Mahoney and Gilbert Roland.

1783 The Last of the Knucklemen. Hexagon, 1981. 93 minutes Color. D-SC: Tim Burstall. WITH Gerard Kennedy, Michael Preston, Peter Hehir, Michael Duffield, Dennis Miller, Stephen Bisley, Michael Caton, Stewart Fatchney, Steve Backman. In frontier Australia a camp boss tries to keep order among his group of rowdy hired hands. Entertaining Australian yarn is a very good character study outing.

1784 The Last of the Mohicans. Associated Producers, 1920. 50 minutes B/W. D: Maurice Tourneur & Clarence Brown. SC: Robert Dillon. WITH Wallace Beery, Albert Roscoe, Barbara Bedford, Lillian Hall, Henry Woodward, Boris Karloff, Harry Lorraine, Nelson McDowell, George Hackathorne, Jack McDonald. The last of the Mohican tribe tries to save the daughters of a British fort commander who have been captured by a rival tribe loyal to the French. Well made silent feature version of the James Fenimore Cooper novel. V: Classic Video Cinema Collectors Club.

1785 The Last of the Mohicans. Mascot, 1932. 12 Chapters B/W. D: Ford Beebe & B. Reeves Eason. SC: Colbert Clark, Jack Natteford, Ford Beebe & Wyndham Gittens. WITH Harry Carey, Hobart Bosworth, Junior Coghlan, Edwina Booth, Lucille Browne, Walter Miller, Robert Kortman, Walter McGrail, Nelson McDowell, Edward Hearn, Mischa Auer, Yakima Canutt, Chief Big Tree, Joan Gale, Tully Marshall, Al Cavan. During the French and Indian War scout Hawkeye and his Indian blood brother try to stop an evil chief and his tribe from aiding the French against British settlers. Slow moving serial version of the James Fenimore Cooper novel although Harry Carey is good as Hawkeye and Robert Kortman makes an excellent evil Magua. V: Cassette Express.

1786 The Last of the Mohicans. United Artists, 1936. 91 minutes B/W. D: George

B. Seitz. SC: Philip Dunne. WITH Randolph Scott, Binnie Barnes, Heather Angel, Hugh Buckler, Henry Wilcoxon, Bruce Cabot, Robert Barrat, Phillip Reed, Willard Robertson, Frank McGlynn, Will Stanton, William V. Mong, Olaf Hytten, Claude King, Lumsden Hare, Reginald Barlow, Lionel Belmore. During the French and Indian War, scout Hawkeye and his Indian friend escort two pretty girls through the wilderness and they fall in love with them. Nicely done screen adaptation of James Fennimore Cooper's often filmed 1826 novel. Earlier versions include the 1920 German production **Lederstrumpf** (Leatherstocking) with Bela Lugosi as Chingachgook; **The Last of the Mohicans** (q.v.) (Associated Producers, 1920) with Wallace Beery, Albert Roscoe and Barbara Bedford; the 1932 Mascot serial **The Last of the Mohicans** (q.v.) starring Harry Carey and Edwina Booth. V: Nostalgia Merchant.

1787 The Last of the Mohicans. International German/Balcazar/Cineproduzione, 1965. 88 minutes Color. D: Harald Reinl. SC: Joachim Bartsch. WITH Joachim Fuchsberger, Karin Dor, Carl Lange, Anthony Steffens, Dan Martin, Jose Marco, Luis Induni. When trouble starts between warring Indian tribes, Hawkeye and Chingachgook try to save the lives of the kidnapped daughters of an army colonel. Despite dubbing, this West German production of the James Fenimore Cooper story is a pretty good one. West German title: **Der Letzte Mohikaner.** Alternate title: **The Last Tomahawk.**

1788 The Last of the Mohicans. NBC-TV/Schick Sunn Classics, 1977. 100 minutes Color. D: James L. Conway. SC: Stephen Lord. WITH Steve Forrest, Ned Romero, Andrew Prine, Don Shanks, Robert Tessier, Jane Actman, Michele Marsh, Robert Easton, Whit Bissell, Beverly Rowland. Hawkeye and Indian ally Chingachgook aid a British major in leading a small party through hostile country during the French and Indian War. Well done "Classics Illustrated" production made for television.

1789 Last of the Pony Riders. Columbia, 1953. 59 minutes B/W. D: George Archainbaud. SC: Ruth Woodman. WITH Gene Autry, Smiley Burnette, Kathleen Case, Dick Jones, Howard Wright, Arthur Space, Gregg Barton, Buzz Henry, Harry Mackin, Harry Hines, Kermit Maynard. Pony Express rider Gene Autry loses his job when he buys a stagecoach and finds

out that crooks are working to sabotage the express operations in order to get its mail contract. Gene Autry's final theatrical feature is a pleasant, leisurely paced affair. V: NTA Home Entertainment, Blackhawk.

1790 Last of the Redmen. Columbia, 1947. 77 minutes Color. D: George Sherman. SC: Herbert Dalmas & George Plympton. WITH Jon Hall, Evelyn Ankers, Michael O'Shea, Julie Bishop, Buster Crabbe, Rick Vallin, Buzz Henry, Frederick Worlock, Emmett Vogan, Chief Many Treaties, Guy Hedlund. An Indian, the last of his Mohican tribe, risks his life to save a group of white settlers led into an ambush by Iroquois. Tame adaptation of The Last of the Mohicans.

1791 Last of the Renegades. Constantin, 1964. 104 minutes Color. D: Harald Reinl. SC: Harald G. Peterson. WITH Lex Barker, Pierre Brice, Anthony Steel, Karin Dor, Klaus Kinski, Mario Girotti, Renato Baldini, Eddi Arent, Marie Noelle. Apache chief Winnetou wants to keep his people from going to war after the death of his father, but a ruthless oilman tries to start an uprising so the Indians will be slaughtered and he can take their lands. Flavorful West German oater from the popular Karl May books series. Issued in Europe by Rialto/Jadran-Film as **Winnetou II.**

1792 Last of the Warrens. Supreme, 1936. 56 minutes B/W. D-SC: Robert North Bradbury. WITH Bob Steele, Margaret Marquis, Charles K. French, Lafe McKee, Charles King, Horace Murphy, Blackie Whiteford, Jim Corey, Steve Clark. After becoming an aviator hero during the war, a cowboy returns home to find a crooked local businessman has stolen his property. Typically actionful and entertaining Bob Steele oater.

1793 Last of the Wild Horses. Lippert, 1948. 86 minutes B/W. D: Robert L. Lippert. SC: Jack Harvey. WITH James Ellison, Mary Beth Hughes, Jane Frazee, Douglass Dumbrille, Reed Hadley, James Millican, Olin Howlin, Grady Sutton, William Haade, Stanley Andrews, Rory Mallinson. A cowboy gets himself in the middle of a range dispute when a crooked businessman and his sheriff henchman try to blame a wealthy, crippled rancher for local cattle thefts. More than passable Lippert production with an extremely brutal fight sequence between hero James Ellison and villain Reed Hadley.

1794 The Last Outlaw. Paramount, 1927. 70 minutes B/W. D: Arthur Rosson. SC: John Stone & J. Walter Ruben. WITH Gary Cooper, Betty Jewel, Jack Luden, Herbert Prior, Jim Corey, Billy Butts, Flash (horse). When a lawman is falsely accused of killing his girl's brother, he tries to bring the real murderers, who are also cattle thieves, to justice. Vintage Gary Cooper silent vehicle which will appeal to his fans.

1795 The Last Outlaw. RKO Radio, 1936. 62 minutes B/W. D: Christy Cabanne. SC: John Twist & Jack Townley. WITH Harry Carey, Hoot Gibson, Tom Tyler, Henry B. Walthall, Margaret Callahan, Ray Mayer, Harry Jans, Frank M. Thomas, Russell Hopton, Frank Jenks, Maxine Jennings, Joseph Sawyer, Fred Scott. A once-famous outlaw is released from prison after a quarter of a century and he returns home to find the West he has known is gone and that he is now up against modern-day gangsters. John Ford cowrote the story for this film and it is a corker, combining a nostalgic look at the genre as well as plenty of action from its veteran stars.

1796 The Last Outpost. Paramount, 1951. 88 minutes Color. D: Lewis R. Foster. SC: Geoffrey Homes, George Worthing Yates & Winston Miller. WITH Ronald Reagan, Rhonda Fleming, Bruce Bennett, Bill Williams, Peter Hanson, Noah Beery Jr., Hugh Beaumont, John Ridgeley, Lloyd Corrigan, Charles Evans. When the girl he loves is staying at a fort threatened by Indians, a Confederate cavalry officer leads his men in helping defend the Union-held garrison. Good, colorful actioner from the Pine-Thomas unit.

1797 The Last Posse. Columbia, 1953. 73 minutes B/W. D: Alfred Werker. SC: Seymour Bennett, Connie Lee Bennett & Kenneth Gamet. WITH Broderick Crawford, John Derek, Charles Bickford, Wanda Hendrix, Warner Anderson, Henry Hull, Will Wright, Tom Powers, Raymond Greenleaf, James Kirkwood, Eddy Waller, Skip Homeier, James Bell, Guy Wilkerson, Mira McKinney, Helen Wallace, Harry Hayden, Monte Blue. When a rancher's money is stolen, a sheriff leads a posse into the desert in pursuit of the culprits. Very good and compact oater from producer Harry Joe Brown.

1798 The Last Rebel. Sterling World Distributors, 1961. 83 minutes Color. D-SC: Miguel Contreras Torres. WITH Carlos Thompson, Ariadne Welter, Rudolpho Acosta, Charles Fawcett, Lee Morgan. The happy-go-lucky leader of a Mexican outlaw band defeats a group of murderous gold hunters but as a result is stalked by the Texas Rangers. Mexican-filmed oater is pretty fair entertainment; reissued in 1968.

1799 The Last Rebel. Columbia, 1971. 89 minutes Color. D: Denys McCoy. SC: Warren Kiefer (Luciano Ricci). WITH Joe Namath, Jack Elam, Woody Strode, Ty Hardin, Victoria George, Renato Romano, Marina Coffa, Anmaria Chio, Mike Forrest, Bruce Ewelle, Jessica Dublin, Larry Laurence, Herb Andress. In a small Missouri town after the Civil War a veteran tries to protect some ex-slaves from being lynched. Very poor Italian production.

1800 The Last Ride of the Dalton Gang. NBC-TV, 1979. 150 minutes Color. D: Dan Curtis. WITH Cliff Potts, Larry Wilcox, Randy Quaid, Dale Robertson, Jack Palance, Bo Hopkins, Sharon Farrell, Harris Yulin. The life and times of the legendary Dalton brothers and their career as outlaws. Overlong and somewhat dull tongue-in-cheek look at the Daltons. V: Warner Home Video.

1801 The Last Ride to Santa Cruz. Casino Films, 1964. 99 minutes Color. D: Rolf Olson. WITH Edmund Purdom, Marion Cook (Marianne Koch), Mario Adorf, Klaus Kinski, Walter Giller. When a crooked lawman unjustly sends a man to prison the man escapes and returns for revenge. Fairly entertaining West German oater issued there by Magnet as **Der Letze Ritt Nach Sante Cruz.**

1802 The Last Round-Up. Columbia, 1947. 77 minutes B/W. D: John English. SC: Jack Townley & Earle Snell. WITH Gene Autry, Jean Heather, Ralph Morgan, Bobby Blake, Bud Osborne, Jay Silverheels, John Cason, Carol Thurston, Mark Daniels, Russ Vincent, Shug Fisher, Trevor Bardette, Lee Bennett, John Halloran, Roy Gordon, Dale Van Sickle, Ed Piel Sr., George Carleton, Nolan Leary, Ted Adams, Steve Clark, Frankie Marvin, Kernan Cripps, Iron Eyes Cody, Blackie Whiteford, Robert Walker, Virginia Carroll, Rodd Redwing, Alex Montoya. A crooked land baron causes troubles with local Indians in order to stop an aqueduct project which would interfere with his takeover of more range land. Modern-day western is too long and Gene Autry is very stiff although the film does utilize an amusing sequence involving television.

1803 Last Stagecoach West. Republic, 1957. 70 minutes B/W. D: Joseph Kane. SC: Barry Shipman. WITH Jim Davis, Mary Castle, Victor Jory, Lee Van Cleef, Grant Withers, Roy Barcroft, John Alderson, Glenn Strange, Francis McDonald, Tristram Coffin, Willis Bouchey, Lewis Martin. When crooks sabotage his stageline so that he loses his mail contract, a man joins with his outlaw pal to get revenge. Just passable action melodrama with a good cast and a mediocre plot and only average production values.

1804 The Last Stand. Universal, 1938. 57 minutes B/W. D: Joseph H. Lewis. SC: Harry O. Hoyt & Norton S. Parker. WITH Bob Baker, Marjorie Reynolds, Fuzzy Knight, Earle Hodgins, Forrest Taylor, Glenn Strange, Jack Kirk, Jimmy Phillips, Sam Flint, Frank Ellis, Jack Montgomery. When his father is murdered a cowpoke pretends to be an outlaw in order to infiltrate the gang responsible for the crime. Fair Bob Baker vehicle in which he croons a trio of tunes.

1805 The Last Sunset. Universal, 1961. 112 minutes Color. D: Robert Aldrich. SC: Dalton Trumbo. WITH Rock Hudson, Kirk Douglas, Dorothy Malone, Joseph Cotten, Carol Lynley, Neville Brand, Regis Toomey, Rad Fulton, Adam Williams, Jack Elam, John Shay, Jose Torvay. A lawman is on the trail of the murderer of his brother-in-law and finds him on a cattle drive with a drunken rancher and romancing the latter's pretty daughter. Complicated Mexican-filmed oater with murder, drunkenness, adultery and incest.

The Last Tomahawk see **The Last of the Mohicans** (1965)

1806 The Last Trail. Fox, 1927. 58 minutes B/W. D: Lewis Seiler. SC: John Stone. WITH Tom Mix, Carmelita Geraghty, William Davidson, Frank Hagney, Lee Shumway, Robert Brower, Jerry the Giant, Oliver Eckhardt. A cowboy aids a man and his pretty daughter in their contest with a crook for the government mail contract. Fast moving and entertaining silent version of the Zane Grey novel, first filmed in 1921 by Fox with Maurice Flynn, Eva Novak, Wallace Beery and Rosemary Theby.

1807 The Last Trail. Fox, 1933. 59 minutes B/W. D: James Tinling. SC: Stuart Anthony.

WITH George O'Brien, Claire Trevor, J. Carrol Naish, El Brendel, Matt McHugh, Lucille LaVerne, Ed LeSaint, Ruth Warren, George Reed. A man finds out that gangsters have taken control of his family's ranch and he sets out to stop them. Pleasant adaptation of the Zane Grey work with as much comedy as action.

1808 Last Train from Gun Hill. Paramount, 1959. 94 minutes Color. D: John Sturges. SC: James Poe. WITH Kirk Douglas, Anthony Quinn, Carolyn Jones, Earl Holliman, Brad Dexter, Brian Hutton, Ziva Rodann, Val Avery, Walter Sande, Lars Henderson, John P. Anderson, Lee Hendry, William Newell, Sid Tomack, Charles Stevens, Julius Tannen, Ken Becker, Courtland Shepard, Ty Hardin, Glenn Strange, Hank Mann, William Benedict. After his wife is brutally murdered by two men, a sheriff tracks them to a small town but finds the locals oppose him taking them away to stand trial. Intense and well made action melodrama.

1809 The Last Wagon. 20th Century-Fox, 1956. 99 minutes Color. D: Delmer Daves. SC: James Edward Grant, Delmer Daves & Gwen Bagni. WITH Richard Widmark, Felicia Farr, Susan Kohner, Tommy Rettig, Stephanie Griffin, Ray Stricklyn, Nick Adams, Carl Benton Reid, Douglas Kennedy, George Mathews, James Drury, Ken Clark, Timothy Carey, Juney Ellis, Abel Fernandez. After killing the two men who raped his wife and murdered his children, a man joins a wagon train but finds he is a wanted man. Very well done psychological melodrama, finely acted, especially by Richard Widmark.

Last Warrior see **Flap**

1810 The Law and Jake Wade. Metro-Goldwyn-Mayer, 1958. 86 minutes Color. D: John Sturges. SC: William Bowers. WITH Robert Taylor, Richard Widmark, Patricia Owens, Robert Middleton, Henry Silva, DeForest Kelley, Burt Douglas, Eddie Firestone. A reformed outlaw is about to marry but he and his fiancée are kidnapped by his ex-partner who wants to know the location of hidden loot. Nicely done action drama with good work by the two stars.

1811 Law and Lawless. Majestic, 1932. 58 minutes B/W. D: Armand Schaefer. SC: Oliver Drake. WITH Jack Hoxie, Hilda Moore, Wally Wales, Yakima Canutt, Julian Rivero, Jack Mower, J. Frank Glendon, Edith Fellows, Helen Gibson,

Bob Burns, Fred Burns, Al Taylor. A cowboy rides into an area which is being plagued by cattle rustlers and he sets out to round up the gang. Jack Hoxie's fans will like this film.

1812 Law and Lead. Colony, 1936. 62 minutes B/W. D: Robert Hill. SC: Basil Dickey. WITH Rex Bell, Wally Wales, Harley Wood, Earl Dwire, Solidad Jiminez, Donald Reed, Roger Williams, Lane Chandler, Lloyd Ingraham, Karl Hackett, Ed Cassidy, Lew Meehan. A cattlemen's association agent is assigned to bring in the Juarez Kid for lawless activities on the border but the operative does not believe the Kid is guilty of the crimes. Okay actioner.

1813 Law and Order. Universal, 1932. 80 minutes B/W. D: Edward L. Cahn. SC: John Huston & Tom Reed. WITH Walter Huston, Harry Carey, Raymond Hatton, Russell Hopton, Ralph Ince, Harry Woods, Richard Alexander, Russell Simpson, Alphonse Ethier, Andy Devine, Dewey Robinson, Walter Brennan, Nelson McDowell, D'Arcy Corrigan, George Dixon, Arthur Wanzer, Neal Hart, Richard Cramer, Art Mix, Hank Bell. A famous lawman and his three pals are hired to clean out the lawless element in a small town, culminating in a shootout. Well made, directed and acted, this is one of the all-time great Western films—a must see! Reissue title: **Guns A' Blazing.**

1814 Law and Order. Universal, 1940. 57 minutes B/W. D: Ray Taylor. SC: Sherman Lowe & Victor McLeod. WITH Johnny Mack Brown, Nell O'Day, Fuzzy Knight, James Craig, Harry Cording, Earle Hodgins, Robert Fiske, Jimmie Dodd, William Worthington, Ted Adams, Ethan Laidlaw, Robert Kortman, Jim Corey, Charles King, The Notables, Harry Humphrey, George Plues, Kermit Maynard, Frank McCarroll, Frank Ellis, Lew Meehan. An ex-lawman is aided by a reformed gambler in cleaning up the lawless element in a small town. Still another screen version of W. R. Burnett's novel Saint Johnson which was done much better in 1932 as **Law and Order** (q.v.). This outing is only average with music to boot!

1815 Law and Order. Producers Releasing Corporation, 1942. 56 minutes B/W. D: Sherman Scott (Sam Newfield). SC: Sam Robins. WITH Buster Crabbe, Al St. John, Tex (Dave) O'Brien, Sarah Padden, Wanda McKay, Charles King, Hal Price,

John Merton, Kenne Duncan, Ted Adams, Budd Buster, Kermit Maynard. In order to save a woman from marrying a crook, Billy the Kid poses as her nephew, an Army officer who has been murdered. An out-of-the-ordinary plotline adds a bit of zest to this otherwise mundane PRC "Billy the Kid" series entry. TV title: **Billy the Kid's Law and Order.**

1816 Law and Order. Universal, 1953. 80 minutes Color. D: Nathan Juran. SC: John Bagni, Owen Bagni & D. D. Beauchamp. WITH Ronald Reagan, Dorothy Malone, Alex Nicol, Preston Foster, Ruth Hampton, Russell Johnson, Barry Kelley, Chubby Johnson, Dennis Weaver, Jack Kelly, Valerie Jackson, Don Garner, Thomas Browne Henry, Richard Garrick, Tristram Coffin, Mike Ragan, John Carpenter, Buddy Roosevelt, Richard Cutting, Britt Wood, Martin Garralaga. A lawman gives up his badge to marry and become a rancher but when his brother, who had taken his job, is killed by badmen he sets out to clean up the town. Still another screen version of Saint Johnson by W. R. Burnett and quite mediocre compared to the classic 1932 version.

1817 Law Beyond the Range. Columbia, 1935. 60 minutes B/W. D-SC: Ford Beebe. WITH Tim McCoy, Billie Seward, Robert Allen, Guy Usher, Harry Todd, Walter Brennan, Si Jenks, Tom London, J. B. Denton, Ben Hendricks Jr., Jack Rockwell. A ranger is falsely accused of murder and a pal lets him escape; he is drummed out of the service and goes to a small town and aids a girl newspaper editor who is opposing the mysterious town boss, El Poder (The Power). One of Tim McCoy's better Columbia outings with a good story by Lambert Hillyer, and an exciting shootout at the climax.

1818 The Law Comes to Gunsight. Monogram, 1947. 56 minutes. D: Lambert Hillyer. SC: J. Benton Cheney. WITH Johnny Mack Brown, Raymond Hatton, Reno Blair, Lanny Rees, William Ruhl, Zon Murray, Frank LaRue, Ernie Adams, Kermit Maynard, Ted Adams, Lee Roberts, Artie Ortego. When the crooked mayor mistakes a lawman for a hired gun, he makes him the town's sheriff and the lawman sets out to round up the outlaws. Predictable but more than passable oater.

1819 The Law Comes to Texas. Columbia, 1939. 55 minutes B/W. D: Joseph Levering. SC: Nate Gatzert. WITH Bill Elliott, Veda Ann Borg, Charles King, Bud Osborne,

Slim Whitaker, Leon Beaumont, Edmund Cobb, Lee Shumway, Frank Ellis, Paul Everton, Jack Ingram, Frank LaRue, David Sharpe, Forrest Taylor, Lane Chandler, Budd Buster, Dan White, Ben Corbett. The state of Texas is plagued by cattle rustling and murder and a man tries to restore law and order and helps form the Texas Rangers. Okay actionful outing from producer Larry Darmour in his Bill Elliott series.

1820 The Law Commands. Crescent, 1937. 58 minutes B/W. D: William Nigh. SC: Bennett Cohen. WITH Tom Keene, Lorraine Hayes (Laraine Day), Budd Buster, Mathew Betz, Robert Fiske, John Merton, Carl Stockdale, David Sharpe, Marie Stoddard, Fred Burns, Horace B. Carpenter. Landgrabbers try to steal farms from settlers who have come to Iowa in 1862 under the Homestead Act. Another entry in Tom Keene's Crescent Pictures historical series and one that is pretty good.

1821 Law for Tombstone. Universal, 1937. 59 minutes B/W. D: Buck Jones. SC: Frances Guihan. WITH Buck Jones, Muriel Evans, Harvey Clark, Carl Stockdale, Earle Hodgins, Alexander Cross, Chuck Morrison, Mary Carney, Charles LeMoyne, Ben Corbett, Francis Walker, Robert Kortman, Slim Whitaker, Tom Forman, Bill Patton, Frank McCarroll. When a stage line is plagued with gold shipment robberies a special agent is hired to stop the lawlessness. Sturdy Buck Jones vehicle produced and directed by the star.

1822 Law Men. Monogram, 1944. 55 minutes B/W. D: Lambert Hillyer. SC: Glenn Tyron. WITH Johnny Mack Brown, Raymond Hatton, Jan Wiley, Kirby Grant, Robert Frazer, Edmund Cobb, Art Fowler, Hal Price, Marshall Reed, Isabel Withers, Ben Corbett, Ted Mapes, Steve Clark, Bud Osborne, Jack Rockwell, George Morrell, Ray Jones. Two lawmen investigate a series of holdups with one joining the gang while the other sets himself up in business in town, both trying to find out who is behind the robberies. Pretty good action entry written by former screen star Glenn Tyron. Also known as **Lawmen.**

1823 Law of the Badlands. RKO Radio, 1951. 60 minutes B/W. D: Lesley Selander. SC: Ed Earl Repp. WITH Tim Holt, Richard Martin, Joan Dixon, Robert Livingston, Leonard Penn, Harry Woods, Larry Johns,

Robert Bray, Kenneth MacDonald, John Cliff. On the trail of a gang of counterfeiters, two Texas Rangers pretend to be outlaws in order to infiltrate the crooks. Fairly actionful Tim Holt vehicle, average for the series.

1824 Law of the Barbary Coast. Columbia, 1949. 65 minutes B/W. D: Lew Landers. SC: Robert Libott & Frank Burt. WITH Gloria Henry, Stephen Dunne, Adele Jergens, Robert Shayne, Stefan Schnabel, Edwin Max, Ross Ford, J. Farrell MacDonald. When her brother is murdered a young girl takes a job in a Barbary Coast gambling house to get the proof needed to convict the killer. Average action melodrama set in frontier times.

1825 Law of the Canyon. Columbia, 1947. 55 minutes B/W. D: Ray Nazarro. SC: Eileen Gary. WITH Charles Starrett, Smiley Burnette, Nancy Saunders, Buzz Henry, Texas Jim Lewis & His Lone Star Cowboys, Fred Sears, George Chesebro, Edmund Cobb, Zon Murray, Jack Kirk, Robert Wilke, Frank Marlo, Stanley Price. The Durango Kid steps in when outlaws try to make people pay protection money or risk having their goods stolen and then be forced to pay a ransom for them. Less than mediocre "Durango Kid" feature.

1826 Law of the 45s. Normandy Pictures/First Division/Grand National, 1935. 56 minutes B/W. D: John McCarthy. SC: Robert (Emmett) Tansey. WITH Guinn Williams, Molly O'Day, Al St. John, Ted Adams, Lafe McKee, Fred Burns, Martin Garralaga, Curly Baldwin, Sherry Tansey, Glenn Strange, Bill Patton, Jack Kirk, Francis Walker, Jack Evans, Tex Palmer, Merrill McCormack, George Morrell, William McCall, Broderick O'Farrell. Tucson Smith and Stony Brooke are on the trail of an outlaw gang terrorizing the territory. The first "Three Mesquiteers" film, from the books by William Colt MacDonald, is minus a Mesquiteer but otherwise is an interesting low budget offering.

1827 Law of the Golden West. Republic, 1949. 59 minutes B/W. D: Philip Ford. SC: Norman S. Hall. WITH Monte Hale, Paul Hurst, Gail Davis, Roy Barcroft, John Holland, Scott Elliott, Lane Bradford, Harold Goodwin, John Hamilton. A group of outlaws have been attacking an area and Buffalo Bill Cody sets out to stop them. Okay costume entry in Monte Hale's Republic series. V: Cumberland Video.

1828 Law of the Land. NBC-TV, 1976. 100 minutes Color. D: Virgil Vogel. SC: John Wilder & Sam Rolfe. WITH Jim Davis, Barbara Parkins, Andrew Prine, Moses Gunn, Glenn Corbett, Charles Martin Smith, Dana Elcar, Don Johnson, Cal Bellini, Nicholas Hammond, Darleen Carr, Ward Costello, Paul Stevens, Barney Phillips. When a madman goes on a rampage killing hookers, a lawman and his deputies go in pursuit of him. Pretty good TV actioner, highlighted by Jim Davis' performance as the old-time sheriff. Alternate title: **The Deputies.**

1829 Law of the Lash. Producers Releasing Corporation, 1947. 54 minutes B/W. D: Ray Taylor. SC: William L. Nolte. WITH Lash LaRue, Al St. John, Lee Roberts, Mary Scott, Jack O'Shea, Charles King, Carl Matthews, Richard Cramer, Slim Whitaker, John Elliott, Ted French, Brad Slaven. Outlaws run the settlers out of a small town and take it over but U.S. marshals arrive on the scene and try to restore law and order. Fairly typical Lash LaRue oater with Charles King a good guy for a change! V: Cassette Express.

1830 Law of the Lawless. Paramount, 1964. 87 minutes Color. D: William F. Claxton. SC: Steve Fisher. WITH Dale Robertson, Yvonne De Carlo, William Bendix, Lon Chaney, Bruce Cabot, Barton MacLane, John Agar, Richard Arlen, Kent Taylor, Jody McCrea, Bill Williams, Rod Lauren, George Chandler, Donald Barry, Romo Vincent, Lorraine Bendix, Joe Forte, Alex Sharp, Leigh Chapman, Laurel Goodwin, Fred Rapport, George Taylor, Lori Campbell, Dick Ryan, Roy Jensen, Jerry Summers, Reg Parton, Wally West. A hanging judge comes to town to try a man accused of murder, the man being the son of an old friend who tries to blackmail the judge. The first in a series of oaters from producer A. C. Lyles with veteran casts, and it is a good one.

1831 Law of the North. Monogram, 1932. 56 minutes B/W. D-SC: Harry Fraser. WITH Bill Cody, Andy Shuford, Nadine Dore, Al St. John, William L. Thorne, Heinie Conklin, Jack Carlyle. A lawman is on the trail of an elusive outlaw who has been able to escape from previous arrest attempts. Slow moving and not very entertaining Bill Cody film.

1832 Law of the Northwest. Columbia, 1943. 57 minutes B/W. D: William Berke.

SC: Luci Ward. WITH Charles Starrett, Shirley Patterson, Arthur Hunnicutt, Stanley Brown, Douglas Leavitt, Donald Curtis, Douglass Drake, Davison Clark, Reginald Barlow. The Mounties are after a crooked contractor trying to stop work on a rival's road in order to get a valuable war contract. Average, but well photographed (by Benjamin Kline), Charles Starrett north woods opus.

1833 Law of the Pampas. Paramount, 1939. 54 (72) minutes B/W. D: Nate Watt. SC: Harrison Jacobs. WITH William Boyd, Russell Hayden, Steffi Duna, Sidney Toler, Sidney Blackmer, Pedro de Cordoba, William Duncan, Anna Demetrio, Eddie Dean, Glenn Strange, Tony Roux, Martin Garralaga, The King's Men, Jojo LaSavio. In South America bringing in cattle for a land owner, Hoppy begins to suspect the ranch foreman of being behind the killing of the owner's two children because he wants the ranch for himself. Nice locations, interesting storyline and some good action make this a fine "Hopalong Cassidy" outing.

1834 Law of the Panhandle. Monogram, 1950. 55 minutes B/W. D: Lewis D. Collins. SC: Joseph Poland. WITH Johnny Mack Brown, Jane Adams, Riley Hill, Marshall Reed, Myron Healey, Ted Adams, Lee Roberts, Carol Henry, Milburn Morante, Bob Duncan, Kermit Maynard, Boyd Stockman, George DeNormand, Tex Palmer, Ray Jones. A small town is being plagued by rustlers out to get range land to be used by the railroad and the sheriff calls in a U. S. marshal. Good Johnny Mack Brown actioner with fine work by Myron Healey as the vicious gang leader.

1835 Law of the Plains. Columbia, 1938. 56 minutes B/W. D: Sam Nelson. SC: Maurice Geraghty. WITH Charles Starrett, Iris Meredith, Robert Warwick, Bob Nolan & The Sons of the Pioneers, Dick Curtis, Ed Le Saint, Edmund Cobb, Art Mix, Jack Rockwell, George Chesebro, Jack Long, John Tyrell, Blackie Whiteford. The foreman of a ranch whose owner is being threatened by an outlaw gang tries to stop the crooks. Well done Charles Starrett vehicle.

1836 Law of the Range. Universal, 1941. 59 minutes B/W. D: Ray Taylor. SC: Sherman Lowe. WITH Johnny Mack Brown, Fuzzy Knight, Nell O'Day, Roy Harris (Riley Hill), Pat O'Malley, Elaine Morey, Ethan Laidlaw, The Texas Rangers, Al

Bridge, Hal Taliaferro, Lucille Walker, Charles King, Bud Osborne, Robert Kortman, Slim Whitaker, Jack Rockwell, Terry Frost, Jim Corey. A cowboy whose family is involved in a range feud over cattle and sheep gets the blame for the death of the man whose daughter he loves. Sturdy Johnny Mack Brown vehicle.

1837 Law of the Rangers. Columbia, 1937. 57 minutes B/W. D: Spencer Gordon Bennet. SC: Nate Gatzert. WITH Bob Allen, Elaine Shepard, Hal Taliaferro, Lafe McKee, John Merton, Tom London, Lane Chandler, Slim Whitaker, Ernie Adams, Bud Osborne, Jimmie Aubrey. Two rangers arrive incognito in a remote area to investigate the intimidation of settlers by a crook and his gang, the badman trying to get the control of all the water rights in the area. Entertaining entry in Bob Allen's brief Columbia series, this one again teaming him with Hal Taliaferro (Wally Wales).

1838 Law of the Rio Grande. Syndicate, 1931. 57 minutes B/W. D: Forrest Sheldon. SC: Betty Burbridge & Bennett Cohen. WITH Bob Custer, Betty Mack, Edmund Cobb, Nelson McDowell, Harry Todd. An ex-outlaw tries to go straight as a ranch foreman, but a former cohort wants to get him back on the wrong side of the law. This outing is a bit better than some Bob Custer vehicles thanks mainly to Edmund Cobb as the bad guy.

1839 Law of the Saddle. Producers Releasing Corporation, 1943. 57 minutes B/W. D: Melville DeLay. SC: Fred Myton. WITH Robert Livingston, Al St. John, Betty Miles, Lane Chandler, John Elliott, Reed Howes, Frank Ellis, Curley Dresden, Al Ferguson, Frank Hagney, Jimmie Aubrey. The Lone Rider is after an outlaw gang which goes from town to town electing one of its members as sheriff, then taking all the town's money. Interesting plot is hurt by low grade production values in this "Lone Rider" series entry.

1840 Law of the Texan. Columbia, 1938. 54 minutes. D: Elmer Clifton. SC: Monroe Shaff & Arthur Hoerl. WITH Buck Jones, Dorothy Fay, Don Douglas, Kenneth Harlan, Joe Whitehead, Matty Kemp, Forrest Taylor, Robert Kortman, Jose Torosa, Melissa Sierra, Tommy Mack, Jack Ingram, Dave O'Brien. The leader of a band of Texas Rangers finds out a cattle rustling attempt was just a ruse to hide the theft of an ore shipment and he tries to find the culprit behind

the robbery, a mysterious figure called El Coyote. A strong script and scenic values add up to a good Buck Jones series entry.

1841 Law of the Timber. Producers Releasing Corporation, 1941. 63 minutes B/W. D: Bernard B. Ray. SC: Jack Natteford. WITH Marjorie Reynolds, Monte Blue, J. Farrell MacDonald, Hal Brazeal, George Humbert, Sven Hugo, Earl Eby, Milt Moroni, Betty Roadman, Eddie Phillips. After the death of her logger father, a girl tries to fulfill his government contract despite sabotage efforts by her foreman. Nice action melodrama from PRC.

1842 Law of the Valley. Monogram, 1944. 59 minutes B/W. D: Howard Bretherton. SC: Joseph O'Donnell. WITH Johnny Mack Brown, Raymond Hatton, Lynne Carver, Kirk Barron, Hal Price, Edmund Cobb, Tom Quinn, Charles King, Marshall Reed, George DeNormand, Steve Clark, George Morrell, Charles McMurphy. Outlaws want range land which controls the area's water supply because the railroad plans to build a spur on it and two marshals are called in to stop their activities. Pleasant entry in the Johnny Mack Brown-Raymond Hatton series.

1843 Law of the West. World Wide, 1932. 50 minutes B/W. D-SC: Robert North Bradbury. WITH Bob Steele, Nancy Drexel, Ed Brady, Hank Bell, Charles West, Earl Dwire, Dick Dickinson, Rose Plummer, Frank Ellis. Kidnapped by an outlaw gang as a baby, a young man believes his father is the gang leader, who is planning to have him shoot his real father, the town marshal. Well written and executed Bob Steele vehicle, with equal emphasis on drama and action.

1844 Law of the West. Monogram, 1949. 60 minutes B/W. D: Ray Taylor. SC: J. Benton Cheney. WITH Johnny Mack Brown, Max Terhune, Bill Kennedy, Gerry Pattison, Jack Ingram, Eddie Parker, Riley Hill, Steve Clark, Jack Harrison, Bob Woodward, Marshall Reed, Kenne Duncan, Bud Osborne, Frank Ellis. A real estate agent is faking deeds to properties and then stealing them from the owners and a vacationing U. S. marshal comes to the rescue. Mediocre series outing for Johnny Mack Brown saved somewhat by Max Terhune's comedy and ventriloquist work.

1845 The Law of the Wild. Mascot, 1934. 12 Chapters B/W. D: B. Reeves Eason

& Armand L. Schaefer. SC: Sherman Lowe & B. Reeves Eason. WITH Rex (horse), Rin-Tin-Tin Jr. (dog), Ben Turpin, Bob Custer, Lucille Browne, Richard Cramer, Ernie Adams, Richard Alexander, Edmund Cobb, Charles "Slim" Whitaker, George Chesebro, Wally Wales, Charles King, Lafe McKee, Hank Bell, Art Mix, Bud Osborne, Glenn Strange, Al Taylor, Jack Evans, Bud McClure, Herman Hack. A rancher owns a beautiful stallion which he tamed but one of his men, along with two cohorts, plot to steal the animal and use him as a race horse. Fun Mascot poverty row cliffhanger with hero Bob Custer getting fourth billing behind the two animal stars and comedy relief Ben Turpin. V: Video Connection.

1846 Law of the Wolf. Ziehm, 1941. 55 minutes B/W. D: Raymond K. Johnson. SC: Joseph Murphy. WITH Rin-Tin-Tin III, Dennis Moore, Luana Walters, George Chesebro, Steve Clark, Jack Ingram, Robert Frazer, Jimmie Aubrey, Martin Spellman, Bobby Gordon. A man is aided by his girl and a dog in a battle with crooks. Low grade but exceedingly action-ful programmer.

1847 The Law Rides. Supreme, 1936. 57 minutes B/W. D: Robert North Bradbury. SC: Al Martin. WITH Bob Steele, Harley Wood, Charles King, Buck Connors, Margaret Mann, Jack Rockwell, Barney Furey, Ted Mapes. A gold strike results in outlaws robbing and killing miners and a cowboy tracks down the culprits. Very actionful Bob Steele series entry, although a bit short on production values.

1848 The Law Rides Again. Monogram, 1943. 58 minutes B/W. D: Alan James. SC: Frances Kavanaugh. WITH Ken Maynard, Hoot Gibson, Betty Miles, Kenneth Harlan, Jack LaRue, Chief Thundercloud, Hank Bell, Bryant Washburn, Emmett Lynn, John Bridges, Fred Hoose, Charles Murray Jr., Chief Many Treaties, John Merton. Two lawmen are on the trail of a man masquerading as an Indian agent and robbing the tribes. Second in the "Trail Blazers" series, this film should please the fans of its two stars.

1849 The Law Vs. Billy the Kid. Columbia, 1954. 73 minutes Color. D: William Castle. SC: John T. Williams. WITH Scott Brady, Betta St. John, James Griffith, Alan Hale Jr., Paul Cavanagh, William Phillips, Benny Rubin, Steve Darrell, William Tannen, Martin Garralaga, Richard Cutting, Frank Sully, William Fawcett. On the run from the law, Billy the Kid is befriended by a rancher and falls in love with his pretty daughter who is also loved by the ranch foreman. Only average fiction about Billy the Kid.

1850 The Law West of Tombstone. RKO Radio, 1938. 72 minutes B/W. D: Glenn Tryon. SC: John Twist & Clarence Upson Young. WITH Harry Carey, Tim Holt, Evelyn Brent, Jean Rouverol, Clarence Kolb, Allan Lane, Esther Muir, Bradley Page, Paul Guilfoyle, Robert Moya, Ward Bond, George Irving, Monte Montague, Robert Kortman, Kermit Maynard. A judge who rules by the gun sets up court in a small town and opposes his daughter's upcoming wedding to a no-good, who is soon dispatched by a young gunman. Top-notch oater which takes a look at the career of Judge Roy Bean, here called Bill Parker. V: Cassette Express, Nostalgia Merchant.

1851 The Lawless. Wrather Corporation, 1956. 75 minutes Color. D: Earl Bellamy & Oscar Rudolph. SC: Thomas Seller & Doane Hoag. WITH Clayton Moore, Jay Silverheels, Myron Healey, Allen Pinson, Wayne Burson, George J. Lewis, Trevor Bardette, Pierce Lyden, Zon Murray, William Fawcett, Tudor Owen, John Beradino, Mickey Simpson, Maria Manay, Joe Vitale, David Armstrong, Rocky Shahan, John Cason, Robert Roark, David Kashner, J. Anthony Hughes, Louise Lewis, Paul Engle, Mercedes Shirley. The Lone Ranger and Tonto are on the trail of an outlaw gang masquerading as cavalrymen, they stop vigilantes from breaking the law and aid a retired lawman in capturing two murderers. Well done telefeature from "The Lone Ranger" (ABC-TV, 1949-57) series from the segments "Return of Don Pedro O'Sullivan," "The Tarnished Star" and "Sam's Boy."

1852 Lawless Borders. Spectrum, 1935. 58 minutes B/W. D: John P. McCarthy. SC: Zara Tazil. WITH Bill Cody, Molly O'Day, Martin Garralaga, Ted Adams, John Elliott, Merrill McCormack, Roger Williams, Budd Buster. After his pal is murdered, a man seeks revenge on the killers. Typically low grade Bill Cody effort from Spectrum.

1853 Lawless Breed. Universal, 1946. 58 minutes B/W. D: Wallace Fox. SC: Robert Williams. WITH Kirby Grant, Fuzzy Knight, Jane Adams, Harry Brown, Dick Curtis, Charles King, Karl Hackett, Hank Worden, Claudia Drake, Ernie Adams,

Harry Wilson, Artie Ortego. Two cowboys ride into a small town where they get mixed up with an outlaw gang and are accused of murdering a banker and are forced to flee a lynch mob. Fairly good finale to Kirby Grant's Universal series. TV title: **Lawless Clan.**

1854 The Lawless Breed. Universal, 1952. 83 minutes Color. D: Raoul Walsh. SC: Bernard Gordon. WITH Rock Hudson, Julia (Julie) Adams, John McIntire, Mary Castle, Hugh O'Brian, Forrest Lewis, Lee Van Cleef, Tom Fadden, William Pullen, Dennis Weaver, Glenn Strange, Richard Garland, Race Gentry, Carl Pitti, Ned Davenport, Robert Anderson, Stephen Chase, Richard Wessel, Emory Parnell, George Wallace, Edward Earle, Michael Ansara, Paul "Tiny" Newlan, Francis Ford, I. Stanford Jolley, Buddy Roosevelt, Ethan Laidlaw, Stanley Blystone, Wheaton Chambers. After sixteen years in prison John Wesley Hardin returns home to find his teenage son idolizes him as a gunman and he decides to take part in one last lawless effort to show the boy the error of his ways. Slick production values and a good story greatly help this oater.

Lawless Clan see **Lawless Breed** (1946)

1855 Lawless Code. Monogram, 1949. 58 minutes B/W. D: Oliver Drake. SC: Basil Dickey. WITH Jimmy Wakely, Dub Taylor, Ellen Hall, Tristram Coffin, Riley Hill, Kenne Duncan, Terry Frost, Myron Healey, Steve Clark, Bud Osborne, Bob Curtis, Frank McCarroll, Beatrice Maude. The nephew of a man murdered by outlaws is accused of the killing and a cowboy comes to his rescue. Not even a good bunch of screen bad guys can save this typically low grade Jimmy Wakely singing oater.

1856 Lawless Cowboys. Monogram, 1951. 58 minutes B/W. D: Lewis D. Collins. SC: Maurice Tombragel. WITH Whip Wilson, Fuzzy Knight, Jim Bannon, Pamela Duncan, Lee Roberts, Marshall Reed, Lane Bradford, I. Stanford Jolley, Bruce Edwards, Stanley Price, Richard Emory, Ace Malloy. An ex-Texas Ranger is hired to look into a scheme where participants are fixing rodeo events. Okay modern day actioner in the Whip Wilson series.

1857 The Lawless Eighties. Republic, 1958. 70 minutes B/W. D: Joseph Kane. SC: Kenneth Gamet. WITH Buster Crabbe, John Smith, Marilyn Saris, Ted De Corsia,

Anthony Caruso, John Doucette, Frank Ferguson, Sheila Bromley, Walter Reed, Buzz Henry. A gunman comes to the aid of a circuit rider who has been beaten by outlaws who he has seen mistreating Indians. Pretty good action melodrama which will please Buster Crabbe fans.

1858 Lawless Empire. Columbia, 1945. 58 minutes B/W. D: Vernon Keays. SC: Bennett Cohen. WITH Charles Starrett, Tex Harding, Dub Taylor, Mildred Law, Bob Wills & The Texas Playboys, Johnny Walsh, John Calvert, Ethan Laidlaw, Forrest Taylor, Jack Rockwell, George Chesebro, Boyd Stockman, Lloyd Ingraham, Jessie Arnold, Tom Chatterton, Ray Jones, Edward Howard, Bud Nelson, Frank LaRue, Joe Galbreath, John Tyrell, Jack Kirk. The Durango Kid aids a minister and his wife who are trying to help settlers harassed by a gang of raiders. Choppy, but fast moving, "Durango Kid" episode.

1859 The Lawless Frontier. Monogram, 1934. 52 minutes B/W. D-SC: Robert North Bradbury. WITH John Wayne, Sheila Terry, George ("Gabby") Hayes, Earl Dwire, Yakima Canutt, Jack Rockwell, Gordon D. Woods, Lloyd Whitlock, Eddie Parker, Artie Ortego, Buffalo Bill Jr. A young man whose parents were murdered by a Mexican bandit leader teams with an old man and his daughter to get revenge. Rather typical entry in the John Wayne "Lone Star" series.

1860 Lawless Land. Republic, 1936. 55 minutes. D: Albert Ray. SC: Andrew Bennison. WITH Johnny Mack Brown, Louise Stanley, Ted Adams, Julian Rivero, Horace Murphy, Frank Ball, Ed Cassidy, Roger Williams, Frances Kellogg. A Texas Ranger comes to a small town to investigate a series of murders and finds out the town marshall is the real culprit. Fairly good Johnny Mack Brown series entry.

1861 The Lawless Nineties. Republic, 1936. 56 minutes B/W. D: Joseph Kane. SC: Joseph Poland. WITH John Wayne, Ann Rutherford, Harry Woods, George ("Gabby") Hayes, Al Bridge, Lane Chandler, Fred "Snowflake" Toones, Etta McDaniel, Tom Brower, Cliff Lyons, Jack Rockwell, Al Taylor, Charles King, George Chesebro, Tom London, Sam Flint, Earl Seaman, Tracy Layne, Philo McCullough. A federal investigator is sent to Wyoming to see that elections there are not rigged and he finds himself up against an outlaw gang opposing statehood. Very actionful and well done John Wayne film. V: NTA Home Entertainment.

1862 Lawless Plainsmen. Columbia, 1942. 59 minutes B/W. D: William Berke. SC: Luci Ward. WITH Charles Starrett, Russell Hayden, Cliff Edwards, Luana Walters, Ray Bennett, Gwen Kenyon, Frank LaRue, Stanley Brown, Nick Thompson, Eddie Laughton, Carl Mathews. When the head of a wagon train is killed by Indians, the man's daughter persuades another man to take over the train and he discovers a crook is behind the attacks. Cheaply made but fast moving Charles Starrett-Russell Hayden vehicle.

1863 The Lawless Range. Republic, 1935. 56 minutes B/W. D: Robert North Bradbury. SC: Lindsley Parsons. WITH John Wayne, Sheila Mannors, Frank McGlynn Jr., Earl Dwire, Yakima Canutt, Jack Curtis, Wally Howe, Glenn Strange, Jack Kirk, Fred Burns, Slim Whitaker, Julia Griffin. A young peace officer goes to a valley plagued by cattle rustling to see who is behind the illegal activities. Okay actionful John Wayne vehicle in which Duke even warbles a (dubbed) tune. V: Discount Video.

1864 The Lawless Rider. United Artists, 1954. 72 minutes B/W. D: Yakima Canutt. SC: John Carpenter. WITH John Carpenter, Texas Rose Bascom, Douglass Dumbrille, Frankie Darro, Frank "Red" Carpenter, Noel Neill, Kenne Duncan, Weldon Bascom, Bud Osborne, Bill Coontz, Tap Canutt, Hank Caldwell & His Saddle Kings, Roy Canada. A gunman takes over a small town and a woman rancher goes to the deputy marshal for help. Poor John Carpenter outing which was Edward D. Wood Jr.'s first released film (he was the associate producer).

1865 Lawless Riders. Columbia, 1935. 60 minutes B/W. D: Spencer Gordon Bennet. SC: Nate Gatzert. WITH Ken Maynard, Geneva Mitchell, Harry Woods, Frank Yaconelli, Hal Taliaferro, Slim Whitaker, Frank Ellis, Jack Rockwell, Bob McKenzie, Hank Bell, Bud Jamison, Horace B. Carpenter, Bud McClure, Pascale Perry, Oscar Gahan. After rescuing the banker's daughter during a stage holdup, a roaming cowboy sets out to capture a notorious outlaw and his gang. Actionful and enjoyable Ken Maynard film.

1866 A Lawless Street. Columbia, 1955. 78 minutes Color. D: Joseph H. Lewis. SC: Kenneth Gamet. WITH Randolph Scott, Angela Lansbury, Warner Anderson, Jean Parker, Wallace Ford, John Emery, James Bell, Ruth Donnelly, Michael Pate, Don Megowan, Jeannete Nolan, Peter Ortiz, Frank Hagney, Frank Ferguson, Harry Tyler, Harry Antrim, Jay Lawrence, Reed Howes, Guy Teague, Hal K. Dawson, Stanley Blystone, Eddie Chandler. The doctor of a frontier town finds out a local businessman has marked him for murder because he loves the physician's estranged wife, a recently imported opera singer. Another film from Randolph Scott with a good plot and fine action.

1867 Lawless Valley. RKO Radio, 1938. 59 minutes B/W. D: David Howard. SC: Oliver Drake. WITH George O'Brien, Kay Sutton, Fred Kohler, Fred Kohler Jr., Walter Miller, George McQuarrie, Lew Kelly, Earle Hodgins, Chill Wills, Dot Farley, Robert Stanton (Kirby Grant), George Chesebro, Carl Stockdale, Ben Corbett, Robert McKenzie. A young man, who was falsely sent to prison, returns home to prove his innocence, find the killer of his father and claim his girl, and he finds himself opposed to a self-appointed town boss and his son. Very good George O'Brien series oater.

1868 Lawman. United Artists, 1971. 99 minutes Color. D: Michael Winner. SC: Gerald Wilson. WITH Burt Lancaster, Robert Ryan, Lee J. Cobb, Sheree North, Joseph Wiseman, Robert Duvall, Albert Salmi, J. D. Cannon, John McGiver, Richard Jordan, John Beck, Ralph Waite, William Watson, Charles Tyner, John Hillerman, Robert Emhardt, Richard Bull, Hugh McDermott, Lou Frizzell, Walter Brooke, Bill Bramley. A marshal arrives in a small town to arrest a local cattle baron for the killing of an old man and finds his actions opposed by the local citizens, including the town's weak-willed sheriff. Average big budget oater somewhat saved by its good cast.

1869 A Lawman Is Born. Republic, 1937. 61 minutes B/W. D: Sam Newfield. SC: George Plympton. WITH Johnny Mack Brown, Iris Meredith, Warner Richmond, Charles King, Dick Curtis, Mary McLaren, Earle Hodgins, Al St. John, Frank LaRue, Steve Clark, Jack C. Smith, Sherry Tansey, Wally West, Budd Buster, Lew Meehan, Tex Palmer. A young man opposed to local crooks becomes the town's sheriff and tries to stop several big ranchers from taking over all of the local cattle trade. This oater suffers from a somewhat complicated plot but it does not lack for action.

Lawmen see **Law Men**

1870 The Law's Lash. Pathe, 1928. 60 minutes B/W. D: Noel Mason Smith. SC: Edward Meagher. WITH Klondike (dog), Robert Ellis, Mary Mayberry, Jack Marsh, Richard R. Meill, LeRoy Mason, William Walters. A mountie, aided by a police dog, searches for the killer of a fellow trooper and the chief suspect is his girl's foster father. Average silent actioner.

1871 Lay That Rifle Down. Republic, 1955. 71 minutes B/W. D: Charles Lamont. SC: Barry Shipman. WITH Judy Canova, Robert Lowery, Jil Jarmyn, Jacqueline de Witt, Richard Deacon, Robert Burton, James Bell, Leon Tyler, Tweeny Canova, Pierre Watkin, Marjorie Bennett, William Fawcett, Paul E. Burns, Edmund Cobb, Donald MacDonald, Mimi Gibson, Rudy Lee. An overworked girl who is a drudge in a small hotel dreams of becoming wealthy. Another genre outing with Judy Canova which will please her fans.

1872 Leadville Gunslinger. Republic, 1952. 54 minutes B/W. D: Harry Keller. SC: M. Coates Webster. WITH Allan "Rocky" Lane, Eddy Waller, Grant Withers, Elaine Riley, Roy Barcroft, Richard Crane, I. Stanford Jolley, Kenneth Mac-Donald, Mickey Simpson, Art Dillard. An outlaw gang has been carrying out a series of robberies and killings and their activities are soon opposed by a U. S. marshal. Another typical entry in the Allan Lane Republic series; average.

1873 The Leather Burners. United Artists, 1943. 54 (66) minutes B/W. D: Joseph Henaberry. SC: Jo Pagano. WITH William Boyd, Andy Clyde, Jay Kirby, Victor Jory, George Givot, Shelley Spencer, Bobby Larson, George Reeves, Hal Talia-ferro, Forbes Murray, Robert Mitchum, Robert Kortman, Herman Hack. Hoppy and California help Johnny and a local rancher in trying to rid the area of rustlers and Hoppy gets in good with a man mixed up in the affair to find out who is really behind the raids. Fairly good "Hopalong Cassidy" actioner with an exciting climax in a mine.

1874 Leave Your Guns at the Door!. Agata Film, 1972. 83 minutes Color.

D: Leopoldo Savona. SC: Norbert Blake & Leopoldo Savona. WITH Mark Damon, Richard Melvill, Veronica Korosec, Pietro Ceccarelli. An Italian immigrant in the West joins forces with two pretty girls and a cowboy in trying to promote pizzas. Undistinguished Italian oater comedy issued in France as **Deposez Les Colts.**

1875 The Left-Handed Gun. Warner Brothers, 1958. 102 minutes B/W. D: Arthur Penn. SC: Leslie Stevens. WITH Paul Newman, Lita Milan, John Dehner, Hurd Hatfield, James Congdon, James Best, Colin Keith-Johnston, John Dierkes, Bob Anderson, Wally Brown, Ainslie Pryor, Martin Garralaga, Denver Pyle, Nestor Paiva, Robert Foulk, Paul Smith, Jo Summers, Anne Barton. Young Billy the Kid is befriended by a ranger who is brutally murdered and Billy seeks revenge for the killing. Psychological approach to the Billy the Kid saga which should appeal to Newman's fans.

1876 Left Handed Law. Universal, 1937. 63 minutes B/W. D: Lesley Selander. SC: Frances Guihan. WITH Buck Jones, Robert Frazer, Noel Francis, Frank LaRue, Lee Phelps, Matty Fain, George Regas, Lee Shumway, Nena Quartero, Charles LeMoyne, Budd Buster, Frank Lackteen, Jim Toney, Bill Wolfe, Jack Evans, Jim Corey. A town plagued by lawlessness hires an army colonel to get rid of the outlaws. Top notch Buck Jones vehicle.

1877 The Legacy of the Incas. Marischka/PEA/Orbita Films, 1966. 100 minutes Color. D: Georg Marischka. SC: Georg Marischka, Winifried Groth & Franz Marischka. WITH Guy Madison, Geula Nuni, Fernando Rey, Rik Battaglia, Chris Howland, Heinz Erhardt, William Rothlein, Carlo Tamberlani, Francesco Rabal. The president of Peru assigns the last descendant of the Incas the task of trying to stop an Indian tribe, which is being aided by a bandit king and a revolutionary, from trying to drive out all whites and re-erect the Inca empire. Entertaining West German feature based on a Karl May work. West German title: **Das Vermachtnis Des Inka.**

1878 Legend of a Gunfighter. Italian-Spanish, 1966. 95 minutes Color. WITH Ron Randell, Judith Dornys, Toni Frisch. Three years after his parents were murdered in a stagecoach ambush, a man returns to his home town seeking revenge on the killers. Better-than-average European oater.

1879 The Legend of Alfred Packer. American National Enterprises, 1980. 95 minutes Color. D: Jim Roberson. WITH Patrick Dray, Ron Haines, Jim Dratfield, Bob Damon, Dave Ellingson, Ron Holiday. A half-dozen men search for gold in Colorado in 1873 but only one of them survives the bitter Rocky Mountain winter. Passably entertaining, but obscure, feature supposedly based on an actual story.

1880 The Legend of Amaluk. Yukon Pictures, 1971. 104 minutes Color. D: James Connor. SC: Leo Rosencrans. WITH Lorne Greene (narrator). The story of a young Eskimo and his way of life, including his fight for survival after being trapped by an ice quake. Nature lovers will enjoy this somewhat overlong documentary. Retitled: **North of the Yukon.**

1881 Legend of Cougar Canyon. James T. Flocker, 1974. 91 minutes Color. Two young boys, searching for their missing goat, find themselves pinned in the forbidden Mammy Cave and stalked by a killer cougar. Family oriented, low budget affair.

1882 The Legend of Custer. Filmways/20th Century-Fox, 1968. 94 minutes Color. D: Sam Wanakamer. WITH Wayne Maunder, Slim Pickens, Robert F. Simon, Peter Palmer, Michael Dante, Mary Ann Mobley, William Mims, Rodolfo Acosta. After troubles with Army brass, General George Armstrong Custer is assigned to a dead-end post in the Dakotas in 1870 but develops his men into the group known as the Fighting Seventh. So-so look at Custer's early years in the West which served as the pilot for the brief "The Legend of Custer" (ABC-TV, 1969) series.

1883 Legend of Death Valley. American National Enterprises, 1977. 90 minutes, Color. D: Kent Durden. WITH Robert Dawson. A young man attempts to trace his great-grandfather's trips to Death Valley in search of gold. Basically a documentary on Death Valley, detailing its history as well as its flora and fauna; nicely photographed and fairly interesting.

1884 The Legend of Earl Durand. Howco-International, 1974. 110 minutes Color. D: John D. Patterson. SC: J. Frank James. WITH Peter Haskell, Slim Pickens, Keenan Wynn, Martin Sheen, Anthony Caruso, Albert Salmi, Ivy Bethune, Phil Lopp, Hal Boker, Howard Wright. During the last days of the Depression, a young man in Wyoming steals game to give to the poor and is hunted by a posse.

Small budget modern-day oater which did not get wide distribution.

1885 The Legend of Frenchy King. SNC/K-Tel, 1973. 97 minutes Color. D: Christian-Jacque & Guy Casaril. SC: Marie-Agnes Anies, Jean Nemours, Guy Casaril, Clement Bywood & Daniel Boulanger. WITH Brigitte Bardot, Claudia Cardinale, Michael J. Pollard, Emma Cohen, Micheline Presle, Patty Shepard. In the 1880s a group of sisters at a French settlement in Mexico turn to lawlessness to get the things they want in life. Mediocre European coproduction although Bardot, et al., are nice on the eyes. French title: **Les Petroleuses.**

1886 The Legend of Lobo. Buena Vista, 1962. 67 minutes Color. SC: Dwight Hauser & James Algar. WITH Rex Allen (narrator/songs), The Sons of the Pioneers (songs). The story of a wolf, from birth to his growing up to lead a pack and save his mate from a rustler. Another documentary winner from Walt Disney; a very good film.

1887 The Legend of Nigger Charley. Paramount, 1972. 98 minutes Color. D: Martin Goldman. SC: Martin Goldman & Larry G. Spangler. WITH Fred Williamson, D'Urville Martin, Don Pedro Colley, Gertrude Jeannette, Marcia McBroom, Alan Gifford, Joe Ryan, Will Hussung, Mill Moor, Thomas Anderson, Jerry Gatlin, Tricia O'Neil, Doug Rowe, Keith Prentice, Tom Pemberton, Joe Santos, Fred Lerner. When a Virginia slave is forced to kill a vicious plantation overseer he finds himself a fugitive hunted by the law. Exploitation black actioner with heavy doses of action and comedy. Sequel: **The Soul of Nigger Charley** (q.v.).

1888 The Legend of the Golden Gun. NBC-TV/Columbia, 1979. 100 minutes Color. D: Alan J. Levi. SC: James D. Parriott. WITH Jeffrey Osterhage, Carl Franklin, Hal Holbrook, Keir Dullea, Robert Davi, Michelle Carey, John McLiam, Elissa Leeds, R. G. Armstrong, R. L. Tolbert, William Bryant, J. Brian Pizer, Rex Holman, Michael Yamaha, Walt Davis. A young farmer, taught to shoot by a legendary gunman, teams with a runaway slave to bring in Quantrill and his raiders. Fairly interesting TV film, with an offbeat premise.

1889 The Legend of the Lone Ranger. Apex Film Corporation, 1949. 75 minutes B/W. D-SC: George B. Seitz Jr. WITH

Clayton Moore, Jay Silverheels, Glenn Strange, Walter Sande, George Chesebro, Jack Clifford, Tristram Coffin, Guy Wilkerson, Ralph Littlefield, George J. Lewis. The lone survivor of an ambushed band of Texas Rangers is brought back to health by an Indian and the two set out to round up the Butch Cavendish gang, the outlaws responsible for the massacre. Excellent recounting of "The Lone Ranger" origins, made up of the first three segments of the long-running and popular TV program, which was on ABC-TV from 1949 to 1957. Clayton Moore and Jay Silverheels are the epitome of the Lone Ranger and Tonto and Glenn Strange is fine as the vicious Butch Cavendish; ten times better than the theatrical misfire of the same title issued in 1981.

1890 The Legend of the Lone Ranger. Universal/Associated Film Distribution, 1981. 98 minutes Color. D: William A. Fraker. SC: Ivan Goff, Ben Roberts, Michael Kane & William Roberts. WITH Klinton Spilsbury, Michael Horse, Jason Robards, Christopher Lloyd, Matt Clark, Juanin Clay, John Bennett Perry, David Hayward, John Hart, Richard Farnsworth, Lincoln Tate, Ted Flicker, Marc Gilpin, Patrick Montoya. A young lawyer becomes the Lone Ranger to combat the evil Butch Cavendish gang's plans to kidnap President Ulysses S. Grant. There is not much to recommend this sad rehash of the famous story although the film does prove one thing: Clayton Moore IS the Lone Ranger. VD: Blackhawk.

1891 Legion of the Lawless. RKO Radio, 1940. 59 minutes B/W. D: David Howard. SC: Doris Schroeder. WITH George O'Brien, Virginia Vale, Herbert Heywood, Norman Willis, Hugh Sothern, Billy Benedict, Eddy Waller, Delmer Watson, Bud Osborne, Monte Montague, Slim Whitaker, Mary Field, Richard Cramer, John Dilson, Martin Garralaga, Ed Piel Sr., Lloyd Ingraham, Wilfred Lucas, Henry Wills. A young lawyer leads the fight to aid homesteaders and ranchers in opposing a vigilante group out to steal land wanted for a railroad right-of-way. Pretty good George O'Brien action outing. V: Nostalgia Merchant.

1892 The Legend of Tom Dooley. Columbia, 1959. 79 minutes B/W. D: Ted Post. SC: Stan Sheptner. WITH Michael Landon, Jo Morrow, Jack Hogan, Richard Rust, Dee Pollack, Ted Lynch, Howard Wright, Ralph Moody, John Cliff. At the end of the Civil War, a young Confederate

soldier attacks a Union stage, unaware the war is over, and becomes a wanted criminal. Pretty good actioner based on the popular hit song of the time.

1893 The Legend of Walks Far Woman. NBC-TV, 1982. 110 minutes Color. D: Mel Damski. SC: Evan Hunter. WITH Raquel Welch, Bradford Dillman, George Clutesi, Nick Mancuso, Nick Ramos. A Blackfoot Indian woman, who is captured by the Sioux, lives to see the end of the way of life of the Plains Indians as she lives to be 102 years of age. Overlong and basically boring TV film.

1894 Lemonade Joe. Allied Artists, 1967. 90 minutes Color. D: Oldrich Lipsky. SC: Jiri Brdeca & Oldrich Lipsky. WITH Carl Fiala, Olga Schoberova, Veta Fialova, Miles Kopeck, Rudy Dale, Joseph Nomaz. The representative of a lemonade franchise teams with a temperance father-daughter team to drum out the evils of liquor in the Old West. Quite amusing Czech-made genre takeoff.

1895 Let Freedom Ring. Metro-Goldwyn-Mayer, 1939. 100 minutes B/W. D: Jack Conway. SC: Ben Hecht. WITH Nelson Eddy, Virginia Bruce, Victor McLaglen, Lionel Barrymore, Edward Arnold, Guy Kibbee, Charles Butterworth, H. B. Warner, Raymond Walburn. A Harvard-educated young man returns home and his family wants him to lead the fight by homesteaders against a crook so he joins the latter's gang as a spy. Dandy entertainment with good work by Nelson Eddy in the lead role; very patriotic.

1896 The Life and Times of Grizzly Adams. Sunn Classic, 1975. 93 minutes Color. D: Richard Friedenberg. SC: Larry Dobkin. WITH Dan Haggerty, Denver Pyle, Don Shanks, Marjorie Harper, Lisa Jones. A fur trapper is hunted by the law for a crime he did not commit and he finds peace and contentment in the wilderness. Popular roadshow production is only mediocre but it spawned a television series of the same title which ran on NBC-TV from 1977-78.

1897 The Life and Times of Judge Roy Bean. National General, 1972. 120 minutes Color. D: John Huston. SC: John Milius. WITH Paul Newman, Jacqueline Bisset, Ava Gardner, Stacy Keach, Anthony Perkins, Tab Hunter, John Huston, Roddy McDowall, Victoria Principal, Anthony Zerbe, Ned Beatty, Roy Jenson, LeRoy Johnson, Matt Clark, Dean Smith, Bill

McKinney, Fred Krone, Jack Colvin, David Sharpe, Gary Combs, Neil Summers. Judge Roy Bean rules as the only law west of the Pecos River as he carries on his one-sided love affair from afar with actress Lily Langtry. Pretty bad tongue-in-cheek look at the Roy Bean legend. V: Warner Home Video.

1898 Life in the Raw. Fox, 1933. 62 minutes B/W. D: Louis King. SC: Stuart Anthony. WITH George O'Brien, Claire Trevor, Greta Nissen, Francis Ford, Warner Richmond, Gaylord (Steve) Pendleton, Alan Edwards, Nigel De Brulier. A cowboy falls for a pretty girl and sets out to reform her no-good brother. Claire Trevor made her screen debut in this fun George O'Brien vehicle based on a Zane Grey work; film has lots of humor.

1899 Life on the Mississippi. PBS-TV, 1980. 120 minutes Color. SC: Philip Reisman Jr. WITH David Knell, Robert Lansing, Donald Madden, James Keane, Bill Holliday, John Pankow, Luke Reilly. Twenty-two year old Samuel L. Clemens signs on a Mississippi riverboat wanting to earn his pilot's license but comes under the tutelage of a stern captain. Fine PBS-TV adaptation of the Mark Twain work set in the pre-Civil War era.

1900 The Light in the Forest. Buena Vista, 1958. 93 minutes Color. D: Herschel Daugherty. SC: Lawrence E. Watkin. WITH James MacArthur, Carol Lynley, Fess Parker, Wendell Corey, Joanne Dru, Jessica Tandy, Joseph Calleia, John McIntire, Rafael Campos, Frank Ferguson, Norman Frederic, Marian Seldes, Stephen Bekassy, Sam Buffington. In 1764 a peace treaty results in a young white boy, who has been raised by Indians, being returned home and he finds it very difficult to adjust to a new life. Pleasant Disney entertainment feature.

1901 The Light of the Western Stars. Paramount, 1930. 80 minutes B/W. D: Otto Brower & Edwin H. Knopf. SC: Grover Jones & William Slavens McNutt. WITH Richard Arlen, Mary Brian, Harry Green, Regis Toomey, Fred Kohler, William LeMaire, George Chandler, Syd Saylor, Guy Oliver, Gus Saville. A cowboy falls in love with the sister of his murdered friend and when a local lawman, in cahoots with the killer, tries to take her ranch for back taxes, the cowboy stages a robbery and steals gold stolen from his dead friend to pay off the ranch. Pleasant early sound adaptation of the Zane Grey

work which was first filmed in 1918 by Sherman/United with Dustin Farnum and remade in 1925 by Paramount with Jack Holt, Billie Dove and Noah Beery. Remade again in 1940. Reissued by Favorite Films as **Winning the West.**

1902 The Light of the Western Stars. Paramount, 1940. 63 minutes B/W. D: Lesley Selander. SC: Norman Houston. WITH Victor Jory, Jo Ann Sayers, Russell Hayden, Noah Beery Jr., J. Farrell MacDonald, Morris Ankrum, Ruth Rogers, Tom Tyler, Rad Robinson, Eddie Dean, Esther Estrella, Alan Ladd. A ranch foreman, on the verge of becoming an outlaw, is helped by a pretty girl who has faith in him as he opposes a dishonest lawman and gun-runners. Although none-too-close to the Zane Grey work, this high class "B" effort provides good entertainment. V: Cumberland Video.

1903 Lightnin' Bill Carson. Puritan, 1936. 71 minutes B/W. D: Sam Newfield. SC: Joseph O'Donnell. WITH Tim McCoy, Lois January, Rex Lease, Harry Worth, Karl Hackett, John Merton, Lafe McKee, Edmund Cobb, Jack Rockwell, Joe Girard, Frank Ellis, Slim Whitaker, Jimmie Aubrey, Oscar Gahan, Artie Ortego, Herman Hack, Franklyn Farnum, George Morrell, Tom Smith. A U. S. marshal is after the outlaw brother of the girl he loves and at the same time is hunted by a notorious gunman. A bit long for a series "B" Western, this pretty good Tim McCoy vehicle introduced the character of G-man Lightnin' Bill Carson, a characterization he would continue with his later Victory series.

1904 Lightnin' Crandall. Republic, 1937. 60 minutes B/W. D: Sam Newfield. SC: Charles Francis Royal. WITH Bob Steele, Lois January, Dave O'Brien, Horace Murphy, Charles King, Ernie Adams, Earl Dwire, Richard Cramer, Frank LaRue, Lew Meehan, Lloyd Ingraham, Ed Carey, Art Felix. After buying a ranch in Arizona a cowboy finds himself in the middle of a range war between two feuding families. Sturdy and entertaining Bob Steele opus.

1905 Lightnin' in the Forest. Republic, 1948. 58 minutes B/W. D: George Blair. SC: John K. Butler. WITH Lynne Roberts, Don Barry, Warren Douglas, Adrian Booth, Lucien Littlefield, Claire DuBrey, Roy Barcroft, Paul Harvey, Al Eben, Jerry Jerome, George Chandler, Eddie Dunn, Dale Van Sickel, Bud Wolfe, Hank Worden.

A gang of crooks, on the run from the law, kidnap a rich and spoiled young socialite and hold her hostage in a mountain cabin. Adequate Republic programmer.

1906 Lightning Bill. Superior, 1934. 46 minutes B/W. D: Victor Adamson (Denver Dixon). SC: L. V. Jefferson. WITH Buffalo Bill Jr., Alma Rayford, Allen Holbrook, George Hazel, Nelson McDowell, Bud Osborne, William McCall, Lafe McKee, Eva McKenzie, Blackjack Ward. A cowboy is on the trail of a notorious horse rustler and his gang. A misspelled title is only the beginning of the fun in this tattered Denver Dixon production; a joy for fans of rock-bottom cinema.

1907 Lightning Bryce. National Film Corporation (Arrow), 1919. 15 Chapters B/W. D: Paul Hurst. WITH Jack Hoxie, Ann Little, Steve Clemente, Ben Corbett, Walter Patterson, George Champion, Slim Lucas, George Hunter, Paul Hurst, Yakima Canutt. Outlaws try to steal valuable clues to the location of a gold mine, discovered by the parents of a man and woman looking for the claim. Rare silent serial which will please fans of Jack Hoxie and Ann Little.

1908 Lightning Carson Rides Again. Victory, 1938. 59 minutes B/W. D: Sam Newfield. SC: Joseph O'Donnell. WITH Tim McCoy, Joan Barclay, Ben Corbett, Bob Terry, Jane Keckley, Ted Adams, Karl Hackett, Sherry Tansey, Frank Wayne, Forrest Taylor, Reed Howes, Frank LaRue, James Flavin. A lawman comes to his nephew's aid when the young man is accused of robbing and murdering his partner, actually the work of an outlaw gang. Tim McCoy resumes the role of Lightnin' Bill Carson in his first effort in his Victory Pictures series for producer Sam Katzman; a fairly good outing.

1909 Lightning Guns. Columbia, 1950. 55 minutes B/W. D: Fred F. Sears. SC: Victor Arthur. WITH Charles Starrett, Smiley Burnette, Gloria Henry, William Norton Bailey, Edgar Dearing, Ken Houchins, Raymond Bond, Jock (Mahoney) O'Mahoney, Chuck Roberson, Frank Griffin, Joel Friedkin, George Chesebro, Merrill McCormack, Billy Williams. The Durango Kid tries to discover who is behind an outlaw gang constantly sabotaging the construction of a new dam. Well done "Durango Kid" series segment.

1910 Lightning Jack. Anchor, 1924. 50 minutes B/W. WITH Jack Perrin, Josephine

Hill, Lew Meehan, Jack Richardson, Jack Phillips. A cowboy, about to enter his fast horse in a race, is framed on a murder charge. There is nothing special about this silent Jack Perrin outing, but it moves fast and is fun to view.

1911 Lightning Range. Superior, 1934. 50 minutes B/W. D: Victor Adamson (Denver Dixon). SC: L. V. Jefferson. WITH Buddy Roosevelt, Patsy Bellamy, Genee Boutell, Betty Butler, Anne Howard, Si Jenks, Denver Dixon, Jack Evans, Boris Bullock, Clyde McClary, Bart Carre, Olin Francis, Lafe McKee, Merrill McCormack, Ken Broeker, Jack Bronston. A cowboy sets out to aid a pretty girl whose money is stolen by a gang of crooks. Tacky Denver Dixon production which will appeal to fans of this kind of fare.

1912 Lightning Raiders. Producers Releasing Corporation, 1945. 61 minutes B/W. D: Sam Newfield. SC: Elmer Clifton. WITH Buster Crabbe, Al St. John, Mady Lawrence, Henry Hall, Steve Darrell, I. Stanford Jolley, Karl Hackett, Roy Brent, Marin Sais, Al Ferguson, John Cason. Billy Carson and Fuzzy Q. Jones uncover a scheme in which a banker leads a gang which steals mail in order to obtain land by foreclosures. Average low grade "Billy Carson" Western containing a funny sequence where Fuzzy accidentally eats Mexican jumping beans. V: Cumberland Video.

1913 Lightning Strikes West. Colony, 1940. 57 minutes B/W. D: Harry Fraser. SC: Martha Chapin. WITH Ken Maynard, Claire Rochelle, Michael Vallon, Charles King, Bob Terry, Reed Howes, Dick Dickinson, George Chesebro, John Elliott, William Gould, Tex Palmer, Carl Mathews, Chick Hannon. A U. S. marshal works undercover to capture an escaped convict who has reteamed with his gang to find buried loot stolen from a government dam project. Ken Maynard's last solo starring series oater is a fast moving and entertaining affair with the star doing a good job masquerading as a vagrant.

1914 Lightning Triggers. Willis Kent/Marcy, 1935. 50 minutes B/W. D: S. Roy Luby. WITH Reb Russell, Fred Kohler, Yvonne Pelletier, Jack Rockwell, Edmund Cobb, Lillian Castle, Lew Meehan, William McCall, Richard Botiller, Olin Francis, Artie Ortego, Steve Clark. A cowboy joins an outlaw gang in order to capture them and then finds out the gang leader is actually his father. Fair Reb Russell vehicle which will please his fans.

1915 The Lightning Warrior. Mascot, 1931. 12 Chapters B/W. D: Armand L. Schaefer & Benjamin Kline. WITH Rin-Tin-Tin, Frankie Darro, George Brent, Hayden Stevenson, Georgia Hale, Pat O'Malley, Theodore Lorch, Lafe McKee, Robert Kortman, George McGrill, Frank Lanning, Frank Brownlee, Kermit Maynard, Dick Dickinson, Helen Gibson, William Desmond, Steve Clemente. A young boy and a German shepherd dog try to find the true identity of the Wolf Man, the person responsible for the murders of the boy's father and the dog's master. Very actionful cliffhanger with excellent stunt work by Yakima Canutt.

1916 Lights of Old Santa Fe. Republic, 1944. 54 (76) minutes B/W. D: Frank McDonald. SC: Gordon Kahn & Bob Williams. WITH Roy Rogers, George "Gabby" Hayes, Dale Evans, Lloyd Corrigan, Richard Powers (Tom Keene), Claire DuBrey, Arthur Loft, Roy Barcroft, Lucien Littlefield, Bob Nolan & The Sons of the Pioneers, Sam Flint, Jack Kirk. Roy Rogers and the Sons of the Pioneers work for a rodeo which is being sabotaged by a rival outfit. Only a fair film with no real dramatic climax, just a big rodeo finale.

1917 Li'l Scratch. American National Enterprises, 1972. 93 minutes Color. D: Larry Jones. WITH Larry Jones. An outdoorsman on a photographic excursion in the wilderness makes friends with an orphaned bear cub. Pleasant and amusing documentary.

1918 The Lion and the Horse. Warner Brothers, 1952. 83 minutes Color. D: Louis King. SC: Crane Wilbur. WITH Steve Cochran, Sherry Jackson, Ray Teal, Bob Steele, Harry Antrim, George O'Hanlon, Ed Hinton, William Fawcett, House Peters Jr., Lee Roberts, Lane Chandler, Frank Nelson (voice), Wildfire (horse). In order to save his beloved stallion from an uncaring new owner, a cowboy takes the horse into the wilds and seeks sanctuary with an old rancher and his little granddaughter. Well written and actionful family fare.

1919 The Lion's Den. Puritan, 1936. 59 minutes B/W. D: Sam Newfield. SC: John T. Neville. WITH Tim McCoy, Joan Woodbury, Don Barclay, J. Frank Glendon, John Merton, Arthur Millet, Karl Hackett, Dick Curtis, Jack Evans, Art Felix, Bud McClure, Jack Rockwell, Frank Ellis. A sharp-shooter, who has agreed to aid ranchers in their fight against terrorism, arrives in a small town and is mistaken for a hired gunman by the man causing the trouble. A bit complicated but still an entertaining Tim McCoy vehicle.

1920 Little Big Horn. Lippert, 1951. 86 minutes B/W. D: Charles Marquis Warren. SC: Charles Marquis Warren & Harold Shumate. WITH Lloyd Bridges, Marie Windsor, John Ireland, Reed Hadley, Jim Davis, Wally Cassell, Hugh O'Brian, Sheb Wooley, King Donovan, Rodd Redwing, Richard Emory, John Pickard, Ted Avery. A group of soldiers attempt to rescue General Custer and his men at the Little Big Horn but become involved with personal differences. Cheaply made but well acted; a different kind of oater. Alternate title: **The Fighting 7th.**

1921 Little Big Man. National General, 1970. 150 minutes Color. D: Arthur Penn. SC: Calder Willingham. WITH Dustin Hoffman, Faye Dunaway, Martin Balsam, Richard Mulligan, Chief Dan George, Jeff Corey, Amy Eccles, Jean Peters, Carole Androsky, Robert Little Star, Cal Bellini, Thayer David, James Anderson, Jesse Vint, Jack Bannon. An aged man recounts his life which included living with the Indians, returning to whites and taking part in the Battle of the Little Big Horn. Overlong and sometimes confusing film which should please Dustin Hoffman fans. V: CBS/Fox.

1922 Little House: Bless All the Dear Children. NBC-TV, 1984. 100 minutes Color. D: Victor French. SC: Chris Abbott-Fish. WITH Melissa Gilbert, Dean Butler, Victor French, Richard Bull, Kevin Hagen, Patricia Pearcy, Robin Clarke, Harvey Vernon, Allison Balson, Robert Casper, Pamela Boylance, Joel Graves, David Friedman, Lindsay Kennedy, Shannon Doherty, Leslie Landon, Michael Landon (narrator). While Christmas shopping in Mankato, the Wilders' small daughter is kidnapped by a woman who has lost her own baby in childbirth. Shown after, but probably filmed before **Little House: The Last Farewell** (q.v.), this telefilm is another segment in the long-running "Little House on the Prairie" (NBC-TV, 1974-83) TV series; passable holiday fare.

1923 Little House: Look Back to Yesterday. NBC-TV, 1983. 100 minutes Color. D: Victor French. SC: Vince R. Gutierrez. WITH Michael Landon, Melissa Gilbert, Victor French, Dean Butler, Richard

Bull, Henry Brandon, Kevin Hagen, Dabbs Greer, Matthew Laborteaux, Melora Hardin, Jonathan Gilbert, Cooper Huckabee, James T. Callahan, Charles Cyphers, Allison Balson, Pamela Boylance, Robert Casper, Leslie Landon. Pa Ingalls returns home to Walnut Grove to find the area in a recession and his adopted son about to die from a blood disease. Telefeature spinoff from the popular long-running series "Little House on the Prairie" (NBC-TV, 1974-83) is a bit maudlin but fans will enjoy it, although Katherine MacGregor's character of Mrs. Oleson is sorely needed to enliven the proceedings.

1924 Little House on the Prairie. NBC-TV, 1974. 96 minutes Color. D: Michael Landon. SC: Blanche Hanalis. WITH Michael Landon, Karen Grassle, Melissa Gilbert, Melissa Sue Anderson, Victor French, Lindsay & Sidney Greenbush, Vic Mohica, Cal Bellini, Sam Vlahos, Richard Alarian, Marian Breedler. A pioneer family tries to adjust to a new life on the Kansas plains. Excellent telefeature based on the popular Laura Ingalls Wilder books and pilot for the very popular and long-running series of the same title on NBC-TV from 1974 to 1982. The TV series ran another season as "Little House: A New Beginning" from 1982-83. V: Warner Home Video.

1925 Little House: The Last Farewell. NBC-TV, 1984. 100 minutes Color. D-SC: Michael Landon. WITH Michael Landon, Karen Grassle, Melissa Gilbert, Victor French, Dean Butler, Richard Bull, Kevin Hagen, Dabbs Greer, James Karen, Dennis Robertson, Roger Torrey, Rod Colbin, Alvy Moore, Bill McLennan, Jonathan Gilbert, Allison Balson, Stan Ivar, Pamela Roylance, Lindsay Kennedy, David Friedman, Leslie Landon, Robert Casper, Sherri Stoner, Shannen Doherty, Diane Kennedy, Steve Rumph, Alex Sharp, Ruth Foster, Jack Lilley. The citizens of Walnut Grove find out they are going to lose their town to a ruthless land baron who has the law on his side. Well done telefeature finale (?) to the long-running "Little House on the Prairie" (NBC-TV, 1974-83) TV series.

1926 Little Joe the Wrangler. Universal, 1942. 64 minutes B/W. D: Lewis D. Collins. SC: Sherman Lowe & Elizabeth Beecher. WITH Johnny Mack Brown, Tex Ritter, Fuzzy Knight, Jennifer Holt, Florine McKinney, James Craven, Hal Taliaferro, Glenn Strange, The Jimmy Wakely Trio (Jimmy Wakely, Johnny Bond, Scotty

Harrell), Ethan Laidlaw. A stranger is framed on a charge of robbery and murder but the local lawman believes him innocent and the duo try to find the real culprits. Too long and involved Johnny Mack Brown-Tex Ritter vehicle with too much music to boot.

1927 Little Moon and Jud McGraw. International Cine Corporation, 1979. 80 minutes Color. D: Bernard Girard. WITH James Caan, Stefanie Powers, Aldo Ray, Sammy Davis Jr., Barbara Werle, Robert Walker (Jr.), Peter Fonda, Mike Lane, Michael Conrad, Kenny Adams, Anne Barton, Paul Bergen, Fred Book, Fabian Dean, Noel Drayton, Anthony Gordon, Pepper Martin, Boyd "Red" Morgan, Chuck Hayward, Reed Sherman, Jay York, Dick Shane, Buck Lee, Bill Foster, Danny Redeznick, Gillian Sampson, Chris Calebrese, James McHale, Benny Dobbins, Julie Ann Johnson, Ginger Irwin, Lenore Stevens, Sherise Roland. A newspaper reporter and his girlfriend visit a ghost town and are told the story of how a young man and an Indian girl team to get revenge on the town boss and his gang. Tacky, rambling feature rounded out with filler material; absolutely awful. Filmed in 1969 by Cinema Releasing Corporation as **Man Without Mercy** and issued briefly in 1975 by International Cinefilm as **Gone with the West.**

1928 The Little Shepherd of Kingdom Come. 20th Century-Fox, 1961. 108 minutes Color. D: Andrew V. McLaglen. SC: Barre Lyndon. WITH Jimmie Rodgers, Luana Patten, Chill Wills, Linda Hutchins, Robert Dix, George Kennedy, Shirley O'Hara, Ken Miller, Neil Hamilton, Lois January, Jack Holland, Edward Faulkner, Morris Ankrum, Nelson Leigh, Lane Chandler, Diana Darien, I. Stanford Jolley, Jerry Summers, Dan Simmons, Helen Scott, Glen Marshall. A young Southern man, who fought for the North during the Civil War, returns to his rural Kentucky home and tries to resume a normal life. Slow moving version of the old chestnut which was first filmed in 1920 with Jack Pickford for Goldwyn and remade in 1928 by First National with Richard Barthelmess.

1929 The Littlest Outlaw. Buena Vista, 1955. 75 minutes Color. D: Roberto Gavaldon. SC: Bill Walsh. WITH Andres Velasquez, Pedro Armendariz, Joseph Calleia, Rodolfo Acosta, Pepe Ortiz, Laila Maley, Gilberto Gonzales, Jose Torvay, Ferrusquilla, Enriqueta Zazueta,

Margarito Luna. A young Mexican boy becomes a fugitive when he runs away with a horse who has been ordered killed by its owner, a general. Charming Walt Disney family film.

1930 The Living Desert. Buena Vista, 1953. 73 minutes Color. D: James Algar. SC: James Algar, Winston Hibler & Ted Sears. WITH Winston Hibler (Narrator). The American desert is shown, zeroing in on its animal life. Academy Award winning documentary feature from Walt Disney; a must-see for fans of such fare.

1931 The Llano Kid. Paramount, 1939. 70 minutes B/W. D: Edward Venturini. SC: Wanda Tuchock. WITH Tito Guizar, Gale Sondergaard, Alan Mowbray, Jane (Jan) Clayton, Emma Dunn, Minor Watson, Chris-Pin Martin, Carlos de Valdez, Anna Demetrio, Glenn Strange, Tony Roux, Harry Worth, Eddie Dean. A Mexican bandit poses as the long lost heir to an old lady's fortune. Okay version of the O. Henry story "Double-Dyed Deceiver" which was first filmed in 1930 as **The Texan** (q.v.) with Gary Cooper.

1932 Loaded Pistols. Columbia, 1949. 70 minutes B/W. D: John English. SC: Dwight Cummings & Dorothy Yost. WITH Gene Autry, Barbara Britton, Chill Wills, Jack Holt, Robert Shayne, Russell Arms, Fred Kohler Jr., Vince Barnett, Leon Weaver, Clem Bevans, Sandy Sanders, Budd Buster, John R. McKee, Stanley Blystone, Hank Bell, Felice Raymond, Richard Alexander, Frank O'Connor, Reed Howes, Snub Pollard, Heinie Conklin, William Sundholm. Gene Autry and his friends find themselves up against a crooked rancher. There is plenty of action in this good Gene Autry vehicle. V: Cumberland Video.

1933 The Local Bad Man. Allied, 1932. 60 minutes B/W. D: Otto Brower. SC: Philip White. WITH Hoot Gibson, Sally Blane, Ed Peil Sr., Hooper Atchley, Skeeter Bill Robbins, Edward Hearn, Milt Brown, Jack Clifford. Two crooked bankers plan to rob their own express shipment and place the blame on their driver. Pretty fair Hoot Gibson outing.

1934 Lock, Stock and Barrel. NBC-TV/ Universal, 1971. 96 minutes Color. D: Jerry Thorpe. SC: Richard Alan Simmons. WITH Tim Matheson, Belinda Montgomery, Claude Akins, Jack Albertson, Neville Brand, Burgess Meredith, Robert Emhardt, John Beck, Charles Dierkop, Joe DiReda,

Mills Watson, Timothy Scott, Dan Jenkins. When a young couple elope and head to Oregon, the girl's father gives chase as they encounter a series of adventures. Passable genre spoof made for television.

1935 The Lone Avenger. World Wide/Fox, 1933. 61 minutes B/W. D-SC: Alan James. WITH Ken Maynard, Muriel Gordon, Jack Rockwell, Charles King, Alan Bridge, Jim Mason, Niles Welch, William N. Bailey, Ed Brady, Clarence Geldert, Lew Meehan, Horace B. Carpenter, Jack Ward, Bud McClure. A cowboy sets out to stop an outlaw gang trying to take over a town by causing a bank panic. A top notch Ken Maynard vehicle with plenty of action to suit his legion of fans.

1936 The Lone Bandit. Empire/Kinematrade, 1934. 60 minutes B/W. D: J. P. McGowan. SC: Ralph Consumana. WITH Lane Chandler, Doris Brook, Wally Wales, Slim Whitaker, Ray Gallagher, Ben Corbett, Jack Prince, Philo McCullough, Forrest Taylor. A masked bandit steals a man's horse and the man is accused of being the outlaw but is cleared and sets out to get back his horse and capture the mystery man. A rather complicated plot does not detract from the overall entertainment value of this low budget affair.

1937 Lone Cowboy. Paramount, 1934. 75 minutes B/W. D: Paul Sloane. SC: Agnes Brand Leahy & Bobby Vernon. WITH Jackie Cooper, Lila Lee, Barton MacLane, Addison Richards, Charles Middleton, Gavin Gordon, Herbert Corthell, John Wray, J. M. Kerrigan, Del Henderson, Irving Bacon, Lillian Harmon, William LeMaine. A delinquent from Chicago is sent to the West to live with his dad's pal, a cowboy, and the two become friends when faced by outlaws. A different kind of genre offering and a good film.

1938 The Lone Defender. Mascot, 1930. 12 Chapters B/W. D: Richard Thorpe. WITH Rin-Tin-Tin, Walter Miller, June Marlowe, Buzz Barton, Josef Swickard, Lee Shumway, Frank Lanning, Robert Kortman, Arthur Morrison, Lafe McKee, Bob Irwin, Arthur Metzeth, Bill McBowan, Victor Metzetti. Crooks murder a dog's master for the map to a secret mine and then try to kidnap the dog because they believe he can lead them to the gold. Mascot's first all-talking serial is a slow affair but it's worth a look to see Rin-Tin-Tin. V: Video Connection.

1939 The Lone Gun. United Artists, 1954. 78 minutes Color. D: Ray Nazarro. SC: Don Martin & Richard Schayer. WITH George Montgomery, Dorothy Malone, Neville Brand, Frank Faylen, Skip Homeier, Douglas Kennedy, Robert Wilke, Douglas Fowley, Fay Roope. While on the trail of a gang of cattle thieves in Texas, a lawman falls in love with a rancher's pretty daughter. Average oater outing with good work by the two stars.

1940 The Lone Hand. Universal-International, 1953. 79 minutes Color. D: George Sherman. SC: Joseph Hoffman. WITH Joel McCrea, Barbara Hale, Alex Nicol, Charles Drake, Jimmy Hunt, James Arness, Wesley Morgan, Roy Roberts, Frank Ferguson. A rancher with a small son and a new wife risks losing their respect when he is forced to secretly work undercover to infiltrate a gang of rustlers. Pretty good Joel McCrea vehicle.

1941 The Lone Hand Texan. Columbia, 1947. 54 minutes B/W. D: Ray Nazarro. SC: Ed Earl Repp. WITH Charles Starrett, Smiley Burnette, Mary Newton, Fred Sears, Frank Rice, Ernest Stokes, Maudie Prickett, George Chesebro, Robert Stevens, Bob Cason, Jim Diehl, George Russell, Jasper Weldon, Mustard & Gravy. Outlaws try to sabotage an oil driller's operation and the Durango Kid tries to stop them and find out who is behind the illegal activities. Okay "Durango Kid" segment.

1942 The Lone Prairie. Columbia, 1942. 58 minutes B/W. D: William Berke. SC: Ed Earl Repp & J. Benton Cheney. WITH Russell Hayden, Bob Wills & The Texas Playboys, Dub Taylor, Lucille Lambert John Merton, John Maxwell, Jack Kirk, Edmund Cobb, Ernie Adams, Kermit Maynard, Art Mix, Steve Clark. Crooks are after a man's ranch because a railroad is going through it and they steal his cattle until a cattle buyer comes to his rescue. Pretty fair Russell Hayden vehicle with some nice musical interludes by Bob Wills and his group.

1943 The Lone Ranger. Republic, 1938. 15 Chapters B/W. D: William Witney & John English. SC: Barry Shipman, George Worthington Yates, Franklyn Adreon, Ronald Davidson & Lois Eby. WITH Chief Thundercloud, Lee Powell, Herman Brix (Bruce Bennett), Lynne Roberts, William Farnum, Stanley Andrews, George Cleveland, Hal Taliaferro (Wally Wales), Lane Chandler, George (Montgomery) Letz,

John Merton, Sammy McKim, Tom London, Ray Bennett, Maston Williams, Frank McGlynn, Reed Howes, Allan Cavan, Walter James, Francis Sayles, Murdock McQuarrie, Ted Adams, Jack Kirk, Art Dillard, Frank Ellis, Carl Stockdale, Bud Osborne, Fred Burns, Forbes Murray, Charles King, Jack Perrin, Slim Whitaker, Edmund Cobb, Jack Rockwell, Frankie Marvin, Lafe McKee, Charles Williams, Robert Kortman, Post Parks, George Plues, Al Taylor, Blackie Whiteford. After the Civil War five lawmen team to combat outlaws in the West and they are aided by a masked man and his Indian friend and it becomes apparent that one of the lawmen is the Lone Ranger. One of the all-time great sound serials; a must-see for genre fans. Issued in a 69 minute feature version by Republic, in 1940 as **Hi-Yo Silver.**

1944 The Lone Ranger. Warner Brothers, 1956. 86 minutes Color. D: Stuart Heisler. SC: Herb Meadow. WITH Clayton Moore, Jay Silverheels, Lyle Bettger, Bonita Granville, Perry Lopez, Robert Wilke, John Pickard, Beverly Washburn, Michael Ansara, Frank DeKova, Charles Meredith, Mickey Simpson, Zon Murray, Lane Chandler. The Lone Ranger and Tonto are assigned to look into unrest between whites and Indians and they find out a rich rancher is opposing efforts for the territory's statehood. Well done theatrical feature with Clayton Moore and Jay Silverheels successfully repeating their TV roles, with fine work by Lyle Bettger as the villainous rancher.

1945 The Lone Ranger and the Lost City of Gold. United Artists, 1958. 80 minutes Color. D: Lesley Selander. SC: Robert Schaefer & Eric Friewald. WITH Clayton Moore, Jay Silverheels, Douglas Kennedy, Charles Watts, Noreen Nash, Lisa Montell, Ralph Moody, Norman Frederic, John Miljan, Maurice Jara, Bill Henry, Lane Bradford, Belle Mitchell. When hooded riders murder members of an Indian tribe, the Lone Ranger and Tonto investigate and find a plot to steal five medallions which reveals the location of a sacred lost city of gold. While not as well produced as the earlier **The Lone Ranger** (q.v.), this is a more than passably enjoyable "Lone Ranger" effort.

1946 The Lone Ranger Rides Again. Republic, 1939. 15 Chapters B/W. D: William Witney & John English. SC: Franklyn Adreon, Ronald Davidson, Sol Shor & Barry Shipman. WITH Robert Livingston, Chief Thundercloud, Duncan Renaldo, Jinx Falken(burg), Ralph Dunn, J. Farrell MacDonald, William Gould, Rex Lease, Ted Mapes, Henry Otho, John Beach, Glenn Strange, Stanley Blystone, Edwin Parker, Al Taylor, Carleton Young, Ernie Adams, Billy Bletcher, Slim Whitaker, David Sharpe, Art Felix, Chick Hannon, Eddie Dean, Duke Lee, Howard Chase, Nelson McDowell, Walter Wills, Jack Kirk, Fred Burns, Lew Meehan, Wheeler Oakman, Forrest Taylor, Frank Ellis, Herman Hack, Bud Wolfe, Duke Taylor, Forrest Burns, George DeNormand, Tommy Coats, Ted Wells, Carl Sepulveda, Roger Williams, Buddy Roosevelt, Jack Montgomery, Post Parks, Art Dillard, Horace B. Carpenter, Cactus Mack, Lafe McKee, Charles Hutchison, Monte Montague, Griff Barnett, Augie Gomez. The Lone Ranger and Tonto come to the aid of a wagon train and settlers thought to be the victims of attacks of a greedy cattleman. Cliffhanger follow-up to **The Lone Ranger** (q.v.) is an exciting and entertaining serial.

1947 The Lone Rider. Columbia, 1930. 60 minutes B/W. D: Louis King. SC: Forrest Sheldon. WITH Buck Jones, Vera Reynolds, Harry Woods, George Pearce. An outlaw quits his gang and thwarts a stage robbery and ends up heading the town's vigilante committee. Fair Buck Jones early talkie, loosely remade four years later as **The Man Trailer.**

1948 The Lone Rider Ambushed. Producers Releasing Corporation, 1941. 68 minutes B/W. D: Sam Newfield. SC: Oliver Drake. WITH George Houston, Al St. John, Maxine Leslie, Frank Hagney, Jack Ingram, Hal Price, Ted Adams, George Chesebro, Ralph Peters, Steve Clark, Charles King, Carl Mathews. The Lone Rider is the double for a wanted outlaw and he pretends to be the man in order to prove the innocence of a bank teller accused of robbing his bank. Entertaining entry in "The Lone Rider" series.

The Lone Rider and Outlaws of Boulder Pass see **Outlaws of Boulder Pass**

1949 The Lone Rider and the Bandit. Producers Releasing Corporation, 1942. 55 minutes B/W. D: Sam Newfield. SC: Steve Braxton. WITH George Houston, Al St. John, Smokey (Dennis) Moore, Vicki Lester, Glenn Strange, Jack Ingram, Milton Kibbee, Kenne Duncan, Eddie Dean, Slim Whitaker, Hal Price, Slim Andrews, Carl Sepulveda, Curley Dresden.

Pretending to be an entertainer, the Lone Rider comes to a small town to aid the sheriff in catching crooks forcing local miners to sell their claims. Okay "Lone Rider" outing.

1950 The Lone Rider Cross the Rio. Producers Releasing Corporation, 1941. 63 minutes B/W. D: Sam Newfield. SC: William Lively. WITH George Houston, Al St. John, Raquell Verrin, Charles King, Alden Chase, Julian Rivero, Thorton Edwards, Howard Masters, Frank Ellis, Phillip Turich, Jay Wilsey (Buffalo Bill Jr.), Frank Hagney, Curley Dresden, Sherry Tansey, Steve Clark. In Mexico, the Lone Rider tries to untangle a romantic problem between two families and ends up solving a kidnapping. Somewhat different "Lone Rider" effort from PRC.

1951 The Lone Rider Fights Back. Producers Releasing Corporation, 1941. 64 minutes B/W. D: Sam Newfield. SC: Joseph O'Donnell. WITH George Houston, Al St. John, Dorothy Short, Dennis Moore, Frank Hagney, Charles King, Frank Ellis, Hal Price, Jack O'Shea, Merrill McCormack. When his pal is killed over a mine, the Lone Rider joins the gang to get the goods on the murderer. No better or no worse than the average film in this PRC series.

The Lone Rider in Border Roundup see **Border Roundup**

1952 The Lone Rider in Cheyenne. Producers Releasing Corporation, 1942. 59 minutes B/W. D: Sam Newfield. SC: Oliver Drake & Elizabeth Beecher. WITH George Houston, Al St. John, Smokey (Dennis) Moore, Ella Neal, Roy Barcroft, Kenne Duncan, Lynton Brent, Milton Kibbee, Karl Hackett, Jack Ingram, George Chesebro, Jack Holmes. An innocent man is accused of murdering an outlaw who took part in a robbery and the Lone Rider sets out to find the real killer. No different than most of the "Lone Rider" entries from PRC.

1953 The Lone Rider in Frontier Fury. Producers Releasing Corporation, 1941. 62 minutes B/W. D: Sam Newfield. SC: Fred Myton. WITH George Houston, Al St. John, Hillary Brooke, Karl Hackett, Ted Adams, Archie Hall, Budd Buster, Virginia Card, Ed Piel, John Elliott, Tom London, Frank Ellis, Reed Howes, Dan White, Tom London, Horace B. Carpenter, Tex Cooper, Tex Palmer, Curley Dresden, Wally West, Herman Hack.

The Lone Rider is falsely convicted of killing a ranch owner but the man's niece begins to suspect his innocence. Fair "Lone Rider" series entry enhanced by a good cast.

1954 The Lone Rider in Ghost Town. Producers Releasing Corporation, 1941. 64 minutes B/W. D: Sam Newfield. SC: William Lively. WITH George Houston, Al St. John, Elaine Brandes, Budd Buster, Frank Hagney, Alden Chase, Reed Howes, Charles King, George Chesebro, Ed Piel Sr., Archie Hall, Karl Hackett, Jay Wilsey (Buffalo Bill Jr.), Curley Dresden, Frank Ellis, Steve Clark, Jack Ingram, Lane Bradford. The Lone Rider tries to find a girl who has been kidnapped by crooks who do not want her father to exercise an option he has on a mine. A good story and a big cast of genre veterans make this a bit better than average in "The Lone Rider" series.

1955 The Lone Rider in Texas Justice. Producers Releasing Corporation, 1942. 60 minutes B/W. S: Sam Newfield. SC: Steve Braxton (Sam Robins). WITH George Houston, Al St. John, Dennis Moore, Wanda McKay, Claire Rochelle, Karl Hackett, Curley Dresden, Steve Clark, Ray Davis, Archie Hall, Slim Whitaker, Ed Piel Sr., Julian Rivero, Dirk Thane, Horace Carpenter, Frank Ellis, Merrill McCormack. Tom Cameron, The Lone Rider and his pal Fuzzy try to buy a man's ranch only to find out the man is being framed as a cattle rustler. Above average PRC Western that moves fast and is fairly exciting; George Houston was a different kind of hero with a very good singing voice. Also called **Texas Justice.**

1956 The Lone Rider Rides On. Producers Releasing Corporation, 1941. 61 minutes B/W. D: Sam Newfield. SC: Joseph O'Donnell. WITH George Houston, Al St. John, Hillary Brooke, Lee Powell, Buddy Roosevelt, Al Bridge, Frank Hagney, Tom London, Karl Hackett, Forrest Taylor, Frank Ellis, Curley Dresden, Harry Harvey, Isabel LaMal, Don Forrest, Robert Kortman, Wally West, Steve Clark. The Lone Rider investigates the murder of a man planning to take possession of land he had purchased and notices the killing was similar to the murder of his parents years before. Pretty good entry in the long-running "Lone Rider" series.

1957 Lone Star. Metro-Goldwyn-Mayer, 1952. 90 minutes B/W. D: Vincent Sherman.

SC: Borden Chase. WITH Clark Gable, Ava Gardner, Broderick Crawford, Lionel Barrymore, Beulah Bondi, William Farnum, Ed Begley, James Burke, Lowell Gilmore, Rex Bell, Lucius Cook, Ralph Reed, Ric Roman, Victor Sutherland, Charles Kane, Nacho Galindo, Trevor Bardette, Harry Woods, Emmett Lynn. President Andrew Jackson asks a trusted friend to persuade Sam Houston to lead the fight for Texas independence. Along the way Sam runs into a badman and a pretty newspaper editor. Good, big budget outing which will appeal to action fans.

1958 Lone Star Law Men. Monogram, 1941. 58 minutes B/W. D: Robert Emmett Tansey. SC: Robert Emmett (Tansey) & Frances Kavanaugh. WITH Tom Keene, Betty Miles, Frank Yaconelli, Sugar Dawn, Glenn Strange, Charles King, Gene Alsace, James Sheridan, Stanley Price, Fred Hoose, Franklyn Farnum, Jack Ingram, Reed Howes. A man and his pal find a sheriff who has been ambushed and left for dead and the cowboy agrees to help him capture the gang by pretending to be an outlaw and infiltrating their operations. Passable Tom Keene vehicle.

Lone Star Lawman see **Texas Lawmen**

1959 Lone Star Pioneers. Columbia, 1939. 56 minutes B/W. D: Joseph Lovering. SC: Nate Gatzert. WITH Bill Elliott, Dorothy Gulliver, Lee Shumway, Slim Whitaker, Charles King, Jack Ingram, Harry Harvey, Buzz Barton, Frank LaRue, Budd Buster, David Sharpe, Frank Ellis, Kit Guard, Merrill McCormack, Jack Rockwell, Tex Palmer. In Texas after the Civil War, guerillas raid supply wagons and a federal marshal is sent to stop the robberies. He joins a gang disguised as an outlaw and finds they are holding a family hostage on their ranch, which the gang uses as its headquarters. Okay Bill Elliott vehicle which tends to be a bit draggy. Jack Ingram is a good guy for a change in this one.

1960 Lone Star Raiders. Republic, 1940. 54 (57) minutes B/W. D: George Sherman. SC: Joseph March & Barry Shipman. WITH Robert Livingston, Bob Steele, Rufe Davis, June Johnson, George Douglas, Sarah Padden, John Elliott, John Merton, Rex Lease, Bud Osborne, Jack Kirk, Tom London, Hal Price. The Three Mesquiteers go to work for the government rounding up wild horses and run into

outlaws who want the horses for themselves. Mediocre entry in the long running
series with too much stock footage.

1961 The Lone Star Ranger. Fox, 1930.
70 minutes B/W. D: A. F. Erickson. SC:
Seton I. Miller & John Hunter Booth.
WITH George O'Brien, Sue Carol, Walter
McGrail, Warren Hymer, Russell Simpson,
Roy Stewart, Lee Shumway, Colin Chase,
Richard Alexander, Joel Franz, Joe Rick-
son, Oliver Eckhardt, Caroline Rankin,
Elizabeth Patterson, Billy Butts, Delmar
Watson, William Steel, Bob Fleming,
Ralph Le Fevre, Joe Chase. Falsely ac-
cused of many crimes, a young man is
given a chance to redeem himself by
capturing an outlaw gang. Strong George
O'Brien vehicle from the 1914 Zane Grey
novel, first filmed by Fox in 1923 with
Tom Mix and Billie Dove.

1962 The Lone Star Ranger. 20th Century-
Fox, 1942. 58 minutes B/W. D: James
Tinling. SC: William Conselman Jr., George
Kane & Irving Cummings Jr. WITH John
Kimbrough, Sheila Ryan, William Farnum,
Truman Bradley, Jonathan Hale, George
E. Stone, Russell Simpson, Dorothy Bur-
gess, Tom Fadden, Fred Kohler Jr., Eddy
Waller, Harry Holden, George Melford,
Tom London. A man quits an outlaw
gang, meets a pretty girl and is given
the chance to get a pardon by capturing
his old gang. Futile attempt to make
a genre star of John Kimbrough; third
film version of the Zane Grey story.

1963 The Lone Star Trail. Universal,
1943. 58 minutes B/W. D: Ray Taylor.
SC: Oliver Drake. WITH Johnny Mack
Brown, Tex Ritter, Fuzzy Knight, Jennifer
Holt, Earle Hodgins, Jack Ingram, Robert
Mitchum, George Eldredge, Michael
Vallon, Ethan Laidlaw, Harry Strang,
The Jimmy Wakely Trio (Jimmy Wakely,
Johnny Bond, Dick Rinehart), William
Desmond, Henry Rocquemore, Denver
Dixon, Billy Engle, Carl Mathews, Bob
Reeves, Eddie Parker, Fred Graham,
Tom Steele, Art Mix. A rancher, falsely
sentenced to jail for a bank robbery,
is paroled and with the aid of a marshal
sets out to find those who framed him.
Johnny Mack Brown-Tex Ritter vehicle,
the last of their Universal series, which
is fast going from start to finish; one
of the first films to bring notice to Robert
Mitchum, cast here as a saloon owner.

1964 The Lone Star Vigilantes. Columbia,
1942. 58 minutes B/W. D: Wallace Fox.
SC: Luci Ward. WITH Bill Elliott, Tex

Ritter, Virginia Carpenter, Frank Mitchell,
Luana Walters, Budd Buster, Forrest
Taylor, Gavin Gordon, Lowell Drew,
Edmund Cobb, Ethan Laidlaw, Rick Ander-
son. After the Civil War two men return
home to Texas to find their town under
the thumb of bandits masquerading as
Army troops. Not an overly distinguished
film in the teaming of Bill Elliott and
Tex Ritter at Columbia although Tex
does sing "Headin' Home to Texas" and
"When the Moon is Shining on the Old
Corral." Reissued by Astor Pictures
in 1950.

1965 The Lone Texan. 20th Century-Fox,
1959. 70 minutes B/W. D: Paul Landres.
SC: James Landis & Jack Thomas. WITH
Willard Parker, Grant Williams, Audrey
Dalton, Douglas Kennedy, June Blair,
Dabbs Greer, Barbara Heller, Rayford
Barnes, Tyler McVey, Lee Farr, Jimmy
Murphy, Dick Monahan, Robert Dix,
I. Stanford Jolley, Gregg Barton, Sid
Melton, Hank Patterson, Tom London,
Frank Marlowe, Boyd Stockman, Jerry
Summers, Bill Coontz, Shirley Haven.
After the Civil War, a Union calvary
officer returns home to Texas to find
himself called a traitor and his younger
brother a corrupt sheriff. Rather interest-
ing drama inhibited by a low budget.

1966 Lone Texas Ranger. Republic, 1945.
54 (56) minutes B/W. D: Spencer Gordon
Bennet. SC: Bob Williams. WITH Bill
Elliott, Bobby Blake, Alice Fleming,
Roy Barcroft, Helen Talbot, Jack Mc-
Clendon, Rex Lease, Tom Chatterton,
Jack Kirk, Nelson McDowell, Dale Van
Sickel, Frank O'Connor, Robert Wilke,
Bud Geary, Budd Buster, Hal Price, Horace
B. Carpenter, Nolan Leary, Tom Steele,
LeRoy Mason (voice). After killing a
highly respected lawman (who was actually
an outlaw leader), Red Ryder faces a
challenge from the man's son. A strong
script highlights this actionful "Red
Ryder" series entry.

The Lone Trail (1932) see **The Sign
of the Wolf**

1967 Lonely Are the Brave. Universal,
1962. 107 minutes B/W. D: David Miller.
SC: Dalton Trumbo. WITH Kirk Douglas,
Gena Rowlands, Walter Matthau, Michael
Kane, Carroll O'Connor, William Schallert,
Karl Swenson, George Kennedy, Dan
Sheridan, Bill Raisch, William Mims,
Martin Garralaga, Lalo Rios. A modern
day, free-spirited, cowboy escapes from
jail and is hunted by a posse. This yester-

day's versus today's values oater is a good one, with excellent work by Kirk Douglas as the cowboy.

1968 The Lonely Man. Paramount, 1957. 87 minutes B/W. D: Henry Levin. SC: Harry Essex. WITH Jack Palance, Anthony Perkins, Neville Brand, Robert Middleton, Elaine Aiken, Elisha Cook Jr., Claude Akins, Lee Van Cleef, Harry Shannon, James Bell, Adam Williams, Denver Pyle, John Doucette, Paul Newlan. A gunman wants to lead a lawful life but is forced into one last showdown. Fairly interesting oater greatly aided by good production values and acting.

1969 The Lonely Trail. Republic, 1936. 56 minutes B/W. D: Joseph Kane. SC: Bernard McConville & Jack Natteford. WITH John Wayne, Ann Rutherford, Cy Kendall, Robert Kortman, Fred "Snowflake" Toones, Etta McDaniel, Sam Flint, Denny Meadows (Dennis Moore), Jim Toney, Yakima Canutt, Lloyd Ingraham, Bob Burns, James Marcus, Rodney Hildebrand, Eugene Jackson, Jack Kirk, Jack Ingram, Bud Pope, Tex Phelps, Tracy Layne. After the Civil War, the governor of Texas asks a rancher, who had fought with the Union, to aid him in ridding the state of carpetbaggers. Extremely good early John Wayne film with nice work from Cy Kendall as the bad guy. V: NTA Home Entertainment.

1970 The Lonesome Trail. Syndicate, 1930. 60 minutes B/W. D: Bruce Mitchell. SC: G. A. Durlam. WITH Charles Delaney, Virginia Brown Faire, George Berlinger, William Von Bricken, George Hackathorne, George Regas, Yakima Canutt, Art Mix, Ben Corbett, Lafe McKee, Jimmie Aubrey, Monte Montague, Bob Reeves, Bill McCall. A cowboy brings a cattle herd to a buyer whose partner is in cahoots with a bandit and his gang. Stilted early talkie with a bunch of wheezy vaudeville gags and hero Charles Delaney singing "Oh, Susannah."

1971 The Lonesome Trail. Monogram, 1945. 57 minutes B/W. D: Oliver Drake. SC: Louise Rosseau. WITH Jimmy Wakely, Lee "Lasses" White, John James, Iris Clive, Horace Murphy, Lorraine Miller, Eddie Majors, The Saddle Pals, The Sunshine Girls, Coleen Sumners (Mary Ford), Zon Murray, Roy Butler, Frank McCarroll, Jack Clifford, Arthur Smith, Carl Mathews, Carl Sepulveda, Jack Rivers. Much to the chagrin of his two pals, one of the three owners of a ghost town sells an interest in it to two crooks who immediately start a false gold rush rumor. The music is good but the plot is weak in this Jimmy Wakely outing.

1972 The Lonesome Trail. Lippert, 1955. 73 minutes B/W. D: Richard Bartlett. SC: Richard Bartlett & Ian MacDonald. WITH Wayne Morris, John Agar, Margia Dean, Edgar Buchanan, Adele Jergens, Earle Lyon, Ian MacDonald, Douglas Fowley, Richard Bartlett, Betty Blythe. When landgrabbers try to steal his land, a man retaliates with a bow and arrow instead of a six gun. Rather interesting low budget outing although top billed Wayne Morris has only a small role as a bartender.

1973 The Long Chase. Universal, 1972. 89 minutes Color. D: Alexander Singer. WITH Roger Davis, Ben Murphy, Rod Cameron, Buddy Ebsen, Sally Field, James Drury, Frank Sinatra Jr., Marie Windsor, J. D. Cannon, Miles Watson, George Keymas, Walt Davis. Made up of two segments of the television series "Alias Smith and Jones" (CBS-TV, 1970-73), this telefeature told of two ex-outlaws trying to go straight and up against a grizzled, villainous bounty hunter. Not bad for a paste-up.

1974 The Long, Long Trail. Universal, 1929. 60 minutes B/W. D: Arthur Rosson. SC: Howard Green. WITH Hoot Gibson, Sally Eilers, Kathryn McGuire, Jim Mason, Archie Ricks, Walter Brennan, Howard Truesdale. A fun-loving cowboy falls for a pretty girl and at the same time uncovers a plot to steal rodeo proceeds. Fun Hoot Gibson early talkie, a remake of his 1923 Universal film **The Ramblin' Kid.**

1975 A Long Ride from Hell. Cinerama, 1970. 94 minutes Color. D: Alex Burks (Camillo Bazzoni). SC: Steve Reeves. WITH Steve Reeves, Wade Preston, Dick Palmer, Silvana Venturelli, Lee Burton, Ted Carter, Rosalba Neri, Mimmo Palmara, Franco Fantasia. A rancher, wrongly sent to prison for a robbery he did not commit, escapes to clear his name and get revenge for the murder of his family. Okay European action oater for Steve Reeves fans. Originally issued in Italy in 1968 by B.R.C. as **Vivo Per la Tua Morte** (I Live for Your Death).

The Long Ride Home see **A Time for Killing**

1976 The Long Riders. United Artists, 1980. 100 minutes Color. D: Walter Hill. SC: Bill Bryden, Steven Phillip Smith, Stacy Keach & James Keach. WITH David Carradine, Keith Carradine, Robert Carradine, James Keach, Stacy Keach, Dennis Quaid, Randy Quaid, Kevin Brophy, Harry Carey Jr., Christopher Guest, Nicholas Guest, Shelby Leverington, Felice Orlandi, Pamela Reed, James Remar, Frank Ryan, Savannah Smith, Amy Stryker, James Whitmore Jr., John Bottoms, West Buchanan. The story of the outlaw activities of the James-Younger-Miller gang culminating in the ill-fated Northfield, Minnesota, raid. Fair look at the famous bandits' lives, interesting for the casting of acting brothers in the main roles.

1977 The Long Rifle and the Tomahawk. International Television Corporation (ITC), 1964. 89 minutes. D: Sam Newfield & Sidney Salkow. WITH John Hart, Lon Chaney, John Vernon. Hawkeye and Chingachgook, his blood brother, aid the English settlers in upper New York State during colonial times. Three episodes of the "Hawkeye and the Last of the Mohicans" (Syndicated, 1956) television series strung together and issued to TV as a feature film; average production from Sigmund Neufeld, filmed on the cheap in Canada.

1978 The Long Rope. 20th Century-Fox, 1961. 61 minutes B/W. D: William Witney. SC: Robert Hamner. WITH Hugh Marlowe, Lisa Montell, Alan Hale (Jr.), Robert Wilke, John Alonzo, Madaleine Holmes, David Renard, Jeffrey Morris, Chris Robinson. A circuit-riding judge enlists the aid of a gunman to protect a young man from townspeople during a murder trial. Short, but compact and entertaining little effort, produced by Margia Dean.

The Long Tomorrow see **Face to the Wind**

The Longest Hunt see **Gringo**

1979 The Longhorn. Allied Artists/Mono-gram, 1951. 70 minutes B/W. D: Lewis D. Collins. SC: Dan Ullman. WITH William Elliott, Phyllis Coates, Myron Healey, John Hart, Marshall Reed, William Faw-cett, Lee Roberts, Carol Henry, Zon Murray, Steve Clark, Lane Bradford, Herman Hack, Carl Mathews. A cowboy sets up a cattle drive in order to cross-breed stock but his so-called friend and his gang plan to rustle the herd along the way. Very fine Bill Elliott vehicle with a good script, cast and fast action; recommended.

1980 Look Out Sister. Astor, 1948. 64 minutes B/W. D: Bud Pollard. SC: John E. Gordon. WITH Louis Jordan, Suzette Harbin, Monte Hawley, Glenn Allen, Tommy Southern, Jack Clisby, Maceo Sheffield, Petty Thomas, Louise Franklin, Bob Scott & Louis Jordan Tympany Six. A bandleader on a dude ranch tries to save it from foreclosure. Music man Louis Jordan, plus eleven good tunes, add some zest to this oater made for the Negro market of the 1940s.

1981 Lost Canyon. United Artists, 1943. 54 (61) minutes B/W. D: Lesley Selander. SC: Harry O. Hoyt. WITH William Boyd, Andy Clyde, Jay Kirby, Lola Lane, Douglas Fowley, Herbert Rawlinson, Guy Usher, Karl Hackett, Hugh Prosser, Robert Kortman, The Sportsmen Quartette, Si Jenks, John Cason, Keith Richards, Herman Hack, Merrill McCormack, George Morrell. Bar 20 wrangler Johnny Travers is accused of a bank robbery but Hoppy soons finds out that a lawyer is behind the theft. Average "Hopalong Cassidy" entry with stock footage from the finale of **Rustler's Valley** (q.v.).

1982 Lost in Alaska. Universal, 1952. 76 minutes B/W. D: Jean Yarbrough. SC: Martin Ragaway & Leonard Stern. WITH Bud Abbott, Lou Costello, Tom Ewell, Mitzi Green, Bruce Cabot, Emory Parnell, Jack Ingram, Rex Lease, Joe Kirk, Minerva Urecal, Howard Negley, Maudie Prickett, Billy Wayne, Paul Newlan, Michael Ross, Iron Eyes Cody, Donald Kerr. Three men head for Alaska to find a fortune in buried gold but meet with opposition from the local inhabitants. Tired Abbot and Costello vehicle; for their fans only.

Lost Island of Kioga see **Hawk of the Wilderness**

1983 Lost Ranch. Victory, 1937. 56 minutes B/W. D: Sam Katzman. SC: Basil Dickey. WITH Tom Tyler, Jeanne Martel, Lafe McKee, Forrest Taylor, Harry Harvey Jr., Marjorie Beebe, Howard Bryant, Theodore Lorch, Slim Whitaker, Roger Williams. A young girl and her friend come West to find the girl's missing father and his "secret" and are attacked by outlaws but saved by a cowboy. Economical but entertaining actioner with mostly outdoor action and few interiors.

1984 The Lost Trail. Monogram, 1945. 60 minutes B/W. D: Lambert Hillyer. SC: Jess Bowers (Adele Buffington). WITH Johnny Mack Brown, Raymond Hatton, Jennifer Holt, Riley Hill, Kenneth MacDonald, Milburn Morante, Steve Clark, Eddie Parker, Lynton Brent, John Ince, Frank LaRue, Frank McCarroll, Dick Dickinson, George Morrell, John Bridges, Cal Shrum & His Rhythm Rangers, Carl Mathews. Two lawmen come to the aid of a young girl whose stage line is being robbed by outlaws. Pretty good Johnny Mack Brown series entry.

1985 Lost Treasure of the Aztecs. American-International, 1966. 87 minutes Color. D-SC: Piero Pierotti. WITH Alan Steel, Mario Petri, Tony Sailer, Anna M. Polani, Pierre Cressoy, Harry Riebauer, Birgit Heiberg, Wolfgang Lukschy, Dada Gallotti. A crooked saloon owner murders a girl's father and puts the blame on another, but the real murderer is suspected by a gambler and his friend who find a lost Inca civilization and its fabulous treasure. Fairly interesting combination of the Western and muscle-men pictures so popular in Europe in the 1960s; despite its U. S. title the film actually deals with Incas and not Aztec Indians. Issued in Italy by Romana Film/Constantin Film (An Italian-West German coproduction) as **Sansone e il Tesoro Degli Incas** (Samson and the Treasure of the Incas). Alternate title: **Hercules and the Treasure of the Incas.**

Lost Women see **Mesa of Lost Women**

1986 The Lottery Bride. United Artists, 1930. 80 minutes B/W. D: Paul S. Stein. SC: Horace Jackson & Howard Emmett Rogers. WITH Jeanette MacDonald, John Garrick, Joe E. Brown, ZaSu Pitts, Robert Chisholm, Joseph Macaulay, Harry Gribbon, Carroll Nye. In order to pay off her brother's gambling debts, a young girl agrees to become a lottery bride in the King's Bay settlement of Northern Norway. Although not a Western in the strictest sense, this early talkie musical does concern the settlement of the northern frontier, although this time in Norway. The film creaks a bit with age but the pleasant Rudolf Friml score holds up very well.

Louisiana Gal see **Old Louisiana**

1987 Love Me Tender. 20th Century-Fox, 1956. 89 minutes B/W. D: Robert D. Webb. SC: Robert Buckner. WITH Richard Egan, Debra Paget, Elvis Presley, Robert Middleton, William Campbell, Neville Brand, Mildred Dunnock, Bruce Bennett, James Drury, Russ Conway, Ken Clark, Barry Coe, L. Q. Jones, Paul Burns, Jerry Sheldon, James Stone, Ed Mundy, Joe Di Reda, Bobby Rose, Tom Greenway, Jay Jostyn, Steve Darrell. Two brothers love the same girl. When one leaves home to fight for the South during the Civil War, the younger brother marries her, causing a conflict when the older brother returns home. Average adaptation of Maurice Geraghty's novel; best known for being Elvis Presley's film debut.

1988 Lovin' Molly. Columbia, 1974. 98 minutes Color. D: Sidney Lumet. SC: Stephen Friedman. WITH Anthony Perkins, Beau Bridges, Blythe Danner, Edward Binns, Susan Sarandon, Conrad Fowkes, Claude Transverse, John Henry Faulk. Two men love the same woman over a four decade period in Texas. Fair drama based on Larry McMurtry's novel Leaving Cheyenne.

1989 The Luck of Roaring Camp. Monogram, 1937. 59 minutes B/W. D: Irvin V. Willat. SC: Harvey Gates. WITH Owen Davis Jr., Joan Woodbury, Charles Brokaw, Forrest Taylor, Robert Kortman, Charles King, Byron Foulger, Bob McKenzie, John Wallace. The birth of a baby boy brings luck to the inhabitants of a gold rush mining town. Expanded version of Bret Harte's short story makes for only average entertainment.

1990 Lucky Boots. Beacon/Equity, 1935. 59 minutes B/W. D: Al Herman. SC: William L. Nolte. WITH Guinn "Big Boy" Williams, Marion Schilling, Frank Yaconelli, Wally Wales, Charles K. French, Tom London, Roger Williams, Gordon Griffith, Barney Beasley, Si Jenks, Dick Botiller, Julian Rivero. Two cowpokes become involved in a treasure hunt after a Mexican bandit leader is killed, his loot is buried on a ranch and one of the cowboys finds the dead man's boots. Pretty good oater considering its poverty row origins; hero Guinn Williams sings "Home on the Range." Original title: **Gun Play.**

1991 Lucky Cisco Kid. 20th Century-Fox, 1940. 68 minutes B/W. D: H. Bruce Humberstone. SC: Robert Ellis & Helen Logan. WITH Cesar Romero, Mary Beth Hughes, Dana Andrews, Evelyn Venable, Chris-Pin Martin, Joseph Sawyer, Dick Rich, Johnny Sheffield, Francis Ford, William Royle.

The Cisco Kid romances two lovely ladies while on the trail of crooks after local ranches. Slow moving and overly romantic "Cisco Kid" series entry.

1992 Lucky Larkin. Universal, 1930. 66 minutes B/W. D: Harry Joe Brown. SC: Marion Jackson. WITH Ken Maynard, Nora Lane, Harry Todd, Charles Clary, Paul Hurst, James Farley, Jack Rockwell, Edgar "Blue" Washington. A cowboy agrees to ride in the big race to save the ranch of the father of the girl he loves. Okay Ken Maynard silent feature, also issued with sound and music effects.

1993 Lucky Larrigan. Monogram, 1932. 58 minutes B/W. D: J. P. McCarthy. SC: Wellyn Totman. WITH Rex Bell, Helen Foster, George Chesebro, John Elliott, Stanley Blystone, Julian Rivero, G. D. Wood, Wilfred Lucas. A self-centered polo player goes out West and ends up aiding his father and his girl's father in fighting outlaws. Poor Rex Bell vehicle.

1994 Lucky Terror. Grand National, 1936. 61 minutes B/W. D-SC: Alan James. WITH Hoot Gibson, Lona Andre, Charles Hill, George Chesebro, Wally Wales, Robert McKenzie, Jack Rockwell, Frank Yaconelli, Charles King, Art Mix, Horace Carpenter, Horace Murphy, Hank Bell, Nelson McDowell. A drifter accidentally stumbles across a cache of gold and hides it. Later he joins a medicine show and tries to aid a girl when crooks try to steal her gold mine. Highly entertaining Hoot Gibson feature; one of his best in the sound era.

1995 The Lucky Texan. Monogram, 1934. 55 minutes B/W. D-SC: Robert North Bradbury. WITH John Wayne, Barbara Sheldon, Yakima Canutt, Lloyd Whitlock, George ("Gabby") Hayes, Gordon D. (De-Main) Woods, Eddie Parker, Earl Dwire, Jack Rockwell, Artie Ortego, Tex Palmer, Tex Phelps, George Morrell. A young man comes West and joins his late father's partner in a mining venture but the duo is challenged by claim jumpers. Average entry in John Wayne's Lone Star series for producer Paul Malvern. V: Video Dimensions.

1996 Lumberjack. United Artists, 1944. 54 (65) minutes B/W. D: Lesley Selander. SC: Norman Houston & Barry Shipman. WITH William Boyd, Andy Clyde, Jimmy Rogers, Ellen Hall, Douglass Dumbrille, Francis McDonald, Herbert Rawlinson, Ethel Wales, John Whitney, Hal Taliaferro,

Henry Wills, Charles Morton, Frances Morris, Jack Rockwell, Bob Burns, Hank Worden, Earle Hodgins, Pierce Lyden. Hopalong Cassidy and the Bar 20 boys fight a gang of outlaws in lumber country. Fast paced and actionful entry in the long-running "Hopalong Cassidy" series; one of the better ones toward the end of the first United Artists period.

Lure of the Range see **Speeding Hoofs**

1997 Lure of the Wasteland. Al Lane Pictures, 1939. 55 minutes Color. D: Harry Fraser. SC: Monroe Talbot. WITH Grant Withers, LeRoy Mason, Marion Arnold, Snub Pollard, Karl Hackett, Henry Rocquemore, Tom London, Sherry Tansey. A federal agent works undercover and infiltrates an outlaw gang to find out what happened to loot stolen from a robbery a few years before. Low grade independent outing mainly of interest because it was filmed in Telco Color.

1998 Lust for Gold. Columbia, 1949. 90 minutes B/W. D: S. Sylvan Simon & (uncredited George Marshall). SC: Ted Sherdeman & Richard English. WITH Ida Lupino, Glenn Ford, Gig Young, William Prince, Edgar Buchanan, Will Geer, Paul Ford, Jay Silverheels, Antonio Moreno, Eddy Waller, Will Wright, Virginia Mullen, Myrna Dell, Tom Tyler, Paul Burns, Hayden Rorke, Elspeth Dudgeon, Si Jenks. A woman who is married to a no-good pretends to be single in order to romance a man who knows the location of the Lost Dutchman gold mine. Interesting but hard to follow oater enhanced by a good cast.

1999 Lust in the Dust. Fox Run, 1984. 87 minutes Color. D: Paul Bartel. SC: Philip Taylor. WITH Tab Hunter, Divine, Lainie Kazan, Geoffrey Lewis, Henry Silva, Cesar Romero, Woody Strode, Pedro Gonzalez-Gonzalez, Gina Gallego, Nedia Volz, Courtney Gains, Daniel Fushman, Erni Shinagawa. A woman attacked by an outlaw gang meets a mysterious gunman and they go to a small town where the populace is after hidden treasure. Outlandish, but surprisingly funny, R-rated genre satire, filmed in New Mexico.

2000 Lust to Kill. Barjul International/ Emerson, 1960. 69 minutes B/W. D: Oliver Drake. SC: Sam Roeca & Tom Hubbard. WITH Jim Davis, Don Megowan, Allison Hayes, Gerald Milton, Toni Turner, Sandra Giles, Tom Hubbard, Claire Carleton,

John Holland, James Maloney, Fred Sherman, Roger Williams, Al Terry, Gene Street. An outlaw's girl friend helps him escape from a lawman so he can get revenge on the gang who killed his brother. Low grade actioner made in 1957. TV title: **Border Lust.**

2001 The Lusty Men. RKO Radio, 1952. 113 minutes B/W. D: Nicholas Ray. SC: Horace McCoy & David Dortort. WITH Robert Mitchum, Susan Hayward, Arthur Kennedy, Arthur Hunnicutt, Frank Faylen, Walter Coy, Carol Nugent, Maria Hart, Lorna Thayer, Burt Mustin, Karen King, Jimmie Dodd, Eleanor Todd, Riley Hill, Robert Bray, Sheb Wooley, Marshall Reed, Paul E. Burns, Dennis Moore, George Wallace, Lane Bradford, Glenn Strange, George Sherwood, Lane Chandler, Ralph Volkie. A veteran rodeo star trains a younger performer while both men vie for the love of a hell-raising girl. Well done tale of the rodeo circuit, especially well acted by its trio of stars.

2002 Lynch Mob. CBS-TV/20th Century-Fox, 1955. 45 minutes B/W. WITH Cameron Mitchell, E. G. Marshall, Robert Wagner, Wallace Ford, Raymond Burr, Hope Emerson, Jay Brooks. When a cattle raiser is murdered three strangers are accused of the crime and threatened with lynching. TV adaptation of The Ox-Bow Incident originally telecast November 2, 1955 on "The Twentieth Century-Fox Hour" (CBS-TV, 1955-57) and available for television as a feature.

M

2003 The Macahans. ABC-TV/Metro-Goldwyn-Mayer, 1976. 125 minutes Color. D: Bernard McEveety. SC: Jim Byrnes. WITH James Arness, Eva Marie Saint, Richard Kiley, Bruce Boxleitner, Kathryn Holcomb, William Kirby Cullen, Vicki Schreck, Gene Evans, Vic Mohica, Frank Ferguson, Ann Doran, Ben Wilson, Mel Stevens, Rudy Diaz, John Crawford, William Conrad (narrator). On the eve of the Civil War, a Virginia farmer decides to move his family West and enlists the aid of his brother, a mountain scout. This telefeature was a spinoff of the popular film How the West Was Won (q.v.) and proved to be a big ratings favorite as well as good, solid entertainment. James Arness as mountain man Zeb Macahan is especially good and the tele-

feature developed into a popular miniseries retitled **How the West Was Won,** which ran on ABC-TV from 1977 to 1979.

Machismo—40 Graves for 40 Guns see **40 Graves for 40 Guns**

2004 Macho Callahan. Avco-Embassy, 1970. 100 minutes Color. D: Bernard Kowalski. SC: Cliff Gould. WITH David Janssen, Jean Seberg, Lee J. Cobb, James Booth, Pedro Armendariz Jr., David Carradine, Anne Revere, Richard Anderson, Matt Clark, Richard Evans, Bo Hopkins, Diane Ladd, Robert Morgan. During the Civil War a man escapes from prison and sets out to kill the man who put him there. None-too-good oater helped by Mexican locales.

2005 MacKenna's Gold. Columbia, 1969. 128 minutes Color. D: J. Lee Thompson. SC: Carl Foreman. WITH Gregory Peck, Omar Sharif, Telly Savalas, Camilla Sparv, Keenan Wynn, Julie Newmar, Eli Wallach, Raymond Massey, Edward G. Robinson, Anthony Quayle, Burgess Meredith, Lee J. Cobb, Eduardo Ciannelli, Rudy Diaz, Ted Cassidy, Dick Peabody, Robert Phillips, J. Robert Porter, Pepe Callahan, Duke Hobbie, Trevor Bardette, Madeleine Taylor Holmes, John Garfield Jr., Shelley Morrison, Victor Jory (narrator). A group of people who try to find a lost canyon filled with gold are not only at odds with themselves but with Apaches and the cavalry. Surprisingly poor big budget oater which was hurt by prerelease cuts.

2006 MacKintosh and T. J. Penland, 1975. 96 minutes Color. D: Marvin Chomsky. SC: Paul Savage. WITH Roy Rogers, Clay O'Brien, Billy Green Bush, Joan Hackett, Andrew Robinson, James Hampton, Walter Barnes, Dean Smith, Larry Mahan. An aging drifter takes a homeless young man under his wing. Together they fight a rabies epidemic and hunt for a madman hiding on a large ranch. Roy Rogers' return to the screen was sadly overlooked when first issued; the film is highly entertaining and well worth watching. Music by Waylon Jennings, Willie Nelson and The Waylors. Reissued in 1984.

2007 Mad Dog. Cinema Shares, 1980. 93 minutes Color. D-SC: Philippe Mora. WITH Dennis Hopper, Jack Thompson, David Culpilil, Frank Thring, Michael Pate. The story of the famous 19th century Australian outlaw "Mad Dog" Morgan.

Relatively entertaining Australian R-rated oater which won the John Ford Memorial Award as Best Western of the Year in 1976. It was originally issued in Australia in 1976 as **Mad Dog Morgan** and U. S. release prints ran 102 minutes.

Mad Dog Morgan see **Mad Dog**

2008 Madron. Four Star/Excelsior, 1971. 92 minutes Color. D: Jerry Hopper. SC: Edward Chappell & Leo McMahon. WITH Richard Boone, Leslie Caron, Sam Red, Paul Smith, Gabi Amrani, Chaim Banai, Avraham Telya, Willy Gafni. A nun, the sole survivor of an Indian attack on a group of French Canadian sisters, is found by an Indian hunter and the two are captured by brutal drifters. Less than mediocre oater filmed in Israel.

2009 The Magnificent Bandits. Tritone/ Medusa, 1969. 90 minutes Color. D: Giovanni Fago. SC: Giovanni Fago, Antonio Troisio, Bernardino Zapponi & Jose Luis Jerez. WITH Tomas Milian, Ugo Pagliani, Eduardo Fajuardo, Howard Ross, Alfredo Santa Cruz, Jesus Guzman. In Brazil, the farmers unite to fight the government over the destruction of their farm lands. Well made Italian feature, originally called **O Cangaceiro**, set in South America.

2010 Magnificent Roughnecks. Columbia, 1956. 75 minutes B/W. D: Sherman A. Rose. SC: Stephen Kandel. WITH Jack Carson, Mickey Rooney, Nancy Gates, Jeff Donnell, Myron Healey, Willis Bouchey, Eric Feldary, Alan Wells, Frank Gerstle, Larry Carr, Matty Fain, Joe Locke. Two oil wildcatters try to bring in a new series of wells but meet with opposition. Very boring "comedy" with surprisingly poor results from the potentially great teaming of Jack Carson and Mickey Rooney.

2011 The Magnificent Seven. United Artists, 1960. 126 minutes Color. D: John Sturges. SC: William Roberts. WITH Yul Brynner, Eli Wallach, Steve McQueen, Horst Buchholz, Charles Bronson, Robert Vaughn, Brad Dexter, James Coburn, Vladimir Sokoloff, Rosenda Monteros, Jorge Martinez de Hoyos, Whit Bissell, Val Avery, Bing Russell, Rico Alaniz, Robert Wilke. The inhabitants of a small rural Mexican village obtain the services of seven hired guns to protect them from the ravages of a gang of bandits. Finely done and near-classic oater which is a refashioning of the famous 1954 Japanese film **Seven Samurai**. V: Cumberland Video. VD: Blackhawk.

2012 The Magnificent Seven Ride! United Artists, 1972. 100 minutes Color. D: George McCowan. SC: Arthur Rowe. WITH Lee Van Cleef, Stefanie Powers, Mariette Hartley, Michael Callan, Luke Askew, Pedro Armendariz Jr., William Lucking, James B. Sikking, Melissa Murphy, Darrell Larson, Ed Lauter, Carolyn Conwell, Jason Wingreen, Allyn Ann McLerie, Elizabeth Thompson, Ralph Waite, Rita Rogers, Robert Jaffe, Gary Busey, Rodolfo Acosta. When his bride is kidnapped by outlaws, an ex-gunman joins a friend in trying to find the bandit leader and ends up helping five escaped convicts defend a town against the bandit's gang. Fourth entry in "The Magnificent Seven" series and a pretty good outing.

2013 Mail Order Bride. Metro-Goldwyn-Mayer, 1964. 83 minutes Color. D-SC: Burt Kennedy. WITH Buddy Ebsen, Keir Dullea, Lois Nettleton, Warren Oates, Barbara Luna, Bill Smith, Jimmy Mathers, Marie Windsor, Paul Fix, Doodles Weaver, Denver Pyle, Kathleen Freeman, Abigail Shelton, Diane Sayer, Ted Ryan. A reckless young man inherits a ranch but his guardian feels he needs to grow up before taking it over so the guardian sends for a bride for him. Fair genre comedy helped by a good cast.

2014 Major Dundee. Columbia, 1965. 124 minutes Color. D: Sam Peckinpah. SC: Harry Julian Fink, Oscar Paul & Sam Peckinpah. WITH Charlton Heston, Richard Harris, Jim Hutton, James Coburn, Michael Anderson Jr., Senta Berger, Mario Adorf, Brock Peters, Warren Oates, Ben Johnson, R. G. Armstrong, L. Q. Jones, Slim Pickens, Karl Swenson, Michael Pate, John Davis Chandler, Dub Taylor, Albert Carter, Jose Carlos Ruiz. With a group of prison volunteers, a Union army major sets out to capture a rampaging Indian leader and his band in New Mexico. Colorful oater with a good cast and script. V: RCA/Columbia.

2015 A Man Alone. Republic, 1955. 96 minutes Color. D: Ray Milland. SC: John Tucker Battle. WITH Ray Milland, Mary Murphy, Ward Bond, Raymond Burr, Arthur Space, Lee Van Cleef, Alan Hale, Douglas Spencer, Thomas Browne Henry, Grandon Rhodes, Martin Garralaga, Kim Spalding, Howard Negley, Julian Rivero, Lee Roberts, Minerva Urecal, Thorpe Whiteman, Dick Rich, Frank Hagney. A loner is mistakenly accused of murder and is hunted by the law in a small town but is sheltered by the sheriff's pretty daughter. Ray Milland made his directorial debut in this film and he did a good job helming and starring in this very fine feature which is basically a silent movie for the first third of its running time; well worth seeing.

2016 Man and Boy. Levitt-Pickman, 1972. 98 minutes Color. D: E. W. Swackhamer. SC: Harry Essex & Oscar Saul. WITH Bill Cosby, George Spell, Floria Foster, Douglas Turner Ward, Yaphet Kotto, Shelley Morrison, Leif Erickson, John Anderson, Henry Silva, Dub Taylor. A black Civil War veteran and his young son set out on the trail of the thief who took their horse. Standard drama aimed at the family trade.

2017 The Man Behind the Gun. Warner Brothers, 1952. 82 minutes Color. D: Felix Feist. SC: John Twist. WITH Randolph Scott, Patrice Wymore, Philip Carey, Dick Wesson, Lina Romay, Roy Roberts, Morris Ankrum, Alan Hale (Jr.), Douglas Fowley, Anthony Caruso, Clancy Cooper, Robert Cabal, James Brown, Reed Howes, Rory Mallinson, John Logan, Vicki Raaf, Lee Morgan, Edward Hearn, Terry Frost, Charles Horvath, Art Millan, Rex Lease, James Bellah, Jack Parker, Billy Vincent, Alberto Morin, Edward Colmans, Ray Spiker, Herbert Deans. In 1850 one of the founders of Los Angeles fights to keep the territory from splitting into slave and non-slave holding areas. Fast moving historial drama for Randolph Scott followers.

2018 A Man Called Gannon. Universal, 1969. 105 minutes Color. D: James Goldstone. SC: Gene Kearney, Borden Chase & D. D. Beauchamp. WITH Tony Franciosa, Michael Sarrazin, Judi West, Susan Oliver, John Anderson, David Sheiner, James Westerfield, Gavin MacLeod, Eddie Firestone, Ed Peck, Harry Davis, Robert Sorrells, Terry Wilson, Eddra Gale, Harry Basch, James Callahan, Cliff Potter, Jason Evers, Jack Perkins. A cowboy makes a young Easterner his protege. When they take a job with a widow ranch owner, they find themselves opposed by neighbors over the size of their herd. Tepid remake of **Man Without a Star** (q.v.).

2019 The Man Called Gringo. International Germania/Procusa/Domiziana, 1964. 90 minutes Color. D: Roy Rowland. SC: Clarke Reynolds & Helmut Harun. WITH Gotz George, Alexandra Stewart, Helmut Schmid, Dan Martin, Sieghardt Rupp,

Sylvia Solar. A stranger arrives in a small Western town to unravel a twenty-year-old mystery involving his father. Another violent oater from Europe, this one a West German-Spanish-Italian coproduction originally issued in West Germany as **Sie Nannten Ihn Gringo**.

2020 A Man Called Horse. National General, 1970. 114 minutes Color. D: Elliott Silverstein. SC: Jack DeWitt. WITH Richard Harris, Judith Anderson, Jean Gascon, Manu Tupou, Dub Taylor, Corinna Tsopei, William Jordan, James Gammon, Eddie Little Sky, Manuel Padilla, Iron Eyes Cody, Lina Marin. While on a hunting expedition in the Dakotas, a British nobleman is captured by the Sioux Indians and made their slave. Interesting but violent and gory oater which resulted in two sequels, **Return of a Man Called Horse** and **Triumphs of a Man Called Horse** (qq.v.).

2021 The Man Called Noon. National General, 1973. 97 minutes Color. D: Peter Collinson. SC: Scott Finch. WITH Richard Crenna, Stephen Boyd, Rosanna Schiaffino, Farley Granger, Patty Shepard, Angel De Pozo, Howard Ross, Aldo Sambrell, Jose Jaspe, Charley Bravo, Ricardo Palacios, Fernando Hilbeck, Bruce Fisher. Aided by the girl who loves him, a gunman who has lost his memory searches for his identity and hidden loot. Based on the novel by Louis L'Amour, this spaghetti Western is better than the usual such fare, aided by good characterizations.

2022 A Man Called Sledge. Columbia, 1971. 92 minutes Color. D: Vic Morrow. SC: Vic Morrow & Frank Kowalsky. WITH James Garner, Dennis Weaver, Claude Akins, John Marley, Laura Antonelli, Paola Barbara, Mario Valgoi, Lorenzo Piani, Wade Preston, Laura Betti, Tony Young, Ken Clark, Franco Giornelli. A wanted outlaw joins three other men in stealing a half-million dollars in gold from a prison and then the group has a falling out over the loot. Okay oater mainly for James Garner fans.

2023 The Man from Bitter Ridge. Universal, 1955. 80 minutes Color. D: Jack Arnold. SC: Lawrence Roman. WITH Lex Barker, Mara Corday, Stephen McNally, Trevor Bardette, John Dehner, Myron Healey, Warren Stevens, Richard Garland, Jennings Miles, John Cliff, Ray Teal, John Harmon. While working undercover to find who is behind a series of stage holdups, a special agent is accused of the crimes by the outlaws. Fast moving Lex Barker vehicle.

2024 The Man from Black Hills. Monogram, 1952. 57 minutes B/W. D: Thomas Carr. SC: Joseph O'Donnell. WITH Johnny Mack Brown, James Ellison, Rand Brooks, Stanley Andrews, Florence Lake, Robert Bray, I. Stanford Jolley, Lane Bradford, Denver Pyle, Stanley Price, Ray Bennett, Joel Allen, Bud Osborne, Merrill McCormack. When a man finds his long-lost father he also discovers another fellow is masquerading as him in order to inherit a mine. Average Johnny Mack Brown film with a bit different plot.

2025 The Man from Button Willow. AFC Filmakers/United Screen Arts, 1965. 81 minutes Color. D-SC: David Detiege. WITH (voices) Dale Robertson, Howard Keel, Edgar Buchanan, Barbara Jean Wong, Hershel Bernardi, Ross Martin, Cliff Edwards, Verna Felton, Edward Platt, Clarence Nash, Buck Buchanan. In 1869 the first undercover agent tries to help settlers who are being fleeced of their lands during the construction of the first intercontinental railroad. Fairly pleasing animated feature aimed mainly at the juvenile set.

2026 Man from Cheyenne. Republic, 1942. 54 (60) minutes B/W. D: Joseph Kane. SC: Winston Miller. WITH Roy Rogers, George "Gabby" Hayes, Sally Payne, Gale Storm, Bob Nolan & The Sons of the Pioneers, Lynne Carver, William Haade, James Seay, Jack Ingram, Jack Kirk, Fred Burns, Jack Rockwell, Al Taylor, Chick Hannon, Art Dillard, Frank Brownlee. An outlaw gang terrorizes a small town and a cowboy hero returns home to stop them. Rather typical Roy Rogers outing with just enough action and songs to keep it going.

2027 The Man from Colorado. Columbia, 1949. 99 minutes Color. D: Henry Levin. SC: Robert D. Andrews & Ben Maddow. WITH Glenn Ford, William Holden, Ellen Drew, Ray Collins, Edgar Buchanan, Jerome Courtland, James Millican, Jim Bannon, Bill Phillips, Denver Pyle, James Bush, Mikel Conrad, David Clarke, Ian MacDonald, Clarence Chase, Stanley Andrews, Myron Healey, Craig Reynolds. A vicious Army officer is appointed a federal judge for the Colorado Territory and he uses his power to destroy his enemies. A different kind of genre offering with good acting and lots of violence.

2028 The Man from Dakota. Metro-Goldwyn-Mayer, 1940. 74 minutes B/W. D: Leslie Fenton. SC: Lawrence Stallings. WITH Wallace Beery, Dolores Del Rio, John Howard, Donald Meek, Robert Barrat, Addison Richards, Frederick Burton, William Haade, John Wray. A Union prisoner of war with a bad past tries to redeem himself by stealing Confederate secret plans, escaping from jail with another man, and heading north to deliver the plans to General Grant. Serio-comedy which will please Wallace Beery followers.

2029 The Man from Death Valley. Monogram, 1931. 64 minutes B/W. D: Lloyd Nosler. SC: G. A. Durlam. WITH Tom Tyler, Betty Mack, Si Jenks, Gino Corrado, John Oscar, Stanley Blystone, Hank Bell. A man arrives home to find his girl engaged to the town's lawyer. He overhears a plan to rob the bank, and does it himself to keep the crooks from getting the money. Confused and low grade Tom Tyler effort.

2030 Man from Del Rio. United Artists, 1956. 82 minutes B/W. D: Harry Horner. SC: Richard Carr. WITH Anthony Quinn, Katy Jurado, Peter Whitney, Douglas Fowley, John Larch, Whit Bissell, Douglas Spencer, Guinn Williams, Barry Atwater. A Mexican bandit wins respect for himself when he tries to save a small town from a brutal outlaw gang. Still another telling of the old story but a film that is not without merit.

2031 The Man from Galveston. Warner Brothers, 1964. 57 minutes B/W. D: William Conrad. SC: Dean Riesner & Michael Zagor. WITH Jeffrey Hunter, Preston Foster, James Coburn, Joanna Moore, Edward Andrews, Kevin Hagen, Martin West, Ed Nelson, Karl Swenson, Grace Lee Whitley, Claude Stroud, Sherwood Price, Arthur Malet, Marjorie Bennett. Sam Houston's lawyer son, Temple Houston, comes to a small Texas town to defend a woman accused of murder. Entertaining pilot to the TV series "Temple Houston" (NBC-TV, 1963-64); issued theatrically.

2032 The Man from God's Country. Phil Goldstone, 1924. 50 minutes B/W. D: Alvin J. Neitz. SC: George C. Hill. WITH William Fairbanks, Dorothy Revier, Lew Meehan, Milton Ross, Carl Silvera, Andrew Waldron. Two pals, an American and his Mexican vaquero buddy, fall for the same pretty girl. The American is blamed when she is brutalized by an American ranch foreman. Okay melodrama from the silent days. Also called **Borderland Rangers.**

2033 Man from God's Country. Allied Artists, 1958. 72 minutes Color. D: Paul Landres. SC: George Waggner. WITH George Montgomery, Susan Cummings, Randy Stuart, House Peters Jr., James Griffith, Kim Charney, Frank Wilcox, Gregg Barton, Philip Terry, Al Wyatt. In Montana a group of ranchers work together to obtain land needed by the railroad. Tame outing mainly for George Montgomery fans.

2034 The Man from Guntown. Puritan, 1935. 60 minutes B/W. D: Ford Beebe. SC: Ford Beebe & Thomas H. Ince Jr. WITH Tim McCoy, Billie Seward, Rex Lease, Jack Clifford, Wheeler Oakman, Bob McKenzie, Jack Rockwell, George Chesebro, Ella McKenzie, Horace B. Carpenter, Hank Bell, George Pierce. Falsely accused of a crime, a man is aided by the town marshal in escaping from jail so he can get the goods on the real culprit. Pretty good Tim McCoy outing with a nice story and direction.

2035 The Man from Hell. Willis Kent, 1934. 58 minutes B/W. D: Lewis Collins. SC: Melville Shyer. WITH Reb Russell, Fred Kohler, Ann D'Arcy, George ("Gabby") Hayes, Jack Rockwell, Yakima Canutt, Slim Whitaker, Roy D'Arcy, Tracey Layne, Mary Gordon, Tommy Bupp, Charles K. French, Murdock McQuarrie. After being released from Yuma Prison, a man tries to get proof that he is innocent and bring in the man who framed him. Pretty good Reb Russell vehicle enhanced by a fine cast.

2036 The Man from Hell's Edges. World Wide, 1932. 60 minutes B/W. D-SC: Robert North Bradbury. WITH Bob Steele, Nancy Drexel, Julian Rivero, Robert Homans, George ("Gabby") Hayes, Pee Wee Holmes, Earl Dwire, Dick Dickinson, Perry Murdock, Blackie Whiteford. A young man escapes from prison and ends up in a small town where he saves the life of the sheriff and becomes his deputy. He begins to suspect that a local caballero is behind an outlaw gang. Above average Bob Steele vehicle with a fine performance by Julian Rivero as the slick villain, Lobo; the words "Hell's Edges" in the title refers to the penitentiary. V: Discount Video.

2037 The Man from Laramie. Columbia, 1955. 104 minutes Color. D: Anthony Mann. SC: Philip Yordan & Frank Burt. WITH James Stewart, Arthur Kennedy, Donald Crisp, Cathy O'Donnell, Alex Nicol, Aline MacMahon, Wallace Ford, Jack Elam, John War Cloud, James Millican, Gregg Barton, Boyd Stockman, Frank De Kova, Frosty Royse, Eddy Waller. A mule-team driver sets out to find the men who murdered his younger brother. Exciting revenge melodrama with fine production values.

2038 The Man from Montana. Universal, 1941. 57 minutes B/W. D: Ray Taylor. SC: Bennett Cohen. WITH Johnny Mack Brown, Fuzzy Knight, Jeanne Kelly (Jean Brooks), Butch & Buddy, Nell O'Day, William Gould, James Blaine, Richard Alexander, Karl Hackett, Edmund Cobb, Kermit Maynard, Murdock MacQuarrie, The Kings Men, Frank Ellis, Blackjack Ward. A crook tries to start a feud between homesteaders and cattlemen because he wants both land and cattle. Okay Johnny Mack Brown series entry with a quartet of tunes, including "Little Joe the Wrangler."

2039 The Man from Monterey. Warner Brothers, 1933. 57 minutes B/W. D: Mack V. Wright. SC: Lesley Mason. WITH John Wayne, Ruth Hall, Luis Alberni, Francis Ford, Nina Quartero, Lafe McKee, Donald Reed, Lillian Leighton, Slim Whitaker, Jim Corey. In Old California a young army captain tries to persuade a landowner to register his property, which is sought by a crooked neighbor. Good costume drama; the last entry in John Wayne's early Warner Brothers series.

2040 The Man from Montreal. Universal, 1940. 60 minutes B/W. D: Christy Cabanne. SC: Owen Francis. WITH Richard Arlen, Andy Devine, Anne Gwynne, Jerry Marlowe, Kay Sutton, Reed Hadley, Addison Richards, Tom Whitten, Lane Chandler, Don Brodie, Karl Hackett, Pat Flaherty, Eddy Waller, William Royle, Eddy Conrad. A trapper falsely arrested for carrying stolen pelts sets out to find the real fur thieves. Fast paced northwoods melodrama; a part of the Richard Arlen-Andy Devine series of action pictures from Universal.

2041 Man from Music Mountain. Republic, 1938. 54 (58) minutes B/W. D: Joseph Kane. SC: Bernard McConville. WITH Gene Autry, Smiley Burnette, Carol Hughes, Sally Payne, Polly Jenkins & Her Plowboys, Ivan Miller, Al Terry, Dick Elliott, Hal Price, Cactus Mack,

Ed Cassidy, Howard Chase, Lew Kelly, Frankie Marvin, Earl Dwire, Lloyd Ingraham, Gordon Hart, Joe Yrigoyen, Harry Harvey, Lillian Drew. Near the site of the Boulder Dam, crooks try to swindle settlers by the supposed revamping of a ghost town but a singing cowboy and his pals arrive on the scene to stop them. Good Gene Autry vehicle with fine interpolation of story, music and action. V: Nostalgia Merchant.

2042 Man from Music Mountain. Republic, 1943. 54 (71) minutes B/W. D: Joseph Kane. SC: J. Benton Cheney & Bradford Ropes. WITH Roy Rogers, Bob Nolan & The Sons of the Pioneers, Ruth Terry, Paul Kelly, Ann Gillis, George Cleveland, Pat Brady, Hal Taliaferro, Jay Novello, Paul Harvey, Roy Barcroft, Renie Riano, Hank Bell, I. Stanford Jolley, Jack O'Shea. Radio singer Roy Rogers' homecoming is spoiled by a crooked rancher who uses a cattlemen vs. sheepmen feud to get control of new grazing licenses. Pretty entertaining Roy Rogers series film. TV title: **Texas Legionaires.**

2043 The Man from New Mexico. Monogram, 1932. 60 minutes B/W. D: J. P. McCarthy. SC: Harry O. Hoyt. WITH Tom Tyler, Caryl Lincoln, Robert Walker, Lafe McKee, Jack Richardson, Frank Ball, Lewis Sargent, Blackie Whiteford, Slim Whitaker, Jack Long, William Nolte. A cattlemen's association detective works undercover to find out who has been rustling area cattle. Okay Tom Tyler vehicle.

2044 The Man from Nowhere. Leone Film/Orphee, 1966. 107 minutes Color. D: Michele Lupo. SC: Martino & Gastaldi. WITH Giuliano Gemma, Corrine Marchand, Fernando Sancho, Robert Camardiel, Rosalba Neri, Giovanni Pazzafini, Gianni Solaro, Mirko Ellis. A saloon owner hires a gunman to kill the man who murdered his daughter, but the gunman's price includes a night with the man's other daughter. Endlessly violent genre effort from Italy, originally called **Arizona Colt.**

2045 Man from Oklahoma. Republic, 1945. 54 (68) minutes B/W. D: Frank McDonald. SC: John K. Butler. WITH Roy Rogers, George "Gabby" Hayes, Dale Evans, Roger Pryor, Bob Nolan & The Sons of the Pioneers, Arthur Loft, Maude Eburne, Sam Flint, Si Jenks, June Bryde, Elaine Lange, Charles Soldani, Edmund Cobb, George Sherwood, Eddie

Kane, George Chandler, Wally West, Tex Terry, Robert Wilke. Roy Rogers becomes involved in a feud between rival ranchers which is secretly being instigated by the supposed friend of one of the ranchers. Typical Roy Rogers fantasy of the time with an exciting wagon chase, good songs and the use of a movie camera to uncover the villain.

2046 The Man from Oklahoma. International Germania/Cineproduction Associates/Balcazar, 1966. 85 minutes Color. D: J. Balcazar. SC: Helmut Harun. WITH Rick Horne, Sabine Bethmann, Tom Fellighi, Karl-Otto Alberty, George Herzig. The newly appointed sheriff of a small town in New Mexico feels a local rancher is behind a hated outlaw gang. Another in the long string of violent oaters from Europe, this one made in West Germany as **Oklahoma John.**

2047 The Man from Painted Post. Paramount-Artcraft, 1917. 55 minutes B/W. D: Joseph Henaberry. SC: Douglas Fairbanks. WITH Douglas Fairbanks, Eileen Percy, Frank Campeau, Herbert Standing, Monte Blue, Charles Stevens, W. E. Lowery. A detective is assigned to investigate the disappearance of cattle in a small Wyoming town. Fun Douglas Fairbanks silent comedy-drama.

2048 Man from Rainbow Valley. Republic, 1946. 56 minutes Color. D: R. G. Springsteen. SC: Betty Burbridge. WITH Monte Hale, Adrian Booth, Jo Ann Marlowe, Ferris Taylor, Emmett Lynn, The Sagebrush Serenaders, Bud Geary, Tom London, Kenne Duncan, Doye O'Dell, Bert Roach. A cowboy comes to the aid of a rancher, also a comic-strip writer, who is being swindled by a crooked rodeo owner. Monte Hale's second film is slow going despite an interesting plotline.

2049 The Man from Snowy River. 20th Century-Fox, 1982. 104 minutes Color. D: George Miller. SC: John Dixon. WITH Kirk Douglas, Jack Thompson, Tom Burlinson, Sigrid Thornton, Lorraine Bayly, Chris Haywood, Terence Donovan, June Jago, Tony Bonner, Bruce Kerr, John Nash. At the turn of the century in Australia, a young man grows into manhood working for a cattle baron and falling in love with the man's daughter. Fine Australian "Western" with good work by Kirk Douglas in dual roles as brothers.

2050 Man from Sonora. Monogram, 1951. 54 minutes B/W. D: Lewis D. Collins.

SC: Maurice Tombragel. WITH Johnny
Mack Brown, Phyllis Coates, House Peters
Jr., Lyle Talbot, Lee Roberts, John Merton,
Stanley Price, Dennis Moore, Ray Jones,
Pierce Lyden, Sam Flint, George De-
Normand. A marshal comes to the aid
of a local sheriff trying to find out who
is behind the theft of a bullion shipment
and the murder of a lawman working
undercover as a traveling salesman.
Tired Johnny Mack Brown vehicle from
the Monogram assembly line.

2051 The Man from Sundown. Columbia,
1939. 58 minutes B/W. D: Sam Nelson.
SC: Paul Franklin. WITH Charles Starrett,
Iris Meredith, Richard Fiske, Bob Nolan
& The Sons of the Pioneers, Jack Rockwell,
Alan Bridge, Richard Botiller, Robert
Fiske, Ed Peil, Clem Horton, Forrest
Dillon, Tex Cooper, Al Haskell, Ed LeSaint,
Kit Guard, George Chesebro, Oscar Gahan,
Frank Ellis. A Texas Ranger sets out
to find out who killed a rancher who
was going to testify against an outlaw
gang. Average Charles Starrett vehicle.

2052 The Man from Texas. Aywon, 1924.
50 minutes B/W. D-SC: Tom Mix. WITH
Tom Mix, Goldie Colwell, Sid Jordan,
Leo Maloney, Roy Watson, Inez Walker,
Pat Christian, Hoot Gibson. Searching
for the man who caused his sister's death,
a cowboy falls in love with the daughter
of a rancher. Tom Mix fans will find
this an interesting curio in that it is
an expanded version of the star's 1915
two reeler. V: Film and Sound Video.

2053 Man from Texas. Monogram, 1939.
60 minutes B/W. D: Al Herman. SC:
Robert Emmett (Tansey). WITH Tex
Ritter, Ruth Rogers, Hal Price, Charles
B. Wood, Kenne Duncan, Vic Demoruelle
Jr., Roy Barcroft, Frank Wayne, Tom
London, Nelson McDowell, Chick Hannon,
Charles King. A lawman tries to aid
a rancher who is being plagued by thefts
and is soon opposing a gunman whose
life he once saved. Pretty good Tex Ritter
vehicle with more emphasis on drama
than music.

2054 The Man from Texas. Eagle-Lion,
1947. 71 minutes B/W. D: Leigh Jason.
SC: Joseph Fields & Jerome Chodorov.
WITH James Craig, Lynn Bari, Johnny
Johnston, Sara Allgood, Una Merkel,
Harry Davenport, Wallace Ford, Vic
Cutler, Reed Hadley, Clancy Cooper,
Bert Conway, King Donovan. A once-
notorious outlaw, the El Paso Kid, weds
and tries to lead a peaceful life but his

past keeps following him. Okay feature
from Eagle-Lion with good work by James
Craig in the lead. Based on the play
by E. B. Ginty.

2055 The Man from the Alamo. Universal-
International, 1953. 79 minutes Color.
D: Budd Boetticher. SC: Steve Fisher
& D. D. Beauchamp. WITH Glenn Ford,
Julia (Julie) Adams, Chill Wills, Victor
Jory, Hugh O'Brian, Jeanne Cooper,
Butch Cavell, Dennis Weaver, John Day,
Dan Poore, Myra Marsh, George Eldredge,
Howard Negley. A man leaves the Alamo
to warn settlers of Santa Anna's advance
and finds himself branded a coward.
Good action melodrama with interesting
historical fiction.

2056 The Man from the Rio Grande.
Republic, 1943. 55 minutes B/W. D: Howard
Bretherton. SC: Norman S. Hall. WITH
Don "Red" Barry, Wally Vernon, Twinkle
Watts, Kirk Alyn, Nancy Gay, Roy Bar-
croft, Harry Cording, Paul Scardon,
LeRoy Mason, Earle Hodgins, Kenneth
Terrell, Robert Homans, Tom London,
Bud Geary, Kenne Duncan, Jack Kirk,
Jack O'Shea. A man murders his brother
in order to inherit a big cattle ranch
but a cowboy and his pal set out to capture
him. Only average Don Barry film and
one of the last of his Republic series.

2057 The Man from Thunder River. Repub-
lic, 1943. 55 minutes B/W. D: John English.
SC: J. Benton Cheney. WITH "Wild Bill"
Elliott, George "Gabby" Hayes, Anne
Jeffreys, Ian Keith, John James, Georgia
Cooper, Jack Ingram, Eddie Lee, Charles
King, Bud Geary, Jack Rockwell, Ed
Cassidy, Roy Brent, Alan Bridge, Al
Taylor, Edmund Cobb, Robert Barron,
Jack O'Shea, Curley Dresden, Frank
McCarroll. Wild Bill Eliott tries to find
who is behind a plot to steal gold ore
and as a result he ends up saving a girl's
life. Strong Bill Elliott series entry at
Republic, well written and directed.
V: Cumberland Video.

2058 The Man from Tumbleweeds. Colum-
bia, 1940. 59 minutes B/W. D: Joseph
H. Lewis. SC: Charles Francis Royal.
WITH Bill Elliott, Iris Meredith, Dub
Taylor, Raphael (Ray) Bennett, Francis
Walker, Ernie Adams, Al Hill, Stanley
Brown, Richard Fiske, Ed LeSaint, Don
Beddoe, Eddie Laughton, John Tyrell,
Edward Cecil, Jack Lowe, Olin Francis,
Jay Lawrence, Bruce Bennett (Herman
Brix), George Chesebro, Hank Bell, Steve
Clark, Ray Jones. Wild Bill Saunders

enlists the aid of paroled prisoners in order to help him bring law and order to a town controlled by a ruthless outlaw gang. Speedy and entertaining Bill Elliott oater with a fine performance by Raphael Bennett as the villainous Powder Kilgore.

2059 The Man from Utah. Monogram, 1934. 55 minutes B/W. D: Robert North Bradbury. SC: Lindsley Parsons. WITH John Wayne, Polly Ann Young, George ("Gabby") Hayes, Yakima Canutt, Ed Piel Sr., Anita Campillo, Lafe McKee, George Cleveland, Earl Dwire, Artie Ortego. A cowboy sets out to get the goods on a gang of crooks who are committing murders on the rodeo circuit. Fairly actionful John Wayne-Lone Star Western hurt by the use of poorly interpolated stock rodeo footage. V: Thunderbird.

2060 The Man in the Saddle. Columbia, 1951. 87 minutes Color. D: Andre De Toth. SC: Kenneth Gamet. WITH Randolph Scott, Ellen Drew, Alexander Knox, John Russell, Richard Rober, Alfonso Bedoya, Guinn Williams, Clem Bevans, Cameron Mitchell, Richard Crane, Frank Sully, George Lloyd, James Kirkwood, Frank Hagney, Don Beddoe. A wealthy rancher swears revenge on a neighbor, who has the love of the man's wife. Nicely made and entertaining Randolph Scott vehicle greatly helped by Tennessee Ernie Ford's singing of the title song throughout the proceedings.

2061 Man in the Shadow. Universal-International, 1957. 80 minutes B/W. D: Jack Arnold. SC: Gene L. Coon. WITH Jeff Chandler, Orson Welles, Colleen Miller, Ben Alexander, Barbara Lawrence, John Larch, James Gleason, Royal Dano, Paul Fix, Leo Gordon, Martin Garralaga, Mario Siletti, Charles Horvath, William Schallert, Joseph J. Greene, Forrest Lewis, Harry Harvey Sr., Joe Schneider, Mort Mills. A Mexican youth dies after being ordered beaten by the owner of a large ranch and the honest local sheriff tries to find out who killed the boy and why. Fairly interesting, but brooding, modern oater from producer Albert Zugsmith.

2062 Man in the Wilderness. Warner Brothers, 1971. 105 minutes Color. D: Richard C. Sarafian. SC: Jack DeWitt. WITH Richard Harris, Henry Wilcoxon, John Huston, Prunella Ransome, John Bindon, Ben Carruthers, James Doohan, Bruce M. Fisher, Percy Herbert, Bryan Marshall, Norman Rossington, Robert Russell, Dennis Waterman, Paul Castro,

Judith Furst, Manolo Landau, William Layton, Sheila Raynor, Joaquin Solis, Peggy (bear). In the northwest in 1820, a trapper is left for dead after being mauled by a bear. He fights to survive and get back to civilization. Rugged outdoor melodrama which will entertain genre fans.

2063 Man of Action. Columbia, 1933. 60 minutes B/W. D: George Melford. SC: Robert Quigley. WITH Tim McCoy, Caryl Lincoln, Julian Rivero, Wheeler Oakman, Walter Brennan, Joe Girard, Stanley Blystone, Ted Adams, Lafe McKee, Charles K. French. A ranger and his pal try to find out who robbed a local bank, and uncover a scheme to steal a girl's ranch. This Tim McCoy oater is quite entertaining and well made and in it Julian Rivero even sings a few love songs.

2064 Man of Conquest. Republic, 1939. 97 minutes B/W. D: George Nichols Jr. SC: Wells Root & E. E. Paramore Jr. WITH Richard Dix, Gail Patrick, Joan Fontaine, Edward Ellis, George ("Gabby") Hayes, Victor Jory, Robert Barrat, C. Henry Gordon, Robert Armstrong, Ralph Morgan, Max Terhune, Janet Beecher, George (Montgomery) Letz, Guy Wilkerson, Charles Stevens, Hal Taliaferro, Lane Chandler, Ethan Laidlaw, Edmund Cobb, Billy Benedict, Tex Cooper, Kathleen Lockhart, Leon Ames, Ferris Taylor. The story of Sam Houston, from his days as governor of Tennessee to his leading the rebellion which lead to Texas independence. Good historical drama enhanced by excellent production values and good performances by the entire cast.

2065 Man of the East. United Artists, 1974. 122 minutes Color. D-SC: E. B. Clucher (Enzo Barbondi). WITH Terence Hill, Gregory Walcott, Harry Carey Jr., Dominic Barton, Yanti Somer. A stuffy young man from New England heads West to take over his father's ranch and runs into trouble. Overlong but somewhat amusing Italian oater issued in that country in 1972 as E **Poi Lo Chiamarono Il Magnifico.**

2066 Man of the Forest. Paramount, 1933. 62 minutes B/W. D: Henry Hathaway. SC: Jack Cunningham & Harold Shumate. WITH Randolph Scott, Harry Carey, Verna Hillie, Noah Beery, Larry "Buster" Crabbe, Barton MacLane, Guinn Williams, Vince Barnett, Blanche Frederici, Tempe Piggot, Tom Kennedy, Frank McGlynn

Jr., Duke Lee, Lew Kelly, Merill Mc-Cormack, Tom London. A crook wants to steal an ex-convict's forest land and plans to kidnap the man's niece so the land cannot be signed over to her. Beautiful scenic locations and excellent photography (by Ben Reynolds) make this Zane Grey series entry a very entertaining film. Reissued as **Challenge of the Frontier.**

Man of the Frontier see **Red River Valley** (1936)

2067 Man of the Law. CBS-TV/20th Century-Fox, 1957. 45 minutes B/W. SC: David Lang. WITH Wendell Corey, Ron Randell, Marsha Hunt, Constance Ford, Johnny Washbrook, John Conte. Three witnesses must come forth to testify after the local sheriff arrests an outlaw for a murder during a holdup. Telefeature originally shown as a segment of "The Twentieth Century Fox Hour" (CBS-TV, 1955-57) on February 20, 1957.

2068 Man of the West. United Artists, 1958. 100 minutes Color. D: Anthony Mann. SC: Reginald Rose. WITH Gary Cooper, Julie London, Lee J. Cobb, Arthur O'Connell, Jack Lord, John Dehner, Royal Dano, Robert Wilke, Jack Williams, Guy Wilkerson, Chuck Roberson, Frank Ferguson, Emory Parnell, Tina Menard, Joe Dominguez. A reformed outlaw is on a stagecoach held up by his former gang members, now led by his uncle. Average oater made on a big scale with star Gary Cooper too old for the lead.

2069 Man or Gun. Republic, 1958. 79 minutes B/W. D: Albert C. Gannaway. SC: Vance Skarstedt & James C. Cassity. WITH Macdonald Carey, James Craig, Audrey Totter, James Gleason, Warren Stevens, Harry Shannon, Jil Jarmyn, Robert Burton, Ken Lynch, Karl Davis. A drifter arrives in a small town ruled by a ruthless family and sets out to free the people of this problem. Well acted but rather dreary oater.

2070 The Man Trailer. Columbia, 1934. 59 minutes B/W. D-SC: Lambert Hillyer. WITH Buck Jones, Cecilia Parker, Arthur Vinton, Clarence Geldert, Steve Clark, Charles West, Tom Forman, Lew Meehan, Richard Botiller, Artie Ortego. On the run from the law for a murder he did not commit, a man saves the money during a stagecoach robbery and is made the local sheriff only to have an outlaw aware of his past blackmail him. One of the all-time best "B" Westerns.

2071 The Man Who Killed a Ghost. NBC-TV/Universal, 1971. 74 minutes Color. WITH Robert Wagner, Lex Barker, Janet Leigh, Kim Stanley, Susan Saint James, David Hartman, Alfred Ryder, Donald Barry, Lurene Tuttle, William Bryant, Jack Soo, Teddy Eccles. A reporter investigates a food franchise and runs into a former Hollywood cowboy star who does not live up to his star image. Episode of the TV series "The Name of the Game" (NBC-TV, 1968-71) issued to television as a feature film.

2072 The Man Who Loved Cat Dancing. Metro-Goldwyn-Mayer, 1973. 114 minutes Color. D: Richard C. Sarafin. SC: Eleanor Perry. WITH Burt Reynolds, Sarah Miles, Lee J. Cobb, Jack Warden, George Hamilton, Bo Hopkins, Robert Donner, Sandy Kevin, Nancy Malone, Jay Silverheels, Jay Varela, Owen Bush, Larry Littlebird. An outlaw gang pulls off a robbery and takes a woman along as hostage. She finds herself falling in love with the gang leader. Fairly entertaining, but rather brutal, adaptation of Marilyn Durham's novel. Jack Warden is especially good as the vicious gang member.

2073 The Man Who Shot Liberty Valance. Paramount, 1962. 122 minutes B/W. D: John Ford. SC: Willis Goldbeck & James Warner Bellah. WITH John Wayne, James Stewart, Vera Miles, Lee Marvin, Edmond O'Brien, Andy Devine, Ken Murray, John Carradine, Jeanette Nolan, John Qualen, Willis Bouchey, Carleton Young, Woody Strode, Denver Pyle, Strother Martin, Lee Van Cleef, Robert F. Simon, O. Z. Whitehead, Paul Birch, Joseph Hoover, Jack Pennick, Anna Lee, Charles Seel, Shug Fisher, Earle Hodgins, Stuart Holmes, Dorothy Phillips, Buddy Roosevelt, Gertrude Astor, Eva Novak, Slim Talbot, Monte Montana, Bill Henry, Helen Gibson, Major Sam Harris, Ted Mapes, Jack Kenny, John B. Whiteford. A noted politician recounts how he came to power through the guise of another man killing a town bully. Extremely well-done John Ford oater with an excellent cast and highly entertaining script. John Ford's last great Western. VD: Blackhawk.

2074 Man with the Golden Pistol. Balcazar, 1966. 107 minutes Color. D: Alfonso Balcazar. WITH Carl Mohner, Gloria Milland, Fernando Sancho, Luis Davilla, Umberto Raho, Pedro Gil, Irene Mir. A wanted man finds the body of a murdered gunman, takes his identity and is hired by villagers to protect them from marauders. Typically violent Italian-Spanish coproduction.

2075 Man with the Gun. United Artists, 1955. 83 minutes B/W. D: Richard Wilson. SC: N. B. Stone Jr. & Richard Wilson. WITH Robert Mitchum, Jan Sterling, Karen Sharpe, Henry Hull, Emile Meyer, John Lupton, Barbara Lawrence, Ted De Corsia, Leo Gordon, James Westerfield, Forenz Ames, Robert Osterloh, Jay Adler, Amzie Strickland, Stafford Repp, Maudie Prickett, Angie Dickinson. A gunman, whose wife has left him, is hired to clean up a town lorded over by a wealthy rancher. Slow moving and brooding oater with good work by Robert Mitchum as the gunfighter.

2076 Man with the Steel Whip. Republic, 1954. 12 Chapters B/W. D: Franklyn Adreon. SC: Ronald Davidson. WITH Richard Simmons, Barbara Bestar, Dale Van Sickel, Mauritz Hugo, Lane Bradford, Pat Hogan, Roy Barcroft, Stuart Randall, Edmund Cobb, I. Stanford Jolley, Guy Teague, Alan Wells, Tom Steele, Art Dillard, Chuck Hayward, Charles Stevens, Jerry Brown, Harry Harvey, Bob Clark, Charles Sullivan, Gregg Barton, Tex Terry, George Eldredge, Herman Hack. A rancher takes on the guise of the masked rider El Latigo in an effort to keep Indians from being blamed for raids caused by a saloon owner after gold rich lands. Republic's final cliffhanger is a hodgepodge of stock footage from previous endeavors.

2077 Man Without a Star. Universal, 1955. 89 minutes Color. D: King Vidor. SC: Borden Chase & D. D. Beauchamp. WITH Kirk Douglas, Jeanne Crain, Claire Trevor, William Campbell, Richard Boone, Jay C. Flippen, Myrna Hansen, Mara Corday, Eddy Waller, Sheb Wooley, George Wallace, Roy Barcroft, James Hayward, Paul Birch, Malcolm Atterbury, William Challee, William Phillips, Ewing Mitchell, Mark Hanna, Frank Chase, Gil Patrick, Casey Macgregor, Jack Ingram, Carl Andre, Jack Elam, Myron Healey, Lee Roberts. A drifter becomes involved in helping a rancher oppose a woman landowner who wants all the range for herself. Fine, stout genre effort from King Vidor. Frankie Laine sings the title song.

2078 Man's Country. Monogram, 1938. 55 minutes B/W. D: Robert Hill. SC: Robert Emmett (Tansey). WITH Jack Randall, Marjorie Reynolds, Ralph Peters, Walter Long, Forrest Taylor, Bud Osborne,

Dave O'Brien, Ernie Adams, David Sharpe, Charles King, Sherry Tansey, Chick Hannon. An undercover agent for the rangers befriends a family by making them think he is a wanted outlaw in order to find out who committed two murders. Standard Jack Randall series vehicle.

2079 A Man's Land. Allied, 1932. 65 minutes B/W. D: Phil Rosen. SC: Adele Buffington. WITH Hoot Gibson, Marion Shilling, Skeeter Bill Robbins, Alan Bridge, Charles King, Ethel Wales, Hal Burney, Robert Ellis, William Nye, Merrill McCormack, Slim Whitaker. A girl and a ranch foreman each inherit one-half of a ranch plagued by rustlers. Okay Hoot Gibson vehicle.

2080 Many Rivers to Cross. Metro-Goldwyn-Mayer, 1955. 92 minutes Color. D: Roy Rowland. SC: Harry Brown & Guy Trosper. WITH Robert Taylor, Eleanor Parker, Victor McLaglen, Rosemary De Camp, Jeff Richards, Russ Tamblyn, James Arness, Alan Hale (Jr.), John Hudson, Rhys Williams, Josephine Hutchinson, Sig Rumann, Russell Johnson, Ralph Moody, Abel Fernandez. In 1798 Kentucky a wild young girl pursues a frontiersman, but their romance is complicated by warring Indians. Likeable frontier satire.

2081 Mara of the Wilderness. Allied Artists, 1966. 90 minutes Color. D: Frank McDonald. SC: Tom Blackburn. WITH Adam West, Linda Saunders, Theo Marcuse, Denver Pyle, Sean McClory, Eve Brent, Roberto Contreras, Ed Kemmer, Stuart Walsh, Lelia Walsh. A seven-year-old girl is left to live with wolves after her parents die in a plane crash. A dozen years later a forest ranger finds her and tries to re-civilize the girl, while a hunter wants to sell her to a sideshow. Entertaining human interest drama.

2082 The Marauders. United Artists, 1947. 64 minutes B/W. D: George Archainbaud. SC: Charles Belden. WITH William Boyd, Andy Clyde, Rand Brooks, Ian Wolfe, Dorinda Clifton, Mary Newton, Harry Cording, Earle Hodgins, Dick Bailey, Richard Alexander, Herman Hack. When the Bar 20 trio find themselves in a terrible storm they take shelter in a town inhabited only by a woman and her daughter, who are being harrassed by an outlaw gang. Tired entry in the long-running "Hopalong Cassidy" series.

2083 The Marauders. Metro-Goldwyn-Mayer, 1955. 81 minutes Color. D: Gerald

Mayer. SC: Jack Leonard & Earl Felton. WITH Dan Duryea, Jarma Lewis, Keenan Wynn, Jeff Richards, John Hudson, Harry Shannon, David Kasday, James Anderson, Richard Lupino, Peter Mamakos, John Mills, Michael Dugan. A small rancher fights to save his spread when a greedy land baron hires gunmen to run him away. Pretty good little programmer with nice production values.

2084 Mark of the Gun. Emerson, 1968. 90 minutes B/W. WITH Ross Hagen, Brad Thomas, Chris Carter, Gabrielle St. Claire, Katye Martine, Joan McCrea, Wallace J. Campodanio, Erick Lindberg. The story of Jack Slade and his outlaw gang as they rampage through the West. Obscure, and violent, low grade actioner.

2085 Mark of the Lash. Screen Guild, 1948. 58 minutes B/W. D: Ray Taylor. SC: Moree Herring & Gloria Welsch. WITH Lash LaRue, Al St. John, Suzi Crandall, Jimmie Martin, John Cason, Marshall Reed, Tom London, Lee Roberts, Steve Dunhill, Harry Cody, Cliff Taylor, Britt Wood, Jack Hendricks. Lash and Fuzzy are out to rid the Red Rock area of an outlaw gang after the local water rights. Another fast actioner from Lash LaRue.

2086 Mark of the Renegade. Universal-International, 1951. 81 minutes Color. D: Hugo Fregonese. SC: Louis Solomon & Robert Hardy Andrews. WITH Ricardo Montalban, Cyd Charisse, J. Carrol Naish, Gilbert Roland, Andrea King, George Tobias, Antonio Moreno, Georgia Backus, Robert Warwick, Armando Silvestre, Bridget Carr, Alberto Morin, Renzo Cesana, Robert Cornthwaite, Edward C. Rios, David Wolfe. In 1824 California a local ruler captures a bandit and forces him to romance the pretty daughter of the area governor. A different kind of frontier drama but one that is none-too-entertaining.

2087 Mark of Zorro. United Artists, 1920. 90 minutes B/W. D: Fred Niblo. SC: Elton Thomas. WITH Douglas Fairbanks, Marguerite de la Motte, Robert McKim, Noah Beery, Charles H. Mailes, Claire McDowell, George Periolat, Walt Whitman, Sidney de Grey. In Old California a young snob takes on the guise of a masked man who fights government oppression. Lively silent with Doug Fairbanks ideal in the role of Zorro; a fun film. V: Cassette Express, Glenn Photo.

2088 Mark of Zorro. 20th Century-Fox, 1940. 93 minutes B/W. D: Rouben Mamoulian. SC: John Tainton Foote. WITH Tyrone Power, Linda Darnell, Basil Rathbone, Gale Sondergaard, Eugene Pallette, J. Edward Bromberg, Montagu Love, Janet Beecher, Robert Lowery, Chris-Pin Martin, George Regas, Belle Mitchell, John Bleifer, Frank Puglia, Pedro de Cordova, Guy D'Ennery, Eugene Borden, Fred Malatesta, Fortunio Bonanova, Harry Worth, Michael (Ted) North, Ralph Byrd, Stanley Andrews, Victor Kilian, Hector Sarno, Franco Corsaro. A foppish-acting nobleman tries to fight government tyranny in Spanish California by wearing a mask and leading the people in their fight for freedom. Remake of the 1920 version (q.v.) is more serious but it is still fine entertainment with a colorful story and lots of action, plus some good dueling sequences.

2089 Mark of Zorro. ABC-TV/20th Century-Fox, 1974. 74 minutes Color. D: Don McDougall. SC: Brian Taggert. WITH Frank Langella, Ricardo Montalban, Gilbert Roland, Yvonne De Carlo, Louise Sorel, Anne Archer, Robert Middleton, Tom Lacy, George Cervera, Jay Hamer, Robert Carricart. Pale TV version of the 1920 and 1940 (qq.v.) filmings of Johnston McCulley's story although this one is greatly aided by Gilbert Roland as the elder Vega, the father of Frank Langella's lacklustre Zorro.

2090 Marked for Murder. Producers Releasing Corporation, 1945. 56 minutes B/W. D-SC: Elmer Clifton. WITH Tex Ritter, Dave O'Brien, Guy Wilkerson, Marilyn McConnell, Ed Cassidy, Henry Hall, Charles King, Jack Ingram, Robert Kortman, The Milo Twins, Kermit Maynard. In the 1880s the trio of the Texas Rangers tries to find out who is behind a range war between cattlemen and sheep herders. Very entertaining and actionful "Texas Rangers" outing with Tex singing "Long Time Gone," "Froggie Went a Courtin'" and "Tears of Regret."

2091 Marked Trails. Monogram, 1944. 58 minutes B/W. D: J. P. McCarthy. SC: J. P. McCarthy & Victor Hammond. WITH Bob Steele, Hoot Gibson, Veda Ann Borg, Ralph Lewis, Mauritz Hugo, Steve Clark, Charles Stevens, Lynton Brent, Bud Osborne, George Morrell, Allen B. Sewell, Ben Corbett. Two lawmen are on the trail of a notorious outlaw gang with one of them posing as a badman

255   The Marksman

in order to infiltrate the gang. Substandard Bob Steele-Hoot Gibson vehicle.

2092 The Marksman. Allied Artists, 1953.
60 (62) minutes B/W. D: Lewis D. Collins.
SC: Dan Ullman. WITH Wayne Morris,
Elean Verdugo, Rick Vallin, Frank Ferguson, I. Stanford Jolley, Tom Powers,
Robert Bice, Stanley Price, Tim Ryan,
Russ Whiteman, William Fawcett, Brad
Johnson, Jack Rice. Because he is an
expert with a telescopic rifle, a man
is hired as the town marshal in order
to track down an outlaw gang. The "B"
Western was on its last legs as a series
format and this vapid oater is a good
example.

2093 Marshal of Amarillo. Republic,
1948. 60 minutes B/W. D: Philip Ford.
SC: Bob Williams. WITH Allan "Rocky"
Lane, Eddy Waller, Mildred Coles, Clayton
Moore, Roy Barcroft, Trevor Bardette,
Minerva Urecal, Denver Pyle, Charles
Williams, Tom Chatterton, Tom London.
A murder takes place at a halfway house
for the stage line and a marshal and
his pal arrive to investigate. Well staged
mystery aura greatly helps this Allan
Lane series entry.

2094 Marshal of Cedar Rock. Republic,
1953. 54 minutes B/W. D: Harry Keller.
SC: M. Coates Webster. WITH Allan
"Rocky" Lane, Eddy Waller, Phyllis Coates,
Roy Barcroft, Bill Henry, Robert Shayne,
John Crawford, John Hamilton, Kenneth
MacDonald, Herbert Lytton. A young
man is falsely accused of taking part
in a bank robbery and a U. S. marshal
steps in to prove his innocence. More
than passably entertaining entry in the
later stages of Allan Lane's Republic
series.

2095 Marshal of Cripple Creek. Republic,
1947. 54 (58) minutes B/W. D: R. G.
Springsteen. SC: Earle Snell. WITH Allan
Lane, Bobby Blake, Martha Wentworth,
Tom London, Trevor Bardette, Roy Barcroft, Gene (Roth) Stutenroth, William
Self, Helen Wallace. Crooks try to take
advantage of the situation when a small
settlement is turned into a boom town
with the discovery of gold. Allan Lane's
last entry in Republic's "Red Ryder"
series and it is hardly one of the best.

2096 Marshal of Gunsmoke. Universal,
1944. 58 minutes B/W. D: Vernon Keyes.
SC: William Lively. WITH Tex Ritter,
Russell Hayden, Jennifer Holt, Fuzzy
Knight, Harry Woods, Herbert Rawlinson,

Ethan Laidlaw, Ray Bennett, Michael
Vallon, Ernie Adams, Slim Whitaker,
George Chesebro, William Desmond,
James Farley, Dan White, Roy Brent,
Bud Osborne, Johnny Bond and His Red
River Valley Boys (Wesley Tuttle, Paul
Sells, Jimmie Dean). A marshal and his
lawyer brother obtain the aid of a saloon
singer in trying to stop her crooked boss
from taking over a town. Appealing Tex
Ritter-Russell Hayden vehicle with Jen-
nifer Holt doing a couple of songs while
Tex Ritter sings "Git Along Little Dog-
gies." British title: **Sheriff of Gunsmoke.**

2097 Marshal of Laredo. Republic, 1945.
54 (56) minutes B/W. D: R. G. Springsteen.
SC: Bob Williams. WITH Bill Elliott,
Bobby Blake, Alice Fleming, Peggy Stewart, Roy Barcroft, Tom London, George
Carleton, Wheaton Chambers, Tom Chatterton, George Chesebro, Don Costello,
Bud Geary, Sarah Padden, Jack O'Shea,
Lane Bradford, Kenneth Terrell, Dorothy
Granger. An honest young lawyer opposes
an outlaw gang and is almost hanged
for his trouble before being rescued
by Red Ryder. Actionful entry in the
popular "Red Ryder" series.

2098 Marshal of Madrid. CBS-TV/20th
Century-Fox, 1972. 100 minutes Color.
D: Richard Donner. SC: Anthony Lawrence
& Jack Turley. WITH Glenn Ford, Edgar
Buchanan, Linda Cristal, Bobby Darin,
Victor Campos, James Gregory, Rodolfo
Acosta, Taylor Lacher. The marshal
of a rural New Mexico county finds himself
involved with two cases: a smuggling
operation resulting in killings and an
ex-convict who is convinced he is Billy
the Kid. Fairly entertaining modern-day
Western culled from two segments of
the television series "Cade's County"
(CBS-TV, 1971-72).

2099 The Marshal of Mesa City. RKO
Radio, 1939. 62 minutes B/W. D: David
Howard. SC: Jack Lait Jr. WITH George
O'Brien, Virginia Vale, Leon Ames, Henry
Brandon, Harry Cording, Lloyd Ingraham,
Slim Whitaker, Joe McGuinn, Mary Gordon,
Frank Ellis, Wilfred Lucas, Carl Stockdale,
Cactus Mack. After saving a girl from
the unwanted attentions of a nearby
city's sheriff, a man is made marshal
of a lawless town and sets out to bring
law and order. A bit complicated but
still fairly interesting and well-made
George O'Brien vehicle.

2100 Marshal of Reno. Republic, 1944.
54 minutes B/W. D: Wallace Grissell.

The Marshal's

SC: Anthony Coldeway. WITH Wild Bill Elliott, Bobby Blake, Alice Fleming, Herbert Rawlinson, Jay Kirby, Tom London, Kenne Duncan, Charles King, Jack Kirk, LeRoy Mason, Robert Wilke, Fred Burns, Tom Steele, Edmund Cobb, Fred Graham, Blake Edwards, Hal Price, Bud Geary, Jack O'Shea, Al Taylor, Marshall Reed, Tom Chatterton, Carl Sepulveda, Kenneth Terrell, Horace B. Carpenter, Charles Sullivan, Roy Barcroft (voice). When two towns resort to violence over the question of which one will be the new county seat, Red Ryder arrives on the scene to restore order. Fast moving adventure in the "Red Ryder" series with a top notch genre cast.

2101 The Marshal's Daughter. United Artists, 1953. 71 minutes B/W. D: William Berke. SC: Bob Duncan. WITH Hoot Gibson, Laurie Anders, Ken Murray, Harry Lauter, Robert Bray, Bob Duncan, Preston Foster, Jimmy Wakely, Johnny Mack Brown, Buddy Baer, Forrest Taylor, Tom London, Cecil Elliot, Bette Lou Walters, Francis Ford, Julian Upton, Bob Gross, Lee Phelps, Ted Jordan, Harry Harvey, Danny Duncan, Tex Ritter (narrator). The daughter of a U. S. marshal takes on the guise of a masked rider to capture an outlaw gang. Fairly amusing genre spoof which should please fans. Produced by Ken Murray.

2102 The Masked Raiders. RKO Radio, 1949. 60 minutes B/W. D: Lesley Selander. SC: Norman Houston. WITH Tim Holt, Richard Martin, Marjorie Lord, Gary Gray, Frank Wilcox, Charles Arnt, Tom Tyler, Harry Woods, Clayton Moore, Houseley Stevenson. When dishonest bankers try to take ranchers' land they form a group of masked riders led by a girl rancher. Typically good entry in Tim Holt's RKO series with nice work by Marjorie Lord as the leader of the title characters.

2103 The Masked Rider. Universal, 1941. 58 minutes B/W. D: Ford Beebe. SC: Sherman Lowe & Victor McLeod. WITH Johnny Mack Brown, Fuzzy Knight, Nell O'Day, Grant Withers, Roy Barcroft, Guy D'Ennery, Virginia Carroll, Richard Botiller, Fred Cordova, The Guadalajara Trio, The Jose Cansino Dancers, Al Haskell, Robert O'Connor, Rico De Montez, Carmela Cansino. In South America two American cowboys get jobs in a silver mine and get on the trail of a masked man stealing the mine's shipments. Pleasant, and somewhat tongue-in-cheek, Johnny Mack Brown vehicle.

2104 Mason of the Mounted. Monogram, 1932. 49 minutes B/W. D-SC: Harry Fraser. WITH Bill Cody, Andy Shuford, Nancy Drexel, Art Smith (Art Mix/George Kesterson), Jack Carlisle, Blackie Whiteford, Nelson McDowell, James Marcus, Joe Dominguez, LeRoy Mason, Dick Dickinson, Frank Hall Crane, Earl Dwire, Jack Long, Gordon McGee. A Mountie arrives in the U. S. to bring back a notorious outlaw, the leader of a horse stealing operation. Fair Bill Cody vehicle.

2105 Masquerade. Wrather Corporation, 1956. 75 minutes Color. D: Earl Bellamy. SC: Wells Root, Charles Carson, Robert E. Schaefer, Eric Friewald & Robert Leslie Bellem. WITH Clayton Moore, Jay Silverheels, Allen Pinson, Wayne Burson, Myron Healey, Helen Marshall, Margaret Stewart, Rand Brooks, Louise Lewis, Don C. Harvey, Pierce Lyden, John Cason, William Fawcett, Zon Murray, Nolan Leary, George Barrows, David Saber, Paul Engle, William Challee, Jason Johnson, John Cliff, Sandy Sanders, John Maxwell. Pretending to be a Mexican with hearing problems, the Lone Ranger tries to stop the robbery of a gold shipment. He and Tonto also help a Mexican revolutionary leader and try to capture a gang of masked robbers. Well made TV movie from "The Lone Ranger" (ABC-TV, 1949-57) series from the episodes "The Turning Point," "Code of Honor" and "Dead Eye."

2106 Massacre. First National, 1934. 70 minutes B/W. D: Alan Crosland. SC: Ralph Block & Sheridan Gibney. WITH Richard Barthelmess, Ann Dvorak, Dudley Digges, Claire Dodd, Henry O'Neill, Robert Barrat, Arthur Hohl, Philip Faversham, George Blackwood, Sidney Toler, Clarence Muse, Charles Middleton, Tully Marshall, Wallis Clark, William V. Mong, DeWitt Jennings, Juliet Ware, James Eagles, Frank McGlynn, Agnes Narcha. An educated Indian chief sets out to remove crooked officials who have been cheating his people. A good look at injustice in the reservation system makes this a film worth viewing; Richard Barthelmess is fine as the caring Indian leader.

2107 Massacre. Lippert, 1956. 76 minutes Color. D: Louis King. SC: D. D. Beauchamp. WITH Dane Clark, James Craig, Marta Roth, Miguel Torruco, Jamie Fernandez, Jose Munoz. Crooked traders sell guns to Indians and it results in the needless killing of settlers. Average actioner filmed in Mexico.

Massacre at Fort Holman see **A Reason to Live, Reason to Die!**

2108 Massacre at Fort Perdition. Avco-Embassy, 1965. 95 minutes Color. D: Jose Maria Elorrieta. WITH Jerry Cobb (German Cobos), Marta May, Ethel Rojo, George Gordon, Hugh Pepper. A soldier dressed in civilian clothes is found by a rescue force at a fort where the rest of the inhabitants have been massacred and the man is branded as a traitor. Another in the long string of dubbed, violent European oaters, this one made in Spain as **Fuerte Perdido.** British title: **Massacre at Fort Grant.**

2109 Massacre at Fort Phil Kearney. NBC-TV/Universal, 1966. 49 minutes Color. WITH Richard Egan, Robert Fuller, Robert Pipe, Peter Duryea, Phyllis Avery, Carroll O'Connor. Two Army officers have different views on how to deal with the Indians; one wants to pacify them while the other believes in force. This telefeature was originally shown as a segment of "The Bob Hope Chrysler Theatre" (NBC-TV, 1963-67) on October 26, 1966.

2110 Massacre at Grand Canyon. Columbia, 1965. 90 minutes Color. D: Alfredo Antonini (Albert Band). SC: E. C. Geltman & Alfred Antonini. WITH James Mitchum, Jill Powers, Eduardo Ciannelli, Giorgio (George) Ardisson, Burt Nelson, G. Rossi Stuart, Andrea Giordana, Mills Sannoner. Feuding families hire gunmen who kill the local sheriff; the man's brother and his fiancée try to get the locals to fight back. Pretty well done European oater with good photography by Enzo Barboni. Rodd Dana sings the title song. Produced in Italy in 1963 as **I Pascoli Rossi** (Red Pastures) by Ultra Film/Prodi Cinematografica.

2111 Massacre at Marble City. Rapid-Film, 1964. 87 minutes Color. D: Paul Martin. SC: Alex Berg, Hans Billian & W. P. Zibaso. WITH Brad Harris, Mario Adorf, Dieter Borsche, Horst Frank, Marianne Hoppe (Dorothy Parker). When Indians bring gold for trade at a frontier settlement, greedy miners try to find the location of the ore and violence results. More bloodshed from Europe in this imitation Western, which was produced in West Germany as **Die Goldsucher Von Arkansas.** V: Marketing Film.

2112 Massacre at Sand Creek. CBS-TV/Columbia, 1956. 74 minutes B/W. SC:

William Sackheim. WITH John Derek, Everett Sloane, Gene Evans, H. M. Wynant. A tribe of ill-armed Cheyenne Indians are attacked by an Indian-hating colonel and his troops. Telefilm which was originally shown December 27, 1956 on "Playhouse 90" (CBS-TV, 1956-61).

2113 Massacre Canyon. Columbia, 1954. 64 minutes B/W. D: Fred F. Sears. SC: David Lang. WITH Philip Carey, Audrey Totter, Douglas Kennedy, Jeff Donnell, Guinn Williams, Charlita, Ross Elliott, Ralph Dumke, Mel Welles, Chris Alcaide, Steven Ritch, John Pickard, James Flavin, Bill Hale. A sergeant and two Army privates must guard a shipment of rifles wanted by marauders. Threadbare actioner from producer Wallace MacDonald.

2114 Massacre River. Allied Artists/Windsor Pictures Corporation, 1949. 75 minutes B/W. D: John Rawlins. SC: Louis Stevens & Otto Englander. WITH Guy Madison, Rory Calhoun, Carole Mathews, Cathy Downs, Johnny Sands, Steve Brodie, Art Baker, Iron Eyes Cody, Gregg Barton, Emory Parnell, Queenie Smith, Eddie Walker, James Bush, John Holland, Douglas Fowley, Harry Brown, Kermit Maynard. A trio of cavalry officers assigned to the West after the Civil War jeopardize their friendship over a colonel's pretty daughter and the machinations of a gambling establishment owner. Routine oater with some star appeal. Based on Harold Bell Wright's novel.

2115 The Master Gunfighter. Taylor-Laughlin Distributing Company, 1975. 120 minutes Color. D: Frank Laughlin. SC: Harold Lapland. WITH Tom Laughlin, Ron O'Neal, Lincoln Kilpatrick, Victor Campos, Geo Anne Sosa, Barbara Carrera, Hector Elias, Michael Lane, Patti Clifton, Henry Wills, Angelo Rossitto, Alberto Morin, Franco Casaro, Robert Tafur, Edward Colmans, Robert Hoy, Burgess Meredith (narrator). A gunman who hates his trade goes after a Spanish landowner who has murdered Indians for their gold so he could pay the taxes on his lands. Very bad psychological Western; a remake of the 1966 Japanese feature **Goyokin.**

2116 Masterson of Kansas. Columbia, 1955. 73 minutes Color. D: William Castle. SC: Douglas Heyes. WITH George Montgomery, Nancy Gates, James Griffith, Jean Willes, Benny Rubin, William Henry, David Bruce, Bruce Cowling, Gregg Barton, Donald Murphy, Sandy Sanders, Gregg

Martell, Jay Silverheels, John Maxwell. Lawmen Bat Masterson, Wyatt Earp and Doc Holliday team to save a negotiator who has made a treaty giving grazing lands to the Indians instead of cattlemen. There is not much to recommend this Sam Katzman production of pseudo-historical pap other than it is competently made.

2117 The Maverick. Allied Artists, 1952. 71 minutes Color. D: Thomas Carr. SC: Sid Theil. WITH Bill Elliott, Phyllis Coates, Myron Healey, Richard Reeves, Terry Frost, Rand Brooks, Russell Hicks, Robert Bray, Florence Lake, Gregg Barton, Denver Pyle, Robert Wilke, Eugene (Gene) Roth, Joel Allen. Cattlemen hire gun-slingers to force settlers off the range and the government sends in the calvary to stop the lawlessness. Another good entry in Bill Elliott's final starring Western series.

2118 The Maverick Queen. Republic, 1956. 90 minutes Color. D: Joseph Kane. SC: Kenneth Gamet & DeVallon Scott. WITH Barbara Stanwyck, Barry Sullivan, Scott Brady, Mary Murphy, Wallace Ford, Jim Davis, Howard Petrie, Emile Meyer, Walter Sande, George Keymas, John Doucette, Taylor Holmes, Pierre Watkin. A woman hotel keeper works with an outlaw gang but finds herself falling in love with a man who is newly arrived in town, not knowing he is working as an undercover Pinkerton agent out to break up the rustlers. The stars and director rise above the mediocre material to make this an entertaining affair.

2119 McCabe and Mrs. Miller. Warner Brothers, 1971. 107 minutes Color. D: Robert Altman. SC: Robert Altman & Brian McVey. WITH Warren Beatty, Julie Christie, Rene Auberjonois, Hugh Naughton, Shelley Duvall, Michael Murphy, John Schuck, Corey Fisher, Keith Carradine, William Devane, Anthony Holland, Bert Remsen, Elizabeth Murphy. At the turn of the century, a gambler and his lady friend set up a successful brothel in a small town but soon hoodlums are trying to take it over. Overrated drama will satisfy Robert Altman followers.

2120 McCloud: Who Killed Miss U.S.A.? NBC-TV/Universal, 1970. 100 minutes Color. D: Richard A. Colla. SC: Stanford Whitmore, Richard Levinson & William Link. WITH Dennis Weaver, Diana Muldaur, Craig Stevens, Mark Richman, Julie Newmar, Terry Carter, Mario Alcalde,

Raul Julia, Shelly Novack, Michael Bow, Nefti Millet, Kathy Stritch, Gregory Sierra, Bill Baldwin. A marshal from the Southwest comes to New York City with a witness who is promptly kidnapped, leading the lawman into a murder case. Telefeature very similar to **Coogan's Bluff** (q.v.) and the pilot for the "McCloud" (NBC-TV, 1971-76) series; better than average for this kind of fare. Retitled **Portrait of a Dead Girl.**

2121 McKenna of the Mounted. Columbia, 1932. 66 minutes B/W. D: D. Ross Lederman. SC: Stuart Anthony. WITH Buck Jones, Greta Grandstedt, James Flavin, Walter McGrail, Niles Welch, Mitchell Lewis, Claude King, Glenn Strange, Bud Osborne, Edmund Cobb. A disgraced Mountie leaves the service and becomes a part of an outlaw gang, but is really out to get the goods on the desperadoes. Not one of Buck Jones' better efforts.

2122 McLintock! United Artists, 1963. 127 minutes Color. D: Andrew V. McLaglen. SC: James Edward Grant. WITH John Wayne, Maureen O'Hara, Yvonne De Carlo, Patrick Wayne, Stefanie Powers, Jack Kruschen, Chill Wills, Jerry Van Dyke, Edgar Buchanan, Bruce Cabot, Perry Lopez, Michael Pate, Strother Martin, Gordon Jones, Robert Lowery, H. W. Gim, Ed Faulkner, Aissa Wayne, Chuck Roberson, Mari Blanchard, John Stanley, Hal Needham, Pedro Gonzales Jr., Hank Worden, Leo Gordon, Kari Noven, Bob Steele, Big John Hamilton, Ralph Volkie. A rich land baron wants state government to get rid of incompetent officials and he also has domestic problems with his estranged wife and daughter. Well done, somewhat tongue-in-cheek, John Wayne vehicle which is sure to delight his fans.

2123 The McMasters. Chevron, 1970. 97 minutes Color. D: Alf Kjellin. SC: Harold Jacob Smith. WITH Burl Ives, Brock Peters, David Carradine, Nancy Kwan, Jack Palance, John Carradine, L. Q. Jones, R. G. Armstrong, Dane Clark, Frank Raiter, Alan Vint, Marian Brash, Neil Davis, William Kiernan, Richard Alden, David Strong. After the Civil War an ex-slave who fought for the North returns home to be given half-interest in the farm he once worked but he finds himself resented by the locals. Unsuccessful melodrama which was issued theatrically in two versions, one running 89 minutes.

2124 Meanwhile, Back at the Ranch. Rancho Films, 1977. D–SC: Richard Patterson. WITH John Wayne, Buck Jones, Ken Maynard, Gene Autry, Roy Rogers, Eddie Dean, Tim McCoy, William Boyd, George "Gabby" Hayes, Smiley Burnette, Bob Steele, George O'Brien, Buster Crabbe, Lash LaRue, Monte Hale, Hoot Gibson, Johnny Mack Brown, Rex Allen, Don "Red" Barry, Iron Eyes Cody. All of the great cowboy stars are united for one mighty feature film but due to contract disputes it is never released. This film attempts to make a completely new movie of film clips from genre features of the past, but it is only of interest due to its oddity value. Shown at the Cannes Film Festival in 1977 but not issued theatrically. Eddie Dean sings the title song.

2125 The Medico of Painted Springs. Columbia, 1941. 58 minutes B/W. D: Lambert Hillyer. SC: Winston Miller. WITH Charles Starrett, Terry Walker, Richard Fiske, Ray Bennett, The Simp-Phonie, Ben Taggert, Bud Osborne, Edmund Cobb, Edith Elliott, Steve Clark, Lloyd Bridges, George Chesebro, Charles Hamilton, Jim Corey. An army doctor recruiting men for the Rough Riders finds himself in the middle of warfare between sheepmen and cattle raiders. Pretty good actioner in Charles Starrett's Columbia series.

2126 Melody of the Plains. Spectrum, 1937. 55 minutes B/W. D: Sam Newfield. SC: Bennett Cohen. WITH Fred Scott, Al St. John, Louise Small, Hal Price, Lew Meehan, Charles "Slim" Whitaker, Lafe McKee, David Sharpe, Bud Jamison, Carl Mathews, George Fiske, George Morrell. A cowpoke, who mistakenly thinks he has killed a young man, goes to work for the young man's father whose ranch is being sought by crooks who were responsible for the killing. Somewhat complicated and low grade but still a fairly pleasant singing sagebrusher with Fred Scott, who was one of the best of the western crooners. V: Cumberland Video.

2127 Melody Ranch. Republic, 1940. 54 (84) minutes B/W. D: Joseph Santley. SC: Jack Moffitt & F. Hugh Herbert. WITH Gene Autry, Jimmy Durante, Ann Miller, Barton MacLane, Barbara Jo Allen (Vera Vague), George "Gabby" Hayes, Jerome Cowan, Mary Lee, Joseph Sawyer, Horace McMahon, Clarence Wilson, William Benedict, Ruth Clifford, Maxine Ardell, Veda Ann Borg, George Chandler, Jack Ingram, Horace Murphy, Lloyd Ingraham, Tom London, John Merton, Edmund Cobb, Slim Whitaker, Curley Dresden, Dick Elliott, Billy Bletcher, Art Mix, George Chesebro, Tiny Jones, Herman Hack, Jack Kirk, Merrill McCormack, Wally West, Bob Wills & His Texas Playboys, Frankie Marvin, Carl Cotner, Tex Cooper, Chick Hannon. Radio star Gene Autry returns home to become honorary sheriff and finds they are plagued with racketeers. Entertaining Gene Autry opus which is badly butchered for TV. V: Blackhawk.

2128 Melody Trail. Republic, 1935. 54 (60) minutes B/W. D: Joseph Kane. SC: Sherman Lowe. WITH Gene Autry, Smiley Burnette, Ann Rutherford, Wade Boteler, Wally Costello, Al Bridge, Marie Quillan, Gertrude Messinger, Tracy Layne, Abe Lefton, George DeNormand, Jane Barnes, Ione Reed, Marion Downing, Buck (dog). Cowpokes Gene Autry and Frog Millhouse get jobs as cooks on a ranch where the owner's hands have quit due to cattle rustling and he uses his daughter's girl friends as ranch hands. Pleasant Gene Autry vehicle with more emphasis on music and comedy than action. V: Blackhawk.

2129 Men of Texas. Universal, 1942. 71 minutes B/W. D: Ray Enright. SC: Harold Shumate. WITH Robert Stack, Anne Gwynne, Broderick Crawford, Jackie Cooper, Ralph Bellamy, Jane Darwell, Leo Carrillo, John Litel, William Farnum, Janet Beecher, J. Frank Hamilton, Kay Linaker, Joseph Crehan, Addison Richards, Frank Hagney. At the end of the Civil War a newspaper reporter and photographer are assigned to go to Texas to look into reports that an uprising may take place. Typically slick melodrama from Universal which should please genre fans.

2130 Men of the North. Metro-Goldwyn-Mayer, 1930. 61 minutes B/W. D: Hal Roach. SC: Richard Schayer. WITH Gilbert Roland, Barbara Leonard, Arnold Korff, George Davis, Robert Elliott, Nina Quartero, Robert Graves Jr. An adventurer in Canada is falsely accused of stealing gold from a mine but his innocence is believed by the mine owner's pretty daughter. Vintage melodrama is worth a look to see a youthful Gilbert Roland. A Spanish language version also starring Gilbert Roland (billed under his real name of Luis Alonso) was filmed simultaneously by the producer-director Hal Roach as **Monsieur Le Fox.**

2131 Men of the Plains. First Division/ Grand National, 1936. 63 minutes B/W. D: Robert Emmett (Tansey). SC: Robert Emmett (Tansey) & Jack Cowell. WITH Rex Bell, Joan Barclay, George Ball, Charles King, Forrest Taylor, Roger Williams, Ed Cassidy, Lafe McKee. A government investigator is assigned to look into a series of gold shipment thefts and finds out that two of the town's leading citizens are behind the lawless activities. Passable action drama produced by Arthur and Max Alexander.

2132 Men of the Timberland. Universal, 1941. 62 minutes B/W. D: John Rawlins. SC: Maurice Tombragel & Griffin Jay. WITH Richard Arlen, Andy Devine, Linda Hayes, Francis McDonald, Willard Robertson, Paul E. Burns, Gaylord (Steve) Pendleton, Hardie Albright, Roy Harris (Riley Hill), John Ellis, Jack Rice. A timberman uncovers a plot by a crook to cut timber over a large area, the illegal scheme having been brought about by the crook's bribing of government officials. Actionful "B" effort from Universal in the popular Richard Arlen-Andy Devine series.

Men with Steel Faces see **The Phantom Empire**

Men with Whips see **Rangle River**

2133 Men Without Law. Columbia, 1930. 60 minutes B/W. D: Louis King. SC: Dorothy Howell. WITH Buck Jones, Tom Carr, Carmelita Geraghty, Lydia Knott, Harry Woods, Fred Burns, Syd Saylor, Fred Kelsey, Lafe McKee, Ben Corbett, Art Mix. Returning home from World War I, a man finds his younger brother has been arrested for taking part in a bank robbery and he is soon captured by an outlaw leader. Good early Buck Jones sound film with a well-lighted climactic fight sequence. Background music includes "La Paloma" and the gang members sing "Bury Me Not on the Lone Prairie."

2134 The Mercenary. United Artists, 1970. 105 minutes Color. D: Sergio Corbucci. SC: Luciano Vincenzoni, Sergio Spina & Sergio Corbucci. WITH Jack Palance, Franco Nero, Tony Musante, Giovanna Ralli, Eduardo Fajardo, Bruno Corazzari, Remo de Angeles, Joe Camel, Franco Giacobini, Vicente Joja, Jose Riesgo, Angel Ortiz, Fernando Villena, Tito Garcia, Angel Alvarez. Two bitter mercenary enemies are after a valuable treasure but it is also sought after by a revolutionary, a peasant girl and a miner. Pretty good Italian oater with the usual violence and some not-so-usual humor. Made by Produzioni Europee Associate/Produzioni Associate Delphos S.P.A./Profilms as **Il Mercenario.**

2135 Mesa of Lost Women. Howco, 1953. 70 minutes B/W. D: Herbert Tevos & Ron Ormond. SC: Herbert Tevos. WITH Jackie Coogan, Richard Travis, Allan Nixon, Mary Hill, Robert Knapp, Tandra Quinn, Harmon Stevens, Samuel Wu, George Barrows, Chris-Pin Martin, John Martin, Angelo Rossitto, Lyle Talbot (Narrator). In the Mexican desert, a mad scientist works on a serum to create a super-race. Low grade and awful. TV title: **Lost Women.**

2136 Mesquite Buckaroo. Metropolitan, 1939. 55 minutes B/W. D: Harry S. Webb. SC: George Plympton. WITH Bob Steele, Carolyn (Clarene) Curtis, Frank LaRue, Charles King, Ted Adams, Joe Whitehead, Ed Brady, Snub Pollard, Carleton Young, John Elliott, Juanita Fletcher, Gordon Roberts, Jimmie Aubrey. A rodeo cowboy gets involved with a gang of crooks and romances a pretty girl. Low grade Bob Steele film plagued with far too much rodeo stock footage.

2137 A Message to Garcia. 20th Century-Fox, 1936. 90 minutes B/W. D: George Marshall. SC: W. P. Lipscomb & Gene Fowler. WITH Wallace Beery, Barbara Stanwyck, John Boles, Herbert Mundin, Martin Garralaga, Enrique Acosta, Jose Luis Tortosa, Joan Torena, Alan Hale, Mona Barrie, Warren Hymer, Frederik Vogeding, Sam Appel, Yorke Sherwood, Iris Adrian, Davidson Clark, Lon Chaney, Del Henderson, John Carradine (voice), Rita (Hayworth) Cansino, Philip Morris. President William McKinley sends an Army officer to Cuba to warn a guerilla leader that the U. S. has declared war on Spain. Silly historical melodrama which not even its stars can save.

Meteor Monster see **Teenage Monster**

2138 The Mexicali Kid. Monogram, 1938. 58 minutes B/W. D: Wallace Fox. SC: Robert Emmett (Tansey). WITH Jack Randall, Eleanor Stewart, Wesley Barry, Ed Cassidy, Bud Osborne, George Chesebro, William von Bricken, Sherry Tansey, Ernie Adams, Frank LaRue, Buzz Barton, Archie Ricks, Denver Dixon, Hal Price,

Glenn Strange, Chester Gan, Fred Parker, Billy Bletcher. A cowboy befriends an outlaw and later learns the man has been hired by a crooked ranch foreman who wants him to aid the crook in taking over a valuable ranch. Fair Jack Randall vehicle.

2139 Mexicali Rose. Republic, 1939. 54 (60) minutes B/W. D: George Sherman. SC: Gerald Geraghty. WITH Gene Autry, Smiley Burnette, Noah Beery, Luana Walters, William Farnum, LeRoy Mason, William Royle, Wally Albright, Kathryn Frey, Roy Barcroft, Richard Botiller, John Beach, Merrill McCormack, Fred "Snowflake" Toones, Sherry Hall, Al Taylor, Josef Swickard, Tom London, Jack Ingram, Eddie Parker, Henry Otho, Joe Dominguez, Al Haskell. Crooked officials of a bogus oil company are out to cheat the public and they hire Gene Autry to aid them although he believes they are honest. Good Gene Autry vehicle with fine work by Noah Berry as a lovable bandit leader.

2140 Mexican Spitfire Out West. RKO Radio, 1941. 76 minutes B/W. D: Leslie Goodwins. SC: Charles E. Roberts & Jack Townley. WITH Lupe Velez, Leon Errol, Donald Woods, Elizabeth Risdon, Cecil Kellaway, Linda Hayes, Lydia Bilbrook, Grant Withers, Charles Coleman, Charles Quigley, Eddie Dunn, Tom Kennedy. After an argument with her husband, the Mexican Spitfire heads West for a divorce but her uncle makes plans to stop her. Average entry in the "Mexican Spitfire" series; basically for fans only.

2141 The Michigan Kid. Universal, 1928. 55 minutes B/W. D: Irvin Willat. SC: Peter Milne, Walter Anthony, J. Grubb Alexander & (uncredited, J. G. Hawks, Charles Logue & Irvin Willat). WITH Renee Adoree, Conrad Nagel, Fred Esmelton, Virginia Grey, Maurice Murphy, Adolph Miler, Lloyd Whitlock, Donald House. Wanting money to marry his girl, a young man heads to Alaska to make his fortune. His rival is also there and sends for the girl so they can get married. The plot is not much but the acting and locales make this silent effort worth watching.

2142 The Michigan Kid. Universal, 1947. 70 minutes B/W. D: Ray Taylor. SC: Roy Chanslor. WITH Jon Hall, Rita Johnson, Victor McLaglen, Andy Devine, Byron Foulger, Stanley Andrews, Milburn Stone, William Brooks, Joan (Shawlee)

Fulton, Leonard East, Ray Teal, Eddy Waller, George Chandler, Edmund Cobb, Karl Hackett, Robert Wilke, Guy Wilkerson. Corrupt town officials are after a girl's ranch but she is aided by four strangers. Pleasant adaptation of Rex Beach's novel.

2143 Midnight Canyon. Berolina Film, 1964. 102 minutes Color. D: Rolf Olsen. SC: Donald Sharp & Paul Clydeburn. WITH Thomas Fritsch, Walter Giller, Judith Dornys, Gustav Knuth, Heidemarie Hatheyer. After his parents are killed in a stagecoach holdup, a young man learns to survive in the West. Fairly interesting West German oater, issued in that country as **Heiss Weht Der Wind.**

2144 The Million Dollar Dixie Deliverance. Buena Vista, 1978. 100 minutes Color. D: Russell Mayberry. WITH Brock Peters, Christian Juttner, Chip Courtland, Alicia Fleer, Joe Dorsey, Christian Berrigan, Kyle Richards, Kip Niven. During the Civil War, a captured Union soldier tries to aid five children captured and held for one million dollars ransom by Confederates. The Disney studios' first feature film developed especially for network TV is a good family drama.

2145 The Mine with the Iron Door. Columbia, 1936. 70 minutes B/W. D: David Howard. SC: Howard Swift & Dan Jarrett. WITH Richard Arlen, Cecilia Parker, Henry B. Walthall, Stanley Fields, Horace Murphy, Spencer Charters, Charles Wilson, Barbara Bedford. A tenderfoot prospector is given the location of a valuable gold mine but is at odds with a bandit who has kidnapped a girl who he wants to ransom for the mine's location. Pretty entertaining adaptation of the 1923 Harold Bell Wright novel which was first filmed by producer Sol Lesser (who also produced this version) in 1924 for his Principal Pictures with Pat O'Malley, Dorothy Mackaill, Raymond Hatton, Charles Murray, Creighton Hale and Mary Carr.

2146 Minnesota Clay. Harlequin International, 1964. 89 minutes Color. D: Sergio Corbucci. SC: Adriano Bolzoni. WITH Cameron Mitchell, Georges Riviere, Diana Martin, Ethel Rojo, Fernando Sancho, Anthony Ross, Antonio Casas, Julio Pena, Gino Pernice. Going blind, a man escapes from prison and returns to the small town where the man who can prove his innocence lives and there he finds rival gangs at war. Good Italian-French-Spanish coproduction with fine work by Cameron Mitchell in the title role.

2147 A Minute to Pray, a Second to Die. Cinerama, 1968. 103 minutes Color. D: Franco Giraldi. SC: Ugo Liberatore & Louis Garfinkle. WITH Alex Cord, Arthur Kennedy, Robert Ryan, Nicoletta Machiavelli, Mario Brega, Renato Romano, Gianpeiro Albertini, Dan Martin, Jose Manuel Martin, Enzo Fiermonte. A wanted outlaw takes refuge in a small town but is soon found by his enemies, including the law, rival badmen and bounty hunters. Well made but basically average European oater, originally called **Escondido** and cut to 97 minutes for U. S. release.

Miracle in the Sand see **The Three Godfathers** (1936)

2148 The Miracle of the Hills. 20th Century-Fox, 1959. 73 minutes B/W. D: Paul Landres. SC: Charles Hoffman. WITH Rex Reason, Theona Bryant, Jay North, June Vincent, Nan Leslie, Betty Lou Gerson, Gilbert Smith, Tracy Stratford, Gene Roth, I. Stanford Jolley, Gene Collins, Paul Wexler, Kenneth Mayer, Pat O'Hara, Tom Daly, Cecil Elliott, Charles Arnt, Claire Carleton. A young minister tries to bring spiritual rebirth to an 1880s mining town run by a wealthy ex-dance hall hostess. Pleasant outing.

2149 The Miracle Rider. Mascot, 1935. 15 Chapters B/W. D: Armand L. Schaefer & B. Reeves Eason. SC: John Rathmell. WITH Tom Mix, Joan Gale, Charles Middleton, Jason Robards, Robert Kortman, Edward Earle, Edward Hearn, Tom London, Niles Welch, Edmund Cobb, Ernie Adams, Max Wagner, Charles King, George Chesebro, Jack Rockwell, Stanley Price, George Barton, Wally Wales, Buffalo Bill Jr., Dick Curtis, Frank Ellis, Richard Alexander, Earl Dwire, Lafe McKee, Hank Bell, Pat O'Malley, Slim Whitaker, Robert Frazer, Art Ardigan, Chief Big Tree, Forrest Taylor, Fred Burns, Chief Standing Bear. A Texas Ranger comes to the aid of an Indian tribe whose lands are being secretly used by a crook and his cohorts to mine a valuable mineral. Somewhat static but actionful cliffhanger; Tom Mix's final film. V: Cassette Express.

2150 The Misfits. United Artists, 1961. 125 minutes B/W. D: John Huston. SC: Arthur Miller. WITH Clark Gable, Marilyn Monroe, Montgomery Clift, Eli Wallach, Thelma Ritter, James Barton, Estelle

Winwood, Kevin McCarthy, Dennis Shaw, Philip Mitchell, Walter Rampage, Peggy Barton, Rex Bell, Ralph Roberts. A divorcee becomes upset at the cruelty toward horses during a roundup and she appeals to new-found cowboy friends to help her stop it. Overlong and overrated feature which does have some appeal, but mainly of interest because it was Clark Gable's and Marilyn Monroe's final feature. VD: Blackhawk.

Missile Base at Taniak see **Canadian Mounties vs. Atomic Invaders**

2151 The Mississippi Gambler. Universal-International, 1953. 99 minutes Color. D: Rudolph Mate. SC: Seton I. Miller. WITH Tyrone Power, Piper Laurie, Julia (Julie) Adams, John McIntire, John Baer, Paul Cavanagh, Ron Randell, William Reynolds, Guy Williams, Robert Warwick, Ralph Dumke, Hugh Beaumont, King Donovan, Gwen Verdon, Alan Dexter, Al Wyatt, Dale Van Sickel, Michael Dale, Bert LeBaron, Dennis Weaver, Frank Wilcox, Edward Earle, Dorothy Bruce, Angela Stevens, Rolfe Sedan, Tony Hughes, Fred Cavens, David Newell, Buddy Roosevelt, Anita Ekberg, Jackie Laughery, Paul Bradley. An honest gambler decides to set up a gambling house in frontier New Orleans. Passable costume melodrama for Tyrone Power fans.

2152 Mississippi Rhythm. Monogram, 1949. 69 minutes B/W. D: Derwin Abrahams. SC: Louise Rosseau. WITH Jimmie Davis, Veda Ann Borg, Lee "Lasses" White, James Flavin, Lyle Talbot, Sue England, Guy Beach, Paul Maxey, Paul Bryar, Joel Marston, Duke York, Wheaton Chambers, Charlie Jordan. When crooked gamblers try to stop land settlement by homesteaders, a land agent comes to the settlers' rescue. Pleasant musical melodrama starring Louisiana governor Jimmie Davis.

2153 The Missouri Breaks. United Artists, 1976. 126 minutes Color. D: Arthur Penn. SC: Thomas McGuane. WITH Marlon Brando, Jack Nicholson, Kathleen Lloyd, Randy Quaid, Frederic Forrest, Harry Dean Stanton, John McLiam, John Ryan, Sam Gilman, Steve Franken, Richard Bradford, James Greene, Luana Anders, R. L. Armstrong, Dan Ades, Charles Wagenheim. When horse thieves attack herds belonging to Montana ranchers, the latter agree to hire a gunman to dispose of the menace. An overlong and surprisingly poor feature with mediocre

263   A Missouri

performances from the two leads. V: 20th Century-Fox Video. VD: CBS/Fox Video.

2154 A Missouri Outlaw. Republic, 1941. 54 minutes B/W. D: George Sherman. SC: Doris Schroeder & Jack Latt Jr. WITH Don "Red" Barry, Lynn Merrick, Noah Beery, Al St. John, Paul Fix, Frank LaRue, Kenne Duncan, John Merton, Carleton Young, Frank Brownlee, Fred "Snowflake" Toones, Karl Hackett, Lee Shumway, Ray Bennett, Bob McKenzie, Kermit Maynard, Frank McCarroll, Curley Dresden, Herman Hack. When his gunman son returns home, the local sheriff is forced to arrest him. Very good entry in Don Barry's Republic series, greatly helped by the presence of pretty Lynn Merrick and the great Noah Beery.

2155 The Missouri Traveler. Buena Vista, 1958. 103 minutes Color. D: Jerry Hopper. SC: Norman Shannon Hall. WITH Brandon de Wilde, Lee Marvin, Gary Merrill, Mary Hosford, Paul Ford, Ken Curtis, Cal Tinney, Frank Cady, Mary Field, Kathleen Freeman, Will Wright, Roy Jensen, Earle Hodgins. In 1915 an orphaned boy tries to make a go of it in a rural Missouri town. Pleasant Walt Disney production of a bucolic nature.

2156 The Missourians. Republic, 1950. 60 minutes B/W. D: George Blair. SC: Arthur Orloff. WITH Monte Hale, Paul Hurst, Lyn Thomas, Roy Barcroft, Howard Negley, Robert Neil, Lane Bradford, John Hamilton, Sarah Padden, Charles Williams, Perry Ivans. A refugee from Poland attempts to go into ranching but local ranchers oppose him although the town marshal tries to stop such prejudice. Mediocre entry in Monte Hale's Republic series. V: Cumberland Video.

2157 Mohawk. 20th Century-Fox, 1956. 80 minutes Color. D: Kurt Neumann. SC: Maurice Geraghty & Milton Krims. WITH Scott Brady, Rita Gam, Neville Brand, Lori Nelson, Allison Hayes, John Hoyt, Vera Vague, Rhys Williams, Ted De Corsia, Mae Clarke, John Hudson, Tommy Cook, Michael Granger. Land owners try to stop settlement in the Mohawk Valley by inciting the Indians to war but their efforts are thwarted by an Easterner and his Indian girlfriend. Okay action melodrama enhanced by footage from **Drums Along the Mohawk** (q.v.).

2158 Mojave Firebrand. Republic, 1944. 55 minutes B/W. D: Spencer Gordon

Bennet. SC: Norman S. Hall. WITH "Wild Bill" Elliott, George "Gabby" Hayes, Anne Jeffreys, LeRoy Mason, Jack Ingram, Harry McKim, Karl Hackett, Forrest Taylor, Hal Price, Marshall Reed, Kenne Duncan, Bud Geary, Jack Kirk, Fred Graham, Tom London, Frank Ellis, Tom Steele, Bob Burns, Art Dillard, Bud Osborne. Crooks try to steal a silver mine from an old prospector but he is helped by a lawman. Well made and fast moving Bill Elliott vehicle.

2159 Molly and Lawless John. Producers Distributing Corporation, 1973. 96 minutes Color. D: Gary Nelson. SC: Terry Kingsley-Smith. WITH Vera Miles, Sam Elliott, Clu Gulager, John Anderson, Cynthia Mayers, Charles A. Pinney, Robert Westmoreland, Melinda Chavaria, George LeBow, Grady Hill. A young outlaw convinces the sheriff's wife to help him escape from jail. They run away together and as they travel, his interest in her wanes. Fair film helped by some good acting but still nothing special.

2160 Money, Women and Guns. Universal, 1958. 80 minutes Color. D: Richard H. Bartlett. SC: Montgomery Pittman. WITH Jock Mahoney, Kim Hunter, Tim Hovey, Gene Evans, William Campbell, Lon Chaney, Tom Drake, James Gleason, Jeffrey Stone, Judi Meredith, Philip Terry, Richard Devon, Ian MacDonald, Don Megowan, Nolan Leary, Kelly Thordsen. When an old prospector is murdered, a detective is hired to find his heirs as well as his killer. Pleasant oater with some good performances although a rather tame film.

2161 Montana. Warner Brothers-First National, 1950. 76 minutes B/W. D: Ray Enright. SC: James R. Webb, Borden Chase & Charles O'Neal. WITH Errol Flynn, Alexis Smith, S. Z. Sakall, Douglas Kennedy, James Brown, Ian MacDonald, Charles Irwin, Paul E. Burns, Tudor Owen, Lester Mathews, Nacho Galindo, Lane Chandler, Monte Blue, Billy Vincent, Warren Jackson. An Australian sheepman comes to Montana to raise sheep and is opposed by a woman cattle rancher. Standard genre outing.

2162 Montana Belle. RKO Radio, 1952. 82 minutes Color. D: Allan Dwan. SC: Horace Webster & Norman S. Hall. WITH Jane Russell, George Brent, Scott Brady, Forrest Tucker, Andy Devine, Jack Lambert, Ray Teal, Rory Mallinson, Roy Barcroft, John Litel, Ned Davenport, Dick

Elliott, Eugene (Gene) Roth, Stanley Andrews, Holly Bane. The notorious Belle Starr expands her lawless activities by joining forces with the Dalton Brothers. Very dull oater not even saved by Jane Russell's good looks.

2163 Montana Desperado. Monogram, 1951. 51 minutes B/W. D: Wallace Fox. SC: Dan Ullman. WITH Johnny Mack Brown, Virginia Herrick, Myron Healey, Marshall Reed, Steve Clark, Edmund Cobb, Lee Roberts, Carl Mathews, Ben Corbett. A masked rider has been killing ranchers in order to get their land and another rancher tries to find out the murderer's identity. Compact oater with a good premise, cheap production values.

2164 Montana Incident. Monogram, 1952. 54 minutes B/W. D: Lewis D. Collins. SC: Dan Ullman. WITH Whip Wilson, Rand Brooks, Noel Neill, Peggy Stewart, Hugh Prosser, Russ Whiteman, William Fawcett, Terry Frost, Marshall Reed, Lyle Talbot, Bruce Edwards, Barbara Woodell, Stanley Price. Two railroad surveyors try to aid the people of a small town being ruled by the ruthless woman. Better-than-average Whip Wilson outing, due mainly to pretty Peggy Stewart as the villain.

2165 The Montana Kid. Monogram, 1931. 60 minutes B/W. D: Harry Fraser. SC: G. A. Durlam. WITH Bill Cody, Andy Shuford, Doris Hill, W. L. Thorne, G. D. Wood, John Elliott, Paul Panzer. A cowboy tries to aid a young man whose father was murdered after he was forced to sign over his ranch to a crooked gambler. Better than average entry in the "Bill and Andy" series.

Montana Mike see **Heaven Only Knows**

2166 Montana Moon. Metro-Goldwyn-Mayer, 1930. 88 minutes B/W. D: Malcolm St. Clair. SC: Sylvia Thalberg. WITH Joan Crawford, John(ny) Mack Brown, Ricardo Cortez, Dorothy Sebastian, Cliff Edwards, Benny Rubin, Karl Dane, Lloyd Ingraham. A spoiled heiress runs away from her father's private train and meets and later marries a cowboy but she is soon romanced by a gigolo. Dated but entertaining Joan Crawford vehicle with songs like "The Moon is Low"; Johnny Mack Brown's first sound Western.

2167 Montana Territory. Columbia, 1952. 64 minutes Color. D: Ray Nazarro. SC:

Barry Shipman. WITH Lon McCallister, Preston Foster, Wanda Hendrix, Hugh Sanders, Clayton Moore, Jack Elam, Robert Griffin, Myron Healey, Eddy Waller, George Russell, Ethan Laidlaw, Ruth Warren, Trevor Bardette, George Chesebro. After witnessing a murder, a young man is made a deputy sheriff and assigned to bring in the killers. Average production with a rather interesting plotline.

2168 Monte Walsh. National General, 1970. 98 minutes Color. D: William Fraker. SC: Lukas Heller & David Zelag Goodman. WITH Lee Marvin, Jack Palance, Jeanne Moreau, Mitchell Ryan, Jim Davis, G. D. Spradlin, John Hudkins, Ray Guth, John McKee, Michael Conrad, Tom Heaton, Ted Gehring, Bo Hopkins, John McLiam, Allyn Ann McLerie, Matt Clark, Billy Green Bush, Charles Tyner, Jack Colvin, Guy Wilkerson, Roy Barcroft. In the 1890s two cowpokes find it hard to get jobs; one becomes a storekeeper who is soon killed by another wrangler forced to become an outlaw, and his buddy sets out to revenge the storekeeper's death. Good account of the end of the wild life of the cowboy as civilization began to take over the West. Worth seeing.

2169 Montezuma's Lost Gold. Bill Burrud Productions/Gold Key Entertainment, 1978. 90 minutes Color. D: John Burrud & Miles Hinshaw. SC: Jeff Fellows & John Schwartz. WITH Miles Hinshaw, Tom Hinshaw, Michael Carr, William Lewis, Bill Burrud (narrator). Adequate docudrama about a drifter-prisoner who knows the whereabouts of the legendary treasure of the Aztecs, buried in North America after the Spanish plundered Mexico. Tod Connor signs the title song, "Gold."

2170 Moonlight and Cactus. Universal, 1944. 60 minutes B/W. D: Edward Cline. SC: Eugene Conrad & Paul Gerard Smith. WITH The Andrews Sisters (Patty, Maxene, LaVerne Andrews), Leo Carrillo, Elyse Knox, Tom Seidel, Shemp Howard, Eddie Quillan, Murray Alper, Tom Kennedy, Frank Lackteen, Minerva Urecal, Jacqueline de Wit, Mary O'Brien. A Naval officer returns home to his Western ranch to find it being run by a trio of girl singers. The Andrews Sisters are out West in this pleasant blend of music, comedy and nonsense.

2171 Moonlight on the Prairie. Warner Brothers, 1935. 63 minutes B/W. D: D.

Ross Lederman. SC: William Jacobs. WITH Dick Foran, Sheila Mannors, George E. Stone, Gordon (Bill) Elliott, Joseph Sawyer, Robert Barrat, Herbert Heywood, Dickie Jones, Joseph King, Milton Kibbee, Raymond Brown, Richard Carle, Bud Osborne, Ben Corbett, Gene Alsace, Glenn Strange, Victor Potel, Cactus Mack, Jack Kirk. The star singing cowboy of a rodeo is led to believe he will be unjustly accused of murder at the show's next stop. Dick Foran's initial series film is a pleasant outing with a good script and cast and enhanced by Foran's brand of singing.

2172 Moonlight on the Range. Spectrum, 1937. 60 minutes B/W. D: Sam Newfield. SC: Fred Myton. WITH Fred Scott, Lois January, Al St. John, Dick Curtis, Frank LaRue, Oscar Gahan, Jimmie Aubrey, Carl Mathews, Wade Walker, William McCall, Shorty Miller, Jack Evans, Rudy Sooter, Lew Meehan, Ed Cassidy, Tex Palmer, George Morrell, Forrest Taylor, Sherry Tansey. A cowboy hits the trail for revenge when his lookalike cattle rustler half-brother murders his best pal. Fred Scott plays both the hero and the lead villain in this fairly good actioner which is highlighted by the star singing four good songs. V: Cumberland Video.

2173 The Moonlighter. Warner Brothers, 1953. 77 minutes B/W. D: Roy Rowland. SC: Niven Busch. WITH Barbara Stanwyck, Fred MacMurray, Ward Bond, William Ching, John Dierkes, Morris Ankrum, Jack Elam, Charles Halton, Norman Leavitt, Sam Flint, Myra Marsh. A cattle rustler returns home for his own funeral and meets his ex-girlfriend and her hate for him soon returns to love. Originally issued in 3-D, this dull oater has little to recommend it other than its stars; the title refers to a cattle rustler.

2174 Moon Over Montana. Monogram, 1946. 56 minutes B/W. D: Oliver Drake. SC: Louise Rousseau & Ande Lamb. WITH Jimmy Wakely, Lee "Lasses" White, Jennifer Holt, Jack Ingram, Terry Frost, Louise Arthur, Woody Woodell & His Riding Rangers, Stanley Blystone, Brad Slaven, Eddie Majors, Bob Duncan, Arthur Smith, John Elliott, Ray Jones, Denver Dixon (Victor Adamson). A cowboy leads a group of cattlemen in opposing the actions of a corrupt rancher out to get controlling interest in a railroad. Poorly done and uninteresting Jimmy Wakely musical vehicle.

2175 More Dead Than Alive. United Artists, 1969. 101 minutes Color. D: Robert Sparr. SC: George Schenck. WITH Clint Walker, Anne Francis, Vincent Price, Paul Hampton, Mike Henry, Craig Littler, Beverly Powers, Clarke Gordon, William Woodson. After eighteen years in prison, an ex-gunman is released and tries to live a peaceful life but his past keeps catching up with him. Mediocre oater highlighted by Vincent Price's performance as the showman who hires the gunman as his star attraction.

2176 More Than Magic. Wrather Corporation, 1956. 75 minutes Color. D: Earl Bellamy & Oscar Rudolph. SC: Thomas Seller, Robert E. Schaefer, Eric Friewald & Hilary Cresen Rhodes. WITH Clayton Moore, Jay Silverheels, Allen Pinson, Wayne Burson, Mary Ellen Kay, Harry Lauter, Rand Brooks, Don C. Harvey, Tom Brown, Ben Welden, Edmond Hashim, Robert Swan, Charles Stevens, Mike Ragan, Louis Lettieri, Sandy Sanders, John Cliff, William Challee, Barbara Ann Knudsdy, Sydney Mason, David Dwight, John Maxwell, Walt LaRue, John Pickard. The Lone Ranger and Tonto try to capture a band of disappearing road agents, get on the trail of an outlaw gang and aid an Indian chief in choosing his heir. Pleasant telefeature from "The Lone Ranger" (ABC-TV, 1949-57) series from the episodes "Outlaws in Greasepaint," "Hot Spell in Panamint" and "White Hawks' Decision."

2177 More Wild Wild West. CBS-TV, 1980. 100 minutes Color. D: Burt Kennedy. SC: William Bowers & Tony Hayden. WITH Robert Conrad, Ross Martin, Jonathan Winters, Harry Morgan, Rene Auberjonois, Liz Torres, Victor Buono, Jack LaLanne, Randi Brough, Candi Brough, Dr. Joyce Brothers. Two federal undercover agents are on the trail of a wily madman. Fans of the TV series "Wild Wild West" (CBS-TV, 1965-70) will enjoy this telefilm, a followup to the 1979 revival **The Wild, Wild West Revisited** (q.v.).

2178 Mosby's Marauders. Buena Vista, 1967. 80 minutes Color. D: Michael O'Herlihy. WITH James MacArthur, Nick Adams, Jack Ging, Kurt Russell, Peggy Lipton, Donald Harron, Jeanne Cooper, James Callahan, Robert Sorrells, E. J. Andre, Michael Forst, Steve Raines, Michael Pate, Michael Kearney, Robert Random, Amzie Strickland. A young Confederate officer joins the forces of Mosby's Marauders in a daring capture of a Union general behind enemy lines in 1863. Exciting, and fairly accurate, Walt Disney historical drama originally shown on ABC-TV on Disney's TV show as "Willie and the Yank" on January 8, 15, and 22, 1967.

2179 Mother Lode. Agamemnon Films, 1982. 101 minutes Color. D: Charlton Heston. SC: Fraser Clarke Heston. WITH Charlton Heston, Nick Mancuso, Kim Basinger, John Marley, Dale Wilson, Ricky Zantolas, Marie George. A bush pilot and a young woman head into the mountains of British Columbia to look for the man's gold-seeking buddy and find a Scottish miner who will stop at nothing to protect his claim. Very entertaining actioner with fine photography, plus good second unit work by Joe Canutt; filmed in the Cassair Mountains of British Columbia.

2180 Mountain Family Robinson. Pacific International, 1979. 98 minutes Color. D: John Cotter. SC: Arthur R. Dubs. WITH Robert Logan, Susan Damante Shaw, Heather Rattray, Ham Larsen, George "Buck" Flower, William Bryant, Calvin Bartlett, Jim Davidson. The government demands the Robinson family move from their cabin home in the Rocky Mountains because the land they are on is a mining, not a homestead, claim. The final film in the "Wilderness Family" trilogy is a good family outing with excellent photography by James Roberson. First two films in the series: **The Wilderness Family** and **Further Adventures of the Wilderness Family** (qq.v.). V: Media Home Video.

2181 Mountain Justice. Universal, 1930. 64 minutes B/W. D: Harry Joe Brown. SC: Bennetth Cohen & Leslie Mason. WITH Ken Maynard, Kathryn Crawford, Otis Harlan, Paul Hurst, Richard Carlyle, Les Bates, Gilbert "Pee Wee" Holmes, Edgar "Blue" Washington, Fred Burns. An Oklahoma cowboy heads to the Kentucky hills pretending to be deaf in order to find the man who shot his father. Good Ken Maynard vehicle originally called **Kettle Creek.**

Mountain Man see **Guardian of the Wilderness**

2182 The Mountain Men. Columbia, 1980. 102 minutes Color. D: Richard Lang. SC: Fraser Clarke Heston. WITH Charlton Heston, Brian Keith, Stephen Macht, Victoria Racimo, Victor Jory, Seymour

Cassell, David Ackroyd, John Glover, Carl Bellini, Bill Lucking, Ken Ruta, Danny Zapien, Tim Haldeman, Bob Terhune, Chuck Roberson, Roy Jenson, Henry Wills. In the 1840s an aging trapper keeps looking for a previously unhunted wilderness and finds trouble with hostile Indians. Well made and beautifully photographed frontier tale, but still only average. V: Columbia Pictures Home Entertainment.

2183 Mountain Rhythm. Republic, 1939. 54 (61) minutes B/W. D: B. Reeves Eason. SC: Gerald Geraghty. WITH Gene Autry, Smiley Burnette, June Storey, Maude Eburne, Ferris Taylor, Walter Fenner, Jack Pennick, Hooper Atchley, Ed Cassidy, Jack Ingram, Tom London, Frankie Marvin, Roger Williams. Eastern crooks want grazing land for a tourist resort and set up a government auction in order to buy the land out from the ranchers who own it. Average Gene Autry vehicle.

2184 Mounted Fury. World Wide, 1931. 63 minutes B/W. D: Stuart Paton. SC: Betty Burbridge. WITH Blanche Mehaffey, John Bowers, Frank Rice, Lina Basquette, Robert Ellis, George Regas, John Ince. A Mountie is assigned to bring in a man wanted for murder. Quickie production that gives viewers a chance to see silent star John Bowers in one of his few sound outings.

2185 The Mounted Stranger. Universal, 1930. 60 minutes B/W. D-SC: Arthur Rosson. WITH Hoot Gibson, Louise Lorraine, Francis Ford, Milton Brown, Buddy Hunter, Fred Burns, Jim Corey, Walter Patterson, Francelia Billington. As a boy a man witnessed the murder of his father by an outlaw gang leader and years later he tries to bring the man to justice. Actionful Hoot Gibson early talkie, more serious than most of his features.

2186 Mr. Horn. CBS-TV, 1979. 200 minutes Color. D: Jack Starrett. SC: William Goldman. WITH David Carradine, Richard Widmark, Karen Black, Richard Masur, Clay Tanner, Pat McCormick, Jack Starrett, John Durren, Jeremy Slate, Enrique Lucero, Stafford Morgan, Don Collier, Lewis James Oliver, John Alderman. The story of Tom Horn, the man who captured Geronimo and then became a bounty hunter. Overlong two-part TV movie enhanced by good work by stars David Carradine and Richard Widmark.

2187 Mrs. Mike. United Artists, 1949. 99 minutes B/W. D: Louis King. SC: Alfred

Lewis & DeWitt Bodeen. WITH Dick Powell, Evelyn Keyes, John Miljan, J. M. Kerrigan, Angela Clarke, Will Wright, Nan Boardman, Frances Morris, Joel Nester, Jean Inness, Chief Yowlachie, Clarence Straight, James Fairfax, Donald Pietro. A Mountie marries a city girl and brings her with him to live at a remote outpost where she learns to face the harsh realities of frontier existence. A wonderful motion picture, deftly written and finely performed by stars Dick Powell and Evelyn Keyes; a must see!

2188 Mrs. Sundance. ABC-TV/20th Century-Fox, 1974. 78 minutes Color. D: Marvin Chomsky. SC: Christopher Knopf. WITH Elizabeth Montgomery, Robert Foxworth, L. Q. Jones, Arthur Hunnicutt, Lurene Tuttle, Claudette Nevins, Robert Donner, Dean Smith, Tod Shelhorse. When school teacher Etta Place learns that the Sundance Kid did not die with Butch Cassidy she sets out to meet him but also knows bounty hunters are on her trail. TV movie followup to **Butch Cassidy and the Sundance Kid** (q.v.) is acceptable due to Elizabeth Montgomery's work in the title role. Sequel: **Wanted: the Sundance Woman.**

Mrs. Sundance Rides Again see **Wanted: the Sundance Woman**

2189 Mule Train. Columbia, 1950. 70 minutes B/W. D: John English. SC: Gerald Geraghty. WITH Gene Autry, Pat Buttram, Sheila Ryan, Robert Livingston, John Miljan, Frank Jacquet, Vince Barnett, Syd Saylor, Sandy Sanders, Gregg Barton, Kenne Duncan, Roy Gordon, Stanley Andrews, Robert Hilton, Robert Wilke, Robert Carson, Pat O'Malley, Eddie Parker, George Morrell, John R. McKee, George Slocum, Frank O'Connor, Norman Leavitt, Evelyn Finley. Marshal Gene Autry comes to the aid of two prospectors who claim a natural cement deposit is stolen by a contractor in cahoots with a crooked female sheriff. Another entertaining Gene Autry vehicle enhanced by the title tune plus a trio of other country/western favorites: "Room Full of Roses," "Cool Water" and "The Old Chisholm Trail."

2190 Murder on the Yukon. Monogram, 1940. 59 minutes B/W. D: Louis Gasnier. SC: Milton Raison. WITH James Newill, Polly Ann Young, Dave O'Brien, Al St. John, William Royle, Chief Thundercloud, Budd Buster, Karl Hackett, Kenne Duncan,

Snub Pollard, Earl Douglas, Jack Clifford. Two Mounties investigate the murders of two prospectors in the Yukon. Nicely paced entry in the "Renfrew of the Mounted" series. Also called **Renfrew of the Mounted in Murder on the Yukon.**

Murieta see **Desperate Mission**

2191 Mustang. United Artists, 1959. 73 minutes B/W. D: Peter Stephens. SC: Tom Gries. WITH Jack Buetel, Madelyn Trahey, Steve Keyes, Milton Swift, Autumn Moon. A rodeo star goes to work for a rancher but becomes at odds with the man when he wants to kill a wild stallion. Poor programmer.

2192 Mustang Country. Universal, 1976. 79 minutes Color. D-SC: John Champion. WITH Joel McCrea, Robert Fuller, Patrick Wayne, Nika Mina, Tiger (horse), Rote (dog). On the Montana-Canadian border an aging cowboy helps a young Indian boy round up a wild stallion. Joel McCrea triumphantly returned to the screen in this very entertaining drama which is a good bet for the entire family; recommended.

2193 Mutiny at Fort Sharp. Walter Manley Enterprises, 1966. 91 minutes Color. D: Fernando Cerchio. SC: Ugo Liberatore & Fernando Cerchio. WITH Broderick Crawford, Elisa Montes, Mario Valdemarin, Umberto Ceriani, Hugo Arden, Julio Pena, Carlos Mendi, Tomas Pico, Nando Angelini. In 1864 French troops accidentally cross into Confederate territory in Texas and are forced to join the rebels at a fort besieged by Indians. Mediocre Spanish-made and poorly dubbed oater; Broderick Crawford is lethargic as the Confederate fort commander.

2194 Mutiny in the Arctic. Universal, 1941. 64 minutes B/W. D: John Rawlins. SC: Maurice Tombragel & Victor McLeod. WITH Richard Arlen, Andy Devine, Anne Nagel, Don Terry, Addison Richards, Oscar O'Shea, Harry Cording. Two Explorers searching for a pitchblende mountain in the Arctic are betrayed by the man financing the venture and they end up stranded on an iceberg. Fair programmer in the Richard Arlen-Andy Devine series.

2195 Mutiny on the Blackhawk. Universal, 1939. 66 minutes B/W. D: Christy Cabanne. SC: Michael L. Simmons. WITH Richard Arlen, Andy Devine, Constance Moore, Noah Beery, Guinn Williams, Mala, Thurston Hall, Sandra Kane, Paul Fix,

Richard Lane, Mabel Albertson, Charles Trowbridge, Bill Moore, Byron Foulger, Francisco Maran, Eddy Waller, Mamo Clark. In 1840 a naval investigator looks into slave running between California and the Sandwich Islands and later the Mexican government tries to wipe out American settlers in California. Two stories in one film highlight this programmer, the first of the series with Richard Arlen and Andy Devine.

2196 My Darling Clementine. 20th Century-Fox, 1946. 97 minutes B/W. D: John Ford. SC: Samuel G. Engel & Winston Miller. WITH Henry Fonda, Linda Darnell, Victor Mature, Walter Brennan, Tim Holt, Ward Bond, Cathy Downs, Alan Mowbray, John Ireland, Grant Withers, Roy Roberts, Jane Darwell, Russell Simpson, Francis Ford, J. Farrell MacDonald, Don Garner, Ben Hall, Arthur Walsh, Jack Pennick, Louis Mercier, Mickey Simpson, Fred Libby, Harry Woods, Charles Stevens, Mae Marsh, Hank Bell. Wyatt Earp and Doc Holliday go after the Clantons when the latter steal the Earp's cattle and murder the youngest Earp brother. Pictorially interesting but historically inaccurate recounting of the events leading up to the gunfight at the O. K. Corral; mainly for John Ford buffs.

2197 My Friend Flicka. 20th Century-Fox, 1943. 89 minutes Color. D: Harold Shumate. SC: Lillie Hayward & Frances Edwards Faragoh. WITH Preston Foster, Rita Johnson, Roddy McDowall, James Bell, Jeff Corey, Diana Hale, Arthur Loft, Jimmie Aubrey. Against his father's will, a young boy sets out to tame the wild horse he has grown to love. Nicely done family film which was the basis for the popular television series of the late 1950s and early 1960s. Sequel: **Thunderhead, Son of Flicka** (q.v.).

2198 My Little Chickadee. Universal, 1940. 83 minutes B/W. D: Edward Cline. SC: Mae West & W. C. Fields. WITH Mae West, W. C. Fields, Joseph Calleia, Dick Foran, Margaret Hamilton, George Moran, Si Jenks, James Conlin, Gene Austin, Candy & Coco (Russell "Candy" Hall & Otto "Coco" Heimel), Fuzzy Knight, Ann Nagel, Ruth Donnelly, Donald Meek, Willard Robertson, William B. Davidson, Addison Richards, Jackie Searle, Fay Adler, Jan Duggan, Morgan Wallace, Wade Boteler, Harlan Briggs, Eddie Butler, Bing Conley, John Kelly, Walter McGrail, Otto Hoffman, Billy Benedict, Delmar

Watson, Chester Gan, George Melford, Lita Chevret, Bob McKenzie, James Morton, Joe Whitehead, Lloyd Ingraham, Dick Rush, Hank Bell, Lane Chandler, Alan Bridge, Edward Hearn. Thrown out of town by snobs, a beautiful woman meets a con man and pretends to marry him in order to get social acceptance. The classic teaming of Mae West and W. C. Fields is hardly a classic comedy but it is a pleasant affair which has delighted audiences for nearly four decades and is well worth viewing.

2199 My Name Is Nobody. Universal, 1974. 115 minutes Color. D: Tonino Valerii. SC: Ernesto Gastaldi. WITH Terence Hill, Henry Fonda, Jean Martin, Piero Lulli, Leo Gordon, R. G. Armstrong, Neil Summers, Steve Kanaly, Geoffrey Lewis. In 1899 an aging gunman heads to New Orleans to retire but comes across a younger gunslinger who soon makes the man his idol. Pleasant take-off of the genre.

2200 My Name Is Pecos. Golden Era, 1968. 83 minutes Color. D: Maurizio Lucidi. WITH Robert Woods, Peter Carsten, Lucia Modugno, Norman Karlk, Cristina Josani, Max Deal. A man sets out to take revenge on the outlaws who murdered his family, the gang now in control of a small town. Violent and bloody spaghetti oater. Issued in Italy in 1966 as **Il Mio Nome E Pecos.**

2201 My Outlaw Brother. Eagle Lion, 1951. 78 minutes B/W. D: Elliott Nugent. SC: Gene Fowler Jr. & Albert L. Levitt. WITH Mickey Rooney, Wanda Hendrix, Robert Preston, Robert Stack, Carlos Muzquiz, Jose Torvay, Fernando Waggner. A young man finds out his brother is an outlaw and he joins the Texas Rangers to fight lawlessness. More than passable actioner based on Max Brand's "South of the Rio Grande."

2202 My Pal the King. Universal, 1932. 63 minutes B/W. D: Kurt Neumann. SC: Jack Natteford & Tom J. Crizer. WITH Tom Mix, Finia Barton, Stuart Holmes, Mickey Rooney, Paul Hurst, Noel Francis, James Kirkwood, Jim Thorpe, Christian Frank, Clarissa Selwynne, Ferdinand Schumann-Heink, Wallis Clark. A cowboy takes his frontier show into a kingdom where plotters are trying to take the throne from a boy king. A different kind of Tom Mix film but one that is well done and quite entertaining.

2203 My Pal Trigger. Republic, 1946. 54 (79) minutes B/W. D: Frank McDonald. SC: Jack Townley & John K. Butler. WITH Roy Rogers, George "Gabby" Hayes, Dale Evans, Jack Holt, Bob Nolan & The Sons of the Pioneers, LeRoy Mason, Roy Barcroft, Sam Flint, Kenne Duncan, Ralph Sanford, Francis McDonald, Harlan Briggs, William Haade, Alan Bridge, Paul E. Burns, Frank Reicher, Fred Graham, Ted Mapes, Tom London, Earle Hodgins. Singing star Roy Rogers comes to the aid of a rancher about to lose his ranch to a crooked rival and ends up in jail on a framed charge and almost loses Trigger. Good Roy Rogers vehicle although Jack Holt steals the show as the dishonest rancher; remade as the Rex Allen vehicle **Rodeo King and the Senorita** (q.v.).

2204 My Side of the Mountain. Paramount, 1969. 100 minutes Color. D: James B. Clark. SC: Ted Sherdeman, Jane Klove & Joanna Crawford. WITH Tommy Eccles, Theodore Bikel, Tudi Wiggins, Frank Perry, Peggi Boder, Gina Dick, Karen Pearson. A boy decides to emulate his hero Thoreau and live close to nature after his father reneges on a promised camping trip. This drama, filmed in Canada, will be especially good for family viewing.

2205 My Uncle Antoine. Gendon/Janus Films, 1972. 110 minutes Color. D: Claude Jutra. SC: Clement Perron & Claude Jutra. WITH Jean Duceppe, Lynde Champagne, Olivette Thibault, Claude Jutra, Jacques Gagnon, Lionel Villeneuve, Helene Loiselle, Mario Dubuc, Lise Brunelle, Alain Legendre, Serge Evers, Robin Marcous, Monique Mercure, Georges Alexander, Rene Aslvatore Catta, Jean Dubost, Benoit Marcoux, Dominique Joly, Lisa Talbot, Michel Talbot, Simeon Dallaire, Sydney Harris, Roger Garand. A teenage boy learns about growing up as he works as a stock boy in his uncle's store in a small backwoods Canadian mining town. Leisurely paced and pleasant Canadian feature.

2206 The Mysterious Avenger. Columbia, 1936. 60 minutes B/W. D: David Selman. SC: Ford Beebe. WITH Charles Starrett, Joan Perry, Wheeler Oakman, Ed LeSaint, Lafe McKee, Hal Price, Charles Lochner (Jon Hall), George Chesebro, Jack Rockwell, Edmund Cobb, Richard Botiller, The Sons of the Pioneers. A Texas Ranger returns home to help end a feud between his father and another rancher which

has been caused by a mysterious rustling operation. Very sturdy Charles Starrett vehicle.

2207 The Mysterious Desperado. RKO Radio, 1949. 61 minutes B/W. D: Lesley Selander. SC: Norman Houston. WITH Tim Holt, Richard Martin, Movita, Robert Livingston, Edward Norris, Frank Wilcox, William Tannen, Robert B. Williams, Kenneth MacDonald, Frank Lackteen. Crooks want land recently inherited by a young man and they try to frame him on a false charge so he will lose the ownership. Better than average Tim Holt vehicle.

2208 The Mysterious Rider. Paramount, 1933. 61 minutes B/W. D: Fred Allen. SC: Harvey Gates & Robert Niles. WITH Kent Taylor, Lona Andre, Gail Patrick, Warren Hymer, Berton Churchill, Irving Pichel, Cora Sue Collins, E. H. Calvert, Sherwood Bailey, Niles Welch, Clarence Wilson. A young cowboy takes on the guise of a hooded rider to protect area ranchers from outlaws. Kent Taylor is good in the lead, aided by a fine supporting cast, but this "B" affair has little to do with the Zane Grey work on which it was supposed to be based. Remade in 1938 (q.v.).

2209 The Mysterious Rider. Paramount, 1938. 78 minutes B/W. D: Lesley Selander. SC: Maurice Geraghty. WITH Douglass Dumbrille, Sidney Toler, Russell Hayden, Charlotte Fields, Weldon Heyburn, Monte Blue, Stanley Andrews, Earl Dwire, Glenn Strange, Jack Rockwell, Leo McMahon, Ben Corbett, Ed Brady, Robert Kortman, Richard Alexander, Arch Hall, Price Mitchell. A drifter rides into an area plagued by outlaw raids and becomes a masked avenger aiding the ranchers. Like its predecessor this film bears little resemblance to the Zane Grey book but it is a corker of a good movie, anyway.

2210 The Mysterious Rider. Producers Releasing Corporation, 1942. 57 minutes B/W. D: Sam Newfield, SC: Steve Braxton, WITH Buster Crabbe, Al St. John, Caroline Burke, John Merton, Edwin Brien, Jack Ingram, Slim Whitaker, Kermit Maynard, Ted Adams, Guy Wilkerson, Frank Ellis. Two children are being cheated out of a mine left to them and Billy the Kid comes to their rescue. Typically fast moving entry in Buster Crabbe's starring series at PRC; also typically cheap looking. Reissued in 1947 by Eagle-Lion in a re-edited 39 minute version called **Panhandle Trail.**

2211 Mystery Brand. Rayart, 1927. 50 minutes B/W. D: Ben Wilson. WITH Ben Wilson, Neva Gerber, Al Ferguson, Ted Henderson, Lafe McKee. A representative from the Cattlemen's Association ends up on the trail of a gang of horse thieves. Nothing to brag about, but this silent effort lets the viewer see the popular serial team of Ben Wilson and Neva Gerber in one of their many oaters. Alternate title: **Lariats' End.**

2212 Mystery Man. United Artists, 1944. 54 (58) minutes B/W. D: George Archainbaud. SC: J. Benton Cheney. WITH William Boyd, Andy Clyde, Jimmy Rogers, Don Costello, Francis McDonald, Forrest Taylor, Eleanor Stewart, Jack Rockwell, Pierce Lyden, John Merton, Bob Burns, Ozie Waters, Art Mix, George Morrell, Bob Baker, Hank Bell, Bill Hunter. Hopalong Cassidy, California Carlson and Jimmy Rogers find themselves at odds with a gang of robbers led by a man pretending to be a respectable citizen. Rather dull series entry with an exciting climax.

2213 Mystery Mountain. Mascot, 1934. 12 Chapters B/W. D: B. Reeves Eason & Otto Brower. SC: Bennett Cohen & Armand L. Schaefer. WITH Ken Maynard, Verna Hillie, Edward Earle, Edmund Cobb, Lynton Brent, Syd Saylor, Carmencita Johnson, Lafe McKee, Alan Bridge, Edward Hearn, Robert Kortman, Wally Wales, Tom London, George Chesebro, Philo McCullough, Frank Ellis, Steve Clark, Gene Autry, Smiley Burnette, Jim Mason, Lew Meehan, Jack Rockwell, Art Mix, William Gould, Curley Dresden, Hooper Atchley, Cliff Lyons. A railroad detective is on the trail of a mysterious figure called "The Rattler" who is trying to sabotage a railroad. Fun Mascot cliffhanger with a good mystery element to heighten the suspense. V: Cassette Express.

2214 The Mystery of Chalk Hill. NBC-TV/Universal, 1973. 98 minutes Color. WITH Richard Boone, Sharon Acker, Bruce Davison, Robert Fuller, Louise Latham, Pat Hingle, John Anderson, Henry Jones, Jeanette Nolan, Lee Paul, Bernie Hamilton, Rick Lenz. Ex-gunman turned detective Hec Ramsey wants to find the killer of a lawman's bride-to-be and her young son. More than competent mystery-Western telefilm first shown as an episode of the "Hec Ramsey" (NBC-TV, 1972-74) television series.

The Mystery of the Golden Eye see **The Golden Eye**

2215 The Mystery of the Green Feather. NBC-TV/Universal, 1972. 98 minutes Color. WITH Richard Boone, Rory Calhoun, Marie Windsor, Lorraine Gary, Alan Hewitt, Morgan Woodward, Lloyd Bochner, Rick Lenz. Indians are blamed for massacring a family after a second medicine bag is found at the scene but detective Hec Ramsey does not believe the Indians are guilty of the crime and tries to prove his belief. Entertaining film which was originally shown as "The Green Feather Mystery," an episode of the "Hec Ramsey" (NBC-TV, 1972-74) television series.

2216 Mystery of the Hooded Horsemen. Grand National, 1937. 60 minutes B/W. D: Ray Taylor. SC: Edmund Kelso. WITH Tex Ritter, Iris Meredith, Horace Murphy, Charles King, Forrest Taylor, Earl Dwire, Joe Girard, Lafe McKee, Heber Snow (Hank Worden), Oscar Gahan, Jack C. Smith, Chich Hannon, Tex Palmer, Lynton Brent, Ray Whitley & His Range Ramblers. A group of hooded horsemen kill a man for his mine and a cowpoke and his pal try to find out who is behind the gang. Well done Tex Ritter film with a nice mystery element and a trio of good songs, including "Ride, Ride, Ride" and "Ridin' Old Paint."

2217 Mystery Ranch. Fox, 1932. 65 minutes B/W. D: David Howard. SC: Al Cohn. WITH George O'Brien, Cecilia Parker, Charles Middleton, Roy Stewart, Charles Stevens, Forrester Harvey, Virginia Herdman, Noble Johnson, Russ Powell. A cowboy attempts to rescue a young girl kidnapped by a vicious rancher. Not one of George O'Brien's better Fox films but Charles Middleton, as always, is a delight as the villain.

2218 Mystery Ranch. Reliable, 1934. 56 minutes B/W. D: Ray Bernard (Bernard B. Ray). SC: Carl Krusada & Rose Gordon. WITH Tom Tyler, Roberta Gale, Jack (Perrin) Gable, Louise Gabo, Frank Hall Crane, Charles King, Jimmie Aubrey, Tom London, Lafe McKee. A mystery writer goes to a ranch where he thwarts all kinds of practical jokes but accidentally becomes involved with crooks who have stolen gold bullion. The light-hearted plot greatly aids this low grade Tom Tyler epic.

2219 Mystery Range. Victory, 1937. 55 minutes B/W. D: Robert Hill. SC:

Basil Dickey. WITH Tom Tyler, Jerry Bergh, Milburn Morante, Lafe McKee, Roger Williams, Richard Alexander, Jim Corey, Slim Whitaker, Steve Clark. A cattleman's protective association agent masquerades as an outlaw to investigate a man who is trying to cheat his niece out of her ranch because the land is wanted by the railroad. Surprisingly good Sam Katzman production with fine work by Lafe McKee as the villainous uncle.

2220 The Mystery Trooper. Syndicate, 1931. 10 Chapters B/W. D: Stuart Paton. SC: Carl Krusada. WITH Buzz Barton, Blanche Mehaffey, Robert Frazer, Al Ferguson, Charles King, William von Brencken, William Bertram, White Cloud (horse). A group of people looking for a lost gold mine are harassed by outlaws, also after the mine, but are protected by a mysterious Mountie. Low grade cliffhanger reissued as **Trail of the Royal Mounted.** V: Cassette Express.

2221 The Mystic Warrior. ABC-TV, 1984. 200 minutes Color. D: Richard T. Heffron. SC: Jeb Rosebrook. WITH Robert Beltran, Nick Ramus, Devon Ericson, Victoria Racimo, Roger Campo, Will Sampson, Ned Romero, Douglas Toby, David Yanez. The story of a Plains Indian tribe in the early 1800s with a young boy destined to grow into a warrior and lead his people. Long, leisurely and probably accurate attempt at receating Indian life on the plains before and during the arrival of the white settlers. Well worth watching.

N

2222 The Naked Dawn. Universal-International, 1955. 82 minutes Color. D: Edgar G. Ulmer. SC: Nina Schneider & Herman Schneider. WITH Arthur Kennedy, Betta St. John, Eugene Iglesias, Roy Engel, Charlita. A bandit robs a train, takes refuge with a Mexican farmer, and schemes to steal the man's pretty wife. Lionized as a classic by Edgar G. Ulmer followers, this film does make good use of color and contains fine performances by Arthur Kennedy (as the bandit) and Betta St. John, but overall it is basically a talky soaper with a few artistic touches.

2223 The Naked Gun. Associated Film Releasing, 1956. 73 minutes B/W. D: Edward (Eddie) Dew. SC: Ron Ormond

& Jack Lewis. WITH Willard Parker, Mara Corday, Barton MacLane, Tom Brown, Chick Chandler, Veda Ann Borg, Timothy Carey, Billy House, Morris Ankrum, Bill Phillips, X Brands, Steve Raines, Rick Vallin, Jim Hayward, Jody McCrea, Tony McCoy, Bill Ward. An insurance agent, attempting to deliver jewels to an estate's heirs, becomes involved with crooks who are after an Aztec treasure. Poor production values hurt this otherwise acceptable drama; director Edward Dew is the Eddie Dew who starred in oaters for Republic and Universal in the 1940s.

2224 The Naked Hills. Allied Artists, 1956. 73 minutes Color. D-SC: Josef Shaftel. WITH David Wayne, Keenan Wynn, James Barton, Jim Backus, Marcia Henderson, Denver Pyle, Myrna Dell, Lewis Russell, Frank Fenton, Fuzzy Knight, Jim Hayward, Steve Terrell. An Indiana farmer deserts his wife and family to prospect for gold in California. More than passable melodrama about gold fever.

2225 Naked in the Sun. Allied Artists, 1957. 88 minutes Color. D: R. John Hugh. SC: John Cresswell. WITH James Craig, Lita Milan, Barton MacLane, Robert Wark, Jim Boles, Tony Hunter, Douglas Wilson, Bill Armstrong, Dennis Cross. The Osceola and Seminole Indian tribes unite to oppose an evil slave trader. Offbeat plot somewhat compensates for mediocre production values.

2226 The Naked Spur. Metro-Goldwyn-Mayer, 1953. 91 minutes Color. D: Anthony Mann. SC: Sam Rolfe & Harold Jack Bloom. WITH James Stewart, Janet Leigh, Robert Ryan, Ralph Meeker, Millard Mitchell. A bounty hunter on the trail of a wanted man plans to use the reward money to buy back land he lost in the Civil War. Relentless chase-type oater with very good work by its compact cast.

2227 Nakia. ABC-TV/Screen Gems/Columbia, 1974. 74 minutes Color. D: Leonard Horn. SC: Christopher Trumbo, Michael Butler & Sy Salkowitz. WITH Robert Forster, Arthur Kennedy, Linda Evans, Stephen McNally, George Nader, Robert Donner, Maria-Elena Cordero, Joe Kapp, Chief George Clutesi, Taylor Lacher, Jay Varella. An Indian deputy sheriff is caught between his tribe's desire to save an historic mission and local citizens wanting to use the spot for a housing

The Narrow 272

development. Fairly interesting television movie which was the pilot for the short-lived 1974 ABC-TV series of the same name.

2228 The Narrow Trail. Paramount-Artcraft, 1917. 55 minutes B/W. D: Lambert Hillyer. SC: Harvey F. Thew. WITH William S. Hart, Sylvia Breamer, Milton Ross, Robert Kortman. An outlaw falls for the niece of a vice king. Later, when he poses as a rich rancher, the man tries to fleece him, but the girl will not go along with the scheme. Well made William S. Hart silent vehicle. V: Classic Video Cinema Collectors Club, Glenn Photo.

2229 Naughty Marietta. Metro-Goldwyn-Mayer, 1935. 106 minutes B/W. D: W. S. Van Dyke. SC: John Lee Mahin, Frances Goodrich & Albert Hackett. WITH Jeanette MacDonald, Nelson Eddy, Frank Morgan, Elsa Lanchester, Douglass Dumbrille, Joseph Cawthorn, Cecilia Parker, Walter Kingsford, Greta Meyer, Akim Tamiroff, Harold Huber, Edward Brophy, Marjorie Main, Mary Doran, Jean Chatburn, Pat Farley, Jane Barnes, Kay English, Linda Parker, Jane Mercer, Walter Long, Olive Carey, William Desmond, Cora Sue Collins, Guy Usher, Louis Mercier, Robert Mc-Kenzie, Ben Hall, Harry Tenbrook, Edward Keane, Edward Norris, Ralph Brooks, Richard Powell, Wilfred Lucas, Arthur Belasco, Tex Driscoll, Edward Hearn, Edmund Cobb, Charles Dunbar, Frank Hagney, Ed Brady, Dr. Edouard Lippe. Fleeing from an unhappy romance in France, a princess arrives in the wilds of Canada where she falls in love with a captain. The first teaming of Jeanette MacDonald and Nelson Eddy is a delightful screen romance filled with good music. V: MGM/United Artists.

2230 Navajo. Lippert, 1951. 70 minutes B/W. D-SC: Norman Foster. WITH Francis Kee Teller, John Mitchell, Billy Draper, Mrs. Teller, Sammy Ogg. A young Navajo Indian boy tries to come to terms with his heritage and modern day life on a reservation. Spendid low budget Hal Bartlett production filmed on location in northern Arizona.

Navajo Coyote see **Birth of a Legend**

2231 Navajo Joe. United Artists, 1967. 89 minutes Color. D: Sergio Corbucci. SC: Mario Pierotti (Dean Craig) & Fernando Di Leo. WITH Burt Reynolds, Aldo Sambrell, Fernando Rey, Nicholetta Machiavelli, Tanya Lopert, Franca Polesello, Lucie Modungo, Pierre Cressoy, Nino Imparato, Alvaro De Luna, Valeria Sabel, Mario Lanfranchi, Lucio Rosator, Simon Arriaga, Chris Huerta, Angel Ortiz, Angel Alvarez, Fianni De Stolfo, Rafael Albaicin. The survivor of a massacre sets out to take revenge on an outlaw gang by systematically killing them one by one. Burt Reynolds fans may be interested in this Italian (and violent) oater but its main asset is a rousing opening music theme by Ennio Morricone. Released in Europe in 1966 as **Un Dollaro a Testa** (A Dollar a Head).

2232 The Navajo Kid. Producers Releasing Corporation, 1945. 59 minutes B/W. D-SC: Harry Fraser. WITH Bob Steele, Syd Saylor, Caren Marsh, Ed Cassidy, Bud Osborne, Henry Hall, Stanley Blystone, Edward Howard, Charles King (Jr.), Budd Buster, Gertrude Glorie, Rex Rossi, Bert Dillard. When his Indian agent foster father is murdered, a young man sets out to find the killer and the identity of his natural father. Fairly good entry in Bob Steele's final starring series. V: Video Connection.

2233 Navajo Run. American-International, 1964. 75 minutes B/W. D: Johnny Seven. SC: Jo Heims. WITH Johnny Seven, Warren Kemmerling, Virginia Vincent, Ron Soble. A young half-breed Navajo is nursed back to health by a frontier family only to be hunted by the mute brother of the girl he loves. Fair low budget actioner.

2234 The Navajo Trail. Monogram, 1945. 60 minutes B/W. D: Howard Bretherton. SC: Jess Bowers (Adele Buffington). WITH Johnny Mack Brown, Raymond Hatton, Jennifer Holt, Riley Hill, Edmund Cobb, Bud Osborne, Charles King, Ray Bennett, Ed Cassidy, Tom Quinn, John Carpenter. When a fellow Texas Ranger is murdered, two rangers try to find his killer. One of them infiltrates a gang out to steal horses belonging to an Indian tribe. Good entry in Johnny Mack Brown's Monogram series.

2235 Navajo Trail Raiders. Republic, 1949. 60 minutes B/W. D: R. G. Springsteen. SC: M. Coates Webster. WITH Allan "Rocky" Lane, Eddy Waller, Barbara Bestar, Robert Emmett Keane, Hal Landon, Dick Curtis, Dennis Moore, Ted Adams, Forrest Taylor, Marshall Reed, Steve Clark, Chick Hannon. A cowboy comes to the aid of some friends being harassed by a band of outlaws. Fast moving film in Allan Lane's Republic series.

2236 Near the Rainbow's End. Tiffany, 1930. 60 minutes B/W. D: J. P. McGowan. SC: Sally Winters & Charles A. Post. WITH Bob Steele, Louise Lorraine, Al Ferguson, Lafe McKee, Alfred Hewston. A rancher and his son fence off their range to prevent cattle thefts. When a sheepman is murdered, the son is blamed. Bob Steele's first talkie is pleasant.

2237 Near the Trail's End. Monogram, 1931. 55 minutes B/W. D: Wallace Fox. SC: G. A. Durlam. WITH Bob Steele, Marion Shockey, Hooper Atchley, Si Jenks, Jay Morley, Murdock McQuarrie, Henry Rocquemore, Fred Burns, Artie Ortego. When a girl witnesses two murders by crooks, a cowboy aids her in finding the culprits. Fair Bob Steele early talkie.

2238 'Neath Arizona Skies. Monogram, 1934. 54 minutes B/W. D: Harry Fraser. SC: B. R. (Burl) Tuttle. WITH John Wayne, Sheila Terry, Shirley Ricketts (Shirley Jane Rickert), Jack Rockwell, Yakima Canutt, Weston Edwards, George ("Gabby") Hayes, Buffalo Bill Jr., Phil Keefer, Frank Hall Crane, Earl Dwire, Artie Ortego, Tex Phelps, Eddie Parker. A young man is the guardian of a small Indian girl who is the heir to oil lands. When outlaws kidnap her, the man comes to her rescue and ends up being mistaken for a bandit. Shoddy production values hurt this otherwise interesting effort in John Wayne's Lone Star series.

2239 'Neath Canadian Skies. Screen Guild, 1946. 41 minutes B/W. D: B. Reeves Eason. SC: Arthur V. Jones. WITH Russell Hayden, Inez Cooper, Douglas Fowley, I. Stanford Jolley, Jack Mulhall, Cliff Nazarro, Richard Alexander, Kermit Maynard, Boyd Stockman, Jimmie Martin, Gil Patrick, Pat Hurst. In the 1890s a Mountie tries to stop claim jumpers in a recently inhabited area. Okay compact melodrama with nice scenic values and a good cast.

2240 'Neath Western Skies. Syndicate, 1930. 60 minutes B/W. D: J. P. McGowan. SC: Sally Winters. WITH Tom Tyler, Lotus Thompson, J. P. McGowan, Harry Woods, Hank Bell, Bobby Dunn, Alfred Hewston, Barney Furey. An outlaw gang tries to sabotage an oil driller's operations and even kidnap his girlfriend. Early Tom Tyler outdoor talkie which should please his fans.

2241 The Nebraskan. Columbia, 1953. 68 minutes Color. D: Fred F. Sears. SC:

David Lang & Martin Berkeley. WITH Phil(ip) Carey, Roberta Haynes, Wallace Ford, Richard Webb, Lee Van Cleef, Maurice Jara, Regis Toomey, Jay Silverheels, Pat Hogan, Dennis Weaver, Boyd "Red" Morgan. An Indian scout is falsely accused of murder and the accusation almost sets off a war. Cheaply made oater originally issued in 3-D.

2242 Ned Kelly. United Artists, 1970. 103 minutes Color. D: Tony Richardson. SC: Tony Richardson & Neil Hartley. WITH Mick Jagger, Allen Bickford, Geoff Gilmour, Mark McManus, Serge Lazareff, Peter Sumner, Ken Shorter, James Elliott, Clarissa Kaye, Diane Craig, Susan Lloyd, Bruce Barry, Janne Wesley, Ken Goodlet, Nigel Lovell, John Gray, Anne Harvey, Frank Thring, Gordon McDougall. The story of the notorious 1870s Australian outlaw Ned Kelly. Worth watching if you are a fan of Mick Jagger; music by Mick Jagger and Waylon Jennings.

2243 Neeka. Wrather Corporation, 1968. 100 minutes Color. WITH Lassie, Jed Allan, Robert Rockwell, Mark Miranda, Jeff Pomerantz, Philip Pine, Douglas Henderson. Lassie and her Forest Ranger master head to Alaska to search for a deranged hunter and soon meet with an adopted Indian boy and his father. Okay family fare filmed in Alaska and made up of four segments of the "Lassie" (CBS-TV, 1954-71) TV series.

2244 Nevada. Paramount, 1927. 75 minutes B/W. D: John Waters. SC: John Stone & L. G. Rigby. WITH Gary Cooper, Thelma Todd, William Powell, Philip Strange, Ernie Adams, Christian Frank, Ivan Christy, Guy Oliver. Two outlaws try to go straight but get mixed up with cattle rustlers. Interesting silent version of the Zane Grey work with the teaming of Gary Cooper and William Powell as the two good-bad guys. Remade in 1935 (q.v.).

2245 Nevada. Paramount, 1935. 70 minutes B/W. D: Charles Barton. SC: Garnett Weston & Stuart Anthony. WITH Larry "Buster" Crabbe, Kathleen Burke, Syd Saylor, Monte Blue, William Duncan, Richard Carle, Stanley Andrews, Frank Sheridan, Raymond Hatton, Glenn (Leif) Erickson, Jack Kennedy, Henry Roquemore, William Desmond, Frank Rice, Barney Furey, William L. Thorne. A gunman and his pal become cowboys on an Englishman's ranch but due to their pasts they get mixed up with outlaws. Programmer remake of the Zane Grey novel with good work by Buster Crabbe as the reformed gunslinger.

2246 Nevada. RKO Radio, 1944. 62 minutes B/W. D: Edward Killy. SC: Norman Houston. WITH Robert Mitchum, Anne Jeffreys, Guinn Williams, Nancy Gates, Richard Martin, Craig Reynolds, Harry Woods, Russell Hopton, Edmund Glover, Alan Ward, Harry McKim, Larry Wheat, Jack Overman, Emmett Lynn, Wheaton Chambers, Philip Morris, Mary Halsey, Patti Brill, Bryant Washburn, Bert Moorehouse, George DeNormand. A young man is nearly lynched for a murder he did not commit and sets out to prove that a gang of claim jumpers are the real culprits. Robert Mitchum is quite good in the title role of this "B" outing based on Zane Grey's novel; a good film.

Nevada (1971) see **The Boldest Job in the West.**

2247 Nevada Badmen. Monogram, 1951. 58 minutes B/W. D: Lewis D. Collins. SC: Joseph O'Donnell. WITH Whip Wilson, Fuzzy Knight, Phyllis Coates, Jim Bannon, I. Stanford Jolley, Kenne Duncan, Bill Kennedy, Marshall Reed, Riley Hill, Lee Roberts, Pierce Lyden, Bud Osborne. Three cattlemen try to find out who murdered the brother of one of them for his hidden gold claim. A good plot helps this otherwise mediocre Whip Wilson vehicle.

2248 Nevada Buckaroo. Tiffany, 1931. 59 minutes B/W. D: John P. McCarthy. SC: Welly Totman. WITH Bob Steele, Dorothy Dix, George ("Gabby") Hayes, Ed Brady, Glen Cavendar, Billy Engle, Artie Ortego. Once on the wrong side of the law, a man changes his ways for a girl but runs into trouble when his old gang murders his sidekick. Well written and fast paced Bob Steele film.

2249 Nevada City. Republic, 1941. 54 (58) minutes B/W. D: Joseph Kane. SC: James R. Webb. WITH Roy Rogers, George "Gabby" Hayes, Sally Payne, Fred Kohler Jr., George Cleveland, Pierre Watkin, Yakima Canutt, Rex Lease, Art Mix, Jack Ingram, Syd Saylor, Hank Bell, Henry Wills, Bob Woodward, Jack Kirk, Fred Burns. When a crooked businessman tries to control freight traffic to California, Roy Rogers tries to stop him. Fast moving and entertaining Roy Rogers series entry.

2250 Nevada Smith. Paramount, 1966. 120 minutes Color. D: Henry Hathaway. SC: John Michael Hayes. WITH Steve McQueen, Karl Malden, Suzanne Pleshette, Brian Keith, Arthur Kennedy, Raf Vallone, Janet Margolin, Howard Da Silva, Pat Hingle, Martin Landau, Paul Fix, Gene Evans, Josephine Hutchinson, John Doucette, Val Avery, Lyle Bettger, Bert Freed, David McLean, Ric Roman, John Litel, Ted De Corsia, Stanley Adams, George Mitchell, Sheldon Allman. A young man seeks revenge on the trio of outlaws who brutally murdered his parents. Well acted and produced melodrama which was a followup to Harold Robbins' **The Carpetbaggers** (Paramount, 1964).

2251 Nevada Smith. NBC-TV/Metro-Goldwyn-Mayer, 1975. 74 minutes Color. D: Gordon Douglas. SC: Martin Rackin & John Michael Hayes. WITH Cliff Potts, Lorne Greene, Adam West, Warren Vanders, Jorge Luke, Jerry Gatlin, Eric Cord, Lorraine Chanel, John McKee, Alan George, Roger Cudney. Two old friends, a half-breed cowboy and his former teacher, band together to carry a shipment of explosives. Telefeature based on the 1966 feature film is only so-so and served as the pilot for an unsold TV series.

2252 The Nevadan. Columbia, 1950. 81 minutes Color. D: Gordon Douglas. SC: George W. George & George P. Slavin. WITH Randolph Scott, Dorothy Malone, Forrest Tucker, Frank Faylen, George Macready, Charles Kemper, Jeff Corey, Tom Powers, Jack O'Mahoney (Jock Mahoney), Stanley Andrews, James Kirkwood, Kate Drain Lawson, Olin Howlin (Howland), Louis Mason. A government agent works undercover with an outlaw to retrieve gold, stolen by the latter, which is now held by a gang. Another good feature starring Randolph Scott with plenty of action coupled with an entertaining story.

2253 Never Cry Wolf. Buena Vista, 1983. 105 minutes Color. D: Carroll Ballard. SC: Curtis Hanson, Sam Hamm & Richard Kletter. WITH Charles Martin Smith, Brian Dennehy, Zachary Ittimangnaq, Samson Jorah, Hugh Webster, Martha Ittimangnaq, Tom Dahlgren, Walker Stuart; C. M. Smith, Eugene Corr, Christina Luescher (narrators). A young biologist learns to survive in the Arctic while studying the habits of the white wolf to see if they are responsible for the disappearance of caribou herds. Location shooting, a good story and fine work by Charles Martin Smith as the biologist make this good entertainment.

Never Give an Inch see **Sometimes a Great Notion**

2254 The New Daughters of Joshua Cabe. ABC-TV, 1976. 74 minutes Color. D: Bruce Bilson. SC: Paul Savage. WITH John McIntire, Jack Elam, Jeanette Nolan, John Dehner, Liberty Williams, Renne Jarrett, Lezlie Dalton, Geoffrey Lewis, Sean McClory, Joel Fabiani, Ford Rainey, Larry Hovis, James Lydon, Randall Carver. When a sheriff is falsely jailed on a murder charge, a trio of girls, who he previously palmed off as his daughters, come to his rescue. Anemic telefeature which followed two previous efforts: **The Daughters of Joshua Cabe** and **The Daughters of Joshua Cabe Return** (qq.v.).

2255 The New Frontier. Republic, 1935. 55 minutes B/W. D: Carl L. Pierson. SC: Robert Emmett (Tansey). WITH John Wayne, Muriel Evans, Warner Richmond, Alan Bridge, Murdock McQuarrie, Alan Cavan, Sam Flint, Mary MacLaren, Glenn Strange, Earl Dwire, Hooper Atchley, Jack Kirk, Frank Ball, Sherry Tansey. A young man finds that his sheriff-father has been murdered by a crooked saloon owner and he enlists the aid of a bandit gang in opposing the murderer and his followers. Very good early John Wayne film with a terrificly staged shootout finale.

2256 The New Frontier. Republic, 1939. 57 minutes B/W. D: George Sherman. SC: Betty Burbridge & Luci Ward. WITH John Wayne, Ray Corrigan, Raymond Hatton, Phyllis Isley (Jennifer Jones), Eddy Waller, Sammy McKim, LeRoy Mason, Harrison Greene, Reginald Barlow, Burr Caruth, Dave O'Brien, Hal Price, Jack Ingram, Bud Osborne, Slim Whitaker. The Three Mesquiteers convince settlers to move to new lands only to find they are getting worthless range but crooked land speculators capture them. John Wayne's last entry in "The Three Mesquiteers" series and this one is not up to par with earlier entries. TV title: **Frontier Horizon.** V: NTA Home Entertainment.

2257 The New Land. Warner Brothers, 1973. 161 minutes Color. D: Jan Troell. SC: Bengi Forslund & Jan Troell. WITH Max von Sydow, Liv Ullman, Eddie Axberg, Hans Alfredson, Halvar Bjork, Allan Edwall, Peter Lindgren, Oscar Ljung. The story of a Swedish immigrant, his wife and brother and their settlement in the 1850s in Minnesota and the hardships they face. Somewhat overlong but interesting followup to Jan Troell's earlier **The Emigrants** (Warner Brothers, 1971); well worth viewing.

2258 The New Maverick. ABC-TV/Warner Brothers, 1978. 100 minutes Color. D: Hy Averback. SC: Juanita Bartlett. WITH James Garner, Jack Kelly, Charles Frank, Susan Blanchard, Eugene Roche, Susan Sullivan, George Loros, Woodrow Parfrey, Gary Allen, Henel Paige Camp, Jack Garner, Graham Jarvis. The British nephew of the notorious Maverick brothers enlists the aid of his famous uncles in a series of misadventures. Watchable TV feature recreation of the popular "Maverick" (ABC-TV, 1957-62) series which, in turn, served as the pilot for the brief "Young Maverick" (CBS-TV, 1979-80) series.

2259 New Mexico. United Artists, 1951. 78 minutes Color. D: Irving Reis. SC: Max Trell. WITH Lew Ayres, Marilyn Maxwell, Andy Devine, Robert Hutton, Raymond Burr, Jeff Corey, Lloyd Corrigan, Verna Felton, Ted de Corsia, John Hoyt, Donald Buka, Robert Osterloh, Ian MacDonald, William Tannen. A captain in the U. S. cavalry tries to prevent warfare in New Mexico with Indians led by Acoma. Mundane plotline is given a good shot in the arm by fine production values and a good cast.

2260 New Moon. Metro-Goldwyn-Mayer, 1940. 105 minutes B/W. D: Robert Z. Leonard. SC: Jacquel Deval & Robert Arthur. WITH Jeanette MacDonald, Nelson Eddy, Mary Boland, George Zucco, H. B. Warner, Grant Mitchell, Stanley Fields, Dick Purcell, John Miljan, Ivan Simpson, William Tannen, Bunty Cutler, Claude King, Cecil Cunningham, Joe Yule, George Irving, Robert Warwick, Hillary Brooke, Rafael Storm, Winifred Harris. During the reign of King Louis XVI a young woman arrives in New Orleans to look over property she has inherited and falls in love with a French political fugitive who is a bondsman. Nice teaming of Jeanette MacDonald and Nelson Eddy with a good Sigmund Romberg score as added dressing for this period piece. The 1930 MGM version, called **Parisian Belle** on TV, with Grace Moore and Lawrence Tibbett, is set in Russia and not frontier Louisiana.

2261 The Night Cry. Warner Brothers, 1926. 55 minutes B/W. D: Herman C. Raymaker. SC: Ewart Adamson, Paul Klein & Edward Meagher. WITH Rin Tin Tin, John Harron, June Marlowe, Gayne Whitman, Heinie Conklin, Don Alvarado, Mary Louise Miller. A dog is unjustly accused of killing sheep when the real culprit is a giant condor who steals his master's baby and the dog sets out to rescue her. Top notch Rin Tin Tin silent actioner.

2262 Night Games. NBC-TV/Paramount, 1974. 74 minutes Color. D: Don Taylor. SC: E. Jack Neumann. WITH Barry Newman, Susan Howard, Stefanie Powers, Anjanette Comer, Joanna Cameron, Albert Salmi, Luke Askew, Jon Cypher, Henry Darrow, Ralph Meeker, William Prince, Dennis Patrick, Robert Emhardt, William Hanson, Larry Thor. A lawyer in a small modern-day Arizona cattle town defends a young, socially prominent woman accused of killing her husband. Fair telefilm which served as the pilot for the "Petrocelli" (NBC-TV, 1974-76) series.

2263 The Night Hawk. W. W. Hodkinson, 1924. 60 minutes B/W. D: Stuart Paton. SC: Joseph Poland. WITH Harry Carey, Claire Adams, Joseph Girard, Fred Malatesta, Nicholas De Ruiz, Lee Shumway, Myles McCarthy, Fred Kelsey. Hired to murder a sheriff in the West, a New York City crook arrives on the scene only to fall in love with the lawman's daughter. Sturdy Harry Carey silent film.

The Night of the Desperado see **Ringo's Big Night**

2264 The Night of the Grizzly. Paramount, 1966. 102 minutes Color. D: Joseph Pevney. SC: Warren Douglas. WITH Clint Walker, Martha Hyer, Keenan Wynn, Nancy Kulp, Kevin Brodie, Ellen Corby, Jack Elam, Ron Ely, Ned Florey, Leo Gordon, Don Haggerty, Sammy Jackson, Victoria Paige Meyerink, Candy Moore, Regis Toomey. Trying to settle down to ranching in Wyoming in the 1880s, a former lawman finds himself up against unexpected bills, former foes and a killer grizzly. Well made action melodrama enhanced by a fine cast.

2265 Night Passage. Universal, 1957. 90 minutes Color. D: James Neilson. SC: Borden Chase. WITH James Stewart, Audie Murphy, Dan Duryea, Dianne Foster, Elaine Stewart, Branden de Wilde, Jay C. Flippen, Herbert Anderson, Robert Wilke, Hugh Beaumont, Jack Elam, Tommy Cook, Paul Fix, Olive Carey, James Flavin, Donald Curtis, Ellen Corby, Ted Mapes, Patsy Novak, Chuck Roberson. A railroad troubleshooter finds that an outlaw gang, to which his younger brother belongs, plans to rob the train of its payroll shipment. Expansive and exceedingly well done entertainment, with Dan Duryea especially good as the gang leader, Whitey Harbin.

2266 Night Raiders. Monogram, 1952. 52 minutes B/W. D: Howard Bretherton. SC: Maurice Tombragel. WITH Whip Wilson, Fuzzy Knight, Lois Hall, Tommy Farrell, Terry Frost, Marshall Reed, Lane Bradford, Steve Clark, Boyd Stockman, Forrest Taylor, Iron Eyes Cody, Carol Henry, Ed Cassidy, Roy Butler, Stanley Price. Two lawmen investigate the mysterious raids on ranches in which nothing is stolen. The mystery angle greatly helps this otherwise pedestrian Whip Wilson vehicle.

2267 Night Rider. Artclass, 1932. 54 minutes B/W. D: William Nigh. SC: Harry (Fraser) P. Crist. WITH Harry Carey, Eleanor Fair, George ("Gabby") Hayes, Robert Kortman, Walter Shumway, Julian Rivero, Jack Weatherby. A lawman takes on the guise of a gunman to stop a murderous outlaw gang. Defective production values hurt this otherwise entertaining Harry Carey vehicle.

2268 The Night Rider. ABC-TV/Universal, 1979. 78 minutes Color. D: Hy Averback. SC: Stephen J. Cannell. WITH David Selby, Kim Cattrall, Percy Rodrigues, George Grizzard, Harris Yulin, Pernell Roberts, Anthony Herrera, Anna Lee, Michael Sharrett, Hildy Brooks, Curt Lowens, Van Williams, Stuart Nisbet, Gary Allen, Whit Bissell, Edward Knight, Susan Davis, Maria Diane, Sydney Penny. When crooks kill his family for its silver mine a New Orleans gentleman turns masked avenger. Passable TV movie.

2269 The Night Riders. Republic, 1939. 56 minutes B/W. D: George Sherman. SC: Betty Burbridge & Stanley Roberts. WITH John Wayne, Ray Corrigan, Max Terhune, Doreen McKay, Ruth Rogers, George Douglas, Tom Tyler, Kermit Maynard, Sammy McKim, Walter Wills, Ethan Laidlaw, Ed Peil, Tom London, Jack Ingram, William Nestell, Yakima Canutt, Glenn Strange, David Sharpe,

Bud Osborne, Lee Shumway, Cactus Mack, Hal Price, Hank Worden, Roger Williams, Olin Francis, Francis Walker, Hugh Prosser, Jack Kirk. A crook uses a forged land grant to make himself the ruler of thousands of acres of land. When he forces settlers, who cannot pay his high taxes, off their properties he is opposed by The Three Mesquiteers. Fast paced and entertaining.

2270 Night Riders. Alameda, 1963. 76 minutes Color. D: Fernando Menez. SC: Ramon Obon. WITH Gaston Santos, Alma Rosa Aguirre, Pedro D'Aguillon, Quentin Bulnes, Guillermo Alvarez, Jose Chavez. A gang of masked night riders terrorize a small town and a government agent, backed by the cavalry, comes to the rescue. Actionful Mexican Western made in that country in 1958 as **Los Diablos de los Terror.**

2271 Night Riders of Montana. Republic, 1951. 60 minutes B/W. D: Fred C. Brannon. SC: M. Coates Webster. WITH Allan "Rocky" Lane, Claudia Barrett, Roy Barcroft, Chubby Johnson, Arthur Space, Myron Healey, Mort Thompson, Marshall Reed, Lane Bradford, Lester Dorr, Ted Adams, George Chesebro, Don C. Harvey, Zon Murray. An outlaw gang plagues ranchers and a ranger working for the state comes to their rescue. Another good actionful outing in the Allan Lane-Republic series.

2272 Night Stage to Galveston. Republic, 1952. 60 minutes B/W. D: George Archainbaud. SC: Norman S. Hall. WITH Gene Autry, Pat Buttram, Virginia Houston, Thurston Hall, Judy Nugent, Robert Livingston, Harry Cording, Robert Bice, Frank Sully, Clayton Moore, Frank Rawls, Steve Clark, Harry Lauter, Robert Peyton, Lois Austin, Kathleen O'Malley, Riley Hill, Richard Alexander, Boyd Stockman, Bob Woodward, Sandy Sanders, Ben Weldon, Gary Goodwin. Two ex-rangers, now newspapermen, go to work on a story about Texas state police corruption and nearly get killed when they try to save the kidnapped daughter of their publisher from crooked officials. A good story highlights this entertaining Gene Autry vehicle. V: Blackhawk.

2273 Night Time in Nevada. Republic, 1948. 54 (67) minutes Color. D: William Witney. SC: Sloan Nibley. WITH Roy Rogers, Andy Devine, Adele Mara, Grant Withers, Marion Harmon, Joseph Crehan, Holly Bane, Bob Nolan & The Sons of

the Pioneers, George Carleton, Steve Darrell, Hank Patterson, Jim Nolan. To cover up a murder he committed sixteen years ago, a man plans to steal Roy Rogers' and The Sons of the Pioneers' cattle to pay off the dead man's daughter. A good, exciting and well directed Roy Rogers feature dominated by Grant Withers as the bad guy. V: Thunderbird.

2274 Nightwing. Columbia, 1979. 103 minutes Color. D: Arthur Hiller. SC: Steve Shagan, Bud Shrake & Martin Cruz Smith. WITH Nick Mancuso, David Warner, Stephan Macht, Kathryn Harrold, Strother Martin, Ben Piazza, George Clutesi, Donald Hotton, Judith Novgrod, Charles Hallahan, Pat Corley, Alice Hirson, Danny Dapien, Jose Toledo, Charlie Bird, Peter Prouse, Richard Romacito, Flavio Martinez III. A mysterious man arrives in the Arizona desert intent on killing an army of vampire bats carrying disease. Overlong and basically boring horror-Western. V: RCA/Columbia.

2275 Nikki, Wild Dog of the North. Buena Vista, 1961. 74 minutes Color. D: Jack Couffer. SC: Ralph Wright & Winston Hibler. WITH Jean Coutu, Emile Genest, Uriel Luft, Robert Rivard; Jacques Fauteux, Dwight Hauser (narrators), Nikki (dog), Neewa (bear). A young wolf dog and a bear cub, separated from their master, are forced to survive in the wilds. Satisfying adaptation of James Oliver Curwood's novel Nomads of the North.

2276 The Nine Lives of Elfego Baca. Buena Vista, 1960. 80 minutes Color. D: Norman Foster. WITH Robert Loggia, Lisa Montell, Robert F. Simon. A New Mexico lawman defies an 80-man lynch mob in order to protect a prisoner. Issued abroad theatrically, this feature was originally shown as part of Walt Disney's TV series in 1958; good entertainment.

No Man's Land see **No Man's Range**

2277 No Man's Law. Pathe, 1927. 60 minutes B/W. D: Fred Jackman. SC: Frank Butler. WITH Rex (horse), Barbara Kent, Theodore von Eltz, Oliver Hardy, Jimmy Finlayson. Two crooks stumble onto a remote cabin where a young girl and her uncle are protected by a wild stallion. Another silent adventure with Rex the Wonder Horse and a pretty good outing. V: Film Classic Exchange.

2278 No Man's Range. Supreme, 1935. 56 minutes B/W. D: Robert North Bradbury.

SC: Forbes Parkhill. WITH Bob Steele, Roberta Gale, Buck Connors, Steve Clark, Charles K. French, Jack Rockwell, Roger Williams, Earl Dwire, Ed Cassidy, Jim Corey. When outlaws rule the range, a cowboy pretends to be one of them in order to put a stop to their lawlessness. Average entry in Bob Steele's lengthy series for producer A. W. Hackel. Also called **No Man's Land.**

2279 No Name on the Bullet. Universal, 1959. 77 minutes Color. D: Jack Arnold. SC: Gene L. Coon. WITH Audie Murphy, Joan Evans, Charles Drake, R. G. Armstrong, Virginia Grey, Warren Stevens, Whit Bissell, Karl Swenson, Willis Bouchey, Edgar Stehli, Jerry Paris, Charles Watts, Simon Scott, John Alderson. Each of the citizens of a small town feel they may be the intended victim when a hired killer arrives on the scene. Okay action melodrama which will satisfy Audie Murphy fans.

2280 No Room to Die. Junior Films, 1969. 88 minutes Color. D-SC: Sergio Garrone. WITH Antonio De Teffe (Anthony Steffen), William Berger, Nicoletta Machiavelli, Mario Brega, Riccardo Garrone, Mariangela Giordano. A preacher and a bounty hunter join forces to get the reward money on a gang smuggling aliens across the border. Very violent Italian oater, but fairly entertaining. Issued in Italy as **Una Lunga Fila di Croci.**

2281 Nomads of the North. Associated First National, 1920. 50 minutes B/W. D: David M. Hartford. SC: David M. Hartford & James Oliver Curwood. WITH Lewis Stone, Betty Blythe, Lon Chaney, Francis McDonald, Milbourne McDowell, Spottiswoode Aitken. A man in the north country tries to win a girl by making her think her trapper lover is dead and when the rival returns the man tries to stop him. Somewhat overacted but still entertaining silent adaptation of a James Oliver Curwood work (coscripted by Curwood) with well staged storm and forest fire sequences.

2282 Noose for a Gunman. United Artists, 1960. 90 minutes B/W. D: Edward L. Cahn. SC: James B. Gordon. WITH Jim Davis, Lyn Thomas, Ted de Corsia, Walter Sande, Barton MacLane, Harry Carey Jr., Lane Chandler, John Hart, Leo Gordon, William Tannen, Jan Arvan, William Remick, Bob Tetrick, Kermit Maynard, William Challee, Cecil Weston. An honest gunman, banished after killing a corrupt

land baron's two sons, returns to tell the citizens that an outlaw, in cahoots with the land baron, is planning a robbery. Well made programmer with a good performance by Jim Davis as the hero.

2283 North Country. American National Enterprises, 1969. 94 (105) minutes Color. D: Ron Hayes. WITH Jeff Graham. A woodsman makes a life for himself in the remote Alaskan wilderness. Pleasant documentary, filmed on location in Alaska, will appeal to nature lovers.

2284 North from the Lone Star. Columbia, 1941. 58 minutes B/W. D: Lambert Hillyer. SC: Charles Francis Royal. WITH Bill Elliott, Dorothy Fay, Dub Taylor, Richard Fiske, Arthur Loft, Jack Roper, Chuck Morrison, Claire Rochelle, Al Rhein, Edmund Cobb, Steve Clark, Art Mix, Hank Bell, Richard Botiller. A crook takes over the town of Deadwood and makes Wild Bill Hickok its marshall but Hickok sets out to clean up the town. Actionful Bill Elliott vehicle with a well staged saloon fight sequence.

2285 North of Arizona. Reliable, 1935. 60 minutes B/W. D: Harry S. Webb. SC: Carl Krusada. WITH Jack Perrin, Blanche Mehaffey, Lane Chandler, Alan Bridge, Murdock MacQuarrie, George Chesebro, Artie Ortego, Budd Buster, Frank Ellis, Blackie Whiteford, Starlight. A cowboy joins a gang of crooks and pretends to help them although he really wants to stop the gang from cheating Indians of gold ore and shipments. Not bad, with Jack Perrin a likable hero.

2286 North of Nome. Columbia, 1936. 62 minutes B/W. D: William Nigh. SC: Albert DeMond. WITH Jack Holt, Evelyn Venable, Guinn Williams, John Miljan, Roger Imhoff, Dorothy Appleby, Paul Hurst, Frank McGlynn, George Cleveland, Ben Hendricks. A seal poacher on the run from the law and hijackers, comes across a shipwreck and tries to rescue the survivors. Average action melodrama which will appeal to Jack Holt followers.

2287 North of the Border. Screen Guild, 1946. 40 minutes B/W. D: B. Reeves Eason. SC: Arthur V. Jones. WITH Russell Hayden, Inez Cooper, Lyle Talbot, Douglas Fowley, Anthony Warde, Jack Mulhall, Guy Beach, I. Stanford Jolley, Richard Alexander. A cowboy crosses into Canada and finds himself suspected of the murder of his partner, a deed actually carried out by a gang of fur thieves and smugglers. Cheaply made but entertaining featurette.

2288 North of the Great Divide. Republic, 1950. 54 (67) minutes Color. D: William Witney. SC: Eric Taylor. WITH Roy Rogers, Penny Edwards, Gordon Jones, Roy Barcroft, Foy Willing & The Riders of the Purple Sage, Jack Lambert, Keith Richards, Douglas Evans, Noble Johnson, Iron Eyes Cody. Indian agent Roy Rogers tries to protect Indian salmon fishing rights from a murderous crook who is damming up the river, catching all the fish, and illegally shipping them to Canadian canneries. Well done Roy Rogers film which is badly butchered for TV; some TV prints are in black and white. V: NTA Home Entertainment.

2289 North of the Rio Grande. Paramount, 1937. 54 (65) minutes B/W. D: Nate Watt. SC: Joseph O'Donnell. WITH William Boyd, George ("Gabby") Hayes, Russell Hayden, Stephen Morris (Morris Ankrum), Bernadene Hayes, John Rutherford, Lorraine Randall, Walter Long, Lee Colt (Lee J. Cobb), John Beach, Al Ferguson, Lafe McKee. Hopalong Cassidy poses as a badman to uncover the identity of "The Lone Wolf," the leader of a gang of robbers who killed his brother. Slow moving series entry which livens up at the finale.

2290 North of the Rockies. Columbia, 1942. 60 minutes B/W. D: Lambert Hillyer. SC: Herbert Dalmas. WITH Bill Elliott, Tex Ritter, Shirley Patterson, Frank Mitchell, Larry Parks, John Miljan, Ian MacDonald, Lloyd Bridges, Gertrude F. Hoffman, Earl Gunn, Boyd Irwin, Art Dillard, David Harper, Francis Sayles. A Canadian Mountie and a U. S. marshal are somewhat at odds with each other as they try to capture a gang of fur smugglers. Well made actioner that is somewhat hurt by having its two stars spending most of their screen time as opponents.

2291 North of the Yukon. Columbia, 1939. 59 minutes B/W. D: Sam Nelson. SC: Bennett Cohen. WITH Charles Starrett, Linda Winters (Dorothy Comingore), Bob Nolan & The Sons of the Pioneers, Lane Chandler, Paul Sutton, Robert Fiske, Vernon Steele, Edmund Cobb, Tom London, Kenne Duncan, Hal Taliaferro, Richard Botiller, Harry Cording, Ed Brady. Two Mountie brothers search for the fur thieves who murdered a trader. Actionful and well made north woods drama.

North of the Yukon see **The Legend of Amaluk**

2292 North to Alaska. 20th Century-Fox, 1960. 122 minutes Color. D: Henry Hathaway. SC: John Lee Mahin, Martin Rackin & Claude Binyon. WITH John Wayne, Stewart Granger, Capucine, Fabian, Ernie Kovacs, Mickey Shaughnessy, Karl Swenson, Kathleen Freeman, John Qualen, Stanley Adams, Stephen Courtleigh, Douglas Dick, Jerry O'Sullivan, Ollie O'Toole, Tudor Owen, Lilyan Chauvin, Marcel Hillaire, Richard Deacon, James Griffith, Max Hellinger, Richard Collier, Esther Dale, Fortune Gordien, Roy Jensen, Charles Seel, Rayford Barnes, Fred Graham, Alan Carney, Peter Bourne, Tom Dillon, Arlene Harris, Paul Maxey, Oscar Beregi, Kermit Maynard, Maurice Delamore. Two prospectors strike it rich in Alaska. When one of them sends his partner South to claim his fiancee, the partner finds the girl has already married, and sets out to find a substitute. Big, brawling, entertaining tongue-in-cheek adventure film. V: CBS/Fox.

2293 North to the Klondike. Universal, 1942. 60 minutes B/W. D: Erle C. Kenton. SC: Clarence Upson Young, Lou Sarecky & George Bricker. WITH Broderick Crawford, Lon Chaney, Evelyn Ankers, Andy Devine, Stanley Andrews, Willie Fung, Keye Luke, Dorothy Granger, Lloyd Corrigan, Riley Hill, Paul Dubov, Armand Cortes, Fred Cordova, Monte Blue, Tony Paton, Jeff Corey, Bob Homans, Lee Phelps, William Ruhl. A mining engineer joins forces with farmers in Alaska who are being run off their lands by a local trader who thinks there is gold in the area. Good adaptation of Jack London's Gold Hunters of the North with a dilly of a brawl between good guy Broderick Crawford and baddie Lon Chaney.

2294 North West Mounted Police. Paramount, 1940. 125 minutes Color. D: Cecil B. DeMille. SC: Alan LeMay, Jesse Lasky Jr. & C. Gardner Sullivan. WITH Gary Cooper, Madeleine Carroll, Paulette Goddard, Preston Foster, Robert Preston, George Bancroft, Lynne Overman, Akim Tamiroff, Walter Hampden, Lon Chaney, Montagu Love, Francis McDonald, George E. Stone, Willard Robertson, Regis Toomey, Richard Denning, Douglas Kennedy, Clara Blandick, Ralph Byrd, Lane Chandler, Julia Faye, Jack Pennick, Rod Cameron, James Seay, Jack Chapin, Eric Alden, Wallace Reid Jr., Bud Geary, Evan Thomas, Davison Clark, Chief Thundercloud, Harry Burns, Lou Merrill, Ynez Seabury, Philip Terry, Soledad Jiminez, Kermit Maynard, Anthony Caruso, Paul Sutton,

James Flavin, Archie Twitchell, Nestor Paiva, Ray Mala, Monte Blue, Chief Yowlachie, David Newell. A Texas Ranger comes to Canada on the trail of a wanted man and becomes involved with the Mounties in stopping an Indian uprising. Much maligned but highly entertaining and well made Cecil B. DeMille production.

2295 Northern Frontier. Ambassador, 1935. 57 minutes B/W. D: Sam Newfield. SC: Barry Barringer. WITH Kermit Maynard, Eleanor Hunt, J. Farrell MacDonald, LeRoy Mason, Charles King, Ben Hendricks Jr., Russell Hopton, Nelson McDowell, Walter Brennan, Gertrude Astor, Dick Curtis, Kernan Cripps, Jack Chisholm, Lloyd Ingraham, Lafe McKee, Tyrone Power (Jr.), Artie Ortego. A Mountie is on the trail of a gang of murderous outlaws engaged in stealing furs and counterfeiting currency. Not the best of Kermit Maynard's series for producer Maurice Conn but still passable, mainly due to a fine cast and nice scenery; look for Tyrone Power in a bit as a fellow Mountie.

2296 Northern Lights. Cine Manifest, 1979. 90 minutes Color. D-SC: John Hanson & Rob Nilsson. WITH Robert Behling, Susan Lynch, Henry Martinson, Joe Spano, Ray Ness, Helen Ness, Marianne Astrom-DeFina, Gary Hanish, Jon Ness, Thorbjorn Rue, Nick Eldridge. Farmers in North Dakota in the 1910s fight the railroads and market monopolies and try to form a union. Interesting historical drama, independently made.

2297 Northern Patrol. Monogram, 1953. 62 minutes B/W. D: Rex Bailey. SC: Warren Douglas. WITH Kirby Grant, Marian Carr, Emmett Lynn, Bill Phipps, Claudia Drake, Frank Sully, Dale Van Sickel, Gloria Talbott, Richard Walsh, Frank Lackteen, Chinook (dog). When crooks plan to plunder an Indian burial group they are opposed by a lone Mountie and his loyal dog. Cheaply made but entertaining northwoods tale supposedly based on the works of James Oliver Curwood.

2298 Northern Pursuit. Warner Brothers, 1943. 94 minutes B/W. D: Raoul Walsh. SC: Frank Gruber & Alvah Bessie. WITH Errol Flynn, Julie Bishop, Helmut Dantine, John Ridgely, Gene Lockhart, Tom Tully, Bernard Nedell, Warren Douglas, Monte Blue, Alec Craig, Tom Fadden, Carl Harbaugh, Fred Kelsey, Herbert Heywood, Arno Frey, Robert Hutton, Robert Kent, John Forsythe, Jay Silverheels, Russell Hicks, Milton Kibbee, Lester Mathews, George Urchel, Joe Herrera. A Mountie pretends to be a turncoat in order to infiltrate a Nazi gang working around Hudson's Bay in Canada during World War II. Surprisingly none-too-entertaining Errol Flynn vehicle.

2299 Northwest Outpost. Republic, 1947. 91 minutes B/W. D: Allan Dwan. SC: Elizabeth Meehan & Richard Sale. WITH Nelson Eddy, Ilona Massey, Joseph Schildkraut, Elsa Lanchester, Hugo Haas, Erno Verebes, Lenore Ulric, Peter Whitney, Tamara Shayne, George Sorel, Rick Vallin, The American G. I. Chorus. In pioneer California, a young Russian girl tries to defeat the crooked plans of her evil husband and ends up fallng in love with a dashing ranger. Republic's attempt to revive the romantic operetta with a new score by Rudolf Friml was defeated by this sadly dull production.

2300 Northwest Passage. Metro-Goldwyn-Mayer, 1940. 126 minutes Color. D: King Vidor. SC: Lawrence Stallings & Talbot Jennings. WITH Spencer Tracy, Robert Young, Walter Brennan, Ruth Hussey, Nat Pendleton, Louis Hector, Robert Barrat, Lumsden Hare, Donald MacBride, Isabel Jewell, Douglas Walton, Addison Richards, Hugh Sothern, Regis Toomey, Montagu Love, Lester Matthews, Truman Bradley, Andrew Pena, Tom London, Eddie Parker, Hank Worden, Don Castle, Rand Brooks, Kent Rogers, Verna Felton, Richard Cramer, Ray Teal, Edward Gargan, John Merton, Gibson Gowland, Frank Hagney, Gwendolen Logan, Addie McPahil, Helen MacKellar, Arthur Aylesworth, Ted Oliver, Lawrence Porter, Tony Guerrero, Ferdinand Munier, George Eldredge, Frederic Worlock. Major Robert Rogers leads his Rogers' Rangers to stop the Indians at St. Francis in Canada to break the French hold on the area during the French and Indian War in 1759. Colorful and entertaining feature based on Kenneth Roberts' best seller; film contains some fine character performances, especially by Addison Richards as the mad ranger.

2301 Northwest Rangers. Metro-Goldwyn-Mayer, 1942. 64 minutes B/W. D: Joe Newman. SC: Gordon Kahn & David Lang. WITH James Craig, William Lundigan, Patricia Dane, John Carradine, Jack Holt, Keenan Wynn, Grant Withers, Darryl Hickman, Drew Roddy, John Butler, Philip Van Zandt, Michael Brown, Luis Alberni, Jim Farley, Alec Craig, Kay

Medford, Hugh Beaumont, Alexander Granach, Mitchell Lewis, Ray Teal, Al Hill, George Carleton, Howard Hickman, Herbert Heyes, Emmett Vogan, Patrick McVey, William Tannen, Roy Barcroft, Ivan "Dusty" Miller, Hubert Brill, LeRoy Mason, Mark Daniels, Hooper Atchley, Howard Mitchell, Dick Rush, Murdock MacQuarrie, Robert Winkler. Two boys grow up together. One becomes a gambler while the other is a ranger, and eventually they are forced into a showdown. Low budget affair from MGM which is a fairly entertaining feature.

2302 Northwest Stampede. Eagle Lion, 1948. 76 minutes Color. D: Albert S. Rogell. SC: Art Arthur & Lillie Hayward. WITH James Craig, Joan Leslie, Jack Oakie, Chill Wills, Victor Kilian, Stanley Andrews, Lane Chandler, Ray Bennett, Harry Shannon, Kermit Maynard. The lady owner of a ranch is at odds with her rodeo champion foreman who wants to corral a wild stallion. The cast and the scenery helps to breathe life into this average feature.

2303 Northwest Territory. Monogram, 1951. 61 minutes B/W. D: Frank McDonald. SC: Bill Raynor. WITH Kirby Grant, Gloria Saunders, Warren Douglas, Pat Mitchell, Tristram Coffin, John Crawford, Duke York, Don C. Harvey, Sam Flint, Chinook (dog). Outlaws murder an old man for his oil claim and a Mountie, who has brought the man's young grandson-heir to the territory, sets out to track down the killers. Actionful and compact little melodrama with good work by Kirby Grant in the lead.

2304 Northwest Trail. Screen Guild, 1945. 66 minutes Color. D: Derwin Abrahams. SC: Harvey Gates & L. J. Swabacher. WITH Bob Steele, Joan Woodbury, John Litel, Ian Keith, Raymond Hatton, Madge Bellamy, Poodles Hanneford, Grace Hanneford, George Meeker, Charles Middleton, John Hamilton, Al Ferguson, Bud Osborne, Bob Duncan, Bill Hammond, Josh (John) Carpenter. When a woman brings money to her uncle for the purchase of timberland, the money is stolen and a Mountie tries to find the thieves. Very colorful action melodrama with a fine performance by Bob Steele as the Mountie.

2305 Not Above Suspicion. Wrather Corporation, 1956. 75 minutes Color. D: Earl Bellamy & Oscar Rudolph. SC: Herbert Purdum, Robert Leslie Bellem,

Thomas Seller & Charles Carson. WITH Clayton Moore, Jay Silverheels, Allen Pinson, Wayne Burson, Dennis Moore, Tristram Coffin, Roy Barcroft, Richard Benedict, Francis McDonald, Florence Lake, Tyler McDuff, Harry Strang, Rick Vallin, Jason Johnson, Alan Wells, Robert Burton, Gregg Barton, Melinda Byron, Joseph Sargent. The Lone Ranger and Tonto try to stop a crook from taking over a town as well as fight renegade Indians and disrupt a plot to murder a rancher. Okay telefeature from "The Lone Ranger" (ABC-TV, 1949-57) series from the episodes "Mission for Tonto," "Journey to San Carlos" and "The Avenger."

2306 Not Exactly Gentlemen. Fox, 1931. 70 minutes B/W. D: Benjamin Stoloff. SC: William Conselman, Dudley Nichols & Emmett Flynn. WITH Victor McLaglen, Fay Wray, Lew Cody, Robert Warwick, Eddie Gribbon, David Worth, Joyce Compton, Louise Huntington, Franklyn Farnum, Carol Wines, James Farley. Three rogues raid a wagon train and ride off with a pretty girl whose father has a map to a gold mine they seek. Average early talkie with some well staged land rush scenes. Original title: **Three Rogues.**

O

2307 Oath of Vengeance. Producers Releasing Corporation, 1944. 50 (57) minutes B/W. D: Sam Newfield. SC: Fred Myton. WITH Buster Crabbe, Al St. John, Mady Lawrence, Karl Hackett, Marin Sais, Jack Ingram, Charles King, Kermit Maynard, Frank Ellis, Hal Price, Budd Buster, Jimmie Aubrey. When Fuzzy Q. Jones purchases a ranch and finds he cannot settle down, he and Billy Carson try to prove the innocence of a young man accused of murder. Another tacky entry in the long-running PRC series.

2308 Oh, Susanna!. Republic, 1936. 56 minutes B/W. D: Joseph Kane. SC: Oliver Drake. WITH Gene Autry, Smiley Burnette, Frances Grant, Donald Kirke, Earle Hodgins, The Light Crust Doughboys, Clara Kimball Young, Boothe Howard, Ed Piel, Frankie Marvin, Carl Stockdale, Gerald Roscoe, Roger Gray, Fred Burns, Walter James, Fred "Snowflake" Toones, Earl Dwire, Bruce Mitchell, Jack Kirk, George Morrell. After a wanted outlaw knocks him out and takes his clothes, Gene Autry is mistaken for the badman.

When pals Frog Millhouse and The Professor help him escape, he becomes the object of a manhunt. More music and pseudo-Western nonsense that made Gene Autry the era's top genre star.

2309 Oh, Susanna. Republic, 1951. 90 minutes Color. D: Joseph Kane. SC: Charles Marquis Warren. WITH Rod Cameron, Adrian Booth, Forrest Tucker, Chill Wills, Jim Davis, William Ching, Wally Cassell, Douglas Kennedy, James Lydon, William Haade, John Compton, James Flavin, Charles Stevens, Alan Bridge, Marshall Reed, John Pickard, Ruth Brennan, Louise Kane, Marion Randolph. At a frontier outpost, two Army rivals battle each other and the possibility of a Sioux uprising. Melodrama leans more toward dialogue than action but the fine cast carries it off okay.

2310 The Oil Raider. Mayfair, 1934. 59 minutes B/W. D: Spencer Gordon Bennet. SC: George Morgan & Homer King Gordon. WITH Buster Crabbe, Gloria Shea, George Irving, Max Wagner, Emmett Vogan, Harold Minjir, Tom London, Wally Wales. A wildcatter borrows money from an investment banker to complete his oil drilling project but when the banker suffers market reverses and needs money, he hires a crooked rival oil driller to sabotage the operation. Fairly good low budget programmer from producer Lester Scott Jr.

2311 Oklahoma!. Magna Corporation, 1955. 143 minutes Color. D: Fred Zinneman. SC: Sonya Levien & William Ludwig. WITH Gordon MacRae, Shirley Jones, Gloria Grahame, Gene Nelson, Charlotte Greenwood, Eddie Albert, James Whitmore, Rod Steiger, Barbara Lawrence, Jay C. Flippen, Roy Barcroft, James Mitchell, Bambi Lynn, Marc Platt. A cowboy falls in love with a pretty girl and asks her to a dance but has troubles with a rival. Enjoyable screen adaptation of the popular Broadway musical. V: MGM/CBS Home Video.

2312 Oklahoma Annie. Republic, 1952. 90 minutes B/W. D: R. G. Springsteen. SC: Jack Townley. WITH Judy Canova, John Russell, Grant Withers, Roy Barcroft, Emmett Lynn, Frank Ferguson, Minerva Urecal, Housely Stevenson, Almira Sessions, Allen Jenkins, Maxine Gates, Emory Parnell, Denver Pyle, House Peters Jr., Andrew Tombes, Fuzzy Knight, Si Jenks, Marion Martin, Herbert Vigran, Hal Price, Fred Hoose, Lee Phelps, Bobby Taylor,

William Fawcett. A backwoods girl running a gunshop falls for the town's new sheriff and wants him to arrest the local saloon owner. He tries to get her out of his hair by making her his deputy and she brings in a robbery suspect. Fun Judy Canova vehicle.

2313 Oklahoma Badlands. Republic, 1948. 59 minutes B/W. D: Yakima Canutt. SC: Bob Williams. WITH Allan "Rocky" Lane, Eddy Waller, Mildred Coles, Roy Barcroft, Gene (Roth) Stutenroth, Earle Hodgins, Jay Kirby, Terry Frost, Hank Patterson, House Peters Jr., Jack Kirk, Bob Woodward, Claire Whitney, Dale Van Sickel. When a man is about to lose his ranch due to rustlers, a lawman pretends to be a friend from the East in order to stop the outlaws. Director Yakima Canutt keeps this Allan Lane vehicle moving at a good clip. V: Cumberland Video.

2314 Oklahoma Blues. Monogram, 1946. 56 minutes B/W. D: Lambert Hillyer. SC: Bennett Cohen. WITH Jimmy Wakely, Dub Taylor, Virginia Belmont, I. Stanford Jolley, Zon Murray, George J. Lewis, Steve Clark, Frank LaRue, Milburn Morante, Charles King, Bob Woodward. A singing cowboy finds himself in between two towns fighting for the location of the county seat. A bit more action than usual for a Jimmy Wakely musical film, but still none too good.

2315 Oklahoma Crude. Columbia, 1973. 105 minutes Color. D: Stanley Kramer. SC: Marc Norman. WITH George C. Scott, Faye Dunaway, Jack Palance, John Mills, William Lucking, Harvey James, Ted Gehring, Cliff Osmond, Rafael Campos, Woodrow Parfrey, John Hudkins, Harvey Parry, Bob Herron, Jerry Brown, Jim Burk, Henry Wills, Hal Smith, Cody Bearpaw, James Jeter, Larry D. Mann, John Dierkes, Karl Lucas, Wayne Storm, Billy Varga. A drifter is hired by the woman owner of an oil well to help her fight the advances of a large petroleum company. Modern-day drama does not seem to know whether it wants to be serious or serio-comedic.

2316 Oklahoma Cyclone. Tiffany, 1930. 60 minutes B/W. D: John P. McCarthy. SC: Ford Beebe. WITH Bob Steele, Nita Ray, Al St. John, Charles L. King, Slim Whitaker, Shorty Hendricks, Emilio Fernandez, Hector Sarno, Fred Burns, Cliff Lyons, John Ince. A young man infiltrates an outlaw gang as he searches for his missing sheriff father and he promptly falls for a pretty senorita. Early talkie is a bit shaky in its production values but Bob Steele's fans won't mind.

2317 Oklahoma Frontier. Universal, 1939. 59 minutes B/W. D-SC: Ford Beebe. WITH Johnny Mack Brown, Anne Gwynne, Fuzzy Knight, Bob Baker, Robert Cummings Sr., James Blaine, Lane Chandler, Anthony Warde, Robert Kortman, Harry Tenbrook, Charles King, Horace Murphy, George Chesebro, Joe de la Cruz, Lloyd Ingraham, The Texas Rangers, Al Bridge, Hank Worden, Hank Bell, Blackie Whiteford, Roy Harris, George Magrill, Tom Smith. Crooks who want the water rights to land frame a cowboy on a fake charge of killing his best friend. The accused man's girl tries to save him. Somewhat complicated oater with a good amount of action.

2318 Oklahoma Jim. Monogram, 1931. 61 minutes B/W. D: Harry Fraser. SC: Harry Fraser & G. A. Durlam. WITH Bill Cody, Marion Burns, Andy Shuford, William Desmond, Si Jenks, Franklyn Farnum, John Elliott, Ed Brady, G. D. Wood, Earl Dwire, Iron Eyes Cody, Ann Ross, Artie Ortego. A saloon owner causes the death of an Indian maiden but tries to place the blame on a gambler, who has fallen in love with the man's late partner's daughter. Less than mediocre Bill Cody talkie, slow moving, poorly recorded and with lots of stock footage.

2319 Oklahoma Justice. Monogram, 1951. 56 minutes B/W. D: Lewis D. Collins. SC: Joseph O'Donnell. WITH Johnny Mack Brown, James Ellison, Phyllis Coates, Barbara Allen, Kenne Duncan, Lane Bradford, Marshall Reed, Zon Murray, I. Stanford Jolley, Stanley Price, Bruce Edwards, Richard Avonde, Lyle Talbot, Carl Mathews, Ed Cassidy, George De-Normand. With the aid of his stagecoach driver pal, a lawman pretends to be an outlaw in order to locate a robbery gang. First feature to team Johnny Mack Brown and James Ellison is an average affair.

2320 The Oklahoma Kid. Warner Brothers, 1939. 85 minutes B/W. D: Lloyd Bacon. SC: Warren Duff, Robert Buckner & Edward E. Paramore. WITH James Cagney, Rosemary Lane, Humphrey Bogart, Donald Crisp, Harvey Stephens, Hugh Sothern, Charles Middleton, Edward Pawley, Ward Bond, Lew Harvey, Trevor Bardette, John Miljan, Arthur Aylesworth, Irving Bacon, Joe Devlin, Wade Boteler, Dan

Wolheim, Ray Mayer, Robert Kortman, Tex Cooper, John Harron, Stuart Holmes, Jeffrey Sayre, Frank Mayo, Jack Mower, Al Bridge, Don Barclay, Horace Murphy, Robert Homans, George Lloyd, Soledad Jiminez, Clem Bevans, Ed Brady, Tom Chatterton, Elliott Sullivan. In the 1890s a daredevil bandit in the Oklahoma Territory robs from the rich and gives to the poor as he tries to avenge his father's murder. Rather strange Western with James Cagney as a singing hero and Humphrey Bogart as the dastardly villain; best viewed as tongue-in-cheek.

2321 Oklahoma Raiders. Universal, 1944. 56 minutes B/W. D: Lewis D. Collins. SC: Betty Burbridge. WITH Tex Ritter, Jennifer Holt, Fuzzy Knight, Dennis Moore, Jack Ingram, George Eldredge, John Elliott, Slim Whitaker, I. Stanford Jolley, Richard Alexander, Herbert Rawlinson, Ethan Laidlaw, Johny Bond & His Red River Valley Boys (Wesley Tuttle, Jimmie Dean, Paul Sells), Steve Keyes, William Desmond, Bob Baker, Lane Chandler, Frank Ellis. A lieutenant in the Union army during the Civil War is sent to Oklahoma in the guise of a drifter to stop a masked bandit called El Vengador who has been leading raids on the cavalry. Very good Tex Ritter vehicle with plenty of action, a good story and supporting cast and five pleasant songs, including "Cowboy's Dream" and "Starlight on the Prairie." British title: **Riders of Oklahoma.**

2322 Oklahoma Renegades. Republic, 1940. 54 (57) minutes B/W. D: Nate Watt. SC: Earle Snell & Doris Schroeder. WITH Robert Livingston, Raymond Hatton, Duncan Renaldo, Florine McKinney, Lee "Lasses" White, Al Herman, William Ruhl, Eddie Dean, James Seay, Harold Daniels, Jack Lescoulie, Frosty Royce, Yakima Canutt. Coming home after serving in the Spanish-American War, The Three Mesquiteers come to the aid of veterans being cheated out of their homesteads. Fairly pleasing effort in "The Three Mesquiteers" series.

2323 Oklahoma Territory. United Artists, 1960. 67 minutes B/W. D: Edward L. Cahn. SC: Orville Hampton. WITH Bill Williams, Gloria Talbott, Ted de Corsia, Grant Richards, Walter Sande, X Brands, Walter Baldwin, Grandon Rhodes. When the local Indian commissioner is murdered, an Indian chief is charged with the crime but the district attorney believes him innocent and tries to find the real killer.

Low budget but adequately entertaining melodrama.

2324 Oklahoma Terror. Monogram, 1938. 50 minutes B/W. D: Spencer Gordon Bennet. SC: Joseph West (George Waggner). WITH Jack Randall, Al St. John, Virginia Carroll, Davison Clark, Nolan Willis, Glenn Strange, Warren McCollum, Tristram Coffin, Ralph Peters, Slim Whitaker, Nelson McDowell, Don Rowan, Brandon Beach. After the Civil War, a man wants to find out who killed his stageline-manager father and he organizes vigilantes to aid in cleaning up lawlessness. Pretty good Jack Randall vehicle.

2325 The Oklahoma Woman. American Releasing Corporation, 1956. 72 minutes B/W. D: Roger Corman. SC: Lou Rusoff. WITH Richard Denning, Peggie Castle, Cathy Downs, Tudor Owen, Martin Kingsley, Touch (Michael) Connors, Jonathan Haze, Richard (Dick) Miller, Tom Dillon, Edmund Cobb. Released from prison, an ex-gunfighter goes home to his Oklahoma ranch but his former girlfriend tries to frame him on a murder charge. Roger Corman's fans will find this early effort of interest but others beware.

2326 The Oklahoman. Allied Artists, 1957. 73 minutes Color. D: Francis D. Lyon. SC: Daniel B. Ullman. WITH Joel McCrea, Barbara Hale, Gloria Talbott, Brad Dexter, Michael Pate, Verna Felton, Douglas Dick, Anthony Caruso, Esther Dale, Adam Williams, Ray Teal, Peter Vitrian, John Pickard, Mimi Gibson, I. Stanford Jolley, Jody Williams, Don Marlowe. When crooks try to cheat an Indian out of his oil lands, a doctor comes to his defense. Somewhat predictable but okay drama.

2327 The Old Barn Dance. Republic, 1938. 54 (60) minutes B/W. D: Joseph Kane. SC: Bernard McConville & Charles Francis Royal. WITH Gene Autry, Smiley Burnette, Helen Valkis, Sammy McKim, Ivan Miller, Earl Dwire, Hooper Atchley, Ray Bennett, Carleton Young, Frankie Marvin, Earle Hodgins, Gloria Rich, Dick Weston (Roy Rogers), Walt Shrum & His Colorado Hillbillies, The Maple City Four, The Stafford Sisters, Denver Dixon (Victor Adamson/Al Mix). Gene Autry and his singing group try to aid farmers being cheated by a company selling tractors but the farmers believe Gene has doublecrossed them when he goes to work for a radio station owned by the company. Entertaining Gene Autry

opus with plenty of good music. V: Cumberland Video.

2328 The Old Chisholm Trail. Universal, 1942. 61 minutes B/W. D-SC: Elmer Clifton. WITH Johnny Mack Brown, Tex Ritter, Fuzzy Knight, Jennifer Holt, Mady Correll, Earle Hodgins, Roy Barcroft, Edmund Cobb, Budd Buster, Michael Vallon, Scoop Martin, The Jimmy Wakely Trio (Jimmy Wakely, Johnny Bond, Scott Harrell). The female owner of a trading post takes on a woman gambler after the latter tries to run a cowboy out of town over water rights. The two male stars are at odds over Jennifer Holt, who is at odds with Mady Correll, and Jimmy Wakely and company do three songs—all in one hour!

2329 The Old Corral. Republic, 1936. 54 minutes B/W. D: Joseph Kane. SC: Joseph Poland & Sherman Lowell. WITH Gene Autry, Smiley Burnette, Hope (Irene) Manning, The Sons of the Pioneers (Bob Nolan, Roy Rogers, Hugh Farr, Karl Farr, Tim Spencer), Cornelius Keefe, Lon Chaney Jr., John Bradford, Milburn Morante, Abe Lefton, Merrill McCormack, Charles Sullivan, Buddy Roosevelt, Lynton Brent, Frankie Marvin, Oscar & Elmer, Jack Ingram. A girl singer witnesses a gangland murder in Chicago and heads West to a small town where the local gambler recognizes her and informs the gangsters who want to silence her. It is Gene Autry versus gangsters out West and the results are pretty entertaining. V: Cumberland Video, Cassette Express.

2330 The Old Frontier. Republic, 1950. 60 minutes B/W. D: Philip Ford. SC: Bob Williams. WITH Monte Hale, Paul Hurst, Claudia Barrett, William Henry, Tristram Coffin, William Haade, Victor Kilian, Lane Bradford, Denver Pyle, Tom London, Almira Sessions. The town's new lawman is after a bank robbery gang which is actually being lead by a local attorney. Average Monte Hale outing.

2331 Old Los Angeles. Republic, 1948. 87 minutes B/W. D: Joseph Kane. SC: Clements Riley & Gerald Adams. WITH William Elliott, John Carroll, Catherine McLeod, Joseph Schildkraut, Andy Devine, Estelita Rodriguez, Grant Withers, Virginia Brissac, Tito Renaldo, Roy Barcroft, Henry Brandon, Julian Rivero, Earle Hodgins. A Missouri lawman comes to Los Angeles to prospect for gold but finds his brother and several miners have been murdered and he tries to find the killers. Fast paced and quite entertaining Bill Elliott "A" effort. Also known as **In Old Los Angeles.** Reissue title: **California Outpost.**

2332 Old Louisiana. Crescent, 1937. 60 minutes B/W. D: Irvin V. Willat. SC: Mary Ireland. WITH Tom Keene, Rita (Hayworth) Cansino, Will Morgan, Robert Fiske, Ray Bennett, Budd Buster, Allan Cavan, Carlos De Valdez, Wally Albright, Ramsay Hill, J. Louis Johnson, Iron Eyes Cody. A frontiersman comes to the aid of American settlers in the Upper Mississippi Valley when a dishonest trader tries to stir up trouble between them and the Spanish so he can have the territory for himself. Cheaply made but rather interesting pseudo-historical drama revolving around the Louisiana Purchase. Reissue title: **Louisiana Gal.**

2333 Old Oklahoma Plains. Republic, 1952. 60 minutes B/W. D: William Witney. SC: Milton Raison. WITH Rex Allen, Slim Pickens, Elaine Edwards, Roy Barcroft, John Crawford, Joel Marston, Russell Hicks, Fred Graham, Stephen Chase, The Republic Rhythm Riders. During the 1920s a former cavalry officer is returned to duty to stop outlaws terrorizing the plains and comes up with the idea of using tanks. More than passable Rex Allen vehicle with overuse of stock footage from **Army Girl** (Republic, 1938).

2334 Old Overland Trail. Republic, 1953. 60 minutes B/W. D: William Witney. SC: Milton Raison. WITH Rex Allen, Slim Pickens, Virginia Hall, Roy Barcroft, The Republic Rhythm Riders, Zon Murray, Harry Harvey, Gil Herman, Wade Crosby, Leonard Nimoy. A cowboy tries to prevent warfare between immigrant settlers and Apaches. Standard Rex Allen vehicle hurt by the decline of the "B" Western of the period.

2335 Old Shatterhand. CCC/Filmkunst/ Avala/Criterion/Serena, 1964. 89 minutes Color. D: Hugo Fregonese. SC: Ladislaus Fodor & Robert A. Stemmle. WITH Lex Barker, Pierre Brice, Daliah Lavi, Guy Madison, Ralf Walter, Bill Ramsey, Gustavo Rojo, Rik Battaglia, Kitti Mattern, Alain Tissier, Charles Fawcett, Nikola Popovic, Mirko Ellis, Burschi Putzgruber, Jim Burk. White renegades try to discredit Apaches by attacking ranchers in hopes of getting Indian lands, but Old Shatterhand and his blood brother Apache chief Winne-

tou come to the native Americans' rescue. Filmed in Yugoslavia in 70mm Superpanorama this German oater is a well done effort that is highly entertaining and will appeal to genre fans because of stars Lex Barker and Guy Madison. Called **La Battaglia Di Fort Apache** in Italy and issued in the United States in 1968 as **Shatterhand** by Goldstone Film Enterprises. TV title: **Apache's Last Battle.**

2336 The Old Texas Trail. Universal, 1944. 60 minutes B/W. D: Lewis D. Collins. SC: William Lively. WITH Rod Cameron, Fuzzy Knight, Eddie Dew, Marjorie Clements, Ray Whitley, Virginia Christine, Edmund Cobb, Joseph J. Greene, George Eldredge, Jack Clifford, Dick Purcell, Harry Strang, Ray Jones, Merle Travis, William Desmond, George Turner, Art Fowler, Henry Wills, Terry Frost, Ray Whitley's Bar-6 Cowboys. Three cowboys come to the aid of a girl who is about to lose the option rights to her stageline thanks to a crook and his gang who are after the contract. Sturdy Rod Cameron vehicle with good entertainment value. V: Cassette Express.

2337 The Old West. Columbia, 1952. 61 minutes B/W. D: George Archainbaud. SC: Gerald Geraghty. WITH Gene Autry, Pat Buttram, Gail Davis, Lyle Talbot, Louis Jean Heydt, House Peters, House Peters Jr., Dick Jones, Kathy Johnson, Don C. Harvey, Dee Pollack, James Craven, Tom London, Frankie Marvin, Syd Saylor, Bob Woodward, Buddy Roosevelt, Tex Terry, John Merton, Pat O'Malley, Bobby Clark, Frank Ellis. After a traveling minister aids him after being attacked, a horse wrangler helps the sky pilot bring religion to a small town. Good, and somewhat offbeat, Gene Autry film.

2338 The Old Wyoming Trail. Columbia, 1937. 56 minutes B/W. D: Folmer Blangstead. SC: Ed Earl Repp. WITH Charles Starrett, Donald Grayson, Barbara Weeks, The Sons of the Pioneers, Dick Curtis, Ed LeSaint, Guy Usher, George Chesebro, Art Mix, Slim Whitaker, Alma Chester, Ernie Adams, Richard Botiller, Frank Ellis, Joe Yrigoyen, Charles Brinley, Fred Burns, Si Jenks, Curley Dresden, Ray Whitley, Blackie Whiteford, Tom London, Art Dillard, Ray Jones, Jerome Ward, Tex Cooper. Two pals try to stop a crook from forcing a man to sell his valuable ranch for little money. Well done Charles Starrett vehicle with emphasis on music from singing costar Donald Grayson, and The Sons of the Pioneers, including Roy Rogers.

2339 Old Yeller. Buena Vista, 1957. 83 minutes Color. D: Robert Stevenson. SC: Fred Gipson & William Tunberg. WITH Dorothy McGuire, Fess Parker, Tommy Kirk, Kevin Corcoran, Jeff York, Beverly Washburn, Chuck Connors, Spike (dog). In Texas in 1869 a stray dog ingratiates himself into the lives of a frontier family. Very entertaining Walt Disney family feature. V: Disney Home Video.

2340 Ole Rex. Universal-International, 1961. 40 minutes Color. D-SC: Robert Hinkle. WITH Billy Hughes, Rex (dog), William Foster, Robert Hinkle, Whitey Hughes, William Hughes, Richard McCarthy, Red Bray, Dale Marlow Jr., Dale Terry. The adventures of a young boy and his German shepherd dog. Fair featurette for the family trade.

2341 The Omaha Trail. Metro-Goldwyn-Mayer, 1942. 62 minutes B/W. D: Edward Buzzell. SC: Jesse Lasky Jr. & Hugh Butler. WITH James Craig, Pamela Blake, Dean Jagger, Edward Ellis, Chill Wills, Donald Meek, Howard DaSilva, Henry (Harry) Morgan, Morris Ankrum, Kermit Maynard. When an ox train race causes the deaths of two Indians, the result is an Indian uprising. Cheaply made and mediocre oater plagued with excessive stock footage.

2342 O'Malley of the Mounted. 20th Century-Fox, 1936. 59 minutes B/W. D: David Howard. SC: Dan Jarrett & Frank Howard Clark. WITH George O'Brien, Irene Ware, Crauford Kent, James Bush, Victor Potel, Charles King, Stanley Fields, Tom London, Reginald Barlow, Richard Cramer, Olin Francis, Black Jack Ward. A Mountie infiltrates an outlaw gang terrorizing U. S. border towns and instigates a plan which leads the badmen into a robbery which results in their capture. Nicely done George O'Brien vehicle which should please north of the border drama fans.

2343 On the Great White Trail. Grand National, 1938. 59 minutes B/W. D: Al Herman. SC: Charles Logue & Joe Pallim. WITH James Newill, Terry Walker, Robert Frazer, Richard Alexander, Richard Tucker, Robert Terry, Eddie Gribbon, Walter McGrail, Philo McCullough, Charles King, Juan Duval, Victor Potel, Carl Mathews, Bruce Warren. When his girl's

father is falsely accused of robbery and murder, a Mountie heads into the wilderness to capture the real culprit. Good entry in the popular "Renfrew of the Mounted" series. Also called **Renfrew of the Royal Mounted on the Great White Trail, Renfrew on the Great White Trail** and **On the Trail.** V: Thunderbird.

2344 On the Night Stage. Mutual, 1915. 60 minutes B/W. D: Reginald Barker. SC: C. Gardner Sullivan & Thomas H. Ince. WITH Robert Edeson, Rhea Mitchell, William S. Hart, Herschel Mayall, Gladys Brockwell, Shorty Hamilton. A good-badman steps aside when the girl he loves weds a parson who has aided him in a fight. When the girl is blackmailed by a former cohort, the man comes to her rescue. Probably the best known of William S. Hart's early films, this silent feature provides plenty of good entertainment. V: Classic Video Cinema Collectors Club.

2345 On the Old Spanish Trail. Republic, 1947. 54 (75) minutes Color. D: William Witney. SC: Sloan Nibley. WITH Roy Rogers, Tito Guizar, Bob Nolan & The Sons of the Pioneers, Jane Frazee, Andy Devine, Estelita Rodriguez, Charles McGraw, Fred Graham, Steve Darrell, Marshall Reed, Wheaton Chambers. When he comes to the aid of The Sons of the Pioneers' failing road show, Roy Rogers runs into "The Gypsy," a mysterious man wanted in connection with oil company robberies. Tito Guizar is about as much of a star of this vehicle as is Roy Rogers and while the film has some nice songs it is a bit draggy.

On the Trail see **On the Great White Trail**

2346 On Top of Old Smoky. Columbia, 1953. 59 minutes B/W. D: George Archainbaud. SC: Gerald Geraghty. WITH Gene Autry, Smiley Burnette, Gail Davis, Sheila Ryan, Cass County Boys, Grandon Rhodes, Kenne Duncan, Robert Bice, Zon Murray, Fred S. Martin, Jerry Scroggins, Pat O'Malley, Bert Dodson. Mistaken for a ranger, a singing star comes to the aid of a girl whose ranch is sought by a crook because it contains rich mica deposits. Good songs and an interesting plot bring some life to this Gene Autry vehicle.

2347 Once upon a Horse. Universal-International, 1958. 85 minutes B/W. D-SC: Hal Kantor. WITH Dan Rowan,

Dick Martin, Martha Hyer, Leif Erickson, Nita Talbot, James Gleason, John McGiver, David Burns, Dick Ryan, Max Baer, Buddy Baer, Bob Steele, Robert Livingston, Tom Keene, Kermit Maynard, Steve Pendleton, Paul Anderson. Two cowpokes steal cattle from a ruthless cattle queen and then find they do not have the money to feed the stock. Comedy does not offer much except to see four genre stars as themselves in a brief scene. Reissue title: **The Hot Horse.**

2348 Once upon a Time in the West. Paramount, 1969. 165 minutes Color. D: Sergio Leone. SC: Sergio Leone & Sergio Donati. WITH Henry Fonda, Claudia Cardinale, Jason Robards, Charles Bronson, Frank Wolff, Gabriele Ferzetti, Keenan Wynn, Paolo Stoppa, Marco Zuanelli, Lionel Stander, Jack Elam, John Frederick, Woody Strode, Enzio Santianello, Dino Mele, Benito Stefanelli, Salvo Basile. In Kansas before the turn of the century, a mysterious harmonica-playing stranger arrives on the scene to avenge the murder of his father as the killer and his hired guns fight for land containing water needed by the railroad. Long, leisurely and violent European oater which has a cult following and is well worth watching. Italian title: **C'era Una Volta Il West.**

2349 One Eyed Jacks. Paramount, 1961. 141 minutes Color. D: Marlon Brando. SC: Guy Trosper & Calder Willingham. WITH Marlon Brando, Karl Malden, Pina Pellicer, Katy Jurado, Ben Johnson, Slim Pickens, Elisha Cook, Rodolfo Acosta, Larry Duncan, Sam Gilman, Timothy Carey, Miriam Colon, Ray Teal, John Dierkes, Hank Worden, Nina Martinez, Margarita Cordova. Released from prison, an outlaw seeks revenge on the partner who betrayed him and finds the man is now a sheriff. Lots of psychological stuff in this overdrawn oater which was cut prior to release, which may explain why it is not as satisfying as it should be.

2350 One Foot in Hell. 20th Century-Fox, 1960. 90 minutes Color. D: James B. Clark. SC: Aaron Spelling. WITH Alan Ladd, Don Murray, Dan O'Herlihy, Dolores Michaels, Larry Gates, Karl Swenson, Barry Cox, John Alexander, Rachel Stephens. When his young wife is killed, a deputy sheriff is determined to take revenge on the three businessmen he feels are responsible. A different kind of oater which will appeal to Alan Ladd fans.

2351 100 Rifles. 20th Century-Fox, 1969. 110 minutes Color. D: Tom Gries. SC: Clair Huffaker & Tom Gries. WITH Jim Brown, Raquel Welch, Burt Reynolds, Fernando Lamas, Dan O'Herlihy, Michael Forest, Soledad Miranda, Alberto Dalbes, Jose Manuel Martin, Hans Gudegast, Aldo Sambrell, Carlos Bravo. A lawman after a bank robber ends up helping a female revolutionary in Mexico defend an Indian village against a tyrant. Fairly actionful oater, but nothing special.

2352 100,000 Dollars for Lassiter. P.E.A./ Centauro Films, 1966. 97 minutes Color. D: Joaquin L. Romero Marchent. SC: Sergio Donati & Joaquin Romero Hernandez. WITH Robert Hundar, Pamela Tudor, Andrew Ray, Luigi Pistilli, Jose Bodalo, Jesus Fuente, Robert Camardiel, Aldo Sambrell, Benito Stefanelli, Robert Johnson Jr. A wheelchair-ridden rancher dominates the area's water supply, aided by an outlaw gang in his service, and he is opposed by a widow and her hired gunman. Typically violent European example of an imitation oater. An Italian-Spanish coproduction filmed as **100,000 Dollari Per Lassiter** and shown on U. S. TV as **Dollars for a Fast Gun.**

2353 $100,000 for Ringo. Balcazar, 1965. 106 minutes Color. D: Alberto De Martino. WITH Richard Harrison, Fernando Sancho, Eleanora Bianchi, Gerard Tichy, John Barracuda, Loris Lotty, Lee Burton. A stranger rides into a small town and tries to bring order between factions after a buried treasure. Another in the extensive series of violent oaters from Europe in the mid-1960s; also called **Three from Texas.**

2354 One Little Indian. Buena Vista, 1973. 90 minutes Color. D: Bernard McEveety. SC: Harry Spalding. WITH James Garner, Vera Miles, Pat Hingle, Morgan Woodward, Jim Davis, John Doucette, Clay O'Brien, Robert Pine, Bruce Glover, Ken Swofford, Jay Silverheels, Andrew Prine, Jodie Foster, Walter Brooke, Rudy Diaz, John Flynn, Tim Simcox, Lois Red Elk, Hal Baylor, Terry Wilson, Paul Sorenson, Boyd "Red" Morgan. Falsely accused of crimes by his superiors, a cavalry soldier escapes from prison, heads into the desert on a camel and befriends a runaway Indian boy. Light oater comedy-drama from Walt Disney studios which should please fans.

2355 One Man Justice. Columbia, 1937. 59 minutes B/W. D: Leon Barsha. SC:

Paul Perez. WITH Charles Starrett, Barbara Weeks, Hal Taliaferro, Jack Clifford, Alan Bridge, Walter Downey, Mary Gordon, Jack Lipson, Edmund Cobb, Dick Curtis, Maston Williams, Art Mix, Hank Bell, Steve Clark, Frank Ellis, Ethan Laidlaw, Eddie Laughton, Ted Mapes, Lew Meehan, Merrill McCormack, Harry Fleischman. Arriving in a small town, a man finds he is the look-alike for a rancher supposedly dead for several years. He agrees to impersonate the man to aid the sheriff combat an outlaw gang who is rustling the cattle belonging to the man's pretty widow. Strong Charles Starrett vehicle making good use of the amnesia gimmick.

2356 One Man Law. Columbia, 1932. 60 minutes B/W. D-SC: Lambert Hillyer. WITH Buck Jones, Shirley Grey, Robert Ellis, Murdock McQuarrie, Harry Todd, Henry Sedley, Ernie Adams, Richard Alexander, Wesley Girard, Ed LeSaint. A crooked land speculator convinces a cowboy to become the local sheriff so his dishonest activities can be protected, but the new sheriff soon becomes wise to his activities. Well done Buck Jones vehicle.

2357 One Man's Law. Republic, 1940. 54 (57) minutes B/W. D: George Sherman. SC: Bennett Cohen & Jack Natteford. WITH Don "Red" Barry, Janet Waldo, George Cleveland, Dub Taylor, Rex Lease, Carleton Young, Edmund Cobb, Robert Frazer, Charles King, Dick Elliott, Jack Ingram, Roy Barcroft, Stanley Price, Ed Piel, Fred "Snowflake" Toones, Bud Osborne, Horace B. Carpenter, Jack Kirk, Cactus Mack, Jim Corey, Curley Dresden, Roy Brent, Guy Usher, William Kellogg, James H. MacNamara. When crooks try to stop a town from getting a railroad franchise, a cowboy comes to the town's rescue. Another fast paced and well produced entry in Don Barry's Republic series.

2358 One Mask Too Many. Wrather Corporation, 1956. 75 minutes Color. D: Earl Bellamy & Oscar Rudolph. SC: Doane Hoag, Thomas Seller, Edmund Kelso & Orville Hampton. WITH Clayton Moore, Jay Silverheels, Allen Pinson, Wayne Burson, Tristram Coffin, Jim Bannon, Roy Barcroft, Virginia Christine, William Challee, Paul Engle, Sydney Mason, John Cliff, Louise Lewis, Sandy Sanders, Walt LaRue, Charles Wagenheim, Robert Closson, Saul M. Gorss, Michael Winkelman, John Ira Hudkins, Paul Stader, Gabor Curtiz, Richard Benedict, Peter Miles, Jason Johnson. The Lone Ranger attempts to clear his name when crimes are committed by a masked bandit. He and Tonto try to stop the assassination of a European nobleman as well as oppose a brutal outlaw gang. Fast paced telefeature from "The Lone Ranger" (ABC-TV, 1949-57) TV series, culled from the segments "Canuck," "Prince of Buffalo Gap" and "Counterfeit Mask."

2359 One More Train to Rob. Universal, 1971. 106 minutes Color. D: Andrew V. McLaglen. SC: Don Tait & Dick Nelson. WITH George Peppard, Diana Muldaur, John Vernon, France Nuyen, Steve Sandor, Soon-Taik Oh, Richard Loo, C. K. Yang, John Doucette, Robert Donner, George Chandler, Pamela McMyler, Merlin Olsen, Phil Olsen, Marie Windsor, Joan Shawlee, Harry Carey Jr., Ben Cooper, Walter Reed, Andy Albin, Charles Seel, Mike Henry, Don ("Red") Barry, Larry J. Blake, Lane Chandler. When he is released from prison, a man sets out to find his partner who double-crossed him and finds the man is the leading citizen of a small town who is trying to cheat a group of Chinese out of a fortune in gold. Average action outing somewhat helped by its supporting cast of veteran players.

2360 One of the Missing. Feigelson Productions, 1971. 56 minutes Color. D: Julius D. Feigelson. WITH Talmadge Armstrong, Gordon Baxter. During the Civil War, a sharpshooter is pinned by heavy beams after an explosion, with his cocked rifle pointed directly between his eyes. Interesting short feature based on the story by Ambrose Bierce.

2361 One Silver Dollar. Warner/Pathe, 1967. 95 minutes Color. D: Kelvin Jackson Padget (Giorgio Ferroni). SC: George Finlay (Giorgio Stegani) & Kelvin Jackson Padget (Giorgio Ferroni). WITH Montgomery Wood (Giuliano Gemma), Evelyn Stewart (Ida Galli), Peter Cross, Frank Farrell, John MacDouglas, Tor Altmayer, Peter Surtees, Max Dean, Nicholas St. John, Frank Liston, Benny Farber, Andrew Scott, Benny Reeves, Jean Martin. When a silver dollar stops a bullet aimed at him, a young man sets out to round up the gang that tried to murder him. Standard and violent spaghetti Western originally issued in 1965 in Italy as **Un Dollaro Bucato.**

2362 $1,000 Reward. Aywon Film Corporation, 1923. 60 minutes B/W. D: Charles R. Seeling. WITH Guinn "Big Boy" Williams. Falsely accused of murder, a cowboy escapes to another town where he becomes a deputy sheriff and ends up arresting the man who accused him. Fairly good silent actioner made by Charles R. Seeling Productions, with a chance to see Guinn Williams in one of his silent films.

2363 One Way Trail. Columbia, 1931. 60 minutes B/W. D: Ray Taylor. SC: George Plympton. WITH Tim McCoy, Doris Hill, Polly Ann Young, Al Ferguson, Carroll Nye, Bud Osborne, Slim Whitaker, Blackjack Ward, Herman Hack. A cowboy suspects a rancher of murdering his brother and tries to ruin the man. Tim McCoy's first Columbia series entry is an okay affair but not up to the standard of some of his later outings.

2364 Only Birds and Fools. NBC-TV/ Universal, 1974. 76 minutes Color. WITH Richard Boone, Robert Foxworth, Cliff Potts, Rick Lenz, Charles Aidman, Harry Morgan, Harold J. Stone. When a stranger in town is murdered, a lawman investigates and is led to two aviators seeking funds from the town council. Turn-of-the-century Western-mystery is a pleasant affair and was originally made as the final episode of the TV series "Hec Ramsey" (NBC-TV, 1972-74) and telecast April 7, 1974.

2365 Only the Brave. Paramount, 1930. 71 minutes B/W. D: Frank Tuttle. SC: Edward E. Paramore Jr. WITH Gary Cooper, Mary Brian, Phillips Holmes, James Neill, Morgan Farley, Guy Oliver, John Elliott, E. H. Calvert, Virginia Bruce, Elda Voelkel, William LeMaire, Freeman S. Wood, Lalo Encinas, Clinton Rosemond. During the Civil War, a young Union officer is rejected by his girl friend and volunteers to work as a spy. Dated melodrama which will mainly appeal to Gary Cooper fans.

2366 Only the Valiant. Warner Brothers, 1951. 107 minutes B/W. D: Gordon Douglas. SC: Charles Marquis Warren. WITH Gregory Peck, Barbara Payton, Gig Young, Ward Bond, Lon Chaney, Warner Anderson, Jeff Corey, Steve Brodie, Neville Brand, Terry Kilburn, Herbert Heyes, Art Baker, Hugh Sanders, Michael Ansara, Nana Bryant, Harvey Udell, Claire James, Clark Howat, Harlan Howe, John Halloran, David Clarke, William Newell, John Doucette, William Phillips. A disciplinarian cavalry officer leads a small group of men who hate him through Indian country.

They fight the Apaches, and feud among themselves over a pretty woman who has joined them. Somewhat offbeat psychological Western is pretty good, especially Lon Chaney as a murderous, mercenary Arab.

2367 The Open Switch. Rayart, 1926. 50 minutes B/W. D: J. P. McGowan. WITH Helen Holmes, Jack Perrin, Slim Whitaker, Mack V. Wright, Arthur Millet, Henry Roquemore, Max Asher, J. P. McGowan. After the theft of an express package, a crook takes on the identity of a railroad agent in order to get a reward but is opposed by a girl and her partner. The teaming of silent serial queen Helen Holmes and oater star Jack Perrin brings some life to this silent programmer.

2368 Operation Haylift. Lippert, 1950. 75 minutes B/W. D: William Berke. SC: Joseph Sawyer & Dean Riesner. WITH Bill Williams, Ann Rutherford, Tom Brown, Jane Nigh, Joseph Sawyer, Richard Travis, Raymond Hatton, James Colin, Tommy Ivo, Dick Dean, Joanna Armstrong, M'liss McClure, Frank Jaron, H. G. Fisher, Roger Norton. When cattle are stranded and starving during a blizzard in Montana, the brother of one of the ranchers aids the Air Force in dropping hay to feed the stock. Very entertaining modern day Western based on an actual event; actor Joseph Sawyer not only appeared in the film but also cowrote and coproduced it.

2369 Operator 13. Metro-Goldwyn-Mayer, 1934. 86 minutes B/W. D: Richard Boleslavsky. SC: Harry Thew, Zelda Sears & Eve Greene. WITH Marion Davies, Gary Cooper, Jean Parker, Katharine Alexander, Ted Healy, Russell Hardie, Henry Wadsworth, Douglass Dumbrille, Willard Robertson, Fuzzy Knight, Sidney Toler, Robert McWade, Marjorie Gateson, Wade Boteler, Walter Long, Hattie McDaniel, Francis McDonald, William H. Griffith, James Marcus, The Mills Brothers, Sam McDaniel, Buddy Roosevelt, Frank McGlynn Jr., Wheeler Oakman, Don Douglas, Si Jenks, Reginald Barlow, Ernie Alexander, Richard Powell, Wilfred Lucas, William Henry, Richard Tucker, Arthur Grant, Sherry Tansey, Charles Lloyd, Sam Ash, Claudia Coleman, Sterling Holloway, Douglas Fowley. A Yankee actress, during the Civil War, heads South in order to spy for the North. Hokey melodrama wastes a good cast.

2370 Oregon Passage. Allied Artists, 1958. 82 minutes Color. D: Paul Landres. SC: Jack DeWitt. WITH John Ericson, Lola Albright, Toni Gerry, Edward Platt, Harvey Stephens, Judith Ames, H. M. Wynant, Jon Shepodd, Walter Barnes, Paul Fierro. A cavalry officer innocently incurs the wrath of a Shoshone Indian chief when he rescues an Indian girl from a tribal ceremony. Depite an interesting plot, this film is on the bland side.

2371 The Oregon Trail. Republic, 1936. 59 minutes B/W. D: Scott Pembroke. SC: Jack Natteford, Robert Emmett (Tansey) & Lindsley Parsons. WITH John Wayne, Ann Rutherford, Yakima Canutt, Ben Hendricks Jr., Joseph Girard, Frank Rice, E. H. Calvert, Harry Harvey, Jack Rutherford, Roland Ray, Ed LeSaint, Octavio Giraud, Fern Emmett, Gino Corrado, Marian Ferrell. A young man is after the bushwackers who murdered his father and troopers, and along the way he falls for a pretty girl. Average Republic actioner from the studio's early days; probably the least seen of all of John Wayne's "B" starring vehicles.

2372 The Oregon Trail. Universal, 1939. 15 Chapters B/W. D: Ford Beebe & Saul A. Goodkind. SC: George H. Plympton, Basil Dickey, Edmund Kelso, W. W. Watson & Dorothy Cormack. WITH Johnny Mack Brown, Louise Stanley, Bill Cody Jr., Fuzzy Knight, Ed LeSaint, James Blaine, Jack C. Smith, Roy Barcroft, Colin Kenny, Charles King. The government hires a scout to stop Indian attacks on a wagon train headed for the Oregon Territory. Actionful, but juvenile, Universal cliffhanger. V: Cassette Express.

2373 The Oregon Trail. Republic, 1945 55 minutes B/W. D: Thomas Carr. SC: Betty Burbridge. WITH Sunset Carson, Peggy Stewart, Frank Jaquet, Si Jenks, Mary Carr, Lee Shumway, Bud Geary, Kenne Duncan, Steve Winston, Tex Terry, Tom London, Earle Hodgins, Monte Hale, Rex Lease. When outlaws murder a man and a group of Mexicans, the murdered man's son vows revenge. Fairly interesting Sunset Carson vehicle. V: Cumberland Video.

2374 The Oregon Trail. 20th Century-Fox, 1959. 82 minutes Color. D: Gene Fowler Jr. SC: Gene Fowler Jr. & Louis Vittes. WITH Fred MacMurray, Gloria Talbott, William Bishop, Nina Shipman, Henry Hull, John Carradine, John Dierkes, Elizabeth Patterson, James Bell, Ralph Sanford, Tex Terry, Oscar Bergei, Addison Richards, Lumsden Hare, Gene H. Fowler, Sherry Spalding, Roxene Wells. A newspaper reporter is sent on a wagon train west to Oregon to investigate reports that the government has sent troops there to fight the British in a dispute over the territory. Film has a lot of promise but not enough budget to fulfill it.

2375 The Oregon Trail. NBC-TV/Universal, 1976. 100 minutes Color. D: Boris Sagal. SC: Michael Gleason. WITH Rod Taylor, Blair Brown, David Huddleston, Douglas V. Fowley, Andrew Stevens, Linda Purl, G. D. Spradlin, Tony Becker, Gina Maria Smika, George Keymas, Eddie Little Sky. An Eastern family gives up their farm to head West for free land and a new life. Well done wagon train drama which lead to the TV series of the same title which ran on NBC-TV in the fall of 1977.

2376 Oregon Trail Scouts. Republic, 1947. 54 minutes B/W. D: R. G. Springsteen. SC: Earle Snell. WITH Allan "Rocky" Lane, Bobby Blake, Martha Wentworth, Roy Barcroft, Emmett Lynn, Edmund Cobb, Earle Hodgins, Ed Cassidy, Frank Lackteen, Jack Kirk, Jack O'Shea, Chief Yowlachie. Red Ryder comes to the aid of Indians whose trapping rights are sought by a gang of hoodlums who kidnap a young Indian boy. Cheaply made and quite juvenile entry in the "Red Ryder" series, but very actionful.

2377 Orphan of the North. Monogram, 1940. 56 minutes B/W. D-SC: Norman Dawn. WITH Bob Webster, Mary Joyce, Ann Hemming, Eleanor Phillips, John Pool. When a small girl's father fails to return from a gold hunt she sets out to find him and a rescue party follows. Low grade, but picturesque, semi-documentary drama. The title refers to bear cubs.

2378 Orphan of the Pecos. Victory, 1937. 55 minutes B/W. D: Sam Katzman. SC: Basil Dickey. WITH Tom Tyler, Jeanne Martel, Forrest Taylor, Lafe McKee, Theodore (Ted) Lorch, Slim Whitaker, John Elliott. A cowboy tries to find out who killed his pal while outlaws are after the dead man's daughter's ranch. Sam Katzman actually directed this cheap affair in which Jeanne Martel makes a comely "orphan" while a neat plot twist has ventriloquism being used to reveal the murderer.

2379 Orphan Train. CBS-TV, 1979. 150 minutes Color. D: William A. Graham. WITH Jill Eikenberry, Kevin Dobson, Linda Manz, Melissa Michaelsen, Graham Fletcher-Cook. A young social worker teams with a newspaper photographer to lead a group of slum children out of New York City to start new lives in the West. Well done TV drama based on Dorothea G. Petrie's book.

2380 Out California Way. Republic, 1946. 67 minutes Color. D: Lesley Selander. SC: Betty Burbridge. WITH Monte Hale, Adrian Booth, Bobby Blake, John Dehner, Nolan Leary, Fred Graham, Tom London, Jimmy Starr, Edward Keane, Robert Wilke, Brooks Benedict, Roy Rogers, Dale Evans, Don "Red" Barry, Allan "Rocky" Lane, Foy Willing & The Riders of the Purple Sage, St. Luke's Choristers. A young cowboy comes to Hollywood hoping to become a film star but is hindered by a jealous fading genre hero. Fans will enjoy this Monte Hale vehicle, both for its plot and for the guest appearances by genre stars.

2381 Out West with the Hardys. Metro-Goldwyn-Mayer, 1938. 90 minutes B/W. D: George B. Seitz. SC: Kay Van Riper, Agnes Christine Johnston & William Ludwig. WITH Mickey Rooney, Lewis Stone, Cecilia Parker, Ann Rutherford, Fay Holden, Sara Haden, Don Castle, Virginia Weidler, Gordon Jones, Ralph Morgan, Nana Bryant, Thurston Hall, Tom Neal. The Hardy family takes a vacation on a ranch where the owner is having problems with water rights. Delightful "Hardy Family" fare for fans of the series.

2382 Out West with the Peppers. Columbia, 1940. 63 minutes B/W. D: Charles Barton. SC: Harry (Sauber) Rebuas. WITH Edith Fellows, Dorothy Peterson, Dorothy Ann Seese, Tommy Bond, Charles Peck, Bobby Larson, Victor Kilian, Helen Brown, Emory Parnell, Pierre Watkin, Ronald Sinclair, Walter Soderling, Roger Gray, Hal Price. A widowed mother takes her five children to redwood country where the youngsters build a raft. While taking it down a river they almost lose their lives. Pleasing family programmer in the series based on the books by Margaret Sidney.

2383 The Outcast. Republic, 1954. 90 minutes Color. D: William Witney. SC: John K. Butler & Richard Wormser. WITH John Derek, Joan Evans, Jim Davis, Catherine McLeod, Ben Cooper, Taylor Holmes, Nana Bryant, Slim Pickens, Frank Ferguson, James Millican, Bob Steele, Nacho Galindo, Harry Carey Jr., Buzz Henry. A young man returns home to claim his inheritance but finds his vicious, crooked uncle is trying to cheat him out of it. Fast moving and well produced feature with especially good work by Jim Davis as the uncle, Taylor Holmes as his crooked partner and Bob Steele as his gunman.

2384 Outcasts of Black Mesa. Columbia, 1950. 54 minutes B.W. D: Ray Nazarro. SC: Barry Shipman. WITH Charles Starrett, Smiley Burnette, Martha Hyer, Richard Bailey, Stanley Andrews, William Haade, Lane Chandler, William Gould, Robert Wilke, Charles "Chuck" Roberson, Ozie Waters. The Durango Kid aids a young woman whose father and two partners have been murdered because of their mine. Another good action entry in "The Durango Kid" series.

2385 The Outcasts of Poker Flat. RKO Radio, 1937. 68 minutes B/W. D: Christy Cabanne. SC: John Twist & Harry Segall. WITH Preston Foster, Jean Muir, Van Heflin, Virginia Weidler, Margaret Irving, Frank M. Thomas, Si Jenks, Dick Elliott, Al St. John, Bradley Page, Richard Lane, Monte Blue, Billy Gilbert, Dudley Clements. A group of people are snowbound in a cabin and some of them find new meaning for living. A combination of Bret Harte's stories "The Outcasts of Poker Flat" and "The Luck of Roaring Camp," this film did a fairly good job in retaining the flavor of the author's work. Filmed before in 1919 by Universal by director John Ford with Harry Carey, Cullen Landis, Gloria Hope and J. Farrell MacDonald.

2386 The Outcasts of Poker Flat. 20th Century-Fox, 1952. 81 minutes B/W. D: Joseph M. Newman. SC: Edmund H. North. WITH Anne Baxter, Dale Robertson, Miriam Hopkins, Cameron Mitchell, Craig Hill, Barbara Bates, Billy Lynn, Dick Rich, Russ Conway, Bob Adler, John Ridgely, Harry Shannon, Lee Phelps, Harry Carter, Tom Greenway, Harry Harvey Jr. A diverse group of people are tossed out of a mining town and take refuge in a mountain cabin during a snowstorm. Good work by Miriam Hopkins as Duchess, a has-been saloon singer.

2387 Outcasts of the Trail. Republic, 1949. 60 minutes B/W. D: Philip Ford.

SC: Oliver Cooper. WITH Monte Hale, Jeff Donnell, Paul Hurst, Roy Barcroft, John Gallaudet, Milton Parsons, Tommy Ivo, Minerva Urecal, Ted Mapes, George Lloyd, Steve Darrell, Tom Steele. When two cowpokes wander into a small town they find they are unwelcome and try to find out why. Good entry in Monte Hale's Republic series with an especially interesting plotline.

2388 The Outlaw. United Artists, 1943. 126 minutes B/W. D: Howard Hughes, Howard Hawks & Otho Lovering. SC: Jules Furthman. WITH Jane Russell, Jack Beutel, Walter Huston, Thomas Mitchell, Mimi Aguglia, Joseph Sawyer, Gene Rizzi, Frank Darien, Pat West, Carl Stockdale, Nena Quartaro, Martin Garralaga, Julian Rivero, Dickie Jones, Ethan Laidlaw, Ed Brady, William Steele, Wallace Reid Jr., Ed Peil Sr., Lee "Lasses" White, Ted Mapes, William Newell, Lee Shumway, Emory Parnell, Arthur Loft, Dick Elliott, John Sheehan. Doc Holliday befriends the notorious Billy the Kid and saves him from Sheriff Pat Garrett. Later when Billy is shot, he leaves him in the care of Rio, and she and the Kid fall in love. Made in 1941 and given brief release in 1943, this Howard Hughes production was reissued in 1946 by RKO Radio and cut by nine minutes due to censorship problems. The film is historically inaccurate and not overly entertaining but Jane Russell is a knockout as Rio. V: Capital Home Video, VCII Film Classics.

2389 Outlaw Brand. Monogram, 1948. 60 minutes B/W. D: Lambert Hillyer. SC: J. Benton Cheney. WITH Jimmy Wakely, Dub Taylor, Kay Morley, Christine Larson, Ray Whitley, John James, Bud Osborne, Nolan Leary, Eddie Majors, Tom Chatterton, Boyd Stockman, Leonard Penn, Frank McCarroll, Jay Kirby, John James, Dick Rinehart. An outlaw stallion has been plaguing area ranchers and a singing cowpoke who sets out to tame him ends up uncovering the activities of a crook. Passable Monogram programmer with star Jimmy Wakely better with a guitar than a gun.

2390 The Outlaw Breaker. Goodwill, 1926. 55 minutes B/W. D: Jacques Jaccard. SC: Jacques Jaccard & Yakima Canutt. WITH Yakima Canutt, Alma Rayford, Nelson McDowell, Harry Northrub, Dick LeReno, Florence Lee, William Bertram, Frank Ellis, Boy (horse). Carrying on a feud with sheepherders which was begun by his late rancher father, a cowboy finds himself framed on a murder charge. Yakima Canutt fans will like this fast paced silent outing.

2391 Outlaw Country. Screen Guild, 1949. 76 minutes B/W. D: Ray Taylor. SC: Ron Ormond & Ira Webb. WITH Lash LaRue, Al St. John, Nancy Saunders, Dan White, House Peters Jr., Steve Dunhill, Lee Roberts, Ted Adams, John Merton, Dee Cooper, Jack O'Shea, Sandy Saunders, Bob Duncan. Lash LaRue and Fuzzy Q. Jones are assigned to break up a counterfeiting gang. They meet an outlaw called The Frontier Phantom, who turns out to be Lash's long, lost brother. A bit overlong, but still a pretty entertaining Lash LaRue vehicle. Footage later used in **The Frontier Phantom** (q.v.).

2392 The Outlaw Deputy. Puritan, 1935. 56 minutes B/W. D: Otto Brower. SC: Dell Andrews. WITH Tim McCoy, Nora Lane, Bud Osborne, George Offerman Jr., Si Jenks, Joe Girard, Hooper Atchley, Richard Botiller, Charles Brinley, Jack Montgomery, Jim Corey, Hank Bell, Eddie Gribbon, Tex Cooper, George Holtz. A cowboy goes to a lawless town to get revenge for the murder of his young pal. Tim McCoy's first Puritan film is an actionful affair and one which will please his fans.

2393 Outlaw Express. Universal, 1938. 57 minutes B/W. D: George Waggner. SC: Norton S. Parker. WITH Bob Baker, Cecilia Callejo, Don Barclay, LeRoy Mason, Forrest Taylor, Nina Campana, Martin Garralaga, Carleton Young, Carlyle Moore Jr., Jack Kirk, Ed Cassidy, Jack Ingram, Julian Rivero, Tex Palmer, Chief Many Treaties, Ray Jones, Joe Dominguez, William McCauley. The government assigns a cavalry captain to investigate the murders of Pony Express riders and the thefts of their mail. Pleasant and actionful entry in Bob Baker's Universal series; well directed by George Waggner.

The Outlaw Gang see **The Dalton Gang**

2394 Outlaw Gold. Monogram, 1950. 51 minutes B/W. D: Wallace Fox. SC: Jack Lewis. WITH Johnny Mack Brown, Jane Adams, Myron Healey, Milburn Morante, Marshall Reed, Hugh Prosser, Carol Henry, Bud Osborne, George De-Normand, Frank Jacquet, Carl Mathews, Ray Jones, Steve Clark, Bob Woodward, Merrill McCormack. A ranger and his pal look into the thefts of Mexican gold shipments and find out that a newspaper publisher is the culprit. Short, but fairly interesting oater enhanced by Myron Healey's work as a good-badman.

2395 The Outlaw Josey Wales. Warner Brothers, 1976. 137 minutes Color. D: Clint Eastwood. SC: Phil Kaufman & Sonia Chernus. WITH Clint Eastwood, Chief Dan George, Sondra Locke, Bill McKinney, John Vernon, Paula Trueman, Sam Bottoms, Geraldine Keams, Woodrow Parfrey, Joyce Jameson, Sheb Wooley, Royal Dano, Matt Clark, John Verros, Will Sampson, William O'Connell, John Quade. A Civil War veteran ends up with a price on his head when he takes revenge on the soldiers who murdered his family. Overlong and too violent, but this oater is of much more interest than most of star-director Clint Eastwood's later vehicles. V: Warner Home Video.

2396 Outlaw Justice. Majestic, 1932. 61 minutes B/W. D: Armand L. Schaefer. SC: Oliver Drake. WITH Jack Hoxie, Dorothy Gulliver, Donald Keith, Chris-Pin Martin, Charles King, Kermit Maynard, Jack Rockwell, Walter Shumway, Tom London, Jack Trent. A cowboy takes on the guise of a notorious outlaw in order to run in a crook. Jack Hoxie's first sound feature is a slow affair, but pretty well made.

2397 Outlaw of Red River. Fenix/Harold Goldman, 1967. 76 minutes Color. D: Maury Dexter. SC: Eduardo Brochero. WITH George Montgomery, Elisa Montes, Joseph (Jose) Nieto, Miguel Castillo, Jesus Tordesillas, Anna Custodio, Gloria Camara, Ricardo Valle, Carmen Procel, Jose Villasante, Franco Brano, Rafael Yaquero. A gunman, now the right-hand man of a Mexican colonel, must oppose the lawlessness of his boss's fiancée's brother as well as that of a bandit and his gang. Lumbering Spanish oater with star George Montgomery, as the good gunman O'Brien, as its main asset.

2398 Outlaw of the Plains. Producers Releasing Corporation, 1946. 56 minutes B/W. D: Sam Newfield. SC: Elmer Clifton. WITH Buster Crabbe, Al St. John, Patti McCarthy, Charles King (Jr.), Karl Hackett, Jack O'Shea, Bud Osborne, Roy Brent, Slim Whitaker, John Cason, Budd Buster. Crooks convince Fuzzy Q. Jones that worthless land contains gold. He persuades others to join him in purchasing it, but Billy Carson comes to his rescue. Another standard entry in PRC's "Billy Carson" series.

2399 Outlaw Roundup. Producers Releasing Corporation, 1944. 56 minutes B/W. D: Harry Fraser. SC: Elmer Clifton. WITH James Newill, Dave O'Brien, Guy Wilkerson, Helen Chapman, Jack Ingram, I. Stanford Jolley, Charles King, Reed Howes, Bud Osborne, Frank Ellis, Budd Buster, Frank McCarroll, Jimmie Aubrey, Cal Shrum, Dan White, Jack Ternak. Three Texas Rangers set up a plan to round up an outlaw gang by starting the rumor that an outlaw who buried stolen loot in the area has escaped from jail, and one of them accuses the other of being the escaped convict. Low grade effort in PRC's "Texas Rangers" series.

2400 The Outlaw Stallion. Columbia, 1954. 64 minutes Color. D: Fred F. Sears. SC: David Lang. WITH Phil(ip) Carey, Dorothy Patrick, Billy Gray, Gordon Jones, Roy Roberts, Trevor Bardette, Morris Ankrum, Chris Alcaide, Robert Anderson, Harry Harvey, Guy Teague. Thieves pretend to befriend a woman and her young son in order to steal their herd of horses. Unambitious juvenile fare from producer Wallace MacDonald.

2401 The Outlaw Tamer. Empire/Kinematrade, 1934. 60 minutes B/W. D: J. P. McGowan. SC: J. Wesley Patterson. WITH Lane Chandler, Janet Morgan (Blanche Mehaffey), Charles "Slim" Whitaker, Ben(ny) Corbett, George S. ("Gabby") Hayes, J. P. McGowan, Tex Palmer, Herman Hack. A cowboy known as the Phantom Rider discovers a murdered man and sets out to find his killer. Well made low budget production; Lane Chandler's last series film.

Outlaw Territory see **Hannah Lee**

2402 Outlaw Trail. Monogram, 1944. 53 minutes B/W. D: Robert Tansey. SC: Alvin J. Neitz (Alan James). WITH Hoot Gibson, Bob Steele, Chief Thundercloud, Jennifer Holt, Cy Kendall, Rocky Camron, George Eldredge, Charles King, Hal Price, John Bridges, Bud Osborne, Jim Thorpe, Warner Richmond, Frank Ellis, Al Ferguson, Tex Palmer. When a cattle buyer disappears on a visit to a town owned by a banker, The Trail Blazers are sent to investigate. Good, fast paced entry in Monogram's popular "Trail Blazers" series. V: Discount Video.

2403 Outlaw Treasure. American Releasing Corporation, 1955. 67 minutes B/W. D: Oliver Drake. SC: John Carpenter. WITH John (Carpenter) Forbes, Adele

Jergens, Glenn Langan, Michael Whalen, Harry Lauter, Frank Jenks, Hal Baylor, Frank "Red" Carpenter. When gold shipments disappear, an army troubleshooter tries to get to the bottom of the problem. Sub-par production from producer John Carpenter.

2404 Outlaw Women. Howco, 1952. 76 minutes Color. D: Sam Newfield & Ron Ormond. SC: Orville Hampton. WITH Marie Windsor, Richard Rober, Allan Nixon, Carla Balenda, Jackie Coogan, Maria Hart, Jacqueline Fontaine, Billy House, Richard Avonde, Leonard Penn, Lyle Talbot, Brad Johnson, Tom Tyler, Angela Stevens, Ted Cooper, Riley Hill. A small Western town is controlled by Iron Mae McLeod and her gang of female hellions but they are opposed by a gambler who is appointed U. S. marshal. Just as bad as it sounds and Cinecolor does not help; sad to see Tom Tyler gunned down early in the proceedings.

2405 The Outlaw's Daughter. 20th Century-Fox, 1954. 75 minutes Color. D: Wesley Barry. SC: Sam Roeca. WITH Jim Davis, Bill Williams, Kelly Ryan, George Cleveland, Elisha Cook Jr., Guinn Williams, Sara Haden, Nelson Leigh, George Barrows, Zon Murray, Zabuda, Dick (Richard) Powers, Regina Gleason, Sam Flint, Paul Stader, Danny Fisher, Eugene Anderson Jr. A young girl is implicated in a stagecoach holdup when the robbers leave a trail leading to her grandfather's ranch, because the old man was once a famous badman. Fairly entertaining programmer made on a modest budget.

2406 The Outlaws is Coming! Columbia, 1965. 89 minutes B/W. D: Norman Maurer. SC: Elwood Ullman. WITH The Three Stooges (Moe Howard, Larry Fine, Joe DaRita), Adam West, Nancy Kovack, Mort Mills, Don Lamond, Rex Holman, Emil Sitka, Henry Gibson, Murray Alper, Tiny Brauer, Joe Bolton, Hal Fryar (Harlow Hickenlooper), Johnny Ginger, Wayne Mack, Bruce Sedley, Paul Shannon, Sally Starr. Three newsroom zanies accompany a reporter West to do a story on the slaughter of buffalos and they become involved with a legion of gunslingers. Very funny Three Stooges feature which will appeal to both adults and kiddies.

2407 Outlaws of Boulder Pass. Producers Releasing Corporation, 1942. 61 minutes B/W. D: Sam Newfield. SC: Steve Braxton. WITH George Houston, Al St. John, Smokey (Dennis) Moore, Marjorie Manners, Charles

King, I. Stanford Jolley, Karl Hackett, Ted Adams, Kenne Duncan, Frank Ellis, Steve Clark, Jimmie Aubrey, Budd Buster. An outlaw gang is charging illegal tolls for cattle transportation and the Lone Rider and his pals try to stop them. Typically passable entry from PRC's series "The Lone Rider." TV title: **The Lone Rider and Outlaws of Boulder Pass.**

2408 Outlaws of Pine Ridge. Republic, 1942. 56 minutes B/W. D: William Witney. SC: Norman S. Hall. WITH Don "Red" Barry, Lynn Merrick, Noah Beery, Emmett Lynn, Clayton Moore, Donald Kirke, Forrest Taylor, Stanley Price, Francis Ford, Wheaton Chambers, George J. Lewis, Roy Brent, Kenneth Terrell, Al Taylor, Tex Terry, Jack O'Shea, Cactus Mack, Tom Steele, Horace B. Carpenter, Duke Green. When he stops a holdup, a young gambler finds himself a hero and he ends up stopping an outlaw gang. William Witney's first directorial entry in the Don Barry series is a fast moving and exciting effort.

2409 Outlaws of Santa Fe. Republic, 1944. 56 minutes B/W. D: Howard Bretherton. SC: Norman S. Hall. WITH Don "Red" Barry, Helen Talbot, Wally Vernon, Twinkle Watts, Charles Morton, Herbert Heyes, Bud Geary, LeRoy Mason, Kenne Duncan, Nolan Leary, Walter Soderling, Edmund Cobb, Frank McCarroll, Robert Kortman, Emmett Lynn, Ernie Adams, Jack Kirk, Pierce Lyden, Forrest Taylor, Bob Burns, Jack O'Shea, Fred Graham. When he finds out he is the son of a murdered lawman, not the son of an outlaw, a young bandit agrees to take the job of sheriff to stop a crook and his gang who control Santa Fe. Pretty good action entry in Don Barry's Republic series, although the addition of Twinkle Watts is dubious.

2410 Outlaws of Sonora. Republic, 1938. 56 minutes B/W. D: George Sherman. SC: Betty Burbridge & Edmund Kelso. WITH Robert Livingston, Ray Corrigan, Max Terhune, Jack Mulhall, Jean Joyce, Stelita Peluffe, Otis Harlan, Tom London, Gloria Rich, Ralph Peters, George Chesebro, Frank LaRue, Jack Ingram, Merrill McCormack, Curley Dresden, Jim Corey, George Cleveland, Earl Dwire, Jack Kirk, Edwin Mordant. An outlaw impersonates Stony Brooke, who is blamed for a series of robberies. He and his pals try to capture the real culprit. Good action entry in "The Three Mesquiteers" series.

2411 Outlaws of Stampede Pass. Monogram, 1943. 55 minutes B/W. D: Wallace Fox. SC: Jess Bowers (Adele Buffington). WITH Johnny Mack Brown, Raymond Hatton, Harry Woods, Ellen Hall, Edmund Cobb, Charles King, Milburn Morante, Sam Flint, Mauritz Hugo, Art Mix, Cactus Mack, Artie Ortego, Hal Price, Dan White, Tex Cooper, Bill Wolfe, Jon Dawson. Two lawmen are aided by a blacksmith's daughter as they try to find out who is behind the rustling of ranchers' cattle. Standarized but entertaining series oater.

2412 Outlaws of Texas. Monogram, 1950. 56 minutes B/W. D: Thomas Carr. SC: Dan Ullman. WITH Whip Wilson, Andy Clyde, Phyllis Coates, Terry Frost, Tommy Farrell, Zon Murray, George DeNormand, Stanley Price, Steve Carr. Two U. S. marshals work undercover to capture a gang of bank robbers. Good Whip Wilson vehicle.

2413 Outlaws of the Cherokee Trail. Republic, 1941. 56 minutes B/W. D: Lester Orlebeck. SC: Albert DeMond. WITH Bob Steele, Tom Tyler, Rufe Davis, Lois Collier, Rex Lease, Tom Chatterton, Roy Barcroft, Joel Friedkin, Philip Trent, Peggy Lynn, Bud Osborne, Chief Yowlachie, John James, Lee Shumway, Karl Hackett, Billy Burtis, Griff Barnett, Bud Geary, Al Taylor, Henry Wills, Sarah Padden, Iron Eyes Cody, Cactus Mack, Chuck Morrison. When the daughter of a ranger captain is kidnapped by outlaws, The Three Mesquiteers come to her rescue. Good action entry in the latter "Three Mesquiteers" grouping.

2414 Outlaws of the Desert. Paramount, 1941. 54 (66) minutes B/W. D: Howard Bretherton. SC: J. Benton Cheney & Bernard McConville. WITH William Boyd, Andy Clyde, Brad King, Forrest Stanley, Jean Phillips, Nina Guilbert, Luci Deste, Albert Morin, George J. Lewis, Duncan Renaldo, Jean Del Val, George Woolsley. The Bar 20 boys go to Arabia to buy horses for a rancher and after he is kidnapped they become involved in desert warfare. Nice desert photography helps this meandering and fairly dull "Hopalong Cassidy" entry. V: Video Connection.

2415 Outlaws of the Panhandle. Columbia, 1941. 60 minutes B/W. D: Sam Nelson. SC: Paul Franklin. WITH Charles Starrett, Frances Robinson, Bob Nolan & The Sons of the Pioneers, Richard Fiske, Ray Teal, Lee Prather, Bud Osborne, Steve Clark, Eddie Laughton, Norman Willis, Blackie Whiteford, Stanley Brown, Jack Low. A cowboy aids cattlemen trying to construct a railroad spur, but the project is opposed by a crooked gambler who robs gold shipments. Good Charles Starrett vehicle.

2416 Outlaws of the Prairie. Columbia, 1937. 59 minutes B/W. D: Sam Nelson. SC: Ed Earl Repp. WITH Charles Starrett, Donald Grayson, Iris Meredith, The Sons of the Pioneers, Ed LeSaint, Hank Bell, Dick Curtis, Norman Willis, Edmund Cobb, Art Mix, Steve Clark, Earle Hodgins, Richard Alexander, Frank Shannon, Fred Burns, Jack Rockwell, Jack Kirk, George Chesebro, Frank Ellis, Charles LeMoyne, Frank McCarroll, Curley Dresden, Vernon Dent, George Morrell, Ray Jones, Jim Corey, Blackie Whiteford, Lee Shumway, Bob Burns. Two Texas Rangers are sent to a small town to investigate a series of stagecoach holdups. One of them is also on the trail of the man who murdered his father and branded him when he was a child. Pretty good Charles Starrett vehicle with a grand supporting cast.

2417 Outlaws of the Range. Spectrum, 1936. 60 minutes B/W. D: Al Herman. SC: Zara Tazil. WITH Bill Cody, Catherine Cotter, Bill Cody Jr., William McCall, Gordon Griffith, Dick Strong, Wally West. A gang, headed by a ranch foreman, rustles a rancher's cattle because a businessman, who pretends to be the rancher's friend, wants his land for its oil deposits. A drifting cowboy, who has saved the rancher's daughter from being dragged by a horse, is blamed when the rancher is murdered. Complicated but formula Bill Cody outing; poorly edited.

2418 Outlaws of the Rio Grande. Producers Releasing Corporation, 1941. 63 minutes B/W. D: Peter Stewart (Sam Newfield). SC: George H. Plympton. WITH Tim McCoy, Virginia Carpenter, Charles King, Ralph Peters, Karl Hackett, Rex Lease, Philip Turich, Frank Ellis, Kenne Duncan, Thorton Edwards, Joe Dominguez, George Chesebro, Sherry Tansey. A gang of counterfeiters force an engraver to work for them and a U. S. marshal sets out to breakup the operation. Well made and nicely paced entry in Tim McCoy's PRC series.

2419 Outlaws of the Rockies. Columbia, 1945. 55 minutes B/W. D: Ray Nazarro. SC: J. Benton Cheney. WITH Charles Starrett, Tex Harding, Dub Taylor, Carole

Matthews, Spade Cooley, Carolina Cotton, Philip Van Zandt, I. Stanford Jolley, George Chesebro, Steve Clark, Jack Rockwell, Frank LaRue, Bud Nelson, Kermit Maynard, Ted Mapes, Frank O'Connor. Two lawmen are accused of aiding an outlaw gang and are forced out of town only to be opposed by the crooks. But the Durango Kid, who is really one of the lawmen, comes to the rescue. Fast moving but somewhat hard to follow "Durango Kid" segment.

2420 Outlaw's Paradise. Victory, 1939. 60 minutes B/W. D: Sam Newfield. SC: Basil Dickey. WITH Tim McCoy, Joan Barclay, Ben Corbett, Ted Adams, Forrest Taylor, Bob Terry, Donald Gallagher, Dave O'Brien, Jack Mulhall, Carl Mathews, Jack C. Smith, George Morrell. Federal investigator Lightnin' Bill Carson, who closely resembles an imprisoned outlaw, decides to take on the identity of the badman in order to infiltrate his gang. Tim McCoy's handling of dual roles is the most interesting aspect of this Sam Katzman production.

2421 Outlaw's Son. United Artists, 1957. 88 minutes B/W. D: Lesley Selander. SC: Richard Alan Simmons. WITH Dane Clark, Ben Cooper, Lori Nelson, Ellen Drew, Charles Watts, Cecile Rogers, Joseph "Bucko" Stafford, Eddie Foy III, John Pickard, Robert Knapp, Guy Preston, George Pembroke, Jeff Daley, James Parnell. A young man comes to the aid of his outlaw father, who deserted him years before, when the latter is falsely accused of committing a robbery. Okay melodrama, well acted by its leading players.

2422 Outlawed Guns. Universal, 1935. 62 minutes B/W. D: Ray Taylor. SC: Jack Neville. WITH Buck Jones, Ruth Channing, Frank McGlynn, Roy D'Arcy, Joseph Girard, Pat O'Brien, Joan Gale, Lee Shumway, Charles King, Jack Rockwell, Monte Montague, Bob Walker, Carl Stockdale, Cliff Lyons, Jack Montgomery. When his younger brother becomes involved with an outlaw gang, a man sets out to stop the gang and save his sibling. Very picturesque Buck Jones oater enhanced by a good story.

2423 Outposts of the Mounties. Columbia, 1939. 63 minutes B/W. D: C. C. Coleman Jr. SC: Charles Francis Royal. WITH Charles Starrett, Iris Meredith, Bob Nolan & The Sons of the Pioneers, Stanley Brown, Kenneth MacDonald, Edmund

Cobb, Lane Chandler, Dick Curtis, Albert Morin, Hal Taliaferro, Pat O'Hara. A Mountie is forced to arrest his girl's brother for the murder of a trading company co-owner but he doubts his guilt and sets out to find the culprit. Another adventure in the north woods with Charles Starrett and it is a fairly exciting one.

2424 The Outrage. Metro-Goldwyn-Mayer, 1964. 97 minutes B/W. D: Martin Ritt. SC: Michael Kanin. WITH Paul Newman, Laurence Harvey, Claire Bloom, Edward G. Robinson, William Shatner, Howard DaSilva, Albert Salmi, Thomas Chalmers, Paul Fix. Three different stories are told about the incident of an outlaw capturing a man and his wife, with the woman raped and the husband dying. Surprisingly sturdy Western adaptation of the Japanese film **Rashomon** (1951).

2425 The Outriders. Metro-Goldwyn-Mayer, 1950. 93 minutes Color. D: Roy Rowland. SC: Irving Ravetch. WITH Joel McCrea, Arlene Dahl, Barry Sullivan, Claude Jarman Jr., James Whitmore, Ramon Novarro, Jeff Corey, Ted De Corsia, Martin Garralaga. Three Confederate spies join a wagon train in Santa Fe during the Civil War and plan to hijack its one million dollars in gold for the Southern cause. Fairly entertaining actioner aided by the MGM gloss.

2426 Over the Border. Monogram, 1950. 58 minutes B/W. D: Wallace Fox. SC: J. Benton Cheney. WITH Johnny Mack Brown, Wendy Waldron, Myron Healey, Marshall Reed, Mike Ragan, House Peters Jr., Pierre Watkin, Hank Bell, George DeNormand, Milburn Morante, Frank Jacquet, Buck Bailey, George Sowards, Carol Henry, Frank McCarroll, Bud Osborne, Artie Ortego, Herman Hack, Ray Jones, Bob Woodward. A Wells Fargo guard uncovers a plot by a businessman to smuggle silver into the U. S. from Mexico and sell it for a profit. Okay Johnny Mack Brown entry enhanced by Myron Healey's villainy.

2427 Over the Santa Fe Trail. Columbia, 1947. 63 minutes B/W. D: Ray Nazarro. SC: Louise Rosseau. WITH The Hoosier Hot Shots, Ken Curtis, Jennifer Holt, Guy Kibbee, Guinn Williams, Noel Neill, Holmes Herbert, George Chesebro, Jim Diehl, Frank LaRue, Steve Clark, Julian Rivero, Nolan Leary, Bud Osborne, The DeCastro Sisters, Art West & His Sunset Riders. A pretty medicine show entertainer falls for a cowpoke who is at odds with an outlaw gang. Tame oater full of musical numbers and comedy but not much genre action; for fans of The Hoosier Hot Shots.

2428 The Overland Express. Columbia, 1938. 55 minutes B/W. D: Drew Eberson. SC: Monroe Shaff. WITH Buck Jones, Marjorie Reynolds, Carlyle Moore, Maston Williams, William Arnold, Lew Kelly, Bud Osborne, Ben Taggart, Ben Corbett, Gene Alsace, Blackie Whiteford, Bob Woodward. At the outbreak of the Civil War a man sets up the cross country pony express, but the operation is opposed by renegades planning to start an Indian uprising. Exciting Buck Jones vehicle.

2429 Overland Mail. Monogram, 1939. 51 minutes B/W. D: Robert Hill. SC: Robert Emmett (Tansey). WITH Jack Randall, Vince Barnett, Jean Joyce, Tristram Coffin, Glenn Strange, Dennis Moore, Merrill McCormack, Joe Garcia, Sherry Tansey, Hal Price, Maxine Leslie, Harry Semels, George Cleveland, Iron Eyes Cody, George Morrell, Hank Bell. A mail rider and a federal agent team to capture a counterfeiting gang responsible for the death of an Indian and thus prevent tribal warfare. Fast moving Jack Randall vehicle.

2430 Overland Mail. Universal, 1942. 15 Chapters B/W. D: Ford Beebe & John Rawlins. SC: Paul Huston. WITH Lon Chaney, Helen Parrish, Noah Beery, Noah Beery Jr., Don Terry, Roy Harris, Robert Barron, Jack Clifford, Tom Chatterton, Harry Cording, Charles Stevens, Carleton Young, Bob Baker, Ethan Laidlaw, William Gould, Ben Taggart, Frank Pershing, Tom Steele, Forrest Taylor, Chief Thundercloud, Jack Rockwell, Bill Moss, Marguerite De La Motte, Ruth Ricksby, Charles Phipps, Eddie Polo, Frosty Royce, George Sherwood, Gene O'Donnell, Jack Shannon. A frontiersman and his pal are assigned to find out who is sabotaging mail shipments in a remote territory and find out a renegade is dressing his gang as Indians when making the raids. Lon Chaney is an appealingly athletic hero in this fast paced chapterplay. V: Video Connection.

2431 Overland Mail Robbery. Republic, 1943. 56 minutes B/W. D: John English. SC: Bob Williams & Robert Yost. WITH Wild Bill Elliott, George "Gabby" Hayes, Anne Jeffreys, Weldon Heyburn, Nancy Gay, Kirk Alyn, Roy Barcroft, Bud Geary, Tom London, Alice Fleming, Jack Kirk, Kenne Duncan, Jack Rockwell, Frank McCarroll, Jack O'Shea, LeRoy Mason, Hank Bell, Cactus Mack, Ray Jones, Tom Steele, Frank Ellis, Maxine Doyle. A young man from Boston comes West to claim his inheritance but is opposed by a crook and Wild Bill Elliott comes to his aid. Standard but past paced and actionful Republic series entry. V: Cumberland Video.

2432 Overland Pacific. United Artists, 1954. 73 minutes Color. D: Fred F. Sears. SC: J. Robert Bren, Gladys Atwater & Martin Goldsmith. WITH Jack (Jock) Mahoney, Peggie Castle, Adele Jergens, William Bishop, Walter Sande, Chubby Johnson, Pat Hogan, Chris Alcaide, Phil Chambers, George Eldredge, Dick Rich, House Peters Jr. A railroad investigator works incognito as he looks into reports of Indian raids on trains. Low budget but effective action drama.

2433 Overland Riders. Producers Releasing Corporation, 1946. 54 minutes B/W. D: Sam Newfield. SC: Ellen Coyle. WITH Buster Crabbe, Al St. John, Patti McCarty, Slim Whitaker, Bud Osborne, Jack O'Shea, Frank Ellis, Al Ferguson, John Cason, George Chesebro, Lane Bradford, Wally West. Billy Carson and Fuzzy Q. Jones investigate a stagecoach robbery and find the money taken was to be used to pay the mortgage on a property where a railroad line will intersect. Typically cheap and fast moving "Billy Carson" series entry.

2434 Overland Stage Raiders. Republic, 1938. 55 minutes B/W. D: George Sherman. SC: Luci Ward. WITH John Wayne, Ray Corrigan, Max Terhune, Louise Brooks, Anthony Marsh, Ralph Bowman (John Archer), Gordon Hart, Roy James, Olin Francis, Fern Emmett, Henry Otho, George Sherwood, Archie Hall, Frank LaRue, Yakima Canutt, Milton Kibbee, Jack Kirk, Slim Whitaker, Bud Osborne, Dirk Thane, Bud McClure, John Beach, Curley Dresden, George Plues, Edwin Gaffney, Tommy Coats. The Three Mesquiteers become partners in an operation that flies ore out of a remote gold mine but their other partner is being blackmailed by the crooked owner of a stage line. Modern day "Three Mesquiteers" outing moves along at a fast clip but is best remembered as silent film siren Louise Brooks' final movie.

2435 Overland Stagecoach. Producers Releasing Corporation, 1942. 61 minutes B/W. D: Sam Newfield. SC: Steve Braxton.

WITH Robert Livingston, Al St. John, Smoky (Dennis) Moore, Julie Duncan, Glenn Strange, Charles King, Art Mix, Budd Buster, Ted Adams, Julian Rivero, John Elliott, Tex Cooper. The Lone Rider is on the trail of a masked stagecoach bandit. Robert Livingston's first, and Dennis Moore's last, entry in "The Lone Rider" series is actionful enough to satisfy fans.

2436 Overland Telegraph. RKO Radio, 1951. 60 minutes B/W. D: Lesley Selander. SC: Adele Buffington. WITH Tim Holt, Richard Martin, Gail Davis, George Nader, Mari Blanchard, Hugh Beaumont, Robert Wilke, Robert Bray, Fred Graham, Cliff Clark, Russell Hicks. An innocent man is falsely blamed for the murder of a worker installing a telegraph line and a cowboy tries to prove his innocence. Typical entry in Tim Holt's fine RKO series.

2437 Overland to Deadwood. Columbia, 1942. 59 minutes B/W. D: William Berke. SC: Paul Franklin. WITH Charles Starrett, Russell Hayden, Cliff Edwards, Leslie Brooks, Norman Willis, Francis Walker, Lynton Brent, Matt Willis, June Pickrell, Gordon DeMain, Art Mix, Herman Hack, Bud Osborne, Bud Geary. Two cowboys come to the rescue of a young woman whose hauling operation is being sabotaged by a rival who wants to obtain an important railroad franchise. The final Charles Starrett-Russell Hayden vehicle is on the mediocre side but Norman Willis is quite good as the villain.

2438 Overland Trails. Monogram, 1948. 60 minutes B/W. D: Lambert Hillyer. SC: Jess Bowers (Adele Buffington). WITH Johnny Mack Brown, Raymond Hatton, Virginia Belmont, Steve Darrell, Bill Kennedy, Holly Bane, Ted Adams, Boyd Stockman, Virginia Carroll, Carl Mathews, Milburn Morante, Bob Woodward, Boyd Stockman, Tom London, Pierce Lyden, Roy Butler, Post Park, Marshall Reed, Artie Ortego, George Peters. A cowboy is in love with the daughter of a man, who with his partner, grubstakes prospectors and then kills them to get their claims. Some interesting plot twists add life to this otherwise typical Monogram series outing.

2439 Overland with Kit Carson. Columbia, 1939. 15 Chapters B/W. D: Sam Nelson & Norman Deming. SC: Morgan Cox, Joseph Poland & Ned Dandy. WITH Bill Elliott, Iris Meredith, Richard Fiske, Bobby Clack, James Craig, Hal Taliaferro, Trevor Bardette, LeRoy Mason, Olin Francis, Francis Sayles, Kenneth MacDonald, Dick Curtis, Richard Botiller, Ernie Adams, Ben Campbell, Joe Garcia, Stanley Brown, Hank Bell, Art Mix, John Tyrell, Lee Prather, Jack Rockwell, Ed LeSaint, Martin Garralaga, Iron Eyes Cody, Carl Stockdale, Robert Fiske, Eddie Foster, Irene Herndon, J. W. Cody, Del Lawrence. Frontier scout Kit Carson tries to locate a mysterious outlaw called Pegleg and his Black Raiders who are raiding settlements west of the Mississippi River in an attempt to rid the area of settlers and set up an empire. There is nothing really special about this cliffhanger other than Bill Elliott holds it all together in good fashion as he essays the title role.

2440 The Overlanders. Universal-International/J. Arthur Rank/Associated British-Pathe, 1946. 91 minutes B/W. D-SC: Harry Watt. WITH Chips Rafferty, John Nugent Howard, Daphne Campbell, Jean Blue, Helen Grieve, John Fernside, Peter Pagan, Frank Ransome, Stan Tolhurst, Marshall Corsby, Clyde Combo, Henry Murdock. In Australia in 1942, cattlemen decide to drive their herds south across the continent to keep them from falling into the hands of possible Japanese invaders. Well done Australian feature based on a true story.

2441 The Over-the-Hill Gang. ABC-TV/Paramount, 1969. 74 minutes Color. D: Jean Yarbrough. SC: Jameson Brewer. WITH Walter Brennan, Edgar Buchanan, Andy Devine, Jack Elam, Gypsy Rose Lee, Rick Nelson, Kris Nelson, Pat O'Brien, Chill Wills, Edward Andrews, William Smith, Dennis Cross, Rex Holman, Burt Mustin, Almira Sessions. Three former Texas Rangers come to the aid of a buddy and end up defending a town against a crooked mayor and his lawless gang. Very amusing and well done TV Western-comedy, expertly directed by Jean Yarbrough and well acted by its cast of veterans.

2442 The Over-the-Hill Gang Rides Again. ABC-TV/Paramount, 1970. 74 minutes Color. D: George McGowan. SC: Richard Carr. WITH Walter Brennan, Fred Astaire, Edgar Buchanan, Andy Devine, Chill Wills, Lana Wood, Paul Richards, Parley Baer, Walter Burke, Jonathan Hole, Lillian Bronson, Burt Mustin, Pepper Martin, Don Wilbanks. A trio of ex-Texas Rangers try to help a friend who is a drunk and after they reform him the group ends up defending the peace in Waco. Tired followup to the delightful **The Over-the-Hill Gang** (q.v.).

2443 The Ox-Bow Incident. 20th Century-Fox, 1943. 76 minutes B/W. D: William A. Wellman. SC: Lamar Trotti. WITH Henry Fonda, Dana Andrews, Mary Beth Hughes, Anthony Quinn, William Eythe, Henry (Harry) Morgan, Jane Darwell, Francis Ford, Harry Davenport, Matt Briggs, Frank Conroy, Marc Lawrence, Victor Kilian, Paul Hurst, Chris-Pin Martin, Ted North, George Meeker, Almira Sessions, Margaret Hamilton, Dick Rich, Stanley Andrews, Billy Benedict, Rondo Hatton, Paul Burns, Leigh Whipper, George Lloyd, George Chandler, Hank Bell, Forrest Dillon, Willard Robertson, Tom London, George Plues. Two drifters get involved with a lynch mob who want to hang three men accused of cattle rustling and murder. Classic adaptation of Walter Van Tilburg Clark's novel, fine character work; a must see! Also done as **Lynch Mob** (q.v.).

P

2444 Pack Train. Columbia, 1953. 57 minutes B/W. D: George Archainbaud. SC: Norman S. Hall. WITH Gene Autry, Smiley Burnette, Gail Davis, Kenne Duncan, Sheila Ryan, Tom London, Harry Lauter, Melinda Plowman, Louise Lorimer, Frankie Marvin, Tex Terry, Kermit Maynard, Frank Ellis, Richard Alexander, Herman Hack. A cowboy tries to get supplies needed by settlers but crooks want to sell the commodities at inflated prices to miners at a gold strike. Fair Gene Autry series vehicle.

2445 Packin' It In. CBS-TV, 1983. 100 minutes Color. D: Jud Taylor. SC: Patricia Jones & Donald Reiker. WITH Richard Benjamin, Paula Prentiss, Andrea Marcovicci, Tony Roberts, Molly Ringwald, David Hollander, Mari Gorman, Kenneth McMillan, Sam Whipple, Clinton Dean, Susan Ruttan, Laura Bruneau. A city family, fed up with urban life, join their former neighbors in the Oregon high country and once there find a truckers' strike is causing food hoarding. Fairly pleasant TV movie along the lines of the theatrical "Wilderness Family" trilogy.

2446 Paint Your Wagon. Paramount, 1969. 151 (166) minutes Color. D: Joshua Logan. SC: Alan Jay Lerner. WITH Lee Marvin, Clint Eastwood, Jean Seberg, Harve Presnell, Ray Walston, Tom Ligon, Ben(ny) Baker, Alan Baxter, Alan Dexter, William O'Connell, Paula Trueman, Robert Easton, Geoffrey Morgan, H. B. Haggerty, Terry Jenkins, Karl Bruck, John Mitchum, Sue Casey, Eddie Little Sky, Harvey Parry, H. W. Gim, William Mims, Roy Jenson, Pat Hawley, The Nitty Gritty Dirt Band. A Mormon girl is bought by a gold miner and she falls in love with his partner and decides to marry both men to the consternation of the locals. Alan Jay Lerner wrote and produced this overlong musical from his Broadway play and the end result is fair entertainment, although the film should probably have been done years before with Nelson Eddy or Howard Keel in the lead. V: Paramount.

2447 The Painted Desert. Pathe, 1931. 75 minutes B/W. D: Howard Higgin. SC: Howard Higgin & Tom Buckingham. WITH William Boyd, Helen Twelvetrees, William Farnum, J. Farrell MacDonald, Clark Gable, William Walling, Wade Boteler, William LeMaire, Richard Cramer, Jim Mason, Charles Sellon, Edward Hearn, James Donlan. A young boy is found on the desert and is adopted by a man, and he grows to manhood as a thirty-year feud between his adopted father and another man continues. Fairly interesting early sound Western mainly known today because of Clark Gable in a supporting role. V: Cassette Express.

2448 The Painted Desert. RKO Radio, 1938. 59 minutes B/W. D: David Howard. SC: John Rathmell & Oliver Drake. WITH George O'Brien, Laraine (Day) Johnson, Ray Whitley, Fred Kohler, Max Wagner, Stanley Fields, Harry Cording, Lee Shumway, Lloyd Ingraham, Maude Allen, William V. Mong, Lew Kelly, Jim Mason, Jack O'Shea, Ray Jones. A young man returns to his feuding home to find out that a crook is trying to steal a tungsten mine. Remake of the 1931 RKO-Pathe film with William Boyd and Clark Gable, this good George O'Brien series entry deftly used stock footage from the earlier feature. Ray Whitley sings the title song.

2449 The Painted Hills. Metro-Goldwyn-Mayer, 1951. 65 minutes Color. D: Harold F. Kress. SC: True Boardman. WITH Lassie, Paul Kelly, Bruce Cowling, Gary Gray, Art Smith, Ann Doran, Chief Yowlachie, Andrea Virginia Lester, Brown Jug (Don Kay) Reynolds. In the California gold fields of the 1880s a boy and his Collie dog try to outwit a crook. Well made and pleasing family fare; also called **Lassie's Adventures in the Gold Rush.**

2450 The Painted Stallion. Republic, 1937. 12 Chapters. D: William Witney, Alan James & Ray Taylor. SC: Barry Shipman & Winston Miller. WITH Ray Corrigan, Hoot Gibson, Julia Thayer (Jean Carmen), LeRoy Mason, Duncan Renaldo, Jack Perrin, Sammy McKim, Hal Taliaferro, Oscar & Elmer, Yakima Canutt, Maston Williams, Duke Taylor, Loren Riebe, George DeNormand, Gordon DeMain, Charles King, Vinegar Roan, Lafe McKee, Frankie Marvin, Chief Big Tree, Pascale Perry, Henry Hall, Ed Peil Sr., Horace B. Carpenter, Joe Yrigoyen, Monte Montague, Roy Bucko, Joe Dominguez, Jack Padjan, Al Haskell, Augie Gomez. A crooked politician tries to stop a wagon train on its way to the New Mexico Territory, hoping to sabotage a trade agreement between the U. S. and Mexico. Top notch Republic serial with beautiful Julia Thayer as the mysterious rider; great fun. V: Cassette Express.

2451 The Painted Trail. Monogram, 1938. 50 minutes B/W. D: Robert Hill. SC: Robert Emmett (Tansey). WITH Tom Keene, Eleanor Stewart, LeRoy Mason, Walter Long, James Eagles, Forrest Taylor, Harry Harvey, Ernie Adams, Bud Osborne, Glenn Strange, Frank Campeau, Robert Kortman, Richard Cramer, Tom London. Masquerading as a wanted outlaw called The Pecos Kid, a federal agent infiltrates an outlaw gang in order to arrest them and stop their smuggling and rustling activities. Short but sturdy actioner providing good entertainment.

2452 The Pal from Texas. Metropolitan, 1939. 55 minutes B/W. D: Harry S. Webb. SC: Carl Krusada. WITH Bob Steele, Claire Rochelle, Jack Perrin, Josef Swickard, Ted Adams, Betty Mack, Carleton Young, Jack Ingram, Robert Walker. A crook tries to cheat the rightful owner out of his gold mine and a cowboy comes to the rescue. Tawdry, low grade series oater; Bob Steele deserves far better.

2453 Pale Rider. Warner Brothers, 1985. 115 minutes Color. D: Clint Eastwood. SC: Michael Butler & Fritz Manes. WITH Clint Eastwood, Michael Moriarty, Carrie Snodgrass, Christopher Penn, John Russell, Richard Dysart, Sydney Penny, Richard Kiel, Doug McGrath. A drifter tries to aid gold prospectors whose land is coveted by a grasping tycoon who brings in hired guns to aid his cause. It has all been done before but this 1980s genre revival attempt is worth watching.

2454 The Paleface. Paramount, 1948. 91 minutes Color. D: Norman Z. McLeod. SC: Edmund Hartmann & Frank Tashlin. WITH Bob Hope, Jane Russell, Robert Armstrong, Iris Adrian, Robert (Bobby) Watson, Jackie Searl, Joseph Vitale, Henry Brandon, Charles Trowbridge, Clem Bevans, Jeff York, Stanley Andrews, Wade Crosby, Chief Yowlachie, Iron Eyes Cody, John Maxwell, Tom Kennedy, Francis McDonald, Frank Hagney, Skelton Knaggs, Olin Howlin, George Chandler, Nestor Paiva, Earle Hodgins, Arthur Space, Edgar Dearing, Dorothy Granger, Charles Cooley, Eric Alden, Jody Gilbert, Al Hill, Harry Harvey, Hall Bartlett, Stanley Blystone, Robert Kortman, Oliver Blake, Lane Chandler, Syd Saylor, Paul E. Burns, Dick Elliott, Sharon McManus. Calamity Jane and a correspondence school dentist team to take on a notorious outlaw gang. Funny spoof of Westerns followed by a sequel, **Son of Paleface** (q.v.).

2455 Palm Springs. Paramount, 1936. 72 minutes B/W. D: Aubrey Scotto. SC: Joseph Fields. WITH Frances Langford, Sir Guy Standing, Smith Ballew, David Niven, Ernest Cossart, E. E. Clive, Spring Byington, Sterling Holloway, Grady Sutton, Sarah Edwards, Ed Moose, Mary Jane Temple, June Horn, Ann Doran, Ella McKenzie, Fred "Snowflake" Toones, Frances Morris, David Worth, Annabelle & Marianne Brudie, Lee Phelps, Maidel Turner, Bert Gale, Cyril Ring. Although the daughter of a wealthy man is supposed to wed an English nobleman she falls in love with a cowboy. This musical comedy will be of interest to "B" Western fans because it gave Smith Ballew his first leading role in a Western, although a peripheral one at best.

2456 The Palomino. Columbia, 1950. 73 minutes Color. D: Ray Nazarro. SC: Tom Kilpatrick. WITH Jerome Courtland, Beverly Tyler, Joseph Calleia, Roy Roberts, Gordon Jones, Robert Osterloh, Trevor Bardette, Tom Trout, Harry Garcia, Juan Duval. Crooks steal a girl's prize horse so she will lose her ranch and a cattle buyer tries to help her retrieve the animal. Okay juvenile melodrama helped somewhat by Technicolor.

2457 Pals of the Golden West. Republic, 1951. 68 minutes B/W. D: William Witney.

SC: Robert DeMond & Eric Taylor. WITH Roy Rogers, Dale Evans, Estelita Rodriguez, Pinky Lee, Roy Barcroft, Anthony Caruso, Eduardo Jiminez, Kenneth Terrell, Emmett Vogan, Roy Rogers Riders, Maurice Jara. When diseased cattle are smuggled into the country, the Border Patrol assigns agent Roy Rogers the task of stopping the operations. Roy Rogers' final series film is a competent affair and a good finale to his Republic tenure.

2458 Pals of the Pecos. Republic, 1941. 56 minutes B/W. D: Lester Orlebeck. SC: Oliver Drake & Herbert Delmas. WITH Robert Livingston, Bob Steele, Rufe Davis, June Johnson, Dennis Moore, Roy Barcroft, Pat O'Malley, Robert Frazer, John Holland, Tom London, Robert Winkler, George Chesebro, Chuck Morrison, Bud Osborne, Jack Kirk, Forrest Taylor, Frank Ellis, Eddie Dean. When a rivalry develops between two stagecoach lines, The Three Mesquiteers come to the aid of one who is being cheated by the other. Only average outing in "The Three Mesquiteers" series.

2459 Pals of the Range. Superior, 1935. 55 minutes B/W. D: Elmer Clifton. SC: Elmer Clifton & George Merrick. WITH Rex Lease, Frances (Morris) Wright, Art Mix, George Chesebro, Yakima Canutt, Blackie Whiteford, Bill Patton, Artie Ortego, Milburn Morante, Tom Forman, Bud Osborne, Ben Corbett, George Morrell, Joey Ray. When a rancher is falsely accused of stealing cattle, he escapes from jail to find the real cattle thieves. Low grade entry in Rex Lease's series for producer Louis Weiss.

2460 Pals of the Saddle. Republic, 1938. 55 minutes B/W. D: George Sherman. SC: Stanley Roberts & Betty Burbridge. WITH John Wayne, Ray Corrigan, Max Terhune, Doreen McKay, George Douglas, Josef (Joe) Forte, Frank Milan, Ted Adams, Harry Depp, Dave Weber, Don Orlando, Charles Knight, Jack Kirk, Monte Montague, Olin Francis, Curley Dresden, Art Dillard, Tex Palmer. The Three Mesquiteers become involved with a female secret agent who is on the trail of foreign agents who are smuggling a secret chemical out of the U. S. John Wayne's first entry in "The Three Mesquiteers" series is a fast paced, actionful affair.

2461 Pals of the Silver Sage. Monogram, 1940. 52 minutes B/W. D: Al Herman.

SC: George Martin. WITH Tex Ritter, Sugar Dawn, Arkansas Slim Andrews, Clarissa Curtis, Carleton Young, Glenn Strange, Joe McGuinn, Chester Gan, Warner Richmond, Gene Alsace, Chick Hannon, Harry Harvey, Sherry Tansey. Two cowhands come to the aid of a little girl who will lose the ranch she has inherited if she cannot get her cattle to market on time. Pretty fair Tex Ritter vehicle. British title: **Roundup Time.**

2462 Panamint's Bad Man. Principal/20th Century-Fox, 1938. 60 minutes B/W. D: Ray Taylor. SC: Luci Ward & Charles A. Powell. WITH Smith Ballew, Evelyn Daw, Noah Beery, Stanley Fields, Harry Woods, Pat O'Brien, Armand Wright. A marshal goes undercover disguised as a badman in order to get the goods on a gang of robbers and their boss. Smith Ballew's final "B" film is a pretty good one. V: Video Dimensions.

2463 Pancho Villa. Scotia International, 1972. 92 minutes Color. D: Gene Martin. SC: Julian Halvey. WITH Telly Savalas, Clint Walker, Anne Francis, Chuck Connors, Jose Maria Prada, Angel Del Pozo, Luis Davila, Monica Randall, Antonio Casas, Alberto Dalbes, Berta Barri, Eduardo Calvo, Dan Van Husen, Norman Bailey, Tony Ross, Art Larkin, Gene Collins, Ralph Neville, Walter Coy. The story of the Mexican bandit leader who led a revolution of the peons against the government and his invasion of the United States, attacking a small border town. Fairly standard European-made actioner.

2464 Pancho Villa Returns. Hispano Continental Films, 1950. 96 minutes B/W. D-SC: Miguel Contreras Torres. WITH Leo Carrillo, Jeanette Comber, Esther Fernandez, Rodolfo Acosta, Rafael Alcayde, Jorge Trevino, Eduardo Gonzales Pliego. Pancho Villa leads the Mexican people in revolt against the government but must contend with personal problems including the ordering of a firing squad for a respected officer who has broken an order. Mexican-made actioner has its main interest in the performance of Leo Carrillo as Pancho Villa.

2465 Panhandle. Allied Artists, 1948. 85 minutes B/W. D: Lesley Selander. SC: John C. Champion & Blake Edwards. WITH Rod Cameron, Cathy Downs, Reed Hadley, Anne Gwynne, Blake Edwards, Dick Crockett, Charles Judels, Alex Gerry, Francis McDonald, J. Farrell MacDonald, Henry Hall, Stanley Andrews,

Jeff York, James Harrison, Charles La-Torre, Frank Dae, Bud Osborne. An ex-gunman takes up his six-shooters to get revenge for the murder of his brother. Top notch action feature with fine work by Rod Cameron as the hero and Blake Edwards as the villain.

Panhandle Trail see **The Mysterious Rider** (1942)

2466 Parade of the West. Universal, 1930. 75 minutes B/W. D: Harry Joe Brown. SC: Bennett Cohen & Lesley Mason. WITH Ken Maynard, Gladys McConnell, Otis Harlan, Frank Rice, Bobby Dunn, Jackie Hanlon, Fred Burns, Frank Yaconelli, Stanley Blystone, Edgar "Blue" Washington. A cowboy, the guardian of a small boy, appears in a wild west show and romances one of the performers, but the owner's right-hand man resents the attention he pays the girl and sets out to sabotage his ride on a wild horse. Ken Maynard part-talkie which will be of interest to his fans.

2467 Paradise Canyon. Monogram, 1935. 55 minutes B/W. D: Carl L. Pierson. SC: Lindsley Parsons & Robert Emmett (Tansey). WITH John Wayne, Marion Burns, Earle Hodgins, Yakima Canutt, Reed Howes, Perry Murdock, Gordon Clifford, Henry Hall, Gino Corrado, Tex Palmer, Earl Dwire, John Goodrich, Herman Hack. An undercover agent is working along the Mexican border trying to capture a gang of counterfeiters. The final entry in John Wayne's Monogram-Lone Star series is a pretty good one, highlighted by Earle Hodgins' barker scenes.

2468 The Paradise Trail. Mark IV Pictures, 1981. 90 minutes Color. D: Donald W. Thompson. WITH Burt Douglas, Robert Somers, Teri Hernandez, Gene Otis, Deborah Trissel, The Chuckwagoneers, Dusty (mule). A blind preacher and a crippled gunfighter meet and both find religious salvation. Religious Western made in Iowa and mainly shown to churches.

2469 Parasite. Embassy, 1982. 85 minutes Color. D: Charles Band. SC: Alan Adler, Michael Shoob & Frank Leverny. WITH Robert Claudini, Demi Moore, Luca Bercovini, Vivian Blaine, James Davidson, Al Fann, Cherie Currie. In the savage West of the future a terrible giant parasite destroys people while a doctor tries to find a way to combat the menace. Absolutely awful 3-D effort.

2470 Pardners. Paramount, 1956. 90 minutes Color. D: Norman Taurog. SC: Sidney Sheldon. WITH Dean Martin, Jerry Lewis, Lori Nelson, Jackie Loughery, John Baragrey, Jeff Morrow, Agnes Moorehead, Lon Chaney, Mickey Finn, Douglas Spencer, Philip Tonge, Bob Steele, Jack Elam, Scott Douglas, Stuart Randall, Richard Aherne, Milton Frome. Two Easterners come to the small Western town where their fathers were once gunned down and clean up the lawless element. Average genre comedy loosely based on **Rhythm on the Range** (q.v.), also directed by Norman Taurog.

2471 Pardon My Gun. Pathe, 1930. 70 minutes B/W. D: Robert De Lacy. SC: Hugh Cummings. WITH Sally Starr, George Duryea (Tom Keene/Richard Powers), Lee Moran, Robert Edeson, Frank MacFarlane, Tom MacFarlane, Harry Woods, Lew Meehan, Ethan Laidlaw, Harry Watson, Al Norman, Ida May Chadwick, Abe Lyman & His Band. A cowboy loves the boss's daughter who is also sought by a rival rancher, and the two are also rivals at an annual relay race. Uneven early talkie which lends its second half to a series of musical numbers in a barn dance setting; mainly for fans of Tom Keene.

2472 Pardon My Gun. Columbia, 1942, 57 minutes B/W. D: William Berke. SC: Wyndham Gittens. WITH Charles Starrett, Alma Carroll, Noah Beery, Arthur Hunnicutt, Texas Jim Lewis & His Lone Star Cowboys, Dick Curtis, Ted Mapes, Lloyd Bridges, Dave Harper, Roger Graves, Guy Usher, Jack Kirk, Steve Clark, Art Mix, George Morrell, Joel Friedkin, Denver Dixon. A surveyor and a sheep rancher's daughter find themselves accused of murder when a man is bushwacked and robbed of a large amount of money he was carrying. Fast moving and well scripted Charles Starrett vehicle with some good western swing music by Texas Jim Lewis and his group.

2473 Park Avenue Logger. RKO Radio, 1937. 67 minutes B/W. D: David Howard. SC: Dan Jarrett & Ewing Scott. WITH George O'Brien, Beatrice Roberts, Willard Robertson, Ward Bond, Bert Hanlon, Gertrude Short, Lloyd Ingraham, George Rosenor, Robert Emmett O'Connor, Al Baffert, Dave Wengren. A playboy is sent to work in a lumber camp and finds out the foreman is a crook. Another good example of the high quality George O'Brien RKO series. TV title: **Tall Timber.**

2474 Paroled to Die. Republic, 1938. 55 minutes B/W. D: Sam Newfield. SC: George Plympton. WITH Bob Steele, Kathleen Eliot, Karl Hackett, Horace Murphy, Steve Clark, Budd Buster, Sherry Tansey, Frank Ball, Jack C. Smith, Horace B. Carpenter. A rancher is blamed for a bank robbery and a series of killings when the real culprit is a local businessman. Quality entry in Bob Steele's series for producer A. W. Hackel. V: Cumberland Video.

2475 The Parson and the Outlaw. Columbia, 1957. 71 minutes Color. D: Oliver Drake. SC: Oliver Drake & John Mantley. WITH Anthony Dexter, Charles "Buddy" Rogers, Marie Windsor, Sonny Tufts, Robert Lowery, Jean Parker, Madalyn Trahey, Bob Steele, Bob Duncan, Bob Gilbert, Jack Owell, John Davis, Joe Sodja, Paul Spahn, Herman Pulver, Richard Reeves. Escaping death at the hands of Sheriff Pat Garrett, Billy the Kid tries to lead a peaceful life but becomes involved with a minister fighting a corrupt land baron and his henchmen. Tacky production with little but curio value; coproduced by Charles "Buddy" Rogers.

2476 The Parson of Panamint. Paramount, 1941. 84 minutes B/W. D: William McGann. SC: Harold Shumate & Adrian Scott. WITH Charles Ruggles, Ellen Drew, Philip Terry, Joseph Schildkraut, Porter Hall, Henry Kolker, Janet Beecher, Clem Bevans, Douglas Fowley, Paul Hurst, Frank Puglia, Minor Watson, Harry Hayden, Russell Hicks, Hal Price. A young man comes to a brawling mining town and tries to reform its citizens. Very pleasant screen adaptation of the Peter B. Kyne story, previously filmed in 1916 by Paramount with Dustin Farnum and again by the same studio in 1922 with Jack Holt.

2477 The Parting of the Trails. Syndicate, 1930. 60 minutes B/W. D: J. P. McGowan. SC: Sally Winters. WITH Bob Custer, Vivian Ray, Bobby Dunn, Henry Roquemore, George A. Miller, Tommy Bay. Two drifters come to the aid of a girl whose millionaire father has been kidnapped by outlaws. Silly Bob Custer silent effort, also issued theatrically with a music score version.

2478 Partners. RKO Radio, 1932. 57 minutes B/W. D: Fred Allen, SC: Donald W. Lee. WITH Tom Keene, Nancy Drexel, Otis Harlan, Victor Potel, Bob Nelson, Lee Shumway, Billy Franey, Carleton Young, Ben Corbett. A horse raiser is blamed for the murder of the man who loaned him the money to buy a ranch, and he sets out to find the real killer. A well made but not very interesting oater with Tom Keene a bit too dramatic as the star; some good desert scenery.

2479 Partners of the Plains. Paramount, 1938. 54 (70) minutes B/W. D: Lesley Selander. SC: Harrison Jacobs. WITH William Boyd, Russell Hayden, Harvey Clark, Gwen Gaze, Hilda Plowright, John Warburton, Alan Bridge, Al Hill, Earle Hodgins, John Beach, Jim Corey. Hoppy and the Bar 20 boys try to aid a snobbish young woman by saving her cattle and land from the evil Scar Lewis. Well photographed and very entertaining entry in the "Hopalong Cassidy" series.

2480 Partners of the Sunset. Monogram, 1948. 53 minutes B/W. D: Lambert Hillyer. SC: J. Benton Cheney. WITH Jimmy Wakely, Dub Taylor, Christine Larson, Steve Darrell, Marshall Reed, Jay Kirby, Leonard Penn, Bob Woodward, Carl Mathews, Carl Sepulveda. A young girl plans to murder her husband but the plot is uncovered by a singing cowboy. Mystery element and songs somewhat help this laggard Jimmy Wakely vehicle.

2481 Partners of the Trail. Monogram, 1931. 63 minutes B/W. D: Wallace Fox. SC: G. A. Durlam. WITH Tom Tyler, Betty Mack, Lafe McKee, Reginald Sheffield, Pat Rooney, Horace B. Carpenter. A man kills his wife's lover but his buddy is convicted of the crime. Very low grade Tom Tyler outing.

2482 Partners of the Trail. Monogram, 1944. 59 minutes B/W. D: Lambert Hillyer. SC: Frank Young. WITH Johnny Mack Brown, Raymond Hatton, Christine McIntyre, Craig Woods, Robert Frazer, Lloyd Ingraham, Marshall Reed, Jack Ingram, Lynton Brent, Steve Clark, Benny Corbett, Ted Mapes, Joe Egenton, Hal Price. Two lawmen come to a small town to discover why ranchers are being murdered and uncover a plot to obtain a rich gold claim. Well written Johnny Mack Brown-Raymond Hatton series entry.

2483 Passage West. Paramount, 1951. 81 minutes Color. D-SC: Lewis R. Foster. WITH John Payne, Dennis O'Keefe, Arleen Whelan, Frank Faylen, Mary Anderson, Peter Hanson, Richard Rober, Griff Barnett, Dooley Wilson, Mary Field,

Richard Travis, Mary Beth Hughes, Arthur Hunnicutt, Lillian Bronson, Susan Whitney, Paul Fierro. A half-dozen escaped convicts take refuge in a wagon train belonging to a religious sect heading West. Average oater which is well produced.

2484 Passion. RKO Radio, 1954. 84 minutes Color. D: Allan Dwan. SC: Joseph Leytes, Beatrice A. Dresher & Howard Estabrook. WITH Cornel Wilde, Yvonne De Carlo, Raymond Burr, Lon Chaney, John Qualen, Rodolfo Acosta, Anthony Caruso, Frank De Kova, Peter Coe, John Dierkes, Richard Hale, Rosa Turich, Stuart Whitman, James Kirkwood, Robert Warwick, Belle Mitchell, Alex Montoya, Zon Murray, Rozene Kemper. In Spanish California, a man finds his wife and daughter murdered by a land-hungry Army officer and his thugs and he teams with his pretty sister-in-law to get revenge. Interesting, violent Western with good work by Yvonne De Carlo in a dual role and Lon Chaney as the vicious henchman Castro; concluding gunfight sequence in the snowy Sierras is a real knockout. V: Disney Home Video.

2485 Pat Garrett and Billy the Kid. Metro-Goldwyn-Mayer, 1973. 106 minutes Color. D: Sam Peckinpah. SC: Rudolph Wurlitzer. WITH James Coburn, Kris Kristofferson, Richard Jaeckel, Katy Jurado, Chill Wills, Jason Robards, Bob Dylan, R. G. Armstrong, Luke Askew, John Beck, Richard Bright, Matt Clark, Rita Coolidge, Jack Dodson, Jack Elam, Emilio Fernandez, Paul Fix, L. Q. Jones, Slim Pickens, Jorge Russek, Charles Martin Smith, Harry Dean Stanton, John Chandler, Rudy Wurlitzer, Elisha Cook Jr., Gene Evans, Dub Taylor, Don Levy, Sam Peckinpah, Rutanya Alda, Walter Kelly, Claudia Bryar, Mike Mikler, Aurora Clavel, Donnie Fritts, Barry Sullivan. Sheriff Pat Garrett is on the trail of his ex-pal Billy the Kid after the outlaw refuses his orders to leave New Mexico Territory. Stagnant version of the final days of the famous outlaw with self-indulgent direction and a lifeless music score by Bob Dylan. Heavily recut for television, including the footage with Barry Sullivan which was deleted for theatrical release. V: MGM/United Artists.

2486 The Pathfinder. Columbia, 1953. 78 minutes Color. D: Sidney Salkow. SC: Robert E. Kent. WITH George Montgomery, Helena Carter, Jay Silverheels, Walter Kingsford, Rodd Redwing, Elena Verdugo, Chief Yowlachie, Ross Conklin,

Bruce Lester. When the French attack his tribe, a young Englishman, raised by the Indians, tries to help the British. Another tepid retelling of James Fenimore Cooper's "Leatherstocking" tales, this time embellished by color.

2487 The Pathfinder and the Mohican. International Television Corporation (ITC), 1964. 90 minutes B/W. D: Sam Newfield. WITH John Hart, Lon Chaney, Jonathan White, Angela Fusco, Larry Solway. When Delaware Indians are falsely accused of various crimes against settlers, Hawkeye and Chingachgook attempt to prove the truth. Paste-up telefeature made from three segments of the cheap "Hawkeye and the Last of the Mohicans" (Syndicated, 1956-57) TV series.

2488 Pawnee. Republic, 1957. 80 minutes Color. D-SC: George Waggner. WITH George Montgomery, Lola Albright, Bill Williams, Francis McDonald, Robert E. Griffin, Dabbs Greer, Kathleen Freeman, Charlotte Austin, Ralph Moody, Anne Barton, Raymond Hatton, Charles Horvath, Robert Nash. A white man raised by the Pawnee Indians must choose between his own race and his adopted one when corrupt whites try to steal Indian lands. Pretty fair action outing.

2489 Payment in Blood. Columbia, 1968. 89 minutes Color. D: E. G. Rowland (Enzo Girolami). SC: Tito Carpi & E. G. Rowland. WITH Guy Madison, Edd Byrnes, Louise Barrett, Enzo Girolami, Mario Donen, Ryk Boyd, Rosella Bergamonti, Alfred Aysanoa, Marco Mariani, Ariana Facchetti, Attillio Severini, Giulio Maculani, Mirella Pamphilio, Piero Vida. During the Civil War a bounty hunter infiltrates a renegade band of Confederates in Texas with tales of a hidden treasure. Violent and bloody Italian Western which may appeal to Guy Madison fans. Made in 1967 by Circus Film/Rono Roma/St. Regis Films as **7 Winchester Per Un Massacro** (7 Winchesters for a Massacre). TV title: **Winchester for Hire.**

2490 Peace for a Gunfighter. Crown-International, 1965. 82 minutes Color. D: Raymond Boley. SC: Michael W. Fuller. WITH Burt Berger, JoAnne Meredith, Everett King, Sterling Walker, Danny Zapien, John Scovern, Mark Farrington, Ray Odom, Mark Sanchez, Allen Wood. A gunman called "The Preacher" tries to give up his trade but meets with resistance in a small town. Low grade actioner.

2491 The Peacemaker. United Artists, 1956. 83 minutes B/W. D: Ted Post. SC: Hal Richards & Jay Ingram. WITH James Mitchell, Rosemarie Bowe, Jan Merlin, Jess Barker, Hugh Sanders, Herbert Patterson, Dorothy Patrick, Taylor Holmes, Robert Armstrong, Philip Tonge, Wheaton Chambers, Harry Shannon, Jack Holland, Nancy Evans. An ex-gunman turned preacher arrives in a small town to find a feud between settlers and ranchers. Very vapid oater; typical example of why the genre declined in the 1950s.

2492 The Pecos Kid. Commodore, 1935. 56 minutes B/W. D: William Berke. SC: Henry Hess. WITH Fred Kohler Jr., Ruth Findlay, Wally Wales, Roger Williams, Francis Walker, Ed Cassidy, Budd Buster, Robert Walker, Clyde McClory, Rose Plummer, Earl Dwire, Jack Evans. When his family is murdered by outlaws, a young boy grows up determined to get revenge on the culprits. Cheaply made but rather interesting Fred Kohler Jr. vehicle; worth a look.

2493 Pecos River. Columbia, 1951. 55 minutes B/W. D: Fred F. Sears. SC: Barry Shipman. WITH Charles Starrett, Smiley Burnette, Jack (Jock) Mahoney, Delores Sidener, Steve Darrell, Harmonica Bill, Edgar Dearing, Frank Jenks, Paul Campbell, Zon Murray, Maudie Prickett, Eddie Fetherston. A post office investigator masquerades as a stage driver as he tries to find out who has been carrying out a series of mail holdups. Okay action entry in the "Durango Kid" series.

2494 Per Un Pugno Nell'occhio. Flora/Variety Film, 1966. 101 minutes Color. D: Giorgio Simonelli. SC: Ciorciolini, Gianviti & Sollazzo. WITH Franco Franchi, Ciccio Ingrassia, George Hilton, Gloria Paul, Pedro Sanchez, Mimmo Palmara, Umberto D'Orsi, Orchidea De Santis, Fulvia Franco. Two dimwits pretend to be a bandit and a sharp-shooter to eke out a living deceiving poor peons until a bounty hunter forces them to join him in his lawless activities. Inane Italian spoof of spaghetti Westerns. Alternate title: **I Due Figli Di Ringo** (Ringo's Two Sons).

2495 The Perfect Alibi. Photo Drama Company, 1924. 55 minutes B/W. D: Ford Beebe. SC: Frances Beebe & Ford Beebe. WITH Leo Maloney, Leonard Clapham, Jim Corey, Bullet (dog). A ranger, who refuses to pursue charges against his girl's brother, is dismissed from the service but tries to find out who really pulled off the robbery for which the young man is blamed. This quickly made and fast moving effort provides a chance to see popular silent cowboy star Leo Maloney in a typical vehicle.

2496 A Perilous Journey. Republic, 1953. 90 minutes B/W. D: R. G. Springsteen. SC: Richard Wormser. WITH Vera Ralston, David Brian, Scott Brady, Charles Winninger, Hope Emerson, Eileen Christy, Leif Erickson, Veda Ann Borg, Virginia Grey, Dorothy Ford, Ben Cooper, Kathleen Freeman, Barbara Hayden, Paul Fierro, Angela Greene, John Dierkes, Alden Aldrich, Fred Graham, Trevor Bardette, Richard Reeves, Bob Carney, Charles Evans, Philip Van Zandt, Byron Foulger, Denver Pyle, Harry Tyler, Emil Sitka, Jack O'Shea, Brandon Beach, Frank Hagney, Stanley Blystone, Richard Alexander, Charles Cane, Gloria Clark. A woman joins four dozen women, all mail order brides on the way to California on a ship via Panama, in order to locate her gambler-husband. Standard Republic feature with Hope Emerson stealing the show as the stern-willed chaperone.

2497 Perils of the Royal Mounted. Columbia, 1942. 15 Chapters B/W. D: James W. Horne. SC: Basil Dickey, Scott Littleton, Jesse A. Duffy & Louis Heifetz. WITH Robert Stevens (Kellard), Nell O'Day, Herbert Rawlinson, Kenneth MacDonald, John Elliott, Nick Thompson, Art Miles, Richard Fiske, Rick Vallin, Forrest Taylor, Kermit Maynard, George Chesebro, Jack Ingram, Iron Eyes Cody. A Mountie finds that Indian attacks are really being made by white men led by a renegade in cahoots with a corrupt Indian medicine man. Standard Columbia cliffhanger.

2498 Perils of the Wilderness. Columbia, 1956. 15 Chapters B/W. D: Spencer Gordon Bennet. SC: George H. Plympton. WITH Dennis Moore, Richard Emory, Eve Anderson, Kenneth MacDonald, Rick Vallin, John Elliott, Don C. Harvey, Terry Frost, Al Ferguson, Bud Osborne, Rex Lease, Pierce Lyden, John Mitchum, Lee Roberts, Stanley Price, Kermit Maynard, Ed Coch. A man poses as an outlaw in order to capture a ruthless crime baron in the Canadian north country and he is aided by a Mountie and a pretty girl. The penultimate cliffhanger is a sadly cheap affair with an unbelievable plotline.

2499 The Persuader. Allied Artists, 1957. 72 minutes B/W. D: Dick Ross. SC: Curtis Kenyon. WITH James Craig, Kristine Miller, William Talman, Darryl Hickman, Georgia Lee, Alvy Moore, Rhoda Williams, Gregory Walcott, Paul Engle, Nolan Leary, Frank Richards. A minister arrives in a small Oklahoma town where outlaws killed his brother and he helps the citizens stand up to the lawlessness. Pretty fair programmer.

2500 Peter Lundy and the Medicine Hat Stallion. NBC-TV, 1977. 100 minutes Color. D: Michael O'Herlihy. SC: Jack Turley. WITH Leif Garrett, Milo O'Shea, John Anderson, Bibi Besch, John Quade, Ann Doran, Brad Rearden, Mitch Ryan, Charles Tyner, Ned Romero, James Lydon. In the early 1860s a youngster becomes a Pony Express rider in the Nebraska Territory. Well made and entertaining juvenile fare for television.

2501 The Petrified Forest. Warner Brothers, 1936. 83 minutes B/W. D: Archie Mayo. SC: Charles Kenyon & Delmer Daves. WITH Leslie Howard, Bette Davis, Genevieve Tobin, Dick Foran, Humphrey Bogart, Joseph Sawyer, Porter Hall, Charley Grapewin, Paul Harvey, Eddie Acuff, Adrian Morris, Nina Campana, Slim Thompson, John Alexander, Addison Richards (voice). A diverse group of people are held prisoner in a way station in the desert by a fleeing gangster and his gang. Top notch screen adaptation of Robert Emmet Sherwood's play, which is really gangster drama in a Western setting.

2502 The Phantom Bullet. Universal, 1926. 60 minutes B/W. D: Clifford Smith. SC: Curtis Benton. WITH Hoot Gibson, Eileen Percy, Alan Forrest, Pat Harmon, William H. Turner, Nelson McDowell, John T. Price, Pee Wee Holmes, Rosemary Cooper. After his father is mysteriously killed a man returns home and takes on the guise of a bumbler in order to find out who did the shooting. Well photographed Hoot Gibson silent feature with lots of comedy and an exciting car chase sequence.

2503 The Phantom Cowboy. Republic, 1941. 56 minutes B/W. D: George Sherman. SC: Doris Schroeder. WITH Don "Red" Barry, Virginia Carroll, Milburn Stone, Neyle Marx, Rex Lease, Nick Thompson, Bud Osborne, Ernest Wilson, Burr Caruth, Frank Ellis, Art Dillard, Jack O'Shea, Chuck Baldra. When a man is murdered

and his niece is cheated out of his ranch, a cowboy becomes a masked phantom in order to restore the girl's property. Star Don Barry and director George Sherman do the best they can in the confines of a script which lacks action.

2504 The Phantom Empire. Mascot, 1935. 12 Chapters. D: Otto Brower & B. Reeves Eason. SC: John Rathmell, Armand L. Schaefer, Wallace MacDonald, Gerald Geraghty & Hy Freedman. WITH Gene Autry, Frankie Darro, Betsy King Ross, Dorothy Christy, Wheeler Oakman, Charles K. French, Warner Richmond, J. Frank Glendon, Smiley Burnette, William Moore, Ed Peil Sr., Jack Carlyle, Frank Ellis, Wally Wales, Buffalo Bill Jr., Fred Burns, Stanley Blystone, Richard Talmadge, Bob Card, Bruce Mitchell. Crooks are after a valuable mineral on a radio singer's ranch and the latter, in fighting the crooks, finds a secret underground civilization. Gene Autry's first starring vehicle is a flavorful affair combining the Western and sci-fi genres. Feature titles: **Men with Steel Faces** and **Radio Ranch.**

2505 The Phantom Flyer. Universal, 1928. 45 minutes B/W. D: Bruce Mitchell. SC: Bruce Mitchell & Gardner Bradford. WITH Al Wilson, Lillian Gilmore, Buck Connors, Billy "Red" Jones, Don Fuller, Myrtis Crinley, Mary Cornwallis, Larry Steers. A homesteader and his family find themselves opposed by a female cattle rancher who wants their water rights. Colorful silent actioner with lots of exciting aerial footage with star Al Wilson, here playing a border patrol aviator. Also called **The Phantom Ranger.**

2506 Phantom Gold. Columbia, 1938. 56 minutes B/W. D: Joseph Levering. SC: Nate Gatzert. WITH Jack Luden, Beth Marion, Barry Downing, Slim Whitaker, Hal Taliaferro, Art Davis, Jack Ingram, Marin Sais, Buzz Barton, Jimmy Robinson, Tuffy (dog). Outlaws plan a gold rush by salting an old mine but are thwarted by a cowboy and his two buddies, as well as a young boy and a dog the three men have rescued. Jack Luden's final series film is a mediocre affair.

2507 The Phantom of Santa Fe. Burroughs-Tarzan Enterprises, 1936. 87 minutes Color. D: Jacques Jaccard. SC: Charles F. Royal. WITH Norman Kerry, Nina Quartero, Frank Mayo, Monte Montague, Tom O'Brien, Carmelita Geraghty, Jack

Mower, Frank Ellis, Merrill McCormack. A young man pretends to be a coward to disguise himself as the "Hawk," a masked man opposed to a crook and his gang. Originally made in 1931 as **The Hawk**, this feature was rerecorded and re-edited before receiving theatrical release; pretty poor stuff.

2508 Phantom of the Desert. Syndicate, 1930. 55 minutes B/W. D: Harry S. Webb. SC: Carl Krusada. WITH Jack Perrin, Eva Novak, Josef Swickard, Lila Eccles, Ben Corbett, Edward Earle, Robert Walker, Pete Morrison. Two cowpokes go to work for a rancher whose horses are supposedly being rustled by a wild stallion and one of the cowboys gets to the bottom of the trouble. Likable Jack Perrin early talkie vehicle.

2509 Phantom of the Plains. Republic, 1945. 54 (56) minutes B/W. D: Lesley Selander. SC: Earle Snell & Charles Kenyon. WITH Bill Elliott, Bobby Blake, Alice Fleming, Ian Keith, William Haade, Virginia Christine, Jack Rockwell, Tom London, Earle Hodgins, Bud Geary, Henry Hall, Fred Graham, Jack Kirk, Rose Plummer. The Duchess falls in love with an Englishman but Red Ryder does not trust the man and finds out he is a wife-murderer. So-so "Red Ryder" episode.

2510 Phantom of the Range. Victory, 1936. 58 minutes B/W. D: Robert Hill. SC: Basil Dickey. WITH Tom Tyler, Beth Marion, Sammy Cohen, Forrest Taylor, Soledad Jiminez, Charles King, John Elliott, Richard Cramer. An investigator for the cattlemen's association is on the trail of a gang after a secret treasure. Shoddy Sam Katzman production which hardly enhances Tom Tyler's genre reputation. V: Video Connection.

2511 The Phantom of the West. Mascot, 1931. 10 Chapters B/W. D: D. Ross Lederman. SC: Ford Beebe. WITH Tom Tyler, Dorothy Gulliver, William Desmond, Tom Santschi, Tom Dugan, Philo McCullough, Joe Bonomo, Kermit Maynard, Frank Lanning, Frank Hagney, Dick Dickinson, Hallee Sullivan, Al Taylor, Ernie Adams. A mysterious figure plagues a small town, murdering several people while a rancher tries to solve the mystery of who killed his father. Mascot's second sound cliffhanger, and Tom Tyler's talkie debut, is an interesting affair with a good mystery angle and the usual genre thrills. V: Cassette Express.

2512 Phantom Patrol. Ambassador, 1936. 60 minutes B/W. D: Charles Hutchison. SC: Stephen Norris. WITH Kermit Maynard, Joan Barclay, Dick Curtis, Harry Worth, George Cleveland, Paul Fix, Julian Rivero, Eddie Phillips, Roger Williams, Lester Dorr. A Mountie impersonates an American detective story writer in order to round up a gang of crooks. Average Kermit Mayanard vehicle for producer Maurice Conn, supposedly based on James Oliver Curwood's Fatal Note. V: Cassette Express.

Phantom Pinto see **Buzzy and the Phantom Pinto**

2513 The Phantom Plainsmen. Republic, 1942. 57 minutes B/W. D: John English. SC: Robert Yost & Barry Shipman. WITH Bob Steele, Tom Tyler, Rufe Davis, Lois Collier, Robert O. Davis, Charles Miller, Alex Callam, Monte Montague, Henry Roland, Richard Crane, Jack Kirk, Ed Cassidy, Vince Barnett, Lloyd Ingraham, Al Taylor, Bud Geary, Herman Hack. The Three Mesquiteers find out a rancher is selling cattle to the Nazis. Interesting "Three Mesquiteers" series entry.

2514 Phantom Rancher. Colony, 1940. 61 minutes B/W. D: Harry Fraser. SC: William Lively. WITH Ken Maynard, Dorothy Short, Harry Harvey, Ted Adams, Dave O'Brien, Tom London, John Elliott, Reed Howes, Steve Clark, Carl Mathews, Sherry Tansey, Wally West, George Morrell, Herman Hack. Ken Mitchell arrives to take over his late uncle's ranch and takes on the guise of a masked phantom in opposing a land grabber. Ken Maynard was getting hefty when he made this entertaining oater but he was still quite agile. V: Video Communications, Discount Video.

The Phantom Ranger (1928) see **The Phantom Flyer**

2515 Phantom Ranger. Monogram, 1938. 54 minutes B/W. D: Sam Newfield. SC: Joseph O'Donnell. WITH Tim McCoy, Suzanne Kaaren, John Merton, Charles King, Karl Hackett, Tom London, Richard Cramer, John St. Polis, Edward Earle, Harry Strang, Bruce Warren, Bob McKenzie, Jimmie Aubrey, Donald Dean, Herb Holcombe, Wally West, Horace Carpenter, Sherry Tansey, George Morrell, Herman Hack. Secret Service agent Tim Hayes is sent West to round up the gang responsible for flooding the country with counterfeit money. Low grade but okay modern sagebrush yarn.

2516 The Phantom Rider. Universal, 1936. 15 Chapters B/W. D: Ray Taylor. SC: George Plympton, Basil Dickey & Ella O'Neill. WITH Buck Jones, Marla Shelton, Diana Gibson, Joey Ray, Harry Woods, Frank La Rue, George Cooper, Eddie Gribbon, Helen Shipman, Jim Mason, Charles Lemoyne, Charles King. When crooks try to steal a girl's ranch a government agent takes on the guise of a masked phantom in order to stop them. Well paced serial sure to delight Buck Jones fans.

2517 The Phantom Rider. Republic, 1946. 12 Chapters B/W. D: Spencer Gordon Bennet & Fred C. Brannon. SC: Albert DeMond, Basil Dickey, Jesse Duffy, Lynn Perkins & Barney A. Sarecky. WITH Robert Kent, Peggy Stewart, LeRoy Mason, George J. Lewis, Kenne Duncan, Hal Taliaferro, Chief Thundercloud, Monte Hale, Tom London, Roy Barcroft, John Hamilton, Hugh Prosser, Jack Kirk, Rex Lease, Tommy Coats, Joe Yrigoyen, Bill Yrigoyen. When outlaws threaten an area and incite Indians, a frontier doctor becomes a masked phantom to bring about justice. Pretty fair cliffhanger. Reissue title: **Ghost Riders of the West.**

2518 The Phantom Stage. Universal, 1939. 58 minutes B/W. D: George Waggner. SC: Joseph West. WITH Bob Baker, Marjorie Reynolds, George Cleveland, Forrest Taylor, Reed Howes, Tex Palmer, Murdock MacQuarrie, Glenn Strange, Jack Kirk, Ernie Adams, Dick Rush. Two cowpokes find out a girl is about to lose her stage line which is being robbed of its gold shipments. Only fair Bob Baker vehicle. V: Cumberland Video.

2519 The Phantom Stagecoach. Columbia, 1957. 69 minutes B/W. D: Ray Nazarro. SC: David Lang. WITH William Bishop, Richard Webb, Kathleen Crowley, Hugh Sanders, John Doucette, Frank Ferguson, Ray Teal, Percy Helton, Maudie Prickett, Lane Bradford, Eddy Waller, Robert Anderson, John Lehmann. Two stage line owners have a dispute over right-of-way, leading to gunplay. Only average "B" second bill feature.

2520 Phantom Stallion. Republic, 1954. 54 minutes B/W. D: Harry Keller. SC: Gerald Geraghty. WITH Rex Allen, Slim Pickens, Carla Balenda, Harry Shannon, Don Haggerty, Peter Price, Rosa Turich, Zon Murray. A cowboy helps a ranch owner whose best horses are disappearing, with a wild horse herd being blamed for the thefts. Standard Rex Allen outing with the plot twist of having the rancher's niece as the main villain.

2521 The Phantom Thunderbolt. World Wide/Fox, 1933. 63 minutes B/W. D-SC: Alan James. WITH Ken Maynard, Frances Dade, Frank Rice, Robert Kortman, William Gould, Harry Holman, Frank Beal, Wilfred Lucas, William Robyns, Nelson McDowell, Lew Meehan. The Thunderbolt Kid is hired by the leaders of Coyote Gulch to stop a lawless gang which is keeping a railroad from going through the area. Rawboned but actionful Ken Maynard vehicle. V: Discount Video.

2522 Phantom Valley. Columbia, 1948. 53 minutes B/W. D: Ray Nazarro. SC: J. Benton Cheney. WITH Charles Starrett, Smiley Burnette, Virginia Hunter, Sam Flint, Ozie Waters & His Colorado Rangers, Joel Friedkin, Robert Filmer, Mikel Conrad, Zon Murray, Fred Sears, Teddy Infuhr, Jerry Jerome. A new sheriff arrives in a small town where ranchers and homesteaders are at war due to attacks by an outlaw gang. Better than average "Durango Kid" film.

2523 Pierre of the Plains. Metro-Goldwyn-Mayer, 1942. 66 minutes B/W. D: George B. Seitz. SC: Lawrence Kimble. WITH John Carroll, Ruth Hussey, Bruce Cabot, Paul Brown, Reginald Owen, Evelyn Ankers, Henry Travers, Patrick McVey, Sheldon Leonard, Lois Ransom, Charles Stevens, Frederick Worlock. A Mountie, in love with a pretty innkeeper, tries to foil lawlessness in the Northwest. John Carroll is okay as the daredevil Mountie and he has to carry this otherwise tame effort.

2524 Pillars of the Sky. Universal-International, 1956. 95 minutes Color. D: George Marshall. SC: Sam Rolfe. WITH Jeff Chandler, Dorothy Malone, Ward Bond, Keith Andes, Lee Marvin, Sydney Chaplin, Willis Bouchey, Michael Ansara, Olive Carey, Charles Horvath, Orlando Rodriguez, Glen Kramer, Floyd Simmons, Pat Hogan, Felix Noriego, Paul Smith, Martin Milner, Robert Ellis, Ralph Votrian, Walter Coy, Alberto Morin, Richard Hale, Frank De Kova, Terry Wilson, Philip Kieffer, Gilbert Connor. A hard-drinking Army sergeant is forced to fight off attacking Indians with men he does not like but he soon learns to respect their skills and bravery. Another of the seemingly aimless 1950s adult oaters about a man reformed by responsibility and a good woman; only fair.

2525 The Pinto Bandit. Producers Releasing Corporation, 1944. 57 minutes B/W. D-SC: Elmer Clifton. WITH James Newill, Dave O'Brien, Guy Wilkerson, Mady Lawrence, James Martin, Jack Ingram, Ed Cassidy, Budd Buster, Karl Hackett, Robert Kortman, Charles King, Jimmie Aubrey. The Texas Rangers trio enter a three-man relay race for a mail contract in order to capture the masked bandit who has been stealing mail shipments between two towns. Fair entry in PRC's long-running "The Texas Rangers" series.

2526 Pinto Canyon. Metropolitan, 1940. 55 minutes B/W. D: Raymond Johnson. SC: Carl Krusada. WITH Bob Steele, Louise Stanley, Kenne Duncan, Ted Adams, Steve Clark, Budd Buster, Murdock McQuarrie, George Chesebro, Jimmie Aubrey, Carl Mathews. A lawman is on the trail of an outlaw gang who steal cattle. Badly made and boring Bob Steele vehicle for producer Harry S. Webb.

2527 Pinto Rustlers. Reliable, 1936. 56 minutes B/W. D: Henri Samuels (Harry S. Webb). SC: Robert Tansey. WITH Tom Tyler, George Walsh, Al St. John, Catherine Cotter, Earl Dwire, William Gould, George Chesebro, Roger Williams, Bud Osborne, Murdock MacQuarrie, Charles King, Slim Whitaker, Milburn Morante, Sherry Tansey. After rustlers kill his father, a man pretends to be an outlaw so he can join the gang and get the goods on them. Pretty fair Tom Tyler oater for which R. G. Springsteen served as the assistant director.

Pioneer Builders see **The Conquerors**

2528 Pioneer Days. Monogram, 1940. 51 minutes B/W. D: Harry S. Webb. SC: Bennett Cohen. WITH Jack Randall, June Wilkins, Frank Yaconelli, Ted Adams, Nelson McDowell, Bud Osborne, Robert Walker, Glenn Strange, Denver Dixon, George Chesebro, Jimmie Aubrey, Lafe McKee, Richard Cramer. A cowboy helps a girl who has inherited half interest in a saloon, while her partner tries to cheat her. Average entry in Jack Randall's Monogram series.

2529 Pioneer Justice. Producers Releasing Corporation, 1947. 56 minutes B/W. D: Ray Taylor. SC: Adrian Page. WITH Lash LaRue, Al St. John, Jennifer Holt, William Fawcett, Jack Ingram, Dee Cooper, Lane Bradford, Henry Hall, Steve Drake, Bob Woodward, Terry Frost, Wally West, Slim Whitaker. U. S. marshals

Cheyenne Davis and Fuzzy Q. Jones come to the aid of homesteaders who have been the victims of killings and property seizures. Very good Lash LaRue vehicle; non-stop action from the start.

2530 Pioneer Marshal. Republic, 1949. 60 minutes B/W. D: Philip Ford. SC: Bob Williams. WITH Monte Hale, Paul Hurst, Nan Leslie, Damian O'Flynn, Roy Barcroft, Myron Healey, Ray Walker, John Hamilton, Clarence Straight, Robert Williams. A lawman infiltrates a town used by outlaws as he tracks down a notorious gunman. Well made Monte Hale film with an exciting gunfight at the climax. V: Cumberland Video.

2531 Pioneer Trail. Columbia, 1938. 55 minutes B/W. D: Joseph Lovering. SC: Nate Gatzert. WITH Jack Luden, Joan Barclay, Hal Taliaferro, Marin Sais, Slim Whitaker, Leon Beaumont, Eva McKenzie, Hal Price, Richard Botiller, Tom London, Bud Osborne, Robert McKenzie, Art Davis, Fred Burns, Pete Palmer, Tuffy (dog). A ranch foreman convinces area ranchers to take all their cattle in one large drive to market for better prices but he is captured by a female outlaw and her gang. Low grade Jack Luden vehicle with more heroics from Tuffy the dog than from Luden.

2532 Pioneer Woman. ABC-TV/Filmways, 1973. 74 minutes Color. D: Buzz Kulik. SC: Suzanne Clauser. WITH Joanna Pettet, William Shatner, David Janssen, Lance LeGault, Helen Hunt, Russell Baer, Linda Kupecek, Lloyd Berry, Robert Koons, Agatha Mercer. In 1867 a woman struggles to keep her family together in the Wyoming Territory and continue homesteading after her husband is killed. Fairly entertaining made-for-TV movie.

2533 The Pioneers. Monogram, 1941. 59 minutes B/W. D: Al Herman. SC: Charles Alderson. WITH Tex Ritter, Wanda McKay, Red Foley & His Saddle Pals, Arkansas Slim Andrews, Doye O'Dell, George Chesebro, Del Lawrence, Post Park, Karl Hackett, Lynton Brent, Chick Hannon, Gene Alsace, Jack C. Smith, Chief Many Treaties, Charles Soldani, Art Dillard. A singing cowboy aids a group of settlers to their destination, fighting Indians and outlaws along the way. Poor Tex Ritter vehicle, supposedly based on James Fenimore Cooper, which is full of stock footage and too much music; the Indian attack portion is from the serial **Fighting with Kit Carson q.v.).**

Pioneers

2534 Pioneers of the Frontier. Columbia, 1940. 58 minutes B/W. D: Sam Nelson. SC: Fred Myton. WITH Bill Elliott, Linda Winters (Dorothy Comingore), Dub Taylor, Dick Curtis, Lafe McKee, Stanley Brown, Richard Fiske, Carl Stockdale, Ralph McCullough, Al Bridge, Edmund Cobb, George Chesebro, Lynton Brent, Jack Kirk, Ralph Peters. A ruthless gunman murders his kindly land baron boss and takes over his range but the dead man's nephew arrives on the scene to aid the settlers. Very good Bill Elliott actioner with an excellent performance by Dick Curtis as the brutal bully.

2535 Pioneers of the West. Bill Mix Productions, 1927. 50 minutes B/W. D-SC: Marcel Perez. WITH Dick Carter, Dorothy Earle, Bud Osborne, Gene Crosby, Olin Francis. A Pony Express rider tries to stop an Indian uprising led by a renegade and his Indian ally, who is the rider's rival for the love of a pretty white squaw. Low grade silent actioner but fun to watch.

2536 Pioneers of the West. Republic, 1940. 54 (56) minutes B/W. D: Lester Orlebeck. SC: Jack Natteford, Karen DeWolf & Gerald Geraghty. WITH Robert Livingston, Raymond Hatton, Duncan Renaldo, Noah Beery, Beatrice Roberts, Lane Chandler, George Cleveland, Hal Taliaferro, Yakima Canutt, John Dilson, Joe McGuinn, Earl Askam, George Chesebro, Jack Kirk, Herman Hack, Bob Burns, Tex Terry, Art Dillard, Ray Jones, Artie Ortego, Chuck Baldra. Settlers are being swindled out of their lands and the Three Mesquiteers aid them as they cross Indian territory via wagon train. Pretty good "Three Mesquiteers" series entry enhanced by a fine cast of veteran players.

2537 Pirates of Monterey. Universal, 1947. 75 minutes Color. D: Alfred Werker. SC: Sam Hellman & Margaret Buell Wilder. WITH Maria Montez, Rod Cameron, Mikhail Rasumny, Philip Reed, Gilbert Roland, Gale Sondergaard, Tamara Shayne, Robert Warwick, Michael Raffetto, Neyle Morrow, Victor Varconi, Charles Wagenheim, George J. Lewis, Joe Barnard, George Navarro, Victor Romito, Don Driggers, George Magrill, Lucius Villegas, Chris-Pin Martin, Julia Andre, Fred Cordova, Dick Dickinson. In California in the 1840s a young Spanish noblewoman arrives to wed a soldier but falls for an American who is aiding the Mexican government in trying to put down a loyalist rebellion. Dull color Maria Montez vehicle with good support from Rod Cameron and Gilbert Roland.

2538 The Pirates of the Mississippi. Rapid Film, 1963. 95 minutes Color. D: Jurgen Roland. WITH Horst Frank, Brad Harris, Hansjorg Felmy, Sabrina Sinjen, Dorothee Parker. River pirates steal an Indian land grant in a mail robbery and then take over a river town, only to have the Cherokees save the settlers and take revenge on the pirates. Far-out West German-made oater (original title: **Die Flusspiraten Vom Mississippi**) for fans of this type of fare only.

2539 Pirates of the Prairie. RKO Radio, 1942. 57 minutes B/W. D: Howard Bretherton. SC: Doris Schroeder & J. Benton Cheney. WITH Tim Holt, Nell O'Day, Cliff Edwards, Roy Barcroft, John Elliott, Karl Hackett, Richard Cramer, Ed Cassidy, Eddie Dew, Merrill McCormack, Reed Howes, Charles King, Bud Geary, Lee Shumway, Russell Wade, Ben Corbett, Frank McCarroll, Artie Ortego, George Morrell. A U. S. marshal is on the trail of a gang of masked riders who are stealing land in order to get a big price out of it when the railroad comes through. Good Tim Holt vehicle with plenty of action.

2540 Pirates on Horseback. Paramount, 1941. 54 (69) minutes B/W. D: Lesley Selander. SC: Ethel La Blanche & J. Benton Cheney. WITH William Boyd, Russell Hayden, Andy Clyde, Eleanor Stewart, Morris Ankrum, William Haade, Dennis Moore, Henry Hall, Britt Wood, Silver-Tip Baker. Hopalong Cassidy and his pals are after a gang of outlaws who are trying to locate a hidden gold mine. Another well made entry in the popular "Hopalong Cassidy" series, this one enhanced by a mystery tinge.

2541 A Pistol for Ringo. Embassy, 1966. 97 minutes Color. D-SC: Duccio Tessari. WITH Montgomery Wood (Giuliano Gemma), Fernando Sancho, Hally Hammond, George Martin, Nieves Navarro, Antonio Casas, Jose Manuel Martin, Paco Sanz. A sheriff enlists the aid of a gunman to save a ranch where his fiancée and her father are being held prisoners by a wounded Mexican bandit and his gang. Another violent spaghetti Western with a plot and cast very similar to its predecessor, **The Return of Ringo** (q.v.). Italian title: **Una Pistola Per Ringo** (A Pistol for Ringo).

2542 Pistol Harvest. RKO Radio, 1951. 60 minutes B/W. D: Lesley Selander. SC: Norman Houston. WITH Tim Holt, Richard Martin, Joan Dixon, Guy Edward Hearn, Mauritz Hugo, Robert Clarke, William Griffith, Lee Phelps, Robert Wilke, Joan Freeman. When their boss is murdered by rustlers, two cowboys set out to track down the killers. Average entry in Tim Holt's RKO series.

2543 A Place Called Glory. Embassy, 1966. 92 minutes Color. D: Sheldon Reynolds. SC: Edward Di Lorenzo, Jerold Hayden Boyd & Fernando Lamas. WITH Lex Barker, Pierre Brice, Marianne Koch, Jorge Rigaud, Gerard Tichy, Angel Del Pozo, Santiago Ontanon, Hans Nielson, Wolfgang Lukschy, Victor Israel. In the town of Glory, two gunmen plan to oppose each other in a duel but end up joining forces to stop a gang of bandits. Pretty good German-made Western with fine work by Lex Barker and Pierre Brice. German title: **Die Holle Von Manitoba,** a Omnia Deutsche Film Export release.

A Place Called Trinity see **Trinity**

2544 The Plainsman. Paramount, 1936. 115 minutes B/W. D: Cecil B. DeMille. SC: Waldemar Young, Harold Lamb & Lynn Riggs. WITH Gary Cooper, Jean Arthur, James Ellison, Charles Bickford, Porter Hall, Helen Burgess, John Miljan, Victor Varconi, Paul Harvey, Frank McGlynn, Granville Bates, Purnell Pratt, Pat Moriarity, Charles Judels, Anthony Quinn, George MacQuarrie, George ("Gabby") Hayes, Fuzzy Knight, George Ernest, Fred Kohler, Frank Albertson, Harry Woods, Francis McDonald, Francis Ford, Irving Bacon, Edgar Dearing, Edwin Maxwell, John Hyams, Bruce Warren, Mark Strong, Charles Stevens, Arthur Aylesworth, Douglas Wood, George Cleveland, Lona Andre, Leila McIntyre, Harry Stubbs, Davison Clark, C. W. Herzinger, William Humphries, Sidney Jarvis, Wadsworth Harris, Dennis O'Keefe, Gail (Ann) Sheridan, Lane Chandler, Hank Bell. Wild Bill Hickok, Calamity Jane and Buffalo Bill Cody team to oppose a gun runner who is selling arms to the Indians out to get General Custer. Highly inaccurate but quite entertaining Cecil B. DeMille epic.

2545 The Plainsman. Universal, 1966. 92 minutes Color. D: David Lowell Rich. SC: Michael Blankfort. WITH Don Murray, Abby Dalton, Guy Stockwell, Bradford Dillman, Henry Silva, Simon Oakland, Leslie Nielsen, Edward Binns, Michael Evans, Percy Rodriguez, Terry Wilson, Walter Berke, Emily Banks. A renegade white man is selling guns to the Indians who plan to attack General Custer and Wild Bill Hickok, Calamity Jane and Buffalo Bill Cody try to stop him. Bland remake of the 1936 Cecil B. DeMille film with little to recommend it.

2546 The Plainsman and the Lady. Republic, 1946. 82 minutes B/W. D: Joseph Kane. SC: Richard Wormser. WITH William Elliott, Vera Ralston, Gail Patrick, Joseph Schildkraut, Donald (Don "Red") Barry, Andy Clyde, Raymond Walburn, Reinhold Schunzel, Paul Hurst, William B. Davidson, Charles Judels, Eva Puig, Jack Lambert, Stuart Hamblen, Noble Johnson, Hal Taliaferro, Byron Foulger, Pierre Watkin, Eddy Waller, Charles Morton, Martin Garralaga, Guy Beach, Joseph Crehan, Grady Sutton, Eddie Parks, Norman Willis, Tex Terry, Chuck Roberson, Rex Lease, Henry Wills, Hank Bell, Roy Barcroft, Jack O'Shea, Carl Sepulveda, Daniel Day Tolman, David Williams, Lola & Fernando. Before the Civil War a rich cattleman aids a banker and his pretty daughter in establishing the Pony Express between St. Joseph, Missouri, and Sacramento, California, despite the machinations of a crooked stagecoach operator and his murderous henchman. Slick Bill Elliott "A" vehicle which benefits from good production values and nice support from Don Barry as the gunman and Gail Patrick as the heroine's social-climbing sister.

2547 Plainsong. Ed Stabile, 1983. 88 minutes Color. D-SC: Ed Stabile. WITH Teresanne Joseph, Jessica Nelson, Lyn Traverse, Steve Geiger, Sandon McCall, Carl Kielblock. A man and a group of women come to Kansas in the 1880s and find themselves in the middle of a range war. Mini-budget New Jersey-filmed melodrama has little to offer genre followers.

2548 Plunder of the Sun. Warner Brothers, 1953. 81 minutes B/W. D: John Farrow. SC: Jonathan Latimer. WITH Glenn Ford, Diana Lynn, Patricia Medina, Francis L. Sullivan, Sean McClory, Eduardo Noreiga, Julio Villareal, Charles Rooner, Douglass Dumbrille. A modern-day expedition in Mexico sets out to find an Aztec treasure. Mystery writer Jonathan Latimer's script would have benefitted from more action and less talk in this otherwise okay melodrama.

2549 The Plunderers. Republic, 1948. 87 minutes Color. D: Joseph Kane. SC: Gerald Geraghty & Gerald Adams. WITH Rod Cameron, Ilona Massey, Adrian Booth, Forrest Tucker, George Cleveland, Grant Withers, Taylor Holmes, Paul Fix, Francis Ford, James Flavin, Maude Eburne, Russell Hicks, Mary Ruth Wade, Hank Bell, Rex Lease, Louis R. Faust. An Army officer is sent to bring in a young outlaw but they join forces when attacked by rampaging Indians. Fairly good and actionful Republic top-budget production.

2550 The Plunderers. Allied Artists, 1960. 94 minutes B/W. D: Joseph Pevney. SC: Bob Barbash. WITH Jeff Chandler, Dolores Hart, Marsha Hunt, John Saxon, Jay C. Flippen, Ray Stricklyn, James Westerfield, Harvey Stephens, Vaughn Taylor, William Challee, Ken Patterson, Dee Pollack, Roger Torrey. A quartet of young hellions tries to take over a small town but are opposed by a Civil War veteran. Nicely done oater from producer Lindsley Parsons.

2551 The Plunderers of Painted Flats. Republic, 1959. 70 minutes B/W. D: Albert C. Gannaway. SC: Phil Shuken & John Greene. WITH John Carroll, Corinne Calvet, Skip Homeier, Edmund Lowe, George Macready, Bea Benadaret, Madge Kennedy, Joe Besser, Allan Lurie, Candy Candido, Herbert Vigran, Burt Topper, Roy Gordon. A town boss wants to run settlers out of the area and he hires a notorious gunman to do his bidding, but one of the settlers is a young man out to kill the gunslinger for the murder of his father. Mediocre production greatly aided by some fine performances, especially Edmund Lowe as an aged shootist and Corinne Calvet as a woman with a past.

2552 The Pocatello Kid. Tiffany, 1931. 61 minutes B/W. D: Phil Rosen. SC: W. Scott Darling. WITH Ken Maynard, Marceline Day, Richard Cramer, Charles King, Lafe McKee, Lew Meehan, Jack Rockwell, Bert Lindley, Bob Reeves, Bud Osborne, Jack Ward. Falsely thinking he was responsible for the death of his dishonest lawman twin brother, a cowboy takes his place and sets out to stop a rustling gang. Slow moving Ken Maynard vehicle which is hardly one of the star's better efforts. V: Video Dimensions.

2553 Pocket Money. National General, 1972. 102 minutes Color. D: Stuart Rosen-berg. SC: Terry Malick. WITH Paul Newman, Lee Marvin, Strother Martin, Christine Belford, Kelly Jean Peters, Fred Graham, Wayne Rogers, Hector Elizondo, Mickey Gilbert. A down-on-his-luck cowpoke heads to Mexico to buy cattle from a crooked dealer and he enlists the aid of a shiftless pal in getting the goods on the man. Poor genre "comedy" saved somewhat by Lee Marvin's mugging.

2554 Poco. Cinema Shares, 1977. 88 minutes Color. D: Dwight Brooks. SC: William E. Carville. WITH Chill Wills, Michaelle Ashburn, Clint Ritchie, Sherry Bain, John Steadman, Tom Roy Lowe. A small dog, lost after a car wreck, treks through the desert in search of his owner, a disabled little girl. Pleasant little feature. V: Children's Video Library.

2555 The Pony Express. Paramount, 1925. 90 minutes B/W. D: James Cruze. SC: Walter Woods. WITH Betty Compson, Ricardo Cortez, Ernest Torrance, Wallace Beery, George Bancroft, Frank Lackteen, Ed Piel Jr., William Turner, Al Hart, Charles Gerson, Rose Tapley, Vondell Darr, Hank Bell, Ernie Adams. During the Civil War a group tries to get California to secede from the Union and the plan is opposed by a Pony Express rider. Fine silent feature with a good story and plenty of action.

2556 The Pony Express. Paramount, 1953. 101 minutes Color. D: Jerry Hopper. SC: Charles Marquis Warren. WITH Charlton Heston, Rhonda Fleming, Forrest Tucker, Jan Sterling, Michael Moore, Porter Hall, Richard Shannon, Henry Brandon, Stuart Randall, Lewis Martin, Pat Hogan, James Davies, Eric Alden, Willard Willingham, Frank Wilcox, Len Hendry, Charles Hamilton, Bob Templeton. Buffalo Bill Cody and Wild Bill Hickok join forces to establish the Pony Express across the West and stop the secession of California from the Union during the Civil War. Okay yarn with colorful characters and good movement.

2557 Pony Express Rider. Doty-Dayton, 1976. 100 minutes Color. D: Robert Totten. SC: Dan Greer, Hal Harrison Jr. & Robert Totten. WITH Stewart Petersen, Jack Elam, Henry Wilcoxon, Joan Caulfield, Slim Pickens, Dub Taylor, Buck Taylor, Maureen McCormack, Ace Reis. While looking for his father's killer, a young man finds a murdered pony express rider and decides to finish his mail run. Okay actioner greatly aided by a good cast.

2558 Pony Post. Universal, 1940. 61 minutes B/W. D: Ray Taylor. SC: Sherman Lowe. WITH Johnny Mack Brown, Nell O'Day, Dorothy Short, Ray Teal, Tom Chatterton, Kermit Maynard, Stanley Blystone, Jack Rockwell, Edmund Cobb, Lloyd Ingraham, Iron Eyes Cody, Charles King, Worth Crouch, Jimmy Wakely & His Rough Riders, Lane Chandler, Frank McCarroll. A Pony Express operator runs into opposition from outlaws and Indians when he tries to open a relay station in an isolated valley. More than passable Johnny Mack Brown vehicle.

2559 Pony Soldier. 20th Century-Fox, 1952. 82 minutes Color. D: Joseph M. Newman. SC: John D. Higgins. WITH Tyrone Power, Cameron Mitchell, Penny Edwards, Thomas Gomez, Robert Horton, Anthony Numken, Adeline De Walt Reynolds, Howard Petrie, Stuart Randall, Richard Shackelford, James Hayward, Muriel Landers, Frank De Kova, Louis Heminger, John War Eagle. A Mountie tries to keep Cree Indians from going on the warpath as he escorts them back to the reservation. Colorful but not exceptional Mountie movie.

2560 Por Mis Pistolas. Columbia/Posa Films, 1968. 123 minutes Color. D: Miguel Delgado. WITH Cantinflas (Mario Moreno), Isela Vega, Jorge Rado, Alfonso Mejia, Gloria Coral, Quintin Bulnes, Manuel Alvarado, Manver. An easygoing druggist heads West where he gets mixed up with Indians, outlaws and a lost mine. Actionful Cantinflas comedy made in Mexico.

2561 Posse. Paramount, 1975. 94 minutes Color. D: Kirk Douglas. SC: William Roberts & Christopher Knopf. WITH Kirk Douglas, Bruce Dern, Bo Hopkins, James Stacy, Alfonso Arau, David Canary, Luke Askew, Beth Brickell, Katherine Woodville, Mark Roberts, Dick O'Neill, Bill Burton. An ambitious, crooked politician tries to get himself elected to the senate by hunting a wanted man, but the outlaw turns the tables on him. Offbeat and interesting oater from producer-director-star Kirk Douglas, with the good guy and the badman changing roles at the finale.

2562 Posse from Heaven. P. M. Films, 1975. 87 minutes Color. D: Phillip Pine. SC: Ward Wood & Phillip Pine. WITH Fanne Foxe, Todd Compton, Sherry Bain, Ward Wood, Dick Burch. A not-too-bright young man is sent to the Old West by God to save it from sin and the Archangel Gabriel comes along, reincarnated as a horse, to protect him. Hard-to-believe Western fantasy made on the cheap.

2563 Posse from Hell. Universal-International, 1961. 89 minutes Color. D: Herbert Coleman. SC: Clair Huffaker. WITH Audie Murphy, John Saxon, Zohra Lampert, Vic Morrow, Robert Keith, Ward Ramsey, Rodolfo Acosta, Royal Dano, Frank Overton, James Bell, Paul Carr, Lee Van Cleef, Ray Teal, Forrest Lewis, Charles Horvath, Harry Lauter, Henry Wills, Stuart Randall, Allan Lane. When four escaped convicts murder the marshall of a small town, an ex-gunman friend of the lawman forms a posse to catch the killers. Clair Huffaker adapted his novel for this film but the end result is nothing exceptional.

2564 Powder River. 20th Century-Fox, 1953. 77 minutes Color. D: Louis King. SC: Geoffrey Holmes. WITH Rory Calhoun, Corinne Calvet, Cameron Mitchell, Penny Edwards, Carl Betz, John Dehner, Raymond Greenleaf, Victor Sutherland, Ethan Laidlaw, Robert Wilke, Harry Carter, Robert Adler, Post Park, Richard Garrick, Frank Ferguson, Henry Kulky, Walter Sande, Zon Murray, Ray Bennett. When his buddy is murdered a man takes the job as town sheriff in order to capture the gambler he suspects of the crime, but he too is killed. Minor, but rather interesting, oater with a good cast.

2565 Powder River Rustlers. Republic, 1949. 60 minutes B/W. D: Philip Ford. SC: Richard Wormser. WITH Allan "Rocky" Lane, Eddy Waller, Gerry Ganzer, Roy Barcroft, Bud Geary, Cliff Clark, Francis McDonald, Douglas Evans, Bruce Edwards, Stanley Blystone, Eddie Parker, Herman Hack. Government agent Rocky Lane investigates a scheme to bilk local citizens through a bridge building project. Although more actionful than some films in the Rocky Lane series, this one is still a bit on the dull side.

2566 Powderkeg. CBS-TV/Filmways, 1971. 93 minutes Color. D-SC: Douglas Heyes. WITH Rod Taylor, Dennis Cole, Fernando Lamas, Luciana Paluzzi, John McIntire, Michael Ansara, Tisha Sterling, Reni Santoni, Melodie Johnson, William Bryant, Joe DeSantis, Jay Novello, Jim L. (James) Brown, Roy Jenson. In 1914 outlaws hijack a train and hold its passengers hostage and two troubleshooters are hired to retrieve the train and capture the crooks. Pretty fair action drama which resulted in the brief TV series "The Bearcats" (CBS-TV, 1971).

2567 Powdersmoke Range. RKO Radio, 1935. 72 minutes B/W. D: Wallace Fox. SC: Adele Buffington. WITH Harry Carey, Hoot Gibson, Guinn Williams, Bob Steele, Tom Tyler, Boots Mallory, Ray Mayer, Sam Hardy, Adrian Mooris, Wally Wales, Art Mix, Buddy Roosevelt, Buffalo Bill Jr., Franklyn Farnum, William Desmond, William Farnum, Buzz Barton, Ethan Laidlaw, Irving Bacon, Henry Roquemore, Bob McKenzie, Frank Rice, Eddie Dunn, Barney Furey, Jim Mason, Nelson McDowell, Frank Ellis. A corrupt saloon owner and his crooked sheriff cohort are out to steal the ranch of three buddies and when the trio aid an outlaw they are framed on a robbery charge. This screen adaptation of the adventures of William Colt McDonald's "Three Mesquiteers" is only average plotwise but since it is literally a who's who of genre stardom it is must viewing for old timers' fans. V: Nostalgia Merchant.

2568 The Prairie. Screen Guild, 1947. 80 minutes B/W. D: Frank Wisbar. SC: Arthur St. Claire. WITH Lenore Aubert, Alan Baxter, Russ Vincent, Jack Mitchum, Charles Evans, Edna Holland, Chief Thundercloud, Fred Colby, Bill Murphy, David Gerber, George Morrell, Don Lynch, Chief Yowlachie, Jay Silverheels, Beth Taylor, Frank Hemingway (narrator). The story of the trials and tribulations of pioneers as they try to settle upstate New York, battling Indians and the elements. Less than mediocre adaptation of the James Fenimore Cooper story.

2569 Prairie Badmen. Producers Releasing Corporation, 1946. 55 minutes B/W. D: Sam Newfield. SC: Fred Myton. WITH Buster Crabbe, Al St. John, Patricia Knox, Charles King, Ed Cassidy, Kermit Maynard, John Cason, Steve Clark, Frank Ellis, Budd Buster. Billy Carson and Fuzzy Q. Jones try to help a medicine showman return gold he found to its owner but an outlaw gang also wants it. Just a typical entry in the PRC "Billy Carson" series.

2570 Prairie Chickens. United Artists, 1943. 46 minutes B/W. D: Hal Roach Jr. SC: Arnold Belgarde & Earle Snell. WITH Noah Beery Jr., Jimmy Rogers, Marjorie Reynolds, Joseph Sawyer, Jack Norton, Raymond Hatton, Rosemary LaPlanche, Edward Gargan, Frank Faylen, Dudley Dickerson, Mary Ann Deighton.

Two cowpokes get involved with a man who has inherited a ranch. Last of a trio of mediocre featurettes Hal Roach produced with Jimmy Rogers (Will's son) and Noah Beery Jr.; the highlight is Jack Norton's usual tipsy portrayal of the ranch owner.

2571 Prairie Express. Monogram, 1947. 60 minutes B/W. D: Lambert Hillyer. SC: Anthony Coldeway & J. Benton Cheney. WITH Johnny Mack Brown, Raymond Hatton, Robert Winkler, Virginia Belmont, William Ruhl, Marshall Reed, Gary Garrett, Ted Adams, Curly Gibson, Frank LaRue, Steve Darrell, Hank Worden, Carl Mathews, Boyd Stockman, Steve Clark, Artie Ortego, I. Stanford Jolley, Jack Hendricks. A respected citizen is behind a gang out to force a family off their ranch so the land can be bought cheaply and then sold to the railroad. Average Johnny Mack Brown-Raymond Hatton series entry.

2572 Prairie Gunsmoke. Columbia, 1942. 56 minutes B/W. D: Lambert Hillyer. SC: Fred Myton. WITH Bill Elliott, Tex Ritter, Virginia Carroll, Frank Mitchell, Hal Price, Tristram Coffin, Joe McGuinn, Frosty Royce, Rich Anderson, Art Mix, Francis Walker, Ray Jones, Ted Mapes, Glenn Strange, Steve Clark. Although Wild Bill Hickok comes to a small town to aid citizens and ranchers harrassed by rustlers he finds that he is distrusted by the locals. Pretty good actioner in the Bill Elliott-Tex Ritter series.

2573 Prairie Justice. Universal, 1938. 58 minutes B/W. D: George Waggner. SC: Joseph West (George Waggner). WITH Bob Baker, Dorothy Fay, Hal Taliaferro, Jack Rockwell, Carleton Young, Jack Kirk, Forrest Taylor, Glenn Strange, Tex Palmer, Slim Whitaker, Murdock MacQuarrie. When cattle rustlers kill his father a young man gets on their trail for revenge. Fair Bob Baker series vehicle.

2574 Prairie Law. RKO Radio, 1940. 58 minutes B/W. D: David Howard. SC: Doris Schroeder & Arthur V. Jones. WITH George O'Brien, Virginia Vale, J. Farrell MacDonald, Slim Whitaker, Dick Hogan, Cy Kendall, Paul Everton, Henry Hall, Monte Montague, Quen Ramsey, Lloyd Ingraham, Bud Osborne, Ferris Taylor, Ben Corbett, Hank Bell, Cactus Mack, Frank O'Connor, Jack O'Shea, Ed Brady, Hank Worden, Frank Ellis, Billy Benedict, Jack Henderson. Crooks bring settlers

315   Prairie Moon

to range land with false promises of
plenty of water and the scheme is soon
opposed by a cattleman who wants to
help the homesteaders. Fine George
O'Brien film with a good plotline and
supporting cast.

2575 Prairie Moon. Republic, 1938. 54
(58) minutes B/W. D: Ralph Staub. SC:
Betty Burbridge & Stanley Roberts. WITH
Gene Autry, Smiley Burnette, Shirley
Deane, Tommy Ryan, Warner Richmond,
Tom London, William Pawley, Walter
Tetley, David Gorcey, Stanley Andrews,
Peter Potter, Bud Osborne, Ray Bennett,
Jack Rockwell, Merrill McCormack,
Hal Price, Lew Meehan, Jack Kirk. Gene
and Frog become the guardians of three
boys whose father was a gangster and
the boys end up helping a gang of rustlers
hide cattle on their ranch. Pretty fair
Gene Autry musical vehicle with the
old plot of having cattle hidden behind
a waterfall. V: Blackhawk.

Prairie Outlaws see **Wild West**

2576 Prairie Pals. Producers Releasing
Corporation, 1942. 60 minutes B/W.
D: Peter Stewart (Sam Newfield). SC:
Patricia Harper. WITH Bill Boyd, Art
Davis, Lee Powell, Esther Estrella, Charles
King, John Merton, Kermit Maynard,
I. Stanford Jolley, Karl Hackett, Bob
Burns, Al St. John, Art Dillard, Curley
Dresden, Frank McCarroll, Bill Patton,
Carl Mathews, Frank Ellis, J. Merrill
Holmes. Outlaws kidnap a scientist who
is working on an important project and
two lawmen set out to rescue him. Tacky
PRC entry teaming musicians Bill Boyd
("The Cowboy Rambler") and Art Davis.
V: Video Connection.

2577 Prairie Pioneers. Republic, 1941.
57 minutes B/W. D: Lester Orlebeck.
SC: Barry Shipman. WITH Robert Liv-
ingston, Bob Steele, Rufe Davis, Esther
Estrella, Robert Kellard, Guy D'Ennery,
Davidson Clark, Jack Ingram, Kenneth
MacDonald, Lee Shumway, Mary MacLaren,
Yakima Canutt, Wheaton Chambers,
Jack Kirk, Carleton Young, Frank Ellis,
Cactus Mack, Curley Dresden, Frank
McCarroll. A half-breed outlaw is trying
to steal a gold mine and The Three
Mesquiteers try to stop him. Not one
of the better "Three Mesquiteers" series
features despite a supporting cast of
genre favorites.

2578 The Prairie Pirate. Producers Distributing Corporation, 1925. 50 minutes

B/W. D: Edmund Mortimer. SC: Anthony
Dillon. WITH Harry Carey, Jean Dumas,
Lloyd Whitlock, Trilby Clark, Robert
Edeson, Tote Du Crow, Evelyn Selbie,
Fred Kohler. After his sister is murdered
a man becomes an outlaw in order to
track down the killer. Entertaining Harry
Carey silent oater.

2579 Prairie Raiders. Columbia, 1947.
54 minutes B/W. D: Derwin Abrahams.
SC: Ed Earl Repp. WITH Charles Starrett,
Smiley Burnette, Nancy Saunders, Robert
Scott, Ozie Waters & His Colorado Rang-
ers, Hugh Prosser, Lane Bradford, Ray
Bennett, Doug Coppin, Steve Clark,
Tommy Coats, Frank LaRue, Bob Cason,
Sam Flint. A rancher leases land from
the Interior Department in order to round
up and sell wild horses but he is faced
with competition from an outlaw gang.
Another lookalike entry in the "Durango
Kid" series.

2580 Prairie Roundup. Columbia, 1951.
53 minutes B/W. D: Fred F. Sears. SC:
Joseph O'Donnell. WITH Charles Starrett,
Smiley Burnette, Mary Castle, Frank
Fenton, The Sunshine Boys, Lane Chandler,
Frank Sully, Paul Campbell, Forrest
Taylor, Don C. Harvey, George Baxter,
John Cason, Al Wyatt, Alan Sears. Falsely
accused of murder by an outlaw gang,
a man escapes from jail with the help
of his pal and the two take a job on a
ranch run by a girl whose cattle the
outlaws plan to rustle. Fast moving entry
in the "Durango Kid" series.

2581 Prairie Rustlers. Producers Releasing
Corporation, 1945. 56 minutes B/W.
D: Sam Newfield. SC: Fred Myton. WITH
Buster Crabbe, Al St. John, Evelyn Finley,
Karl Hackett, Bud Osborne, Marin Sais,
I. Stanford Jolley, Kermit Maynard,
Herman Hack, George Morrell, Tex Cooper,
Dorothy Vernon. Because of his close
resemblance to his outlaw cousin, a man
is falsely accused of the desperado's
crimes. No better or no worse than most
of the PRC "Billy Carson" films.

2582 Prairie Schooners. Columbia, 1940.
58 minutes B/W. D: Sam Nelson. SC:
Robert Lee Johnson & Fred Myton. WITH
Bill Elliott, Evelyn Young, Dub Taylor,
Kenneth Harlan, Ray Teal, Bob Burns,
Netta Parker, Richard Fiske, Edmund
Cobb, Jim Thorpe, George Morrell, Merrill
McCormack, Sammy Stein. Wild Bill
Hickok leads a wagon train of settlers,
who have lost their lands due to fore-
closures, west to search for gold and

along the way they are attacked by Indians. Actionful Bill Elliott vehicle.

2583 Prairie Stranger. Columbia, 1941. 58 minutes B/W. D: Lambert Hillyer. SC: Winston Miller. WITH Charles Starrett, Cliff Edwards, Patti McCarty, Lew Preston & His Ranch Hands, Forbes Murray, Frank LaRue, Archie Twitchell, Francis Walker, Edmund Cobb, Jim Corey, Russ Powell, George Morrell. A doctor opens his practice in a small Nevada town and is opposed by a rival and accused of poisoning cattle. Average Charles Starrett vehicle.

2584 Prairie Thunder. Warner Brothers, 1937. 54 minutes B/W. D: B. Reeves Eason. SC: Ed Earl Repp. WITH Dick Foran, Ellen Clancy (Janet Shaw), Wilfred Lucas, Frank Orth, Frank Ellis, Yakima Canutt, Arthur J. Smith, George Chesebro, J. P. McGowan, John Harron, Frank McCarroll, Slim Whitaker, Henry Otho, Art Mix, Jim Corey, Iron Eyes Cody. A cavalry scout finds out a freight operator has been inciting Indians to disrupt the construction of telegraph lines. Dick Foran's final Warner Brothers' series film is a pretty fair outing.

2585 Prescott Kid. Columbia, 1934. 60 minutes B/W. D: David Selman. SC: Ford Beebe. WITH Tim McCoy, Sheila Mannors, Alden Chase, Hooper Atchley, Joseph (Sawyer) Sauers, Albert J. Smith, Carlos De Valdez, Ernie Adams, Steve Clark, Slim Whitaker, Charles King, Bud Osborne, Art Mix, Tom London, Edmund Cobb, Walter Brennan, Lew Meehan, Jack Rockwell. A man rides into a small town and is mistaken for the expected marshal and runs up against a gang of crooks. Exceedingly well done Tim McCoy vehicle; worth watching.

2586 The Price of Power. Golden Era, 1969. 96 (122) minutes Color. D: Tonino Valerii. SC: Massimo Patrizi. WITH Giuliano Gemma, Van Johnson, Warren Vanders, Fernando Rey, Jose Suarez, Benito Stefanelli, Maria Cuadra, Ray Saunders, Maria Luisa Sala. In post-Civil War Texas a man wants revenge on the men who falsely accused his buddy of killing the governor, resulting in his friend's death by a mob. Interesting Italian actioner issued in that country by Patry Film/Film Montana as **Il Prezzo del Potere** (The Price of Power).

2587 Pride of the Plains. Republic, 1944. 54 (56) minutes B/W. D: Wallace Fox.

SC: John K. Butler & Bob Williams. WITH Robert Livingston, Smiley Burnette, Nancy Gay, Steven Barclay, Kenneth MacDonald, Charles Miller, Kenne Duncan, Jack Kirk, Bud Geary, Yakima Canutt, Budd Buster, Bud Osborne. A lawman is on the trail of an outlaw gang rustling cattle which is sold to be canned for animal food. Bob Livingston's first entry in the "John Paul Revere" series is a good one.

2588 Pride of the West. Paramount, 1938. 54 (56) minutes B/W. D: Lesley Selander. SC: Nate Watt. WITH William Boyd, Russell Hayden, George ("Gabby") Hayes, Charlotte Field, Earle Hodgins, Billy King, Kenneth Harlan, Glenn Strange, James Craig, Bruce Mitchell, Willie Fung, George Morrell, Earl Askam, Jim Toney, Horace B. Carpenter, Henry Otho. A realty agent uses a stagecoach robber to help defraud citizens and Hopalong Cassidy gets on their trail. Action packed entry in the "Hopalong Cassidy" series.

2589 Prince of the Plains. Republic, 1949. 60 minutes B/W. D: Philip Ford. SC: Louise Rosseau & Albert DeMond. WITH Monte Hale, Paul Hurst, Shirley Davis, Roy Barcroft, Rory Mallinson, Harry Lauter, Lane Bradford, George Carleton. An outlaw gang raids and terrorizes ranchers and a cowboy tries to stop them. More than passable entry in Monte Hale's series for Republic; should please the star's fans.

2590 The Professionals. Columbia, 1966. 117 minutes Color. D-SC: Richard Brooks. WITH Burt Lancaster, Lee Marvin, Robert Ryan, Jack Palance, Claudia Cardinale, Ralph Bellamy, Woody Strode, Joe De Santis, Rafael Bertrand, Jorge Martinez De Hoyos, Maria Gomez, Jose Chavez, Carlos Romero, Vaugh Taylor, Robert Conteras, Don Carlos, John Lopez, John McKee, Eddie Little Sky, Leigh Chapman, Elizabeth Campbell, Phil Parslow. A quartet of mercenaries is hired by a rich man to return his young wife who has been kidnapped by a bandit-outlaw during the 1917 Mexican Revolution. More than adequate action melodrama. V: RCA/Columbia.

2591 The Proud and the Damned. Prestige, 1972. 97 minutes Color. D-SC: Ferde Grofe Jr. WITH Chuck Connors, Aron Kincaid, Cesar Romero, Jose Greco, Henry Capps, Peter Ford, Smoky Roberds, Maria Grimm, Dana Lorca, Anita Quinn, Conrad Parkman, Alvaro Ruiz. Four

Civil War veterans drifting in Latin America find themselves forced into aiding a military dictator. Fair drama helped by Chuck Connors and Cesar Romero.

2592 The Proud Ones. 20th Century-Fox, 1956. 94 minutes Color. D: Robert D. Webb. SC: Edmund North & Joseph Petracca. WITH Robert Ryan, Virginia Mayo, Jeffrey Hunter, Robert Middleton, Walter Brennan, Arthur O'Connell, Ken Clark, Rodolfo Acosta, George Mathews, Fay Roope, Edward Platt, Whit Bissell, Paul Burns, Richard Deacon, Lois Ray, Jack Low, Kenneth Terrell, Don Brodie, Jackie Coogan, Juanita Close, I. Stanford Jolley, Jack Mather, Steve Darrell. A young man and two gunmen arrive in a small town to take revenge on the local lawman for having killed the young man's father. Fairly interesting psychological yarn, enhanced by good performances.

2593 The Proud Rebel. Buena Vista, 1958. 103 minutes Color. D: Michael Curtiz. SC: Joseph Petracca & Lillie Hayward. WITH Alan Ladd, Olivia de Havilland, Dean Jagger, David Ladd, Cecil Kellaway, Dean Stanton, Thomas Pittman, Henry Hull, Eli Mintz, James Westerfield, John Carradine, King (dog). A woman who refuses to sell out to a rich sheep farmer hires a convict, falsely imprisoned by the man, to help her work her farm and fight the sheep raiser. Rather interesting Walt Disney feature with a good cast and acceptable plotline.

2594 Public Cowboy No. 1. Republic. 1937. 54 (59) minutes B/W. D: Joseph Kane. SC: Oliver Drake. WITH Gene Autry, Smiley Burnette, Ann Rutherford, William Farnum, James C. Morton, Maston Williams, Arthur Loft, Frankie Marvin, House Peters Jr., Frank LaRue, Milburn Morante, Hal Price, Jack Ingram, Rafael Bennett, Frank Ellis, George Plues, Jim Mason, Bob Burns. Ranchers are stymied by the loss of cattle until a singing cowboy discovers the rustlers are using modern methods like radios, airplanes and refrigerated trucks. Popular and well done Gene Autry film. V: Cumberland Video.

2595 The Purple Hills. 20th Century-Fox, 1961. 60 minutes Color. D: Maury Dexter. SC: Edith Cash Pearl & Russell (Russ) Bender. WITH Gene Nelson, Kent Taylor, Joanna Barnes, Russ Bender, Jerry Summers, Jack Carr, Danny Zapien, Jack Riggs, Medford Salway. When a cowboy kills a wanted man in Indian territory

he finds he is hunted by the Indians as he tries to take the man's body in for the reward. Compact little "B" outing.

2596 The Purple Vigilantes. Republic, 1938. 54 (58) minutes B/W. D: George Sherman. SC: Betty Burbridge & Oliver Drake. WITH Robert Livingston, Ray Corrigan, Max Terhune, Joan Barclay, Earle Hodgins, Earl Dwire, Jack Perrin, Frances Sayles, George Chesebro, Robert Fiske, Ernie Adams, William Gould, Harry Strang, Ed Cassidy, Frank O'Connor. Outlaws use the guise of a vigilante group to terrorize the locals until the Three Mesquiteers get on their trail. Well made entry in the popular "Three Mesquiteers" series. V: Cumberland Video.

Pursued (1928) see **The Arizona Kid** (1928)

2597 Pursued. Warner Brothers, 1947. 100 minutes B/W. D: Raoul Walsh. SC: Niven Busch. WITH Teresa Wright, Robert Mitchum, Judith Anderson, Dean Jagger, Alan Hale, John Rodney, Harry Carey Jr., Clifton Young, Ernest Severn, Charles Bates, Peggy Miller, Norman Jolley, Lane Chandler, Elmer Ellingwood, Jack Montgomery, Ian MacDonald, Kathy Jeanne Johnson, Mickey Little, Scotty Hugenberg, Ray Teal, Eddy Waller, Russ Clark, Jack Davis, Crane Whitley, Carl Harbough, Lester Dorr, Bill Sundholm, Paul Scardon, Harry Lamont, Erville Alderson, Sherman Saunders, Al Kundee, Ben Corbett, Charles Miller, Tom Fadden, Virginia Brissac, Ervin Richardson, Louise Volding, Ian Wolfe, Ed Coffey. A young man haunted by his past sets out to find the murderer of his father. Psychological oater which is a bit hard to follow but is fairly entertaining with fine work by Robert Mitchum as the young Spanish-American War veteran.

2598 Pursuit. Key International, 1975. 86 minutes Color. D: Thomas Quillen. SC: DeWitt Lee & Jack Lee. WITH Ray Danton, DeWitt Lee, Troy Nabors, Diane Taylor, Eva Kovacs, Jason Clark. An Army scout wounded by a bear is tracked through the desert by an Indian brave who plans to kill him. Suspenseful R-rated Western thriller.

2599 Pursuit Across the Desert. Cinematografica Intercontinental, 1960. 75 minutes Color. D: Gilberto Gazcon. SC: Gilberto Gazcon, Fernando Mendez & Raul de Anda. WITH Pedro Armendariz, Teresa Velasquez (Tere Velazquez), Sonia

Furio, Agustin de Anda, Andres Soler, Carlos Lopez Moctezunna, Felix Gonzales, Jose Chavez. Although he knows his quarry is innocent, a lawman gives chase to an accused murderer. Well done Mexican-made melodrama, originally called **La Carcel de Cananea** (The Prisoner of Cananea).

Q

2600   Quantez. Universal-International, 1957. 80 minutes Color. D: Harry Keller. SC: R. Wright Campbell. WITH Fred MacMurray, Dorothy Malone, John Gavin, James Barton, Sydney Chaplin, John Larch, Michael Ansara. Several people are held prisoner in a saloon by a group of bank robbers who are heading into Mexico. Compact little melodrama which is well acted.

2601 Quantrill's Raiders. Allied Artists, 1958. 71 minutes Color. D: Edward Bernds. SC: Polly James. WITH Steve Cochran, Diane Brewster, Leo Gordon, Gale Robbins, Will Wright, Kim Charney, Myron Healey, Robert Foulk, Glenn Strange, Lane Chandler, Guy Prescott, Thomas Browne Henry, Dan White. General Robert E. Lee sends a Confederate captain to contact Quantrill about raiding a Kansas arsenal but the man soon turns against the evil guerilla leader. Not much historical fact here but the film provides action entertainment with Leo Gordon giving a good performance as Quantrill.

2602 Quebec. Paramount, 1951. 85 minutes Color. D: George Templeton. SC: Alan LeMay. WITH John Barrymore Jr., Corinne Calvet, Barbara Rush, Patric Knowles, John Hoyt, Arnold Moss, Don Haggerty, Patsy Ruth Miller, Howard Joslin, Paul Guevremont, Adrian Belanger. During the 1837 Canadian rebellion against Great Britain a rebel leader falls in love with a woman who is the wife of the British commander. Average historical effort with little interest for genre followers.

2603 Queen of the Yukon. Monogram, 1940. 73 minutes B/W. D: Phil Rosen. SC: Joseph West. WITH Charles Bickford, Irene Rich, Melvin Long, George Cleveland, Guy Usher, June Carlson, Dave O'Brien, Tristram Coffin. An aging dance hall hostess tries to protect her young daughter from her way of life during the gold rush days in the Yukon. Taken from Jack London's story, this is a low budget affair which offers a fine performance from veteran star Irene Rich in the title role.

2604   The   Quest. NBC-TV/Columbia, 1976. 100 minutes Color. D: Lee H. Katzin. SC: Tracy Keenan Wynn. WITH Tim Matheson, Kurt Russell, Brian Keith, Keenan Wynn, Will Hutchins, Neville Brand, Cameron Mitchell, Morgan Woodward, Art Lund, Mark Lambert, Gregory Walcott, Iron Eyes Cody, Luke Askew, Irene Yah-Ling Sun. Two brothers search for their sister who was taken from them as a child and now lives with the Indians. Pretty fair made-for-television oater which resulted in a series of the same title which had a brief run on NBC-TV in 1976.

2605 Quick on the Trigger. Columbia, 1948. 55 minutes B/W. D: Ray Nazarro. SC: Elmer Clifton. WITH Charles Starrett, Smiley Burnette, Lyle Talbot, Helen Parrish, George Eldredge, The Sunshine Boys, Ted Adams, Alan Bridge, Russell Arms, Budd Buster, Blackie Whiteford, Tex Cooper, Bud Osborne, Russell Meeker. Outlaws plague a girl's stage line and the local sheriff captures a gang member who turns out to be the girl's brother, and when he is murdered in his cell the lawman is accused of the crime. Well written "Durango Kid" series entry.

2606 The Quiet Gun. 20th Century-Fox, 1957. 79 minutes B/W. D: William F. Claxton. SC: Eric Norden. WITH Forrest Tucker, Mara Corday, Jim Davis, Cleo Moore, Kathleen Crowley, Lee Van Cleef, Tom Brown, Lewis Martin, Hank Worden, Everett Glass, Edith Evanson, Gerald Milton. A saloon owner and his girlfriend hatch a plot which forces a rancher into committing murder. Strangely violent Western with a good cast and fine direction.

2607 The Quiet Gun. Columbia, 1964. 88 minutes Color. D: Sidney Salkow. SC: Robert E. Kent. WITH Audie Murphy, Merry Anders, James Best, Ted De Corsia, Walter Sande, Rex Holman, Charles Meredith, Frank Ferguson, Mort Mills, Gregg Palmer, Frank Gerstle, Stephen Roberts, Paul Bryar, Raymond Hatton, William Fawcett. A young cowboy returns home to find rejection because two years before he was forced to kill the local land baron's son in self defense. Nothing special about this redemption-plotted Audie Murphy film.

2608 Quincannon, Frontier Scout. United Artists, 1956. 83 minutes Color. D: Lesley Selander. SC: John C. Higgins & Don Martin. WITH Tony Martin, Peggie Castle, John Bromfield, John Smith, Ron Randell, John Doucette, Morris Ankrum, Peter Mamakos, Ed Hashim. A former Army officer, now a scout, agrees to lead an expedition into hostile territory in order to find stolen rifles. Tony Martin is very good in the title role of this rather interesting outing.

R

2609 Rachael and the Stranger. RKO Radio, 1948. 92 minutes B/W. D: Norman Foster. SC: Waldo Salt. WITH Loretta Young, William Holden, Robert Mitchum, Gary Gray, Tom Tully, Sara Haden, Frank Ferguson, Walter Baldwin, Regina Wallace, Fran Conlan. A frontier farmer buys a bond servant for a wife but finds out she is attracted to his vagabond hunter pal. Well modulated frontier fare with just the right amounts of drama and humor plus excellent work from its trio of stars.

2610 Racing Blood. 20th Century-Fox, 1954. 76 minutes Color. D: Wesley Barry. SC: Sam Roeca & Wesley Barry. WITH Bill Williams, Jean Porter, Jimmy Boyd, George Cleveland, Frankie Darro, John Eldredge, Sam Flint, Fred Kohler Jr., Fred Kelsey. A colt, which was supposed to have been destroyed at birth due to a split hoof, is raised by a stable boy and his uncle. Fair family oriented film trading on the popularity of child singing star Jimmy Boyd.

Racketeer Round-Up see **Gunners and Guns**

2611 Racketeers of the Range. RKO Radio, 1939. 62 minutes B/W. D: D. Ross Lederman. SC: Oliver Drake. WITH George O'Brien, Marjorie Reynolds, Chill Wills, Ray Whitley, Gay Seabrook, Robert Fiske, Ben Corbett, Bud Osborne, John Dilson, Monte Montague, Cactus Mack, Frankie Marvin, Ed Peil Sr., Frank O'Connor, Mary Gordon, Stanley Andrews, Wilfred Lucas, Harry Cording, Dick Hunter. A dishonest lawyer tries to cheat a girl out of her packing plant and another meat packer takes over her operations to save the local ranchers from being fleeced by the crook. Exceedingly well

done and very entertaining George O'Brien vehicle. V: Nostalgia Merchant.

Radio Ranch see **The Phantom Empire**

2612 Rage. Columbia, 1967. 103 minutes Color. D: Gilberto Gazcon. SC: Teddi Sherman & Gilberto Gazcon. WITH Glenn Ford, Stella Stevens, David Reynoso, Armando Silvestre, Ariadna Welter, Jose Elias Moreno, David Silva, Valentin Trujillo. A physician makes a desperate flight through the Mexican desert as he heads to a medical clinic after being bitten by a rabid dog. Pretty entertaining screen fare, enhanced by Glenn Ford's fine work as the doctor.

2613 Rage. Warner Brothers, 1972. 100 minutes Color. D: George C. Scott. SC: Philip Friedman & Dan Kleinman. WITH George C. Scott, Richard Basehart, Martin Sheen, Barnard Hughes, Nicholas Beauvy, Paul Stevens, Stephen Young, Kenneth Tobey, Robert Walden, William Jordan, Dabbs Greer, John Dierkes, Lou Frizzell, Ed Lauter, Terry Wilson, Fielding Greaves. A rancher sets out to get revenge on those responsible for the death of his son, who was killed as a result of an Army chemical experiment. Fair melodrama which promises more than it delivers.

2614 Rage at Dawn. RKO Radio, 1955. 87 minutes Color. D: Tim Whelan. SC: Horace McCoy. WITH Randolph Scott, Forrest Tucker, Mala Powers, J. Carrol Naish, Edgar Buchanan, Kenneth Tobey, Howard Petrie, Myron Healey, Ralph Moody, Guy Prescott, Mike Ragan, Phil Chambers. Two undercover agents pose as outlaws to capture the Reno Brothers and they arrive at the ranch of the gang's sister, who is shielding them against her better judgment. Pretty good Randolph Scott vehicle with a good script, direction and cast. Original title: **Seven Bad Men.**

2615 Ragtime Cowboy Joe. Universal, 1940. 60 minutes B/W. D: Ray Taylor, SC: Sherman Lowe. WITH Johnny Mack Brown, Fuzzy Knight, Nell O'Day, Marilyn (Lynn) Merrick, Dick Curtis, Walter Soderling, Roy Barcroft, Harry Tenbrook, Wilfred Lucas, Harold Goodwin, Ed Cassidy, Buck Moulton, George Plues, Viola Vonn, Kermit Maynard, Jack Clifford, William Gould, Bud Osborne, Bob O'Connor, Eddie Parker, Frank McCarroll, The Texas Rangers. A detective for the cattle association is on the trail of a crook lawyer and his cohort who are rustling cattle from a ranch so they can obtain it to sell to the railroad. The hackneyed plot gets pretty good service from this Universal actioner.

2616 The Raid. 20th Century-Fox, 1954. 83 minutes Color. D: Hugo Fregonese. SC: Sidney Boehm. WITH Van Heflin, Anne Bancroft, Richard Boone, Lee Marvin, Tommy Rettig, Peter Graves, Douglas Spencer, Paul Cavanagh, Will Wright, James Best, John Dierkes, Helen Ford, Harry Hines, Simon Scott, Claude Akins. During the Civil War a young widow and her son try to thwart the plans of several Confederate soldiers, who have escaped from a nearby military prison to loot their town. Pretty good melodrama with an interesting plotline.

2617 The Raiders. Universal-International, 1952. 80 minutes Color. D: Lesley Selander. SC: Polly James & Lillie Hayward. WITH Richard Conte, Viveca Landfors, Barbara Britton, Hugh O'Brian, Richard Martin, Palmer Lee, William Reynolds, William Bishop, Morris Ankrum, Dennis Weaver, Margaret Field, John Kellogg, Lane Bradford, Riley Hill, Neyle Morrow, Carlos Rivero, George J. Lewis, Francis Mc-Donald. In 1849 California two men who have been wronged by the local authorities team up to destroy a crooked judge who is the leader of an outlaw gang. Nice melodrama which delivers in the entertainment department. Reissue and TV title: **Riders of Vengeance.**

2618 The Raiders. Universal, 1964. 75 minutes Color. D: Herschel Daugherty. SC: Gene L. Coon. WITH Brian Keith, Robert Culp, Judi Meredith, James McMullan, Alfred Ryder, Simon Oakland, Ben Cooper, Trevor Bardette, Harry Carey Jr., Richard Cutting, Addison Richards, Cliff Osmond, Paul Birch, Richard Deacon, Michael Burns. Texans try to drive their cattle herds to the Kansas railheads and are ambushed, but Wild Bill Hickok, Buffalo Bill Cody and Calamity Jane come to their rescue. Actionful little oater which has the look of a TV movie.

2619 Raiders of Ghost City. Universal, 1944. 13 Chapters B/W. D: Ray Taylor & Lewis D. Collins. SC: Luci Ward & Morgan Cox. WITH Dennis Moore, Wanda McKay, Lionel Atwill, Joseph Sawyer, Regis Toomey, Virginia Christine, Eddy Waller, Emmett Vogan, Addison Richards, Charles Wagenheim, Edmund Cobb, Jack Ingram, Jack Rockwell, Ernie Adams, George Eldredge, Gene Garrick, Chief

Thundercloud, Herman Hack, Chick Hannon. Near the end of the Civil War a Union Secret Service operative gets on the trail of a gang of supposedly Confederate soldiers who have been raiding gold shipments in California. Pretty good Universal cliffhanger enhanced by a fine cast.

2620 Raiders of Old California. Republic, 1957. 72 minutes B/W. D: Albert C. Gannaway. SC: Sam Roeca & Thomas C. Hubbard. WITH Jim Davis, Arleen Whelan, Faron Young, Marty Robbins, Louis Jean Heydt, Harry Lauter, Douglas Fowley, Lee Van Cleef, Larry Dobkin, Bill Coontz, Don Diamond, Rick Vallin, Tom Hubbard. At the end of the Mexican War, a group of Cavalry officers in California try to set up their own empire. Low budget but not uninteresting drama; okay for action fans.

2621 Raiders of Red Gap. Producers Releasing Corporation, 1943. 60 minutes B/W. D: Sam Newfield. SC: Joseph O'Donnell. WITH Robert Livingston, Al St. John, Myrna Dell, Ed Cassidy, Charles King, Kermit Maynard, Roy Brent, Frank Ellis, George Chesebro, Reed Howes, Bud Osborne, Jimmie Aubrey, Merrill McCormack, George Morrell, Wally West, Slim Whitaker. A crooked and greedy rancher wants all the cattle in the area and he hires the Lone Rider, thinking he is an outlaw, to kill off other ranchers but has the tables turned on him. Pretty fair entry in PRC's popular "Lone Rider" series.

Raiders of Red Rock see **Fugitive of the Plains**

2622 Raiders of San Joaquin. Universal, 1943. 60 minutes B/W. D: Lewis D. Collins. SC: Elmer Clifton & Morgan Cox. WITH Johnny Mack Brown, Tex Ritter, Fuzzy Knight, Jennifer Holt, Henry Hall, Joseph Bernard, George Eldredge, Henry Roquemore, John Elliott, Michael Vallon, Jack O'Shea, Jack Ingram, Carl Sepulveda, Budd Buster, The Jimmy Wakely Trio (Jimmy Wakely, Johnny Bond, Scotty Harrell), Slim Whitaker, Roy Brent, Earle Hodgins. A man becomes a fugitive when his father is murdered by railroaders trying to burn out area ranchers, but he gets help from the son of the railroad's vice president. Actionful teaming of Johnny Mack Brown and Tex Ritter plus some nice songs composed by Oliver Drake.

2623 Raiders of Sunset Pass. Republic, 1943. 56 minutes B/W. D: John English. SC: John K. Butler. WITH Eddie Dew, Smiley Burnette, Jennifer Holt, Roy Barcroft, Charles Miller, LeRoy Mason, Maxine Doyle, Kenne Duncan, Jack Kirk, Jack Rockwell, Hank Bell, Budd Buster, Jack Ingram, Frank McCarroll, Fred Burns, Al Taylor, Mozelle Gravens, Nancy Worth. During World War II there is a manpower shortage on the range and a lawman rounds up a group of cowgirls to bring in needed cattle but they are opposed by an outlaw gang. Novel idea is used to good advantage in this oater but a weak hero does not help.

2624 Raiders of the Border. Monogram, 1944. 53 minutes B/W. D: John P. Mc-Carthy. SC: Jess Bowers (Adele Buffing-ton). WITH Johnny Mack Brown, Raymond Hatton, Craig Woods, Ellen Hall, Raphael (Ray) Bennett, Edmund Cobb, Ernie Adams, Richard Alexander, Lynton Brent, Stanley Price, Kermit Maynard. Outlaws along the Mexican border rustle cattle and trade them for stolen jewels, but are tracked by two lawmen. Well written and acted oater, an early entry in Johnny Mack Brown-Raymond Hatton's Monogram series.

2625 Raiders of the Range. Republic, 1942. 55 minutes B/W. D: John English. SC: Barry Shipman. WITH Bob Steele, Tom Tyler, Rufe Davis, Lois Collier, Frank Jacquet, Fred Kohler Jr., Dennis Moore, Tom Chatterton, Charles Miller, Max Malzman, Hal Price, Bud Geary, Jack Ingram, Al Taylor, Chuck Morrison, Bob Woodward, Monte Montague, Tom Steele, Kenneth Terrell, Richard Alexan-der, Cactus Mack, John Cason, Charles Phillips, Joel Friedkin. Outlaws are after a man's range because it contains rich oil deposits and the Three Mesquiteers come to his aid when the crooks sabotage the man's oil drilling efforts. Fair entry in the latter days of "The Three Mesquiteers" series.

2626 Raiders of the South. Monogram, 1947. 55 minutes B/W. D: Lambert Hillyer. SC: J. Benton Cheney. WITH Johnny Mack Brown, Raymond Hatton, Evelyn Brent, Marshall Reed, Reno Blair, John Merton, John Hamilton, Pierce Lyden, Cactus Mack, Eddie Parker, Ted Adams, Frank LaRue, George Morrell, Curt Barrett & The Trailsmen, Ray Jones, Artie Ortego, Dee Cooper. In Texas during Reconstruc-tion a Secret Service agent poses as an ex-Confederate in order to stop a

lawyer's scheme to start an empire by a land grab. Pretty interesting melodrama with a small budget compensated by series stars Johnny Mack Brown and Raymond Hatton and leading lady Evelyn Brent.

2627 Raiders of the West. Producers Releasing Corporation, 1942. 64 minutes B/W. D: Peter Stewart (Sam Newfield). SC: Oliver Drake. WITH Bill Boyd, Art Davis, Lee Powell, Virginia Carroll, Rex Lease, Glenn Strange, Charles King, Slim Whitaker, Milton Kibbee, Lynton Brent, John Elliott, Eddie Dean, Curley Dresden, William Desmond, Dale Sherwood, Kenne Duncan, Bill Cody Jr., Reed Howes, Hal Price, Fred "Snowflake" Toones, Carl Sepulveda, Frank Ellis, John Cason. In order to capture an outlaw gang, two range detectives pretend to be entertainers and get a job with the man they suspect is the gang leader. Overlong and vapid entry in the brief "Frontier Marshals" series; this entry wastes an extremely fine supporting cast. V: Cumberland Video.

2628 Raiders of Tomahawk Creek. Colum-bia, 1950. 55 minutes B/W. D: Fred F. Sears. SC: Barry Shipman. WITH Charles Starrett, Smiley Burnette, Kay Buckley, Edgar Dearing, Billy Kimbley, Paul Marion, Paul McGuire, Bill Hale, Ted Mapes, Lee Morgan. A new Indian agent tries to find out the reason for the killings of several area ranchers, deeds committed by the ex-agent who wants Indian lands because he has discovered a valuable silver deposit. Okay "Durango Kid" series actioner.

2629 Rails into Laramie. Universal-Interna-tional, 1954. 81 minutes Color. D: Jesse Hibbs. SC: D. D. Beauchamp & Joseph Hoffman. WITH John Payne, Mari Blanchard, Dan Duryea, Joyce MacKenzie, Barton MacLane, Harry Shannon, Ralph Dumke, Lee Van Cleef, Myron Healey, James Griffith, Alexander Campbell, George Chandler, Charles Horvath, Steve Chase. In the 1870s an Army sergeant tries to get the railroad through to Lara-mie, Wyoming, in spite of local crooks and sabotage. Entertaining and colorful oater.

Rainbow see Gringo

2630 Rainbow Over Texas. Monogram, 1940. 62 minutes B/W. D: Al Herman. SC: Roland Lynch, Roger Merton & Robert Emmett (Tansey). WITH Tex

Ritter, Dorothy Fay, Warner Richmond, Dennis Moore, Arkansas Slim Andrews, James Pierce, Chuck Morrison, John Merton, Romaine Loudermilk & His Ranch House Cowboys, Tommy Southworth, Steve Lorber. When outlaws try to take over a town and close its school, a lawman comes to the rescue. Fairly good Tex Ritter vehicle in which he does a trio of songs, including the title tune.

2631 Rainbow Over Texas. Republic, 1946. 54 (65) minutes B/W. D: Frank McDonald. SC: Gerald Geraghty. WITH Roy Rogers, George "Gabby" Hayes, Dale Evans, Bob Nolan & The Sons of the Pioneers, Sheldon Leonard, Robert Emmett Keane, Gerald Oliver Smith, Minerva Urecal, George J. Lewis, Kenne Duncan, Pierre Lyden, Dick Elliott, Bud Osborne, George Chesebro. Movie star Roy Rogers and The Sons of the Pioneers return to a small Texas town and try to rid it of crooks. Mediocre Roy Rogers effort.

2632 Rainbow Over the Rockies. Monogram, 1947. 54 minutes B/W. D: Oliver Drake. SC: Elmer Clifton. WITH Jimmy Wakely, Lee "Lasses" White, Dennis Moore, Pat Starling, Wesley Tuttle & His Texas Stars, Budd Buster, Zon Murray, Carl Sepulveda, Bob Gilbert, Billy Dix, Jack Baxley. Two ranchers get into a feud which is caused by rustlers wanting their herds. Low grade Jimmy Wakely musical vehicle.

2633 Rainbow Ranch. Monogram, 1933. 55 minutes B/W. D: Harry Fraser. SC: Phil Dunham. WITH Rex Bell, Cecilia Parker, Robert Kortman, Henry Hall, George Nash, Gordon DeMain, Phil Dunham, Tiny Sanford, Jerry Storm. A man returns home to find his uncle murdered and his girl and water rights stolen by a crook. So-so Rex Bell vehicle.

2634 The Rainbow Trail. Fox, 1925. 58 minutes B/W. D-SC: Lynn Reynolds. WITH Tom Mix, Anne Cornwall, George Bancroft, Lucien Littlefield, Mark Hamilton, Vivien Oakland, Thomas Delmar, Fred De Silva, Steve Clemento, Carol Halloway, Diana Miller. A man sets out to free his uncle who has been trapped in a canyon by an outlaw and his gang. Tom Mix plays a dual role in this Zane Grey followup to **Riders of the Purple Sage** (q.v.) and it is an entertaining silent effort. Initially filmed in 1918 by Fox with William Farnum.

2635 Rainbow Valley. Monogram, 1935. 56 minutes B/W. D: Robert North Bradbury. SC: Lindsley Parsons. WITH John Wayne, Lucille Browne, LeRoy Mason, George ("Gabby") Hayes, Buffalo Bill Jr., Bert Dillard, Lloyd Ingraham, Lafe McKee, Frank Ellis, Art Dillard, Frank Ball, Fern Emmett, Henry Rocquemore, Eddie Parker, Herman Hack. An undercover agent pretends to be an escaped convict in order to get the goods on a gang after a tract of valuable land. A rather complicated plot does not hurt the overall entertainment value of this pleasant Lone Star Production from Paul Malvern.

2636 Rainbow's End. First Division, 1935. 59 minutes B/W. D: Norman Spencer. SC: Rollo Ward. WITH Hoot Gibson, June Gale, Oscar Apfel, Warner Richmond, Buddy Roosevelt, Ada Ince, Stanley Blystone, John Elliott, Henry Rocquemore, Fred Gilman. A cowpoke has a falling out with his businessman father and becomes foreman of a ranch on which his father holds the mortgage, and a crooked lawyer tries to get the old man to foreclose so he can get possession of the land. Modern Western with a good story and lots of comedy, the latter typical for Hoot Gibson.

2637 The Rainmaker. Paramount, 1956. 121 minutes Color. D: Joseph Anthony. SC: N. Richard Nash. WITH Katharine Hepburn, Burt Lancaster, Wendell Corey, Lloyd Bridges, Earl Holliman, Cameron Prud'Homme, Wallace Ford, Yvonne Lime, Dottie Bee Baker, Dan White, Stan Jones, John Benson, James Stone, Tony Merrill, Joe Brown, Ken Becker. A fake rainmaker comes to a drought-striken ranch in the Southwest and remains to romance a lonely spinster. Talkative but pleasantly entertaining offbeat drama.

2638 Ramona. 20th Century-Fox, 1936. 94 minutes Color. D: Henry King. SC: Lamar Trotti. WITH Loretta Young, Don Ameche, Kent Taylor, Pauline Frederick, Jane Darwell, Katherine DeMille, J. Carrol Naish, Victor Kilian, John Carradine, Pedro de Cordoba, Charles Waldron, Claire DuBrey, Russell Simpson, William Benedict, Chief Thundercloud, Erville Alderson, Donald Reed, Cecil Weston, D'Arcy Corrigan, Ethan Laidlaw, Kathryn Sheldon, Charles Middleton, Tom London, Richard Botiller, Sam Appel, Anita Ray, Carmen Bailey, Solidad Gonzales, Allan Jones. A half-breed Indian girl and a chief's son marry in Old California but find themselves the victims of prejudice. Colorful but somewhat miscast third screen version of the Helen Hunt Jackson novel.

2639 Rampage at Apache Wells. Columbia, 1966. 91 minutes Color. D: Harald Philipp. SC: Fred Denger & Harald Philipp. WITH Stewart Granger, Pierre Price, Macha Meril, Harald Leipnitz, Antje Weisgerber, Mario Girotti, Walter Barnes, Heinz Erhardt, Gerhard Frickhoffer, Peter Poetrovic. Frontiersman Old Surehand and his Indian friend Winnetou oppose an outlaw and his gang who have been cheating whites and Comanches out of their land. One of the better European Westerns from the 1960s with fine work by Stewart Granger as Old Surehand. Made in West Germany in 1965 by Rialto-Film/Jadran-Film as **Der Olprinz.**

2640 Ramrod. United Artists, 1947. 94 minutes B/W. D: Andre De Toth. SC: John Moffitt, Graham Baker & Cecile Kramer. WITH Joel McCrea, Veronica Lake, Preston Foster, Charles Ruggles, Arleen Whelan, Donald Crisp, Lloyd Bridges, Don DeFore, Ian McDonald, Sarah Padden, Nestor Paiva, Trevor Bardette, Hal Taliaferro, Wally Cassell, Ray Teal, Jeff Corey, Rose Higgens, Chic York, Cliff Parkinson, Ward Wood, John Powers. A rebellious young woman who owns a sheep ranch feuds with her father and hires a cowboy to do her bidding. Well done oater which is good for passing time.

2641 Ranchers and Rascals. Steiner, 1925. 55 minutes B/W. WITH Leo Maloney, Josephine Hill, Whitehorse, Evelyn Thatcher, Barney Furey, Patricia Darling, Tom London, Bud Osborne, Bullet (dog). A cowboy, who wants only a peaceful life while planning to get married, gets involved with a runaway wife, two malicious neighbors and a small baby. Amusing silent Leo Maloney vehicle.

2642 Rancho Deluxe. United Artists, 1975. 93 minutes Color. D: Frank Perry. SC: Thomas McGuane. WITH Jeff Bridges, Sam Waterston, Elizabeth Ashley, Slim Pickens, Clifton James, Charlene Dallas, Harry Dean Stanton, Richard Bright, Patti D'Arbanville, Maggie Wellman, Bert Conway, Anthony Palmer, Sandy Kenyon, Helen Craig. Two pals pick off cattle from a rich rancher and then decide to rustle the entire herd. Passable entertainment with several defects although Slim Pickens is sheer delight as the supposedly bumbling range investigator.

2643 Rancho Grande. Republic, 1940. 68 minutes B/W. D: Frank McDonald. SC: Bradford Ropes, Betty Burbridge & Peter Milne. WITH Gene Autry, Smiley Burnette, June Storey, Mary Lee, Dick Hogan, Ellen Lowe, Ferris Taylor, Joseph DeStefani, Roscoe Ates, Rex Lease, Ann Baldwin, Roy Barcroft, The Pals of the Golden West, Edna Lawrence, Jack Ingram, Bud Osborne, Slim Whitaker, Richard Webb, Hank Bell, Eddie Parker, Horace B. Carpenter, Jim Corey, Cactus Mack, The Brewer Kids, St. Joseph's School Boys' Choir. A ranch foreman and his pal try to help the heirs of the ranch from a gang of crooks who want the land for an irrigation project. Too much music and not enough action hamper this Gene Autry vehicle despite the presence of an extraordinarily good supporting cast of genre veterans. TV title: **El Rancho Grande.**

2644 Rancho Notorious. RKO Radio, 1952. 89 minutes Color. D: Fritz Lang. SC: Daniel Taradash. WITH Marlene Dietrich, Arthur Kennedy, Mel Ferrer, Gloria Henry, William Frawley, Lisa Ferraday, John Raven, Jack Elam, George Reeves, Frank Ferguson, Francis McDonald, Dan Seymour, John Kellogg, Redd Redwing, Stuart Randall, Roger Anderson, I. Stanford Jolley, Felipe Turich, John Doucette, Jose Dominguez. A man hunts for the killer of his girlfriend and ends up at a place run by a woman who protects outlaws. There is not much to recommend this attempt to re-establish the Marlene Dietrich image from **Destry Rides Again** (q.v.). V: VCI Home Video.

2645 Randy Rides Alone. Monogram, 1934. 53 minutes B/W. D: Harry Fraser. SC: Lindsley Parsons. WITH John Wayne, Alberta Vaughn, George ("Gabby") Hayes, Yakima Canutt, Earl Dwire, Tex Phelps, Artie Ortego, Herman Hack, Mack V. Wright. A drifter is falsely accused of robbery and murder but with the help of a young girl he tries to find the real culprits. Rawboned Monogram-Lone Star Production greatly helped by George "Gabby" Hayes' work as the villain.

2646 Range Beyond the Blue. Producers Releasing Corporation, 1947. 53 minutes B/W. D: Ray Taylor. SC: Patricia Harper. WITH Eddie Dean, Roscoe Ates, Helen Mowery, Ted Adams, Bob Duncan, Bill Hammond, George Turner, Ted French, Brad Slavin, Steve Clark, The Sunshine Boys. A stage line is being robbed only when gold shipments are aboard and an investigator is called into corral the culprits. Dreary oater, except for Eddie Dean singing the title song and the novelty ditty "The Pony With the Uncombed Hair."

2647 The Range Busters. Monogram, 1940. 55 minutes B/W. D: S. Roy Luby. SC: John Rathmell. WITH Ray Corrigan, John King, Max Terhune, Luana Walters, LeRoy Mason, Earle Hodgins, Frank LaRue, Kermit Maynard, Bruce King, Duke Matthews, Horace Murphy, Karl Hackett. A crook kills a man for his ranch and gold mine and the Range Busters arrive on the scene looking for a mysterious figure called "The Phantom," who hides out on the dead man's spread. First entry in "The Range Busters" series, this film provides good action and a mystery angle.

2648 Range Defenders. Republic, 1937. 54 minutes B/W. D: Mack V. Wright. SC: Joseph Poland. WITH Robert Livingston, Ray Corrigan, Max Terhune, Eleanor Stewart, Harry Woods, Yakima Canutt, Earle Hodgins, Thomas Carr, John Merton, Harrison Greene, Horace B. Carpenter, Frank Ellis, Fred "Snowflake" Toones, Jack O'Shea, Ernie Adams, Jack Rockwell, Merrill McCormack, Curley Dresden, Jack Kirk, George Morrell, Donald Kirke, Milburn Morante, Al Taylor. Crooks cause a feud between cattle ranchers and sheepmen and the Three Mesquiteers try to cool the situation. Action packed and entertaining entry in the popular "The Three Mesquiteers" series; well directed by Mack V. Wright.

2649 Range Feud. Columbia, 1931. 56 (64) minutes B/W. D: D. Ross Lederman. SC: George Plympton. WITH Buck Jones, Susan Fleming, John Wayne, Ed Le Saint, William Walling, Wallace MacDonald, Harry Woods, Frank Austin, Glenn Strange, Lew Meehan, Jim Corey, Frank Ellis, Bob Reeves. The town's new sheriff is forced to arrest his own foster brother who is accused of killing his girl's rancher father. Nicely done Buck Jones vehicle with John Wayne in a supporting role of the falsely accused brother.

2650 Range Justice. Monogram, 1949. 57 minutes B/W. D: Ray Taylor. SC: Ronald Davidson. WITH Johnny Mack Brown, Max Terhune, Sarah Padden, Felice Ingersoll, Riley Hill, Tristram Coffin, Fred Kohler Jr., Eddie Parker, Kenne Duncan, Bill Hale, Myron Healey, Bill Potter, Bob Woodward. A ranch

foreman joins an outlaw gang to get the goods on the hoodlums who have been rustling his woman boss's cattle. Fair Johnny Mack Brown Monogram film from the latter days of the star's long-running series.

2651 Range Land. Monogram, 1949. 60 minutes B/W. D: Lambert Hillyer. SC: Adele Buffington. WITH Whip Wilson, Andy Clyde, Reno Browne, Reed Howes, Kenne Duncan, Kermit Maynard, Stanley Blystone, Steve Clark, Leonard Penn, John Cason, Carol Henry. A cowboy tries to stop an outlaw gang from stealing a vast amount of range land. Below average oater.

2652 Range Law. Tiffany, 1931. 60 minutes B/W. D: Phil Rosen. SC: Earle Snell. WITH Ken Maynard, Frances Dade, Lafe McKee, Frank Mayo, Charles King, Jack Rockwell, Tom London, William Duncan, Blackjack Ward, Aileen Manning. A man is falsely put in jail for a crime he did not commit but his friends arrange his rescue and he rounds-up the real culprits. Fairly actionful early Ken Maynard talkie with Lafe McKee in a comedy relief role for a change. V: Discount Video.

2653 Range Law. Monogram, 1944. 57 minutes B/W. D: Lambert Hillyer. SC: Frank H. Young. WITH Johnny Mack Brown, Raymond Hatton, Ellen Hall, Sarah Padden, Lloyd Ingraham, Marshall Reed, Steve Clark, Jack Ingram, Hugh Prosser, Stanley Price, Art Fowler, Hal Price, Ben Corbett, Bud Osborne, Tex Palmer, George Morrell, Lynton Brent, Forrest Taylor, Horace B. Carpenter. Two marshals come to the aid of a woman whose friend has been falsely accused of cattle rustling. Average Monogram oater.

2654 Range Renegades. Monogram, 1948. 54 minutes B/W. D: Lambert Hillyer. SC: Ronald Davidson & William Lively. WITH Jimmy Wakely, Dub Taylor, Jennifer Holt, Dennis Moore, Riley Hill, John James, Frank LaRue, Steve Clark, Milburn Morante, Bob Woodward, Carl Mathews, Roy Garrett. A marshal is on the trail of an outlaw gang led by a woman. Typically low grade Jimmy Wakely singing oater.

2655 Range Riders. Superior, 1934. 46 minutes. SC: Victor Adamson (Denver Dixon). SC: L. V. Jefferson. WITH Buddy Roosevelt, Barbara Starr, Merrill Mc-

Cormack, Horace B. Carpenter, Herman Hack, Lew Meehan, Denver Dixon, Clyde McClary, Fred Parker. A lawman masquerades as a fop in order to get the goods on a gang of cutthroats. About as low grade as an oater can go; production values are totally absent.

2656 Range War. Paramount, 1939. 54 (64) minutes B/W. D: Lesley Selander. SC: Sam Robins. WITH William Boyd, Russell Hayden, Willard Robertson, Matt Moore, Pedro de Cordoba, Betty Moran, Britt Wood, Kenneth Harlan, Eddie Dean, Earle Hodgins, Glenn Strange, Jason Robards, Stanley Price, George Chesebro, Raphael Bennett. In trying to help a girl stop the destruction of a railroad, Hoppy takes money from a stagecoach so outlaws won't get it and ends up being arrested, so he joins the outlaw gang to get the goods on them. Nice locations and photography highlight this "Hopalong Cassidy" feature.

2657 Range Warfare. Willis Kent, 1935. 55 minutes B/W. D: S. Roy Luby. SC: E. B. Mann. WITH Reb Russell, Lucille Lund, Wally Wales, Lafe McKee, Roger Williams, Slim Whitaker, Ed Boland, Richard Botiller, Chief Blackhawk, Ed Porter, Gene Alsace, Bart Carre. A cowboy is on the trail of an outlaw gang wanted for cattle rustling and murder. Pretty fair Reb Russell vehicle that will please his fans. Reissued as **Vengeance.**

Rangeland Empire see **West of the Brazos**

2658 The Ranger and the Lady. Republic, 1940. 54 (59) minutes B/W. D: Joseph Kane. SC: Stuart Anthony & Gerald Geraghty. WITH Roy Rogers, George "Gabby" Hayes, Jacqueline Wells (Julie Bishop), Harry Woods, Henry Brandon, Noble Johnson, Si Jenks, Ted Mapes, Yakima Canutt, Herman Hack, Art Dillard. In Texas, ranger Roy Rogers fights outlaws trying to hijack settlers' wagons in order to take over the country—until General Sam Houston comes to the rescue. Lots of action, a very good plot and pleasant songs in this Roy Rogers entry.

2659 Ranger Courage. Columbia, 1937. 58 minutes B/W. D: Spencer Gordon Bennet. SC: Nate Gatzert. WITH Bob Allen, Martha Tibbets, Walter Miller, Buzz Henry, Bud Osborne, Robert Kortman, Harry Strang, William Gould, Horace Murphy, Franklyn Farnum, Buffalo Bill Jr., Gene Alsace. A ranger comes to

the rescue of a wagon train attacked by outlaws disguised as Indians and he sets out to round up the gang. Mediocre entry in Bob Allen's brief Columbia series.

2660 Ranger of Cherokee Strip. Republic, 1949. 60 minutes B/W. D: Philip Ford. SC: Bob Williams. WITH Monte Hale, Alice Talton, Paul Hurst, Roy Barcroft, Douglas Kennedy, George Meeker, Frank Fenton, Monte Blue, Lane Bradford. A renegade Indian is blamed for the death of his chief by cattlemen who want to lease the Indian's land; set in the Cherokee Indian Nation in the 1890s, with Monte Hale as a ranger out to stop the trouble. Average outing with Douglas Kennedy more colorful than hero Monte Hale.

2661 Ranger of the Law. American, 1935. 50 minutes B/W. D: R. J. Renroh (Robert J. Horner). SC: Royal Hampton. WITH Buffalo Bill Jr., Jeanee (Genee) Boutell, George Chesebro, Jack Long, Boris Bullock, Benny Corbett, Frank Clark, Duke Lee, Lake Reynolds. A rodeo rider opposes a crook who is out to steal a ranch from a pretty girl. Very cheaply made with lots of stock rodeo footage and a poor soundtrack with muffled dialogue.

2662 The Rangers. NBC-TV/Universal, 1974. 74 minutes Color. D: Christian Nyby II. SC: Robert A. Cinader, Michael Donavan & Preston Wood. WITH James G. Richardson, Colby Chester, Jim B. Smith, Laraine Stephens, Laurence Delaney, Michael Conrad, Roger Bowen, Carl Roger Breedlove, David Birkoff. U. S. Forest Service park rangers work to preserve the forests and wildlife as well as rescue those in danger. Passable telefeature which evolved into the brief "Sierra" (NBC-TV, 1974) television series.

2663 The Ranger's Code. Monogram, 1933. 60 minutes B/W. D: Robert North Bradbury. SC: Harry O. (Fraser) Jones. WITH Bob Steele, Doris Hill, George ("Gabby") Hayes, George Nash, Frank Ball, Ed Brady, Hal Price, Ernie Adams, Dick Dickinson. A lawman finds out his girl's brother is hooked up with an outlaw gang. So-so Bob Steele vehicle.

2664 Rangers of Fortune. Paramount, 1940. 80 minutes B/W. D: Sam Wood. SC: Frank Butler. WITH Fred MacMurray, Albert Dekker, Gilbert Roland, Patricia Morison, Joseph Schildkraut, Dick Foran, Betty Brewer, Arthur Allen, Bernard

Nedell, Brandon Tynan, Minor Watson, Rosa Turich, Frank Puglia, Frank Milan, Matt McHugh, Erville Alderson, Fern Emmett, Joseph Eggenton, Ed LeSaint, Rod Cameron, Fred Malatesta, Harry Fleischmann, Martin Garralaga, Paul "Tiny" Newlan, Charles Middleton, Charles Irwin, Frank Hagney, Dewey Robinson, Jack Robinson. Three desperadoes, on the run from a firing squad, befriend a newspaper editor and a small girl in a small town and help get rid of the local outlaw element. Breezy actioner with the three leads making a good team.

2665 The Rangers Ride. Monogram, 1948. 56 minutes B/W. D: Derwin Abrahams. SC: Basil Dickey. WITH Jimmy Wakely, Dub Taylor, Virginia Belmont, Riley Hill, Marshall Reed, Steve Clark, Pierce Lyden, Milburn Morante, Jim Diehl, Cactus Mack, Carol Henry, Bud Osborne, Bob Woodward, Boyd Stockman. When a former Texas Ranger is falsely accused of murder a friend comes to his rescue. Not much to brag about.

2666 The Ranger's Round-Up. Spectrum, 1938. 57 minutes B/W. D: Sam Newfield. SC: George Plympton. WITH Fred Scott, Al St. John, Christine McIntyre, Earle Hodgins, Steve Ryan, Karl Hackett, Robert Owen, Syd Chatan, Carl Mathews, Richard Cramer, Jimmie Aubrey, Lew Porter, Cactus Mack, Steve Clark, Chick Hannon, Milburn Morante. An undercover agent joins a medicine store which outlaws have been using as a front for their activities, a fact not known by its proprietor. Pretty fair Fred Scott vehicle; this one includes the classic song "The Terror of Termite Valley."

2667 The Rangers Step In. Columbia, 1937. 58 minutes B/W. D: Spencer Gordon Bennet. SC: Nate Gatzert. WITH Bob Allen, Eleanor Stewart, Hal Taliaferro, John Merton, Jay Wilsey (Buffalo Bill Jr.), Jack Ingram, Jack Rockwell, Lafe McKee, Robert Kortman, Billy Townsend, Ray Jones, Lew Meehan, Tommy Thompson, Herman Hack, Richard Cramer, Joe Girard, George Plues, Harry Harvey, Tex Palmer, Francis Walker. A crook revives a feud between two families in order to get a ranch, and the local sheriff calls in a Texas Ranger to help stop the fighting. Bob Allen's final series film is a pleasant affair and a good finale to his all-too-brief genre career.

2668 The Rangers Take Over. Producers Releasing Corporation, 1942. 62 minutes

B/W. D: Albert Herman. SC: Elmer Clifton. WITH Dave O'Brien, James Newill, Guy Wilkerson, Iris Meredith, Forrest Taylor, I. Stanford Jolley, Charles King, Carl Mathews, Harry Harvey, Lynton Brent, Bud Osborne, Cal Shrum & The Rhythm Rangers. When he is discharged from the Texas Rangers a man joins an outlaw gang, but he works as an informant for the Rangers. Another typical entry in PRC's "The Texas Rangers" series; mediocre.

2669 Rangle River. J. H. Hoffenberg, 1936. 75 minutes B/W. D: Clarence Badger. SC: Zane Grey. WITH Victor Jory, Margaret Dare, Robert Coote, George Bryant, Rita Paucefort, Leo Crackwell, Cecil Perry, Georgia Sterling, Stewart McColl, Phil Smith. Crooks try to put a rancher out of business by cheating him of his water rights. Interesting Zane Grey film made in Australia. TV title: **Men with Whips.**

2670 Ransom for Alice. NBC-TV/Universal, 1977. 78 minutes Color. D: David Lowell Rich. SC: Jim Byrnes. WITH Yvette Mimieux, Gil Gerard, Charles Napier, Gene Barry, John Dennan, Laurie Prange, Barnard Hughes, Robert Logan, Harris Yulin, Marc Vahanian, Mills Watson, Gavin MacLeod, Anthony James. In 1890s' Seattle a deputy marshall and his pretty partner try to find a young girl caught in a white slavery ring. Average TV movie with a good cast.

2671 The Rare Breed. Universal, 1966. 97 minutes Color. D: Andrew V. McLaglen. SC: Ric Hardman. WITH James Stewart, Maureen O'Hara, Brian Keith, Juliet Mills, Don Galloway, David Brian, Jack Elam, Ben Johnson, Harry Carey Jr., Perry Lopez, Larry Domasin, Alan Caillou, Bob Gravage, Wayne Van Horn, Leroy Johnson, John Harris, Ted Mapes, Larry Blake, Charles Lampkin, Tex Armstrong. A woman cattle breeder and her daughter bring their prize bull to the U. S. to start a new breed but the woman becomes involved with an ex-rancher and his pal. Well made production that is on the dull side.

2672 Raton Pass. Warner Brothers, 1951. 84 minutes B/W. D: Edwin L. Marin. SC: Tom Blackburn & James Webb. WITH Dennis Morgan, Patricia Neal, Steve Cochran, Dorothy Hart, Scott Forbes, Basil Ruysdael, Louis Jean Heydt, Roland Winters, James Burke, Elvira Curci, Carlos Conde, John Crawford, Rodolfo

Hoyos Jr. A husband and wife are at odds over their cattle empire and when the woman gets the upper hand, the husband organizes area homesteaders against her. More than passable Western melodrama with good performances by its leads.

2673 Raw Edge. Universal-International, 1956. 76 minutes Color. D: John Sherwood. SC: Harry Essex & Robert Hill. WITH Rory Calhoun, Yvonne De Carlo, Mara Corday, Rex Reason, Neville Brand, Emile Meyer, Herbert Rudley, Robert J. Wilke, John Gilmore, Gregg Barton, Ed Fury, Francis McDonald, Julia Montoya, Paul Fierro, William Schallert, Richard James, Robert Hoy. A beautiful woman taken by the first man who claimed her in Oregon in the 1840s finds herself attracted to the man out to kill her husband in revenge for his brother's murder. Complicated Albert Zugsmith production saved by good photography and fetching Yvonne De Carlo.

2674 Raw Timber. Crescent, 1937. 63 minutes B/W. D: Ray Taylor. SC: Bennett Cohen & John T. Neville. WITH Tom Keene, Peggy Keys, Budd Buster, Robert Fiske, Lee Phelps, John Rutherford, Rafael Bennett, Slim Whitaker, Bart Carre. A timber baron murders a forest ranger who finds out he is destroying the forests for his own gain but another ranger arrives on the scene to investigate. Pretty fair entry in Tom Keene's historical series for Crescent Pictures with nice locales and good photography by Arthur Martinelli.

2675 Rawhide. Principal/20th Century-Fox, 1938. 60 minutes B/W. D: Ray Taylor. SC: Dan Jarrett & Jack Natteford. WITH Smith Ballew, Lou Gehrig, Evalyn Knapp, Carl Stockdale, Cy Kendall, Slim Whitaker, Arthur Loft, Si Jenks, Lafe McKee, Lee Shumway, Dick Curtis, Tom Forman, Cliff Parkinson, Harry Tenbrook, Ed Cassidy. Baseball star Lou Gehrig finds crooks trying to take his sister's ranch and he teams with her lawyer to stop them. Interesting oater with the curio value of Lou Gehrig's sturdy performance which overshadows (somewhat) star Smith Ballew as the attorney. V: Blackhawk, Cassette Express.

2676 Rawhide. 20th Century-Fox, 1951. 86 minutes B/W. D: Henry Hathaway. SC: Dudley Nichols. WITH Tyrone Power, Susan Hayward, Hugh Marlowe, Dean Jagger, Edgar Buchanan, Jack Elam, George Tobias, Jeff Corey, James Millican, Louis Jean Heydt, William Haade, Milton Corey Sr., Kenneth Tobey, Dan White, Max Terhune, Robert Adler, Judy Ann Dunn, Vincent Neptune, Walter Sande, Si Jenks, Dick Curtis, Edith Evanson. Outlaws hole up at a lonely way station and kill the owner and hold his assistant and a young woman with a small child hostages. Well modulated and entertaining melodrama with fine work by Hugh Marlowe as the gang leader. Alternate TV title: **Desperate Siege.**

2677 Rawhide Rangers. Universal, 1941. 56 minutes B/W. D: Ray Taylor. SC: Ed Earl Repp. WITH Johnny Mack Brown, Fuzzy Knight, Nell O'Day, Kathryn Adams, Roy Harris, Harry Cording, Al Bridge, Frank Shannon, Ed Cassidy, Robert Kortman, Chester Gan, James Farley, Jack Rockwell, Frank Ellis, Fred Burns, Tex Palmer, Tex Terry, The Pickard Family, The Texas Rangers. After the murder of his brother, a Texas Ranger supposedly resigns and becomes an outlaw but he is only trying to infiltrate the gang responsible for the killing. Standard, but slick, Johnny Mack Brown vehicle.

2678 Rawhide Romance. Superior, 1934. 47 minutes B/W. D: Victor Adamson (Denver Dixon). SC: L. V. Jefferson. WITH Buffalo Bill Jr., Genee Boutell, Lafe McKee, Si Jenks, Bart Carre, Boris Bullock, Jack Evans, Marin Sais, Clyde McClary. A cowboy finds himself involved with a pretty girl when he sets out to rid the area of outlaws. Bottom of the barrel Denver Dixon production; a delight for camp followers.

2679 The Rawhide Terror. Security, 1934. 52 minutes B/W. D: Jack Nelson & Bruce Mitchell. SC: Jack Nelson. WITH Art Mix, William Desmond, Edmund Cobb, William Barrymore (Boris Bullock), Frances Morris, Bill Patton, Tommy Bupp, Herman Hack, George Holt, George Gyton, Ed Carey, Ernest Scott, Fred Parker, Denver Dixon. A lawman is on the trail of an outlaw who is really his orphaned brother. This Victor Adamson (Denver Dixon) production has to be seen to be believed; a treat for grade-Z movie freaks. Genre fans will appreciate the fact it gives the great Art Mix (George Kesterson) one of his few talkie starring roles.

2680 The Rawhide Trail. Allied Artists, 1950. 60 (67) minutes B/W. D: Robert Gordon. SC: Alexander Wells. WITH

Rex Reason, Nancy Gates, Richard Erdman, Rusty Lane, Frank Chase, Ann Doran, Robert Knapp, Richard Warren, Al Wyatt. Two men falsely accused of leading settlers into an Indian ambush prove their innocence as they await hanging and the Indians attack the fort where they are imprisoned. Low budget affair which is nothing to shout about.

2681 The Rawhide Years. Universal-International, 1956. 85 minutes Color. D: Rudolph Mate. SC: Earl Felton, Robert Presnell Jr. & D. D. Beauchamp. WITH Tony Curtis, Colleen Miller, Arthur Kennedy, William Demarest, William Gargan, Peter Van Eyck, Minor Watson, Donald Randolph, Chubby Johnson, James Anderson, Robert Wilke, Trevor Bardette, Robert Foulk, Leigh Snowden, Don Beddoe, Malcolm Atterbury, Charles Evans, I. Stanford Jolley, Rex Lease, Chuck Roberson, Marlene Felton, Clarence Lung, Lane Bradford. A reformed gambler in the 1870s is falsely accused of a riverboat murder. More than passably entertaining melodrama.

R.C.M.P. and the Treasure of Genghis Khan see **Dangers of the Canadian Mounted**

2682 The Reason Nobody Hardly Ever Seen a Fat Outlaw in the Old West is as Follows: NBC-TV/Universal, 1967. 49 minutes Color. WITH Don Knotts, Arthur Godfrey, Percy Helton, Mary-Robin Redd, Jack Lambert. A bumbling outlaw called The Curly Kid finds he cannot get himself arrested or even break the law despite the fact he desires to be the most famous outlaw in the West. Fair comedy-Western originally telecast as a segment of the "Bob Hope Chrysler Theatre" (NBC-TV, 1963-67).

2683 A Reason to Live, A Reason to Die! K-Tel, 1974. 92 minutes Color. D-SC: Tonino Valeri. WITH James Coburn, Telly Savalas, Bud Spencer, Georges Geret, Robert Burton. During the Civil War a Union officer and seven prisoners try to capture a fort held by the Confederates. Violent European coproduction which must depend on the name value of its stars rather than any innate quality. TV title: **Massacre at Fort Holman.** V: Video Gems.

2684 Rebel City. Allied Artists, 1953. 60 minutes B/W. D: Thomas Carr. SC: Sid Theil. WITH Bill Elliott, Marjorie Lord, Robert Kent, Ray Walker, I. Stanford

Jolley, Keith Richards, Henry Rowland, Denver Pyle, John Crawford, Otto Waldis, Stanley Price, Michael Vallon. A man arrives in a Kansas town to find out who murdered his father and uncovers a conspiracy with copperheads aiding the Confederate cause. Compact and entertaining Bill Elliott vehicle.

2685 Rebel in Town. United Artists, 1956. 78 minutes Color. D: Alfred Werker. SC: Danny Arnold. WITH John Payne, Ruth Roman, J. Carrol Naish, Ben Cooper, John Smith, James Griffith, Mary Adams, Bobby Clark, Mimi Gibson, Ben Johnson, Joel Ashley. After a bank robbery, an ex-soldier accidentally kills a small boy but ends up having his life saved by the boy's father. Different kind of plotline for this type of fare; above average.

2686 Rebellion. Crescent, 1936. 62 minutes B/W. D: Lynn Shores. SC: John T. Neville. WITH Tom Keene, Rita (Hayworth) Cansino, Duncan Renaldo, William Royle, Gino Corrado, Roger Gray, Bob McKenzie, Allen Cavan, Jack Ingram, Lita Cortez, Theodore Lorch, Merrill McCormack. President Zachary Taylor sends an army officer to California after its acquisition from Mexico to stop lawlessness against Spanish land owners. Pretty fair entry in the historical film series Tom Keene made for producer E. B. Derr. Reissued in 1946 as **Lady from Frisco.**

2687 Rebels on the Loose. Fenix Film, 1966. 92 minutes Color. D: Bruno Corbucci. SC: Vighi, Guerra, Scarnicci & Tarabusi. WITH Raimondo Vianello, Lando Buzzanca, Maria Martinez, Monica Randal, Gino Buzzanca, Alfonso Rojos, Emilio Rodrigues, Giovanna Lenzi, Miguel del Castillo, Santiago Rivero, Mario Castellani, Mario De Simone, Antonio Albaisin. Two Southern soldiers at an isolated fortress still believe the war is going on although it has been over for eight years and they meet two girls who urge them to continue their sabotage activities. Limp comedy takeoff of spaghetti Westerns. Italian title: **Ringo e Gringo Contro Tutti** (Ringo and Gringo Against All).

2688 Reckless Ranger. Columbia, 1937. 56 minutes B/W. D: Spencer Gordon Bennet. SC: Nate Gatzert. WITH Bob Allen, Louise Small, Mary MacLaren, Harry Woods, Jack Perrin, Buddy Cox, Jack Rockwell, Slim Whitaker, Roger Williams, Jay Wilsey (Buffalo Bill Jr.), Bud Osborne, Jim Corey, Tom London, Hal Price, Al Taylor, Tex Cooper, Bob

McKenzie, Lane Chandler, Frank Ball, George Plues, Lafe McKee, Tex Palmer, Chick Hannon. A ranger investigates the killing of his twin brother who was murdered by a gang controlled by a crook who wants to run off all the sheepmen in order to use government grazing lands for his cattle. Fast moving Bob Allen vehicle although Jack Perrin just about steals the show as a secondary hero.

2689 The Red Badge of Courage. Metro-Goldwyn-Mayer, 1951. 69 minutes B/W. D-SC: John Huston. WITH Audie Murphy, Bill Mauldin, Douglas Dick, Royal Dano, John Dierkes, Arthur Hunnicutt, Andy Devine, Robert Easton Burke, Smith Ballew, Glenn Strange, Dan White, Frank McGraw, Tim Durant, Emmett Lynn. I. Stanford Jolley, William Phillips, House Peters Jr., Frank Sully, George Offerman Jr., Joel Marston, Robert Nichols, Lou Nova, Fred Kohler Jr., Dick Curtis, Guy Wilkerson, Buddy Roosevelt, Jim Hayward, Gloria Eaton, Robert Cherry, Whit Bissell, William Phipps, Ed Hinton, Lynn Farr. During the Civil War a young recruit panics during his first battlefield encounter but later garners courage enough to fight and ends up a hero. John Huston's truncated version of the Stephen Crane novel is fairly interesting, especially for its look at the effects of battle on individuals. Look for Andy Devine's dynamic cameo as the optimistic soldier.

2690 The Red Badge of Courage. NBC-TV/20th Century-Fox, 1974. 78 minutes Color. D: Lee Philips. SC: John Gay. WITH Richard Thomas, Michael Brandon, Wendell Burton, Charles Aidman, Warren Berlinger, Lee DeBroux, Francesca Jarvis, George Sawaya, Hank Hendrick, John Cox, Tiny Wells, Norman Stone, Jack DeLeon (narrator). A frightened Union soldier during the Civil War learns the meaning of courage after running from the enemy during his first battle. Okay TV adaptation of the famous Stephen Crane story.

2691 Red Blood. Anchor, 1926. 50 minutes B/W. D: J. P. McGowan. SC: G. A. Durlam. WITH Al Hoxie, Nayone Warfield, Lew Meehan, Eddie Barry, J. P. McGowan, Frances Kellogg, Walter Patterson, Len Sewards. A cowboy, who is always getting into trouble, is in love with his boss' daughter, who is also sought by a crooked gambler who is blackmailing the girl's brother. Although it contains lots of fight sequences, this Al Hoxie silent horse opera is pretty dull going.

2692 Red Blood of Courage. Ambassador, 1935. 55 minutes B/W. D: Jack (John) English. SC: Barry Barringer. WITH Kermit Maynard, Ann Sheridan, Reginald Barlow, Charles King, Ben Hendricks Jr., George Regas, Nat Carr. A Mountie uncovers a plot where crooks kidnap a man for his land while one of them impersonates the kidnapped man for his visiting niece. Entertaining Kermit Maynard vehicle. V: Cassette Express.

2693 Red Desert. Lippert, 1949. 60 minutes B/W. D: Ford Beebe. SC: Daniel B. Ullman & Ron Ormond. WITH Don Barry, Tom Neal, Jack Holt, Margia Dean, Byron Foulger, Joseph Crehan, John Cason, Tom London, Holly Bane, Hank Bell, George Slocum. Two gambling house operators use their business as a front for the sale of stolen government money and President Grant assigns the Pecos Kid to uncover the culprits. Actionful and well acted Don Barry vehicle; ten times better than the 1964 Michelangelo Antonioni Italian film with the same title.

2694 Red Fork Range. Big 4, 1931. 60 minutes B/W. D-SC: Alvin J. Neitz (Alan James). WITH Wally Wales, Ruth Mix, Al Ferguson, Cliff Lyons, Bud Osborne, Lafe McKee, Jim Corey, Chief Big Tree, Will Armstrong, George Gerwin. A cowboy tries to win a stagecoach race but is opposed by an outlaw gang. Bottom rung and torpid Wally Wales outing.

2695 Red Garters. Paramount, 1954. 91 minutes Color. D: George Marshall. SC: Michael Fessier. WITH Rosemary Clooney, Jack Carson, Guy Mitchell, Pat Crowley, Gene Barry, Buddy Ebsen, Cass Daley, Reginald Owen, Frank Faylen, Joanne Gilbert, Richard Hale. A man rides into a small town looking for his brother's killer and finds the citizens celebrating the event. Strange conglomerate of music and drama; definitely a curio.

2696 Red Mountain. Paramount, 1951. 84 minutes Color. D: William Dieterle. SC: John Meredyth Lucas, George F. Slavin & George W. George. WITH Alan Ladd, Lizabeth Scott, Arthur Kennedy, John Ireland, Jeff Corey, James Bell, Bert Freed, Walter Sande, Neville Brand, Carleton Young, Whit Bissell, Jay Silverheels, Francis McDonald, Iron Eyes Cody, Dan White, Ralph Moody, Crane Whitley, Herbert Belles. Quantrill and his band of raiders, pretending to fight for the

Confederacy, go on looting and murder raids in Kansas and Missouri during the Civil War. Actionful accounting of the career of the notorious Quantrill, well played by John Ireland.

2697 The Red Pony. Republic, 1949. 89 minutes Color. D: Lewis Milestone. SC: John Steinbeck. WITH Robert Mitchum, Myrna Loy, Louis Calhern, Shepperd Strudwick, Peter Miles, Margaret Hamilton, Patty King, Jackie Jackson, Beau Bridges, Don Kay Reynolds, Wee Willie Davis, Tommy Sheridan, George Tyne, Nino Tempo, Poodles Hanneford, Gracie Hanneford, Eddie Borden, Max Wagner, Alvin Hammer, Dolores Castle, William Quinan. A young boy longs for his own pony and after his stern father gets him one, he neglects it and the animal wanders away and dies. John Steinbeck adapted this uneven version of his novella, although the film makes for pleasant entertainment.

2698 The Red Pony. NBC-TV/Universal, 1973. 100 minutes Color. D: Robert Totten. SC: Robert Totten & Ron Bishop. WITH Henry Fonda, Maureen O'Hara, Ben Johnson, Jack Elam, Clint Howard, Julian Rivero, Richard Jaeckel, Roy Jenson, Woodrow Chambliss, Warren Douglas, Yvonne Wood, Victor Sen Yung, Lieux Dressler, Link Wyler, Rance Howard, Sally Carter-Ihnat, Heather Totten, Kurt Sled. A young boy feels more kinship with his pony than with his hard-to-understand father. Well made version of the John Steinbeck work, although the character of Billy Buck (played by Robert Mitchum in the 1949 screen version [q.v.]) is deleted.

2699 The Red Raiders. First National, 1927. 63 minutes B/W. D: Albert Rogell. SC: Marion Jackson. WITH Ken Maynard, Ann Drew, J. P. McGowan, Paul Hurst, Harry Shutan, Ben Corbett, Chief Yowlachie, Tom Bay, Lafe McKee, Hal Salter. A young Army lieutenant is sent to a fort in the Sioux Territory and there he manages to subdue a wild horse, fall in love with a beautiful girl and try to thwart the war intentions of a chief who does not want his people on a reservation. One of Ken Maynard's very best films in which he does a great deal of impressive stunt work; a highly entertaining feature.

2700 The Red Rider. Universal, 1934. 15 Chapters B/W. D: Louis Friedlander (Lew Landers). SC: George Plympton, Vin Moore, Ella O'Neill & George Morgan.

WITH Buck Jones, Marion Shilling, Grant Withers, Walter Miller, J. P. McGowan, Richard Cramer, Margaret LaMarr, Charles K. French, Edmund Cobb, William Desmond, Mert Lavarre (John Merton), Frank Rice, Jim Thorpe, Monte Montague, Denny Meadows (Dennis Moore), Jim Corey, Bud Osborne, Al Ferguson, Artie Ortego, Tom Ricketts, J. Frank Glendon, Charles Brinley, Bill Steele, Fred Burns, Hank Bell, Chester Gan, Jim Toney, Art Mix, Jack Rockwell, Jack O'Shea, Frank Ellis. A sheriff loses his job because he refuses to believe his pal committed a murder and near the Mexican border he comes across clues to support his belief. Top notch Buck Jones cliffhanger.

2701 Red River. United Artists, 1948. 125 minutes B/W. D: Howard Hawks. SC: Borden Chase & Charles Schnee. WITH John Wayne, Montgomery Clift, Joanne Dru, Walter Brennan, Coleen Gray, John Ireland, Noah Beery Jr., Harry Carey, Harry Carey, Jr., Chief Yowlachie, Mickey Kuhn, Paul Fix, Hank Worden, Ivan Parry, Hal Taliaferro, Paul Fiero, Billy Self, Ray Hyke, Glenn Strange, Tom Tyler, Lane Chandler, Dan White, Lee Phelps, George Lloyd, Shelley Winters. A cattle baron leads a rough cattle drive, forming the Chisholm Trail, but along the way his methods are questioned by his foster son, who takes command away from him. Classic Western; one of the very best. VD: Blackhawk.

2702 Red River Range. Republic, 1938. 56 minutes B/W. D: George Sherman. SC: Stanley Roberts, Betty Burbridge & Luci Ward. WITH John Wayne, Ray Corrigan, Max Terhune, Polly Moran, Lorna Gray (Adrian Booth), Kirby Grant, Sammy McKim, William Royle, Perry Ivins, Stanley Blystone, Lenore Bushman, Burr Caruth, Roger Williams, Earl Askam, Olin Francis, Ed Cassidy, Fred "Snowflake" Toones, Bob McKenzie, Theodore Lorch, Al Taylor, Jack Montgomery. Outlaws use a dude ranch as a base for cattle rustling via trucks and the Three Mesquiteers are called in to get to the bottom of the situation with Stony Brooke pretending to be an outlaw to get in with the gang. Fast moving entry in the popular "The Three Mesquiteers" series.

2703 Red River Renegades. Republic, 1946. 55 minutes B/W. D: Thomas Carr. SC: Norman S. Hall. WITH Sunset Carson, Peggy Stewart, Tom London, Bruce Langley, Kenne Duncan, LeRoy Mason, Ted

Adams, Edmund Cobb, Stanley Price, Fred Graham, Jack Rockwell, Tex Terry. Two postal inspectors investigate a rash of stagecoach robberies and disappearances and one of them is murdered. Typically actionful Sunset Carson film with speed making up for lack of finesse. V: Cumberland Video.

2704 Red River Robin Hood. RKO Radio, 1943. 57 minutes B/W. D: Lesley Selander. SC: Bennett Cohen. WITH Tim Holt, Cliff Edwards, Barbara Moffett, Eddie Dew, Otto Hoffman, Russell Wade, Tom London, Earle Hodgins, Bud McTaggart, Reed Howes, Kenne Duncan, David Sharpe, Bob McKenzie, Jack Rockwell, Jack Montgomery. A masked figure called "Mr. Justice" fights for the rights of ranchers who are being bilked in taxes by crooks holding a faked land grant claim. Satisfying Tim Holt vehicle.

2705 Red River Shore. Republic, 1953. 54 minutes B/W. D: Harry Keller. SC: Arthur Orloff & Gerald Geraghty. WITH Rex Allen, Slim Pickens, Lyn Thomas, Bill Phipps, Douglas Fowley, Trevor Bardette, William Haade, Emmett Vogan, John Cason, Rayford Barnes. A marshal is forced to kill a crooked businessman in a gunfight but vows to keep the man's guilt a secret and when the latter's son arrives trouble develops between him and the lawman over the dead man's bogus oil drilling operation. A complicated plot keeps this Rex Allen film moving along well despite dropping production values.

2706 Red River Valley. Republic, 1936. 54 (56) minutes B/W. D: B. Reeves Eason. SC: Dorrell McGowan & Stuart McGowan. WITH Gene Autry, Smiley Burnette, Frances Grant, Booth Howard, George Chesebro, Charles King, Frankie Marvin, Lloyd Ingraham, Hank Bell, Earl Dwire, Jack Kinney, Sam Flint, Eugene Jackson, Edward Hearn, Frank LaRue, Ken Cooper, C. E. "Cap" Anderson, George Morrell. Singing cowpoke Gene Autry tries to find out who is the culprit in dynamiting ditches, the action endangering a big irrigation project. Colorful and fast moving Gene Autry musical vehicle. Alternate title: **Man of the Frontier.** V: Discount Video.

2707 Red River Valley. Republic, 1941. 54 (62) minutes B/W. D: Joseph Kane. SC: Malcolm Stuart Boylan. WITH Roy Rogers, George "Gabby" Hayes, Sally Payne, Gale Storm, Hal Taliaferro, Bob Nolan & The Sons of the Pioneers, Trevor Bardette, Robert Homans, Lynton Brent, Ed Piel Sr., Dick Wessell, Jack Rockwell, Ted Mapes. Racketeers set out to obtain water rights and cattle in a valley where a dam project is being built. Fair Roy Rogers series entry.

2708 Red Rock Outlaw. Friedgen, 1950. 56 minutes B/W. D-SC: Elmer Pond. WITH Bob Gilbert, Lee "Lasses" White, Ione Nixon, Forrest Matthews, Virginia Jackson, Wanda Cantlon. A murderous outlaw tries to kill his honest rancher twin brother and take his place. Rock bottom oater.

2709 The Red Rope. Republic, 1937. 60 minutes B/W. D: S. Roy Luby. SC: George Plympton. WITH Bob Steele, Lois January, Horace Murphy, Charles King, Bobby Nelson, Ed Cassidy, Lew Meehan, Frank Ball, Karl Hackett, Jack Rockwell, Forrest Taylor. A cowboy comes to the rescue of a young couple who want to marry but whose plans are altered by a man who holds the mortgage to the girl's father's ranch and wants her for himself. Well written Bob Steele film.

2710 Red Skies of Montana. 20th Century-Fox, 1952. 96 minutes Color. D: Joseph M. Newman. SC: Harry Kleiner. WITH Richard Widmark, Constance Smith, Jeffrey Hunter, Richard Boone, Warren Stevens, James Griffith, Joseph Sawyer, Gregory Walcott, Richard Crenna, Bob Nichols, Ralph Reed, Walter Murphy, Robert Adler, Charles (Bronson) Buchinsky, Mike Mahoney, Larry Dobkin, John Close, Grady Galloway, Henry Kulky, Harry Carter, Charles Tannen, Ron Hargrave, Robert Osterloh, Ted Ryan, John Kennedy, Parley Baer, Barbara Woodell, Ray Hyke, Wilson Hood, Ann Morrison. A young firefighter working for the U. S. Forestry Service plans revenge on a superior who he feels caused his father's death during a mission. A dull plot handicaps the otherwise well staged fire sequences in this action melodrama. Also called **Smoke Jumpers.**

2711 The Red Stallion. Eagle-Lion, 1947. 82 minutes Color. D: Lesley Selander. SC: Robert E. Kent & Crane Wilbur. WITH Robert Paige, Noreen Nash, Ted Donaldson, Jane Darwell, Ray Collins, Guy Kibbee, Willie Best, Robert Bice, Pierre Watkin, Bill Carledge, Big Red (horse), Daisy (dog). When his grandmother is about to lose her ranch, a young boy desperately tries to use his beloved horse to make the money to save it. Well made and nicely entertaining family feature.

2712 Red Stallion in the Rockies. Eagle-Lion, 1949. 85 minutes Color. D: Ralph Murphy. SC: Francis Rosenwald. WITH Arthur Franz, Jean Heather, Wallace Ford, Jim Davis, Ray Collins, Leatrice Joy, James Kirkwood, Dynamite (horse). Two circus performers go to work on a ranch and one of them falls in love with the owner's niece. Good drama enhanced by Jim Davis' performance as the ranch owner's grasping son.

2713 Red Sun. National General, 1972. 112 minutes Color. D: Terence Young. SC: Laird Koenig, Denne Bart Petitclerc, William Roberts & Lawrence Roman. WITH Charles Bronson, Toshiro Mifune, Alain Delon, Ursula Andress, Capucine, Satoshi Nakamoura, Bart Barry, Lee Burton, Anthony Dawson, John Hamilton, George W. Lycan, Jose Nieto, Julio Pena, Monica Randall, Luc Merenda. A Japanese Samurai travels to the U. S. and eventually joins forces with a westerner in retrieving a valuable sword stolen by outlaws. Fairly interesting teaming of Charles Bronson and Toshiro Mifune adds zest to this melodrama. Issued in Europe in 1971 as **Soleil Rouge** (Red Sun) by Cornoa Films/Oceania Films/Balcazar Films.

2714 Red Sundown. Universal-International, 1956. 81 minutes Color. D: Jack Arnold. SC: Martin Berkeley. WITH Rory Calhoun, Martha Hyer, Dean Jagger, Robert Middleton, James Millican, Lita Baron, Grant Williams, Trevor Bardette, David Kasday, Leo Gordon, Steve Darrell, Stevie Wootton, John Carpenter, Henry Wills, Alex Sharp, Lee Van Cleef. An ex-gunman becomes a deputy sheriff in a small town and opposes a land baron and his hired killer. Nothing exceptional in this Albert Zugsmith production.

2715 The Red Tomahawk. Paramount, 1967. 82 minutes Color. D: R. G. Springsteen. SC: Steve Fisher. WITH Howard Keel, Joan Caulfield, Broderick Crawford, Scott Brady, Wendell Corey, Richard Arlen, Tom Drake, Ben Cooper, Tracy Olsen, Donald (Don "Red") Barry, Reg Parton, Roy Jenson, Dan White, Henry Wills. Following the massacre at the Little Big Horn, an Army captain tries to warn the citizens of Deadwood of a possible Indian attack and he uncovers four Gatling guns to hold off the marauders. The veteran cast tries hard

but they can do nothing with an indifferent script and few production values.

The Red, White and Black see **Soul Soldier**

2716 The Redhead and the Cowboy. Paramount, 1951. 82 minutes B/W. D: Leslie Fenton. SC: Jonathan Latimer & Liam O'Brien. WITH Glenn Ford, Rhonda Fleming, Edmond O'Brien, Alan Reed, Morris Ankrum, Edith Evanson, Perry Ivins, Janine Perreau, Douglas Spencer, Ray Teal, Ralph Byrd, King Donovan, Tom Moore. A pretty girl takes on the task of being a courier for the Confederacy during the closing days of the Civil War and she is pursued by a cowboy, who needs her testimony to clear himself of a murder charge, and another man, who is actually a Union spy. Pretty fair screen entertainment.

2717 The Redhead from Wyoming. Universal-International, 1953. 80 minutes Color. D: Lee Sholem. SC: Polly James & Herb Meadow. WITH Maureen O'Hara, Alex Nicol, Robert Strauss, Jeanne Cooper, William Bishop, Alexander Scourby, Jack Kelly, Palmer Lee, Claudette Thornton, Ray Bennett, Joe Bailey, Rush Williams, Dennis Weaver, Stacy Harris, Larry Hudson. A pretty woman operates a front shielding cattle rustlers but finds herself falling in love with the lawman after a rustler she is protecting. Okay action feature with Maureen O'Hara doing a good job in the title role.

2718 The Redmen and the Renegades. International Television Corporation, 1964. 89 minutes B/W. D: Sam Newfield. WITH John Hart, Lon Chaney, George Barnes, John Vernon, Brian Smyth. Ethan Allen is accused of treason and Hawkeye and Chingachgook try to help him. Telefeature made up of three segments of the series "Hawkeye and the Last of the Mohicans" (Syndicated, 1957); below average.

2719 Redwood Forest Trail. Republic, 1950. 68 minutes B/W. D: Philip Ford. SC: Bradford Ropes. WITH Rex Allen, Jeff Donnell, Jane Darwell, Marten Lamont, Carl ("Alfalfa") Switzer, Pierre Watkin, Jimmy Ogg, Dick Jones, John Cason, Jack Larson, Robert Burns, Joseph Granby. When the boys at a ranch to rehabilitate delinquents are accused of being involved in a murder a cowboy attempts to prove their innocence. Pretty good Rex Allen vehicle with a fine supporting cast.

The Refugee see Three Faces West

2720 Relentless. Columbia, 1948. 93 minutes Color. D: George Sherman. SC: Winston Miller. WITH Robert Young, Marguerite Chapman, Willard Parker, Akim Tamiroff, Barton MacLane, Mike Mazurki, Robert Barrat, Clem Bevans, Frank Fenton, Hank Patterson, Paul E. Burns, Emmett Lynn, Will Wright. Framed for a murder he did not commit and chased by a posse, a cowboy gets help from a girl. Well done chase melodrama.

2721 Relentless. CBS-TV, 1977. 74 minutes Color. D: Lee H. Katzin. SC: Sam Rolfe. WITH Will Sampson, Monte Markham, John Hillerman, Marianna Hill, Larry Wilcox, Antony Ponzini, John Lawlor, Ted Markland, David Pendleton, Ron Foster, Don Starr, Danny Zapian, Mel Todd, Dick Armstrong, Teddy (dog). An Arizona state policeman tracks a gang of bank robbers who have pulled a heist, murdered his uncle and taken a woman hostage into the mountains. Actionful and well produced telefeature.

2722 The Relentless Four. Astor, 1965. 90 minutes Color. D: Primo Zeglio. SC: Sebares De Caso & Primo Zeglio. WITH Adam West, Robert Hundar, Robert Baards, Red Ross, Robert Camardiel, Ralph Baldwyn, John Bartha, Robert Johnson Jr., Dina Loy, Luis Induni, Jose Jaspe. A quartet of bandits, secretly supported by a corrupt deputy sheriff, commit a series of lawless acts and place the blame on a lawman. Better-than-average spaghetti Western with star Adam West for domestic appeal. Released in Italy by P.E.A./Astorfilms as **I Quattro Inesorabili** (The Inexorable Four).

Remember the Alamo see **Heroes of the Alamo**

2723 The Renegade. Producers Releasing Corporation, 1943. 58 minutes B/W. D: Sam Newfield. SC: Joseph O'Donnell. WITH Buster Crabbe, Al St. John, Lois Ransom, Karl Hackett, Ray Bennett, Frank Hagney, Jack Rockwell, Tom London, George Chesebro, Jimmie Aubrey, Dan White, Carl Sepulveda, Wally West. Billy the Kid and his sidekick Fuzzy Q. Jones are on the trail of a vicious lawbreaker. Standard "Billy the Kid" series entry. Reissued by Eagle-Lion in 1947 in a re-edited 38 minute version called **Code of the Plains.**

2724 Renegade Girl. Screen Guild, 1946. 65 minutes B/W. D: William Berke. SC: Edwin K. Westrate. WITH Alan Curtis, Ann Savage, Jack Holt, Edward Brophy, Russell Wade, Ray Corrigan, John King, Chief Thundercloud, Edmund Cobb, Claudia Drake, Dick Curtis, Nick Thompson, James Martin, Harry Cording. During the Civil War the girl leader of a band of raiders is stalked by a special Union investigator. Fairly actionful oater with a supporting cast of ex-genre stars.

2725 Renegade Gunfighter. Tirso/Petruka Film, 1966. 76 minutes Color. D-SC: Silvio Amadio. WITH Zachary Hatcher, Dick Palmer, Pier Angeli (Annamaria Pierangeli), Ruben Rojo, Mirko Ellis, Manuel Gil. A peace loving young man learns to become a vengeful killer after his parents are murdered by two evil land-grabbing brothers. Typically violent and mediocre dubbed oater from Italy where it was called **Per Mille Dollari Al Giorno** (For a Thousand Dollars a Day).

2726 Renegade Ranger. RKO Radio, 1939. 60 minutes B/W. D: David Howard. SC: Oliver Drake. WITH George O'Brien, Rita Hayworth, Tim Holt, Ray Whitley, William Royle, Neal Hart, Monte Montague, Robert Kortman, Charles Stevens, Jim Mason, Tom London, Guy Usher, Lucio Villegas, Cecilia Callejo. A Texas Ranger is sent to capture a female bandit leader but ends up saving her life and then discovers she and her fellow honest ranchers have been forced into a life of crime by a crooked tax collector. Good production values and an entertaining story make this a good George O'Brien vehicle, with lovely Rita Hayworth costarring as the bandit queen. The film was a remake of Tom Keene's 1932 RKO film **Come On, Danger** (q.v.) and in 1942 it was filmed for the third time under its original title with Tim Holt and Ray Whitley again starring, this time Holt having the lead role.

2727 The Renegade Trail. Paramount, 1939. 54 (61) minutes B/W. D: Lesley Selander. SC: John Rathmell & Harrison Jacobs. WITH William Boyd, George ("Gabby") Hayes, Russell Hayden, Charlotte Wynters, Russell Hopton, Sonny Bupp, Jack Rockwell, Roy Barcroft, John Merton, Robert Kortman, Eddie Dean, The King's Men. The Bar 20 trio aids a woman and her son whose cattle are the target of an outlaw gang which includes the woman's ex-convict husband, who the boy thinks died a good man. A bit slower than the average "Hopalong Cassidy" feature and somewhat less scenic but still pretty good with a pleasant musical interlude by The King's Men. V: Cumberland Video.

2728 Renegades. Columbia, 1946. 88 minutes Color. D: George Marshall. SC: Melvin Levy & Francis Edwards Faragoh. WITH Evelyn Keyes, Willard Parker, Larry Parks, Edgar Buchanan, Forrest Tucker, Jim Bannon, Ludwig Donath, Willard Robertson, Paul E. Burns, Frank Sully, Eddy Waller, Virginia Brissac, Francis Ford, Vernon Dent, Addison Richards. The youngest son of a family of outlaws tries to lead a peaceful life but finds his family's reputation too great to conquer. Okay oater, well acted by its good cast.

2729 Renegades of Sonora. Republic, 1948. 60 minutes B/W. D: R. G. Springsteen. SC: M. Coates Webster. WITH Allan "Rocky" Lane, Eddy Waller, William Henry, Douglas Fowley, Roy Barcroft, George J. Lewis, Frank Fenton, Mauritz Hugo, Marshall Reed, Holly Bane, Dale Van Sickel, Art Dillard, House Peters Jr. A cowboy is framed on a murder charge by crooks when he stops in a small town on his way to Wyoming to buy a ranch. Nothing special here but entertaining nonetheless.

2730 Renegades of the Rio Grande. Universal, 1945. 56 minutes B/W. D: Howard Bretherton. SC: Ande Lamb. WITH Rod Cameron, Fuzzy Knight, Jennifer Holt, Eddie Dew, Ray Whitley & His Bar-6 Cowboys, Glenn Strange, Ethan Laidlaw, Edmund Cobb, Richard Alexander, John James, Richard Botiller, Iris Clive. A ranger is assigned to stop an outlaw gang which is rustling cattle along the Mexican border. Solid Rod Cameron vehicle, which shows why he went on to bigger things.

2731 Renegades of the Sage. Columbia, 1949. 56 minutes B/W. D: Ray Nazarro. SC: Earle Snell. WITH Charles Starrett, Smiley Burnette, Leslie Banning, Douglas Fowley, Trevor Bardette, Fred Sears, Jock (Mahoney) O'Mahoney, Jerry Hunter, George Chesebro, Frank McCarroll, Selmer Jackson. Following the Civil War a government undercover agent is sent West to find out who is responsible for sabotaging a telegraph line and suspicion falls on a trader who is an ex-Confederate guerilla leader. Fair "Durango Kid" series segment.

2732 Renegades of the West. RKO Radio, 1932. 55 minutes B/W. D: Casey Robinson. SC: Albert LeVine. WITH Tom Keene, Betty Furness, Rosco(e) Ates, Rockcliffe Fellows, Jim Mason, Jack Pennick, Max Wagner, Joseph Girard, Billy Franey. When cattle rustlers murder his rancher father, a young man sets out to get even with them. Well directed Tom Keene film; above average.

2733 Renfrew of the Royal Mounted. Grand National, 1937. 57 minutes B/W. D: Al Herman. SC: Charles Logue. WITH James Newill, Carol Hughes, William Royle, Herbert Corthell, Kenneth Harlan, Dickie Jones, Chief Thundercloud, William Austin, Donald Reed, Bob Terry, William Gould, David Barclay (Dave O'Brien), Dwight Frye, Lightning (dog). A Mountie is appointed to look into the smuggling of counterfeit currency across the U.S.-Canadian border and learns a former counterfeiter, who has gone straight, is being held prisoner and forced to engrave plates. Good opener for the long-running "Renfrew of the Royal Mounted" series; a pleasing film.

Renfrew of the Royal Mounted in Fighting Mad see **Fighting Mad**

Renfrew of the Royal Mounted in Murder on the Yukon see **Murder on the Yukon**

Renfrew of the Royal Mounted in Yukon Flight see **Yukon Flight**

Renfrew of the Royal Mounted on the Great White Trail see **On the Great White Trail**

Renfrew on the Great White Trail see **On the Great White Trail**

2734 Reno. RKO Radio, 1939. 73 minutes B/W. D: John Farrow. SC: John Twist. WITH Richard Dix, Gail Patrick, Anita Louise, Paul Cavanagh, Laura Hope Crews, Louis Jean Heydt, Hobart Cavanaugh, Charles Halton, Astrid Allwyn, Joyce Compton, Frank Faylen, William Haade. A smart lawyer turns Reno, Nevada, from a rough mining town into the country's divorce capital but lives to regret it. Entertaining medium-budget Richard Dix vehicle.

2735 Reprisal! Columbia, 1956. 74 minutes Color. D: George Sherman. SC: David P. Harmon, Raphael Hayes & David Dortort. WITH Guy Madison, Felicia Farr, Kathryn Grant, Michael Pate, Edward

Platt, Otto Mulett, Wayne Mallory, Robert Burton, Ralph Moody, Frank De Kova, Paul McGuire, Don Rhoes, Philip Breedlove, Malcolm Atterbury, Eve McVeagh, Addison Richards, Jack Lomas, John Zaremba. When a man is falsely accused of murdering a local cattle baron, he is saved from a lynch mob by the two women who love him. Compact actioner provides good viewing.

2736 Requiem for a Gunfighter. Embassy, 1965. 91 minutes Color. D: Spencer Gordon Bennet. SC: R. Alexander. WITH Rod Cameron, Stephen McNally, Mike Mazurki, Tim McCoy, Olive Sturgess, Bob Steele, Johnny Mack Brown, Lane Chandler, Raymond Hatton, Dick Jones, Rand Brooks, Dale Van Sickel, Frank Lackteen, Zon Murray, Edmund Cobb, Richard Alexander, Boyd "Red" Morgan, Fred Carson, Chet Douglas, Chris Hughes. When a judge is murdered in order to prevent a trial, a gunman mistaken for the judge makes plans to see that justice is carried out. A cast full of genre veterans adds zest to this Alex Gordon production.

2737 The Restless Breed. 20th Century-Fox, 1957. 81 minutes Color. D: Allan Dwan. SC: Steve Fisher. WITH Scott Brady, Anne Bancroft, Jim Davis, Jay C. Flippen, Leo Gordon, Rhys Williams, Myron Healey, Scott Marlowe, Eddy Waller, Harry V. Cheshire, Gerald Milton, Dennis King Jr., James Flavin, Billy Miller, Evelyn Rudie, Clegg Hoyt, Joe Devlin, Fred Graham. When a gang leader murders his father, who was a secret service agent, a man sets out for revenge. Average melodrama; well made but nothing exciting.

2738 The Return of a Man Called Horse. United Artists, 1976. 129 minutes Color. D: Irvin Kerschner. SC: Jack DeWitt. WITH Richard Harris, Ana DeSade, Gale Sondergaard, Geoffrey Lewis, Bill Lucking, Jorge Luke, Claudio Brook, Enrique Lucerno, Jorge Russek, Pedro Damien. A titled Englishman, who became a Sioux after many trials, returns to the Indians to aid them in their struggle against the whites. A bit long, but still quite good sequel to **A Man Called Horse** (q.v.), followed by the vapid **Triumphs of a Man Called Horse** (q.v.).

2739 Return of Daniel Boone. Columbia, 1941. 56 minutes B/W. D: Lambert Hillyer. SC: Paul Franklin & Joseph Hoffman. WITH Bill Elliott, Dub Taylor, Betty Miles, Ray Bennett, Walter Soderling,

Carl Stockdale, Bud Osborne, Francis Walker, Lee Powell, Tom Carter, Edmund Cobb, Roy Butler, Art Miles, Edwin Bryant, Steve Clark, Murdock McQuarrie, Hank Bell, Rodik Twins. A young man goes to work as a tax collector but finds out his boss is a crook cheating settlers of their properties. Okay Bill Elliott vehicle, which has nothing to do with Daniel Boone.

2740 The Return of Draw Egan. Triangle, 1916. 55 minutes B/W. D: William S. Hart. SC: C. Gardner Sullivan. WITH William S. Hart, Louise Glaum, Margery Wilson, Robert McKim, J. P. Lockney. A badman becomes the reform sheriff of a small town and brings about law and order only to be blackmailed by his old gang. Very entertaining William S. Hart silent effort which was often reworked plotwise in the sound era; film also benefits from the presence of beautiful Margery Wilson. V: Classic Video Cinema Collectors Club.

2741 The Return of Frank James. 20th Century-Fox, 1940. 92 minutes Color. D: Fritz Lang. SC: Sam Hellman. WITH Henry Fonda, Gene Tierney, Jackie Cooper, Henry Hull, J. Edward Bromberg, Donald Meek, John Carradine, Eddie Collins, George Barbier, Ernest Whitman, Charles Tannen, Lloyd Corrigan, Russell Hicks, Victor Kilian, Edward McWade, George Chandler, Irving Bacon, Frank Shannon, Barbara Pepper, Louis Mason, Matthew "Stymie" Beard, William Pawley, Frank Sully, Davidson Clark, Nelson McDowell, Lee Phelps, Lillian Yarbo, Adrian Morris, Lester Dorr, Milton Kibbee, Frank Melton. When a judge sets Bob Ford free on the charge of murdering Jesse James, Frank James vows revenge. Not much history here but lots of entertainment value; John Carradine makes the film as the villainous Bob Ford.

2742 The Return of Grey Wolf. Ambassador, 1925. 60 minutes B/W. D: Jacques Rollens. SC: Jay Arr. WITH Leader (dog), James Pierce, Helen Lynch, Walter Shumway, Edward Coxen, Harry Belmore, Whitehorse. A dog aids a man and a woman fight crooks in the Canadian Rockies. The scenery is the best part of this silent effort, although Jim Pierce fans will enjoy seeing him in a starring role.

2743 The Return of Jack Slade. Allied Artists, 1955. 79 minutes B/W. D: Harold Schuster. SC: Warren Douglas. WITH

John Ericson, Mari Blanchard, Neville Brand, Casey Adams (Max Showalter), Jon Shepodd, Howard Petrie, John Dennis, Angie Dickinson, Donna Drew, Mike Ross, Alan Wells, Raymond Bailey, Lyla Graham. The son of famous outlaw Jack Slade becomes a lawman in order to redeem his family name and sets out to capture a gang of outlaws. Fair low budget affair with good work by John Ericson as Slade's son.

2744 The Return of Jesse James. Lippert, 1950. 77 minutes B/W. D: Arthur Hilton. SC: Carl K. Hittleman. WITH John Ireland, Ann Dvorak, Henry Hull, Reed Hadley, Hugh O'Brian, Carleton Young, Barbara Woodell, Margia Dean, Sid Melton, Victor Kilian, Byron Foulger, Sam Flint, Robin York, Paul Maxey. A lookalike for Jesse James takes on the guise of the dead outlaw and is used by a gang to rob banks, but he is overcome by his own greed and the ambition of the saloon singer he loves. An odd kind of oater, more psychological than actionful, but pretty good anyway.

2745 The Return of Rin Tin Tin. Eagle Lion, 1947. 86 minutes Color. D: Max Nosseck. SC: Jack DeWitt. WITH Rin Tin Tin III, Donald Woods, Bobby Blake, Claudia Drake, Gaylord (Steve) Pendleton, Earle Hodgins. A priest brings a boy from Europe to his Western mission hoping to restore his faith and the boy becomes attached to a dog whose return is demanded by its master. Pleasant family fare originally made by Producers Releasing Corporation.

2746 The Return of Ringo. Rizzoli Film, 1965. 104 minutes Color. D: Duccio Tessair. SC: Duccio Tessari & Fernando De Leo. WITH Montgomery Wood (Giuliano Gemma), Fernando Sancho, Hally Hammond, George Martin, Nieves Navarro, Antonio Casas, Pajarito. Returning home from the Civil War, a Northern army captain takes revenge on the Mexican who had taken his land, and his family hostage. Very violent spaghetti Western; a Spanish-Italian coproduction issued in Europe as **Il Ritorno di Ringo.** Sequel: **A Pistol for Ringo** (q.v.).

2747 Return of Sabata. United Artists, 1972. 106 minutes Color. D: Frank Kramer (Gianfranco Parolini). SC: Renato Izzo & Gianfranco Parolini. WITH Lee Van Cleef, Reiner Schone, Annabelle Incontrera, Gianni Rizzo, Gianpiero Albertini, Jacqueline Alexandre, Pedro Sanchez,

Nick Jordan, Gunther Stoll. An ex-Confederate major, now a sharpshooter with a circus, arrives in a small town to get even with those who bilked him out of money and settles the score by exposing a corrupt politician. Extremely violent Italian-made oater which will satisfy Lee Van Cleef fans; a sequel to **Sabata** (q.v.).

2748 Return of the Bad Men. RKO Radio, 1948. 90 minutes B/W. D: Ray Enright. SC: Charles O'Neal, Jack Natteford & Luci Ward. WITH Randolph Scott, Robert Ryan, Anne Jeffreys, George "Gabby" Hayes, Jacqueline White, Steve Brodie, Richard Powers (Tom Keene), Robert Bray, Lex Barker, Walter Reed, Michael Harvey, Dean White, Robert Armstrong, Tom Tyler, Lew Harvey, Gary Gray, Walter Baldwin, Minna Gombell, Warren Jackson, Robert Clarke, Jason Robards, Harry Shannon, Charles McAvoy, Larry McGrath, Billy Vincent, Ernie Adams, Sam Flint, Lane Chandler, Earle Hodgins, Charles Stevens, Kenneth MacDonald, John Hamilton, Frank O'Connor, Cy King, Dan Foster, Ida Moore. In the 1880s in Oklahoma a town marshal and a female desperado fall in love while the lawman fights such outlaws as The Sundance Kid, the Younger and Dalton brothers, Wild Bill Doolin and Billy the Kid. Nicely produced "A" actioner; quasi-sequel to **Badman's Territory** (q.v.) and followed by **Best of the Badmen** (q.v.). V: Blackhawk, Nostalgia Merchant.

2749 Return of the Durango Kid. Columbia, 1945. 58 minutes B/W. D: Derwin Abrahams. SC: J. Benton Cheney. WITH Charles Starrett, Tex Harding, Jean Stevens, John Calvert, Betty Roadman, Britt Wood, The Jesters, Hal Price, Richard Botiller, Ray Bennett, Elmo Lincoln, Paul Conrad, Steve Clark, Carl Sepulveda, Ted Mapes, Herman Hack, Bud Nelson, Dan White. The passenger on a stagecoach robbed by outlaws takes on the guise of the masked Durango Kid and steals the money back from the gang leader. Mediocre film which nonetheless started Charles Starrett playing "The Durango Kid" in a series of more than three score features; despite its title this film is not a sequel to **The Durango Kid** (q.v.).

2750 Return of the Frontiersman. Warner Brothers, 1950. 74 minutes Color. D: Richard L. Bare. SC: Edna Anhalt. WITH Gordon MacRae, Julie London, Rory Calhoun, Jack Holt, Fred Clark, Edwin Raynd, Raymond Bond, Matt McHugh,

Britt Wood. A sheriff is forced to jail his own son when he is falsely accused of murder, but the son escapes, aided by the real killer. Okay oater with fine work by Jack Holt as the sheriff-father.

2751 Return of the Gunfighter. ABC-TV/ Metro-Goldwyn-Mayer, 1967. 98 minutes Color. D: James Neilson. SC: Robert Buckner. WITH Robert Taylor, Chad Everett, Ana Martin, Lyle Bettger, Mort Mills, John Davis Chandler, Michael Pate, Barry Atwater, John Crawford, Willis Bouchey, Rodolfo Hoyos, Read Morgan, Henry Wills, Robert Shelton. When a young Mexican girl's parents are murdered for their land she enlists the aid of an aging gunman and a wounded cowboy to help her get revenge. One of the first, and best, movies made for network television; Robert Taylor is outstanding as the gunslinger. Alternate title: **As I Rode Down to Laredo.**

2752 Return of the Lash. Producers Releasing Corporation, 1947. 53 minutes B/W. D: Ray Taylor. SC: Joseph O'Donnell. WITH Lash LaRue, Al St. John, Mary Maynard, Brad Slaven, George Chesebro, Lane Bradford, Bud Osborne, George DeNormand, Lee Morgan, Carl Mathews, Slim Whitaker, Kermit Maynard, Frank Ellis, Bob Woodward. Two marshals arrive in a small town in order to stop a range war caused by a crook who wants the land because the railroad is coming through. Mediocre "Cheyenne Kid" entry, but not as dull as some in the series.

2753 Return of the Rangers. Producers Releasing Corporation, 1943. 61 minutes B/W. D-SC: Elmer Clifton. WITH James Newill, Dave O'Brien, Guy Wilkerson, Nell O'Day, Glenn Strange, Emmett Lynn, Robert Barron, Henry Hall, Harry Harvey, I. Stanford Jolley, Richard Alexander, Charles King. In order to capture a gang of rustlers, Texas Rangers arrive in a small town incognito with one pretending to be a criminal and the other the judge planning to try his case. A good script puts some life into this "Texas Rangers" series entry from PRC.

2754 Return of the Seven. United Artists, 1966. 96 minutes Color. D: Burt Kennedy. SC: Larry Cohen. WITH Yul Brynner, Robert Fuller, Warren Oates, Julian Mateos, Jordan Christopher, Claude Akins, Fernando Rey, Emilio Fernandez, Elisa Montes, Virgilio Texera, Rodolfo Acosta. When outlaws kidnap a former member of a gang, his wife asks the other two living members to aid him and they do so with the aid of four other men. Adequate sequel to **The Magnificent Seven** (q.v.).

2755 Return of the Texan. 20th Century-Fox, 1952. 87 minutes B/W. D: Delmer Daves. SC: Dudley Nichols. WITH Dale Robertson, Joanne Dru, Walter Brennan, Richard Boone, Tom Tully, Robert Horton, Helen Westcott, Lannie Thomas, Robert Adler, Kathryn Sheldon, Dennis Ross. A widower returns to his family home hoping to take up ranching again, but finds he is opposed by local crooks. Fair oater for Dale Robertson fans.

2756 The Return of Wild Bill. Columbia, 1940. 59 minutes B/W. D: Joseph H. Lewis. SC: Robert Lee Johnson & Fred Myton. WITH Bill Elliott, Iris Meredith, Dub Taylor, Luana Walters, George Lloyd, Ed LeSaint, Frank LaRue, Francis Walker, Chuck Morrison, Buel Bryant, William Kellogg, Jack Rockwell, Jim Corey, John Ince, Tex Cooper. Crooks are after two ranches and they try to get the owners to gun down each other but one of them sends for his son, a feared gunman, but is shot before he can arrive on the scene. Well made Bill Elliott vehicle.

2757 The Return of Wildfire. Screen Guild, 1948. 83 minutes Color. D: Ray Taylor. SC: Betty Burbridge & Carl K. Hittleman. WITH Richard Arlen, Patricia Morison, Mary Beth Hughes, Reed Hadley, James Millican, Stanley Andrews, Edmund Cobb, Chris-Pin Martin. A drifter arrives at a ranch where he is hired to capture a wild horse and he also becomes mixed up with a gambler and one of the ranch owner's daughters. Well done low budget effort with plenty of excitement and a nice performance by Richard Arlen as the drifter. Patricia Morison sings "Just an Old Sombrero".

2758 Return to Warbow. Columbia, 1958. 67 minutes B/W. D: Ray Nazarro. SC: Les Savage Jr. WITH Phil(ip) Carey, Catherine McLeod, Andrew Duggan, William Leslie, Robert Wilke, James Griffith, Jay Silverheels, Chris Olsen, Francis de Sales, Harry Lauter, Paul Picerni, Joe Forte. Three outlaws return to the spot where they buried loot only to learn the brother of one of them has already taken the money. Fair low budget oater from producer Wallace MacDonald.

2759 The Returning. Willow Films, 1983. 80 minutes Color. D: Joel Bender. SC:

Patrick Nash. WITH Gabriel Walsh, Susan Strasberg, Brian Foleman, Victor Arnold, Ruth Warrick, H.E.D. Redford, Mostea Oshley, Rick Barker. While on a trip to the Mojave Desert, a Utah family acquires a rock with strange powers controlled by the spirits of dead Indian warriors. Fair combination of modern-day Western and horror genres; on the cerebral side.

2760 Revenge in El Paso. Paramount, 1969. 103 minutes Color. D: Giuseppe Colizzi. SC: Giuseppe Colizzi. WITH Eli Wallach, Terence Hill, Bud Spencer, Brock Peters, Kevin McCarthy, Steffen Zacharias, Livio Lorenzon, Tiffany Hoyveld, Remo Capitani. Three enemies after a shipment of money decide to team in order to get the loot. A somewhat different spaghetti Western with more plot and humor than violence. Italian title: **Quattro Dell'Ave Maria.**

2761 The Revenge Rider. Columbia, 1935. 60 minutes. D: David Selman. SC: Ford Beebe. WITH Tim McCoy, Robert Allen, Billie Seward, Edward Earle, Frank Sheridan, Jack Clifford, Jack Mower, George Pierce, Alan Sears, Harry Semels, Joseph (Sawyer) Sauers, Lafe McKee, Tom London, Charles King. Returning home, a man finds his sheriff brother has been murdered and the culprits appear to belong to the local cattlemen's association. Good Tim McCoy vehicle with a dandy finale of the star piecing clues together a la Charlie Chan, plus a corker of a shootout.

2762 The Revengers. National General, 1971. 107 minutes Color. D: Daniel Mann. SC: Wendell Mayes. WITH William Holden, Susan Hayward, Ernest Borgnine, Woody Stroke, Roger Hanin, Rene Koldehoff, Jorge Luke, Jorge Martinez De Hoyos, Arthur Hunnicutt, Warren Vanders, Larry Pennell, John Kelly, Scott Holden, James Daughton, Lorraine Chanel, Raul Prieto. After his wife and children are massacred by renegade whites and Indians a rancher sets out for revenge. Pretty fair actioner unjustly overlooked when first released.

2763 The Reverend Colt. R. M. Films, 1971. 90 minutes Color. D: Leon Klimowsky. SC: T. Carpi & Manuel Martinez Remis. WITH Guy Madison, Richard Harrison, Thomas Moore, Maria Martin, Pedro Sanchez, Perla Cristina, Alfonso Royas, Marta Moterei. A minister comes to a small town to build a church but is blamed when outlaws rob the bank,

and he is forced to clear his name by tracking down the desperadoes. Guy Madison is good in the title role of this better-than-average Italian oater. An Italian-Spanish coproduction issued in Italy as **Reverendo Colt.**

2764 Revolt at Fort Laramie. United Artists, 1957. 72 minutes B/W. D: Lesley Selander. SC: Robert C. Dennis. WITH John Dehner, Frances Helm, Gregg Palmer, Don Gordon, Robert Keys, William Phillips, Robert Knapp, Cain Mason, Eddie Little, Dean Stanton, Bill Barker, Kenne Duncan, Clay Randolph. When the Civil War breaks out Southern soldiers at a remote fort want to leave to join the Confederacy despite the threat of an Indian attack. An interesting plot and good direction highlight this "B" oater.

2765 Revolt in Canada. Embassy, 1964. 107 minutes Color. D: Mando De Ossurio. WITH George Martin, Pamela Tudor, Luis Marin. In frontier Canada a trapper protected by the British commits a series of crimes and puts the blame on rebel trappers. Rather typical European-made dubbed action drama.

2766 The Reward. 20th Century-Fox, 1965. 92 minutes Color. D: Serge Bourguignon. SC: Serge Bourguignon & Oscar Millard. WITH Max Von Sydow, Yvette Mimieux, Efrem Zimbalist Jr., Gilbert Roland, Nino Castelnuovo, Emilio Fernandez, Henry Silva, Rodolfo Acosta, Julian Rivero, Rafael Lopez. Bounty hunters capture a wanted criminal but during a trek through the desert they have a falling out over the division of the reward money. Fairly interesting melodrama enhanced by a good cast.

Rex, King of the Wild Horses see **King of the Wild Horses** (1924)

2767 Rhythm of the Rio Grande. Monogram, 1940. 53 minutes B/W. D: Al Herman. SC: Robert Emmett (Tansey). WITH Tex Ritter, Suzan Dale, Warner Richmond, Martin Garralaga, Arkansas Slim Andrews, Frank Mitchell, Tristram Coffin, Earl Douglas, Forrest Taylor, Mike Rodriguez, Glenn Strange, James McNally, Juan Duval, Chick Hannon, Sherry Tansey. A cowboy teams with a Mexican outlaw to prove that a respected rancher is behind all the lawlessness in the territory. Okay Tex Ritter musical vehicle which includes the tune "Mexicali Moon." British title: **Lonesome Trail to the Rio Grande.**

2768 Rhythm of the Saddle. Republic, 1938. 54 (58) minutes B/W. D: George Sherman. SC: Paul Franklin. WITH Gene Autry, Smiley Burnette, Peggy Moran, Pert Kelton, LeRoy Mason, Arthur Loft, Ethan Laidlaw, Walter De Palma, Archie Hill, Eddie Hart, Eddie Acuff, Douglas Wright, Kelsey Sheldon, Lola Monte, Alan Gregg, Rudy Shooter, William Norton Bailey, Tom London, Roger Williams, Curley Dresden, Jim Mason, Jack Kirk, Emmett Vogan. A crooked nightclub owner bribes the chairman of the annual rodeo into helping him get the next year's contract, and in doing so fixes a halter rope which causes the injury of a rider in the bucking contest and Gene Autry investigates. A strong plotline greatly aids this Gene Autry film.

2769 Rhythm on the Range. Paramount, 1936. 87 minutes B/W. D: Norman Taurog. SC: John C. Moffitt, Sidney Salkow, Walter DeLeon & Francis Martin. WITH Bing Crosby, Frances Farmer, Bob "Bazooka" Burns, Martha Raye, Samuel S. Hinds, Warren Hymer, Lucille Webster Gleason, George E. Stone, James Burke, Martha Sleeper, Clem Bevans, The Sons of the Pioneers, Leonid Kinsky, Charles Williams, Beau Baldwin, Emmett Vogan, Billy Bletcher, Eddy Waller, Bud Flanagan (Dennis O'Keefe), Duke York, James Blaine, Herbert Ashley, James "Slim" Thompson, Robert E. Homans, Jim Toney, Ed LeSaint, Sam McDaniel, Syd Saylor, Oscar Smith, Charles Arnt, Harry C. Bradley, Otto Yamaoka, Bob McKenzie, Irving Bacon, Heinie Conklin, Frank Dawson. The owners of a dude ranch in California, on their way West with a prize bull they have won, meet an heiress on the run from her fiancée and ask her to join them. Very pleasant musical comedy.

Riata see **The Deadly Trackers**

2770 Ricochet Romance. Universal-International, 1954. 80 minutes B/W. D: Charles Lamont. SC: Kay Lenard. WITH Marjorie Main, Chill Wills, Rudy Vallee, Benay Venuta, Pedro Gonzales Gonzales, Alfonso Bedoya, Marjorie Bennett, Judith (Rachel) Ames, Darryl Hickman, Lee Aaker, Irene Ryan, Philip Tonge, Phillip Chambers, Charles Watt, Ruth Hampton. A woman is hired as the cook at a dude ranch and soon she involves herself in everyone's business. This attempt at making a movie team of Marjorie Main and Chill Wills is a bit forced but Main fans will like it and Rudy Vallee is great, as usual, as the stuffed-shirt guest.

2771 Riddle Ranch. Beaumont, 1935. 63 minutes B/W. D: Charles Hutchison. SC: E. J. Thornton. WITH Black King (horse), David Worth, June Marlowe, Baby Charlene Barry, Julian Rivero, Richard Cramer, Fred "Snowflake" Toones, Budd Buster, Art Felix, Henry Sylvester, Ray Gallagher, Ace Cain. The owner of a beautiful stallion is framed for a murder by a Mexican outlaw, who poses as a horse buyer and who wants the man's horse. Bottom rung actioner for fans of such fare.

2772 Ride a Crooked Mile. Paramount, 1938. 78 minutes B/W. D: Alfred E. Green. SC: Ferdinand Reyher & John C. Moffitt. WITH Akim Tamiroff, Frances Farmer, Leif Erickson, Lynne Overman, John Miljan, J. M. Kerrigan, Eva Novak, Ethel Clayton. A Russian Cossack flees his homeland and becomes a cattle rustler in the West until he discovers he has a grown son who has been jailed for the same crime. The three stars do their best but are bogged down by the script.

2773 Ride a Crooked Trail. Universal-International, 1958. 87 minutes Color. D: Jesse Hibbs. SC: Borden Chase. WITH Audie Murphy, Gia Scala, Walter Matthau, Henry Silva, Joanna Moore, Eddie Little, Mary Field, Leo Gordon, Mort Mills, Frank Chase, Bill Walker, Ned Weaver, Richard Cutting. An outlaw takes on the identity of a dead lawman in order to pull off a bank robbery. Fairly good Audie Murphy vehicle.

2774 Ride a Northbound Horse. Buena Vista, 1969. 79 minutes Color. D: Robert Totten. SC: Herman Groves. WITH Michael Shea, Carroll O'Connor, Ben Johnson, Andy Devine, Edith Atwater, Jack Elam, Dub Taylor, Harry Carey Jr. A young man wins and loses a horse in the Old West and sets out to regain the animal. Minor, but entertaining, Walt Disney film from Richard Wormser's novel.

2775 Ride a Violent Mile. 20th Century-Fox, 1957. 79 minutes B/W. D-SC: Charles Marquis Warren. WITH John Agar, Penny Edwards, John Pickard, Richard Shannon, Charles Gray, Bing Russell, Helen Wallace, Richard Gilden, Sheb Wooley, Patrick O'Moore, Rush Williams, Roberto Contreras, Eva Novak, Mary Townsend, Rocky Shahan. During the Civil War a cowboy and a girl become involved in an attempt to break the Union blockade of Confederate seaports. Fair actioner.

2776 Ride a Wild Pony. Buena Vista, 1976. 91 minutes Color. D: Don Chaffey. SC: Rosemary Anne Sisson. WITH Michael Craig, Robert Bettles, Eva Griffith, John Meillon, Graham Rouse. In Australia the poor son of homesteaders battles a rich polio-crippled girl for the possession of a beautiful Welsh pony. Delightful Walt Disney family film made in Australia.

2777 Ride and Kill. P.E.A./Fenix Film, 1964. 94 minutes Color. D: J. L. Boraw. SC: Jose Mallorqui. WITH Alex Nicol, Robert Hundar, Margaret Grayson, Lawrence Palmer, Pauline Baards, John McDouglas, Anthony Gradwell. When outlaws over-run a small Arizona town and murder the sheriff, the town drunk puts down the bottle and takes up the badge to defend the girl he loves. Fair Italian-Spanish coproduction with a nice music score by Riz Ortolani. Italian title: **Cavalca de Uccidi** (Ride and Kill).

2778 The Ride Back. United Artists, 1957. 79 minutes B/W. D: Allen H. Miner. SC: Anthony Ellis. WITH Anthony Quinn, William Conrad, Lita Milan, George Trevino, Victor Millan, Ellen Hope Monroe, Joe Dominguez, Louis Towers. A lawman and his prisoner trek through hostile Indian country and learn they need each other to survive. William Conrad produced this interesting low budget suspense Western; worth viewing.

2779 Ride Beyond Vengeance. Columbia, 1966. 100 minutes Color. D: Bernard McEveety. SC: Andrew J. Fenady. WITH Chuck Connors, Michael Rennie, Kathryn Hays, Joan Blondell, Gloria Grahame, Gary Merrill, Bill Bixby, Claude Akins, Paul Fix, Marrisa Mathes, Harry Harvey Sr., William Bryant, Jamie Farr, Larrie Domasin, William Catching, James MacArthur, Ruth Warrick, Buddy Baer, Frank Gorshin, Robert Q. Lewis, Arthur O'Connell (narrator). After being separated from his wife for eleven years, a buffalo hunter returns home only to be attacked and branded and then rejected by his wife, so he sets out to get revenge on his attackers. Fair actioner with a good cast.

2780 Ride Clear of Diablo. Universal-International, 1953. 80 minutes Color. D: Jesse Hibbs. SC: George Zuckerman. WITH Audie Murphy, Dan Duryea, Susan Cabot, Abbe Lane, Russell Johnson,

Paul Birch, William Pullen, Jack Elam, Lane Bradford, Mike Ragan, Denver Pyle. To avenge the murders of his father and brother a young man becomes a deputy sheriff to a man who is in cahoots with the outlaws who committed the killings. Better-than-average Audie Murphy vehicle, mainly due to Dan Duryea's villainy.

2781 Ride 'em Cowboy. Universal, 1936. 59 minutes B/W. D: Lesley Selander. SC: Frances Guihan. WITH Buck Jones, Luana Walters, George Cooper, William Lawrence, J. P. McGowan, Joseph Girard, Donald Kirk, Charles LeMoyne, Edmund Cobb, Lester Dorr. A happy-go-lucky cowboy ends up becoming a race driver to help a pal and also to save a girl who has promised to marry a wealthy man to save her father's ranch. Buck Jones wrote the original story and produced this film which shows his penchant for comedy and auto racing but the overall results are somewhat disappointing. TV title: **Cowboy Roundup.**

2782 Ride 'em Cowboy. Universal, 1942. 82 minutes B/W. D: Arthur Lubin. SC: True Boardman & John Grant. WITH Bud Abbott, Lou Costello, Johnny Mack Brown, Dick Foran, Anne Gwynne, Samuel S. Hinds, Richard Lane, Douglass Dumbrille, Charles Lane, Ella Fitzgerald, Judd McMichael, Ted McMichael, Joe McMichael, Mary Lou Cook, Jody Gilbert, Morris Ankrum, Russell Hicks, Wade Boteler, James Flavin, Boyd Davis, Eddie Dunn, Isabel Randolph, Tom Hanlon, James Seay, Harold Daniels, Ralph Peters, Linda Brent, Lee Sunrise, Chief Yowlachie, Harry Monty, Sherman E. Sanders, Carmelo Cansino. Two hot dog vendors head West to a dude ranch and become involved in a romance between a pseudo-cowboy and the rodeo rider daughter of the ranch owner. Good Abbott & Costello vehicle in which Dick Foran sings "I'll Remember April."

2783 Ride 'em Cowgirl. Grand National, 1939. 52 minutes B/W. D: Samuel Diege. SC: Arthur Hoerl. WITH Dorothy Page, Milton Frome, Vince Barnett, Lynn Mayberry, Joe Girard, Frank Ellis, Merrill McCormack, Fred Berhle, Harrington Reynolds, Pat Henning, Fred Cordova, Lester Dorr, Snowey (horse). A girl is blamed for having contraband silver on her property but escapes from jail to prove a silver smuggler has framed her father in order to acquire his ranch as a front for his operations. Okay entry in the brief Dorothy Page cowgirl series for Grand National. V: Cassette Express.

2784 Ride Him Cowboy. Warner Brothers, 1932. 56 minutes B/W. D: Fred Allen. SC: Scott Mason. WITH John Wayne, Ruth Hall, Henry B. Walthall, Harry Gribbon, Otis Harlan, Frank Hagney, Charles Sellon, Lafe McKee, Ben Corbett, Glenn Strange, Fred Burns. A cowboy saves a horse from being shot and then sets out to capture a notorious bandit leader called "The Hawk," but ends up being accused of being the outlaw himself. John Wayne's first starring "B" series Western is a good one which moves along at a steady clip; remake of **The Unknown Cavalier** (First National, 1926) starring Ken Maynard. British title: **The Hawk.**

2785 Ride in the Whirlwind. Jack H. Harris Enterprises, 1971. 83 minutes Color. D: Monte Hellman. SC: Jack Nicholson. WITH Jack Nicholson, Millie Perkins, Cameron Mitchell, Harry Dean Stanton, Rupert Crosse, Katherine Squire, George Mitchell. A trio of cowpokes are mistaken for outlaws by a posse after they meet the real bad guys on their way home from a long trail drive. Watchable feature which was originally made in 1966 and issued to television before the advent of Jack Nicholson's popularity brought it to theaters. V: Capital Home Video.

2786 Ride, Kelly, Ride. 20th Century-Fox, 1941. 59 minutes B/W. D: Norman Foster. SC: William Conselman Jr. & Irving Cummings Jr. WITH Eugene Pallette, Marvin Stephens, Rita Quigley, Mary Healy, Richard Lane, Charles D. Brown, Chick Chandler, Dorothy Peterson, Lee Murray, Frankie Burke, Cy Kendall, Hamilton MacFadden, Walter O'Donnell, Ernie Adams. With the aid of a young girl a cowboy is taught to become a top jockey. Actionful programmer.

2787 Ride Lonesome. Columbia, 1959. 73 minutes Color. D: Budd Boetticher. SC: Burt Kennedy. WITH Randolph Scott, Karen Steele, Pernell Roberts, James Best, Lee Van Cleef, James Coburn, Dyke Johnson, Boyd Stockman, Roy Jenson, Boyd "Red" Morgan, Bonnie Dubbins. A lawman is transporting a prisoner across the desert and he enlists the aid of two bounty hunters for a share of the reward, since they all are being hunted by the prisoner's brother and his outlaw gang. Really good Randolph Scott vehicle; well written and produced.

2788 Ride On, Vaquero. 20th Century-Fox, 1941. 64 minutes B/W. D: Herbert I. Leeds. SC: Samuel G. Engel. WITH Cesar Romero, Mary Beth Hughes, Chris-Pin Martin, Robert Lowery, William Demarest, Ben Carter, Robert Shaw, Edwin Maxwell, Paul Sutton, Don Costello, Arthur Hohl, Irving Bacon, Joan Woodbury, Paul Harvey, Dick Rich. The Cisco Kid is after a gang of kidnapping outlaws. Cesar Romero's final "Cisco Kid" adventure is an average affair.

2789 Ride Out for Revenge. United Artists, 1957. 79 minutes B/W. D-SC: Norman Retchin. WITH Rory Calhoun, Gloria Grahame, Lloyd Bridges, Vincent Edwards, Joanne Gilbert, Frank De Kova, Michael Winkelman, Richard Shannon, Cyril Delevanti, John Merrick. A sheriff tries to aid Indians who are being forced off their lands by a corrupt Army officer who has discovered gold there. Run-of-the-mill oater for Rory Calhoun fans.

2790 Ride, Ranger, Ride. Republic, 1936. 56 minutes B/W. D: Joseph Kane. SC: Dorrell McGowan & Stuart McGowan. WITH Gene Autry, Smiley Burnette, Kay Hughes, Monte Blue, Max Terhune, George J. Lewis, Robert Homans, Chief Thundercloud, The Tennessee Ramblers, Frankie Marvin, Iron Eyes Cody, Bud Pope, Nelson McDowell, Robert Thomas. Former Texas Rangers become scouts for the cavalry and set out to stop a half-breed's attempts to start an Indian uprising. Lots of action, music and comedy highlight this pretty good Gene Autry vehicle. V: Thunderbird, Video Yesteryear, Nostalgia Merchant.

2791 Ride, Tenderfoot, Ride. Republic, 1940. 54 (65) minutes B/W. D: Frank McDonald. SC: Winston Miller. WITH Gene Autry, Smiley Burnette, June Storey, Warren Hull, Mary Lee, Si Jenks, Forbes Murray, Joe Frisco, Joe McGuinn, Isabel Randolph, Herbert Clifton, Mildred Shay, Cindy Walker, Jack Kirk, Slim Whitaker, Fred Burns, Patty Saks, The Pacemakers, Bob Burns, Fred "Snowflake" Toones, Chuck Morrison, Frank O'Connor, Curley Dresden. When Gene Autry becomes the owner of a packing company the boyfriend of a rival tries to merge the two businesses and then dissolve Gene's operations. This Gene Autry opus does not have enough action to sustain its storyline.

2792 Ride the High Country. Metro-Goldwyn-Mayer, 1962. 94 minutes Color.

D: Sam Peckinpah. SC: N. B. Stone Jr. WITH Randolph Scott, Joel McCrea, Mariette Hartley, Ronald Starr, Edgar Buchanan, R. G. Armstrong, John Anderson, L. Q. Jones, Warren Oates, James Drury, John Davis Chandler, Jenie Jackson. Two aging former lawmen are hired to protect a gold shipment and they are joined by a young hellion and a girl trying to escape her new husband and his brothers. This teaming of genre stars Randolph Scott (in his final film) and Joel McCrea is a near-classic Western; very, very good.

2793 Ride the Man Down. Republic, 1953. 90 minutes Color. D: Joseph Kane. SC: Mary McCall Jr. WITH Brian Donlevy, Rod Cameron, Ella Raines, Forrest Tucker, Barbara Britton, Chill Wills, J. Carrol Naish, Jim Davis, Taylor Holmes, James Bell, Paul Fix, Roy Barcroft, Douglas Kennedy, Chris-Pin Martin, Jack LaRue, Al Caudebec, Roydon Clark, Claire Carleton. When a rich rancher dies, a feud develops between his daughter and local land grabbers and the ranch foreman tries to protect the property. Fine direction and a good cast make this "A" feature a good one to watch.

2794 Ride the Wind. NBC-TV, 1966. 120 minutes Color. D: William Witney. WITH Lorne Greene, Rod Cameron, Victor Jory, Michael Landon, Dan Blocker, DeForrest Kelly, Ray Teal, Victor Sen Yung, Wolfe Brazell, Stewart Moss, Warren Vanders, Richard Hale, Clay Tanner, Jack Bighead, James Novak. A rancher tries to aid a man in setting up Pony Express riders despite opposition, including Indian attacks on the final leg of the route. Well made and entertaining feature made up of two segments of the "Bonanza" (NBC-TV, 1959-73) TV series and issued theatrically in Europe.

2795 Ride to Glory. NBC-TV/Columbia, 1965. 90 minutes Color. WITH Chuck Connors, Robert Lansing, David Brian, Kathie Browne, Noah Beery Jr., H. M. Wynant, Michael Pate, Lee Van Cleef, William Bryant. A former Army officer, falsely accused of cowardice, tries to prove his innocence as well as prevent an Indian uprising. Sturdy TV film made from three segments of the "Branded" (NBC-TV, 1965-66) series and issued abroad theatrically under its episode title of **Call to Glory.**

2796 Ride to Hangman's Tree. Universal, 1967. 90 minutes Color. D: Alf Rafkin.

SC: Luci Ward, Jack Natteford & William Bowers. WITH Jack Lord, James Farentino, Don Galloway, Melodie Johnson, Richard Anderson, Robert Yuro, Ed Peck, Paul Reed, Richard Cutting, Bing Russell, Virginia Capers, Robert Sorrells, Robert Cornthwaite. A notorious road agent terrorizes local citizens after escaping from a lynch mob. Vapid remake of **Black Bart** (q.v.).

2797 Ride, Vaquero! Metro-Goldwyn-Mayer, 1953. 90 minutes Color. D: John Farrow. SC: Frank Fenton. WITH Robert Taylor, Ava Gardner, Howard Keel, Anthony Quinn, Kurt Kasznar, Ted De Corsia, Charlita, Jack Elam, Frank McGrath, Joe Dominguez, Walter Baldwin, Charles Stevens, Rex Lease, Tom Greenway. A young couple try to settle a ranch but are opposed by half-brothers who both end up falling for the wife. A good cast does its best with this oater but it is still nothing to brag about.

2798 Rider from Tucson. RKO Radio, 1950. 60 minutes B/W. D: Lesley Selander. SC: Ed Earl Repp. WITH Tim Holt, Richard Martin, Elaine Riley, Douglas Fowley, Veda Ann Borg, Robert Shayne, William Phipps, Harry Tyler, Marshall Reed, Stuart Randall, Dorothy Vaughn. In order to obtain a valuable gold claim, crooks turn to murder and kidnapping but are opposed by a cowpoke. Average Tim Holt vehicle.

2799 The Rider of Death Valley. Universal, 1932. 78 minutes B/W. D: Albert Rogell. SC: Jack Cunningham. WITH Tom Mix, Lois Wilson, Fred Kohler, Forrest Stanley, Willard Robertson, Edith Fellows, Mae Busch, Max Asher, Pete Morrison, Edmund Cobb, Otis Harlan, Francis Ford, Richard Cramer, Robert McKenzie, Lloyd Whitlock, Iron Eyes Cody. Crooks murder a man for his Death Valley gold mine claim and the dead man's rancher friend tries to protect his small daughter's interest in the mine and bring the murderers to justice. One of Tom Mix's best sound features, this "A" outing is highly entertaining and contains some beautiful Death Valley photography by Daniel Clark; well worth seeing. TV title: **Riders of the Desert.**

2800 Rider of the Law. Supreme, 1935. 56 minutes B/W. D: Robert North Bradbury. SC: Jack Natteford. WITH Bob Steele, Gertrude Messinger, Si Jenks, Earl Dwire, Forrest Taylor, Lloyd Ingraham, John Elliott, Sherry Tansey, Tex

343 Rider of the Plains

Palmer, Chuck Baldra. Posing as a dude, a government agent sets out to round up an outlaw gang. Typically entertaining Bob Steele vehicle.

2801 Rider of the Plains. Syndicate, 1931. 57 minutes B/W. D: J. P. McCarthy. SC: Wellyn Totman. WITH Tom Tyler, Andy Shuford, Lillian Bond, Alan Bridge, Gordon DeMain, Jack Perrin, Slim Whitaker, Ted Adams, Fern Emmett. An outlaw befriends a young boy and is reformed by him and a pretty girl. Draggy Tom Tyler vehicle; not much.

2802 Rider on a Dead Horse. Allied Artists, 1962. 67 minutes B/W. D: Herbert L. Strock. SC: Stephen Longstreet. WITH John Vivyan, Lisa Lu, Bruce Gordon, Kevin Hagen, Charles Lampkin. A trio of gold prospectors divides their diggings but one murders one of them and tries to prove the third man is the real killer, with the latter finding out that love is more important than riches. Tacky, talky feature.

Riders for Justice see **Westward Ho** (1942)

2803 Riders from Nowhere. Monogram, 1940. 47 minutes B/W. D: Raymond K. Johnson. SC: Carl Krusada. WITH Jack Randall, Margaret Roach, Charles King, Ernie Adams, Tom London, Nelson McDowell, George Chesebro, Ted Adams, Dorothy Adams, Carl Mathews, Jack Evans, Herman Hack, Archie Ricks, Ray Henderson. A stranger tries to find who murdered a lawman and robbed a gold shipment. Average Jack Randall series affair.

2804 Riders in the Sky. Columbia, 1949. 70 minutes B/W. D: John English. SC: Gerald Geraghty. WITH Gene Autry, Pat Buttram, Gloria Henry, Mary Beth Hughes, Robert Livingston, Steve Darrell, Alan Hale Jr., Tom London, Hank Patterson, Ben Welden, Kenne Duncan, Dennis Moore, Joe Forte, Frank Jacquet, Roy Gordon, Boyd Stockman, Pat O'Malley, John Parrish, Kermit Maynard, Bud Osborne, Lynton Brent, Isabel Withers, Sandy Sanders, Denver Dixon, Robert Walker. When a rancher is framed on false charges by a crooked gambler, Gene Autry plans to clear the man and bring the crook to justice. Fine Gene Autry film with good use of songs, including the title tune made famous by Vaughn Monroe.

2805 Riders of Black Mountain. Producers Releasing Corporation, 1940. 59 minutes B/W. D: Peter Stewart (Sam Newfield). SC: Joseph O'Donnell. WITH Tim McCoy, Pauline Haddon, Ed Peil, Frank LaRue, Rex Lease, Ralph Peters, Ted Adams, Julian Rivero, Jack Rutherford, George Chesebro, Dirk Thane, Carl Mathews. A local banker, involved in an insurance fraud, is behind a series of stagecoach robberies and his gang is pursued by a federal marshal disguised as a gambler. Okay Tim McCoy PRC vehicle. Alternate title: **Black Mountain Stage.**

2806 Riders of Black River. Columbia, 1939. 59 minutes B/W. D: Norman Deming. SC: Bennett Cohen. WITH Charles Starrett, Iris Meredith, Bob Nolan & The Sons of the Pioneers, Dick Curtis, Edmund Cobb, Stanley Brown, Francis Sayles, Forrest Taylor, George Chesebro, Olin Francis, Lew Meehan, Maston Williams, Carl Sepulveda. A former Texas Ranger returns home and plans to marry a girl whose brother is under the thumb of an outlaw gang which has been rustling area cattle. Competent remake of **The Revenge Rider** (q.v.), a Tim McCoy vehicle.

2807 Riders of Death Valley. Universal, 1941. 15 Chapters B/W. D: Ray Taylor & Ford Beebe. SC: Sherman Lowe, Basil Dickey, George Plympton & Jack Connell. WITH Dick Foran, Leo Carrillo, Buck Jones, Charles Bickford, Lon Chaney, Noah Beery Jr., Guinn Williams, Jeanne Kelly (Jean Brooks), Monte Blue, James Blaine, Glenn Strange, Roy Barcroft, Ethan Laidlaw, Richard Alexander, Jack Rockwell, Frank Austin, Charles Thomas, William Hall, James Guilfoyle, Ernie Adams, Edmund Cobb, William Pagan, Jack Clifford, Richard Travis, Ivar McFadden, Jack Perrin, Slim Whitaker, Bud Osborne, Frank Brownlee, Art Miles, Ed Payson, James Farley, Ted Adams, Dick Rush, Gil Perkins, Duke York. A vigilante group tries to aid miners against a protection racket and ends up opposing a notorious outlaw after all the gold mines in the district. A top notch cast is the chief asset of this otherwise mediocre serial. V: Video Connection.

2808 Riders of Destiny. Monogram, 1933. 52 minutes B/W. D-SC: Robert North Bradbury. WITH John Wayne, Cecilia Parker, George ("Gabby") Hayes, Forrest Taylor, Al St. John, Heinie Conklin, Earl Dwire, Yakima Canutt, Lafe McKee, Fern Emmett, Hal Price, Si Jenks, Horace B. Carpenter. Posing as a notorious bandit, a government agent tries to get the goods on a businessman who is trying to rob settlers of their land by denying them needed water. The only "Singin' Sandy" film, this initial entry in John Wayne's Monogram-Lone Star series for producer Paul Malvern is a good one, when the star is not singing, dubbed or not. V: Discount Video, Video Dimensions.

2809 Riders of Pasco Basin. Universal, 1940. 56 minutes B/W. D: Ray Taylor. SC: Ford Beebe. WITH Johnny Mack Brown, Bob Baker, Fuzzy Knight, Frances Robinson, Lafe McKee, Arthur Loft, Frank LaRue, James Guilfoyle, Chuck Morrison, Ed Cassidy, Robert Winkler, William Gould, Ted Adams, Kermit Maynard, David Sharpe, Rudy Sooter's Californians, Hank Bell, Ed Piel, Gordon Hart. A rodeo rider returns home to find promoters of an irrigation project trying to force themselves on the locals and he leads the vigilantes to stop them. Well done Johnny Mack Brown vehicle.

2810 Riders of the Badlands. Columbia, 1941. 57 minutes B/W. D: Howard Bretherton. SC: Betty Burbridge. WITH Charles Starrett, Russell Hayden, Cliff Edwards, Ilene Brewer, Kay Hughes, Roy Barcroft, Rick Anderson, Edith Leach, Ethan Laidlaw, Harry Cording, Hal Price, Ted Mapes, George J. Lewis, John Cason, Edmund Cobb, Francis Walker. A ranger and his dentist pal set out to bring in an outlaw and his gang but the ranger is a lookalike for the bad man and ends up being arrested by another ranger whose wife was murdered by the bandit. The plot is complicated but this Charles Starrett-Russell Hayden vehicle is actionful from start to finish.

2811 Riders of the Black Hills. Republic, 1938. 54 (55) minutes B/W. D: George Sherman. SC: Betty Burbridge & Bernard McConville. WITH Robert Livingston, Ray Corrigan, Max Terhune, Ann Evers, Roscoe Ates, Maude Eburne, Frank Melton, Johnny Lang Fitzgerald, Jack Ingram, John P. Wade, Fred "Snowflake" Toones, Edward Earle, Monte Montague, Ben Hall, Frank O'Connor, Tom London, Bud Osborne, Milburn Morante, Jack O'Shea, Art Dillard. When a young woman's valuable race horse is stolen, the Three Mesquiteers aid her in finding it and capturing the thieves. High grade entry in the popular Republic series.

2812 Riders of the Cactus. Big 4, 1931. 60 minutes B/W. D-SC: David Kirkland.

WITH Wally Wales, Buzz Barton, Lorraine LaVal, Fred Church, Ed Cartwright, Don Wilson. A cowboy is on the trail of an outlaw gang after a man searching for buried treasure. Bottom-of-the-barrel.

2813 Riders of the Dawn. Monogram, 1937. 53 minutes B/W. D: Robert North Bradbury. SC: Robert Emmett (Tansey). WITH Jack Randall, Peggy Keys, Warner Richmond, James Sheridan, George Cooper, Earl Dwire, Lloyd Ingraham, Ed Brady, Tim Davis, Yakima Canutt, Frank Hagney, Tex Cooper, Oscar Gahan, Forrest Taylor, Chick Hannon, Ella McKenzie, Ed Coxen, Jim Corey, Augie Gomez. Two lawmen are assigned to clean up a lawless town plagued by an outlaw gang led by the notorious gunman Danti. Jack Randall's first series film is a pretty good one, greatly aided by Warner Richmond's usual excellence as the villain.

2814 Riders of the Dawn. Monogram, 1945. 58 minutes B/W. D: Oliver Drake. SC: Louise Rosseau. WITH Jimmy Wakely, Lee "Lasses" White, John James, Phyllis Adair, Sarah Padden, Horace Murphy, Jack Baxley, Bob Shelton, Wesley Tuttle & His Texas Stars, Arthur Smith, Bill Hammond. Three medicine show entertainers find a young couple murdered and rescue their baby and find out a local doctor killed them for oil on their property. The plot is pretty good but overall just another dull Jimmy Wakely vehicle.

2815 Riders of the Deadline. United Artists, 1943. 54 (68) minutes B/W. D: Lesley Selander. SC: Bennett Cohen. WITH William Boyd, Andy Clyde, Jimmy Rogers, Richard Crane, Frances Woodward, William Halligan, Tony (Anthony) Warde, Robert Mitchum, Jim Bannon, Hugh Prosser, Herbert Rawlinson, Monte Montana, Earle Hodgins, Bill Beckford, Pierce Lyden, Art Felix. A gang of gun runners murders a Texas Ranger and Hopalong Cassidy, disguised as an outlaw, tries to locate them. The fiftieth entry in the popular "Hopalong Cassidy" series is only an average outing.

2816 Riders of the Desert. World Wide, 1932. 57 minutes B/W. D: Robert North Bradbury. SC: Wellyn Totman. WITH Bob Steele, Gertrude Messinger, George ("Gabby") Hayes, Al St. John, Horace B. Carpenter, Louise Carter, Joe Dominguez, Greg Whitespear, John Elliott, Earl Dwire. An Arizona Ranger is on the trail of an outlaw gang terrorizing the vicinity. Fine Bob Steele film with plenty of action for his fans.

Riders of the Desert (1932) see **The Rider of Death Valley**

2817 Riders of the Dusk. Monogram, 1949. 60 minutes B/W. D: Lambert Hillyer. SC: Jess Bowers (Adele Buffington) & Robert Emmett Tansey. WITH Whip Wilson, Andy Clyde, Reno Browne, Tristram Coffin, Marshall Reed, Myron Healey, John Merton, Holly Bane, Lee Roberts, Dee Cooper, Thornton Edwards, Ray Jones, John Cason. A deputy marshal heads for a small town to aid the local lawman in capturing a mysterious cattle rustler but along the way he is mistaken for the badman. Pretty fair Whip Wilson vehicle.

2818 Riders of the Frontier. Monogram, 1939. 58 minutes B/W. D: Spencer Gordon Bennet. SC: Jesse Duffy & Joseph Levering. WITH Tex Ritter, Jean Joyce, Hal Taliaferro, Jack Rutherford, Mantan Moreland, Marin Sais, Olin Francis, Nolan Willis, Roy Barcroft, Merrill McCormack, Edward Cecil, Bruce Mitchell, Maxine Leslie, Charles King, Forrest Taylor, Nelson McDowell. Outlaws hold a woman prisoner at her ranch but a lawman pretends to be a wanted criminal to gain access to the place and save its owner. One of the better Tex Ritter Monogram efforts, which includes the traditional folk song "Boll Weevil," a tune closely associated with the star. British title: **Ridin' the Frontier.**

2819 Riders of the Golden Gulch. West Coast, 1932. 52 minutes B/W. D: Clifford Smith. SC: Yakima Canutt. WITH Buffalo Bill Jr., Yakima Canutt, Mary Dunn, Pete Morrison, Edmund Cobb. A cowboy gets involved in a plot to rob his girl's father. Just about as bad as they get.

2820 Riders of the Law. Sunset, 1922. 55 minutes B/W. D-SC: Robert North Bradbury. WITH Jack Hoxie, Marin Sais. A government ranger, working undercover, saves the life of a sheriff who has been wounded by a gang of liquor smugglers. Fast moving Jack Hoxie silent film.

2821 Riders of the Lone Star. Columbia, 1947. 55 minutes B/W. D: Derwin Abrahams. SC: Barry Shipman. WITH Charles Starrett, Smiley Burnette, Virginia Hunter, Steve Darrell, Curley Williams & His Georgia Peach Pickers, Edmund Cobb, Mark Dennis, Lane Bradford, Ted Mapes,

George Chesebro, Peter Perkins, Eddie Parker, Bud Osborne, Nolan Leary. Two Texas Rangers are on the trail of a notorious badman who has returned to an area he once terrorized to stop the reopening of a mine. Pretty good "Durango Kid" film.

2822 Riders of the North. Syndicate, 1931. 59 minutes B/W. D: J. P. McGowan. SC: G. A. Durlam. WITH Bob Custer, Blanche Mehaffey, Frank Rice, Eddie Dunn, George Regas, Buddy Shaw, William Walling. A Canadian Mountie is on the trail of an outlaw gang in the north woods. Shoddy Bob Custer vehicle with the star his usual stoical self.

2823 Riders of the Northland. Columbia, 1942. 58 minutes B/W. D: William Berke. SC: Paul Franklin. WITH Charles Starrett, Russell Hayden, Cliff Edwards, Shirley Patterson, Lloyd Bridges, Bobby Larson, Kenneth MacDonald, Paul Sutton, Robert O. Davis, Joe McGuinn, Francis Walker, George Piltz, Blackjack Ward, Dick Jensen. A trio of Texas Rangers are sent to Alaska to investigate enemy activities and find a group of saboteurs trying to construct a runway for enemy planes. Sturdy Charles Starrett vehicle.

2824 Riders of the Northwest Mounted. Columbia, 1943. 57 minutes B/W. D: William Berke. SC: Fred Myton. WITH Russell Hayden, Dub Taylor, Bob Wills & His Texas Playboys, Adele Mara, Dick Curtis, Richard Bailey, Jack Ingram, Vernon Steele. A mountie is assigned to stop fur thieves working in the Red River district, the gang being led by a corrupt and vicious trading post operator. Probably the best of Russell Hayden's Columbia films with nice photography by Benjamin Kline, pretty Adele Mara as the leading lady and grand nastiness from Dick Curtis as the villain.

2825 Riders of the Purple Sage. Fox, 1925. 56 minutes B/W. D: Lynn Reynolds. SC: Edfrid Bingham. WITH Tom Mix, Beatrice Burnham, Arthur Morrison, Seesel Ann Johnson, Warner Oland, Fred Kohler, Charles Newton, Joe Rickson, Mabel Ballin, Charles Le Moyne, Harold Goodwin, Marion Nixon, Dawn O'Day (Anne Shirley), Wilfred Lucas. When a crooked lawyer kidnaps his sister and niece a Texas Ranger sets out to find them. Great photography (by Dan Clark) and a good story make this Tom Mix silent feature a good viewing bet. Followed by a sequel, **The Rainbow Trail**

(q.v.), this Zane Grey story was first filmed in 1918 by Fox with William Farnum. V: Classic Video Cinema Collectors Club.

2826 Riders of the Purple Sage. Fox, 1931. 58 minutes B/W. D: Hamilton MacFadden. SC: John F. Goodrich, Philip Klein & Barry Connors. WITH George O'Brien, Marguerite Churchill, Noah Beery, Yvonne Pelletier, James Todd, Stanley Fields, Lester Dorr, Frank McGlynn Jr., Shirley Nails. A man becomes an outcast by killing the man who kidnapped his sister but he later saves a girl and her ranch from outlaws. Good screen version of the Zane Grey novel, filmed previously by Fox in 1918 with William Farnum and in 1925 starring Tom Mix; 20th Century-Fox produced still another version in 1941 (q.v.) with George Montgomery. Also the book's sequel, The Rainbow Trail, was filmed in 1918, 1925 and 1931 as sequels to the Farnum, Mix and O'Brien films.

2827 Riders of the Purple Sage. 20th Century-Fox, 1941. 56 minutes B/W. D: James Tinling. SC: William Bruckner & Robert Metzler. WITH George Montgomery, Mary Howard, Robert Barrat, Lynne Roberts, Kane Richmond, Patsy Peterson, Richard Lane, Oscar O'Shea, James Gillette, Frank McGrath, LeRoy Mason. A young cowboy helps a pretty young ranch owner fight a gang of vicious vigilantes. Still another fine screen adaptation of the Zane Grey work.

2828 Riders of the Range. Truart, 1923. 50 minutes B/W. D-SC: Otis B. Thayer. WITH Edmund Cobb, Clare Hatton, Frank Gallagher, Roy Langdon, Harry Ascher, E. Glendower, B. Bonaventure, Levi Simpson, Dolly Dale, Helen Hayes, Mae Dean, Ann Drew. The president of the cattlemen's association believes local sheepmen are behind a series of rustlings but he begins to change his mind when he falls in love with the pretty daughter of a sheepherder. Okay silent actioner which gives the viewer a chance to see the great Edmund Cobb in a starring role.

2829 Riders of the Range. RKO Radio, 1950. 60 minutes B/W. D: Lesley Selander. SC: Norman Houston. WITH Tim Holt, Richard Martin, Jacqueline White, Reed Hadley, Robert Barrat, Tom Tyler, Robert Clarke, William Tannen. Two cowpokes aid a young girl whose cattle are being stolen by a crook who is blackmailing

the girl's brother. Nice Tim Holt outing with a fine supporting cast.

2830 Riders of the Rio Grande. Syndicate, 1929. 55 minutes B/W. D: J. P. McGowan. SC: Sally Winters. WITH Bob Custer, Edna Aslin, Horace B. Carpenter, Kip Cooper, Bob Erickson, Martin Cichy, Merrill McCormack. A cowboy comes to the aid of a girl and an engraver who have been kidnapped by the Quantrill gang. Slow moving Bob Custer silent vehicle also issued with a music score.

2831 Riders of the Rio Grande. Republic, 1943. 55 minutes B/W. D: Howard Bretherton. SC: Albert DeMond. WITH Bob Steele, Tom Tyler, Jimmie Dodd, Lorraine Miller, Edward Van Sloan, Rick Vallin, Harry Worth, Roy Barcroft, Charles King, Jack Ingram, John James, Jack O'Shea, Henry Hall, Bud Osborne. Outlaws threaten a town and its leading citizens and the Three Mesquiteers come to the rescue. Final entry in the popular and long-running "Mesquiteers" series; nothing exceptional but it does entertain.

2832 Riders of the Rockies. Grand National, 1937. 59 minutes B/W. D: Robert North Bradbury. SC: Robert Emmett (Tansey). WITH Tex Ritter, Louise Stanley, Horace Murphy, Snub Pollard, Heber Snow (Hank Worden), Charles King, Yakima Canutt, Earl Dwire, Martin Garralaga, Jack Rockwell, Paul Lopez, Tex Palmer, Clyde McClary, The Texas Tornados. When two Texas Rangers are falsely accused of a crime, another ranger resigns his commission and sets out to prove their innocence. Average Tex Ritter vehicle with a quartet of songs, including the title tune, "Song of the Open Range" and "Home on the Range." V: Cumberland Video, Video Communications.

2833 Riders of the Sage. Metropolitan, 1939. 55 minutes B/W. D: Harry S. Webb. SC: Carl Krusada. WITH Bob Steele, Claire Rochelle, Ralph Hoopes, James Whitehead, Earl Douglas, Ted Adams, Dave O'Brien, Frank LaRue, Bruce Dane, Jerry Sheldon, Reed Howes, Bud Osborne, Gordon Roberts (Carleton Young). A cowboy stops two outlaws from killing a man and finds himself in the middle of a sheepmen versus cattlemen feud with a sheep rancher trying to take over the area. Pretty tattered Bob Steele vehicle. V: Thunderbird.

2834 Riders of the Timberline. Paramount, 1941. 54 (59) minutes B/W. D: Lesley

Selander. SC: J. Benton Cheney. WITH William Boyd, Andy Clyde, Brad King, J. Farrell MacDonald, Eleanor Stewart, Anna Q. Nilsson, Edward Keene, Hal Taliaferro, Tom Tyler, Victor Jory, Mickey Eissa, Hank Bell, The Guardsmen Quartet. Hopalong Cassidy, Johnny Nelson and California Carlson come to the aid of the owner of a logging operation when a crook plans to blow up a dam to ruin the man's business. A fast moving plot and nice north woods locations and photography (by Russell Harlan) highlight this "Hopalong Cassidy" series entry.

2835 Riders of the West. Monogram, 1942. 60 minutes B/W. D: Howard Bretherton. SC: Jess Bowers (Adele Buffington). WITH Buck Jones, Tim McCoy, Raymond Hatton, Christine McIntyre, Dennis Moore, Harry Woods, Sarah Padden, Walter Mc-Grail, Harry Frazer, Bud Osborne, Charles King, Lee Phelps, Kermit Maynard, Milburn Morante, Ed Piel Sr., Lynton Brent, George Morrell, Tom London, J. Merrill Holmes. A trio of crooks are trying to steal a woman's ranch and The Rough Riders try to aid her, with one of them infiltrating the gang. Pleasant series entry for the popular "Rough Riders" trio. V: Video Connection.

2836 Riders of the Whistling Pines. Columbia, 1949. 70 minutes B/W. D: John English. SC: Jack Townley. WITH Gene Autry, Patricia White, Jimmy Lloyd, Douglass Dumbrille, Damian O'Flynn, Clayton Moore, Harry V. Chesire, Leon Weaver, Loie Bridge, Jerry Scroggins, Fred S. Martin, Bert Dodson, Roy Gordon, Jason Robards, Britt Wood, Len Torrey, The Cass County Boys, The Pinafores, Lane Chandler, Lynn Farr, Al Thompson, Emmett Vogan, Virginia Carroll, Nolan Leary, Steve Benton. A man falsely believes he accidentally killed a forest ranger when the ranger was actually murdered because he had discovered a moth infestation in the forest which would have profited two crooked businessmen. Colorful and entertaining Gene Autry vehicle. V: Video Connection, Nostalgia Merchant.

2837 Riders of the Whistling Skull. Republic, 1937. 54 minutes B/W. D: Mack V. Wright. SC: Oliver Drake. WITH Robert Livingston, Ray Corrigan, Max Terhune, Mary Russell, Fern Emmett, Roger Williams, C. Montague Shaw, Yakima Canutt, John Ward, George Godfrey, Frank Ellis, Earle Ross, Chief Thundercloud, John Van Pelt, Ed Peil, Jack Kirk, Iron Eyes

Cody, Tom Steele, Wally West, Tracy Layne, Ken Cooper. An archeologist searching for a lost Indian city is missing and the Three Mesquiteers try to locate him. One of the most entertaining segments in the popular "The Three Mesquiteers" series; reworked into the Charlie Chan vehicle, **The Feather Serpent** (q.v.). V: Cassette Express, Video Dimensions.

Riders of Vengeance see **The Raiders** (1952)

2838 Ridin' Down the Trail. Monogram, 1947. 53 minutes B/W. D: Howard Bretherton. SC: Bennett Cohen. WITH Jimmy Wakely, Dub Taylor, Beverly Jons, Douglas Fowley, John James, Doug Aylesworth, Charles King, Matthew (Brad) Slaven, Kermit Maynard, Harry Carr, Milburn Morante, Ted French, Post Park, Dick Rinehart, Don Weston. Arriving at a ranch, members of a medicine show find the people there murdered and they end up being blamed for the crime. One of the better Jimmy Wakely vehicles.

2839 The Ridin' Fool. Tiffany, 1931. 58 minutes B/W. D: J. P. McCarthy. SC: Wellyn Totman. WITH Bob Steele, Frances Morris, Florence Turner, Ted Adams, Al Bridge, Eddie Fetherston, Jack Henderson, Gordon DeMain, Josephine Velez, Fern Emmett, Artie Ortego. A cowboy who saved a gambler from being hung for a crime he did not commit becomes at odds with the man in a new town when they both fall for the same girl and then are accused of robbing a stage and murdering its driver. This Bob Steele vehicle should satisfy the star's fans although it is a bit slow with a somewhat complicated plot; Ted Adams is fine as the good-bad man while Bob Steele croons the song "I Fell in Love with You, Can't You Fall in Love with Me?".

2840 Ridin' Law. Big 4/Biltmore, 1930. 55 minutes B/W. D: Harry S. Webb. SC: Carl Krusada. WITH Jack Perrin, Renee Borden, Yakima Canutt, Jack Mower, Ben Corbett, Robert Walker, Pete Morrison, Fern Emmett, Olive Young. While looking for the murderer of his father in Mexico a young cowboy is captured by a gang of smugglers. Tacky early talkie.

2841 Ridin' Mad. Ben Wilson Productions, 1924. 60 minutes B/W. D-SC: Jacques Jaccard. WITH Yakima Canutt, Lorraine

Eason, Wilbur McGaugh, Helen Rosson, Annabelle Lee, Dick LaReno. Forced to kill a man in self-defense, a cowboy finds out his sister is in love with a crooked oil promoter who plans to leave her. Low grade but actionful Yakima Canutt silent programmer.

2842 Ridin' On. Reliable, 1936. 60 minutes B/W. D: Bernard B. Ray. SC: John T. Neville. WITH Tom Tyler, Geraine Greear (Joan Barclay), Rex Lease, John Elliott, Earl Dwire, Robert McKenzie, Roger Williams, Slim Whitaker, Jimmie Aubrey, Francis Walker, Wally West, Richard Cramer. Two range families engage in a feud but romance complicates the situation when the son of one family falls for the daughter of the other. Low grade Tom Tyler film.

2843 Ridin' On a Rainbow. Republic, 1941. 74 minutes B/W. D: Lew Landers. SC: Bradford Ropes & Doris Malloy. WITH Gene Autry, Smiley Burnette, Mary Lee, Carol Adams, Ferris Taylor, Georgia Caine, Byron Foulger, Ralf Harolde, James Conlin, Guy Usher, Anthony Warde, Forrest Taylor, Burr Caruth, Ed Cassidy, Ben Hall, Tom London, William V. Mong. After completing a cattle drive a rancher puts the profits in a bank only to have it robbed, and to investigate the matter he joins the entertainment group aboard a steamboat where an old-time performer, suspected in the robbery, works. A good script highlights this Gene Autry actioner. V: Blackhawk, NTA Home Entertainment.

2844 Ridin' the Cherokee Trail. Monogram, 1941. 60 minutes B/W. D: Spencer Gordon Bennet. SC: Edmund Kelso. WITH Tex Ritter, Arkansas Slim Andrews, The Tennessee Ramblers, Betty Miles, Forrest Taylor, Jack Roper, Fred Burns, Bruce Nolan, Gene Alsace, Ed Cassidy, Bob Card, Nolan Willis, Chuck Baldra, Sherry Tansey. A Texas Ranger heads into the Cherokee Strip to stop a crooked empire builder who tries to control the land before it is open to settlement. Nicely done Tex Ritter vehicle with several good songs. British title: **Cherokee Trail.**

2845 Ridin' the Lone Trail. Republic, 1937. 56 minutes B/W. D: Sam Newfield. SC: E. B. Mann. WITH Bob Steele, Claire Rochelle, Charles King, Ernie Adams, Lew Meehan, Julian Rivero, Steve Clark, Hal Price, Frank Ball, Jack Kirk. A Texan aids a sheriff in trying to apprehend a band of road agents who use a ranch-

owner's daughter's white horses in their killing and robbery sprees. Bob Steele is great in this very exciting and well done film which contains nice underplayed comedy and well staged fight sequences.

2846 Ridin' the Outlaw Trail. Columbia, 1951. 54 minutes B/W. D: Fred F. Sears. SC: Victor Arthur. WITH Charles Starrett, Smiley Burnette, Sunny Vickers, Jim Bannon, Pee Wee King & His Golden West Cowboys, Edgar Dearing, Peter Thompson, Lee Morgan, Chuck Roberson, Ethan Laidlaw, Frank McCarroll. The Durango Kid is on the trail of a man who stole gold pieces worth $20,000 but the man is killed by a crook who plans to have the gold melted so he can claim it was recently discovered. Fairly complicated, but okay, "Durango Kid" actioner.

2847 Ridin' the Trail. Arthur Ziehm, 1940. 57 minutes B/W. D: Raymond K. Johnson. SC: Phil Dunham. WITH Fred Scott, Iris Lancaster, Harry Harvey, Jack Ingram, John Ward, Bud Osborne, Carl Mathews, Gene Howard, Ray Lenhart, Buddy Kelly, Elias Gamboa, Denver Dixon. A masked avenger aids the side of the law when he takes on an outlaw gang. Followup to **Two Gun Troubador** (q.v.) this outing was originally made for Spectrum but the studio folded before its release; fairly good Fred Scott singing oater.

2848 Ridin' Thru. Reliable, 1934. 55 minutes B/W. D: Harry S. Webb. SC: Rose Gordon & Carl Krusada. WITH Tom Tyler, Ruth Hiatt, Lafe McKee, Philo McCullough, Ben Corbett, Lew Meehan, Bud Osborne, Colin Chase, Jayne Regan, Buck Morgan. Two cowpokes investigate a series of cattle thefts which have forced a rancher to turn his place into a dude ranch. There is not much to brag about in this less than mediocre Tom Tyler vehicle.

2849 The Riding Avenger. Diversion, 1936. 58 minutes B/W. D: Harry Fraser. SC: Norman Houston. WITH Hoot Gibson, Ruth Mix, June Gale, Buzz Barton, Stanley Blystone, Roger Williams, Francis Walker, Slim Whitaker, Budd Buster, Blackie Whiteford, Jack Evans. Appointed by the governor to round up a notorious rustler and his gang, a marshal takes on the guise of a gunman. Hoot Gibson does his best but poor production values hurt this modest vehicle.

2850 Riding High. Paramount, 1944.
88 minutes B/W. D: George Marshall.
SC: Walter De Leon, Arthur Phillips
& Art Arthur. WITH Dorothy Lamour,
Dick Powell, Victor Moore, Gil Lamb,
Bill Goodwin, Cass Daley, Rod Cameron,
Glenn Langan, Milt Britton & His Band,
George Carleton, Andrew Tombes, Douglas
Fowley, Pierre Watkin, James Burke,
Roscoe Karns, Patricia Mace, Gwen
Kenyon, Lorraine Miller, Stanley Andrews,
Wade Boteler, Fred Kelsey, Russell Simp-
son, Matt McHugh, Tom Kennedy, Stanley
Price, Lane Chandler, Ray Spiker, Charles
Soldani, Hal K. Dawson. A mining engineer
trying to capture a gang of counterfeiters
romances a burlesque dancer, the daughter
of a local miner. Not one of your better
Western musical comedies.

2851 Riding Shotgun. Warner Brothers,
1954. 75 minutes Color. D: Andre DeToth.
SC: Tom Blackburn. WITH Randolph
Scott, Wayne Morris, Joan Weldon, Joseph
Sawyer, James Millican, Charles (Bronson)
Buchinsky, James Bell, Fritz Feld, Richard
Garrick, Victor Perrin, John Baer, William
Johnstone, Ken Dibbs, Alvin Freeman,
Edward Coch Jr., Eva Pweis, Lonnie
Pierce, Mary Lou Holloway, Boyd "Red"
Morgan, Richard Benjamin, Jay Lawrence,
George Ross, Ray Bennett, Jack Kenney,
Dub Taylor, Jack Woody, Frosty Royce,
Ruth Whitney, Phil Chambers, Clem
Fuller, Bud Osborne, Frank Ferguson,
Budd Buster, Dick Dickinson, Buddy
Rossevelt, Mira McKinney. In an attempt
to find the outlaw responsible for his
wife's death, a man takes a job as a stage-
coach guard hoping to locate the man
when he pulls a robbery. Well paced
and entertaining Randolph Scott vehicle.

2852 Riding Speed. Superior, 1934. 50
minutes B/W. D: Jay Wilsey (Buffalo
Bill Jr.). SC: Delores Booth. WITH Buffalo
Bill Jr., Joile Benet, Bud Osborne, Lafe
McKee, Clyde McClary, Allen Holbrook,
Ernest Scott, Denver Dixon. A cowboy
opposes a gang of smugglers working
along the Mexican border. Rock bottom,
but fun, Victor Adamson (Denver Dixon)
production, written by Mrs. Adamson.

2853 Riding the California Trail. Mono-
gram, 1947. 60 minutes B/W. D: William
Nigh. SC: Clarence Upson Young. WITH
Gilbert Roland, Teala Loring, Inez Cooper,
Frank Yaconelli, Martin Garralaga, Ted
Hecht, Marcelle Granville, Eve Whitney,
Frank Marlowe, Alex Montoya, Rosa
Turich, Julia Kent. The Cisco Kid is
on the trail of a gang of crooks. Typically
pleasant and light-hearted "Cisco Kid"
series adventure.

2854 Riding the Sunset Trail. Monogram,
1941. 56 minutes B/W. D: Robert Emmett
Tansey. SC: Robert Emmett (Tansey)
& Frances Kavanaugh. WITH Tom Keene,
Betty Miles, Frank Yaconelli, Sugar
Dawn, Arkansas Slim Andrews, Kenne
Duncan, Tom London, Tom Seidel, James
Sheridan, Earl Douglas, Gene Alsace,
Fred Hoose. A crook tries to murder
his half-brother for his ranch but a cowboy
and his pal find the wounded man and
set out to stop the illegal activities.
Film has a stronger plot than production
values.

2855 Riding the Wind. RKO Radio, 1942.
60 minutes B/W. D: Edward Killy. SC:
Morton Grant & Earle Snell. WITH Tim
Holt, Ray Whitley, Lee "Lasses" White,
Eddie Dew, Mary Douglas, Ernie Adams,
Earle Hodgins, Kate Harrington, Charles
Phipps, Bud Osborne, Karl Hackett, Hank
Worden, Frank McCarroll, Bob Burns,
Larry Steers. A rancher and his pals
come to the aid of another rancher who
tries to build a windmill to provide water
for his cattle after crooks block his water
supply with a dam. Pretty good Tim
Holt series entry.

2856 Riding Through Nevada. Columbia,
1942. 55 minutes B/W. D: William Berke.
SC: Gerald Geraghty. WITH Charles
Starrett, Arthur Hunnicutt, Shirley Patterson, Jimmie Davis & His Rainbow Ramblers, Davidson Clark, Clancy Cooper,
Minerva Urecal, Edmund Cobb, Ethan
Laidlaw, Kermit Maynard, Art Mix, Stanley
Brown. A postal inspector investigates
the causes of stagecoach stickups and
takes on the job of shotgun guard to
uncover the culprits. Pretty thin entry
in the long-running Charles Starrett-
Columbia series.

2857 Riding Tornado. Columbia, 1932.
59 minutes B/W. D: D. Ross Lederman.
SC: Burt Kempler. WITH Tim McCoy,
Shirley Grey, Wallace MacDonald, Wheeler
Oakman, Russell Simpson, Montagu Love,
Lafe McKee, Art Mix, Vernon Dent,
Bud Osborne, Hank Bell, Silver Tip Baker,
Tex Palmer, Artie Ortego. A championship
rodeo rider is at odds with a local boss
who he believes is actually the mastermind
behind a gang of rustlers. Very good
and actionful Tim McCoy vehicle.

2858 Riding West. Columbia, 1944. 58
minutes B/W. D: William Berke. SC:

Luci Ward. WITH Charles Starrett, Shirley Patterson, Arthur Hunnicutt, Wheeler Oakman, Clancy Cooper, Steve Clark, Ernest Tubb, Johnny Bond, Blackie Whiteford, Bill Wilkerson. A gambler tries to prevent a man from setting up a Pony Express operation. Good Charles Starrett actioner with some pleasing music from Ernest Tubb and Johnny Bond.

2859 Riding Wild. Aywon, 1925. 60 minutes B/W. D: Leon Dela Mothe. SC: Robert L. Horner & Matilda Smith. WITH Kit Carson, Pauline Curley, Jack Richardson, Walter Maly, C. L. James. Recovering from a lung disease, a man sets out to avenge his mistreatment at the hands of a leader of a rustling gang. Fast paced poverty row oater with lots of plot twists.

2860 Riding Wild. Columbia, 1935. 57 minutes B/W. D: David Selman. SC: Ford Beebe. WITH Tim McCoy, Billie Seward, Niles Welch, Ed Le Saint, Richard Alexander, Richard Botiller, Eddie (Edmund) Cobb, Jack Rockwell, Bud Osborne, Wally West, Al Haskell, Si Jenks, Lafe McKee. A crooked rancher sells land to nestors to keep from going broke and then tries to run them off but they are helped by a cattle ranch foreman. Good Tim McCoy drama with some brief, but well done, night riding sequences.

2861 Riding with Buffalo Bill. Columbia, 1954. 15 Chapters B/W. D: Spencer Gordon Bennet. SC: George H. Plympton. WITH Marshall Reed, Rick Vallin, Joanne Rio, Shirley Whitney, Jack Ingram, William Fawcett, Gregg Barton, Ed Cotch, Steven Ritch, Pierce Lyden, Michael Fox, Lee Roberts, Zon Murray. Buffalo Bill Cody comes to the aid of a miner-rancher whose property has been attacked by a gang led by a man trying to keep out the expansion of the railroad. Latter day serial has little to recommend it; for genre fans only.

2862 Rim of the Canyon. Columbia, 1949. 70 minutes B/W. D: John English. SC: John K. Butler. WITH Gene Autry, Nan Leslie, Thurston Hall, Clem Bevans, Walter Sande, Jock Mahoney, Francis McDonald, Alan Hale Jr., Amelita Ward, Denver Pyle, Bobby Clark, Boyd Stockman, Sandy Sanders, Rory Mallinson, Frankie Marvin, John R. McKee, Lynn Farr. Gene Autry and his pals try to defend a small town from three ex-convicts who return there for revenge. More than adequate Gene Autry vehicle.

2863 Rimfire. Screen Guild, 1949. 66 minutes B/W. D: B. Reeves Eason. SC: Arthur St. Clair & Fred Wisbar. WITH James Millican, Marty Beth Hughes, Henry Hull, Reed Hadley, Fuzzy Knight, Glenn Strange, Chris-Pin Martin, Richard Alexander, George Cleveland, John Cason, Ray Bennett, Margia Dean, I. Stanford Jolley, Victor Kilian, Jason Robards, Don C. Harvey, Lee Roberts, Stanley Price. In Texas after the Civil War a cavalry officer opposes a gang of crooked gamblers in a boom town. Fairly interesting actioner with a fine cast.

2864 Ringo and His Golden Pistol. Metro-Goldwyn-Mayer, 1967. 88 minutes Color. D: Sergio Corbucci. SC: Adriano Bolzoni & Franco Rossetti. WITH Mark Damon, Valeria Fabrizi, Franco Derosa, Ettore Manni. In Mexico a deadly bounty hunter is on the trail of a number of outlaws with prices on their heads. Another in the long series of violent and bloody spaghetti Westerns, no better or no worse than most of its ilk. Issued in Italy in 1966 as **Johnny Oro.**

2865 Ringo's Big Night. Fenix Film, 1965. 95 minutes Color. D: Mario Maffei. SC: Emo Bistolfi. WITH William Berger, Adriana Ambesi, Eduardo Fajardo, Walter Maestosi, Guido Da Salvi, Tom Felleghy. A federal agent is arrested along with an outlaw in order to find out the hiding place of $200,000 stolen on its way to Tombstone. Typically violent and actionful Italian oater; interesting music score by Carlo Rustichelli. Italian title: **La Notte del Desperado** (The Night of the Desperado).

2866 Rio Bravo. Warner Brothers, 1959. 141 minutes Color. D: Howard Hawks. SC: Jules Furthman & Leigh Brackett. WITH John Wayne, Dean Martin, Ricky Nelson, Walter Brennan, Angie Dickinson, Ward Bond, John Russell, Pedro Gonzalez Gonzalez, Estelita Rodriguez, Claude Akins, Harry Carey Jr., Malcolm Atterbury, Bob Steele, Bing Russell, Myron Healey, Eugene Iglesias, Fred Graham, Tom Monroe, Riley Hill. A sheriff, aided only by four other people, tries to keep a murderer in jail while his powerful rancher brother and hired guns plan to break him out. Classic genre film is well worth watching; Walter Brennan steals the show as the colorful Stumpy. V: Cumberland Video. VD: Blackhawk.

2867 Rio Conchos. 20th Century-Fox, 1964. 107 minutes Color. D: Gordon

Douglas. SC: Joseph Landon & Clair Huffaker. WITH Richard Boone, Stuart Whitman, Tony Franciosa, Edmond O'Brien, Wende Wagner, Warner Anderson, Jim Brown, Rodolfo Acosta, Barry Kelly, Vito Scotti, House Peters Jr., Kevin Hagen. Four men trek across the Texas desert after the Civil War in search of stolen rifles and are attacked by Indians and outlaws. Well acted and entertaining outing.

2868 Rio Grande. Columbia, 1939. 58 minutes B/W. D: Sam Nelson. SC: Charles Francis Royal. WITH Charles Starrett, Ann Doran, Bob Nolan & The Sons of the Pioneers, Dick Curtis, Hal Taliaferro, Stanley Brown, Hank Bell, Forrest Taylor, Harry Strang, Ed LeSaint, Ed Piel Sr., Ted Mapes, Art Mix, George Chesebro, Lee Prather, Fred Burns, George Morrell, John Tyrell. A cowboy and his pals come to the aid of a girl being forced off her ranch by land grabbers. Average Charles Starrett actioner.

2869 Rio Grande. Astor, 1949. 56 minutes B/W. D: Norman Sheldon. SC: Hugh Jamison & Norman Sheldon. WITH Sunset Carson, Evohn Keyes, Lee Morgan, Bobby Clark, Bob Deats, Henry Garcia, Walter Calmback Jr., Maria Louisa Marulanda, Don Gray. A cowboy comes to the aid of a rancher and his pretty sister when two crooked brothers try to cheat them out of their water rights. Sunset Carson's final theatrically released film is rock bottom all the way; filmed in Texas by Lautem Productions.

2870 Rio Grande. Republic, 1950. 105 minutes B/W. D: John Ford. SC: James Kevin McGuinness. WITH John Wayne, Maureen O'Hara, Ben Johnson, Claude Jarman Jr., Harry Carey Jr., Chill Wills, J. Carrol Naish, Victor McLaglen, Grant Withers, Peter Ortiz, Steve Pendleton, Karolyn Grimes, Alberto Morin, Stan Jones, Jack Pennick, Fred Kennedy, The Sons of the Pioneers, Chuck Roberson, Patrick Wayne, Cliff Lyons. A cavalry lieutenant stationed near the Mexican border must deal with raiding Apaches as well as his estranged wife and new recruit son. Entertaining John Ford feature, but not as good as his other cavalry films of the period, **Fort Apache** (q.v.) and **She Wore a Yellow Ribbon** (q.v.). V: Blackhawk, Cumberland Video.

2871 Rio Grande Patrol. RKO Radio, 1950. 60 minutes B/W. D: Lesley Selander. SC: Norman Houston. WITH Tim Holt,

Richard Martin, Jane Nigh, Douglas Fowley, Cleo Moore, Tom Tyler, Rick Vallin, John Holland, Larry Johns, Harry Harvey, Forrest Burns. An official with the Border Patrol finds out that two members of the service are aiding Mexican bandits in a gun-smuggling scheme. Pretty good Tim Holt vehicle.

2872 Rio Grande Raiders. Republic, 1946. 56 minutes B/W. D: Thomas Carr. SC: Norton S. Parker. WITH Sunset Carson, Linda Stirling, Bob Steele, Tom London, Tristram Coffin, Edmund Cobb, Jack O'Shea, Tex Terry, Kenne Duncan, Al Taylor. A cowboy tries to aid his ex-convict brother who is being used as a pawn in a battle between two stage lines for a mail contract. Sunset Carson's final Republic vehicle is pretty good although the stock footage hurts as does the casting of the star as Bob Steele's "older" brother! V: Cumberland Video.

2873 Rio Grande Ranger. Columbia, 1936. 54 minutes B/W. D: Spencer Gordon Bennet. SC: Nate Gatzert. WITH Bob Allen, Iris Meredith, Hal Taliaferro, Paul Sutton, Buzz Henry, John Elliott, Tom London, Slim Whitaker, Jack Rockwell, Richard Botiller, Art Mix, Frank Ellis, Jack Ingram, Al Taylor, Jim Corey, Henry Hall, Jack C. Smith, Ed Cassidy, Ray Jones. Two rangers are assigned to a small border town to round up a gang of outlaws plaguing the area. Pretty good actioner with Bob Allen and Hal Taliaferro (Wally Wales) making a good team.

2874 Rio Grande Romance. Victory, 1936. 70 minutes B/W. D: Robert Hill. SC: Al Martin. WITH Eddie Nugent, Maxine Doyle, Fuzzy Knight, Don Alvarado, Nick Stuart, George Walsh, Forrest Taylor, Lucille Lund, Ernie Adams, George Cleveland, Joyce Kay. An FBI agent is on the trail of a gang of crooks. Pleasant, but average, programmer.

2875 Rio Lobo. Cinema Center, 1970. 114 minutes Color. D: Howard Hawks. SC: Burton Wohl & Leigh Brackett. WITH John Wayne, Jennifer O'Neill, Jorge Rivero, Jack Elam, Victor French, Christopher Mitchum, Susana Dosamantes, Mike Henry, David Huddleston, Bill Williams, Edward Faulkner, Sherry Lansing, Dean Smith, Robert Donner, Jim Davis, Peter Jason, Robert Rothwell, Chuck Courtney, George Plympton, Bob Steele, Boyd "Red" Morgan, Hank Worden, Chuck Roberson, John Ethan Wayne, Don "Red"

Barry. Betrayed during the Civil War, an ex-Union colonel sets out to find the culprits and discovers one of them trying to cheat an old man out of his ranch. Colorful actioner with good second unit direction by Yakima Canutt.

2876 Rio Rita. Metro-Goldwyn-Mayer, 1942. 91 minutes B/W. D: S. Sylvan Simon. SC: Richard Connell & Gladys Lehman. WITH Bud Abbott, Lou Costello, Kathryn Grayson, John Carroll, Patricia Dane, Tom Conway, Peter Whitney, Arthur Space, Joan Valerie, Dick Rich, Barry Nelson, Eva Puig, Mitchell Lewis, Eros Volusia, Julian Rivero, Douglass Newland, Lee Murray, Inez Cooper, Frank Penny. Two pet shop workers get stranded at a ranch which is actually a headquarters for Nazi spies. This pleasant Abbott & Costello musical comedy is a remake of the 1929 film which starred Bert Wheeler and Robert Woolsey; better than average.

2877 Rip Roarin' Buckaroo. Victory, 1936. 51 minutes B/W. D: Robert Hill. SC: William Buchanan. WITH Tom Tyler, Beth Marion, Sammy Cohen, Charles King, Forrest Taylor, Richard Cramer, John Elliott. A boxer, who is framed in a crooked match, voluntarily leaves the ring and heads West in order to get the culprits. Very poor production values make this Tom Tyler vehicle a low grade affair.

2878 River Lady. Universal, 1948. 78 minutes Color. D: George Sherman. SC: D. D. Beauchamp & William Bowers. WITH Yvonne De Carlo, Rod Cameron, Dan Duryea, Helena Carter, Lloyd Gough, Florence Bates, John McIntire, Jack Lambert, Esther Somers, Anita Turner, Edmund Cobb, Dewey Robinson, Eddy Waller, Milton Kibbee, Billy Wayne, Jimmy Ames, Edward Earle, Paul Maxey, Dick Wessel, Charles Sullivan, Mickey Simpson, Reed Howes, George Magrill, Carl Sepulveda, John McGuire, Howard Negley, Charles Wagenheim, Robert Wilke, Perc Launders, Al Hill, Harold Goodwin, Paul Fierro, Beverly Warren, Jack Shutta, Jerry Jerome, Frank Hagney. The beautiful owner of a Mississippi River gambling ship wants a lumberman who is in love with a timber king's daughter and in order to get her man, the gambling lady forms a syndicate to buy all of the timberland. Colorful, brawling action melodrama.

River of Destiny see **Forlorn River**

2879 River of No Return. 20th Century-Fox, 1954. 91 minutes Color. D: Otto Preminger. SC: Frank Fenton. WITH Robert Mitchum, Marilyn Monroe, Rory Calhoun, Tommy Rettig, Murvyn Vye, Will Wright, Douglas Spencer, Ed Hinton, Don Beddoe, Claire Andre, Jack Mather, Edmund Cobb, Jarma Lewis, Hal Baylor, Barbara Nichols, Fay Morley, John Doucette, Arthur Shields, Geneva Gray, Larry Chance, Paul Newlan. A beautiful woman hires a man and his young son to take her down a dangerous river in pursuit of her husband and they are tracked by a gambler and attacked by Indians. Otto Preminger smartly keeps the film moving, otherwise it is only average.

2880 The River's Edge. 20th Century-Fox, 1957. 87 minutes Color. D: Allan Dwan. SC: Harold Jacob Smith & James Leicester. WITH Ray Milland, Debra Paget, Anthony Quinn, Harry Carey Jr., Chubby Johnson, Byron Foulger, Tom McKee, Frank Gerstle. A crook enlists the aid of his ex-girlfriend's Mexican farmer husband in helping him cross the Mexican border with a cache of stolen money. Sadly underrated melodrama, this one is well worth viewing.

2881 River's End. Warner Brothers, 1930. 74 minutes B/W. D: Michael Curtiz. SC: Charles Kenyon. WITH Charles Bickford, Evelyn Knapp, J. Farrell MacDonald, ZaSu Pitts, Walter McGrail, David Torrence, Junior Coughlan, Tom Santschi. A man falsely accused of a crime takes over the identity of the lawman sent to capture him and he falls in love with the dead man's girlfriend, but trouble develops. Early talkie still holds good entertainment value; remade a decade later with Dennis Morgan in the dual role played here by Charles Bickford.

2882 River's End. Warner Brothers, 1940. 69 minutes B/W. D: Ray Enright. SC: Barry Trivers & Bertram Milhauser. WITH Dennis Morgan, Elizabeth Earl, Victor Jory, George Tobias, James Stephenson, Steffi Duna, Edward Pawley, John Ridgely, Frank Wilcox, David Bruce, Gilbert Emery. A man, falsely convicted of murder, escapes from prison and takes on the guise of his dead Mountie brother in order to find the real killer. Okay remake of the James Oliver Curwood story which Warner Bros. originally filmed in 1930 with Charles Bickford in the leading role. TV title: **Double Identity.**

2883 The Road Agent. Rayart, 1926. 50 minutes B/W. D: J. P. McGowan.

SC: Charles Saxton. WITH Al Hoxie, Ione Reed, Lew Meehan, Leon de la Mothe, Florence Lee, Cliff Lyons. Running from the law, a cowpoke is hired by a crook to impersonate a man about to inherit a ranch. Bottom-of-the-barrel silent film.

2884 Road Agent. Universal, 1941. 69 minutes B/W. D: Charles Lamont. SC: Morgan Cox, Arthur Strawn & Maurice Tombragel. WITH Dick Foran, Leo Carrillo, Andy Devine, Anne Gwynne, Samuel S. Hinds, Richard Davies, Anne Nagel, Morris Ankrum, John Gallaudet, Reed Hadley, Eddy Adams, Ernie Adams, Lew Kelly, Luana Walters. Three pals arrive in a small town and are promptly jailed on a fake murder charge but they are later released to fight outlaws. Typically fast moving, actionful and slick Universal programmer. Reissue title: **Texas Road Agent.** V: Thunderbird.

2885 Road Agent. RKO Radio, 1952. 60 minutes B/W. D: Lesley Selander. SC: Norman Houston. WITH Tim Holt, Richard Martin, Noreen Nash, Mauritz Hugo, Dorothy Patrick, Robert Wilke, Tom Tyler, Guy Edward Hearn, William Tannen, Sam Flint, Forbes Murray, Stanley Blystone, Tom Kennedy. When crooks steal money from the locals, a young man takes on the guise of a Robin Hood-type character to right the wrongs. Pretty good Tim Holt vehicle, one of the last of his long-running RKO series.

2886 The Road to Denver. Republic, 1955. 90 minutes Color. D: Joseph Kane. SC: Horace McCoy & Allen Rivkin. WITH John Payne, Mona Freeman, Lee J. Cobb, Ray Middleton, Skip Homeier, Andy Clyde, Lee Van Cleef, Karl Davis, Glenn Strange, Buzz Henry, Dan White, Robert Burton, Anne Carroll, Tex Terry. A stage line operator tries to tell his younger brother the man he works for is a crook and the two brothers eventually meet in a showdown. Well produced melodrama which provides good entertainment.

2887 The Road to Fort Alamo. World Entertainment Corporation, 1966. 82 minutes Color. D: John M. Old (Mario Bava). SC: Vincent Thomas, Charles Price & Jane Brisbane. WITH Ken Clark, Jany Clair, Michel Lexmoine, Andreina Paul, Kirk Bert, Antonio Gratoldi, Dean Ardow. After a disagreement a man is left to die in the desert by his outlaw gang partners and after his rescue he pretends to be a federal officer but soon

proves to be a hero when he tries to save a wagon train from Indians. Actionful and entertaining spaghetti Western greatly aided by steady direction by Mario Bava. Issued in Italy in 1965 by Protor/Piazzi/Comptori as **La Strada per Fort Alamo** (The Road to Fort Alamo). French title: **Arizona Bill.**

2888 Road to Utopia. Paramount, 1945. 89 minutes B/W. D: Hal Walker. SC: Norman Panama & Melvin Frank. WITH Bing Crosby, Bob Hope, Dorothy Lamour, Hillary Brooke, Douglass Dumbrille, Jack LaRue, Robert Barrat, Nestor Paiva, Will Wright, Jimmy Dundee, Billy Benedict, Arthur Loft, Stanley Andrews, Alan Bridge, Romaine Callender, Paul Newlan, Jack Rutherford, Al Hill, Edward Emerson, Ronnie Rondell, Allen Pomeroy, Jack Stoney, George McKay, Larry Daniels, Charles Gemora, Claire James, Maxine Fife, Ferdinand Munier, Edgar Dearing, Charles C. Wilson, Jim Thorpe, Robert Benchley (narrator). Two vaudevillians head to the Klondike where they get mixed up with a map to a gold claim, crooks after the map and a pretty dance hall girl. One of the better outings in the "Road" series.

2889 Roamin' Wild. Reliable, 1936. 58 minutes B/W. D: Bernard B. Ray. SC: Robert Emmett Tansey. WITH Tom Tyler, Carol Wyndham, Max Davidson, Al Ferguson, George Chesebro, Fred Parker, Slim Whitaker, Bud Osborne, Wally West, Earl Dwire, Lafe McKee, Sherry Tansey, Frank Ellis, John Elliott. Crooks pose as government men and try to bilk miners out of their earnings but a U. S. marshal investigates the situation. Tacky Tom Tyler vehicle with a maximum of outdoor activity supplemented by fights, gunplay, etc. to cover up the lack of script and budget.

2890 The Roaming Cowboy. Spectrum, 1937. 60 minutes B/W. D: Robert Hill. SC: Fred Myton. WITH Fred Scott, Al St. John, Lois January, Forrest Taylor, Roger Williams, Budd Cox, Art Miles, George Morrell, George Chesebro, Carl Mathews, Richard Cramer, Lew Meehan, Oscar Gahan. After finding a rancher murdered and his son orphaned, two cowpokes join another outfit and get involved in a range war caused by a man who wants to buy up all the area land. Good low budget Fred Scott series film highlighted by Scott's fine singing of several Stephen Foster songs.

2891 Roar of the Iron Horse. Columbia, 1950. 15 Chapters B/W. D: Spencer Gordon Bennet & Thomas Carr. SC: George H. Plympton, Sherman Lowe & Royal K. Cole. WITH Jock (Mahoney) O'Mahoney, Virginia Herrick, William Fawcett, Hal Landon, Jack Ingram, Mickey Simpson, George Eldredge, Myron Healey, Rusty Wescoatt, Frank Ellis, Pierce Lyden, Dick Curtis, Hugh Prosser, Rick Vallin, Bud Osborne. A special investigator from Washington is assigned to find out who is causing a series of mishaps to the construction of a government-financed railroad. Jock Mahoney fans will enjoy this actionful cliffhanger.

2892 Roarin' Guns. Puritan, 1936. 60 minutes B/W. D: Sam Newfield. SC: Joseph O'Donnell. WITH Tim McCoy, Rosalinda Rice, Wheeler Oakman, Karl Hackett, John Elliott, Tommy Bupp, Jack Rockwell, Lew Meehan, Rex Lease, Frank Ellis, Ed Cassidy, Richard Alexander, Artie Ortego, Tex Phelps, Al Taylor. A cowboy comes to the aid of several ranchers who are being cheated by a group heading a cattle combine. Low budget but appealing Tim McCoy vehicle.

2893 Roarin' Lead. Republic, 1936. 54 minutes B/W. D: Mack V. Wright & Sam Newfield. SC: Oliver Drake & Jack Natteford. WITH Robert Livingston, Ray Corrigan, Max Terhune, Christine Maple, Hooper Atchley, Yakima Canutt, George Chesebro, Tommy Bupp, Grace Kern, George Plues, Harry Tenbrook, Newt Kirby, Pascale Perry, Baby Jane Keckley. A crook uses his outlaw rustling gang like a military unit but their activities are opposed by the Three Mesquiteers. Typically fast, entertaining action entry in "The Three Mesquiteers" series.

2894 Roaring Frontiers. Columbia, 1941. 60 minutes B/W. D: Lambert Hillyer. SC: Robert Lee Johnson. WITH Bill Elliott, Tex Ritter, Ruth Ford, Frank Mitchell, Hal Taliaferro, Bradley Page, Tristram Coffin, Francis Walker, Joe McGuinn, George Chesebro, Charles Stevens, Charles King, Lew Meehan, Hank Bell, George Eldredge, Fred Burns, Ernie Adams. A marshall is sent to a small town to arrest a cowboy for killing the local sheriff but ends up saving him from a lynch mob instigated by the real murderer. Solid entertainment in the Bill Elliott-Tex Ritter Columbia series.

Roaring Mountain see **Thunder Mountain** (1935)

2895 Roaring Ranch. Universal, 1930. 70 minutes B/W. D-SC: B. Reeves Eason. WITH Hoot Gibson, Sally Eilers, Wheeler Oakman, Bobby Nelson, Frank Clark, Leo White. A geologist and a rancher both love the same girl and when the geologist discovers oil on his rival's ranch he schemes to get the property cheap. Well done Hoot Gibson early talkie; one which will please his fans.

2896 Roaring Rangers. Columbia, 1946. 55 minutes B/W. D: Ray Nazarro. SC: Barry Shipman. WITH Charles Starrett, Smiley Burnette, Adelle Roberts, Merle Travis & His Bronco Busters, Jack Rockwell, Ed Cassidy, Mickey Kuhn, Edmund Cobb, Ted Mapes, Robert Wilke, Herman Hack, Gerald Mackey, Teddy Infuhr, Roger Williams, John Tyrell, Nolan Leary, Ethan Laidlaw, Frank Fanning, Frank O'Connor, Jack Kirk, Kermit Maynard, Tommy Coates, Chick Hannon, Carol Henry. Upon the request of the sheriff's young son, the Durango Kid comes to a small town to investigate a series of lawless acts and finds out the lawman's brother is behind the activities. Pretty good "Durango Kid" segment.

Roaring Rider see **Wyoming Whirlwind**

2897 Roaring Six Guns. Ambassador, 1937. 55 minutes B/W. D: J. P. McGowan. SC: Arthur Everett. WITH Kermit Maynard, Mary Hayes, Sam Flint, John Merton, Budd Buster, Robert Fiske, Ed Cassidy, Curley Dresden, Dick Moorehead, Slim Whitaker, Earle Hodgins, Rene Stone. A rancher is in love with a neighbor's pretty daughter but the neighbor opposes the match and also joins forces with a crook in trying to force the rancher to lose a lease he has obtained on government grazing land. Standard Kermit Maynard vehicle, but not up to par with some of his previous films. V: Thunderbird.

2898 Roaring Timber. Columbia, 1937. 65 minutes B/W. D: Phil Rosen. SC: Paul Franklin & Robert James Cosgriff. WITH Jack Holt, Grace Bradley, Ruth Donnelly, Raymond Hatton, Willard Robertson, J. Farrell MacDonald, Charles Wilson, Fred Kohler Jr., Tom London, Philip Ahn, Ben Hendricks, Ernest Wood. A timber boss struggles to complete a job, in spite of his opposition's sabotage, to get a bonus and win the heart of his pretty boss. Rugged and very actionful.

2899 The Roaring West. Universal, 1935. 15 Chapters B/W. D: Ray Taylor. SC:

George Plympton, Nate Gatzert, Basil Dickey, Robert C. Rothafel & Ella O'Neill. WITH Buck Jones, Muriel Evans, Walter Miller, Frank McGlynn, Harlan E. Knight, William Desmond, William Thorne, Eole Galli, Pat O'Brien, Charles King, Slim Whitaker, Tom London, Edmund Cobb, Dick Rush, Cecil Kellogg, Paul Palmer, Harry Tenbrook, Buffalo Bill Jr., Tiny Skelton, George Ovey, Fred Humes, Cliff Lyons, John Bose, Lafe McKee. Two men plan to file a claim on mineral-rich land during a land rush but crooks steal their map and file on the same claim only to learn the map was incorrect and they begin a reign of terror to find the real map. Actionful serial starring Buck Jones; should please his fans.

2900 Roaring Westward. Monogram, 1949. 55 minutes B/W. D: Oliver Drake. SC: Ronald Davidson. WITH Jimmy Wakely, Dub Taylor, Lois Hall, Dennis Moore, Jack Ingram, Claire Whitney, Kenne Duncan, Buddy Swan, Holly Bane, Marshall Reed, Nolan Leary, Bud Osborne, Bob Woodward, Al Haskell, Denver Dixon, Tom Smith. A singing cowboy is on the trail of crooks who have stolen money intended for a school headed by a sheriff's association. Jimmy Wakely's penultimate series oater is nothing to roar about, despite its title.

2901 Robbers of the Range. RKO Radio, 1941. D: Edward Killy. SC: Morton Grant & Arthur V. Jones. WITH Tim Holt, Ray Whitley, Virginia Vale, Emmett Lynn, LeRoy Mason, Howard Hickman, Ernie Adams, Frank LaRue, Ray Bennett, Tom London, Ed Cassidy, Bud Osborne, George Melford, Bud McTaggart, Harry Harvey, Lloyd Ingraham. When a young rancher refuses to sell his land to a corrupt railroad land agent, he is framed on a murder charge, but escapes and aids another rancher to get the money to pay off his mortgage. Very good Tim Holt vehicle.

2902 Robbers' Roost. Fox, 1933. 64 minutes B/W. D: Louis King. SC: Dudley Nichols. WITH George O'Brien, Maureen O'Sullivan, Walter McGrail, Reginald Owen, Doris Lloyd, Maude Eburne, Walter Pawley, Ted Oliver, Frank Rice, Bill Nestell, Clifford Santley, Gilbert "Pee Wee" Holmes, Vinegar Roan. When his boss's cattle are rustled, a ranch hand suspects the foreman is the culprit. Entertaining George O'Brien actioner.

2903 Robber's Roost. United Artists, 1955. 82 minutes Color. D: Sidney Salkow.

SC: John O'Dea, Sidney Salkow & Maurice Geraghty. WITH George Montgomery, Richard Boone, Bruce Bennett, Peter Graves, Sylvia Findley, Warren Stevens, William Hopper, Leo Gordon, Tony Romano, Stanley Clements, Joe Bassett, Leonard Geer, Al Wyatt, Boyd "Red" Morgan. Two outlaw gangs battle each other for valuable range land. Standard, supposedly based on Zane Grey.

2904 Robbery Under Arms. Lopert, 1958. 83 minutes Color. D: Jack Lee. WITH Peter Finch, Ronald Lewis, Maureen Swanson, David McCallum, Jill Ireland, Laurence Naismith, Vincent Ball, Dudy Nimmo, Jean Anderson, Ursula Finlay, Johnny Dacell, Larry Taylor, Russell Napier, Yvonne Buckingham, George Cormack, Doris Goddard. In frontier Australia in the 1870s two brothers become involved in a robbery while romancing two pretty sisters. Pleasantly paced British production filmed in Australia.

2905 Robin Hood of El Dorado. Metro-Goldwyn-Mayer, 1936. 86 minutes B/W. D: William A. Wellman. SC: William A. Wellman & Joseph Calleia. WITH Warner Baxter, Ann Lording, Bruce Cabot, Margo, J. Carrol Naish, Soledad Jiminez, Carlos De Valdez, Eric Linden, Edgar Kennedy, Charles Trowbridge, Harvey Stephens, Ralph Remley, George Regas, Harry Woods, Francis McDonald, Kay Hughes, Paul Hurst, Boothe Howard. A Mexican farmer becomes a notorious bandit and rebel leader after his wife dies when they are beaten and thrown off their lands. Well made and exciting, if a bit romantic, account of the life of Joaquin Murieta.

2906 Robin Hood of Monterey. Monogram, 1947. 55 minutes B/W. D: Christy Cabanne. SC: Bennett R. Cohen. WITH Gilbert Roland, Chris-Pin Martin, Evelyn Brent, Jack LaRue, Pedro de Cordoba, Donna DeMario, Travis Kent, Thornton Edwards, Nestor Paiva, Ernie Adams, Julian Rivero, Alex Montoya, Fred Cordova, Felipe Turich. The Cisco Kid and Pancho (dubbed Chico and Pablo in TV prints) come to the aid of a young man accused of killing his father, a Spanish rancher. Star Gilbert Roland is given credit for additional dialogue in this entertaining "Cisco Kid" outing which includes fine villainous work by Evelyn Brent and Jack LaRue.

2907 Robin Hood of Texas. Republic, 1947. 71 minutes B/W. D: Lesley Selander.

SC: John Butler & Earle Snell. WITH Gene Autry, Lynne Roberts, Adele Mara, Sterling Holloway, The Cass County Boys, James Cardwell, John Kellogg, Ray Walker, Michael Brandon, Paul Bryar, James Flavin, Dorothy Vaughn, Stanley Andrews, Alan Bridge, Hank Patterson, Edmund Cobb, Lester Dorr, William Norton Bailey, Irene Mack, Eva Novak, Frankie Marvin, Billy Wilkerson, Kenneth Terrell, Joe Yrigoyen. Gene Autry and his pals fix up an old spread and turn it into a dude ranch while aiding the local sheriff capture a gang of bank robbers. Very pleasant and entertaining Gene Autry opus. V: Blackhawk.

2908 Robin Hood of the Pecos. Republic, 1941. 59 (54) minutes B/W. D: Joseph Kane. SC: Olive Cooper. WITH Roy Rogers, George "Gabby" Hayes, Marjorie Reynolds, Cy Kendall, Leigh Whipper, Sally Payne, Eddie Acuff, Robert Strange, Jay Novello, William Haade, Roscoe Ates, Jim Corey, Chick Hannon. A crook runs the territory in post-Civil War Texas and the citizens band together and form a group of masked night riders to combat the carpetbaggers who are harassing them. Very entertaining Roy Rogers oater.

2909 Robin Hood of the Range. Columbia, 1943. 57 minutes B/W. D: William Berke. SC: Betty Burbridge. WITH Charles Starrett, Kay Harris, Arthur Hunnicutt, The Jimmy Wakely Trio, Johnny Bond, Stanley Brown, Kenneth MacDonald, Douglas Drake, Bud Osborne, Ed Piel Sr., Frank LaRue, Frank McCarroll, Ray Jones, Merrill McCormack. The mysterious Vulcan rides to the aid of homesteaders about to lose their homes to the railroad. Actionful Charles Starrett vehicle.

2910 Rock Island Trail. Republic, 1950. 90 minutes B/W. D: Joseph Kane. SC: James Edward Grant. WITH Forrest Tucker, Adele Mara, Adrian Booth, Bruce Cabot, Chill Wills, Jeff Corey, Grant Withers, Barbara Fuller, Roy Barcroft, Pierre Watkin, Valentine Perkins, Jimmy Hunt, Olin Howlin, Sam Flint, John Holland, Emory Parnell, Dick Elliott, Jack Pennick. A railroad engineer battles competition from a rival stagecoach operation. Fairly good Republic "A" production enhanced by a typically good studio cast.

2911 Rock River Renegades. Monogram, 1942. 59 minutes B/W. D: S. Roy Luby. SC: John Vlahos & Earle Snell. WITH Ray Corrigan, John King, Max Terhune,

Christine McIntyre, John Elliott, Weldon Heyburn, Kermit Maynard, Frank Ellis, Carl Mathews, Richard Cramer, Tex Palmer, Hank Bell, Budd Buster, Steve Clark. The Range Busters come to the aid of a sheriff battling a band of mysterious road agents as well as a saloon owner who is after his girl. One of the lesser entries in "The Range Busters" series due to lack of plot development.

2912 Rockin' in the Rockies. Columbia, 1945. 65 minutes B/W. D: Vernon Keays. SC: J. Benton Cheney & John Gray. WITH Mary Beth Hughes, The Three Stooges (Moe Howard, Larry Fine, Jerry "Curly" Howard), Jay Kirby, Gladys Blake, Tim Ryan, Vernon Dent, The Hoosier Hotshots, The Cappy Barra Boys, Spade Cooley, Forrest Taylor, Jack Clifford. A rancher trying to sell his ranch gets mixed up with three zanies and some show business people trying to make it to Broadway. Broad musical Western farce, but lots of fun.

2913 Rocky. Monogram, 1946. 76 minutes B/W. D: Dave Milton. WITH Roddy McDowell, Edgar Barrier, Nita Hunter. The adventures of a young man and his dog in the early days of the West. Pleasing programmer for which star Roddy McDowell and Monogram editor Ace Herman were the associate producers.

2914 Rocky Mountain. Warner Brothers, 1950. 83 minutes B/W. D: William Keighley. SC: Winston Miller & Alan LeMay. WITH Errol Flynn, Patrice Wymore, Scott Forbes, Guinn Williams, Dick Jones, Howard Petrie, Slim Pickens, Chubby Johnson, Buzz Henry, Sheb Wooley, Peter Coe, Rush Williams, Steve Dunhill, Alex Sharp, Yakima Canutt, Nakai Snez. A Confederate officer and his band of men are ordered to get outlaws on their side for the South to get control of California. Errol Flynn's final Western is a fairly good affair with nice locales and some well-staged action sequences.

2915 Rocky Mountain Mystery. Paramount, 1935. 63 minutes B/W. D: Charles Barton. SC: Edward E. Paramore Jr. & Ethel Doherty. WITH Randolph Scott, Charles "Chic" Sale, Mrs. Leslie Carter, Kathleen Burke, George Marion, Ann Sheridan, James C. Eagles, Howard Wilson, Willie Fung, Florence Roberts. A young lawman joins forces with the local sheriff in order to solve several murders at an isolated radium mine. Nicely entertaining drama which really has little to do with

357   **Rocky Mountain**

the Zane Grey novel Golden Dreams, upon which it is supposedly based. The film does afford a chance to see the famous stage actress Mrs. Leslie Carter. Alternate titles: **The Fighting Westerner** and **Vanishing Pioneer.**

2916 Rocky Mountain Rangers. Republic, 1940. 54 (58) minutes B/W. D: George Sherman. SC: Barry Shipman & Earle Snell. WITH Robert Livingston, Raymond Hatton, Duncan Renaldo, Rosella Towne, Sammy McKim, LeRoy Mason, Pat O'Malley, Dennis Moore, John St. Polis, Robert Blair, Burr Caruth, Jack Kirk, Hank Bell, Budd Buster. The Three Mesquiteers, now working as Texas Rangers, are on the trail of a notorious outlaw gang. Okay action outing in "The Three Mesquiteers" series, but nothing special.

2917 Rocky Rhodes. Universal, 1934. 64 minutes B/W. D: Al Raboch. SC: Edward Churchill. WITH Buck Jones, Sheila Terry, Stanley Fields, Walter Miller, Alf P. James, Paul Fix, Lydia Knott, Lee Shumway, Jack Rockwell, Carl Stockdale, Monte Montague, Bud Osborne, Harry Samuels. A cowboy and a Chicago hood team to stop land grabbers in a small Arizona town. Nice blend of action and comedy make this a very good Buck Jones outing. Reissued by Realart.

2918 Rodeo. Monogram, 1952. 70 minutes B/W. D: William Beaudine. SC: Charles R. Marion. WITH John Archer, Jane Nigh, Wallace Ford, Gary Gray, Frances Rafferty, Sara Haden, Frank Ferguson, Myron Healey, Fuzzy Knight, Robert Karnes, Jim Bannon, I. Stanford Jolley. When crooked promoters run out on a rodeo owing her father money, a young woman takes over the show and makes it a success. Competently made and entertaining "B" drama.

2919 Rodeo Girl. CBS-TV, 1980. 100 minutes Color. D: Jackie Cooper. WITH Katharine Ross, Bo Hopkins, Candy Clark, Jacqueline Brookes, Wilford Brimley, Parley Baer. Bored with her rodeo husband's way of life, a woman goes into business for herself by forming an all-female rodeo and becomes a world champion. Entertaining TV flick based on the actual experiences of rodeo champion Sue Pirtle.

2920 Rodeo King and the Senorita. Republic, 1951. 67 minutes B/W. D: Philip Ford. SC: John K. Butler. WITH Rex Allen, Mary Ellen Kay, Buddy Ebsen,

Roy Barcroft, Tristram Coffin, Bonnie DeSimone, Don Beddoe, Jonathan Hale, Harry Harvey, Rory Mallinson, Joe Forte. A rodeo star tries to aid a rancher being harrassed by a crooked fellow rancher and ends up not being able to join the rodeo show. Entertaining remake of the Roy Rogers vehicle **My Pal Trigger** (q.v.).

2921 Rodeo Rhythm. Producers Releasing Corporation, 1942. 68 minutes B/W. D: Fred Neymeyer. SC: Gene Tuttle & Eugene Allen. WITH Fred Scott, The Ray Knapp Rough Riders, Patricia Redpath, Lori Bridge, Pat Dunn, Jack Cooper, John Frank, Doc Hartley, Landon Laird, Raylene Smith, Vernon Brown, Donna Lee Meinke, Gloria Morse. When they are in danger of losing their home, a group of orphans appear in a rodeo to get the money to save their orphanage. Although top billed Fred Scott sings a few songs, this Kansas City-filmed outing is basically a vehicle for a group of rodeo youngsters.

2922 Rogue of the Range. Supreme, 1936. 60 minutes B/W. D: S. Roy Luby. SC: Earle Snell. WITH Johnny Mack Brown, Lois January, Phyllis Hume, Alden (Stephen) Chase, George Ball, Jack Rockwell, Horace Murphy, Frank Ball, Lloyd Ingraham, Fred Hoose, Forrest Taylor, George Morrell, Blackie Whiteford, Slim Whitaker, Tex Palmer, Horace B. Carpenter, Max Davidson, Art Dillard. A secret service agent, after rescuing a woman preacher from a runaway wagon, hires out as a gunman in order to get the goods on outlaws and ends up romancing a saloon girl. A meandering plot detracts from this Johnny Mack Brown series entry for producer A. W. Hackel.

2923 Rogue of the Rio Grande. Sono Art/World Wide, 1930. 70 minutes B/W. D: Spencer Gordon Bennett. SC: Oliver Drake. WITH Jose Bohr, Raymond Hatton, Myrna Loy, Carmelita Geraghty, Walter Miller, Gene Morgan, William P. Burt, Florence Dudley. A dashing Mexican bandit, El Malo, falls in love with a pretty cantina dancer and she urges him to reform. Dated and labored early talkie which includes the song "Argentine Moon." V: Cassette Express.

2924 Rogue River. Eagle Lion, 1950. 84 minutes Color. D: John Rawlins. SC: Louis Lantz. WITH Rory Calhoun, Peter Graves, Ellye Marshall, Frank Fenton, Ralph Sanford, George Stern, Roy Engel,

Jane Liddell, Robert Rose, Stephen Roberts, Duke York. A state policeman and his no-account cousin get involved in a robbery. Somewhat talkative but nonetheless entertaining melodrama.

2925 Roll Along, Cowboy. 20th Century-Fox/Principal, 1937. 57 minutes B/W. D: Gus Meins. SC: Dan Jarrett. WITH Smith Ballew, Cecilia Parker, Stanley Fields, Gordon (William) Elliott, Wally Albright, Ruth Robinson, Frank Milan, Monte Montague, Bud Osborne, Harry Bernard, Budd Buster, Buster Fite & His Six Saddle Tramps. A cowboy inherits a ranch and falls in love with a pretty girl but is plagued by rustlers. Smith Ballew's second series vehicle is none-too-good, being a poor remake of George O'Brien's **The Dude Ranger** (q.v.).

2926 Roll On, Texas Moon. Republic, 1946. 54 (68) minutes B/W. D: William Witney. SC: Paul Gangelin & Mauri Grashin. WITH Roy Rogers, George "Gabby" Hayes, Dale Evans, Dennis Hoey, Elisabeth Risdon, Bob Nolan & The Sons of the Pioneers, Francis McDonald, Edward Keane, Kenne Duncan, Harry Strang, Lee Shumway, Tom London, Ed Cassidy, Steve Darrell, Pierce Lyden. Roy Rogers is sent by a cattle syndicate to stop a long-time feud between sheep herders and cattlemen. Complicated plot, but fairly interesting oater with lots of action. V: Cumberland Video.

2927 Roll, Thunder, Roll. Eagle Lion, 1949. 60 minutes Color. D: Lewis D. Collins. SC: Paul Franklin. WITH Jim Bannon, Don Kay Reynolds, Nancy Gates, Marin Sais, Emmett Lynn, Glenn Strange, I. Stanford Jolley, Lee Morgan, Lane Bradford, Steve Pendleton, George Chesebro, Charles Stevens, William Fawcett, Rocky Shahan, Carol Henry, Jack O'Shea, Dorothy Latta. Bandits try to blame El Coujo, a Mexican Robin Hood, for a series of robberies but Red Ryder believes he is innocent. Okay "Red Ryder" segment.

2928 Roll Wagons Roll. Monogram, 1939. 52 minutes B/W. D: Al Herman. SC: Victor Adamson. WITH Tex Ritter, Muriel Evans, Nelson McDowell, Tom London, Nolan Willis, Steve Clark, Reed Howes, Frank Ellis, Kenne Duncan, Frank LaRue, Chick Hannon, Charles King. An army officer, trying to find out who is supplying Indians with weapons, joins a wagon train headed for Oregon. Actionful Tex Ritter film. British title: **Roll, Covered Wagon.**

2929 Rollin' Home to Texas. Monogram, 1940. 53 minutes B/W. D: Al Herman. SC: Robert Emmett (Tansey). WITH Tex Ritter, Virginia Carpenter, Arkansas Slim Andrews, Eddie Dean, Cal Shrum & His Rhythm Rangers, I. Stanford Jolley, Harry Harvey, Gene Alsace, John Rutherford, Olin Francis, Sherry Tansey, Charles Phipps, Minta Durfee. Two men are asked by a prison warden to find out how prisoners are escaping to pull area robberies. Okay Tex Ritter actioner. British title: **Ridin' Home to Texas.**

2930 Rollin' Westward. Monogram, 1939. 55 minutes B/W. D: Al Herman. SC: Fred Myton. WITH Tex Ritter, Dorothy Fay, Horace Murphy, Slim Whitaker, Herbert Corthell, Harry Harvey, Charles King, Hank Worden, Dave O'Brien, Tom London, Bob Terry, Rudy Sooter, Estrellita Novarro. A cowboy opposes the crooked activities of a land baron who tries to force small ranchers off their range. Fair Tex Ritter outing. British title: **Rollin' West.**

2931 Rolling Caravans. Columbia, 1938. 55 minutes B/W. D: Joseph Levering. SC: Nate Gatzert. WITH Jack Luden, Eleanor Stewart, Harry Woods, Slim Whitaker, Lafe McKee, Buzz Barton, Bud Osborne, Richard Cramer, Jack Rockwell, Franklyn Farnum, Cactus Mack, Tex Palmer, Sherry Tansey, Oscar Gahan, Curley Dresden, Horace Murphy, Francis Walker, Tuffy (dog). Pioneers plan to settle a new area but crooks try to stop them and a cowboy comes to their rescue. Bland oater with a bland hero (who even uses a bland ventriloquist doll) although Eleanor Stewart is a fetching heroine and Harry Woods a dastardly villain.

2932 Rolling Down the Great Divide. Producers Releasing Corporation, 1942. 62 minutes B/W. D: Peter Stewart (Sam Newfield). SC: George Milton. WITH Art Davis, Bill Boyd, Lee Powell, Wanda McKay, Glenn Strange, Karl Hackett, J. Merrill Holmes, Ted Adams, Ted Ingram, John Elliott, George Chesebro, Horace B. Carpenter, Jack Roper, Curley Dresden, Dennis Moore, Tex Palmer. A marshal is aided by two singing cowboys in trying to locate a short wave station employed by rustlers in their illegal activities. Tattered entry in the Art Davis-Bill "Cowboy Rambler" Boyd-Lee Powell series.

2933 Rolling Home. Screen Guild, 1946. 69 minutes B/W. D-SC: William Berke.

WITH Jean Parker, Russell Hayden, Pamela Blake, Raymond Hatton, Jo Ann Marlowe, Buzz Henry, James Conlin, William Farnum, Jonathan Hale, Milton Parsons, Elmo Lincoln, Jimmie Dodd. A minister who is about to lose his church befriends an old cowboy and his grandson and their lame horse. Although basically an equestrian drama this film does include scenes of Raymond Hatton riding the range and even Jimmie Dodd singing a campfire cowboy song; very pleasant.

2934 Romance of the Redwoods. Columbia, 1939. 67 minutes B/W. D: Charles Vidor. SC: Michael L. Simmons. WITH Charles Bickford, Jean Parker, Alan Bridge, Gordon Oliver, Alan Mowbray, Lloyd Hughes, Pat O'Malley. Two loggers both love the camp's pretty dishwasher but when one of them is killed under mysterious circumstances the other is blamed. Fair programmer from a Jack London story, with fine photography.

2935 Romance of the Rio Grande. Fox, 1929. 90 minutes B/W. D: Alfred Santel. SC: Marion Orth. WITH Warner Baxter, Mona Maris, Antonio Moreno, Mary Duncan, Robert Edeson, Agostino Borgato, Albert Roccardi, Solidad Jiminez, Majel Coleman, Charles Byer, Merrill McCormack. Following an attack by bandits a railroad construction supervisor is injured and taken to the home of the grandfather he has always disliked and there he meets a girl with whom he falls in love. Dated early talkie.

2936 Romance of the Rio Grande. 20th Century-Fox, 1941. 73 minutes B/W. D: Herbert I. Leeds. SC: Harold Shumate & Samuel G. Engel. WITH Cesar Romero, Patricia Morison, Ricardo Cortez, Lynne Roberts, Chris-Pin Martin, Richard Lane, Ray Bennett, Joseph McDonald. The Cisco Kid comes to the aid of a girl whose ranch is sought by two crooks. Average "Cisco Kid" series outing.

2937 Romance of the Rockies. Monogram, 1937. 53 minutes B/W. D: Robert North Bradbury. SC: Robert Emmett (Tansey). WITH Tom Keene, Beryl Wallace, Don Orlando, Bill Cody Jr., Franklyn Farnum, Earl Dwire, Russell Paul, Steve Clark, Jim Corey, Tex Palmer, Jack C. Smith, Blackie Whiteford, Frank Ellis. In cattle country a young doctor gets mixed up in a battle over water rights. Good Tom Keene vehicle; well made.

2938 Romance of the West. Producers Releasing Corporation, 1946. 58 minutes Color. D: Robert Emmett (Tansey). SC: Frances Kavanaugh. WITH Eddie Dean, Joan Barton, Emmett Lynn, Robert McKenzie, Forrest Taylor, Jerry Jerome, Stanley Price, Chief Thundercloud, Don Reynolds, Laurie Harrison, Rocky Camron, Lee Roberts, Don Williams, Jack Richardson, Matty Roubert, Forbes Murray, Jack O'Shea, Tex Cooper. An Indian agent investigates attacks by renegades and finds out that outlaws are encouraging them in order to steal Indian lands. Average Eddie Dean vehicle with some good music.

2939 Romance on the Range. Republic, 1942. 54 (63) minutes B/W. D: Joseph Kane. SC: J. Benton Cheney. WITH Roy Rogers, George "Gabby" Hayes, Linda Hayes, Bob Nolan & The Sons of the Pioneers, Sally Payne, Ed Pawley, Hal Taliaferro, Harry Woods, Glenn Strange, Roy Barcroft, Jack Kirk, Jack O'Shea, Dick Wessel, Richard Alexander. Roy Rogers is on the trail of an outlaw gang leader and finds out the man he is looking for is a highly respected citizen. Typical Roy Rogers film with the advantage of more action than music or romance.

2940 Romance Rides the Range. Spectrum, 1936. 59 minutes B/W. D: Harry Fraser. SC: Tom Gibson. WITH Fred Scott, Marion Shilling, Cliff Nazarro, Buzz Barton, Robert Kortman, Theodore Lorch, Frank Yaconelli, Bill Steele, Allen Greer. An opera star goes West and stops crooks from swindling a girl and her brother out of their money. Pleasant Fred Scott outing with the star singing "Only You," and the villains are more inept than evil.

2941 Rooster Cogburn. Universal, 1975. 107 minutes Color. D: Stuart Millar. SC: Martin Julien (Martha Hyer). WITH John Wayne, Katharine Hepburn, Anthony Zerbe, Richard Jordan, John McIntire, Paul Koslo, Strother Martin, Jack Colvin, Jon Lormer, Richard Romancito, Lane Smith, Warren Vanders, Jerry Gatlin, Mickey Gilbert, Chuck Hayward, Gary McLarty, Tommy Lee. An aging missionary teams with a hard-drinking, one-eyed lawman to find the outlaw gang who killed her father. This sequel to **True Grit** (q.v.) is not nearly as good as the original, but the teaming of John Wayne and Katharine Hepburn, plus some good action sequences, make this film good entertainment. Also called **Rooster Cogburn and the Lady.** V: Cumberland Video.

Rooster Cogburn and the Lady see Rooster Cogburn

2942 Rootin' Tootin' Rhythm. Republic, 1937. 54 (60) minutes B/W. D: Mack V. Wright. SC: Jack Natteford. WITH Gene Autry, Smiley Burnette, Armida, Monte Blue, Ann Pendleton, Hal Taliaferro, Charles King, Max Hoffman Jr., Frankie Marvin, Nina Campana, Charles Mayer, Karl Hackett, Jack Rutherford, Henry Hall, Curley Dresden, Art Davis, Al Clauser & His Oklahoma Outlaws. An outlaw gang is actually run by the head of the cattlemen's association and a singing cowboy and his partner find out about the culprit. Standard Gene Autry vehicle with more emphasis on music than action.

2943 Rose Marie. Metro-Goldwyn-Mayer, 1936. 113 minutes B/W. D: W. S. Van Dyke. SC: Frances Goodrich, Albert Hackett & Alice Duer Miller. WITH Jeanette MacDonald, Nelson Eddy, Allan Jones, Gilda Gray, Reginald Owen, James Stewart, George Regas, Robert Freig, Una O'Connor, Lucien Littlefield, Alan Mowbray, David Niven, Herman Bing, James Conlin, Dorothy Gray, Mary Anita Loos, Aileen Carlyle, Halliwell Hobbes, Paul Porcasi, Edgar Dearing, Pat West, David Clyde, Russell Hicks, Milton Owen, Rolfe Sedan, Jack Pennick, Leonard Carey, Major Sam Harris, Jim Mason, Agostino Borgato, Fred Graham, Lee Phelps. An opera singer arrives in the northwest to see her brother who has committed a murder and is being hunted by a Mountie and the girl winds up falling in love with the lawman. Classic Rudolf Friml-Otto A. Harbach-Oscar Hammerstein II operetta successfully brought to the screen as a vehicle for Jeanette MacDonald and Nelson Eddy, who sing their famous duet, "Indian Love Call." TV title: **Indian Love Call.**

2944 Rose Marie. Metro-Goldwyn-Mayer, 1954. 104 minutes Color. D: Mervyn LeRoy. SC: Ronald Miller & George Froeschel. WITH Ann Blyth, Howard Keel, Fernando Lamas, Bert Lahr, Marjorie Main, Joan Taylor, Ray Collins, Chief Yowlachie, James Logan, Turl Ravenscroft, Abel Fernandez, Billy Dix, Al Ferguson, Frank Hagney, Marshall Reed, Sheb Wooley, Dabbs Greer, John Pickard, John Damler, Sally Yarnell, Gordon Richards, Lumsden Hare, Mickey Simpson, Paul Lanzi. A Mountie tries to civilize a wild backwoods Canadian girl and ends up vying for her affections with an adven-

turer. Glossy screen adaptation of the aging operetta with the songs better than the plot.

2945 Rose of Cimarron. 20th Century-Fox, 1952. 77 minutes Color. D: Harry Keller. SC: Maurice Geraghty. WITH Mala Powers, Jack Buetel, Bill Williams, Jim Davis, Dick Curtis, Lane Bradford, William Phipps, Bob Steele, Alex Gerry, Lillian Bronson, Art Smith, Monte Blue, Argentina Brunetti, John Doucette. A young woman raised by Indians sets out to take revenge on the white outlaws who killed her foster parents. Fair actioner with a good cast.

2946 Rose of the Rancho. Paramount, 1936. 85 minutes B/W. D: Marion Gering. SC: Frank Parton, Charles Brackett, Arthur Sheekmand & Nat Perrin. WITH Gladys Swarthout, John Boles, Charles Bickford, Willie Howard, Benny Baker, Herb Williams, Grace Bradley, H. B. Warner, Charlotte Granville, Don Alvarado, Minor Watson, Louise Carter, Pedro de Cordoba, Paul Harvey, Arthur Aylesworth, Harry Woods, Russell Hopton. A government agent in Old California is assigned to capture a masked guerilla leader who in reality is the daughter of a nobleman who is working against a land grabber. Pleasant operetta more for music fans than Western addicts.

2947 Rose of the Rio Grande. Monogram, 1938. 60 minutes B/W. D: William Nigh. SC: Ralph Bettinson. WITH John Carroll, Movita, Antonio Moreno, Don Alvarado, Lina Basquette, George Cleveland, Duncan Renaldo, Gino Corrado, Martin Garralaga, Rosa Turich. A young man takes on the guise of a bandit in order to find the men who murdered his family. Mediocre costume actioner with John Carroll as a singing (dubbed) cowboy.

2948 Rose of the Yukon. Republic, 1948. 61 minutes B/W. D: George Blair. SC: Norman S. Hall. WITH Steve Brodie, Myrna Dell, William Wright, Benny Baker, Emory Parnell, Jonathan Hale, Gene Gary, Dick Elliott, Lotus Long, Eugene Signaloff. While prospecting for gold in the Yukon, two men are framed on a murder charge when they find a rich pitchblend deposit. Fair Republic action melodrama.

2949 Rough Night in Jericho. Universal, 1967. 104 minutes Color. D: Arnold Laven. SC: Sidney Boehm & Marvin H. Albert. WITH Dean Martin, Jean Simmons, George Peppard, John McIntire, Slim Pickens,

Don Galloway, Brad Weston, Richard O'Brien, Carol Anderson, John Napier. A former lawman has taken control of a small town and proves to be ruthless and is forced into a showdown by a female stage line owner. Very violent oater with only average entertainment value.

2950 Rough Riders of Cheyenne. Republic, 1945. 56 minutes B/W. D: Thomas Carr. SC: Elizabeth Beecher. WITH Sunset Carson, Peggy Stewart, Mira McKinney, Monte Hale, Wade Crosby, Michael Sloane, Kenne Duncan, Tom London, Eddy Waller, Jack O'Shea, Robert Wilke, Tex Terry, Jack Rockwell, Rex Lease, Hank Bell, Henry Wills, Cactus Mack, Artie Ortego, Jack Luden. A mysterious figure perpetuates a feud between two families so they will eventually wipe each other out so he can grab their ranches for use in a cattle rustling scheme. Fairly good Sunset Carson vehicle with a good script.

2951 Rough Riders of Durango. Republic, 1950. 60 minutes B/W. D: Fred C. Brannon. SC: M. Coates Webster. WITH Allan Lane, Aline Towne, Walter Baldwin, Steve Darrell, Ross Ford, Denver Pyle, Stuart Randall, Tom London, Hal Price, Russ Whiteman, Dale Van Sickel, Bob Burns. A special courier comes to the rescue when outlaws hijack ranchers' grain shipments and money. Some good fights, but production values were declining in this Allan "Rocky" Lane entry, which also utilized lots of stock footage.

2952 Rough Riders Roundup. Republic, 1939. 54 (58) minutes B/W. D: Joseph Kane. SC: Jack Natteford. WITH Roy Rogers, Mary Hart, Raymond Hatton, Eddie Acuff, Edward Pawley, Dorothy Sebastian, George Meeker, Guy Usher, Duncan Renaldo, George Chesebro, Glenn Strange, Jack Rockwell, Jack Kirk, Hank Bell, Dorothy Christy, Fred Kelsey, Eddy Waller, John Merton, George (Montgomery) Letz, Frank Ellis, Frank McCarroll, Dan White. A band of ex-Rough Riders regroup to combat a gang involved in a gold shipment robbery. Plenty of action and a good story make this a nice Roy Rogers entry.

2953 Rough Ridin' Justice. Columbia, 1945. 58 minutes B/W. D: Derwin Abrahams. SC: Elizabeth Beecher. WITH Charles Starrett, Dub Taylor, Betty Jane Graham, Jimmy Wakely & His Oklahoma Cowboys, Wheeler Oakman, Jack Ingram, Forrest Taylor, Jack Rockwell,

Edmund Cobb, Dan White, Robert Kortman, George Chesebro, Robert Ross. The man who is leading a gang harassing cattlemen is hired by the ranchers when they are opposed by an outlaw gang. Sturdy Charles Starrett vehicle; well done.

2954 Rough Riding Ranger. Superior, 1935. 57 minutes B/W. D: Elmer Clifton. SC: Elmer Clifton & George M. Merrick. WITH Rex Lease, Janet Chandler, Bobby Nelson, Yakima Canutt, Mabel Strickland, David Horsley, George Chesebro, William Desmond, Robert Walker, Carl Mathews, Artie Ortego, Allen Greer, George Morrell, Milburn Morante, Johnny Luther's Cowboy Band. A cowboy tries to help a family being bothered by a mysterious letter writer and outlaw attacks. Low grade Rex Lease film.

2955 Rough Riding Rhythm. Ambassador, 1937. 57 minutes B/W. D: J. P. McGowan. SC: Arthur Everett. WITH Kermit Maynard, Beryl Wallace, Ralph Peters, Olin Francis, Betty Mack, Curley Dresden, Cliff Parkinson, Dave O'Brien, Newt Kirby, J. P. McGowan. The leader of a gang of crooks accidentally kills his wife in an argument and a cowboy and his pal, the latter the brother of the murdered woman, go after the man who has also shot a sheriff in a recent holdup. Sub-standard effort in Kermit Maynard's Ambassador series.

2956 Rough Romance. Fox, 1930. 55 minutes B/W. D: A. F. Erickson. SC: Elliott Lester & Donald Davis. WITH George O'Brien, Helen Chandler, Antonio Moreno, Roy Stewart, Harry Cording, David Hartford, Eddie Borden, Noel Francis, Frank Lanning, John Wayne. In the Oregon timber country a young lumberjack fights, for the girl he loves, with a notorious outlaw. Poorly done George O'Brien early talkie interspersed with musical interludes.

2957 The Rough, Tough West. Columbia, 1952. 54 minutes B/W. D: Ray Nazarro. SC: Barry Shipman. WITH Charles Starrett, Smiley Burnette, Jack (Jock) Mahoney, Carolina Cotton, Pee Wee King & His Band, Marshall Reed, Fred F. Sears, Bert Arnold, Tommy Ivo, Boyd "Red" Morgan, Valerie Fisher, Tommy Kingston. When his pal, the local saloon owner, makes a man the town's sheriff he begins to suspect his friend may be behind a scheme to cheat miners out of their property. Fast moving and actionful "Durango Kid" film.

2958 Roughshod. RKO Radio, 1949. 88 minutes B/W. D: Mark Robson. SC: Geoffrey Homes & Hugo Butler. WITH Robert Sterling, Gloria Grahame, Claude Jarman Jr., John Ireland, Jeff Donnell, Myrna Dell, Martha Hyer, George Cooper, Jeff Corey, Sara Haden, James Bell, Sean McClory, Robert B. Williams, Steve Savage, Ed Cassidy. A young farmer, in love with a saloon girl, fears that three outlaws on the run from the law are after him. Pretty good action melodrama.

2959 The Rounders. Metro-Goldwyn-Mayer, 1965. 85 minutes Color. D-SC: Burt Kennedy. WITH Glenn Ford, Henry Fonda, Sue Anne Langdon, Hope Holiday, Chill Wills, Edgar Buchanan, Kathleen Freeman, Joan Freeman, Denver Pyle, Barton MacLane, Doodles Weaver, Allegra Varron. Two aging cowboys try to tame a wild horse and two equally wild women. Very pleasant genre action comedy.

2960 Rounding Up the Law. Aywon, 1922. 50 minutes B/W. D: Charles R. Seeling. SC: W. H. Allen. WITH Guinn Williams, Russell Gordon, Patricia Palmer, Chet Ryan, William McCall. A cowboy wins a sheriff's ranch in a poker game and the lawman and his crooked pal plan to run the cowpoke out of the country. Low budget Guinn "Big Boy" Williams silent offering; it should please his fans.

2961 The Roundup. Paramount, 1941. 90 minutes B/W. D: Lesley Selander. SC: Harold Shumate. WITH Richard Dix, Patricia Morison, Preston Foster, Don Wilson, Ruth Donnelly, Betty Brewer, Douglass Dumbrille, Jerome Cowan, William Haade, Morris Ankrum, Clara Kimball Young, Dick Curtis, Weldon Heyburn, Lane Chandler, Lee "Lasses" White, The King's Men. A rancher plans to wed the girl he loves only to find her ex-lover, who she thought dead, has returned on their wedding day. Nonetoo-actionful romantic oater, filmed originally in 1920 with Fatty Arbuckle.

2962 Roundup Time in Texas. Republic, 1937. 54 (58) minutes B/W. D: Joseph Kane. SC: Oliver Drake. WITH Gene Autry, Smiley Burnette, Maxine Doyle, LeRoy Mason, Buddy Williams, Earle Hodgins, Dick Wessell, Cornie Anderson, Frankie Marvin, Ken Cooper, Elmer Fain, Al Ferguson, Slim Whitaker, Al Knight, Carleton Young, Jack C. Smith, Jim Corey, Jack Kirk, George Morrell, The Cabin Kids. Two cowboys take a horse herd to South Africa and discover a mine and a smuggling operation. Offbeat plotline adds some color to this Gene Autry musical vehicle.

2963 Rovin' Tumbleweeds. Republic, 1939. 64 minutes B/W. D: George Sherman. SC: Betty Burbridge, Dorrell McGowan & Stuart McGowan. WITH Gene Autry, Smiley Burnette, Mary Carlisle, Douglass Dumbrille, Pals of the Golden West, William Farnum, Lee "Lasses" White, Ralph Peters, Victor Potel, Jack Ingram, Sammy McKim, Gordon Hart, Horace Murphy, Fred "Snowflake" Toones, Forrest Taylor, Reginald Barlow, Eddie Kane, Guy Usher, David Sharpe, Jack Kirk, Bob Burns, Art Mix, Horace Carpenter, Frank Ellis, Fred Burns, Ed Cassidy, Tom Chatterton, Crauford Kent, Maurice Costello, Charles K. French, Lee Shumway, Bud Osborne, Harry Semels, Chuck Morrison, Rose Plummer, Nora Lou Martin, Hal Taliaferro. Corrupt politicians fail to pass a flood control bill and a flood causes great damage to farm land and singer Gene Autry is elected to Congress in order to get a flood bill passed. A very good Gene Autry film which has Gene getting married at the finale; film introduced song "Back in the Saddle Again" and also contains a takeoff on the popular "Lum 'n Abner" radio program. Also called **Washington Cowboy.**

2964 Roy Colt and Winchester Jack. Libert, 1975. 90 minutes Color. D: Mario Bava. SC: Di Nardo & Agrin. WITH Brett Halsey, Marilu Tolo, Charles Southwood, Teodoro Corra. Two friends battle for the leadership of their outlaw gang and when one wins the other becomes a lawman and when the gang teams with a renegade looking for a valuable treasure map the sheriff must stop them. Another violent spaghetti oater with good direction by the stylish Mario Bava. Originally issued in Italy in 1971 by P.A.C./Tigielle 33.

2965 The Royal Mounted Patrol. Columbia, 1941. 59 minutes B/W. D: Lambert Hillyer. SC: Winston Miller. WITH Charles Starrett, Russell Hayden, Wanda McKay, Donald Curtis, Lloyd Bridges, Kermit Maynard, Evan Thomas, Ted Adams, Harrison Greene, Ted Mapes, George Morrell. Two Mounties both like the same girl, a teacher at a remote post and the sister of a crooked lumber camp boss. The initial entry in the series is a likable effort.

2966 The Royal Mounted Rides Again. Universal, 1945. 13 Chapters B/W. D:

Ray Taylor & Lewis D. Collins. SC: Joseph O'Donnell & Harold C. Wire. WITH Bill Kennedy, George Dolenz, Daun Kennedy, Paul E. Burns, Milburn Stone, Robert Armstrong, Danny Morton, Addison Richards, Tom Fadden, Joseph Haworth, Helen Bennett, Joseph Crehan, Selmer Jackson, Daral Hudson, George Lloyd, George Eldredge. A Mountie is assigned to find out who murdered a mill owner and soon finds out his mining operator father is the chief suspect. Fairly entertaining Universal serial.

2967 The Royal Rider. First National, 1929. 67 minutes B/W. D: Harry Joe Brown. SC: Nate Gatzert. WITH Ken Maynard, Olive Hasbrouck, Philippe De Lacey, Theodore Lorch, Joseph Burke, Harry Semels, William Franey, Frank Rice, Bobby Dunn, Johnny Sinclair, Ben Corbett. Members of a Wild West show become palace guards for a Balkan boy king and aid him in putting down a palace revolt. Ken Maynard silent (one version was issued with music and sound effects) with a Grustarkian background finds the cowboy star a bit out of place although the action is plentiful.

2968 Ruggles of Red Gap. Paramount, 1935. 90 minutes B/W. D: Leo McCarey, SC: Walter De Leon, Harlan Thomson & Humphrey Pearson. WITH Charles Laughton, Charles Ruggles, Mary Boland, ZaSu Pitts, Roland Young, Leila Hyams, Maude Eburne, Lucien Littlefield, Leota Lorraine, James Burke, Dell Henderson, Baby Ricardo Lord Cezon, Brenda Fowler, Augusta Anderson, Sarah Edwards, Clarence H. Wilson, Rafael Storm, George Burton, Victor Potel, Frank Rice, William J. Welsh, Lee Kohlmar, Harry Bernard, Alice Ardell, Rolfe Sedan, Jack Norton, Willie Fung, Libby Taylor, Armand Kaliz, Henry Roquemore, Heinie Conklin, Ed Le Saint, Charles Fallon, Isabelle La Mal, Ernie Adams, Frank O'Connor, Jim Welch. An uncouth Western family wins a debonair British butler in a poker game and he makes a big change in their lives. Very pleasant comedy. First produced in the silent era by Essanay in 1918 and Paramount in 1923 and remade in 1950 as **Fancy Pants** (q.v.).

The Rumpo Kid see **Carry On Cowboy**

2969 Run, Cougar, Run. Buena Vista, 1973. 100 minutes Color. D: Jerome Courtland. WITH Stuart Whitman, Alfonso Arau, Harry Carey Jr., Douglas V. Fowley, Frank Aletter, Lonny Chapman. An easy-going sheep herder opposes a professional hunter out to kill a cougar. Fine Walt Disney production originally telecast on Disney's NBC-TV program.

2970 Run for Cover. Paramount, 1955. 92 minutes Color. D: Nicholas Ray. SC: Winston Miller. WITH James Cagney, John Derek, Viveca Lindfors, Jean Hersholt, Grant Withers, Jack Lambert, Ernest Borgnine, Irving Bacon, Trevor Bardette, Ray Teal, John Miljan, Denver Pyle, Emerson Tracey, Gus Schilling, Phil Chambers, Harold Kennedy, Joe Hayworth, Henry Wills. A former outlaw becomes the sheriff of a small town, much to the chagrin of his young friend. Rather interesting psychological oater from action producers William H. Pine and William C. Thomas.

2971 Run for the Hills. Realart, 1953. 72 minutes B/W. D: Lew Landers. SC: Leonard Neubrauer. WITH Sonny Tufts, Barbara Payton, John Harmon, Mauritz Hugo, Vici Raaf, Jack Wrightson, Paul Maxey, John Hamilton, Byron Foulger, Charles Victor, William Fawcett, Ray Parsons, Jean Wills, Richard Benedict, Michael Fox. An insurance company actuary becomes worried about an H-bomb attack and he and his wife take refuge in a cave. A silly script and unfunny situations make this film a real loser.

2972 Run Home Slow. Emerson, 1965. 66 minutes B/W. D: Tim Sullivan. WITH Mercedes McCambridge, Linda Gaye Scott, Allen Richards, Gary Kent. To avenge her father's hanging, a woman organizes her family into a brutal outlaw gang. Obscure feature, with music score by Frank Zappa, which will not appeal to the average genre viewer.

2973 Run of the Arrow. RKO Radio/ Universal-International, 1957. 85 minutes Color. D-SC: Samuel Fuller. WITH Rod Steiger, Sarita Montiel, Brian Keith, Ralph Meeker, Jay C. Flippen, Charles Bronson, Tim McCoy, Olive Carey, H. M. Wynant, Neyle Morrow, Frank De Kova, Stuart Randall, Frank Warner, Billy Miller, Chuck Hayward, Chuck Roberson, Carleton Young, Don Orlando, Bill White Jr., Frank Baker, Emile Avery, Angie Dickinson (voice). An embittered Confederate soldier joins the Sioux Indians in their fight with the U. S. government. Rather strange pyschological Western with solid performances to give it strength.

Run or Burn see **White-Water Sam**

2974 Run, Simon, Run. ABC-TV, 1970. 74 minutes Color. D: George McGowan. SC: Lionel E. Siegel. WITH Burt Reynolds, Inger Stevens, Royal Dano, James Best, Rodolfo Acosta, Don Dubbins, Joyce Jameson, Barney Phillips, Herman Budin, Eddie Little Sky, Marsha Moore, Ken Lynch, Martin G. Soto, Rosemary Eliot. Falsely sent to prison, an Indian returns home after a decade to find the man who murdered his mother. Fairly good melodrama made for television.

2975 Run to the High Country. Sun International, 1972. 97 minutes Color. D-SC: Keith Larsen. WITH Erik Larsen, Keith Larsen, Karen Steele, Alvin Redmond, Rodney Burt. A young boy tries to protect wildlife from hunters. Filmed on location in Utah, this feature is short on plot but heavy on scenery.

2976 The Runaway Barge. NBC-TV, 1975. 75 minutes Color. D: Boris Sagal. SC: Stanford Whitmore. WITH Bo Hopkins, Tim Matheson, Jim Davis, Nick Nolte, Devon Ericson, Christina Hart, James Best, Lucille Henson, Clifton James, Dom Plumley, Beau Gibson, Bill Rowley. Three boatmen try to make a living on a modern-day Mississippi riverboat and find themselves involved in a hijacking and kidnapping. Okay action drama made for the small screen.

2977 Running Target. United Artists, 1956. 83 minutes Color. D: Marvin R. Weinstein. SC: Marvin R. Weinstein, Jack Couffer & Conrad Hall. WITH Arthur Franz, Doris Dowling, Richard Reeves, Myron Healey, James Parnell, Charles Delaney, Gene Roth, James Anderson, Frank Richards. Four escaped convicts head into the Colorado Rockies and are pursued by a sheriff and his posse. Standard action yarn with the plot twist of having the lawman opposed to killing.

2978 Running Wild. Golden Circle, 1973. 104 minutes Color. D-SC: Robert McChaon. WITH Lloyd Bridges, Dina Merrill, Gilbert Roland, Pat Hingle, Morgan Woodward, R. G. Armstrong, Lonny Chapman, Fred Betts, Slavio Martinez. While in Colorado doing a photo story, a woman journalist becomes alarmed at the treatment given to wild horses. Sturdy and entertaining drama, reissued in 1976 by Dimension Pictures as **Deliver Us from Evil.**

2979 The Rustlers. RKO Radio, 1949. 61 minutes B/W. D: Lesley Selander. SC: Jack Natteford & Luci Ward. WITH Tim Holt, Richard Martin, Martha Hyer, Lois Andrews, Steve Brodie, Francis McDonald, Harry Shannon, Addison Richards, Frank Fenton, Robert Bray, Don Haggerty, Monte Montague, Stanley Blystone, Pat Patterson, George Ross. Two cowpokes are framed on charges of theft and murder and set out to find the real culprits. Another entertaining film in Tim Holt's RKO series.

2980 Rustlers' Hideout. Producers Releasing Corporation, 1944. 60 minutes B/W. D: Sam Newfield. SC: Joseph O'Donnell. WITH Buster Crabbe, Al St. John, Patti McCarty, Charles King, John Merton, Lane Chandler, Terry Frost, Hal Price, Al Ferguson, Frank McCarroll, Ed Cassidy, Bud Osborne, Steve Clark, John Cason, Lane Chandler. Billy Carson and Fuzzy Q. Jones lead a large Wyoming cattle herd to market and come up against outlaws wanting to take the herd to start their own cattle business. A good storyline and some nice camera work make this a better than average entry in the PRC "Billy Carson" series.

Rustler's Hideout (1946) see **Rustler's Roundup**

2981 Rustlers of Devil's Canyon. Republic, 1947. 54 (58) minutes B/W. D: R. G. Springsteen. SC: Earle Snell. WITH Allan "Rocky" Lane, Peggy Stewart, Bobby Blake, Martha Wentworth, Arthur Space, Emmett Lynn, Roy Barcroft, Tom London, Harry Carr, Pierce Lyden, Forrest Taylor, Bob Burns. Red Ryder tries to stop hostilities between ranchers and homesteaders in a range war arranged by rustlers. Average "Red Ryder" series film.

2982 Rustlers of Red Dog. Universal, 1935. 12 Chapters B/W. D: Louis Friedlancer (Lew Landers). SC: George H. Plympton, Basil Dickey, Ella O'Neill, Nate Gatzert & Vin Moore. WITH Johnny Mack Brown, Joyce Compton, Walter Miller, Raymond Hatton, Harry Woods, Frederick MacKaye, Charles K. French, Lafe McKee, William Desmond, J. P. McGowan, Edmund Cobb, Bud Osborne, Monte Montague, Jim Thorpe, Chief Thundercloud, Wally Wales, Slim Whitaker, Art Mix, Bill Patton, Cliff Lyons, Tex Cooper, Ben Corbett, Hank Bell, Artie Ortego, Ann D'Arcy, Fritzi Burnette, Grace Cunard. A trio of cowboys sets out to protect a wagon train from ruthless outlaws and marauding Indians. Actionful and entertaining Johnny Mack Brown cliffhanger; his second serial outing.

2983 Rustlers of the Badlands. Columbia, 1945. 55 minutes B/W. D: Derwin Abrahams. SC: J. Benton Cheney. WITH Charles Starrett, Tex Harding, Dub Taylor, Sally Bliss, George Eldredge, Edward Howard, Ray Bennett, Al Trace & His Silly Symphonists, Ted Mapes, Karl Hackett, Bud Nelson, Frank McCarroll, Carl Sepulveda, Steve Clark, Ted French, Frank LaRue, Bud Osborne, Edmund Cobb, Nolan Leary, Frank Ellis, Jack Ingram. Three Army scouts are assigned to find out who murdered a lieutenant and they come across a rash of cattle rustling which seems tied to the killing. Standard "Durango Kid" offering.

2984 Rustlers' Paradise. Ajax, 1935. 61 minutes B/W. D: Harry Fraser. SC: Weston Edwards. WITH Harry Carey, Gertrude Messinger, Edmund Cobb, Carmen Bailey, Theodore Lorch, Slim Whitaker, Roger Williams, Chuck Morrison, Allen Greer, Chief Thundercloud. A man searches for his wife and daughter who were kidnapped by an outlaw years before and he poses as a crook in order to infiltrate a gang whose leader he suspects of the kidnapping. Pretty good Harry Carey vehicle.

2985 Rustlers' Rhapsody. Paramount, 1985. 88 minutes Color. D-SC: Hugh Wilson. WITH Tom Berenger, G. W. Bailey, Marilu Henner, Andy Griffith, Fernando Rey, Sela Ward, Patrick Wayne, Brant Van Hoffman, Christopher Malcolm, Jim Carter, Billy J. Mitchell. A singing cowboy and his pal wander through the Old West and in a small town aid sheepherders against a corrupt cattle baron. Pleasant satire on the musical Westerns of yore.

2986 Rustlers' Roundup. Universal, 1933. 56 minutes B/W. D: Henry MacRae. SC: Frank Clark & Jack Cunningham. WITH Tom Mix, Dianne Sinclair, Noah Beery Jr., Douglass Dumbrille, Roy Stewart, William Desmond, Gilbert "Pee Wee" Holmes, Bud Osborne, Frank Lackteen, William Wanger, Nelson McDowell, Walter Brennan. A rancher tries to help a young man and his sister when an outlaw gang is after their land because it contains an underground spring they want to use for their rustling operation. Tom Mix's final series feature is not up to the others in his Universal series, although it is still above average.

2987 Rustler's Roundup. Universal, 1946. 57 minutes B/W. D: Wallace Fox. SC:

Jack Natteford. WITH Kirby Grant, Jane Adams, Fuzzy Knight, Edmund Cobb, Ethan Laidlaw, Earle Hodgins, Charles Miller, Mauritz Hugo, Eddy Waller, Roy Brent, Frank Marlo, Hank Bell, Rex Lease, Budd Buster, Steve Clark, Bud Osborne, Jack Curtis, George Morrell, Ray Spiker, Alfred Wagstaff. A cowboy and his pals set out to round up a gang of rustlers plaguing area ranchers. Nicely paced and actionful Kirby Grant vehicle. TV title: **Rustler's Hideout.**

2988 Rustler's Valley. Paramount, 1937. 54 (60) minutes B/W. D: Nate Watt. SC: Harry O. Hoyt. WITH William Boyd, George ("Gabby") Hayes, Russell Hayden, John St. Polis, Lee Colt (Lee J. Cobb), Stephen Morris (Morris Ankrum), Muriel Evans, Ted Adams, Al Ferguson, John Beach, Oscar Apfel, Bernadine Hayes. Hoppy aids pal Lucky when he is accused of a bank robbery which was really masterminded by a crooked lawyer who is out to get a ranch from his fiancée and her father. A bit slow for "Hopalong Cassidy" but the scenery is nice and the finale exciting. V: Video Connection.

2989 Rusty Rides Alone. Columbia, 1933. 58 minutes B/W. D: D. Ross Lederman. SC: Robert Quigley. WITH Tim McCoy, Barbara Weeks, Dorothy Burgess, Wheeler Oakman, Edmund Cobb, Ed Burns, Rockcliffe Fellows, Clarence Gildert, Silver King (dog). A cowboy opposes the crooked activities of a sheepman who wants to set up an empire for himself by driving all the cattle ranchers from their ranges. A weak script hurts this series effort.

2990 The Ruthless Four. Metro-Goldwyn-Mayer, 1968. 97 minutes Color. D: Giorgio Capitani. SC: Fernando Di Leo. WITH Van Heflin, Gilbert Roland, George Hilton, Klaus Kinski, Sarah Ross. An old prospector teams with his grandson and a friend, and join an old comrade, in treking to the man's rich gold claim but they fall out among themselves over the gold. Pretty good Spanish-Italian Western which will appeal to the two stars' fans. Also called **Each Man for Himself** and **Sam Cooper's Gold.** Italian title: **Ognuno per se** (Each One for Himself).

2991 Sabata. United Artists, 1970. 106 minutes Color. D: Gianfranco Parolini

The Sacketts 366

(Frank Kramer). SC: Gianfranco Parolini (Frank Kramer) & Renato Izzo. WITH Lee Van Cleef, William Berger, Pedro Sanchez, Nick Jordan, Franco Ressel, Linda Veras, Antonio Gradoli, Robert Hundar, Gianni Rizzo, Spanny Convery, Marco Zuanelli, John Bartha. Three crooked businessmen hire a gunman to steal a safe for them and then try to double-cross him when he demands a higher payment. Lee Van Cleef is very good in the title role of this ultra-violent European oater which resulted in two sequels: **Adios, Sabata** and **The Return of Sabata** (qq.v.). Released in Italy in 1969 as ...**Ehi, Amico, C'e Sabata...Hai Chiuso!** (Hey, Friend, Here's Sabata... You're Finished).

2992 The Sacketts. NBC-TV, 1979. 200 minutes Color. D: Robert Totten. SC: Jim Byrnes. WITH Sam Elliott, Tom Sellack, Jeff Osterhage, Glenn Ford, Ben Johnson, Gilbert Roland, John Vernon, Ruth Roman, Jack Elam, Gene Evans, L. Q. Jones, Paul Kolso, Mercedes McCambridge, Slim Pickens, Pat Buttram, James Gammon, Buck Taylor, Lee DeBroux, Marcy Hanson, Ana Alicia, Wendy Rastatter, Shug Fisher, Frank Ramirez, Ramon Chavez, Don Collier, Billy Cardi, Rusty Lane. After the Civil War a trio of brothers try to bring law and order to the New Mexico Territory after avenging a family murder. Glossy TV adaptation of Louis L'Amour's works; entertaining for the author's followers.

2993 Sacred Ground. Pacific-International, 1983. 100 minutes Color. D-SC: Charles B. Pierce. WITH Tim McIntire, Jack Elam, L. Q. Jones, Mindi Miller, Serene Hedin, Eloy Phil Casados. In the 1860s trouble results when a frontiersman and his Indian wife settle in sacred Paiute territory with their new baby. Fairly entertaining drama. V: CBS/Fox.

2994 The Sad Horse. 20th Century-Fox, 1959. 81 minutes Color. D: James B. Clark. SC: Charles Hoffman. WITH David Ladd, Chill Wills, Rex Reason, Patrice Wymore, Gregg Palmer. A lonely little boy develops a close relationship with a racehorse. Pleasant and entertaining family fare.

2995 Saddle Aces. Resolute, 1935. 56 minutes B/W. D: Harry Fraser. SC: Harry C. (Fraser) Crist. WITH Rex Bell, Ruth Mix, Buzz Barton, Stanley Blystone, Earl Dwire, Chuck Morrison, Mary MacLaren, John Elliott, Roger Williams,

Chief Thundercloud, Allen Greer, Bud Osborne. Two men falsely convicted of crimes they did not commit escape from a prison train and aid a girl whose ranch is sought by the crook really responsible for the crimes for which they were accused. Last of the Rex Bell-Ruth Mix-Buzz Barton vehicles; cheaply made and it shows.

2996 The Saddle Buster. RKO Radio, 1932. 60 minutes B/W. D: Fred Allen. SC: Oliver Drake. WITH Tom Keene, Helen Forest, Charles Quigley, Marie Quillan, Ben Corbett, Fred Burns, Richard Carlyle, Robert Frazer, Harry Bowen, Al Taylor, Slim Whitaker. A Montana cowboy leaves his home to join a rodeo and he becomes a big success but is almost thwarted due to the jealousy of another performer. Very fine and well made Tom Keene vehicle; quite exciting.

2997 Saddle Leather Law. Columbia, 1944. 55 minutes B/W. D: Benjamin Kline. SC: Elizabeth Beecher. WITH Charles Starrett, Dub Taylor, Vi Athens, Lloyd Bridges, Jimmy Wakely & His Saddle Pals, Salty Holmes, Reed Howes, Robert Kortman, Frank LaRue, Ted French, Ed Cassidy, Steve Clark, Frank O'Connor, Budd Buster, Franklyn Farnum, Nolan Leary. When a rancher is killed two cowboys are blamed and they find out a girl, working for a crooked syndicate after the man's spread for a dude ranch, is the culprit. Pretty fair entry in Charles Starrett's series with the leading lady turning out to be the villain.

2998 Saddle Legion. RKO Radio, 1951. 61 minutes B/W. D: Lesley Selander. SC: Ed Earl Repp. WITH Tim Holt, Richard Martin, Dorothy Malone, Robert Livingston, James Bush, Mauritz Hugo, Cliff Clark, George J. Lewis, Robert Wilke, Stanley Andrews. Crooks try to obtain cattle by falsely making the herd appear to be diseased but two cowpokes see through the ruse. Well done entry in Tim Holt's RKO series.

2999 Saddle Mountain Roundup. Monogram, 1941. 61 minutes B/W. D: S. Roy Luby. SC: Earle Snell & John Vlahos. WITH Ray Corrigan, John King, Max Terhune, Jack Mulhall, Lita Conway, Willie Fung, John Elliott, George Chesebro, Jack Holmes, Harold Goodwin, Carl Mathews, Al Ferguson, Steve Clark, Slim Whitaker, Tex Palmer. A crusty rancher hires the Range Busters to protect him from death threats and after he is murdered they

Saddle Pals

try to find his killer. Dandy entry in "The Range Busters" series, enhanced by its mystery element.

3000 Saddle Pals. Republic, 1947. 54 (72) minutes B/W. D: Lesley Selander. SC: Bob Williams & Jerry Sackheim. WITH Gene Autry, Lynne Roberts, Sterling Holloway, Irving Bacon, Damian O'Flynn, The Cass County Boys, Charles Arnt, Jean Van, Tom London, Charles Williams, Francis McDonald, Edward Gargan, Carl Sepulveda, George Chandler, LeRoy Mason, Paul E. Burns, Joel Friedkin, Larry Steers, Nolan Leary, Edward Keane, Maurice Cass, Minerva Urecal, Sam Ash, Frank O'Connor, Neal Hart, Ed Piel Sr., Bob Burns, Bob Yrigoyen. Gene Autry comes to the aid of area ranchers whose rents have been suddenly raised by the local land company. Tired Gene Autry film with little action and limp comedy.

3001 Saddle Serenade. Monogram, 1945. 60 minutes B/W. D: Oliver Drake. SC: Frances Kavanaugh. WITH Jimmy Wakely, Lee "Lasses" White, John James, Nancy Brinckman, Foy Willing & The Riders of the Purple Sage, Jack Ingram, Claire James, Pat Gleason, Gay Deslys, Roy Butler, Alan Foster, Elmer Napier, Frank McCarroll, Dee Cooper, Jack Hendricks, Jack Spear, Carl Mathews. Two cowpokes go to work at a dude ranch which is actually a front for eastern jewel thieves. Tepid Jimmy Wakely vehicle with some good musical interludes.

3002 Saddle the Wind. Metro-Goldwyn-Mayer, 1958. 84 minutes Color. D: Robert Parrish. SC: Thomas Thompson. WITH Robert Taylor, Julie London, John Cassavetes, Donald Crisp, Charles McGraw, Royal Dano, Richard Erdman, Douglas Spencer, Ray Teal. A one-time gunman settles down to a peaceful life as a rancher but he is soon faced with a showdown with his gunslinger younger brother. Well done and quite entertaining; Robert Taylor is especially good as the rancher.

3003 Saddle Tramp. Universal-International, 1950. 76 minutes Color. D: Hugo Fregonese. SC: Harold Shumate. WITH Joel McCrea, Wanda Hendrix, John Russell, John McIntire, Jeannette Nolan, Russell Simpson, Ed Begley, Jimmy Hunt, Orley Lindgren, Gordon Gebert, Gregory Moffett, Antonio Moreno, John Ridgely, Walter Coy, Joaquin Garay, Peter Leeds, Michael Steele, Paul Picerni. A saddle tramp becomes the guardian of four orphans

and when he gets a job as a ranch hand he becomes involved in lots of trouble. Very pleasant and good viewing Joel McCrea vehicle.

3004 Saddlemates. Republic, 1941. 56 minutes B/W. D: Lester Orlebeck. SC: Albert DeMond & Herbert Dalmas. WITH Robert Livingston, Bob Steele, Rufe Davis, Gale Storm, Forbes Murray, Cornelius Keefe, Peter George Lynn, Marin Sais, Glenn Strange, Iron Eyes Cody, Chief Yowlachie, Henry Wills, Matty Faust, Ellen Lowe. The Three Mesquiteers aid the army in trying to control a band of hostile Indians led by a half-breed. Fair entry in the popular Republic series. V: Cumberland Video.

3005 Saddles and Sagebrush. Columbia, 1943. 57 minutes B/W. D: William Berke. SC: Ed Earl Repp. WITH Russell Hayden, Dub Taylor, Bob Wills & The Texas Playboys, Ann Savage, William Wright, Frank LaRue, Wheeler Oakman, Edmund Cobb, Jack Ingram, Joe McGuinn, Ray Jones, Art Mix, Blackie Whiteford, Ben Corbett, Bob Burns. A cowboy and his pals come to the aid of a rancher and his daughter who are being victimized by crooks. Pretty sturdy Russell Hayden vehicle.

3006 Saga of Death Valley. Republic, 1939. 54 (58) minutes B/W. D: Joseph Kane. SC: Karen DeWolf & Stuart Anthony. WITH Roy Rogers, George "Gabby" Hayes, Donald (Don "Red") Barry, Doris Day, Frank M. Thomas, Jack Ingram, Hal Taliaferro, Lew Kelly, Fern Emmett, Tommy Baker, Buzz Buckley, Horace Murphy, Lane Chandler, Fred Burns, The Jimmy Wakely Trio (Jimmy Wakely, Johnny Bond, Dick Rinehart), Ed Brady, Pasquel Perry, Cactus Mack, Art Dillard, Horace B. Carpenter, Hooper Atchley, Frankie Marvin. A young man returns to the ranch where his father was murdered to take revenge on his killer and he finds the man's chief henchman is actually his younger brother. Very good Roy Rogers vehicle; well worth viewing.

3007 The Saga of Hemp Brown. Universal-International, 1959. 80 minutes Color. D: Richard Carlson. SC: Bob Williams. WITH Rory Calhoun, Beverly Garland, John Larch, Russell Johnson, Fortunio Bonanova, Marjorie Stapp, Morris Ankrum, Yvette Vickers, Charles Boaz, Allan Lane, Victor Sen Yung, Trevor Bardette, Addison Richards, Francis McDonald, Theodore Newton. Framed on a payroll robbery charge, a soldier is dismissed from the army and he sets out to find those who actually committed the crime. Average melodrama.

Saga of the West see **When a Man's a Man**

3008 The Sagebrush Family Trails West. Producers Distribution Corporation, 1940. 62 minutes B/W. D: Peter Stewart (Sam Newfield). SC: William Lively. WITH Bobby Clark, Earle Hodgins, Nina Guilbert, Joyce Bryant, Minerva Urecal, Archie Hall, Kenneth (Kenne) Duncan, Forrest Taylor, Carl Mathews, Wally West, Byron Vance, Augie Gomez. The young son of a kidnapped inventor comes to his rescue when a gang is after the man's secret formula. Shoddy effort which mercifully did not make it as a series; the star, Bobby Clark, is not the famous comic, but a teenage world's junior champion cowboy.

3009 Sagebrush Law. RKO Radio, 1943. 56 minutes B/W. D: Sam Nelson. SC: Bennett Cohen. WITH Tim Holt, Joan Barclay, Cliff Edwards, John Elliott, Ed Cassidy, Karl Hackett, Roy Barcroft, Ernie Adams, John Merton, Bud McTaggart, Edmund Cobb, Otto Hoffman, Cactus Mack Ben Corbett, Frank McCarroll, Bob McKenzie, Dick Rush. When his father, the town banker, is falsely accused of embezzlement and is murdered, his son wants to prove his innocence and find his killers. A fine script and cast make this Tim Holt vehicle a good one.

3010 Sagebrush Trail. Monogram, 1933. 55 minutes B/W. D: Armand L. Schaefer. SC: Lindsley Parsons. WITH John Wayne, Nancy Schubert, Lane Chandler, Yakima Canutt, Henry Hall, Wally Wales, Art Mix, Bob Burns, Bill Dwyer, Earl Dwire, Hank Bell, Slim Whitaker, Hal Price. Falsely accused of murder a young man escapes from jail and joins an outlaw gang hoping to find the real killer, not realizing the gang member who befriends him is the man he is seeking. John Wayne's second Lone Star oater for producer Paul Malvern is a speedy affair and will appeal to Duke's fans. V: Electric Video.

3011 The Sagebrush Troubador. Republic, 1935. 54 minutes B/W. D: Joseph Kane. SC: Oliver Drake & Joseph Poland. WITH Gene Autry, Smiley Burnette, Barbara Pepper, J. Frank Glendon, Hooper Atchley, Dennis Moore, Fred Kelsey, Julian Rivero, Tom London, Frankie Marvin, Art Davis, Wes Warner. When an elderly, nearly

blind rancher is murdered, a singing cowboy tries to discover who committed the crime. Pretty fair Gene Autry early vehicle with just the right blend of music, action and mystery.

3012 Saginaw Trail. Columbia, 1953. 56 minutes B/W. D: George Archanbaud. SC: Dorothy Yost & Dwight Cummings. WITH Gene Autry, Smiley Burnette, Connie Marshall, Eugene Borden, Myron Healey, John Merton, Ralph Reed, Henry Blair, Mickey Simpson, John War Eagle, Rodd Redwing, Billy Wilkerson, Gregg Barton, John Parrish. In 1827 in Michigan the captain of Hamilton's Rangers is out to stop a fur magnate from murdering settlers. Pretty good, and different, Gene Autry film.

3013 The Sagittarius Mine. Gold Key, 1972. 91 minutes Color. WITH Steve Forrest, Diane Baker, Ray Danton, Richard Basehart. A sheriff suspects an invisible force is stopping prospectors after the Lost Dutchman gold mine. Obscure sci-fi/Western.

3014 Salome, Where She Danced. Universal, 1945. 90 minutes Color. D: Charles Lamont. SC: Laurence Stallings. WITH Yvonne De Carlo, Rod Cameron, David Bruce, Walter Slezak, Albert Dekker, Marjorie Rambeau, J. Edward Bromberg, Abner Biberman, John Litel, Kurt Katch, Arthur Hohl, Nestor Paiva, Gavin Muir, Will Wright, Joseph Haworth, Matt McHugh, Jane Adams, Barbara Bates, Daun Kennedy, Kathleen O'Malley, Karen Randle, Jean Trent, Kerry Vaughn, Jan Williams, Doreen Tryden, Bert Dole, Emmett Casey, Eddie Dunn, Charles Wagenheim, Gene Garrick, Eric Feldary, George Sherwood, Colin Campbell, Charles McAvoy, Al Ferguson, Edmund Cobb, Jack Clifford, Bud Osborne, George Morrell, Hank Bell, George Chesebro, Budd Buster, Richard Alexander, Cecilia Callejo. A beautiful dancer flees from Europe and begins a dance tour of the U. S. and in a small Arizona town she convinces an outlaw gang to go straight. Amusing tongue-in-cheek melodrama with Yvonne De Carlo a knockout in the title role. V: National Cinema Service.

3015 Salt Lake Raiders. Republic, 1950. 60 minutes B/W. D: Fred C. Brannon. SC: M. Coates Webster. WITH Allan "Rocky" Lane, Eddy Waller, Martha Hyer, Roy Barcroft, Byron Foulger, Myron Healey, Clifton Young, Stanley Andrews, Rory Mallinson, Kenneth MacDonald,

George Chesebro. When a convict escapes from prison, a U. S. Deputy Marshal is assigned to bring him back. Pretty entertaining Allan Lane vehicle.

3016 Sam Cade. CBS-TV/20th Century-Fox, 1972. 100 minutes Color. WITH Glenn Ford, Edgar Buchanan, Darren McGavin, Loretta Swit, Edward Asner, Shelley Fabares, H. M. Wynant, Richard Anderson, Taylor Lacher, Victor Campos, Peter Ford, Betty Ann Carr, Myron Healy, Jean Fowler, Ralph James, Ed Flanders, Larry Casey, William H. Bassett, Felice Orlandi, Philip Kenneally, Ann Randell, Gene Lebell. A New Mexico sheriff must face a wartime friend who comes home to kill him and then stop the proposed assassination of an ex-syndicate boss. Two segments of the television series "Cade's County" (CBS-TV, 1971-72), strung together into a feature, makes for pretty good viewing.

Sam Cooper's Gold see **The Ruthless Four**

3017 Sam Hill: Who Killed the Mysterious Mr. Foster? NBC-TV/Universal, 1971. 100 minutes Color. D: Fiedler Cook. SC: Richard Levinson & William Link. WITH Ernest Borgnine, Judy Geeson, Stephen Hudis, Will Geer, J. D. Cannon, Bruce Dern, Sam Jaffe, Carmen Mathews, John McGiver, Slim Pickens, G. D. Spradlin, Jay C. Flippen, Woodrow Parfrey, George Furth, Dub Taylor, Milton Selzer, Ted Gehrig, Dennis Fimple, Robert Gooden. In order to win re-election as the sheriff of a small town a sheriff must find the man who murdered a minister. Mediocre TV-made Western which has been retitled **Who Killed the Mysterious Mr. Foster?**

3018 Sam Whiskey. United Artists, 1969. 95 minutes Color. D: Arnold Laven. SC: William W. Norton. WITH Burt Reynolds, Clint Walker, Angie Dickinson, Ossie Davis, Del Reeves, Rick Davis, William Schallert, Woodrow Parfrey, Anthony James, Bud Adler, Ayllene Gibbons, Amanda Harley, Tracey Roberts, Virgil Warner, William Boyett, Sidney Clute, Chubby Johnson, John Damler. A rogue comes under the spell of a beautiful widow who convinces him to take a million dollars in gold bars from a sunken riverboat and return it to the U. S. mint before the theft, which was perpetrated by her late husband, is discovered. Burt Reynolds fans may like this mediocre film but others beware.

3019 Samson and the Slave Queen. American-International, 1964. 86 minutes Color. D: Umberto Lenzi. SC: Guido Malatesta & Umberto Lenzi. WITH Pierre Brice, Alan Steel, Massimo Serato, Moira Orfel, Maria Grazia Spina, Andrea Aureli. Two young women both want to become the queen of Navarre after the death of their uncle-king and one of them enlists the aid of Zorro while the other seeks help from mighty-man Samson. Below par Italian swashbuckler issued in Europe in 1963 as **Zorro Control Maciste** (Zorro Against Maciste).

3020 San Antone. Republic, 1953. 90 minutes B/W. D: George Sherman. SC: Steve Fisher. WITH Rod Cameron, Arleen Whelan, Forrest Tucker, Katy Jurado, Rodolfo Acosta, Roy Roberts, Bob Steele, Harry Carey Jr., James Lilburn, Andrew Brennan, Richard Hale, Martin Garralaga, Argentina Brunetti, Douglas Kennedy, Paul Fierro, George Cleveland. During the Civil War, a rancher agrees to lead a cattle drive through enemy country, not realizing he is being used by his so-called allies. Sedate oater provides good entertainment.

3021 San Antone Ambush. Republic, 1949. 60 minutes B/W. D: Philip Ford. SC: Norman S. Hall. WITH Monte Hale, Paul Hurst, Roy Barcroft, Bette Daniels, James Cardwell, Trevor Bardette, Lane Bradford, Tommy Coats, Francis Ford, Tom London, Edmund Cobb, Carl Sepulveda. When an army pay wagon is attacked and robbed a cavalry officer is falsely accused of being the tip-off man for the job. Monte Hale fans will enjoy this fairly exciting outing.

3022 San Antonio. Warner Brothers-First National, 1945. 111 minutes Color. D: David Butler. SC: Alan LeMay & W. R. Burnett. WITH Errol Flynn, Alexis Smith, S. Z. Sakall, Florence Bates, John Litel, Paul Kelly, Robert Shayne, John Alvin, Monte Blue, Robert Barrat, Pedro de Cordoba, Tom Tyler, Chris-Pin Martin, Charles Stevens, Poodles Hanneford, Doodles Weaver, Dan White, Ray Spiker, William Gould, Harry Seymour, Norman Willis, Eddy Waller, James Flavin, Henry Hall, Al Hill, Harry Cording, Chalky Williams, Wallis Clark, Bill Steele, Allen E. Smith, Howard Hill, Arnold Dent, Dan Seymour, Don McGuire, Brad King, Francis Ford, Lane Chandler, Hal Taliaferro, Jack Mower. Returning to San Antonio from Mexico in 1877, a cattleman brings proof a saloon owner is behind a gang of cattle rustlers. Colorful Errol Flynn vehicle.

3023 The San Antonio Kid. Republic, 1944. 54 (59) minutes B/W. D: Howard Bretherton. SC: Norman S. Hall. WITH Bill Elliott, Bobby Blake, Alice Fleming, Linda Stirling, Tom London, Earle Hodgins, Glenn Strange, Duncan Renaldo, LeRoy Mason, Jack Kirk, Robert Wilke, Jack O'Shea, Tex Terry, Bob Woodward, Herman Hack, Henry Wills, Tom Steele, Billy Vincent, Bud Geary, Cliff Parkinson. Crooks try to run ranchers off their lands before news of an oil strike is announced but Red Ryder arrives on the scene to get to the bottom of the trouble. Average outing in the popular "Red Ryder" series.

3024 San Fernando Valley. Republic, 1944. 54 (74) minutes B/W. D: John English. SC: Dorrell McGowan & Stuart McGowan. WITH Roy Rogers, Dale Evans, Jean Porter, Bob Nolan & The Sons of the Pioneers, Andrew Tombes, Edward Gargan, Dot Farley, LeRoy Mason, Charles Smith, Pierce Lyden, Maxine Doyle, Helen Talbot, Pat Starling, Kay Forrester, Hank Bell, The Morell Trio. When outlaws plague the San Fernando Valley, Roy Rogers sets out to stop them. Top-notch Roy Rogers vehicle, the one where he gets his first screen kiss from Jean Porter.

3025 San Francisco. Metro-Goldwyn-Mayer, 1936. 115 minutes B/W. D: W. S. Van Dyke. SC: Anita Loos. WITH Clark Gable, Jeanette MacDonald, Spencer Tracy, Jack Holt, Ted Healy, Margaret Irving, Jessie Ralph, Harold Huber, Al Shean, William Ricciardi, Kenneth Harlan, Roger Imhof, Frank Mayo, Tom Dugan, Charles Judels, Russell Simpson, Bert Roach, Warren Hymer, Edgar Kennedy, Adrienne d'Ambricourt, Nigel de Brulier, Mae Digges, Tudor Williams, Tandy MacKenzie, Nyas Berry, Tom Mahoney, Gertrude Astor, Jason Robards, Vernon Dent, Jack Baxley, Anthony Jowitt, Carl Stockdale, Richard Carle, Oscar Apfel, Frank Sheridan, Ralph Lewis, Chester Gan, Jack Kennedy, Cy Kendall, Don Rowan. In 1905 San Francisco a Barbary Coast saloon owner and a priest both keep a watchful eye on a beautiful young singer. This big production feature still provides good entertainment but the plot is secondary to the grand special effects of the San Francisco earthquake.

3026 The San Francisco Story. Warner Brothers, 1952. 80 minutes B/W. D: Robert

Parrish. SC: D. D. Beauchamp. WITH Joel McCrea, Yvonne De Carlo, Sidney Blackmer, Richard Erdman, Florence Bates, Onslow Stevens, John Raven, O. Z. Whitehead, Ralph Dumke, Robert Foulk, Lane Chandler, Trevor Bardette, John Doucette, Peter Virgo, Tor Johnson, Frank Hagney, Fred Graham. The pretty mistress of a corrupt politician in 1856 San Francisco falls in love with a mine owner out to stop her keeper. Fairly good action melodrama; Tor Johnson is the scariest bartender in the history of the genre.

3027 Sand. 20th Century-Fox, 1949. 77 minutes Color. D: Louis King. SC: Martin Berkeley & Jerome Cady. WITH Mark Stevens, Coleen Gray, Rory Calhoun, Charley Grapewin, Bob Patten, Mikel Conrad, Tom London, Paul Hogan, Jack Gallagher, William Walker, Davison Clark, Ben Erway, Harry V. Cheshire, Iron Eyes Cody, Jay Silverheels, Joseph Cody. A show horse escapes during a fire and his trainer tries to find him before he becomes wild. Mediocre outing which may appeal to juvenile viewers. Also called **Will James' Sand.**

3028 Sandflow. Universal, 1937. 58 minutes B/W. D: Lesley Selander, SC: Frances Guihan. WITH Buck Jones, Lita Chevret, Robert Kortman, Arthur Aylesworth, Robert Terry, Enrique DeRosas, Josef Swickard, Lee Phelps, Harold Hodge, Tom Chatteron, Arthur Van Slyke, Malcolm Graham, Ben Corbett. The two sons of a cattle rustler try to make good on losses to ranchers whose cattle their father rustled but one of them is falsely accused of killing a lawman. Somewhat meandering Buck Jones vehicle.

3029 Sandy Burke of the U-Bar-U. Betzwood Films, 1919. 55 minutes B/W. D: Ira M. Morgan. SC: J. Allen Dunn. WITH Louis Bennison, Virginia Lee, Alphonse Ethier, Herbert Horton Patlee, Echlin C. Gayer, Lucy Beaumont, Wilma Bayley, Nadia Gery. A young cowboy fights a gang of crooks on his boss's ranch. Early silent feature oater is worth a look.

3030 Sangaree. Paramount, 1953. 95 minutes Color. D: Edward Ludwig. SC: David Dovean. WITH Fernando Lamas, Arlene Dahl, Patricia Medina, Francis L. Sullivan, Charles Korvin, Tom Drake, John Sutton, Willard Parker, Charles Evans, Lester Mathews, Russell Gaige, William Walker, Felix Nelson, Voltaire Perkins. In frontier Georgia of 1781 a doctor, managing his late friend's estate, uncovers piracy and battles the plague. Handsomely mounted but basically dull costumer.

3031 Santa Fe. Columbia, 1951. 89 minutes Color. D: Irving Pichel. SC: Kenneth Gamet. WITH Randolph Scott, Janis Carter, Jerome Courtland, Peter Thompson, John Archer, Warner Anderson, Roy Roberts, Billy House, Olin Howlin, Alice Roberts, Jack O'Mahoney (Jock Mahoney), Harry Cording, Sven Hugo Borg, Frank Ferguson, Irving Pichel, Harry Tyler, Chief Thundercloud, Paul E. Burns, Reed Howes, Charles Meredith, Paul Stanton, Richard Cramer, William Haade, Francis McDonald, Frank O'Connor, Harry Tenbrook, Jim Mason, Guy Wilkerson, Frank Hagney, William Tannen, James Kirkwood, Stanley Blystone, Edgar Dearing, Al Junde, Art Loeb, Blackie Whiteford, Bud Fine, Lane Chandler, Charles Evans, George Sherwood, Louis Mason, Roy Butler, Ralph Sanford, William McCormack, Chuck Hamilton. After the Civil War several brothers head West and one goes to work building the Santa Fe Railroad while the others become outlaws. Average action melodrama for Randolph Scott fans.

3032 Santa Fe Bound. Reliable, 1936. 56 minutes B/W. D: Henri Samuels (Harry S. Webb). SC: Carl Krusada. WITH Tom Tyler, Jeanne Martel, Richard Cramer, Charles King, Slim Whitaker, Ed Cassidy, Lafe McKee, Wally West, Earl Dwire, Dorothy Woods, Ray Henderson. Falsely accused of murdering an old man actually bushwacked by bandits, a cowboy pretends to be a crook in order to infiltrate and capture the gang responsible for the crime. A trifle better than most of his Reliable outings, this was Tom Tyler's final series film for that outfit. V: Thunderbird.

3033 Santa Fe Marshal. Paramount, 1940. 54 (65) minutes B/W. D: Lesley Selander. SC: Harrison Jacobs. WITH William Boyd, Russell Hayden, Marjorie Rambeau, Bernadine Hayes, Earle Hodgins, Britt Wood, Kenneth Harlan, William Pagan, George Anderson, Jack Rockwell, Eddie Dean, Fred Graham, Matt Moore, Tex Phelps, Cliff Parkinson. Hopalong Cassidy goes undercover as a doctor in order to find an outlaw gang. Okay "Hopalong Cassidy" series entry, but nothing special.

3034 Santa Fe Passage. Republic, 1955. 90 minutes Color. D: William Witney.

SC: Lillie Hayward. WITH John Payne, Rod Cameron, Faith Domergue, Slim Pickens, Anthony Caruso, Leo Gordon, Irene Tedrow, George Keymas. A wagon train heading to Santa Fe is menaced by Kiowa Indians and gun runners and the wagon boss, despite his hatred of Indians, finds himself falling in love with a half-breed girl passenger. Standard, but actionful, Republic "A" effort.

3035 Santa Fe Rides. Reliable, 1937. 58 minutes B/W. D: Raymond Samuels (Bernard B. Ray). SC: Pliny Goodfriend. WITH Bob Custer, Eleanor Stewart, Ed Cassidy, David Sharpe, Roger Williams, Slim Whitaker, Lafe McKee, Snub Pollard, The Singing Cowboys (Lloyd Perryman, Rudy Sooter, Curley Hogg), Nelson McDowell, John Elliott. A rival tries to stop a cowboy and his musical group from getting a radio contract and he frames a girl's father and brother on a charge of having stolen cattle. Bob Custer's final film tries to interpolate the then-popular fad of having music in Westerns but the overall result is dismal.

3036 Santa Fe Saddlemates. Republic, 1945. 56 minutes B/W. D: Thomas Carr. SC: Bennett Cohen. WITH Sunset Carson, Linda Stirling, Olin Howlin, Roy Barcroft, Bud Geary, Kenne Duncan, George Chesebro, Robert Wilke, Henry Wills, Forbes Murray, Frank Jacquet, Josh (John) Carpenter, Rex Lease, Edmund Cobb, Nolan Leary, Fred Graham, George Magrill, Jack O'Shea, Carol Henry, Billy Vincent. The government sends an investigator to the U. S.-Mexican border to locate a diamond smuggling ring believed to be headquartered at a local ranch. Action from start to finish makes this one of the best of the Republic-Sunset Carson series.

3037 Santa Fe Scouts. Republic, 1943. 55 minutes B/W. D: Howard Bretherton. SC: Morton Grant & Betty Burbridge. WITH Bob Steele, Tom Tyler, Jimmie Dodd, Lois Collier, John James, Tom Chatterton, Elizabeth Valentine, Tom London, Budd Buster, Jack Ingram, Kermit Maynard, Rex Lease, Ed Cassidy, Yakima Canutt, Jack Kirk, Curley Dresden, Reed Howes, Bud Geary, Carl Sepulveda, Kenne Duncan, Al Taylor. The Three Mesquiteers work for a rancher whose son has been framed on a murder charge and the trio sets out to obtain his freedom. This next-to-last entry in the long-running "The Three Mesquiteers" series is more than passable entertainment.

3038 Santa Fe Stampede. Republic, 1938. 56 minutes B/W. D: George Sherman. SC: Luci Ward & Betty Burbridge. WITH John Wayne, Ray Corrigan, Max Terhune, William Farnum, June Martel, LeRoy Mason, Martin Spellman, Genee Hall, Walter Wills, Ferris Taylor, Tom London, Dick Rush, James F. Cassidy, George Chesebro, Yakima Canutt, Bud Osborne, Richard Alexander, Nelson McDowell, Curley Dresden, Bill Wolfe, Charles King. When crooks kill a miner whose successful claim was grubstaked by The Three Mesquiteers, Stony Burke is falsely accused of the crime and his pals set out to clear him. Actionful entry in "The Three Mesquiteers" series with the murder of the miner and his granddaughter in a buckboard wreck especially well staged.

3039 The Santa Fe Trail. Paramount, 1930. 80 minutes B/W. D: Edwin Knopf & Otto Brower. SC: Sam Mintz & Edward E. Paramore Jr. WITH Richard Arlen, Rosita Moreno, Eugene Pallette, Mitzi Green, Junior Durkin, Hooper Atchley, Luis Alberni, Lee Shumway, Chief Yowlachie, Jack Byron, Blue Cloud, Chief Standing Bear. Three men lead a large herd of sheep tended by Indians and arrange to graze the herd on a Spaniard's ranch but when his barn is burned he blames the Indians. Early talkie of interest to Richard Arlen fans. V: VCII Film Classics, Capital Home Video.

3040 Santa Fe Trail. Warner Brothers-First National, 1940. 110 minutes B/W. D: Michael Curtiz. SC: Robert Buckner. WITH Errol Flynn, Olivia de Havilland, Raymond Massey, Ronald Reagan, Alan Hale, William Lundigan, Van Heflin, Gene Reynolds, Henry O'Neill, Guinn Williams, Alan Baxter, John Litel, Moroni Olsen, David Bruce, Hobart Cavanaugh, Charles D. Brown, Joseph Sawyer, Frank Wilcox, Ward Bond, Russell Simpson, Charles Middleton, Erville Alderson, Spencer Charters, Suzanne Carnahan (Susan Peters), William Marshall, George Haywood, Wilfred Lucas, Russell Hicks, Napoleon Simpson, Roy Barcroft, Lane Chandler, Richard Kipling, Nestor Paiva, Trevor Bardette, Eddy Waller, Libby Taylor, Edmund Cobb, Creighton Hale, William Hopper, Addison Richards, Rev. Neal Dodd. West Point graduates Jeb Stuart and George A. Custer are stationed in Kansas during the fight over the free soil question and they both fall for the same girl and eventually become involved in the capture of abolitionist John Brown. Pseudo-historical drama which makes

for big scale entertainment. V: Nostalgia Merchant.

3041 Santa Fe Uprising. Republic, 1946. 54 minutes B/W. D: R. G. Springsteen. SC: Earle Snell. WITH Allan "Rocky" Lane, Bobby Blake, Martha Wentworth, Barton MacLane, Jack LaRue, Tom London, Dick Curtis, Forrest Taylor, Emmett Lynn, Hank Patterson, Edmund Cobb, Pat Michaels, Kenne Duncan, Edythe Elliott, Frank Ellis, Art Dillard. In order to keep the Duchess from taking over a toll road she has inherited, outlaws kidnap Little Beaver but Red Ryder comes to his rescue. Allan Lane's first entry as "Red Ryder" is an average affair.

3042 Santee. Crown-International, 1973. 93 minutes Color. D: Gary Nelson. SC: Tom Blackburn. WITH Glenn Ford, Dana Wynter, Michael Burns, Jay Silverheels, Harry Townes, John Larch, Robert Wilke, Robert Donner, Taylor Lacher, Lindsay Crosby, Chuck Courtney, X. Brands, John Hart, Boyd "Red" Morgan, Robert Mellard, Ben Zeller. A bounty hunter, whose son has been killed, becomes the father figure to a young man whose outlaw father was shot by the man. Genre fans will enjoy this fairly good melodrama.

3043 Saskatchewan. Universal-International, 1954. 87 minutes Color. D: Raoul Walsh. SC: Gil Doud. WITH Alan Ladd, Shelley Winters, Robert Douglas, J. Carrol Naish, Hugh O'Brian, Richard Long, Jay Silverheels, Antonio Moreno, Lowell Gilmore, George J. Lewis, Frank Chase, John Cason, Henry Wills. A Canadian Mountie tries to prevent the Sioux Indians from forcing the peaceful Cree tribe in joining them in a rebellion. The story doesn't amount to much but the scenic locales and fine photography (by John Seitz) make up for it. British title: **O'Rourke of the Royal Mounted.**

3044 Sasquath. NAFP, 1976. 94 minutes Color. D: Ed Ragozzini. SC: Ed Hawkins. WITH George Lauris, Jim Bradford, William Emmons, Steve Boergadine, Ken Kenzie. Seven men trek into the wilds of British Columbia in search of the legendary Bigfoot creature. Average semi-documentary speculation feature. Alternate title: **Sasquath, The Legend of Bigfoot.**

Sasquath, The Legend of Bigfoot see **Sasquath**

3045 Satan's Cradle. Monogram, 1949. 60 minutes B/W. D: Ford Beebe. SC:

J. Benton Cheney. WITH Duncan Renaldo, Leo Carrillo, Ann Savage, Douglas Fowley, Byron Foulger, Buck Bailey, George DeNormand, Claire Carleton, Wesley Hudman. In a small town the Cisco Kid and Pancho find themselves up against a crooked lawyer and his pretty saloon owner accomplice. More than adequate "Cisco Kid" programmer.

3046 Satan's Harvest. Killarney Studios, 1970. 104 minutes Color. D: George Montgomery. WITH George Montgomery, Tippi Hedren, Matt Munro, Davy Kaye, Brian O'Shaughnessy, Roland Robinson, Tromp Terreblanche, Melody O'Brian. An American detective heads to South Africa to take over the ranch he has inherited but finds the place is actually being used as a headquarters by drug smugglers. Colorful modern-day actioner filmed in South Africa and Rhodesia.

3047 The Savage. Paramount, 1952. 95 minutes Color. D: George Marshall. SC: Sidney Boehm. WITH Charlton Heston, Susan Morrow, Joan Taylor, Peter Hanson, Don Porter, Ted De Corsia, Milburn Stone, Richard Rober, Howard Negley, Ian MacDonald. A young white man, raised by the Indians, is torn between loyalties when war breaks out between the two peoples. Pretty engrossing tale, with Charlton Heston handling the lead role in good fashion.

The Savage American see **The Talisman**

3048 The Savage Eye. NBC-TV/Universal, 1971. 74 minutes Color. WITH Robert Stack, Jim Hutton, Peter Duel, Marianna Hill, Susan St. James. An investigator for a large publishing company looks into reports that an ecology documentary film made by his employers has caused trouble among lumberjacks. Average drama which was originally telecast February 19, 1971 as a segment of "The Name of the Game" (NBC-TV, 1968-71) television series.

3049 Savage Frontier. Republic, 1953. 54 minutes B/W. D: Harry Keller. SC: Dwight Babcock & Gerald Geraghty. WITH Allan "Rocky" Lane, Eddy Waller, Bob Steele, Dorothy Patrick, Roy Barcroft, Richard Avonde, William Phipps, Jimmy Hawkins, Lane Bradford, John Cason, Kenneth MacDonald, Bill Henry John Hamilton, Gerry Flash. A former convict, now a farmer, risks losing his parole when he tries to prove to a U. S. marshal that a local prominent citizen is behind

a gang of outlaws. A solid entry near the end of Allan Lane's Republic series, highlighted by Bob Steele as the reformed gunman.

3050 Savage Gringo. Italian International Film/Castilla Cinematografica, 1965. 82 minutes Color. D-SC: Antonio Roman. WITH Ken Clark, Yvonne Bastien, Piero Lulli, Renato Rossini, Alfonso Rojas, Antonio Gradoli, Angel Ortiz, Livio Lorenzon, Aldo Sambrell, Renato Terra, Paco Saenz. A cowboy goes to work for a rancher who is hated by both his wife and a rival and is soon accused of killing the local sheriff. Ken Clark, as the cowboy, adds some life to this Italian oater. Italian title: **Nebraska il Pistolero** (A Gunman Called Nebraska).

3051 The Savage Guns. Metro-Goldwyn-Mayer, 1961. 83 minutes Color. D: Michael Carreras. SC: Edmund Morris. WITH Richard Basehart, Don Taylor, Alex Nicol, Pacquita Rico, Maria Granada, Jose Nieto, Fernando Rey, Felix Fernandez, Francisco Camoiras, Antonio Fuentes, Sergio Mendizabal, Jose Manuel Martin, Pilar Caballero, Rafael Albaicin, Victor Bayo. A Civil War veteran, tired of violence, rides into a small Mexican town where he joins forces with a former Confederate officer to combat an evil land-grabber and his gang. Adequate actioner made by the British in Spain.

3052 The Savage Horde. Republic, 1950. 90 minutes B/W. D: Joseph Kane. SC: Kenneth Gamet. WITH William Elliott, Adrian Booth, Grant Withers, Jim Davis, Barbara Fuller, Noah Beery Jr., Douglass Dumbrille, Bob Steele, Will Wright, Roy Barcroft, Earle Hodgins, Stuart Hamblen, Hal Taliaferro, Lloyd Ingraham, Marshall Reed, Crane Whitley, Charles Stevens, James Flavin, Ed Cassidy, Kermit Maynard, George Chesebro, Jack O'Shea, Monte Montague, Bud Osborne, Reed Howes. A reformed gunman sides with small ranchers who are being menaced by a landgrabber while members of his former gang join with the crook. William Elliott's final big budget Western is a fine action drama.

3053 The Savage Innocents. Paramount, 1960. 110 minutes Color. D-SC: Nicholas Ray. WITH Anthony Quinn, Yoko Tani, Peter O'Toole, Anna May Wong. Carlo Guistini, Marie Yang, Marco Guglielmi, Lee Montague, Andy Ho, Anthony Chin. Two Canadian Mounties are assigned to bring in an eskimo who has accidentally killed a missionary. Good photography aids this rather mundane story.

Savage Justice see Bitter Springs

The Savage Land see This Savage Land

3054 Savage Pampas. Comet, 1967. 99 minutes Color. D: Hugo Fregonese. SC: Hugo Fregonese & John Melson. WITH Robert Taylor, Ron Randell, Marc Lawrence, Ty Hardin, Rosenda Monteros, Felicia Roc, Angel De Pozo, Mario Lozano, Enrique Avila, Laura Granados, Milo Quesada, Charles Fawcett, Julio Pena, Jose Nieto, Lucia Prado, George Rigaud. In the Argentine Pampas an army captain tracks an outlaw gang made up of deserters and Indians. Pretty fair action film made in South America and a remake of the 1946 Argentine feature **Pampa Barbara.**

3055 Savage Sam. Buena Vista, 1963. 103 minutes Color. D: Norma Tokar. SC: Fred Gipson & William Tunberg. WITH Brian Keith, Tommy Kirk, Kevin Corcoran, Dewey Martin, Jeff York, Royal Dano, Marta Kristen, Rafael Campos, Slim Pickens, Rodolfo Acosta, Pat Hogan, Dean Fredericks, Brad Weston. Two young brothers, along with a neighbor girl, are kidnapped by Indians and it is up to the boys' dog to lead a rescue party to them. Standard Walt Disney followup to **Old Yeller** (q.v.).

3056 The Savage Seven. American-International, 1968. 96 minutes Color. D: Richard Rush. SC: Michael Fisher. WITH Robert Walker, Larry Bishop, Adam Roarke, Joanna Frank, John Garwood, Max Julien, Richard Anders, Duane Eddy, Chuck Bail, Mel Berger, Billy Rush, John Cardos, Susannah Darrow, Beach Dickerson, Gary Kent, Penny Marshall, Walt Robles. Indians ally themselves with a motorcycle gang in order to stop the town boss who controls their lives. Violent combination of the Western and cycle genres by producer Dick Clark—the result is nothing special to fans of either type of film.

3057 The Savage Wild. American-International, 1970. 103 minutes Color. D-SC: Gordon Eastman. WITH Gordon Eastman, Carl Spore, Maria Eastman, Arlo Curtis, Jim Timiaough, Robert Wellington Kirk, John Payne, Charles Abou, Alex Dennis, Charley Davis, Wilber O'Brian. A filmmaker and his crew film the wildlife in Northern Canada, just below the Arctic Circle, and begin raising baby wolves. Very well made and entertaining British docudrama.

3058 Savages. ABC-TV, 1974. 74 minutes Color. D: Lee H. Katzin. SC: William Wood. WITH Andy Griffith, Sam Bottoms, Noah Beery, James Best, Randy Boone, Jim Antonio, Jim Chandler. A New York City attorney accidentally kills an old prospector while on a hunting trip and to cover up his crime he tries to hunt down and kill his young guide. The story has been told many times before with all kinds of variations but this TV movie is nonetheless entertaining.

3059 Scalawag. Paramount, 1973. 93 minutes Color. D: Kirk Douglas. SC: Albert Maltz & Sid Fleishman. WITH Kirk Douglas, Mark Lester, Neville Brand, George Eastman, Don Stroud, Lesley Anne Down, Danny DeVito, Mel Blanc, Phil Brown, Davor Antolic, Stole Arandjelovic, Fabijan Sovagovic, Shaft Douglas. In the 1840s a lovable peg-legged pirate leads his gang of cutthroats on a treasure hunt in California. Less than mediocre family film made in Yugoslavia; not enhanced by too many songs.

3060 The Scalphunters. United Artists, 1968. 102 minutes Color. D: Sydney Pollack. SC: William Norton. WITH Burt Lancaster, Shelley Winters, Telly Savalas, Ossie Davis, Armando Silvestre, Dan Vadis, Dabney Coleman, Paul Picerni, Nick Cravat, John Epper, Jack Williams, Chuck Roberson, Tony Epper, Agapito Roldan, Gregorio Acosta, Marco Antonio. A trapper has his furs stolen by Indians and he joins forces with a runaway slave to get them back. Fairly actionful oater-comedy with plenty of plot twists to satisfy most viewers.

3061 Scalplock. ABC-TV/Columbia, 1966. 100 minutes Color. D: James Goldstone. SC: Steven Kandel. WITH Dale Robertson, Diana Hyland, Lloyd Bochner, Gary Collins, David Sheiner, Steve Ihnat, Robert Random, Roger Torrey, Sandra Smith, James Westerfield, John Anderson, Todd Armstrong, Robert Cinder, Cliff Hall, Woodrow Parfrey, James Doohan, Herbert Voland, Eddie Firestone, Stephanie Hill, Harry Basch, Paul Sorensen, Jerry Summers. A notorious gambler wins a railroad in a poker game and learns that running a big business is more than giving orders. One of the first movies-made-for-network television and a mediocre one at that; the pilot for "The Iron Horse" (ABC-TV, 1966-68) series.

3062 Scalps. 21st Century, 1983. 82 minutes Color. D-SC: Fred Olen Ray. WITH

Kirk Alyn, Carroll Borland, Jo Anne Robinson, Richard Hench, Barbara Magnusson, Frank MacDonald, Roger Maycock, Forrest J. Ackerman, Carol Flockhart. A group of college students on an archaeological dig in the desert are possessed by the spirit of an Indian sorcerer. Low budget, but fairly interesting modern-day horror-Western, and it is nice to see the screen's original "Superman", Kirk Alyn, in a major role.

3063 Scandalous John. Buena Vista, 1971. 117 minutes Color. D: Robert Butler. SC: Bill Walsh & Don DaGradi. WITH Brian Keith, Michele Carey, Alfonso Arau, Rick Lenz, Harry Morgan, Simon Oakland, Bill Williams, Christopher Dark, Fran Ryan, Bruce Glover, Richard Hale, James Lydon, John Ritter, Iris Adrian, Larry D. Mann, Jack Raine, Booth Colman, Edward Faulkner, Bill Zuckert, John Zaremba, Robert Padilla, Alex Tinne, Ben(ny) Baker, Paul Koslo, William O'Connell, Sam Edwards, Lenore Stevens, Jose Nieto, Margarita Mendoza, Joseph Gutierrez, Freddie Hernandez. An aging man who basically lives in a fantasy world goes against a land baron trying to take over and flood his property. Overlong and minor-league Disney Western.

3064 Scar Tissue. NBC-TV/Universal, 1974. 76 minutes Color. WITH Richard Boone, Kurt Russell, Dick Haymes, Chill Wills, Tom Drake, Rick Lenz, Harry Morgan, Dennis Rucker. A sheriff and his deputies hunt for a young man who plans to kill the father who deserted him as an infant. Entertaining telefilm originally shown as a segment of the "Hec Ramsey" (NBC-TV, 1972-74) television series.

3065 Scarlet Angel. Universal-International, 1952. 81 minutes Color. D: Sidney Salkow. SC: Oscar Brodney. WITH Yvonne De Carlo, Rock Hudson, Richard Denning, Bodil Miller, Amanda Blake, Henry O'Neill, Henry Brandon, Maude Wallace, Dan Riss, Whitfield Connor, Tol Avery, Arthur Page, George Hamilton, Dale Van Sickel, Mickey Pfleger, Harry Harvey, George Spaulding, Thomas Browne Henry, Fred Graham, Fred Coby, Eddie Dew, Nolan Leary, Wilma Francis, Leo Curley, Dabbs Greer, Joe Forte, Coleman Francis, Charles Horvath, Bud Wolfe, Creighton Hale, Carl Saxe. After stealing money from a sea captain, a pretty girl befriends a woman and her child and when the woman dies she takes the child and assumes the woman's identity and becomes a

member of society on San Francisco's Nob Hill. Fair remake of **Flame of New Orleans** (q.v.).

3066 The Scarlet Horseman. Universal, 1946. 13 Chapters B/W. D: Ray Taylor & Lewis D. Collins. SC: Joseph O'Donnell, Tom Gibson & Patricia Harper. WITH Paul Guifoyle, Peter Cookson, Virginia Christine, Victoria Horne, Danny Morton, Fred Coby, Janet Shaw, Jack Ingram, Edward M. Howard, Harold Goodwin, Ralph Lewis, Edmund Cobb, Cy Kendall. A government agent takes on the guise of "The Scarlet Horseman," an ancient idol of the Indians, in order to prevent an uprising. Pleasantly actionful chapterplay.

3067 Scarlet River. RKO Radio, 1933. 57 minutes B/W. D: Otto Brower. SC: Harold Shumate. WITH Tom Keene, Dorothy Wilson, Roscoe Ates, Edgar Kennedy, Creighton (Lon Jr.) Chaney, Hooper Atchley, Betty Furness, Billy Butts, Yakima Canutt, Joel McCrea, Myrna Loy, Bruce Cabot, Julie Haydon. On location shooting a movie, a cowboy star tries to help a pretty ranch owner who is being swindled by her corrupt foreman. Highly actionful and very entertaining Tom Keene series entry, with a look at movie making (including some guest stars) as well as the usual genre fare.

3068 Scott Free. NBC-TV/Universal, 1976. 74 minutes Color. D: William Wiard. SC: Stephen J. Cannell. WITH Michael Brandon, Stephan Nathan, Susan Saint James, Robert Loggia, Ken Swofford, Allan Rich, Paul Koslo, Cal Bellini, Michael Lerner. A gambler wins a few acres of desert land in a poker game and soon finds to his dismay that it is sought by both gangsters and Indians. Mundane pilot for a TV series that was never produced.

3069 Scream of the Wolf. ABC-TV/Metromedia, 1974. 74 minutes Color. D: Dan Curtis. SC: Richard Matheson. WITH Peter Graves, Clint Walker, Jo Ann Pflug, Philip Carey, Don Megowan, Brian Richards, Lee Paul, James Storm, Bonnie Van Dyke, Dean Smith, Orville Sherman, Grant Owens, William Baldwin. A noted hunter emerges from retirement to hunt a man-killing wolf and evidence mounts that the quarry might be a werewolf. Mediocre combination of the horror and Western genres; made for television.

3070 Sea of Grass. Metro-Goldwyn-Mayer, 1947. 131 minutes B/W. D: Elia Kazan. SC: Marguerite Roberts. WITH Spencer Tracy, Katharine Hepburn, Melvyn Douglas, Robert Walker, Phyllis Thaxter, Edgar Buchanan, Harry Carey, Ruth Nelson, William "Bill" Phillips, Robert Armstrong, James Bell, Robert Barrat, Charles Trowbridge, Russell Hicks, Trevor Bardette, Morris Ankrum, Dan White, Glenn Strange, Douglas Fowley, Guy Wilkerson, Buddy Roosevelt, Earle Hodgins, Robert Bice, John Rice, Hank Worden, George Reed, Dorothy Vaughn, Vernon Dent, Erville Alderson, Leota Lorraine, Wyndham Standing, William Holmes, Henry Adams, Joseph Crehan, John Hamilton, John Vosper, Bud Fine, Chief Many Treaties, Nora Cecil, Fred Graham, Frank Hagney, Frank Austin, Ray Teal, Eddie Acuff, Davidson Clark, Fred Gilman, Dick Rush, Charles Middleton, Carol Nugent, Jimmie Hawkins, Wheaton Chambers, George Magrill, Nolan Leary, Charles McAvoy, Eddy Waller, Forrest Taylor, Gene (Roth) Stutenroth, Joe Bernard, Frank Darien, William Challee, Stanley Andrews, Ralph Littlefield. A feud develops over grassland between ranchers while a cattle baron learns that his son was actually fathered by a long-time rival. Ponderous Western which is well made and acted but dull.

3071 The Search. Wrather Corporation, 1956. 75 minutes Color. D: Earl Bellamy. SC: Thomas Seller, Robert E. Schaefer, Eric Friewald, Hilary Creston Rhodes & Robert Leslie Bellem. WITH Clayton Moore, Jay Silverheels, Allen Pinson, Wayne Burson, Aline Towne, Richard Crane, Denver Pyle, Lane Bradford, John Crawford, Jeanne Bates, Terry Frost, Bill Henry, Keith Richards, Charles Wagenheim, House Peters Jr., Tom Steele, Brad Morrow, Don Turner, David T. Armstrong, Baynes Barron, Steve Raines, James Baird, Mary Newton, Gregg Barton, Robert Burton, Ric Roman, Larry Jans. The Lone Ranger and Tonto, at Christmas, aid a boy in protecting his dog, look for a lost father and try to find a stolen jewel encrusted cross. Nicely done telefeature from "The Lone Ranger" (ABC-TV, 1949-57) TV series from the episodes "The Cross of Santo Domingo," "The Christmas Story" and "The Breaking Point."

3072 The Searchers. Warner Brothers, 1956. 119 minutes Color. D: John Ford. SC: Frank S. Nugent. WITH John Wayne, Jeffrey Hunter, Vera Miles, Ward Bond, Natalie Wood, John Qualen, Olive Carey, Henry Brandon, Ken Curtis, Harry Carey Jr., Antonio Moreno, Hank Worden, Lana Wood, Walter Coy, Dorothy Jordan, Pippa Scott, Patrick Wayne, Beulah Archuletta, Jack Pennick, Peter Mamakos, Chuck Roberson, Nacho Galindo, Robert Lyden, Chief Thundercloud, Mae Marsh, Don Borzage, Cliff Lyons, Terry Wilson, Frank McGrath, Chuck Hayward, Fred Kennedy, Slim Hightower, Billy Cartledge, Dale Van Sickel, Henry Wills. A Civil War veteran and the fiancée of his niece spend years searching for the other niece who was kidnapped by Indians. One of the all-time great classic Westerns; a must-see feature film. V: Warner Home Video, Cumberland Video. VD: Blackhawk.

3073 Second Chance. ABC-TV/Metromedia, 1972. 74 minutes Color. D: Peter Tewksbury. SC: Michael Morris. WITH Brian Keith, Elizabeth Ashley, Kenneth Mars, William Windom, Pat Carroll, Avery Schreiber, Rosey (Roosevelt) Grier, Juliet Prowse, Ann Morgan Builbert, Mark Savage, Ned Wertimer, Bret Parker, Emily Yancy. A stockbroker buys a Nevada ghost town and turns it into a resort for people who never had a chance in life. Passable modern day TV feature.

3074 The Second Time Around. 20th Century-Fox, 1961. 99 minutes Color. D: Vincent Sherman. SC: Oscar Saul & Dan Hansen. WITH Debbie Reynolds, Steve Forrest, Andy Griffith, Thelma Ritter, Juliet Prowse, Ken Scott, Isobel Elsom, Rodolfo Acosta, Timothy Carey, Tom Greenway, Eleanor Audley, Blossom Rock, Tracy Stratford, Jimmy Garrett, Lisa Pons, Nicky Blair. A young widow and her children come to Arizona in 1912 and she quickly is romanced by two local men, including the sheriff. Very pleasant Western-comedy.

Secret Barriers see **The Great Barrier**

3075 The Secret of Convict Lake. 20th Century-Fox, 1951. 83 minutes B/W. D: Michael Gordon. SC: Oscar Paul & Victor Trivas. WITH Glenn Ford, Gene Tierney, Ethel Barrymore, Zachary Scott, Ann Doran, Barbara Bates, Cyril Cusack, Richard Hylton, Helen Westcott, Jeanette Nolan, Ruth Donnelly, Harry Carter, Jack Lambert, Mary Carroll, Houseley Stevenson, Charles Flynn, David Post, Max Wagner, Raymond Greenleaf, Ray Teal, Tom London. A group of escaped convicts arrive in a town populated by women with one of the men out to find the man who sent him to jail while another is after hidden money and the accuser's sister. Murky melodrama which is well acted and fairly entertaining.

3076 Secret of Navajo Cave. Key International, 1976. 87 minutes Color. D-SC: James T. Flocker. WITH Rex Allen (narrator), Holger Kasper, Steven Benally Jr., Johnny Guerro. Two boys fight with a cougar while pursuing their stray goat. Fairly pleasant outdoor film with long prologue which somewhat detracts from the adventure aspects of the feature.

3077 The Secret of the Pueblo. William Steiner, 1923. 55 minutes B/W. D: Neal Hart. SC: Alvin J. Neitz. WITH Neal Hart, Hazel Deane, Tom Grimes, Monte Montague. When a girl is abducted by renegade Indians and taken to their secret altar room, a cowboy comes to her rescue. Typical low budget oater of the 1920s; one of the few available Neal Hart vehicles.

3078 Secret of Treasure Mountain. Columbia, 1956. 68 minutes B/W. D: Seymour Friedman. SC: David Lang. WITH Valerie French, Raymond Burr, William Prince, Lance Fuller, Susan Cummings, Pat Hogan, Reginald Sheffield, Rodolfo Hoyos, Paul McGuire, Tom Hubbard, Boyd Stockman. Several men hunt for Indian treasure in the desert and find an old prospector and his daughter living next to the guardian of the treasure. Producer Wallace MacDonald made a fairly interesting film here although the fact it is a low budget affair is more than evident.

3079 Secret Patrol. Columbia, 1936. 60 minutes B/W. D: David Selman. SC: J. P. McGowan & Robert Watson. WITH Charles Starrett, Finis Barton, J. P. McGowan, Henry Mollinson, LeStrange Millman, James McGrath, Arthur Kerr, Reginald Hincks, Ted Mapes. A Mountie works undercover as a woodsman to find the killer of a comrade as well as the person who has been trying to sabotage a lumber mill. Colorful and entertaining Charles Starrett film.

3080 Secret Valley. 20th Century-Fox, 1936. 60 minutes B/W. D: Howard Bretherton. SC: Earle Snell, Dan Jarrett & Paul Franklin. WITH Richard Arlen, Virginia Grey, Jack Mulhall, Syd Saylor, Russell Hicks. A western farmer decides to raise horses and soon finds them coveted by an outlaw gang. Standard programmer from the Harold Bell Wright story.

3081 Secrets. United Artists, 1933. 90 minutes B/W. D: Frank Borzage. SC: Frances Marion. WITH Mary Pickford, Leslie Howard, C. Aubrey Smith, Blanche Frederici, Doris Lloyd, Herbert Evans, Ned Sparks, Allan Sears, Mona Maris, Huntley Gordon, Ethel Clayton, Bessie Barriscale, Theodore Von Eltz, Virginia Grey. A young couple elope and take a wagon train West and settle down to cattle ranching with the husband rising in politics until the news of a love affair ruins his career. Heavy, but well made, melodrama which is best remembered as Mary Pickford's screen swan song.

3082 Secrets of the Wasteland. Paramount, 1941. 54 (66) minutes B/W. D: Derwin Abrahams. SC: Gerald Geraghty. WITH William Boyd, Andy Clyde, Brad King, Barbara Britton, Douglas Fowley, Keith Richards, Soo Young, Gordon Hart, Hal Price, Earl Gunn, Ian MacDonald, Richard Loo, Jack Rockwell, John Rawlings. A group of Chinese try to stop an expedition to a lost ruins where they have a hidden city and Hoppy, as the leader of the expedition, tries to rescue a girl on the trip who has been kidnapped. A fairly interesting story and nice scenery add up to make this a better than average "Hopalong Cassidy" outing.

3083 The Seekers. Rank/Universal-International, 1966. 75 minutes Color. D: Ken Annakin. SC: William Fairchild. WITH Jack Hawkins, Glynis Johns, Noel Purcell, Laya Raki, Inia Te Wiata, Patrick Warbrick, Kenneth Williams, Tony Estrich, Edward Baker. A Britisher, falsely convicted of smuggling, and his school teacher wife are sent to New Zealand in the 1820s and endure the hardships of pioneering there. Good British-made pioneer melodrama. U. S. theatrical title: **Land of Fury.**

3084 Seminole. Universal-International, 1953. 86 minutes Color. D: Budd Boetticher. SC: Charles K. Peck Jr. WITH Rock Hudson, Barbara Hale, Anthony Quinn, Richard Carlson, Hugh O'Brian, Russell Johnson, Lee Marvin, Ralph Moody, James Best, Dan Poore, Frank Chase, Earl Spainard, Scott Lee, Fay Roope, Don Gibson, John Day, Howard Erskine, Duane Thorsen, Walter Reed, Robert Karns, Robert Dane, John Phillips, Soledad Jiminez, Don Garrett, Robert Bray, Alex Sharpe, William Janssen. In Florida Seminole Indians refuse to sign a treaty with whites, preferring to live their own lives, and a West Point graduate returns to find his girlfriend engaged to a member of the tribe. Fairly interesting melodrama bolstered by a fine cast.

3085 Seminole Uprising. Columbia, 1955. 74 minutes Color. D: Earl Bellamy. SC: Robert E. Kent. WITH George Montgomery, Karin Booth, William Fawcett, Steven Ritch, Ed Hinton, John Pickard, Jim Maloney, Rory Mallinson, Howard Wright, Russ Conklin, Richard Cutting, Paul McGuire, Kenneth MacDonald. An army man raised by Indians is torn between orders to bring in the tribe's chief and the safety of his girl, who the braves have kidnapped. Sam Katzman produced this one and the threadbare production values show it.

3086 Señor Americano. Universal, 1929. 71 minutes B/W. D: Harry Joe Brown. SC: Bennett Cohen & Lesley Mason. WITH Ken Maynard, Kathryn Crawford, Gino Corrado, J. P. McGowan, Frank Yaconelli, Frank Beal. The government sends an army lieutenant to California to investigate land grabbers and he wins a golden bridle in a riding contest and learns of plans to steal a man's land. Actionful Ken Maynard part-talkie.

3087 Señorita from the West. Universal, 1945. 63 minutes B/W. D: Frank Strayer. SC: Howard Dinsdale. WITH Allan Jones, Bonita Granville, Jess Barker, George Cleveland, Fuzzy Knight, Spade Cooley & Orchestra, Oscar O'Shea, Benny McEvoy, Olin Howlin, Danny Mummert, Bob Merrill, Emmett Vogan, Billy Nelson, Jack Clifford, Gwen Donovan, Ralph Dunn, Ann Lawrence, Richard Alexander, Al Ferguson, Frank Hagney, Lane Chandler, Cyril Ring. A pretty girl from the West, wanting to become a singer, runs away from home and meets the "ghost singer" for a famous radio star. Typically amusing and glossy Universal World War II product.

3088 September Gun. CBS-TV, 1983. 100 minutes Color. D: Don Taylor. SC: William Norton. WITH Robert Preston, Patty Duke Astin, Christopher Lloyd, Geoffrey Lewis, Sally Kellerman, David Knell, Jacques Aubuchon, Jonathan Gries, Clayton Landey, Pat Anderson. An aging gunfighter reluctantly becomes the protector of a nun and her orphaned Apache charges in a wild Colorado town. Spritely TV movie vehicle for Robert Preston as the good-hearted gunman.

3089 Sequoia. Metro-Goldwyn-Mayer, 1935. 73 minutes B/W. D: Chester M.

Franklin. SC: Anna Cunningham, Sam Armstrong & Carey Wilson. WITH Jean Parker, Russell Hardie, Samuel S. Hinds, Paul Hurst, Ben Hall, Willie Fung, Harry Lowe Jr., Malibu (deer), Gato (puma). In the High Sierras a young girl who loves animals protects a puma cub and a fawn from hunters. Pretty fair outdoor drama.

3090 Sergeant Rutledge. Warner Brothers, 1960. 111 minutes Color. D: John Ford. SC: Willis Goldbeck & James Warner Bellah. WITH Jeffrey Hunter, Constance Towers, Woody Strode, Billie Burke, Juano Hernandez, Willis Bouchey, Carleton Young, Judson Pratt, Bill Henry, Walter Reed, Chuck Hayward, Mae Marsh, Fred Libby, Toby Richards, Jan Styne, Cliff Lyons, Charles Seel, Jack Pennick, Hank Worden, Chuck Roberson, Eva Novak, Estelle Winwood, Shug Fisher. When a black cavalry officer is falsely accused of rape and murder, a lieutenant defends him at his courtmartial. Tense and well acted melodrama from John Ford.

3091 Sergeants 3. United Artists, 1962. 112 minutes Color. D: John Sturges. SC: W. R. Burnett. WITH Frank Sinatra, Dean Martin, Sammy Davis Jr., Peter Lawford, Joey Bishop, Henry Silva, Ruta Lee, Buddy Lester, Philip Crosby, Dennis Crosby, Lindsay Crosby, Hank Henry, Richard Simmons, Michael Pate, Richard Hale, Mickey Finn, Sonny King, Eddie Little Sky, Rodd Redwing, Madge Blake, Dorothy Abbott, Walter Merrill. A former slave is rescued from Indians by a trio of army sergeants and due to their aiding him the trio become heroes when the Indians plan to murder incoming settlers. Comedy reworking of **Gunga Din** (RKO Radio, 1939); not much.

3092 Seven Alone. Doty-Dayton, 1974. 97 minutes Color. D: Earl Bellamy. SC: Eleanor Lamb & Douglas C. Stewart. WITH Dewey Martin, Aldo Ray, Stewart Petersen, Anne Collings, James Griffith, Dehl Berti, Bea Morris, Dean Smith. On the way to Oregon in 1843 seven children are orphaned when their parents are killed, and the oldest, a 13-year-old boy, leads them on a 2,000 mile trek from Missouri to their destination. Well-staged and acted family Western which is quite entertaining. V: Children's Video Library.

3093 Seven Angry Men. Allied Artists, 1958. 90 minutes B/W. D: Charles Marquis Warren. SC: Daniel B. Ullman. WITH

Raymond Massey, Debra Paget, Jeffrey Hunter, Larry Pennell, Leo Gordon, John Smith, James Best, Dennis Weaver, Guy Williams, Tom Irish, James Anderson, James Edwards, John Pickard, Smoki Whitfield, Jack Lomas, Robert Simon, Dabbs Greer, Ann Tyrell, Robert Osterloh. Abolitionist John Brown and his sons fight to free the slaves, resulting in a massacre of slave holders and their being hunted as fugitives. Fine drama about John Brown, who is excellently portrayed by Raymond Massey.

Seven Bad Men see **Rage at Dawn**

3094 Seven Brides for Seven Brothers. Metro-Goldwyn-Mayer, 1954. 103 minutes Color. D: Stanley Donen. SC: Albert Hackett, Frances Goodrich & Dorothy Kingsley. WITH Howard Keel, Jane Powell, Jeff Richards, Russ Tamblyn, Tommy Rall, Marc Platt, Julie (Newmar) Newmeyer, Nancy Kilgas, Betty Carr, Virginia Gibson, Matt Mattox, Jacques d'Amboise, Ruta Kilmonis, Norma Doggett, Ian Wolfe, Howard Petrie, Earl Burton, Dante Dipaolo, Kelly Brown, Matt Moore, Dick Rich, Marjorie Wood, Russell Simpson, Anna Q. Nilsson, Larry Blake, Phil Rich, Lois Hall, Russ Aunders, Terry Wilson, George Robothom, Walter Beaver, Jarma Lewis, Sheila James, I. Stanford Jolley, Tim Graham. When a young Oregon farmer brings home a pretty bride, his six brothers go out and kidnap girls for themselves. Delightful M-G-M Western musical with good songs by Johnny Mercer and Gene de Paul. V: MGM/United Artists.

3095 Seven Cities of Gold. 20th Century-Fox, 1955. 103 minutes Color. D: Robert D. Webb. SC: Richard L. Breen & John C. Higgins. WITH Richard Egan, Anthony Quinn, Michael Rennie, Jeffrey Hunter, Rita Moreno, Eduardo Noriega, Leslie Bradley, John Doucette, Kathleen Crowley, Victor Junco, Julio Villareal, Yerye Beirute, Jack Mower. In the 18th century, a Spanish expedition sets out to find the legendary seven cities of gold in the Southwest. Average adventure saga highlighted by Michael Rennie's performance as Father Junipero Serra.

3096 The 7 Faces of Dr. Lao. Metro-Goldwyn-Mayer, 1964. 100 minutes Color. D: George Pal. SC: Charles Beaumont. WITH Tony Randall, Barbara Eden, Arthur O'Connell, John Ericson, Kevin Tate, Argentina Brunetti, Noah Beery, Royal Dano, John Doucette, Frank Cady, Lee Patrick, John Qualen, Douglas Fowley,

Minerva Urecal, Eddie Little Sky, Peggy Rae, Dal McKennon, Chubby Johnson. The crooked denizens of a small Western town are brought to their senses by the acts in a small touring circus. Excellent fantasy in a Western setting, this feature is based on Charles G. Finney's sadly neglected novel, The Circus of Dr. Lao.

3097 Seven from Texas. PEA, 1964. 93 minutes Color. D-SC: Joaquin L. Romero Marchent. WITH Paul Paiget, Robert Hundar, Gloria Milland, Claudio Undari, Fernando Sancho. A young bride sways between the love of her husband and her feelings toward a former lover, a gunman, who is part of an escort taking them to a settlement through Indian country. More dramatic than violent European oater, originally titled **Camino Del Sur.**

3098 Seven Guns for the MacGregors. Columbia, 1968. 97 minutes Color. D: Frank Garfield (Franco Giraldi). SC: Enzo Dell'Aquila, Fernando Di Leo, David Moreno & Duccio Tessari. WITH Robert Wood, Fernando Sancho, Manolo Zarzo, Nick Anderson, Paul Carter, Julio Perez Tabernero, Saturno Cerra, Albert Waterman, Agata Flori, Leo Anchoriz, Perla Cristal, Harold Cotton, Anne-Marie Noe, Margaret Horowitz, Ralphael Bardem, Antonio Molino Rojo, Chris Huerta. The seven sons of two Scot pioneers are arrested after a cattle drive by a crooked sheriff in cahoots with a bandit and the seven escape and plan their revenge. There is nothing very special about this Italian-Spanish coproduction other than it has more humor and less violence than most spaghetti Westerns. Sequel: **Up the MacGregors** (q.v.). Issued in Italy in 1965 as **Sette Pistole Per I MacGregor** (Seven Pistols for the MacGregors).

3099 Seven Guns to Mesa. Allied Artists, 1958. 69 minutes B/W. D: Edward Dein. SC: Myles Wilder, Edward Dein & Mildred Dein. WITH Charles Quinlivan, Lola Albright, James Griffith, Jay Adler, John Cliff, Burt Nelson, John Merrick, Charles Keane, Jack Carr, Don Sullivan, Rush Williams, Neil Grant, Reed (Howes) Hawes, Mauritz Hugo, Harvey Russell. Stagecoach passengers are taken prisoners by an outlaw gang planning to rob a gold shipment. Very dull oater.

3100 7 Men from Now. Warner Brothers, 1956. 78 minutes Color. D: Budd Boetticher. SC: Burt Kennedy. WITH Randolph Scott, Gail Russell, Lee Marvin, Walter

Reed, John Larch, Donald (Don "Red") Barry, Fred Graham, John Barradino, John Phillips, Chuck Roberson, Steve Mitchell, Pamela Duncan, Stuart Whitman. An ex-lawman hunts for the outlaws who murdered his wife during a robbery. Most entertaining, and well written, action drama which will more than please Randolph Scott fans.

3101 Seven Ways from Sundown. Universal-International, 1960. 86 minutes Color. D: Harry Keller. SC: Clair Huffaker. WITH Audie Murphy, Barry Sullivan, Venetia Stevenson, John McIntire, Kenneth Tobey, Mary Field, Teddy Rooney, Suzanne Lloyd, Ken Lynch, Wade Ramsey, Don Collier, Jack Kruschen, Claudia Barrett, Don Haggerty, Robert Burton, Fred Graham, Dale Van Sickel. A Texas Ranger becomes fast friends with a murderous outlaw and eventually realizes he will have to hunt him down. Pretty fair oater with Audie Murphy and Barry Sullivan good in the leads.

3102 The 7th Cavalry. Columbia, 1956. 75 minutes Color. D: Joseph H. Lewis. SC: Peter Packer. WITH Randolph Scott, Barbara Hale, Jay C. Flippen, Jeanette Nolan, Frank Faylen, Leo Gordon, Denver Pyle, Harry Carey Jr., Michael Pate, Donald Curtis, Frank Wilcox, Pat Hogan, Russell Hicks, Peter Ortiz, William Leslie, Jack Parker, Al Wyatt. An officer returns from a furlough to find his regiment, Custer's 7th Cavalry, has been wiped out by the Indians and he sets out to find the true cause of the massacre. Very fine genre film with the star excellent as the officer.

3103 Shadow of Chikara. Howco-International, 1977. 114 minutes Color. D-SC: Earl E. Smith. WITH Joe Don Baker, Sondra Locke, Slim Pickens, Ted Neeley, Dennis Fimple, John Chandler, Joy Houck Jr., Linda Dano. Survivors of the final battle of the Civil War set out to find a hidden treasure but the area is protected by hawk demons. Surprisingly good blend of the Western and horror film genres. Original title: **Wishbone Cutter.**

3104 Shadow of the Hawk. Columbia, 1976. 92 minutes Color. D: George McGowan. SC: Norman Thaddeus Vane & Herbert J. Wright. WITH Jan-Michael Vincent, Marilyn Hassett, Chief Dan George, Pia Shandel, Marianne Jones, Jacques Hubert. The grandson of an Indian chief and a newspaperwoman returns to the man's reservation where

his grandfather wants him to use tribal rituals to combat evil forces in the form of a 200-year-old sorceress. Rather unpleasant combination of Western and horror film genres filmed in the backwoods of Vancouver, British Columbia.

3105 Shadow of Zorro. Allied Artists, 1962. 90 minutes Color. WITH Frank Latimore, Marie Gale. A crook tries to capture Zorro by committing acts of violence and blaming them on the masked avenger. Pretty good adventure outing originally issued in Spain by Copercines/Explorer as **La Sombra de Zorro** (The Shadow of Zorro).

3106 Shadow Ranch. Columbia, 1930. 55 minutes B/W. D: Louis King. SC: Frank Clark. WITH Buck Jones, Marguerite De La Motte, Kate Price, Al Smith, Frank Rice, Slim Whitaker, Ben Wilson, Robert McKenzie, Lafe McKee, Fred Burns, Ben Corbett, Frank Ellis, Hank Bell. A crooked saloon owner wants to control the water supply in a valley and all he needs is a girl's ranch and he murders her foreman but the man's pal comes looking for revenge. Slow moving and poorly recorded early Buck Jones talkie with some nice locations and the songs "When It's Roundup Time in Texas" and "Ragtime Cowboy Joe" are sung early in the film.

3107 The Shadow Riders. CBS-TV, 1982. 100 minutes Color. D: Andrew V. McLaglen. SC: Jim Byrnes. WITH Tom Selleck, Sam Elliott, Katharine Ross, Ben Johnson, Geoffrey Lewis, Gene Evans, Jeff Osterhage, R. G. Armstrong, Harry Carey Jr. Two brothers who fought on opposite sides in the Civil War unite to oppose renegade soldiers in postwar Texas. Exceedingly well-done television oater.

3108 Shadow Valley. Eagle Lion, 1947. 58 minutes B/W. D: Ray Taylor. SC: Arthur Sherman. WITH Eddie Dean, Roscoe Ates, Jennifer Holt, Andy Parker & The Plainsmen, George Chesebro, Eddie Parker, Lee Morgan, Lane Bradford, Carl Mathews, Budd Buster, Forrest Taylor. A cowboy tries to help a girl whose ranch is coveted by a train robber masquerading as a lawyer. Fair Eddie Dean musical opus.

3109 Shadows of Death. Producers Releasing Corporation, 1945. 60 minutes B/W. D: Sam Newfield. SC: Fred Myton. WITH Buster Crabbe, Al St. John, Donna Dax, Ed Hall, Charles King, Frank Ellis, Emmett Lynn, Karl Hackett, Ed Piel Sr., Bob

(John) Cason, Frank McCarroll. Marshals Billy Carson and Fuzzy Q. Jones learn that outlaws have murdered a man in order to get land which they plan to sell to the railroad. Typically mediocre entry in the long-running "Billy Carson" PRC series.

3110 Shadows of the West. Monogram, 1949. 60 minutes B/W. D: Ray Taylor. SC: Adele Buffington. WITH Whip Wilson, Andy Clyde, Reno Browne, Riley Hill, Bill Kennedy, Pierce Lyden, Keith Richards, William Ruhl, Ted Adams, Curt Barrett, Red Egner, Lee Phelps, Bert Hamilton, Bud Osborne, Donald Curr, Billy Hammond, Clem Fuller, Carol Henry, Bob Woodward, Edmund Glover, Dee Cooper. A lawman takes a vacation in a town where his pal is the ex-sheriff and the new peacemaker appears to be involved with an outlaw gang. Okay Whip Wilson vehicle.

3111 Shadows of Tombstone. Republic, 1953. 54 minutes B/W. D: William Witney. SC: Gerald Geraghty. WITH Rex Allen, Slim Pickens, Jeanne Cooper, Roy Barcroft, Emory Parnell, Ric Roman, Richard Avonde, Julian Rivero. A cowboy running for sheriff gets aid from a woman newspaper editor. Fair Rex Allen vehicle, well written and directed.

3112 Shadows on the Range. Monogram, 1946. 56 minutes B/W. D: Lambert Hillyer. SC: Jess Bowers (Adele Buffington). WITH Johnny Mack Brown, Raymond Hatton, Jan Bryant, John Merton, Marshall Reed, Steve Clark, Ted Adams, Terry Frost, Pierce Lyden, Cactus Mack, Roy Butler, Jack Perrin, Lane Bradford. An investigator for the cattlemen's association works undercover to expose a gang of rustlers by taking a job as a ranch foreman and then pretending to join the outlaws. Compact and fast-moving Johnny Mack Brown series entry with fine direction by Lambert Hillyer.

3113 Shadows on the Sage. Republic, 1942. 55 minutes B/W. D: Lester Orlebeck. SC: J. Benton Cheney. WITH Bob Steele, Tom Tyler, Jimmie Dodd, Bryant Washburn, Yakima Canutt, Cheryl Walker, Harry Holman, Tom London, Griff Barnett, Freddie Mercer, Rex Lease, Curley Dresden, Eddie Dew, Horace B. Carpenter, Frank Brownlee, John Cason, Pascale Perry. Outlaws have been stealing from miners and the Three Mesquiteers try to find out who is behind the thieves. Well written and actionful, this is a good

entry in the later stages of "The Three Mesquiteers" series.

3114 The Shakiest Gun in the West. Universal, 1966. 101 minutes Color. D: Alan Rafkin. SC: Jim Fritzell & Everett Greenbaum. WITH Don Knotts, Barbara Rhodes, Jackie Coogan, Donald (Don "Red") Barry, Ruth McDevitt, Frank McGrath, Terry Wilson, Carl Ballantine, Pat Morita, Robert Yuro, Herbert Voland, Fay DeWitt, Dub Taylor, Hope Summers, Dick Wilson, Vaughn Taylor, Ed Peck, Ed Faulkner, Arthur Space, Greg Mullavey, Benny Rubin, E. J. Andre. A meek dentist goes West to set up practice and gets involved with a woman bandit who is now working for the government trying to capture gun smugglers. Okay Don Knotts vehicle, a remake of **The Paleface** (q.v.).

3115 Shalako. Cinerama, 1968. 116 minutes Color. D: Edward Dmytryk. SC: J. J. Griffith, Hal Hopper & Scot Finch. WITH Sean Connery, Brigitte Bardot, Stephen Boyd, Jack Hawkins, Peter Van Eyck, Honor Blackman, Woody Strode, Eric Sykes, Alexander Knox, Valerie French, Julian Mateos, Donald (Don "Red") Barry, Rodd Redwing, Chief Tug Smith, Hans De Vries, Walter Brown, Charles Stalnaker, Bob Cunningham, John Clark, Bob Hall. A group of European nobles on a hunting trip in the West are attacked by Indians and a loner tries to rescue them. Well made but slow moving and not very interesting costumer.

3116 Shane. Paramount, 1953. 118 minutes Color. D: George Stevens. SC: A. B. Guthrie Jr. WITH Alan Ladd, Jean Arthur, Van Heflin, Brandon De Wilde, Jack Palance, Ben Johnson, Edgar Buchanan, Emile Meyer, Elisha Cook Jr., Douglas Spencer, John Dierkes, Ellen Corby, Paul McVey, John Miller, Edith Evanson, Leonard Strong, Ray Spiker, Janice Carroll, Martin Mason, Helen Brown, Nancy Kulp, Howard Negley, Beverly Washburn, George J. Lewis, Charles Quirk, Jack Sterling, Henry Wills, Rex Moore, Ewing Brown. A one-time gunman, wanting to lead a peaceful life as a ranch-hand in Wyoming, is forced to take up his guns again when homesteaders are threatened by range warfare. One of the all-time classic Westerns; grand performances by Alan Ladd, Van Heflin and Jack Palance. VD: Blackhawk.

3117 Shanghai Joe. Beacon Releasing, 1975. 98 minutes Color. D: Mario Caiano. SC: Carlo A. Alfieri, F. T. Trecca &

Mario Caiano. WITH Robert Hundar, John Stuart (Giacomo Rossi), Gordon Mitchell, Klaus Kinski, Chen Lee, Pancho del Rio, Carla Romanelli, Piero Lulli, Umberto D'Orsi, Dante Maggio, Rick Boyd, Andrea Aurelli, Carla Mancini. A young Chinaman goes to the American West to become a cowboy but his polite ways cause him trouble from brutal cowboys. Violent, but fairly interesting, Italian oater originally issued in Italy in 1972 by C.B.A. as **Mezzogiorno de Fucco Per An Hao** and also called **Il Mio Nome e Shangay Joe** (My Name is Shanghai Joe).

3118 Shark River. United Artists, 1953. 80 minutes Color. D: John Rawlins. SC: Joseph Carpenter & Lewis Meltzer. WITH Steve Cochran, Carole Matthews, Steve Warren, Robert Cunningham, Spencer Fox, Ruth Foreman. Following the Civil War, a man tries to elude the law in the Florida swamps. Okay action-romance melodrama.

Shatterhand see **Old Shatterhand**

3119 She Wore a Yellow Ribbon. RKO Radio, 1949. 103 minutes Color. D: John Ford. SC: Frank S. Nugent & Laurence Stallings. WITH John Wayne, Joanne Dru, John Agar, Ben Johnson, Harry Carey Jr., Victor McLaglen, Mildred Natwick, George O'Brien, Arthur Shields, Francis Ford, Harry Woods, Chief Big Tree, Cliff Lyons, Noble Johnson, Tom Tyler, Michael Dugan, Mickey Simpson, Fred Graham, Frank McGrath, Don Summers, Fred Libby, Jack Pennick, Billy Jones, Bill Gettinger, Post Park, Fred Kennedy, Rudy Bowman, Ray Hyke, Lee Bradley, Chief Sky Eagle, Dan White, Irving Pichel (narrator). An Army captain, on his last mission, tries to prevent Indian warfare while escorting his commanding officer's wife and daughter out of dangerous territory. One of the most enduring of Western classics; well worth viewing. V: Nostalgia Merchant, Cumberland Video.

3120 The Sheepman. Metro-Goldwyn-Mayer, 1958. 85 minutes Color. D: George Marshall. SC: William Bowers & James Edward Grant. WITH Glenn Ford, Shirley MacLaine, Leslie Nielsen, Mickey Shaughnessy, Edgar Buchanan, Willis Bouchey, Pernell Roberts, Slim Pickens, Buzz Henry, Pedro Gonzales Gonzales. A cattle baron tries to destroy a sheep farmer who has moved into his area and attracted the attentions of his fiancée. Likable Western with more than a touch of humor.

3121 Shenandoah. Universal, 1965. 105 minutes Color. D: Andrew V. McLaglen. SC: James Lee Barrett. WITH James Stewart, Doug McClure, Glenn Corbett, Patrick Wayne, Rosemary Forsyth, Phillip Alford, Katharine Ross, Charles Robinson, Paul Fix, Denver Pyle, George Kennedy, Tim McIntire, James McMullan, James Best, Warren Oates, Strother Martin, Dabbs Greer, Harry Carey Jr., Kevin Hagen, Tom Simcox, Berkeley Harris, Edward Faulkner, Peter Wayne, Gregg Palmer, Bob Steele, James Heneghan Jr., Eugene Jackson Jr., Rae Miller, Rayford Barnes, Dave Cass, Hoke Howell, Kelly Thordsen, Lane Bradford, Shug Fisher, John Daheim, Joe Yrigoyen, Henry Wills, Buzz Henry, James Carter, Leroy Johnson. During the Civil War a Virginia farmer tries not to get involved in the conflict, but this ends in tragic results for his family. Well made, interesting and poignant melodrama with James Stewart giving a powerful performance as the patriarch. V: MCA.

3122 The Shepherd of the Hills. Paramount, 1941. 98 minutes Color. D: Henry Hathaway. SC: Grover Jones & Stuart Anthony. WITH John Wayne, Betty Field, Harry Carey, Beulah Bondi, James Barton, Marjorie Main, Samuel S. Hinds, John Qualen Marc Lawrence, Tom Fadden, Ward Bond, Dorothy Adams, Olin Howland, Fuzzy Knight, John Harmon, Carl Knowles, Fern Emmett, Vivita Campbell, William Haade, Robert Kortman, Henry Brandon, Jim Corey, Selmer Jackson. A stranger arrives in the Ozark Mountains resulting in changes in people's lives, including that of his long unseen son. Nice screen adaptation of Harold Bell Wright's novel, highlighted by good photography (Charles Lang, W. Howard Greene) and especially fine performances by John Wayne, Harry Carey, Beulah Bondi, and Marjorie Main. First filmed in 1919 by Wright Films with George Hackathorne and remade in 1928 by First National with Alec B. Francis, Molly O'Day and John Boles, and done again in 1964 (q.v.) with Richard Arlen.

3123 Shepherd of the Hills. Howco-International, 1964. 105 minutes Color. D-SC: Ben Parker. WITH Richard Arlen, James W. Middleton, Sherry Lynn, James Collie, Lloyd Durre, Hal Meadows, James Bradford, Joy N. Houck Jr., Gilbert Elmore, George Jackson, Delores James, Danny Spurlock, Reubin Egan, Tom Pope, Roy Idom, Jim Teague, Roger Nash, Jim Greene. A man tries to end a feud between mountain families and aids a drought striken community. Cheaply made version of the 1907 Harold Bell Wright novel with Richard Arlen very good in the role of Old Matt. Reissue and TV title: **Thunder Mountain.**

3124 Sheriff of Cimarron. Republic, 1945. 54 minutes B/W. D: Yakima Canutt. SC: Bennett Cohen. WITH Sunset Carson, Linda Stirling, Olin Howlin, Riley Hill, Jack Ingram, Tom London, Jack Kirk, Robert Wilke, Jack O'Shea, Ed Cassidy, George Chesebro, Hal Price, Carol Henry. A young man is made the sheriff of a town but his crooked brother is actually responsible for all the crimes there and the crook tries to frame his honest lawman brother and send him to jail. Nicely directed, actionful outing greatly helped by pretty Linda Stirling, in deference to Sunset Carson's acting.

3125 Sheriff of Fractured Jaw. 20th Century-Fox, 1959. 103 minutes Color. D: Raoul Walsh. SC: Arthur Dales. WITH Kenneth More, Jayne Mansfield, Henry Hull, William Campbell, Bruce Cabot, Robert Morley, Ronald Squire, David Horne, Eynon Evans, Sidney James, Donald Stewart, Reed De Rouen, Clancy Cooper, Charles Irwin, Gordon Tamer, Tucker McGuire, Nick Brady, Larry Taylor, Jack Lester, Nicholas Stuart, Sheldon Lawrence, Susan Denny, Charles Farrell, Chief Jonas Applegarth, Chief Joe Buffalo. An unsuccessful British inventor heads to the American West to sell guns, is mistaken for a gunman and ends up the sheriff of a rowdy town. Fairly pleasant British-made genre satire.

3126 Sheriff of Las Vegas. Republic, 1944. 54 minutes B/W. D: Lesley Selander. SC: Norman S. Hall. WITH Bill Elliott, Bobby Blake, Alice Fleming, Peggy Stewart, Selmer Jackson, William Haade, Jay Kirby, John Hamilton, Kenne Duncan, Bud Geary, Jack Kirk, Frank McCarroll. A young man, who was estranged from his judge father, is blamed for the man's murder but Red Ryder tries to prove his innocence. Well written "Red Ryder" series entry with a bang-up finale.

3127 The Sheriff of Medicine Bow. Monogram, 1948. 55 minutes B/W. D: Lambert Hillyer. SC: J. Benton Cheney. WITH Johnny Mack Brown, Raymond Hatton, Max Terhune, Evelyn Finley, George J. Lewis, Bill Kennedy, Frank LaRue, Peter Perkins, Carol Henry, Bob Woodward, Ted Adams. A sheriff comes to the

aid of a paroled convict when crooks try to steal gold hidden on his ranch. Okay Johnny Mack Brown vehicle.

3128 The Sheriff of Redwood Valley. Republic, 1946. 54 minutes B/W. D: R. G. Springsteen. SC: Earle Snell. WITH Bill Elliott, Bobby Blake, Alice Fleming, Bob Steele, Peggy Stewart, Arthur Loft, James Craven, Tom London, Kenne Duncan, Bud Geary, Tom Chatterton, Budd Osborne, Frank McCarroll. Red Ryder comes to the aid of an innocent rancher falsely accused of a crime and uncovers an outlaw gang. More than competent "Red Ryder" series film greatly aided by Bob Steele in the supporting cast.

3129 Sheriff of Sage Valley. Producers Releasing Corporation, 1942. 56 minutes B/W. D: Sherman Scott (Sam Newfield). SC: Milton Raison & George W. Sayre. WITH Buster Crabbe, Al St. John, Maxine Leslie, Tex (Dave) O'Brien, Charles King, John Merton, Kermit Maynard, Hal Price, Curley Dresden, Lynton Brent, Jack Kirk. Billy the Kid is asked by the mayor of a small town to round up the gang responsible for killing the sheriff during a holdup. Average PRC "Billy the Kid" entry with Buster Crabbe. TV title: **Billy the Kid, Sheriff of Sage Valley.**

3130 Sheriff of Sundown. Republic, 1944. 57 minutes B/W. D: Lesley Selander. SC: Norman S. Hall. WITH Allan Lane, Linda Stirling, Max Terhune, Duncan Renaldo, Roy Barcroft, Herbert Rawlinson, Bud Geary, Jack Kirk, Twinkle Watts, Tom London, Robert Wilke, Kenne Duncan, Rex Lease, Herman Hack, Jack O'Shea, Carl Sepulveda, Nolan Leary, Horace B. Carpenter, Cactus Mack. Cowboys leading a herd into a small town find themselves opposing the corrupt activities of a murderous town boss. Entertaining and well done Republic oater in the Allan Lane series.

3131 Sheriff of Tombstone. Republic, 1941. 54 (56) minutes B/W. D: Joseph Kane. SC: Olive Cooper. WITH Roy Rogers, George "Gabby" Hayes, Elyse Knox, Addison Richards, Sally Payne, Harry Woods, Hal Taliaferro, Jay Novello, Roy Barcroft, Jack Rockwell, Zeffie Tilbury, Jack Ingram, George Rosenor, Jack Kirk, Frank Ellis, Art Dillard, Herman Hack, Vester Pegg, Al Haskell, Ray Jones, Jess Cavan. Crooked businessmen hire a tough cowpoke to be the sheriff of Tombstone but he turns on them when the crooks try to cheat an old lady and her family out of their mine. Actionful and entertaining Roy Rogers opus chock full of favorite villains.

3132 Sheriff of Wichita. Republic, 1949. 60 minutes B/W. D: R. G. Springsteen. SC: Bob Williams. WITH Allan "Rocky" Lane, Eddy Waller, Lyn Wilde, Clayton Moore, Roy Barcroft, Gene Roth, Trevor Bardette, Edmund Cobb, House Peters Jr., Earle Hodgins, John Hamilton, Jack O'Shea, Dick Curtis, Lane Bradford, Steve Raines. A sheriff agrees to help a girl find out who murdered her father. Too much obvious indoor scenery but still a fair Allan Lane outing with a good mystery flavor.

3133 The Sheriff Was a Lady. Arthur Brauner, 1964. 88 minutes Color. D: Sobey Martin. SC: Gustav Kampendonk. WITH Freddy Quinn, Mamie Van Doren, Rik Battaglia, Carlo Croccolo, Otto Waldis, Klaus Dahlen, Beba Lancar. Pretending to be a greenhorn, a young man hunts for the gang who killed his parents and enlists the aid of a pretty saloon girl. West German vehicle for popular singer Freddy Quinn with some appeal for TV viewers via costar Mamie Van Doren; okay dubbed European oater. West German title: **Freddy Und Das Lied Per Prarie** (CCC Filmkunst/Avala-Film).

3134 Sheriff Won't Shoot. Hispamer, 1965. 85 minutes Color. WITH Mickey Hargitay, Pilar Clemens, Vincent Cashino, Alche Nana. A sheriff is forced into a showdown when he learns his younger brother is behind the activities of an outlaw band. Okay Spanish-made actioner.

3135 Shine on Harvest Moon. Republic, 1938. 54 (57) minutes B/W. D: Joseph Kane. SC: Jack Natteford. WITH Roy Rogers, Mary Hart, William Farnum, Lulu Belle & Scotty (Wiseman), Stanley Andrews, Frank Jaquet, Chester Gunnels, Matty Roubert, Pat Henning, Jack Rockwell, Joe Whitehead, David Sharpe. An outlaw tries to convince his former partner to join him in a cattle rustling scheme and when the latter refuses the crook sets out to frame him for his crimes. Too many novelty tunes bog down this outing which (fortunately) is dominated by William Farnum, as the ex-outlaw turned good-guy rancher, and Stanley Andrews as the villain.

3136 Shipwreck! Pacific International, 1979. 102 minutes Color. D-SC: Stewart Raffill. WITH Robert Logan, Heather Rattray, Shannon Saylor, Mikki-Jamison Olsen, Cjon Damitri Patterson. A man, his two young daughters, one of their friends and a black stowaway set out on a boat trip and end up being marooned on a remote Alaskan island. Well done family-oriented feature from the makers of "The Wilderness Family" trilogy.

3137 Shoot Out. Universal, 1971. 94 minutes Color. D: Henry Hathaway. SC: Marguerite Roberts. WITH Gregory Peck, Pat Quinn, Robert F. Lyons, Susan Tyrell, Jeff Corey, James Gregory, Rita Gam, Dawn Lyn, Pepe Serna, John Chandler, Paul Fix, Arthur Hunnicutt, Nicholas Beauvy, Arthur Space, Lane Bradford, Willis Bouchey. After six years in prison a man sets out to get revenge on the now-prosperous partner who betrayed him and along the way he is adopted by a small girl. Interesting premise goes awry due to lack of action; remake of **Lone Cowboy** (q.v.).

3138 Shoot Out at Big Sag. Parallel, 1962. 64 minutes B/W. D-SC: Roger Kay. WITH Walter Brennan, Leif Erickson, Luana Patten, Chris Robinson, Constance Ford, Virginia Gregg, Les Tremayne, Don O'Kelly, Andy Brennan, William Foster, Robert Beecher, Lennie Geer. In a remote Montana area a cowardly preacher tries to run off a recently settled Texan and his son. Okay film which was actually a 1960 pilot for a TV series, "Barbed Wire," which did not sell; based on Walt Coburn's 1931 novel Barb Wire.

3139 Shoot-Out at Medicine Bend. Warner Brothers, 1957. 87 minutes B/W. D: Richard L. Bare. SC: John Tucker Battle & D. D. Beauchamp. WITH Randolph Scott, James Craig, Angie Dickinson, James Garner, Dani Crayne, Gordon Jones, Trevor Bardette, Don Beddoe, Myron Healey, John Alderson, Harry Harvey Sr., Robert Warwick, Howard Negley, Marshall Bradford, Ann Doran, Daryn Hinton, Dickie Bellis, Edward Hinton, Lane Bradford, Frances Morris, Robert Lynn, Sam Flint, Philip Van Zandt, Guy Wilkerson, Syd Saylor, Harry Rowland, Marjorie Bennett, Jesslyn Fax, Marjorie Stapp, Nancy Kulp, George Meader, Rory Mallinson, Dee Carroll, Dale Van Sickel, Gil Perkins, Harry Lauter, Carol Henry, George Pembroke, Tom Monroe, Buddy Roosevelt, George Bell. Three men whose families were massacred by Indians due to the use of faulty ammunition, set out to get revenge on the trader who sold them the defective merchandise. Fairly good horse opera although not up to the standards of Randolph Scott's usual 1950s fare.

3140 Shoot Out in a One-Dog Town. ABC-TV, 1974. 74 minutes Color. D: Burt Kennedy. SC: Larry Cohen & Dick Nelson. WITH Richard Crenna, Stefanie Powers, Jack Elam, Richard Egan, Arthur O'Connell, Michael Ansara, Dub Taylor, Gene Evans, Michael Anderson Jr., John Pickard, Jay Ripley, Jerry Gatlin, Henry Wills. When outlaws threaten to rob his bank, a small-town banker takes drastic measures to protect the money. Fairly good action made-for-TV Western with a cast of familiar faces.

3141 Shoot the Sun Down. JAD Films International, 1981. 93 minutes Color. D: David Leeds. SC: Richard Rothstein & David Leeds. WITH Margot Kidder, Christopher Walken, Geoffrey Lewis, Bo Brundin, A. Martinez, Sacheen Little-feather. In the West in 1836, a gunman joins a bounty hunter and a retired sea captain in searching for lost gold and he falls in love with the captain's pretty indentured girl. Slow moving, uninteresting oater which is a pretty pointless effort. V: Video Communications.

Shootin' Irons see **West of Texas**

3142 Shootin' Square. Anchor, 1924. 50 minutes B/W. WITH Jack Perrin, Peggy O'Day, Bud Osborne, Alfred Hewston, S. J. Bingham, Horace B. Carpenter, Milburn Morante, David Dunbar, Starlight (horse). A crooked foreman, actually wanted for murder, is at odds with a cowboy over the affections of the ranch owner's pretty daughter. The lighthearted-ness of this otherwise competent Jack Perrin silent film is somewhat hurt by a too complicated plotline.

3143 The Shooting. Jack H. Harris, 1971. 82 minutes Color. D: Monte Hellman. SC: Adrien Joyce. WITH Jack Nicholson, Millie Perkins, Warren Oates, Will Hutchins, B. J. Merholz, Charles Eastman, Guy El Tsosie. A woman persuades two miners to be her guides on a journey which leads to revenge. Watchable West-ern, which like **Ride in the Whirlwind** (q.v.), was given TV release before making it to theaters. V: Capital Home Video.

3144 Shooting High. 20th Century-Fox, 1940. 65 minutes B/W. D: Alfred E. Green. SC: Lou Breslow & Owen Francis. WITH Jane Withers, Gene Autry, Marjorie Weaver, Frank M. Thomas, Robert Lowery, Katharine (Kay) Aldridge, Hobart Cava-naugh, Jack Carson, Hamilton MacFadden, Charles Middleton, Ed Brady, Tom London, Eddie Acuff, Pat O'Malley, George Chand-ler. The grandson of a famous outlaw takes over the part of his grandfather in a movie and ends up winning the girl he loves and captures bank robbers. Gene Autry's loan-out to 20th Century-Fox and teaming with Jane Withers results in an uneven film.

3145 The Shootist. Paramount, 1976. 100 minutes Color. D: Don Siegel. SC: Miles Hood Swarthout & Scott Hale. WITH John Wayne, Lauren Bacall, James Stewart, Ron Howard, Harry Morgan, Richard Boone, John Carradine, Hugh O'Brian, Sheree North, Richard Lenz, Scatman Crothers, Bill McKinney, Gregg Palmer, Alfred Dennis, Dick Winslow, Melody Thomas, Kathleen O'Malley. An aging, and famous, gunman dying of cancer at the turn of the century finds his reputation getting in the way of his wish to die a peaceful death. The best Western of the 1970s, and one of the all-time best of the genre. Had the political climate of Hollywood not been so hostile, John Wayne would have won his second Oscar for this film; as it was he was not even nominated. V: Cumberland Video. VD: Blackhawk.

The Short and Happy Life of the Brothers Blue see **Brothers Blue**

3146 Short Grass. Allied Artists, 1950. 82 minutes B/W. D: Lesley Selander. SC: Tom W. Blackburn. WITH Rod Cam-eron, Cathy Downs, Johnny Mack Brown, Alan Hale Jr., Morris Ankrum, Jeff York, Raymond Walburn, Jonathan Hale, Riley Hill, Harry Woods, Stanley Andrews, Tristram Coffin, Myron Healey, Jack Ingram, Rory Mallinson, Marlo Dwyer, Felipe Turich, George J. Lewis, Lee Tung Foo, Lee Roberts, Frank Ellis, Tom Monroe, Kermit Maynard. A sheriff joins forces with a rancher to stop a crooked land scheme. A good script, direction and a fine cast all add up to a very fine little oater.

3147 Shotgun. Allied Artists, 1955. 80 minutes Color. D: Lesley Selander. SC: John Champion, Clark E. Reynolds & Rory Calhoun. WITH Sterling Hayden, Yvonne De Carlo, Zachary Scott, Robert Wilke, Guy Prescott, Ralph Sanford, John Pickard, Ward Wood, Rory Mallinson,

Paul Marion, Harry Harvey Jr., Lane Chandler, Angela Greene, Robert E. Griffin, Al Wyatt, Bob Morgan, Peter Coe, Charles Morton, James Parnell, Richard Cutting, Fiona Hale, Francis McDonald. A showgirl joins forces with a sheriff and a bounty hunter to track a killer only to find themselves stalked by Apaches. Rory Calhoun, who cowrote the script, was originally scheduled to star in this minor oater, best recommended for Yvonne De Carlo's bathing sequence.

3148 Shotgun Pass. Columbia, 1931. 60 minutes B/W. D: J. P. McGowan. SC: Robert Quigley. WITH Tim McCoy, Virginia Lee Corbin, Frank Rice, Dick Stewart, Joe Marba, Monty Vandergrift, Ben Corbett, Albert J. Smith, Archie Ricks. Two dishonest brothers own a pass and refuse to let a cowboy, with an army contract, lead a herd of horses through it and trouble follows, including murder. There is enough action in this Tim McCoy vehicle to delight his fans.

3149 Showdown. Paramount, 1940. 54 (65) minutes B/W. D: Howard Bretherton. SC: Howard Kusel & Donald Kusel. WITH William Boyd, Russell Hayden, Britt Wood, Morris Ankrum, Jan Clayton, Wright Kramer, Donald Kirk, Roy Barcroft, Eddie Dean, Kermit Maynard, Walter Shumway, The King's Men. Hoppy and Lucky are at odds when Lucky sides with a girl ranch owner while Hoppy believes a European baron, who is actually a fake, is out to rustle her cattle. Average entry in the "Hopalong Cassidy" series without much action until its finale.

3150 The Showdown. Republic, 1950. 86 minutes B/W. D-SC: Dorrell McGowan & Stuart McGowan. WITH William Elliott, Walter Brennan, Marie Windsor, Harry Morgan, Rhys Williams, Jim Davis, William Ching, Nacho Galindo, Leif Erickson, Henry Rowland, Charles Stevens, Victor Kilian, Yakima Canutt, Guy Teague, William Steele, Jack Sparks. A cattle trail herd driver, a former lawman, tracks down the outlaw who murdered his brother. Distinguished adult Western starring William Elliott, who was its coproducer.

3151 Showdown. Universal, 1963. 79 minutes B/W. D: R. G. Springsteen. SC: Bronson Howitzer. WITH Audie Murphy, Kathleen Crowley, Charles Drake, Skip Homeier, Harold J. Stone, L. Q. Jones, Strother Martin, Charles Horvath, John McKee, Henry Wills, Joe Haworth, Kevin Brodie, Carol Thurston, Dabbs Greer,

Harry Lauter. Two convicts escape from prison and head for the Mexican border and get involved in a robbery. Audie Murphy fans will like this programmer but for others it is only of passing interest.

3152 The Showdown. NBC-TV/Universal, 1971. 74 minutes Color. WITH Gene Barry, Jessica Walter, Warren Oates, Jack Albertson, Albert Salmi, Ron Turbeville, Jack Garner, Daniel Kemp, William Bramley, Jack Collins, Martin Garralaga. A magazine publisher is tipped off to the fake account of a famous gunfight and investigates the claim and in flashbacks returns to the old West. Originally a segment of "The Name of the Game" (NBC-TV, 1968-71) television series, this telefeature is for avid series fans only.

3153 Showdown. Universal, 1973. 90 minutes Color. D: George Seaton. SC: Theodore Taylor. WITH Dean Martin, Rock Hudson, Susan Clark, Donald Moffat, John McLiam, Charles Baca, Jackson Kane, Ben Zeller, John Richard Gill, Phillip L. Mead, Rita Rogers, Vic Mohica, Raleigh Gardenhire, Ed Begley Jr., Dan Boydston. Two men who once loved the same girl find themselves on the opposite sides when one of them, a lawman, hunts the other, an outlaw. Fair teaming of Rock Hudson and Dean Martin makes this an okay time passer.

3154 Showdown at Abilene. Universal-International, 1956. 80 minutes Color. D: Charles Haas. SC: Bernie Giler. WITH Jock Mahoney, Martha Hyer, David Janssen, Lyle Bettger, Grant Williams, Ted De Corsia, Harry Harvey Sr., Dayton Lummis, Richard Cutting, Robert G. Anderson, John Maxwell, Lane Bradford. Returning home to Texas after the Civil War, a gun-shy ex-lawman finds his girl, who thought him dead, engaged to a dishonest cattleman. Nicely entertaining Jock Mahoney vehicle, remade in 1967 as **Gunfight in Abilene** (q.v.).

3155 Showdown at Boot Hill. Republic, 1957. 72 minutes B/W. D: Gene Fowler Jr. SC: Louis Vittes. WITH Charles Bronson, Robert Hutton, John Carradine, Carole Mathews, Paul Maxey, Thomas Browne Henry, William Stevens, Martin Smith, Joseph McGuinn, George Douglas, Michael Mason, George Pembroke, Argentina Brunetti, Ed Wright, Fintan Meyler, Dan Simmons, Barbara Woodell, Norman Leavitt. A bounty hunter arrives in a small town and kills a wanted man but must face the wrath of angry citizens. Sadly neglected "B" melodrama, enhanced by good direction and top flight performances by Charles Bronson, John Carradine and Carole Mathews.

3156 Shut My Big Mouth. Columbia, 1942. 71 minutes B/W. D: Charles Barton. SC: Oliver Drake, Karen D. Wolf & Francis Martin. WITH Joe E. Brown, Adele Mara, Victor Jory, Don Beddoe, Lloyd Bridges, Forrest Tucker, Earle Hodgins, Fritz Feld, Russell Simpson, Pedro De Cordoba, Joan Woodbury, Ralph Peters, Joe McGuinn, Noble Johnson, Chief Thundercloud. A timid man from the East accidentally knocks out a desperado and is made the local sheriff and has to stand up to an outlaw gang leader. Amusing Joe E. Brown vehicle with a good story and direction.

3157 Sidekicks. CBS-TV/Warner Brothers, 1974. 75 minutes Color. D: Burt Kennedy. SC: William Bowers. WITH Larry Hagman, Lou Gossett, Blythe Danner, Jack Elam, Harry Morgan, Gene Evans, Noah Beery, Hal Williams, Dick Peabody, Denver Pyle, John Beck, Dick Haynes, Tyler McVey, Bill Shannon. After the Civil War, two con men out West try to collect bounty on an outlaw. Television version of **Skin Game** (q.v.) which never made it as a series.

3158 The Siege at Red River. 20th Century-Fox, 1954. 86 minutes Color. D: Rudolph Mate. SC: Sydney Boehm. WITH Van Johnson, Joanne Dru, Richard Boone, Milburn Stone, Jeff Morrow, Craig Hill, Rico Alaniz, Robert Burton, Pilar Del Rey, Ferris Taylor. During the Civil War a Confederate spy masquerades as a showman in order to steal a Gatling gun and becomes involved with a pretty Yankee nurse, a Pinkerton agent and marauding Indians. Fairly entertaining oater. Alternate title: **The Siege of Red River.**

The Seige of Red River see **The Siege at Red River**

3159 Sierra. Universal-International, 1950. 83 minutes Color. D: Alfred E. Green. SC: Edna Anhalt. WITH Audie Murphy, Wanda Hendrix, Dean Jagger, Burl Ives, Richard Rober, Anthony Caruso, Houseley Stevenson, Elliott Reid, Griff Barnett, Elizabeth Risdon, Roy Roberts, Gregg Martell, Sara Allgood, James Arness, Ted Jordan, I. Stanford Jolley, Jack Ingram. A young female lawyer stumbles across the hideout of a man and his son, the former on the run from the law after being falsely accused of murder. Pretty good remake of **Forbidden Valley** (q.v.).

3160 Sierra Baron. 20th Century-Fox, 1958. 80 minutes Color. D: James B. Clark. SC: Houston Branch. WITH Brian Keith, Rick Jason, Rita Gam, Mala Powers, Allan Lewis, Pedro Calvan, Fernando Wagner, Steve Brodie, Carlos Muzquiz, Lee Morgan, Reed Howes, Alberto Mariscal. In 19th century California a ruthless man hires a gunman to kill a Mexican in order to get his vast land holdings. More than passable entertainment, enhanced by good photography.

3161 Sierra Passage. Monogram, 1951. 81 minutes B/W. D: Frank McDonald. SC: Tom W. Blackburn, Warren D. Wandberg & Sam Rosca. WITH Wayne Morris, Lola Albright, Lloyd Corrigan, Alan Hale Jr., Roland Winters, Jim Bannon, Billy Gray, Paul McGuire, Richard Karlan, George Eldredge. A man postpones his marriage in order to hunt down the man who murdered his father. Grade B actioner that provides its allotted modicum of entertainment.

3162 Sierra Stranger. Columbia, 1957. 78 minutes B/W. D: Lee Sholem. SC: Richard J. Dorso. WITH Howard Duff, Gloria McGhee, Dick Foran, John Hoyt, Barton MacLane, George E. Stone, Ed Kemmer, Robert Foulk, Eve McVeagh, Henry Kulky, Byron Foulger. A wild young man is saved from a lynching by a prospector and the two end up in still more trouble. Barely passable second-bill feature although it is nice to see Dick Foran in a costarring role.

3163 Sierra Sue. Republic, 1941. 54 (64) minutes B/W. D: William Morgan. SC: Earl Fenton & Julian Zimet. WITH Gene Autry, Smiley Burnette, Fay McKenzie, Frank M. Thomas, Robert Homans, Earle Hodgins, Dorothy Christy, Jack Kirk, Eddie Dean, Kermit Maynard, Budd Buster, Rex Lease, Hugh Prosser, Vince Barnett, Hal Price, Syd Saylor, Roy Butler, Sammy Stein, Bob McKenzie, Marin Sais, Ray Davis, Frankie Marvin, Art Dillard. The state agricultural commission sends inspector Gene Autry to a devil weed-infested area to study the problem but he meets opposition from the head of the local cattlemen's association. Pretty dreary Gene Autry vehicle except for a few songs.

3164 The Sign of the Wolf. Metropolitan, 1931. 10 Chapters B/W. D: Harry S. Webb & Forrest Sheldon. SC: Carl Krusada. WITH King (dog), Rex Lease, Virginia Browne Faire, Joe Bonomo, Jack Mower, Josephine Hull, Al Ferguson, Robert Walker, Edmund Cobb, Harry Todd, Billy O'Brien, Jack Perrin. In Tibet, an explorer steals chains which can turn sand into jewels and years later crooks in the West try to steal them from him and his daughter. Very low grade, but fun, cliffhanger; issued in a feature version in 1932 by Syndicate called **The Lone Trail.**

3165 Sign of the Wolf. Monogram, 1941. 69 minutes B/W. D: Howard Bretherton. SC: Elizabeth Hopkins & Edmond Kelso. WITH Michael Whelan, Grace Bradley, Mantan Moreland, Darryl Hickman, Louise Beavers, Wade Crosby, Tony Paton, Smoky & Shadow (dogs). Two dogs are raised together in the north country and one becomes a thief while the other stays loyal to his master who is beset by fur grabbers. Fair adaptation of a Jack London story by producer Paul Malvern.

3166 The Sign of Zorro. Buena Vista, 1960. 91 minutes B/W. D: Norman Foster & Lewis R. Foster. SC: Norman Foster, Lowell S. Hawley, Bob Wehling & John Meredyth Lucas. WITH Guy Williams, George J. Lewis, Henry Calvin, Gene Sheldon, Britt Lomond, Tony Russo, John Dehner, Lisa Gay, Romney Brent, Than Wyenn, Elvira Corona, Eugenia Paul. In 1820 the son of a California nobleman arrives from Spain and pretends to be a fop in order to hide his disguise as the avenger Zorro, out to right wrongs of a local despot. Made up of episodes of the popular "Zorro" (ABC-TV, 1957-59) TV series, this Walt Disney production was issued theatrically both in the U. S. and abroad; fairly entertaining. V: Disney Home Video.

3167 Silence of the North. Universal, 1981. 94 minutes Color. D: Allan Winton King. SC: Patricia Louisiana Knop. WITH Ellen Burstyn, Tom Skerritt, Gordon Pinsent, Jennifer McKinney, Donna Dobrijevic, Colin Fox, Chapelle Jaffe, Ken Pogue, Tom Hauff, Murray Westgate, Ken James, Booth Savage, Louis Banks, Sean McCann, Frank Adamson. In 1919 a young woman marries a vagabondish trapper and goes to live with him in the wilds of Canada. Based on a true story, this drama holds some interest but the scenery is better than the plot.

3168 The Silent Call. 20th Century-Fox, 1961. 63 minutes B/W. D: John Bushelman. SC: Tom Maruzzi. WITH Gail Russell, Roger Mobley, David McClean, Joe Besser, Jack Younger, Rusty Westcoatt, Roscoe Ates, Sherwood Keith, Milton Parsons, Dal McKennon. Separated from his young master, a faithful dog makes the dangerous 600 mile trek from Reno to Los Angeles. Pleasant family programmer.

3169 The Silent Code. Stage & Screen, 1935. 55 minutes B/W. D: Stuart Paton. SC: George Morgan. WITH Kane Richmond, Blanche Mehaffey, J. P. McGowan, Joe Girard, Barney Furey, Pat Harmon, Ben Corbett, Carl Mathews, Ed Coxen, Bud Osborne, Ted Mapes, Wolfgang (dog). A miner is murdered and the blame for the crime is placed on a Canadian Mountie. Low grade actioner.

3170 Silent Conflict. United Artists, 1948. 61 minutes B/W. D: George Archainbaud. SC: Charles Earl Belden. WITH William Boyd, Andy Clyde, Rand Brooks, Virginia Belmont, Earle Hodgins, James Harrison, Forbes Murray, John Butler, Herbert Rawlinson, Richard Alexander, Don Haggerty. A fake doctor uses hypnotism to get Lucky to steal cattle association funds from Hopalong Cassidy and when they find out, Hoppy and California get on his trail. Very dull entry from the tail-end of the "Hopalong Cassidy" series.

3171 The Silent Gun. ABC-TV/Paramount, 1969. 74 minutes Color. D: Michael Caffey. SC: Clyde Ware. WITH Lloyd Bridges, John Beck, Ed Begley, Edd Byrnes, Pernell Roberts, Susan Howard, Michael Forrest, Trace Evans, Bob Diamond, Barbara Rhoades. A once-famous gunman, who has vowed never to take up arms again, is made the sheriff of a small town and has to deal with the hatred between a politician and a settler. Mediocre made-for-television oater with far more talk than action.

3172 The Silent Man. Paramount-Artcraft, 1917. 60 minutes B/W. D: William S. Hart. SC: Charles Kenyon. WITH William S. Hart, Vola Vale, Robert McKim, Harold Goodwin, J. P. Lockney, George P. Nichols, Gertrude Claire, Milton Ross, Dorcas Matthews. A miner, cheated out of his rich mining claim by a crooked saloon owner, sets out for revenge. Entertaining William S. Hart silent vehicle. V: Classic Video Cinema Collectors Club.

3173 Silent Men. Columbia, 1933. 60 minutes B/W. D: D. Ross Lederman. SC: Jack Cunningham, Stuart Anthony & Gerald Geraghty. WITH Tim McCoy, Florence Britton, Wheeler Oakman, J. Carrol Naish, Matthew Betz, Lloyd Ingraham, Steve Clark, William V. Mong, Walter Brennan, Syd Saylor, Joseph Girard. A special agent for cattlemen loses his job when it is found out he is an escaped convict and is suspected of being the leader of a gang of rustlers. Eerie and atmospheric Tim McCoy vehicle with a complicated, and sometimes hard to follow, plot.

3174 Silent Rage. Columbia, 1982. 90 minutes Color. D: Michael Miller. SC: Joseph Fraley. WITH Chuck Norris, Ron Silver, Steven Keats, Toni Kalem, William Finley, Brian Libby, Stephen Furst, Stephanie Dunnam, Joyce Ingle. The sheriff of a small Texas community tries to protect his town from a psychotic killer. Fair modern-day action melodrama starring six-time World Karate Champion Chuck Norris.

3175 Silent Valley. Reliable, 1935. 56 minutes B/W. D: Bernard B. Ray. SC: Rose Gordon. WITH Tom Tyler, Nancy DeShon, Alan Bridge, Wally Wales, Charles King, Charles "Slim" Whitaker, Art Miles, Murdock McQuarrie, Jimmie Aubrey, Frank Ellis. A lawman, on the trail of cattle rustlers, suspects the brother of the girl he likes of being in the gang which is led by a supposedly respectable citizen. Alan Bridge is very good as the slick villain as is Slim Whitaker as his murderous henchman but overall this Tom Tyler vehicle is on the tacky side.

3176 Silent Wilderness. Ted Leverfech, 1976. 92 minutes Color. WITH Dr. Roger Latham. A naturalist explores Alaska, from abandoned gold mines to oil pipelines, and encounters a grizzly bear near Mt. McKinley and whales near the Arctic. Well made and entertaining documentary.

3177 Silly Billies. RKO Radio, 1936. 64 minutes B/W. D: Fred Guiol. SC: Al Boasberg & Jack Townley. WITH Bert Wheeler, Robert Woolsey, Dorothy Lee, Harry Woods, Ethan Laidlaw, Chief Thunderbird, Delmar Watson, Richard Alexander, Lafe McKee, Tommy Bond. Two silly dentists head West on a wagon train and end up saving it from an Indian attack. Very weak Wheeler-Woolsey comedy vehicle.

3178 Silver Bandit. Friedgen, 1950. 54 minutes B/W. D: Elmer Clifton. SC: Elmer S. Pond (Clifton). WITH Spade Cooley, Bob Gilbert, Virginia Jackson, Richard Elliott, Billy Dix, Jene Gray. When silver has been stolen from a mine, its owners send a bookkeeper to investigate and he uncovers an outlaw gang behind the robberies. Bottom-of-the-barrel Spade Cooley vehicle.

3179 The Silver Bullet. Reliable, 1935. 53 minutes B/W. D: Bernard B. Ray. SC: Rose Gordon & Carl Krusada. WITH Tom Tyler, Jayne Regan, Lafe McKee, Charles King, George Chesebro, Slim Whitaker, Lew Meehan, Franklyn Farnum, Walt Williams (Wally Wales), Blackie Whiteford, Hank Bell, Nelson McDowell, Robert Brower, Allen Smith, Tom Smith, Tex Palmer, Fern Emmett, Jack Evans, Murray Horn. A prospector agrees to become the sheriff of a small town plagued by outlaws and he tries to find out who is the leader of the gang. Cheaply made but more than passable Tom Tyler oater.

3180 The Silver Bullet. Universal, 1942. 56 minutes B/W. D: Joseph H. Lewis. SC: Elizabeth Beecher. WITH Johnny Mack Brown, Fuzzy Knight, William Farnum, Jennifer Holt, LeRoy Mason, Rex Lease, Grace Lenard, Claire Whitney, Slim Whitaker, William Desmond, Merrill McCormack, Michael Vallon, James Farley, Lloyd Ingraham, The Pals of the Golden West & Nora Lou Martin, Harry Holman, Hank Bell. A man searches for the outlaw who shot him in the back with a silver bullet and murdered his father. A bit complicated but well done Johnny Mack Brown vehicle.

3181 Silver Canyon. Republic, 1951. 70 minutes B/W. D: John English. SC: Gerald Geraghty. WITH Gene Autry, Pat Buttram, Gail Davis, Jim Davis, Bob Steele, Edgar Dearing, Richard Alexander, Terry Frost, Peter Mamakos, Steve Clark, Stanley Andrews, Duke York, Eugene Borden, Bobby Clark, Frankie Marvin, Boyd Stockman, Sandy Sanders, Kenne Duncan, Bill Hale, Jack O'Shea, Stanley Blystone, John Merton, Jack Pepper, Pat O'Malley, Jim Magill, John Daheim, Eddie Parker. During the Civil War an Army scout is on the trail of a Union renegade leader and his band whose activities have also been denounced by the Confederacy. Top notch Gene Autry vehicle with splendid work by Jim Davis as the villain.

3182 Silver City. Paramount, 1951. 90 minutes Color. D: Byron Haskin. SC: Frank Gruber. WITH Yvonne De Carlo, Edmond O'Brien, Richard Arlen, Barry Fitzgerald, Gladys George, Laura Elliot, Edgar Buchanan, Michael Moore, John Dierkes, Don Dunning, Warren Earl Fisk, James Van Horn, John Mansfield, Harvey Parry, Boyd "Red" Morgan, Frank Cordell, Leo J. McMahon, Howard Joslin, Robert G. Anderson, Frank Fenton, Myron Healey, James R. Scott, Paul E. Burns, Cliff Clark, Billy House, Howard Negley, Ray Hyke, Slim Gaut. A miner tries to help a pretty girl and her father develop their claim but the trio is opposed by a wealthy rancher who wants the gold and the girl for himself. A good cast does what it can for a mediocre story. British title: **High Vermillion.**

3183 Silver City Bonanza. Republic, 1951. 67 minutes B/W. D: George Blair. SC: Bob Williams. WITH Rex Allen, Buddy Ebsen, Mary Ellen Kay, Billy Kimbley, Bill Kennedy, Alix Ebsen, Gregg Barton, Clem Bevans, Frank Jenks, Hank Patterson, Harry Lauter, Harry Harvey. When a blind man is murdered at a supposedly "haunted" ranch, a cowboy sets out to find the killer. Fast paced and well written Rex Allen film.

3184 Silver City Kid. Republic, 1944. 56 minutes B/W. D: John English. SC: Taylor Cavan. WITH Allan Lane, Peggy Stewart, Wally Vernon, Twinkle Watts, Frank Jacquet, Harry Woods, Glenn Strange, Lane Chandler, Bud Geary, Tom London, Tom Steele, Jack Kirk, Sam Flint, Frank McCarroll, Hal Price, Ed Piel Sr., Fred Graham, Frank O'Connor, Horace B. Carpenter. When valuable ore is stolen by an outlaw gang, a ranch foreman suspects the town's judge is behind the operation. Allan Lane's first series film is a quick moving affair. V: Cumberland Video.

3185 Silver City Raiders. Columbia, 1943. 55 minutes B/W. D: William Berke. SC: Ed Earl Repp. WITH Russell Hayden, Dub Taylor, Alma Carroll, Bob Wills & The Texas Playboys, Paul Sutton, Edmund Cobb, Jack Ingram, Art Mix, Luther Wills, Jack Rockwell, John Tyrell, Merrill McCormack, George Morrell, Tex Palmer, Horace B. Carpenter. A group of ranchers find out they may lose their lands to a land office operator who claims he has a Spanish land grant giving him claim to their properties. Better than average outing in Russell Hayden's Columbia series.

Silver Devil see **Wild Horse**

3186 Silver Dollar. First National, 1932. 84 minutes B/W. D: Alfred E. Green. SC: Carl Erickson & Harvey Thew. WITH Edward G. Robinson, Bebe Daniels, Aline MacMahon, Jobyna Howland, De Witt Jennings, Robert Warwick, Russell Simpson, Harry Holman, Charles Middleton, John Marston, Marjorie Gateson, Emmett Corrigan, Wade Boteler, William Le Maire, David Durand, Lee Kohlmar, Theresa Conover, Leon Ames, Virginia Edwards, Christian Rub, Walter Rogers, Niles Welch, Wilfred Lucas, Herman Bing, Bonita Granville, Walter Long, Charles Coleman, Frederick Burton, Willard Robertson, Alice Wetherfield. A Kansas farmer moves to Colorado for the gold rush but goes broke only to become rich in a silver strike and rise politically but then becomes involved in a scandal. Entertaining soap opera.

3187 The Silver Horde. RKO Radio, 1930. 75 minutes B/W. D: George Archainbaud. SC: Wallace Smith. WITH Evelyn Brent, Joel McCrea, Louis Wolheim, Raymond Hatton, Jean Arthur, Gavin Gordon, Blanche Sweet, Prunell Pratt, William B. Davidson, Ivan Linow. A saloon entertainer comes to the aid of a young salmon fisherman whose business is being threatened by a crook. Good production values for this Rex Beach adaptation make this early talkie good entertainment.

3188 Silver Lode. RKO Radio, 1954. 80 minutes Color. D: Allan Dwan. SC: Karen De Wolfe. WITH John Payne, Lizabeth Scott, Dan Duryea, Dolores Moran, Emile Meyer, Harry Carey Jr., Morris Ankrum, John Hudson, Robert Warwick, Stuart Whitman, Alan Hale Jr., Frank Sully, Paul Birch, Florence Auer, Roy Gordon, Edgar Barrier, John Dierkes, Myron Healey, Hugh Sanders, Roy Jordan. On his wedding day, a man is falsely accused of murder and he runs away to prove his innocence. Sturdy action melodrama. V: Disney Home Video.

3189 Silver on the Sage. Paramount, 1939. 54 (66) minutes B/W. D: Lesley Selander. SC: Harrison Jacobs. WITH William Boyd, George ("Gabby") Hayes, Russell Hayden, Stanley Ridges, Ruth Rogers, Frederick Burton, Jack Rockwell, Roy Barcroft, Ed Cassidy, Jim Corey, Sherry Tansey, Bruce Mitchell, William Wright, George Morrell, Frank O'Connor, Buzz Barton, Herman Hack, Dick Dickinson, Hank Bell. Lucky is falsely accused of murder and Hoppy and Windy help him escape the law as Hoppy seeks to uncover the real culprit who is also behind a cattle rustling gang. Actionful entry in the "Hopalong Cassidy" series with an amusing finale. V: Video Connection.

3190 Silver Queen. United Artists, 1942. 81 minutes B/W. D: Lloyd Bacon. SC: Bernard Schulbert & Cecile Kramer. WITH George Brent, Priscilla Lane, Bruce Cabot, Lynne Overman, Eugene Pallette, Janet Beecher, Guinn Williams, Roy Barcroft, Eleanor Stewart, Arthur Hunnicutt, Sam McDaniel, Spencer Charters, Cy Kendall, Georges Renavent, Francis X. Bushman, Franklyn Farnum, Marietta Canty, Herbert Rawlinson, George Eldredge, Earle Hodgins, Fred "Snowflake" Toones, Frederick Burton, Ed Cassidy, Jason Robards. A girl gambles in order to raise the money to pay off her father's debts while her fiancée invests her winnings in a silver mine. Passable entertainment—nothing more.

3191 Silver Raiders. Allied Artists, 1950. 55 minutes B/W. D: Wallace Fox. SC: Dan Ullman. WITH Whip Wilson, Andy Clyde, Virginia Herrick, Leonard Penn, Dennis Moore, Patricia Rice, Reed Howes, Riley Hill, Marshall Reed, George De-Normand, Kermit Maynard, Ed Cassidy, Frank Hagney, Frank Ellis. A Texas Ranger infiltrates a gang smuggling silver ore across the Mexican border into the United States. Pretty good Whip Wilson vehicle.

3192 Silver Range. Monogram, 1946. 53 minutes B/W. D: Lambert Hillyer. SC: J. Benton Cheney. WITH Johnny Mack Brown, Raymond Hatton, Jan Bryant, I. Stanford Jolley, Terry Frost, Eddie Parker, Ted Adams, Frank LaRue, Cactus Mack, Lane Bradford, Bill Willmering, George Morrell, Dee Cooper. A cattleman aids a former lawman in finding a kidnapped man and the culprits behind a silver smuggling operation. Nicely done and compact actioner.

3193 Silver River. Warner Brothers-First National, 1948. 110 minutes B/W. D: Raoul Walsh. SC: Stephen Longstreet & Harriet Frank Jr. WITH Errol Flynn, Ann Sheridan, Thomas Mitchell, Bruce Bennett, Tom D'Andrea, Barton MacLane, Monte Blue, Jonathan Hale, Alan Bridge, Arthur Space, Art Baker, Joseph Crehan. A one-time Civil War officer becomes a gambler and then a rancher who almost loses everyone he cares for due to his greed. Okay Errol Flynn vehicle, but

not up to the standard of his earlier genre vehicles.

3194 Silver Spurs. Universal, 1936. 60 minutes B/W. D: Ray Taylor, SC: Joseph Poland. WITH Buck Jones, Muriel Evans, J. P. McGowan, George ("Gabby") Hayes, Dennis Moore, Beth Marion, Robert Frazer, Bruce Lane, Charles K. French, William Lawrence, Earl Askam, Kernan Cripps. A cowboy aids a rancher plagued by rustlers. Very good Buck Jones vehicle, produced by the star.

3195 Silver Spurs. Republic, 1943. 54 (65) minutes B/W. D: Joseph Kane. SC: John K. Butler & J. Benton Cheney. WITH Roy Rogers, Smiley Burnette, John Carradine, Phyllis Brooks, Jerome Cowan, Joyce Compton, Dick Wessel, Hal Taliaferro, Forrest Taylor, Charles Wilson, Byron Foulger, Bob Nolan & The Sons of the Pioneers, Kermit Maynard, Tom London, Jack Kirk, Jack O'Shea, Slim Whitaker, Arthur Loft, Eddy Waller, Bud Osborne, Fred Burns, Henry Wills. Roy Rogers is blamed for the killing of his ex-boss by a swindler who is responsible for the murder. Villain John Carradine adds some class to this entertaining Roy Rogers entry which boasts an exciting shootout finale and good stunt work. V: Video Connection.

3196 Silver Stallion. Monogram, 1941. 59 minutes B/W. D: Edward Finney. SC: Robert Emmett (Tansey). WITH David Sharpe, LeRoy Mason, Chief Thundercloud, Walter Long, Janet Waldo, Thornton Edwards, Fred Hoose, Thunder (horse), Captain Boots (dog). Three men are forced to become thieves as one of them tries to find the man who framed his brother. Modest actioner marred by too much stock footage, although David Sharpe, LeRoy Mason and Chief Thundercloud are likable triad heroes.

3197 The Silver Star. Lippert, 1955. 73 minutes B/W. D: Richard Bartlett. SC: Richard Bartlett & Ian MacDonald. WITH Edgar Buchanan, Marie Windsor, Lon Chaney, Earle Lyon, Richard Bartlett, Barton MacLane, Morris Ankrum, Edith Evanson, Michael Whalen, Steve Rowland, Jimmy Wakely (voice). A pacifistic sheriff does not want to face three gunmen hired to kill him and an old-time lawman comes to his defense. Low grade production has little to offer except for some good work by veterans Edgar Buchanan, Marie Windsor, Lon Chaney, etc. and a title tune sung by Jimmy Wakely.

3198 The Silver Trail. Reliable, 1937. 58 minutes B/W. D: Raymond Samuels (Bernard B. Ray). SC: Bennett Cohen & Forrest Sheldon. WITH Rin-Tin-Tin Jr., Rex Lease, Mary Russell, Ed Cassidy, Roger Williams, Steve Clark, Oscar Gahan, Sherry Tansey, Tom London. A man and a dog join forces to stop crooks who are murdering miners in order to put together a silver combine. Low grade dual biller.

3199 Silver Trails. Monogram, 1948. 53 minutes B/W. D: Christy Cabanne. SC: J. Benton Cheney. WITH Jimmy Wakely, Dub Taylor, Christine Larson, George J. Lewis, Pierce Lyden, Whip Wilson, William Norton Bailey, Fred Edwards, Robert Strange, Bob Woodward, Bud Osborne. In California crooks try to steal land by causing a feud between settlers and ranchers. One of the better Jimmy Wakely films thanks to good direction and a flashy performance by Whip Wilson in a supporting role.

3200 The Silver Whip. 20th Century-Fox, 1953. 73 minutes B/W. D: Harmon Jones. SC: Jesse Lasky Jr. WITH Dale Robertson, Rory Calhoun, Robert Wagner, Kathleen Crowley, James Millican, Lola Albright, J. M. Kerrigan, John Kellogg, Harry Carter, Ian MacDonald, Robert Adler, Clancy Cooper, Burt Mustin, Dan White, Paul Wexler, Bobby Diamond, Jack Rice, Charles Watts. Wanting to be like two men, a sheriff and a stage guard he admires, a young man takes on the job of a stage driver and runs into outlaws. A good cast adds some life to this otherwise average outing.

3201 Silverado. Columbia, 1985. 132 minutes Color. D: Lawrence Kasdan. SC: Lawrence Kasdan & Mark Kasdan. WITH Kevin Kline, Scott Glenn, Kevin Costner, Danny Glover, John Cleese, Rosanna Arquette, Brian Dennehy, Linda Hunt, Jeff Goldblum. Two drifters join forces and arrive in the town of Silverado where they fight a corrupt man who controls the law. Overlong but pretty good look at the mythical Old West.

3202 Sin Town. Universal, 1942. 74 minutes B/W. D: Ray Enright. SC: W. Scott Darling & Gerald Geraghty. WITH Constance Bennett, Broderick Crawford, Anne Gwynne, Patric Knowles, Andy Devine, Leo Carrillo, Ward Bond, Arthur Aylesworth, Ralf Harolde, Charles Wagenheim, Billy Wayne, Hobart Bosworth, Jack Mulhall, Paul Bryar, Rebel Randall, Jean Trent, Oscar O'Shea, Eddy Waller, Clarence Muse, Ben Erdway, Ed Peil Sr., Harry Strang, Guy Usher, Victor Zimmerman, George J. Lewis, Larry McGrath, Murray Parker, Frank Hagney, Neeley Edwards, Jack C. Smith, Kernan Cripps, Art Miles, Charles Marsh, Frank Coleman. A pair of confidence operators arrive in a small town where a lynch mob is after the murderer of the newspaper editor. A good cast and fast pacing make this potboiler adequate diversion.

3203 Sing, Cowboy, Sing. Grand National, 1937. 60 minutes B/W. D: Robert North Bradbury. SC: Robert Emmett (Tansey). WITH Tex Ritter, Louise Stanley, Al St. John, Karl Hackett, Charles King, Bob McKenzie, Budd Buster, Heber Snow (Hank Worden), Chick Hannon, Horace Murphy, Snub Pollard, Tex Palmer, Jack C. Smith, Oscar Gahan, Herman Hack, Milburn Morante, Tex Ritter's Tornadoes. Two cowpokes masquerade as entertainers in order to find who killed a girl's father who ran a shipping franchise. Good scenic locations and a very actionful climax help this Tex Ritter vehicle which also has the benefit of a quartet of songs, including the very good title tune.

3204 The Singer Not the Song. Warner Brothers/Rank, 1961. 129 minutes Color. D: Roy Baker. SC: Nigel Balchin. WITH Dirk Bogarde, John Mills, Mylene Demongeot, Laurence Naismith, John Bentley, Leslie French, Eric Pohlmann, Nyall Florenz, Roger Delgado, Philip Gilbert, Sheila Gallagher, Selma Vaz Dias, Laurence Payne, Jacqueline Evans, Lee Montague, Serafina DiLeo. In a small Mexican village a new priest vies for control of the people with a bandit while trying to fend off the lust of a local beauty. Overlong and dull melodrama.

3205 Singin' in the Corn. Columbia, 1946. 65 minutes B/W. D: Del Lord. SC: Richard Weil. WITH Judy Canova, Allen Jenkins, Guinn Williams, Alan Bridge, Charles Halton, Robert Dudley, Nick Thompson, George Chesebro, Ethan Laidlaw, Francis Rel, Frank Lackteen, Guy Beach, Jay Silverheels, Rod Redwing, Dick Stanley, Charles Reynolds, Si Jenks, Pat O'Malley, Chester Conklin, Mary Gordon. A carnival mindreader inherits a ranch and tries to stop crooks from cheating local Indians. More comedy corn from Judy Canova; for her fans only.

3206 The Singing Buckaroo. Spectrum, 1937. 60 minutes B/W. D-SC: Tom Gibson.

WITH Fred Scott, Cliff Nazarro, Victoria Vinton, William Faversham, Howard Hill, Roger Williams, Rosa Caprino, Carl Mathews, Dick Curtis, Augie Gomez, Shorty Miller, Wade Walker, Oscar Gahan, The Singing Buckaroos. A cowboy comes to the aid of a girl who has taken money for safekeeping but whose father is a hostage of crooks after the currency. Entertaining Fred Scott musical opus. V: Video Images.

3207 The Singing Cowboy. Republic, 1936. 56 minutes B/W. D: Mack V. Wright. SC: Dorrell McGowan & Stuart McGowan. WITH Gene Autry, Smiley Burnette, Lois Wilde, Lon Chaney Jr., Ann Gillis, John Van Pelt, Earle Hodgins, Earl Eby, Ken Cooper, Harrison Greene, Wes Warner, Jack Rockwell, Tracy Layne, Fred "Snowflake" Toones, Oscar Gahan, Frankie Marvin, Jack Kirk, Audrey Davis, George Pearce, Charlie McAvoy, Alfred P. James, Pat Carson, Harvey Clark. A singing cowboy becomes the guardian of a young girl after her mine-owner father is murdered and he needs to earn the money for an operation the girl needs. Fine interpolation of music, story line and action make this Gene Autry vehicle a good one.

3208 The Singing Cowgirl. Grand National, 1939. 59 minutes B/W. D: Samuel Diege. SC: Arthur Hoerl. WITH Dorothy Page, Dave O'Brien, Vince Barnett, Ed Peil, Dix Davis, Stanley Price, Warner Richmond, Dorothy Short, Paul Barrett, Lloyd Ingrahan, Ethan Allen, Ed Gordon, Merrill McCormack. A young woman rancher takes in a boy whose parents have been killed by rustlers and she sets out to help round up the gang. Last of the trio of cowgirl actioners starring Dorothy Page; an okay series entry. V: Cassette Express.

3209 Singing Guns. Republic, 1950. 91 minutes Color. D: R. G. Springsteen. SC: Dorrell McGowan & Stuart McGowan. WITH Vaughn Monroe, Ella Raines, Walter Brennan, Ward Bond, Jeff Corey, Barry Kelley, Harry Shannon, Tom Fadden, Ralph Dunn, Rex Lease, George Chandler, Billy Gray, Mary Baer, Jimmie Dodd. A notorious outlaw ends up saving the life of the lawman tracking him and with a new identity becomes the sheriff of a small town. Bandleader-singer Vaughn Monroe makes a very convincing Western star in this entertaining "A" production and he manages to sing a little, too!

3210 The Singing Hill. Republic, 1941. 54 (61) minutes B/W. D: Lew Landers. SC: Olive Cooper. WITH Gene Autry, Smiley Burnette, Virginia Dale, Mary Lee, Spencer Charters, Gerald Oliver Smith, George Meeker, Wade Boteler, Harry Stubbs, Cactus Mack, Jack Kirk, Chuck Morrison, Monte Montague, Sam Flint, Hal Price, Fred Burns, Herman Hack, Jack O'Shea. When a young girl wants to sell the ranch she inherited, neighboring ranchers fear the sale will bring an end to their open range. Average Gene Autry vehicle.

3211 The Singing Outlaw. Universal, 1938. 56 minutes B/W. D: Joseph H. Lewis. SC: Harry O. Hoyt. WITH Bob Baker, Joan Barclay, Fuzzy Knight, Carl Stockdale, Harry Woods, LeRoy Mason, Ralph Lewis, Glenn Strange, Georgia O'Dell, Jack Rockwell, Ed Peil Sr., Jack Kirk, Robert McKenzie, Budd Buster, Lafe McKee, Hank Worden, Art Mix, Chick Hannon, Herman Hack, Jack Montgomery, Curley Gibson, Francis Walker. In order to find out who murdered a U. S. marshal, a cowboy takes on the identity of the lawman and gets on the trail of a gang of rustlers. Despite a fine supporting cast, this Bob Baker musical vehicle is substandard entertainment-wise.

3212 The Singing Sheriff. Universal, 1944. 60 minutes B/W. D: Leslie Goodwins. SC: Henry Blankfort & Eugene Conrad. WITH Bob Crosby, Fay McKenzie, Fuzzy Knight, Iris Adrian, Samuel S. Hinds, Edward Norris, Andrew Tombes, Joseph Sawyer, Walter Sande, Doodles Weaver, Jean Trent, Donald Kerr, Pat Starling, Louis Da Pron, Spade Cooley & Orchestra. The son of a prominent citizen arrives in town incognito and immediately gets involved with the sheriff and outlaws. Slim musical vehicle for bandleader Bob Crosby.

3213 The Singing Vagabond. Republic, 1935. 54 minutes B/W. D: Carl L. Pierson. SC: Oliver Drake & Betty Burbridge. WITH Gene Autry, Smiley Burnette, Ann Rutherford, Barbara Pepper, Warner Richmond, Frank LaRue, Grace Goodall, Niles Welch, Tom Bower, Robinson Neeman, Henry Rocquemore, Ray (Corrigan) Bernard, Alan Sears, Bob Burns, Charles King, Chief Big Tree, Chief Thundercloud, Marie Quillan, Elaine Shepherd, Edmund Cobb, George (Montgomery) Letz. A young girl, who has run away from home to join a traveling show, is rescued by a cavalry captain when her wagon train is attacked. Okay Gene Autry film, with more music than action.

3214 Single Handed Sanders. Monogram, 1932. 61 minutes B/W. D: Lloyd Nosler. SC: Charles A. Post. WITH Tom Tyler, Margaret Morris, Lois Bridge, Robert Manning, G. D. Woods, John Elliott, Hank Bell, Fred "Snowflake" Toones. A blacksmith, whose brother is a crook, tries to save his girl and their town from a gang led by a senator. Poorly made and creaky Tom Tyler vehicle.

3215 Sinister Journey. United Artists, 1948. 59 minutes B/W. D: George Archainbaud. SC: Doris Schroeder. WITH William Boyd, Andy Clyde, Rand Brooks, Elaine Riley, John Kellogg, Don Haggerty, Stanley Andrews, Harry Strang, Herbert Rawlinson, John Butler, Wayne Treadway. The Bar 20 trio helps a young man clear himself of a murder charge and get him reunited with his girl. Mild "Hopalong Cassidy" feature which plays better as a 27-minute segment of the Hoppy TV series.

3216 Sioux City Sue. Republic, 1946. 54 (68) minutes B/W. D: Frank McDonald. SC: Olive Cooper. WITH Gene Autry, Lynne Roberts, Sterling Holloway, The Cass County Boys, Richard Lane, Ralph Sanford, Ken Lundy, Helen Wallace, Pierre Watkin, Edwin Wills, Minerva Urecal, Frank Marlowe, LeRoy Mason, Harry V. Cheshire, George Carleton, Sam Flint, Tex Terry, Tristram Coffin, Frankie Marvin. In order to pay off his debts and save his ranch, a singing cowboy is persuaded by a pretty talent scout to make a movie but he finds out only his voice is used in an animated feature for a donkey. Gene Autry's first feature after World War II service is a pleasant affair, although more for comedy and music than traditional genre values. V: Blackhawk.

3217 Sitting Bull. United Artists, 1954. 105 minutes Color. D: Sidney Salkow. SC: Jack DeWitt & Sidney Salkow. WITH Dale Robertson, Mary Murphy, J. Carrol Naish, Iron Eyes Cody, John Litel, William Hopper, Douglas Kennedy, Bill Tannen, Joel Fluellen, John Hamilton, Thomas Browne Henry, Felix Gonzalez, Al Wyatt. A young pro-Indian soldier is falsely accused of aiding Chief Sitting Bull at the time of the Custer massacre. Silly, boring, and over-long, this pseudo-historical piece is notable only for J. Carrol Naish's fine performance in the title role.

3218 Sitting Bull at the Spirit Lake Massacre. Sunset, 1927. 72 minutes B/W. D: Robert North Bradbury. SC: Ben Allah. WITH Bryant Washburn, Ann Schaeffer, Jay Morley, Shirley Palmer, Thomas Lingham, Chief Yowlachie, James O'Neil, Bob (Steele) Bradbury Jr., Fred Warren, Leon Kent, Lucille Ballart. A young scout falls for a pretty girl but their romance is interrupted by an Indian uprising led by Chief Sitting Bull. Pretty good low budget actioner with a chance to see Bob Steele in his pre-series days. Also called **With Sitting Bull at the Spirit Lake Massacre.**

3219 Six Black Horses. Universal-International, 1962. 80 minutes Color. D: Harry Keller. SC: Burt Kennedy. WITH Audie Murphy, Dan Duryea, Joan O'Brien, George Wallace, Roy Barcroft, Bob Steele, Henry Wills, Phil Chambers, Richard Pasco, Charles Regis, Dale Van Sickel. A woman hires two men to lead her through Indian lands as she plans to kill one of them, a gunman who murdered her husband. Pretty good melodrama highlighted by Dan Duryea's slick villain portrayal.

3220 Six Foot Four. American Film Company, 1919. 50 minutes B/W. SC: Stephen Fox. WITH William Russell, Vola Vale, Harvey Clark, Al Garcia, Charles K. French, Jack Brammal, Jack Collins, John Gough. A crooked sheriff teams with a rancher in trying to blame two robberies on another cattleman whose ranch is wanted by them. Actionful silent outing and a chance to see William Russell at his peak.

3221 Six Gun Gold. RKO Radio, 1941. 57 minutes B/W. D: David Howard. SC: Norton S. Parker. WITH Tim Holt, Ray Whitley, Jan Clayton, Lee "Lasses" White, Lane Chandler, LeRoy Mason, Eddy Waller, Davidson Clark, Harry Harvey Sr., Slim Whitaker, Jim Corey, Fern Emmett. A young man, whose marshal brother has been kidnapped by gold thieves, tries to find him and get to the bottom of the robberies. Interesting Tim Holt vehicle.

3222 Six Gun Gospel. Monogram, 1943. 54 minutes B/W. D: Lambert Hillyer. SC: Ed Earl Repp & Jess Bowers (Adele Buffington). WITH Johnny Mack Brown, Raymond Hatton, Inna Gest, Kenneth MacDonald, Roy Barcroft, Edmund Cobb, Mary McLaren, Eddie Dew, Bud Osborne, Milburn Morante, Artie Ortego, Lynton Brent, Kernan Cripps, Jack Daley. Two lawmen, one masquerading as a preacher, try to find out who is behind the hijacking of gold shipments. The same old plot is given a fairly good treatment in this Johnny Mack Brown film.

3223 Six Gun Law. Columbia, 1948. 54 minutes B/W. D: Ray Nazarro. SC: Barry Shipman. WITH Charles Starrett, Smiley Burnette, Nancy Saunders, Paul Campbell, Hugh Prosser, George Chesebro, Curley Clements & His Rodeo Rangers, Billy Dix, Robert Wilke, Bob Cason, Ethan Laidlaw, Pierce Lyden, Bud Osborne, Budd Buster, Slim Gault. A rancher is falsely accused of murdering the local sheriff and forced to sign a confession by the gang leader who then makes him the new sheriff, thinking he can control him, not realizing the rancher is really the Durango Kid. Fair "Durango Kid" film.

3224 Six-Gun Law. Buena Vista, 1963. 78 minutes Color. D: Christian Nyby. WITH Robert Loggia, James Dunn, Lynn Bari, Annette (Funicello), Jay C. Flippen, Patrick Knowles, Audrey Dalton, James Drury, Kenneth Tobey, R. G. Armstrong, Grant Withers, Edward Colmans. When a notorious rustler is murdered an English rancher is charged with the shooting. Entertaining Western issued in Europe and originally a segment of Walt Disney's TV series on ABC-TV, telecast on February 6, 1959 as "Attorney at Law" in "The Nine Lives of Elfego Baca" mini-series.

3225 Six Gun Man. Producers Releasing Corporation, 1946. 59 minutes B/W. D-SC: Harry Fraser. WITH Bob Steele, Syd Saylor, Jean Carlin, Bud Osborne, Brooke Temple, I. Stanford Jolley, Budd Buster, Roy Brent, Jimmie Martin, Stanley Blystone, Steve Clark, Dorothy Whitmore, Ray Jones. Rustlers are terrorizing the citizens of a small town and two U. S. marshals try to stop them. Ragged PRC effort, mainly for Bob Steele fans.

3226 Six Gun Mesa. Monogram, 1950. 57 minutes B/W. D: Wallace Fox. SC: Adele Buffington. WITH Johnny Mack Brown, Gail Davis, Riley Hill, Leonard Penn, Marshall Reed, Steve Clark, Milburn Morante, Carl Mathews, Bud Osborne, George DeNormand, Stanley Blystone, Holly Bane, Frank Jacquet, Artie Ortego, Merrill McCormack. A town boss tries to blame the foreman of a cattle herd for the murder of its wranglers but a lawman suspects the plot. Fair Johnny Mack Brown vehicle; shows the wear on the genre with the coming of the 1950s.

3227 Six-Gun Rhythm. Grand National/ Arcadia, 1939. 55 minutes B/W. D: Sam Newfield. SC: Fred Myton. WITH Tex Fletcher, Joan Barclay, Ralph Peters, Reed Howes, Bud McTaggert, Ted Adams, Walter Shumway, Slim Hacker, Carl Mathews, Art Davis, Robert Frazer, Sherry Tansey, Kit Guard, Art Mix, Jack O'Shea, Frank Ellis. A singing football player returns home to Texas to find his sheriff-father missing and the area infested with outlaws. Tex Fletcher's only oater is a fairly pleasant affair except for an obtrusive canned music track although Tex does get to warble several tunes, including "Lonesome Cowboy" and "Git Along Little Doggies." V: Video Dimensions.

3228 Six Gun Serenade. Monogram, 1947. 55 minutes B/W. D: Ford Beebe. SC: Bennett Cohen. WITH Jimmy Wakely, Lee "Lasses" White, Jimmie Martin, Kay Morley, Steve Clark, Pierce Lyden, Bud Osborne, Chick Hannon, Cactus Mack. Ranchers get a group of cowboys out of jail in order to stop a gang of cattle thieves. Good direction and script lift this Jimmy Wakely vehicle a bit above the usual for the musical star.

3229 Six-Gun Trail. Victory, 1938. 60 minutes B/W. D: Sam Newfield. SC: Joseph O'Donnell. WITH Tim McCoy, Nora Lane, Alden Chase, Ben Corbett, Karl Hackett, Donald Gallagher, Ted Adams, Kenne Duncan, Sherry Tansey, Bob Terry, Jimmie Aubrey, George Morrell. A Justice Department investigator, masquerading as a Chinaman, heads to a small town to capture an outlaw gang trying to sell stolen gems. Surprisingly good Sam Katzman production, although more for plot, acting and direction than budget.

3230 Six-Shootin' Sheriff. Grand National, 1938. 59 minutes B/W. D: Harry Fraser. SC: Weston Edwards. WITH Ken Maynard, Marjorie Reynolds, Jane Keckley, Bob Terry, Harry Harvey Sr., Walter Long, Earl Dwire, Ben Corbett, Lafe McKee, Tom London, Warner Richmond, Richard Alexander, Glenn Strange, Roger Williams, Bud Osborne, Ed Piel Sr., Milburn Morante, Carl Mathews, Herb Holcombe. An outlaw is accidentally made the sheriff of a small town and when his old gang arrives on the scene he tries to warn them away but when they pull a robbery he goes after them. Poor production values hurt this Ken Maynard vehicle; hardly one of his better efforts. V: Video Communications.

3231 Skin Game. Warner Brothers, 1971. 102 minutes Color. D: Paul Bogart. SC: Pierre Marton. WITH James Garner, Lou Gossett, Susan Clark, Brenda Sykes, Edward Asner, Andrew Duggan, Henry Jones, Neva Patterson, Parley Baer, George Tyne, Royal Dano, Pat O'Malley, Joel Fluellen, Napoleon Whiting, Juanita Moore, Cort Clark, Jim Boles, George Wallace, Robert Foulk, Bill Henry, Tom Monroe, Don Haggerty, Claude Stroud, Forrest Lewis, James McCallion, Dan Borgaze, Reg Parton, Bob Steele. Before the Civil War, two con men, one black and the other white, travel around the South with the latter "selling" the former and the two split the proceeds. Entertaining genre comedy which was later done as a TV movie called **Sidekicks** (q.v.).

3232 Skipalong Rosenbloom. United Artists, 1951. 72 minutes B/W. D: Sam Newfield. SC: Dean Riesner & Eddie Forman. WITH Maxie Rosenbloom, Max Baer, Jackie Coogan, Hillary Brooke, Fuzzy Knight, Jacqueline Fontaine, Raymond Hatton, Ray Walker, Sam Lee, Al Shaw, Joseph Greene, Dewey Robinson, Whitey Haupt, Carl Mathews, Artie Ortego. An Eastern gunman sets out to put an end to the lawlessness caused by a bad man. Broad genre take-off, starring the two boxing greats, with lots of slapstick. Reissue title: **The Square Shooter.**

3233 Skull and Crown. Reliable, 1935. 60 minutes B/W. D: Elmer Clifton. SC: Bennett Cohen & Carl Krusada. WITH Rin-Tin-Tin Jr., Regis Toomey, Jack Mulhall, Molly O'Day, James Murray, Lois January, Jack Mower, Tom London, Robert Walker, John Elliott. A dog and a lawman are on the trail of smugglers working on the Mexican border. Poverty row effort of interest mainly due to its cast.

3234 Sky Bandits. Monogram, 1940. 56 minutes B/W. D: Ralph Staub. SC: Edward Halperin. WITH James Newill, Louise Stanley, Dave O'Brien, William Pawley, Ted Adams, Bob Terry, Dwight Frye, Joseph Stefani, Dewey Robinson, Jack Clifford, Kenne Duncan. Looking into the disappearance of a plane carrying gold from a Yukon mine, Canadian Mounties uncover crooks using a mysterious ray. The use of sci-fi in the plot makes this "Renfrew of the Royal Mounted" series interesting although most of the plot is very similar to the same series' **Yukon Flight** (q.v.).

3235 Sky High. Fox, 1922. 72 minutes B/W. D-SC: Lynn Reynolds. WITH Tom Mix, Eva Novak, J. Farrell MacDonald, Sid Jordan, William Buckley, Adele Warner, Wynn Mace, Pat Chrisman. An immigration officer is assigned to find out who is smuggling Chinese immigrants across the Mexican border. Thrill-packed and entertaining Tom Mix silent film. V: Glenn Photo.

3236 The Sky Pilot. Associated First National, 1921. 45 minutes B/W. D: King Vidor. SC: John McDermott. WITH John Bowers, Colleen Moore, David Butler, Harry Todd, James Corrigan, Donald MacDonald, Kathleen Kirkham. In the Canadian northwest a minister gets a rough reception from the local cowboys but he later saves the life of the ranch owner's daughter. This silent melodrama still holds up rather well. V: Film Classic Exchange.

3237 Slaughter Trail. RKO Radio, 1951. 78 minutes Color. D: Irving Allen. SC: Sid Kuller. WITH Brian Donlevy, Gig Young, Virginia Grey, Andy Devine, Robert Hutton, Terry Wilkerson, Lew Bedell, Myron Healey, Ken Kountik, Eddie Parker, Ralph Peters, Ric Roman, Lois Hall. Escaping after a robbery, and aided by a woman, an outlaw gang murders three Indians and the commander of a fort. Passable action melodrama with "A" trappings.

3238 Slay Ride. CBS-TV/20th Century-Fox, 1972. 100 minutes Color. D: Robert Day. SC: Anthony Wilson & Rick Husky. WITH Glenn Ford, Edgar Buchanan, Victor Campos, Peter Ford, Leslie Parrish, Gerald S. O'Loughlin, Tony Bill, John Schuck, Anne Seymour, Sam Chew, Harry Lauter, Bernie Casey, Hunter Von Leer, Mark Jenkins, Jill Banner, Dehl Berti. A sheriff in a small southwestern community tries to solve a murder case but finds the situation complicated by an Apache who is a chronic confessor. Well done telefeature originally telecast as two segments of the program "Cade's County" (CBS-TV, 1971-72).

3239 Slim Carter. Universal-International, 1957. 82 minutes Color. D: Richard Bartlett. SC: Montgomery Pittman. WITH Jock Mahoney, Julie Adams, Tim Hovey, William Hopper, Ben Johnson, Joanna Moore, Walter Reed, Bill Williams, Barbara Hale, Maggie Mahoney, Roxanne Arlen, Jean Moorehead, Donald Kerr, Jim Healey. A young orphan, who has won a contest, spends a month with his favorite Western star, and the latter changes from an egotist who eventually wants to adopt the boy. Surprisingly good satirical look at Hollywood and cowboy stars with a fine performance by Jock Mahoney.

3240 Smith. Buena Vista, 1969. 102 minutes Color. D: Michael O'Herlihy. SC: Louis Pelletier. WITH Glenn Ford, Nancy Olson, Dean Jagger, Keenan Wynn, Warren Oates, Chief Dan George, Frank Ramirez, Jay Silverheels. A rancher tries to help an Indian boy falsely accused of murder. Easygoing Disney feature filmed in Washington and Oregon.

3241 Smoke in the Wind. Adelphi Film Distributors, 1976. 94 minutes Color. D: Joseph Kane. SC: Eric Allen. WITH Walter Brennan, John Ashley, John Russell, Myron Healey, Susan Houston, Linda Weld, Henry Kingi, Adair Jameson, Dan White, Lorna Thayer, Billy Hughes Jr., Bill Foster, Jack Horton, Bill McKenzie. Following the Civil War Confederate veterans return to their Arkansas mountain homeland only to be attacked as traitors to the cause. Originally made in 1971, director Joseph Kane's final feature is mainly of interest due to his direction and the film's cast

3242 Smoke Jumpers. CBS-TV/20th Century-Fox, 1956. 45 minutes B/W. WITH Dan Duryea, Joan Leslie, Dean Jagger, Richard Jaeckel, John Conte. When the leader of a fire-fighting unit is the only survivor of a forest fire, he is accused of sacrificing his men in order to save himself. Well acted drama, a television remake of **Red Skies of Montana** (q.v.), originally shown as part of "The Twentieth Century Fox Hour" (CBS-TV, 1955-57) on November 14, 1956.

3243 Smoke Lightning. Fox, 1933. 63 minutes B/W. D: David Howard. SC: Gordon Rigby & Sidney Mitchell. WITH George O'Brien, Nell O'Day, Betsy King Ross, Frank Atkinson, Virginia Sale, Douglass Dumbrille, Morgan Wallace, Clarence Wilson, George Burton, Fred Wilson. When a small orphan girl is about to be cheated by her crooked uncle and his lawman cohort a cowboy protects her. Entertaining adaptation of Zane Grey's Canyon Walls.

3244 Smoke Signal. Universal-International, 1955. 88 minutes Color. D: Jerry Hopper. SC: George F. Slavin & George W. George.

WITH Dana Andrews, Piper Laurie, Rex Reason, William Talman, Milburn Stone, Douglas Spencer, Gordon Jones, William Schallert, Bill Phipps, Robert Wilke, Pat Hogan, Peter Coe. After Indians attack and destroy a frontier post, the survivors head for safety aboard flatboats on the Colorado River. Actionful and entertaining drama.

3245 Smoke Tree Range. Universal, 1937. 60 minutes B/W. D: Lesley Selander. SC: Arthur Henry Gordon. WITH Buck Jones, Muriel Evans, John Elliott, Edmund Cobb, Robert Kortman, Donald Kirke, Ted Adams, Ben Hall, Dickie Jones, Lee Phelps, Charles King, Earle Hodgins, Mabel Concord, Eddie Phillips, Bob McKenzie, Slim Whitaker. A cowboy aids an orphaned girl whose cattle are being rustled by an outlaw gang. Fine Buck Jones vehicle, produced by the star.

3246 Smokey Smith. Supreme, 1935. 58 minutes B/W. D-SC: Robert North Bradbury. WITH Bob Steele, Mary Kornman, George ("Gabby") Hayes, Warner Richmond, Earl Dwire, Horace B. Carpenter, Tex Phelps, Archie Ricks. A cowboy sets out to find the outlaws who murdered his parents. Another revenge-angle oater for Bob Steele, but a fairly good one. V: Cassette Express.

3247 Smoking Guns. Universal, 1934. 65 minutes B/W. D: Alan James. SC: Ken Maynard. WITH Ken Maynard, Gloria Shea, Jack Rockwell, Walter Miller, William Gould, Harold Goodwin, Robert Kortman, Edward Coxen, Edgar "Blue" Washington, Etta McDaniel, Slim Whitaker, Bob Reeves, Jim Corey, Wally Wales, Edmund Cobb, Fred McKaye, Martin Turner, Hank Bell, Horace B. Carpenter, Roy Bucko, Buck Bucko, Ben Corbett, Blackjack Ward, Bud McClure, Cliff Lyons. Falsely accused of a crime, a cowboy heads to the jungles of South America but is followed by a Texas Ranger and the two become friends and when the latter dies after being attacked by crocodiles the cowboy takes over his identity and returns home to clear himself. Ken Maynard's final Universal vehicle, which he also wrote, is actually rather fun if taken tongue-in-cheek.

3248 Smoky. Fox, 1933. 69 minutes B/W. D: Eugene Forde. SC: Stuart Anthony & Paul Perez. WITH Victor Jory, Irene Manning, LeRoy Mason, Hank Mann, Frank Campeau, Leonard Snegoff, Will James. A cowboy befriends and tames a beautiful stallion who has been made hostile by crooks. Okay programmer, the first of a trio of features based on the Will James book; the author appears in this version.

3249 Smoky. 20th Century-Fox, 1946. 87 minutes Color. D: Louis King. SC: Lillie Hayward, Dwight Cummings & Dorothy Yost. WITH Fred MacMurray, Anne Baxter, Burl Ives, Bruce Cabot, Esther Dale, Roy Roberts, J. Farrell MacDonald, Max Wagner, Guy Beach, Howard Negley, Bud Geary, Harry Carter, Bob Adler, Victor Kilian, Herbert Heywood, Douglas Spencer, Stanley Andrews. A man befriends, tames and trains a wild stallion who has a hatred of humans. Satisfying drama based on Will James' novel.

3250 Smoky. 20th Century-Fox, 1966. 103 minutes Color. D: George Sherman. SC: Howard Medford. WITH Fess Parker, Diana Hyland, Katy Jurado, Hoyt Axton, Robert Wilke, Armando Silvestre, Jose Hector, Ted White, Chuck Roberson, Bob Terhune. A wrangler captures and trains a black stallion but his brother beats the animal, who tramples him and escapes. Fair remake of the 1946 version (q.v.).

3251 Smoky Canyon. Columbia, 1951. 55 minutes B/W. D: Fred F. Sears. SC: Barry Shipman. WITH Charles Starrett, Smiley Burnette, Jack (Jock) Mahoney, Dani Sue Nolan, Tristram Coffin, Larry Hudson, Chris Alcaide, Sandy Sanders, Forrest Taylor, Charles Stevens, LeRoy Johnson, Boyd "Red" Morgan. Sheepmen are being blamed for the slaughter of cattle and a government agent investigates and finds out the cause is actually crooked cattlemen trying to deplete herds in order to raise prices. Fast moving and compact "Durango Kid" series episode.

3252 Smoky Mountain Melody. Columbia, 1948. 61 minutes B/W. D: Ray Nazarro. SC: Barry Shipman. WITH Roy Acuff, Guinn Williams, Russell Arms, Sybil Merritt, Jason Robards, Harry V. Cheshire, Fred Sears, Trevor Bardette, Carolina Cotton, Tommy Ivo, Jock Mahoney, John Elliott, Sam Flint, Ralph Littlefield, Eddie Acuff, Heinie Conklin, Olin Howlin, The Smoky Mountain Boys. A singer gets a three month trial run at running a ranch and the late owner's son tries to sabotage his chances. Pleasant country music-Western starring the great Roy Acuff and His Smoky Mountain Boys,

including Bashful Brother Oswald (Pete Kirby).

3253 Smoky Trails. Metropolitan, 1939. 55 minutes B/W. D: Bernard B. Ray. SC: George Plympton. WITH Bob Steele, Jean Carmen, Murdock McQuarrie, Jimmie Aubrey, Frank LaRue, Ted Adams, George Chesebro, Frank Wayne, Bob Terry, Bruce Dane. A cowpoke is on the trail of an outlaw gang, trying to capture them before they commit murder. Barely passable Bob Steele vehicle from producer Harry S. Webb.

3254 Snake River Desperadoes. Columbia, 1951. 54 minutes B/W. D: Fred F. Sears. SC: Barry Shipman. WITH Charles Starrett, Smiley Burnette, Monte Blue, Don Kay Reynolds (Little Brown Jug), Tommy Ivo, Boyd "Red" Morgan, George Chesebro, John Pickard, Charles Horvath, Sam Flint, Duke York. The Durango Kid tries to keep peace when a series of Indian raids, actually caused by white men dressed as Indians, take place. Well done actioner in the "Durango Kid" series.

3255 Snarl of Hate. Bischoff Productions, 1927. 60 minutes B/W. D: Noel Mason Smith. SC: Ben Bellah. WITH Johnnie Walker, Mildred June, Jack Richardson, Wheeler Oakman, Silverstreak (dog). When his prospector brother is murdered a man sets out to track down the killer. Johnnie Walker plays both the hero and victim in this average silent melodrama.

3256 Snow Dog. Monogram, 1950. 63 minutes B/W. D: Frank McDonald. SC: William Raynor. WITH Kirby Grant, Elena Verdugo, Rick Vallin, Milburn Stone, Richard Karlan, Jane Adrian, Hal Gerard, Richard Avonde, Duke York, Guy Zanette, Chinook (dog). While trailing the killer of a fellow officer, a Mountie uncovers an outlaw gang using wolves to murder their victims. Average outing in Kirby Grant's Monogram-Mountie series.

3257 Snowbeast. NBC-TV, 1977. 96 minutes Color. D: Herb Wallerstein. SC: Joseph Stefano. WITH Bo Svenson, Yvette Mimieux, Robert Logan, Clint Walker, Sylvia Sidney, Michael J. London, Thomas Babson, Kathy Christopher, Ann McEncroe, Richard Jamison, Prentiss Rowe. At a Western ski resort during a winter carnival, the resort owners try to suppress evidence that a murderous monster is on the rampage. Fair made-for-TV horror film.

3258 Snowfire. Allied Artists, 1958. 73 minutes Color. D-SC: Dorrell McGowan & Stuart McGowan. WITH Don Megowan, Molly McGowan, Claire Kelly, John Cason, Michael Vallon, Melody McGowan. When her father captures a wild white stallion, a young girl sets him free and earns his friendship. Pretty good low budget family film.

Snowman see **Land of No Return**

3259 Soft Boiled. Fox, 1923. 78 minutes B/W. D-SC: John G. Blystone. WITH Tom Mix, Billie Dove, Joseph Girard, L. C. Shumway, Tom Wilson, Frank Beal, Jack Curtis, Charles Hill Mailes, Harry Dunkinson, Wilson Hummell. A cowboy tries to control his temper and his uncle bets him he cannot do so for a month and during that time he has to endure insults to his sweetheart without becoming angry. Interesting Tom Mix comedy will please his fans.

3260 Soldier Blue. Avco-Embassy, 1970. 114 minutes Color. D: Ralph Nelson. SC: John Gay. WITH Candice Bergen, Peter Strauss, Donald Pleasence, Bob Carraway, Mort Mills, Jorge Rivero, Dana Elcar, John Anderson, Martin West, Jorge Russek, Marco Antonio Arzate, Ron Fletcher, Barbara Turner, Aurora Clavell. Indians attack a paymaster's detachment and leave only two survivors, a private and a woman planning to wed a lieutenant for his money. Pro-Indian feature is excessively violent and has little to offer.

3261 The Soldiers of Pancho Villa. Unifilms-Cimex, 1958. 90 minutes Color. D: Ismael Rodriguez. SC: Ricardo Garibay. WITH Dolores Del Rio, Maria Felix, Emilio Fernandez, Pedro Armendariz, Antonio Aguilar. During the Mexican Revolution two women of different social classes love a peasant general follower of Pancho Villa. Pretty good Mexican feature, with some well staged battle sequences, which is hurt by mediocre dubbing. Mexican title: **La Cucaracha.**

3262 The Sombrero Kid. Republic, 1942. 56 minutes B/W. D: George Sherman. SC: Norman S. Hall. WITH Don "Red" Barry, Lynn Merrick, Robert Homans, John James, Joel Friedkin, Rand Brooks, Stuart Hamblen, Bob McKenzie, Lloyd "Slim" Andrews, Anne O'Neal, Kenne Duncan, I. Stanford Jolley, Bud Geary, Frank Brownlee, William Nestell, Hank Bell, Curley Dresden, Jack O'Shea, Pascale

Perry, Griff Barnett, Chick Hannon, Merrill McCormack, Ed Cassidy. A young man is forced to become an outlaw by the man who murdered the lawman he thought was his father. Rather complicated and grim Don Barry vehicle, but full of action nonetheless. Bob McKenzie just about steals the show as the jovial Judge Tater. V: Video Dimensions.

3263 Something Big. National General, 1971. 108 minutes Color. D: Andrew V. McLaglen. SC: James Lee Barrett. WITH Dean Martin, Brian Keith, Honor Blackman, Carol White, Ben Johnson, Albert Salmi, Don Knight, Joyce Van Patten, Denver Pyle, Merlin Olsen, Robert Donner, Harry Carey Jr., Judi Meredith, Edward Faulkner, Paul Fix, David Huddleston, Bob Steele, Chuck Hicks, John Kelly. During the Mexican War outlaws battle each other for the possession of a Gatling gun. There is nothing to brag about in this big budget affair.

Something Is Out There see **Day of the Animals**

3264 Something for a Lonely Man. NBC-TV/Universal, 1968. 98 minutes Color. D: Don Taylor. SC: John Fante & Frank Fenton. WITH Dan Blocker, Susan Clark, John Dehner, Warren Oates, Paul Petersen, Don Stroud, Henry Jones, Sandy Kenyon, Edgar Buchanan, Tom Nolan, Dub Taylor, Grady Sutton, Joan Shawlee, Iron Eyes Cody, Ralph Neff, Conlan Carter. A blacksmith tries to redeem himself in the eyes of the people he brought West only to have their town bypassed by the railroad. Dan Blocker fans will like this light affair; made for TV.

3265 Sometimes a Great Notion. Universal, 1971. 113 minutes Color. D: Paul Newman. SC: John Gay. WITH Paul Newman, Henry Fonda, Lee Remick, Michael Sarrazin, Richard Jaeckel, Linda Lawson, Cliff Potts, Sam Gilman, Lee De Broux, Jim Burk, Roy Jenson, Joe Maross, Roy Poole, Charles Tyner, Hal Needham, Dean Smith. An old-time logging baron refuses to take part in a strike against a big lumber company and ends up in a great deal of trouble as a result. Poor modern-day actioner although its cast tries hard. TV title: **Never Give an Inch.**

3266 Somewhere in Sonora. Warner Brothers, 1933. 57 minutes B/W. D: Mack V. Wright. SC: Joe Roach. WITH John Wayne, Henry B. Walthall, Shirley Palmer,

J. P. McGowan, Ann Fay, Frank Rice, Billy Franey, Paul Fix, Ralph Lewis, Slim Whitaker, Jim Corey, Blackie Whiteford. Falsely accused of wrongdoing during a stagecoach race, a cowboy goes to Mexico where he uncovers a plot to rob the mine of the father of the girl he loves. John Wayne fans will enjoy this remake of the 1927 Ken Maynard-First National film of the same title.

3267 Son of a Bad Man. Screen Guild, 1949. 64 minutes B/W. D: Ray Taylor. SC: Ron Ormond & Ira Webb. WITH Lash LaRue, Al St. John, Noel Neill, Michael Whalen, Zon Murray, Frank Lackteen, Francis McDonald, Jack Ingram, Steve Raines, Chuck (Bob/John) Cason, Don C. Harvey, Edna Holland, Bill Bailey, Sandy Sanders, Doye O'Dell, William Norton Bailey. U. S. marshals Lash LaRue and Fuzzy Q. Jones head for a small town whose citizens have been plagued by a gang led by the mysterious El Sombre. Lash LaRue's final Screen Guild series film is fast on the action and sure to please his fans.

3268 The Son of a Gun. G. M. Anderson, 1919. 68 minutes B/W. D: Richard Jones. WITH G. M. "Broncho Billy" Anderson. The town's lovable no-good becomes a hero when he stops a gang of swindlers. Broncho Billy Anderson's final film is worth a look just to see the screen's first cowboy star; otherwise an average silent Western feature.

3269 Son of a Gunfighter. Metro-Goldwyn-Mayer, 1966. 92 minutes Color. D: Paul Landres. SC: Clarke Reynolds. WITH Russ Tamblyn, Kieron Moore, James Philbrook, Fernando Rey, Maria Granada, Aldo Sambrell, Antonio Casas, Ralph Browne. A young man teams with a bounty hunter to get revenge on his father but eventually father and son team to fight a gang of outlaws after a girl's ranch. Mediocre Spanish-made oater.

3270 Son of Belle Starr. Allied Artists, 1953. 70 minutes Color. D: Frank McDonald. SC: D. D. Beauchamp & William Raynor. WITH Keith Larsen, Dona Drake, Peggie Castle, Regis Toomey, James Seay, Myron Healey, Frank Puglia, Robert Keys, I. Stanford Jolley, Paul McGuire, Lane Bradford, Mike Ragan, Joe Dominguez, Alex Montoya. Growing to adulthood, Belle Starr's son attempts to prove he is not an outlaw like his famous mother. There is very little to recommend this tired outing.

3271 Son of Billy the Kid. Screen Guild, 1949. 64 minutes B/W. D: Ray Taylor. SC: Ron Ormond & Ira Webb. WITH Lash LaRue, Al St. John, Marion Colby, June Carr, George Baxter, Terry Frost, John James, House Peters Jr., Clarke Stevens, Bob Duncan, Cliff Taylor, William Perrott, Felipe Turich, Rosa Turich, I. Stanford Jolley, Bud Osborne, Eileen Dixon, Jerry Riggio, Frazer McMinn. A special U. S. marshal heads to a small town to stop an outlaw gang terrorizing the area in order to get mortgages for land wanted by the incoming railroad. Lash LaRue's fans will go for this one which moves along fast enough to cover its budget and script deficits.

3272 Son of Davy Crockett. Columbia, 1941. 59 minutes B/W. D-SC: Lambert Hillyer. WITH Bill Elliott, Iris Meredith, Dub Taylor, Richard Fiske, Kenneth MacDonald, Eddy Waller, Don Curtis, Edmund Cobb, Steve Clark, Harrison Greene, Lloyd Bridges, Curley Dresden, Paul Scanlon, Frank Ellis, Dick Botiller, Ray Jones, Tom London, Merrill McCormack, Martin Garralaga, Lew Meehan, Jack Ingram, Frank LaRue. President Ulysses S. Grant sends Davy Crockett's son to the unclaimed territory of Yucca Valley as the government's unofficial representative to overthrow a tyrant and his hired killers. Well written and directed segment in the pseudo-historical series of films Bill Elliott did for Columbia.

3273 Son of Geronimo. Columbia, 1952. 15 Chapters B/W. D: Spencer Gordon Bennet. SC: Arthur Hoerl, Royal K. Cole & George H. Plympton. WITH Clay(ton) Moore, Bud Osborne, Tommy Farrell, Rodd Redwing, Marshall Reed, Eileen Rowe, John Crawford, Zon Murray, Rick Vallin, Lyle Talbot, Chief Yowlachie, Sandy Sanders, Bob Cason, Wally West, Frank Matta. A frontier scout tries to bring peace between settlers and Indians, the latter led by a brave who claims to be Geronimo's son and who is in cahoots with renegade whites. Clayton Moore fans should enjoy this cliffhanger although the star is its main benefit and it's nice to see Bud Osborne (as wagon train boss Tulsa) in a major role.

3274 Son of God's Country. Republic, 1948. 60 minutes B/W. D: R. G. Springsteen. SC: Paul Gangelin. WITH Monte Hale, Pamela Blake, Paul Hurst, Jason Robards, Jay Kirby, Jim Nolan, Steve Darrell, Francis McDonald, Fred Graham, Herman Hack. In order to capture an outlaw gang, a U. S. marshal pretends to be a crook in order to locate the bad men. Pretty fair Monte Hale vehicle. V: Cumberland Video.

3275 Son of Jesse James. P.E.A./Apolofilm, 1965. 90 minutes Color. D: A. Del Amo. SC: Passalacqua & Fondato. WITH Robert Hundar (Claudio Undari), Mercedes Alonso, Adrian Hoven, Ralph Baldwin, Robert Camardiel, Janos Bartha, Joe Kamel, Robert Johnson Jr. Jesse James' grown son is falsely accused of murder and the man who put the blame on him is Bob Ford, the murderer of his famous father. As a pseudo-historical feature, this Italian production may hold some interest. Italian title: **Solo Contro Tutti** (One Against All).

3276 Son of Oklahoma. World Wide, 1932. 57 minutes B/W. D: Robert North Bradbury. SC: Burl Tuttle & George Hull. WITH Bob Steele, Josie Sedgwick, Julian Rivero, Carmen LaRoux, Earl Dwire, Robert Homans, Henry Rocquemore. A cowboy, separated from his family for seventeen years by an outlaw, sets out to find them. Pretty good Bob Steele vehicle with plenty of action.

3277 Son of Paleface. Paramount, 1952. 95 minutes Color. D: Frank Tashlin. SC: Frank Tashlin, Robert L. Welch & Joseph Quillan. WITH Bob Hope, Jane Russell, Roy Rogers, Bill Williams, Lloyd Corrigan, Paul E. Burns, Douglass Dumbrille, Harry Von Zell, Iron Eyes Cody, Wee Willie Davis, Charley Cooley, Charles Morton, Don Dunning, Leo J. McMahon, Felice Richmond, Charmeinne Harker, Isabel Cushin, Jane Easton, Homer Dickinson, Lyle Moraine, Hank Mann, Michael A. Cirillo, Chester Conklin, Flo Stanton, John George, Charles Quirk, Frank Cordell, Willard Willingham, Warren Fiske, Jean Willes, Jonathan Hale, Cecil B. DeMille, Bing Crosby, Robert L. Welch. A tenderfoot goes West to collect an inheritance and when he ends up with only debts he decides to marry a buxom, and rich, young woman. Amusing followup to **The Paleface** (q.v.).

3278 Son of Roaring Dan. Universal, 1940. 63 minutes B/W. D: Ford Beebe. SC: Clarence Upson Young. WITH Johnny Mack Brown, Fuzzy Knight, Nell O'Day, Jeanne Kelly (Jean Brooks), Robert Homans, Tom Chatterton, John Eldredge, Ethan Laidlaw, Lafe McKee, Richard Alexander, Eddie Polo, Bob Reeves, Frank McCarroll, The Texas Rangers,

Chuck Morrison, Lloyd Ingraham, Jack Shannon, Ben Taggert, Ralph Peters, Ralph Dunn, Jack Montgomery. When his father is murdered a man pretends to be the tenderfoot son of a fellow rancher in order to catch the culprits. Well done Johnny Mack Brown vehicle with a trio of well interpolated songs.

3279 Son of the Border. RKO Radio, 1933. 55 minutes B/W. D: Lloyd Nosler. SC: Wellyn Totman & Harold Shumate. WITH Tom Keene, Julie Haydon, Edgar Kennedy, David Durand, Creighton (Lon Jr.) Chaney, Charles King, Al Bridge, Claudia Coleman. When a cowboy shoots her fiancée during a gunfight with bank robbers, a young girl vows revenge and later uses the man's younger brother to carry out her plan. Well made drama with strong performances from its cast.

3280 A Son of the Plains. Syndicate, 1931. 59 minutes B/W. D-SC: Robert North Bradbury. WITH Bob Custer, Doris Phillips, J. P. McGowan, Edward Hearn, Gordon DeMain, Al St. John. A deputy sheriff is torn between his duty and the love of a girl whose father aids another man in a holdup. Very poor Western made worse by Bob Custer's BAD acting. Film does contain an amusing sequence at the Yucca Saloon where a gal sings the film's theme song, "On the Banks of the Wabash"(!) and Al St. John has a few good comic moments as a drunk.

3281 Son of the Renegade. United Artists, 1953. 57 minutes B/W. D: Reg Browne. SC: John Carpenter. WITH John Carpenter, Lori Irving, Joan McKellan, Valley Keene, Jack Ingram, Verne Teters, Bill Coonz, Bill Ward, Roy Canada, Whitney Hughes, Ewing Brown, Freddie Carson, Pat McGeehan (narrator). Returning home, the son of a notorious outlaw meets with resentment from the locals until he uncovers a robbery plan. Low grade John Carpenter outing, but worth a look for his followers.

3282 Son of Zorro. Republic, 1947. 13 Chapters B/W. D: Spencer Gordon Bennet & Fred C. Brannon. SC: Franklin Adreon, Basil Dickey, Jesse Duffy & Sol Shor. WITH George Turner, Peggy Stewart, Roy Barcroft, Ed Cassidy, Ernie Adams, Stanley Price, Edmund Cobb, Kenneth Terrell, Wheaton Chambers, Fred Graham, Eddie Parker, Si Jenks, Jack O'Shea, Jack Kirk, Tom Steele, Dale Van Sickel. After the Civil War, a cavalry officer returns home to find the area controlled by crooked politicians and he revives the character of Zorro to stop them. Pretty good pseudo-Zorro cliffhanger; the previous year Republic used the Zorro plot motif in an entirely modern-day detective cliffhanger, **Daughter of Don Q** starring Adrian Booth and Kirk Alyn.

3283 Song of Arizona. Republic, 1946. 54 (68) minutes B/W. D: Frank McDonald. SC: M. Coates Webster. WITH Roy Rogers, George "Gabby" Hayes, Dale Evans, Lyle Talbot, Tommy Cook, Bob Nolan & The Sons of the Pioneers, Edmund Cobb, Johnny Calkins, Sarah Edwards, Tommy Ivo, Michael Chapin, Dick Curtis, Tony Quinn, Noble "Kid" Chissell, The Robert Mitchell Boychoir. An outlaw is killed by his own gang and his son is told Gabby committed the crime and when Gabby tries to protect the boy from the gang he is shot but the youngster uses bank robbery money left by his father to pay off Gabby's debts. Fairly lively actioner in the Roy Rogers series.

3284 Song of Idaho. Columbia, 1948. 70 minutes B/W. D: Ray Nazarro. SC: Barry Shipman. WITH Kirby Grant, The Hoosier Hot Shots, June Vincent, The Sunshine Boys & Girls, Tommy Ivo, Emory Parnell, The Starlighters, Eddie Acuff, Dorothy Vaughn, Maudie Prickett. A radio singer has to please his sponsor's brat son in order to get his contract renewed. Average Columbia country music-Western programmer.

3285 Song of Nevada. Republic, 1944. 54 (75) minutes B/W. D: Joseph Kane. SC: Gordon Kahn & Oliver Cooper. WITH Roy Rogers, Dale Evans, Mary Lee, Bob Nolan & The Sons of the Pioneers, Thurston Hall, Lloyd Corrigan, John Eldredge, Forrest Taylor, LeRoy Mason, George Meeker, Emmett Vogan, William B. Davidson, Kenne Duncan, Si Jenks, Frank McCarroll, Henry Wills, Jack O'Shea, Helen Talbot. A millionaire tries to stop his daughter from marrying a man he dislikes by pretending he is dead and having a cowboy romance her. Music outweighs action in this mediocre Roy Rogers vehicle which is saved somewhat by Thurston Hall as the millionaire; TV version is really butchered. V: Cumberland Video.

3286 Song of Old Wyoming. Producers Releasing Corporation, 1945. 65 minutes Color. D: Robert Emmett (Tansey). SC: Frances Kavanaugh. WITH Eddie Dean, Jennifer Holt, Sarah Padden, Al ("Lash") LaRue, Emmett Lynn, Ray Elder, John

Carpenter, Ian Keith, Robert Barron, Horace Murphy, Rocky Camron, Richard Cramer, Steve Clark, Lee Bennett. A singing cowboy comes to the aid of his woman rancher-newspaper owner-boss when rustlers steal her cattle and try to bankrupt her. Lash LaRue steals the show as the rancher's outlaw-nephew but attractive Cinecolor and Eddie Dean's singing also help make this good viewing.

3287 Song of Texas. Republic, 1943. 54 (69) minutes B/W. D: Joseph Kane. SC: Winston Miller. WITH Roy Rogers, Sheila Ryan, Bob Nolan & The Sons of the Pioneers, Barton MacLane, Harry Shannon, Arline Judge, William Haade, Hal Taliaferro, Yakima Canutt, Tom London, Forrest Taylor, Eve March. Roy Rogers tries to help a drunken once-famous rodeo star, who is being used by crooks, in fooling his visiting daughter into thinking he is still a success. Western reworking of **Lady for a Day** (Warner Brothers, 1933), this Roy Rogers vehicle is a very good one and Harry Shannon is quite effective as the down-on-his-luck old man. V: Cumberland Video.

3288 Song of the Buckaroo. Monogram, 1938. 58 minutes B/W. D: Al Herman. SC: John Rathmell. WITH Tex Ritter, Jinx Falkenberg, Mary Ruth, Tom London, Frank LaRue, Charles King, Bob Terry, Horace Murphy, Snub Pollard, Dave O'Brien, Dorothy Fay, George Chesebro, Ernie Adams. A desperado finds a dead man and assumes his identity and raises his little girl and becomes a respected citizen but his old gang recognizes him and tries to blackmail him. Pretty fair Tex Ritter vehicle with the tune "Texas Dan" written by Carson Robison.

3289 Song of the Caballero. Universal, 1930. 72 minutes B/W. D: Harry Joe Brown. SC: Bennett Cohen & Lesley Mason. WITH Ken Maynard, Doris Hill, Francis Ford, Gino Corrado, Evelyn Sherman, Josef Swickard, Frank Rice, William Irving, Joyzelle Joyner. Because of abuse to his mother, a man becomes a bandit who preys only on a rich family until he saves the life of the family's pretty daughter. Okay Ken Maynard early talkie with a Mexican setting.

3290 Song of the Drifter. Monogram, 1948. 55 minutes B/W. D: Lambert Hillyer. SC: Frank Young. WITH Jimmy Wakely, Dub Taylor, Mildred Coles, Patsy Moran, William Ruhl, Marshall Reed, Frank LaRue, Carl Mathews, Jimmie Martin,

Steve Clark, Wheaton Chambers, Bud Osborne, Bob Woodward, Dick Rinehart, Cliffie Stone. A singing cowboy tries to combat crooks who try to pollute water in order to get range land for themselves. Lambert Hillyer's direction tries hard but can't really help this Jimmy Wakely vehicle.

3291 Song of the Gringo. Grand National, 1936. 57 minutes B/W. D: John McCarthy. SC: John McCarthy, Robert Emmett (Tansey) & Al Jennings. WITH Tex Ritter, Joan Woodbury, Monte Blue, Fuzzy Knight, Richard (Ted) Adams, Warner Richmond, Al Jennings, Martin Garralaga, William Desmond, Glenn Strange, Budd Buster, Murdock MacQuarrie, Ethan Laidlaw, Slim Whitaker, Ed Cassidy, Earl Dwire, Jack Kirk, Bob Burns, Forrest Taylor, Robert Fiske, Rosa Rey, Jose Pacheco & His Continental Orchestra. Cowpoke Tex infiltrates an outlaw gang which poses as cowboys and he ends up being accused of murdering the ranch owner. More drama and music than action in Tex Ritter's film debut but it does contain an exciting finale with a courtroom shootout.

3292 Song of the Range. Monogram, 1944. 55 minutes B/W. D: Wallace Fox. SC: Betty Burbridge. WITH Jimmy Wakely, Dennis Moore, Lee "Lasses" White, Kay Forrester, Sam Flint, Hugh Prosser, George Eldredge, Steve Clark, Johnny Bond, Edmund Cobb, Pierre Watkin, Bud Osborne, Ken Terrell, Carl Mathews, Carl Sepulveda, The Sunshine Girls, The Red River Valley Boys. Falsely accused of murder, a cowpoke escapes from jail and assumes the guise of a federal agent in order to capture a gang of gold smugglers. Jimmy Wakely's first starring Western but he has little to do as Dennis Moore dominates throughout as the wrongly accused cowboy. Okay production that moves fairly quickly but contains too much music. V: Cumberland Video.

3293 Song of the Saddle. Warner Brothers, 1936. 58 minutes B/W. D: Louis King. SC: William Jacobs. WITH Dick Foran, Alma Lloyd, Charles Middleton, Addison Richards, Eddie Shubert, Monte Montague, Victor Potel, Kenneth Harlan, Myrtle Stedman, George Ernest, Pat West, James Farley, Julian Rivero, William Desmond, Bud Osborne, Robert Kortman, Bonita Granville, The Sons of the Pioneers. Fifteen years after the murder of his father, a young man returns to find the killers. Typically good Dick Foran vehicle.

3294 Song of the Sierras. Monogram, 1946. 55 minutes B/W. D: Oliver Drake. SC: Elmer Clifton. WITH Jimmy Wakely, Lee "Lasses" White, Jean Carlin, Jack Baxley, Iris Clive, Zon Murray, Budd Buster, Bob Duncan, Brad Slaven, Ben Corbett, Ray Jones, Carl Sepulveda, Wesley Tuttle & His Texas Stars. In order to win a big race, a cowboy trains wild horses but his activities are opposed by crooks. Another anemic Jimmy Wakely vehicle.

3295 Song of the Trail. Ambassador, 1936. 65 minutes B/W. D: Russell Hopton. SC: George Sayre & Barry Barrington. WITH Kermit Maynard, Evelyn Brent, Fuzzy Knight, George ("Gabby") Hayes, Antoinette Lees (Andrea Leeds), Wheeler Oakman, Lee Shumway, Roger Williams, Ray Gallagher, Charles McMurphy, Horace Murphy, Lynette London, Bob McKenzie, Frank McCarroll, Artie Ortego. A rodeo star falls in love with a pretty girl whose father is being harrassed by crooks over his valuable mine. One of the best of Kermit Maynard's vehicles for producer Maurice Conn; full of action and well made. V: Video Dimensions, Cassette Express.

3296 Song of the Wasteland. Monogram, 1947. 58 minutes B/W. D: Thomas Carr. SC: J. Benton Cheney. WITH Jimmy Wakely, Lee "Lasses" White, Dottye Brown, Holly Bane, John James, Henry Hall, Marshall Reed, Gary Garrett, Ted Adams, Pierce Lyden, George Chesebro, Chester Conklin, John Carpenter, Ray Jones, The Saddle Pals (Johnny Bond, Dick Rinehart, River Lewis). Vigilantes are formed to combat outlaws but a singing cowpoke finds out they are the real cause of the area's lawlessness. A fine supporting cast can do little to retrieve this Jimmy Wakely film from boredom.

3297 Songs and Bullets. Spectrum, 1938. 58 minutes B/W. D: Sam Newfield. SC: Joseph O'Donnell & George Plympton. WITH Fred Scott, Al St. John, Alice Ardell, Karl Hackett, Charles King, Frank LaRue, Richard Cramer, Carl Mathews, Jimmie Aubrey, Budd Buster, Lew Porter, Sherry Tansey. A corrupt murderer businessman heads a gang, including the local sheriff, which pulls off a robbery but he is trailed by a singing lawman and his partner. Better-than-average Fred Scott outing with the lovely theme song "Prairie Moon" deftly sung by the star who also belts out "My Old

Ten Gallon Hat" and "Back in Arkansas."
When villain Karl Hackett meets pretty
French schoolmarm Alice Ardell one
of his cohorts exclaims, "That's the first
time Shelton's smiled since he dispossessed
the Higgins family."

3298 Songs and Saddles. Colony, 1938.
65 minutes B/W. D: Harry Fraser. SC:
Wayne Carter. WITH Gene Austin, Joan
Brooks, Lynne Barkeley, Henry Rocquemore, Walter Willis, Charles King, Karl
Hackett, Ted Claire, John Merton, Ben
Corbett, Bob Terry, John Elliott, Lloyd
Ingraham, Russell "Candy" Hall, Otto
"Coco" Heimel, Darryl Harper. An entertainer and his troupe find themselves
captured by a gang of outlaws. Gene
Austin's solo starring film is a low budget
affair but his fans will like him as a
singing cowboy and the film is loaded
with good songs.

3299 Sonny and Jed. K-Tel, 1974. 91
minutes Color. D: Sergio Corbucci. SC:
Sabatino Ciuffini, Mario Amendola, Adri-
ano Bolzoni, Jose Maria Forque & Sergio
Corbucci. WITH Tomas Milian, Susan
George, Telly Savalas, Rossana Yanni,
Franco Giacobini, Eduardo Fajardo,
Herbert Fux, Laura Betti, Alvaro De
Luna. An escaped convict teams with
a pretty free-spirited young girl as they
rob their way across Mexico and are
tracked by a determined lawman. Some-
what tongue-in-cheek Italian-Spanish-West
German coproduction which is made
to work by its trio of stars. Issued in
Italy in 1972 as **J. & S.—Storia Criminale
Del Far West** (J. and S.—A Criminal
Story of the Far West).

3300 Sonora Stagecoach. Monogram,
1944. 61 minutes B/W. D: Robert Emmett
Tansey. SC: Frances Kavanaugh. WITH
Hoot Gibson, Bob Steele, Chief Thunder-
cloud, Rocky Camron, Betty Miles, Glenn
Strange, George Eldredge, Karl Hackett,
Henry Hall, Charles King, Bud Osborne,
Charley Murray Jr., John Bridges, Al
Ferguson, Forrest Taylor, Frank Ellis,
Hal Price, Rodd Redwing, John Cason,
Horace B. Carpenter. The Trail Blazers
are assigned to take an accused killer
to stand trial and the men who really
committed the crime try to ambush
them. Fast paced and well done entry
in "The Trail Blazers" series.

3301 Sons of Adventure. Republic, 1948.
68 minutes B/W. D: Yakima Canutt.
SC: Franklin Adreon & Sol Shor. WITH
Lynne Roberts, Russell Hayden, Gordon

Jones, Grant Withers, George Chandler,
Roy Barcroft, John Newland, Stephanie
Bachelor, John Holland, Gilbert Frye,
Richard Irving, Joan Blair, John Crawford,
Keith Richards, James Dale. When a
Western star is killed on the set of his
new film, a stuntman is blamed for the
killing and his pal sets out to find the
real murderer. Out-of-the-ordinary film
which is well directed by Yakima Canutt
with an added bonus of a look at the
Republic film factory.

3302 The Sons of Katie Elder. Paramount,
1965. 122 minutes Color. D: Henry Hatha-
way. SC: William H. Wright, Allen Weiss
& Harry Essex. WITH John Wayne, Dean
Martin, Martha Hyer, Michael Anderson
Jr., Earl Holliman, Jeremy Slate, James
Gregory, Paul Fix, George Kennedy,
Dennis Hopper, Sheldon Allman, John
Litel, John Doucette, James Westerfield,
Rhys Williams, John Qualen, Rodolfo
Acosta, Strother Martin, Percy Helton,
Karl Swenson. Four brothers return home
after their mother's death only to be
falsely blamed for a killing by the crooks
who cheated their father. Very entertaining
John Wayne vehicle. VD: RCA. V: Cumber-
land Video.

3303 Sons of New Mexico. Columbia,
1950. 71 minutes B/W. D: John English.
SC: Paul Gangelin. WITH Gene Autry,
Gail Davis, Robert Armstrong, Dick
Jones, Clayton Moore, Frankie Darro,
Irving Bacon, Russell Arms, Marie Blake,
Sandy Sanders, Roy Gordon, Frankie
Marvin, Pierce Lyden, Paul Raymond,
Kenne Duncan, Harry Mackin, Bobby
Clark, Gaylord (Steve) Pendleton, Billy
Lechner. When he is appointed the executor
of an estate, Gene Autry tries to get
the dead man's son from under the influ-
ence of a crooked rancher by sending
him to military school. Pleasant Gene
Autry opus, but this one is mainly geared
to juveniles.

3304 Sons of the Pioneers. Republic,
1942. 54 (61) minutes B/W. D: Joseph
Kane. SC: M. Coates Webster, Mauri
Grashin & Robert T. Shannon. WITH
Roy Rogers, George "Gabby" Hayes,
Maris Wrixon, Bob Nolan & The Sons
of the Pioneers, Bradley Page, Hal Tali-
aferro, Tom London, Minerva Urecal,
Jack O'Shea, Frank Ellis, Tom London,
Bob Woodward, Fern Emmett, Chester
Conklin, Karl Hackett, Fred Burns. Roy
Rogers returns home to aid Gabby and
the townspeople in stopping ruthless
land grabbers who know that valuable

minerals are beneath the soil. Fairly good Roy Rogers entry although the title singing group has little to do in the feature.

3305 Sons of the Saddle. Universal, 1930. 76 minutes B/W. D: Harry Joe Brown. SC: Bennett Cohen & Lesley Mason. WITH Ken Maynard, Doris Hill, Joseph Girard, Carroll Nye, Francis Ford, Harry Todd. The foreman of a ranch loves the boss's daughter, but so does his pal, and when she rejects the latter he joins an outlaw gang planning to raid the ranch's cattle herd. Entertaining Ken Maynard vehicle.

3306 Sons of Vengeance. P.E.A./Centauro Films, 1965. 98 minutes Color. D: Joaquin L. Romero Marchent. SC: Jesus Navarro & Joaquin L. Romero Marchent. WITH Richard Harrison, Robert Hundar (Claudio Undari), Gloria Milland, Fernando Sancho, Andrew Scott, Evelyn Merrill, Billy Hyden. A bandit leader murders the father of three young boys and their mother vows revenge and years later two of the boys set out to get the killer while the third son, a federal marshal, wants to capture him lawfully. Better than average European Western with a good plot and cast. Italian title: **I Tre Spietati** (The Three Ruthless Ones). Spanish title: **El Sabor de la Venganza.** British title: **Gunfight at High Noon.**

3307 The Soul of Nigger Charley. Paramount, 1973. 104 minutes Color. D: Larry G. Spangler. SC: Harold Stone. WITH Fred Williamson, D'Urville Martin, Denise Nicholas, Pedro Armendariz Jr., Kirk Calloway, George Allen, Kevin Hagen, Michael Cameron, Johnny Greenwood, James Garbo, Nai Bonet, Robert Minor, Fred Lerner, Joe Henderson, Richard Farnsworth, Tony Brubaker, Boyd "Red" Morgan, Al Hassan, Ed Hice, Henry Wills, Phil Avenetti. A former slave heads to Mexico in order to free a group of his people held there by a former Confederate officer. Overlong and none-too-entertaining sequel to **The Legend of Nigger Charley** (q.v.).

3308 Soul Soldier. Fanfare/Metromedia, 1971. 78 (97) minutes Color. D: John Cardos. SC: Marlene Weed. WITH Rafer Johnson, Barbara Hale, Cesar Romero, Robert Doqui, Isaac Fields, Lincoln Kilpatrick, Isabel Sanford, Otis Taylor, Steve Drexel, Robert Dix, James Michelle, Bobby Clark, John Pace, John Nettles, John Fox. After the Civil War a regiment of black soldiers are assigned to border duty in Texas but find themselves hated by both whites and Indians. Bombed out effort which was originally issued in 1970 as **The Red, White and Black.**

3309 South of Arizona. Columbia, 1938. 55 minutes B/W. D: Sam Nelson. SC: Bennett Cohen. WITH Charles Starrett, Iris Meredith, Bob Nolan & The Sons of the Pioneers, Dick Curtis, Robert Fiske, Edmund Cobb, Art Mix, Richard Botiller, Lafe McKee, Ed Coxen, Hank Bell, Hal Taliaferro, John Tyrell, Merill McCormack. Crooks want a range for themselves and rustle the ranchers' cattle and murder a government ranger sent to help them. Another streamlined entry in Charles Starrett's Columbia series.

3310 South of Caliente. Republic, 1951. 67 minutes B/W. D: William Witney. SC: Eric Taylor. WITH Roy Rogers, Dale Evans, Pinky Lee, Douglas Fowley, Pat Brady, Charlita, Ric Roman, Leonard Penn, Willie Best, Frank Richards, George J. Lewis, Roy Rogers Riders. Crooks steal a racehorse that Roy Rogers is taking to a Mexican racetrack and he sets out to recover the animal. Pretty good Roy Rogers vehicle if you can overlook the "comedy" of Pinky Lee and Pat Brady.

3311 South of Death Valley. Columbia, 1949. 54 minutes B/W. D: Ray Nazarro. SC: Earle Snell. WITH Charles Starrett, Smiley Burnette, Gail Davis, Clayton Moore, Fred Sears, Lee Roberts, Tommy Duncan & His Western All Stars, Richard Emory, Jason Robards. Trying to find out who murdered his gold mine-owning brother-in-law, a cowboy rides into an area and finds himself in the middle of a range war. Another assembly line "Durango Kid" segment.

3312 South of Hell Mountain. Cannon Films, 1971. 92 minutes Color. D: William Sachs & Louis Lehman. WITH Anna Stewart, Martin J. Kelly. A young woman and her stepmother are held hostage in their cabin by three outlaws but the leader of the band and the girl fall in love. Somewhat obscure, violent drama.

3313 South of Monterey. Monogram, 1946. 63 minutes B/W. D: William Nigh. SC: Charles Belden. WITH Gilbert Roland, Martin Garralaga, Frank Yaconelli, Marjorie Reynolds, George H. Lewis, Terry Frost, Harry Woods, Iris Flores, Wheaton Chambers, Rose Turich. The Cisco Kid

South of Rio   406

tries to stop two crooks from carrying
out a land swindle. Pleasant "Cisco Kid"
series adventure.

3314 South of Rio. Republic, 1949. 60
minutes B/W. D: Philip Ford. SC: Norman
S. Hall. WITH Monte Hale, Kay Chris-
topher, Paul Hurst, Roy Barcroft, Douglas
Kennedy, Don Haggerty, Rory Mallinson,
Lane Bradford, Emmett Vogan, Myron
Healey, Tom London. Outlaws are terror-
izing a frontier area and a newly appointed
ranger tries to stop them. Okay Monte
Hale vehicle.

3315 South of Santa Fe. World Wide,
1932. 60 minutes B/W. D: Bert Glennon.
SC: G. A. Durlam. WITH Bob Steele,
Janis Elliott, Chris-Pin Martin, Jack
Clifford, Eddie Dunn, Bob Burns, Hank
Bell, Allan Garcia. On the Mexican Border
a cowboy tries to combat a gang of outlaws. Bob Steele's first World Wide release
is a good one, thanks to fine direction
and a good script.

3316 South of Santa Fe. Republic, 1942.
54 (56) minutes B/W. D: Joseph Kane.
SC: James R. Webb. WITH Roy Rogers,
George "Gabby" Hayes, Linda Hayes,
Bob Nolan & The Sons of the Pioneers,
Paul Fix, Bobby Beers, Arthur Loft,
Charles Miller, Sam Flint, Jack Kirk,
Jack Ingram, Hank Bell, Carleton Young,
Lynton Brent, Robert Strange, Henry
Wills, Jack O'Shea, Merrill McCormack.
Roy Rogers invites three industrialists
to appear in a town celebration, hoping
they will back the opening of a gold
mine which will keep the town from
ruin, but a gangster kidnaps the men
and the blame is placed on Rogers. There
is lots of action in this Roy Rogers film
and it is a pretty good vehicle for him.

3317 South of St. Louis. Warner Brothers,
1949. 88 minutes Color. D: Ray Enright.
SC: Zachary Gold & James R. Webb.
WITH Joel McCrea, Alexis Smith, Zachary
Scott, Dorothy Malone, Douglas Kennedy,
Alan Hale, Victor Jory, Bob Steele, Art
Baker, Monte Blue, Nacho Galindo, Warren
Jackson, Russell Hicks, Harry Woods,
Art Smith. During the Civil War three
ranchers run blockades for the South
but they break up when one gets greedy
and kills several soldiers for a gun ship-
ment. Well made action melodrama.

3318 South of the Border. Republic,
1939. 54 (71) minutes B/W. D: George
Sherman. SC: Dorrell McGowan & Stuart
McGowan. WITH Gene Autry, Smiley

Burnette, June Storey, Lupita Tovar,
Mary Lee, Duncan Renaldo, Frank Reicher,
Alan Edwards, Claire DuBrey, Richard
Botiller, William Farnum, Selmar Jackson,
Sheila Darcy, Rex Lease, Charles King,
Reed Howes, Jack O'Shea, Slim Whitaker,
Hal Price, Julian Rivero, Curley Dresden,
The Checkerboard Band. Gene Autry
is sent to Mexico to squelch a revolution
and when he gets there he finds foreign
agents at work. Although one of Gene
Autry's best known features, this outing
is nothing to brag about except for the
title tune. V: Blackhawk.

3319 South of the Chisholm Trail. Colum-
bia, 1947. 58 minutes B/W. D: Derwin
Abrahams. SC: Michael Simmons. WITH
Charles Starrett, Smiley Burnette, Nancy
Saunders, Frank Sully, Hank Newman
& The Georgia Crackers, Jim Diehl,
Jack Ingram, George Chesebro, Frank
LaRue, Jacques O'Mahoney (Jock Ma-
honey), Eddie Parker, Kit Guard, Ray
Elder, Victor Holbrook, Fred Sears, Thomas
Kingston. When the members of a musical
troupe recapture money stolen by an
outlaw gang they are mistaken for the
gang and nearly hung until rescued by
the Durango Kid. Complicated and hard
to follow "Durango Kid" entry starring
Charles Starrett.

3320 South of the Rio Grande. Columbia,
1932. 60 minutes B/W. D: Lambert Hillyer.
SC: Harold Shumate. WITH Buck Jones,
Mona Maris, George J. Lewis, Doris
Hill, Philo McCullough, Paul Fix, Charles
Reque, James Durkin, Harry Semels,
Charles Stevens. A lawman comes to
the aid of a pal who is in love with the
girl who caused the death of the peace-
keeper's brother. Well produced and
directed Buck Jones vehicle but the
star is not as good in a Mexican getup
as Tim McCoy.

3321 South of the Rio Grande. Monogram,
1945. 62 minutes B/W. D: Lambert Hillyer.
SC: Victor Hammond & Ralph Bettinson.
WITH Duncan Renaldo, Martin Garralaga,
George J. Lewis, Armida, Francis McDonald, Lillian Molieri, Charles Stevens,
Pedro Regas, Soledad Jiminez, The Guadalajara Trio. The Cisco Kid is opposed
to a corrupt military leader trying to
control the countryside. Passable "Cisco
Kid" series entry. V: VCI Home Video.

3322 South Pacific Trail. Republic, 1952.
60 minutes B/W. D: William Witney.
SC: Arthur Orloff. WITH Rex Allen,
Estelia Rodriguez, Slim Pickens, Roy

Barcroft, Nestor Paiva, Douglas Evans, Forrest Taylor, Joe McGuinn, The Republic Rhythm Riders. A cowboy finds that his ranch foreman is planning a gold hijack scheme. Pretty fair Rex Allen film.

3323 Southward Ho! Republic, 1939. 54 (57) minutes B/W. D: Joseph Kane. SC: Jack Natteford & John Rathmell. WITH Roy Rogers, Mary Hart, George "Gabby" Hayes, Wade Boteler, Arthur Loft, Lane Chandler, Tom London, Charles Moore, Edwin Brady, Hal Taliaferro, Fred Burns, Frank Ellis, Jack Ingram, Frank McCarroll, Curley Dresden, Jim Corey, George Chesebro. In post-Civil War Texas Roy and Gabby are at odds with renegade Yankee soldiers, working as the military governor's men, who ransack the territory. Nicely made early Roy Rogers series entry.

3324 Southwest Passage. United Artists, 1954. 75 minutes Color. D: Ray Nazarro. SC: Harry Essex. WITH Rod Cameron, Joanne Dru, John Ireland, Guinn Williams, John Dehner, Darryl Hickman, Stuart Randall, Morris Ankrum, Kenneth MacDonald, Stanley Andrews, Mark Hanna. A caravan testing the use of camels in the West is joined by a banker and an outlaw and his girl and the group face an Indian attack. A different kind of oater and one which provides pretty good entertainment.

3325 Spawn of the North. Paramount, 1938. 110 minutes B/W. D: Henry Hathaway. SC: Jules Furthman & Talbot Jennings. WITH George Raft, Dorothy Lamour, Henry Fonda, Akim Tamiroff, Lynne Overman, John Barrymore, Louise Platt, Fuzzy Knight, Vladimir Sokoloff, Duncan Renaldo, John Wray, Michio Ito, Stanley Andrews, Richard Ung, Alex Woloshin, Archie Twitchell, Lee Shumway, Wade Boteler, Galan Galt, Arthur Aylesworth, Rollo Lloyd, Guy Usher, Henry Brandon, Egon Brecher, Harvey Clark, Monte Blue, Irving Bacon, Robert Middlemass, Eddie Marr, Frank Puglia, Leonid Snegoff, Edmund Elton, Aids Kutzenoff, Slicker (seal). Two Alaskan fisherman pals have a falling out when one joins forces with Russian pirates. Sturdy melodrama in which George Raft out-acts Henry Fonda but it is sad to see John Barrymore wasted in a supporting role. Remade as **Alaska Seas** (q.v.).

3326 Special Agent. Paramount, 1949. 70 minutes B/W. D: William C. Thomas.

SC: Milton Raison. WITH William Eythe, Laura Elliot, Paul Valentine, George Reeves, Carole Mathews, Tom Powers, Raymond Bond, Frank Puglia, Walter Baldwin. An unhappy agent in a small cattle town suddenly finds himself in the middle of a crime wave. Fairly interesting programmer from the Pine-Thomas unit.

3327 Speeding Hoofs. Rayart, 1927. 50 minutes B/W. D: Louis Chaudet. WITH Dick Hatton, Elsa Benham, Roy Watson, William Ryno, Bud Osborne. Crooks hiding a treasure on a ranch start rumors that the spread is haunted while the rightful owner and her boyfriend search for the riches. Standard low grade actioner from the silent era. Alternate title: **Lure of the Range.**

3328 Spencer's Mountain. Warner Brothers, 1963. 118 minutes Color. D-SC: Delmer Daves. WITH Henry Fonda, Maureen O'Hara, James MacArthur, Donald Crisp, Wally Cox, Mimsy Farmer, Virginia Gregg, Lillian Bronson, Whit Bissell, Hayden Rorke, Kathy Bennett, Dub Taylor, Hope Summers, Ken Mayer, Bronwyn Fitzsimmons, Barbara McNair, Larry Mann, Buzz Henry, Jim O'Hara, Victor French, Michael Greene, Med Flory, Ray Savage, Mike Henry, Gary Young, Michael Young, Veronica Cartwright, Ricky Young, Susan Young, Rocky Young, Kym Karath, Michelle Daves, William Breen. A Wyoming mountain couple, with a large family, decides to use the money intended to build their dream house for their eldest son's college education. Folksy, but pleasant, drama from Earl Hamner Jr.'s novel, later the basis for the fine TV series "The Waltons" (CBS-TV, 1972-81).

3329 The Spikes Gang. United Artists, 1974. 96 minutes Color. D: Richard Fleischer. SC: Irving Ravetch & Harriet Frank Jr. WITH Lee Marvin, Gary Grimes, Ron Howard, Charlie Martin Smith, Arthur Hunnicutt, Noah Beery, Marc Smith, Don Fellows, Elliott Sullivan, Robert Beatty, Ralph Brown, Bill Curran, Bert Conway, Frances O'Flynn. Three farm boys nurse a wounded bank robber back to health and he takes them along with him on his robbery exploits. Okay pass-time viewing but nothing special.

3330 The Spirit of the West. Allied, 1932. 59 minutes B/W. D: Otto Brower. SC: Jack Natteford. WITH Hoot Gibson, Doris Hill, Hooper Atchley, Alan Bridge, George Mendoza, Walter Perry, Lafe

McKee, Charles Brinley, Tiny Sanford. A rodeo champion comes to the aid of his brother, the foreman of a ranch whose owner has been murdered by a crooked banker and sheriff who want his range. Typical sound era Hoot Gibson vehicle with Hoot masquerading as a simpleton in order to capture the bad guys.

3331 Spirit of the Wind. Raven Pictures, 1980. 103 minutes Color. D: Ralph Liddle. SC: Ralph Liddle & John Logue. WITH Pius Savage, Chief Dan George, Slim Pickens, George Clutesi. A young handicapped boy sets out to fulfill his goals without letting his physical problems stop him. Fair outdoor drama.

3332 The Spoilers. Segli-Poliscope, 1914. 90 minutes B/W. D-SC: Colin Campbell. WITH William Farnum, Kathlyn Williams, Bessie Eyton, Tom Santschi, Frank Clark, Jack McDonald, Wheeler Oakman, Norvel MacGregor, William Ryno. Two gold prospectors in the Klondike are cheated out of their valuable claim by a crooked politician. The first, and still the best, of the five versions of the Rex Beach novel, famous for its reel-long fight sequence between William Farnum and Tom Santschi. A true cinema classic. The second version was done in 1923 by Goldwyn with Lambert Hillyer directing Milton Sills, Anna Q. Nilsson and Barbara Bedford in the leading roles.

3333 The Spoilers. Paramount, 1930. 81 minutes B/W. D: Edwin Carewe. SC: Agnes Brand Leahy & Bartlett Cormack. WITH Gary Cooper, Kay Johnson, Betty Compson, William "Stage" Boyd, Harry Green, James Kirkwood, Slim Summerville, Lloyd Ingraham, Oscar Apfel, Edward Coxen, Jack Trent, Edward Hearn, Hal David, Knute Erickson, John Beck, Jack N. Holmes. In the Klondike gold rush days a young man romances two girls while he and his partners fight claim jumpers. Initial sound version of Rex Beach's novel is little seen today although it is a fairly good adaptation of the famous work. Gary Cooper replaced George Bancroft in the lead and the stars of the 1914 version, William Farnum and Tom Santschi, were technical advisors for the film's restaging of the big fight scene. Ironically the two older stars did a better job redoing the fight sequence the next year in the non-Western **Ten Nights in a Barroom** (Road Show, 1931).

3334 The Spoilers. Universal, 1942. 87 minutes B/W. D: Ray Enright. SC: Lawrence Hazard & Tom Reed. WITH Marlene Dietrich, Randolph Scott, John Wayne, Margaret Lindsay, Harry Carey, Richard Barthelmess, George Cleveland, Samuel S. Hinds, Russell Simpson, William Farnum, Marietta Canty, Jack Norton, Ray Bennett, Forrest Taylor, Charles Halton, Bud Osborne, Drew Demarest, Robert W. Service, Charles McMurphy, Art Miles, William Haade, Robert Homans. Two prospectors are at odds with a crooked gold commissioner in the Klondike in the 1890s and they are aided by a saloon girl. The slickest of the five versions of the Rex Beach novel although Harry Carey and Richard Barthelmess steal the acting honors. V: MCA, Blackhawk, Cumberland Video.

3335 The Spoilers. Universal-International, 1955. 84 minutes Color. D: Jesse Hibbs. SC: Oscar Brodney & Charles Hoffman. WITH Anne Baxter, Jeff Chandler, Rory Calhoun, Ray Danton, Barbara Britton, John McIntire, Wallace Ford, Carl Benton Reid, Raymond Walburn, Ruth Donnelly, Willis Bouchey, Forrest Lewis, Roy Barcroft, Dayton Lummis, John Harmon, Paul McGuire, Frank Sully, Bob Steele, Byron Foulger, Arthur Space, Lane Bradford, Terry Frost. A saloon-owning gal vies for the attentions of a prospector with a respectable woman who works for the crook trying to cheat the man and his partner out of their gold claim. The use of color is the only asset to this fifth, and final, screen version of Rex Beach's novel; mediocre.

3336 Spoilers of the Forest. Republic, 1957. 70 minutes Color. D: Joe (Joseph) Kane. SC: Bruce Manning. WITH Rod Cameron, Vera Ralston, Ray Collins, Hillary Brooke, Edgar Buchanan, Carl Benton Reid, Sheila Bromley, Hank Worden, John Compton, Angela Greene, Paul Stader, Mary Alan Hokanson, Raymond Greenleaf, Eleanor Audley, Don Haggerty, William Haade, Jo Ann Lilliquist, Bucko Stafford, Robert Karns, Ken Dibbs, Rory Mallinson, Virginia Carroll, John Patrick, Bob Swan, Mack Williams, Theresa Harris, Helen Wallace, Pauline Moore, Judd Holdren. A timber company owner uses his handsome foreman to woo a young girl in order to take the timber from her Montana ranch. Cheaply made but entertaining melodrama.

3337 Spoilers of the North. Republic, 1947. 66 minutes B/W. D: Richard Sale. WITH Paul Kelly, Adrian Booth, Evelyn Ankers, James Millican, Roy Barcroft,

Louis Jean Heydt. A crooked salmon tycoon and his Indian girl friend enlist the aid of an unsuspecting city girl in their schemes to defraud fishermen. Standard, entertaining Republic effort.

3338 Spoilers of the Plains. Republic, 1951. 68 minutes B/W. D: William Witney. SC: Sloan Nibley. WITH Roy Rogers, Penny Edwards, Gordon Jones, Foy Willing & The Riders of the Purple Sage, Grant Withers, Fred Kohler Jr., William Forrest, Don Haggerty, House Peters Jr., George Meeker, Keith Richards. The foreman of an oil supply company suspects that a rival firm has planted spies in his operation. There is lots of action in this fast moving Roy Rogers film.

3339 Spoilers of the Range. Columbia, 1939. 58 minutes B/W. D: C. C. Coleman Jr. SC: Paul Franklin. WITH Charles Starrett, Iris Meredith, Bob Nolan & The Sons of the Pioneers, Dick Curtis, Kenneth MacDonald, Hank Bell, Ed Le Saint, Forbes Murray, Art Mix, Edmund Cobb, Ed Peil, Horace B. Carpenter, Charles Brinley, Carl Sepulveda, Ethan Laidlaw, Joe Weaver. Crooks try to stop ranchers' cattle from going to market in order to keep them from repaying a loan which will save their lands. Average Charles Starrett vehicle.

3340 Spook Town. Producers Releasing Corporation, 1944. 59 minutes B/W. D-SC: Elmer Clifton. WITH James Newill, Dave O'Brien, Guy Wilkerson, Mady Lawrence, Dick Curtis, Harry Harvey, Ed Cassidy, Charles King, Robert Barron, Richard Alexander, John Cason. The captain of the rangers is forced to resign when money entrusted to him by ranchers is stolen but a trio of rangers find the real thief. The mystery element adds some flavor to this otherwise mundane "Texas Rangers" series film.

3341 Springfield Incident. CBS-TV/20th Century-Fox, 1957. 45 minutes B/W. WITH Ann Harding, Tom Tryon, Marshall Thompson, Alan Hale, John Conte. In frontier Illinois, young lawyer Abraham Lincoln defends a widow's two sons accused of murder. Adequate television adaptation of the film **Young Mr. Lincoln** (q.v.), originally telecast February 6, 1957 as "Young Man from Kentucky" on "The Twentieth Century-Fox Hour" (CBS-TV, 1955-57).

3342 Springfield Rifle. Warner Brothers, 1952. 93 minutes Color. D: Andre De Toth. SC: Charles Marquis Warren & Frank Davis. WITH Gary Cooper, Phyllis Thaxter, David Brian, Paul Kelly, Philip Carey, Lon Chaney, James Millican, Martin Milner, Guinn Williams, James Brown, Jack Woody, Alan Hale, Vince Barnett, Fess Parker, Richard Lightner, Ewing Mitchell, Poodles Hanneford, George Ross, Eric Hoeg, Wilton Graff, Ned Young, William Fawcett, Richard Hale, Ben Corbett, Guy E. Hearn, George Eldredge, Ralph Sanford, Rory Mallinson, Ric Roman, Jack Mower, Michael Chapin. Renegades rustle horses intended for the Union cause and an Army officer is sent West to stop the problem. Slightly better than average Civil War Western yarn.

3343 Springtime in Texas. Monogram, 1945. 55 minutes B/W. D: Oliver Drake. SC: Frances Kavanaugh. WITH Jimmy Wakely, Dennis Moore, Lee "Lasses" White, Marie Harmon, Rex Lease, The Callahan Brothers & Their Blue Ridge Mountain Folks, Pearl Early, Horace Murphy, I. Stanford Jolley, Hal Taliaferro, Budd Buster, Roy Butler, Ted French, Johnny Bond, Frankie Marvin, Lloyd Ingraham, Pat Patterson, Rust McDonald, Spud Goodall. Three pals are suspected of murder when one of the candidates for mayor of a small town is murdered. Jimmy Wakely's second film is not much better than his first (**Song of the Range,** [q.v.]) but this outing does offer a chance to see country music veterans The Callahan Brothers.

3344 Springtime in the Rockies. Republic, 1937. 60 minutes B/W. D: Joseph Kane. SC: Betty Burbridge & Gilbert Wright. WITH Gene Autry, Smiley Burnette, The Sons of the Pioneers, Polly Rowles, Ula Love, Ruth Bacon, Jane Hunt, George Chesebro, Lew Meehan, Edmund Cobb, Jack Rockwell, Alan Bridge, Tom London, Edward Hearn, Frankie Marvin, William Hale, Fred Burns, Art Davis, Jack Kirk, Frank Ellis, George (Montgomery) Letz, Oscar Gahan, Jim Corey. Singer Gene Autry gets involved in a range feud between ranchers and sheepherders by telling a female ranch owner, who has just bought sheep he wants her to sell, that her ranch is rundown. Entertaining Gene Autry outing enhanced by the title song and "You're the Only Star in My Blue Heaven."

3345 Springtime in the Sierras. Republic, 1947. 54 (75) minutes Color. D: William Witney. SC: Sloan Nibley. WITH Roy

Rogers, Andy Devine, Jane Frazee, Bob Nolan & The Sons of the Pioneers, Roy Barcroft, Stephanie Bachelor, Hal London, Harry V. Chesire, Chester Conklin, Hank Patterson, Bob Woodward. Roy Rogers goes on the trail of professional hunters who are killing outlawed game after they murder his long-time friend, a game warden. Only so-so Roy Rogers entry highlighted by a fight between two gals at the finale. V: Video Yesteryear.

3346 Spurs. Universal, 1930. 59 minutes B/W. D-SC: B. Reeves Eason. WITH Hoot Gibson, Helen Wright, Buddy Hunter, Pee Wee Holmes, Robert Homans, Frank Clark, William Bertram, Philo McCullough, Pete Morrison, Art Ardigan, Cap Anderson. A cowboy and a young boy team to try to track down a group of outlaws while the cowboy vies for a large purse and silver spurs in a rodeo as well as for the love of a pretty girl. Exciting and well-done early Hoot Gibson sound film, one which will appeal to his fans.

3347 Square Dance Jubilee. Lippert, 1949, 80 minutes B/W. D: Paul Landres. SC: Ron Ormond & Dan Ullman. WITH Don Barry, Wally Vernon, Mary Beth Hughes, Max Terhune, Thurston Hall, Britt Wood, Spade Cooley & His Band, John Eldredge, Marshall Reed, Tom Tyler, Tom Kennedy, Chester Clute, Clarke Stevens, Lee Roberts, Slim Gault, Cliff Taylor, Ralph Moody, Hazel Nilsen, Alex Montoya, Hal King, Lloyd "Cowboy" Copas, Johnny Downs, The Broome Brothers, Smiley & Kitty, Herman the Hermit, Ray Vaughn, The Tumbleweed Tumblers, The Elder Lovelies, Claude Casey, Buddy McDowell, Dana Gibson, Dot Remey. A TV promoter sends two talent scouts West to find real Western talent for his program and the two run across a gang trying to cheat a girl out of her ranch. Interesting curio full of old-time country music acts with Don Barry even singing a song; worth a look.

3348 The Square Deal Man. Triangle, 1917. 45 minutes B/W. D: William S. Hart. SC: J. G. Hawks. WITH William S. Hart, Mary McIvor, Joseph J. Dowling, Mary Jane Irving, J. Frank Burke, Darrell Foss, Thomas Kirihara, Milton Ross, Charles O. Rush. An honest gambler wins a ranch from a man who is later killed and the man's daughter is made to think the gambler murdered her father, when the actual murderer is his rival for her affections. Entertaining William S. Hart silent film. V: Classic Video Cinema Collectors Club.

3349 Square Deal Sanderson. Paramount-Artcraft, 1919. 60 minutes B/W. D: William S. Hart & Lambert Hillyer. SC: Lambert Hillyer. WITH William S. Hart, Ann Little, Lloyd Bacon, Frank Whitson, Andrew Robson, Edwin Wallach. A man finds the bodies of two murdered men and learns from a letter that one of them is the long-lost brother of a girl who is being persecuted by a rejected suitor, so the man sets out to defend the girl who mistakes him for her brother. Highly melodramatic William S. Hart silent effort; his fans will enjoy it. V: Classic Video Cinema Collectors Club.

3350 Square Shooter. Columbia, 1935. 57 minutes B/W. D: David Selman. SC: Harold Shumate. WITH Tim McCoy, Jacqueline Wells (Julie Bishop), Wheeler Oakman, J. Farrell MacDonald, Charles Middleton, John Darrow, Erville Alderson, Steve Clark, William V. Mong, Eddie Chandler, Ernie Adams, Bud Osborne, Art Mix. Returning home after being in prison for five years for falsely being accused of murdering his uncle, a cowboy tries to find the real culprits. Another finely written, directed and acted Tim McCoy vehicle for Columbia.

The Square Shooter (1951) <u>see</u> **Skipalong Rosenbloom**

3351 The Squaw Man. Metro-Goldwyn-Mayer, 1931. 106 minutes B/W. D: Cecil B. DeMille. SC: Lucien Hubbard, Lenore Coffee & Elsie Janis. WITH Warner Baxter, Eleanor Boardman, Paul Cavanagh, Lawrence Grant, Roland Young, Charles Bickford, Desmond Roberts, Mitchell Lewis, Luke Cosgrove, J. Farrell Mac-Donald, DeWitt Jennings, Frank Rice, Raymond Hatton, Frank Hagney, Victor Potel, Dickie Moore, Harry Northrup, Julia Faye, Eva Dennison, Ed Brady, Lillian Bond. After being disinherited an Englishman comes to Wyoming where he sets up a cattle empire and marries an Indian girl who has his child. Early sound version of Edwin Milton Royle's famous play is a bit on the creaky side but genre fans will still want to watch it. This is the third screen Paramount version of the play by director Cecil B. DeMille, who first filmed it in 1914 with Dustin Farnum and again in 1918 with Elliott Dexter, Thurston Hall and Katherine MacDonald.

3352 Stacked Cards. Circle Productions/ Fred J. Balshoffer, 1926. 55 minutes B/W. D: Robert Eddy. SC: Guy C. Cleve-

411 Stage to Blue

land & William De Geiger. WITH Fred Church, Katherine McGuire, Robert Thurston, John Watson, Artie Ortego. A crooked ranch foreman tries to cheat a girl out of her rightful inheritance but a cowboy comes to her aid. Low grade, but actionful, quickie from the silent days.

3353 Stage to Blue River. Monogram, 1951. 55 minutes B/W. D: Lewis D. Collins. SC: Joseph Poland. WITH Whip Wilson, Fuzzy Knight, Phyllis Coates, Lee Roberts, Lane Bradford, Pierce Lyden, John Hart, Terry Frost, I. Stanford Jolley, William Fawcett, Steve Clark, Stanley Price, Bud Osborne. U. S. marshals try to help a girl whose stageline is coveted by a crook and his lawman henchman. Average Whip Wilson vehicle.

3354 Stage to Chino. RKO Radio, 1940. 59 minutes B/W. D: Edward Killy. SC: Morton Grant & Arthur V. Jones. WITH George O'Brien, Virginia Vale, Hobart Cavanaugh, Roy Barcroft, William Haade, Carl Stockdale, Glenn Strange, Harry Cording, Martin Garralaga, Ethan Laidlaw, Tom London, Billy Benedict, John Dilson, Bob Burns, Frank Ellis, Hank Bell, Jack O'Shea, The Pals of the Golden West. A postal inspector stops a stage holdup and takes a job as a driver for the girl owner of the stage line in order to investigate a series of robberies. Very good George O'Brien film.

3355 Stage to Mesa City. Producers Releasing Corporation, 1947. 52 minutes B/W. D: Ray Taylor. SC: Joseph Poland. WITH Lash LaRue, Al St. John, Jennifer Holt, George Chesebro, Brad Slavin, Marshall Reed, Terry Frost, Carl Mathews, Bob Woodward, Steve Clark, Frank Ellis, Lee Morgan, Wally West, Russell Arms. U. S. marshals Cheyenne Davis and Fuzzy Q. Jones are sent to Mesa City to investigate a stage line being harassed by bandits. A very good Lash LaRue film which is fast moving with realistic fight sequences.

3356 Stage to Thunder Rock. Paramount, 1964. 82 minutes Color. D: William F. Claxton. SC: Charles Wallace. WITH Barry Sullivan, Marilyn Maxwell, Scott Brady, Lon Chaney, Anne Seymour, John Agar, Keenan Wynn, Wanda Hendrix, Ralph Taeger, Allan Jones, Laurel Goodwin, Robert Strauss, Robert Lowery, Rex Bell Jr., Argentina Brunetti, Suzanne Cupito, Paul E. Burns, Wayne Peters, Roy Jenson. A lawman arrives at a stage-coach station with a prisoner and learns the man's father is planning to rescue his son and kill the sheriff. The best of A. C. Lyles' Westerns for Paramount in the 1960s, well made with a good cast and an especially fine performance by Lon Chaney as the drunken way station owner.

3357 Stage to Tucson. Columbia, 1951. 82 minutes Color. D: Ralph Moody. SC: Bob Williams, Frank Burt & Robert Libott. WITH Rod Cameron, Wayne Morris, Kay Buckley, Sally Eilers, Carl Benton Reid, Roy Roberts, Harry Bellaver, Douglas Fowley, John Pickard, Olin Howlin, Boyd Stockman, John Sheehan, Reed Howes, James Kirkwood. The government sends two men to the Southwest to find out about the numerous hijackings of government stagecoaches and finds secessionists behind the problem. Actionful melodrama highlighted by the work of its two likable stars.

3358 Stagecoach. United Artists, 1939. 96 minutes B/W. D: John Ford. SC: Dudley Nichols. WITH Claire Trevor, John Wayne, Thomas Mitchell, Andy Devine, George Bancroft, John Carradine, Donald Meek, Louise Platt, Tim Holt, Berton Churchill, Tom Tyler, Chris-Pin Martin, Francis Ford, Elvira Rios, Yakima Canutt, Chief Big Tree, Harry Tenbrook, Jack Pennick, Paul McVey, Walter McGrail, Brenda Fowler, Florence Lake, Cornelius Keefe, Vester Pegg, Bryant Washburn, Nora Cecil, Bill Cody, Buddy Roosevelt, Chief White Horse, Duke Lee, Mary Kathleen Walker, Helen Gibson, Dorothy Appleby, Joe Rickson. An assorted group of passengers are on a stagecoach for Lordsburg and along the way they learn they are in the path of Geronimo's warring Apaches. One of the all-time great classic Westerns and a must-see for all genre followers. The entire cast is superb, especially Andy Devine as the stage driver, John Carradine's gambler and Louise Platt as the pregnant passenger. Excellent. V: Cumberland Video. VD: Blackhawk.

3359 Stagecoach. 20th Century-Fox, 1966. 114 minutes Color. D: Gordon Douglas. SC: Joseph Landon. WITH Alex Cord, Ann-Margret, Red Buttons, Michael Connors, Bing Crosby, Bob (Robert) Cummings, Van Heflin, Slim Pickens, Stefanie Powers, Keenan Wynn, Brad Weston, Joseph Hoover, Oliver McGowan, David Humphreys Miller, Bruce Mars, Edwin Mills, Hal Lynch, Norman Rockwell, Muriel Davidson, Brett Pearson. A saloon girl, a gambler, a drunken doctor, a pregnant girl and a wanted outlaw are among the passengers on a stagecoach heading into Indian country. Bland remake of the famous 1939 John Ford film; its only compensation is fine performances by Van Heflin as the stage driver and Slim Pickens as his shotgun rider.

3360 Stagecoach Buckaroo. Universal, 1942. 58 minutes B/W. D: Ray Taylor. SC: Al Martin. WITH Johnny Mack Brown, Fuzzy Knight, Nell O'Day, Anne Nagel, Herbert Rawlinson, Glenn Strange, Ernie Adams, Henry Hall, Lloyd Ingraham, Kermit Maynard, Frank Brownlee, Jack C. Smith, Harry Tenbrook, Frank Ellis, Blackie Whiteford, Hank Bell, Ray Jones, Jim Corey, William Nestell, Carl Sepulveda, The Guardsman. A young woman tries to carry on her father's stagecoach operation after he is killed by outlaws and she hires two men to help her. Pretty actionful Johnny Mack Brown vehicle with the unique plot device of using a bullet-proof stagecoach to thwart holdups.

3361 Stagecoach Days. Columbia, 1938. 58 minutes B/W. D: Joseph Levering. SC: Nate Gatzert. WITH Jack Luden, Eleanor Stewart, Hal Taliaferro, Harry Woods, Slim Whitaker, Jack Ingram, Lafe McKee, Robert Kortman, Dick Botiller, Blackjack Ward, Tom London, Tuffy (dog). A cowboy comes to the aid of a girl and her father who are trying to acquire a government mail contract for their stage line. Crude and low-grade but passable Jack Luden vehicle with good work by Hal Taliaferro as the father.

3362 Stagecoach Driver. Monogram, 1951. 52 minutes B/W. D: Lewis D. Collins. SC: Joseph O'Donnell. WITH Whip Wilson, Fuzzy Knight, Jim Bannon, Gloria Winters, Lane Bradford, Marshall Reed, Barbara Allen, Leonard Penn, John Hart, Stanley Price, George DeNormand. A lawman and his pals try to stop the lawlessness caused when the telegraph begins putting the pony express and freight lines out of business. Pleasant effort in the Whip Wilson series.

3363 Stagecoach Express. Republic, 1942. 56 minutes B/W. D: George Sherman. SC: Doris Schroeder. WITH Don "Red" Barry, Lynn Merrick, Charles King, Al St. John, Robert Kent, Emmett Lynn, Guy Kingsford, Ethan Laidlaw, Eddie Dean, Cyclone (horse), Duke (dog). A man and his pal agree to help a girl by

driving her stagecoach which has been attacked by bandits. Pleasant but slow Don Barry effort with several well staged riding and chase sequences involving holdups.

3364 Stagecoach Kid. RKO Radio, 1949. 60 minutes B/W. D: Lew Landers. SC: Norman Houston. WITH Tim Holt, Richard Martin, Jeff Donnell, Joseph Sawyer, Thurston Hall, Carol Hughes, Robert Bray, Robert B. Williams, Kenneth MacDonald, Harry Harvey. Outlaws plan to murder a wealthy man and kidnap his daughter but their plot is stopped by a stageline owner. Another good entry in Tim Holt's RKO series.

3365 Stagecoach Outlaws. Producers Releasing Corporation, 1945. 58 minutes B/W. D: Sam Newfield. SC: Fred Myton. WITH Buster Crabbe, Al St. John, Frances Gladwin, Ed Cassidy, Kermit Maynard, I. Stanford Jolley, Steve Clark, Robert Kortman, Bob Cason, George Chesebro, Hank Bell. Marshal Billy Carson pretends to be a wanted outlaw in order to stop a gang from destroying a stage line. Typically cheap but watchable PRC "Billy Carson" series film.

3366 Stagecoach to Dancer's Rock. Universal-International, 1962. 72 minutes B/W. D: Earl Bellamy. SC: Kenneth Darling. WITH Warren Stevens, Jody Lawrence, Martin Landau, Judy Dan, Del Moore, Don Wilbanks, Bob Anderson, Rand Brooks, Gene Roth, Charles Tannen, Mike Ragan, Mauritz Hugo, Tim Bolton. When a stage driver discovers one of his passengers has smallpox he leaves all of them stranded in the desert. Nothing special but worth viewing.

3367 Stagecoach to Denver. Republic, 1946. 54 (56) minutes B/W. D: R. G. Springsteen. SC: Earle Snell. WITH Allan Lane, Bobby Blake, Martha Wentworth, Peggy Stewart, Roy Barcroft, Emmett Lynn, Ted Adams, Edmund Cobb, Tom Chatterton, Bobbie Hyatt, George Chesebro, Ed Cassidy, Wheaton Chambers, Forrest Taylor, Britt Wood, Tom London, Stanley Price. Wanting a woman's property, a supposedly good citizen has her kidnapped and then murders a local official and has his henchman put in his place. Fairly actionful "Red Ryder" series entry. V: Video Connection.

3368 Stagecoach to Fury. 20th Century-Fox, 1956. 76 minutes B/W. D: William F. Claxton. SC: Eric Norden. WITH

Forrest Tucker, Mari Blanchard, Wallace Ford, Rodolfo Hoyos, Paul Fix, Rico Alaniz, Wright King, Margia Dean, Ian MacDonald. Passengers aboard a stage are held hostage by Mexican bandits who await the arrival of the next stagecoach in order to steal its gold. Dreary melodrama with too much talk.

3369 Stagecoach to Monterey. Republic, 1944. 54 minutes B/W. D: Lesley Selander. SC: Norman S. Hall. WITH Allan Lane, Peggy Stewart, Wally Vernon, Twinkle Watts, Roy Barcroft, LeRoy Mason, Tom London, Kenne Duncan, Bud Geary, Carl Sepulveda, Jack O'Shea, Jack Kirk, Fred Graham, Henry Wills, Cactus Mack. Treasury agents are on the trail of gangsters who plan to counterfeit currency. Okay addition to Allan Lane's Republic series.

3370 Stagecoach War. Paramount, 1940. 54 (63) minutes B/W. D: Lesley Selander. SC: Norman Houston. WITH William Boyd, Russell Hayden, Julie Carter, Harvey Stephens, J. Farrell MacDonald, Rad Robinson, Eddy Waller, Frank Lackteen, Jack Rockwell, Eddie Dean, Robert Kortman, The King's Men. Hopalong Cassidy and the Bar 20 boys find themselves in the middle of a contract war between two stagecoach lines. Good "Hopalong Cassidy" film, made when the series was near its peak. V: Video Connection.

3371 The Stalking Moon. National General, 1968. 109 minutes Color. D: Robert Mulligan. SC: Wendell Mayes & Alvin Sargent. WITH Gregory Peck, Eva Marie Saint, Robert Forster, Nolan Clay, Russell Thorsen, Frank Silvera, Lonny Chapman, Lou Frizzell, Henry Beckman, Charles Tyner, Richard Bull, Sandy Wyeth, Joaquin Martinez, Boyd "Red" Morgan. An Apache warrior comes in search of the white woman and his son who were taken from him by a man who has settled down with them on his New Mexico ranch. Well produced oater is basically dull due to lack of suspense.

3372 Stallion Canyon. Astor, 1949. 72 minutes Color. D: Harry Fraser. SC: Hy Heath. WITH Ken Curtis, Carolina Cotton, Shug Fisher, Forrest Taylor, Ted Adams, Billy Hammond, Roy Butler. A cowboy tries to help an Indian framed on a murder charge and he also tries to win the big purse at an annual race. Low grade affair.

3373 Stallion Road. Warner Brothers, 1947. 97 minutes B/W. D: James V. Kern. SC: Stephen Longstreet. WITH Ronald Reagan, Alexis Smith, Zachary Scott, Peggy Knudsen, Patti Brady, Harry Davenport, Angela Greene, Frank Puglia, Ralph Byrd, Lloyd Corrigan, Fernando Alvarado, Matthew Boulton, Mary Gordon, Nina Campana, Dewey Robinson, Paul Panzer, Bobby Valentine, Ralph Littlefield, Tom Wilson, Oscar O'Shea, Leon Lenoir, Monte Blue, Fred Kelsey, Major Sam Harris, Joan Winfield, Danny Dowling, Douglas Kennedy, Creighton Hale, Elaine Lange, Roxanne Stark, Vera Lewis. A veterinarian and his novelist pal both fall in love with a woman who breeds horses but the doctor almost loses her when her herd contracts anthrax. Only fair modern-day melodrama; not even uncredited direction by Raoul Walsh could help it.

3374 The Stampede. Victor Kremer Films, 1921. 50 minutes B/W. D: Francis Ford. SC: Kingsley Benedict & Eugenie Kremer. WITH Texas Guinan, Francis Ford, Frederick Moore, Jean Carpenter, Vale Rio, Fred Kohler, Cecil McLean, Kingsley Benedict, Snowflake (horse). A young woman, in love with a cowboy who does not return her affections, sets out to claim a section of government land only to be opposed by crooks who want the land for themselves. This actionful silent entry will give viewers a chance to see famous night club hostess Texas Guinan in one of her several starring Westerns.

3375 Stampede. Columbia, 1936. 58 minutes B/W. D: Ford Beebe, SC: Robert Watson. WITH Charles Starrett, Finis Barton, J. P. McGowan, LeStrange Millman, Reginald Hincks, James McGrath, Arthur Kerr, Jack Atkinson, Michael Heppell, Ted Mapes. A rancher wants the spread of a rival and kills a buyer for the man's cattle but the murdered man's brother arrives on the scene looking for the killer. Mediocre Charles Starrett vehicle, not up to the usual good standards of his Columbia series.

3376 Stampede. Allied Artists, 1949. 78 minutes B/W. D: Lesley Selander SC: John C. Champion & Blake Edwards. WITH Rod Cameron, Gale Storm, Don Castle, Johnny Mack Brown, Don Curtis, John Eldredge, John Miljan, Jonathan Hale, James Harrison, Ted Elliott, Jack Parker, Chuck Roberson, Tim Ryan, Kenne Duncan, Carol Henry, Adrian Wood, I. Stanford Jolley, Marshall Reed,

Philo McCullough, Charles King, Duke York, Wes Christensen. Two feuding cattlemen brothers become involved with settlers who are being cheated out of their water rights. This nicely made compact oater moves along at a nice clip.

3377 Stampede at Bitter Creek. Buena Vista, 1966. 81 minutes Color. D: Harry Keller. SC: D. P. Harmon. WITH Tom Tryon, Stephen McNally, Sidney Blackmer, Bill Williams, John Larch, Harold J. Stone, Norma Moore, Grant Williams, H. M. Wynant, Don Kelly. After marrying the girl he loves, a Texas Ranger finds himself caught between both Indians on the warpath and outlaws and ends up a wanted man. Actionful Walt Disney Western originally shown on his TV program on March 6, 1959 as "The Man from Bitter Creek" segment of the "Texas John Slaughter" miniseries.

3378 The Stand at Apache River. Universal-International, 1953. 77 minutes Color. D: Lee Sholem. SC: Arthur Ross. WITH Stephen McNally, Julia (Julie) Adams, Hugh Marlowe, Jaclynne Greene, Hugh O'Brian, Russell Johnson, Jack Kelly, Edgar Barrier, Forrest Lewis. Eight people are stranded at a way station with Apache Indians about to attack. Mediocre actioner which may appeal to diehard genre fans.

3379 Stand Up and Fight. Metro-Goldwyn-Mayer, 1939. 97 minutes B/W. D: W. S. Van Dyke. SC: James M. Cain, Jane Murtin & Harvey Fergusson. WITH Wallace Beery, Robert Taylor, Florence Rice, Helen Broderick, Charles Bickford, Barton MacLane, Charles Grapewin, John Qualen, Robert Glecker, Clinton Rosemond, Cy Kendall, Paul Everton, Claudia Morgan, Selmar Jackson, Robert Middlemass. A young man is hired by the railroad to investigate slave running and he becomes at odds with a stagecoach operator involved in the trade. Slick pre-Civil War melodrama sure to delight Wallace Beery fans.

3380 Standing Tall. NBC-TV, 1978. 100 minutes Color. D: Harvey Hart. SC: Franklin Thompson. WITH Robert Forster, Will Sampson, L. Q. Jones, Robert Donner, Ron Hayes, Buck Taylor, Linda Evans, Chuck Connors, Faith Quabius, Dani Janssen, Robert Gentry, Eddie Firestone, David Lewis. During the Depression a half-breed cattleman runs into trouble when he refuses to sell his spread to

a ruthless cattle baron. Typically mediocre made-for-TV film.

3381 Star in the Dust. Universal-International, 1956. 80 minutes Color. D: Charles Haas. SC: Oscar Brodney. WITH John Agar, Mamie Van Doren, Richard Boone, Coleen Gray, Leif Erickson, James Gleason, Randy Stuart. When a gunman kills three farmers the local sheriff plans to hang him for the crimes but the town's citizens refuse to support him. Passable Albert Zugsmith production, but nothing special.

3382 Star of Texas. Allied Artists, 1953. 68 minutes B/W. D: Thomas Carr. SC: Dan Ullman. WITH Wayne Morris, Paul Fix, Rick Vallin, Robert Bice, Frank Ferguson, Jack Larson, James Flavin, Lyle Talbot, William Fawcett, Mickey Simpson, George Wallace, John Crawford, Stanley Price. When an outlaw gang begins recruiting its members from prisons, a Texas Ranger pretends to be an escaped convict to track down the crooks. Documentary-like atmosphere makes this Wayne Morris film (the first entry in his Allied Artists series and the final official "B" Western series) good entertainment.

3383 The Star Packer. Monogram, 1934. 54 minutes B/W. D-SC: Robert North Bradbury. WITH John Wayne, Verna Hillie, George ("Gabby") Hayes, Yakima Canutt, Earl Dwire, Ed (Eddie) Parker, George Cleveland, Tom Lingham, Artie Ortego, David Aldrich, Tex Palmer, Billy Franey. A young cowboy takes the job of the sheriff of a small town in order to combat an outlaw gang led by a mysterious figure called The Shadow. Hidden tunnels, a hooded gang leader and lots of action make this Lone Star production a good one. V: Electric Video.

3384 Starbird and Sweet William. Howco-International, 1975. 95 minutes Color. D: Jack B. Hively. SC: Axel Gruenberg. WITH Dan Haggerty, Skip Homeier, A. Martinez, Louise Fitch, Skeeter Vaughn, Roger Bear, Ancil Cook. An Indian youth takes an unauthorized solo flight in a plane and ends up crashing it in the wilderness where he has to fight to survive and is befriended by a bear cub and other animals. Pleasant little outdoor drama; well directed.

3385 Stardust on the Sage. Republic, 1942. 54 (65) minutes B/W. D: William Morgan. SC: Stuart McGowan & Dorrell

McGowan. WITH Gene Autry, Smiley Burnette, Edith Fellows, Bill Henry, Louise Currie, George Ernest, Emmett Vogan, Vince Barnett, Betty Farrington, Roy Barcroft, Frankie Marvin, Tom London, Rex Lease, Frank Ellis, Ed Cassidy, Fred Burns, Frank LaRue, Franklyn Farnum, Edmund Cobb, Merrill McCormack, Monte Montague, George DeNormand, George Sherwood, William Nestell, Frank O'Connor, Griff Barnett, Lee Shumway. When crooks frame a young man on an embezzlement charge, Gene Autry comes to his rescue. Not even some good songs, including "Deep in the Heart of Texas," and an excellent supporting cast can stop the tedium of this Gene Autry effort.

3386 Starlight Over Texas. Monogram, 1938. 56 minutes B/W. D: Al Herman. SC: John Rathmell. WITH Tex Ritter, Carmen LaRoux, Snub Pollard, Horace Murphy, Karl Hackett, Charles King, Martin Garralaga, George Chesebro, Carlos Villarias, Ed Cassidy, Sherry Tansey, Bob Terry, Horace B. Carpenter, Dave O'Brien, Denver Dixon, Chick Hannon, Tex Palmer, Rosa Turich, Carmen Alvarez, Jerry Gomez, The Northwesterners. When outlaws plague Spanish ranchers, a cowboy and his pals bring them to justice. Standard Tex Ritter vehicle somewhat hurt by a long mid-way musical segment, although it is well staged, with Tex singing the rousing "A Viva Tequila." British title: **Moonlight Over Texas.**

3387 Stars in My Crown. Metro-Goldwyn-Mayer, 1950. 89 minutes B/W. D: Jacques Tourneur. SC: Margaret Fitts. WITH Joel McCrea, Ellen Drew, Dean Stockwell, Alan Hale, Lewis Stone, James Mitchell, Amanda Blake, Juano Hernandez, Charles Kemper, Connie Gilchrist, Ed Begley, Jack Lambert, Arthur Hunnicutt, James Arness. A new minister comes to the pulpit in a small rural community and finds he needs a gun to carry out his mission. Homey episodic film about life in rural 19th century America; good viewing.

3388 Stars Over Arizona. Monogram, 1937. 62 minutes B/W. D: Robert North Bradbury. SC: Robert Emmett (Tansey). WITH Jack Randall, Kathleen Eliot, Horace Murphy, Warner Richmond, Tom Herbert, Hal Price, Earl Dwire, Chick Hannon, Jack Rockwell, Forrest Taylor, Bob McKenzie, Sherry Tansey, Tex Palmer. When a crooked town boss tries to keep a girl rancher from selling her cattle she is aided by a federal marshal sent to the area to stop the lawlessness. Okay Jack Randall vehicle, but nothing special.

3389 Stars Over Texas. Producers Releasing Corporation, 1946. 59 minutes B/W. D: Robert Emmett Tansey. SC: Frances Kavanaugh. WITH Eddie Dean, Shirley Patterson, Roscoe Ates, Lee Bennett, Lee Roberts, Kermit Maynard, Jack O'Shea, Hal Smith, Matty Roubert, Carl Matthews, William Fawcett, The Sunshine Boys. Outlaws are murdering citizens and rustling cattle in a small community and the local cattlemen hire a detective to stop the activities. Plotwise this Eddie Dean vehicle is not much but the film does include two of the star's lovely compositions: the title tune and "Sands of the Old Rio Grande," the latter written with Glenn Strange.

3390 Station West. RKO Radio, 1948. 92 minutes B/W. D: Sidney Lanfield. SC: Frank Fenton & Winston Miller. WITH Dick Powell, Jane Greer, Agnes Moorehead, Burl Ives, Tom Powers, Steve Brodie, Gordon Oliver, Guinn Williams, Raymond Burr, Regis Toomey, Michael Steele, Olin Howlin, John Berkes, Dan White, John Kellogg, Charles Middleton, John Doucette, Suzi Crandall. An Army officer works undercover in a small town to find out who is behind a series of hijackings which have led to murder. Spritely action melodrama which moves at a good clip. V: Blackhawk.

3391 Stay Away, Joe. Metro-Goldwyn-Mayer, 1968. 101 minutes Color. D: Peter Tewksbury. SC: Burt Kennedy & Michael A. Hoey. WITH Elvis Presley, Burgess Meredith, Joan Blondell, Katy Jurado, Thomas Gomez, Henry Jones, L. Q. Jones, Quentin Dean, Anne Seymour, Angus Duncan, Douglas Henderson, Michael Lane, Susan Trustman, Warren Vanders, Buck Kartalian, Maurishka, Caitlin Wyles, Marya Christen, Del "Sonny" West, Jennifer Peak, Brett Parker, Michael Keller, Dick Wilson, David Cadiente, Harry Harvey, Joe Esposito, Robert Lieb, The Jordanaires. A half-blood Cree Indian rodeo rider returns to his reservation to help his people in a government rehabilitation program to set them up as cattle ranchers. Pretty poor Elvis Presley vehicle.

3392 Steel Cowboy. NBC-TV/EMI Television, 1978. 100 minutes Color. D: Harvey Laidman. SC: Douglas Wheeler & Bill Kerby. WITH James Brolin, Jennifer Warren, Rip Torn, Melanie Griffith, Julie Cobb, Lou Frizzell, Strother Martin,

Albert Popwell, John Dennis Johnston, Bob Schott, Don Calfa, Rudy Diaz, Bob Hoy, Scott Thompson, Larry Spalding. Despite opposition from his wife, a trucker tries to save his rig by agreeing to haul stolen cattle for a pal. TV movie which should please James Brolin's fans, but otherwise mediocre.

3393 Stick to Your Guns. Paramount, 1941. 54 (63) minutes B/W. D: Lesley Selander. SC: J. Benton Cheney. WITH William Boyd, Andy Clyde, Brad King, Jacqueline (Jennifer) Holt, Dick Curtis, Weldon Heyburn, Henry Hall, Joe Whitehead, Bob Card, Jack C. Smith, Herb Holcombe, Tom London, Kermit Maynard, Frank Ellis, Jack Rockwell, The Jimmy Wakely Trio (Jimmy Wakely, Johnny Bond, Dick Rinehart). When a gang of rustlers proves elusive, Hopalong Cassidy takes on the guise of a wanted man in order to infiltrate the gang. Pretty slow "Hopalong Cassidy" series entry.

3394 The Still Trumpet. CBS-TV/20th Century-Fox, 1957. 45 minutes B/W. WITH Dale Robertson, Victor Jory, Regis Toomey, Carol Ohmart, John Conte. When Indians threaten the citizens of a remote Western fort, imprisoned Confederate soldiers are used to protect them. Okay television remake of the film **Two Flags West** (q.v.), originally telecast as a segment of "The Twentieth Century-Fox Hour" (CBS-TV, 1955-57) on April 3, 1957.

3395 The Sting of the West. Film Ventures, 1976. 98 minutes Color. D: Enzo G. Castellari. SC: Gianni Simonelli, Tito Carpi, J. Maesso & Enzo G. Castellari. WITH Jack Palance, Timothy Brent, Lionel Stander, Francesca Romana Coluzzi, Renzo Palmer, Eduardo Fajardo, Mabel Karr, Ricardo Garrone, Maria Vico Villardo, Miguel Pedreghosa, Dante Clari, Carla Calo, Franco Borelli, Rocco Lerro, Bruno Boschetti, Carla Mancini. When a family inherits a mine from their deceased con man uncle, they try to sell it believing the property is worthless. Okay Italian-made genre comedy originally issued in 1972 as **Te Deum** by F. P. Cinematografica/Canaria Film.

3396 Stone of Silver Creek. Universal, 1935. 61 minutes B/W. D: Nick Grinde. SC: Earle Snell. WITH Buck Jones, Noel Francis, Niles Welch, Murdock McQuarrie, Marion Shilling, Peggy Campbell, Rodney Hildebrand, Harry Semels, Grady Sutton, Bob McKenzie, Lew Meehan, Frank Rice,

Kernan Cripps. A saloon owner gets religion but finds he is at odds with the town's preacher over a pretty girl. A different kind of Buck Jones actioner with touches of the kind of fare William S. Hart did in the silent days, although not nearly so austere.

3397 The Storm. Universal, 1930. 90 minutes B/W. D: William Wyler. SC: Wells Root & Tom Reed. WITH Lupe Velez, Paul Cavanaugh, William Boyd, Alphonse Ethier, Ernie Adams, Tom London, Nick Thompson, Erin La Bissoniere. Two war buddies both fall in love with the same girl and are snowed in with her in the wilds of Canada and the men become bitter enemies for her hand in marriage. Standard screen version of the 1919 Landgon McCormick novel with a well staged avalanche sequence; first filmed in 1922 by Universal with Matt Moore, House Peters and Virginia Valli.

3398 The Storm Rider. 20th Century-Fox, 1957. 70 minutes B/W. D: Edward Bernds. SC: Edward Bernds & Don Martin. WITH Scott Brady, Mala Powers, Bill Williams, John Goddard, William Fawcett, Roy Engel, George Keymas, Olin Howlin, Hank Patterson, James Dobson, John Close, Jim Hayward, Rocky Shanan, Frank Richards, Rick Vallin, Lane Chandler, Tom London. A big rancher, in order to stop competition, hires a vicious gunman while the Cattle Association sends an agent to help those under attack. Moody and fairly actionful oater highlighted by Byrdon Baker's photography; especially good early sequence of agent riding into town during a dust storm.

3399 Storm Over Wyoming. RKO Radio, 1950. 60 minutes B/W. D: Lesley Selander. SC: Ed Earl Repp. WITH Tim Holt, Richard Martin, Noreen Nash, Richard Powers, Betty Underwood, Kenneth MacDonald, Leo MacMahon, Bill Kennedy, Holly Bane, Don Haggerty, Richard Kean. A dishonest foreman of a sheep ranch causes trouble between cattlemen and sheep herders. Despite more than adequate production values, this Tim Holt vehicle is only average.

3400 Stormy. Universal, 1935. 68 minutes B/W. D: Louis Friedlander (Lew Landers). SC: George Plympton & Ben Grauman Kohn. WITH Noah Beery Jr., Jean Rogers, J. Farrell MacDonald, Raymond Hatton, Walter Miller, Fred Kohler, James P. Burtis, The Arizona Wranglers, (Charles

Hunter, L. F. Costello, Cal Short, John Jackson, Glenn Strange, John Luther), Bud Osborne, Kenny Cooper, James Phillips, Jack Sanders, Cecil Kellogg, Jack Shannon, Robert E. Homans, Wilfred Lucas, Samuel R. McDaniel, Eddie (Edmund) Cobb, Charles Murphy, James Welch, Shirley Marks, Chester Gan, William Welsh, Jack Leonard, Monte Montague, W. H. Davis, Rex (horse). A young man searches for a beautiful stallion lost during a train wreck and ends up saving a herd of wild horses. Well made and entertaining melodrama.

3401 Stormy Trails. Colony/Grand National, 1937. 59 minutes B/W. D: Sam Newfield. SC: Phil Dunham. WITH Rex Bell, Bob Hodges, Lois Wilde, Lane Chandler, Earl Dwire, Lloyd Ingraham, Karl Hackett, Earle Ross, Murdock MacQuarrie, Jimmie Aubrey, Roger Williams, George Morrell. Two brothers own a ranch with a mortgage on it and bad men are after the land for the gold it contains. Low grade production with a complicated plot and some good action.

3402 Straight Shooter. Victory, 1939. 60 minutes B/W. D: Sam Newfield. SC: Basil Dickey & Joseph O'Donnell. WITH Tim McCoy, Julie Sheldon, Ben Corbett, Forrest Taylor, Carl Mathews, Ted Adams, Budd Buster, Reed Howes, Wally West, Jack Ingram. Lawman Lightnin' Bill Carson pretends to be a rancher trying to buy a property where he suspects an outlaw gang has hidden stolen loot. Not one of Tim McCoy's best, mainly due to budget considerations.

3403 Straight Shooting. Universal/Butterfly, 1917. 53 minutes B/W. D: Jack (John) Ford. SC: George Hively. WITH Harry Carey, Molly Malone, Duke Lee, Vester Pegg, Hoot Gibson, George Berrell, Ted Brooks, Milt Brown. Cattlemen hire an outlaw to aid them in their fight against settlers but the gunman soon changes sides due to the brutality of his employers and his love for a nester girl. John Ford's first feature film is crude and simplistic by today's standards but it is entertaining and well worth viewing. Reissued as a two reel short in 1925 called **Straight Shootin'.** V: Cassette Express.

3404 Strange Gamble. United Artists, 1948. 61 minutes B/W. D: George Archainbaud. SC: J. Benton Cheney, Bennett Cohen & Ande Lamb. WITH William Boyd, Andy Clyde, Rand Brooks, Elaine Riley, Francis McDonald, Paul Fix, William

Leicester, Joan Barton, James Craven, Joel Friedkin, Herbert Rawlinson, Robert Williams, Alberto Morin, Lee Tung Foo. The government hires Hopalong Cassidy to investigate the appearance of counterfeit currency in a small border town. Turgid "Hopalong Cassidy" entry from the twilight of the theatrical series.

3405 Strange Lady in Town. Warner Brothers, 1955. 112 minutes Color. D: Mervyn LeRoy. SC: Frank Butler. WITH Greer Garson, Dana Andrews, Cameron Mitchell, Lois Smith, Walter Hampden, Pedro Gonzales-Gonzales, Joan Camden, Jose Torvay, Adele Jergens, Robert Wilke, Frank DeKova, Russell Johnson, Gregory Walcott, Douglas Kennedy, Ralph Moody, Nick Adams, Jack Williams, The Trianas. A woman doctor arrives in Santa Fe in 1879 to find her brother is an outlaw. Overlong and none-too-successful oater vehicle for Greer Garson; Frankie Laine sings the title song.

3406 The Strange Vengeance of Rosalie. 20th Century-Fox, 1972. 107 minutes Color. D: Jack Starrett. SC: Anthony Greville-Bell & John Kohn. WITH Bonnie Bedelia, Ken Howard, Anthony Zerbe. A young Indian girl forces a traveling salesman to keep her company in her large, isolated New Mexico desert home. Strange melodrama which is not likely to appeal to genre fans.

3407 The Stranger and the Gunfighter. Columbia, 1976. 107 minutes Color. D: Anthony M. Dawson (Antonio Margheriti). SC: Barth Jules Sussman. WITH Lee Van Cleef, Lo Lieh, Julian Ugarte, Patty Shepard, Karen Yeh, Femi Benussi, Erika Blanc, George Rigaud, Richard Palacios, Goyo (Gregorio) Peralta, Al Tung, Alfred Boreman, Bart Barry, Paul Costello. In order to obtain a fortune once belonging to a Chinese war lord, a gunman joins forces with a kung fu expert as they search for clues tatooed on the backsides of four young ladies. Elaborate genre put-on is lots of fun for fans of spaghetti Westerns.

3408 Stranger at My Door. Republic, 1956. 85 minutes B/W. D: William Witney. SC: Barry Shipman. WITH Macdonald Carey, Patricia Medina, Skip Homeier, Stephen Wootton, Louis Jean Heydt, Howard Wright, Slim Pickens, Fred Sherman, Malcolm Atterbury. A minister tries to help an outlaw and ends up putting his family in danger. Upbeat and pretty good melodrama with especially fine work by Macdonald Carey as the preacher.

3409 The Stranger from Arizona. Columbia, 1938. 60 minutes B/W. D: Elmer Clifton. SC: Monroe Shaff. WITH Buck Jones, Dorothy Fay, Hank Mann, Roy Barcroft, Hank Worden, Bob Terry, Horace Murphy, Budd Buster, Dot Farley, Stanley Blystone, Ralph Peters, Horace B. Carpenter, Walter Anthony. A fast-talking cowpoke is actually a railroad detective looking into a series of robberies and killings. Although well done this Buck Jones film is not as appealing as some of his other efforts.

3410 The Stranger from Pecos. Monogram, 1943. 58 minutes B/W. D: Lambert Hillyer. SC: Jess Bowers (Adele Buffington). WITH Johnny Mack Brown, Raymond Hatton, Kirby Grant, Christine McIntyre, Steve Clark, Sam Flint, Roy Barcroft, Robert Frazer, Edmund Cobb, Charles King, Bud Osborne, Artie Ortego, Tom London, Kermit Maynard, Milburn Morante, Lynton Brent, Carol Henry, George Morrell. Investigating a series of robberies in a small town, lawmen discover the local sheriff and banker are the real culprits. Johnny Mack Brown's second series vehicle for Monogram is an actionful affair.

3411 The Stranger from Ponca City. Columbia, 1947. 56 minutes B/W. D: Derwin Abrahams. SC: Ed Earl Repp. WITH Charles Starrett, Smiley Burnette, Virginia Hunter, Paul Campbell, Texas Jim Lewis & His Lone Star Cowboys, Jim Diehl, Forrest Taylor, Ted Mapes, Jacques O'Mahoney (Jock Mahoney), Tom McDonough, John Carpenter, Charles Hamilton, Ted Wells, Herman Hack, Roy Bucko. A cowboy arrives in a small town which is torn between peaceful and lawless elements. Fair "Durango Kid" series segment.

3412 Stranger from Santa Fe. Monogram, 1945. 60 minutes B/W. D: Lambert Hillyer. SC: Frank Young. WITH Johnny Mack Brown, Raymond Hatton, Beatrice Gray, Lewis Hart, Jack Ingram, Ray Elder, Jimmie Martin, Bud Osborne, Tom Quinn, Hal Price, Steve Clark, Jack Rockwell, Eddie Parker, Joann Curtis, John Merton. Impersonating a cowpoke, a lawman is forced by an outlaw gang to take part in a stage holdup and they frame him for the murder of the guard. Good script enhances this good Johnny Mack Brown vehicle.

3413 The Stranger from Texas. Columbia, 1939. 54 minutes B/W. D: Sam Nelson.

SC: Paul Franklin. WITH Charles Starrett, Lorna Gray, Richard Fiske, Bob Nolan & The Sons of the Pioneers, Dick Curtis, Edmund Cobb, Alan Bridge, Jack Rockwell, Hal Taliaferro, Ed LeSaint, Art Mix, George Chesebro. A rancher's son, a lawman working incognito, tries to find out who is behind a series of fence cuttings and cattle rustling which a rancher blames on his father. Passable remake of star Charles Starrett's earlier film **The Mysterious Avenger** (q.v.).

3414 Stranger in Town. Metro-Goldwyn-Mayer, 1968. 86 minutes Color. D: Vance Lewis (Luigi Vanzi). SC: Warren Garfield. WITH Tony Anthony, Dan Vadis, Iolenda Modio, Gia Sandri, Raf Baldassaree, Aldo Berti, Antonio Marsina, Enrico Capoloni. A mysterious stranger is double-crossed by a ruthless bandit and sets out for revenge. Empty and violent Italian oater but one of the few that proved to be popular box office in the U. S. Issued in Italy in 1966 by Primex-Italiana as **Un Dollaro Tia I Denti.** Sequel: **The Stranger Returns** (q.v.). Alternate title: **Donde Vas Extranjero?.**

3415 Stranger on Horseback. United Artists, 1955. 66 minutes Color. D: Jacques Tourneur. SC: Herb Meadow & Don Martin. WITH Joel McCrea, Miroslava, Kevin McCarthy, John McIntire, Nancy Gates, John Carradine, Emile Meyer, Robert Cornthwaite, James Bell, Jaclynne Greene. A circuit-riding judge is sent to a small town to restore law and order and to do so he arrests the son of the local cattle baron on a murder charge. Compact and entertaining little feature with good work by Joel McCrea as the peacemaker.

3416 Stranger on the Run. NBC-TV/Universal, 1967. 97 minutes Color. D: Donald Siegel. SC: Dean Riesner. WITH Henry Fonda, Anne Baxter, Dan Duryea, Michael Parks, Sal Mineo, Lloyd Bochner, Michael Burns, Tom Reese, Bernie Hamilton, Madlyn Rhue, Zalman King, Walter Burke, Rodolfo Acosta, George Dunn, Pepe Hern. A drifter, taking a message from a prisoner to his sister, is falsely accused of murder and chased into the desert by a sheriff and his posse. Don Siegel followers will like this made-for-TV feature but others will find it nothing special.

3417 The Stranger Returns. Metro-Goldwyn-Mayer, 1968. 90 minutes Color. D: Vance Lewis (Luigi Vanzi). SC: Bob Ensecalle Jr. & Ione Mang. WITH Tony

Anthony, Dan Vadis, Daniele Vargas, Marco Guglielmi, Jill Banner, Ettore Manni, Marina Berti, Ralf Baldassaree, Anthony Freeman. A mysterious stranger runs across a murdered postal inspector and impersonates him in order to track down an outlaw band who stole a gold plated stagecoach. Star Tony Anthony wrote the original story for this violence-for-violence's sake oater, a sequel to **Stranger in Town** (q.v.). Issued in Italy by Primex/Juventus/Reverse as **Un Uomo, Un Cavallo, Una Pistola.**

3418 The Stranger Wore a Gun. Columbia, 1953. 83 minutes Color. D: Andre De Toth. SC: Kenneth Gamet. WITH Randolph Scott, Claire Trevor, Joan Weldon, George Macready, Alfonso Bedoya, Lee Marvin, Clem Bevans, Roscoe Ates, Ernest Borgnine, Pierre Watkin, Joseph Vitale, Paul Maxey, Frank Scannell, Reed Howes, Edward Earle, Guy Wilkerson, Mary Newton, Franklyn Farnum, Barry Brooks, Tap Canutt, Al Haskell, Frank Hagney, Frank Ellis, Francis McDonald, Al Hill, Terry Frost, Herbert Rawlinson, Britt Wood, James Millican, Jack Woody, Rayford Barnes, Edith Evanson, Guy Teague. After his life is saved by an outlaw, a stage line employee must choose between loyalty to the man who saved him and his job when the bandit plans to rob a gold shipment. An interesting script and good production values make this Randolph Scott film add up to good entertainment.

3419 Strangers at Sunrise. Commonwealth United, 1971. 91 minutes Color. D: Percival Roberts. SC: Lee Marcus & Percival Roberts. WITH George Montgomery, Deanna Martin, Brian O'Shaughnessy, Tromp Terreblanche. A fugitive American mining engineer in South Africa during the Boer War tries to aid a farm family threatened by three British Army deserters. George Montgomery gives a very good performance in the starring role of this well-made and entertaining South African production.

3420 The Stranger's Gundown. New Line Cinema, 1974. 107 minutes Color. D: Sergio Garrone. SC: Sergio Garrone & Antonio De Teffe. WITH Anthony Steffan (Antonio De Teffe), Teodoro Corra, Rada Rassimov, Lu Kamante, Paolo Gozlino. When his fellow soldiers sell out his regiment during the Civil War, the lone survivor of the massacre swears revenge and plots to wipe out a town full of culprits. Very violent, but well made, spa-

ghetti oater, originally issued in Italy in 1969 as **Django il Bastardo** (Django the Bastard).

3421 The Strawberry Roan. Universal, 1933. 60 minutes B/W. D: Alan James. SC: Nate Gatzert. WITH Ken Maynard, Ruth Hall, Harold Goodwin, Frank Yaconelli, Charles King, William Desmond, James Marcus, Jack Rockwell, Robert Walker, Ben Corbett, Bill Patton, Art Mix, Bud McClure. A cowboy comes to the aid of a beautiful stallion who is accused of horse rustling, an activity actually being carried out by a local citizen. This film was said to be Ken Maynard's personal favorite and it is easy to understand why as it is full of action, music and good humor.

3422 The Strawberry Roan. Columbia, 1948. 79 minutes Color. D: John English. SC: Dwight Cummings & Dorothy Yost. WITH Gene Autry, Pat Buttram, Gloria Henry, Jack Holt, Dick Jones, Rufe Davis, Eddy Waller, John McGuire, Rodd Harper, Jack Ingram, Ted Mapes, Eddie Parker, Sam Flint. A horse breaker tries to protect a roan from being killed by a ranch owner whose son was injured by the animal. One of Gene Autry's best Columbia outings.

3423 Streets of Ghost Town. Columbia, 1950. 54 minutes B/W. D: Ray Nazarro. SC: Barry Shipman. WITH Charles Starrett, Smiley Burnette, Mary Ellen Kay, Ozie Waters & His Colorado Rangers, George Chesebro, Stanley Andrews, Frank Fenton, John Cason, Little Brown Jug (Don Kay Reynolds), Jack Ingram. Three lawmen come to a ghost town to investigate a series of mysterious happenings caused by a now-blind outlaw using his young nephew to help him find the stolen loot he once hid there. The mystery element adds some life to this "Durango Kid" outing.

3424 Streets of Laredo. Paramount, 1949. 92 minutes Color. D: Leslie Fenton. SC: Charles Stevens & Elizabeth Hill. WITH William Holden, Macdonald Carey, Mona Freeman, William Bendix, Stanley Ridges, Alfonso Bedoya, Ray Teal, Clem Bevans, James Bell, Dick Foote, Joe Dominguez, Grandon Rhodes, Perry Ivins, James Davies, Robert Kortman, Byron Foulger, Wade Crosby, Carl Andre. Two outlaws end up joining the Texas Rangers and after being converted to the side of the law are forced to hunt down their ex-partner. Mediocre remake of the much better **The Texas Rangers** (q.v.).

3425 Strictly in the Groove. Universal, 1943. 60 minutes B/W. D: Vernon Keays. SC: Kenneth Higgens & Warren Wilson. WITH Richard Davies, Mary Healy, Leon Errol, Franklin Pangborn, Ozzie Nelson, Jimmie Davis, The Dinning Sisters, The Jimmy Wakely Trio (Jimmy Wakely, Johnny Bond, Eddie Synder), Diamond's Solid-Aires, Russell Hicks, Martha Tilton, Shemp Howard, Grace MacDonald, Eddie Johnson, Charles Lang, Holmes Herbert, Tim Ryan, Ralph Dunn, Ken Stevens, Lloyd Ingraham, Neeley Edwards, Francis Morris, Drew Demarest, Grace Lenard, Jim Lucas, Joey Ray, Francis Sayles, Jack Gardner. When a young man fails to join his father in the restaurant business and instead forms a band, the old man banishes him to a Western dude ranch. Fair Universal programmer musical Western mainly of interest due to its vocalists and songs like "You Are My Sunshine," "Chisholm Trail," "Happy Cowboy," etc.

3426 Strike It Rich. Monogram, 1949. 81 minutes B/W. D: Lesley Selander. SC: Francis Rosenwald. WITH Rod Cameron, Bonita Granville, Don Castle, Stuart Erwin, Lloyd Corrigan, Ellen Corby, Emory Parnell, Harry Tyler, Virginia Dale, William Haade, Edward Gargan, Robert Dudley. Two Texas oil drillers make a big strike and then fight the law limiting the amount of oil they can produce. Actionful and well directed drama.

3427 Strike Me Deadly. Medallion, 1963. 81 minutes B/W. D: Herbert L. Strock. WITH Gary Clarke, Jeannine Riley. A forest ranger and his young bride are hunted by a man who has murdered a hunter and the three get caught in an out-of-control fire. Low budget but fairly fast moving affair.

3428 Strong Medicine. NBC-TV, 1956. 54 minutes B/W. SC: William Mourne. WITH Patrick O'Neal, Mary Webster, Myron Healey, Joe Maross. An Easterner has trouble taking possession of the ranch land he inherited. Fair telefeature originally telecast as a segment of "Matinee Theatre" (NBC-TV, 1955-58) on December 28, 1956.

3429 Strongheart. Biograph, 1914. 45 minutes B/W. D: James Kirkwood. WITH Blanche Sweet, Henry B. Walthall, Antonio Moreno, Lionel Barrymore, Alan Hale, Gertrude Robinson. An Indian brave saves a young man's life and his sister falls in love with the Indian. Supervised by D. W. Griffith, this early silent melodrama is quite entertaining, especially because of its stars.

3430 Stronghold. Lippert, 1952. 72 minutes B/W. D: Steve Sekely. SC: Wells Root. WITH Veronica Lake, Zachary Scott, Arturo de Cordova, Rita Lacedo, Alfonso Bedoya, Yadiro Jiminez, Fanny Schiller, Gilberto Gonzales, Carlos Muzquiz. The pretty owner of several Mexican silver mines is kidnapped by a rebel-bandit leader and the woman soon warms to his cause but her crooked foreman plans to dynamite her mines in order to insure the bandit's capture. The trio of stars do a lot to keep this low budget actioner going.

3431 Sudden Bill Dorn. Universal, 1938. 60 minutes B/W. D: Ray Taylor. SC: Frances Guihan. WITH Buck Jones, Evelyn Brent, Noel Francis, Frank McGlynn, Harold Hodge, Ted Adams, William Lawrence, Lee Phelps, Tom Chatterton, Carlos Valdez, Ezra Pallette, Red Hightowner, Charles LeMoyne, Adolph Milar. A cowboy gets on the trail of crooks who arrive in a small town after the discovery of gold. Buck Jones produced this fair actioner made at the close of his Universal tenure.

Sudden Death see **Fast on the Draw**

3432 Sugarfoot. Warner Brothers, 1951. 80 minutes Color. D: Edwin L. Marin. SC: Russell Hughes. WITH Randolph Scott, Raymond Massey, Adele Jergens, S. Z. Sakall, Robert Warwick, Gene Evans, Hugh Sanders, Hope Landin, Hank Worden, Arthur Hunnicutt, Edward Hearn, John Hamilton, Cliff Clark, Kenneth MacDonald, Dan White, Paul Newlan, Philo McCullough. A former Confederate officer tries to settle down peacefully as a rancher in Arizona but he soon finds he is the sworn enemy of a local crook, a one-time rival. Actionful Randolph Scott vehicle. TV title: **A Swirl of Glory.**

3433 The Sugarland Express. Universal, 1974. 109 minutes Color. D: Steven Spielberg. SC: Hal Barwood & Matthew Boulton. WITH Goldie Hawn, Ben Johnson, Michael Sacks, William Atherton, Gregory Walcott, Harrison Zanuck, Steve Kanaly, Louise Latham, A. L. Camp, Jessie Lee Fuller, Dean Smith, Ted Grossman, Billy Thurman, Kenneth Hudgins, Buster Daniels, Jim Harrell, Frank Steggall, Roger Ernest, Gene Rader, Gordon Hurst, George Hagy, John Hamilton. A police official leads a chase across Texas in 1968 for a fugitive couple who have escaped from prison to find their small daughter who has been adopted against their will. Overrated chase thriller, although Ben Johnson is good as the police captain.

3434 Sun Valley Cyclone. Republic, 1946. 54 (56) minutes B/W. D: R. G. Springsteen. SC: Earle Snell. WITH Bill Elliott, Bobby Blake, Alice Fleming, Roy Barcroft, Monte Hale, Kenne Duncan, Eddy Waller, Tom London, Edmund Cobb, Ed Cassidy, George Chesebro, Rex Lease, Hal Price, Jack Kirk, Frank O'Connor, Jack Sparks. A gang of outlaws are stealing horses intended for the Army and Red Ryder tries to stop them. Well written and paced "Red Ryder" series entry.

Sundown Fury see **Jesse James Jr.**

3435 Sundown in Santa Fe. Republic, 1948. 60 minutes B/W. D: R. G. Springsteen. SC: Norman S. Hall. WITH Allan "Rocky" Lane, Eddy Waller, Roy Barcroft, Jean Dean, Russell Simpson, Minerva Urecal, Rand Brooks, Trevor Bardette, Lane Bradford, Joseph Crehan, Kenne Duncan, Robert Wilke. An army intelligence agent tries to find out who is behind an outlaw band. Fairly interesting film with a good plot which makes this better than the average Allan Lane series entry.

3436 Sundown Jim. 20th Century-Fox, 1942. 58 minutes B/W. D: James Tinling. SC: Robert F. Metzler & William Bruckner. WITH John Kimbrough, Virginia Gilmore, Arleen Whelan, Moroni Olsen, Paul Hurst, Cliff Edwards, Joseph Sawyer, Don Costello, Tom Fadden, Frank McGrath, LeRoy Mason, James Bush, Lane Chandler, Charles Tannen, Paul Sutton, Eddy Waller. A new sheriff in a small town finds out its citizens do not support his efforts to bring a land baron to justice when his gang commits a murder. Production values are okay but this effort to make a genre star of John Kimbrough is only average.

3437 Sundown Kid. Republic, 1942. 55 minutes B/W. D: Elmer Clifton. SC: Norman S. Hall. WITH Don Barry, Linda Johnson, Ian Keith, Helen MacKellar, Emmett Lynn, Wade Crosby, Robert Kortman, Ted Adams, Kenne Duncan, Bud Geary, Fern Emmett, Kenneth Harlan, Jack Ingram, Jack Rockwell, Joe McGuinn, Cactus Mack. A cowboy teams with a pretty girl newspaper reporter to oppose a gang of counterfeiters. Spritely Don Barry series entry. V: Cumberland Video.

3438 Sundown on the Prairie. Monogram, 1939. 53 minutes B/W. D: Al Herman. SC: William Nolte & Edmund Kelso. WITH Tex Ritter, Dorothy Fay, Horace Murphy, Hank Worden, Charles King, Dave O'Brien, Karl Hackett, Bob Terry, Frank LaRue, Ed Peil, Bud Osborne. When rustlers plague the area around Santa Fe, two government men are sent to stop them. Fair Tex Ritter actioner. British title: **Prairie Sundown.**

3439 The Sundown Rider. Columbia, 1933. 56 minutes B/W. D-SC: Lambert Hillyer. WITH Buck Jones, Barbara Weeks, Wheeler Oakman, Pat O'Malley, Niles Welch, Bradley Page, Frank LaRue, Ward Bond, Ed Brady, Harry Todd. A cowboy is falsely accused of rustling and he uncovers a plot by local crooks to steal a girl's ranch because it contains oil deposits. Really good Buck Jones vehicle, well written and directed by Lambert Hillyer, one of the most underrated of film directors.

3440 Sundown Riders. Film Enterprises, 1948. 60 minutes Color. D: Lambert Hillyer. SC: Rodney J. Graham. WITH Russell Wade, Andy Clyde, Jay Kirby, Evelyn Finley, Marshall Reed, Jack Ingram, Steve Clark, Hal Price, Ted Mapes, Bud Osborne, Ted Wells, Henry Wills, Cliff Parkinson, Cactus Mack, Chief Many Treaties. A trio of cowpokes gets involved with a gang of outlaws and nearly end up getting hanged. Okay action feature originally made in 16mm in 1944 for non-theatrical release and issued to theatres in 1948.

3441 Sundown Saunders. Supreme, 1936. 64 minutes B/W. D-SC: Robert North Bradbury. WITH Bob Steele, Catherine Cotter, Earl Dwire, Milburn Morante, Ed Cassidy, Jack Rockwell, Frank Ball, Hal Price, Charles King, Horace Murphy, Edmund Cobb, Bob McKenzie, Jack Kirk, Herman Hack. A cowboy wins a big horse race and ends up with a ranch but crooks try to cheat him out of it. Actionful Bob Steele vehicle.

3442 Sundown Trail. RKO Radio, 1931. 55 minutes B/W. D-SC: Robert Hill. WITH Tom Keene, Marion Shilling, Nick Stuart, Hooper Atchley, Louise Beavers, Stanley Blystone, William Welsh, Murdock McQuarrie, Alma Chester. A cowboy opposes a crook who wants the same girl who is loved by the cowpoke. Tom Keene's first series film is pretty good.

3443 Sundown Valley. Columbia, 1944. 55 minutes B/W. D: Benjamin Kline. SC: Luci Ward. WITH Charles Starrett, Dub Taylor, Jeanne Bates, Jimmy Wakely, Clancy Cooper, Jessie Arnold, Wheeler Oakman, Jack Ingram, Forrest Taylor, Joel Friedkin, Grace Lenard, Eddie Laughton, The Tennessee Ramblers. A war hero wants to close a gambling den in a small town because its owners are causing absenteeism at the local gun manufacturing plant. Fairly good Charles Starrett vehicle with a different kind of plot, one geared to World War II audiences.

3444 The Sundowners. Eagle Lion, 1950. 83 minutes Color. D: George Templeton. SC: Alan LeMay & George Templeton. WITH Robert Preston, Robert Sterling, Chill Wills, Cathy Downs, John Barrymore Jr., John Litel, Jack Elam, Don Haggerty, Stanley Price. Two brothers fight to keep their property against a gunman who is really their third brother. Pretty well done action melodrama.

3445 The Sundowners. Warner Brothers, 1960. 141 minutes Color. D: Fred Zinneman. SC: Isobel Lennart. WITH Deborah Kerr, Robert Mitchum, Peter Ustinov, Glynis Johns, Dina Merrill, Chips Rafferty, Michael Anderson Jr., Lola Brooks, Wylie Watson, John Meillon, Ronald Fraser, Mervyn Johns, Molly Urquhart, Ewen Solon. An Australian sheepherder must choose between his love of being a wanderer and the love of his wife and son. Excellent on-location production of Jon Cleary's novel with a magnificent performance by Robert Mitchum as the sheepherder, Paddy Carmody.

3446 Sunrise Trail. Tiffany, 1931. 65 minutes B/W. D: J. P. McCarthy. SC: Wellyn Totman. WITH Bob Steele, Blanche Mehaffey, Jack Clifford, Richard Alexander, Eddie Dunn, Fred Burns, Germaine DeNeel. A man, secretly working with the local sheriff, pretends to be a gunman to expose a rustling gang. Pretty good Bob Steele early talkie.

3447 Sunscorched. Creole/Production Cinema, 1964. 77 minutes Color. D: Mark Stevens. SC: Mark Stevens & Irving Dennis. WITH Mark Stevens, Marianne Koch, Mario Adorf, Vivien Dodds, Albert Bessler, Antonio Iranzo, Frank Oliveras. Four outlaws terrorize a small town where the local sheriff, once a member of their gang, is helpless in stopping them. West German-made oater, directed and written by star Mark Stevens, is a pretty good action affair. West German title: **Vergeltung in Catano.**

3448 Sunset Carson Rides Again. Astor, 1948. 63 minutes Color. D: Oliver Drake. SC: Elmer Clifton. WITH Sunset Carson, Pat Starling, Al Terry, Bob (John) Cason, Dan White, Pat Gleason, Steven Keyes, Ron Ormond, Bob Curtis, Joe Hiser, Forrest Matthews, The Rodeo Revelers. A cowboy's ranch partner is actually behind an outlaw gang trying to cheat the cowpoke out of his land and steal money he has raised for a new school. Sunset Carson's first film for Astor is a bottom rung affair, due more to budget limitations than to its direction, script or cast. V: Video Connection, Sunland Enterprises, Cassette Express.

3449 Sunset in El Dorado. Republic, 1945. 54 (65) minutes B/W. D: Frank McDonald. SC: John K. Butler. WITH Roy Rogers, George "Gabby" Hayes, Dale Evans, Hardie Albright, Margaret Dumont, Roy Barcroft, Tom London, Hal Price, Robert Wilke, Ed Cassidy, Dorothy Granger, Bob Nolan & The Sons of the Pioneers, Edmund Cobb, Hank Bell, Jack Kirk, Gino Corrado, Frank Ellis, Tex Cooper, Tex Terry, Bud Osborne. The granddaughter of a famous saloon singer dreams of the events that caused her to throw over her crooked partner for a cowboy who was framed for murder. Only fair, with too many musical numbers. V: Discount video.

3450 Sunset in the West. Republic, 1950. 67 minutes Color. D: William Witney. SC: Gerald Geraghty. WITH Roy Rogers, Penny Edwards, Estelita Rodriguez, Gordon Jones, Foy Willing & The Riders of the Purple Sage, Will Wright, Pierre Watkin, Charles La Torre, William Tannen, Gaylord Pendleton, Paul E. Burns. An outlaw gang is wrecking trains as they smuggle weapons out of the country and Roy Rogers tries to aid the elderly sheriff who is trying to stop them. There is lots of action and good fun in this Roy Rogers vehicle.

3451 Sunset in Wyoming. Republic, 1941. 65 minutes B/W. D: William Morgan. SC: Ivan Goff & Anne Morrison Chapin. WITH Gene Autry, Smiley Burnette, Maris Wrixon, George Cleveland, Robert Kent, Sarah Edwards, Monte Blue, Dick Elliott, John Dilson, Stanley Blystone, Earle Hodgins, Eddie Dean, Reed Howes, Fred Burns, Ralph Peters, Syd Saylor, Tex

Terry, Lloyd Whitlock, Herman Hack. Gene Autry tries to get a mountain made into a state park after a lumber company cuts too much timber, causing floods. Good Gene Autry film with nice scenery and photography.

3452 The Sunset Legion. Paramount, 1928. 70 minutes B/W. D: Lloyd Ingraham & Alfred L. Werker. SC: Frank M. Clifton & Garrett Graham. WITH Fred Thompson, Edna Murphy, William Courtright, Harry Woods. In order to capture an outlaw gang a Texas Ranger takes on the guise of a masked man as well as a gun peddler. Entertaining Fred Thompson silent opus with his horse Silver King in a dual role!

3453 Sunset of Power. Universal, 1936. 66 minutes B/W. D: Ray Taylor. SC: Earle Snell. WITH Buck Jones, Dorothy Dix, Charles Middleton, Donald Kirk, Charles King, Ben Corbett, William Lawrence, Joe de la Cruz, Nina Campana, Murdock McQuarrie, Alan Sears, Glenn Strange, Monty Vandergrift, Eumenco Blanco. A ranch foreman tries to find out who is stealing a rancher's cattle while romancing the granddaughter of his boss, who resents the fact his only grandchild is a girl. Interesting and well made Buck Jones vehicle.

3454 Sunset on the Desert. Republic, 1942. 54 minutes B/W. D: Joseph Kane. SC: Gerald Geraghty. WITH Roy Rogers, George "Gabby" Hayes, Lynne Carver, Bob Nolan & The Sons of the Pioneers, Frank M. Thomas, Beryl Wallace, Glenn Strange, Douglas Fowley, Fred Burns, Roy Barcroft, Henry Wills, Forrest Taylor, Bob Woodward, Ed Cassidy, Cactus Mack. When a group of wicked land grabbers try to take over Roy Rogers' home town he sets out to stop them. Average Roy Rogers action-musical vehicle. V: Video Images.

3455 Sunset Pass. Paramount, 1933. 64 minutes B/W. D: Henry Hathaway. SC: Jack Cunningham & Gerald Geraghty. WITH Randolph Scott, Tom Keene, Kathleen Burke, Harry Carey, Noah Beery, Leila Bennett, Fuzzy Knight, Kent Taylor, George Barbier, Vince Barnett, Patricia Farley, Charles Middleton, Christian J. Frank, Tom London, Frank Beal, Al Bridge, Robert Kortman, Jim Mason, Nelson McDowell. A government agent, working undercover as a cowpoke, falls in love with a girl whose brother is suspected of being behind a rustling operation. A top flight cast highlights this remake

of Zane Grey's novel, first filmed by Paramount in 1929 with Jack Holt and remade by RKO Radio in 1946.

3456 Sunset Pass. RKO Radio, 1946. 59 minutes B/W. D: William Berke. SC: Norman Houston. WITH James Warren, Nan Leslie, Jane Greer, Steve Brodie, John Laurenz, Robert Clarke, Harry Woods, Harry Harvey, Slim Balch, Roy Bucko, Steve Stevens, George Plues, Clem Fuller, Artie Ortego, Buck Bucko, Bob Dyer, Slim Hightower, Boyd Stockman, Frank O'Connor, Robert Bray, Florence Pepper, Vonne Lester, Dennis Waters, Marcia Dodd, Dorothy Curtiss. Agents for an express company are on the trail of a stolen gold shipment. Fair third screen version of the Zane Grey novel.

3457 Sunset Range. First Division, 1935. 59 minutes B/W. D: Ray McCarey. SC: Paul Schofield. WITH Hoot Gibson, Mary Doran, James Eagles, Walter McGrail, John Elliott, Ralph Lewis, Eddie Lee, Kitty McHugh, Lee Fong, Martha Sleeper, Fred Gilman. A man involved with a robbery gang gives his sister title to a ranch and Hoot Gibson gets on the trail of the outlaws after the man is shot trying to protect the girl. Pleasant film with heavy emphasis on comedy, including a sequence where the girl ranch owner tries to dress the ranch hands like Hollywood cowboys.

3458 Sunset Serenade. Republic, 1942. 54 (58) minutes B/W. D: Joseph Kane. SC: Earl Fenton. WITH Roy Rogers, George "Gabby" Hayes, Joan Woodbury, Helen Parrish, Onslow Stevens, Frank M. Thomas, Bob Nolan & The Sons of the Pioneers, Roy Barcroft, Jack Kirk, Dick Wessell, Rex Lease, Jack Ingram, Fred Burns, Budd Buster, Jack Rockwell. Roy Rogers suspects a housekeeper and her boyfriend are trying to murder a young heir and his pretty guardian. Fair.

3459 The Sunset Trail. Tiffany, 1932. 62 minutes B/W. D: B. Reeves Eason. SC: Bennett Cohen. WITH Ken Maynard, Ruth Hiatt, Frank Rice, Philo McCullough, Buddy Hunter, Richard Alexander, Frank Ellis, Slim Whitaker, Jack Rockwell, Lew Meehan, Bud Osborne, Bud McClure. Two cowboys are in love with the same girl, whose ranch is being sought by crooks. Pretty good Ken Maynard actioner. V: Discount Video.

3460 Sunset Trail. Paramount, 1938. 54 (60) minutes B/W. D: Lesley Selander.

SC: Norman Houston. WITH William Boyd, George ("Gabby") Hayes, Russell Hayden, Charlotte Wynters, Jan Clayton, Robert Fiske, Kathryn Sheldon, Maurice Cass, Anthony Nace, Kenneth Harlan, Alphonse Ethier, Glenn Strange, Jack Rockwell, Tom London. Hopalong Cassidy poses as a dude in order to thwart a crook who is trying to steal a guest ranch from a woman and her daughter. Very well done "Hopalong Cassidy" series entry.

3461 Support Your Local Gunfighter. United Artists, 1971. 92 minutes Color. D: Burt Kennedy. SC: James Edward Grant. WITH James Garner, Suzanne Pleshette, Jack Elam, Joan Blondell, Harry Morgan, Marie Windsor, Henry Jones, John Dehner, Chuck Connors, Dub Taylor, Kathleen Freeman, Willis Bouchey, Walter Burke, Gene Evans, Dick Haymes, John (Day) Daheim, Ellen Corby, Ben Cooper, Grady Sutton, Pedro Gonzales-Gonzales, Roy Glenn, Herbert Vigran, Terry Wilson, Jim Nolan, Guy Way. A con man escapes from his planned wedding and is mistaken for a gunman and gets involved with a small town whose citizens are divided over rival mine operations. Lukewarm sequel to **Support Your Local Sheriff** (q.v.); mediocre except for a fine supporting cast.

3462 Support Your Local Sheriff. United Artists, 1969. 93 minutes Color. D: Burt Kennedy. SC: William Bowers. WITH James Garner, Joan Hackett, Walter Brennan, Harry Morgan, Jack Elam, Bruce Dern, Henry Jones, Walter Burke, Dick Peabody, Gene Evans, Willis Bouchey, Kathleen Freeman, Gayle Rogers, Richard Hoyt, Marilyn Jones. A soldier-of-fortune is hired by a small town to be its sheriff and defeat a local family who is charging a heavy toll to use the road out of town since gold has been discovered there. Clever genre comedy which provides amusing entertainment. Sequel: **Support Your Local Gunfighter** (q.v.).

3463 Susanna Pass. Republic, 1949. 67 minutes Color. D: William Witney. SC: Sloan Nibley & John K. Butler. WITH Roy Rogers, Dale Evans, Estelita Rodriguez, Foy Willing & The Riders of the Purple Sage, Martin Garralaga, Robert Emmett Keane, Lucien Littlefield, Douglas Fowley, David Sharpe, Robert Bice. A game warden tries to stop the destruction of local animal life by crooks who are out to sabotage a fish hatchery. Entertaining Roy Rogers series entry.

3464 Susannah of the Mounties. 20th Century-Fox, 1939. 78 minutes B/W. D: William A. Seiter. SC: Fidel LaBarba, Walter Ferris, Robert Ellis & Helen Logan. WITH Shirley Temple, Randolph Scott, Margaret Lockwood, J. Farrell MacDonald, Maurice Moscovitch, Martin Good Rider, Moroni Olsen, Victor Jory, Lester Mathews, Leyland Hodgson, Herbert Evans, Jack Luden, Charles Irwin, John Sutton, Chief Big Tree. A small orphan girl is raised by a Mountie at a remote outpost and she aids in his romance with a pretty girl as well as warning the post of an Indian attack. This Shirley Temple vehicle is a pleasant affair which will also appeal to Randolph Scott fans.

3465 Sutter's Gold. Universal, 1936. 94 minutes B/W. D: James Cruze. SC: Jack Kirkland, Walter Woods & George O'Neil. WITH Edward Arnold, Lee Tracy, Binnie Barnes, Katherine Alexander, Addison Richards, Montagu Love, John Miljan, Robert Warwick, Harry Carey, Mitchell Lewis, William Janney, Ronald Cosbey, Nan Grey, Joanne Smith, Billy Gilbert, Aura Da Silva, Allen Vincent, Harry Cording, Sidney Bracy, Bryant Washburn, Gaston Glass. Swiss immigrant Johann August Sutter builds an empire in the West only to have it destroyed when gold is discovered on his California lands in 1849. Gigantic screen effort which was a financial failure in its time but a film that deserves viewing.

3466 Swamp of Lost Monsters. Trans-International, 1965. 80 minutes Color. D: Raphael Baledon. SC: Ramon Obon. WITH Gaston (Sands) Santos, Manola Savedra, Manuel Dondi. In a remote area the inhabitants are being terrorized by a monster from a deep lake. Unbelievable Mexican horror-Western which is made even worse by its dubbing. TV title: **Swamp of Lost Souls.**

Swamp of Lost Souls see Swamp of Lost Monsters

3467 Swifty. Diversion/Grand National, 1935. 62 minutes B/W. D: Alan James. SC: Bennett Cohen. WITH Hoot Gibson, June Gale, George ("Gabby") Hayes, Ralph Lewis, Wally Wales, Robert Kortman, William Gould, Lafe McKee, Art Mix, Duke Lee, Starlight (horse). A drifter is falsely accused of the murder of a rancher and he escapes to find the real murderer. The lack of good production values greatly hinders this otherwise fair Hoot Gibson vehicle.

3468 Swing, Cowboy, Swing. Three Crown, 1944. 60 minutes B/W. D-SC: Elmer Clifton. WITH Max Terhune, Cal Shrum & His Rhythm Rangers, Alta Lee, Walt Shrum & His Colorado Hillbillies, I. Stanford Jolley, Frank Ellis, Ed Cassidy, Ted Adams, Tom Hubbard, Shorty Woodward, Don Weston, Ann Roberts, Phil Dunham, Ace Dehne. In a small town a musical troupe gets involved with a gang of crooks. Fans of old-time country music will go for this low budget affair (others beware) which Astor reissued in 1949 as **Bad Man from Big Bend.**

3469 Swing in the Saddle. Columbia, 1944. 68 minutes B/W. D: Lew Landers. SC: Elizabeth Beecher, Morton Grant & Radford Ropes. WITH Jane Frazee, Guinn Williams, Red River Dave (McEnery), Slim Summerville, Mary Treen, Sally Bliss, Carole Mathews, Byron Foulger, The Hoosier Hotshots, (Nat) King Cole Trio, Jimmy Wakely & His Oklahoma Cowboys, Cousin Emmy. A pretty girl, who comes to a ranch through a misunderstanding, ends up engaged to the ranch foreman and winning a local singing contest. Fun film with far more emphasis on music than action. This is the only feature film starring the sadly neglected singer-songwriter Red River Dave McEnery, who also starred in two 1948 Universal Western featurettes, **Echo Ranch** and **Hidden Valley Days,** as well as the short **Pretty Women** (Sack Amusements, 1949), plus fourteen three-minute Western songfests for the Soundies Corporation of America between 1942 and 1946.

A Swirl of Glory see **Sugarfoot**

T

3470 Taggart. Universal, 1964. 85 minutes Color. D: R. G. Springsteen. SC: Robert Creighton Williams. WITH Tony Young, Dan Duryea, Dick Foran, Elsa Gardenas, Emile Meyer, Jean Hale, Peter Duryea, David Carradine, Harry Carey Jr., Bob Steele, Ray Teal, Arthur Space, Sarah Selby, Stuart Randall, Bill Henry, Tom Reese, George Murdock. A young man hunting for the outlaws who murdered his parents is tracked through Indian country by gunmen. Well made and entertaining adaptation of the Louis L'Amour novel.

3471 Take a Hard Ride. 20th Century-Fox, 1975. 108 minutes Color. D: Anthony M. Dawson (Antonio Margheritti). SC: Eric Bercovici & Jerry Ludwig. WITH Jim Brown, Lee Van Cleef, Fred Williamson, Jim Kelly, Catherine Spaak, Dana Andrews, Barry Sullivan, Harry Carey Jr., Robert Donner. After his boss is murdered by outlaws, a black cowboy teams with a gambler and an Indian scout in taking money across the desert to be delivered to its rightful owners in Mexico. Fairly exciting actioner filmed in the Canary Islands.

3472 Take Me to Town. Universal-International, 1953. 81 minutes Color. D: Douglas Sirk. SC: Richard Morris. WITH Ann Sheridan, Sterling Hayden, Philip Reed, Lee Patrick, Lee Aaker, Phyllis Stanley, Harvey Grant, Dusty Henley, Guy Williams, Alice Kelley, Lane Chandler, Larry Gates, Frank Sully, Forrest Lewis, Ann Tyrell, Dorothy Neumann, Robert Anderson. A saloon singer escapes from a lawman and ends up at a logging camp where she is taken in by a lumberjack minister and his three orphan boys. Likable musical comedy vehicle for Ann Sheridan.

3473 Tale of Gold. Wrather Corporation, 1956. 75 minutes Color. D: Earl Bellamy. SC: Jack Natteford, Thomas Seller & Herbert Purdum. WITH Clayton Moore, Jay Silverheels, Allen Pinson, Wayne Burson, Harry Lauter, Louise Lewis, Trevor Bardette, Charles Stevens, Mike Ragan, John Cason, Pat O'Malley, Ralph Sanford, Pierce Lyden, Robert Roark, Bill Ward, Walt LaRue, Jerry Brown, Sandy Sanders, Robert Swan, George Mather, William J. Tanner, Mae Morgan. The Lone Ranger and Tonto try to prevent violence resulting from a horse race wager between the citizens of a small town and a tribe of Cheyenne Indians and the duo also go after gold thieves and help a farmer get back his savings. Pleasant telefilm from "The Lone Ranger" (ABC-TV, 1949-57) series from the segments "Quarterhorse War," "Decision for Chris McKeever" and "A Harp for Hannah."

3474 Tales of Adventure. Pathe, 1954. 80 minutes B/W. D: Herbert Kline. WITH Lon Chaney, Don DeFore, Rita Moreno, Robert Hutton, Robert Lowery, Eve McVeagh, Coleen Gray, Frank Silvera. Three Jack London stories including the trial of an evil man in the northwoods and the marriage of an Indian maiden. This film was issued only to television and was made up of three 1952 segments of the series "The Schlitz Playhouse of Stars" (CBS-TV, 1951-55); the episode with Lon Chaney was filmed near Mexico City. Also called **Jack London's Tales of Adventure** and **Flight from Adventure.**

3475 The Talisman. Universal Entertainment/Gillman Film Corporation, 1970. 93 minutes Color. D-SC: John Carr. WITH Ned Romero, Linda Hawkins, Richard Thies, Jerald Cormier, Raymond Brown, Raymonda de Anda, Louis Bacigalupi. An Indian warrior and a white woman, the survivors of a wagon train massacre, form an uneasy alliance until three renegade Confederates rape and murder the woman and the Indian swears revenge. Violent, and somewhat obscure, oater, also called **The Savage American.** Average.

3476 Tall in the Saddle. RKO Radio, 1944. 87 minutes B/W. D: Edwin L. Marin. SC: Michael Hogan & Paul Fix. WITH John Wayne, Ella Raines, Ward Bond, George "Gabby" Hayes, Audrey Long, Elizabeth Risdon, Russell Wade, Don Douglas, Frank Puglia, Emory Parnell, Raymond Hatton, Paul Fix, Harry Woods, Cy Kendall, Bob McKenzie, Wheaton Chambers, Walter Baldwin, Russell Simpson, Frank Orth, Russell Hopton, George Chandler, Eddy Waller, Frank Darien, Clem Bevans, Erville Alderson. A cowboy goes to work for a ranch and the owner suddenly dies and the new owner, a young girl who has a guardian aunt, feels she is being cheated by a local judge. Rugged and adventuresome John Wayne vehicle with a good blend of action and mystery; well done. V: Nostalgia Merchant, Cumberland Video, Blackhawk.

3477 Tall Man Riding. Warner Brothers, 1955. 83 minutes Color. D: Lesley Selander. SC: Joseph Hoffman. WITH Randolph Scott, Dorothy Malone, Peggie Castle, Robert Barrat, William Ching, John Baragrey, John Dehner, Paul Richards, Mickey Simpson, Lane Chandler, Joe Bassett, Charles Watts, Russ Conway, Mike Ragan, Carl Andre, John Logan, Guy Hearn, William Fawcett, Nolan Leary, Phil Rich, Eva Novak, Buddy Roosevelt, Jack Henderson, Bob Peoples, Dub Taylor, William Bailey, Bob Stephenson, Roger Creed, Vernon Rich. After fourteen years a man returns home to take revenge on the land baron who stole his land and ruined his intended marriage. Entertaining Randolph Scott film with a good script.

3478 The Tall Men. 20th Century-Fox, 1955. 122 minutes Color. D: Raoul Walsh. SC: Sydney Boehm & Frank Nugent. WITH Clark Gable, Jane Russell, Robert Ryan, Cameron Mitchell, Juan Garcia, Emile Meyer, Harry Shannon, Steve Darrell, Will Wright, Robert Adler, Russell Simpson, Tom Wilson, Tom Fadden, Tom White, Argentina Brunetti, Doris Kemper, Carl Harbaugh, Post Park, Jack Mather. After the Civil War two brothers head West and become involved with a crooked cattleman and rescue a pretty woman from Indians. Rugged and lusty melodrama with the fine teaming of Clark Gable and Jane Russell.

3479 The Tall Stranger. Allied Artists, 1957. 83 minutes Color. D: Thomas Carr. SC: Christopher Knopf. WITH Joel McCrea, Virginia Mayo, Barry Kelley, Michael Ansara, Whit Bissell, James Dobson, George Neise, Adam Kennedy, Michael Pate, Leo Gordon, Ray Teal, Robert Foulk, George J. Lewis, Guy Prescott. After having his life saved by the passengers of a wagon train, a man agrees to help them with the settlement of their new lands in opposition to crooks. Colorful, if not overly exciting, Joel McCrea vehicle which will please his fans.

3480 The Tall T. Columbia, 1957. 78 minutes Color. D: Budd Boetticher. SC: Burt Kennedy. WITH Randolph Scott, Maureen O'Sullivan, Richard Boone, Arthur Hunnicutt, Skip Homier, Henry Silva, John Hubbard, Robert Burton, Robert Anderson, Fred E. Sherman, Chris Olsen. Three outlaws kidnap the wife of a rich rancher and hold her hostage at the ranch of another man who tries to help her. Exceedingly fine Randolph Scott film, well written and taut.

3481 Tall Texan. Lippert, 1953. 81 minutes B/W. D: Elmo Williams. SC: Samuel Roeca. WITH Lloyd Bridges, Lee J. Cobb, Marie Windsor, Luther Adler, Syd Saylor, Samuel Herrick, George Steele, Dean Train. A group of wagon passengers, including a lady of easy virtue and a lawman with his prisoner, go into sacred Indian lands in search of gold. Low budget but entertaining action drama.

Tall Timber see **Park Avenue Logger**

3482 The Tall Women. Allied Artists, 1967. 95 minutes Color. D: Cechet Grooper. SC: Mino Rolli. WITH Anne Baxter, Maria Perschy, Gustavo Rojo,

Rossella Como, Adriana Ambesi, Mara Cruz, Christa Linder, John Clarke. Seven women survive an Indian massacre of their wagon train and are forced to trek across the desert and learn to fight in order to stay alive. Better-than-average European-made Western originally issued in 1966 as **Donne Alla Frontiera** (Women at the Frontier) by Danny/L. M./Danubia Film.

3483 Taming of the West. Columbia, 1939. 55 minutes B/W. D: Norman Deming. SC: Robert Lee Johnson & Charles Francis Royal. WITH Bill Elliott, Iris Meredith, Dub Taylor, Dick Curtis, James Craig, Stanley Brown, Kenneth MacDonald, Ethan Allen, Victor Wong, Charles King, Lane Chandler, Jack Kirk, George Morrell, Art Mix, Don Beddoe, Richard Fiske, John Tyrell, Bob Woodward, Hank Bell. The new sheriff of a lawless town tries to bring peace but is opposed by supposedly honest businessmen who are actually behind the outlaws terrorizing the area. Bill Elliott fans will enjoy this actionful outing.

3484 Tap Roots. Universal-International, 1948. 109 minutes Color. D: George Marshall. SC: Alan LeMay. WITH Van Heflin, Susan Hayward, Boris Karloff, Julie London, Ward Bond, Whitfield Connor, Richard Long, Arthur Shields, Griff Barnett, Sondra Rodgers, Ruby Dandridge, Russell Simpson, Gregg Barton, Jonathan Hale, Arthur Space, Kay Medford, William Haade, Harry Cording, George Lewis, Helen Mowery, William Challee, John James, Keith Richards, Hank Worden, Elmo Lincoln. A family in Mississippi tries to keep their vast estate neutral when the Civil War breaks out but find only trouble. Colorful, but dramatically empty, soaper.

3485 Tarantula. Universal-International, 1955. 80 minutes B/W. D: Jack Arnold. SC: Martin Berkeley. WITH John Agar, Mara Corday, Leo G. Carroll, Nestor Paiva, Ross Elliott, Ed Rand, Raymond Bailey, Clint Eastwood, Jane Howard, Billy Wayne, Hank Patterson, Dee Carroll, Bert Holland, Steve Darrell, Tom London, Edgar Dearing, James J. Hyland, Stuart Wade, Vernon Rich, Bob Nelson, Eddie Parker, Bing Russell, Ray Quinn, Robert R. Stephenson, Don Dillaway, Bud Wolfe, Jack Stoney, Rusty Wescoatt. In a desert area a scientist working on a serum to grow gigantic crops causes a tarantula to become a giant and the insect goes on a rampage. Another big bug monster

caper in the West, but nicely made and satisfying for sci-fi fans.

3486 Target. RKO Radio, 1952. 60 minutes B/W. D: Stuart Gilmore. SC: Norman Houston. WITH Tim Holt, Richard Martin, Linda Douglas, Walter Reed, Harry Harvey, John Hamilton, Lane Bradford, Riley Hill, Mike Ragan. Two cowboys find themselves up against a dishonest land agent and his outlaw gang. One of the last of the Tim Holt-RKO series, this one is fast on action from beginning to end.

3487 Taza, Son of Cochise. Universal-International, 1954. 79 minutes Color. D: Douglas Sirk. SC: Gerald Grayson Adams. WITH Rock Hudson, Barbara Rush, Gregg Palmer, Bart Roberts, Morris Ankrum, Ian MacDonald, Richard Cutting, Joseph Sawyer, Robert Burton, Eugene Iglesias, Lance Fuller, Brad Jackson, James Van Horn, Charles Horvath, Robert Hoy, William Leslie, Dan White, Edna Parrish, Seth Bigman, John Kay Hawks, Barbara Burck, Jeff Chandler. Cochise's son is made head of the Apaches after his father's death but he is at odds with his brother over how to deal with the whites as well as a pretty maiden. Passable programmer with Jeff Chandler briefly reprising his Cochise role from **Broken Arrow** and **The Battle of Apache Pass** (qq.v.).

3488 Teenage Monster. Howco-International, 1957. 73 minutes B/W. D: James Marquette. SC: Ray Buffum. WITH Anne Gwynne, Stuart Wade, Gloria Castillo, Charles Courtney, Gilbert Perkins, Frank Davis, Stephen Parker, Norman Leavitt, Jim McCullough, Gabye Mooradian, Arthur Berkeley. In a small Western town a young boy is turned into a rampaging monster by a crashing meteor and he is hunted by a posse. Low grade feature mixes horror and Western genres with mediocre results. TV title: **Meteor Monster.**

3489 The Telegraph Trail. Warner Brothers, 1933. 55 minutes B/W. D: Tenny Wright. SC: Kurt Kempler. WITH John Wayne, Marceline Day, Frank McHugh, Otis Harlan, Albert J. Smith, Yakima Canutt, Lafe McKee, Clarence Geldert, Slim Whitaker, Frank Ellis, Jack Kirk. An Army scout organizes the citizens of a town in stringing a telegraph wire after his best friend has been killed by Indians as he tried to complete the job. Patchwork John Wayne vehicle with most of his best action footage culled from the Ken Maynard silent **The Red Raiders** (q.v.); below average.

3490 Tell Them Willie Boy Is Here. Universal, 1970. 98 minutes Color. D-SC: Abraham Polonsky. WITH Robert Redford, Katharine Ross, Robert Blake, Susan Clark, Barry Sullivan, Charles McGraw, Charles Aidman, John Vernon, Shelly Novack, Ned Romero, John Day, Lee De Broux, George Tyne, Robert Lipton, Steve Shemayne, Lloyd Gough, John Hudkins, Jerry Velasco, Gary Walberg, Jerome Raphel, Johnny Coons, Stanley Torres, Kenneth Holzman, Joseph Mandel, Spencer Lyons, Everett Creach. A Paiute Indian accidentally kills the father of the girl he loves and the two try to elude a posse led by a young assistant sheriff. Oater with all kinds of political undertones, but only average.

3491 Ten Days to Tulara. United Artists, 1958. 77 minutes B/W. D: George Sherman. SC: Lawrence Mascott. WITH Sterling Hayden, Grace Raynor, Rodolfo Hoyos, Carlos Muzquiz, Tony Caravaijal, Juan Garcia. Mexican police pursue an American pilot and his Mexican outlaw friend through the desert in order to retrieve the gold the two are carrying. Passable melodrama filmed in Mexico.

3492 $10,000 Blood Money. Golden Era, 1967. 97 minutes Color. D: Romolo Guerrieri. WITH Gary Hudson (Gianni Garko), Claudio Camasco, Fernando Sancho, Lorenda Nusiak, Adriana Camasco, Pinuccio Ardia, Fidel Gonzales, Franco Lantieri. A bounty hunter and a kidnapper are forced into an uneasy alliance with each eventually trying to double-cross the other. Highly violent Italian Western issued in Europe in 1966 as **10,000 Dollari Per Un Massacro** ($10,000 for a Massacre).

3493 Ten Wanted Men. Columbia, 1955. 80 minutes Color. D: H. Bruce Humberstone. SC: Kenneth Gamet. WITH Randolph Scott, Jocelyn Brando, Richard Boone, Alfonso Bedoya, Donna Martell, Skip Homeier, Clem Bevans, Leo Gordon, Minor Watson, Lester Mathews, Tom Powers, Dennis Weaver, Lee Van Cleef, Louis Jean Heydt, Kathleen Crowley, Boyd "Red" Morgan, Denver Pyle, Francis McDonald, Pat Collins, Paul Maxey, Julian Rivero, Edna Holland, Reed Howes, Terry Frost, Franklyn Farnum, George Boyce, Jack Perrin. A crook frames a cattle baron's nephew on a murder charge because he wants the young man's girl. Better-than-average theatrical

programmer, made so by an impressive cast.

3494 Ten Who Dared. Buena Vista, 1960. 92 minutes Color. D: William Beaudine. SC: Lawrence E. Watkin. WITH Brian Keith, John Beal, James Drury, R. G. Armstrong, Ben Johnson, L. Q. Jones, Dan Sheridan, David Stollery, Stan Jones, David Frankham, Pat Hogan, Ray Walker, Jack Bighead, Roy Barcroft, Dawn Little Sky. A motley crew of men join Major John Wesley Powell on his expedition exploring the Colorado River in 1869. Surprisingly poor historical film from Walt Disney.

3495 Tenderfoot. Buena Vista, 1966. 80 minutes Color. D: Byron Paul. SC: Maurice Tombragel. WITH Brandon de Wilde, James Whitmore, Richard Long, Donald May, Christopher Dark, Judson Pratt, Carlos Romero, Angela Dorian (Victoria Vetri), Rafael Campos, Harry Harvey Jr. A young man learns the values of growing up in Arizona in the 1850s. Pretty good family drama originally telecast in three parts on Walt Disney's ABC-TV program in 1964.

3496 A Tenderfoot Goes West. Hoffberg, 1937. 65 minutes B/W. D: Maurice O'Neill. WITH Jack LaRue, Virginia Carroll, Russell Gleason, Ralph Byrd, Chris-Pin Martin, Si Jenks, John Merton, Joseph Girard, John Ince, Ray Turner, Glenn Strange. An outlaw saves an Easterner mistaken for him from a lynch mob. Fair oater comedy from poverty row.

3497 Tennessee Johnson. Metro-Goldwyn-Mayer, 1942. 100 minutes B/W. D: William Dieterle. SC: John Balderson & Wells Root. WITH Van Heflin, Ruth Hussey, Lionel Barrymore, Marjorie Main, Regis Toomey, J. Edward Bromberg, Grant Withers, Alec Craig, Charles Dingle, Carl Benton Reid, Russell Hicks, Noah Beery, Robert Warwick, Montagu Love, Lloyd Corrigan, William Farnum, Charles Trowbridge, Morris Ankrum, Sheldon Leonard, Harry Worth, Dane Clark, Robert Emmett O'Connor, Lee Phelps, Brandon Hurst, Charles Ray, Harlan Briggs, Hugh Sothern, Frederick Burton, Allen Pomeroy, Duke York, Roy Barcroft, Ed O'Neill, Jack Norton, Russell Simpson, Louise Beavers, James Davis, William Roberts, Frank Jaquet, Emmett Vogan, Pat O'Malley, Will Wright, William Davidson, John Hamilton. Runaway frontier bond servant Andrew Johnson works his way up the political ladder to eventually become one of the most controversial of U. S. presidents. Excellent biographical film with great work by Van Heflin in the title role.

3498 Tennessee's Partner. RKO Radio, 1955. 87 minutes Color. D: Allan Dwan. SC: Allan Dwan, Milton Krims & D. D. Beauchamp. WITH John Payne, Rhonda Fleming, Ronald Reagan, Coleen Gray, Anthony Caruso, Leo Gordon, Myron Healey, Morris Ankrum, Chubby Johnson, Joe Devlin, John Mansfield, Angie Dickinson. A cowboy saves a crook from being bushwacked and the two become pals, with the latter after the former's girl. Mediocre Western which is a bit on the dull side. V: Disney Home Video.

3499 Tension at Table Rock. RKO Radio, 1956. 93 minutes Color. D: Charles Marquis Warren. SC: Winston Miller. WITH Richard Egan, Dorothy Malone, Cameron Mitchell, Billy Chapin, Royal Dano, Edward Andrews, John Dehner, DeForrest Kelley, Angie Dickinson, Joe De Santis. After killing his partner in self-defense, an outlaw is forced to change his identity. Fair screen adaptation of Frank Gruber's Bitter Sage.

3500 Tentacles of the North. Rayart, 1926. 50 minutes B/W. D: Louis Chaudet. SC: Leslie Curtis. WITH Gaston Glass, Alice Calhoun, Al Ferguson, Albert Roscoe, Joseph Girard, T. Hohai. A young man finds a girl stranded on a ship where the crew have all died and the men on his ship chase them into the Arctic. Low budget silent adaptation of James Oliver Curwood's "In the Tentacles of the North."

3501 Tenting Tonight on the Old Camp Ground. Universal, 1943. 59 minutes B/W. D: Lewis D. Collins. SC: Elizabeth Beecher. WITH Johnny Mack Brown, Tex Ritter, Fuzzy Knight, Jennifer Holt, John Elliott, Earle Hodgins, The Jimmy Wakely Trio (Jimmy Wakely, Johnny Bond, Scott Harrell), Rex Lease, Lane Chandler, Alan Bridge, Dennis Moore, Tom London, Reed Howes, Bud Osborne, Lynton Brent, Hank Worden, George Plues, Ray Jones, George Eldredge. A crooked saloon operator tries to tempt workers, who are actually prisoners, from their jobs building a bridge for a stagecoach route carrying the mail. Sufficient Universal programmer.

3502 Territory of Others. Gold Key, 1974. 93 minutes Color. Wildlife in the American desert have developed interdependent relationships over thousands of years and among those presented in this documentary are the jaguar, a poisonous lizard and the rattlesnake. Well done documentary.

3503 Terror at Black Falls. Beckman, 1962. 76 minutes B/W. D-SC: Richard Sarafian. WITH House Peters Jr., Sandra Knight, John Alonso, Peter Mamakos, Gary Gray, I. Stanford Jolley, Marshall Bradford, Jim Hayward. Seeking revenge for the death of his son and the loss of a hand, a madman takes hostages in a remote area before doing battle with the local sheriff. Slow moving and not very interesting poverty row melodrama.

3504 Terror in a Texas Town. United Artists, 1958. 81 minutes B/W. D: Joseph H. Lewis. SC: Ben L. Perry. WITH Sterling Hayden, Carol Kelly, Sebastian Cabot, Victor Millan, Eugene Martin, Ned Young, Ann Verela, Sheb Wooley, Fred Kohler Jr., Steve Mitchell, Tyler McVey, Ted Stanhope, Gil Lamb, Frank Ferguson, Hank Patterson. Returning home to his father's Texas ranch, a man finds the area terrorized by a land baron who wants the land for its rich oil deposits. Standard oater yarn given some atmosphere by Joseph H. Lewis' direction.

3505 Terror of the Black Mask. Embassy, 1967. 97 minutes Color. D: Umberto Lenzi. SC: Gino De Santis, Guido Malatesta & Umberto Lenzi. WITH Pierre Brice, Helene Chanel, Daniele Vargas, Adolf Bufi-Landi, Carlo Latimer, Giselle Arden, Massimo Serato. The timid stepson of a 17th century despot is actually the masked Don Diego, alias Zorro, who attacks his stepfather's army and weakens his control over the people. Typical dubbed European oater included here because of the Zorro character. Issued in Europe in 1963 by Romana Film.

3506 The Terror of Tiny Town. Columbia, 1938. 62 minutes B/W. D: Sam Newfield. SC: Fred Myton. WITH Billy Curtis, Yvonne Moray, Little Billy, Billy Platt, Johnny Rambary, Charles Becker, Joseph Herbert, Nita Krebs, George Ministeri, Karl Casitzky, Fern McDill, W. H. O'Dogharty. A bad man pits two families against each other so they will kill each other off and he can get their lands. Outside the novelty of this being an all-midget cast film, there is not much here for the viewer. V: Video Yesteryear, Admit One Video.

3507 Terror Trail. Universal, 1933. 58 minutes B/W. D: Armand L. Schaefer. SC: Jack Cunningham. WITH Tom Mix, Naomi Judge, Arthur Rankin, Raymond Hatton, Francis McDonald, Robert Kortman, John St. Polis, Francis Brownlee, Harry Tenbrook, Lafe McKee, W. J. Holmes, Hank Bell, Leonard Trainer, Jim Corey, Jay Wilsey. A cowboy sets out to retrieve his horse which has been stolen by an outlaw gang led by the local sheriff. Entertaining Tom Mix vehicle, although not up to par with some of his other Universal works.

3508 Terror Trail. Columbia, 1946. 55 minutes B/W. D: Ray Nazarro. SC: Ed Earl Repp. WITH Charles Starrett, Smiley Burnette, Barbara Pepper, Lane Chandler, Zon Murray, Elvin Eric Feld, Ozie Waters & His Colorado Rangers, Tommy Coats, George Chesebro, Robert Barron, Budd Buster, Bill Clark, Ted Mapes. When a dishonest rancher tries to start a range war by secretly placing sheep on cattlemen's land, the Durango Kid tries to stop the hostilities. Pretty fair "Durango Kid" episode with good supporting work by Lane Chandler and Barbara Pepper.

3509 Terrors on Horseback. Producers Releasing Corporation, 1946. 55 minutes B/W. D: Sam Newfield. SC: George Milton. WITH Buster Crabbe, Al St. John, Patti McCarthy, I. Stanford Jolley, Henry Hall, Kermit Maynard, Karl Hackett, Marin Sais, Budd Buster, Steve Darrell, Steve Clark, Bud Osborne, Al Ferguson, George Chesebro, Frank Ellis, Jack Kirk, Lane Bradford. To avenge the murder of his niece, a cowboy sets out to kill off the outlaw gang responsible for her death during a stagecoach robbery. One of the last of the "Billy Carson" series and one of the best films in the series; actionful from start to finish.

3510 The Test. Reliable, 1935. 55 minutes B/W. D: Bernard B. Ray. SC: L. V. Jefferson. WITH Rin-Tin-Tin Jr., Grant Withers, Grace Ford, Monte Blue, Lafayette (Lafe) McKee, James (Jimmie) Aubrey, Artie Ortego, Dorothy Vernon, Jack Evans, Tom London, Nanette (dog). Two north woods fur trappers vie for the daughter of the trading post owner and one of them has his men steal the other's valuable furs. Low budget actioner; picturesque due to its mostly outdoor shooting.

3511 The Testing Block. Paramount-Artcraft, 1920. 60 minutes B/W. D-SC: Lambert Hillyer. WITH William S. Hart, Eva Novak, Gordon Russell, Florence Carpenter, Richard Headrick, Ira McFadden. An outlaw gang leader falls in love with a pretty entertainer and they later marry and settle down but one of the gang arrives on the scene and plans to steal the girl. Melodramatic and sombre, this silent drama was based on star William S. Hart's original story.

3512 Tex Granger. Columbia, 1948. 12 Chapters B/W. D: Derwin Abrahams. SC: Arthur Hoerl, Lewis Clay, Harry Fraser & Royal K. Cole. WITH Robert Kellard, Peggy Stewart, Buzz Henry, Smith Ballew, Jack Ingram, I. Stanford Jolley, Terry Frost, Jim Diehl, Britt Wood, William Fawcett. A cowboy joins a boy and a young woman in opposing the crooked activities of a man who has become the town sheriff. Standard cliffhanger highlighted by Smith Ballew's portrayal of villain Blaze Talbot.

3513 Tex Rides with the Boy Scouts. Grand National, 1937. 66 minutes B/W. D: Ray Taylor. SC: Edmund Kelso. WITH Tex Ritter, Marjorie Reynolds, Horace Murphy, Snub Pollard, Tommy Bupp, Charles King, Forrest Taylor, Karl Hackett, Lynton Brent, Philip Ahn, Ed Cassidy, Timmy Davis, Heber Snow (Hank Worden), The Beverly Hillbillies. A mine ore geologist and his two pals are aided by a Boy Scout troop in capturing a gang of train robbers masquerading as gold mine operators. Pretty good Tex Ritter film with lots of action and good music with the introduction relating the history of the Boy Scouts, to whom the film is dedicated.

3514 Tex Takes a Holiday. First Division, 1932. 60 minutes Color. D: Alvin J. Neitz (Alan James). SC: Robert Walker. WITH Wallace MacDonald, Virginia Brown Faire, George Chesebro, Ben Corbett, Jack Perrin, James Dillon, Claude Peyton, George Gerwing. A mysterious stranger is blamed for a series of local crimes but uncovers the real culprit. Poor Natural Color mystery-Western.

3515 The Texan. Paramount, 1930. 79 minutes B/W. D: John Cromwell. SC: Daniel N. Rubin. WITH Gary Cooper, Fay Wray, Emma Dunn, Oscar Apfel, James Marcus, Donald Reed, Soledad Jiminez, Veda Buckland, Cesar Vanoni, Edwin J. Brady, Enrique Acosta, Romualdo Tirado, Russ Columbo. The Llano Kid, a wanted outlaw, pretends to be the long-lost son of an old woman. Early

Gary Cooper talking film is dated and fairly bland. Remade as **The Llano Kid** (q.v.).

3516 The Texan. Principal, 1932. 64 minutes B/W. D: Cliff Smith. WITH Buffalo Bill Jr., Lucille Browne, Bobby Nelson, Lafe McKee, Jack Mower, Art Mix, Yakima Canutt. A fugitive joins two crooks in cheating townspeople out of their money in a fixed horse race but is redeemed by the love of a local girl. Better than might be expected.

3517 The Texan Meets Calamity Jane. Columbia, 1950. 71 minutes Color. D-SC: Andre Lamb. WITH James Ellison, Evelyn Ankers, Lee "Lasses" White, Jack Ingram, Ruth Whitney, Frank Pharr, Sally Weidman, Rudy de Saxe, Hugh Hooker, Ray Jones. A Texan comes to the aid of Calamity Jane as she tries to prove the validity of her ownership of a saloon. Unbelievably poor oater which is neither straight drama nor satire.

3518 The Texans. Paramount, 1938. 90 minutes B/W. D: James Hogan. SC: Paul Sloane & William Wister Haines. WITH Joan Bennett, Randolph Scott, May Robson, Walter Brennan, Robert Cummings, Robert Barrat, Harvey Stephens, Francis Ford, Bill Roberts, Clarence Wilson, Raymond Hatton, Jack Moore, Francis McDonald, Alan Ladd, Chris-Pin Martin, Anna Demetrio, Richard Tucker, Edward Gargan, Otis Harlan, Spencer Charters, Archie Twitchell, William Haade, Irving Bacon. A cowboy leads a cattle drive, which includes the pretty daughter of the herd's owner, from Texas to Kansas after the Civil War. Too much stock footage mars this remake of Emerson Hough's novel North of '36 which Paramount first filmed in 1924 with Jack Holt under its original title.

3519 Texans Never Cry. Columbia, 1951. 70 minutes B/W. D: Frank McDonald. SC: Norman S. Hall. WITH Gene Autry, Pat Buttram, Gail Davis, Mary Castle, Russell Hayden, Richard Powers, Don C. Harvey, Mike Ragan, Roy Gordon, I. Stanford Jolley, Frank Fenton, Sandy Sanders, John McKee, Harry McKim, Minerva Urecal, Duke York. A Texas Ranger is on the trail of a gang counterfeiting Mexican lottery tickets. Fair Gene Autry opus with good work by Richard Powers (Tom Keene) as the villain.

3520 Texas. Columbia, 1941. 94 minutes B/W. D: George Marshall. SC: Horace McCoy, Lewis Meltzer & Michael Blankfort. WITH William Holden, Glenn Ford, Claire Trevor, George Bancroft, Edgar Buchanan, Don Beddoe, Andrew Tombes, Addison Richards, Edmund MacDonald, Joseph Crehan, Willard Robertson, Pat Moriarity, Edmund Cobb, Lyle Latell, Raymond Hatton, Ralph Peters, Duke York, James Flavin, Carleton Young, Jack Ingram, Ethan Laidlaw, William Gould. After the Civil War, two ex-Confederates head to Texas, one going to work for a woman cattle rancher while the other joins an outlaw gang. Entertaining and actionful oater, originally filmed in Sepia.

3521 Texas Across the River. Universal, 1966. 101 minutes Color. D: Michael Gordon. SC: Wells Root, Harold Green & Ben Starr. WITH Dean Martin, Alain Delon, Joey Bishop, Rosemary Forsyth, Tina (Aumont) Marquand. Peter Graves, Michael Ansara, Andrew Prine, Linden Chiles, Roy Barcroft, Stuart Anderson, George Wallace, Richard Farnsworth, John Harmon. When he is accused of murdering the fiancée of the girl he loves, a Spanish nobleman heads for Texas and falls for an Indian maiden while the girl follows him and is attracted to a cattleman. Fairly amusing genre satire.

3522 Texas Bad Man. Universal, 1932. 60 minutes B/W. D: Edward Laemmle. SC: Jack Cunningham. WITH Tom Mix, Lucille Powers, Fred Kohler, Ed Le Saint, Willard Robertson, Richard Alexander, C. E. Anderson, Lynton Brent, Franklyn Farnum, Joe Girard, Buck Moulton, James Burtis, Slim Cole, Boothe Howard, Francis Sayles, Theodore Lorch, George Magrill, Bud Osborne, Buck Bucko. A lawman pretends to go bad in order to infiltrate an outlaw gang. Very good Tom Mix vehicle.

3523 Texas Bad Man. Allied Artists, 1953. 62 minutes B/W. D: Lewis D. Collins. SC: Joseph Poland. WITH Wayne Morris, Elaine Riley, Frank Ferguson, Sheb Wooley, Denver Pyle, Myron Healey, Mort Mills, Nelson Leigh. A lawman tries to stop his outlaw father and his gang from robbing the proceeds from the spring cleanup of a gold mine. Average programmer.

3524 Texas Buddies. World Wide, 1932. 57 minutes B/W. D-SC: Robert North Bradbury. WITH Bob Steele, Nancy Drexel, Francis McDonald, Harry Semels, George ("Gabby") Hayes, Bill Dyer, Dick Dickinson,

Earl Dwire. In 1919 a young man returns home from the war and teams up with his late dad's pal to work a mine and they end up trying to trap crooks who tried to rob a payroll and murder a pilot. Entertaining, but somewhat rambling Bob Steele vehicle with such disparate plot elements as aviation, a horse race, robbery and murder and a runaway tin lizzy.

3525 Texas Carnival. Metro-Goldwyn-Mayer, 1951. 77 minutes Color. D: Charles Walters. SC: Dorothy Kingsley. WITH Esther Williams, Red Skelton, Howard Keel, Ann Miller, Paula Raymond, Keenan Wynn, Tom Tully, Red Norvo Trio, Foy Willing & The Riders of the Purple Sage, Glenn Strange, Dick Wessell, Donald MacBride, Marjorie Wood, Hans Conreid, Thurston Hall, Duke Johnson, Wilson Wood, Michael Dugan. The managers of a large Texas resort hotel mistakenly believe a circus bum is a big cattle and oil tycoon. There is not much to recommend this glossy musical comedy outside the presence of Red Skelton.

3526 Texas City. Monogram, 1952. 54 minutes B/W. D: Lewis D. Collins. SC: Joseph Poland. WITH Johnny Mack Brown, James Ellison, Lois Hall, Lorna Thayer, Lane Bradford, Marshall Reed, Terry Frost, Lyle Talbot, Pierce Lyden, John Hart, Lennie Osborne, Stanley Price. An ex-calvary officer is falsely accused of giving secret information about army gold shipments to outlaws and a U. S. marshal tries to find the real culprit. Okay Johnny Mack Brown vehicle from near the end of his long-term Monogram series.

3527 Texas Cowboy. Syndicate, 1929. 50 minutes B/W. D: J. P. McGowan. WITH Bob Steele, Edna Aslin, J. P. McGowan, Grace Stevens, Bud Osborne, Perry Murdock, Alfred Hewston, Cliff Lyons. A young man returns to his California ranch home to find his mother has married a brute who is trying to control her property and cheat him out of his rightful inheritance. Nicely done Bob Steele silent film enhanced by the presence of pretty Edna Aslin as the neighbor girl in love with the hero.

3528 Texas Cyclone. Columbia, 1932. 63 minutes B/W. D: D. Ross Lederman. SC: Randall Faye. WITH Tim McCoy, Shirley Grey, Wheeler Oakman, John Wayne, Wallace MacDonald, James Farley, Harry Cording, Vernon Dent, Walter Brennan, Mary Gordon. A cowboy rides into a small Arizona town where he is mistaken for another man, almost winds up being murdered and then tries to solve the mystery. Interesting Tim McCoy vehicle with John Wayne along in a supporting role.

Texas Desperadoes see **Drift Fence**

3529 Texas Detour. Arista Films, 1978. 92 minutes Color. D-SC: Hikmet Avedis. WITH Patrick Wayne, Mitch Vogel, Priscilla Barnes, Cameron Mitchell, Lindsay Bloom, R. G. Armstrong. A stuntman in the southwest joins forces with a pretty girl as they are chased by a gang of crooks. Cheaply made action melodrama.

3530 Texas Dynamo. Columbia, 1950. 54 minutes B/W. D: Ray Nazarro. SC: Barry Shipman. WITH Charles Starrett, Smiley Burnette, Lois Hall, John Dehner, Jock O'Mahoney (Mahoney), Marshall Reed, George Chesebro, Lane Bradford, Slim Duncan, Emil Sitka, Fred Sears, Greg Barton. The Durango Kid takes on the guise of the notorious gunman Texas Dynamo in order to infiltrate a gang led by a ruthless town boss. Pretty fair Charles Starrett series entry with strong work by John Dehner as the town boss.

3531 Texas Gunfighter. Tiffany, 1932. 63 minutes B/W. D: Phil Rosen. SC: Bennett Cohen. WITH Ken Maynard, Sheila Mannors, Harry Woods, Bob Fleming, Jim Mason, Edgar Lewis, Lloyd Ingraham, Jack Rockwell, Frank Ellis, Blackjack Ward, Bob Burns, Bud McClure. A member of an outlaw gang tries to go straight and becomes a lawman but his former cohorts want him to rob a safe. Mediocre Ken Maynard vehicle. V: Discount Video.

3532 Texas Jack. Reliable, 1932. 52 minutes B/W. D: Bernard B. Ray. SC: Carl Krusada. WITH Jack Perrin, Jayne Regan, Nelson McDowell, Robert Walker, Lew Meehan, Cope Borden, Blackie Whiteford, Budd Buster, Oscar Gahan, Jim Oates, Steve Clark. Using a medicine show as a front, a man searches for the crook who lured his sister south of the border in a shady operation which resulted in her suicide. Low grade Jack Perrin vehicle; a poor proposition.

Texas Justice see **The Lone Rider in Texas Justice**

3533 The Texas Kid. Monogram, 1943. 57 minutes B/W. D: Lambert Hillyer.

SC: Jess Bowers (Adele Buffington). WITH Johnny Mack Brown, Raymond Hatton, Marshall Reed, Shirley Patterson, Robert Fiske, Edmund Cobb, Stanley Price, Lynton Brent, Bud Osborne, Kermit Maynard, John Judd, Cyril Ring, George J. Lewis, Charles King. Two lawmen come to the aid of an ex-outlaw whose old gang is after a gold shipment from the man's stage line. Pretty good Johnny Mack Brown film from an original story by character actor Lynton Brent.

3534 Texas Lady. RKO Radio, 1955. 86 minutes Color. D: Tim Whelan. SC: Horace McCoy. WITH Claudette Colbert, Barry Sullivan, Ray Collins, Gregory Walcott, Walter Sande, James Bell, Horace McMahon, John Litel, Douglas Fowley, Don Haggerty, Celia Lovsky. After winning big gambling and paying off her father's debts, a woman takes over a newspaper and opposes a local crook. Claudette Colbert out West provides some charm in this otherwise mundane drama.

3535 Texas Lawmen. Monogram, 1951. 57 minutes B/W. D: Lewis D. Collins. SC: Joseph Poland. WITH Johnny Mack Brown, James Ellison, I. Stanford Jolley, Lee Roberts, Lane Bradford, Marshall Reed, Terry Frost, Lyle Talbot, Pierce Lyden, Stanley Price, John Hart. A federal marshal enlists the aid of a sheriff in helping him round up the culprits who robbed a mining payroll. Stale Johnny Mack Brown-James Ellison outing; also called **Lone Star Lawman.**

Texas Legionaires see **Man from Music Mountain** (1943)

3536 Texas Manhunt. Producers Releasing Corporation, 1942. 61 minutes B/W. D: Peter Stewart (Sam Newfield). SC: William Lively. WITH Lee Powell, Art Davis, Bill Boyd, Julie Duncan, Dennis Moore, Frank Hagney, Karl Hackett, Frank Ellis, Arno Frey, Eddie Phillips, Kenne Duncan. When cattle operations are being sabotaged, federal marshals suspect two cattlemen of being enemy agents. The plot of having spies on the range adds some life to this PRC series film.

3537 The Texas Marshal. Producers Releasing Corporation, 1941. 58 minutes B/W. D: Peter Stewart (Sam Newfield). SC: William Lively. WITH Tim McCoy, Art Davis, Kay Leslie, Karl Hackett, Ed Piel, Charles King, Dave O'Brien, Budd Buster, John Elliott, Frank Ellis,

Byron Vance, Wilson Edwards, Art Davis' Rhythm Riders. A lawman is called in to investigate terrorism against local ranchers caused by three crooks who use a legitimate business as a front and his problems are compounded by his singing partner who is taken in by the organization. Mediocre PRC oater with too much music and too little action; Tim McCoy's final solo series film.

3538 Texas Masquerade. United Artists, 1944. 54 (59) minutes B/W. D: George Archainbaud. SC: Norman Houston. WITH William Boyd, Andy Clyde, Jimmy Rogers, Mady Correll, Don Costello, Russell Simpson, Nelson Leigh, Francis McDonald, J. Farrell MacDonald, June Pickerell, John Merton, Pierce Lyden, Robert McKenzie, Bill Hunter, George Morrell, Keith Richards. Hoppy masquerades as an Eastern dude lawyer to get the goods on a murderous band of outlaws. Novel idea wears thin as the film progresses although this "Hopalong Cassidy" entry does have a different ending with the villain dying in quicksand. V: Thunderbird.

3539 Texas Panhandle. Columbia, 1945. 57 minutes B/W. D: Ray Nazarro. SC: Ed Earl Repp. WITH Charles Starrett, Tex Harding, Dub Taylor, Nanette Parks, Carolina Cotton, Space Cooley, Forrest Taylor, Edward Howard, Ted Mapes, George Chesebro, Jody Gilbert, William Gould, Jack Kirk, Budd Buster, Tex Palmer, Hugh Hooker. An ex-Secret Service agent joins a wagon train to investigate a robbery, using his guise as the Durango Kid to round up the outlaws. Okay "Durango Kid" series entry.

3540 Texas Pioneers. Monogram, 1932. 58 minutes B/W. D: Harry Fraser. SC: Wellyn Totman & Harry Fraser. WITH Bill Cody, Andy Shuford, Sheila Mannors, Harry Allen, LeRoy Mason, Frank Lackteen, John Elliott, Ann Ross, Hank Bell, Iron Eyes Cody, Chief Standing Bear. When an outlaw gang attacks a remote frontier post a scout tries to defend it. Just passable Billy Cody vehicle. V: Video Dimensions.

3541 The Texas Rambler. Spectrum, 1935. 59 minutes B/W. D: Robert Hill. SC: Oliver Drake. WITH Bill Cody, Cathrine Cotter, Earle Hodgins, Stuart James, Mildred Rogers, Budd Buster, Ace Cain, Roger Williams, Buck Morgan, Colin Chase, Allen Greer. A mysterious figure enlists the aid of a cowboy called "The

Rambler" to help a girl who crooks want to kidnap for her inheritance, which is one-half interest in a ranch. Better than average Bill Cody vehicle, due to Bob Hill's direction, Oliver Drake's script and Earle Hodgins' villainy.

3542 The Texas Ranger. Columbia, 1931. 60 minutes B/W. D: D. Ross Lederman. SC: Forrest Sheldon. WITH Buck Jones, Carmelita Geraghty, Harry Woods, Ed Brady, Nelson McDowell, Billy Bletcher, Harry Todd, Budd Fine, Ed Piel, Blackie Whiteford, Lee Meehan, Bert Woodruff. A Texas Ranger tries to stop a feud between two factions in Texas cattle country, the trouble being caused by a crook and his gang. Exciting and fast moving Buck Jones early talkie.

3543 The Texas Rangers. Paramount, 1936. 98 minutes B/W. D: King Vidor. SC: Louis Stevens. WITH Fred MacMurray, Jack Oakie, Jean Parker, Lloyd Nolan, Edward Ellis, Bennie Bartlett, Frank Shannon, Frank Cordell, Richard Carle, Jed Prouty, Fred Kohler, George ("Gabby") Hayes, Elena Martinez, Kathryn Bates, Rhea Mitchell, Hank Bell, Jack Montgomery, Howard Joslin, Joe Dominguez, Joseph Rickman, Frank Ellis, Bill Gillis, Neal Hart, Cecil Kellogg, Frank Cordell, Lloyd A. Saunders, Homer Farra, Ray Burgess, Gayne Whitman, Bobby Caldwell, Dell Henderson, Stanley Andrews, William Strauss, Irving Bacon. Two outlaws reform and join the Texas Rangers and take part in a manhunt for their ex-partner. Sturdy saga of the Texas Rangers, remade in 1949 as **Streets of Laredo** (q.v.).

3544 The Texas Rangers. Columbia, 1951. 74 minutes Color. D: Phil Karlson. SC: Richard Schayer. WITH George Montgomery, Gale Storm, Jerome Courtland, Noah Beery Jr., John Litel, William Bishop, Douglas Kennedy, John Dehner, Ian MacDonald, John Doucette, Jock (Mahoney) O'Mahoney, Joseph Fallon, Myron Healey, Julian Rivero, Trevor Bardette, Stanley Andrews, Edward Earle. Two former outlaws join the Texas Rangers in trying to find and bring in a notorious gang. Dull George Montgomery film.

3545 The Texas Rangers Ride Again. Paramount, 1940. 68 minutes B/W. D: James Hogan. SC: William Lipman & Horace McCoy. WITH John Howard, Ellen Drew, Akim Tamiroff, Broderick Crawford, May Robson, Charles Grapewin, John Miljan, Anthony Quinn, Tom Tyler, Donald Curtis, Eddie Acuff, Ruth Rogers,

Robert Ryan, Eva Puig, Monte Blue, James Pierce, William Duncan, Harvey Stephens, Harold Goodwin, Edward Pawley, Eddie Foy Jr., Joseph Crehan, Stanley Price, Charles Lane, Jack Perrin, Gordon Jones, John Miller, Henry Rocquemore, Franklin Parker, Chuck Hamilton, Paul Kruger. Members of the Texas Rangers pretend to be rustlers in order to infiltrate an outlaw gang. Minor big studio oater enhanced by a fine cast.

3546 Texas Renegades. Producers Distributing Corporation, 1940. 56 minutes B/W. D: Peter Stewart (Sam Newfield). SC: Joseph O'Donnell. WITH Tim McCoy, Nora Lane, Harry Harvey, Kenne Duncan, Lee Prather, Earl Gunn, Hal Price, Joe McGuinn, Raphael (Ray) Bennett, Ed Cassidy. Posing as an outlaw, a lawman attempts to clean up a wild western town. Tim McCoy's initial vehicle for producer Sigmund Neufeld at PDC (soon to become Producers Releasing Corporation) is a pretty good affair.

Texas Road Agent see **Road Agent**

3547 Texas Stagecoach. Columbia, 1940. 59 minutes B/W. D: Joseph H. Lewis. SC: Fred Myton. WITH Charles Starrett, Iris Meredith, Bob Nolan & The Sons of the Pioneers, Dick Curtis, Kenneth MacDonald, Ed LeSaint, Don Beddoe, George Becinita, Harry Cording, George Chesebro, George Morrell, Francis Walker, Blackie Whiteford, Lillian Lawrence, Eddie Laughton, Fred Burns, Carl Stockdale. A crooked banker promotes trouble between two rival stage lines in the hopes of taking over both operations. Fairly good Charles Starrett series entry.

3548 Texas Stampede. Columbia, 1939. 59 minutes B/W. D: Sam Nelson. SC: Charles Francis Royal. WITH Charles Starrett, Iris Meredith, Bob Nolan & The Sons of the Pioneers, Fred Kohler Jr., Lee Prather, Ray Bennett, Blackjack Ward, Hank Bell, Edmund Cobb, Edward Hearn, Ed Coxen, Ernie Adams, Blackie Whiteford, Charles Brinley. A lawman attempts to keep the peace between cattlemen and sheepmen when the latter shuts off rights-of-way to water during a drought. Nicely done remake of Buck Jones' early talkie **The Dawn Trail** (q.v.).

3549 Texas Terror. Monogram, 1935. 58 minutes B/W. D-SC: Robert North Bradbury. WITH John Wayne, Lucille Browne, LeRoy Mason, Fern Emmett, John Ince, George ("Gabby") Hayes, Henry

Rocquemore, Buffalo Bill Jr., Bert Dillard, Jack Duffy, Lloyd Ingraham, Bobby Nelson, Yakima Canutt. Falsely believing that he killed his best pal, a young lawman resigns his job and becomes a prospector but after he saves the dead man's sister in a stage holdup attempt he begins to realize the truth. Average John Wayne Monogram-Lone Star production, but entertaining none-the-less. V: Video Dimensions.

3550 Texas Terrors. Republic, 1940. 54 (57) minutes B/W. D: George Sherman. SC: Doris Schroeder & Anthony Coldeway. WITH Don "Red" Barry, Julie Duncan, Al St. John, Arthur Loft, Ann Pennington, Eddy Waller, William Ruhl, Sammy McKim, Reed Howes, Robert Fiske, Fred "Snowflake" Toones, Hal Taliaferro, Edmund Cobb, Al Haskell, Jack Kirk, Ruth Robinson, Blackjack Ward, Curley Dresden, Jimmy Wakely & His Rough Riders (Johnny Bond, Dick Rinehart). A young Western lawyer is on the trail of the outlaws who murdered his folks. Another fast paced and well made Don Barry vehicle; the plot is nothing new but the star and production values keep it moving. Look for one-time Broadway and early talkies star Ann Pennington in a brief production number.

3551 Texas to Bataan. Monogram, 1942. 58 minutes B/W. D: Robert (Emmett) Tansey. SC: Arthur Hoerl. WITH John King, David Sharpe, Max Terhune, Marjorie Manners, Budd Buster, Escolastico Baucin, Kenne Duncan, Frank Ellis, Carl Mathews, Guy Kingsford, Steve Clark, Al Ferguson, Tom Steele, Tex Palmer. Assigned to take a shipment of horses to the Philippine Islands for the Army, the Range Busters find themselves opposed by enemy agents. Fans of "The Range Busters" will enjoy this patriotic romp.

3552 Texas Tornado. Willis Kent, 1932. 55 minutes B/W. D-SC: Oliver Drake. WITH Lane Chandler, Doris Hill, Buddy Roosevelt, Yakima Canutt, Robert Hale, Ben Corbett, Edward Hearn, Bart Carre, Mike Brand, Fred Burns, J. Frank Glendon, Wes Warner, Pat Herly. A Texas Ranger gets involved with gangsters who have kidnapped a girl and killed her father. Okay poverty row outing in Lane Chandler's series for Willis Kent.

3553 Texas Trail. Paramount, 1937. 54 (58) minutes B/W. D: David Selman. SC: Joseph O'Donnell. WITH William Boyd, George ("Gabby") Hayes, Russell

Hayden, Judith Allen, Billy King, Alexander Cross, Karl Hackett, Robert Kortman, Jack Rockwell, John Beach, Ray Bennett, Philo McCullough, Earle Hodgins, Ben Corbett, John Judd, Clyde Kinney, Leo McMahon. A fort commander asks Hopalong Cassidy to round up 500 horses for government use in the Spanish-American War and an outlaw leader and his gang plan to rustle the herd. Compact and entertaining "Hopalong Cassidy" series film.

3554 Texas Trouble Shooters. Monogram, 1942. 58 minutes B/W. D: S. Roy Luby. SC: Arthur Hoerl. WITH Ray Corrigan, John King, Max Terhune, Julie Duncan, Roy Harris (Riley Hill), Eddie Phillips, Frank Ellis, Ted Mapes, Kermit Maynard, Gertrude W. Hoffman, Steve Clark, Jack Holmes, Glenn Strange, Richard Cramer. The Range Busters set out to aid a man who has been dry-gulched while trying to claim a ranch he inherited. Fairly actionful Range Busters entry including such old-time favorites "Deep in the Heart of Texas" and "Light of the Western Skies."

3555 Texas Wildcats. Victory, 1939. 57 minutes B/W. D: Sam Newfield. SC: George Plympton. WITH Tim McCoy, Joan Barclay, Forrest Taylor, Ted Adams, Dave O'Brien, Frank Ellis, Carl Mathews, Bob Terry, Slim Whitaker, Reed Howes, George Morrell, Avando Reynaldo. Taking on the guise of the mysterious Phantom, a lawman seeks to trap the man who murdered his pal and he also aids a girl and her brother whose mortgage is held by the crook. Tim McCoy fans should enjoy this outing although it is a bit slight on production values; a "Lightning Bill Carson" adventure.

3556 The Texican. Columbia, 1966. 90 minutes Color. D: Lesley Selander. SC: John C. Champion. WITH Audie Murphy, Broderick Crawford, Diana Lorys, Luz Marquez, Antonio Casas, Molino Rojo, Aldo Sambrell, Antonio Peral, Jorge Rigaud, Martha May, Juan Carlos Torres, Gerald Tichy, Luis Induni, Helga Genth. A cowboy seeks revenge from the ruthless town boss who falsely accused him of murder. Mediocre remake of director Lesley Selander's earlier success **Panhandle** (q.v.), filmed in Spain.

3557 Them! Warner Brothers, 1954. 93 minutes B/W. D: Gordon Douglas. SC: Ted Sherdeman. WITH James Whitmore, Edmund Gwenn, James Arness, Joan

Weldon, Onslow Stevens, Chris Drake, Sean McClory, Sandy Descher, Mary Alan Hokanson, Frederick J. Foote, Olin Howlin, Scott Correll, Richard Bellis, Joel Smith, John Close, William Schallert, Cliff Ferre, Matthew McCue, Marshall Bradford, Joe Forte, Ann Doran, Willis Bouchey, John Maxwell, Leonard Nimoy, Fess Parker, Dick Wessell, Dub Taylor, Russell Gage, Robert Burger, Harry Tyler, Harry Wilson, Eddie Dew, Dorothy Green, Dean Cromer, Lawrence Dobkin, James Cardwell, Booth Colman, Walter Coy, Victor Sutherland, Jack Perrin, Royden Clark, Hubert Kerns. Due to atomic testing, ants develop into huge giants which plague the Arizona desert. One of the all-time best science fiction films, in a Western setting.

3558 There Was a Crooked Man. Warner Brothers-Seven Arts, 1970. 126 minutes Color. D: Joseph L. Mankiewicz. SC: David Newman & Robert Benton. WITH Kirk Douglas, Henry Fonda, Hume Cronyn, Warren Oates, Burgess Meredith, John Randolph, Arthur O'Connell, Martin Gabel, Michael Blodgett, Claudia McNeil, Alan Hale, Victor French, Lee Grant, C. K. Yang, Pamela Hensley, Bert Freed, Barbara Rhoades, J. Edward McKinley, Gene Evans, Jeanne Cooper. A lawman becomes the warden of an Arizona territorial prison and matches wits with an inmate who has hidden away $500,000 from a robbery. Sturdy comedy-drama with a twist ending.

3559 These Thousand Hills. 20th Century-Fox, 1959. 96 minutes Color. D: Richard Fleischer. SC: Alfred Hayes. WITH Don Murray, Richard Egan, Lee Remick, Patricia Owens, Stuart Whitman, Albert Dekker, Harold J. Stone, Royal Dano, Jean Willes, Douglas Fowley, Fuzzy Knight, Robert Adler, Barbara Morris, Ned Weaver. An ambitious young rancher deserts the girl he loves to marry a banker's daughter but eventually learns the meaning of loyalty and responsibility. Well written, directed and acted drama.

3560 They Call Me Trinity. Avco-Embassy, 1971. 117 minutes Color. D-SC: E. B. Clucher (Enzo Barboni). WITH Terence Hill, Bud Spencer, Farley Granger, Steffan Zacharias, Dan Sturkie, Gisela Hahn, Elena Pedemonte, Ezio Marano, Luciano Rossi, Michelle Spaeara, Remo Capitani, Michele Cimarosa. Two rather bumbling outlaws agree to protect a Mormon town against a band of marauding Mexican bandits. Funny take-off on the genre,

especially the European variety. Sequel: **Trinity Is Still My Name** (q.v.).

3561 They Came to Cordura. Columbia, 1959. 123 minutes Color. D: Robert Rossen. SC: Ivan Moffat & Robert Rossen. WITH Gary Cooper, Rita Hayworth, Van Heflin, Richard Conte, Tab Hunter, Michael Callan, Dick York, Robert Keith, Carlos Romero, Jim Bannon, Edward Platt, Maurice Jara, Sam Buffington, Arthur Hanson. During the conflict with Pancho Villa, a demoted Army officer is assigned to find recipients for the Congressional Medal of Honor and during a trek across the Mexican desert they are accompanied by a woman accused of giving aid to Villa's soldiers. Overlong and complicated melodrama, this unsatisfying film was Gary Cooper's final Western.

3562 They Died with Their Boots On. Warner Brothers, 1941. 140 minutes B/W. D: Raoul Walsh. SC: Wally Kline & Aeneas MacKenzie. WITH Errol Flynn, Olivia de Havilland, Arthur Kennedy, Charles Grapewin, Gene Lockhart, Anthony Quinn, Sydney Greenstreet, Stanley Ridges, John Litel, Walter Hampden, Regis Toomey, Hattie McDaniel, G. P. Huntlet Jr., Frank Wilcox, Joseph Sawyer, Minor Watson, Gig Young, John Ridgely, Joseph Crehan, Aileen Pringle, Anna Q. Nilsson, Harry Lewis, Tod Andrews, William Hopper, Selmer Jackson, Patrick McVey, Renie Riano, Minerva Urecal, Virginia Sale, Vera Lewis, Frank Orth, Hobart Bosworth, Irving Bacon, Roy Barcroft, Lane Chandler, Ed Keane, Francis Ford, Frank Ferguson, Herbert Heywood. The story of George Armstrong Custer, from his graduation from West Point, through the Civil War to his final stand at the Little Big Horn. Overlong and historically inaccurate, but still a fun film.

3563 They Ran for Their Lives. Columbia/Masterpiece, 1969. 92 minutes Color. D: John Payne. SC: Monrow Mowsley. WITH John Payne, Luana Patten, Scott Brady, John Carradine, Jim Davis, Anthony Eisley, Darwin Lamb, Boyd Stockman, Bravo (dog). A man camping in the Nevada desert with his dog comes to the aid of a girl who is being tracked by three crooks who are after important papers she is carrying. A good cast helps cover the production deficiencies in this little-seen melodrama made near Las Vegas in 1967.

3564 They Rode West. Columbia, 1954. 84 minutes Color. D: Phil Karlson. SC:

DeVallon Scott & Frank Nugent. WITH Robert Francis, Donna Reed, May Wynn, Phil(ip) Carey, Onslow Stevens, Peggy Converse, Roy Roberts, Jack Kelly, Stuart Randall, Eugene Iglesias, Frank De Kova, Ralph Dumke, James Best, George Keymas, Maurice Jara, John War Eagle. An Army camp commander and his post doctor are at odds when the latter wants to treat a local Indian tribe during a malaria outbreak. Pretty fair action melodrama.

3565 Thirteen Fighting Men. 20th Century-Fox, 1960. 71 minutes B/W. D: Harry Gerstad. SC: Robert Hammer & Jack Thomas. WITH Grant Williams, Carole Mathews, Brad Dexter, Robert Dix, Richard Garland, Rayford Barnes, John Erwin, Richard Crane, Rex Holman, Bob Palmer, Mauritz Hugo, Dick Monohan, Ted Knight, Fred Kohler Jr., I. Stanford Jolley, Walter Reed, John Merrick, Brad Harris. Near the end of the Civil War a Union patrol tries to prevent Confederates from taking a fortune in gold coins they are transporting. Standard melodrama with a good supporting cast.

3566 30 Winchester for El Diablo. Foreign Studios, 1965. 91 minutes Color. D: Frank G. Carrol. WITH Carl Mohner, Topsy Collins, John Heston. The mysterious El Diablo heads a cattle rustling gang which operates around Canyon City and a federal agent is sent to stop them. Average West German-made oater.

3567 This Is My Alaska. Alaskan Adventure, 1969. 120 minutes Color. D-SC: Leroy Shebal. WITH Leroy Shebal, Vivian Shebal, Gary Okahal. Leroy Shebal photographed and narrates this sportsman's guide to Alaska including exploration by bush plane, wolf hunting, snowmobile racing and Eskimos after polar bear. For fans of this type of fare.

3568 This Man Can't Die. Fine Products, 1970. 90 minutes Color. D: Gianfranco Baldanello. SC: Luigi Emmanuele & Gino Mangina. WITH Guy Madison, Peter Martell, Rik Battaglia, Lucienne Birdou, Steve Merrich, Rosalba Neri, John Bartha. Working for the government, two adventurers pose as outlaws to infiltrate a gun-running gang. Pretty good spaghetti actioner which should please Guy Madison fans.

3569 This Rugged Land. NBC-TV, 1962. 60 minutes Color. D: Arthur Hiller. SC: Frank S. Nugent. WITH Richard Egan, Charles Bronson, Terry Moore, Ryan O'Neal, Anne Seymour, Denver Pyle, Oliver McGowan. A ranch hand on a New Mexico ranch is accused of the murder of a coworker's daughter. Shown in Europe around 1970 as a feature film, this production was actually a segment of the television series "Empire" (NBC-TV, 1962-63/ABC-TV, 1963-64).

3570 This Savage Land. Universal, 1969. 98 minutes Color. D: Vincent McEveety. SC: Richard Fielder. WITH Barry Sullivan, George C. Scott, Kathryn Kays, Brenda Scott, Andrew Prine, Kelly Corcoran, Katherine Square, Glenn Corbett, Charles Seel, John Drew Barrymore, Roy Roberts, Rex Holman. A widower moves his family West from Ohio and in a small Western town they are terrorized by vigilantes. Strong melodrama, issued theatrically, although it was originally the first two-part episode of the TV series "The Road West" (NBC-TV, 1966-67) on September 12 & 19, 1966. Also called **The Savage Land.**

3571 This Was the West That Was. NBC-TV/Universal, 1974. 74 minutes Color. D: Fiedler Cook. SC: Sam H. Rolfe. WITH Ben Murphy, Kim Darby, Matt Clark, Jane Alexander, Anthony Franciosa, Stuart Margolin, Stefan Gierasch, Bill McKinney, W. L. LeGault, Roger Robinson, Luke Askew, Woodrow Parfrey, Milton Selzer, Bruce Glover, Wayne Sutherlin, Ronnie Clair Edwards, Dimitra Arliss, Roger Davis (narrator). Gunmen are out to get even with Wild Bill Hickok, who also must contend with a romantic Calamity Jane. There is not much to recommend this TV-made satire of the Wild Bill Hickok-Calamity Jane-Buffalo Bill Cody legends.

3572 Thomasine and Bushrod. Columbia, 1974. 95 minutes B/W. D: Gordon Parks Jr. SC: Max Julien. WITH Max Julien, Vonetta McGee, George Murdock, Glynn Turman, Juanite Moore, Joel Fluellen, Jackson D. Kane, Ben Zeller, Jason Bernard. In Texas in 1911 a black man and woman form a robbery team and are hunted by the law. Okay black exploitation drama.

3573 Thorobred. Clark-Cornelius Corporation, 1922. 50 minutes B/W. D-SC: George Halligan. WITH Helen Gibson, Bob Burns, Otto Nelson, Jack Ganzhorn. A girl takes over her father's duties as a sheriff and tracks an outlaw, eventually using the guise of a saloon girl to capture him. This silent Helen Gibson vehicle is lots of fun.

3574 Those Dirty Dogs. Cinema Financial of America, 1974. 89 minutes Color. D: Giuseppe Rosati. SC: Carl (Carlos) Veo, Giuseppe Rosati & Henry Lovett (Enrique Llovet). WITH Stephen Boyd, Johnny (Gianni) Garko, Helga Line, Simon Andreu, Howard Ross, Harry Boird, Teresa Gimpera, Alfredo Mayo, Daniele Vargas. Three officers, whose convoy has been mostly wiped out by Mexican bandits, try to exchange the kidnapped daughter of the fort's doctor for the gang's leader, who they have captured. Well made but very violent Spanish-Italian coproduction; issued in Spain by Plata Films/San Bernardo/Horse Film as **Los Cuatro de Fort Apache.**

3575 Those Redheads from Seattle. Paramount, 1953. 90 minutes Color. D: Lewis R. Foster. SC: Lewis R. Foster, Geoffrey Homes & George Worthington Yates. WITH Rhonda Fleming, Gene Barry, Agnes Moorehead, Guy Mitchell, Teresa Brewer, Jean Parker, Cynthia Bell, Kay Bell, Bill Pullen, John Kellogg, Frank Wilcox, Roscoe Ates, Michael Ross, Walter Reed, Ed Rand. A widow and her four lovely daughters head to Alaska during the Gold Rush to join her newspaper-editor husband, and when they get there they find he has been murdered. Originally issued in 3-D, this light affair is fairly enjoyable and it also provides a chance to see two of the all-time top recording artists, Guy Mitchell and cute Teresa Brewer, who is quite good as the youngest of the four girls.

3576 Three Bad Men. Fox, 1926. 87 minutes B/W. D: John Ford. SC: John Stone. WITH George O'Brien, Olive Borden, Lou Tellegen, J. Farrell MacDonald, Tom Santschi, Frank Campeau, George Harris, Jay Hunt, Priscilla Bonner, Otis Harlan, Walter Perry, Grace Gordon, Alec B. Francis, George Irving, Phyllis Haver, Vester Pegg. During the Dakota land rush of 1876 a former West Point cadet joins a family planning to settle there and helps them oppose outlaws and a crooked sheriff. Very good John Ford silent Western with just the right mixture of action, romance and sentiment.

3577 Three Bullets for a Long Gun. Avco-Embassy, 1973. 89 minutes Color. D: Peter Henkel. WITH Beau Brummell, Keith Van Der Wat, Patrick Mynhardt, Tulio Moneta. Two men, one of them a Mexican bandit, team to find a hidden treasure only to become enemies during the quest. Okay action Western.

3578 Three Desperate Men. Lippert, 1951, 71 minutes B/W. D: Sam Newfield. SC: Orville Hampton. WITH Preston Foster, Jim Davis, Virginia Grey, Monte Blue, Ross Latimer, Sid Melton, Rory Mallinson, John Brown, Margaret Seddon, House Peters Jr., Joel Newfield, Lee Bennett, Steve Belmont, Carol Henry, Kermit Maynard, Bert Dillard, Milton Kibbee, William N. Bailey, Gene Randall. Three brothers, who were once on the side of the law, are forced to become outlaws with prices on their heads. Pretty fair action drama with an especially good performance by Monte Blue as the lawman forced to hunt down his pals.

3579 Three Faces West. Republic, 1940. 83 minutes B/W. D: Bernard Vorhaus. SC: F. Hugh Herbert, Joseph Moncure March & Samuel Ornitz. WITH John Wayne, Sigrid Gurie, Charles Coburn, Spencer Charters, Roland Varno, Trevor Bardette, Helen MacKellar, Sonny Bupp, Wade Boteler, Russell Simpson, Charles Waldron, Wendell Niles, Dewey Robinson. A refugee doctor and his daughter arrive in a small North Dakota town and eventually aid a local farmer in moving the community to Oregon after drought ruins their land. Underrated John Wayne vehicle provides good entertainment value. Original title: **The Refugee.** V: Cumberland Video.

3580 The Three Godfathers. Metro-Goldwyn-Mayer, 1936. 82 minutes B/W. D: Richard Boleslawski. SC: Edward E. Paramore Jr. & Manuel Seff. WITH Chester Morris, Lewis Stone, Walter Brennan, Irene Hervey, Dorothy Tree, Robert Livingston, Joseph Marievsky, Jean Kirchner, Sidney Toler, Roger Imhoff, Willard Robertson, John Sheehan, Victor Potel, Harvey Clark, Helen Brown, Virginia Brissac. Three outlaws rob a small town bank of its Christmas savings and head into the desert where they find a dying woman and her baby and when their horses drink poison water they return to civilization with the child. Well done and glossy version of the Peter B. Kyne story which was first filmed in 1908 as **Broncho Billy and the Baby** starring G. M. "Broncho Billy" Anderson. In 1916 Universal filmed a six reel version of **The Three Godfathers** starring Harry Carey, with Hart (Jack) Hoxie in the supporting cast; Edward J. LeSaint, later a character actor in Westerns, directed. The first sound version of the Kyne novel was **Hell's Heroes** (q.v.). TV title: **Miracle in the Sand.**

3581 The Three Godfathers. Metro-Gold-wyn-Mayer, 1948. 108 minutes Color. D: John Ford. SC: Laurence Stallings & Frank S. Nugent. WITH John Wayne, Pedro Armendariz, Harry Carey Jr., Ward Bond, Mildred Natwick, Guy Kibbee, Jane Darwell, Mae Marsh, Charles Halton, Dorothy Ford, Ben Johnson, Michael Dugan, Don Summers, Fred Libby, Hank Worden, Jack Pennick, Francis Ford. After robbing a small town bank, three outlaws flee into the desert where they find a woman and her newborn baby and they agree to her dying wish that they take the baby to safety. Filmed in Monument Valley and dedicated to the memory of Harry Carey, this John Ford classic is one very fine Western.

3582 Three Guns for Texas. Universal, 1968. 99 minutes Color. D: David Lowell Rich, Paul Stanley & Earl Bellamy. WITH Neville Brand, Peter Brown, William Smith, Martin Milner, Philip Carey, Albert Salmi, Cliff Osmond, Michael Conrad, Shelley Morrison, John Abbott, Richard Devon, Ralph Manza, Dub Taylor. Texas Rangers are on the trail of an outlaw gang led by an Indian woman while one of the rangers is romanced by a pretty Indian maiden. Theatrical dual biller sewn together from three segments of the "Laredo" (NBC-TV, 1965-67) television series.

3583 Three Hours to Kill. Columbia, 1954. 77 minutes Color. D: Alfred Werker. SC: Richard Alan Simmons, Roy Huggins & Maxwell Shane. WITH Dana Andrews, Donna Reed, Diane Foster, Stephen Elliott, Richard Coogan, Laurence Hugo, James Westerfield, Richard Webb, Carolyn Jones, Charlotte Fletcher, Whit Bissell, Felipe Turich, Arthur Fox, Francis Mc-Donald. Years after he is falsely accused of killing his fiancée's brother, a man returns home to prove his innocence. Taut melodrama which is well acted, especially by Dana Andrews as the man trying to find the real killer.

3584 Three in the Saddle. Producers Releasing Corporation, 1945. 61 minutes B/W. D: Harry Fraser. SC: Elmer Clifton. WITH Tex Ritter, Dave O'Brien, Guy Wilkerson, Lorraine Miller, Charles King, Edward Howard, Ed Cassidy, Bud Osborne, Frank Ellis. Three Texas Rangers come to the aid of a young woman whose ranch is being sought by a land grabber. Ragged PRC "The Texas Ranger" series entry although Tex Ritter does sing a couple of fair songs.

3585 Three Men from Texas. Paramount, 1940. 54 (70) minutes B/W. D: Lesley Selander. SC: Norton S. Parker. WITH William Boyd, Russell Hayden, Andy Clyde, Morris Ankrum, Morgan Wallace, Thornton Edwards, Esther Estrella, Davison Clark, Dick Curtis, Glenn Strange, Bob Burns, Jim Corey, George Morrell, Frank McCarroll. Hoppy tries to reform outlaw California Carlson by taking him to a small town where they, along with Lucky Jenkins, are soon at odds with a criminal who is trying to steal land from its owners. A nice story and exciting climax makes this one of the best entries in the "Hopalong Cassidy" series although it is more brutal than most Hoppy films. This film introduced Andy Clyde as California Carlson.

3586 The Three Mesquiteers. Republic, 1936. 54 (61) minutes B/W. D: Ray Taylor. SC: Jack Natteford. WITH Robert Livingston, Ray Corrigan, Syd Saylor, Kay Hughes, J. P. McGowan, Frank Yaconelli, Al Bridge, Stanley Blystone, John Merton, Jean Marvey, Milburn Stone, Duke York, Allen Connor. Three cowboy pals find themselves in the middle of a feud between rival cattlemen. Fast paced initial entry in the popular and long running "The Three Mesquiteers" series.

3587 Three on the Trail. Paramount, 1936. 54 (60) minutes B/W. D: Howard Bretherton. SC: Doris Schroeder & Vernon Smith. WITH William Boyd, James Ellison, Onslow Stevens, George ("Gabby") Hayes, Muriel Evans, Claude King, William Duncan, Clara Kimball Young, Ernie Adams, Ted Adams, Lew Meehan, John St. Polis, Al Hill, Jack Rutherford, Lita Cortez, Artie Ortego, Franklyn Farnum. The Bar 20 boys oppose a ruthless saloon owner who is in cahoots with the local sheriff in cattle rustling and stage holdups. Sturdy "Hopalong Cassidy" series entry.

3588 The Three Outlaws. Associated Film Releasing, 1956. 75 minutes B/W. D: Sam Newfield. SC: Orville Hampton. WITH Neville Brand, Bruce Bennett, Alan Hale (Jr.), Jeanne Carmen, Jose Gonzales Gonzales, Rodolfo Hoyos, Robert Tafur, Bill Henry. A federal lawman is after Butch Cassidy and his gang who have gone into Mexico and are pretending to be honest citizens. Pretty dreary.

Three Rogues see **Not Exactly Gentlemen**

3589 The Three Swords of Zorro. Hispamer/ Rodes, 1963. 88 minutes Color. D: Richard

Blasco. WITH Guy Stockwell, Gloria Milland, Mikaela. In Spanish California in the 1830s Zorro's son and daughter aid him in fighting a corrupt governor. Actionful Spanish-made melodrama. Spanish title: **Las Tres Espadas del Zorro.**

3590 3:10 to Yuma. Columbia, 1957. 92 minutes B/W. D: Delmer Daves. SC: Halsted Welles. WITH Glenn Ford, Van Heflin, Felicia Farr, Leora Dana, Henry Jones, Richard Jaeckel, Robert Emhardt, Sheridan Comerate, George Mitchell, Robert Ellenstein, Ford Rainey, Barry Curtis, Jerry Hartleben. When a peaceable cowboy witnesses a holdup he tries to hold the gang leader prisoner until the arrival of a train to take him to justice. Sturdy actioner is good entertainment; Frankie Laine sings the haunting title song.

3591 Three Texas Steers. Republic, 1939. 57 minutes B/W. D: George Sherman. SC: Betty Burbridge & Stanley Roberts. WITH John Wayne, Ray Corrigan, Max Terhune, Carole Landis, Ralph Graves, Roscoe Ates, Colette Lyons, Billy Curtis, Ted Adams, Stanley Blystone, David Sharpe, Ethan Laidlaw, Lew Kelly, Dave Willock, John Merton, Ted Mapes, Naba (gorilla). Crooks sabotage a girl's circus in order to force her to sell her ranch so they can use it to build a dam to control area water supplies. Fair entry in "The Three Mesquiteers" series, but not one of the best. British title: **Danger Rides the Range.** V: NTA Home Entertainment.

3592 Three Violent People. Paramount, 1957. 100 minutes Color. D: Rudolph Mate. SC: James Edward Grant. WITH Charlton Heston, Anne Baxter, Gilbert Roland, Forrest Tucker, Bruce Bennett, Tom Tryon, Elaine Stritch, Barton MacLane, Peter Hansen, John Harmon, Ross Bagdasarian, Bobby (Robert) Blake, Raymond Greenleaf, Don Devlin, Roy Engel, Argentina Brunetti, Leo Castillo. In Texas during the Reconstruction period, an ex-Confederate and his brother try to oppose the carpetbaggers while facing a romantic triangle involving one of their wives. Okay romantic action melodrama.

3593 Three Warriors. United Artists/ Fantasy Films, 1978. 105 minutes Color. D: Keith Merrill. SC: Sy Gomberg. WITH Randy Quaid, Byron Patt, Charlie White Eagle, Lois Red Elk, McKee Redwing. A 14-year-old Indian boy leaves his mother and two sisters to learn the ways of his people and he meets a rawbone Indian agent recruit who is also trying to adapt to his new job. Overlong but fairly pleasing drama.

3594 Three Word Brand. Paramount-Artcraft, 1921. 70 minutes B/W. D-SC: Lambert Hillyer. WITH William S. Hart, Jane Novak, Gordon Russell, S. J. Bingham, George C. Pearce, Colette Forbes, Ivor McFadden, Herschel Mayall, Leo Willis. After their father is killed fighting Indians two boys grow up as strangers, one being the governor of the state while the other is a rancher opposed to a crooked water rights bill. Well produced William S. Hart silent entertainment with the star performing three roles, that of the two grown brothers and their father.

3595 Three Young Texans. 20th Century-Fox, 1954. 76 minutes Color. D: Henry Levin. SC: Gerald Drayson Adams. WITH Mitzi Gaynor, Jeffrey Hunter, Keefe Brasselle, Harvey Stephens, Dan Riss, Michael Ansara, Aaron Spelling, Morris Ankrum, Frank Wilcox, Helen Wallace, John Harmon, Alex Montoya. When outlaws try to force his father to commit a robbery, a young man commits the crime himself but cannot return the money because his friend hides it. Average oater with nothing special to offer.

3596 The Thrill Hunter. Columbia, 1933. 58 minutes B/W. D: George B. Seitz. SC: Harry O. Hoyt. WITH Buck Jones, Dorothy Revier, Ed LeSaint, Eddie Kane, Arthur Rankin, Frank LaRue, Robert Ellis, Harry Semels, Al Smith, John Ince, Alf James, Harry Todd, Willie Fung, Jim Corey, Frank Ellis, Hank Bell, Joe Ryan, Glenn Strange, Art Mix, Buddy Roosevelt, Buffalo Bill Jr. A long-winded cowboy ends up starring in a movie and eventually rounds up the remaining members of a notorious outlaw gang. Speedy actioner which pokes some fun at the genre.

3597 The Throwback. Universal, 1935. 61 minutes B/W. D: Ray Taylor. SC: Frances Guihan. WITH Buck Jones, Muriel Evans, George F. ("Gabby") Hayes, Eddie Phillips, Paul Fix, Frank LaRue, Earl Pinegree, Robert Walker, Charles K. French, Bryant Washburn, Allan Ramsay, Margaret Davis, Bobby Nelson, Mickey Martin. Fifteen years after his father was falsely accused of thievery, a man returns to find himself framed on the same charge. Buck Jones fans will go for this well scripted action melodrama.

3598 Thunder at the Border. Columbia, 1967. 98 minutes Color. D: Alfred Vohrer. SC: David De Reszke, C. B. Taylor & Harald G. Petersson. WITH Rod Cameron, Pierre Brice, Marie Versini, Harald Leipnitz, Todd Armstrong, Viktor de Kowa, Nadia Gray, Rik Battaglia, Jorg Marquard. Frontiersman Old Firehand and his blood-brother, Apache chief Winnetou, aid the settlers in a small town besieged by a gang of cutthroats. Nifty and violent West German oater with a fine performance by Rod Cameron as Old Firehand. Issued in Europe in 1966 by Rialto/Jadran-Film as **Winnetou Und Sein Freund Old Firehand** (Winnetou and His Friend Old Firehand).

Thunder Cloud see **Colt .45**

3599 Thunder in God's Country. Republic, 1951. 67 minutes B/W. D: George Blair. SC: Arthur Orloff. WITH Rex Allen, Buddy Ebsen, Mary Ellen Kay, Ian MacDonald, Paul Harvey, Harry Lauter, John Doucette, Harry V. Cheshire, John Ridgely, Frank Ferguson, Wilson Wood. An escaped convict arrives in a small town and begins taking advantage of the peaceful community until he is thwarted by a cowboy. Rex Allen fans will go for this one, with a good plot and lots of action. V: Cumberland Video.

3600 Thunder in the Desert. Republic, 1937. 60 minutes B/W. D: Sam Newfield. SC: George Plympton. WITH Bob Steele, Louise Stanley, Don Barclay, Ed Brady, Charles King, Horace Murphy, Steve Clark, Lew Meehan, Ernie Adams, Richard Cramer, Budd Buster, Sherry Tansey. Pals Bob and Rusty join an outlaw gang while searching for the man who killed Bob's uncle, the rightful owner of a ranch the gang wants. Bob Steele is great in this otherwise fair Western which has some well done comedy and even has villain Charles King as an early romantic interest for the leading lady! "Thunder" in the title refers to dynamite used to blow up waterholes.

3601 Thunder in the Pines. Screen Guild, 1948. 62 minutes B/W. D: Robert Edwards. SC: Maurice Tombragel. WITH George Reeves, Ralph Byrd, Denise Darcel, Greg McClure, Michael Whalen, Marion Martin, Lyle Talbot, Vince Barnett, Roscoe Ates, Tom Kennedy. Two rival lumberjacks put their hostilities aside when outsiders endanger their interests. Okay north woods actioner with a chance to see Denise Darcel early in her career.

3602 Thunder in the Sun. Paramount, 1959. 81 minutes Color. D-SC: Russell Rouse. WITH Susan Hayward, Jeff Chandler, Jacques Bergerac, Blanche Yurka, Carl Esmond, Fortunio Bonanova, Felix Locher, Bertrand Castelli. In 1850 a wagon train of French Basques heads to California to plant vineyards and along the way a pretty girl is romanced by two men, including the wagonmaster. The plot is not much but the overall feature is colorful and entertaining.

3603 Thunder Mountain. Fox, 1935. 68 minutes B/W. D: David Howard. SC: Dan Jarrett & Don Swift. WITH George O'Brien, Barbara Fritchie, Frances Grant, Morgan Wallace, George ("Gabby") Hayes, Ed Le Saint, Dean Benton, William N. Bailey. In the north country, a man is cheated out of his portion of a mining claim and he sets out to right the wrong. Okay George O'Brien vehicle which tends to be a bit draggy. TV title: **Roaring Mountain.**

3604 Thunder Mountain. RKO Radio, 1947. 60 minutes B/W. D: Lew Landers. SC: Norman Houston. WITH Tim Holt, Martha Hyer, Richard Martin, Steve Brodie, Richard Powers, Virginia Owen, Harry Woods, Jason Robards, Robert Clarke, Harry Harvey. Returning home from college a young man finds himself in the middle of a feud instigated by a dishonest saloon owner and his cohort, the sheriff. Supposedly based on the Zane Grey novel, this film has little to do with the famous author but it is a rip-roaring good actioner.

Thunder Mountain (1964) see **The Shepherd of the Hills** (1964)

3605 A Thunder of Drums. Metro-Goldwyn-Mayer, 1961. 97 minutes Color. D: Joseph M. Newman. SC: James Warner Bellah. WITH Richard Boone, George Hamilton, Luana Patten, Arthur O'Connell, Charles Bronson, Richard Chamberlain, Duane Eddy, James Douglas, Tammy Marihugh, Carole Wells, Slim Pickens, Clem Harvey, Casey Tibbs, Irene Tedrow, Marjorie Bennett, J. Edward McKinley. A young lieutenant is assigned to a remote cavalry post where he has troubles with his tough captain. Fans of the performers in this melodrama should enjoy it although it is fairly average.

3606 Thunder over Arizona. Republic, 1956. 75 minutes Color. D: Joseph Kane. SC: Sloan Nibley. WITH Skip Homeier,

Kristine Miller, George Macready, Wallace Ford, Jack Elam, Gregory Walcott, Nacho Galindo, George Keymas, John Doucette, John Compton, Bob Swain, Julian Rivero, Francis McDonald. When a rich silver strike is discovered a crooked politician tries to get control of the mine. Well made and entertaining melodrama.

3607 Thunder over Texas. Beacon, 1934. 61 minutes B/W. D: John Warner (Edgar G. Ulmer). SC: Eddie Granemann. WITH Guinn Williams, Marion Shilling, Helen Westcott, Richard Botiller, Philo McCullough, Ben Corbett, Bob McKenzie, Victor Potel, Jack Kirk, Hank Bell, Tiny Skelton, Claude Peyton. A girl, whose father was murdered over valuable maps, is kidnapped by outlaws after the treasure maps but is rescued by a cowboy. Actionful Guinn "Big Boy" Williams series vehicle directed by Edgar G. Ulmer under a pseudonym with the original story by Ulmer's wife Shirley.

3608 Thunder over the Plains. Warner Brothers, 1953. 82 minutes Color. D: Andre De Toth. SC: Russell Hughes. WITH Randolph Scott, Phyllis Kirk, Lex Barker, Henry Hull, Elisha Cook Jr., Charles McGraw, Hugh Sanders, James Brown, Lane Chandler, Fess Parker, Richard Benjamin, Trevor Bardette, Mark Dana, Frank Matts, Steve Darrell, Earle Hodgins, Jack Woody, John Cason, Monte Montague, Carl Andre, Charles Horvath, John McKee, Gail Robinson, Boyd "Red" Morgan, Gayle Kellogg. In post-Civil War Texas an Army officer is assigned the duty of bringing in a bandit who has been terrorizing carpetbaggers although the soldier sympathizes with him. Pretty good Randolph Scott actioner.

3609 Thunder over the Prairie. Columbia, 1941. 60 minutes B/W. D: Lambert Hillyer. SC: Betty Burbridge. WITH Charles Starrett, Eileen O'Hearn, Cliff Edwards, Ca(r)l Shrum & His Rhythm Rangers, Stanley Brown, David Sharpe, Joe McGuinn, Donald Curtis, Ted Adams, Jack Rockwell, Budd Buster, Horace B. Carpenter, Danny Mummert. A doctor comes to the aid of an Indian medical student falsely accused of murder and dynamiting a dam. Okay Charles Starrett series entry.

3610 Thunder Pass. Lippert, 1954. 80 minutes B/W. D: Frank McDonald. SC: Tom Hubbard & Fred Eggers. WITH Dane Clark, Dorothy Patrick, Andy Devine, Raymond Burr, John Carradine, Mary Ellen Kay, Raymond Hatton, Nestor Paiva, Charles Fredericks, Tom Hubbard. A cavalry captain has two days in which to lead settlers out of Indian territory but they are soon surrounded by Indians supported by a gun runner. Standard oater with an average amount of excitement and sporting a good cast.

3611 Thunder River Feud. Monogram, 1942. 58 minutes B/W. D: S. Roy Luby. SC: John Vlahos & Earle Snell. WITH Ray Corrigan, John King, Max Terhune, Jan Wiley, Jack Holmes, Rick Anderson, Carleton Young, George Chesebro, Carl Mathews, Budd Buster, Ted Mapes, Steve Clark, Richard Cramer. The Range Busters follow a pretty girl to her Wyoming ranch and get mixed up with a feud being instigated by a crook and his pals. Fans of "The Range Busters" may like it but otherwise this feature is on the poor side, both in plot and execution. V: Cassette Express.

3612 Thunder Town. Producers Releasing Corporation, 1946. 57 minutes B/W. D: Harry Fraser. SC: James Oliver. WITH Bob Steele, Ellen Hall, Syd Saylor, Bud Geary, Charles King, Edward Howard, Steve Clark, Bud Osborne, Jimmie Aubrey, Pascale Perry. Released from prison after serving time when framed for a crime, a man returns home to save the girl he loves from one of the men responsible for sending him to jail. While nothing to brag about, this Bob Steele vehicle (from his final starring series) should please the star's legion of fans.

3613 Thunder Trail. Paramount, 1937. 58 minutes B/W. D: Charles Barton. SC: Robert Yost & Stuart Anthony. WITH Gilbert Roland, Charles Bickford, Marsha Hunt, J. Carrol Naish, James Craig, William Duncan, Billy Lee, Monte Blue, Gene Reynolds, Barlowe Borland. Two young brothers are separated by outlaws and fifteen years later one of them rides the desperado trail until he learns who was really behind the separation. Outstanding "B" adaptation of Zane Grey's Arizona Ames; action packed and very entertaining.

3614 Thunderbolt. Regal, 1935. 55 minutes B/W. D: Stuart Paton. SC: Jack Gevne. WITH Kane Richmond, Fay McKenzie, Lobo (dog), Bobby Nelson, Hank Bell, Frank Hagney, Barney Furey, Lafe McKee, Frank Ellis, George Morrell, Wally West, Jack Kirk, Blackie Whiteford, Bob Burns. A boy and his dog try to stop a murderous outlaw gang whose leader is trying to force a pretty girl to marry him. Unbelievably bad independent melodrama from producer Sherman S. Krellberg.

3615 Thunderbolt's Tracks. Rayart, 1927. 55 minutes B/W. D: J. P. McGowan. SC: Bennett Cohen. WITH Jack Perrin, Pauline Curley, Jack Henderson, Billy Lamar, Harry Tenbrook, Ethan Laidlaw, Ruth Royce. Two Marines find the family of a dead friend in Mexico and there they are duped into buying a worthless ranch. Standard independent silent oater.

Thundergap Outlaws see **Bad Men of Thunder Gap**

3616 Thunderhead, Son of Flicka. 20th Century-Fox, 1945. 78 minutes Color. D: Louis King. SC: Dwight Cummings & Dorothy Yost. WITH Preston Foster, Rita Johnson, Roddy McDowall, James Bell, Diana Hale, Carleton Young, Ralph Sanford, Robert Filmer, Alan Bridge. A young boy trains the colt of his own horse and wants to make him a show horse champion. Colorful sequel to **My Friend Flicka** (q.v.).

3617 Thunderhoof. Columbia, 1948. 77 minutes B/W. D: Phil Karlson. SC: Hal Smith. WITH Preston Foster, Mary Stuart, William Bishop. Three people, two men and a girl, trek into Mexico in search of a wild stallion. Compact cast and good scenic values make this pretty fair entertainment.

3618 Thundering Caravans. Republic, 1952. 54 minutes B/W. D: Harry Keller. SC: M. Coates Webster. WITH Allan "Rocky" Lane, Eddy Waller, Mona Knox, Roy Barcroft, Isabel Randolph, Richard Crane, Bill Henry, Edward Clark, Pierre Watkin, Stanley Andrews, Boyd "Red" Morgan. When valuable ore shipments get hijacked a U. S. marshal is called in to investigate. Another actionful entry in Allan Lane's Republic series.

3619 Thundering Frontier. Columbia, 1940. 57 minutes B/W. D: D. Ross Lederman. SC: Paul Franklin. WITH Charles Starrett, Irish Meredith, Bob Nolan & The Sons of the Pioneers, Carl Stockdale, Fred Burns, John Dilson, Alex Callam, Ray Bennett, Blackie Whiteford, John Tyrell, Francis Walker. A cowboy aids a girl whose contractor father's business is being sabotaged. Poor Charles Starrett vehicle with too much music.

3620 Thundering Gunslingers. Producers Releasing Corporation, 1944. 61 minutes

B/W. D: Sam Newfield. SC: Fred Myton. WITH Buster Crabbe, Al St. John, Frances Gladwin, George Chesebro, Karl Hackett, Charles King, Jack Ingram, Kermit Maynard, Budd Buster. When Billy Carson's uncle is murdered he and Fuzzy try to find the real killer but when a suspect is also murdered Billy gets the blame. Average "Billy Carson" series entry.

3621 The Thundering Herd. Paramount, 1933. 62 minutes B/W. D: Henry Hathaway. SC: Jack Cunningham & Mary Flannery. WITH Randolph Scott, Judith Allen, Larry "Buster" Crabbe, Noah Beery, Raymond Hatton, Blanche Frederici, Harry Carey, Monte Blue, Barton MacLane, Alan Bridge, Dick Rush, Frank Rice, Buck Connors, Charles McMurphy. A buffalo hunter joins a wagon train heading West and tries to help them from attacking Indians who have been incited to war by the needless slaughter of the buffalo. Programmer remake of the 1925 Paramount feature starring Jack Holt and Lois Wilson, this version is hurt by too much stock footage from the original. Noah Beery (repeating his role from the original) is great as the lecherous villain Randall Jett and he is equaled by Blanche Frederici as his vengeful wife. Reissued as **Buffalo Stampede.** V: Thunderbird.

3622 Thundering Hoofs. Films Booking Office (FBO), 1924. 5 reels B/W. D: Al Rogell. SC: Marion Jackson. WITH Fred Thompson, Ann May, Charles Mailes, Fred Huntley, Charles De Revenna, Carrie Clark Ward, William Lowery, Silver King (horse). A rancher's son wins a prize horse from a man who mistreated him and then thwarts the man's plans to steal money from a Spanish land baron. Good photography, lots of action and nice comedy relief highlight this silent Fred Thompson film in which his horse, Silver King, plays a big part in the plot. A very good film.

3623 Thundering Hoofs. RKO Radio, 1942. 61 minutes B/W. D: Lesley Selander. SC: Paul Franklin. WITH Tim Holt, Ray Whitley, Luana Walters, Lee "Lasses" White, Fred Scott, Archie Twitchell, Gordon DeMain, Charles Phipps, Monte Montague, Joe Bernard, Frank Fanning, Frank Ellis, Robert Kortman, Lloyd Ingraham. A young man would rather be a rancher than run his father's stage line and he comes to the aid of a rival stage operator when his father's business is threatened by outlaws. Okay Tim Holt series entry which rates no better than average.

3624 The Thundering Trail. Western Adventure, 1951. 55 minutes B/W. D: Ron Ormond. SC: Alexander White. WITH Lash LaRue, Al St. John, Sally Anglim, Archie Twitchell, Ray Bennett, Reed Howes, Bud Osborne, John Cason, Clarke Stevens, Jimmie Martin, Mary Lou Webb, Sue Hussey, Ray Broome, Cliff Taylor. Marshals Lash and Fuzzy are assigned to protect the new territorial governor whose life is threatened by an outlaw gang. Tacky production with long, boring sequences of little action; lots of footage from previous Lash LaRue Screen Guild efforts.

3625 Thundering Trails. Republic, 1943. 56 minutes B/W. D: John English. SC: Norman S. Hall & Robert Yost. WITH Bob Steele, Tom Tyler, Jimmie Dodd, Nell O'Day, Vince Barnett, Karl Hackett, Sam Flint, Charles Miller, John James, Forrest Taylor, Ed Cassidy, Forbes Murray, Reed Howes, Bud Geary, Budd Buster, Lane Bradford, Cactus Mack, Eddie Parker, Al Taylor, Art Mix, Jack O'Shea. The Three Mesquiteers come to the aid of a Texas Ranger whose brother is hooked up with a gang of outlaws. There is lots of action in this fast paced entry in "The Three Mesquiteers" series.

3626 The Thundering West. Columbia, 1939. 58 minutes B/W. D: Sam Nelson. SC: Bennett Cohen. WITH Charles Starrett, Iris Meredith, Bob Nolan & The Sons of the Pioneers, Hal Taliaferro, Dick Curtis, Hank Bell, Ed LeSaint, Robert Fiske, Edmund Cobb, Slim Whitaker, Blackie Whiteford, Art Mix, Steve Clark, Fred Burns, Ed Peil, Art Dillard. A reformed outlaw becomes the sheriff of a small town but soon is plagued by his former gang who tries to blackmail him. Pretty fair remake of Buck Jones' **The Man Trailer** (q.v.).

3627 A Ticket to Tomahawk. 20th Century-Fox, 1950. 90 minutes Color. D: Richard Sale. SC: Mary Loos & Richard Sale. WITH Dan Dailey, Anne Baxter, Rory Calhoun, Walter Brennan, Charles Kemper, Connie Gilchrist, Arthur Hunnicutt, Will Wright, Chief Yowlachie, Victor Sen Yung, Mauritz Hugo, Raymond Greenleaf, Harry Carter, Harry Seymour, Robert Adler, Chief Thundercloud, Marion Marshall, Joyce McKenzie, Marilyn Monroe. Upon his arrival in a small Western town, a drummer gets caught in the middle of a fight for a railroad franchise. Zesty musical comedy.

3628 Tickle Me. Allied Artists, 1965. 90 minutes Color. D: Norma Taurog. SC: Elwood Ullman & Edward Bernds. WITH Elvis Presley, Julie Adams, Jocelyn Lane, Jack Mullaney, Merry Anders, Connie Gilchrist, Edward Faulkner, Bill Williams, Louis Elias, John Dennis, Laurie Benton, Linda Rogers, Ann Morell, Lilyna Chauvin, Jean Ingram, Francine York, Eve Bruce, Jackie Russell, Angela Greene, Peggy Ward, Dorian Brown, Inez Pedroza, Grady Sutton, Dorothy Conrad, Barbara Werle, Allison Hayes. A rodeo star seeks refuge as a wrangler at a dude ranch for women. The songs are okay but the plot is not in this Elvis Presley vehicle.

3629 A Tiger Walks. Buena Vista, 1964. 91 minutes Color. D: Norman Tokar. SC: Lowell S. Hawley. WITH Brian Keith, Vera Miles, Pamela Franklin, Sabu, Kevin Corcoran, Peter Brown, Edward Andrews, Una Merkel, Arthur Hunnicutt, Connie Gilchrist, Theodore Marcuse, Merry Anders, Frank McHugh, Doodles Weaver, Frank Aletter, Jack Albertson, Donald May, Robert Shayne, Hal (Harold) Peary, Ivor Francis, Michael Fox, Richard O'Brien. A tiger escapes from a circus truck and panics a small town where the sheriff's daughter tries to save the animal. Often overlooked, but well done, Disney feature.

3630 Timber. Universal, 1942. 60 minutes B/W. D: Christy Cabanne. SC: Griffin Jay. WITH Leo Carrillo, Andy Devine, Dan Dailey (Jr.), Marjorie Lord, Edmund MacDonald, Wade Boteler, Nestor Paiva, Paul E. Burns, James Seay, Jean Phillips, William Hall, Walter Sande. When sabotage takes place at a lumber camp two FBI agents are called into the case. Standard Universal programmer.

3631 Timber Fury. Eagle Lion, 1950. 63 minutes B/W. D: Bernard B. Ray. SC: Michael Hanson. WITH David Bruce, Laura Lee, Nichle Di Bruno, Sam Flint, George Slocum, Lee Phelps, Gilbert Gryl, Paul Hoffman, Spencer Chan. In the north woods, a young girl and her father fight crooks who try to steal their valuable timber. Low budget actioner.

3632 Timber Queen. Paramount, 1944. 66 minutes B/W. D: Frank McDonald. SC: Maxwell Shane & Edward T. Lowe. WITH Richard Arlen, Mary Beth Hughes, June Havoc, Sheldon Leonard, George E. Stone, Dick Purcell, Tony Hughes,

Edmund McDonald, Horace McMahon. When crooks threaten to steal the timberland of his dead buddy's widow, an ex-pilot tries to help her save the business. Fairly flavorful action melodrama.

3633 Timber Stampede. RKO Radio, 1939. 59 minutes B/W. D: David Howard. SC: Morton Grant. WITH George O'Brien, Marjorie Reynolds, Chill Wills, Morgan Wallace, Guy Usher, Earl Dwire, Frank Hagney, Monte Montague, Robert Fiske, Bob Burns, Tom London, Billy Benedict, Bud Osborne, Robert Kortman, Ben Corbett, Cactus Mack, Hank Worden, Elmo Lincoln. A cattleman opposes the actions of a lumber baron and the head of a railroad to build a road through his area. Okay George O'Brien vehicle but not as good as some of his other efforts.

3634 Timber Terrors. Stage & Screen, 1935. 50 minutes B/W. D-SC: Robert Emmett (Tansey). WITH John Preston, Marla Bratton, William Desmond, James Sheridan, Tiny Skelton, Fred Parker, Tom London, Tex Jones, Captain (dog), Dynamite (horse). When his partner is brutally murdered, a Mountie sets out to bring in the killers. Bottom rung actioner.

3635 The Timber Trail. Republic, 1948. 67 minutes Color. D: Philip Ford. SC: Bob Williams. WITH Monte Hale, Lynne Roberts, James Burke, Roy Barcroft, Foy Willing & The Riders of the Purple Sage, Francis Ford, Robert Emmett Keane, Steve Darrell, Fred Graham, Wade Crosby, Eddie Acuff. A Mountie comes to the aid of a girl whose property is prized by a power-mad gunslinger. Colorful Monte Hale vehicle.

3636 Timber Tramps. Howco-International, 1975. 90 minutes Color. D: Tay Garnett. SC: Chuck Keen. WITH Claude Akins, Joseph Cotten, Patricia Medina, Cesar Romero, Tab Hunter, Leon Ames, Eve Brent, Rosie (Roosevelt) Grier, Bob Easton, Stash Clemmens, Hal Baylor, Shug Fisher. Timbermen fight the elements and crooks in the Alaskan wilderness to complete a lumber contract. Colorful actioner filmed in Alaska in 1972 by Alaska Pictures.

3637 Timber War. Ambassador, 1935. 58 minutes B/W. D: Sam Newfield. SC: Joseph O'Donnell. WITH Kermit Maynard, Lucille Lund, Lawrence Gray, Robert Warwick, Lloyd Ingraham, Wheeler Oakman, Roger Williams, George Morrell, James Pierce, Patricia Royal. At a remote lumber camp a Mountie tries to make a man out of a playboy as he also battles timber thieves. A rather weak effort in Kermit Maynard's generally good Ambassador series.

3638 Timberjack. Republic, 1955. 94 minutes Color. D: Joe (Joseph) Kane. SC: Allen Rivkin. WITH Sterling Hayden, Vera Ralston, David Brian, Adolphe Menjou, Hoagy Carmichael, Chill Wills, Jim Davis, Howard Petrie, Ian Macdonald, Wally Cassell, Elisha Cook Jr., Karl Davis, Tex Terry, George Marshall. A ruthless land baron tries to cheat a man out of the timberland he inherited but the man's cause is aided by a saloon singer. Fair Republic actioner, but not up to the studio's usual standards.

3639 A Time for Dying. Corinth Films, 1982. 73 minutes Color. D-SC: Budd Boetticher. WITH Richard Lapp, Anne Randall, Bob Random, Victor Jory, Audie Murphy. A young man trained by his father to be a fast gun travels through the West and saves a girl from a prostitution ring, only to be forced to marry her by Judge Roy Bean. Filmed in 1969 and produced by Audie Murphy (who does an excellent cameo as Jesse James), this obscure oater got some brief release in 1982 and is an interesting feature for Budd Boetticher followers; Victor Jory is entertainingly hammy as Judge Roy Bean.

3640 A Time for Every Season. Gold Key, 1972. 95 minutes Color. A man and a young boy become the first people to explore the awesome Alaskan Tundra, marveling at its dangers and beauty. Picturesque documentary.

3641 A Time for Killing. Columbia, 1967. 88 minutes B/W. D: Phil Karlson. SC: Halsted Welles. WITH Glenn Ford, Inger Stevens, George Hamilton, Kenneth Tobey, Paul Petersen, Timothy Carey, Richard X. Slattery, Harrison J. Ford, Kay E. Kuter, Dick Miller, Emile Meyer, Marshall Reed, Max Baer (Jr.), Todd Armstrong, (Harry) Dean Stanton, Charlie Briggs, James Davidson. Near the end of the Civil War several Confederate prisoners escape from their Union captors and take the fiancée of the Union captain as their hostage. Average actioner. Alternate title: **The Long Ride Home.**

3642 Timerider. Manson-International, 1983. 93 minutes Color. D: William Dear.

SC: William Dear & Michael Nesbitt. WITH Fred Ward, Belinda Bauer, Peter Coyote, L. Q. Jones, Ed Lauter, Tracey Walker, Bruce Gordon, Richard Masur, Chris Mulkey. While competing in a cross country bike contest, a rider gets caught in a time transference experiment and is sent back to the West of the 1870s where he gets involved with outlaws. Fairly interesting combination of the sci-fi and Western genres, but it could have been better.

3643 The Tin Star. Paramount, 1957. 93 minutes B/W. D: Anthony Mann. SC: Dudley Nichols. WITH Henry Fonda, Anthony Perkins, Betsy Palmer, Michael Ray, Neville Brand, John McIntire, Mary Webster, Peter Baldwin, Richard Shannon, Lee Van Cleef, James Bell, Howard Petrie, Russell Simpson, Hal K. Dawson, Jack Kenney, Mickey Finn, Frank Cady, Frank Kensaton, Frank Cordell, Frank McGrath, Tim Sullivan, Allan Gettel. A bounty hunter arrives in a small town with a dead outlaw and finds the inexperienced sheriff unable to cope with an outlaw gang terrorizing the community. Solidly entertaining melodrama.

3644 The Tioga Kid. Eagle Lion, 1948. 54 minutes B/W. D: Ray Taylor. SC: Ed Earl Repp. WITH Eddie Dean, Roscoe Ates, Jennifer Holt, Andy Parker & The Plainsmen, Dennis Moore, Lee Bennett, Terry Frost, William Fawcett, Eddie Parker, Bob Woodward, Tex Palmer. A Texas Ranger pretends to be a notorious outlaw and he tries to horn in on a gang's operations in order to bring them to justice. Good Eddie Dean series vehicle; well made.

3645 The Titled Tenderfoot. Allied Artists, 1955. 52 minutes B/W. D: Frank McDonald. SC: Bill Raynor & Maurice Tombragel. WITH Guy Madison, Andy Devine, Jeanne Cagney, Clayton Moore, Marshall Reed, I. Stanford Jolley, Dick Cavendish, Hal Gerard, James Bell, Jack Reynolds, Gerald O. Smith, Park MacGregor, Russ Whiteman, Guy Teague. Wild Bill Hickok and his deputy Jingles oppose a gang of fur thieves in the north woods. Adequate programmer made up of two episodes of the popular "Wild Bill Hickok" (Syndicated, 1952-55).

3646 To Find A Rainbow. American National Enterprises/Gold Key, 1972. 90 minutes Color. D-SC: The Staff of American National Enterprises. WITH Lawrence Dobkin (narrator); Jerry, Lucille, Jeff & Jenny Romney; Jerry, Angela, Donna, David & Danny Pimm. A real life Utah family explores the Teton Mountains of Wyoming and Bryce Canyon, the stomping grounds of Butch Cassidy and his gang. Pleasant enough family-oriented documentary with some nice footage of Zion National Park.

3647 To the Last Man. Paramount, 1933. 70 minutes B/W. D: Henry Hathaway. SC: Jack Cunningham, from the novel by Zane Grey. WITH Randolph Scott, Esther Ralston, Noah Beery, Jack LaRue, Larry "Buster" Crabbe, Fuzzy Knight, Barton MacLane, Gail Patrick, Muriel Kirkland, Egon Brecher, James Eagles, Eugenie Besserer, Harlan Knight, Shirley Temple, John Carradine. The story of a family feud which extended from Kentucky to Nevada, is excellently told in this well-made, excellent drama. Among the highlights are Esther Ralston's raw sex appeal and the murder of a family member, played by Buster Crabbe. Highly recommended. V: Video Connection.

3648 Today We Kill, Tomorrow We Die! Cinerama, 1971. 95 minutes Color. D: Tonino Cervi. SC: Dario Argento. WITH Montgomery Ford, Bud Spencer, Tatsuya Nakadai, William Berger, Wayde Preston, Stanley Gordon. After an outlaw falsely frames a rancher and sends him to prison, the man gets out and hires mercenaries to get revenge for him. Another in the long line of violent Westerns from Italy; average.

3649 Toklat. Sun International, 1971. 100 minutes Color. D: Robert W. Davison. SC: Hugh Hogle. WITH Leon Ames. A sheepherder who has watched a bear grow from a cub, must hunt the animal when he thinks it was responsible for his brother's death. Typical family-oriented outdoor adventure film of the 1970s, shy on plot but heavy on beautiful scenery.

3650 The Toll Gate. Paramount-Artcraft, 1920. 55 minutes B/W. D: Lambert Hillyer. SC: Lambert Hillyer & William S. Hart. WITH William S. Hart, Anna Q. Nilsson, Jack Richardson, Joseph Singleton, Richard Headrick. An outlaw gang leader finds one of his men has betrayed the gang for a reward and he follows him to a small town where he burns down the man's cantina and is chased by both the crook and the law but is saved by a woman whose small child he has rescued. William S. Hart wrote the story on which this sombre, but very entertaining, silent feature was based. V: Cassette Express, Classic Video Cinema Collectors Club.

3651 Toll of the Desert. Commodore, 1935. 55 minutes B/W. D: Lester Williams (William Berke). SC: Miller Easton. WITH Fred Kohler Jr., Betty Mack, Tom London, Earl Dwire, Ted Adams, Ed Cassidy, Roger Williams, George Chesebro, Billy Stevens, John Elliott, Ace Cain, Blackie Whiteford, Blackjack Ward, Iron Eyes Cody, Herman Hack, Budd Buster. A young lawman is forced to hunt down the outlaw whose personal code he has always admired, unaware the man is really his father. Dandy little actioner.

3652 Tom Horn. Warner Brothers, 1980. 97 minutes Color. D: William Wiard. SC: Thomas McGuane & Bud Shrake. WITH Steve McQueen, Linda Evans, Richard Farnsworth, Billy Green Bush, Slim Pickens, Peter Canon, Elisha Cook, Roy Jenson, James Kline, Geoffrey Lewis, Harry Northup, Steve Oliver. Tom Horn, the scout who captured Geronimo, is a drifter hired by a group of ranchers to stop cattle rustlers and ends up being framed on a murder charge. Slow moving biopic, not as good as the TV movie **Mr. Horn** (q.v.). V: Warner Home Video.

3653 Tomahawk. Universal-International, 1951. 82 minutes Color. D: George Sherman. SC: Silvia Richards & Maurice Geraghty. WITH Van Heflin, Yvonne De Carlo, Preston Foster, Jack Oakie, Alex Nicol, Tom Tully, Ann Doran, Rock Hudson, Susan Cabot, Arthur Space, Stuart Randall, John Peters, Russell Conway, Ray Montgomery, David Sharpe, David H. Miller, John War Eagle, Regis Toomey, Sheila Darcey, Chief American Horse, Chief Bad Bear. Scout Jim Bridger tries to avoid violence when the government fails to heed his warnings of not letting settlers in Sioux Indian territory. Weak plot detracts from the cast and use of color in this "A" drama. British title: **Battle of Powder River.**

3654 Tomboy and the Champ. Universal-International, 1962. 77 minutes Color. D: Francis D. Lyon. SC: Virginia M. Cooke. WITH Candy Moore, Ben Johnson, Christine Smith, Jess Kirkpatrick, Jesse White, Casey Tibbs, Jerry Naill. A young girl raises a calf until it is grown and wins first prize at a cattle show and then realizes he will be killed. Standard programmer for the family trade.

3655 Tombstone Canyon. World Wide, 1932. 62 minutes B/W. D: Alan James. SC: Claude Rister & Earle Snell. WITH Ken Maynard, Cecilia Parker, Sheldon

Lewis, Frank Brownlee, Bob Burns, George Gerring, Lafe McKee, Jack Clifford, Ed Peil Sr., George Chesebro, Jack Kirk, Merrill McCormack, Bud McClure. A cowboy, looking into the secrecy behind his parentage, comes to an area being terrorized by a mysterious hooded phantom. Actionful Ken Maynard vehicle benefitting from the use of the mystery angle in its interesting plot.

3656 Tombstone Terror. Supreme, 1935. 55 minutes B/W. D-SC: Robert North Bradbury. WITH Bob Steele, Kay McCoy, John Elliott, George ("Gabby") Hayes, Earl Dwire, Hortense Petro, Ann Howard, Frank McCarroll, Artie Ortego, George Morrell, Herman Hack, Nancy DeShon. A young cowboy is mistaken for an outlaw and tries to prove his rightful identity. Average Bob Steele vehicle, for producer A. W. Hackel, which means lots of action and good entertainment for his fans.

3657 Tombstone, the Town Too Tough to Die. Paramount, 1942. 80 minutes B/W. D: William McGann. SC: Albert Shelby Le Vino & Edward E. Paramore. WITH Richard Dix, Kent Taylor, Frances Gifford, Don Castle, Edgar Buchanan, Clem Bevans, Victor Jory, Rex Bell, Charles Halton, Harvey Stephens, Beryl Wallace, Chris-Pin Martin, Jack Rockwell, Charles Stevens, Hal Taliaferro, Wallis Clark, Paul Sutton, Dick Curtis, Charles Middleton, Don Curtis. When a gunfight accidentally results in the killing of a child, Wyatt Earp agrees to become the sheriff of Tombstone and clean up the town. Another retelling of the Wyatt Earp saga, no more historically accurate than the others but worth watching.

3658 Tonka. Buena Vista, 1958. 97 minutes Color. D: Lewis R. Foster. SC: Lewis R. Foster & Lillie Hayward. WITH Sal Mineo, Philip Carey, Jerome Courtland, Rafael Campos, H. M. Wynant, Joy Page, Britt Lomond, Herbert Rudley, Sydney Smith, John War Eagle, Gregg Martell, Slim Pickens, Robert "Buzz" Henry. A young Indian brave captures and tames a wild horse but the animal is claimed by his cruel cousin and is eventually sold to the cavalry. Fairly interesting Walt Disney film which evolves into a tepid retelling of the Battle of the Little Big Horn. TV title: **A Horse Called Comanche.**

3659 Tonto Basin Outlaws. Monogram, 1941. 60 minutes B/W. D: S. Roy Luby. SC: John Vlahos. WITH Ray Corrigan,

John King, Max Terhune, Tristram Coffin, Jan Wiley, Ted Mapes, Art Fowler, Rex Lease, Reed Howes, Carl Mathews, Budd Buster, Ed Peil Sr., Tex Palmer, Jim Corey, Hank Bell, Denver Dixon. During the Spanish-American War, the Range Busters are assigned to find rustlers in Montana stealing cattle contracted to feed government troops. Standard entry in "The Range Busters" series. V: Video Connection.

3660 The Tonto Kid. Resolute, 1934. 61 minutes B/W. D: Harry Fraser. SC: Harry C. (Fraser) Crist. WITH Rex Bell, Ruth Mix, Buzz Barton, Theodore Lorch, Joseph Girard, Barbara Roberts, Jack Rockwell, Murdock McQuarrie, Bert Lindsley, Jane Keckley, Stella Adams, Bud Pope. A crooked lawyer wants a man's ranch and he blames a young man for his shooting and gets a circus performer to pose as the dying man's missing daughter. Poor actioner, the first of a quartet of films starring Rex Bell, Ruth Mix and Buzz Barton. V: Thunderbird.

3661 Too Much Beef. First Divisiion/Grand National, 1936. 66 minutes B/W. D: Robert Hill. SC: Rock Hawley (Robert Hill). WITH Rex Bell, Connie Bergen, Forrest Taylor, Lloyd Ingraham, Jimmie Aubrey, Jack Cowell, Peggy O'Connell, Horace Murphy, George Ball, Fred Burns, Steve Clark, Jack Kirk, Denny Meadows (Dennis Moore), Frank Ellis. Crooks are after a rancher's land because it is in the path of a railroad and a cowboy aids the cattleman in saving his ranch from them. Rex Bell's fans should like this fairly interesting outing from his series for producers Max and Arthur Alexander.

3662 Top Gun. United Artists, 1955. 73 minutes B/W. D: Ray Nazarro. SC: Richard Schayer & Steve Fisher. WITH Sterling Hayden, William Bishop, Karin Booth, James Millican, Regis Toomey, Hugh Sanders, John Dehner, Rod Taylor, Denver Pyle, William Phillips, Richard Reeves. A man is cleared of a murder charge and ends up being elected the town's sheriff and the job brings about a change in his character. More than passable melodrama.

3663 Topeka. Allied Artists, 1953. 60 (69) minutes B/W. D: Thomas Carr. SC: Milton Raison. WITH Bill Elliott, Phyllis Coates, Rick Vallin, Fuzzy Knight, John James, Denver Pyle, Dick Crockett, Harry Lauter, Dale Van Sickel, Ted Mapes, Henry Rowland, Edward Clark. An outlaw becomes sheriff of a lawless town and his former gang members aid him in bringing peace. Well done little actioner with a strong script and performances.

3664 Topeka Terror. Republic, 1945. 55 minutes B/W. D: Howard Bretherton. SC: Patricia Harper & Norman S. Hall. WITH Allan Lane, Linda Stirling, Twinkle Watts, Roy Barcroft, Earle Hodgins, Bud Geary, Frank Jacquet, Jack Kirk, Tom London, Eva Novak, Hank Bell, Robert Wilke, Monte Hale, Jess Cavan, Fred Graham. On the trail of outlaws, a special investigator takes on the guise of a vagabond cowboy in order to conceal his identity. Typically fine actionful Republic "B" entry.

3665 The Torch. Eagle Lion, 1950. 90 minutes B/W. D: Emilio Fernandez. SC: Inigo de Martino Noriega & Emilio Fernandez. WITH Paulette Goddard, Pedro Armendariz, Gilbert Roland, Walter Reed, Julio Villareal, Carlos Musquiz, Margarito Luna, Jose Torvay, Garcia Pena, Antonio Kaneem. In Mexico a small town is captured by a rebel leader and his army and the leader falls in love with the pretty daughter of a nobleman. Fairly interesting remake of director Emilio Fernandez's 1946 Mexican feature **Enamorada.**

3666 A Tornado in the Saddle. Columbia, 1942. 59 minutes B/W. D: William Berke. SC: Charles Francis Royal. WITH Russell Hayden, Bob Wills & His Texas Playboys, Dub Taylor, Alma Carroll, Tristram Coffin, Don Curtis, Jack Baxley, Tex Cooper, John Merton, Ted Mapes, Blackie Whiteford, Art Mix, Carl Sepulveda, Jack Kirk, Jack Evans, George Morrell. A new lawman is at odds with a crooked saloon keeper who tries to steal a gold claim. Threadbare oater with only asset being Wills and the boys performing "Dusty Skies."

3667 Tornado Range. Eagle Lion, 1948. 56 minutes B/W. D: Ray Taylor. SC: William Lively. WITH Eddie Dean, Roscoe Ates, Jennifer Holt, Andy Parker & The Plainsmen, George Chesebro, Brad Slavin, Marshall Reed, Terry Frost, Lane Bradford, Russell Arms, Steve Clark, Hank Bell, Jack Hendricks, Ray Jones. The U. S. Land Office assigns an agent to stop warfare between ranchers and homesteaders. Minor league Eddie Dean musical.

3668 Tough Assignment. Lippert, 1949. 66 minutes B/W. D: Willliam Beaudine.

SC: Carl K. Hittleman. WITH Don Barry, Marjorie Steele, Steve Brodie, Marc Lawrence, Sid Melton, Ben Welden, Iris Adrian, Michael Whalen, Fred Kohler Jr., Dewey Robinson, J. Farrell MacDonald, John Cason, Frank Richards, Stanley Andrews, Leander de Cordova, Stanley Price, Gayle Kellogg, Hugh Simpson. When an outlaw gang forces meat suppliers to buy an inferior product a newspaper reporter and his bride go after them. Fairly efficient actioner with good direction; produced by Don Barry's company.

3669 The Tougher They Come. Columbia, 1950. 69 minutes B/W. D: Ray Nazarro. SC: George Bricker. WITH Wayne Morris, Preston Foster, Kay Buckley, William Bishop, Frank McHugh, Joseph Crehan, Mary Castle, Frank O'Connor, Al Thompson, Al Bridge. Attempts by a lumberjack to work a track of forest land he has inherited are foiled by a gang of timber thieves. Standard northwoods programmer from producer Wallace MacDonald.

3670 Toughest Gun in Tombstone. United Artists, 1958. 72 minutes B/W. D: Earl Bellamy. SC: Orville Hampton. WITH George Montgomery, Beverly Tyler, Jim Davis, Don Beddoe, Scott Morrow, Harry Lauter, Charles Wagenheim, Jack Kenney, John Merrick, Al Wyatt, Lane Bradford, Gregg Barton, Tex Terry, Hank Worden, Rodolfo Hoyos, Alex Montoya, Rico Alaniz, Jack Carr, William Forrest, Harry Strang, Mary Newton, Joey Ray, Gerald Milton. A Texas Ranger captain pretends to be an outlaw in order to formulate a plan to capture the Johnny Ringo gang. Plot possibilities are not carried out well in this mediocre outing.

3671 Toughest Man in Arizona. Republic, 1952. 90 minutes Color. D: R. G. Springsteen. SC: John K. Butler. WITH Vaughn Monroe, Joan Leslie, Edgar Buchanan, Victor Jory, Jean Parker, Henry (Harry) Morgan, Ian MacDonald, Diana Christian, Lee MacGregor, Bobby Hyatt, Charlita, Nadene Ashdown, Francis Ford, Paul Hurst, John Doucette. A widower sheriff is on the trail of a notorious outlaw and at the same time he falls in love with a beautiful girl. Vaughn Monroe's second "A" film for Republic is a pleasant affair.

A Town Called Bastard see **A Town Called Hell**

3672 A Town Called Hell. Scotia International, 1971. 95 minutes Color. D: Robert Parrish. SC: Richard Aubrey. WITH Robert Shaw, Stella Stevens, Telly Savalas, Martin Landau, Fernando Rey, Michael Craig, Al Lettieri, Dudley Sutton, Aldo Sambrell. A small Mexican town ruled by a cruel bandit gang leader is the scene of a manhunt for a revolutionary leader as well as for the killer of a woman's husband. Exceedingly violent Spanish-made horse opera which will have little appeal to genre fans. Original title: **A Town Called Bastard.**

3673 Town Tamer. Paramount, 1965. 89 minutes Color. D: Lesley Selander. SC: Frank Gruber. WITH Dana Andrews, Terry Moore, Lon Chaney, Bruce Cabot, Lyle Bettger, Richard Arlen, Barton MacLane, Pat O'Brien, Richard Jaeckel, Philip Carey, Sonny Tufts, Coleen Gray, Jeanne Cagney, Roger Torrey, Don Barry, Robert Ivers, James Brown, Richard Webb, Bob Steele, DeForrest Kelley, Dale Van Sickel, Dinny Powell, Frank Gruber. When a gunman murders his wife a man travels from town to town bringing peace and searching for the killer, who he finally finds as the marshal of a small community. A top notch cast of veteran players is the main highlight of this screen version of Frank Gruber's novel.

3674 Track of the Cat. Warner Brothers, 1954. 102 minutes Color. D: William A. Wellman. SC: A. I. Bezzerides. WITH Robert Mitchum, Teresa Wright, Diana Lynn, Tab Hunter, Beulah Bondi, Philip Tonge, William Hopper, Carl ("Alfalfa") Switzer. A mountain family, torn by bitter personal conflicts, is harassed by a cougar and the two sons set out to kill the animal. Strangely compelling psychological melodrama.

3675 Track of the Moon Beast. Derio, 1977. 90 minutes Color. D: Dick Ashe. SC: William Finder & Charles Sinclair. WITH Chase Cordell, Donna Leigh Drake, Gregorio Sala, Patrick Wright. A mineralogist turns into a giant lizard after being hit by particles of a meteor. Low budget, but effective, thriller filmed in the southwest.

3676 Tracked by the Police. Warner Brothers, 1927. 60 minutes B/W. D: Ray Enright. SC: John Grey. WITH Rin-Tin-Tin, Jason Robards, Virginia Browne Faire, Tom Santschi, David Morris, Theodore Lorch, Ben Walker, Wilfred North, Nanette (dog). An escaped police dog aids the foreman of an Arizona irrigation project which is being sabotaged by a rival camp.

Very good and actionful Rin-Tin-Tin silent vehicle.

3677 Trackers. Wrather Corporation, 1956. 75 minutes Color. D: Earl Bellamy & Oscar Rudolph. SC: Robert E. Schaefer, Eric Friewald, Charles Larsay & Melvin Levy. WITH Clayton Moore, Jay Silverheels, Mary Ellen Kay, Harry Lauter, Mike Ragan, Charles Stevens, Allen Pinson, Wayne Burson, Terry Frost, Bill Henry, Frank Hagney, Tyler McDuff, Francis McDonald, John Pickard, Robert Burton, Gregg Barton, Molly Wrather, Don Turner, Steve E. Raines, Charles Aldridge, Tom Brocon, Ben Wilder, Edmond Hashim, Robert Swan. The Lone Ranger and Tonto stop a lynch mob, get on the trail of two renegade Confederates charged with murder and try to find out who is behind the mysterious goings-on in a ghostly canyon. Fans of "The Lone Ranger" (ABC-TV, 1949-57) will like this trilogy made up of three series segments: "Ghost Canyon," "The Trouble at Tylerville" and "Twisted Track."

3678 The Trackers. ABC-TV, 1971. 73 minutes Color. D: Earl Bellamy, SC: Gerald Gaiser. WITH Sammy Davis Jr., Ernest Borgnine, Julie Adams, Jim Davis, Connie Kreski, Arthur Hunnicutt, Caleb Brooks, Norman Alden, Leo Gordon, Ross Elliott, David Reynard. A rancher is forced to team with a black tracker in order to find out who murdered his son and kidnapped his daughter. Ordinary TV movie.

3679 Tracy Rides. Reliable, 1935. 59 minutes B/W. D: Harry S. Webb. SC: Rose Gordon & Betty Burbridge. WITH Tom Tyler, Virginia Brown Faire, Edmund Cobb, Charles K. French, Carol Shandrew, Lafe McKee, Jimmie Aubrey, Art Dillard, Jack Evans. A lawman is caught in the middle of a feud between cattlemen and sheepmen and when one of the latter is shot he is forced to arrest his girl's rancher father. Poor Tom Tyler vehicle benefitting from the presence of the lovely and talented Virginia Brown Faire.

3680 The Trail Beyond. Monogram, 1934. 57 minutes B/W. D: Robert North Bradbury. SC: Lindsley Parsons. WITH John Wayne, Verna Hillie, Noah Beery, Iris Lancaster, Noah Beery Jr., Robert Frazer, Earl Dwire, Eddie Parker, James Marcus, Reed Howes, Artie Ortego. A man saves his buddy from cardsharps and then uncovers a map to a hidden gold mine and is pursued by the crooks who also want the map. Perhaps the best of producer Paul Malvern's Lone Star productions, this adaptation of James Oliver Curwood's The Wolf Hunters is very entertaining and sports beautiful photography by Archie Stout. First filmed by Ben Wilson Productions for Rayart in 1926 with Robert McKim and Virginia Browne Faire as **The Wolf Hunters** and that title was again used for a third version (q.v.) in 1949.

3681 The Trail Blazers. Republic, 1940. 54 (58) minutes B/W. D: George Sherman. SC: Barry Shipman. WITH Robert Livingston, Bob Steele, Rufe Davis, Pauline Moore, Rex Lease, Weldon Heyburn, Carroll Nye, Tom Chatterton, Si Jenks, Mary Field, John Merton, Bob Blair, Pascale Perry, Harry Strang, Barry Hays. The Three Mesquiteers try to stop an outlaw gang trying to sabotage the establishment of a telegraph line. Typically swift entry in "The Three Mesquiteers" series.

3682 The Trail Drive. Universal, 1933. 65 minutes B/W. D: Alan James. SC: Nate Gatzert & Alan James. WITH Ken Maynard, Cecilia Parker, William Gould, Lafe McKee, Robert Kortman, Alan Bridge, Frank Rice, Fern Emmett, Jack Rockwell, Slim Whitaker, Frank Ellis, Hank Bell, Wally Wales, Ben Corbett. The foreman for a large rancher agrees to lead a cattle drive with combined herds of all the local ranchers but after the drive is underway he finds out his boss is a crook who is out to cheat his neighbors. A good story and typical Ken Maynard high standards of action makes this top notch feature a must for the star's fans.

3683 Trail Dust. Paramount, 1936. 54 (77) minutes B/W. D: Nate Watt. SC: Al Martin. WITH William Boyd, James Ellison, George ("Gabby") Hayes, Gwynne Shipman, Stephen Morris (Morris Ankrum), Britt Wood, Dick Dickinson, Earl Askam, Al Bridge, John Beach, Ted Adams, Al St. John, Harold Daniels, Kenneth Harlan, John Elliott, George Chesebro, Robert Drew. During a cattle drive the Bar 20 boys find themselves against an outlaw gang with plans to steal their cattle by dynamiting a pass. A bit overlong, but still a satisfying entry in the "Hopalong Cassidy" series.

3684 Trail Guide. RKO Radio, 1952. 60 minutes B/W. D: Lesley Selander. SC: William Lively. WITH Tim Holt,

Richard Martin, Linda Douglas, Frank Wilcox, Robert Sherwood, John Pickard, Kenneth MacDonald, Tom London, Mauritz Hugo. A scout leading a wagon train of settlers finds crooks are out to steal the land intended for the homesteaders. Average Tim Holt vehicle from near the end of his RKO tenure.

3685 Trail of Kit Carson. Republic, 1945. 56 minutes B/W. D: Lesley Selander. SC: Albert DeMond & Jack Natteford. WITH Allan Lane, Helen Talbot, Twinkle Watts, Roy Barcroft, Tom London, Kenne Duncan, Jack Kirk, Bud Geary, Tom Dugan, George Chesebro, Robert Wilke, Herman Hack, John Carpenter, Henry Wills, Tom Steele. Although the death of his partner appears to be an accident, Kit Carson sets out to find out the truth. Fair Allan Lane actioner, the final entry in his first starring series for Republic.

3686 Trail of Robin Hood. Republic, 1950. 67 minutes Color. D: William Witney. SC: Gerald Geraghty. WITH Roy Rogers, Penny Edwards, Gordon Jones, Jack Holt, Foy Willing & The Riders of the Purple Sage, Rex Allen, George Chesebro, Ray Corrigan, Monte Hale, William Farnum, Allan "Rocky" Lane, Tom Keene, Kermit Maynard, Tom Tyler, Emory Parnell, Clifton Young, James Magill, Carol Nugent, Ed Cassidy. When Christmas tree thieves make trouble for a once famous cowboy movie star, now a Christmas tree rancher, Roy Rogers and other screen cowboys come to his rescue. Sturdy entertainment with good nostalgia value.

3687 Trail of Terror. Supreme, 1935. 59 minutes B/W. D-SC: Robert North Bradbury. WITH Bob Steele, Beth Marion, Forrest Taylor, Charles King, Lloyd Ingraham, Charles K. French, Richard Cramer. Trying to get evidence to convict an outlaw gang, a federal man pretends to be an escaped convict. Entertaining Bob Steele vehicle.

3688 Trail of Terror. Producers Releasing Corporation, 1943. 64 minutes B/W. D-SC: Oliver Drake. WITH James Newill, Dave O'Brien, Guy Wilkerson, Patricia Knox, Jack Ingram, I. Stanford Jolley, Budd Buster, Kenne Duncan, Frank Ellis, Robert Hill, Dan White, Jimmie Aubrey, Rose Plummer, Tom London, Artie Ortego. When his twin brother is killed helping robbers hold up a stage, a ranger takes his place to capture the gang. Low grade entry in the PRC "Texas Rangers" series.

3689 Trail of the Mounties. Screen Guild, 1947. 41 minutes B/W. D: Howard Bretherton. SC: Elizabeth (Betty) Burbridge. WITH Russell Hayden, Jennifer Holt, Emmett Lynn, Harry Cording, Terry Frost, Zon Murray, Frank Lackteen, Britt Wood, Charles Bedell. A Mountie is sent to a small village to capture the man who killed a comrade and he discovers the killer is his twin brother, the leader of a gang of fur thieves. Russell Hayden is good in a dual role in this cheaply made but picturesque and entertaining featurette.

Trail of the Royal Mounted see **The Mystery Trooper**

3690 Trail of the Rustlers. Columbia, 1950. 55 minutes B/W. D: Ray Nazarro. SC: Victor Arthur. WITH Charles Starrett, Smiley Burnette, Gail Davis, Eddie Cletro & His Roundup Boys, Tommy Ivo, Myron Healey, Don C. Harvey, Mira McKinney, Chuck Roberson, Gene Roth, Blackie Whiteford. A woman and her two sons discover a secret water source in a valley and they plot to run off the other ranchers to get their land but their secret is solved by the Durango Kid. Fair "Durango Kid" actioner; although Jock Mahoney does not appear in this film (outside of stunt work) it is interesting that the name of the villainous family is Mahoney.

3691 Trail of the Silver Spurs. Monogram, 1941. 58 minutes B/W. D: S. Roy Luby. SC: Elmer Clifton. WITH Ray Corrigan, John King, Max Terhune, I. Stanford Jolley, Dorothy Short, Milburn Morante, George Chesebro, Eddie Dean, Kermit Maynard, Frank Ellis, Carl Mathews, Steve Clark. The government sends the Range Busters on the trail of a gold thief and they wind up in a ghost town where a man and his daughter are being harrassed by a mysterious figure using "ghost writing." Nice addition to the "Range Busters" series, enhanced by a mystery motif.

3692 Trail of the Vigilantes. Universal, 1940. 75 minutes B/W. D: Allan Dwan. SC: Harold Shumate. WITH Franchot Tone, Broderick Crawford, Peggy Moran, Andy Devine, Warren William, Mischa Auer, Porter Hall, Samuel S. Hinds, Charles Trowbridge, Paul Fix, Harry Cording, Max Wagner. A lawman from the East is sent West with the assignment to bring in an outlaw gang. Pleasant blend of humor and action.

3693 Trail of the Wild. A.N.E., 1974.
94 minutes Color. WITH Gordon Eastman.
An outdoorsman leads an expedition
to the northern reaches of Canada to
study the life of the Eskimo. Well made
documentary.

3694 Trail of the Yukon. Monogram,
1949. 67 minutes B/W. D: William Crowley.
SC: Oliver Drake. WITH Kirby Grant,
Suzanne Dalbert, Anthony Warde, Iris
Adrian, Bill Edwards, Dan Seymour,
William Forrest, Maynard Hoffman, Peter
Mamakos, Jay Silverheels, Guy Beach,
Stanley Andrews, Dick Elliott, Bill Ken-
nedy, Alan Bridge, Chinook (dog). A
gang of bank robbers are tracked in the
Canadian Yukon by a Mountie and his
dog. Kirby Grant's first series film for
Monogram is an over-long, lumbering
affair adapted from James Oliver Cur-
wood's The Gold Hunters.

3695 Trail of Vengeance. Republic, 1937.
60 minutes. D: Sam Newfield. SC: George
Plympton & Fred Myton. WITH Johnny
Mack Brown, Iris Meredith, Warner Rich-
mond, Earle Hodgins, Richard Cramer,
Dick Curtis, Karl Hackett, Frank LaRue,
Frank Ellis, Lew Meehan, Frank Ball,
Horace Murphy, Steve Clark, Budd Buster,
Jack Kirk, Tex Palmer, Jim Corey. Dude
Ramsey becomes involved in a range
war and also finds that he is the heir
to a mine, his brother having been
murdered by an outlaw gang leader.
Well made action drama with Warner
Richmond a most effective villain.

3696 Trail Riders. Monogram, 1942.
55 minutes B/W. D: Robert Tansey. SC:
Frances Kavanaugh. WITH John King,
David Sharpe, Max Terhune, Evelyn Finley,
Forrest Taylor, Lynton Brent, Charles
King, Kermit Maynard, John Curtis,
Steve Clark, Kenne Duncan, Frank LaRue,
Bud Osborne, Tex Palmer, Richard Cramer,
Frank Ellis. After his sheriff son is killed
trying to stop a bank robbery, a marshal
sends for the Range Busters to help him
round up the gang. Only average entry
in "The Range Busters" series. V: Video
Connection.

3697 Trail Street. RKO Radio, 1947.
84 minutes B/W. D: Ray Enright. SC:
Norman Houston & Gene Lewis. WITH
Randolph Scott, Anne Jeffreys, Robert
Ryan, George "Gabby" Hayes, Madge
Meredith, Steve Brodie, Billy House,
Virginia Sale, Harry Woods, Phil Warren,
Harry Harvey, Jason Robards, Elena
Warren, Betty Hill, Larry McGrath, Warren

Jackson, Billy Vincent, Glen McCarthy,
Ernie Adams, Kit Guard, Al Murphy,
Lew Harvey, Roy Butler, Frank Austin,
Carl Webster, Jessie Arnold, Si Jenks,
Donald Kerr, Stanley Andrews, Sarah
Padden, Frank McGlynn Jr., Sam Lufkin.
Marshal Bat Masterson teams with a
land agent to battle cattle rustlers plaguing
a Kansas town. Pretty good action melo-
drama. V: Blackhawk, Nostalgia Merchant.

3698 Trail to Gunsight. Universal, 1944.
58 minutes B/W. D: Vernon Keays. SC:
Bennett Cohen. WITH Eddie Dew, Fuzzy
Knight, Maris Wrixon, Lyle Talbot, Ray
Whitley & His Bar-6 Cowboys, Buzzy
Henry, Marie Austin, Sarah Padden,
Glenn Strange, Ray Bennett, Charles
Morton, Forrest Taylor, Terry Frost,
Jack Clifford, Henry Wills. When outlaws
murder a boy's father, a lawman takes
the boy home only to find the gang is
plaguing the family ranch. Passable Eddie
Dew vehicle with the slick Universal
look; at its best when Ray Whitley sings
"Old Nevada Trail."

3699 Trail to Laredo. Columbia, 1948.
54 minutes B/W. D: Ray Nazarro. SC:
Barry Shipman. WITH Charles Starrett,
Smiley Burnette, Jim Bannon, Virginia
Maxey, Tommy Ivo, Hugh Prosser, The
Cass County Boys, George Chesebro,
John Merton, Bob Cason, Robert Wilke,
Ted Mapes, Ethan Laidlaw, Mira McKinney.
Forced to become a fugitive by his crooked
partner, who is in cahoots with a saloon
owner in smuggling gold, a stageline
operator is aided by the Durango Kid.
Actionful "Durango Kid" film.

3700 Trail to Mexico. Monogram, 1946.
57 minutes B/W. D-SC: Oliver Drake.
WITH Jimmy Wakely, Lee "Lasses" White,
Dolores Castelli, Julian Rivero, Dora
Del Rio, Terry Frost, Forrest Matthews,
Brad Slaven, Alex Montoya, Jonathan
McCall, Juan Duval, Arthur Smith, The
Saddle Pals, The Guadalajara Trio. A
singing investigator goes to Mexico to
find out who is behind a series of robberies
plaguing a mining outfit. The music is
good and the plot is fair in this average
Jimmy Wakely opus.

3701 Trail to San Antone. Republic,
1947. 67 minutes B/W. D: John English.
SC: Luci Ward & Jack Natteford. WITH
Gene Autry, Peggy Stewart, Sterling
Holloway, William Henry, The Cass County
Boys, Tristram Coffin, John Duncan,
Dorothy Vaughn, Edward Keane, Ralph
Peters. A horse breeder tries to aid an

injured jockey while he also fights a wild stallion trying to steal his horse herd. Routine Gene Autry vehicle.

3702 Trail to Vengeance. Universal, 1945. 54 minutes B/W. D: Wallace Fox. SC: Bob Williams. WITH Kirby Grant, Poni (Jane) Adams, Fuzzy Knight, Tom Fadden, John Kelly, Frank Jaquet, Stanley Andrews, Walter Baldwin, Roy Brent, Pierce Lyden, Dan White, Beatrice Gray, William Sundholm, Carey Loftin. While investigating his brother's murder a man finds a crooked banker is about to foreclose the mortgage on his property. Standard Kirby Grant vehicle for Universal.

3703 Trailin' Trouble. Universal, 1930. 60 minutes B/W. D: Arthur Rosson. SC: Arthur Rosson & Harold Tarshis. WITH Hoot Gibson, Margaret Quimby, Pete Morrison, Olive Young, William McCall, Robert Perry. A ranch worker, who is in love with the boss's daughter, plans to take a herd of horses to market and his rival plans to have him robbed so he will be discredited in the girl's eyes. Pleasant Hoot Gibson vehicle, not too complicated but plenty of fun for his fans.

3704 Trailin' Trouble. Grand National, 1937. 60 minutes B/W. D: Arthur Rosson. SC: Philip Graham White. WITH Ken Maynard, Lona Andre, Roger Williams, Vince Barnett, Grace Woods, Fred Burns, Phil Dunham, Ed Cassidy, Horace B. Carpenter, Marin Sais, Tex Palmer. Due to a case of mistaken identity, a cowboy finds himself in lots of trouble and has to round up a gang of rustlers in order to prove his innocence. Well done low budget Ken Maynard film with a nice balance of comedy.

3705 Trailin West. Warner Brothers, 1936. 59 minutes B/W. D: Noel Smith. SC: Anthony Coldeway. WITH Dick Foran, Paula Stone, Addison Richards, Robert Barrat, Joseph Crehan, Gordon (William) Elliott, Fred Lawrence, Eddie Shubert, Henry Otho, Stuart Holmes, Milton Kibbee, Carlyle Moore Jr., Jim Thorpe, Edwin Stanley, Bud Osborne, Glenn Strange, Gene Alsace, Tom Wilson. During the Civil War a Secret Service agent is assigned to track down an outlaw band in the West. Plentiful action highlights this musical Dick Foran film.

3706 Trailing Danger. Monogram, 1947. 58 minutes B/W. D: Lambert Hillyer. SC: J. Benton Cheney. WITH Johnny Mack Brown, Raymond Hatton, Marshall Reed, Peggy Wynne, Bonnie Jean Bartley, Steve Darrell, Eddie Parker, Pat Desmond, Bud Osborne, Ernie Adams, I. Stanford Jolley, Artie Ortego, Cactus Mack, Dee Cooper. An outlaw is out to get revenge on the stage line superintendent who sent him to jail but he is opposed by a U. S. marshal. Thin Johnny Mack Brown vehicle.

3707 Trailing Double Trouble. Monogram, 1940. 56 minutes B/W. D: S. Roy Luby. SC: Oliver Drake. WITH Ray Corrigan, John King, Max Terhune, Lita Conway, Roy Barcroft, Kenne Duncan, Tom London, William Kellogg, Carl Mathews, Forrest Taylor, Nancy Louise King, Jimmy Wakely & His Rough Riders (Johnny Bond, Dick Rinehart), Texas Rex Felker. The Range Busters get involved in trying to find out who killed a rancher and kidnapped his sister. Very good entry in "The Range Busters" series with plenty of action and good humor. V: Thunderbird.

3708 Trailing North. Monogram, 1933. 60 minutes B/W. D: J. P. McCarthy. SC: John Morgan. WITH Bob Steele, Doris Hill, Arthur Rankin, George ("Gabby") Hayes, Dick Dickinson, Fred Burns, Norma Fensler. A Texas Ranger heads to Canada to bring back a prisoner. Mediocre Bob Steele series outing.

3709 Trailing the Killer. B. F. Ziedman, 1932. 64 minutes B/W. D: Herman C. Raymaker. SC: Jackson Richards. WITH Francis McDonald, Heinie Conklin, Jose De La Cruz, Peter Rigas, Caesar (dog). A wolf dog is falsely accused of killing his master, the deed actually committed by a mountain lion. Well done action drama, filmed in Canada and made in a semi-documentary vein. Alternate title: **Call of the Wilderness.**

3710 Trail's End. Beaumont, 1935. 57 minutes B/W. D: Al Herman. SC: Jack Jevne. WITH Conway Tearle, Claudia Dell, Baby Charlotte Barry, Fred Kohler, Ernest (Ernie) Adams, Pat Harmon, Victor Potel, Gaylord (Steve) Pendleton, Stanley Blystone, Jack Duffy. Framed and sent to prison, a man gets out seeking revenge on his enemies and ends up being made the sheriff of a small town plagued by his old gang. Despite low grade production values, this Conway Tearle series vehicle is pretty good.

3711 Trail's End. Monogram, 1949. 57 minutes B/W. D: Lambert Hillyer. SC:

J. Benton Cheney. WITH Johnny Mack Brown, Max Terhune, Kay Morley, Myron Healey, Douglas Evans, Zon Murray, George Chesebro, Keith Richards, William Norton Bailey, Carol Henry, Boyd Stockman, Eddie Majors. A crook finds gold on a man's ranch and when he cannot convince him to sell he trumps up a murder charge against him but a lawman believes in the man's innocence. Mediocre Johnny Mack Brown vehicle; the title is sadly prophetic for the "B" genre as a whole at the time.

3712 Trails of Peril. Big 4, 1930. 55 minutes B/W. D-SC: Alvin J. Neitz. WITH Wally Wales, Virginia Browne Faire, Frank Ellis, Lew Meehan, Jack Perrin, Joe Rickson, Buck Connors, Bubby Dunn, Pete Morrison, Hank Bell. Mistaken for an outlaw, a cowboy decides to capture the badman for the reward but the hoodlum gets the same idea. Bottom-of-the-barrel.

3713 Trails of the Wild. Ambassador, 1935. 60 minutes B/W. D: Sam Newfield. SC: Joseph O'Donnell. WITH Kermit Maynard, Billie Seward, Fuzzy Knight, Monte Blue, Matthew Betz, Theodore Von Eltz, Frank Rice, Robert Frazer, Wheeler Oakman, Roger Williams, Charles Delaney, John Elliott, Dick Curtis. A Canadian Mountie is on the trail of the man who murdered his pal. Surprisingly poor adaptation of James Oliver Curwood's Caryl of the Mountains.

3714 The Train Robbers. Warner Brothers, 1973. 92 minutes Color. D-SC: Burt Kennedy. WITH John Wayne, Ann-Margret, Rod Taylor, Ben Johnson, Chris(topher) George, Ricardo Montalban, Bobby Vinton, Jerry Gatlin. A cowboy and his pals team with a beautiful widow in trying to recover gold stolen by her late husband. Okay actioner filmed in Mexico but it is not one of John Wayne's best. V: Warner Home Video.

3715 Train to Tombstone. Lippert, 1950. 60 minutes B/W. D-SC: William Berke. WITH Don Barry, Robert Lowery, Tom Neal, Wally Vernon, Judith Allen, Nan Leslie, Minna Philips, Barbara Stanley, Claude Stroud, Bill Kennedy. The passengers aboard a Tombstone-bound train are first robbed by outlaws and then attacked by marauding Indians. **Stagecoach**-on-a-train provides some excitement in this low budget outing.

3716 The Traitor. Puritan, 1936. 58 minutes B/W. D: Sam Newfield. SC:

Joseph O'Donnell. WITH Tim McCoy, Frances Grant, Karl Hackett, Dick Curtis, Jack Rockwell, Wally Wales, Pegro Regas, Frank Melton, Richard Botiller, Edmund Cobb, Tina Menard, Soledad Jiminez, J. Frank Glendon, Frank McCarroll, Wally West. A Texas Ranger pretends to get thrown out of the service in order to masquerade as an outlaw and join a gang hiding across the border in Mexico. The time-honored plot gets pretty thin in this rather ragged low budget affair. V: Video Communications.

3717 The Tramplers. Avco-Embassy, 1966. 90 minutes Color. D: Alfredo Antonini & Mario Sequi. SC: Alfred Antonini & Ugo Liberatore. WITH Joseph Cotten, Gordon Scott, James Mitchum, Ilaria Occhini, Franco Nero, Emma Vannoni, Georges Lycan, Muriel Franklin, Aldo Cecconi, Franco Balducci, Claudio Gora, Romano Puppo, Dario Michaelis, Ivan Scratuglia, Carla Calo. After the Civil War a Confederate veteran returns home to the terrible aftermath of the conflict and finds his stern-willed father wants to keep the war going. One of the better of the 1960s European oaters with a good plot and plenty of action. Italian title: **Gli Uomini Dal Passo Pesante.**

3718 The Trap. Continental, 1968. 106 minutes Color. D: Sidney Hayers. SC: David Osborn. WITH Oliver Reed, Rita Tushingham, Rex Sevenoaks, Barbara Chilcott, Linda Goranson, Blain Fairman, Walter Marsh, Jo Golland. A Canadian trapper reluctantly takes a deaf-mute girl in a wife auction and her loyalty to him eventually saves his life. Well made Canadian melodrama with nice scenic values in addition to a good plotline.

3719 Trap on Cougar Mountain. Sun International, 1972. 94 minutes Color. D-SC: Keith Larsen. WITH Eric Larsen, Keith Larsen, Karen Steele, Alvin Keeswood, Randy Burt, Lawrence J. Rink, Gene Merlino (songs). A young boy is befriended by a cougar and together they fight to survive in a mountain wilderness. More than adequate family adventure drama.

3720 Trapped. Columbia, 1937. 55 minutes B/W. D: Leon Barsha. SC: John Rathmell. WITH Charles Starrett, Peggy Stratford, Robert Middlemass, Alan Sears, Ted Oliver, Lew Meehan, Ed Piel, Jack Rockwell, Ed LeSaint, Francis Sayles, Art Mix. When his brother is murdered a man believes a neighboring rancher committed the crime in order to get the dead man's land but he cannot prove it because the man he suspects is a helpless cripple. A good mystery element highlights this well done and entertaining Charles Starrett vehicle.

3721 The Traveling Saleslady. Columbia, 1950. 75 minutes B/W. D: Charles F. Riesner. SC: Howard Dinsdal. WITH Joan Davis, Andy Devine, Adele Jergens, Joseph Sawyer, Dean Riesner, John Cason, Chief Thundercloud, Harry Hayden, Charles Halton, Minerva Urecal, Eddy Waller, Teddy Infuhr, Robert Cherry, William Newell, Harry Woods, Ethan Laidlaw, Harry Tyler, Alan Bridge, Gertrude Charre, Emmett Lynn, Stanley Andrews, George Chesebro, Heinie Conklin, Chief Yowlachie, Bill Wilkerson, Nick Thompson, George McDonald, Fred Aldrich, Louis Mason, Jessie Arnold, Robert Wilke. A girl sets out with her boyfriend to sell her dad's soap so his business will survive and the two go West and get involved with crooks and an Indian uprising. Stilted comedy filled with wheezy gags; not even Joan Davis and Andy Devine can do much to save this weak feature.

3722 Treachery Rides the Range. Warner Brothers, 1936. 56 minutes B/W. D: Frank McDonald. SC: William Jacobs. WITH Dick Foran, Paula Stone, Monte Blue, Craig Reynolds, Carlyle Moore Jr., Henry Otho, Jim Thorpe, Milton Kibbee, Bud Osborne, Monte Montague, Don Barclay, Gene Alsace, Richard Botiller, Iron Eyes Cody, William Desmond, Frank McCarroll, Frank Ellis, Artie Ortego, Nick Copeland, Frank Bruno. Crooks try to defraud the Plains Indians and they threaten to go on the warpath but a cowboy tries to bring about continued peace. Top notch Dick Foran vehicle with a good balance between action and music.

3723 Treason. Columbia, 1933. 57 minutes B/W. D: George B. Seitz. SC: Gordon Battle. WITH Buck Jones, Shirley Grey, Robert Ellis, Ed Le Saint, Frank Lackteen, Edwin Stanley, Art Mix, Frank Ellis, T. C. Jacks, Charles Brinley, Charles Hill Mailes, Ivar McFadden. In 1870 an Army scout tries to infiltrate a group of Confederate sympathizers led by a woman who wants to get lands unjustly taken from her in Kansas. High grade Buck Jones melodrama.

3724 The Treasure of Lost Canyon. Universal-International, 1951. 82 minutes Color. D: Ted Tetzlaff. SC: Brainerd Duffield & Emerson Crocker. WITH William Powell, Julia Adams, Rosemary De Camp, Henry Hull, Charles Drake, Tommy Ivo, Chubby Johnson, John Doucette, Marvin Press, Frank Wilcox, Griff Barnett, Jack Perrin, Virginia Mullen, Philo McCullough, Paul "Tiny" Newlan, George Taylor, Jimmy Ogg, Ed Hinkle, Hugh Prosser. A young boy, adopted by a middle-aged couple, accidentally finds a hidden treasure which nearly brings tragedy to everyone it touches. Fairly good screen adaptation of Robert Louis Stevenson's The Treasure of Franchard with good work by William Powell as Doc, the old prospector.

3725 Treasure of Matecumbe. Buena Vista, 1976. 117 minutes Color. D: Vincent McEveety. SC: Don Tait. WITH Peter Ustinov, Robert Foxworth, Joan Hackett, Vic Morrow, Jane Wyatt, Johnny Duran, Billy "Pop" Attmore, Dub Taylor, Don Knight, Virginia Vincent, Dick Van Patten, Mills Watson, Val De Vargas, Robert Doqui. In the Florida Everglades two young boys, using a treasure map, search for hidden riches with the help of three others while a bad guy is on their trail. Average Walt Disney Studio outing.

3726 The Treasure of Pancho Villa. RKO Radio, 1955. 96 minutes Color. D: George Sherman. SC: Niven Busch. WITH Rory Calhoun, Shelley Winters, Gilbert Roland, Joseph Calleia, Fanny Schiller, Tony Carvajal, Pasquel Pena, Carlos Mosquiz. An American mercenary working for Pancho Villa plans the robbery of gold from a government train but the loot is stolen before it reaches the revolutionary. Standard action effort.

The Treasure of Pancho Villa (1966) see **The Vengeance of Pancho Villa**

3727 Treasure of Ruby Hills. Allied Artists, 1955. 71 minutes B/W. D: Frank McDonald. SC: Tom Hubbard & Fred Eggers. WITH Zachary Scott, Carole Mathews, Dick Foran, Barton MacLane, Lola Albright, Lee Van Cleef, Raymond Hatton, Gordon Jones, Steve Darrell, Rick Vallin, Charles Fredericks, Stanly Andrews, James Alexander. Crooked cattlemen fight for control of range land with a rancher trying to stop them and their greed. Pretty fair little actioner with good work by Zachary Scott as the hero.

3728 The Treasure of Sierra Madre. Warner Brothers, 1948. 126 minutes B/W. D-SC: John Huston. WITH Humphrey Bogart, Walter Huston, Tim Holt, Bruce Bennett,

Barton MacLane, Alfonso Bedoya, Martin Garralaga, Jack Holt, John Huston, A. Soto Rangel, Manuel Donde, Jose Torvay, Margarito Luna, Jacqueline Dalya, Bobby Blake, Spencer Chan, Julian Rivero, Harry Vejar, Pat Flaherty, Clifton Young, Ralph Dunn, Guillermo Calleo, Roberto Canedo, Ernesto Escoto, Ignacio Villalbajo, Ann Sheridan, David Sharpe. Three men head into the mountains of Mexico looking for gold but one of them is turned into a madman due to greed. A bit overlong, but still near-classic screen adaptation of B. Traven's novel with fine photography (by Ted McCord) and some magnificent character work, specifically Walter Huston's old prospector, Barton MacLane as the big-mouth McCormick and Alfonso Bedoya's maniac, Gold Hat. V: Key Video.

3729 The Treasure of Silver Lake. Rialtox/ Jadran Film, 1962. 111 minutes Color. D: Harald Reinl. SC: Harald G. Peterson. WITH Lex Barker, Pierre Brice, Herbert Lom, Gotz George, Karin Dor, Marianne Hoppe, Eddi Arent, Ralf Wolter. Frontiersman Old Shatterhand and his Indian blood brother Winnetou try to stop the pillage of Indian lands by crooks looking for hidden treasure. Another well done West German oater based on the works of Karl May. West German title: **Der Schatz Im Silbersee.**

3730 Treasure of Tayopa. Reina Productions, 1974. 85 minutes Color. D: Bob Cawley. WITH Gilbert Roland, Rena Winters, Bob Corrigan, Phil Trapani, Frank Hernandez, Arthur Farnsworth. A woman leads an expedition into the Mexican wilderness looking for a fabulous treasure but one of the party turns out to be a madman set on killing the others. Poor melodrama which will disappoint Gilbert Roland fans in that he appears only at the beginning and end of the feature as its host.

3731 The Treasure of the Aztecs. CCC Filmkunst/ Franco-London/ Serena/ Avala-Film, 1965. 102 minutes Color. D: Robert Siodmak. SC: Ladislas Fodor, R. A. Stemmle & Georg Marischka. WITH Lex Barker, Gerard Barray, Rik Battaglia, Michele Girardon, Ralf Wolter, Allesandra Panaro, Theresa Lorca, Fausto Tozzi, Hans Nielsen. In Mexico in 1864 both followers of Benito Juarez and the Emperor Maximillian search for the lost treasure of the Aztecs in order to use the riches for their causes. Pretty exciting West German film hurt by being cut to 90 minutes and dubbed for U. S. TV. West

German titles: **Der Schatz der Azteken** and **Die Pyramide des Sonnengottes** (The Pyramid of the Sun-God).

3732 The Trial of Billy Jack. Warner Brothers, 1974. 170 minutes Color. D: Frank Laughlin. SC: Frank Christian & Teresa Christian. WITH Delores Taylor, Tom Laughlin, Victor Izay, Teresa Laughlin, Riley Hill, Sparky Watt, Russell Lane, William Wellman Jr., Michelle Wilson, Geo Anna Sosa, Lynn Baker, Guy Greymountain, Sacheen Littlefeather, Michael Bolland, Jack Stanley, Sandra Ego, Trinidad Hopkins, Marianne Hill, Jason Clark, Johnny West, Buffalo Horse, Dennis O'Flaherty, Bong Soo Han, Michael J. Singezone, Kathy Cronkite, Alexandra Nicholson, Rolling Thunder. Released from prison, an Indian rights activist returns to the mountains to search for the meaning of life. Third film in the "Billy Jack" series, this outing is a pretentious bore.

3733 Tribute to a Bad Man. Metro-Goldwyn-Mayer, 1956. 95 minutes Color. D: Robert Wise. SC: Michael Blankfort. WITH James Cagney, Don Dubbins, Stephen McNally, Irene Papas, Vic Morrow, James Griffith, Onslow Stevens, James Bell, Royal Dano, Jeanette Nolan, Chubby Johnson, Lee Van Cleef, Peter Chong, James McCallion, Tony Hughes, Roy Engel, Bud Osborne, John Halloran, Tom London, Dennis Moore, Buddy Roosevelt. A young drifter saves a wealthy horse rancher from bushwackers and soon finds the man is ruthless regarding his property and his woman, who the young man falls for. Highly competent Western with a powerful performance by James Cagney as the rancher.

3734 Trigger Fingers. Victory, 1939. 60 minutes. D: Sam Newfield. SC: Basil Dickey. WITH Tim McCoy, Jill Martin, Joyce Bryant, Ben Corbett, Kenne Duncan, John Elliott, Ralph Peters, Ted Adams, Bud McTaggert, Forrest Taylor, Carleton Young, Carl Mathews. A lawman masquerades as a gypsy in order to get the goods on a band of outlaws. Slow moving, low grade Sam Katzman production.

3735 Trigger Fingers. Monogram, 1946. 60 minutes B/W. D: Lambert Hillyer. SC: Frank H. Young. WITH Johnny Mack Brown, Raymond Hatton, Jennifer Holt, Riley Hill, Ed Cassidy, Ted Adams, Steve Clark, Eddie Parker, Cactus Mack, George Morrell, Pierce Lyden, Ray Jones, Frank McCarroll. A marshal comes to the aid of a young hot-head who shoots a crook during a card game and who is framed for murder by the man's gang. Average Johnny Mack Brown series entry.

3736 Trigger Jr. Republic, 1950. 68 minutes Color. D: William Witney. SC: Gerald Geraghty. WITH Roy Rogers, Dale Evans, Pat Brady, Gordon Jones, Foy Willing & The Riders of the Purple Sage, Grant Withers, Peter Miles, George Cleveland, Frank Fenton, I. Stanford Jolley, Stanley Andrews, The Raymor Lehr Circus. A rodeo show owner finds that a range protection service is actually fleecing local ranchers. Good Roy Rogers vehicle. V: NTA Home Entertainment.

3737 Trigger Law. Monogram, 1944. 56 minutes B/W. D: Vernon Keays. SC: Victor Hammond. WITH Bob Steele, Hoot Gibson, Beatrice Gray, Ralph Lewis, Ed Cassidy, Jack Ingram, George Eldredge, Pierce Lyden, Lane Chandler, Bud Osborne, George Morrell. Two men search for the killer of the father of one of them, the dead man having been the manager of a stagecoach line. Slow moving, low budget actioner.

3738 Trigger Pals. Grand National, 1939. 56 minutes B/W. D: Sam Newfield. SC: George Plympton. WITH Art Jarrett, Lee Powell, Al St. John, Dorothy Fay, Ted Adams, Nina Guilbert, Ernie Adams, Earl Douglas, Stanley Blystone, Frank LaRue, Ethan Allen. A cowboy not only finds a part of the cattle herd he was guarding is stolen but also that his female boss plans to turn her property into a dude ranch. Passable comedy actioner starring crooner Art Jarrett. V: Video Connection.

3739 Trigger Smith. Monogram, 1939. 51 minutes B/W. D: Alan James. SC: Robert Emmett (Tansey). WITH Jack Randall, Joyce Bryant, Frank Yaconelli, Ed Cassidy, Bobby Clark, Warner Richmond, Dave O'Brien, Forrest Taylor, Sherry Tansey, Jim Corey, Reed Howes, Bud Osborne, Dennis Moore. When outlaws murder his brother during a holdup a young man, at the request of his marshal father, sets out to bring in the culprits. Average Jack Randall vehicle.

3740 Trigger Tom. Reliable, 1935. 57 minutes B/W. D: Henri Samuels (Harry S. Webb). SC: Tom Gibson. WITH Tom Tyler, Al St. John, Bernadine Hayes, William Gould, Jack Evans, John Elliott, Bud Osborne, Wally Wales, Lloyd Ingraham.

A cattle buyer and his pal get mixed up with an outlaw gang with one of the head men posing as a deputy sheriff. Low grade, strung out and somewhat hard to follow Tom Tyler vehicle with the asset of having Al St. John as his comedy sidekick.

3741 Trigger Trail. Universal, 1944. 59 minutes B/W. D: Lewis D. Collins. SC: Ed Earl Repp & Patricia Harper. WITH Rod Cameron, Fuzzy Knight, Eddie Dew, Vivian Austin, Ray Whitley, Lane Chandler, George Eldredge, Buzzy Henry, Davidson Clark, Michael Vallon, Richard Alexander, Jack Rockwell, Budd Buster, Bud Osborne, Ray Jones, Jack Ingram, Artie Ortego, Ray Whitley's Bar-6 Cowboys. Returning home from law school, a young man finds a crook is trying to steal land from area ranchers before it becomes a legal territory. Well produced and entertaining Rod Cameron series vehicle.

3742 Trigger Tricks. Universal, 1930. 60 minutes B/W. D-SC: B. Reeves Eason. WITH Hoot Gibson, Sally Eilers, Robert Homans, Jack Richardson, Monte Montague, Neal Hart, Walter Perry, Max Asher. Out to avenge the murder of his brother, a man intervenes in a dispute between a cattle rancher and a sheep herder. Lighthearted Hoot Gibson film topical at the time of its release due to the much publicized Hoot Gibson-Sally Eilers romance.

3743 The Trigger Trio. Republic, 1937. 54 (60) minutes B/W. D: William Witney. SC: Joseph Poland & Oliver Drake. WITH Ray Corrigan, Max Terhune, Ralph Byrd, Sandra Corday, Hal Taliaferro, Robert Warwick, Cornelius Keefe, Sammy McKim, Jack Ingram, Willie Fung. A rancher, trying to prevent authorities from finding out his cattle has hoof-and-mouth disease, kills a range inspector. Exciting "Three Mesquiteers" series entry (this is the one where Ralph Byrd replaced ailing Robert Livingston) which marked the feature directorial debut of William Witney.

3744 Triggerman. Monogram, 1948. 58 minutes B/W. D: Howard Bretherton. SC: Ronald Davidson. WITH Johnny Mack Brown, Raymond Hatton, Virginia Carroll, Bill Kennedy, Marshall Reed, Forrest Mathews, Bob Woodward, Dee Cooper. A Wells Fargo agent goes to work for a woman rancher and finds a crooked real estate agent is after the spread because gold is hidden on it. Better-than-average Johnny Mack Brown Monogram feature, due mainly to an interesting script.

3745 Trinity. Fernando Piazza, 1975. 92 minutes Color. D: James London. SC: Renzo Senti. WITH Richard Harrison, Anna Zinneman, Donal O'Brien, George Wang. A gold strike near a small town causes trouble between two brothers, one a ladies' man and the other a Mormon. Tongue-in-cheek European oater, from a story by star Richard Harrison. Also called **A Place Called Trinity.** Made in Italy in 1972 as **Due Fratelli In Un Posto Chiamato Trinita.** British title: **Jesse and Lester, Two Brothers in a Place Called Trinity.**

Trinity Is My Name see **Trinity Is Still My Name**

3746 Trinity Is Still My Name. Avco-Embassy, 1973. 117 minutes Color. D-SC: E. B. Clucher (Enzo Barboni). WITH Terence Hill, Bud Spencer, Harry Carey Jr., Jessica Dublin, Yanti Somero, Enzo Tarascio, Pupo De Luca. Two bumbling brother outlaws, now on the right side of the law, set out to right all the wrongs they can find. Funny followup to **They Call Me Trinity** (q.v.), this Italian feature also offers Harry Carey Jr. in a good role as the father.

3747 Triple Justice. RKO Radio, 1940. 66 minutes B/W. D: David Howard. SC: Morton Grant & Arthur V. Jones. WITH George O'Brien, Virginia Sale, Peggy Shannon, Harry Woods, Paul Fix, LeRoy Mason, Glenn Strange, Bud McTaggert, Bob McKenzie, Wilfred Lucas, Herman Nolan, John Judd, Lloyd Ingraham, Lew Meehan, Steve Pendleton, Hank Worden, Fern Emmett, George Mendoza, Henry Rocquemore, Paul Everton, Walter Patterson, Jean Del Val, Henrique Valdez, Elenda Lindeman, Clothidle Lindeman, Bertha Lindeman. A rancher, on the way to a friend's wedding, meets a trio of men who rob the local bank and the rancher is blamed for the crime. George O'Brien's final series film is a fast paced and exciting affair and a fine finale to his "B" starring career.

3748 Triumphs of a Man Called Horse. Jensen Farley Pictures, 1982. 90 minutes Color. D: John Hough. SC: Ken Blackwell & Carlos Aured. WITH Richard Harris, Michael Beck, Ana De Sade, Vaughn Armstrong, Anne Seymour, Buck Taylor,

Simon Andreu, Lautaco Murua, Roger Cudney, Jerry Gatlin, John Chandler, Jacqueline Evans. Following the murder of his father, John Morgan, Sioux half-breed Koda tries to protect his people from gold seekers swarming into their sacred Black Hills. Picturesque but tepid third entry in the trilogy preceded by **A Man Called Horse** and **Return of a Man Called Horse** (qq.v.); best thing in feature is Rita Coolidge's singing the title theme, "He's Comin' Back."

3749 Trooper Hook. United Artists, 1957. 82 minutes B/W. D-SC: Charles Marquis Warren. WITH Joel McCrea, Barbara Stanwyck, Earl Holliman, Edward Andrews, John Dehner, Susan Kohner, Royal Dano, Terry Lawrence, Celia Lovsky, Rodolfo Acosta, Stanley Adams, Pat O'Moore, Jeanne Bates, Rush Williams, Dick Shannon, Sheb Wooley, Cyril Delevanti, D. J. Thompson. A trooper falls in love with a woman who has been rescued from the Apaches but is scorned by her own kind because she bore the tribe's chief a son. Sturdy melodrama with Tex Ritter performing the title song.

3750 Trouble at Midnight. Universal, 1938. 68 minutes B/W. D: Ford Beebe. SC: Maurice Geraghty & Ford Beebe. WITH Noah Beery Jr., Catherine (Kay) Hughes, Larry Blake, Bernadene Hayes, Louis Mason, Earl Dwire, Charles Halton, Frank Melton, George Humbert, Edward Hearn, Harlan Briggs, Henry Hunter, Harry Bradley, Virginia Sale. A young man tries to combat a gang of cattle rustlers who use modern methods such as freight trucks to hijack cattle from the ranches near a small town. Highly efficient and entertaining "B" melodrama which was the first to initiate the plotline so often used in other genre outings.

3751 Trouble Busters. Majestic, 1933. 55 minutes B/W. D: Lewis D. Collins. SC: Oliver Drake. WITH Jack Hoxie, Lane Chandler, Kay Edwards, Harry Todd, Ben Corbett, William T. Burt, Roger Williams, Charles "Slim" Whitaker. A cowboy comes to the aid of a girl who is about to be cheated out of her oil-rich land by a crook. Pleasant Jack Hoxie vehicle with enough action and humor to please his fans.

3752 Trouble in High Timber Country. ABC-TV, 1980. 100 minutes Color. D: Vincent Sherman. WITH Eddie Albert, Joan Goodfellow, Martin Kove, Robin Dearden, Belinda J. Montgomery, Kevin

Brophy, Steve Doubet, Scott Yeager, James Sikking, Bettye Ackerman, Richard Sanders. A large corporation stops at nothing to absorb a family's lumber and mining business. Fairly good TV movie.

3753 Trouble in Sundown. RKO Radio, 1939. 60 minutes B/W. D: David Howard. SC: Oliver Drake, Dorrell McGowan & Stuart McGowan. WITH George O'Brien, Rosalind Keith, Ray Whitley, Chill Wills, Ward Bond, Cy Kendall, Howard Hickman, Monte Montague, John Dilson, Otto Yamaoka, Ken Card, Slim Whitaker, Bob Burns, Lafe McKee, Earl Dwire, The Phelps Brothers. A man comes to the rescue of his girlfriend's father, a banker falsely accused of robbing his own bank and murdering the night watchman. Exceedingly good George O'Brien vehicle with a solid script.

3754 Trouble in Texas. Grand National, 1937. 64 minutes B/W. D: Robert North Bradbury. SC: Robert Emmett (Tansey). WITH Tex Ritter, Rita (Hayworth) Cansino, Horace Murphy, Earl Dwire, Yakima Canutt, Charles King, Dick Palmer, Tom Cooper, Hal Price, Fred Parker, Chick Hannon, Oral Zumalt, Fox O'Callahan, Henry Knight, Bob Corsby, Jack Smith, Shorty Miller, Milburn Morante, George Morrell, Jack C. Smith, Glenn Strange, The Texas Tornados. When his brother is murdered a rodeo performer teams with a girl undercover agent and finds an outlaw gang working the rodeo circuit. Pleasingly actionful (and tuneful) Tex Ritter vehicle.

3755 True Grit. Paramount, 1969. 128 minutes Color. D: Henry Hathaway. SC: Marguerite Roberts. WITH John Wayne, Glen Campbell, Kim Darby, Jeremy Slate, Robert Duvall, Dennis Hopper, Alfred Ryder, Strother Martin, Jeff Corey, Ron Soble, John Fiedler, James Westerfield, John Doucette, Donald Woods, Edith Atwater, Carlos Rivas, Isabel Boniface, H. W. Gim, John Pickard, Elizabeth Harrower, Ken Renard, Jay Ripley, Kenneth Becker, Myron Healey, Hank Worden, Guy Wilkerson, Boyd "Red" Morgan, Robin Morse. After outlaws murder her father, a teenage girl convinces a one-eyed, hard drinking rogue lawman to help her hunt down the killers. Outstanding genre drama which won John Wayne his highly deserved Academy Award as Rooster Cogburn, although Glen Campbell's performance as Texas Ranger Le Boeuf is best forgotten. Sequel: **Rooster Cogburn** (q.v.). V: Cumberland Video. VD: Blackhawk.

3756 True Grit. ABC-TV/Paramount, 1978. 100 minutes Color. D: Richard T. Heffron. SC: Sandor Stern. WITH Warren Oates, Lisa Pelikan, Lee Meriwether, James Stephens, Jeff Osterhage, Lee Harourt Montgomery, Ramon Bieri, Jack Fletcher, Parley Baer, Lee DeBroux, Fred Cook, Fredmond Gleeson. A young girl tries to make a hard-drinking lawman tow the straight-and-narrow while they track down the lawless. Pale TV movie based on Charles Portis' characters.

3757 The True Story of Jesse James. 20th Century-Fox, 1957. 92 minutes Color. D: Nicholas Ray. SC: Walter Newman. WITH Robert Wagner, Jeffrey Hunter, Hope Lange, Agnes Moorehead, Alan Hale, Alan Baxter, John Carradine, Rachel Stephens, Barney Phillips, Biff Elliot, Frank Overton, Marian Seldes, Barry Atwater, Chubby Johnson, Frank Gorshin, Carl Thayler, John Doucette. When the James Gang fails in its bank holdup attempt at Northfield, Minnesota, the story of Jesse and Frank is told by those who knew them. Psychological approach to the James boys works fairly well although one does get tired of all the flashbacks.

3758 The Trumpet Blows. Paramount, 1934. 72 minutes B/W. D: Stephen Roberts. SC: Bartlett Cormack & Wallace Smith. WITH George Raft, Adolphe Menjou, Frances Drake, Sidney Toler, Edward Ellis, Nydia Westman, Douglas Wood, Lillian Elliott, Katharine De Mille, Francis McDonald, Morgan Wallace, Gertrude Norman, Aleth "Speed" Hanson, Howard Brooks, E. Alyn Warren, Joyce Compton, Charles Stevens, Hooper Atchley, Al Bridge, Mischa Auer. The younger brother of a Mexican bandit wants to be a bullfighter and at the same time falls for his sibling's dancer girlfriend. Unbelievably poor melodrama with Adolphe Menjou as a Pancho Villa-type.

3759 The Trusted Outlaw. Republic, 1937. 60 minutes B/W. D: Robert North Bradbury. SC: George Plympton & Fred Myton. WITH Bob Steele, Lois January, Joan Barclay, Charles King, Earl Dwire, Richard Cramer, Hal Price, Budd Buster, Frank Ball, Oscar Gahan, George Morrell, Chick Hannon, Sherry Tansey, Clyde McClary. A young man, who is the only surviving member of a family of outlaws, tries to stick to the side of the law but crooks are out to make him their patsy. Sturdy Bob Steele actioner.

3760 The Truth. Wrather Corporation, 1956. 75 minutes Color. D: Oscar Rudolph & Earl Bellamy. SC: Wells Root, Thomas Seller, Charles Larson & Robert Leslie Bellem. WITH Clayton Moore, Jay Silverheels, Allen Pinson, Wayne Burson, Jim Bannon, Claire Carleton, Slim Pickens, Dennis Moore, Hank Worden, Buddy Baer, Victor Sen Yung, Judy Dan, Joseph Vitale, Lee Roberts, John Beradino, Mickey Simpson, Tudor Owen, Florence Lake, Brad Jackson, Ron Hagerthy, Ewing Mitchell, Pat Lawless. The Lone Ranger and Tonto try to aid an innocent man, stop an old lady from inciting an Indian massacre and help a Chinese laundryman fight discrimination in a small town. Well done telefeature from "The Lone Ranger" (ABC-TV, 1949-57) series from the segments "The Law and Miss Aggie," "The Banker's Son" and "Letter Bride."

3761 Tucson Raiders. Republic, 1944. 54 minutes B/W. D: Spencer Gordon Bennet. SC: Anthony Coldeway. WITH Bill Elliott, George "Gabby" Hayes, Bobby Blake, Alice Fleming, Peggy Stewart, LeRoy Mason, Ruth Lee, Stanley Andrews, John Whitney, Bud Geary, Karl Hackett, Tom Steele, Tom Chatterton, Ed Cassidy, Fred Graham, Frank McCarroll, Marshall Reed, Stanley Andrews. A crooked banker and governor try to control a territory but are thwarted by Red Ryder, Gabby and Little Beaver, but not until after Red is falsely accused of murder. Mediocre plot, but lots of action in this "Red Ryder" series entry.

3762 Tulsa. Eagle Lion/Pathe Industries, 1949. 90 minutes B/W. D: Stuart Heisler. SC: Frank Nugent & Curtis Kenyon. WITH Susan Hayward, Robert Preston, Pedro Armendariz, Lloyd Gough, Chill Wills, Ed Begley, Roland Jack, Harry Shannon. A beautiful woman becomes wealthy as an oil wildcatter and her greed for riches almost costs her the man she loves. Entertaining melodrama which moves along at a good clip. V: Cumberland Video, Nostalgia Merchant.

3763 The Tulsa Kid. Republic, 1940. 54 (57) minutes B/W. D: George Sherman. SC: Oliver Drake & Anthony Coldeway. WITH Don "Red" Barry, Noah Beery, Luana Walters, David Durand, George Douglas, Ethan Laidlaw, Stanley Blystone, John Elliott, Jack Kirk, Fred "Snowflake" Toones, Charles Murphy, Art Dillard, Cactus Mack, Jimmy Wakely & His Rough Riders (Johnny Bond, Dick Rinehart). A young rancher almost loses his property

in a dispute with a famous gunfighter, who is actually his father. Exciting Don Barry vehicle with Noah Beery stealing the show as the likable gunman.

3764 Tumbledown Ranch in Arizona. Monogram, 1941. 60 minutes B/W. D: S. Roy Luby. SC: Milton Raison. WITH Ray Corrigan, John King, Max Terhune, Sheila Darcy, Marian Kirby, James Craven, Quen Ramsey, John Elliott, Jack Holmes, Steve Clark, Carl Mathews, Tex Palmer, Tex Cooper, Frank Ellis, Frank McCarroll, Chick Hannon, The University of Arizona Glee Club. A young college student suffers a fall and reverts back to a former time when his ancestor was one of the Range Busters who were mixed up with a crooked politician and his saloon-owner henchman. Fast moving entry in "The Range Busters" series with a good blend of music.

3765 Tumbleweed. Universal-International, 1953. 79 minutes Color. D: Nathan Juran. SC: John Meredyth Lucas. WITH Audie Murphy, Lori Nelson, Chill Wills, K. T. Stevens, Russell Johnson, Madge Blake, Roy Roberts, I. Stanford Jolley, Lee Van Cleef, Ralph Moody, Ross Elliott. When Indians attack a wagon train, a guard hides two women and then goes to the Indian chief and tries to negotiate a peace and later is blamed for the killings. Despite its premise, this is a rather tame Audie Murphy vehicle.

3766 Tumbleweed Trail. Producers Releasing Corporation, 1942. 57 minutes B/W. D: Peter Stewart (Sam Newfield). SC: Fred Myton. WITH Art Davis, Bill Boyd, Lee Powell, Marjorie Manners, Jack Rockwell, Charles King, Karl Hackett, George Chesebro, Frank Hagney, Reed Howes, Curley Dresden, George Morrell, Art Dillard, Steve Clark, Dan White, Augie Gomez, Jack Montgomery. Three Texas marshals are on the trail of the man who murdered their pal and they trace him to a town run by a crooked lawman. Barely passable PRC entry in the "Frontier Marshals" series. V: Video Connection.

3767 Tumbleweed Trail. Producers Releasing Corporation, 1946. 59 minutes B/W. D: Robert Emmett Tansey. SC: Frances Kavanaugh. WITH Eddie Dean, Roscoe Ates, Shirley Patterson, Bob Duncan, Johnny McGovern, Ted Adams, Jack O'Shea, Kermit Maynard, William Fawcett, Carl Mathews, Lee Roberts, Frank Ellis, The Sunshine Boys. A singing cowboy comes to the rescue of a pretty girl whose ranch is sought by a gang of cattle rustlers. Fair Eddie Dean film, greatly helped by the title tune and pretty Shirley Patterson.

3768 Tumbleweeds. United Artists, 1925. 81 minutes B/W. D: King Baggott. SC: C. Gardner Sullivan. WITH William S. Hart, Barbara Bedford, Lucien Littlefield, J. Gordon Russell, Richard R. Neill, Jack Murphy, Lillian Leighton, Gertrude Claire, George F. Marion, Captain T. E. Duncan, James Gordon, Fred Gamble, Turner Savage, Monte Collins. A drover meets and falls in love with a pretty girl and they decide to stake a claim in the Oklahoma Territory when it is opened up to settlers. One of the truly great silent Westerns, with its well staged landrush sequence. The film was reissued in 1939 by Astor with music and sound effects along with an eight-minute prolog starring William S. Hart. V: Blackhawk, Sunland Enterprises.

3769 Tumbling Tumbleweeds. Republic, 1935. 54 minutes B/W. D: Joseph Kane. SC: Ford Beebe. WITH Gene Autry, Smiley Burnette, Lucille Browne, Norma Taylor, George ("Gabby") Hayes, Jack Rockwell, George Chesebro, Frankie Marvin, Charles King, Slim Whitaker, Edward Hearn, Tom London, Cornelius Keefe, Cliff Lyons, Tracy Layne, Bud McClure, George Morrell, Oscar Gahan. A young medicine show entertainer returns home to find out who killed his rancher father after his best friend is accused of the crime. Gene Autry's first feature film is a pleasant, fast paced affair.

Tundra see **Arctic Fury**

3770 Twenty Mule Team. Metro-Goldwyn-Mayer, 1940. 84 minutes B/W. D: Richard Thorpe. SC: Cyril Hume, E. E. Paramore & Richard Maibaum. WITH Wallace Beery, Leo Carrillo, Marjorie Rambeau, Anne Baxter, Douglas Fowley, Noah Beery Jr., Berton Churchill, Arthur Hohl, Clem Bevans, Charles Halton, Minor Watson, Oscar O'Shea, Ivan Miller, Lew Kelly, Lloyd Ingraham, Sam Appel. In Death Valley a crook tries to blackmail a miner into revealing the location of his valuable borax mine as he romances the innocent daughter of the local female tavern keeper. Fans of Wallace Beery and Leo Carrillo will enjoy them as the borax-digging partners.

3771 The Twilight Avengers. P.A.C./ Caravel Film, 1970. 89 minutes Color.

D-SC: Al Albert (Alberto Albertini). WITH Tony Kendall, Peter Thorris, Alberto Dell'Acqua, Ida Meda, Albert Farley, Helen Parker, Spartaco Conversi, Attilio Dottesio. A ruthless man takes over a small Mexican town and the members of a traveling circus arrive on the scene and try to get an old soldier and his men to help them free the area. Violent Italian film which is on the mediocre side. Issued in Italy as **I Vendicatori Dell'Ave Maria** (The Avengers of the Ave Maria).

3772 Twilight in the Sierras. Republic, 1950. 54 (67) minutes Color. D: William Witney. SC: Sloan Nibley. WITH Roy Rogers, Dale Evans, Estelita Rodriguez, Pat Brady, Russ Vincent, George Meeker, Fred Kohler Jr., Edward Keane, House Peters Jr., Pierce Lyden, Foy Willing & The Riders of the Purple Sage, Joe Carro, William Lester, Bob Burns, Robert Wilke. On a sheep ranch which employs parolees, parole officer Roy Rogers gets mixed up with crooks who are making counterfeit money and he is falsely accused of murdering one of the gang. Fairly well done Roy Rogers entry, but not too interesting.

3773 Twilight on the Prairie. Universal, 1944. 62 minutes B/W. D: Jean Yarbrough. SC: Clyde Bruckman. WITH Johnny Downs, Vivian Austin, Eddie Quillan, Connie Haines, Leon Errol, Jack Teagarden, Milburn Stone, Jimmie Dodd, Olin Howland, Perc Launders, Dennis Moore, Ralph Peters, Foy Willing & The Riders of the Purple Sage, The Eight Buckaroos. On its way to Hollywood to break into the movies, a cowboy band gets stranded on a ranch and agrees to work there through harvest time. Plenty of songs fill this typically glossy Universal programmer.

3774 Twilight on the Rio Grande. Republic, 1947. 54 (71) minutes B/W. D: Frank McDonald. SC: Dorrell McGowan & Stuart McGowan. WITH Gene Autry, Adele Mara, Sterling Holloway, Bob Steele, George J. Lewis, Charles Evans, Martin Garralaga, Howard Negley, Nacho Galindo, Tex Terry, The Cass County Boys, Frankie Marvin, Bob Burns, George Magril, Enrique Acosta, Barry Norton, Gil Perkins, Nina Campana, Kenne Duncan, Tom London, Alberto Morin, Keith Richards, Jack O'Shea, Bud Osborne, Frank McCarroll, Robert Wilke, Alex Montoya, Connie Henard. Gene Autry gets mixed up with a gang of jewel thieves and a beautiful knife-thrower. Not even a sterling cast can save this slow moving Gene Autry vehicle, his next-to-last for Republic, which actually plays better in its truncated TV version.

3775 Twilight on the Trail. Paramount, 1941. 54 (58) minutes B/W. D: Howard Bretherton. SC: J. Benton Cheney, Ellen Corby & Cecile Kramer. WITH William Boyd, Andy Clyde, Brad King, Wanda McKay, Jack Rockwell, Norman Willis, Robert Kent, Tom London, Robert Kortman, Frank Austin, Clem Fuller, Frank Ellis, Bud Osborne, Johnny Powers, The Jimmy Wakely Trio (Jimmy Wakely, Johnny Bond, Dick Rinehart). In order to round up a gang of rustlers, Hopalong Cassidy masquerades as a dandified Englishman. Just an average outing in the "Hopalong Cassidy" series.

3776 The Twinkle in God's Eye. Republic, 1955. 75 minutes B/W. D: George Blair. SC: P. J. Wolfson. WITH Mickey Rooney, Coleen Gray, Hugh O'Brian, Don "Red" Barry, Touch (Michael) Connors, Joey Forman, Jil Jarmyn, Kem Dibbs, Tony Garcen, Raymond Hatton, Ruta Lee. In a tough Western town, the new parson tries to spread the word of the Lord via humor. A pleasant enough little feature but still a bit sad to contemplate when one considers the stature cinematically of Mickey Rooney just a decade before.

3777 Twisted Trails. Aywon, 1924. 45 minutes B/W. D: Tom Mix. SC: Edwin Ray Coffin. WITH Tom Mix, Bessie Eyton, Eugenie Besserer, Al W. Wilson, Will Machin, Pat Chrisman, Sid Jordan, George Clark, Frank LeRoy, Olcott Byrnes. Two crooked lawmen try to blame their cattle rustling operations on a ranch foreman who has fallen in love with a girl wanted by a corrupt gambler. There is lots of action but a hard-to-follow plot in this Tom Mix feature, which is made up of his 1916 Selig three reeler of the same title and padded out with footage from some of his other Selig short films.

3778 Two-Fisted Justice. Arrow, 1924. 50 minutes B/W. D: Dick Hatton. SC: Bennett Cohen. WITH Dick Hatton, Marilyn Mills. A man seeking revenge for the murder of his doctor brother ends up falling in love with the wife of the killer. Poverty row silent effort which will appeal to fans of this kind of fare.

3779 Two-Fisted Justice. Monogram, 1931. 63 minutes B/W. D-SC: G. A. Durlam.

WITH Tom Tyler, Barbara Weeks, Bobby Nelson, Yakima Canutt, John Elliott, G. D. Wood, Kit Guard, William Walling, Si Jenks, Pedro Regas. President Lincoln sends a scout to the frontier to protect settlers and he uncovers an outlaw gang. Average Tom Tyler outing.

3780 Two-Fisted Justice. Monogram, 1943. 61 minutes B/W. D: Robert Tansey. SC: William L. Nolte. WITH John King, David Sharpe, Max Terhune, Gwen Gaze, Joel Davis, John Elliott, Charles King, George Chesebro, Frank Ellis, Cecil Weston, Hal Price, Carl Mathews, Lynton Brent, Kermit Maynard, Richard Cramer, Tex Palmer, John Curtis. The Range Busters arrive in a small town to bring an outlaw gang to justice and after a run-in with the leader of the gang they are made the community's lawmen. Only a fair outing in the popular "Range Busters" series.

3781 Two-Fisted Law. Columbia, 1932. 64 minutes B/W. D: D. Ross Lederman. SC: Kurt Kempler. WITH Tim McCoy, Alice Day, Wheeler Oakman, John Wayne, Wallace MacDonald, Tully Marshall, Richard Alexander, Walter Brennan. A man, who has been cheated out of his ranch, makes a gold strike and returns home to try and save the ranch of a girl who is being cheated by the same man who took his spread. Generally good Tim McCoy vehicle, based on a William Colt MacDonald story, with fine photography by Benjamin Kline. John Wayne has a small role as one of Tim McCoy's loyal ranch hands.

3782 Two-Fisted Rangers. Columbia, 1940. 62 minutes B/W. D: Joseph H. Lewis. SC: Fred Myton. WITH Charles Starrett, Iris Meredith, Bob Nolan & The Sons of the Pioneers, Bill Cody Jr., Hal Taliaferro, Kenneth MacDonald, Dick Curtis, Ethan Laidlaw, Bob Woodward, James Craig. A cowboy sets out to bring in the land baron who was responsible for the murder of his sheriff brother. Pretty good Charles Starrett vehicle.

3783 Two-Fisted Sheriff. Columbia, 1937. 60 minutes B/W. D: Leon Barsha. SC: Paul Perez. WITH Charles Starrett, Barbara Weeks, Bruce Lane, Ed Peil, Alan Sears, Walter Downing, Ernie Adams, Claire McDowell, Frank Ellis, Robert Walker, George Chesebro, Art Mix, Alan Bridge, Richard Botiller, George Morrell, Merrill McCormack, Edmund Cobb, Tex Cooper, Richard Cramer, Richard Alexander, Maston Williams, Ethan Laidlaw, Steve Clark, Wally West, Fred Burns. A lawman loses his job when his pal is accused of killing his girl's father and is allowed to escape and the ex-sheriff sets out to find the real killer and clear his friend. Sturdy Charles Starrett vehicle enhanced by a superb supporting cast.

3784 Two-Fisted Stranger. Columbia, 1945. 50 minutes B/W. D: Ray Nazarro. SC: Robert Lee Johnson. WITH Charles Starrett, Smiley Burnette, Doris Houck, Zeke Clements, Charles Murray, Lane Chandler, Ted Mapes, George Chesebro, Jack Rockwell, Herman Hack, I. Stanford Jolley, Edmund Cobb, Davidson Clark, Maudie Prickett, Nolan Leary, Frank Ellis, Frank O'Connor, Matty Roubert. Outlaws try to force miners off their properties but find opposition from the Durango Kid. Short, but not much of an effort in the "Durango Kid" series.

3785 Two Flags West. 20th Century-Fox, 1950. 92 minutes B/W. D: Robert Wise. SC: Frank S. Nugent & Casey Robinson. WITH Joseph Cotten, Linda Darnell, Jeff Chandler, Cornel Wilde, Dale Robertson, Jay C. Flippen, Noah Beery Jr., Harry Von Zell, John Sands, Arthur Hunnicutt, Jack Lee, Robert Adler, Harry Carter, Ferris Taylor, Sally Corner, Everett Glass, Marjorie Bennett, Lee MacGregor, Roy Gordon, Aurora Castillo, Stanley Andrews, Don Garner. A group of captured Confederate soldiers agree to fight Indians in the West in order to get out of prison but the commander of the fort they are assigned to hates all rebels. Fair melodrama enhanced by a fine cast.

3786 Two-Gun Justice. Monogram, 1938. 58 minutes B/W. D: Alan James. SC: Fred Myton. WITH Tim McCoy, Betty Compson, Joan Barclay, John Merton, Lane Chandler, Al Bridge, Tony Paton, Alan Cavan, Harry Strang, Earl Dwire, Enid Parrish, Olin Francis, Curley Dresden, Jack Ingram. Lawman Tim Carson takes on the guise of a Mexican bandit "The Vulture" in order to break up the notorious Kane gang. Cheap, quick on action and shouldered with an obtrusive canned music score, this Tim McCoy vehicle boasted two leading ladies, silent star Betty Compson and Joan Barclay. V: Video Dimensions.

3787 Two-Gun Lady. Associated Film Releasing, 1956. 75 minutes B/W. D: Richard Bartlett. SC: Norman Jolley.

WITH Peggie Castle, William Talman, Marie Windsor, Earle Lyon, Robert Lowery, Joe Besser, Ian MacDonald, Barbara Turner, Norman Jolley, Susan Lang, Kit Carson, Arvo Ojala, Karl Hansen, Dave Tomack, Sid Lopez, Gregory Moffet, Ben Cameron. A gun-toting girl teams with a lawman in hunting down the men who murdered her father. Low budget actioner for fans of Peggie Castle and Marie Windsor.

3788 Two-Gun Law. Columbia, 1937. 56 minutes B/W. D: Leon Barsha. SC: John Rathmell. WITH Charles Starrett, Peggy Stratford, Hank Bell, Ed LeSaint, Charles Middleton, Alan Bridge, Lee Prather, Dick Curtis, Victor Potel, George Chesebro, Art Mix, George Morrell, Tex Cooper. An outlaw wants his adopted son to go straight and the young man and his pal go to a ranch to get jobs but overhear the foreman and some men planning to rustle their boss' cattle. Entertaining entry in the well made Charles Starrett early Columbia series.

3789 The Two-Gun Man. Tiffany, 1931. 60 minutes B/W. D: Phil Rosen. SC: John (Jack) Natteford. WITH Ken Maynard, Lucille Powers, Nita Martin, Charles King, Lafe McKee, Tom London, Murdock McQuarrie, Walter Perry, Will Stanton, William Jackie, Ethan Allen, Jim Corey, Blackjack Ward, Roy Bucko, Buck Bucko. A cowboy opposes a group of crooked cattlemen who are behind the rustling of area herds. Fast moving Ken Maynard oater. V: Discount Video.

3790 Two-Gun Sheriff. Republic, 1941. 54 minutes B/W. D: George Sherman. SC: Doris Schroeder. WITH Don "Red" Barry, Lynn Merrick, Lupita Tovar, Fred Kohler Jr., Jay Novello, Marin Sais, Fred "Snowflake" Toones, Milton Kibbee, Dirk Thane, Archie Hall, Charles Thomas, Lee Shumway, John Merton, Carleton Young, Curley Dresden, Buck Moulton, Bud McClure, Tex Parker, Herman Nolan, George Plues. An outlaw is used by a gang of cattle thieves to take the place of a sheriff, but the two men turn out to be brothers and the outlaw double-crosses the gang leader. A complicated plot and plenty of action in this Don Barry film, with a good musical score by Cy Feuer.

3791 Two-Gun Troubador. Spectrum, 1939. 58 minutes B/W. D: Raymond K. Johnson. SC: Richard L. Bare & Phil Dunham. WITH Fred Scott, Claire

Rochelle, Harry Harvey, John Merton, Buddy Lenhart, Carl Mathews, Buddy Kelly, Harry Harvey Jr., Gene Howard, William Woods, Jack Ingram, Bud Osborne, John Ward, Cactus Mack. Years after his uncle killed his father for his property, a young man returns to claim his inheritance and in doing so takes on the guise of a masked avenger. Pleasant Fred Scott vehicle with some good tunes.

3792 Two Guns and a Badge. Allied Artists, 1954. 69 minutes B/W. D: Lewis D. Collins. SC: Dan Ullman. WITH Wayne Morris, Beverly Garland, Morris Ankrum, Roy Barcroft, William Phipps, Damian O'Flynn, I. Stanford Jolley, Robert Wilke, Chuck Courtney, Henry Rowland. An ex-convict is mistaken for a deputy sheriff when he arrives in a small town and soon finds himself up against a corrupt rancher while falling in love with the man's daughter. Considered the final "B" series Western effort, this little film is a fit finale to a wonderful genre.

3793 Two Guys from Texas. Warner Brothers, 1948. 86 minutes Color. D: David Butler. SC: I. A. L. Diamond & Allen Boretz. WITH Dennis Morgan, Jack Carson, Dorothy Malone, Penny Edwards, Forrest Tucker, Fred Clark, Gerald Mohr, John Alvin, Andrew Tombes, Monte Blue, The Philharmonic Trio. Two vaudeville entertainers find themselves stranded on a Texas ranch where they fight crooks and meet two pretty girls. Okay reworking of **The Cowboy from Brooklyn** (Warner Brothers, 1938).

3794 Two in Revolt. RKO Radio, 1936. 65 minutes B/W. D: Glenn Tyron. SC: Frank Howard Clark, Ferdinand Reyher & Jerry Hutchinson. WITH John Arledge, Louise Latimer, Moroni Olsen, Emmett Vogan, Harry Jans, Murray Alper, Willie Best, Max Wagner, Ethan Laidlaw, Lightning (dog), Warrior (horse). Two animals team to help a man in his battle with outlaws. Fair juvenile matinee fare.

3795 Two Mules for Sister Sara. Universal, 1970. 105 minutes Color. D: Donald Siegel. SC: Albert Maltz. WITH Shirley MacLaine, Clint Eastwood, Armando Silvestre, Manolo Fabregas, John Kelly, Enrique Lucero, Jose Chavez. A mercenary fighting for the cause of Juarez leads a free-wheeling anti-Juarez nun across the Mexican desert. Uneven but rather fun teaming of Clint Eastwood and Shirley MacLaine. V: MCA.

3796 Two Rode Together. Columbia, 1961. 109 minutes Color. D: John Ford. SC: Frank Nugent. WITH James Stewart, Richard Widmark, Shirley Jones, Linda Cristal, Andy Devine, John McIntire, Paul Birch, Willis Bouchey, Henry Brandon, Harry Carey Jr., Ken Curtis, Olive Carey, Chet Douglas, Annelle Hayes, David Kent, Anna Lee, Jeanette Nolan, Edward Brophy, John Qualen, Ford Rainey, Woody Strode, O. Z. Whitehead, Cliff Lyons, Mae Marsh, Frank Baker, Ruth Clifford, Ted Knight, Major Sam Harris, Jack Pennick, Chuck Roberson, Dan Borzage, Bill Henry, Chuck Hayward. A lawman and a cavalry lieutenant form an uneasy alliance in a mission to negotiate the return of settlers kidnapped by the Comanches. Generally good John Ford film highlighted by a number of fine performances, especially Mae Marsh as the captured woman who explains why she does not want to return to her people.

3797 Two Violent Men. P.E.A./Arturo Gonzales, 1965. 94 minutes Color. D: Anthony Greepy (Primo Zeglio). SC: Jesus Navarro & Primo Zeglio. WITH Alan Scott, George (Jorge) Martin, Susy Andersen, Mary Badmayev, Andrew Scott, Pauline Baards, Sylvia Solar, Mike Brendell. A lawman and the friend he is assigned to arrest on a murder charge team to stop the siege of a ranch by outlaws. Better-than-average Italian oater with a fairly literate script. Italian title: **I Due Violenti** (Two Violent Men). Spanish title: **Los Rurales de Texas.** British title: **Two Gunmen.**

U

3798 The Ugly Ones. United Artists, 1968. 96 minutes Color. D: Eugenio Martin. SC: Jose G. Maesso & Eugenio Martin. WITH Richard Wyler, Tomas Milian, Mario Brega, Hugo Blanco, Glenn Foster, Ella Karin, Manolo Zarzo, Lola Gaos, Ricardo Canales. A young woman aids an outlaw in escaping from a bounty hunter only to learn the criminal has actually turned into a murderer due to his hard and roving life as a bandit. Very violent Italian Western issued originally in that country in 1966 as **The Bounty Killer.**

3799 Ulzana's Raid. Universal, 1972. 103 minutes Color. D: Robert Aldrich. SC: Alan Sharp. WITH Burt Lancaster,

Bruce Davison, Jorge Luke, Richard Jaeckel, Joaquin Martinez, Lloyd Bochner, Karl Swenson, Douglas Walton, Dran Hamilton, John Pearce, Gladys Holland, Margaret Fairchild, Aimee Eccles, Richard Bull, Otto Reichow, Dean Smith, Larry Randles. Three men, an aging Indian fighter, a young lieutenant and an Indian scout hunt a raiding party which has been terrorizing local citizens. Fair melodrama, which is well acted but too violent.

3800 Uncle Sam Magoo. U.P.A., 1969. 55 minutes Color. WITH Jim Backus (voice). Mr. Magoo takes on the guise of Uncle Sam and looks back at the nation's history, including his being national heroes like Paul Revere and Davy Crockett. Fans of Mr. Magoo will get a kick out of this animated feature.

3801 Unconquered. Paramount, 1947. 146 minutes Color. D: Cecil B. DeMille. SC: Charles Bennett, Frederick M. Frank & Jesse Lasky Jr. WITH Gary Cooper, Paulette Goddard, Howard Da Silva, Boris Karloff, Cecil Kellaway, Ward Bond, Katherine De Mille, Henry Wilcoxon, C. Aubrey Smith, Victor Varconi, Virginia Grey, Porter Hall, Mike Mazurki, Richard Gaines, Virginia Campbell, Gavin Muir, Alan Napier, Nan Sutherland, Marc Lawrence, Jane Nigh, Robert Warwick, Lloyd Bridges, Oliver Thorndike, Russ Conklin, John Mylong, George Kirby, Leonard Carey, Frank R. Wilcox, Davison Clark, Griff Barnett, Raymond Hatton, Julia Faye, Paul E. Burns, Mary Field, Clarence Muse, Matthew Boulton, Chief Thundercloud, Jack Pennick, Lex Barker, Charles Middleton. In the frontier of the 1760s a Virginia militiaman opposes a corrupt trader who is selling guns to Chief Pontiac's followers while they both vie for the same beautiful girl, a bond servant. There is not much here in the way of real history, but this Cecil B. DeMille production is colorful and exciting.

3802 Unconquered Bandit. Reliable, 1935. 57 minutes B/W. D: Harry S. Webb. SC: Rose Gordon & Lou C. Borden. WITH Tom Tyler, Lillian Gilmore, Charles "Slim" Whitaker, William Gould, John Elliott, Earl Dwire, Joe de la Cruz, George Chesebro, Richard Alexander, Lew Meehan, George Hazel, Wally Wales, Ben Corbett, Colin Chase. When his dad is murdered by a gang secretly led by a policeman, a cowboy plans to use the cop's pretty niece to get revenge for the crime. Better than average Tom Tyler-Reliable vehicle.

3803 The Undefeated. 20th Century-Fox, 1969. 118 minutes Color. D: Andrew V. McLaglen. SC: James Lee Barrett. WITH John Wayne, Rock Hudson, Tony Aguilar, Roman Gabriel, Marian McCargo, Lee Meriwether, Merlin Olsen, Melissa Newman, Bruce Cabot, Michael Vincent, Ben Johnson, Edward Faulkner, Harry Carey Jr., Paul Fix, Royal Dano, Richard Mulligan, Carlos Rivas, John Agar, Guy Raymond, Don Collier, Big John Hamilton, Dub Taylor, Henry Beckman, Victor Junco, Robert Donner, Pedro Armendariz Jr., James Dobson, Rudy Diaz, Richard Angarola, James McEachin, Gregg Palmer, Juan Garcia, Kiel Martin, Bob Gravage, Chuck Roberson. Veterans of the Civil War, both Union and Confederate, form an uneasy alliance as they head for Mexico to start new lives. Not one of John Wayne's best vehicles, but still an entertaining one with a fine supporting cast, especially Dub Taylor as the wagon train cook.

3804 Under a Texas Moon. Warner Brothers, 1930. 82 minutes Color. D: Michael Curtiz. SC: Gordon Rigby. WITH Frank Fay, Raquel Torres, Myrna Loy, Armida, Noah Beery, George E. Stone, George Cooper, Fred Kohler, Betty Boyd, Charles Sellon, Jack Curtis, Sam Appel, Tully Marshall, Mona Maris, Francisco Maran, Tom Dix, Jerry Barrett, Inez Gomez, Edythe Kramera, Bruce Covington. A dashing Mexican adventurer and his pals romance two pretty girls at a ranch and plan to get the reward for the outlaws rustling the owner's cattle. Creaky and badly dated musical Western.

3805 Under Arizona Skies. Monogram, 1946. 60 minutes B/W. D: Lambert Hillyer. SC: J. Benton Cheney. WITH Johnny Mack Brown, Raymond Hatton, Reno Blair, Riley Hill, Tristram Coffin, Reed Howes, Ted Adams, Ray Bennett, Frank LaRue, Steve Clark, Jack Rockwell, Bud Geary, Ted Mapes, Dusty Rhodes, Kermit Maynard, Smith Ballew, Leonard St. Leo, Lynton Brent, Ray Jones, The Sons of the Sage. A rancher who heads an outlaw rustling gang is out to get another rancher's land but two men come to his rescue. Pretty fair Johnny Mack Brown vehicle with Smith Ballew along for a couple of tunes.

3806 Under California Stars. Republic, 1948. 54 (70) minutes Color. D: William Witney. SC: Sloan Nibley & Paul Gagelin. WITH Roy Rogers, Jane Frazee, Andy Devine, Bob Nolan & The Sons of the Pioneers, Michael Chapin, Wade Crosby,

George Lloyd, House Peters Jr., Steve Clark, Joseph Carro, Paul Powers, John Wald. Crooks steal movie star Roy Rogers' horse Trigger and demand a $100,000 ransom. Colorful Roy Rogers actioner which is badly cut for TV; Roy reprises the song "Dust," which he sang in his first starrer, **Under Western Stars** (q.v.).

3807 Under Colorado Skies. Republic, 1947. 65 minutes Color. D: R. G. Springsteen. SC: Louise Rousseau. WITH Monte Hale, Adrian Booth, Foy Willing & The Riders of the Purple Sage, Paul Hurst, William Haade, John Alvin, LeRoy Mason, Tom London, Steve Darrell, Gene Evans, Ted Adams, Steve Raines, Hank Patterson. From the knowledge he received at medical school, a cowboy is able to track down a gang of outlaws. Okay Monte Hale effort.

3808 Under Fiesta Stars. Republic, 1941. 54 (64) minutes B/W. D: Frank McDonald. SC: Karl Brown & Eliot Gibbons. WITH Gene Autry, Smiley Burnette, Carol Hughes, Frank Darien, Joe Straugh Jr., Pauline Drake, Ivan Miller, Sam Flint, John Merton, Jack Kirk, Curley Dresden, Hal Taliaferro, Frankie Marvin, Pascale Perry, Elias Gamboa, Inez Palange. Gene Autry manages a mine but half-interest is controlled by a girl who wants to sell the property and who is being bilked by two corrupt lawyers. There is not much fiesta in this slow moving Gene Autry vehicle.

3809 Under Mexicali Stars. Republic, 1950. 67 minutes B/W. D: George Blair. SC: Bob Williams. WITH Rex Allen, Buddy Ebsen, Dorothy Patrick, Roy Barcroft, Percy Helton, Walter Coy, Steve Darrell, Alberto Morin, Ray Walker, Frank Ferguson, Stanley Andrews, Robert Bice. A Treasury agent, who is also a cowboy, searches for a counterfeit operation and discovers they are using helicopters to smuggle gold. Exciting Rex Allen vehicle.

3810 Under Montana Skies. Tiffany, 1930. 60 minutes B/W. D: Richard Thorpe. SC: Bennett Cohen & James A. Aubrey. WITH Kenneth Harlan, Dorothy Gulliver, Slim Summerville, Nita Martan, Christian Frank, Harry Todd, Ethel Wales, Lafe McKee. A cowboy falls for a girl in a theatrical troupe and helps save the show but a cattle rustler who he sent to jail is released and robs the show's box office. Antiquated early genre musical comedy.

3811 Under Nevada Skies. Republic, 1946. 54 (69) minutes B/W. D: Frank McDonald. SC: Paul Gengelin & J. Benton Cheney. WITH Roy Rogers, George "Gabby" Hayes, Dale Evans, Bob Nolan & The Sons of the Pioneers, Douglass Dumbrille, Tristram Coffin, Leyland Hodgson, Rudolph Anders, LeRoy Mason, George J. Lewis, Iron Eyes Cody. Radio singer Roy Rogers tries to get to the bottom of the mystery of who killed his friend, the manager of a nightclub in a small Western town. Mystery element and the use of an A-bomb component in the plot greatly helps this fast-moving Roy Rogers vehicle, which is somewhat hurt by losing 15 minutes for TV.

3812 Under Strange Flags. Crescent, 1937. 61 minutes B/W. D: I. V. Willat. SC: Mary Ireland. WITH Tom Keene, Lana (Luana) Walters, Budd Buster, Maurice Black, Roy D'Arcy, Paul Sutton, Paul Barrett, Donald Reed, Jane Wolfe. Americans mining silver in Mexico find their shipments being hijacked by Pancho Villa and his followers. Fair entry in the Crescent historical series starring Tom Keene.

3813 Under Texas Skies. Syndicate, 1930. 60 minutes B/W. D: J. P. McGowan. SC: G. A. Durlam. WITH Bob Custer, Natalie Kingston, Bill Cody, Tom London, Lane Chandler, Bob Roper, William McCall, Joseph Marba. When a young woman rancher plans to sell her horses to the government, an agent claims one of her wranglers is working with Mexican revolutionaries. Slow moving Bob Custer vehicle.

3814 Under Texas Skies. Republic, 1940. 54 (57) minutes B/W. D: George Sherman. SC: Anthony Coldeway & Betty Burbridge. WITH Robert Livingston, Bob Steele, Rufe Davis, Lois Ranson, Henry Brandon, Wade Boteler, Rex Lease, Yakima Canutt, Jack Ingram, Earle Hodgins, Walter Tetley, Curley Dresden, Jack Kirk, Ted Mapes, Vester Pegg. When a lawman is murdered the Three Mesquiteers try to find the culprit. Fast paced entry in "The Three Mesquiteers" series.

3815 Under the Pampas Moon. Fox, 1935. 78 minutes B/W. D: James Tinling. SC: Ernest Pascal & Bradley King. WITH Warner Baxter, Ketti Gallian, J. Carroll Naish, John Miljan, Armida, Ann Codee, Jack LaRue, George Irving, Rita (Hayworth) Cansino, Veloz & Yolanda, Tito Guizar, Chris-Pin Martin, Max Wagner,

Philip Cooper, Sam Appel, Arthur Stone, George Lewis, Paul Porcasi, Lona Andre, Martin Garralaga, Tommy Coates, Frank Cordel, Joseph Rickson, Catherine Cotter, Charles Stevens, Pedro Regas, Fred Malatesta, Juan Ortiz, Joe Dominguez, Nick Thompson, Manuel Perez, Soledad Jiminez, John Eberts. In Argentina a gaucho's horse is stolen by crooks who want to run him in a big race in Buenos Aires and the South American cowboy heads to the big city to get him back. Mediocre attempt to transfer Warner Baxter's characterization of a Cisco Kid-type to the Pampas; noteworthy only as Rita Hayworth's first film.

3816 Under the Tonto Rim. Paramount, 1928. 6 reels. D: Herman C. Raymaker. SC: J. Walter Ruben. WITH Richard Arlen, Mary Brian, Alfred Allen, Jack Luden, Harry T. Morey, William Franey, Harry Todd, Bruce Gordon, Jack Byron. A man is blackmailed by a murderer but is aided by a miner who loves his sister. Pretty good adaptation of the Zane Grey novel makes this silent film worth a look.

3817 Under the Tonto Rim. Paramount, 1933. 63 minutes B/W. D: Henry Hathaway. SC: Jack Cunningham & Gerald Geraghty. WITH Stuart Erwin, Verna Hillie, Fred Kohler, Fuzzy Knight, John Lodge, George Barbier, Patricia Farley, Edwin J. Brady, Marion Burdell, Allan Garcia. A cowpoke who operates on the slow side ends up capturing a murderer and winning the love of his boss's daughter. First sound version of the Zane Grey work which is not quite as good as the silent film but still entertaining, especially for Stuart Erwin fans.

3818 Under the Tonto Rim. RKO Radio, 1947. 61 minutes B/W. D: Lew Landers. SC: Norman Houston. WITH Tim Holt, Nan Leslie, Richard Martin, Richard Powers, Carol Forman, Tony Barrett, Harry Harvey Jason Robards, Robert Clarke, Jay Norris, Lex Barker, Steve Savage. A mysterious outlaw gang is trailed by a young cowboy who is determined to capture them. Although this film bears little resemblance to the Zane Grey novel it is a fast effort with fine photography by Anent Hunt.

3819 Under Western Skies. Universal, 1945. 57 minutes B/W. D: Jean Yarbrough. SC: Stanley Roberts & Clyde Bruckman. WITH Martha O'Driscoll, Noah Berry Jr., Leo Carrillo, Leon Errol, Irving Bacon,

Ian Keith, Jennifer Holt, Edna May Wonacott, Earle Hodgins, Shaw & Lee, Dorothy Granger, Jack Rice, Gladys Blake, George Lloyd, Claire Whitney, Frank Lackteen, Jack Ingram, Patsy O'Bryne, Nan Leslie, Eddy Waller, Perc Launders, Donald Kerr, Warren Jackson, Charles Sherlock. The denizens of a small Western town oppose the staging of a traveling show especially when the pretty leading lady gets involved with the town's school teacher and a masked outlaw. Entertaining oater musical programmer.

3820 Under Western Stars. Republic, 1938. 54 (65) minutes B/W. D: Joseph Kane. SC: Dorrell McGowan, Stuart McGowan & Betty Burbridge. WITH Roy Rogers, Smiley Burnette, Carol Hughes, The Maple City Four, Guy Usher, Earl Dwire, Dick Elliott, Jack Rockwell, Frankie Marvin, Earle Hodgins, Jack Ingram, Kenneth Harlan, Tom Chatterton, Alden Chase, Brandon Beach, Slim Whitaker, Jean Fowler, Jack Kirk, Fred Burns, Tex Cooper, Curley Dresden, Bill Woolfe. Roy Rogers is drafted into running for Congress when the incumbent proves to be the pawn of a large water company which is overcharging ranchers for water during a drought. Roy Rogers' first starring vehicle is a good one and in it he sings "That Pioneer Mother of Mine" and Johnny Marvin's Academy Award nominated "Dust."

3821 Under Cover Man. Republic, 1936. 56 minutes B/W. D: Albert Ray. SC: Andrew Bennison. WITH Johnny Mack Brown, Suzanne Kaaren, Ted Adams, Frank Darien, Lloyd Ingraham, Horace Murphy, Dick Moorehead, Ed Cassidy, Margaret Mann, Frank Ball, George Morrell. A Wells Fargo agent saves a girl and gold during a holdup and the local bar owner, who is the leader of the outlaw gang, plans revenge. Johnny Mack Brown's initial Republic series oater is a pleasantly paced affair. V: Cumberland Video.

3822 Undercover Man. United Artists, 1942. 54 (68) minutes B/W. D: Lesley Selander. SC: J. Benton Cheney. WITH William Boyd, Andy Clyde, Jay Kirby, Antonio Moreno, Nora Lane, Chris-Pin Martin, Esther Estrella, John Vosper, Eva Puig, Alan Baldwin, Jack Rockwell, Pierce Lyden, Martin Garralaga, Earle Hodgins, Frank Ellis, Ted Wells, Joe Dominguez. Hopalong Cassidy is falsely accused of robbery and sets out to get the real culprits, a gang operating along the Mexican border. The first United

Artists' "Hopalong Cassidy" release is a bit on the slow side and plays better in its shorter TV version.

3823 Undercover Men. Booth Dominions Pictures, 1935. 60 minutes B/W. D: Sam (Newfield) Neufield. WITH Charles Starrett, Adrienne Dore, Kenneth (Kenne) Duncan, Wheeler Oakman, Eric Clavering, Phil Brandon, Muriel Dean. A Mountie, working as an undercover agent, is on the trail of an outlaw in the wilds of Canada. Canadian-made feature of interest to Charles Starrett fans since it predates his Columbia series.

3824 Undercover Woman. Republic, 1946. 56 minutes B/W. D: Thomas Carr. SC: Jerry Sackheim & Sherman Lowe. WITH Stephanie Bachelor, Robert Livingston, Richard Fraser, Isabel Withers, Helen Heigh, Edythe Elliott, John Dehner, Elaine Lange, Betty Blythe, Tom London, Larry Blake. When a murder is committed at a dude ranch in the West a female detective tries to solve the crime. Pleasing Republic programmer.

3825 Underground Rustlers. Monogram, 1941. 59 minutes B/W. D: S. Roy Luby. SC: Bud Tuttle, Elizabeth Beecher & John Vlahos. WITH Ray Corrigan, John King, Max Terhune, Gwen Gaze, Robert Blair, Forrest Taylor, Bud Osborne, Steve Clark, Tom London, Carl Mathews, John Elliott, Richard Cramer, Tex Palmer, Ed Piel Sr., Tex Cooper, Frank McCarroll. The Range Busters are called in to capture a gang of gold smugglers. Fairly good entry in "The Range Busters" series although the show belongs to the wonderful Max Terhune who disguises himself as a suspender salesman.

3826 Unexpected Guest. United Artists, 1947. 60 minutes B/W. D: George Archainbaud. SC: Ande Lamb. WITH William Boyd, Andy Clyde, Rand Brooks, Una O'Connor, Pamela Tate, Ian Wolfe, John Parrish, Robert Williams, Earle Hodgins, Ned Young, Joel Friedkin. Hopalong Cassidy tries to find out who is behind a series of mysterious incidents, including the framing of Lucky on a murder charge, when California inherits a portion of his late cousin's ranch. Acceptable later entry in the "Hopalong Cassidy" series helped by its use of the mystery element.

3827 The Unforgiven. United Artists, 1960. 120 minutes Color. D: John Huston. SC: Ben Maddow. WITH Burt Lancaster, Audrey Hepburn, Audie Murphy, John Saxon, Charles Bickford, Lillian Gish, Albert Salmi, Joseph Wiseman, June Walker, Kipp Hamilton, Arnold Merritt, Carlos Rivas, Doug McClure. In a remote area the inhabitants resent an Indian girl who has been raised as white and she is threatened by them when the Kiowa Indians go on the warpath. Overwrought melodrama which should have been much better than it is although any film with Lillian Gish is always worth seeing.

3828 Union Pacific. Paramount, 1939. 133 minutes B/W. D: Cecil B. DeMille. SC: Walter DeLeon, C. Gardner Sullivan & Jesse Lasky Jr. WITH Barbara Stanwyck, Joel McCrea, Robert Preston, Akim Tamiroff, Lynne Overman, Brian Donlevy, Robert Barrat, Anthony Quinn, Stanley Ridges, Henry Kolker, Francis McDonald, Willard Robertson, Harold Goodwin, Evelyn Keyes, Richard Lane, William Haade, Regis Toomey, Lon Chaney Jr., J. M. Kerrigan, Fuzzy Knight, Harry Woods, Joseph Crehan, Julia Faye, Sheila Darcy, Joseph Sawyer, Earl Askam, John Marston, Byron Foulger, Selmer Jackson, Morgan Wallace, Russell Hicks, May Beatty, Ernie Adams, William J. Worthington, Guy Usher, James McNamara, Gus Glassmire, Stanley Andrews, Paul Everton, Jack Pennick. A troubleshooter for the Union Pacific Railroad romances an engineer's daughter and tries to combat sabotage to the railroad in its competition with the Central Pacific for the completion of the first transcontinental line. Brawling, and typically entertaining, Cecil B. DeMille epic.

3829 Unknown Ranger. Aywon, 1920. 45 minutes B/W. WITH Rex Ray, Marie Newall, Ben Hill. Texas Rangers are on the trail of a gang smuggling opium across the Mexican border. Fairly interesting silent outing not only for its plot but because the villain escapes scot-free at the end.

3830 Unknown Ranger. Columbia, 1936. 58 minutes B/W. D: Spencer Gordon Bennet. SC: Nate Gatzert. WITH Bob Allen, Martha Tibbets, Harry Woods, Henry Hall, Hal Taliaferro, Buzzy (Buzz) Henry, Edward Hearn, Robert Kortman, Lew Meehan, Bob McKenzie, Art Mix. Rustlers plan to use a wild stallion to steal a rancher's horse herd but a cowboy (actually a ranger) working on the ranch gets wind of the plan. Bob Allen's first series film is a good one and in it Hal Taliaferro (Wally Wales) even sings a novelty tune.

3831 Unknown Valley. Columbia, 1933. 69 minutes B/W. D-SC: Lambert Hillyer. WITH Buck Jones, Cecilia Parker, Bert Black, Carlotta Warwick, Arthur Wanzer, Wade Boteler, Frank McGlynn, Charles Thurston, Ward Bond, Gaylord (Steve) Pendleton, Alf James, Frank Ellis. While searching for his father, an ex-Army scout becomes lost in the desert and is rescued by a girl belonging to a strange religious sect. Out-of-the-ordinary "B" Western which relies far more on its well written script than usual genre action; a very good film.

3832 Unknown Wilderness. American National Enterprises, 1973. 94 minutes Color. D: Austin Green. SC: Roger Davis & Austin Green. Two teenage boys learn to survive in the mountain wilderness of Montana and Wyoming as they search for the legendary treasure of Frency Latrek. Cheaply made but eye-pleasing docudrama.

3833 The Unsinkable Molly Brown. Metro-Goldwyn-Mayer, 1964. 128 minutes Color. D: Charles Walters. SC: Helen Deutsch. WITH Debbie Reynolds, Harve Presnell, Ed Begley, Jack Kruschen, Hermione Baddeley, Martita Hunt, Vassili Lambrinos, Fred Essler, Harvey Lembeck, Kathryn Card, Hayden Rorke, Harry Holcombe, Amy Douglas, George Mitchell, Vaughn Taylor, Anthony Eustrel, Audrey Christie, Lauren Gilbert. In the late 1800s a young orphan girl marries a miner and they strike it rich but are snubbed in Denver but go to Europe where they become the toast of society. Zesty musical with Meredith Willson-Richard Morris score.

3834 Untamed. Paramount, 1940. 83 minutes Color. D: George Archainbaud. SC: Frederick Hazlett Brennan & Frank Butler. WITH Ray Milland, Patricia Morison, Akim Tamiroff, William Frawley, Jane Darwell, J. M. Kerrigan, J. Farrell MacDonald, Esther Dale, Eily Malyon, Fay Helm, Clem Bevans, Sibyl Harris, Roscoe Ates, Gertrude W. Hoffman, Charles Waldron, Darryl Hickman, Charlene Wyatt, Bahe Denetdeel, Donna Jean Lester, Byron Foulger, Helen Brown, Guy Wilkerson, Charles Stevens, Brenda Fowler, Ann Doran, Pauline Haddon, Dorothy Adams, Betsy Ross Clarke. An alcoholic New York City surgeon goes to the north woods to recover and decides to stay after falling in love with his guide's pretty wife. Very well made melodrama enhanced by scenic locales and good use of Technicolor.

3835 Untamed. 20th Century-Fox, 1955. 111 minutes Color. D: Henry King. SC: Talbot Jennings, Frank Fenton & Michael Blankfort. WITH Tyrone Power, Susan Hayward, Richard Egan, John Justin, Agnes Moorehead, Rita Moreno, Hope Emerson, Brad Dexter, Henry O'Neill, Paul Thompson, Alexander D. Havemann, Louis Mercier, Emmett Smith, Jack Macy, Bobby Diamond, Gary Diamond, Brian Corcoran, Kevin Corcoran, Eleanor Audley, Cecil Weston, Forest Burns, Leonard Carey. In South Africa a Dutchman saves a wagon train of settlers from a Zulu attack and falls in love with the pretty wife of a man who is killed in the attack. Entertaining melodrama with beautiful South African scenery although the plot tends more toward the Susan Hayward character than to Tyrone Power's character, who wants to set up a Dutch state.

3836 The Untamed Breed. Columbia, 1948. 79 minutes Color. D: Charles Lamont. SC: Tom Reed. WITH Sonny Tufts, Barbara Britton, George "Gabby" Hayes, Edgar Buchanan, William Bishop, George E. Stone, Joseph Sawyer, Gordon Jones, James Kirkwood, Harry Tyler, Virginia Brissac, Reed Howes. In order to enhance their cattle herds, ranchers along the Pecos River in Texas go along with a man's plan to purchase a Brahma bull. Passable but fairly standard drama.

3837 Untamed Frontier. Universal-International, 1952. 75 minutes Color. D: Hugo Fregonese. SC: Gerald Drayson Adams, John Bagni & Gwen Bagni. WITH Joseph Cotten, Shelley Winters, Scott Brady, Suzan Ball, Minor Watson, Katherine Emery, Antonio Moreno, Douglas Spencer, John Alexander, Richard Garland, Lee Van Cleef, Robert Anderson, Fess Parker. A wealthy cattle baron uses any means he can to stop settlers from taking free government land which he wants for his herds. Okay actioner carried along by good direction and performances.

3838 Untamed Heiress. Republic, 1954. 70 minutes B/W. D: Charles Lamont. SC: Barry Shipman. WITH Judy Canova, Donald (Don "Red") Barry, Taylor Holmes, George Cleveland, Chick Chandler, Jack Kruschen, Hugh Sanders, Douglas Fowley, William Haade, Ellen Corby. A millionaire hires two talent agents to find a woman who once gave him money and they find out she has died and that her daughter is in an orphanage. Typical Judy Canova corn pone effort which will appeal to her followers.

3839 Up the MacGregors. Columbia, 1968. 98 minutes Color. D: Frank Garfield (Franco Giraldi). SC: Fernand Lion (Fernando Di Leo), Vincent Eagle (Enzo Dell-Aquila), Paul Levy (Paolo Levi), Jose Marie Rodriguez & Frank Garfield. WITH David Bailey, Agatha Flory, Leo Anchoriz, Robert Camardiel, Cole Kitosh, Nick Anderson, Paul Carter, Julio Perez Tabernero, Hugo Blanco, Saturnino Cerra, George Rigaud, Roy Bossier, Victor Israel, Ann Casares, Francesco Tensi, Jesus Guzman, King Black, Antonio Vico, Enlena Montoya, Tito Garcia, Anne-Marie Noe, Margaret Horowitz, Margaret Merritt, Kathleen Parker, Ana Maria Mendoza. The seven MacGregor brothers are on the trail of an outlaw gang which stole all of their families' possessions. Pleasant sequel to **Seven Guns for the MacGregors** (q.v.) and, like its predecessor, less violent and more amusing than most of its ilk. Released in Italy in 1966 as **Sette Donne Per I MacGregor** (Seven Women for the MacGregors) by Produzione D.S./Jolly/Talia Film.

3840 Utah. Republic, 1945. 54 (78) minutes B/W. D: John English. SC: Jack Townley & John K. Butler. WITH Roy Rogers, George "Gabby" Hayes, Dale Evans, Peggy Stewart, Beverly Lloyd, Grant Withers, Hal Taliaferro, Bob Nolan & The Sons of the Pioneers, Jack Rutherford, Emmett Vogan, Ed Cassidy, Vivien Oakland, Jill Browning, Ralph Colby. Roy and Gabby try to stop an out-of-work show girl from selling a ranch she inherited to sheep herders. Fairly entertaining with a dull production number finale. V: Video Dimensions.

3841 Utah Blaine. Columbia, 1957. 75 minutes B/W. D: Fred F. Sears. SC: Robert E. Kent & James B. Gordon. WITH Rory Calhoun, Susan Cummings, Max Baer, Angela Stevens, Paul Langton, George Keymas, Ray Teal, Gene Roth, Terry Frost, Dennis Moore, Jack Ingram, Steve Darrell, Norman Fredric, Ken Christy. A gunman comes to the aid of a rancher who is being harassed by marauders out to control the territory. Rory Calhoun fans will go for this better-than-average Sam Katzman production.

3842 The Utah Kid. Tiffany, 1930. 60 minutes B/W. D: Richard Thorpe. SC: Frank Howard Clark. WITH Rex Lease, Dorothy Sebastian, Tom Santschi, Mary Carr, Walter Miller, Lafe McKee, Boris Karloff, Bud Osborne. An outlaw returns to his gang's hideout to find a gang member trying to take advantage of a pretty school teacher who has wandered into their den and he defends the girl, who is actually loved by the local sheriff, and marries her. Rather interesting Rex Lease early talkie film; Boris Karloff has a minor role as a gang member.

3843 The Utah Kid. Monogram, 1944. 54 minutes B/W. D: Vernon Keays. SC: Victor Hammond. WITH Bob Steele, Hoot Gibson, Beatrice Grey, Evelyn Eaton, Ralph Lewis, Mauritz Hogo, Jamesson Shade, Mike G. Letz, Dan White, Bud Osborne, George Morrell. A U. S. marshal and his new deputy investigate a gang who always wins the events on the rodeo circuit. An abundance of rodeo stock footage does not help this rather rag-tag double biller.

3844 Utah Trail. Grand National, 1937. 57 minutes B/W. D: Albert Herman. SC: Edmund Kelso. WITH Tex Ritter, Adele Pearce, Dave O'Brien, Horace Murphy, Snub Pollard, Karl Hackett, Charles King, Ed Cassidy, Bud Osborne, Lynton Brent, Rudy Sooter & Tex Ritter's Tornados, Oscar Gahan, Ray Jones, Denver Dixon, George Morrell, Horace B. Carpenter, Herman Hack, Chick Hannon. An investigator is called in by the railroad to locate a stolen cattle train and find out who is behind the sabotage of the company's trains. Tex Ritter's final Grand National release is a ragged affair with average tunes. British title: **Trail to Utah.**

3845 Utah Wagon Train. Republic, 1951. 67 minutes B/W. D: Philip Ford. SC: John K. Butler. WITH Rex Allen, Penny Edwards, Buddy Ebsen, Roy Barcroft, Sarah Padden, Grant Withers, Arthur Space, Edwin Rand, Robert Karnes, William Holmes, Stanley Andrews, Frank Jenks. A rancher gets himself made trail boss of a modern day wagon train, searching for the route West used a century before by their ancestors, in order to find out who murdered his uncle, the group's original trail guide. Very fine Rex Allen vehicle with an entertaining script. V: Cumberland Video.

V

The Valdez Horses see **Chino**

3846 Valdez Is Coming. United Artists, 1971. 90 minutes Color. D: Edwin Sherin.

SC: Roland Kibbee & David Rayfiel. WITH Burt Lancaster, Susan Clark, Jon Cypher, Barton Heyman, Richard Jordan, Frank Silvera, Hector Elizondo, Phil Brown, Ralph Brown, Roberta Haynes, Jose Garcia, Michael Hinn, Joaquin Parra, Rudy Ugland, Vic Albert, Allan Russell, Juan Fernandez, Tony Eppers, Nick Cravat, Raul Castro, Jose Morales, Mario Sanz. A gunman forced into a shootout is hunted by a posse and he plans to turn the tables on his trackers. Average theatrical affair.

3847 Valerie. United Artists, 1957. 84 minutes B/W. D: Gerd Oswald. SC: Leonard Heideman & Emmett Murphy. WITH Sterling Hayden, Anita Ekberg, Anthony Steel, Peter Walker, John Wengraf, Iphigenie Castiglioni, Robert Adler, Gage Clarke. A man's wife is wounded and her parents murdered and the trial for the crimes becomes a conflicting affair until the girl agrees to testify. A different kind of oater but one that hardly seems worth the effort.

3848 The Valiant Hombre. United Artists, 1948. 60 minutes B/W. D: Wallace Fox. SC: Adele Buffington. WITH Duncan Renaldo, Leo Carrillo, Barbara Billingsley, John Litel, Lee "Lasses" White, Stanley Andrews, Frank Ellis, Ralph Peters, Herman Hack, Daisy (dog). The Cisco Kid and Pancho try to locate a mining engineer who disappeared after making a big strike. Good entry in the long-running "The Cisco Kid" series.

3849 Valley of Fear. Monogram, 1947. 54 minutes B/W. D: Lambert Hillyer. SC: J. Benton Cheney. WITH Johnny Mack Brown, Raymond Hatton, Christine McIntyre, Ed Cassidy, Tristram Coffin, Ted Adams, Steve Darrell, Pierce Lyden, Eddie Parker, Gary Garrett, Cactus Mack, Robert O'Byrne, Ed Piel Sr., Budd Buster. A cowpoke returns home to find his uncle dead and himself accused of taking money the dead man embezzled. Standard, but entertaining, Johnny Mack Brown series sagebrusher.

3850 Valley of Fire. Columbia, 1951. 63 (70) minutes B/W. D: John English. SC: Earle Snell. WITH Gene Autry, Pat Buttram, Gail Davis, Russell Hayden, Christine Larsen, Harry Lauter, Terry Frost, Riley Hill, Barbara Stanley, Duke York, Bud Osborne, Teddy Infur, Victor Sen Yung, Gregg Barton, Sandy Sanders, Fred Sherman, James Magill, Frankie Marvin, Pat O'Malley, Wade Crosby, William Fawcett, Syd Saylor, John Miller,

Marjorie Liszt. In the town of Quantz Creek in the 1850s sheriff Gene Autry runs out a crooked gambler and his cohorts and the latter vows revenge by trying to hijack a wagon train bringing brides to the community. Pretty good Gene Autry vehicle in which Gene sings "On Top of Old Smoky." V: Blackhawk.

3851 The Valley of Gwangi. Warner Brothers-Seven Arts, 1969. 95 minutes Color. D: James O'Connolly. SC: William E. Bast. WITH James Franciscus, Gila Golan, Richard Carlson, Laurence Naismith, Curtis Arden, Freda Jackson, Gustavo Rojo, Dennis Kilbane, Marion De Barros, Jose Burgos. A group in Mexico discover a hidden valley and capture a huge dinosaur and decide to display the reptile to make money. Basically dull combination of Western and sci-fi genres with fine special effects by Ray Harryhausen; Gwangi is a very likable monster.

3852 Valley of Hunted Men. Republic, 1942. 56 minutes B/W. D: John English. SC: Albert DeMond & Morton Grant. WITH Bob Steele, Tom Tyler, Jimmie Dodd, Anna Marie Stewart, Edward Van Sloan, Roland Varno, Edythe Elliott, Arno Frey, Richard French, Kenne Duncan, Jack Kirk, Budd Buster, Hal Price, Rand Brooks, Billy Benedict, George Neiss, Robert Stevenson, Duke Aldon, Charles Flynn. The Three Mesquiteers are on the trail of an escaped Nazi who is actually posing as the nephew of a scientist who is working on a formula for making rubber from culebra plants. Topical entry in "The Three Mesquiteers" series which is not very dated and still entertaining.

3853 Valley of Terror. Ambassador, 1937. 59 minutes B/W. D: Al Herman. SC: Stanley Roberts. WITH Kermit Maynard, Harley Wood, John Merton, Jack Ingram, Dick Curtis, Roger Williams, Frank McCarroll, Hank Bell, Hal Price, Slim Whitaker, George Morrell, Blackie Whiteford, Herman Hack, Jack Casey. A crook is after the mineral deposits on a girl's ranch and he has her boyfriend framed on a rustling charge to get him out of the way. Standard, but actionful, Kermit Maynard vehicle for producer Maurice Conn. V: Blackhawk.

3854 Valley of the Giants. Warner Brothers, 1938. 79 minutes Color. D: William Keighley. SC: Seton I. Miller & Michael Fessler. WITH Wayne Morris, Claire Trevor, Frank McHugh, Alan Hale, Donald Crisp, Charles Bickford, Jack LaRue, John Litel, Dick

Purcell, El Brendel, Russell Simpson, Cy Kendall, Harry Cording, Wade Boteler, Helen McKellar, Addison Richards, Jerry Colonna. A lumberman, with the aid of a saloon girl, fights a rival who wants to take the timber and destroy the north woods in the process. Highly actionful melodrama with plenty of entertainment value. The film was based on Peter B. Kyne's novel and was first filmed in 1919 by Artcraft-Paramount with Wallace Reid, and Warner Brothers remade it in 1927 with Milton Sills. It was done again as **The Big Trees** (q.v.).

3855 Valley of the Lawless. Supreme, 1936. 59 minutes B/W. D-SC: Robert North Bradbury. WITH Johnny Mack Brown, Joyce Compton, George ("Gabby") Hayes, Frank Hagney, Denny Meadows (Dennis Moore), Bobby Nelson, Charles King, Jack Rockwell, Frank Ball, Forrest Taylor, Blackie Whiteford, Horace Murphy, Steve Clark, Ed Cassidy, Bob McKenzie, George Morrell, Jack Evans. In order to retrieve a gold map for which his grandfather was killed, a man must penetrate an area used as a refuge for outlaws. Actionful Johnny Mack Brown vehicle; well written.

3856 Valley of the Redwoods. 20th CenturyFox/Associated Producers, 1960. 63 minutes B/W. D: William Witney. SC: Gene Corman. WITH John Hudson, Lynn Bernay, Ed Nelson, Michael Forest, Robert Shayne, John Brinkley, Bruno VeSoto, Hal Torey, Chris Miller. Three people, two men and a woman, plan a payroll robbery and escape through the valley of the redwoods but their plan is foiled when one of them is injured. Compact and pleasing little action melodrama.

3857 Valley of the Sun. RKO Radio, 1942. 79 minutes B/W. D: George Marshall. SC: Horace McCoy. WITH Lucille Ball, James Craig, Sir Cedric Hardwicke, Dean Jagger, Peter Whitney, Billy Gilbert, Tom Tyler, Antonio Moreno, George Cleveland, Hank Bell, Richard Fiske, Don Terry, Chris Willow Bill, Fern Emmett, Al St. John, Harry Lamont, Al Ferguson, Chester Conklin, Ed Brady, Lloyd Ingraham, Frank Coleman, Francis McDonald, Harry Hayden, Bud Osborne, Steve Clemento. A government agent pretends to be a renegade Indian scout to get the goods on a crooked Indian agent in the Arizona Territory. The cast is the best thing about this slow moving melodrama; Tom Tyler plays Geronimo.

3858 Valley of Vanishing Men. Columbia, 1942. 15 Chapters B/W. D: Spencer Gordon Bennett. SC: Harry Fraser, George Grey & Lewis Clay. WITH Bill Elliott, Slim Summerville, Carmen Morales, Kenneth MacDonald, Jack Ingram, George Chesebro, John Shay, Tom London, Arno Frey, Julian Rivero, Roy Barcroft, I. Stanford Jolley, Ted Mapes, Lane Chandler, Ernie Adams, Michael Vallon, Robert Fiske, Davidson Clark, Lane Bradford, Chief Thundercloud, Blackie Whiteford. A man and his pal search for the former's missing father and learn he and others are being worked as slaves in a mine operated by an outlaw and a renegade European general. Bill Elliott's final Columbia assignment is a sadly cheap and dull cliffhanger.

3859 Valley of Vengeance. Producers Releasing Corporation, 1944. 57 minutes B/W. D: Sam Newfield. SC: Joseph O'Donnell. WITH Buster Crabbe, Al St. John, Evelyn Finley, Glenn Strange, Donald Mayo, Charles King, John Merton, Lynton Brent, Jack Ingram, Bud Osborne, Nora Bush, Steve Clark, David Polonsky, Budd Buster, Ben Corbett, Artie Ortego, John Cason, Tex Cooper, Wally West, George Morrell, Herman Hack, Buck Bucko, Pasquale Perry, Morgan Flowers, Ray Henderson, Merrill McCormack, Tom Smith. Years after their parents were murdered in a wagon train massacre, Billy Carson and Fuzzy Q. Jones stumble onto the crooks responsible for the killings in a small town. Standard "Billy Carson" series entry with a supporting cast full of familiar faces. British title: **Vengeance.**

3860 Valley of Wanted Men. Conn Pictures, 1935. 62 minutes B/W. D: Alan James. SC: Barry Barringer & Forrest Barnes. WITH Frankie Darro, Grant Withers, Drue Layton, (Le)Roy Mason, Paul Fix, Russell Hopton, Walter Miller, Fred "Snowflake" Toones, Al Bridge, William Gould, Jack Rockwell, Slim Whitaker. A young man tries to bring peace to his home, a valley populated by outlaws with prices on their heads. Fast paced low budget dual biller.

3861 The Vanishing American. Paramount, 1926. 110 minutes B/W. D: George B. Seitz. SC: Ethel Doherty & Lucien Hubbard. WITH Richard Dix, Lois Wilson, Noah Beery, Malcolm McGregor, Nocki, Shannon Day, Charles Crockett, Bert Woodruff, Bernard Siegel, Guy Oliver, Joe Ryan, Charles Stevens, Bruce Gordon, Richard Howard, John Webb Dillon. After fighting heroically in World War I an Indian brave returns home only to find the land barren and his people being cheated by corrupt government bureaucrats. A true silent film classic and one of the very first dramas to show the harsh treatment of the American Indian. V: Video Yesteryear.

3862 The Vanishing American. Republic, 1955. 90 minutes B/W. D: Joseph Kane. SC: Alan LeMay. WITH Scott Brady, Audrey Totter, Forrest Tucker, Gene Lockhart, Jim Davis, John Dierkes, Gloria Castillo, Julian Rivero, Lee Van Cleef, George Keymas, Charles Stevens, Jay Silverheels, James Millican, Glenn Strange. When crooks try to steal lands belonging to Navajo Indians, a young brave tries to stop them. Republic's remake of the silent classic is only an average outing, due mainly to budget restrictions.

3863 The Vanishing Frontier. Paramount, 1932. 65 minutes B/W. D: Phil Rosen. SC: Stuart Anthony. WITH Johnny Mack Brown, Evalyn Knapp, ZaSu Pitts, J. Farrell MacDonald, Raymond Hatton, Wallace MacDonald, Ben Alexander, George Irving, Joyzelle Joyner, Deacon McDaniels. In old California an American tries to aid officials in stopping military abuse. Johnny Mack Brown's followers will go for this early actioner, his last pre-series feature film in the genre.

3864 The Vanishing Land. Gold Key, 1975. 91 minutes Color. D: John Elmore. WITH John Elmore. Photographer/guide John Elmore goes on a trek through Alaska photographing its wilderness and people. Top flight documentary.

3865 The Vanishing Legion. Mascot, 1931. 12 Chapters B/W. D: B. Reeves Eason. SC: Wyndham Gittens, Ford Beebe & Helmer Bergman. WITH Harry Carey, Edwina Booth, Rex (horse), Frankie Darro, Philo McCullough, William Desmond, Joe Bonomo, Edward Hearn, Al Taylor, Lafe McKee, Dick Hatton, Pete Morrison, Dick Dickinson, Robert Kortman, Paul Weigel, Frank Brownlee, Yakima Canutt, Tom Dugan, Bob Walker, Olive Fuller Golden (Carey), Charles "Rube" Schaeffer. The mysterious "Voice" and his gang falsely frame a man of a murder charge as they try to take over an oil company. Fun Mascot cliffhanger with a good cast and lots of action. V: Cassette Express.

3866 Vanishing Outpost. Western Adventure, 1951. 56 minutes B/W. D: Ron Ormond. SC: Alexander White. WITH Lash LaRue, Al St. John, Riley Hill, Archie Twitchell, Lee Morgan, Ted Adams, Bud Osborne, Clarke Stevens, Ray Broome, Cliff Taylor, Sharon Hall, Sue Hussey, Johnny Paul. A Pinkerton agent enlists the aid of Lash and Fuzzy in stopping a notorious outlaw gang. Rag-tag Lash LaRue vehicle hurt by the excessive use of footage from previous features.

Vanishing Pioneer see **Rocky Mountain Mystery**

3867 The Vanishing Prairie. Buena Vista, 1954. 75 minutes Color. D: James Algar. SC: James Algar, Winston Hibler & Ted Sears. WITH Winston Nibler (narrator). Life on the American prairie is presented, revolving around such wildlife as the buffalo, antelope, big-horn sheep, coyote and the prairie dog. Top notch Walt Disney documentary for the entire family.

3868 The Vanishing Riders. Spectrum, 1935. 58 minutes B/W. D: Robert Hill. SC: Oliver Drake. WITH Bill Cody, Ethel Jackson, Bill Cody Jr., Wally Wales, Budd Buster, Milburn Morante, Donald Reed, Francis Walker, Roger Williams, Bert Young, Buck Morgan, Colin Chase, Bud Osborne. A cowpoke and his young pal set out to round up a rustling gang plaguing area ranchers. Average oater of note only for its teaming of the Bill Cody's, father and son.

3869 The Vanishing Westerner. Republic, 1950. 60 minutes B/W. D: Philip Ford. SC: Bob Williams. WITH Monte Hale, Aline Towne, Paul Hurst, Roy Barcroft, Arthur Space, Richard Anderson, William Phipps, Don Haggerty, Dick Curtis, Rand Brooks, Edmund Cobb, Harold Goodwin. Two wanted cowpokes are sent by a sheriff to a rancher to get a job but the man is actually a killer who plans to use them as a front for his robbery activities and then have them murdered. A complicated scenario and plenty of action keep this Monte Hale vehicle going at a fast clip. V: Cumberland Video.

3870 Vanishing Wilderness. Pacific International, 1974. 90 minutes Color. D: Arthur R. Dubs & Heinz Seilmann. WITH Rex Allen (narrator). The flora and fauna of North America, from Florida to Alaska, are reviewed in this theatrical documentary. Recommended for fans of this type of entertainment.

3871 The Vanquished. Paramount, 1953. 84 minutes Color. D: Edward Ludwig. SC: Winston Miller, Frank Moss & Lewis R. Foster. WITH John Payne, Jan Sterling, Coleen Gray, Lyle Bettger, Willard Parker, Roy Gordon, John Dierkes, Charles Evans, Ellen Corby, Ernestine Barrie, Russell Gaige, Leslie Kimmell, Voltaire Perkins, Sam Flint, Louis Jean Heydt, Freeman Morse, Richard Shannon, Karen Sharpe, Howard Joslin, Llewellyn Johnson, John Halloran, Harry Cody, William Berry, Major Sam Harris, Jack Hill, Richard Beedle, Richard Bartell, Brad Mora. After the Civil War an ex-Confederate returns home, working undercover, to get the goods on local corrupt officials. Although well produced by the Pine-Thomas unit, this feature has a plot that has been used too many times to make it very interesting.

Vengeance (1935) see **Range Warfare**

3872 Vengeance. Crown-International, 1965. 80 minutes B/W. D: Dene Hilyard. SC: Alex Sharp & Ed Erwin. WITH William Thourlby, Melora Conway, Owen Pavitt, Donald Cook, Ed Cook, Byrd Holland, John Bliss, James Cavanaugh, Tiger Joe Marsh. A man released from a Yankee prison after the Civil War kills one of the men who murdered his brother and then finds himself hunted by the man's fiancée and family. Average low budget melodrama.

3873 Vengeance. Metro-Goldwyn-Mayer/EMI/Cinevision Films, 1971. 100 minutes Color. D: Anthony Dawson (Antonio Margharetti). SC: Antonio Margharetti & Renato Savino. WITH Richard Harrison, Claudio Camaso, Alan Collins. When his friend is murdered by an outlaw gang a man sets out to take revenge. Exceedingly violent spaghetti Western issued in Italy in 1968 as **Joko, Invoco Dio...E Muori.**

3874 The Vengeance of Pancho Villa. Lacy, 1966. 83 minutes Color. D: Jose Elorrieta. WITH John Ericson, James Philbrook, Gustavo Rojo. Believing that government soldiers murdered his parents, a man agrees to aid Pancho Villa in stealing gold from the government. Violent and actionful Spanish-Italian coproduction. Alternate title: **The Treasure of Pancho Villa.**

3875 Vengeance of Rannah. Reliable, 1936. 59 minutes B/W. D: Franklin Shamray (Bernard B. Ray). SC: Joseph O'Donnell.

WITH Bob Custer, Rin-Tin-Tin Jr., John Elliott, Victoria Vinton, Roger Williams, Eddie Phillips, Ed Cassidy, Wally West, Oscar Gahan. An insurance detective investigates a stage payroll robbery and finds the driver murdered with the dead man's dog holding the clue to his killing. Tacky affair supposedly based on a work by James Oliver Curwood.

3876 Vengeance of the West. Columbia, 1942. 60 minutes B/W. D: Lambert Hillyer. SC: Luci Ward. WITH Bill Elliott, Tex Ritter, Adele Mara, Frank Mitchell, Dick Curtis, Richard Fiske, Ted Mapes, Eva Puig, Jose Tortosa, Guy Wilkerson, Edmund Cobb, Eddie Laughton, Stanley Brown, John Tyrell, Steve Clark. When his family is murdered rancher Joaquin Murietta begins raiding gold shipments and eventually he teams with a ranger who has been sent to capture him and together they try to stop the gang responsible for the killings. Fair entry in the Bill Elliott-Tex Ritter Columbia series which treads very lightly on history with Tex singing "Along the Trail Somewhere" and "Only Yesterday."

3877 Vengeance Trail. Filmes, 1972. 98 minutes Color. D-SC: William Redford (Pasquale Squintieri). WITH Leonard Mann, Ivan Rassimov, Elizabeth Eversfield, Klaus Kinski, Steffan Zacharias. Seeking revenge for the murder of his parents by Indians, a young boy kidnaps an Indian girl he plans to sell but ends up falling in love with her and tries to save her after she is captured by an outlaw gang. This Italian film is long on action and violence but short on story. Italian title: **La Vendetta E Un Piatto Che Si Serve Freddo** (Vengeance is a Plate Served Cold).

3878 Vengeance Valley. Metro-Goldwyn-Mayer, 1951. 83 minutes Color. D: Richard Thorpe. SC: Irving Ravetch. WITH Burt Lancaster, Joanne Dru, Robert Walker, Sally Forrest, John Ireland, Carleton Carpenter, Ray Collins, Ted De Corsia, Hugh O'Brian, Will Wright, Grace Mills, James Hayward, James Harrison, Stanley Andrews, Glenn Strange, Paul E. Burns, Robert E. Griffin, Harvey B. Dunne, John McKee, Tom Fadden, Monte Montague, Al Ferguson, Roy Butler, Margaret Bert, Norman Leavitt, Dan White, Robert Wilke, Louis Nicoletti. A ranch foreman always tries to protect his no-good foster brother until the latter fathers an illegitimate child and tries to palm it off as the foreman's, thus leading to a showdown between the two men. Burt Lancaster's first Western is a stout affair and good viewing.

3879 Vengeance Vow. Wrather Corporation, 1956. 75 minutes Color. D: Earl Bellamy. SC: Doane Hoag, De Vallon Scott & Thomas Seller. WITH Clayton Moore, Jay Silverheels, Allen Pinson, Wayne Burson, Jim Bannon, Francis McDonald, James J. Griffith, Ewing Mitchell, Maurice Jara, Joel Ashley, Jerry Brown, Walt LaRue, Mauritz Hugo, Harry Strang, Don C. Harvey, Margaret Aldrich, Gary Murray, Eugenia Paul, Baynes Barron, Robert Homans. An escaped convict plans to murder the Lone Ranger and Tonto as the duo also try to aid an ex-convict and stop an Indian uprising. Action-ful TV movie from "The Lone Ranger" (ABC-TV, 1949-57) series from the segments "Courage of Tonto," "A Message for Abe" and "Two Against Two."

3880 Vera Cruz. United Artists, 1954. 94 minutes Color. D: Robert Aldrich. SC: Roland Kibbee & James R. Webb. WITH Gary Cooper, Burt Lancaster, Denise Darcel, Cesar Romero, Sarita Montiel, George Macready, Ernest Borgnine, Henry Brandon, Charles (Bronson) Buchinsky, Morris Ankrum, James McCallion, Jack Lambert, Jack Elam, James Seay, Archie Savage, Charles Horvath, Juan Garcia. In 1866 in Mexico two American mercenaries agree to accompany a countess to Vera Cruz as she is carrying a gold shipment for Emperor Maximillian's forces. Nicely photographed (by Ernest Laszlo) but basically mundane melodrama. V: Blackhawk. VD: Blackhawk.

3881 Via Pony Express. Majestic, 1933. 60 minutes B/W. D: Lewis D. Collins. SC: Lewis D. Collins & Oliver Drake. WITH Jack Hoxie, Marceline Day, Lane Chandler, Doris Hill, Julian Rivero, Charles K. French, Matthew Betz, Joe Girard. A pony express rider tries to aid a girl whose land grant is sought by outlaws. Poor Jack Hoxie series outing.

3882 The Vigilante. Columbia, 1947. 15 Chapters B/W. D: Wallace Fox. SC: George H. Plympton, Lewis Clay & Arthur Hoerl. WITH Ralph Byrd, Ramsay Ames, Lyle Talbot, George Offerman Jr., Robert Barron, Hugh Prosser, Jack Ingram, Eddie Parker, George Chesebro, Edmund Cobb, Terry Frost, Frank Ellis, Frank Marlo, Bill Brauer. A Western movie star also works as an undercover agent and in that capacity he goes to a ranch where

a gang is after a mysterious string of pearls. The plot is outlandish but this is a fun cliffhanger.

3883 Vigilante Hideout. Republic, 1950. 60 minutes B/W. D: Fred C. Brannon. SC: Richard Wormser. WITH Allan "Rocky" Lane, Eddy Waller, Virginia Herrick, Roy Barcroft, Cliff Clark, Don Haggerty, Paul Campbell, Guy Teague, Art Dillard, Chick Hannon, Bob Woodward. Ranchers plagued by a rash of cattle thefts call in a range detective to stop the rustlers. Fairly exciting outing for the Allan Lane series.

3884 Vigilante Terror. Allied Artists, 1953. 60 (70) minutes B/W. D: Lewis D. Collins. SC: Sid Theil. WITH Bill Elliott, Mary Ellen Kay, Myron Healey, Fuzzy Knight, I. Stanford Jolley, Henry Rowland, George Wallace, Zon Murray, Richard Avonde, Michael Colgan, Denver Pyle, Robert Bray, Al Haskell, John James. Masked vigilantes carry off a successful gold hijacking and put the blame on a storekeeper but a cowboy comes to his defense. The plot is nothing new but good acting and production values makes this Bill Elliott vehicle a pleasing one.

3885 The Vigilantes Are Coming. Republic, 1936. 12 Chapters B/W. D: Mack V. Wright & Ray Taylor. SC: John Rathmell, Maurice Geraghty & Leslie Swabacker. WITH Robert Livingston, Kay Hughes, Guinn Williams, Raymond Hatton, Fred Kohler, Robert Warwick, William Farnum, Robert Kortman, John Merton, Ray Corrigan, Lloyd Ingraham, William Desmond, Yakima Canutt, Tracy Layne, Bud Pope, Steve Clemente, Bud Osborne, John O'Brien, Henry Hall, Philip Armenta, Stanley Blystone, Joe de la Cruz, Fred Burns, Frankie Marvin, Wally West, Wes Warner, Ken Cooper, Frank Ellis, Jerome Ward, Al Taylor, Herman Hack, Jack Ingram, Jack Kirk, Pascale Perry. In 1840 a young man returns to his California home to find the ranch has been taken over by a general who is using Cossacks to aid him in exploiting the land's gold and making an empire. Outstanding Republic serial with a very fine cast; based on the Rudolph Valentino feature **The Eagle** (United Artists, 1925) which had its locale in Russia.

3886 Vigilantes of Boomtown. Republic, 1947. 54 minutes B/W. D: R. G. Springsteen. SC: Earle Snell. WITH Allan "Rocky" Lane, Bobby Blake, Martha Wentworth, John Dehner, Roscoe Karns,

Roy Barcroft, Peggy Stewart, George Chesebro, Ted Adams, George Lloyd, Earle Hodgins, George Turner, Harlan Briggs, Budd Buster, Jack O'Shea, Tom Steele. In Carson City in 1897 factions oppose the sanctioning of the heavyweight boxing bout between James J. Corbett and Bob Fitzsimmons and Red Ryder gets into the fracas to keep the peace. Weak "Red Ryder" entry that doesn't even bother to re-stage the famous title fight; Red Ryder presented as none-too-levelheaded at times.

3887 Vigilantes of Dodge City. Republic, 1944. 54 minutes B/W. D: Wallace Grissell. SC: Norman S. Hall & Anthony Coldeway. WITH Bill Elliott, Bobby Blake, Alice Fleming, Linda Stirling, LeRoy Mason, Tom London, Hal Taliaferro, Kenne Duncan, Bud Geary, Stephen Barclay, Robert Wilkie, Stanley Andrews, Horace B. Carpenter. In Dodge City a group of outlaws try to destroy the Duchess's freight line but Red Ryder and Little Beaver come to her rescue. Fast paced and actionful "Red Ryder" series entry.

3888 The Vigilantes Return. Universal, 1947. 67 minutes Color. D: Ray Taylor. SC: Roy Chanslor. WITH Jon Hall, Margaret Lindsay, Andy Devine, Robert Wilcox, Paula Drew, Jonathan Hale, Arthur Hohl, Wallace Scott, Joan (Shawlee) Fulton, Lane Chandler, George Chandler, Jack Lambert, Robert J. Wilke, Monte Montague, John Hart. A federal marshal is assigned to a lawless region and crooks try to implicate him in a murder charge. Average programmer enhanced by Cinecolor.

3889 The Vigilantes Ride. Columbia, 1944. 55 minutes B/W. D: William Berke. SC: Ed Earl Repp. WITH Russell Hayden, Dub Taylor, Bob Wills & His Texas Playboys, Shirley Patterson, Tristram Coffin, Jack Rockwell, Robert Kortman, Richard Botiller, Jack Kirk, Stanley Brown, Blackie Whiteford. Leaving the rangers when his younger brother is killed by outlaws, a man pretends to become a bandit in order to infiltrate and bring in the gang. Russell Hayden fans will like this actioner, complemented by the music of the Bob Wills group and the meanness of a host of genre villains.

3890 Villa. 20th Century-Fox, 1958. 72 minutes Color. D: James B. Clark. SC: Louis Vittes. WITH Brian Keith, Cesar Romero, Margia Dean, Rodolfo Hoyos, Carlos Muzquiz, Mario Navarro, Ben Wright, Elisa Loti, Enrique Lucero, Rosenda Monteros, Felix Gonzales, Jose Espinoza, Alberto Gutierrez, Jorge Trevino, Lee Morgan, Jose Lopez, Jose Trowe, Jorge Russek. In order to find a better life for himself and his people Pancho Villa turns to banditry and begins harassing the soldiers of Mexico's government. Mediocre accounting of the famous bandit's early years although Rodolfo Hoyos is good in the title role.

3891 Villa Rides! Paramount, 1968. 125 minutes Color. D: Buzz Kulik. SC: Robert Towne & Sam Peckinpah. WITH Yul Brynner, Robert Mitchum, Charles Bronson, Grazia Buccella, Robert Viharo, Frank Wolff, Herbert Lom, Alexander Knox, Diana Lorys, Robert Carricart, Fernando Rey, Regina De Julian, Andres Monreal, Antonio Ruiz, John Ireland, Jill Ireland. An American gunrunner, captured by the forces of Pancho Villa, joins the revolutionary in his assault against the Mexican government. There is more mayhem than melodrama in this overwrought European Western-imitation.

3892 The Villain. Columbia, 1979. 93 minutes Color. D: Hal Needham. SC: Robert O. Kane. WITH Kirk Douglas, Ann-Margret, Arnold Schwarzenegger, Paul Lynde, Ruth Buzzi, Jack Elam, Strother Martin, Robert Tessier. An outlaw is on the trail of a girl and her muscle-bound protector. Fast moving but absurd Western.

3893 The Violent Men. Columbia, 1955. 96 minutes Color. D: Rudolph Mate. SC: Harry Kleiner. WITH Glenn Ford, Barbara Stanwyck, Edward G. Robinson, Dianne Foster, Brian Keith, May Wynn, Warner Anderson, Basil Ruysdael, Lita Milan, Richard Jaeckel, James Westerfield, Jack Kelly, Willis Bouchey, Harry Shannon, Peter Hanson, Don C. Harvey, Robo Bechi, Carl Andre, James Anderson, Katharine Warren, Thomas Browne Henry, Frank Ferguson, Raymond Greenleaf, Edmund Cobb, William "Bill" Phipps. A Civil War veteran opposes a ruthless land baron who is trying to take over a fertile valley in order to expand his holdings. Another psychological Western from the 1950s, although this one has a bit more action than others of its ilk.

3894 The Violent Ones. Feature Film Corporation of America, 1967. 96 minutes Color. D: Fernando Lamas. SC: Doug Wilson & Charles Davis. WITH Fernando Lamas, Aldo Ray, Tommy Sands, David

Carradine, Lisa Gaye, Melinda Marx.
The sheriff of a small New Mexico town
has trouble controlling the Mexican population when three men are apprehended
as suspects in the rape and murder of
a young girl. Low grade modern day
Western melodrama.

3895 Virginia City. Warner Brothers,
1940. 121 minutes B/W. D: Michael Curtiz.
SC: Robert Buckner. WITH Errol Flynn,
Miriam Hopkins, Randolph Scott, Humprey
Bogart, Frank McHugh, Alan Hale, Guinn
Williams, John Litel, Douglass Dumbrille,
Moroni Olsen, Russell Hicks, Dickie
Jones, Frank Wilcox, Russell Simpson,
Victor Kilian, Charles Middleton, Monte
Montague, George Regas, Paul Fix, Thurs-
ton Hall, Charles Trowbridge, Howard
Hickman, Charles Halton, Ward Bond,
Sam McDaniel, Harry Cording, Trevor
Bardette, Tom Dugan, Spencer Charters,
George Reeves. Escaping from a Southern
prison camp, a Union soldier is sent to
Virginia City to stop the shipment of
gold to the Confederacy and there he
falls for a pretty saloon singer who is
a Southern spy. Pretty fair actioner
based on historical fact.

3896 The Virginian. Preferred Pictures,
1923. 60 minutes B/W. D: Tom Forman.
SC: Hope Loring & Louis D. Lighton.
WITH Kenneth Harlan, Florence Vidor,
Russell Simpson, Pat O'Malley, Raymond
Hatton, Milton Ross, Sam Allen, Bert
Hadley, Fred Gambold. A young cowboy
is forced to hang his best pal for stealing
cattle and in doing so loses the affections
of the girl he loves. Very good, and much
underrated, second screen version (first
filmed in 1914 by Paramount with Dustin
Farnum) of Owen Wister's famous novel;
well worth seeing.

3897 The Virginian. Paramount, 1929.
90 minutes B/W. D: Victor Fleming.
SC: Edward E. Paramore Jr. & Howard
Estabrook. WITH Gary Cooper, Walter
Huston, Richard Arlen, Mary Brian, Eugene
Pallette, Chester Conklin, E. H. Calvert,
Helen Ware, Victor Potel, Tex Young,
Charles Stevens, Jack Pennick, George
Chandler, Ernie Adams, Fred Burns,
Randolph Scott. A cowboy fights with
a man over a saloon girl and the man
later has the cowpoke's pal rustle cattle,
thus causing the cowboy to have to hang
his friend. Flavorful early sound adaptation
of the Owen Wister play and book and
a film that still holds up very well today;
Richard Arlen is especially good as Steve.

3898 The Virginian. Paramount, 1946.
87 minutes Color. D: Stuart Gilmore.
SC: Frances Goodrich & Albert Hackett.
WITH Joel McCrea, Brian Donlevy, Sonny
Tufts, Barbara Britton, Fay Bainter,
Tom Tully, Henry O'Neill, Bill Edwards,
William Frawley, Paul Guifoyle, Marc
Lawrence, Vince Barnett. A cowboy
falls for a pretty girl but loses her love
when he hangs his pal after the latter
joins a bad man in rustling cattle. A
good cast and Technicolor cannot bring
this fourth screen version of the famous
novel above the level of average. Owen
Wister's 1902 book also spawned the
TV series "The Virginian" (NBC-TV, 1962-
70) and its followup "The Men from
Shiloh" (NBC-TV, 1970-71).

3899 Viva Cisco Kid. 20th Century-Fox,
1940. 70 minutes B/W. D: Norman Foster.
SC: Samuel G. Engel & Hal Long. WITH
Cesar Romero, Jean Rogers, Chris-Pin
Martin, Minor Watson, Stanley Fields,
Nigel de Brulier, Harold Goodwin, Francis
Ford, Charles Judels. The Cisco Kid
is on the trail of an outlaw gang wanted
for robbery. Well made and entertaining
"Cisco Kid" series film.

3900 Viva Maria! United Artists, 1965.
114 minutes Color. D: Louis Malle. SC:
Louis Malle & Jean-Claude Carriere.
WITH Brigitte Bardot, Jeanne Moreau,
George Hamilton, Claudio Brook, Paulette
Dubost, Gregor von Rezzori, Poldo Benani,
Carlos Lopez Moctezuma, Luis Rizo.
Two entertainers team with an Irish
rebel to aid the revolutionary cause
in Mexico. Pleasant blend of action and
comedy in this French-produced film.

3901 Viva Max! Commonwealth United,
1969. 96 minutes Color. D: Jerry Paris.
SC: Elliott Baker. WITH Peter Ustinov,
Pamela Tiffin, Jonathan Winters, John
Astin, Keenan Wynn, Harry Morgan,
Alice Ghostley, Kenneth Mars, Morgan
Guilford, Bill McCutcheon. A Mexican
general sets out with a small band of
confederates to retake the Alamo, but
163 years after the initial siege. Forced
comedy has its amusing moments mainly
thanks to an excellent cast.

3902 Viva Villa! Metro-Goldwyn-Mayer,
1934. 115 minutes B/W. D: Jack Conway.
SC: Ben Hecht. WITH Wallace Beery,
Fay Wray, Leo Carrillo, Donald Cook,
Stuart Erwin, George E. Stone, Joseph
Schildkraut, Henry B. Walthall, Katherine
De Mille, David Durand, Phillip Cooper,
Frank Puglia, John Merkel, Charles Stev-

ens, Steve Clemento, Pedro Regas, Carlos De Valdez, George Regas, Harry Cording, Nigel De Brulier, Charles Requa, Tom Ricketts, Clarence Wilson, James Martin, Anita Gordiana, Francis McDonald, Harry Semels, Julian Rivero, Bob McKenzie, Dan Dix, Paul Stanton, Mischa Auer, Belle Mitchell, John Davidson, Brandon Hurst, Leonard Moody, Herbert Prior, Emile Chautard, Henry Armetta, Hector Sarno, Ralph (Francis X. Jr.) Bushman, Arthur Treacher, William Von Bricken, Andre Cheron, Michael Visaroff, Shirley Chambers, Chris-Pin Martin. Pancho Villa rises from a petty bandit to revolutionary leader in Mexico. Overlong but passable biopic with a delightfully hammy performance by Wallace Beery in the title role.

3903 Viva Zapata! 20th Century-Fox, 1952. 113 minutes B/W. D: Elia Kazan. SC: John Steinbeck. WITH Marlon Brando, Jean Peters, Anthony Quinn, Joseph Wiseman, Arnold Moss, Alan Reed, Margo, Lou Gilbert, Harold Gordon, Mildred Dunnock, Frank Silvera, Nina Varela, Florenz Ames, Fay Roope, Will Kuluva, Bernie Gozier, Frank De Kova, Pedro Regas, Richard Garrick, Ross Bagdasarian, Leonard George, Abner Biberman, Philip Van Zandt, Henry Silva, Guy Thomajan, George J. Lewis, Peter Mamakos, Ric Roman, Nestor Paiva. A peasant, aided by his brother, rises above his surroundings and leads a revolution against the government of Mexico. Pretty fair biography of Zapata which will satisfy Marlon Brando fans.

W

3904 Waco. Monogram, 1952. 60 (68) minutes B/W. D: Lewis D. Collins. SC: Dan Ullman. WITH Bill Elliott, Pamela Blake, Rand Brooks, I. Stanford Jolley, Richard Avonde, Stanley Andrews, Paul Pierce, Lane Bradford, Pierce Lyden, Terry Frost, Michael Whalen, Stanley Price, Ray Bennett, House Peters Jr., Ray Jones, Ed Cassidy, Russ Whiteman, Richard Paxton. After killing a dishonest gambler in a fair fight, a man is forced on the run when he escapes after being denied a proper trial. Sturdy Bill Elliott vehicle with an entertaining and literate script.

3905 Waco. Paramount, 1966. 85 minutes Color. D: R. G. Springsteen. SC: Steve

Fisher. WITH Howard Keel, Jane Russell, Brian Donlevy, Terry Moore, Wendell Corey, John Agar, Richard Arlen, John Smith, Gene Evans, Ben Cooper, Tracy Olsen, DeForrest Kelley, Anne Seymour, Robert Lowery, Willard Parker, Jeff Richards, Fuzzy Knight, Reg Parton. A former gunslinger is hired to bring peace to a Wyoming community but he finds his ex-girl is now married to the local preacher. Excellent cast lends some credence to this otherwise mediocre horse opera.

3906 The Wagon Master. Universal, 1929. 70 minutes B/W. D: Harry Joe Brown. SC: Marion Jackson & Leslie Mason. WITH Ken Maynard, Edith Roberts, Frederick Dana, Tom Santschi, Al Ferguson, Jack Hanlon, Bobby Dunn, Frank Rice, Whitehorse, Frank Dana. A cowboy joins a wagon train organized to oppose a crook's food monopoly and when the wagon master is murdered by the crook's men the cowboy takes command. This Ken Maynard part-talkie is a pleasant affair which showed the star could adapt well to the sound medium.

3907 Wagon Team. Columbia, 1952. 61 minutes B/W. D: George Archainbaud. SC: Gerald Geraghty. WITH Gene Autry, Pat Buttram, Gail Davis, Dick Jones, Gordon Jones, Harry Harvey, Henry Rowland, George J. Lewis, John Cason, The Cass County Boys, Fred S. Martin, Bert Dodson, Jerry Scroggins, Gregg Barton, Pierce Lyden, Carlo Tircoli, Syd Saylor, Sandy Sanders. Special investigator Gene Autry joins a medicine show while looking for money taken in the holdup of an army payroll. Not one of Gene Autry's better outings although he does sing "Back in the Saddle Again."

3908 Wagon Tracks. Paramount-Artcraft, 1919. 60 minutes B/W. D: Lambert Hillyer. SC: C. Gardner Sullivan. WITH William S. Hart, Jane Novak, Robert McKim, Lloyd Bacon, Leo Pierson, Bertholde Sprotte, Charles Arling. When his brother is shot for supposedly trying to molest a girl a wagon master tries to get to the truth as he leads a wagon train carrying both the girl and the men who shot the young man. Well made and entertaining William S. Hart silent melodrama. V: Classic Video Cinema Collectors Club.

3909 Wagon Tracks West. Republic, 1943. 55 minutes B/W. D: Howard Bretherton. SC: William Lively. WITH Bill Elliott, George ("Gabby") Hayes, Anne Jeffreys,

Tom Tyler, Rick Vallin, Robert Frazer, Roy Barcroft, Charles Miller, Tom London, Cliff Lyons, Jack Rockwell, Kenne Duncan, Minerva Urecal, Hal Price, Frank Ellis, Hank Bell, William Nestell, Jack Ingram, Jack O'Shea, Ray Jones, Curley Dresden, Frank McCarroll, Marshall Reed, Ben Corbett, Jack Montgomery, Tom Steele, Roy Butler. A crooked Indian agent tries to cheat a tribe of its lands and a cowboy tries to help them although he meets opposition from a medicine man. A superb supporting cast is one of the many plus factors in this good Bill Elliott vehicle.

3910 Wagon Trail. Ajax, 1935. 55 minutes B/W. D: Harry Fraser. SC: Monroe Talbot. WITH Harry Carey, Gertrude Messinger, Edward Norris, Earl Dwire, Roger Williams, John Elliott, Chief Thundercloud, Chuck Morrison, Lew Meehan, Francis Walker, Allen Greer, Silver Tip Baker, Richard Botiller. A lawman comes to the aid of his gambler-son when the young man is falsely accused of murder. A bit slow moving but otherwise entertaining Harry Carey oater. V: Thunderbird, Video Connection.

3911 Wagon Train. RKO Radio, 1940. 59 minutes B/W. D: Edward Killy. SC: Morton Grant. WITH Tim Holt, Martha O'Driscoll, Ray Whitley, Emmett Lynn, Bud McTaggart, Cliff Clark, Ellen Lowe, Wade Crosby, Ethan Laidlaw, Monte Montague, Carl Stockdale, Glenn Strange, Bruce Dane. The young owner of a wagon train is the target of the operator of a trading post who has killed the man's father and wants to buy his business. Tim Holt's first series film is a fine sagebrusher and a good start to his RKO tenure.

3912 Wagon Wheels. Paramount, 1934. 57 minutes B/W. D: Charles Barton. SC: Jack Cunningham, Charles Logan & Carl Buss. WITH Randolph Scott, Gail Patrick, Billy Lee, Monte Blue, Raymond Hatton, Jan Duggan, Leila Bennett, Olin Howlin, J. P. McGowan, James Marcus, Helen Hunt, James N. "Pop" Kenton, Alfred Delcambre, John Marston, Sam McDaniel, Michael Visaroff, Howard Wilson, Colin Tapley, E. Alyn Warren, Pauline Moore, Earl Conert & The Singing Guardsmen. Three scouts lead settlers on a wagon train trip to Oregon while a half-breed tries to stop them in order to keep his fur trade. Entertaining remake of Zane Grey's **Fighting Caravans** (Paramount, 1931) with stock footage from that production.

3913 Wagon Wheels Westward. Republic, 1945. 54 minutes B/W. D: R. G. Springsteen. SC: Earle Snell. WITH Bill Elliott, Bobby Blake, Alice Fleming, Linda Stirling, Roy Barcroft, Emmett Lynn, Jay Kirby, Dick Curtis, George J. Lewis, Bud Geary, Tom London, Kenne Duncan, George Chesebro, Tom Chatterton, Frank Ellis, Bob McKenzie, Jack Kirk. When crooks try to sabotage the Duchess's stage line in an isolated area, Red Ryder and Little Beaver come to her aid. Well written "Red Ryder" series vehicle.

3914 Wagonmaster. RKO Radio, 1950. 86 minutes B/W. D: John Ford. SC: Frank S. Nugent & Patrick Ford. WITH Ben Johnson, Joanne Dru, Harry Carey Jr., Ward Bond, Charles Kemper, Alan Mowbray, Jane Darwell, Ruth Clifford, Russell Simpson, Kathleen O'Malley, James Arness, Fred Libby, Hank Worden, Mickey Simpson, Francis Ford, Cliff Lyons, Don Summers, Movita Castenada, Jim Thorpe, Chuck Hayward, The Sons of the Pioneers. Two young cowboys lead a Mormon wagon train across the plains, fighting Indians, outlaws and the harsh elements. Sombre, leisurely wagon train melodrama which is not one of John Ford's best features but is still better than many other genre efforts. V: Nostalgia Merchant.

3915 Wagons West. Monogram, 1952. 73 minutes Color. D: Ford Beebe. SC: Dan Ullman. WITH Rod Cameron, Peggie Castle, Noah Beery Jr., Michael Chapin, Henry Brandon, Sara Haden, Frank Ferguson, Anne Kimball, Wheaton Chambers, Riley Hill, I. Stanford Jolley, Almira Sessions, Harry Tyler, Effie Laird. While leading a train from Missouri across the plains a wagonmaster finds that some of his passengers are selling guns to the Indians. Cheaply made but entertaining action effort with stock footage from **Fort Osage** (q.v.).

3916 Wagons Westward. Republic, 1940. 54 (70) minutes B/W. D: Lew Landers. SC: Joseph M. March & Harrison Jacobs. WITH Chester Morris, Anita Louise, Buck Jones, George "Gabby" Hayes, Guinn Williams, Ona Munson, Douglas Fowley, John Gallaudet, Virginia Brissac, Trevor Bardette, Selmer Jackson, Charles Stevens, James Conlin, Richard Cramer, Edmund Cobb, Bill Woolf, The Hull Twins, Tex Cooper. Twins grow up on the opposite sides of the law with the crooked one being protected by a dishonest sheriff and when the latter twin is arrested his honest brother takes his place in order to round up the remainder of his gang. A well-made, adult Western with Chester Morris quite good in a dual role, although it is sad to see Buck Jones and Silver on the wrong side of the law.

3917 Walk Like a Dragon. Paramount, 1960. 95 minutes B/W. D: James Clavell. SC: James Clavell & Daniel Mainwaring. WITH Jack Lord, Nobu McCarthy, Mel Torme, James Shigeta, Josephine Hutchinson, Rodolfo Acosta, Benson Fong, Michael Pate, Don Kennedy, Donald Barry, Natalie Trundy, Lilyan Chauvin. After saving a young Chinese girl from a prostitution ring, a man takes her to his hometown where she is snubbed by the local citizens. Passable melodrama dealing with racial prejudice.

3918 Walk Tall. 20th Century-Fox, 1960. 60 minutes Color. D: Maury Dexter, SC: Stephen Kandel. WITH Willard Parker, Kent Taylor, Joyce Meadows, Russ Bender, Ron Soble, Alberto Monte, Bill Mims, Felix Locher, Dave De Paul. When a renegade military man and his three cohorts murder women and children of the Shoshone Indian tribe an Army captain is assigned to bring them to justice. Despite its compact running time, this dual biller is a trite affair.

3919 Walk the Proud Land. Universal-International, 1956. 88 minutes Color. D: Jesse Hibbs. SC: Gil Doud & Jack Sher. WITH Audie Murphy, Anne Bancroft, Patricia Crowley, Charles Drake, Tommy Rail, Jay Silverheels, Robert Warwick, Victor Milan, Anthony Caruso, Morris Ankrum, Addison Richards. An Indian agent, wanting to bring peace to warring whites and Apaches, sets out to capture Geronimo. Pretty good Audie Murphy actioner.

3920 The Walking Hills. Columbia, 1949. 78 minutes B/W. D: John Sturges. SC: Alan LeMay. WITH Randolph Scott, Ella Raines, William Bishop, Edgar Buchanan, Arthur Kennedy, John Ireland, Jerome Courtland, Russell Collins, Charles Stevens, Houseley Stevenson, Reed Howes, Josh White. A wanted killer and six other men and a woman trek into Death Valley in search of a wagon train carrying a fortune in gold which was lost in a sand storm years before. Underrated and highly entertaining melodrama; well worth viewing.

3921 Wall Street Cowboy. Republic, 1939. 54 (66) minutes B/W. D: Joseph

Kane. SC: Gerald Geraghty & Norman S. Hall. WITH Roy Rogers, George "Gabby" Hayes, Raymond Hatton, Ann Baldwin, Pierre Watkin, Craig Reynolds, Louisiana Lou, Ivan Miller, Reginald Barlow, Adrian Morris, Jack Roper, Jack Ingram, Hugh Sothern, Paul Fix, George Chesebro, Ted Mapes, Fred Burns. A cowboy tries to obtain money in the East to pay off the mortgage on his ranch since he suspects it contains a rich gold deposit. Despite its title and lack of continuing action, this is pretty fair entertainment.

3922 Wanda Nevada. United Artists, 1979. 95 (107) minutes Color. D: Peter Fonda. SC: Dennis Hackin. WITH Peter Fonda, Brooke Shields, Luke Askew, Fiona Lewis, Ted Markland, Severn Darden, Paul Fix, Henry Fonda, Larry Golden, John Demos, Bert Williams, Danny Zapien, Riley Hill. A gambler wins a young girl in a poker game and the two head for a sacred Indian burial ground to prospect for gold. There is not much here to recommend this 1950-era oater except for seeing Henry Fonda in a bit as a grizzled prospector.

3923 Wanderer of the Wasteland. Paramount, 1935. 62 minutes B/W. D: Otho Lovering. SC: Stuart Anthony. WITH Dean Jagger, Gail Patrick, Edward Ellis, Benny Baker, Larry "Buster" Crabbe, Trixie Friganza, Monte Blue, Raymond Hatton, Fuzzy Knight, Charles Waldron, Anna Q. Nilsson, Stanley Andrews, Pat O'Malley, Glenn (Leif) Erickson, Jim Thorpe. A man who mistakenly thinks he murdered his brother in an argument heads for the desert where he meets and falls in love with a pretty girl. Okay remake of the Zane Grey story which was first filmed by Paramount in 1924 with Jack Holt in two-color Technicolor.

3924 Wanderer of the Wasteland. RKO Radio, 1945. 67 minutes B/W. D: Edward Killy & Wallace Grissell. SC: Norman Houston. WITH James Warren, Richard Martin, Audrey Long, Robert Barrat, Robert Clarke, Harry Woods, Minerva Urecal, Harry D. Brown, Tommy Cook, Harry McKim, Jason Robards. When his father is killed a young man grows up vowing to get revenge on the murderer and he spends years tracking him down. Slow moving adaptation of the Zane Grey novel; James Warren's first series vehicle.

3925 Wanderers of the West. Monogram, 1941. 58 minutes B/W. D: Robert Hill.

SC: Robert Emmett (Tansey). WITH Tom Keene, Betty Miles, Sugar Dawn, Arkansas Slim Andrews, Tom Seidel, Stanley Price, Gene Alsace, Tom London, Fred Hoose, James Sheridan. A cowboy, searching for his father's killer, befriends a man not knowing he is the person he is trailing. A somewhat complicated plot is about the only highlight of this otherwise average actioner.

3926 Wanted. Documento, 1969. 104 minutes Color. D: Giorgio Ferroni. SC: Fernando Di Leo & Augosto Finocchi. WITH Giuliano Gemma, Teresa Gimpera, Serge Marquand, German Cobos, Daniele Vargas, Gia Sandri. Falsely branded an outlaw by a crook, a lawman tries to clear his name. Okay spaghetti oater.

3927 Wanted by the Law. Sunset, 1924. 50 minutes B/W. D-SC: Robert North Bradbury. WITH J. B. Warner, Dorothy Woods. A cowboy takes the blame for a killing committed by his weakling brother and heads to Montana where he finds out his girl's father is being swindled. Actionful, but low budget, silent effort.

3928 Wanted - Dead or Alive. Monogram, 1951. 59 minutes B/W. D: Thomas Carr. SC: Clint Johnston. WITH Whip Wilson, Jim Bannon, Fuzzy Knight, Christine McIntyre, Leonard Penn, Lane Bradford, Zon Murray, Marshall Reed, Stanley Price. A U. S. marshal and his two buddies are after a gang who captures and murders wanted men for the reward money. Better than average entry in the Whip Wilson series.

3929 Wanted: The Sundance Woman. ABC-TV/20th Century-Fox, 1976. 100 minutes Color. D: Lee Philips. SC: Richard Fielder. WITH Katharine Ross, Steve Forrest, Stella Stevens, Michael Constantine, Katherine Helmond, Hector Elizondo, Hector Elias, Warren Berlinger, Jorge Cervera, Lucille Benson. After the deaths of Butch Cassidy and the Sundance Kid, Etta Place finds herself a wanted woman and forms an uneasy alliance with Pancho Villa. Telefilm has Katharine Ross repeat her Etta Place role from the theatrical film **Butch Cassidy and the Sundance Kid** (q.v.) but that is about the only appeal this mediocre outing contains. Alternate title: **Mrs. Sundance Rides Again.**

Wanted Woman see **Jessi's Girls**

3930 War Arrow. Universal-International, 1953. 78 minutes Color. D: George Sher-

man. SC: John Michael Hayes. WITH Maureen O'Hara, Jeff Chandler, Suzan Ball, John McIntire, Charles Drake, Dennis Weaver, Noah Beery Jr., Henry Brandon, Steve Wyman, Jim Bannon, Jay Silverheels, Brad Jackson, Lance Fuller, Bill Ward, Dee Carroll, Roy Whatley, Darla Ridgeway. When the Kiowa tribe threatens to engulf their Seminole neighbors, the U. S. cavalry sends a soldier to help train the Seminole to fight their traditional enemies. Although the plot is a bit different with Indians vs. Indians, the overall film is still only average.

3931 War Drums. United Artists, 1957. 75 minutes Color. D: Reginald LeBorg. SC: Gerald Drayson Adams. WITH Lex Barker, Joan Taylor, Ben Johnson, Larry Chance, Richard Cutting, James Parnell, John Pickard, John Colicos, Tom Monroe, Jil Jarmyn, Jeanne Carmen, Mauritz Hugo, Ward Ellis, Fred Sherman, Paul Fierro, Alex Montoya, Stuart Whitman, Barbara Perry, Boyd "Red" Morgan. At the beginning of the Civil War, Apache Indians go on the warpath when gold seekers invade their lands and a cavalry officer is assigned to stop the trouble. Fairly exciting, and well directed actioner.

3932 War of the Wildcats. Republic, 1943. 102 minutes B/W. D: Albert S. Rogell. SC: Ethel Hill & Eleanore Griffin. WITH John Wayne, Martha Scott, Albert Dekker, George "Gabby" Hayes, Marjorie Rambeau, Grant Withers, Sidney Blackmer, Paul Fix, Dale Evans, Cecil Cunningham, Irving Bacon, Byron Foulger, Anne O'Neal, Richard Graham, Robert Warwick, Stanley Andrews, Will Wright, Harry Shannon, Emmett Vogan, Charles Arnt, Edward Gargan, Harry Woods, Tom London, Dick Rich, Slim Whitaker, LeRoy Mason, Lane Chandler, Arthur Loft, Bud Geary, Kenne Duncan, Hooper Atchley, Wade Crosby, George Chandler, Curley Dresden, Jack Kirk, Roy Barcroft, Yakima Canutt, Shirley Jean Rickert, Linda Scott, Jess Cavan, Pat Hogan, Charles Agnew, Linda Brent, Rhonda Fleming, Fred Graham. A cowboy comes to the aid of an Oklahoma Indian tribe in 1906 when a crooked oil man wants to drill on their lands but keep the profits for himself. Big, brawling action melodrama which packs a lot of entertainment. Original title: **In Old Oklahoma.** V: NTA Home Entertainment, Blackhawk, Cumberland Video.

3933 War Paint. United Artists, 1953. 90 minutes Color. D: Lesley Selander. SC: Richard Alan Simmons & Martin

Berkeley. WITH Robert Stack, Joan Taylor, Charles McGraw, Peter Graves, Keith Larsen, William Pullen, Richard Cutting, Douglas Kennedy, Walter Reed, Charles Nolte, James Farrell, Paul Richards, John Doucette, Robert Wilke. A madman tries to prevent the delivery of a peace treaty with the Indians by first murdering a commissioner and then by trying to lead a cavalry unit into an ambush. Pretty fair action melodrama.

3934 War Party. 20th Century-Fox, 1965. 72 minutes B/W. D: Lesley Selander. SC: George Williams & William Marks. WITH Michael T. Mikler, Donald (Don "Red") Barry, Davey Davison, Laurie Mack, Dennis Robertson, Charles Horvath, Guy Wilkerson, Michael Carr, Fred Krone. A rescue party sets out to reach an army patrol under attack by warring Comanches. Standard, but effective, action programmer.

3935 The War Wagon. Universal, 1967. 101 minutes Color. D: Burt Kennedy. SC: Clair Huffaker. WITH John Wayne, Kirk Douglas, Howard Keel, Robert Walker, Keenan Wynn, Bruce Cabot, Valora Noland, Gene Evans, Joanna Barnes, Bruce Dern, Terry Wilson, Don Collier, Sheb Wooley, Ann McCrea, Emilio Fernandez, Frank McGrath, Chuck Roberson, Boyd "Red" Morgan, Hal Needham, Marco Antonio Arzate, Perla Walter. After being released from prison after being framed by the man who stole his gold-rich lands, a man joins forces with the badman's ex-employee to get revenge by stealing his armor-plated war wagon. Actionful, light-hearted and amusing drama which will delight fans of John Wayne and Kirk Douglas. V: MCA, Blackhawk, Cumberland Video.

3936 Warlock. 20th Century-Fox, 1959. 122 minutes Color. D: Edward Dmytryk. SC: Robert Alan Arthur. WITH Richard Widmark, Henry Fonda, Anthony Quinn, Dorothy Malone, Dolores Michaels, Wallace Ford, Tom Drake, Richard Arlen, DeForrest Kelley, Regis Toomey, Vaughn Taylor, Don Beddoe, Whit Bissell, J. Anthony Hughes, Donald Barry, Frank Gorshin, Ian MacDonald, Robert Osterloh, Mickey Simpson, James Philbrook, Robert Adler, Saul Gross, Ann Doran, Bartlett Robinson. A lawman tries to bring peace to a small town with the aid of a gambler and a member of the gang he has to combat. Although no classic, this feature is entertaining and will appeal to fans of its stars.

3937 Warpath. Paramount, 1951. 95 minutes Color. D: Byron Haskin. SC: Frank Gruber. WITH Edmond O'Brien, Dean Jagger, Forrest Tucker, Polly Bergen, Harry Carey Jr., James Millican, Wallace Ford, Paul Fix, Louis Jean Heydt, Paul Lees, Walter Sande, Charles Dayton, Robert Bray, Douglas Spencer, James Burke, Chief Yowlachie, Monte Blue, Frank Ferguson, Cliff Clark, Charles Stevens, Paul Burns, John Hart, John Mansfield. A man sets out to track down the three outlaws who killed the girl he loved and ends up getting involved in an Indian attack. A superb cast greatly helps this otherwise standard melodrama.

Washington Cowboy see **Rovin' Tumbleweeds**

3938 Water Rustlers. Grand National, 1939. 54 minutes B/W. D: Samuel Diege. SC: Arthur Hoerl. WITH Dorothy Page, Dave O'Brien, Vince Barnett, Ethan Allen, Leonard Trainer, Merrill McCormack, Stanley Price, Warner Richmond, Lloyd Ingraham. A woman rancher and her foreman oppose the crooked activities of a land owner who tries to take control by damming the only creek in the valley. Initial entry in the short-lived cowgirl series starring Dorothy Page; genre fans will enjoy it. V: Cassette Express.

3939 Waterhole #3. Paramount, 1967. 100 minutes Color. D: William Graham. SC: Joseph T. Steck & R. R. Young. WITH James Coburn, Carroll O'Connor, Margaret Blye, Claude Akins, Joan Blondell, James Whitmore, Timothy Carey, Bruce Dern, Harry Davis, Roy Jenson, Robert Cornthwaite, Jim Boles, Steve Whitaker, Ted Markland, Robert Crosse, Buzz Henry. A trio of Confederates rob the Union army of a fortune in gold and bury it at a deserted waterhole and a gambler gets the map showing the location of the buried loot. Takeoff on genre films provides some amusing moments.

3940 Way of a Gaucho. 20th Century-Fox, 1952. 91 minutes B/W. D: Jacques Tourneur. SC: Philip Dunne. WITH Gene Tierney, Rory Calhoun, Richard Boone, Hugh Marlowe, Everett Sloane, Enrique Chaico, Roland Dumas, Lidia Campos, John Henchley, Douglas Poole, Mario Abdah, John Paris. In 1875 a young gaucho and the girl he loves try to find happiness together on the Argentine pampas. Standard drama.

3941 The Way of the West. First Division/ Superior, 1934. 52 minutes B/W. D: Robert Emmett (Tansey). SC: Larry Berringer & Al Lane. WITH The American Rough Riders, Wally Wales, Myrla Bratton, William Desmond, "Little" Bobbie Nelson, Fred Baker, Jim Sheridan, Art Mix, Billy Patton, Tex Jones, Harry Berry, Art Mix, Jimmie Aubrey, Helen Gibson, Gene Layman. A federal investigator tries to stop cattlemen from using an outlaw to harass sheepherders leasing government lands. This raw-boned sagebrusher was Wally Wales' final starring effort and is recommended for his fans. V: Thunderbird.

3942 Way Out West. Metro-Goldwyn-Mayer, 1930. 80 minutes B/W. D: Fred Niblo. SC: Byron Morgan, Alfred Block, Joe Farnham & Ralph Spence. WITH William Haines, Leila Hyams, Polly Moran, Francis X. Bushman Jr., Cliff Edwards, Vera Marsh, Charles Middleton, Jack Pennick, Buddy Roosevelt, Jay Wilsey (Buffalo Bill Jr.). A crooked sideshow barker cheats some cowboys and is forced to work off his debt on a ranch where he falls for the boss's daughter but is hated by her suitor. Badly dated William Haines comedy-drama; today it is hard to understand the popularity of the star's brand of smart-aleck comedy.

3943 Way Out West. Metro-Goldwyn-Mayer, 1936. 65 minutes B/W. D: James W. Horne. SC: Charles Rogers, Felix Adler & James Parrott. WITH Stan Laurel, Oliver Hardy, Sharon Lynne, James Finlayson, Rosina Lawrence, Stanley Fields, Jim Mason, James C. Morton, Frank Mills, Dave Pepper, Vivien Oakland, Harry Bernard, Mary Gordon, May Wallace, The Avalon Boys (Chill Wills, Art Green, Walter Trask, Don Brookins), Jack Hill, Sam Lufkin, Tex Driscoll, Flora Finch, Fred "Snowflake" Toones, Bobby Dunn, John Ince, Fritzi Brunette, Frank Montgomery, Fred Cady, Eddie Borden, Helen Holmes, Lester Dorr, Ham Kinsey, Bill Wolf, Art Mix, Ben Corbett, Buffalo Bill Jr., Cy Slocum, Dinah (mule). Two bumblers arrive in a small town to give their late partner's daughter the deed to a gold mine but the town's crooked saloon owner tries to pass his pretty partner off as the deserving girl. Laurel & Hardy comedy classic which is a delight from start to finish. V: Blackhawk, Nostalgia Merchant.

3944 The Way West. United Artists, 1967. 122 minutes Color. D: Andrew V. McLaglen. SC: Ben Maddow & Mitch Lindemann. WITH Kirk Douglas, Robert Mitchum, Richard Widmark, Lola Albright, Michael Witney, Sally Field, Katherine Justice, Stubby Kaye, William Lundigan, Paul Lukather, Roy Barcroft, Jack Elam, Patric Knowles, Ken Murray, John Mitchum, Nick Cravat, Harry Carey Jr., Roy Glenn, Anne Barton, Eve McVeagh, Peggy Stewart, Stefan Arngrim, Hal Lynch, Timothy Scott, Gary Morris, Eddie Little Sky, Michael Keep, Clarke Gordon, Mitchell Schollars, Jack Coffer, Everett Creach, Jim Burk, Gary McLarty, Paul Wexler. An aging trail scout aids a widowed senator in leading a wagon train across the northwest during the 1840s. Although this drama contains all the ingredients for being entertaining fare the result is a sadly vapid outing.

3945 Welcome to Blood City. EMI, 1977. 96 minutes Color. D: Peter Sasdy. SC: Stephen Schneck & Michael Winder. WITH Jack Palance, Keir Dullea, Samantha Eggar, Barry Morse, Hollis McLaren, Chris Wiggins, Allan Royale, Ken James, Henry Ramer, John Evans. Several people are tested by a research group to see how well they can survive in the environment of the Old West. A silly premise makes for a disappointing feature—watch **Westworld** (q.v.) instead.

3946 Welcome to Hard Times. Metro-Goldwyn-Mayer, 1967. 103 minutes Color. D-SC: Burt Kennedy. WITH Henry Fonda, Janice Rule, Aldo Ray, Keenan Wynn, Janis Paige, John Anderson, Warren Oates, Lon Chaney, Edgar Buchanan, Fay Spain, Denver Pyle, Michael Shea, Arlene Golonka, Royal Dano, Alan Baxter, Paul Birch, Dan Ferrone, Paul Fix, Elisha Cook, Kalen Liu, Ann McCrea, Bob Terhune, Ron Burke. A sadist killer terrorizes and destroys a small town and its survivors try to rebuild the community. Originally made-for-TV, this feature was deemed too violent and was issued theatrically; it is a good drama with some interesting performances, especially Lon Chaney as the saloon owner and Aldo Ray as the Big Bad Man from Bodie. British title: **Killer on a Horse.**

3947 Wells Fargo. Paramount, 1937. 94 (116) minutes B/W. D: Frank Lloyd. SC: Paul Schoefield, Gerald Geraghty & Frederick Jackson. WITH Joel McCrea, Frances Dee, Bob Burns, Lloyd Nolan, Johnny Mack Brown, Henry O'Neill, Porter Hall, Robert Cummings, Ralph Morgan, Mary Nash, Barlowe Borland, Stanley

Fields, Lane Chandler, Clarence Kolb,
Jack Clark, Frank McGlynn, Peggy Stewart,
Bernard Siegel. During the Civil
War a northern Wells Fargo worker believes
his wife has betrayed him to her
former suitor, a Confederate officer.
Epic-scale oater details the history of
the Wells Fargo but overall it is rather
mediocre.

3948 Wells Fargo Gunmaster. Republic,
1951. 60 minutes B/W. D: Philip Ford.
SC: M. Coates Webster. WITH Allan
"Rocky" Lane, Mary Ellen Kay, Chubby
Johnson, Michael Chapin, Roy Barcroft,
Walter Reed, Stuart Randall, William
Bakewell, George Meeker, Anne O'Neal,
James Craven, Forrest Taylor, Lee Roberts.
When a series of robberies plague
the Wells Fargo, a special investigator
is called in to halt them and round up
the gang responsible. Typically entertaining
Allan Lane vehicle.

3949 West of Abilene. Columbia, 1940.
57 minutes B/W. D: Ralph Cedar. SC:
Paul Franklin. WITH Charles Starrett,
Marjorie Cooley, Bruce Bennett, Bob
Nolan & The Sons of the Pioneers, William
Pawley, Don Beddoe, George Cleveland,
Forrest Taylor, William Kellogg, Francis
Walker, Eddie Laughton, Vester Pegg,
Bud Osborne, Frank Ellis. Settlers who
bought land from an irrigation company
find themselves up against land grabbers
who plan to re-sell their properties for
a big profit. Pretty fair Charles Starrett
actioner.

3950 West of Carson City. Universal,
1940. 57 minutes B/W. D: Ray Taylor.
SC: Milton Raison, Sherman Lowe &
Jack Bernhard. WITH Johnny Mack Brown,
Bob Baker, Fuzzy Knight, Peggy Moran,
Harry Woods, Robert Homans, Roy Barcroft,
Ted Wells, Charles King, Frank
Mitchell, Al Hall, Edmund Cobb, Jack
Roper, Jack Shannon, Ernie Adams, Kermit
Maynard, Donald Kerr, The Notables
Quartet, Dick Carter, Al Bridge, Victor
Potel. A rancher returns home to find
a gold strike has taken place in a nearby
town and crooks have taken over the
area. Entertaining and well made Johnny
Mack Brown vehicle.

3951 West of Cheyenne. Syndicate, 1931.
56 minutes B/W. D: Harry S. Webb. SC:
Bennett Cohen & Oliver Drake. WITH
Tom Tyler, Josephine Hill, Harry Woods,
Ben Corbett, Robert Walker, Fern Emmett.
A father and son framed for a crime
set out to bring in the real culprits. Very
minor league Tom Tyler oater.

3952 West of Cheyenne. Columbia, 1938.
53 minutes B/W. D: Sam Nelson. SC:
Ed Earl Repp. WITH Charles Starrett,
Irish Meredith, Bob Nolan & The Sons
of the Pioneers, Dick Curtis, Ed LeSaint,
Edmund Cobb, Art Mix, John Tyrell,
Ernie Adams, Jack Rockwell, Tex Cooper,
Frank Ellis, George Chesebro, Ed Peil
Sr. The new owner of a ranch finds the
place nearly deserted due to a number
of mysterious raids by an outlaw gang
and he and his pals set out to find the
culprits. Fine Charles Starrett film.

3953 West of Cimarron. Republic, 1942.
56 minutes B/W. D: Lester Orlebeck.
SC: Albert DeMond & Don Ryan. WITH
Bob Steele, Tom Tyler, Rufe Davis, Lois
Collier, James Bush, Guy Usher, Roy
Barcroft, Budd Buster, Hugh Prosser,
Cordell Hickman, John James, Bud Geary,
Stanley Blystone, Mickey Rentschiler.
In Texas after the Civil War the Three
Mesquiteers come across crooked Union
soldiers harassing the locals and set
out to right this wrong. Fairly exciting
Three Mesquiteers entry which moves
well but contains a rather dull plot.

3954 West of Dodge City. Columbia,
1947. 57 minutes B/W. D: Ray Nazarro.
SC: Bert Horswell. WITH Charles Starrett,
Smiley Burnette, Nancy Saunders, Fred
Sears, Glenn Stuart, I. Stanford Jolley,
George Chesebro, Robert Wilke, Nolan
Leary, Steve Clark, Zon Murray, Marshall
Reed, Tom Chatterton, Bud Osborne,
Maudie Prickett, Mustard & Gravy. A
crook trying to set up a phoney power
plant scheme murders a rancher for
his land and then tries to force the man's
daughter to sell but the Durango Kid
appears to investigate the crime. Fair
"Durango Kid" entry.

3955 West of El Dorado. Monogram,
1949. 58 minutes B/W. D: Ray Taylor.
SC: Adele Buffington. WITH Johnny
Mack Brown, Max Terhune, Reno Browne,
Teddy Infuhr, Milburn Morante, Marshall
Reed, Willilam Norton Bailey, Terry
Frost, Bud Osborne, Kenne Duncan, Bill
Potter, Bob Woodward, Boyd Stockman,
Artie Ortego. An outlaw gang tries to
find the hiding place of loot stolen by
one of their gang, who was killed by
the man who has custody of the outlaw's
kid brother, who knows the location
of the money. Good plot, but this Johnny
Mack Brown vehicle shows signs of wear.

3956 West of Nevada. Colony, 1936.
59 minutes B/W. D: Robert Hill. SC:

Rock Hawkey (Robert Hill). WITH Rex Bell, Joan Barclay, Al St. John, Steve Clark, Georgia O'Dell, Richard Botiller, Frank McCarroll, Forrest Taylor, Bob Woodward. A senator sends his son and his pal to investigate the thefts of gold from a mine on an Indian reservation. Passable Rex Bell vehicle enhanced by the comedy of Al St. John as the hero's buddy, especially the scenes where he romances the ranch cook.

3957 West of Pinto Basin. Monogram, 1940. 60 minutes B/W. D: S. Roy Luby. SC: Earle Snell. WITH Ray Corrigan, John King, Max Terhune, Gwen Gaze, Tristram Coffin, Bud Osborne, George Chesebro, Jack Perrin, Carl Mathews, Dirk Thane, Phil Dunham, Richard Cramer, Jerry Smith, Budd Buster. The Range Busters are on the trail of a gang whose holdups are causing money and supplies not to reach a dam construction site. Another fast action entry in "The Range Busters" series.

3958 West of Rainbow's End. Monogram, 1938. 57 minutes B/W. D: Alan James. SC: Stanley Roberts & Gennard Rea. WITH Tim McCoy, Kathleen Elliot, Walter McGrail, Frank LaRue, George Chang, Mary Carr, Ed Coxen, George Cooper, Robert Kortman, Jimmie Aubrey, Reed Howes, Ray Jones, Sherry Tansey. When his foster father is murdered while investigating a series of train robberies, an ex-ranger comes out of retirement to capture the killers. Pretty good Tim McCoy vehicle.

3959 West of Santa Fe. Columbia, 1938. 60 minutes B/W. D: Sam Nelson. SC: Bennett Cohen. WITH Charles Starrett, Iris Meredith, Dick Curtis, Robert Fiske, Bob Nolan & The Sons of the Pioneers, LeRoy Mason, Hank Bell, Edmund Cobb, Richard Botiller, Edward Hearn, Ed Le Saint, Buck Connors, Bud Osborne, Clem Horton. Rustlers murder a rancher and a U. S. marshal arrives to aid his daughter and capture the culprits. Entertaining Charles Starrett Columbia series entry.

3960 West of Sonora. Columbia, 1948. 52 minutes B/W. D: Ray Nazarro. SC: Barry Shipman. WITH Charles Starrett, Smiley Burnette, Steve Darrell, George Chesebro, Anita Castle, The Sunshine Boys, Hal Taliaferro, Robert Wilke, Emmett Lynn, Lynn Farr, Lloyd Ingraham. A sheriff asks his pal to become his deputy and find a notorious outlaw and his gang who have kidnapped the badman's little

granddaughter from a stage. Pretty good "Durango Kid" segment enhanced by a well written, mystery-laden script.

3961 West of Texas. Producers Releasing Corporation, 1943. 61 minutes B/W. D-SC: Oliver Drake. WITH Dave O'Brien, James Newill, Guy Wilkerson, Frances Gladwin, Marilyn Hare, Robert Barron, Tom London, Jack Rockwell, Jack Ingram, Art Fowler. Outlaws want a man's property and frame him on a murder charge but his daughter convinces the Texas Rangers to help his cause. One of the better entries in "The Texas Rangers" series but still on the slow side. Reissued by Eagle Lion in 1947 as **Shootin' Irons.**

3962 West of the Alamo. Monogram, 1946. 58 minutes B/W. D: Oliver Drake. SC: Louise Rosseau. WITH Jimmy Wakely, Lee "Lasses" White, Iris Clive, Ray Whitley, Jack Ingram, Earl Cantrell, Betty Lou Head, Budd Buster, Eddie Majors, Billy Dix, Arthur Smith, Ted French, Ray Jones, Steven Keys. A ranger works undercover to find who is behind a series of crimes. Slight Jimmy Wakely vehicle.

West of the Badlands see **The Border Legion** (1940)

3963 West of the Brazos. Lippert, 1950. 60 minutes B/W. D: Thomas Carr. SC: Ron Ormond & Maurice Trombragel. WITH James Ellison, Russell Hayden, Raymond Hatton, Fuzzy Knight, Betty (Julie) Adams, Tom Tyler, Stanley Price, Dennis Moore, George J. Lewis, John Cason, Bud Osborne, George Chesebro, Gene Roth, Jimmie Martin, Stephen Carr, Judith Webster. Two cowboys try to stop a crook out to fleece a man of his oil-rich lands. Cheap but fast moving oater with the twist of hero Russell Hayden being deaf throughout the proceedings. TV title: **Rangeland Empire.**

3964 West of the Divide. Monogram, 1934. 55 minutes B/W. D-SC: Robert North Bradbury. WITH John Wayne, Virginia Browne Faire, Lloyd Whitlock, George ("Gabby") Hayes, Billy O'Brien, Yakima Canutt, Lafe McKee, Blackie Whiteford, Earl Dwire, Dick Dickinson, Tex Palmer, Artie Ortego, Horace B. Carpenter, Hal Price, Archie Ricks. A young man, finding the crook who years before murdered his parents and kidnapped his baby brother, pretends to be an outlaw in order to infiltrate the man's gang. Well paced Lone Star oater with a fine performance by Lloyd

Whitlock as the dastardly villain Gentry. V: Electric Video, Video Dimensions.

3965 West of the Law. Monogram, 1942. 60 minutes B/W. D: Howard Bretherton. SC: Jess Bowers (Adele Buffington). WITH Buck Jones, Tim McCoy, Raymond Hatton, Harry Woods, Evelyn Cook, Milburn Morante, Roy Barcroft, Bud McTaggart, George DeNormand, Jack Daley, Bud Osborne, Lynton Brent. Three marshals work incognito in a small town where outlaws have made attacks on the local newspaper and uncover a gold smuggling operation. The final entry in the popular "Rough Riders" series is a good one with an entertaining plot and lots of fast action. V: Discount Video.

3966 West of the Pecos. RKO Radio, 1934. 68 minutes B/W. D: Phil Rosen. SC: Milton Krims & John Twist. WITH Richard Dix, Martha Sleeper, Samuel S. Hinds, Fred Kohler, Louise Beavers, Maria Alba, Sleep 'n Eat (Willie Best), Pedro Regas, Russell Simpson, Irving Bacon, Maurice Black, G. Pat Collins, George Cooper. A cowboy fights lawlessness in post-Civil War Texas. Well mounted adaptation of the Zane Grey novel; remade in 1945 (q.v.).

3967 West of the Pecos. RKO Radio, 1945. 66 minutes B/W. D: Edward Killy. SC: Norman Houston. WITH Robert Mitchum, Barbara Hale, Richard Martin, Thurston Hall, Rita Corday, Russell Hopton, Bill Williams, Bruce Edwards, Harry Woods, Perc Launders, Bryant Washburn, Philip Morris, Martin Garralaga, Sammy Blum, Robert Anderson, Italia De Nublia, Carmen Granada, Ariel Sherry, Virginia Wave, Ethan Laidlaw, Jack Gargan, Allan Lee, Larry Wheat. When outlaws hold up the stagecoach carrying a rich meat packer and his pretty daughter, a cowpoke and his pal set out to capture the villains. Well produced oater which sent Bob Mitchum onto bigger budget films.

3968 West of the Rio Grande. Monogram, 1944. 57 minutes B/W. D: Lambert Hillyer. SC: Betty Burbridge. WITH Johnny Mack Brown, Raymond Hatton, Christine McIntyre, Dennis Moore, Lloyd Ingraham, Kenneth MacDonald, Frank LaRue, Art Fowler, Hugh Prosser, Edmund Cobb, Steve Clark, Jack Rockwell, Hal Price, John Merton, George Morrell, Bud Osborne, Al Ferguson, Robert Kortman, Pierce Lyden, Lynton Brent. Lawmen pose as a gunslinger and a teacher in order to

work in a town where the head politician has been using a gang to force citizens to give up their voting rights. Pretty entertaining Johnny Mack Brown-Raymond Hatton vehicle.

3969 West of Tombstone. Columbia, 1942. 59 minutes B/W. D: Howard Bretherton. SC: Maurice Geraghty. WITH Charles Starrett, Russell Hayden, Cliff Edwards, Marcella Martin, Gordon DeMain, Clancy Cooper, Jack Kirk, Budd Buster, Tom London, Francis Walker, Ray Jones, Eddie Laughton, Lloyd Bridges, Ernie Adams, George Morrell. After a stagecoach robbery the citizens of a town believe that Billy the Kid is still alive and the doubting sheriff opens the Kid's grave to find it empty. Actionful entry in the Charles Starrett-Russell Hayden series.

3970 West of Wyoming. Monogram, 1950. 57 minutes B/W. D: Wallace Fox. SC: Adele Buffington. WITH Johnny Mack Brown, Gail Davis, Myron Healey, Dennis Moore, Stanley Andrews, Milburn Morante, Mary Gordon, Carl Mathews, Paul Cramer, John Merton, Holly Bane, Steve Clark, Frank McCarroll, Bud Osborne. A lawman is on the trail of a gang which tries to keep settlers out of newly opened territory. The plot is okay but this Johnny Mack Brown vehicle is a rather tired effort.

3971 West to Glory. Producers Releasing Corporation, 1947. 61 minutes B/W. D: Ray Taylor. SC: Elmer Clifton & Robert Churchill. WITH Eddie Dean, Roscoe Ates, Dolores Castle, Gregg Barton, Jimmie Martin, The Sunshine Boys, Zon Murray, Alex Montoya, Ted French, Carl Mathews. Two cowpokes go after a couple of crooks who have stolen a man's gold and are also after his famous diamond. A dull Eddie Dean outing with an unfunny dream sequence where Soapy Jones (Roscoe Ates) dreams he is hero Eddie Dean. Film is partially saved by Eddie Dean's singing of three nice songs, including "Cry, Cry, Cry."

3972 Westbound. Warner Brothers, 1959. 72 minutes Color. D: Budd Boetticher. SC: Berne Giler. WITH Randolph Scott, Virginia Mayo, Karen Steele, Michael Pate, Andrew Duggan, Michael Dante, Wally Brown, John Day, Walter Barnes, Fred Sherman, Mack Williams, Ed Prentiss, Rory Mallinson, Rudi Dana, Tom Monroe, Jack Perrin, Buddy Roosevelt, Charles Morton, John Epper, Gary Epper, Kermit Maynard, Mary Boss, William A. Green, Jack E. Henderson, Felice Richmond,

Creighton Hale, Gertrude Keeler, Walter Reed, Jack C. Williams, Gerald Roberts, John Hudkins. During the Civil War a Union officer is assigned to start a stage line to ship gold from California to aid the Union cause and he is opposed by a rich rancher whose beautiful wife was once his girlfriend. Very well made and entertaining Randolph Scott vehicle.

3973 Westbound Limited. Universal, 1937. 66 minutes B/W. D: Ford Beebe. SC: Maurice Geraghty. WITH Lyle Talbot, Polly Rowles, Henry Brandon, Frank Reicher, Henry Hunter, William Lundigan, William Royale, Tom Steele, Charles Murphy, Monte Vandegrift, J. P. McGowan. Falsely accused of a crime and sent to prison, a railroad agent escapes to prove his innocence. Dandy "B" programmer.

3974 Westbound Mail. Columbia, 1937. 54 minutes B/W. D: Folmer Blangsted. SC: Frances Guihan. WITH Charles Starrett, Rosalind Keith, Edward Keane, Arthur Stone, Ben Weldon, Al Bridge, George Chesebro, Art Mix. An FBI agent masquerades as a mule skinner to help a young woman whose property is being sought by a miner who thinks his gold vein may extend into her land. Top notch, well written Charles Starrett vehicle.

3975 Westbound Stage. Monogram, 1939. 56 minutes B/W. D: Spencer Gordon Bennet. SC: Robert Emmett (Tansey). WITH Tex Ritter, Muriel Evans, Reed Howes, Kenne Duncan, Nelson McDowell, Nolan Willis, Steve Clark, Tom London, Frank Ellis, Chick Hannon, Frank LaRue, Chester Gan, Hank Bell, Phil Dunham. After an outlaw gang massacres an army patrol which included his cousin, a man takes the job as guard on a stage carrying a gold shipment in order to round up the bandits. Pretty sturdy Tex Ritter vehicle.

3976 Western Caravans. Columbia, 1939. 58 minutes B/W. D: Sam Nelson. SC: Bennett Cohen. WITH Charles Starrett, Iris Meredith, Bob Nolan & The Sons of the Pioneers, Russell Simpson, Hal Taliaferro, Dick Curtis, Hank Bell, Sammy McKim, Edmund Cobb, Ethan Laidlaw, Steve Clark, Herman Hack, Charles Brinley. Rustlers try to cause range warfare between ranchers and incoming settlers and the local sheriff tries to maintain peace. Okay Charles Starrett actioner.

3977 The Western Code. Columbia, 1932. 60 minutes B/W. D: J. P. McCarthy. SC: Milton Krims. WITH Tim McCoy, Nora Lane, Wheeler Oakman, Mathew Betz, Dwight Frye, Mischa Auer, Gordon DeMain, Bud Osborne, Emilio Fernandez, Chuck Baldra, Cactus Mack. A cowboy tries to help a girl whose stepfather has stolen her ranch and who has plans to marry her and murder her brother. Pretty entertaining Tim McCoy opus which will interest horror film fans in that Dwight Frye plays a pal of the hero who is framed by the villains.

3978 Western Courage. Columbia, 1936. 61 minutes B/W. D: Spencer Gordon Bennet. SC: Nate Gatzert. WITH Ken Maynard, Geneva Mitchell, Charles K. French, Betty Blythe, Cornelius Keefe, Ward Bond, E. H. Calvert, Renee Whitney, Dick Curtis, Bob Reeves, Bud McClure, Bart Carre, Wally West. The foreman of a dude ranch likes another guest but she is a spoiled rich girl who is being courted by a no-good and later the girl is held for ransom by outlaws. The story is very silly but this Ken Maynard vehicle is fun, anyway.

3979 Western Cyclone. Producers Releasing Corporation, 1943. 65 minutes B/W. D: Sam Newfield. SC: Patricia Harper. WITH Buster Crabbe, Al St. John, Marjorie Manners, Karl Hackett, Milton Kibbee, Glenn Strange, Charles King, Hal Price, Kermit Maynard, Frank Ellis Frank McCarroll, Artie Ortego, Herman Hack, Al Haskell. A young woman, the leader of an outlaw gang, has herself kidnapped and then blames Billy Carson in an attempt to discredit the lawman. Passable, but low grade, entry in PRC's "Billy Carson" series. Reissued by Eagle Lion in 1947 in a 39 minute version called **Frontier Fighters.**

3980 Western Frontier. Columbia, 1935. 56 minutes B/W. D: Al Herman. SC: Nate Gatzert. WITH Ken Maynard, Lucille Browne, Nora Lane, Robert Henry, Otis Harlan, Frank Yaconelli, Harold Goodwin, Frank Hagney, Gordon Griffith, James Marcus, Tom Harris, Nelson McDowell, Frank Ellis, Art Mix, Slim Whitaker, William Gould, Dick Curtis, Budd Buster, Herman Hack, Horace B. Carpenter, Oscar Gahan. Using a medicine show as a front, a lawman arrives in a small town trying to track down an outlaw gang and he finds out his long-lost sister is actually the gang's leader. Ken Maynard wrote the original story for this film, his first Columbia series entry, and overall the picture is quite good.

3981 Western Gold. Principal/20th Century-Fox, 1937. 60 minutes B/W. D: Howard Bretherton. SC: Forrest Barnes. WITH Smith Ballew, Heather Angel, LeRoy Mason, Ben Alexander, Howard Hickman, Alan Bridge, Bud Osborne, Victor Potel, Otis Harlan, Frank McGlynn, Horace Murphy, Tom London, Steve Clark, Paul Fix. A Union officer is sent West by President Lincoln to find out why gold shipments are not reaching the East. Smith Ballew's first series vehicle, based on a Harold Bell Wright book, is a good one and nicely showcases the star's fine singing voice.

3982 Western Heritage. RKO Radio, 1948. 61 minutes B/W. D: Wallace Grissell. SC: Norman Houston. WITH Tim Holt, Richard Martin, Nan Leslie, Lois Andrews, Tony Barrett, Richard Powers, Harry Woods, Walter Reed, Jason Robards, Robert Bray, Perc Launders, Emmett Lynn. A cowpoke finds himself in double trouble, with outlaws and with the saloon girl he loves. Average Tim Holt effort.

3983 Western Jamboree. Republic, 1938. 54 (56) minutes B/W. D: Ralph Staub. SC: Gerald Geraghty. WITH Gene Autry, Smiley Burnette, Jean Rouveral, Esther Muir, Frank Darien, Joe Frisco, Kermit Maynard, Jack Perrin, Jack Ingram, Margaret Armstrong, Harry Holman, Edward Raquello, Ray Teal, Frank Ellis, Eddie Dean, Davidson Clark. Gene Autry and his pals fix up a ranch to make a young woman think her father, a broke prospector, is the owner, while crooks want the land for its valuable helium deposits. Slight Gene Autry film.

3984 Western Justice. Supreme, 1935. 56 minutes B/W. D-SC: Robert North Bradbury. WITH Bob Steele, Renee Bordon, Julian Rivero, Lafe McKee, Perry Murdock, Arthur Loft, Jack Cowell, Vane Calvert. A cowboy comes to the aid of ranchers who are being forced off their lands by an outlaw gang. Entertaining Bob Steele vehicle.

3985 Western Mail. Monogram, 1942. 55 minutes B/W. D: Robert Emmett Tansey. SC: Robert Emmett (Tansey) & Frances Kavanaugh. WITH Tom Keene, Jean Trent, Frank Yaconelli, LeRoy Mason, Glenn Strange, Fred Kohler Jr., James Sheridan, Gene Alsace, Karl Hackett, Tex Palmer. A U. S. marshal

works undercover to find who is behind an outlaw gang and he aids one of the gang members with an alibi in order to infiltrate their activities. Fair Tom Keene vehicle.

3986 Western Pacific Agent. Lippert, 1950. 64 minutes B/W. D: Sam Newfield. SC: Milton Raison. WITH Kent Taylor, Sheila Ryan, Mickey Knox, Morris Carnovsky, Robert Lowery, Sid Melton, Frank Richards, Dick Elliott, Anthony Jochim, Lee Phelps, Ted Jacques, Vera Marshe, Carla Martin, Margia Dean, Gloria Gray. When a railroad detective is murdered during a robbery, a fellow agent hunts for the killer. Fairly good "B" programmer set in the modern-day West.

3987 Western Renegades. Monogram, 1949. 58 minutes B/W. D: Wallace Fox. SC: Adele Buffington. WITH Johnny Mack Brown, Max Terhune, Jane Adams, Riley Hill, Steve Clark, Marshall Bradford, Hugh Prosser, Marshall Reed, Constance Worth, James H. Harrison, Terry Frost, William Ruhl, Myron Healey, Milburn Morante, John Merton, Dee Cooper, Chuck Roberson, Bill Potter, Lane Bradford. A U. S. marshal tries to puzzle out the events surrounding the murder of a banker. A complicated plot somewhat helps this later Johnny Mack Brown effort.

Western Terror see **Buzzy and the Phantom Pinto**

3988 Western Trails. Universal, 1938. 57 minutes B/W. D: George Waggner. SC: Norton S. Parker. WITH Bob Baker, Marjorie Reynolds, Carlyle Moore Jr., John Ridgely, Franco Casarro, Jack Rockwell, Bob Burns, Jack Kirk, Jimmy Phillips, Murdock McQuarrie, Jack Ingram, Hank Worden, Forrest Taylor, Tex Palmer, Herman Hack, Oscar Gahan, Jack Montgomery. An undercover agent attempts to stop a vicious outlaw gang. Okay singing oater in the Bob Baker series; loose remake of **The Dawn Rider** (q.v.). V: Cumberland.

3989 Western Union. 20th Century-Fox, 1941. 93 minutes Color. D: Fritz Lang. SC: Robert Carson. WITH Randolph Scott, Robert Young, Dean Jagger, Virginia Gilmore, John Carradine, Slim Summerville, Chill Wills, Barton MacLane, Russell Hicks, Victor Kilian, Minor Watson, George Chandler, Chief Big Tree, Chief Thundercloud, Dick Rich, Addison Richards, Irving Bacon, Harry Strang, Reed Howes, Tom London, Steve O'Brien, Cliff Clark, Arthur Aylesworth, Paul Burns, Francis

Ford, Eddy Waller. An ex-outlaw joins the gang stringing the Western Union telegraph lines and becomes romantically involved with the sister of the project's chief engineer but has a rival in a fellow worker, a Harvard graduate. Well made but undistinguished historical oater.

3990 The Westerner. Columbia, 1934. 58 minutes B/W. D: David Selman. SC: Harold Shumate. WITH Tim McCoy, Marion Shilling, Joseph (Sawyer) Sauers, Hooper Atchley, Ed Le Saint, John Dilson, Eddie (Edmund) Cobb, Albert J. Smith, Harry Todd, Bud Osborne, Slim Whitaker, Merrill McCormack, Art Mix, Lafe McKee, Hank Bell. A cowboy finds out his ranch foreman and the local sheriff are in cahoots rustling cattle and they try to pin a murder charge on him. Complicated plot twists somewhat take away from this well-made Tim McCoy vehicle which has a well done pseudo-execution sequence.

3991 The Westerner. United Artists, 1939. 99 minutes B/W. D: William Wyler. SC: Jo Swerling & Niven Busch. WITH Gary Cooper, Walter Brennan, Doris Davenport, Fred Stone, Paul Hurst, Chill Wills, Charles Halton, Forrest Tucker, Tom Tyler, Arthur Aylesworth, Lupita Tovar, Julian Rivero, Lillian Bond, Dana Andrews, Roger Gray, Jack Pennick, Art Mix, Helen Foster, Trevor Bardette, Connie Leon, Charles Coleman, Lew Kelly, Heinie Conklin, Lucien Littlefield, Corbet Morris, Stanley Andrews, Henry Roquemore, Hank Bell. A drifter falls in love with a homesteader's daughter and when the father is killed by Judge Roy Bean's men, he goes gunning for the maverick lawman. Not much history here, but this feature is entertaining nonetheless.

3992 Westward Bound. Syndicate, 1931. 60 minutes B/W. D: Harry S. Webb. SC: Carl Krusada. WITH Buffalo Bill Jr., Allene Ray, Buddy Roosevelt, Ben Corbett, Yakima Canutt, Fern Emmett, Tom London, Robert Walker, Pete Morrison. A playboy is sent West by his father who hopes the wide open spaces will reform him and the job gets done when he comes to the rescue of a young woman whose ranch is sought by crooks. Boring and tacky—one of the all-time worst "B" Westerns.

3993 Westward Bound. Monogram, 1944. 59 minutes B/W. D: Robert Emmett Tansey. SC: Frances Kavanaugh. WITH Ken Maynard, Hoot Gibson, Bob Steele,

Betty Miles, John Bridges, Harry Woods, Karl Hackett, Weldon Heyburn, Hal Price, Roy Brent, Frank Ellis, Curley Dresden, Dan White, Al Ferguson, Horace B. Carpenter. The Trail Blazers trio of marshals come to the aid of ranchers who are being forced off their lands by an outlaw gang led by a government official who wants the area for its resale value once Montana becomes a state. Very entertaining entry in the popular "Trail Blazers" series with all three stars used to good advantage.

3994 Westward Ho! Republic, 1935. 55 minutes B/W. D: Robert North Bradbury. SC: Lindsley Parsons, Robert Emmett (Tansey) & Harry Friedman. WITH John Wayne, Sheila Mannors, Frank McGlynn Jr., James Farley, Jack Curtis, Bradley Metcalfe Jr., Dickie Jones, Mary Mac-Laren, Yakima Canutt, Hank Bell, Glenn Strange, The Singing Riders, Lloyd Ingraham, Frank Ellis, Earl Dwire, Fred Burns, Jack Kirk, Tex Palmer. A young man, separated from his younger brother years before when outlaws attacked their wagon and murdered their parents, goes West with settlers and becomes friends with another man working as a spy for outlaws, not knowing he is really his brother. Highly entertaining and actionful production from producer Paul Malvern; John Wayne's first Republic Western.

3995 Westward Ho. Republic, 1942. 56 minutes B/W. D: John English. SC: Morton Grant & Doris Schroeder. WITH Bob Steele, Tom Tyler, Rufe Davis, Evelyn Brent, Donald Curtis, Lois Collier, Emmett Lynn, John James, Jack Kirk, Kenne Duncan, Tom Seidel, Milton Kibbee, Edmund Cobb, Monte Montague, Al Taylor, Bud Osborne, Horace B. Carpenter, John Cason, Jack O'Shea, Ray Jones, Tex Palmer, Jack Montgomery, Curley Dresden, Budd Buster. A gang of desperadoes, led by a woman banker, is trailed by the Three Mesquiteers. Good entry in the popular series bolstered by an excellent genre cast. TV title: **Riders for Justice.**

3996 Westward Ho the Wagons. Buena Vista, 1956. 90 minutes Color. D: William Beaudine. SC: Tom Blackburn. WITH Fess Parker, Kathleen Crowley, George Reeves, Jeff York, David Stollery, Sebastian Cabot, Doreen Tracey, Barbara Woodell, John War Eagle, Cubby O'Brien, Tommy Cole, Leslie Bradley, Morgan Woodward, Iron Eyes Cody, Anthony Numkena, Karen Pendleton, Jane Liddell, Jon Locke. A wagon train filled with

Westward 490

settlers moves West under the leadership of their likable head scout and along the way has many adventures. Leisurely paced Walt Disney drama laced with songs.

3997 Westward the Women. Metro-Goldwyn-Mayer, 1952. 112 minutes B/W. D: William A. Wellman. SC: Charles Schnee. WITH Robert Taylor, Denise Darcel, Hope Emerson, Marilyn Erskine, Julie Bishop, John McIntire, Beverly Dennis, Lenore Lonegan, Henry Nakamura, Renata Vanni. A wagon train filled with women heads to California led by a wagonmaster who has to contend with them as well as Indians, outlaws and the elements. Frank Capra wrote the original story for this rather lighthearted wagon train drama but the overall results are mild.

3998 The Westward Trail. Eagle Lion, 1948. 56 minutes B/W. D: Ray Taylor. SC: Robert Alan Miller. WITH Eddie Dean, Roscoe Ates, Phyllis Blanchard, Eileen Hardin, Andy Parker & The Plainsmen, Steve Drake, Bob Duncan, Carl Mathews, Lee Morgan, Bob Woodward, Budd Buster, Slim Whitaker, Frank Ellis. A U. S. marshal works incognito to aid a woman whose ranch is sought by crooks. Poor Eddie Dean musical Western.

3999 Westworld. Metro-Goldwyn-Mayer, 1973. 89 minutes Color. D-SC: Michael Crichton. WITH Yul Brynner, Richard Benjamin, James Brolin, Norman Bartold, Alan Oppenheimer, Victoria Shaw, Dick Van Patten, Linda Scott, Steve Franklin, Michael Mikler, Terry Wilson, Majel Barrett, Anna Randall, Julie Marcus, Sharyn Wynters, Anne Bellamy, Chris Holter, Charles Seel, Wade Crosby, Lin Henson, Nora Marlow, Lauren Gilbert, Howard Platt, Jared Martin. Two businessmen take a vacation in a fantasy world where the old West of the 1880s is recreated but a robot gunman goes haywire and begins killing the tourists. Interesting sci-fi effort which spawned a less satisfying sequel, **Futureworld** (American-International, 1976) in which Yul Brynner briefly recreated his gunman-robot character.

4000 Wetbacks. Banner, 1956. 89 minutes Color. D: Hank McCune. SC: Peter LaRoche. WITH Lloyd Bridges, Nancy Gates, Barton MacLane, John Hoyt, Harold Peary, Nacho Galindo, Robert Keys, David Colmans, Jose Gonzales Gonzales, Louis Jean Heydt, Tom Keene. The U. S. government border patrol tries

to stop the influx of Mexicans being illegally smuggled across the Texas border for cheap labor. Low grade programmer.

4001 Wheels of Destiny. Universal, 1934. 64 minutes B/W. D: Alan James. SC: Nate Gatzert. WITH Ken Maynard, Dorothy Dix, Philo McCullough, Fred McKay, Fred Sale Jr., Buffalo Bill Jr., Jack Rockwell, Frank Rice, Nelson McDowell, William Gould, Ed Coxen, Merrill McCormack, Slim Whitaker, Hank Bell, Bob Burns, Artie Ortego, Wally Wales, Helen Gibson, Jack Evans, Bud McClure, Fred Burns, Chief Big Tree, Marin Sais, Chuck Baldra, Blackjack Ward, Bobby Dunn, Roy Bucko. A cowboy leads a wagon train of settlers across Mt. Whitney's great salt flats and along the way they battle outlaws, Indians and the harsh environment. Top notch Ken Maynard film which Ken also produced and wrote the music.

4002 When a Man Rides Alone. Monarch, 1933. 60 minutes B/W. D: J. P. McGowan. SC: Oliver Drake. WITH Tom Tyler, Adele Lacy, Alan Bridge, Bob Burns, Frank Ball, Alma Chester, Duke Lee, Barney Furey, Lee Cordova, Jack Rockwell, Bud Osborne, Jack Kirk, Herman Hack. A mysterious bandit robs a gold shipment and then gives the money to settlers who have invested in a bogus mine. Average Tom Tyler outing with low grade production values.

4003 When a Man's a Man. Associated First National, 1924. 55 minutes B/W. D: Edward F. Cline. SC: Walter Anthony & Harry Carr. WITH John Bowers, Marguerite De La Motte, Robert Frazer, June Marlowe, Forrest Robinson, Elizabeth Rhodes, Fred Stanton, George Hackathorne, Edward Hearn, John Fox Jr., Arthur Hoyt, Ray Thompson, Charles Mailes. When his girl refuses his marriage proposal a man heads West where he is mistaken for a cattle rustler but learns to become a man. Fairly good silent adaptation of the Harold Bell Wright novel.

4004 When a Man's a Man. Fox, 1935. 70 minutes B/W. D: Edward F. Cline. SC: Dan Jarrett. WITH George O'Brien, Dorothy Wilson, Paul Kelly, Harry Woods, Jimmy Butler, Richard Carlisle, Edgar Norton, Clarence Wilson. In a small town, a cowboy comes to the aid of a girl ranch owner whose water supply has been taken over by outlaws. Well acted and entertaining George O'Brien vehicle. TV title: **Saga of the West.**

4005 When the Daltons Rode. Universal, 1940. 74 minutes B/W. D: George Marshall. SC: Harold Shumate. WITH Randolph Scott, Kay Francis, Brian Donlevy, Broderick Crawford, George Bancroft, Stuart Erwin, Andy Devine, Frank Albertson, Mary Gordon, Harry Stephens, Edgar Deering, Quen Ramsey, Dorothy Granger, Bob McKenzie, Fay McKenzie, June Wilkins, Walter Soderling, Edgar Buchanan, Sally Payne, Mary Ainslee, Erville Alderson. Four brothers are forced to become outlaws and they befriend a lawyer who falls in love with a girl one of the Dalton's plans to marry. Slick Universal feature that has more action than plot.

4006 When the Legends Die. 20th Century-Fox, 1972. 104 minutes Color. D: Stuart Miller. SC: Robert Dozier. WITH Richard Widmark, Frederick Forrest, Luana Anders, Vito Scotti, Herbert Nelson, John War Eagle, John Gruber, Garry Walberg, Jack Mullaney, Malcolm Curley, Roy Engel, Rex Holman. An aging rodeo circuit rider befriends an orphaned Indian boy who eventually rejects his friendship. Rather interesting melodrama with an excellent performance by Richard Widmark as the rodeo rider.

4007 When the North Wind Blows. Sunn Classic Pictures, 1974. 100 minutes Color. D-SC: Stewart Raffill. WITH Henry Brandon, Dan Haggerty, Herbert Nelson. In the early 1900s two rare Siberian tigers attack near a small Alaskan village and an old-time trapper and a group of youths hunt them and when one of the boys is accidentally wounded by the trapper the man flees into the wilderness where he is befriended by a tigress and her cubs. Pleasant and easy-to-take family fare with good wilderness locations.

4008 When the Redskins Rode. Columbia, 1951. 77 minutes Color. D: Lew Landers. SC: Robert E. Kent. WITH Jon Hall, Mary Castle, James Seay, John Ridgely, Sherry Moreland, Pedro De Cordoba, John Dehner, Lewis L. Russell, William Bakewell, Gregory Gay, Rusty Westcoatt, Milton Kibbee, Rick Vallin. In 1753 Virginia's Governor Dinwiddie and George Washington try to get local Indian tribes to ally with the British against the French but a pretty spy tries to convince the Indian chief's son to do the opposite. Standard historical melodrama set in the pre-Revolutionary War period.

When the West Was Young see **Heritage of the Desert** (1932)

4009 Where the Buffalo Roam. Monogram, 1938. 60 minutes B/W. D: Al Herman. SC: Robert Emmett (Tansey). WITH Tex Ritter, Dorothy Short, Snub Pollard, Horace Murphy, John Merton, Richard Alexander, Karl Hackett, Dave O'Brien, Louise Massey & Her Westerners, Bob Terry, Charles King, Blackie Whiteford, Denver Dixon, Curt Massey, Ernie Adams, Hank Worden. A man is on the trail of the murderers of his mother, an outlaw gang killing buffalo and trying to wreck a stage line. A complicated plot is somewhat offset by some good action and music in this Tex Ritter vehicle.

4010 Where the Lilies Bloom. United Artists, 1974. 96 minutes B/W. D: William A. Graham. SC: Earl Hamner. WITH Julie Gholson, Jan Smithers, Mathew Burrill, Helen Harmon, Harry Dean Stanton, Sudie Bond, Rance Howard, Tom Spratley, Helen Bragdon, Alice Beardsley. In the mountain region of North Carolina, youngsters try to keep their parents' death a secret so they will not be separated. Well made family film, produced in North Carolina.

4011 Where the North Begins. Screen Guild, 1947. 42 minutes B/W. D: Howard Bretherton. SC: Betty Burbridge & Les Swabacker. WITH Russell Hayden, Jennifer Holt, Tristram Coffin, Denver Pyle, Stephen Barclay, Keith Richards, Anthony Warde, Frank Hagney, Artie Ortego. A Canadian Mountie battles a gang of outlaws in a small town while romancing a pretty local girl. Low budget featurette which moves along fairly quickly.

4012 Where the Red Fern Grows. Howco-International/Westamerica, 1974. 97 minutes Color. D: Norman Tokar. SC: Douglas Stewart & Eleanor Lamb. WITH James Whitmore, Beverly Garland, Jack Ging, Lonny Chapman, Stewart Petersen, Jill Clark, Jeanna Wilson. In Oklahoma in the 1930s a young boy raises two redbone hounds and trains them for two years to be champion coon hunters but during the big contest, held in the rugged Cherokee countryside, the dogs are called off the hunt to rescue the boy from a mountain lion. Pleasing family film based on Wilson Rawls' book with soundtrack songs by the Osmond Brothers and Andy Williams.

4013 Where the West Begins. Monogram, 1938. 54 minutes B/W. D: J. P. McGowan. SC: Stanley Roberts & Gennaro Rea. WITH Jack Randall, Luana Walters, Fuzzy

Knight, Richard Alexander, Budd Buster, Arthur Houseman, Ralph Peters, Ray Whitley, The Phelps Brothers, Kit Guard, Ken Card. A crook wants a girl's ranch and he has a cowboy thrown in jail so he cannot persuade her not to sell. Pleasant Jack Randall vehicle.

4014 Where Trails Divide. Monogram, 1937. 60 minutes B/W. D: Robert North Bradbury. SC: Robert Emmett (Tansey). WITH Tom Keene, Eleanor Stewart, Warner Richmond, David Sharpe, Lorraine Randall, Charles K. French, Steve Clark, Hal Price, Richard Cramer, James Sheridan (Sherry Tansey), Bud Osborne, Horace B. Carpenter, Jim Mason, Forrest Taylor, Oscar Gahan, Wally West. An express company lawyer is made sheriff of a small town in order to stop an outlaw gang. Austere Tom Keene film; well done.

4015 Where Trails End. Monogram, 1942. 55 minutes B/W. D: Robert Emmett Tansey. SC: Robert Emmett (Tansey) & Frances Kavanaugh. WITH Tom Keene, Joan Curtis, Frank Yaconelli, Charles King, Donald Stewart, Steve Clark, William Vaughn, Horace B. Carpenter, Nick Moro, Gene Alsace, Fred Hoose, James Sheridan, Tex Palmer, Chick Hannon, Tom Seidel. When settlers are driven from their homes by a mysterious outlaw gang's terrorism a U. S. marshal is sent to investigate and finds that enemy agents are after recently discovered tungsten. Average oater with a prophetic title as it was Tom Keene's final series film.

4016 The Whirlwind. Columbia, 1933. 60 minutes B/W. D: D. Ross Lederman. SC: Stuart Anthony. WITH Tim McCoy, Alice Dahl, Pat O'Malley, Matthew Betz, J. Carrol Naish, Joseph Girard, Lloyd Whitcomb, William McCall, Stella Adams, Theodore Lorch, Hank Bell, Mary Gordon, Joe Dominguez. A man returns home with his two pals to find his father and friends have been turned against him by a crooked lawman. Fair Tim McCoy vehicle with rodeo and boxing sequences in addition to the usual action.

4017 Whirlwind. Columbia, 1951. 70 minutes B/W. D: John English. SC: Norman S. Hall. WITH Gene Autry, Smiley Burnette, Gail Davis, Harry Lauter, Thurston Hall, Dick Curtis, Harry Harvey, Kenne Duncan, Tommy Ivo, Gregg Barton, Al Wyatt, Gary Goodwin, Pat O'Malley, Bud Osborne, Boyd Stockman, Frankie Marvin, Stan Jones. Postal inspector

Gene Autry is on the trail of a gang led by a dishonest rancher. Pleasing Gene Autry vehicle.

4018 Whirlwind Horseman. Grand National, 1938. 60 minutes B/W. D: Robert Hill. SC: George Plympton. WITH Ken Maynard, Joan Barclay, Dave O'Brien, Kenny Dix, Roger Williams, Walter Shumway, Budd Buster, Lew Meehan, Joseph Girard, Bill Griffith, Glenn Strange. When their pal disappears two men go looking for him and find a group of ranchers are being menaced by outlaws. Low budget but entertaining Ken Maynard vehicle with a good sprinkling of comedy.

4019 Whirlwind Raiders. Columbia, 1948. 54 minutes B/W. D: Vernon Keays. SC: Norman S. Hall. WITH Charles Starrett, Smiley Burnette, Nancy Saunders, Fred Sears, Little Brown Jug (Don Kay Reynolds), Doye O'Dell & His Radio Rangers, Jack Ingram, Philip Morris, Patrick Hurst, Eddie Parker, Lynn Farr, Arthur Loft, Maudie Prickett, Frank LaRue, Russell Meeker, Herman Hack. The Durango Kid is on the trail of the corrupt State Police, a group of crooks hiding behind official badges after the disbandment of the Texas Rangers. "Durango Kid" fans will like this actionful series entry.

Whirlwind Rider <u>see</u> **Ranger of the Law**

4020 The Whispering Skull. Producers Releasing Corporation, 1944. 56 minutes B/W. D: Elmer Clifton. SC: Harry Fraser. WITH Tex Ritter, Dave O'Brien, Guy Wilkerson, Denny Burke, I. Stanford Jolley, Henry Hall, George Morrell, Ed Cassidy, Robert Kortman, Wen Wright, Frank Ellis. The Texas Rangers trio are on the trail of a masked killer known as "The Whispering Skull," who is looking for a cache of diamonds. Slow moving and cheaply made series entry which is lacking in atmosphere. Tex Ritter sings "It's Never Too Late" and "In Case You Change Your Mind."

4021 Whispering Smith. Paramount, 1948. 88 minutes Color. D: Leslie Fenton. SC: Frank Butler & Karl Lamb. WITH Alan Ladd, Robert Preston, Brenda Marshall, Donald Crisp, William Demarest, Fay Holden, Murvyn Vye, Frank Faylen, John Eldredge, Robert Wood, J. Farrell MacDonald, Don Barclay, Will Wright, Eddy Waller, Gary Gray, Robert Kortman, Ashley Cowan, Ray Teal, Jimmy Dundee. A special agent is called in by the railroad to investigate a series of robberies and he finds that a friend is involved with the outlaws. Well done drama for Alan Ladd and Robert Preston fans. The film was the basis for a TV series of the same name on NBC-TV in 1961 starring Audie Murphy and Guy Mitchell.

4022 Whistlin' Dan. Tiffany, 1932. 60 minutes B/W. D: Phil Rosen. SC: Stuart Anthony. WITH Ken Maynard, Joyzelle Joyner, Georges Renavent, Harlan E. Knight, Don Terry, Jack Rockwell, Lew Meehan, Bud McClure, Merrill McCormack, Wally Wales, Jessie Arnold, Frank Ellis, Hank Bell. When outlaw Serge Karloff kidnaps and murders his pal, cowboy Whistlin' Dan joins the gang to get revenge on the gunman. Quite interesting Ken Maynard vehicle; leisurely paced. V: Discount Video.

4023 Whistling Bullets. Ambassador, 1937. 58 minutes B/W. D: John English. SC: Joseph O'Donnell. WITH Kermit Maynard, Harlene (Harley) Wood, Jack Ingram, Maston Williams, Bruce Mitchell, Karl Hackett, Sherry Tansey, Cliff Parkinson. Two Texas Rangers are on the trail of a gang of bond thieves. Good production values and direction heighten the affect of this Kermit Maynard vehicle, supposedly based on the works of James Oliver Curwood.

4024 Whistling Hills. Monogram, 1951. 59 minutes B/W. D: Derwin Abrahams. SC: Fred Myton. WITH Johnny Mack Brown, Jimmy (James) Ellison, Pamela Duncan, Noel Neill, I. Stanford Jolley, Lee Roberts, Marshall Reed, Lane Bradford, Bud Osborne, Pierce Lyden, Frank Ellis, Ray Jones, Merrill McCormack. A masked outlaw who uses a mysterious whistle to signal his gang is hunted by the local sheriff and a cowboy who agrees to help him. A bit better than some of the later Johnny Mack Brown series entries.

4025 The White Buffalo. United Artists, 1977. 97 minutes Color. D: J. Lee Thompson. SC: Richard Sale. WITH Charles Bronson, Will Sampson, Jack Warden, Kim Novak, Clint Walker, Stuart Whitman, Slim Pickens, John Carradine, Cara Williams, Shay Duffin, Douglas V. Fowley, Cliff Pellow, Ed Lauter, Martin Kove, Scott Walker, Ed Bakey, Richard Gilliland, David Roy Chandler, Philip Montgomery, Linda Moon Redfearn, Chief Tug Smith, Douglas Hume, Cliff Carnell, Ron Thompson, Eve Brent, Joe Roman, Bert Williams,

Dan Vadis, Christopher Cary, Larry Martindale, Scott Bryson, Will Walker, Gregg White, Hal Southern, Harold Hensley. Wild Bill Hickok and Crazy Horse team in an uneasy alliance in an effort to kill a legendary white buffalo. Strange, almost supernatural-like, Western with dark photography; mainly for fans of Charles Bronson. Alternate TV title: **Hunt to Kill.**

4026 White Comanche. International Producers Corporation, 1969. 90 minutes Color. D: Gilbert Lee Kay (Jose Briz). SC: Robert Holt & Frank Gruber. WITH Joseph Cotten, William Shatner, Rossana Yani, Perli Cristal. Taking place in the town of Rio Hondo, this melodrama tells of a sheriff trying to stop two feuding half-breed brothers from killing each other. Made in Italy as **Comancho Blanco,** this is one of the better 1960s European westerns, enhanced by good work by Joseph Cotten and William Shatner, the latter in a dual role.

4027 The White Dawn. Paramount, 1974. 109 minutes Color. D: Philip Kaufman. SC: James Houston & Tom Rickman. WITH Warren Oates, Timothy Bottoms, Lou Gossett, Simonie Kopapik, Joanasie Salomonie, Pilitak, Munamee Sake. In 1896 on a whaling expedition three men get lost in the Arctic and are saved by Eskimos who they later use to their own advantage. Overlong, but nicely photographed, melodrama.

4028 White Eagle. Columbia, 1932. 60 (67) minutes B/W. D: Lambert Hillyer. SC: Fred Myton. WITH Buck Jones, Barbara Weeks, Ward Bond, Robert Ellis, Jason Robards, Russell Simpson, Frank Campeau, Robert Kortman, Robert Elliott, Jim Thorpe, Frank Hagney, Jimmy House, Clarence Geldert. An Indian brave, who is really white, tries to protect his tribe from crooks who are out to steal their horses. Sturdy Buck Jones vehicle which was later remade as a serial of the same title in 1941 with the star again essaying the title role.

4029 White Eagle. Columbia, 1941. 15 Chapters B/W. D: James W. Horne. SC: Arch Heath, Morgan B. Cox, John Cutting & Lawrence Taylor. WITH Buck Jones, Raymond Hatton, Dorothy Fay, James Craven, Chief Yowlachie, Jack Ingram, Charles King, John Merton, Roy Barcroft, Edward Hearn, Al Ferguson, J. Paul Jones, Edward Cecil, Chick Hannon, Bob Woodward, Horace B. Carpenter,

Steve Clark, Merrill McCormack, Yakima Canutt, Kit Guard, Constantine Romanoff, Harry Tenbrook, Ed Piel, Hank Bell, Lloyd Whitlock, Eddie Featherston, George Chesebro, Kenne Duncan, Bud Osborne, Edmund Cobb, Richard Cramer, Jack O'Shea, Robert Elliott. An Indian pony express rider opposes a gang of renegades who dress like Indians to rob stagecoaches. Slim serial remake of the 1932 Columbia Buck Jones feature vehicle, but still worth viewing, especially for his fans.

4030 White Fang. 20th Century-Fox, 1936. 70 minutes B/W. D: David Butler. SC: Hal Long & Sam Duncan. WITH Michael Whalen, Jean Muir, Charles Winninger, Slim Summerville, Jane Darwell, Thomas Beck, John Carradine, George Cucount, Joe Herrick, Edward Thorpe, Steve Clemento, Marie Chorre, Jack Curtis, Ken Evans, Robert St. Angelo, Nick De Ruiz, Desmond Gallagher, Walter James, Jack Stoney, Joe Brown, Ward Bond, William Wagner, Francis McDonald, Herbert Heywood. A girl promises to marry a man if he will guide her brother to a gold mine during the harsh Yukon winter. Average follow-up to **Call of the Wild** (q.v.); based on the Jack London novel.

4031 White Fang. Titanus, 1972. 97 minutes Color. D-SC: Lucio Fulci. WITH Franco Nero, Virna Lisi, Fernando Rey, Rik Battaglia. A beautiful husky dog aids his master, a sourdough in the Klondike, in fighting both crooks and villains when he strikes gold. Very well done French-Italian-Spanish coproduction based on the work by Jack London. Italian title: **Zanna Bianca.**

4032 White Feather. 20th Century-Fox, 1955. 100 minutes Color. D: Robert Webb. SC: Delmer Daves & Leo Townsend. WITH Robert Wagner, John Lund, Debra Paget, Jeffrey Hunter, Eduard Franz, Noah Beery Jr., Virginia Leith, Emile Meyer, Hugh O'Brian, Milburn Stone. A prospector, in love with an Indian maiden, tries to aid the government in getting the Indians to move to a reservation. Standard melodrama enhanced by some good performances.

4033 White Fury. American National Enterprises, 1969. 100 minutes Color. D-SC: Arthur R. Dubs. WITH Arthur R. Dubs (narrator). Documentary about the wilderness actually made up of three short films: **White Fury, Baja Big Horn** and **High Desert.** Sequel to **Alaskan Safari** (q.v.).

4034 White Gold. Producers Distributing Corporation, 1927. 65 minutes B/W. D: William K. Howard. SC: Marion Orth, Garrett Fort & Tay Garnett. WITH Jetta Goudal, Kenneth Thomson, George Bancroft, George Nichols, Robert Perry, Clyde Cook. A pretty Mexican dancer marries a sheep rancher and moves with him to his remote ranch where she is distrusted by his father and lusted after by the hired hand. Highly regarded silent melodrama; well worth watching.

4035 White Oak. Paramount-Artcraft, 1921. 70 minutes B/W. D: Lambert Hillyer. SC: Bennet Musson. WITH William S. Hart, Vola Vale, Alexander Gaden, Robert Walker, Bertholde Sprotte, Helen Holly, Chief Standing Bear. A gambler seeks revenge on the man who took advantage of his younger sister. Typically dramatic William S. Hart silent effort based on his original story.

4036 The White Outlaw. Universal, 1925. 50 minutes B/W. D: Clifford Smith. SC: Isadore Bernstein. WITH Jack Hoxie, Marceline Day, William Welsh, Duke Lee, Floyd Shackelford, Charles Brinley, Scout (horse). A cowboy befriends and trains a wild stallion who is later accused of stealing area horses. Actionful and pleasing Jack Hoxie silent film.

4037 The White Outlaw. Exhibitors Film Corporation, 1929. 50 minutes B/W. D: Robert L. Horner. SC: Bob McKenzie. WITH Art Acord, Vivian May, Bill Patton, Al Hoxie, Dick Nores, Betty Carter, Howard Davies, Lew Meehan, Walter Maly, Slim Mathews. An outlaw gets the blame for a robbery he did not commit and he sets out to track down the real culprits. Silent Art Acord feature made at the end of his career; cheap, short on action but entertaining.

4038 The White Squaw. Columbia, 1956. 73 minutes B/W. D: Ray Nazarro. SC: Lee Savage Jr. WITH David Brian, May Wynn, William Bishop, Nancy Hale, William Leslie, Myron Healey, Robert C. Ross, Frank De Kova, George Keymas, Roy Roberts, Grant Withers, Wally Vernon, Paul Birch, Neyle Morrow, Guy Teague. A rancher seeks revenge when the government tells him he did not properly file his land claim and they are going to use the area for an Indian reservation. Mediocre programmer from producer Wallace MacDonald.

White Stallion see **The Harmony Trail**

4039 White-Water Sam. Manson International, 1979. 87 minutes Color. D-SC: Keith Larsen. WITH Keith Larsen, Lorne Greene (narrator). A man faces danger from the elements and Indians in the great northwest. Another outdoor actioner from producer-director-writer-star Keith Larsen and it should please his fans. Original title: **Run or Burn.** V: Family Home Entertainment.

4040 White Wilderness. Buena Vista, 1958. 73 minutes Color. D-SC: James Algar. WITH Winston Hibler (narrator). Life in the Arctic is presented both in the warm and frigid months, dealing with the animal life of the region. Another top-notch Walt Disney documentary feature for the entire family.

4041 Who Killed Johnny R? CCC Filmkunst/Tilma Films, 1966. 91 minutes Color. D: Jose Luis Madrid. SC: Ladislaus Fodor & Paul Jarrico. WITH Lex Barker, Joachim Fuchsberger, Marianne Koch, Ralf Wolter, Barbara Bold, Sieghardt Rupp. A hunted Arizona outlaw is thought to be dead until a gun salesman is mistaken for him and is almost lynched. Pretty fair West German-Spanish-made Lex Barker vehicle. Alternate title: **Kill Johnny R.** West German title: **5000 Dollar Fur Der Kopf Von Jonny R.** Spanish title: **La Balada de Johnny Ringo.**

Who Killed the Mysterious Mr. Foster? see **Sam Hill: Who Killed the Mysterious Mr. Foster?**

4042 Why Kill Again? Balcazar, 1965. 92 minutes Color. D: Jose A. de la Loma. WITH Anthony Steffan, Evelyn Stewart (Ida Galli), Gemma Cuervo, Pepe Calvo. Swearing vengeance on the men who crippled him a man ends up causing a feud between two families. Another in the long string of oaters from Spain, this one originally called **Stop the Slayings.**

4043 Wichita. Allied Artists, 1955. 81 minutes Color. D: Jacques Tourneur. SC: Daniel B. Ullman. WITH Joel McCrea, Vera Miles, Lloyd Bridges, Wallace Ford, Edgar Buchanan, Peter Graves, Keith Larsen, Carl Benton Reid, John Smith, Walter Coy, Walter Sande, Robert Wilke, Rayford Barnes, Jack Elam, Mae Clarke, Gene Wesson. In 1874 Wyatt Earp agrees to take on the job as sheriff of the lawless town of Wichita. Strong oater with fine work by Joel McCrea as Wyatt Earp; Tex Ritter sings the title song.

4044 Wide Open Town. Paramount, 1941. 54 (78) minutes B/W. D: Lesley Selander. SC: Harrison Jacobs & J. Benton Cheney. WITH William Boyd, Andy Clyde, Russell Hayden, Evelyn Brent, Victor Jory, Maurice Ankrum, Bernice Kay (Cara Williams), Kenneth Harlan, Roy Barcroft, Glenn Strange, Ed Cassidy, Jack Rockwell, Robert Kortman, George Cleveland, Charles Stevens. Hoppy, Lucky and California ride into a town looking for stolen Bar 20 cattle and find that a local lady saloon owner and another crook are trying to get rid of the town's mayor-newspaperman. Very good "Hopalong Cassidy" series entry with nice production values, fine performances and excellent photography (by Sherman A. Rose).

4045 The Wild and the Innocent. Universal-International, 1959. 85 minutes Color. D: Jack Sher. SC: Sy Gomberg. WITH Audie Murphy, Joanne Dru, Gilbert Roland, Sandra Dee, Jim Backus, Peter Breck, Strother Martin, George Mitchell, Wesley Marie Tackett, Betty Harford, Mel Leonard, Lillian Adams, Val Benedict. A peace loving trapper becomes involved with a young runaway girl and during a town festival is forced to defend her in a gunfight. Well made and surprisingly entertaining drama.

4046 Wild and Woolly. 20th Century-Fox, 1937. 64 minutes B/W. D: Alfred Werker. SC: Lynn Root & Frank Fenton. WITH Jane Withers, Walter Brennan, Pauline Moore, Carl "Alfalfa" Switzer, Jackie Searl, Berton Churchill, Douglas Fowley, Robert Wilcox, Douglas Scott, Lon Chaney Jr., Frank Melton, Syd Saylor, John Beck, Joseph E. Bernard, Sidney Fields, Fred Kelsey, Roger Gray, Eddy Waller, Josephine Drimmer, Alice Armand, Sidney Jarvis, Romaine Callender, Russ Clark, Vester Pegg, Alex Palasthy, Erville Alderson. During an annual Pioneer Day celebration crooks use a feud between two families as a blind for their plans to rob the local bank. Too much Jane Withers and not enough action hamper this comedy Western.

4047 Wild and Wooly. Artcraft-Paramount, 1917. 70 minutes B/W. D: John Emerson. SC: Anita Loos. WITH Douglas Fairbanks, Eileen Percy, Sam De Grasse, Monte Blue, Walter Bytell, J. W. Jones, Forest Seabury, Joseph Singleton, Tom Wilson, Charles Stevens. A young man goes West and finds quite a difference from the real West and the one he encountered in books. Fun silent Douglas Fairbanks feature, based on a story by Horace B. Carptenter. V: Video Images.

4048 Wild and Wooly. ABC-TV, 1978. 100 minutes Color. D: Philip Leacock. SC: Earl W. Wallace. WITH Chris DeLisle, Susan Bigelow, Elyssa Davalos, Doug McClure, Ross Martin, Vic Morrow, David Doyle, Paul Burke, Jessica Walter, Sherry Bain, Kenneth Tobey, Robert Wilke, Charles Siebert, Med Florey, Joan Crosby. Three beautiful women escape from an Arizona territorial prison and try to prevent an assassination attempt against President Theodore Roosevelt. Poor TV movie.

4049 Wild Beauty. Universal, 1927. 60 minutes B/W. D: Henry MacRae. SC: Edward Meagher & Tom Reed. WITH Rex (horse), June Marlowe, Hugh Allan, Scott Seaton, Hayes Robinson, William Bailey, J. Gordon Russell, Jack Pratt, Valerie (horse). A soldier brings a horse suffering from shellshock home and plans to use her to help his girl's father in a big race but the man's enemies capture a wild stallion to help them win the race. Okay Universal silent actioner.

4050 Wild Beauty. Universal, 1946. 59 minutes B/W. D: Wallace Fox. SC: Adele Buffington. WITH Don Porter, Lois Collier, Jacqueline De Wit, Robert Wilcox, George Cleveland, Buzz Henry, Dick Curtis, Eva Puig, Pierce Lyden, Roy Brent, Isabel Withers, Hank Patterson, Wild Beauty (horse). A school teacher from the East goes to work on an Arizona Indian reservation where she befriends a young boy and tries to help him save a herd of wild horses. Pretty fair family-oriented programmer.

4051 Wild Bill Hickok. Paramount-Artcraft, 1923. 70 minutes B/W. D: Clifford S. Smith. SC: J. G. Hawk. WITH William S. Hart, Ethel Grey Terry, Kathleen O'Connor, James Farley, Jack Gardner, Carl Gerard, William Dyer, Bert Sprotte, Leo Willis, Nada Carle, Herschel Mayall. After the Civil War gunman Bill Hickok heads for Dodge City to become a gambler but ends up the town's sheriff and opposed to an outlaw gang leader. Star William S. Hart wrote the original story to this sentimental screen biopic, which is not one of his better efforts.

4052 Wild Bill Hickok Rides. Warner Brothers, 1942. 81 minutes B/W. D: Ray Enright. SC: Charles Grayston, Paul Gerald Smith & Raymond Schrock. WITH Constance Bennett, Bruce Cabot, Warren William, Walter Catlett, Betty Brewer, Ward Bond, Russell Simpson, Frank Wilcox, Howard da Silva, Trevor Bardette, Lillian Yarbo, Lucia Carroll, Faye Emerson, Elliott Sullivan, Richard Botiller, Ray Teal, J. Farrell MacDonald, Cliff Clark. Marshal Wild Bill Hickok tries to stop a ruthless man from setting up his own empire. Despite a good cast and production values this is a pedestrian effort.

4053 Wild Brian Kent. Principal/RKO Radio, 1936. 60 minutes B/W. D: Howard Bretherton. SC: Earle Snell, Don Swift & James Gruen. WITH Ralph Bellamy, Mae Clarke, Helen Lowell, Stanley Andrews, Lew Kelly, Eddie Chandler, Richard Alexander, Jack Duffy. A self-centered playboy learns to become a man when he helps a young woman save her ranch from a gang of crooks. Adequate programmer from Harold Bell Wright's The Re-creation of Brian Kent and first filmed under that title by Principal in 1925 with Kenneth Harlan, Helene Chadwick, Mary Carr, Zasu Pitts and Rosemary Theby.

4054 The Wild Bunch. Warner Brothers-Seven Arts, 1969. 123 (140) minutes Color. D: Sam Peckinpah. SC: Walon Green & Sam Peckinpah. WITH William Holden, Ernest Borgnine, Robert Ryan, Edmond O'Brien, Warren Oates, Jaime Sanchez, Ben Johnson, Emilio Fernandez, Strother Martin, L. Q. Jones, Albert Dekker, Bo Hopkins, Dub Taylor, Jorge Russek, Alfonso Arau, Aurora Clavel, Elsa Cardenas, Fernando Wagner, Paul Harper, Constance White, Lilia Richards. A trail-tired outlaw gang is forced to agree to rob a gun supply train for an enemy of Pancho Villa and end up in a massacre. Exceedingly bloody and violent horse opera which has its main appeal for Sam Peckinpah followers. VD: Blackhawk.

4055 Wild Country. Producers Releasing Corporation, 1947. 59 minutes B/W. D: Ray Taylor. SC: Arthur Orloff. WITH Eddie Dean, Roscoe Ates, Peggy Wynne, Douglas Fowley, I. Stanford Jolley, Steve Clark, Henry Hall, Lee Roberts, Forrest Mathews, William Fawcett, Richard Cramer, The Sunshine Boys, Charles Jordan. Two marshals are on the trail of an escaped convict who has killed the lawman who sent him to jail and has taken over his ranch. Standard Eddie Dean vehicle in which the title tune (which he cowrote) is better than the film.

4056 The Wild Country. Buena Vista, 1971. 100 minutes Color. D: Robert Totten. SC: Calvin Clements Jr. & Ralph Moody. WITH Steve Forrest, Vera Miles, Jack Elam, Ronny Howard, Frank DeKova, Morgan Woodward, Clint Howard, Dub Taylor, Woodrow Chambliss, Karl Swenson, Mills Watson. The story of a Pittsburgh, Pennsylvania, family and its trek to Wyoming in the 1880s. Pretty fair Walt Disney film for the family trade.

4057 The Wild Dakotas. Associated Film, 1956. 75 minutes B/W. D: Sam Newfield. SC: Thomas W. Blackburn. WITH Bill Williams, Coleen Gray, Jim Davis, John Litel, Dick Jones, Lisa Montell, John Miljan, I. Stanford Jolley, Wally Brown, Iron Eyes Cody, Bill Dix. A trail guide is at odds with a corrupt wagon train leader who wants to settle down in a valley belonging to Indians who will fight to protect their land. A good cast can do little to help this sub-standard programmer.

4058 The Wild Frontier. Republic, 1947. 59 minutes B/W. D: Philip Ford. SC: Albert Demond. WITH Allan "Rocky" Lane, Jack Holt, Eddy Waller, Pierre Watkin, John James, Roy Barcroft, Wheaton Chambers, Tom London, Sam Flint, Budd Buster, Ted Mapes, Bob Burns, Art Dillard, Bud McClure. A lawman comes to the aid of an old sheriff and his sons who are fighting a gang run by the town's dishonest saddle shop owner. First film in which Allan Lane was billed as Allan "Rocky" Lane; good start to a new series enhanced by the appearance of Jack Holt as the villain. V: Cumberland Video.

4059 Wild Fury. Ambassador Releasing, 1975. 90 minutes Color. SC: Richard Wiles. Three men trek across the Alaskan wilderness in quest of a killer bear. Okay documentary.

4060 Wild Geese Calling. 20th Century-Fox, 1941. 77 minutes B/W. D: John Brahm. SC: Horace McCoy. WITH Henry Fonda, Joan Bennett, Warren William, Ona Munson, Barton MacLane, Russell Simpson, Iris Adrian, James Morton, Paul Sutton, Mary Field, Stanley Andrews, Jody Gilbert, Robert Emmett Keane, Michael (Adrian) Morris, George Watts, Charles Middleton, Paul Burns, Jack Pennick, Nestor Paiva, George Melford, Tom London, Alan Bridge, Lee Phelps, Captain Anderson, Joe Bernard. A lumberjack with wanderlust is aided by a saloon girl as they battle crooks in Oregon and Alaska in the 1890s. One of those pictures which seems to care more about budget and detail instead of plot.

4061 Wild Gold. Fox, 1934. 75 minutes B/W. D: George Marshall. SC: Dudley Nichols & Lamar Trotti. WITH John Boles, Claire Trevor, Harry Green, Roger Imhof, Ruth Gillette, Monroe Owsley, Edward Gargan, Suzanne Kaaren, Blanca Vischer, Elsie Larson, Gloria Roy, Winifred Shaw, Myra Bratton. During the California Gold Rush an engineer loses his job due to his infatuation with a saloon girl whose husband arrives with an old prospector's gold claim. Fair melodrama with good work by the two leads.

4062 Wild Heritage. Universal-International, 1958. 78 minutes Color. D: Charles Haas. SC: Paul King & Joseph Stone. WITH Will Rogers Jr., Maureen O'Sullivan, Troy Donahue, Gigi Perreau, Paul Birch, George Winslow, Casey Tibbs, Judy Meredith, Rod McKuen, Gary Gray, Jeanette Nolan, John Beradino, Phil Harvey, Lawrence Dobkin, Stephen Ellsworth, Ingrid Goude, Christopher Dark, Guy Wilkerson. Two families find their lives become involved as they migrate to the West. Sentimental stuff, but well made.

4063 Wild Horse. Allied, 1931. 57 (77) minutes B/W. D: Richard Thorpe & Sidney Algier. SC: Jack Natteford. WITH Hoot Gibson, Alberta Vaughn, Stepin Fetchit, Edmund Cobb, Skeeter Bill Robbins, Neal Hart, George Bunny, Ed Piel, Joe Rickson, Glenn Strange. A dishonest rodeo bronc buster murders a cowboy who, with his partner, has captured a wild horse, and the partner is falsely blamed for the crime. A bit raw boned, but still an ingratiating Hoot Gibson vehicle. Reissue title: **Silver Devil.**

4064 Wild Horse Ambush. Republic, 1952. 54 minutes B/W. D: Fred C. Brannon. SC: William Lively. WITH Michael Chapin, Eilene Janssen, James Bell, Richard Avonde, Roy Barcroft, Julian Rivero, Movita, Drake Smith, Scott Lee, Alex Montoya, John Daheim, Ted Cooper, Wayne Burson. Two youngsters aid the law in tracking down a counterfeiting operation. Mediocre juvenile fare; the final entry in the "Rough Ridin' Kids" series.

4065 Wild Horse Canyon. Goodwill, 1925. 50 minutes B/W. WITH Yakima Canutt, Helene Rosson, Edward Cecil, Jay Talbot,

Boy (horse), Lad (dog). While looking for the murderer of his father, a cowboy tames a wild horse who the killer, a ranch foreman, plans to blame for horse thefts he plans to commit. Rather standard, but fast paced, Yakima Canutt silent effort. Reissued by Hollywood Film Enterprises.

4066 Wild Horse Canyon. Monogram, 1938. 50 minutes B/W. D: Robert Hill. SC: Robert Emmett (Tansey). WITH Jack Randall, Dorothy Short, Frank Yaconelli, Dennis Moore, Warner Richmond, Ed Cassidy, Walter Long, Charles King, Earl Douglas, Sherry Tansey. A man, who is looking for his brother's killer, and his pal happen upon a ranch where a man and his daughter are having their horses rustled by a mysterious gang. Pretty good Jack Randall vehicle.

4067 Wild Horse Hank. Film Consortium of Canada, 1979. 94 minutes Color. D: Eric Till. SC: James Lee Barrett. WITH Linda Blair, Richard Crenna, Michael Wincott, Al Waxman, Pace Bradford. A young college student works to keep horses from being butchered for dog food and finally tries to move a herd of horses north in order for them to escape capture. Filmed in Canada, this is a scenic and fairly entertaining adventure drama.

4068 Wild Horse Mesa. Paramount, 1933. 61 minutes B/W. D: Henry Hathaway. SC: Harold Shumate & Frank Howard Clark. WITH Randolph Scott, Sally Blane, Fred Kohler, Lucille LaVerne, James Bush, Charles Grapewin, Jim Thorpe, George F. ("Gabby") Hayes, Buddy Roosevelt, E. H. Calvert. A horse trainer objects to roundup methods using barbed wire which may injure and kill a wild horse herd. Okay programmer with liberal use of footage from the first screen version of this Zane Grey story, produced by Paramount in 1925 with Jack Holt.

4069 Wild Horse Mesa. RKO Radio, 1947. 60 minutes B/W. D: Wallace Grissell. SC: Norman Houston. WITH Tim Holt, Richard Martin, Nan Leslie, Richard Powers, Jason Robards, Tony Barrett, Harry Woods, William Gould, Robert Bray, Richard Foote, Frank Yaconelli. Three cowpokes round up a herd of wild horses to sell but crooks try to take the animals for themselves. Well produced Tim Holt vehicle but it has little resemblance to the Zane Grey work.

4070 Wild Horse Phantom. Producers Releasing Corporation, 1944. 56 minutes B/W. D: Sam Newfield. SC: George Milton. WITH Buster Crabbe, Al St. John, Elaine Morey, Hal Price, Kermit Maynard, Budd Buster, Frank Ellis, Frank McCarroll, Robert Meredith, John Elliott, Bob Cason. Ranchers put their mortgage payment money in the local bank which is robbed and the banker threatens to foreclose on them as Billy Carson and Fuzzy Q. Jones investigate the situation. Average outing for the "Billy Carson" series.

4071 Wild Horse Range. Monogram, 1940. 58 minutes B/W. D: Raymond K. Johnson. SC: Carl Krusada. WITH Jack Randall, Phyllis Ruth, Frank Yaconelli, Charles King, Tom London, Marin Sais, Ralph Hoopes, Forrest Taylor, George Chesebro, Carl Mathews, Ted Adams, Steve Clark, Tex Palmer. A cowboy gets on the trail of a group of rustlers. Jack Randall fans will like this pleasing entry in his Monogram series.

4072 Wild Horse Rodeo. Republic, 1937. 54 minutes B/W. D: George Sherman. SC: Betty Burbridge. WITH Robert Livingston, Ray Corrigan, Max Terhune, June Martel, Walter Miller, Edmund Cobb, William Gould, Jack Ingram, Henry Isabell, Art Dillard, Ralph Robinson, Fred "Snowflake" Toones, Dick Weston (Roy Rogers), Jack Kirk. The Three Mesquiteers capture a wild horse as the chief attraction for a small rodeo and crooks try to steal the prize animal. Actionful entry in "The Three Mesquiteers" series.

4073 Wild Horse Roundup. Ambassador, 1936. 55 minutes B/W. D: Alan James. SC: Joseph O'Donnell. WITH Kermit Maynard, Betty Lloyd, Dickie Jones, Budd Buster, John Merton, Frank Hagney, Roger Williams, Dick Curtis, Jack Ingram. A cowboy and his pals come to the aid of a girl rancher who is being forced off her property by the mysterious "Night Riders," who are headed by a man trying to buy all the nearby property which will be needed for a railroad right-of-way. Pretty fair Kermit Maynard vehicle.

4074 Wild Horse Rustlers. Producers Releasing Corporation, 1943. 58 minutes B/W. D: Sam Newfield. SC: Steve Braxton. WITH Robert Livingston, Al St. John, Linda Johnson, Lane Chandler, Stanley Price, Frank Ellis, Karl Hackett, Jimmie Aubrey. The Lone Rider discovers a plot where a Nazi spy has taken his twin brother's place as the foreman of a ranch in order to sabotage the government's horse procurement program. The plot of the Axis-out-West adds a bit of zest to this otherwise routine "Lone Rider" series film.

4075 Wild Horse Stampede. Monogram, 1943. 59 minutes B/W. D: Alan James. SC: Elizabeth Beecher. WITH Ken Maynard, Hoot Gibson, Betty Miles, Ian Keith, Bob Baker, I. Stanford Jolley, Forrest Taylor, Glenn Strange, Si Jenks, Donald Stewart, John Bridges, Reed Howes, Kenneth Harlan, Tom London, Tex Palmer, Kenne Duncan, Bob McKenzie, Chick Hannon. Ken and Hoot come to the aid of a sheriff after a gang of cattle rustlers. The two stars are colorful and help pull together this minor opener for "The Trail Blazers" series but Bob Baker is poor as the sheriff.

4076 Wild Horse Valley. Metropolitan, 1940. 55 minutes B/W. D: Ira Webb. SC: Carl Krusada. WITH Bob Steele, Phyllis Adair, George Chesebro, Ted Adams, Lafe McKee, Buzz Barton, Jimmie Aubrey, Bud Osborne. Outlaws steal a prize Arabian stallion and a cowboy sets out to get him back. Very low grade Bob Steele outing for producer Harry S. Webb.

4077 Wild Mustang. Ajax, 1935. 62 minutes B/W. D: Harry Fraser. SC: Weston Edwards. WITH Harry Carey, Barbara Fritchie, Del Gordon, Kathryn Johns, Robert Kortman, George Chesebro, Chuck Morrison, Richard Botiller, George Morrell, Milburn Morante, Francis Walker, Budd Buster, Sonny (horse). When an outlaw gang brands his son so the young man will be forced to work with them, an old-time lawman takes up his badge to round up the crooks. Poor production values hurt this otherwise pleasant Harry Carey vehicle in which Robert Kortman is excellent as the wicked gang leader.

4078 The Wild North. Metro-Goldwyn-Mayer, 1952. 97 minutes Color. D: Andrew Marton. SC: Frank Fenton. WITH Stewart Granger, Wendell Corey, Cyd Charisse, Morgan Farley, Howard Petrie, Houseley Stevenson, Lewis Martin, John War Eagle, Ray Teal, Clancy Cooper, J. M. Kerrigan, Henry Corden, Robert Stephenson, G. Pat Collins, Russ Conklin, Brad Morrow, Emile Meyer, Henri Letondal, Holmes Herbert, Cliff Taylor, Rex Lease. A trapper is falsely accused of murder and is tracked in the north country by a Mountie and along the way the trapper meets and falls in love with an Indian

girl. Idaho locales and color photography (by Robert Surtees) are the main assets of this otherwise pedestrian drama. Alternate title: **The Big North.**

4079 Wild Prairie. American National Enterprises, 1975. 92 minutes Color. WITH Larry Jones. Explorer Larry Jones roams the territory of the Southwestern United States looking at its terrain and wildlife. Well done documentary.

4080 Wild Rovers. Metro-Goldwyn-Mayer, 1971. 106 minutes Color. D-SC: Blake Edwards. WITH William Holden, Ryan O'Neal, Karl Malden, Lynn Carlin, Tom Skerritt, Joe Don Baker, James Olson, Leora Dana, Moses Gunn, Victor French, Rachel Roberts, Charles Gray, Sam Gilman, William Bryant, Jack Garner, Caitlin Wyles, Mary Jackson, William Lucking, Ed Bakey, Ted Gehring, Alan Carney, Ed Long, Lee De Broux, Bennie Dobbins, Boyd "Red" Morgan, Bob Beck, Geoffrey Edwards, Studs Tanney, Hal Lynch, Dick Crockett, Bruno VeSota. Two bored cattle drovers pull a bank robbery as a lark and after a wild spree find themselves being relentlessly hunted by a posse. This Western tries hard to be a classic but merely defeats its own purpose and ends up slightly better than mediocre, although it is not without interest.

4081 Wild Stallion. Monogram, 1952. 72 minutes B/W. D: Lewis D. Collins. SC: Dan Ullman. WITH Ben Johnson, Edgar Buchanan, Martha Hyer, Hayden Rorke, Hugh Beaumont, Orley Indgren, Don Haggerty, Susan Odin, I. Stanford Jolley, Barbara Woodell, John Halloran. A young cavalry lieutenant recalls his life in a military school and how another military man helped him settle into the service. Flashback drama which is a sad waste of a good cast.

4082 Wild Stampede. Prodicceones Raul de Anda, 1962. 77 minutes Color. D-SC: Raul de Anda. WITH Luis Aguilar, Christiane Martel, Augustin de Anda, Jose Elias Moreno, Armando Soto la Marina "Chicote," Jose Eduardo Perez, Yerye Beirute, Jose Chavez, Guillermo Alvarez Bianchi. A herd of wild horses are fought over by an outlaw gang and a band of revolutionaries. Actionful Mexican production, originally issued in that country in 1958 as **Estampida.**

4083 Wild West. Producers Releasing Corporation, 1946. 75 minutes Color. D: Robert Emmett Tansey. SC: Frances

Kavanaugh. WITH Eddie Dean, Roscoe Ates, Al "Lash" LaRue, Robert "Buzzy" Henry, Louise Currie, Jean Carlin, Sarah Padden, Lee Bennett, Terry Frost, Warner Richmond, Lee Roberts, Chief Yowlachie, Bob Duncan, Frank Pharr, Matty Roubert, John Bridges, Al Ferguson, Bud Osborne. A singing cowboy tries to stop outlaws from stirring up local Indians against the building of telegraph lines. Eddie Dean's final Cinecolor outing is a fast moving affair. Reissued in 1948 in black and white and minus fifteen minutes as a new film called **Prairie Outlaws** (q.v.). V: Cassette Express.

4084 The Wild West. Filmways, 1977. WITH Charles Bronson, Clint Eastwood, Steve McQueen, John Wayne, Ernest Borgnine, William Boyd, Raymond Burr, Lee Van Cleef, Broderick Crawford, John Derek, Angie Dickinson, Bill Elliott, Henry Fonda, Glenn Ford, William Holden, Rita Hayworth, Ben Johnson, Lash La-Rue, Fred MacMurray, Joel McCrea, Robert Mitchum, Gregory Peck, Roy Rogers, Randolph Scott, Barbara Stanwyck. A compilation feature made up of clips from Westerns of the past, issued briefly in the U. S. as well as in Australia and New Zealand.

4085 Wild West Days. Universal, 1937. 13 Chapters B/W. D: Cliff Smith & Ford Beebe. SC: Wyndham Gittens, Norman S. Hall & Ray Trampe. WITH Johnny Mack Brown, Lynn Gilbert, Frank McGlynn Jr., Walter Miller, Russell Simpson, Frank Yaconelli, Robert Kortman, George Shelley, Bob McClung, Bud Osborne, Lafe McKee, Iron Eyes Cody, Francis McDonald, Charles Stevens, Joe Girard, Sidney Bracey, Alan Bridge, Ed LeSaint, Bruce Mitchell, Frank Ellis, Chief Thundercloud, Jack Clifford, Hank Bell, William Royle, Mike Morita, Chief Thunderbird. Three frontiersmen aid a girl and her brother whose ranch is being raided by an outlaw gang trying to find gold and they also have framed the brother on a murder charge. Fast moving cliffhanger which is an exaggerated version of W. R. Burnett's novel Saint Johnson previously filmed as **Law and Order** (q.v.) in 1932. V: Cassette Express.

4086 Wild West Whoopee. Cosmos, 1931. 57 minutes B/W. D-SC: Robert J. Horner. WITH Jack Perrin, Josephine Hill, Buzz Barton, Fred Church, John Ince, George Chesebro, Horace B. Carpenter, Henry Rocquemore, Ben Corbett. A rodeo rider

tries to save a pretty girl from the attentions of a badman. Really bad, with a plethora of stock rodeo footage.

4087 The Wild Westerners. Columbia, 1962. 70 minutes Color. D: Oscar Rudolph. SC: Gerald Drayson Adams. WITH James Philbrook, Nancy Kovack, Guy Mitchell, Duane Eddy, Hugh Sanders, Elizabeth MacRae, Marshall Reed, Nestor Paiva, Harry Lauter, Bob Steele, Lisa Burkert, Terry Frost, Don C. Harvey, Francis Osborne, Tim Sullivan, Pierce Lyden, Joe McGuinn, Charles Horvath. A marshal and his new wife try to carry gold across the desert for the Northern cause during the Civil War and find themselves opposed by Indians and a renegade lawman and his cohorts. Genre fans will like the cast better than the story.

4088 The Wild Wild West Revisited. CBS-TV, 1979. 100 minutes Color. D: Burt Kennedy. SC: William Bowers. WITH Robert Conrad, Ross Martin, Paul Williams, Harry Morgan, Rene Auberjonois, Jo Ann Harris, Trisha Noble, Alberto Morin, Skip Homeier, Joyce Jameson, Robert Shields, Lorene Yarnell, Jeff McKay, Susan Blu, Paula Ustinov, Wilford A. Brimley, Ted Hartley, Jacqueline Hyde, John Wheeler, Mike Wagner, Jeff Redford. Two government agents investigate a plot in which clones are being used to replace royalty in Europe. Fun, tongue-in-cheek telefeature recreation of the long-running "The Wild Wild West" (CBS-TV, 1965-70) series, followed by **More Wild Wild West** (q.v.).

4089 Wild Women. ABC-TV, 1970. 74 minutes Color. D: Don Taylor. SC: Lou Morheim & Richard Carr. WITH Hugh O'Brian, Anne Francis, Marilyn Maxwell, Marie Windsor, Sherry Jackson, Robert F. Simon, Richard Kelton, Cynthia Hull, Pepe Callahan, Ed Call, Chuck Hicks, Jim Boles, Pedro Regas, Troy Melton. The government orders the Army Corps of Engineers to secretly map the Texas-Mexican border in the mid-1840s in case of war and five women convicts are recruited as a blind for the operation. Mediocre TV movie Western.

4090 The Wild Women of Chastity Gulch. ABC-TV, 1982. 100 minutes Color. D: Philip Leacock. SC: Earl W. Wallace. WITH Priscilla Barnes, Joan Collins, Donny Osmond, Lee Horsley, Howard Duff, Lisa Whelchel, Phyllis Davis, Pamela Bellwood, Jeanette Nolan, Morgan Brittany, Susan Kellerman. When the men go off to Civil War, the women of a small Mississippi town, both respectable and otherwise, join forces to fight a Yankee raiding party. Fair TV-made comedy.

4091 The Wildcat. Aywon, 1926. 50 minutes B/W. D: Harry L. Fraser. SC: David M. Findlay. WITH Gordon Griffith, Charlotte Moore, Irwin Renard, Frank Bond, Hooper Phillips, Arthur Milleton. Going West to a ranch to train for a boxing match, a man finds a cache of diamonds stolen in an express holdup and hides them from the thief in order to capture him. Fairly picturesque and actionful poverty row silent feature.

4092 Wildcat. Paramount, 1942. 73 minutes B/W. D: Frank McDonald. SC: Maxwell Shane & Richard Murphy. WITH Richard Arlen, Arline Judge, Larry "Buster" Crabbe, William Frawley, Arthur Hunnicutt, Elisha Cook Jr., Ralph Sanford, Alec Craig, John Dilson, Will Wright, Jessica Newcombe, Billy Benedict. A wildcatter and his pals drill for oil but find their operations being sabotaged by a rival driller. This William H. Pine-William C. Thomas production packs a lot of action.

4093 Wildcat of Tucson. Columbia, 1941. 55 minutes B/W. D: Lambert Hillyer. SC: Fred Myton. WITH Bill Elliott, Dub Taylor, Evelyn Young, Stanley Brown, Kenneth MacDonald, Ben Taggart, Edmund Cobb, George Lloyd, Sammy Stein, Francis Walker, Robert Winkler, Forrest Taylor, Dorothy Andre, Bert Young, Newt Kirby, Johnny Daheim, Murdock McQuarrie. Wild Bill Hickok and his brother come to the aid of settlers who are being cheated out of their lands by a speculator hooked up with a crooked judge. Fairly actionful Bill Elliott vehicle.

4094 Wildcat Saunders. Atlantic, 1936. 60 minutes B/W. D: Harry Fraser. SC: Monroe Talbot. WITH Jack Perrin, Blanche Mehaffey, Roger Williams, William Gould, Fred "Snowflake" Toones, Tom London, Ed Cassidy, Earl Dwire, Jim Corey, Bud Osborne. A boxer goes West and gets mixed up with an outlaw gang. Passable action entertainment in Jack Perrin's series for producer William Berke.

4095 Wildcat Trooper. Ambassador, 1936. 60 minutes B/W. D: Elmer Clifton. SC: Joseph O'Donnell. WITH Kermit Maynard, Lois Wilde, Hobart Bosworth, Fuzzy Knight, Yakima Canutt, Eddie Phillips,

John Merton, Frank Hagney, Roger Williams, Dick Curtis, Theodore Lorch, Hal Price, Jim Thorpe. A Canadian Mountie is on the trail of an outlaw gang which is actually masterminded by a crooked doctor. Better-than-average Kermit Maynard vehicle, mainly thanks to Hobart Bosworth's good natured hamming as the villain.

4096 The Wildcatter. Universal, 1937. 58 minutes B/W. D: Lewis D. Collins. SC: Charles A. Logue. WITH Scott Colton, Jean Rogers, Jack Smart, Suzanne Kaaren, Russell Hicks, Ward Bond, Wallis Clark, Jack Powell. Two pals leave their roadside cafe business to head for Texas and drill for oil. Okay Universal dual bill item.

4097 Wilderness Calling. Aaro Films, 1969. 102 minutes Color. D-SC: Paul O. Hansen. WITH Art Mercier (narrator). A young man follows the call of the wild from the Dakota prairies through Alaska and British Columbia to the Bering Sea. Interesting documentary shot on location.

Wilderness Family, Part Two see **The Further Adventures of the Wilderness Family**

4098 Wilderness Journey. Gold Key Entertainment, 1970. 92 minutes Color. WITH Tony Tucker Williams, Jimmy Kane. A young Indian boy searches the Alaskan wilds for his father who he fears was injured in an accident. Well made semi-documentary with lots of beautiful scenery.

4099 Wilderness Mail. Ambassador, 1935. 60 minutes B/W. D: Forrest Sheldon. SC: Bennett Cohen & Robert Dillon. WITH Kermit Maynard, Doris Brook, Fred Kohler, Paul Hurst, Dick Curtis, Syd Saylor, Nelson McDowell, Kernan Cripps. A Mountie, assigned to bring in the mail, finds his twin brother in the clutches of crooks. Good scenic shots of heavy snow and dogsled action adds zest to this Kermit Maynard vehicle.

4100 Wildfire. Screen Guild, 1945. 57 minutes Color. D: Robert Tansey. SC: W. H. Tuttle. WITH Bob Steele, Sterling Holloway, William Farnum, John Miljan, Eddie Dean, Virginia Mapes, Sarah Padden, Al Ferguson, Wee Willie Davis, Rocky Camron, Francis Ford, Frank Ellis, Hal Price, Wildfire (horse). Cinecolor outing about a man who tries to save a beautiful wild horse.

Will James' Sand see **Sand**

4101 Will Penny. Paramount, 1968. 106 minutes Color. D-SC: Tom Gries. WITH Charlton Heston, Joan Hackett, Donald Pleasence, Lee Majors, Ben Johnson, Bruce Dern, Slim Pickens, Clifton James, Anthony Zerbe, Roy Jenson, G. D. Spradlin, Quentin Dean, William Schallert, Lydia Clarke, Matt Clark, Luke Askew, Anthony Costello, Chanin Hale. Looking for a new job after a cattle drive, a veteran cowboy finds himself at odds with vicious rawhiders who later torture him when he is hired to be a line rider. Highly atmospheric account of the cowboy's lone existence with an especially poignant love relationship between the title character and a widow. Very good film.

4102 Winchester '73. Universal-International, 1950. 92 minutes Color. D: Anthony Mann. SC: Robert L. Richards & Borden Chase. WITH James Stewart, Shelley Winters, Dan Duryea, Stephen McNally, Millard Mitchell, Charles Drake, John McIntire, Will Geer, Jay C. Flippen, Rock Hudson, John Alexander, Steve Brodie, James Millican, Abner Biberman, Tony Curtis, James Best, Gregg Martell, Frank Chase, Chuck Roberson, Carol Henry, Ray Teal, John Doucette, Chief Yowlachie, Edmund Cobb, Ethan Laidlaw, Jennings Miles. In 1873 in Dodge City a cowboy wins a prize Winchester rifle in a contest only to have it stolen from him by the man who murdered his father. High grade and very entertaining class "A" Western.

4103 Winchester '73. NBC-TV/Universal, 1967. 97 minutes Color. D: Herschel Daugherty. SC: Stephen Kandel & Richard L. Adams. WITH Tom Tryon, John Saxon, Dan Duryea, John Drew Barrymore, Joan Blondell, John Dehner, Barbara Luna, John Doucette, David Pritchard, Paul Fix, John Hoyt, Jack Lambert, Jan Arvan, Robert Bice, Ned Romero, George Keymas. An ex-convict returns home and steals a valuable rifle from his marshal brother who tries to get it back. Poor telefeature reworking of the 1950 near-classic.

4104 Wind Across the Everglades. Warner Brothers, 1958. 93 minutes Color. D: Nicholas Ray. SC: Budd Schulberg. WITH Burl Ives, Christopher Plummer, Gypsy Rose Lee, George Koskovec, Tony Galento, Howard I. Smith, Emmett Kelly, Pat Henning, Chana Eden, Curt Conway, Peter Falk, Fred Grossinger, Sammy Renick, Toch Brown, Frank Rothe, MacKinlay Kantor. At the turn of the century a Florida game warden tries to protect animal life in the Everglades from the encroachment of civilization. Fairly entertaining drama although a bit oddly cast.

4105 The Winds of Autumn. Howco-International, 1976. 104 minutes Color. D: Charles B. Pierce. SC: Earl E. Smith. WITH Jack Elam, Jeannette Nolan, Andrew Prine, Dub Taylor, Charles B. "Chuck" Pierce Jr., Earl E. Smith, Belinda Palmer, Jimmy Clem, Charles B. Pierce. In 1884 a young Quaker boy treks across the Montana grasslands in order to take revenge on the brutal family who murdered his parents. Overlong, but well photographed, melodrama.

4106 Winds of the Wasteland. Republic, 1936. 54 minutes B/W. D: Mack V. Wright. SC: Joseph Poland. WITH John Wayne, Phyllis Fraser, Lane Chandler, Yakima Canutt, Douglas Cosgrove, Sam Flint, Lew Kelly, Robert Kortman, Ed Cassidy, Merrill McCormack, Bud McClure, Jack Ingram, Charles Lochner (Jon Hall), Joe Yrigoyen, Chris Franke, Jack Rockwell, Art Mix. Two pals buy and fix up an old stagecoach and plan to race a rival operation for a valuable government mail contract. Exceedingly fine early John Wayne vehicle, well directed and full of action; well worth watching. V: Cassette Express.

4107 The Windwalker. Pacific International, 1980. 108 minutes Color. D: Keith Merrill. WITH Trevor Howard, Nick Ramus, James Remar, Serene Hedin, Dusty Iron Wing McCrea. An old Indian chief returns to life to save his tribe from his twin son who was stolen at birth by a rival tribe. Mystical film of interest since it deals with Indians in the 1700s prior to contact with whites and because it was filmed in the Cheyenne and Crow languages and subtitled for theatrical showings.

4108 Wings of an Eagle. Martin Green, 1976. 90 minutes Color. WITH Ed Durden. The story of the rare California Golden Eagle, from her life in the nest through adulthood, as told by wild bird trainer Ed Durden. Well done documentary.

4109 Wings of Chance. Universal, 1961. 76 minutes Color. D: Edward Dew. SC:

Patrick Whyte. WITH James Brown, Frances Rafferty, Richard Tretter, Patrick Whyte. A pilot is forced down in the Canadian wilderness by the carelessness of a copilot who is jealous of his attentions toward the pretty girl they both love. Standard drama made in Canada.

4110 Wings of the Hawk. Universal-International, 1953. 81 minutes Color. D: Budd Boetticher. SC: James E. Mosier. WITH Van Heflin, Julia (Julie) Adams, Abbe Lane, Noah Beery Jr., Rodolfo Acosta, George Dolenz, Pedro Gonzales, Antonio Moreno, Paul Fierro, Mario Siletti, Rico Alaniz, John Daheim, Richardo Alba, Nancy Westbrook. While working in Mexico, a mining engineer becomes involved with a pretty bandit queen and her efforts to overthrow the government. Originally issued in 3-D, this actioner is fairly entertaining.

Wings over Wyoming see **Hollywood Cowboy**

4111 Winners of the West. Universal, 1940. 13 Chapters B/W. D: Ford Beebe & Ray Taylor. SC: George H. Plympton, Basil Dickey & Charles R. Condon. WITH Dick Foran, Anne Nagel, James Craig, Tom Fadden, Harry Woods, Charles Stevens, Trevor Bardette, Chief Yowlachie, Edward Keane, William Desmond, Edmund Cobb, Roy Barcroft. The assistant to the president of a railroad line tries to stop a land baron who wants to keep the transcontinental line from crossing his domain. Lightning fast Universal cliffhanger marred by excessive stock footage. V: Cumberland Video, Video Yesteryear, Video Connection.

Winnetou I see **Apache Gold**

Winnetou II see **Last of the Renegades**

Winnetou III see **The Desperado Trail**

4112 Winnetou and Shatterhand in the Valley of Death. CCC Filmkunst/Super International/Jadran-Film, 1968. 90 minutes Color. D: Harald Reinl. SC: Herbert Reinecker. WITH Lex Barker, Pierre Brice, Karin Dor, Ralf Wolter, Eddi Arent, Rik Battaglia. Shatterhand and Winnetou come to the aid of the daughter of a fort commander who is accused of stealing a fortune in gold. The final film in the series based on Karl May's works; does not have the big budget of its predecessors but still provides good entertainment. West German title:

Winnetou Und Shatterhand Im Tal Der Toten.

4113 Winning of the West. Columbia, 1953. 57 minutes B/W. D: George Archainbaud. SC: Norman S. Hall. WITH Gene Autry, Smiley Burnette, Gail Davis, Richard Crane, Robert Livingston, House Peters Jr., Gregg Barton, Ewing Mitchell, Rodd Redwing, George Chesebro, Frank Jacquet, Charles Delaney, Charles Soldani, Eddie Parker, Terry Frost, James Kirkwood, Boyd "Red" Morgan, Bob Woodward. A ranger loses his job when he refuses to shoot his brother who is a member of an outlaw gang terrorizing local miners and ranchers. Fast paced but rather tepid Gene Autry vehicle. V: Blackhawk.

Winning the West see **The Light of the Western Stars** (1930)

4114 Winter Kill. ABC-TV/Metro-Goldwyn-Mayer, 1974. 100 minutes Color. D: Jud Taylor. SC: Joseph Michael Hayes. WITH Andy Griffith, John Larch, Tim O'Connor, Lawrence Pressman, Eugene Roche, Charles Tyner, Joyce Van Patten, Sheree North, John Calvin, Louise Latham, Robert F. Simon, Elayne Heilveil, Nick Nolte, Ruth McDevitt, Walter Brooke, David Frankham, Wes Stern, Vaughn Taylor, Devra Korwin. The sheriff of a small Western ski resort community is baffled by a series of murders in which the killer leaves clues in spray paint. Interesting TV-made Western-mystery which failed to sell as a continuing series; made by Andy Griffith Enterprises.

4115 Winterhawk. Howco-International, 1975. 90 minutes Color. D-SC: Charles B. Pierce. WITH Leif Erickson, Michael Dante, Dawn Wells, Woody Strode, Denver Pyle, Arthur Hunnicutt, Elisha Cook, L. Q. Jones, Charles B. Pierce Jr., Sacheen Littlefeather, Dennis Fimple, Seamon Glass. An Indian chief comes to a white settlement for smallpox serum and is treated badly and in revenge abducts a woman and her small brother. Fairly exciting Western made on a limited budget.

Wishbone Cutter see **Shadow of Chikara**

4116 The Wistful Widow of Wagon Gap. Universal, 1947. 78 minutes B/W. D: Charles Barton. SC: Robert Lees, Frederic I. Rinaldo & John Grant. WITH Bud Abbott, Lou Costello, Marjorie Main, Audrey Young, George Cleveland, Gordon Jones, William Ching, Peter Thompson, Olin Howlin, Bill Clauson, Billy O'Leary, Pamela

Wells, Jimmie Bates, Paul Dunn, Diane Florentine, Rex Lease, Glenn Strange, Dewey Robinson, Edmund Cobb, Wade Crosby, Murray Leonard, Emmett Lynn, Iris Adrian, Lee "Lasses" White, George J. Lewis, Charles King, Jack Shutta, Harry Evans, Mickey Simpson, Frank Marlow, Ethan Laidlaw. Two salesmen arrive in a small Montana town and one of them is falsely accused of shooting the town drunk and a crooked lawyer gets him off by using the state law which says he has to support the man's widow and pay off his debts. A good plotline, Abbott and Costello, and Marjorie Main, make this an amusing genre spoof.

With Buffalo Bill on the U.P. Trail see **Buffalo Bill on the U.P. Trail**

With Custer at the Little Big Horn see **General Custer at the Little Big Horn**

With Daniel Boone in the Wilderness see **Daniel Boone in the Wilderness**

With General Custer at the Little Big Horn see **General Custer at the Little Big Horn**

With Sitting Bull at the Spirit Lake Massacre see **Sitting Bull at the Spirit Lake Massacre**

4117 Without Honors. Artclass, 1932. 62 minutes B/W. D: William Nigh. SC: Harry (Fraser) P. Crist. WITH Harry Carey, Mae Busch, Gibson Gowland, George ("Gabby") Hayes, Lafe McKee, Mary Jane Irving, Tom London, Ed Brady, Jack Richardson. Returning home a man finds his brother has been murdered and in order to capture the culprit he enlists with the rangers. Shaggy production values detract from this otherwise okay Harry Carey vehicle.

4118 Wolf Call. Monogram, 1939. 60 minutes B/W. D: George Waggner. SC: Joseph West. (George Waggner). WITH John Carroll, Polly Ann Young, Movita, George Cleveland, Wheeler Oakman, Guy Usher, Holmes Herbert, Peter George Lynn, John Sheehan, Charles Irwin, Roger Williams, Pat O'Malley. While inspecting his father's Western radium mine, a playboy discovers a group of crooks are trying to steal the property. Paul Malvern produced this average dual biller based on a Jack London story.

4119 Wolf Dog. 20th Century-Fox, 1958. 69 minutes B/W. D: Sam Newfield. SC:

Louis Stevens. WITH Jim Davis, Allison Hayes, Tony Brown, Austin Willis, Don Garrard, Juan Root, Lloyd Chester, Jay MacDonald, B. Braithwaite. An ex-convict and his family move to a ranch in a remote area of Canada but find difficulties with a neighbor who wants the land for himself. Filmed in Canada, this drama is passable entertainment, due mainly to Jim Davis' fine work.

4120 The Wolf Hunters. Monogram, 1950. 70 minutes B/W. D: Oscar "Budd" Boetticher. SC: W. Scott Darling. WITH Kirby Grant, Jan Clayton, Helen Parrish, Edward Norris, Ted Hecht, Charles Lang, Luther Crockett, Elizabeth Root. A Mountie, on the trail of murderous fur thieves, uncovers a plot concerning a lost gold mine. Supposedly based on the James Oliver Curwood work, this film bears little resemblance to it but is still entertaining.

4121 Wolf Riders. Reliable, 1935. 56 minutes B/W. D: Harry S. Webb. SC: Carl Krusada. WITH Jack Perrin, Lillian Gilmore, Lafe McKee, Nancy Deshon, William Gould, George Chesebro, Earl Dwire, Budd Buster, Slim Whitaker, Frank Ellis, Robert Walker, George Morrell, Blackie Whiteford. An Indian agency inspector tries to protect the local tribe from a ruthless gang of fur thieves. Mediocre production values and a strung-out plot hamper this Jack Perrin vehicle.

4122 Wolf Song. Paramount, 1929. 80 minutes B/W. D: Victor Fleming. SC: John Farrow & Keene Thompson. WITH Gary Cooper, Lupe Velez, Louis Wolheim, Constantine Romanoff, Michael Vavitch, Ann Brody, Russ Columbo, Augustina Lopez, George Regas, Leona Lane. The daughter of a Spanish don marries a backwoods Kentucky trapper and they live in a mountain settlement but the husband gets wanderlust and the wife returns home but they still long for each other. Location filming in the California Sierra mountains is the chief highlight of his early talkie.

4123 Wolf Tracks. Sunset, 1923. 40 minutes B/W. D: Robert North Bradbury. SC: William Lester. WITH Jack Hoxie, Andree Tourneur, Jim Welsh, Tom Lingham, William Lester, Marin Sais. Mistaken for an outlaw called "The Wolf," a cowpoke tries to capture the villain not only to save himself but to protect a girl whose father has left her a mine The Wolf is trying to steal. Fast moving silent Jack Hoxie vehicle—a good film.

4124 Wolfheart's Revenge. Aywon, 1925. 55 minutes B/W. D: Charles L. Seeling. WITH Wolfheart (dog), Guinn Williams, Kathleen Collins, Captain Bingham, Larry Fischer, Helen Walton, John Williams. After committing a murder, a ranch foreman attempts to put the blame on an innocent cowboy. Pretty good action entry in Guinn "Big Boy" Williams' silent series for producer Charles L. Seeling with dog star Wolfheart.

4125 Wolves of the Range. Producers Releasing Corporation, 1943. 69 minutes B/W. D: Sam Newfield. SC: Joseph O'Donnell. WITH Robert Livingston, Al St. John, Frances Gladwin, I. Stanford Jolley, Karl Hackett, Ed Cassidy, Jack Ingram, Kenne Duncan, Budd Buster, Bob Hill, Slim Whitaker, Jack Holmes, Roy Bucko. While trying to aid ranchers who are being forced off their land because it is needed for a government irrigation project, the Lone Rider becomes the victim of amnesia. Pretty good entry in the popular "Lone Rider" series.

4126 Woman Obsessed. 20th Century-Fox, 1959. 102 minutes Color. D: Henry Hathaway. SC: Sidney Boehm. WITH Susan Hayward, Stephen Boyd, Arthur Franz, Dennis Holmes, Ken Scott, Theodore Bikel, James Philbrook, Florence MacMichael, Jack Raine, Barbara Nichols, Mary Carroll, Fred Graham, Mike Wally. After the accidental death of her husband a woman struggles to make a living on her remote Saskatchewan ranch and when she remarries she finds her young son resentful of his stepfather. Well made but not overly interesting drama.

4127 Woman of the North County. Republic, 1952. 90 minutes Color. D: Joseph Kane. SC: Norman Reilly Raine. WITH Rod Cameron, Ruth Hussey, John Agar, Gale Storm, J. Carrol Naish, Jim Davis, Jay C. Flippen, Taylor Holmes, Barry Kelley, Grant Withers, Howard Petrie, Hank Worden, Virginia Brissac, Stephen Bekassy. A mining engineer finds himself opposed by a ruthless woman rival miner in the north country and she will stop at nothing to destroy him. Good melodrama with a fine script and performances.

4128 Woman of the Town. United Artists, 1943. 89 minutes B/W. D: George Archainbaud. SC: Aeneas MacKenzie. WITH Claire Trevor, Albert Dekker, Barry Sullivan, Henry Hull, Marion Martin, Porter Hall, Percy Kilbride, Beryl Wallace, Arthur Hohl, Clem Bevans, George Cleveland, Russell Hicks, Herbert Rawlinson, Dorothy Granger, Dewey Robinson, Hal Taliaferro, Wade Crosby, Glenn Strange, Claire Whitney, Russell Simpson, Frances Morris, Teddi Sherman, Marlene Mains, Charley Foy, Eula Gray. Sheriff Bat Masterson is forced to choose between his job and his love for saloon girl Dora Hand. Underrated Harry Sherman production with fine work by Albert Dekker and Claire Trevor in the leading roles ably supported by an outstanding cast.

4129 The Woman They Almost Lynched. Republic, 1953. 90 minutes B/W. D: Allan Dwan. SC: Steve Fisher. WITH Brian Donlevy, Joan Leslie, John Lund, Audrey Totter, Jim Davis, Ben Cooper, James Brown, Ellen Corby, Reed Hadley, Virginia Christine, Richard Simmons, Gordon Jones, Nina Varela, Frank Ferguson, Ann Savage, Richard Crane, Ted Ryan, James Kirkwood, Fern Hall, Minerva Urecal, Marilyn Lindsey, Nacho Galindo, Post Park, Tom McDonough, Carl Pitti, Joe Yrigoyen, Jimmie Hawkins, Paul Livermore, Hal Baylor. After inheriting a saloon in a town controlled by crooks, a city girl becomes a bandit and is almost hung. Despite its exploitation title, this outing is pretty good fare and includes interesting performances, especially Brian Donlevy as Quantrill and Audrey Totter as Kate Quantrill.

4130 The Wonderful Country. United Artists, 1959. 96 minutes Color. D: Robert Parrish. SC: Robert Ardrey. WITH Robert Mitchum, Julie London, Gary Merrill, Pedro Armendariz, Jack Oakie, Albert Dekker, Charles McGraw, Satchel Paige, Victor Mendoza, Tom Lea, Jay Novello, Mike Kellin, Max Slaten, Joe Haworth, Chester Hayes, Chuck Roberson, Anthony Caruso, Claudio Brook, Judy Marsh, Mike Luna. A gun runner working for a Mexican revolutionary is sent to the U. S. for arms and gets involved with a pretty woman, outlaws and rampaging Indians. Sprawling adaptation of Tom Lea's novel provides good entertainment.

4131 Wrangler's Roost. Monogram, 1941. 57 minutes B/W. D: S. Roy Luby. SC: John Vlahos & Robert Finkle. WITH Ray Corrigan, John King, Max Terhune, Gwen Gaze, Forrest Taylor, George Chesebro, Frank Ellis, Walter Shumway, Jack Holmes, Frank McCarroll, Carl Mathews, Hank Bell, Tex Palmer, Jim Corey, Al Haskell, Ray Jones, Horace B. Carpenter, Tex Cooper, Herman Hack, Chick Hannon. The Range Busters are called in to investigate a series of stage holdups and suspect an old-time outlaw who they believe is masquerading as a deacon. Passable entry in "The Range Buster" series, but nothing special.

4132 The Wrath of God. Metro-Goldwyn-Mayer, 1971. 111 minutes Color. D-SC: Ralph Nelson. WITH Robert Mitchum, Rita Hayworth, Frank Langella, Victor Buono, John Calicos, Ken Hutcheson, Paula Pritchett, Gregory Sierra, Frank Ramirez, Enrique Lucero, Jorge Russek, Chano Urueta, Jose Luis Parades, Aurora Clavel, Victor Eberg, Pancho Cordova, Guillermo Hernandez, Ralph Nelson. In the late 1920s a loose-living priest and his two pals come to the aid of a Mexican revolutionary when a small village is threatened by government forces. Not overly good tongue-in-cheek drama although Robert Mitchum is a delight as the priest.

4133 Wyoming. Metro-Goldwyn-Mayer, 1940. 88 minutes B/W. D: Richard Thorpe. SC: Jack Jevne & Hugh Butler. WITH Wallace Beery, Leo Carrillo, Ann Rutherford, Lee Bowman, Joseph Calleia, Bob Watson, Paul Kelly, Marjorie Main, Henry Travers, Addison Richards, Stanley Fields, William Tannen, Clem Bevans, Donald MacBride, Russell Simpson, Dick Curtis, Richard Alexander, Chief Thundercloud, Glenn Lucas, Francis McDonald, Edgar Dearing, Glenn Strange, Ted Adams, Lee Phelps, Howard Mitchell. After the Civil War, a Missouri outlaw and his pal head West and get involved with an earthy female blacksmith and end up on the right side of the law. This initial teaming of Wallace Beery and Marjorie Main, along with Leo Carrillo as Beery's sidekick, makes for good entertainment.

4134 Wyoming. Republic, 1947. 84 minutes B/W. D: Joseph Kane. SC: Lawrence Hazard & Gerald Geraghty. WITH William Elliott, Vera Ralston, John Carroll, George "Gabby" Hayes, Albert Dekker, Virginia Grey, Maria Ouspenskaya, Grant Withers, Harry Woods, Minna Gombell, Dick Curtis, Roy Barcroft, Trevor Bardette, Paul Harvey, Louise Kane, Linda Green, Tom London, George Chesebro, Jack O'Shea, Charles Middleton, Eddy Waller, Olin Howlin, Glenn Strange, Charles King, Eddie Acuff, Marshall Reed, Rex Lease, Charles Morton, Tex Terry, Dale Fink, Ed Peil Sr., Roque Ybarra, James Archuletta, David Williams, Lee Shumway. A Wyoming land baron finds nesters encroaching on his property and when his foreman quits in their defense he also finds his college-educated daughter deserting his cause. Grand scale (for Republic) drama with a great cast and lots of action; Yakima Canutt did the second unit work.

4135 The Wyoming Bandit. Republic, 1949. 60 minutes B/W. D: Philip Ford. SC: M. Coates Webster. WITH Allan "Rocky" Lane, Eddy Waller, Trevor Bardette, Victor Kilian, Rand Brooks, Reed Hadley, Harold Goodwin, Lane Bradford, Robert Wilke, John Hamilton, Edmund Cobb, William Haade. An outlaw teams with a lawman to get those responsible for the murder of his son. Trevor Bardette as good-badman Wyoming Dan steals the show in this above average Allan Lane vehicle.

4136 Wyoming Hurricane. Columbia, 1944. 58 minutes B/W. D: William Berke. SC: Fred Myton. WITH Russell Hayden, Dub Taylor, Bob Wills & His Texas Playboys, Alma Carroll, Tristram Coffin, Joel Friedkin, Paul Sutton, Benny Petti, Robert Kortman, Hal Price. A dishonest cafe operator murders the local lawman and the blame is placed on the marshal's daughter's boyfriend. Lesser Russell Hayden vehicle, with fine villainy from Tristram Coffin.

The Wyoming Kid see **Cheyenne**

4137 The Wyoming Mail. Universal-International, 1950. 87 minutes Color. D: Reginald LeBorg. SC: Harry Essex & Leonard Lee. WITH Stephen McNally, Alexis Smith, Howard Da Silva, Ed Begley, Dan Riss, Roy Roberts, Whit Bissell, Armando Silvestre, James Arness, Richard Jaeckel, Frankie Darro, Felipe Turich, Richard Egan, Gene Evans, Frank Fenton, Emerson Treacy. A former boxer is hired as an undercover agent for the railroad and he infiltrates a gang in Wyoming Territory and falls in love with its female member. The story is a bit farfetched but otherwise this film is all right.

4138 Wyoming Outlaw. Republic, 1939. 56 minutes B/W. D: George Sherman. SC: Jack Natteford & Betty Burbridge. WITH John Wayne, Ray Corrigan, Raymond Hatton, Donald Barry, Adele Pearce (Pamela Blake), LeRoy Mason, Charles Middleton, Elmo Lincoln, Katharine Kentworthy, Jack Ingram, David Sharpe, Jack Kenney, Yakima Canutt, Dave O'Brien, Curley Dresden, Tommy Coates,

Ralph Peters, Jack Kirk, Al Taylor, Bud McTaggart, Budd Buster, Ed Payson. The Three Mesquiteers are at odds with crooked politicians who are cheating small ranchers and they are forced to hunt down a young man forced to break the law in self defense. Exceedingly well done "Three Mesquiteers" series entry with a finale that predates **High Sierra** (Warner Brothers, 1941) by two years.

4139 Wyoming Renegades. Columbia, 1955. 73 minutes Color. D: Fred F. Sears. SC: David Lang. WITH Phil(ip) Carey, Martha Hyer, Gene Evans, William Bishop, Douglas Kennedy, Roy Roberts, Don Beddoe, Aaron Spelling, George Keymas, Harry Harvey, Mel Welles, Henry Rowland, Boyd Stockman, Guy Teague, Bob Woodward, Don C. Harvey, John Cason, Don Carlos. Released from prison a man finds his past causes people to dislike him but he is aided by the girl he loves. Standard programmer from producer Wallace MacDonald.

4140 Wyoming Roundup. Monogram, 1952. 53 minutes B/W. D: Thomas Carr. SC: Dan Ullman. WITH Whip Wilson, Tommy Farrell, Phyllis Coates, Henry Rowland, House Peters Jr., I. Stanford Jolley, Dick Emory, Robert Wilke, Stanley Price. After stopping a gunfight, two cowpokes are made the law in a small town where someone is hiring gunmen to run out rival ranchers. Average Whip Wilson outing.

4141 Wyoming Whirlwind. Willis Kent, 1932. 55 minutes B/W. D: Armand L. Schaefer. SC: Wallace MacDonald. WITH Lane Chandler, Adele Tracy, Harry Todd, Alan Bridge, Yakima Canutt, Lois Bridge, Bob Roper, Harry Semels, Hank Bell, Ted Adams, Fred Burns, Raven (horse). The Lone Wolf, a wanted highwayman, is actually the son of a rancher who was murdered years before and he returns home to capture the killer, the foreman who inherited the ranch. Cheaply made, strung-out and low grade Lane Chandler vehicle. TV title: **Roaring Rider.**

4142 Wyoming Wildcat. Republic, 1941. 54 (56) minutes B/W. D: George Sherman. SC: Bennett Cohen & Anthony Coldeway. WITH Don "Red" Barry, Julie Duncan, Syd Saylor, Frank M. Thomas, Edmund Cobb, Ed Brady, Richard Botiller, Ed Cassidy, George Sherwood, Ethan Laidlaw, Al Haskell, Frank Ellis, Curley Dresden, Art Dillard, Kermit Maynard, Cactus

Mack, Frank O'Connor, Fred Burns. A wanted outlaw gets a job as the guard on a Wells Fargo stagecoach and is hunted by the law after a holdup. Average Don Barry actioner.

Y

4143 Yankee Don. Capitol, 1931. 60 minutes B/W. D: Noel Madison. SC: Frances Jackson. WITH Richard Talmadge, Lupita Tovar, Julian Rivero, Sam Appel, Gayne Whitman, Alma Reat, Victor Stanford. A Bowery desperado heads West and aids a Spanish don whose ranch is threatened by outlaws. Actionful poverty row feature produced by star Richard Talmadge.

4144 Yaqui Drums. Republic, 1957. 70 minutes B/W. D: Jean Yarbrough. SC: Jo Pagano & D. D. Beauchamp. WITH Rod Cameron, Mary Castle, J. Carrol Naish, Robert Hutton, Roy Roberts, Keith Richards, Denver Pyle, Ray Walker, Donald Kerr, John Merrick, Paul Fierro, G. Pat Collins. A rancher fighting a corrupt saloon owner is aided by a Mexican outlaw gang thwarted in a stagecoach holdup attempt. Standard programmer enhanced by the performances of Rod Cameron and J. Carrol Naish.

4145 The Yearling. Metro-Goldwyn-Mayer, 1946. 134 minutes Color. D: Clarence Brown. SC: Paul Osborn. WITH Gregory Peck, Jane Wyman, Claude Jarman Jr., Chill Wills, Clem Bevans, Margaret Wycherly, Henry Travers, Forrest Tucker, Don Gift, Daniel White, Matt Willis, George Mann, Arthur Hohl, June Lockhart, June Wells, Jeff York, Chick York, Housely Stevenson, Jane Green, Victor Kilian, Robert Porterfield, John Eldredge. A young Florida farm boy becomes attached to a fawn which his father must destroy. Award winning classic family film; well worth seeing.

4146 Yellow Dust. RKO Radio, 1936. 68 minutes B/W. D: Wallace Fox. SC: Cyril Hume & John Twist. WITH Richard Dix, Leila Hyams, Moroni Olsen, Jessie Ralph, Andy Clyde, Onslow Stevens, Victor Potel, Ethan Laidlaw, Art Mix, Ted Oliver. A miner falls in love with a saloon girl and tries to win her affections from the saloon owner, even after he is falsely accused of robbing a stage. Surprisingly poor Richard Dix vehicle.

4147 The Yellow Mountain. Universal-International, 1954. 78 minutes Color. D: Jesse Hibbs. SC: George Zuckerman & Russell Hughes. WITH Lex Barker, Mala Powers, Howard Duff, William Demarest, John McIntire, Leo Gordon, Hal K. Dawson, Dayton Lummis. Two men vie for the same girl as well as for a valuable gold claim. Fair Universal feature.

4148 Yellow Rose of Texas. Republic, 1944. 54 (69) minutes B/W. D: Joseph Kane. SC: Jack Townley. WITH Roy Rogers, Dale Evans, Bob Nolan & The Sons of the Pioneers, George Cleveland, Harry Shannon, Grant Withers, William Haade, Weldon Heyburn, Hal Taliaferro, Tom London, Richard Botiller, Janet Martin, Robert Wilke, Jack O'Shea, Rex Lease, Emmett Vogan, John Dilson, Don Kay Reynolds. A man is falsely accused of robbing a stagecoach and goes on the run only to be sought after by his daughter, who is an entertainer on a showboat, and an insurance investigator who masquerades as a fellow entertainer to see if the girl knows her father's whereabouts. Dandy Roy Rogers film with a good story and plenty of music in a showboat setting.

4149 Yellow Sky. 20th Century-Fox, 1948. 95 minutes B/W. D: William A. Wellman. SC: Lamar Trotti. WITH Gregory Peck, Anne Baxter, Richard Widmark, Robert Arthur, John Russell, Henry (Harry) Morgan, James Barton, Charles Kemper, Robert Adler, Victor Kilian, Paul Hurst, William Gould, Norman Leavitt, Chief Yowlachie, Eula Guy. After robbing a bank, six outlaws ride into an Arizona ghost town inhabited only by a man and his granddaughter and trouble erupts when the old man hides their stolen loot. Highly entertaining action drama from the novel by W. R. Burnett.

4150 The Yellow Tomahawk. United Artists, 1954. 82 minutes B/W. D: Lesley Selander. SC: Richard Alan Simmons. WITH Rory Calhoun, Peggie Castle, Noah Beery Jr., Warner Anderson, Peter Graves, Lee Van Cleef, Rita Moreno, Walter Reed, Dan Riss, Adam Williams, Ned Glass. In order to prevent a planned attack on white settlers, an Indian guide plans hand-to-hand combat with his tribe's chief. Okay actioner but nothing special.

4151 Yellowneck. Republic, 1955. 83 minutes Color. D: R. John Hough. SC: Nat S. Linden. WITH Lin McCarthy, Stephen Courtleigh, Barry Kroeger, Harold Gordon, Bill Mason. Five escaped Confederate prisoners make their way through the Florida Everglades in an effort to stay alive and reach the safety of the ocean. Surprisingly atmospheric and entertaining melodrama.

4152 Yellowstone. Universal, 1936. 63 minutes B/W. D: Arthur Lubin. SC: Jefferson Parker, Stuart Palmer & Houston Branch. WITH Henry Hunter, Judith Barrett, Ralph Morgan, Alan Hale, Andy Devine, Monroe Owsley, Michael Loring, Paul Fix, Rollo Lloyd, Paul Harvey, Raymond Hatton, Diana Gibson, Mary Gordon, Claud Allister. A young man searches for bank loot his father supposedly hid there two decades before, while an ex-convict is found murdered and the man becomes a suspect. Fairly good actioner with some nice mystery elements, cowritten by the famous detective story author Stuart Palmer.

4153 Yellowstone Kelly. Warner Brothers, 1959. 91 minutes Color. D: Gordon Douglas. SC: Burt Kennedy. WITH Clint Walker, Edward (Edd) Byrnes, John Russell, Ray Danton, Andra Martin, Claude Akins, Rhodes Reason, Gary Vinson, Warren Oates. A fur trapper finds himself in the middle of Indian warfare after whites take a pretty Indian girl as their prisoner. Clint Walker handles the title role of this actionful Western in good form.

4154 The Yodelin' Kid from Pine Ridge. Republic, 1937. 61 minutes B/W. D: Joseph Kane. SC: Dorrell McGowan, Stuart McGowan & Jack Natteford. WITH Gene Autry, Smiley Burnette, Betty Bronson, LeRoy Mason, Charles Middleton, Russell Simpson, The Tennessee Ramblers, Jack Dougherty, Guy Wilkerson, Frankie Marvin, Henry Hall, Fred "Snowflake" Toones, Bud Osborne, Jack Kirk, Bob Burns, Al Taylor, George Morrell, Lew Meehan, Jim Corey, Jack Ingram, Art Dillard, Art Mix, Oscar Gahan. After being called a traitor by his father and joining a traveling wild west show, Gene Autry returns home to the Turpentine Pine Forest of Florida and Georgia to try and stop a feud between cattle ranchers and turpentine makers. Fine Gene Autry vehicle with lots of action, an interesting story, good photography and location shooting and fine musical interludes. In this one Smiley Burnette is Colonel Millhouse, the carnival chief, and not his usual Frog Millhouse character. V: Cumberland Video.

4155 Young and Free. Manson International, 1978. 90 minutes Color. D-SC: Keith Larsen. WITH Erik Larsen, Ivy Angustain, Keith Larsen, Carrol McCall. A boy grows to manhood learning the ways of the wilderness and how to survive. Keith Larsen strikes again in this outdoor melodrama starring his son; for fans of lots of scenic values.

4156 Young Bill Hickok. Republic, 1940. 54 (59) minutes B/W. D: Joseph Kane. SC: Olive Cooper & Norton S. Parker. WITH Roy Rogers, George "Gabby" Hayes, Jacqueline Wells (Julie Bishop), John Miljan, Sally Payne, Monte Blue, Hal Taliaferro, Ethel Wales, Jack Ingram, Iron Eyes Cody, Dick Elliott, Monte Montague, Fred Burns, Frank Ellis, Slim Whitaker, Jack Kirk, Hank Bell, Henry Wills, William Desmond, John Elliott, Jack Rockwell, Bill Woolfe. Pony Express rider Bill Hickok is out to stop a foreign agent using a gang of marauders in taking part of California during the Civil War. Good, actionful early entry in the Roy Rogers series.

4157 Young Billy Young. United Artists, 1969. 89 minutes Color. D-SC: Burt Kennedy. WITH Robert Mitchum, Angie Dickinson, Robert Walker (Jr.), David Carradine, Jack Kelly, John Anderson, Deana Martin, Paul Fix, Willis Bouchey, Parley Baer, Bob Anderson, Rodolfo Acosta, Christopher Mitchum. A man arrives in a New Mexico town and becomes its sheriff in order to bring in the man who murdered his son. Good finale showdown adds some life to this leisurely paced drama.

4158 Young Blood. Monogram, 1932. 60 minutes B/W. D: Phil Rosen. SC: Wellyn Totman. WITH Bob Steele, Helen Foster, Charles King, Naomi Judge, Art Mix, Henry Roquemore, Hank Bell, Harry Semels, Lafe McKee, Perry Murdock, Roy Bucko. A young man who steals from crooks to aid the oppressed gets involved with a foreign actress. This Bob Steele vehicle has a plot that is hard to believe; below average.

4159 Young Buffalo Bill. Republic, 1940. 54 (59) minutes B/W. D: Joseph Kane. SC: Harrison Jacobs, Robert Yost & Gerald Geraghty. WITH Roy Rogers, George "Gabby" Hayes, Pauline Moore, Hugh Sothern, Trevor Bardette, Chief Thundercloud, Julian Rivero, Gaylord (Steve) Pendleton, Wade Boteler, George Chesebro, Hank Bell, William Kellogg,

Jack O'Shea, Iron Eyes Cody, Anna Demetrio, Estrelita Zarco. A young Bill Cody comes to the aid of both settlers and Indians about to be defrauded by Spanish land grant claimants. Typically actionful early Roy Rogers "historical" saga.

4160 The Young Country. ABC-TV/Universal, 1970. 73 minutes Color. D-SC: Roy Huggins. WITH Roger Davis, Joan Hackett, Walter Brennan, Peter Deuel, Wally Cox, Skip Young, Steve Sandor, Robert Driscoll Miller, Richard Van Fleet, Elliott Street, Barbara Gates, Luis Delgado, Thomas Ballin. A gambler suddenly turns honest when he finds stolen bank money but when he tries to return it no one will claim the loot. Fair genre comedy made for television.

4161 Young Daniel Boone. Monogram, 1950. 60 (71) minutes B/W. D: Reginald LeBorg. SC: Clint Johnson & Reginald LeBorg. WITH David Bruce, Kristine Miller, Damian O'Flynn, Don Beddoe, Mary Treen, John Mylong, William Roy, Stanley Logan, Richard Foote. Daniel Boone rescues the survivors of an Indian attack and uncovers the fact that a French spy has been responsible for the uprising. This dual biller tries hard but lack of a sufficient budget hurts its efforts.

4162 Young Fury. Paramount, 1965. 79 minutes Color. D: Christian Nyby. SC: Steve Fisher. WITH Rory Calhoun, Virginia Mayo, Lon Chaney, Richard Arlen, William Bendix, John Agar, Preston Pierce, Linda Foster, Robert Biheller, Jody McCrea, Merry Anders, Rex Bell Jr., Joan Huntington, Reg Parton, Marc Covell, Jay Ripley, Kevin O'Neal, Dal Jenkins, Fred Alexander, Jerry Summers, William Wellman Jr., Steve Condit, Dave Dunlop, Bill Clark, William J. Vincent, Jesse Wayne, Robert Miles, Eddie Rice, Fred Krone, Joe Finnegan, Kent Hays, Jorge Moreno. A group of young hellions take over a small town and the gang leader learns the saloon hostess is his mother while his ex-gunman father is being chased by the Dalton gang. Mediocre production which is one of the least satisfying of the mid-1960s A. C. Lyles productions, despite a fine cast.

4163 The Young Guns. Allied Artists, 1956. 84 minutes B/W. D: Albert Band. SC: Louis Garfinkle. WITH Russ Tamblyn, Gloria Talbott, Perry Lopez, Scott Marlowe, Wright King, Walter Coy, Chubby Johnson, Myron Healey, James Goodwin, Rayford Barnes, I. Stanford Jolley. The son of a famous gunman tries to lead a peaceful life in a small Wyoming town but his father's reputation makes life difficult for him. Only average outing with Guy Mitchell singing the title tune.

4164 Young Guns of Texas. 20th Century-Fox, 1963. 78 minutes Color. D: Maury Dexter. SC: Harry Cross. WITH James Mitchum, Alana Ladd, Jody McCrea, Chill Wills, Gary Conway, Barbara Mansell, Robert Lowery, Troy Melton, Fred Krone, Alex Sharp, Robert Hinkle, Will Wills. Two men, a young soldier searching for stolen army gold and a father looking for his eloping daughter, join forces when caught in an Indian attack. Entertaining outing with a good script and the gimmick of having for its leads the children of famous stars.

4165 Young Jesse James. 20th Century-Fox, 1960. 73 minutes B/W. D: William F. Claxton. SC: Orville H. Hampton & Jerry Sackheim. WITH Ray Stricklyn, Willard Parker, Merry Anders, Robert Dix, Emile Meyer, Jacklyn O'Donnell, Rayford Barnes, Rex Holman, Bob Palmer, Sheila Bromley, Johnny O'Neill, Leslie Bradley, Norman Leavitt, Lee Kendall. During the Civil War Jesse and Frank James join forces with Quantrill's raiders and become outlaws when Yankees hang their father. Still another retelling of the James Brothers saga, but this one is a bit tattered although it does contain good performances by Willard Parker as Cole Younger and Emile Meyer as Quantrill.

4166 The Young Land. Columbia, 1959. 89 minutes Color. D: Ted Tetzlaff. SC: Norman Shannon Hall. WITH Pat(rick) Wayne, Yvonne Craig, Dennis Hopper, Dan O'Herlihy, Roberto de la Madrid, Cliff Ketchum, Ken Curtis, Pedro Gonzales Gonzales, Edward Sweeney, Miguel Camacho, Cliff Lyons, Randy Sparks, Mario Arteaga, Charles Heard, Carlos Romero, Tom Tiner, John Quijada. Trouble brews in the Republic of Texas when a citizen is to be tried for the murder of a Mexican. Well modulated and entertaining effort.

4167 Young Mr. Lincoln. 20th Century-Fox, 1939. 101 minutes B/W. D: John Ford. SC: Lamar Trotti. WITH Henry Fonda, Alice Brady, Marjorie Weaver, Arleen Whelan, Eddie Collins, Pauline Moore, Richard Cromwell, Eddie Quillan, Ward Bond, Donald Meek, Spencer Charters, Judith Dickens, Milburn Stone, Cliff

Clark, Robert Lowery, Charles Tannen, Francis Ford, Fred Kohler Jr., Kay Linaker, Russell Simpson, Charles Halton, Edwin Maxwell, Robert Homans, Jack Kelly, Dickie Jones, Harry Tyler, Louis Mason, Jack Pennick, Steven Randall, Clarence Wilson, Elizabeth Jones. In frontier Illinois young attorney Abraham Lincoln agrees to act as defense council for two backwoods youths accused of murder. Top notch study of the early life of Abraham Lincoln; a near classic.

4168 Young Pioneers. ABC-TV, 1976. 96 minutes Color. D: Michael O'Herlihy. SC: Blanche Hanalis. WITH Roger Kern, Linda Purl, Robert Hays, Shelly Juttner, Robert Donner, Frank Marth, Brendan Dillon, Charles Tyner, Jonathan Kidd, Arnold Soboloff, Bernice Smith, Janis Famison, Dennis Fimple. A young teenage married couple leave their family home in Iowa and head West to settle in the rugged Dakotas in the 1870s. Fairly good TV movie adaptation of the works of Rose Wilder Lane.

4169 Young Pioneers' Christmas. ABC-TV, 1976. 100 minutes Color. D: Michael O'Herlihy. SC: Blanche Hanalis. WITH Roger Kern, Linda Purl, Robert Hays, Kay Kimler, Robert Donner, Britt Leach, Arnold Soboloff, Brendan Dillon, Rand Bridges, Brian Melrose, Sherri Wagner. A young couple try to overcome the grief of losing their infant and bring a happy Christmas to others trying to settle the Dakota Territory. Okay sequel to **Young Pioners** (q.v.) although this TV movie, like its predecessor, failed to make it as a series.

4170 The Younger Brothers. Warner Brothers, 1949. 77 minutes Color. D: Edwin L. Marin. SC: Edna Anhalt. WITH Wayne Morris, Janis Paige, Bruce Bennett, Geraldine Brooks, Robert Hutton, Alan Hale, Fred Clark, James Brown, Monte Blue, Tom Tyler, William Forrest, Ian Wolfe. While awaiting a pardon from the governor, the Younger Brothers are forced into lawlessness when the youngest brother kills in self defense. Good production values and cast overcome a mundane script in this actioner.

4171 You're Fired. Goodwill, 1925. 50 minutes B/W. D: Paul Hurst. SC: William Lester. WITH Bill Bailey, Alma Rayford, Robert McKenzie, Theodore Lorch, Sam Bloom, Velma Watkins, Floyce Brown, Victor Allen. When his sister tries to civilize a ranch owner by sending a group of dudes to his spread, the owner pretends to be a hired hand and gets fired but comes to the rescue when outlaws kidnap the dudes. Pleasant silent tongue-in-cheek actioner.

4172 Yukon Flight. Monogram, 1939. 57 minutes B/W. D: Ralph Staub. SC: Edward Halperin. WITH James Newill, Louise Stanley, Warren Hull, Dave O'Brien, William Pawley, Karl Hackett, Jack Clifford, Roy Barcroft, Bob Terry, Earl Douglas. Renfrew of the Mounted asks a former Mountie to aid him in stopping an outlaw gang which is carrying gold out of Canada via airplanes. Entertaining effort in the popular "Renfrew of the Mounted" series. Also called **Renfrew of the Royal Mounted in Yukon Flight.** V: Video Connection.

4173 Yukon Gold. Monogram, 1952. 62 minutes B/W. D: Frank McDonald. SC: William Raynor. WITH Kirby Grant, Martha Hyer, Harry Lauter, Philip Van Zandt, Frances Charles, Mauritz Hugo, James Parnell, Sam Flint, I. Stanford Jolley, Chinook (dog). A Mountie arrives in a rugged mining camp searching for a killer and meets a pretty female gambler. Average outing in Kirby Grant's series for Monogram supposedly based on the works of James Oliver Curwood.

4174 Yukon Manhunt. Monogram, 1951. 63 minutes B/W. D: Frank McDonald. SC: William Raynor. WITH Kirby Grant, Gail Davis, Margaret Field, Rand Brooks, Nelson Leigh, John Doucette, Paul McGuire, Chinook (dog). A Mountie and his faithful husky try to find who is behind a series of payroll messenger robberies. Standard outing for the Kirby Grant Mountie series.

The Yukon Patrol see **King of the Royal Mounted**

4175 Yukon Safari. American National Enterprises, 1976. 95 minutes Color. Adventurers explore the Yukon from the Arctic south and look at its land and people. Very well done documentary on the Yukon.

4176 Yukon Vengeance. Allied Artists, 1954. 68 minutes B/W. D: William Beaudine. SC: William Raynor. WITH Kirby Grant, Mary Ellen Kay, Monte Hale, Henry Kulky, Carol Thurston, Marshall Bradford, Park MacGregor, Fred Gabourie, Billy Wilkerson, Chinook (dog). A Mountie and his dog travel to remote Bear Creek

to look into the robbery and murder of three mail carriers. Fair actioner in the Kirby Grant series of James Oliver Curwood-based films with the added treat of Monte Hale in a villainous role.

4177 Yuma. ABC-TV, 1971. 73 minutes Color. D: Ted Post. SC: Charles Wallace. WITH Clint Walker, Barry Sullivan, Kathryn Hays, Edgar Buchanan, Morgan Woodward, Peter Mark Richman, John Kerr, Robert Phillips, Miguel Alejandro, Neil Russell, Bruce Glover. The marshal of a rough town faces opposition from crooked officials as well as from the brother of a prisoner. More than passable made-for-TV oater.

Z

4178 Zachariah. Cinerama Releasing Corporation, 1971. 93 minutes Color. D: George Englund. SC: Joe Massot. WITH John Rubinstein, Pat Quinn, Don Johnson, Elvin Jones, County Joe & The Fish, Doug Kershaw, William Challee, Robert Ball, Dick Van Patten, The James Gang, White Lightnin', The New York Rock Ensemble. Two gunfighter friends go separate ways with one giving up his guns for a life of peace but eventually the two are forced into a showdown. Rock musical-Western which will not appeal to most genre fans.

4179 Zandy's Bride. Warner Brothers, 1974. 116 minutes Color. D: Jan Troell. SC: Marc Norman. WITH Gene Hackman, Liv Ullman, Eileen Heckart, Harry Dean Stanton, Joe Santos, Frank Cady, Sam Bottoms, Susan Tyrell, Bob Simpson, Fabian Gregory Cordova, Don Wilbanks, Vivian Gordon, Alf Kjellin. A frontiersman decides to buy a mail order bride in order to have children but the woman he gets is strong willed and he fears she may be too old for child bearing. Somewhat sluggish effort from the director and star of **The Emigrants** (Warner Brothers, 1971) and **The New Land** (q.v.) although Frank Cady is quite good as Gene Hackman's nasty father.

4180 Zorro. Titanus, 1975. 100 minutes Color. D: Duccio Tessari. SC: Giorgio Arlorio. WITH Alain Delon, Stanley Baker, Ottavia Piccolo, Moustache, Enzo Cerusico, Adriana Asti. In 19th century Latin America the foppish Don Diego takes on the guise of the masked hero

Zorro to avenge his friend's murder. Fairly entertaining French-Italian production about the famous screen hero; originally ran 125 minutes.

Zorro Against Maciste see **Samson and the Slave Queen**

4181 Zorro and the Three Musketeers. Golden Era, 1962. 99 minutes Color. D: Marino Vacca. WITH Gordon Scott, Jose Greci, Giacomo Rossi Stuart, Livio Lorenzon, Franco Fantasia, Nazzareno Zamperla. In the 17th century Zorro joins forces with the Three Musketeers to combat villains. For loyal Zorro fans only!

4182 Zorro in the Court of Spain. Italian, 1968. 90 minutes Color. D: Guido Zurli. WITH George Ardisson, Jack Stuart, Femi Benussi, Carol Wells, Barbara Carroll, Daniele Vargas, Spyros Focas. Zorro aids the people in a revolt against a corrupt governor's injustice. Typically fast paced Italian actioner, originally called **El Zorro el Volpe** (Zorro the Fox).

4183 Zorro, Marquis of Navarra. Romana Film, 1971. 91 minutes Color. D: Jean Monty. SC: Pierotti & Montemurra. WITH Nadior Moretti, Maria Luisa Longo, Daniele Vargas, Loris Gizzi, Renato Montalbano, Gisella Arden. Zorro, allied with the exiled Spanish king, tries to aid the oppressed people of his country against their French conquerors. Although this Euopean made actioner takes place in Spain it is included here because of the Zorro character; average dubbed costumer. Italian title: **Zorro, Marchese di Navarra.** Spanish title: **Zorro, Marquis de Navarre.**

4184 Zorro Rides Again. Republic, 1937. 12 Chapters B/W. D: William Witney & John English. SC: Barry Shipman, John Rathmell, Franklyn Adreon, Ronald Davidson & Morgan B. Cox. WITH John Carroll, Helen Christina, Reed Howes, Duncan Renaldo, Richard Alexander, Noah Beery, Nigel De Brulier, Robert Kortman, Jack Ingram, Roger Williams, Tony Martelli, Edmund Cobb, Mona Rico, Tom London, Harry Strang, Jerry Frank, Paul Lopez, George Mari, Yakima Canutt, Frank Ellis, Al Haskell, Dirk Thane, Lane Chandler, Murdock MacQuarrie, Chris-Pin Martin, Frank McCarroll, Frankie Marvin, Jack Kirk, Ray Teal, Merrill McCormack, Rosa Turich, Art Felix, Josef Swickard, Forrest Burns, Jason Robards, Jack Hendricks. Zorro comes to the aid of a family whose railroad is sought by

a ruthless man and his henchmen. This action packed serial is a real treat. Issued in a 70 minute feature version in 1958 by Republic. V: Video Images, Cassette Express.

4185 Zorro the Avenger. Norberto Solino, 1963. 90 minutes Color. D: Joaquin Luis Romero Marchent. WITH Frank Latimore, Mary Anderson, Howard Vernon, Maria Luz Galicia, Ralph Marsch. In Old California the masked avenger Zorro leads the fight against the tyranny of crooked officials. Pretty fair Spanish-made "Zorro" adventure.

4186 Zorro, the Gay Blade. 20th Century-Fox, 1981. 93 minutes Color. D: Peter Medak. SC: Hal Dresner. WITH George Hamilton, Lauren Hutton, Brenda Vaccaro, Ron Liebman, Donovan Scott, James Booth, Helen Burns, Clive Revill. When an evil tyrant tries to oppress the people in frontier California, the two sons of a nobleman try to stop him but the foppish Don Diego is sidelined by an injury and replaced by his gay brother. Comic travesty of the "Zorro" character not likely to please genre fans. V: 20th Century-Fox Video.

4187 Zorro the Rebel. Romana Film, 1966. 90 minutes Color. D-SC: Pierro Pierotti. WITH Howard Ross, Dina De Santis, Charles Borromel, Arturo Dominici, Gabriella Andreini, Ted Carter. Zorro comes to the aid of a beautiful girl who is being forced to marry the son of the local governor against her will. Italian production which is not one of the better "Zorro" efforts.

4188 Zorro's Black Whip. Republic, 1944. 12 Chapters B/W. D: Spencer Gordon Bennet & Wallace Grissell. SC: Basil Dickey, Jesse Duffy, Grant Nelson & Joseph Poland. WITH George J. Lewis, Linda Stirling, Lucien Littlfield, Francis McDonald, Hal Taliaferro, John Merton, John Hamilton, Tom Chatterton, Tom London, Jack Kirk, Jay Kirby, Si Jenks, Stanley Price, Tom Steele, Duke Green, Dale Van Sickel, Cliff Lyons, Roy Brent, Bill Yrigoyen, Forrest Taylor, Fred Graham, Marshall Reed, Augie Gomez, Carl Sepulveda, Horace B. Carpenter, Herman Hack, Carey Loftin, Cliff Parkinson, Kenneth Terrell, Duke Taylor. After her newspaper editor brother is murdered by elements opposing statehood and promoting lawlessness, a young woman takes over his job as well as his guise as the Black Whip, the masked leader of vigilantes opposing the outlaws. Fast moving and entertaining Republic cliffhanger with pretty Linda Stirling as a female Zorro. V: Cassette Express.

4189 Zorro's Fighting Legion. Republic, 1939. 12 Chapters B/W. D: William Witney & John English. SC: Ronald Davidson, Franklyn Adreon, Morgan Cox, Sol Shor & Barney A. Sareckey. WITH Reed Hadley, Sheila Darcy, William Corson, Leander de Cordova, Edmund Cobb, C. Montague Shaw, John Merton, Budd Buster, Carleton Young, Guy D'Ennery, Paul Marion, Joe Molina, James Pierce, Helen Mitchell, Curley Dresden, Charles King, Al Taylor, Charles B. Murphy, Billy Bletcher, Joe de la Cruz, Jason Robards, Theodore Lorch, Jack O'Shea, Jerome Ward, Augie Gomez, Cactus Mack, Bud Geary, George Plues, Jack Carrington, Victor Cox, John Wallace, Bert Dillard, Kenneth Terrell, Wylie Grant, Carl Sepulveda, Yakima Canutt, Ernest Sarracino, Reed Howes, Joe McGuinn, Bill Yrigoyen, Gordon Clark, Frank Ellis, Joe Yrigoyen, Ted Mapes, Henry Wills. Three crooks try to block gold shipments to the government of Mexican president Benito Juarez and one of them takes on the guise of Don Del Oro to make the Indians think their deity has come to life but their activities are opposed by young nobleman Don Diego as the masked avenger Zorro. Top notch serial, one of the best cliffhangers of the sound era. V: Video Dimensions.

The Cowboys
and Their Horses

Although they are not listed in the casts of the individual entries of this book, the horses of the cowboy stars were often big attractions and as much the star of the film as the humans. Sometimes films were built around the talents of the star's horse, as in the case of Tom Mix's Tony or Ken Maynard's Tarzan. The following list does not include every film cowboy's movie horse but it does list the main equestrian stars of the Western cinema. Listed are the film stars and their horses.

Rex Allen—Koko
Gene Autry—Champion, Champion Jr.
Smith Ballew—Sheik
William Boyd—Topper
Harry Carey—Sonny
Lane Chandler—Raven
Bill Cody—Chico
Eddie Dean—Copper, Flash, White Cloud
William S. Hart—Fritz
Jack Hoxie—Scout
Buck Jones—Silver
Tom Keene—Flash, Prince
Allan Lane—Black Jack

Ken Maynard—Tarzan
Kermit Maynard—Rocky
Tom Mix—Tony, Tony Jr.
Dorothy Page—Snowey
Jack Perrin—Starlight
Jack Randall—Rusty
Tex Ritter—White Flash
Roy Rogers—Trigger
Reb Russell—Rebel
Fred Scott—White King
Charles Starrett—Raider
Fred Thompson—Silver King
John Wayne—Duke

Screen Names

Often people working in motion pictures have used more than one name. Since this book contains thousands of credits the following listing hopefully will help in the confusion resulting from the use of pseudonyms. Listed are the mostly commonly used screen name followed by alternate(s) names.

Jane Adams—Poni Adams
Julie Adams—Betty Adams, Julia Adams
Richard Alexander—Dick Alexander
Barbara Jo Allen—Vera Vague
Gene Alsace—Rocky Camron, Buck Coburn
Arkansas Slim Andrews—Lloyd Andrews
Morris Ankrum—Stephen Morris
John Archer—Ralph Bowman
Vivian Austin—Vivian Coe
Holly Bane—Michael Ragan, Mike Ragan
Joan Barclay—Geraine Greer
Don Barry—Don "Red" Barry, Donald Barry
Hank Bell—Hank Cole
Bruce Bennett—Herman Brix
Raphael Bennett—Ray Bennett
William Berke—Lester Williams
Willie Best—Sleep 'n Eat
Julie Bishop—Diane Duval, Jacqueline Wells
Pamela Blake—Adele Pearce
Adrian Booth—Lorna Gray
Charles Bronson—Charles Buchinsky
Jean Brooks—Jeanne Kelly, Jeannie Kelly
Reno Browne—Reno Blair
Buffalo Bill Jr.—Jay Wilsey
Boris Bullock—William Barrymore
Adele Buffington—Jess Bowers
Francis X. Bushman Jr.—Ralph Bushman
Budd Buster—George Selk
Jean Carmen—Julia Thayer
John Carpenter—Josh Carpenter, John Forbes
John Cason—Bob Cason, Chuck Cason, John L. Cason
Ed Cassidy—Edward Cassidy
Lon Chaney Jr.—Creighton Chaney
Alden Chase—Guy Chase, Stephen Chase
Jan Clayton—Jane Clayton
Elmer Clifton—Elmer S. Pond
Junior Coghlan—Frank Coghlan
Lewis D. Collins—Cullen Lewis

Dorothy Comingore—Linda Winters
Michael Connors—Mike Connors, Touch Connors
Ray Corrigan—Ray Bernard
Bob Custer—Raymond Glenn
Laraine Day—Lorraine Hayes, Laraine Johnson
Art Davis—Larry Mason
Gordon DeMain—G.D. Wood, Gordon Wood
Dick Dickinson—Pete Palmer
Denver Dixon—Victor Adamson, Art Mix, Al Mix, Art James
Cliff Edwards—Ukulele Ike
Bill Elliott—William Elliott, Gordon Elliott, Wild Bill Elliott
Harry Fraser—Harry C. Crist, Weston Edwards, Harry O. Jones
Chip Gorman—Andrea Giordana
Kirby Grant—Robert Stanton
James Griffith—James J. Griffith
Brett Halsey—Montgomery Ford
Jon Hall—Charles Locher
Rita Hayworth—Rita Cansino
Buzz Henry—Buzzy Henry, Robert Henry
Riley Hill—Roy Harris
Robert Hill—Rock Hawley
Pee Wee Holmes—Gilbert Holmes
Olin Howlin—Olin Howland
Robert Hundar—Claudio Undari
Alan James—Alan J. Neitz
Jennifer Jones—Phyllis Isley
Tom Keene—Richard Powers, George Duryea
Robert Kellard—Robert Stevens
Charles King—Charles King Jr., Charles L. King
Ed LeSaint—Edward J. LeSaint
Jack Luden—John Luden

Cactus Mack—Taylor Curtis McPeters
Jock Mahoney—Jack Mahoney, Jock
  O'Mahoney, Jacques J. O'Mahoney,
  Jacques O'Mahoney
Chris-Pin Martin—King Martin
Carl Mathews—Duke Mathews
Stephen McNally—Horace McNally
Bud McTaggert—Malcolm McTaggert
Blanche Mehaffey—Janet Morgan
Lynn Merrick—Marilyn Merrick
John Merton—Mert Lavarre, Morton Laverre
George Milton—Milton Raison, George Sayre
Art Mix—George Kesterson, Art Smith
George Montgomery—George Letz
Dennis Moore—Dennis Meadows, Denny
  Meadows, Smoky Moore
Bud Nelson—James T. Nelson
Sam Newfield—Peter Stewart, Sherman
  Scott, Sam Neufeld
Dave O'Brien—David Barclay, Tex O'Brien
Artie Ortego—Art Ardigan
Calvin Jackson Paget—Giorgio Ferroni
John Payne—Jack Payne
Jack Perrin—Richard Terry, Jack Gable
Hal Price—Harry Price, Harry F. Price
Bernard B. Ray—B.B. Ray, Ray Bernard,
  Franklin Shamray
Rhodes Reason—Rex Reason, Bart Roberts

Duncan Renaldo—Renault Duncan
Lynne Roberts—Mary Hart
Roy Rogers—Dick Weston
Gene Roth—Gene Stutenroth, Eugene Roth
Joseph Sawyer—Joe Sawyer, Joseph Sauers
Bud Spencer—Carlo Pedersoli
Harry Dean Stanton—Dean Stanton
Alan Steel—Sergio Ciani
Anthony Steffan—Antonio De Teffe
Evelyn Stewart—Ida Galli
Robert Emmett Tansey—Robert Emmett
Sherry Tansey—James Sheridan
Virginia Vale—Dorothy Howe
George Waggner—Joseph West
Wally Wales—Hal Taliaferro, Walt Williams
Harry S. Webb—Harry Samuels, Henri
  Samuels
John Wells—Gian Maria Volonte
Slim Whitaker—Charles Whitaker
Robert Wilke—Robert J. Wilke, Bob Wilke
Guinn Williams—Big Boy Williams, Guinn
  "Big Boy" Williams
Norman Willis—Jack Norman
Montgomery Wood—Guiliano Gemma
Hank Worden—Hebert Snow
Victor Sen Yung—Sen Yung, Victor Sen
  Young
Carleton Young—Gordon Roberts

Video Sources

The following is a list of various video sources for the collector. The list is not comprehensive and since new titles are being added all the time, and others deleted, the collector would be wise to check with a local video outlet regarding the availability of videocassettes. Several publications also include information on new releases, two of the best being *The Big Reel* (Route 3, Box 83, Madison, North Carolina 27025) and *Classic Images* (P.O. Box 4079, Davenport, Iowa 52808). Persons interested in the availability of Western movies on film (16mm, 8mm, Super 8mm) should check the various editions of James L. Limbacher's book *Feature Films on 8mm and 16mm*, published by R.R. Bowker Company.

As stated in the book's introduction, this listing is included as a service to the reader and the author, nor the publisher, has not knowingly included information pertaining to any films which may be sold in copyright violation.

Blackhawk Films—1 Old Eagle Brewery, P.O. Box 3990, Davenport, Iowa 52800
Budget Video—4590 Santa Monica Boulevard, Los Angeles, California 90029
Capital Home Video—12812 Garden Grove Boulevard, Suite B, Garden Grove, California 92643
Cassette Express—3123 Sylvania Avenue, Toledo, Ohio 43613
CBS/Fox Video—23434 Industrial Park Ct., Farmington Hills, Michigan 48024
Children's Video Library—P.O. Box 4995, Stamford, Connecticut 06907
Classic Cinema Video Collectors Club—17240 Goldwin, Southfield, Michigan 48975
Columbia Pictures Home Entertainment—Columbia Plaza South, Burbank, California 91505
Cumberland Video—4120 W. Alameda Avenue, Suite 9104, Burbank California 91505
Direct Video—1800 North Highland Avenue, Suite 709, Hollywood, California 90028
Discount Video—1117 N. Hollywood Way, Burbank, California 91505
Disney Home Video—*see* Walt Disney Home Video
Electric Video Inc. (EVI)—85A Bloomingdale Road, Bethpage, New York 11801
Embassy Home Entertainment—424 North Center Street, Northville, Michigan 48167
Film Classic Exchange—P.O. Box 77568, Dockweiler Station, Los Angeles, California 90007
Glenn Photo—6924 Canby Avenue, No. 103, Reseda, California 91335
King Enterprises—23047 Schoolcraft Street, Canoga Park, California 91307
Marketing Film—45 W. 45th Street, New York, N.Y. 10046
MCA Videocassette, Inc.—100 Universal City Plaza, Universal City, California 91608
MGM/United Artists Home Video—1700 Broadway, New York, N.Y. 10019
Morecraft Films/Penguin Video—837 Cahuenga Boulevard, Hollywood, California 90038
National Cinema Service—P.O. Box 43, Ho-Ho-Kus, New Jersey 07423
NTA Home Entertainment—42636 Beatrice Street, Suite 1019, Hollywood, California 90028
Nostalgia Merchant—6255 Sunset Boulevard, Suite 1019, Hollywood, California 90028
Program Releasing Corporation, 2375 E. Tropicana Avenue, Ste. 242, Las Vegas, Nevada 89109
RCA SelectaVision (Video Disc)—30 Rockefeller Plaza, New York, N.Y. 10020
Reel Images—495 Monroe Turnpike, Monroe, Connecticut 06468
Sunland Enterprises—1123 Ohio Avenue, Alamagordo, New Mexico 88310
Thorn EMI—800 Third Avenue, New York, N.Y. 10022
Thunderbird Films—P.O. Box 65157, Los Angeles, California 90065
Unicorn—P.O. Box 1084, Reseda, California 91305
Universal 8—445 Park Avenue, New York, N.Y. 10023
VCII Film Classics—7313 Varna Avenue, North Hollywood, California 91605

Vestron Video—911 Hope Street, Box 4000, Stamford, Connecticut 06907
VID America—235 E. 55th Street, New York, N.Y. 10022
Video Gems—731 North LaBrea Avenue, Los Angeles, California 90038
Video Communications (VCI)—6585 East Skelly Drive, Tulsa, Oklahoma 74145
Video Connection—1920 Sylvania Avenue, Ste. 101, Toledo, Ohio 43613
Video Dimensions—110 East 23rd Street, New York, N.Y. 10010
Video Yesteryear/Video Images—Box C, Sandy Hook, Connecticut 06482
Walt Disney Home Video—500 South Buena Vista Street, Burbank, California 91521
Warner Home Video—75 Rockefeller Plaza, New York, N.Y. 10019

Selected Bibliography

Books

Adams, Les and Rainey, Buck. *The Shoot-Em-Ups*. New Rochelle, N.Y.: Arlington House, 1978.

American Film Institute Catalog, Feature Films 1921–30. New York City: Bowker, 1971.

American Film Institute Catalog, Feature Films 1961–70. New York City: Bowker, 1976.

Aros, Andrew. *An Actor Guide to the Talkies 1965–74*. Metuchen, N.J.: Scarecrow Press, 1977.

Aros, Andrew. *A Title Guide to the Talkies 1964–74*. Metuchen, N.J: Scarecrow Press, 1977.

Baer, D. Richard (ed.). *The Film Buff's Checklist 1912–79*. Hollywood, California: Hollywood Film Archives, 1979.

Barbour, Alan G. (ed.). *Old Movies 1: The B Western*. Kew Gardens, N.Y.: Screen Facts Press, 1969.

Blum, Daniel. *A Pictorial History of the Silent Film*. New York City: Grosset & Dunlap, 1953.

Bond, Johnny. *The Tex Ritter Story*. New York City: Chappel & Co., 1976.

Brooks, Tim and Marsh, Earle. *The Complete Directory to Prime Time Network TV Shows 1946–Present*. New York City: Ballantine, 1979.

Carman, Bob and Scapperotti, Dan. *The Western Films of Sunset Carson*. Lindenhurst, N.Y.: Bob Carman, 1981.

Die Deutschen Filme (German Pictures). Langenbeckstrasse, West Germany: Export-Union Der Deutschen Filmindustrie, 1963–72.

Dimmitt, Richard. *An Actor Guide to the Talkies*. Metuchen, N.J.: Scarecrow Press, 1967.

Dimmitt, Richard. *A Title Guide to the Talkies*. Metuchen, N.J.: Scarecrow Press, 1965.

Eyles, Allen. *The Western*. London & New York City: The Tantivy Press, 1975.

Film Daily Yearbook of Motion Pictures. 1920–70.

Fitzgerald, Michael B. *Universal Pictures*. New Rochelle, N.Y.: Arlington House, 1977.

Fuente, Maria Isabel de la (ed.). *Indice Bibliografico Del Cine Mexicano 1930–65*. Mexico: Talleves de Editorial America, 1967.

Italian Production. Rome, Italy: Unitalia Film Organization, 1963–72.

Lahue, Kalton C. *Continued Next Week*. Norman, Oklahoma: The University of Oklahoma Press, 1964.

Limbacher, James L. *Feature Films on 8mm and 16mm*. New York City: Bowker, 1977.

Maltin, Leonard. *The Disney Films*. New York City, Crown, 1973.

Maltin, Leonard. *TV Movies 1983–84*. New York City, Signet, 1982.

Marrill, Alvin H. *Movies Made for Television*. Westport, Connecticut: Arlington House, 1980.

Michael, Paul (ed.). *The American Movies Reference Book*. Englewood Cliffs, N.J.: Prentice-Hall, 1969.

Miller, Don. *B Movies*. New York City: Curtis Books, 1973.

Miller, Don. *Hollywood Corral*. New York City: Popular Library, 1976.

Parish, James Robert and Pitts, Michael R. *The Great Western Pictures*. Metuchen, N.J.: The Scarecrow Press, 1976.

Rainey, Buck. *The Fabulous Holts*. Nashville, Tennessee: Western Film Collector Press, 1976.

Rainey, Buck. *Saddle Aces of the Cinema*. San Diego, California: A.S. Barnes, 1980.

Rainey, Buck. *The Saga of Buck Jones*. Nashville, Tennessee: Western Film Collector Press, 1975.

Scaramazza, Paul A. *Ten Years in Paradise*. Arlington, Virginia: The Pleasant Press, 1974.

Speed, F. Maurice. *Film Review*. New York City: A.S. Barnes, 1966–73.

Stanley, John. *Creature Features Movie Guide*. New York City: Warner Books, 1984.

TV Feature Film Sourcebook, Volume 19, 1978. New York City: Broadcasting Information Bureau, 1978.

Turner, George H. and Price, Michael H. *Forgotten Horrors: Early Talkie Chillers from Poverty Row*. Cranbury, N.J.: A.S. Barnes, 1979.

Tuska, Jon. *The Vanishing Legion: A History of Mascot Pictures 1927–35*. Jefferson, N.C.: McFarland & Co., 1982.

Variety Reviews (15 volumes). New York City & London: Garland Publishing, 1983.

Weiss, Ken & Goodgold, Ed. *To Be Continued*. New York City: Crown, 1972.

Weldon, Michael. *The Psychotronic Encyclopedia of Film*. New York City: Ballantine Books, 1983.

Wilson, Arthur (ed.). *The Warner Brothers Golden Anniversary Book*. New York City: Dell, 1973.

Periodicals

The Big Reel (Madison, North Carolina)

Classic Images, formerly *Classic Film Collector* (Davenport, Iowa)

Film Collectors Registry (Knoxville, Tennessee)

Film Fan Monthly (Teaneck, New Jersey)

Filmograph (Orlean, Virginia)

Films in Review (New York City)

The Films of Yesteryear. (Waynesville, North Carolina)

Focus on Film (London, England)

Screen Facts (Ken Gardens, New York)

Screen Thrills Illustrated (Philadelphia, Pennsylvania)

Under Western Skies (Waynesville, North Carolina)

Variety (New York City)

Views & Reviews (Milwaukee, Wisconsin)

Western Film Collector (Nashville, Tennessee)

Westerns All' Italiana (Keyport, New Jersey)

Wild West Stars (Knoxville, Tennessee)

Wildest Westerns (Philadelphia, Pennsylvania)

Yesterday's Saturdays (Lubbock, Texas)

Index

Henry, Carol 11, 65, 113, 134, 517, 681, 699, 822, 1354, 1356, 1361, 1401, 1407, 1447, 1503, 1834, 1979, 2266, 2394, 2426, 2651, 2665, 2896, 2927, 3036, 3110, 3124, 3127, 3139, 3376, 3410, 3711, 4102

Henry, Charlotte 1271

Henry, David Lee 1440

Henry, Gloria 20, 34, 1824, 1909, 2644, 2804, 3422

Henry, Louise 971

Henry, Mike 14, 2175, 2359, 2875, 3328

Henry, Robert "Buzzy/Buzz" 472, 473, 509, 689, 986, 1467, 1542, 1604, 1658, 1659, 1789, 1790, 1825, 1857, 2383, 2873, 2886, 2914, 2933, 3120, 3121, 3328, 3412, 3658, 3698, 3741, 3830, 3939, 4050, 4083

Henry, Thomas Browne 208, 1779, 1816, 2015, 2601, 3065, 3155, 3217, 3893

Hensley, Harold 4025

Hensley, Pamela 3558

Hepburn, Audrey 3827

Hepburn, Katharine 2637, 2941, 3070

Herbert, F. Hugh 766, 2127, 3579

Herbert, Holmes 675, 1615, 1657, 2427, 3425, 4078, 4118

Herbert, Hugh 155, 205

Herbert, Percy 525, 536, 2062

Herchey, Barbara 1473, 1771

Herman, Ace 2913

Herman, Al 99, 151, 235, 298, 905, 1289, 1532, 1990, 2053, 2343, 2417, 2461, 2533, 2630, 2668, 2733, 2767, 2928, 2929, 2930, 3208, 3288, 3386, 3438, 3710, 3844, 3853, 3980, 4009

Herman's Mountaineers 1466

Hern, Pepe 169, 1644, 1659, 3416

Hernandez, Juano 3090, 3387

Herrick, Virginia 1173, 1575, 2163, 2891, 3191, 3883

Herrmann, Edward 812

Hersholt, Jean 892, 1489, 2970

Herter, Gerard 16, 68

Hervey, Irene 861, 931, 1434, 3580

Hessler, Gordon 722

Hessman, Howard 1682

Heston, Alfred 2236, 2240, 3142, 3527

Heston, Charlton 122, 238, 503, 1001, 1771, 2014, 2179, 2182, 2556, 3047, 3592, 4101

Heston, Fraser Clarke 2179, 2182

Heston, John 3566

Heyburn, Weldon 297, 372, 620, 622, 814, 816, 1165, 1220, 1261, 1593, 2209, 2911, 2431, 2961, 3393, 3681, 3993, 4148

Heydt, Louis Jean 34, 152, 153, 393, 922, 1187, 1319, 2337, 2620, 2672, 2676, 2734, 3337, 3408, 3493, 3871, 3937, 4000

Heyes, Douglas 186, 196, 1549, 2116, 2566

Heyes, Herbert 509, 814, 1001, 2366, 2401

Heymann, Arthur 820

Heywood, Herbert 108, 1709, 1891, 2171, 2298, 3249, 3562, 4030

Hiatt, Ruth 948, 2848, 3459

Hibbs, Jesse 284, 2629, 2773, 2880, 3335, 3719, 4147

Hibler, Winston 571, 1706, 1930, 2775, 3867, 4040

Hickman, Cordell 234

Hickman, Darryl 279, 395, 1232, 1614, 1625, 2301, 2499, 2770, 3165, 3224, 3834

Hickman, Dwayne 545

Hickman, Howard 210, 213, 452, 1574, 1673, 2901, 3753, 3895, 3981

Hicks, Catherine 812

Hicks, Russell 120, 208, 1199, 1548, 1704, 1708, 2117, 2298, 2333, 2436, 2476, 2549, 2741, 2782, 2943, 3040, 3070, 3080, 3102, 3317, 3425, 3497, 3828, 3895, 3989, 4096, 4128

Higgens, Kenneth 3425

Higgins, Howard 195, 1516, 2447

Higgins, John 349, 423, 2559, 2608, 3095

Hildebrand, Rodney 3396

Hill, Al 355, 499, 1189, 1532, 2301, 2454, 2479, 2878, 2888, 3022, 3418, 3587

Hill, Craig 919, 1107, 3158

Hill, Doris 711, 1202, 2165, 2363, 2663, 2898, 3289, 3320, 3330, 3552, 3708

Hill, Elizabeth 3424

Hill, Ethel 3932

Hill, Josephine 75, 364, 1686, 1910, 2641, 3164, 3951, 4086

Hill, Mariana 954, 1515, 2721, 3048, 3732

Hill, Ramsey 197

Hill, Riley 11, 112, 338, 433, 523, 625, 832, 1012, 1087, 1098, 1155, 1235, 1358, 1407, 1445, 1642, 1834, 1836, 1844, 1856, 1984, 2001, 2132, 2234, 2247, 2272, 2293, 2317, 2404, 2617, 2650, 2654, 2665, 2677, 2866, 3110, 3124, 3146, 3191, 3226, 3486, 3554, 3732, 3735, 3805, 3850, 3866, 3915, 3922, 3987 see also Harris, Roy

Hill, Robert 203, 386, 583, 649, 703, 740, 753, 825, 915, 1016, 1037, 1158, 1195, 1583, 1812, 2078, 2219, 2429, 2451, 2510, 2673, 2874, 2877, 2890, 3442, 3541, 3661, 3868, 3925, 3956, 4018, 4066, 4125

Hill, Roy William 470

Hill, Terence 3, 331, 1267, 2065, 2199, 2760, 3560, 3546

Hill, Walter 1976

Hiller, Arthur 2274, 3569

Hillerman, John 299, 1608, 1868, 2721

Hilliard, Ernest 387

Hillie, Verna 2066, 2213, 3383, 3680, 3817

Hillyer, Lambert 204, 229, 233, 338, 491, 791, 795, 876, 1031, 1034, 1036, 1051, 1087, 1098, 1108, 1159, 1235, 1352, 1356, 1361, 1422, 1447, 1486, 1701, 1746, 1748, 1817, 1818, 1822, 1984, 2070, 2125, 2228, 2284, 2290, 2314, 2356, 2389, 2438, 2480, 2482, 2571, 2572, 2583, 2626, 2651, 2653, 2654, 2739, 2817, 2894, 2965, 3112, 3127, 3192, 3222, 3272, 3290, 3320, 3321, 3332, 3349, 3410, 3412, 3439, 3440, 3511, 3533, 3594, 3609, 3650, 3706, 3711, 3735, 3805, 3831, 3849, 3876, 3908, 3968, 4028, 4035, 4093

Hilton, Arthur 2744

Hilton, George 68, 431, 456, 2494, 2990

Hinds, Samuel S. 155, 861, 977, 1111, 1150, 1305, 1736, 2769, 2782, 2884, 3089, 3122, 3212, 3334, 3692, 3966

Hingle, Pat 1423, 1609, 2214, 2250, 2354, 2978

Hinkle, Robert 1368, 2340, 4164

MacRae, Henry 1710, 2986, 4049
MacRae, Leslie 1011
Macready, George 667, 896, 1391, 2252, 2551, 3118, 3606, 3880
Maddow, Ben 3944
Madison, Guy 19, 178, 203, 464, 568, 656, 922, 1080, 1399, 1432, 1767, 1877, 2114, 2335, 2489, 2735, 2763, 3568, 3645
Madison, Mae 248
Madison, Noel 4143
Madrid, Jose Luis 4041
Maffei, Mario 2865
Magill, James 891
Magrill, George 763, 1451, 2317, 2537, 2878, 3036, 3070, 3522
Maharis, George 849, 1751
Mahin, John Lee 330, 1559, 2229, 2292
Mahon, John 427
Mahon, Larry 1306, 1547, 2006
Mahoney, Jack see Mahoney, Jock
Mahoney, Jock 174, 177, 293, 306, 481, 565, 621, 688, 896, 1172, 1388, 1453, 1530, 1560, 1643, 1687, 1755, 1782, 1909, 2160, 2252, 2430, 2493, 2731, 2862, 2891, 2957, 3031, 3154, 3239, 3251, 3252, 3319, 3411, 3530, 3544
Mahoney, Maggie 292
Main, Marjorie 138, 241, 766, 1146, 1226, 1441, 1548, 1619, 1625, 2229, 2770, 2949, 3122, 3497, 4116, 4133
Mainwaring, Daniel 629, 3917 see also Homes, Geoffrey
Majors, Eddie 2174
Majors, Lee 1514, 4101
Mala, Ray 506, 1252, 1254, 1304, 1452, 2195, 2294
Malatesta, Fred 2263
Malcolm, Robert 531
Malden, Karl 21, 318, 581, 1385, 1425, 1566, 2250, 2349, 4080
Malick, Terry 2553
Malko, George 750
Malle, Louis 3900
Mallinson, Rory 152, 406, 537, 561, 687, 827, 957, 1119, 1314, 1483, 1639, 1680, 1719, 1755, 1793, 2017, 2162, 2589, 2862, 2920, 3015, 3085, 3139, 3146, 3147, 3314, 3336, 3342, 3578, 3972
Mallory, Boots 2567
Malloy, Doris 2843

Malone, Dorothy 123, 468, 638, 1082, 1623, 1805, 1816, 1939, 2252, 2524, 2600, 2998, 3317, 3477, 3499, 3793, 3936
Malone, Joe 90
Malone, Molly 3403
Malone, Nancy 2072
Maloney, Leo 591, 1462, 2052, 2495, 2641
Maltz, Albert 3059, 3795
Malvern, Paul 778, 1995, 2635, 2808, 3610, 3165, 3680
Malyon, Eily 120, 3834
Mamakos, Peter 2608, 3503, 3694, 3903
Mamelok, Emil 820
Mamoulian, Rouben 1223, 1517, 2088
Mancuso, Nick 1893, 2179, 2274
Mander, Miles 79
Manduke, Joe 1695
Manes, Fritz 2453
Mankiewicz, Joseph L. 3558
Mann, Anthony 219, 347, 603, 869, 999, 1187, 1767, 2037, 2068, 2226, 3643, 4102
Mann, Daniel 1567, 2762
Mann, E.B. 2657, 2845
Mann, Hank 103, 499, 779, 1170, 1808, 3248, 3277, 3409
Mann, Larry 85, 3063, 3328
Mann, Leonard 3877
Mann, Margaret 1847, 3821
Mann, Stanley 908
Manners, Marjorie 296, 2407, 3551, 3979
Manning, Bruce 1659, 3336
Manning, Hope see Manning, Irene
Manning, Irene 977, 2329, 3248
Manning, Monroe 1760
Mannors, Sheila 701, 837, 1750, 1863, 2171, 2585, 3531, 3540, 3994
Mansfield, Jayne 3125
Mantee, Paul 313, 782
Mantooth, Randolph 408
Many Treaties, Chief 274, 441, 446, 763, 821, 1718, 1790, 1848, 2393, 2533, 3070, 3440
Manzanoo, Eduardo 1444
Mapes, Ted 104, 152, 218, 272, 277, 305, 350, 393, 509, 661, 688, 704, 739, 759, 794, 808, 842, 851, 914, 957, 985, 1087, 1159, 1161, 1189, 1195, 1211, 1217, 1538, 1592, 1638, 1701, 1712, 1742, 1772, 1822, 1847,

1946, 2073, 2203, 2265, 2355, 2387, 2388, 2419, 2472, 2482, 2572, 2628, 2658, 2671, 2749, 2810, 2821, 2868, 2896, 2965, 2983, 3169, 3375, 3411, 3422, 3440, 3508, 3539, 3554, 3591, 3611, 3659, 3663, 3666, 3699, 3784, 3805, 3814, 3858, 3876, 3921, 4058, 4189
Mapes, Virginia 4100
Maple, Christine 2893
The Maple City Four 1261, 2327, 3820
Mara, Adele 127, 215, 291, 490, 673, 1086, 1199, 2273, 2824, 2907, 2910, 3156, 3774, 3876
March, Alex 755
March, Fredric 1535, 1619
March, Joseph 1960, 3916
March, Sally 104
Marchent, Joaquim L. Romero 161, 732, 2352, 3097, 3306, 4185
Marcovicci, Andrea 2445
Marcus, James 253, 353, 555, 1029, 1551, 1610, 1702, 1750, 1969, 2104, 2369, 3515, 3680, 3911, 3980
Marcus, Lee 3419, 3421
Marcuse, Theodore 2081, 3629
Margheriti, Antonio 946
Margo 1153, 2905, 3902
Margolin, Janet 2250
Marin, Edwin L. 1, 512, 532, 641, 1045, 1126, 1284, 1491, 2672, 3433, 3476, 4170
Marion, Beth 130, 223, 981, 1106, 1176, 2506, 2510, 2877, 3194, 3687
Marion, Charles R. 78, 2918
Marion, Frances 3081
Marion, George 2915, 3768
Marion, Paul 683, 2628, 2681, 3147, 4189
Marischka, Georg 1877
Mark, Robert 1268, 1697
Markey, Enid 768
Markham, Monte 1565, 2721
Markland, Ted 1523, 1654, 1774, 2721, 3922, 3939
Marks, William 193, 3934
Maris, Mona 103, 127, 3081, 3320, 3804
Marlen, Gloria 344
Marley, John 545, 1654, 1695, 2022, 2178
Marlo, Frank 1825
Marlo, Steve 1424, 1545
Marlow, Rex 802
Marlowe, Don 2326

Index   614